D0163807

Students,

If your instructor is using CourseBank, the code below will allow you to register for free. To register, use the URL and directions provided by your instructor.

Scratch off to reveal access code

This code is only valid for a single user for one semester. This code may be invalid if the protective scratch-off coating covering the code has been removed and redeemed by the book's previous owner.

Instructors,

CourseBank is a pre-built online course for your LMS, with learning assets and auto-graded assignments. CourseBank easily integrates with Blackboard, Canvas, D2L, Moodle, and any other LMS for a single sign-on and single grade book experience.

support@chicagobusinesspress.com

BUSINESS
and
SOCIETY

A Strategic Approach to Social Responsibility & Ethics

Seventh Edition

O. C. Ferrell
Auburn University

Debbie Thorne
Texas State University

Linda Ferrell
Auburn University

CHICAGO
BUSINESS PRESS

CHICAGO
BUSINESS PRESS

BUSINESS & SOCIETY:
A STRATEGIC APPROACH TO SOCIAL RESPONSIBILITY & ETHICS

© 2021 Chicago Business Press

ALL RIGHTS RESERVED. No part of this work covered by the copyright herein may be reproduced, transmitted, stored or used in any form or by any means graphic, electronic, or mechanical, including by not limited to photocopying, recording, scanning, digitizing, taping, web distribution, information networks, or information storage and retrieval systems, except as permitted under Section 107 or 108 of the 1976 United States Copyright Act, without the prior written permission of the publisher.

For product information or assistance, contact us at
www.chicagobusinesspress.com

ISBN: 978-1-948426-22-0

Printed in Canada

Brief Table of Contents

Table of Contents

7 Strategic Approaches to Improving Ethical Behavior 178

11 Technology Issues   306

12 Sustainability Issues   340

13 Social Responsibility in a Global Environment 378

Preface

This edition of *Business and Society: A Strategic Approach to Social Responsibility* has been thoroughly updated to capture new challenges and evolving opportunities. We were one of the first business and society textbooks to use a strategic framework that integrates business and society into organizational strategies, and now we are pleased to introduce our seventh edition. Today in corporate America, social responsibility is a major consideration in strategic planning. Most boards of directors face issues related to sustainability, legal responsibilities, employee well-being, consumer protection, corporate governance, philanthropy, as well as emerging social issues. Social responsibility has been linked to financial performance, and business and society courses are as important as other functional areas in preparing students for their careers.

In this text, we demonstrate and help the instructor prove that social responsibility is a theoretically grounded yet highly actionable and practical field of interest. The relationship between business and society is inherently controversial and complex, yet the intersection of its components, such as corporate governance, workplace ethics, community needs, and technology, is experienced in every organization. For this reason, we developed this text to effectively assist decision-making and inspire the application of social responsibility principles to a variety of situations and organizations.

Because of this transformation of corporate responsibility, the seventh edition of *Business and Society: A Strategic Approach to Social Responsibility* is designed to fully reflect these changes. We have been diligent in this revision about discussing the most current knowledge and describing best practices related to social responsibility. The innovative text, cutting-edge cases, and comprehensive teaching and learning package for *Business and Society* ensure that business students understand and appreciate concerns about philanthropy, employee well-being, corporate governance, consumer protection, social issues, and sustainability.

We also address how technology, including artificial intelligence (AI) and its enablers, such as blockchain, drones, and robotics, is impacting the world we live in. AI is rapidly changing business as we know it and raises many ethical concerns about how the technology is used. For example, without ethical decision-making abilities and parameters, AI could result in accidental or intentional discrimination. Businesses must establish checks and balances to make public safety and security a priority. Additionally, AI is quickly changing the workforce as more automated tasks are performed by robots and drones. We address all of these advancements in technology and the benefits and threats they bring.

Business and Society is a highly readable and teachable text that focuses on the reality of social responsibility in the workplace. We have revised the seventh edition to be the most practical and applied business and society text available. A differentiating feature of this book is its focus on the role that social responsibility takes in strategic business decisions. We demonstrate that studying social responsibility provides knowledge and insights that positively contribute to organizational performance and professional success. This text prepares students for the social responsibility challenges and opportunities they will face throughout their careers.

We provide the latest examples, stimulating cases, and unique learning tools that capture the reality and complexity of social responsibility. Students and instructors prefer this book because it presents examples, tools, and practices needed to develop and implement a socially responsible business strategy. Finally, this book makes the assumption that students will be working in an organization trying to improve social responsibility and will not be just critics of business.

Important Changes to the Seventh Edition

The seventh edition has been revised to include new examples, vignettes, and cases. A new full-color design is more engaging and helps the student better understand the visual supports in the book.

Each chapter of the text has been updated to include recent social responsibility issues related to the economy, ethical decision-making, and concerns about corporate governance. Chapter 4 has been broken out into two chapters: Chapter 4, Business, Government, and Regulation and Chapter 5, The Impact of Business on Government and the Political Environment. This allowed us to expand the content and include more real-world examples to help students better understand the concepts. Chapter 11, Technology Issues, has been updated to include a new section on artificial intelligence, introducing key terms such as machine learning and deep learning.

Opening cases at the start of each chapter address a variety of issues related to the chapter content, including strategic philanthropy, fraud, corporate culture, and sustainability. Companies featured in these cases include IKEA, the NFL, Cascade Engineering, and Alibaba. Additional real-world examples of corporate social responsibility are provided in the Ethical Responsibilities and The Earth in Balance boxed readings. The Ethical Responsibilities boxed readings include ethical challenges in different areas of business, including human resources, marketing, banking, and technology. Topics discussed in these vignettes include blockchain technology, the legalization of marijuana, and minimum wage. The Earth in the Balance boxed readings focus on social responsibility related to sustainability issues. These vignettes discuss green initiatives at companies such as Evrnu and Patagonia.

The Responsible Business Debate exercise at the end of each chapter introduces a business-related issue and presents two competing perspectives. The debate is positioned so that class teams can defend a position and analyze topics, giving students the opportunity to engage in active learning. Topics discussed include the U.S.-China trade war, the sustainability of nuclear energy, and the downside of technology.

We have provided 15 case studies at the back of book for use as assignments and for class discussion. All of the cases are new or significantly updated. They include Google and privacy solutions, Volkswagen and sustainability, and ethics at Apple.

Content and Organization

Professors who teach business and society courses come from diverse backgrounds, including law, management, marketing, philosophy, and many others. Such diversity affords great opportunities to the field of business and society and showcases the central role that social responsibility occupies within various academic, professional, and community circles. Because of the widespread interest and multiplicity of stakeholders, the philosophy and practice of social responsibility is both exciting and debatable; it is in a constant state of discussion and refinement—just like all important business concepts and practices.

We define social responsibility in Chapter 1, "Social Responsibility Framework," as *the strategic focus for fulfilling economic, legal, ethical, and philanthropic responsibilities.* To gain the benefits of social responsibility, effective and mutually beneficial relationships must be developed with customers, employees, investors, the government, communities, and others who have a stake in the company. We believe that social responsibility must be fully valued and championed by top managers and granted the same planning time, priority, and management attention as any company initiative. Therefore, the framework for the text reflects a process that begins with the social responsibility philosophy, includes the four types of responsibilities, involves many types of stakeholders, and ultimately results in both short- and long-term performance gains. We also provide a strategic orientation, so students will develop the knowledge, skills, and attitudes for understanding how organizations achieve many benefits through social responsibility.

Chapter 2, "Strategic Management of Stakeholder Relationships," examines the types and attributes of stakeholders, how stakeholders become influential, and the processes for integrating and managing their influence on a firm. The chapter introduces the stakeholder interaction model and examines the impact on global business, corporate reputation, and crisis situations on stakeholder relationships.

Chapter 3, "Corporate Governance," examines the rights of shareholders, the accountability of top management for corporate actions, executive compensation, and strategic-level processes for ensuring that economic, legal, ethical, and philanthropic responsibilities are satisfied. Because both daily and strategic decisions affect a variety of stakeholders, companies must maintain a governance structure for ensuring proper control and responsibility for their actions. Corporate governance is an integral element for social responsibility, which, until the recent scandals, had not received the same level of emphasis as issues such as environment and human rights.

Chapter 4, "Business, Government, and Regulation," and Chapter 5, "The Impact of Business on Government and the Political Environment," explore the complex relationship between business and government. Every business must be aware of and abide by the laws and regulations that dictate required business conduct. Chapter 5 also examines how businesses can participate in public policy to influence government. A strategic approach for legal compliance, based on the Federal Sentencing Guidelines for Organizations, is also provided.

Chapter 6, "Business Ethics and Ethical Decision-Making," and Chapter 7, "Strategic Approaches to Improving Ethical Behavior," are devoted to exploring the role of ethics and ethical leadership in business decision-making. Business ethics relates to responsibilities and expectations that exist beyond legally prescribed levels. We examine the factors that influence ethical decision-making and consider how companies can apply this understanding to improve ethical conduct. We fully describe the components of an organizational ethics program and detail the implementation plans needed for effectiveness.

Chapter 8, "Employee Relations," and Chapter 9, "Consumer Relations," explore relationships with two pivotal stakeholders—consumers and employees. These constituencies, although different by definition, have similar expectations of the economic, legal, ethical, and philanthropic responsibilities that must be addressed by businesses.

Chapter 10, "Community Relations and Strategic Philanthropy," examines companies' synergistic use of organizational core competencies and resources to address key stakeholders' interests and achieve both organizational and social benefits. While traditional benevolent philanthropy involves donating a percentage of sales to social causes, a strategic approach aligns employees and organizational resources and expertise with the needs and concerns of stakeholders. Strategic philanthropy involves both financial and nonfinancial contributions to stakeholders, but it also directly benefits the company.

Chapter 11, "Technology Issues," covers the unique issues that arise as a result of enhanced technology in the workplace and business environment, including its effects on privacy, intellectual property, and health. This chapter explores the ethical concerns raised by artificial intelligence and its enablers such as big data, blockchain, drones, and robotics. The strategic direction for technology depends on the government's and businesses' ability to plan, implement, and audit the influence of technology on society.

Chapter 12, "Sustainability Issues," explores the significant environmental issues business and society face today, including air pollution, global warming, water pollution and water quantity, land pollution, waste management, deforestation, urban sprawl, biodiversity, genetically modified organisms, and alternative energy. This chapter also considers the impact of government environmental policy and regulation and examines how some companies are going beyond these laws to address environmental issues and act in an environmentally responsible manner.

Chapter 13, "Social Responsibility in a Global Environment," is a chapter that addresses the unique issues found in a global business environment. Emerging trends and standards are placed in a global context.

Features

Chapter Opening Cases and Real Company Examples

Company examples and anecdotes from all over the world are found throughout the text. The purpose of these tools is to take students through a complete strategic planning and implementation perspective on business and society concerns by incorporating an active and team-based learning perspective. Every chapter opens with a vignette and includes examples that shed more light on how social responsibility works in today's business. In this edition, all boxed readings focus on managerial and global dimensions of social responsibility. Chapter opening objectives, a chapter summary, boldfaced key terms, and discussion questions at the end of each chapter help direct students' attention to key points.

Experiential Exercises

Experiential exercises at the end of each chapter help students apply social responsibility concepts and ideas to business practice. Most of the exercises involve research on the activities, programs, and philosophies that companies and organizations are using to implement social responsibility today. These exercises are designed for higher-level learning and require students to apply, analyze, synthesize, and evaluate knowledge, concepts, practices, and possibilities for social responsibility. At the same time, the instructor can generate rich and complex discussions from student responses to exercises. For example, the experiential exercise for Chapter 1 asks students to examine *Fortune* magazine's annual list of the Most Admired Companies. This exercise sets the stage for a discussion on the broad context in which stakeholders, business objectives, and responsibilities converge.

"What Would You Do?" exercises depict people in real-world scenarios who are faced with decisions about social responsibility in the workplace. One exercise (see Chapter 5) discusses the dilemma faced by a nutritional supplement company that hired an advertising agency to promote its products. The agency and the supplement company came under fire of the Federal Trade Commission for making unsubstantiated claims. At the end of the exercise, students are asked to examine liability and damage control.

A new debate issue is also located at the end of each chapter. The topic of each debate deals with a real-world company or dilemma that is both current and controversial. Many students have not had the opportunity to engage in a debate and to defend a position related to social responsibility. This feature highlights the complexity of ethical issues by creating a dialog on the advantages and disadvantages surrounding various issues. The debates also help students develop their critical thinking, research, and communication skills.

Cases

So that students learn more about specific practices, problems, and opportunities in social responsibility, 15 cases are provided at the end of the book. The cases represent a comprehensive collection for examining social responsibility in a multidimensional way. The 15 cases allow students to consider the effects of stakeholders and responsibility expectations on larger and well-known businesses. These cases represent the most up-to-date and compelling issues in social responsibility. All of the cases used in this book are original and have been updated with all developments that have occurred through 2019. Students will find these cases to be pivotal to their understanding of the complexity of social responsibility in practice. The following provides an overview of the 15 cases:

- **Case 1: Uber Fuels Controversy.** This case discusses the success of Uber and the regulatory challenges they face as they expand globally. One of the biggest controversies is the fact that Uber drivers do not always have to be professionally licensed, unlike taxi company drivers. This has led several cities worldwide to place bans on certain Uber services. This case also examines Uber's new product offerings.
- **Case 2: Fixer Upper: Home Depot Works on Stakeholder Relationships.** Although Home Depot faced a decrease in customer satisfaction in the past, they have implemented a number of initiatives to restore their ethical reputation with stakeholders. Some major initiatives include their diversity supplier program, their use of wood certified by the Forest Stewardship Council, and their philanthropic involvement with Habitat for Humanity. Above all, Home Depot has adopted a stakeholder orientation that considers how they can best meet the needs of their various stakeholders.
- **Case 3: Big-Box Retailer Walmart Manages Big Responsibility.** This case examines the ups and downs of retail giant Walmart. Many feel that Walmart has had a negative impact on many communities by putting small business owners out of business, a sensation called the "Walmart Effect." Additionally, Walmart has faced ongoing criticism for the treatment and pay of their employees. Additionally, this case explores Walmart's strides in sustainability and robotics.
- **Case 4: Google Searches for Solutions to Privacy Issues.** This case describes Google's path to success, their product mix, and their company culture. It dives deep into the ongoing data privacy concerns Google has created as well as the legal trouble the company faces worldwide.
- **Case 5: CVS Smokes the Competition in Corporate Social Responsibility.** This case examines the corporate social responsibility initiatives of CVS as well as ethical challenges they have faced. Of particular interest is CVS's decision to drop profitable tobacco products from stores to better align themselves as a health services company.
- **Case 6: Volkswagen Charts a New Course: The Road to Sustainability.** This case explores the origin of Volkswagen and the company's rise in popularity. This case focuses on the emissions scandal that undermined the

firm's previous reputation for quality and integrity. The case also examines Volkswagen's attempts to rebuild their reputation.

- **Case 7: Wells Fargo Banks on Recovery.** This case discusses what mistakes Wells Fargo made that led to the creation of more than 3.5 million fake customer accounts. Wells Fargo employees faced unrealistic goals, which created a toxic corporate culture that fueled the fraud for years. The case also explores the company's struggle to regain the trust of their customers.

- **Case 8: A Brew Above the Rest: New Belgium Brewing.** This case examines the background of New Belgium Brewing and their social responsibility initiatives. The company's strong emphasis on sustainability and employee involvement are discussed as examples of how the craft brewery has been able to maintain their corporate values since their founding.

- **Case 9: Starbucks Takes on Coffee Culture.** This case examines Starbucks' foundation for a socially responsible culture. It describes how Starbucks strives to meet the needs of different stakeholders and how this stakeholder emphasis has led to the development of successful products and a strong brand image. This case also explores recent challenges the company has faced with racial bias.

- **Case 10: If the Shoe Fits: TOMS and the One for One Movement.** TOMS Shoes is a for-profit business with a large philanthropic component. This case examines the One for One model and the movement TOMS created with their product mix and promotion strategies. This case also explores how TOMS is evolving both their mission and business model.

- **Case 11: Apple Bites into Ethics.** This case examines Apple's early struggles as a computer company as well as the company's peak popularity. The case considers Apple's continued innovation and efforts to stay ahead of the pack. This case also explores privacy concerns and antitrust issues faced by the tech giant.

- **Case 12: The Hershey Company's Bittersweet Success.** This case explores Hershey's success and considers the inherent ethical conflicts that come from operating in the cocoa industry. It also examines Hershey's commitment to ethics and social responsibility as wells as the challenges the firm faces.

- **Case 13: Corporate Social Responsibility from the Outside In at Patagonia.** Patagonia has integrated core beliefs and values into every product they produce and is known for their innovative designs, exceptional quality, and environmental ingenuity. This case examines Patagonia's unique promotion strategies and how their corporate culture aligns with their values.

- **Case 14: Johnson & Johnson Experiences the Pain of Recalls.** This case examines the struggle of Johnson & Johnson, one of the world's most admired companies, as they faced multiple product recalls of their Tylenol product and legal issues with their baby powder.

- **Case 15: Herbalife Nutrition: Managing Risks and Achieving Success.** This case considers the accusations levied against Herbalife by activist investor William Ackman charging Herbalife's business model as being a pyramid scheme. It also highlights the difference between a pyramid scheme and a multilevel marketing compensation model and applies this distinction to Herbalife's business model.

Role-Play Exercises

In addition to many examples, end-of-chapter exercises, and the cases, we provide three role-play exercises in the *Instructor's Manual*. The role-play exercises, built around a fictitious yet plausible scenario or case, support higher-level learning objectives, require group decision-making skills, and can be used in classes of any size. Implementation of the exercises can be customized to the time frame, course objectives, student population, and other unique characteristics of a course. These exercises are aligned with trends in higher education toward teamwork, active learning, and student experiences in handling real-world business issues. For example, the National Farm & Garden exercise places students in a crisis situation involving a product defect that requires an immediate response and consideration of changes over the long term. The Soy-Dri exercise requires students to come up with an action plan for how to deal with customer confusion over the appropriate use of different products. The Shockvolt exercise places students in a situation in which they must determine the ethics and potential legal implications for marketing an energy drink. The role-play simulations (1) give students the opportunity to practice making decisions that have consequences for social responsibility, (2) utilize a team-based approach, (3) recreate the pressures, power, information flows, and other factors that affect decision-making in the workplace, and (4) incorporate a debriefing and feedback period for maximum learning and linkages to course objectives. We developed the role-play exercises to enhance more traditional learning tools and to complement the array of resources provided to users of this text. Few textbooks offer this level of teaching support and proprietary learning devices.

Supplements

The comprehensive Instructor's Manual includes chapter outlines, answers to the discussion questions at the end of each chapter, comments on the experiential exercises at the end of each chapter, comments on each case, and a sample syllabus. The role-play exercises are included in the manual along with specific suggestions for using and implementing them in class.

The Test Bank provides multiple choice and true-false questions for each chapter and includes a mix of descriptive and application questions.

A PowerPoint slide program is available for easy downloading and provides a recap of the highlights in each chapter.

Visit www.chicagobusinesspress.com to request access to the instructor supplements.

The book is also available with *CourseBank*, a pre-built online course of assets and auto-graded assignments that easily integrates with Blackboard, Canvas, D2L, Moodle, or any other LMS.

Authors' Website

O. C. Ferrell and Linda Ferrell have established a teaching resource website with the Center for Ethical Organizational Cultures at Auburn University's Raymond J. Harbert College of Business. Their publicly accessible website contains original cases, debate issues, and role-play simulations on select business and society topics as well as other resources such as articles on ethics and social responsibility education. It is possible to access this website at http://harbert.auburn.edu/research-and-centers/center-for-ethical-organizational-cultures/.

Acknowledgments

A number of individuals provided reviews and suggestions that helped improve the text and related materials, specifically, Justin Blount at Stephen F. Austin State University, Martha Broderick at University of Maine, Bienvenido Cortes at Pittsburg State University, Kathryn Coulter at Mount Mercy University, William Ferris at Western New England University, David Jacobs at Morgan State University, Ricki Ann Kaplan at East Tennessee State University, Velvet Landingham at Kent State

University, Vitaly Nishanov at University of Washington, Laura Rifkin at Pace University, Sandra Roberts at Barry University, Brandon Shamim at Woodbury University, Patricia Smith at North Carolina Wesleyan College, and Dan Thoman at George Mason University. We sincerely appreciate their time, expertise, and interest in this project.

We wish to acknowledge the many people who played an important role in the development of this book. Kelsey Reddick, Sarah Sawayda, Jennifer Sawayda, and Dr. Catherine Helmuth played a key role in research, writing, editing, and project management. We would like to thank Paul and Jane Ducham at Chicago Business Press for their leadership and support of this edition. Finally, we express much appreciation to our colleagues and the administration at Texas State University-San Marcos and Auburn University. Our goal is to provide materials and resources that enhance and strengthen teaching, learning, and thinking about social responsibility. We invite your comments, concerns, and questions. Your suggestions will be sincerely appreciated and utilized.

O. C. Ferrell
Debbie M. Thorne
Linda Ferrell

Social Responsibility Framework

Shutterstock/Nut Witchuwatanakorn

IKEA Puts It All on the Table with Social Responsibility

IKEA is a favorite among customers searching for well-designed products at low prices. IKEA stores sell ready-to-assemble furniture, appliances, and household goods. Today the firm is the largest furniture retailer in the world, with 139,000 employees operating in 43 countries. Germany is the firm's largest market, followed by the United States and France. Its diverse variety of products includes furniture, food, large items such as cabinetry, and smaller items such as kitchenware, decor, and small plants. IKEA also operates restaurants within its stores.

IKEA is highly focused on design, viewing it as a competitive advantage. For instance, IKEA stores have been designed intentionally to what some describe as a maze that encourages shoppers to go through the entire store. Some customers find themselves lost or retracing their steps. This strategy allows shoppers to see a wide variety of IKEA items, possibly leading to impulse or add-on purchases.

IKEA was founded in Sweden in 1943 by Ingvar Kamprad. The culture of the company heavily reflects Swedish culture, which values hard-working, friendly, and helpful people. These values helped create IKEA's vision, which is "to create a better everyday life for the many people," according to the company's website. IKEA aims to accomplish this not only through selling affordable home furnishing products, but also by helping people around the world. One way that IKEA hopes to help people is by helping the planet, by reducing carbon emissions and creating sustainable energy through solar panels that they sell.

Corporate social responsibility (CSR) is a large factor in IKEA's company culture. IKEA uses CSR to expose its employees to new challenges. Employees at IKEA are encouraged to mentor young students, assist senior citizens, and other altruistic actions. By volunteering for these tasks, employees can learn valuable skills that they can transfer to their jobs.

IKEA has also found that CSR is a powerful recruiting tool. Many potential employees look for employers who share their values. Through CSR, IKEA can help its community while attracting better talent.

In 1982, IKEA launched the IKEA Foundation. Initially, the foundation focused on architecture and interior design, but then it expanded to fight for children's rights and education. Recently, the IKEA Foundation awarded a grant of $2.3 million to the World Resources Institute to help bring clean electricity to 1 million people in India and East Africa. In these areas, many schools, clinics, and agricultural facilities are without power. The grant will be used to create a map that shows the demand for electricity in these areas. Once this map is created, the World Resources Institute will be able to better identify areas in need of electricity and other resources.

Another focus for IKEA is reducing carbon emissions. In fact, IKEA's long-term goal is to become carbon positive, which means they will remove more carbon dioxide than they create. IKEA is already moving toward this goal by switching to electric delivery trucks. The company plans to switch to only electric trucks in major cities like New York and Paris and is committed to completely switching over to electric trucks in every location by 2025. IKEA has already invested around $2 billion in renewable energy. By 2030, IKEA plans to cut emissions from stores by 80 percent and reduce emissions from deliveries and customer travel by 50 percent. These are lofty goals, but the company has invested considerable resources into becoming carbon positive.

For IKEA, CSR is at the very core of its heritage and current culture. IKEA aims to create value for customers by selling stylish, low-cost home furnishing products. However, the company doesn't stop there. It also feels that to sustain the planet, it must reduce its environmental impact and encourage its customers to do the same.[1]

Chapter Objectives
- Define the concept of social responsibility
- Trace the development of social responsibility
- Examine the global nature of social responsibility
- Discuss the benefits of social responsibility
- Introduce a framework for understanding social responsibility

Businesses today must cope with challenging decisions related to their interface with society. Consumers and other stakeholders are increasingly emphasizing the importance of companies' reputations, which are often based on ethics and social responsibility. The meaning of the term "social responsibility" goes beyond being philanthropic or environmentally sustainable. Recent research has concluded that a clear majority (75 percent) of consumers feel that social responsibility is important in developing their attitudes toward the brands they purchase. Social responsibility actions are often quite visible and discoverable, unlike other types of actions that companies take.[2] In an era of intense global competition and increasing media scrutiny, consumer activism, and government regulation, all types of organizations need to become adept at fulfilling these expectations. Like IKEA, many companies are trying, with varying results, to meet the many economic, legal, ethical, and philanthropic responsibilities they now face. Satisfying the expectations of social responsibility is a never-ending process of continuous improvement that requires leadership from top management, buy-in from employees, and good relationships across the community, industry, market, and government. Companies must plan, allocate, and use resources properly to satisfy the demands placed on them by investors, employees, customers, business partners, the government, the community, and others. Those who have an interest or stake in the company are referred to as "stakeholders."

In this chapter, we examine the concept of social responsibility and how it relates to today's complex business environment. First, we define social responsibility. Next, we consider the development of social responsibility, its benefits to organizations, and the changing nature of expectations in our increasingly global economy. Finally, we introduce the framework for studying social responsibility used in this text, which includes such elements as strategic management for stakeholder relations; legal, regulatory, and political issues; business ethics; corporate governance; consumer relations; employee relations; philanthropy and community relations; technology issues; sustainability issues; and global relations.

Social Responsibility Defined

Business ethics, corporate volunteerism, philanthropic activities, going green, sustainability, corporate governance, reputation management—these are concepts that you may have heard used, or even used yourself, to describe the various rights and responsibilities of business organizations. You may have thought about what these concepts actually mean for business practice. You may also have wondered how businesses engage in these behaviors or contribute to these outcomes. In this chapter, we clarify some of the confusion that exists in the terminology that people use when they talk about expectations for business. To this end, we begin by defining social responsibility.

license to operate
permission to conduct a business activity, subject to regulation by the licensing authority

In most societies, businesses are granted a **license to operate** and the right to exist through a combination of social and legal institutions. Businesses are expected to provide quality goods and services, abide by laws and regulations, treat employees fairly, follow through on contracts, protect the natural environment, meet warranty obligations, and adhere to many other standards of good business conduct. Companies that continuously meet and exceed these standards are often rewarded with customer satisfaction, employee dedication, investor loyalty, strong relationships in the community, positive news and social media reports, and the time and energy to continue focusing on business-related concerns. Firms that fail to meet these responsibilities can face penalties, both formal and informal, and may have their attention diverted from core business practice. For example, Volkswagen received a number of penalties, negative media coverage, and criticisms for installing so-called defeat devices into its diesel vehicles, which were intended to fool regulators. While the cars were undergoing emissions testing, they ran below their actual emissions performance to meet requirements. However, when on the road, these same cars emitted 40 times the allowable limit of emissions in the United States. Perhaps most damaging to the firm is that this scandal was a clear and deliberate attempt to bypass environmental rules. German prosecutors launched an investigation to determine whether top executives also misled investors by failing to inform them about complaints filed against the company in a timely manner. Overall, recent reports estimate that Volkswagen has paid $25 billion due to the firm's unlawful actions in the "dieselgate" scandal.[3] The goal is to prevent these negative outcomes in the future.

A large multinational corporation may be faced with protestors who voice their disdain publicly. More firms realize when their products are used in controversially debated activities, they assume the burden. For example, international tensions erupted when Caterpillar and Volvo's bulldozers were scheduled to be used to destroy a Palestinian village. Activists and humanitarian groups took to social media to demand a boycott of Caterpillar and Volvo due to their products' involvement in the planned destruction of Palestinian homes and structures.[4] Whether the public attacks are physical or virtual, companies often spend significant resources in explaining and defending their business decisions.

Finally, a company engaged in alleged deceptive practices may face formal investigation by a government agency and spend years defending itself. In many cases, these strategies have proved unsuccessful and led to significant penalties, oversight and monitoring agreements, investor lawsuits, and new regulations for the company's entire industry. For example, the Federal Trade Commission (FTC) opened an investigation in 2017 after Equifax disclosed that the firm suffered a major data breach that affected approximately 143 million Americans by allowing hackers unfettered access to their social security numbers, birth dates, and home addresses.[5] While the FTC does not always publicly confirm its investigations, the enormity of Equifax's data breach and subsequent public outcry led the FTC to disclose its plan. Members of Equifax's executive leadership team added insult to injury when reports surfaced that top managers sold large qualities of stock before the data breach was disclosed to the public. The Equifax example demonstrates that governmental agencies will use their full authority to investigate dubious corporate activities.[6]

Businesses today are expected to look beyond their self-interest and recognize that they belong to a larger group, or society, that expects responsible participation. Therefore, if any group, society, or institution is to function, there must be a delicate interplay between rights (i.e., what people expect to get) and responsibilities (i.e., what people are expected to contribute) for the common good. Research indicates that the most ethical and socially responsible companies are the most profitable.[7] Therefore, responsible conduct and policies yield significant benefits to society, as well as to shareholders and other investors. While the media provide much coverage of misconduct and illegal activities in business, most businesses try to act in an ethical and socially responsible manner.

The term *social responsibility* came into widespread use in the business world during the 1970s. It has evolved to emphasize seven main areas: social issues, consumer protection, sustainability, corporate governance, philanthropy, legal responsibilities, and employee well-being.

We identify seven issues within social responsibility. First, social issues are linked with the idea of **common good**. The common good is associated with the development of social conditions that allow societal welfare and fulfillment to be achieved. In other words, social issues involve the ethical responsibilities a firm owes to society. Equal rights, gender roles, marketing to vulnerable populations, data protection, and internet tracking are examples of social issues common in business.

Second, **consumer protection laws** were enacted to protect vulnerable members of society. Consumer protection laws were necessary because they created

common good
the development of social conditions that allow for societal welfare and fulfillment to be achieved

consumer protection laws
regulations enacted to protect vulnerable members of society with formal safeguards for consumers

formalized safeguards for unsuspecting consumers. For example, the FTC's Bureau of Consumer Protection attempts to limit prejudicial and deceitful business practices by gathering consumer complaints of deceptive conduct. From a legal perspective, the Bureau of Consumer Protection researches unlawful behavior, sues perpetrating organizations, ensures just marketplace practices, and teaches consumers and companies of their responsibilities and rights. As a society, it is important to provide legal protection and education for consumers and businesses alike.[8]

sustainability
a company's economic, environmental, and social performance

Third, **sustainability** has also become a growing area of concern in society. In the United States, the term is used more often to refer to the environmental impact on stakeholders. Green marketing practices, consumption of resources, and greenhouse gas emissions are important sustainability considerations that socially responsible businesses will have to address.

corporate governance
a company's formal system of accountability, oversight, and control

Fourth, **corporate governance** refers to formal systems of accountability, oversight, and control. Corporate governance is becoming an increasingly important topic in light of the number of business scandals over the last 10 to 15 years. Issues in corporate governance include concerns over executive compensation, internal control mechanisms, and risk management.

philanthropy
the desire to improve the welfare of others through donations of money, resources, or effort

Fifth, **philanthropy** is a key element of social responsibility. Corporate philanthropy is demonstrated in many forms. For example, corporations can contribute financially through cash donations or organizational members can gift their time through volunteerism. Another way that organizations undertake philanthropic initiatives is through outside partnerships with nonprofit firms and charities. Alternatively, corporations may establish in-house philanthropic programs, thereby overseeing their own socially responsible works, when executives feel that their firms' philanthropic giving and strategic direction are aligned.[9]

legal responsibility
the most basic expectation that a company must comply with the law

Sixth, **legal responsibility** is a central factor of social responsibility. Legal responsibility is often thought of as the most basic expectation. Accordingly, organizations must show that they have exceeded their legal responsibilities before they can address their ethical purposes and standards. Legal responsibility is a key foundational issue that affects firms' stakeholder evaluations.[10]

employee well-being
the health and wellness of employees, including how workers feel about their work and their working environment

Finally, **employee well-being** occurs when organizations create a safe and healthy employment environment for their workforce. Such activities include protecting employees' health and safety while creating job opportunities for development and growth. Employees thrive when their managers treat them with dignity and provide an atmosphere that emphasizes dynamic opportunities to contribute to the firm's overall mission and vision.[11] Taken together, social responsibility issues speak to the diverse array of corporate practices that affect firms' decision-making processes. Figure 1.1 discusses the social responsibility issues that we will be covering in this text.

Figure 1.1 Major Emphases of Social Responsibility

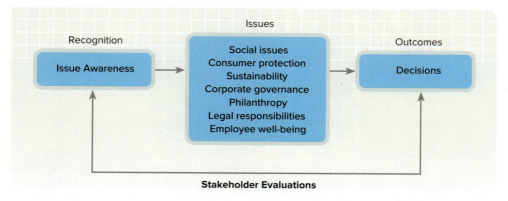

Source: © O.C. Ferrell, 2019.

These seven areas of social responsibility tend to conflict with the traditional or neoclassical view of a business's responsibility to society. The traditional view of social responsibility, articulated in the famous economist Milton Friedman's 1962 *Capitalism and Freedom,* asserts that a business has one purpose—satisfying its investors or shareholders—and that any other considerations are outside its scope.[12] Although this view still exists today, it has lost credibility as more and more companies have assumed a social responsibility orientation.[13] Companies see social responsibility as part of their overall corporate strategy and a benefit that directly increases the bottom line. We define **social responsibility** as a strategic focus for fulfilling economic, legal, ethical, and philanthropic responsibilities. Social responsibility can also be referred to as corporate social responsibility (CSR) when adopted by a business. This definition encompasses a wide range of objectives and activities, including both historical views of business and perceptions that have emerged in the last decade. Let's take a closer look at the parts of this definition.

social responsibility
a strategic focus for fulfilling economic, legal, ethical, and philanthropic responsibilities, can also be referred to as corporate social responsibility (CSR) when adopted by a business

Social Responsibility Applies to All Types of Businesses

It is important to recognize that all types of businesses—small and large, sole proprietorships and partnerships, and large corporations—implement social responsibility initiatives to further their relationships with their customers, their employees, and their community at large. For example, the automaker BMW is often regarded as a socially responsible corporate partner. It earned this reputation by forming educational programs that emphasize key social and environmental issues. BMW has pledged to help over 1 million people through various pro-social initiatives, such as the "The Schools Environmental Education Development Project."[14] Thus, the ideas advanced in this book are equally relevant and applicable across a wide variety of businesses and nonprofits.

Nonprofit organizations are expected to be socially responsible. Relationships with stakeholders—including employees, those that are served, and the community—affect their reputation. For example, the Southern California chapter of the Better Business Bureau was expelled from the organization after evidence emerged that it had been operating a pay-for-play scheme. The Better Business Bureau is a nonprofit self-regulatory organization that objectively rates businesses on how they treat consumers and handle consumer complaints. Investigations revealed that employees at the Southern California bureau were awarding businesses high rankings only if they paid to become members. The bureau is the largest ever expelled for misconduct.[15] This example demonstrates that nonprofit organizations must also develop strategic plans for social responsibility. In addition, government agencies are expected to uphold the common good and act in an ethical and responsible manner.

Although the social responsibility efforts of large corporations usually receive the most attention, the activities of small businesses may have a greater impact on local communities.[16] Owners of small businesses often serve as community leaders, provide goods and services for customers in smaller markets that larger corporations are not interested in serving, create jobs, and donate resources to local community causes. Medium-sized businesses and their employees have similar roles and functions on both a local and a regional level. Although larger firms produce a substantial portion of the gross national output of the United States, small businesses represent more than 47 percent of U.S. employees and generate more than 32 percent of U.S. exports.[17] In addition to these economic outcomes, small businesses present an entrepreneurial opportunity to many people, some of whom have been shut out of the traditional labor force. Women, minorities, and veterans are increasingly interested in self-employment and other forms of small business activity. It is vital that all businesses consider the relationships and expectations that our definition of social responsibility suggests.

Social Responsibility Needs a Strategic Focus

Social responsibility is an important business concept and involves significant planning and implementation. Our definition of social responsibility requires a formal commitment, or a way of communicating the company's social responsibility philosophy. For example, Herman Miller, a multinational provider of office, residential, and healthcare furniture and services, established a set of values that create a strong culture both within and outside the company (shown in Table 1.1). This statement declares Herman Miller's core values and the way it will fulfill its responsibilities to its customers, its shareholders, its employees, the community, and the natural environment. Because this statement takes into account all of Herman Miller's constituents and applies directly to all of the company's operations, products, markets, and business relationships, it demonstrates the company's strategic focus on social responsibility. Other companies that embrace social responsibility have incorporated similar elements into their strategic communications, including **mission** and **vision statements**, annual reports, and websites. For example, Hershey Entertainment & Resorts focuses on four pillars of CSR: (1) the environment and the goal to reduce the ecological footprint; (2) the community and being a positive, productive, and informed partner; (3) the workplace, in fostering one that is safe, inclusive, desirable, and respectful; and (4) a marketplace and guest focus that considers the ethical treatment of all stakeholders.[18]

In addition to a company's verbal and written commitment to social responsibility, our definition requires action and results. To implement its social responsibility philosophy, Herman Miller has developed and implemented several corporate-wide strategic initiatives, including research on improving work furniture and environment, innovation in the area of ergonomically correct products, progressive employee development opportunities, volunteerism, and an environmental stewardship program.[19] As this example demonstrates, effective social responsibility requires both words and action.

If any such initiative is to have strategic importance, it must be fully valued and championed by top management. Leaders must believe in and support the integration of stakeholder interests and economic, legal, ethical, and philanthropic responsibilities into every corporate decision. For example, company objectives for brand awareness and loyalty can be developed and measured from both a marketing and a social responsibility standpoint because researchers have documented a relationship between consumers' perceptions of a firm's social responsibility and their intentions to purchase that firm's brands.[20] There are various ways that companies align stakeholder interests and social responsibility into business decisions. For example, engineers can integrate consumers' desires for reduced negative environmental impact into product design, and marketers can ensure that a brand's advertising campaign incorporates this product benefit. Finally, consumers' desire for an environmentally sustainable product may stimulate a stronger company interest in assuming environmental leadership in all aspects of its operations. Years ago, for example, Home Depot responded to demands by consumers and environmentalists for environmentally friendly wood products by launching a new initiative that

Table 1.1 Herman Miller's Values in Action

- Operational excellence
- Better World Report
- Environmental advocacy
- Inclusiveness and diversity
- Supplier diversity
- Health and well-being
- Community service

Source: "Our Values," Herman Miller, Inc., https://www.hermanmiller.com/our-values/ (accessed July 31, 2019). Courtesy of Herman Miller, Inc.

mission statement
a summary of a company's aims and values

vision statement
a description of a company's current and future objectives to help align decisions with their philosophy and goals

Shutterstock/JuShoot

gives preference to wood products certified as having been harvested responsibly over those taken from endangered forests.[21] With this action, the company—which has long touted its environmental principles—has chosen to take a leadership role in the campaign for environmental responsibility in the home improvement industry. Although social responsibility depends on collaboration and coordination across many parts of the business and among its constituencies, it also produces effects throughout these same groups. We discuss some of these benefits later in this chapter.

Because of the need for coordination, a large company that is committed to social responsibility often creates specific positions or departments to spearhead the various components of its program. For example, Starbucks has a department of global responsibility that focuses on responsible and ethical behaviors regarding the environment, employee relations, customer interactions, suppliers, and communities. Starbucks practices conservation through its Ethical Sourcing of Sustainable Products initiative. Under chief executive officer (CEO) Kevin Johnson's leadership, Starbucks believes that its success is linked to the farmers and suppliers who cultivate and harvest their products. Accordingly, the company's goal is to produce 100 percent ethically sourced tea and cocoa over the next few years.[22] A smaller firm may give an executive, perhaps in human resources or the business owner, the ability to make decisions regarding community involvement, ethical standards, philanthropy, and other areas. Regardless of the formal or informal nature of the structure, this department or executive should ensure that social responsibility initiatives are aligned with the company's **corporate culture**, integrated with companywide goals and plans, fully communicated within and outside the company, and measured to determine their effectiveness and strategic impact. In sum, social responsibility must be given the same planning time, priority, and management attention that are given to any other company initiative, such as continuous improvement, cost management, investor relations, research and development, human resources, or marketing research.

corporate culture
shared values, attitudes, and beliefs that characterize members of an organization

Social Responsibility Fulfills Society's Expectations

Another element of our definition of social responsibility involves society's expectations of business conduct. Many people believe that businesses should accept and abide by four types of responsibility: financial, legal, ethical, and philanthropic (see Table 1.2). To varying degrees, the four types are required, expected, and/or desired by society.[23]

In Stage 1, businesses have a responsibility to be financially viable so that they can provide a return on investment for their owners, create and sustain jobs for the community, and contribute goods and services to the economy. The economy is influenced by the ways that organizations relate to their shareholders, their customers, their employees, their suppliers, their competitors, their community, and even the natural environment. For example, in nations with corrupt businesses and industries, the negative effects often pervade the entire society. Transparency International, a German organization dedicated to curbing national and international corruption, conducts an annual survey on the effects of business and government corruption on a country's economic growth and prospects. The organization reports that corruption reduces economic growth, inhibits foreign investment, and often channels investment and funds into "pet projects" that may create little benefit other than high returns to the corrupt decision-makers. There are a host of practical implications for the four levels of social responsibility, business, and its effects on society.

In Stage 2, companies are required to maintain compliance with legal and regulatory requirements specifying the nature of responsible business conduct.

Table 1.2 Social Responsibility Requirements

Stages	Examples
Stage 1: Financial Viability	Starbucks offers investors a healthy return on investment, including paying dividends.
Stage 2: Compliance with Legal and Regulatory Requirements	Starbucks specifies in its code of conduct that payments made to foreign government officials must be lawful according to the laws of the United States and the foreign country.
Stage 3: Ethics, Principles, and Values	Starbucks offers healthcare benefits to part-time employees and supports coffee growers so they get a fair price.
Stage 4: Philanthropic Activities	Starbucks created the Starbucks Foundation to award grants to eligible nonprofits and to give back to their communities.

Society enforces its expectations regarding the behavior of businesses through the legal system. If a business chooses to behave in a way that customers, special-interest groups, or other businesses perceive as irresponsible, these groups may ask their elected representatives to draft legislation to regulate the business's behavior, or they may sue the firm in a court of law in an effort to force it to "play by the rules." For example, Coca-Cola faced backlash from consumers and special-interest groups alike after reports surfaced that its delivery trucks released 3.7 million metric tons of greenhouse gases into the atmosphere. Such public outcries caused Coca-Cola to transform its supply chain, including an investment in new delivery trucks that utilize alternative fuels, which should reduce its gas emissions by 25 percent.[24]

Beyond financial viability and legal compliance, companies must decide what they consider to be just, fair, and right—the realm of ethics, principles, and values—in Stage 3. **Business ethics** refers to the principles and standards that guide behavior in the world of business. Principles are specific and universal boundaries for behavior that should never be violated. Principles such as fairness and honesty are determined and expected by the public, government regulators, special-interest groups, consumers, industry, and individual organizations. The most basic of these principles have been codified into laws and regulations to require that companies conduct themselves in ways that conform to society's expectations. Ethical issues exist in most managerial decisions. A firm needs to create an ethical culture with values and norms that meet the expectations of stakeholders. *Values* are enduring beliefs and ideals that are socially enforced. Freedom of speech, for example, is a strong value in the Western world. For example, Marriott, a leading hospitality company, values include putting people first, pursuing excellence, embracing change, acting with integrity, and serving our world.[25]

Many firms and industries have chosen to go beyond these basic laws in an effort to act responsibly. The Direct Selling Association (DSA), for example, has established a code of ethics that applies to all individual and company members of the association. Because direct selling involves personal contact with consumers, there are many ethical issues that can arise. For this reason, the DSA code directs the association's members to go beyond legal standards of conduct in areas such as product representation, appropriate ways of contacting consumers, and warranties and guarantees. In addition, the DSA actively works with government agencies and consumer groups to ensure that ethical standards are pervasive in the direct selling industry. The World Federation of Direct Selling Associations (WFDSA) also maintains a **code of conduct** that addresses dealing with consumers, conduct toward direct sellers, and interactions within the industry. This code provides guidance for direct sellers around the world in countries as diverse as Argentina, Canada, Finland, Taiwan, and Poland.[26]

business ethics
the principles and standards that guide behavior in the world of business

code of conduct
a written collection of the rules, principles, values, and expectations of employee behavior

In Stage 4 are **philanthropic activities**, which promote human welfare and goodwill. By making philanthropic donations of money, time, and other resources, companies can contribute to their communities and society and improve the quality of life. For example, the UPS Foundation has been active in the global community since 1951. It offers programs in philanthropy under its aptly named philosophy, "The Logistics of Caring." Donations total approximately $120 million worldwide annually. In addition to the monetary contributions, 2.9 million annual volunteer hours by UPS employees have been given on an annual basis. The foundation focuses its efforts on education, disaster preparedness and resiliency, urgent response to unexpected disasters, post-disaster recovery, in-kind disaster relief, skill-based volunteering, partnerships with humanitarian organizations, and thought leadership.[27]

When these dimensions of social responsibility were first introduced, many people assumed that there was a natural progression from financial viability to philanthropic activities, meaning that a firm had to be financially viable before it could properly consider the other three elements. Today, social responsibility is viewed in a more holistic fashion, with all four dimensions seen as related and integrated, and this is the view that we will use in this book.[28] In fact, companies demonstrate varying degrees of social responsibility at different points in time. Figure 1.2 depicts the social responsibility continuum. Companies' fulfillment of their responsibilities can range from a minimal to a strategic focus that results in a **stakeholder orientation**. Firms that focus only on shareholders and the bottom line operate from a legal or compliance perspective.[29] Activists argue that the so-called opioid epidemic started, in part, because of the pharmaceutical industry's profit-driven focus. While the opioid epidemic has sparked national debate, Harvard University researchers found that the pharmaceutical industry has been incentivizing doctors to prescribe opioids and downplaying the long-term patient risks to the public. The pharmaceutical industry's profit-maximization strategy, which resulted in high investor returns, may have also led to a lethal consequence for another stakeholder group: unintended consumer deaths.[30]

Resource advantage theory stresses that a firm's resources provide competitive advantage. Promoting social trust and social responsibility develops the foundation for economic growth in a firm as well as a society. Customers are often motivated to enhance organizations that exhibit socially responsible behavior. For example, Warby Parker provides designer eyeglasses at a fraction of the cost of its competitors. The firm also makes eyewear available at very low price points to individuals in developing countries. In addition, Warby Parker donates one pair for every pair sold. This illustrates how consumers with strong ethical values are attracted to the brand. Thus, a company's socially responsible behavior can become a resource advantage.[31]

Strategic social responsibility is realized when a company has integrated a range of expectations, desires, and constituencies into its strategic direction and planning processes. In this case, an organization considers social responsibility an

philanthropic activities
efforts made by a company to improve human welfare

stakeholder orientation
the aim to benefit all parties affected by the success or failure of an organization

resource advantage theory
a theory stating that the value of a resource is viewed relative to its potential to create competitive differentiation or customer value

Figure 1.2 Social Responsibility Continuum

Minimal

Considerations that focus
solely on shareholders

Strategic

Financial, legal, ethical, and
philanthropic considerations
targeted at selected stakeholders

essential component of its vision, mission, values, and practices. Method, a popular cleaning product business, demonstrates a high degree of social responsibility by updating its corporate policies to help the environment. It made a strategic decision to modify its dish and hand soap packaging by using plastic recovered from the ocean, which aligns with the company's goal of "creating beautiful cleaning products that are as kind to the planet as they are tough on dirt." By using recycled packaging and biodegradable soap, Method's corporate vision aligns with its founder's strategic goal of "changing the world" through their promise to produce effective consumer products that are safe for the environment.[32] Executives with this philosophy often maintain that customers will be lost, employees will become dissatisfied, and other detrimental effects will occur if a firm abandons its strategic responsibilities.

In this book, we will give many examples of firms that are at different places along this continuum to show how the pursuit of social responsibility is never ending.

Social Responsibility Requires a Stakeholder Orientation

The final element of our definition involves those to whom an organization is responsible, including customers, employees, investors and shareholders, suppliers, governments, communities, and many others. These constituents have a stake in, or a claim on, some aspect of a company's products, industry, markets, and outcomes and are thus known as **stakeholders**. We explore the roles and expectations of stakeholders in Chapter 2. Companies that consider the diverse perspectives of these constituents in their daily operations and strategic planning are said to have a stakeholder orientation, meaning that they are focused on stakeholders' concerns. Adopting this orientation is part of the social responsibility philosophy, which implies that business is fundamentally connected to other parts of society and must take responsibility for its effects in those areas.

stakeholders
constituents who have an interest or stake in a company's products, industry, markets, and outcomes

R. E. Freeman, a developer of stakeholder theory, maintains that business and society are "interpenetrating systems," in that each affects and is affected by the other.[33] For the common good to be achieved, cross-institutional and cross-organizational interactions must move society toward shared partnerships. Research suggests interorganizational networks can be an important element of a successful corporate strategy that creates shared value. By definition, **interorganizational networks** are a set of organizations that are associated through shared or mutual affiliations and interests. For example, interorganizational networks include strategic business alliances, supply chains, human and health services consortia, public-private partnerships, and others. Identifying businesses that are committed to similar environmental and societal issues and that promote a shared operating environment can help create not only financial success, but also socially responsible actions.[34] Overall, companies may affect their communities and beyond through partnering with other organizations with similar value systems.[35]

interorganizational networks
a set of organizations that are associated through shared or mutual affiliations and interests

Development of Social Responsibility

In 1959, Harvard economist Edward Mason asserted that business corporations are "the most important economic institutions."[36] His declaration implied that companies probably affect the community and society in social terms as much as (or perhaps more than) in monetary, or financial, terms. Employment and the benefits associated with a living wage are necessary to develop a sustainable economy. The opportunity for individuals and businesses to attain economic success is necessary to create a society that can address social issues. Today, some question our economic system, but without economic resources, little progress can be made in developing society. Social responsibility has always been a part of our economic system. The history of American capitalism relates to the economic, technological, political, and social development of the country. In the early and mid-nineteenth century, most people lived in rural communities and were largely reliant on trade surpluses and commodity exchanges for substance. In 1850s, for instance, approximately 20 million of the 23 million Americans in the population lived in rural areas where few businesses had more than 300 employees. As industrialization advanced, rail systems and new technology provided an opportunity for manufacturing and retail institutions to develop. Finally, by the twentieth century, businesses were developed and their impact on society was much greater.

Although some firms have more of a social impact than others, companies influence many aspects of our lives, from the workplace to the natural environment. This influence has led many people to conclude that companies' actions should be designed to benefit employees, customers, business partners, and the community as well as shareholders. Social responsibility has become a benchmark for companies today.[37] However, these expectations have changed over time. For example, the first corporations in the United States were granted charters by various state governments because they were needed to serve an important function in society, such as transportation, insurance, water, or banking services. In addition to serving as a license to operate, these charters specified the internal structure of these firms, allowing their actions to be more closely monitored.[38] During this period, corporate charters were often granted for a limited period of time because many people, including legislators, feared the power that corporations could potentially wield. It was not until the mid-1800s and early 1900s that profit and responsibility to stockholders became major corporate goals.[39]

Historical Review of Social Responsibility

After World War II, as many large U.S. firms came to dominate the global economy, their actions inspired imitation in other nations. The definitive external characteristic of these firms was their economic dominance. Internally, they were marked by the virtually unlimited autonomy afforded to their top managers. This total discretion meant that these firms' top managers had the luxury of not having to answer for some of their actions.[40] In the current business mindset, such total autonomy would be viewed as a hindrance to social responsibility because there is no effective system of checks and balances. In a later chapter, we elaborate on *corporate governance,* the process of control and accountability in organizations that is necessary for social responsibility.

In the 1950s, the 130 or so largest companies in the United States provided more than half of the country's manufacturing output. The top 500 firms accounted for almost two-thirds of the country's nonagricultural economic activity.[41] U.S. productivity and technological advancements dramatically outpaced those of global competitors, such as Japan and Western Europe. For example, the level of production in the United States was twice as high as that in Europe and quadruple that in Japan. The level of research and development carried out by U.S. corporations was also well ahead of overseas firms. For these reasons, the United States was perceived as setting a global standard for other nations to emulate.

During the 1950s and 1960s, these companies provided benefits that are often overlooked. Their contributions to charities, the arts, culture, and other community activities were beneficial to the industry or to society rather than simply to the companies' own profitability. For example, the lack of competition meant that companies had the profits to invest in higher-quality products for consumer and industrial use. Although the government passed laws that required companies to take actions to protect the natural environment, make products safer, and promote equity and diversity in the workplace, many companies voluntarily adopted responsible practices rather than constantly fighting government regulations and taxes. These corporations once provided many of the services that are now provided by the government in the United States. For example, during this period, the U.S. government spent less than the government of any other industrialized nation on such things as pensions and health benefits, as these were provided by companies rather than by the government.[42] In the 1960s and 1970s, however, the business landscape changed.

Economic turmoil during the 1970s and 1980s changed the role of corporations. Venerable firms that had dominated the economy in the 1950s and 1960s became less important as a result of bankruptcies, takeovers, mergers, or other threats, including high energy prices and an influx of foreign competitors. The stability experienced by the U.S. firms of midcentury dissolved. During the 1960s and 1970s, the Fortune 500 had a relatively low turnover of about 4 percent. By 1990, however, one-third of the companies in the Fortune 500 of 1980 had disappeared, primarily as a result of takeovers and bankruptcies. The threats and instability led companies to protect themselves from business cycles by becoming more focused on their **core competencies** and reducing their product diversity. To combat takeovers, many companies adopted flatter organizational hierarchies. Flatter organizations meant workforce reduction but also entailed increasing empowerment of lower-level employees.

Thus, the 1980s and 1990s brought a new focus on profitability and economies of scale. Efficiency and productivity became the primary objectives of business. This fostered a wave of downsizing and restructuring that left some people and communities without financial security. Before 1970, large corporations employed about one of every five Americans, but by the 1990s, they employed only one in ten. The familial relationship between employee and employer disappeared, and along with it went employee loyalty and company promises of lifetime employment. Companies slashed their payrolls to reduce costs, and employees changed jobs more often. Workforce reductions and "job hopping" were almost unheard of in the 1960s but had become commonplace two decades later. These trends made temporary employment and contract work the fastest-growing forms of employment throughout the 1990s.[43]

Along with these changes, top managers were largely stripped of their former freedom. Competition intensified, and both consumers and stockholders grew more demanding. The increased competition led business managers to worry more and more about the bottom line and about protecting the company. Escalating use of the internet provided unprecedented access to information about corporate decisions and conduct and fostered communication among once unconnected groups, furthering consumer awareness and shareholder activism. Consumer demands put more pressure on companies and their employees. The education and activism of stockholders had top management fearing for their jobs. Throughout the last two decades of the twentieth century, legislators and regulators initiated more and more regulatory requirements every year. These factors resulted in difficult trade-offs for management.

Corporate responsibilities were renewed in the 1990s. Partly as a result of business scandals and Wall Street excesses in the 1980s, many industries and companies decided to pursue and expect more responsible and respectable business practices. Many of these practices focused on creating value for stakeholders through more effective processes and decreased the narrow and sole emphasis on corporate profitability. At the same time, consumers and employees became less interested in making money for its own sake and turned toward intrinsic

core competencies
unique advantages that differentiate a firm from its competitors

rewards and a more holistic approach to life and work.[44] This resulted in increased interest in the development of human and intellectual capital; the installation of corporate ethics programs; the development of programs to promote employee volunteerism in the community; strategic philanthropy efforts and trust in the workplace; and the initiation of a more open dialogue between companies and their stakeholders.

Despite major advances in the 1990s, the sheer number of corporate scandals at the beginning of the twenty-first century prompted a new era of social responsibility. The downfall of Enron, WorldCom, and other corporate stalwarts in the beginning of the 2000s caused regulators, former employees, investors, nongovernmental organizations (NGOs), and ordinary citizens to question the role and integrity of big business and the underlying economic system. Federal legislators passed the Sarbanes-Oxley Act to overhaul securities laws and governance structures. A new Public Company Accounting Oversight Board was implemented to regulate the accounting and auditing profession after Enron and WorldCom failed due to accounting scandals. Newspapers, business magazines, and news websites devoted entire sections—often titled "Corporate Scandal," "Year of the Apology," or "Year of the Scandal"—to the trials and tribulations of executives, their companies and auditors, and stock analysts.

Recent Developments in Social Responsibility

In 2007 and 2008, a housing boom in the United States collapsed, setting off a financial crisis. Homeowners could not afford to pay their mortgages. Because of the housing boom, in many cases the mortgages were higher than the houses were worth. People all across the United States began to walk away from their mortgages, leaving banks and other lenders with hundreds of thousands of houses that had decreased in value.

Meanwhile, companies such as AIG were using complex financial instruments known as "derivatives" to transfer the risks of securities such as mortgages, almost as a type of insurance policy. The housing collapse created a number of demands on financial firms that had sold these derivatives to pay their insurance contracts on the defaulted debt securities, but financial firms did not have enough of a safety net to cover so many defaults. The housing collapse created a chain reaction that led to the worst recession since the Great Depression. The government was forced to step in to bail out financial firms in order to keep the economy going and prevent the economy from collapsing further. Many established organizations such as Bear Stearns, Lehman Brothers, and Countrywide Financial went bankrupt or were acquired by other firms at a fraction of what they were originally worth. Table 1.3 describes some of the corporations and banks that collapsed in the financial crisis.

In 2010, Congress passed the Dodd-Frank Wall Street Reform and Consumer Protection Act, the most sweeping legislation since Sarbanes-Oxley. Dodd-Frank is intended to protect the economy from similar financial crises in the future by creating more transparency in the financial industry. This complex law required legislators to develop hundreds of laws to increase transparency and create financial stability. The Dodd-Frank Act will be discussed in more detail in Chapter 4. The financial crisis and the collapse of many well-known institutions have led to a renewed interest in business ethics and social responsibility.

In the last five years, the economy has stabilized and the stock market has recovered. Even though many banks failed during the financial crisis, today banks and the other financial institutions are much larger. The largest five banks are twice as large as they were a decade ago.[45] Rather than getting rid of too-big-to-fail financial institutions, they seem to be growing much larger, despite recent legislation.

Table 1.3 Corporations and Banks Involved in the Financial Crisis

Organization	Outcome
General Motors (GM)	Declared bankruptcy and required a government bailout of $49.5 billion to reorganize. The government sold their last shares in GM in 2013 and is estimated to have lost more than $10 billion on its investment.
AIG	Received a government bailout of $182 million and was criticized for using bailout money to pay executives large bonuses. AIG repaid the last of its loans in 2013.
Bank of America	Received $42 billion in bailout money as part of the Troubled Asset Relief Program (TARP). It paid back its loans in 2009.
Washington Mutual	Its banking subsidiaries were sold by the Federal Deposit Insurance Corporation to J. P. Morgan for $1.9 billion.
Chrysler	Declared bankruptcy and required a government bailout of $12.5 billion. By 2011, Chrysler had repaid most of the debt, and Fiat agreed to purchase the rest of the U.S. Treasury's shares in Chrysler for $500 million.
Countrywide Financial	Acquired by Bank of America for $4.1 billion. Bank of America inherited many of the lawsuits against Countrywide claiming it had engaged in fraudulent and discriminatory lending practices.

Future Developments in Social Responsibility

Technology includes the methods and processes creating applications to solve problems, perform tasks, and make decisions. New technology associated with artificial intelligence (AI) and blockchain are changing the way work is accomplished. The result is driverless cars, drones, robotics and machines that can communicate and make decisions like humans. This creates opportunities for new business models and job opportunities.

artificial intelligence
machines learning and performing tasks that typically require human intelligence by using algorithms

Artificial Intelligence   AI relates to machine (computer) learning that can perform activities and tasks that usually require human intelligence, such as decisions, visual perceptions, and speech recognition. In short, AI allows computers to perform humanlike functions. Recent advances within the literature suggest that AI will influence both job creation and development. It is predicted that by 2025, AI will perform half of all workplace jobs, as opposed to about 30 percent today. AI has the potential to make the world more efficient by transforming the food preparation, packaging, and welding industries by changing how firms source repetitive tasks such as assembly-line activities.

Research suggests that AI may create new roles and professional opportunities across a myriad of organizations.[46] The computer science industry, for example, uses robotic processes, including software bots with AI capabilities, to perform tasks such as object recognition. In the automotive industry, AI is an important element of autonomous driving systems. Indeed, industry experts are using AI to program autonomous, self-driving cars to understand predictable encounters on the open road. Finally, major changes are underway in the consumer service industry. Firms are using machine technology to effectively analyze thousands of consumer service emails with more robust response times compared to traditional human-run responses. In fact, approximately 40 percent of Americans that use the internet indicate they would rather use digital customer services than speak to a service provider on the phone.[47] Following this trend, corporations such as Google and Amazon have introduced personal digital assistants that utilize AI technologies to manage their consumer service needs.

AI has the potential to not only provide higher-quality consumer service, but also create new challenges. Opponents of AI fear that it will reduce job prospects because firms may use AI technologies to replace positions currently held by humans. For example, in the accounting industry, employees who collect, record, and reconcile payments could be replaced with advanced AI computer programs. KPMG LLP, one of the largest accounting firms expects to have fewer entry-level accountants in the future.[48] Additionally, AI can be used in surveillance. Surveillance is a sensitive issue related to privacy. Tracking communication, profiles, and other searchable information will accelerate with AI. While AI's impact on surveillance and privacy issues needs to be addressed, machine learning opens opportunities to perform crucial tasks with greater efficiency and be a catalyst for innovation.

AI has made significant advancements in recent years allowing companies to perform and track all types of business activities through machine learning. A firm can use these technologies to improve its CSR as well. AI, if developed properly, allows for decisions and recommendations that benefit all parties, promoting the idea that businesses can increase productivity while also helping the community and environment. Ethical issues such as increasing unemployment and introducing potential bias must be considered to ensure that AI's benefits are maximized. Both AI and blockchain have the potential to promote significant improvement in business ethics and CSR.

Blockchain Blockchain will enable AI through the development of databases that can be used in computer learning. Blockchain, discussed more thoroughly in Chapter 11, is a linked group of ordered transactions that are a subset of a database. The key is that no single authority can make changes to fit its needs, improving the integrity of the data. The finance industry, supply chain, marketing, human resource management, and most other areas of business will become more efficient in developing and tracking information.[49] This means that there will be more tracking and transparency to prevent misconduct and manage CSR activities.

blockchain
decentralized record-keeping technology that stores an immutable record of data blocks over time

Blockchain has the potential to make databases and the digital infrastructures more secure and trustworthy. For example, scanning data in a blockchain database and tracking products from a point of production to consumption. This means that the movement of agricultural products can be tracked from the farm to the table. This will allow complete knowledge and the ability to trace the source of products. For example, Walmart is requiring produce suppliers to track their products through the entire supply chain to each store.[50]

Blockchain represents transactions and data that could provide services, identity, verification, and almost any other activity.[51] Blockchain combined with AI can enable new business models. For example, cryptocurrency such as bitcoin is based on blockchain technology. The ability to verify identities and chronicle events can become an important information source to guide service providers. These shared databases can then be combined with AI machine learning to interact and provide important information and even decisions on key issues.

Blockchain acts as a distributed, incorruptible ledger. It is a decentralized database with data that is unforgeable and permanent. For these reasons, blockchain can serve as a powerful tool to confirm that money donated to a company's CSR projects is being used properly. With blockchain serving as the medium between the donors and the organization, financial ledgers will be transparent, and people will be able to confirm that the money is being funneled and used properly. Blockchain can also be used to track the progress and success of these projects, serving as another method of confirmation that companies are following through with their stated initiatives.

While AI has been deployed to solve many business problems, it raises ethical issues of its own. The rise of AI could increase unemployment as bots and computer systems take jobs. Bots are being used in consumer service, telemarketing, analytics, and sales and could spread further. In addition, the use of AI would widen the pay gap between executives and other employees, where companies use AI to strategize and make more money without having to pay employees more (or at all). Unintended consequences are another concern with AI. If not developed properly, an AI system would make poor decisions if it is not programmed to consider consequences correctly.

Critics often describe the potential disaster of uncontrolled AI that chooses optimal business decisions without considering ethical consequences, but AI can actually be used to promote ethical decisions while still benefiting the interests of the firm. An intelligent system has the potential to understand positive outcomes for multiple parties. AI can remove bias from decision-making and provide the best decisions and strategies based on their merits. AI also can assist with fraud detection, deterring employees and customers from committing unethical acts. More than ever, firms feel the need to broadcast a positive image of their brand, and AI and blockchain can provide tools to improve CSR and promote ethics inside as well as outside the organization.

Global Nature of Social Responsibility

Although many forces have shaped the debate on social responsibility, the increasing globalization of business has made it an international concern. A common theme is criticism of the increasing power and scope of business and income differences among executives and employees. Questions of corruption, environmental protection, fair wages, safe working conditions, and the income gap between rich and poor are posed. Many critics and protesters believe that global business involves exploitation of the working poor, destruction of the planet, and a rise in inequality.[52] After the financial crisis, global trust in business dropped significantly. More recent polls indicate that trust is rebounding in certain countries, but companies are still vulnerable to the ramifications of distrust. Approximately 50 percent of the general public among global consumers indicate that they trust business. This is even lower in the United States, where only 49 percent trust business overall.[53] In an environment where consumers distrust business, greater regulation and lower brand loyalty are the likely results. We discuss more of the relationship between social responsibility and business outcomes later in this chapter.

The globalization of business has critics who believe that the movement is detrimental because it destroys the unique cultural elements of individual countries, concentrates power within developed nations and their corporations, abuses natural resources, and takes advantage of people in developing countries. Multinational corporations are perhaps most subject to criticism because of their size and scope. Table 1.4 shows the world's largest companies, which are more powerful than many of the countries in which they do business. Because of the economic and political power that they potentially wield, the actions of large, multinational companies are under scrutiny by many stakeholders. Most allegations by antiglobalization protestors are not extreme, but the issues are still consequential. For example, the pharmaceutical industry has long been criticized for excessively high pricing, interference with clinical evaluations, some disregard for developing nations, and aggressive promotional practices. Critics have called on governments, as well as public health organizations, to influence the industry toward changing some of its practices.[54]

Advocates of the global economy counter these allegations by pointing to increases in overall economic growth, new jobs, new and more effective products, and other positive effects of global business. Although these differences of opinion provide fuel for debate and discussion, the global economy probably "holds much greater potential than its critics think, and much more disruption than its advocates admit. By definition, a global economy is as big as it can get. This

Table 1.4 World's 10 Largest Corporate Giants

Rank	Company Name	Headquarters	Age (Years)	Number of Employees
1	Apple	United States	41	66,000
2	Alphabet	United States	2	69,953
3	Microsoft	United States	42	114,000
4	Berkshire Hathaway	United States	128	360,000
5	Exxon Mobil	United States	135	73,500
6	Amazon	United States	22	222,400
7	Facebook	United States	13	15,724
8	Johnson & Johnson	United States	131	128,000
9	General Electric	United States	139	333,000
10	China Mobile	China	20	438,645

Source: Alex Gray, "These Are the World's 10 Biggest Corporate Giants," *We Forum*, https://www.weforum.org/agenda/2017/01/worlds-biggest-corporate-giants/ (accessed July 31, 2019).

means that the scale of both the opportunity and the consequences are at an apex."[55] In responding to this powerful situation, companies around the world are increasingly implementing programs and practices that strive to achieve a balance between economic responsibilities and other social responsibilities. Nestlé, a global foods manufacturer and marketer, published the Nestlé Corporate Business Principles in 1998 and has continually revised them. These principles serve as a management tool for decision-making at Nestlé and have been translated into over 50 languages. The updated principles are consistent with the Global Compact, an accord by the United Nations that covers environmental standards, human rights, and labor conditions.[56] We explore the global context of social responsibility more fully throughout this book.

In most developed countries, social responsibility involves stakeholder accountability and the financial, legal, ethical, and philanthropic dimensions discussed earlier in the chapter. However, a key question for implementing social responsibility on a global scale is: Who decides on these responsibilities? Many executives and managers face the challenge of doing business in diverse countries while attempting to maintain their employers' corporate culture and satisfy their expectations. Some companies have adopted an approach in which broad corporate standards can be adapted at a local level. For example, a corporate goal of demonstrating environmental leadership could be met in a number of different ways, depending on local conditions and needs. The Coca-Cola Company releases sustainability and social responsibility reports for each region in which it conducts business. In Eurasia and Africa, the company highlights initiatives and progress achieved regarding women's empowerment, water conservation, and improvement of communities. In Greece, the company contributed toward reforestation and to active lifestyles for youth in the Netherlands. While some of the sustainability and social responsibility initiatives are similar among countries, Coca-Cola's focus on each individual region allows them to make the most relevant contributions to their stakeholders.[57]

Global social responsibility also involves the confluence of government, business, trade associations, and other groups. For example, countries that belong to the Asia-Pacific Economic Cooperation (APEC) are responsible for half the world's annual production and trade volume. As APEC works to reduce trade barriers and tariffs, it has also developed meaningful projects in the areas of sustainable development, clean technologies, workplace safety, management of human resources, and the health of the marine environment. This powerful trade group has demonstrated that financial, social, and ethical concerns can be tackled simultaneously.[58] Like APEC, other trade groups are also exploring ways to enhance economic productivity within the context of legal, ethical, and philanthropic responsibilities.

Another trend involves business leaders becoming so-called cosmopolitan citizens by simultaneously harnessing their leadership skills, worldwide business connections, access to funds, and beliefs about human and social rights. Bill Gates, the cofounder of Microsoft, is no longer active day to day in the company, as he and his wife spearhead the Bill and Melinda Gates Foundation to tackle AIDS, poverty, malaria, and the need for educational resources. Golfer Jack Nicklaus and his business partner, Jack Milstein, designed a line of golf balls whose proceeds are designated to children's health care.[59] SurveyMonkey has a platform called SurveyMonkey Contribute that allows people to earn rewards for taking surveys. Every week, for each survey completed, SurveyMonkey will donate to a participating charity of the survey taker's choice.[60] Patagonia donates 1 percent of its profits to environmental organizations. These business leaders are acting as agents to ensure that the economic promises of globalization are met with true concern for social and environmental considerations. In many cases, such efforts supplant those historically associated with government responsibility and programs.[61]

In sum, progressive global businesses and executives recognize the shared bottom line that results from the partnership among businesses, communities, government, customers, and the natural environment. In a Nielsen survey of more than 28,000 citizens in 56 countries, 76 percent of the respondents indicated that they consult others online regarding the social responsibility of companies before they make a purchase. The top three issues that are most important to consumers include environmental sustainability, advancements in science, technology, engineering, mathematics (STEM) education, and relieving hunger and poverty.[62] Thus, our concept of social responsibility is applicable to businesses around the world, although adaptations of implementation and other details on the local level are definitely required. In companies around the world, there is also the recognition of a relationship between strategic social responsibility and benefits to society and organizational performance.

Benefits of Social Responsibility

The importance of social responsibility initiatives in enhancing stakeholder relationships, improving performance, and creating other benefits has been debated from many perspectives.[63] Many business managers view such programs as costly activities that provide rewards only to society, at the expense of their company's bottom line. Another view holds that some costs of social responsibility can be recovered through improved performance. If social responsibility is strategic and aligned with a firm's mission and values, then improved performance can be achieved. It is hard to measure the reputation of a firm, but it is important to build trust and achieve success. Moreover, ample research evidence demonstrates that companies which implement strategic social responsibility programs are more profitable.

Some of the specific benefits include increased efficiency in daily operations, greater employee commitment, higher product quality, improved decision-making, and increased customer loyalty, as well as improved financial performance. In short, companies that establish a reputation for trust, fairness, and integrity develop a valuable resource advantage that fosters success, which then translates to greater financial performance (see Figure 1.3). This section provides evidence that resources invested in social responsibility programs reap positive outcomes for both organizations and their stakeholders.

Figure 1.3 The Role of Social Responsibility in Performance

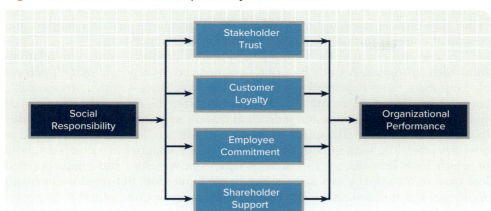

Trust

Trust is the glue that holds organizations together and allows them to focus on efficiency, productivity, and profits. According to Stephen R. Covey, author of *The 7 Habits of Highly Effective People*, "Trust lies at the very core of effective human interactions. Compelling trust is the highest form of human motivation. It brings out the very best in people, but it takes time and patience, and it doesn't preclude the necessity to train and develop people so their competency can rise to that level of trust." When trust is low, organizations decay and relationships deteriorate, resulting in infighting, playing politics within the organization, and general inefficiency. Employee commitment to the organization declines, product quality suffers, employee turnover skyrockets, and customers turn to more trustworthy competitors.[64] Any stakeholder that loses trust can create a missing link necessary for success.

In a trusting work environment, however, employees can reasonably expect to be treated with respect and consideration by both their peers and their superiors. They are also more willing to rely and act on the decisions and actions of their coworkers. Thus, trusting relationships between managers and their subordinates and among peers contribute to greater decision-making efficiency. Research by the Ethics & Compliance Initiative indicates that this trust is pivotal for supporting an ethical climate. Employees of an organization with a strong ethical culture are much more likely to report misconduct but also much less likely to observe misconduct than employees in firms with a weak ethical culture.[65] Table 1.5 shows

Table 1.5 Indicators of Support, Trust, and Transparency

Employees believe that top management is open and honest.
Employees feel that they can openly disagree with their supervisor or raise issues of concern without fear of retaliation.
Managers talk about values frequently and make them a regular and public part of business decision-making.
Supervisors care about their employees as people.
Top managers do the right thing, even if it means that the company loses money, business, and/or clients.

Source: Ethics & Compliance Initiative, "Building Companies Where Values and Ethical Conduct Matter," https://43wli92bfqd835mbif2ms9qz-wpengine.netdna-ssl.com/wp-content/uploads/2018/10/Q3GBESFinal.pdf (accessed July 31, 2019).

five indicators of trust, support, and transparency that have a strong impact on whether employees will report ethical issues. As the table demonstrates, a key factor that inspires trust and transparency in organizations involves support and consistent communication from senior leadership and supervisors.

Trust is also essential for a company to maintain positive long-term relationships with customers. A study by Cone Communications reported that 42 percent of consumers have boycotted companies that have demonstrated irresponsible behavior in the last 12 months.[66] For example, after the *Deepwater Horizon* oil spill in 2010, certain groups and individual citizens aggressively boycotted BP due to the vast environmental damage in the Gulf of Mexico. Stakeholders engaged in boycotts often lose faith in both the competence and integrity of a company, both of which have been shown to influence trust. Communities and regulators that lose trust in a company can damage the firm's reputation and relationships with additional stakeholders, including shareholders, investors, and others.[67]

Customer Loyalty

The prevailing business philosophy about customer relationships is that a company should strive to market products that satisfy customers' needs through a coordinated effort that also allows the company to achieve its own objectives. It is well accepted that customer satisfaction is one of the most important factors for business success. Although companies must continue to develop and adapt products to keep pace with consumers' changing desires, it is also crucial to develop long-term relationships with customers. Relationships built on mutual respect and cooperation facilitate the repeat purchases that are essential for success. By focusing on customer satisfaction, a business can continually strengthen its customers' trust in the company, and as their confidence grows, this in turn increases the firm's understanding of their requirements.

In a Cone survey of consumer attitudes, 89 percent of consumers indicated that they would be likely to switch to brands associated with a good cause if price and quality were equal. These results show that consumers take for granted that they can buy high-quality products at low prices; therefore, companies need to stand out as doing something—something that demonstrates their commitment to society.[68] A study by Harris Interactive Inc. and the Reputation Institute reported that one-quarter of the respondents had boycotted a firm's products or lobbied others to do so when they did not agree with the firm's policies or activities.[69] Another way of looking at these results is that irresponsible behavior could trigger disloyalty and refusals to buy, whereas good social responsibility initiatives could draw customers to a company's products. For example, many firms use cause-related marketing programs to donate part of a product's sales revenue to a charity that is meaningful to the product's target market. Among the best-known cause-related marketing programs is Avon's "pink ribbon."

Employee Commitment

Employee commitment stems from employees who are empowered with training and autonomy. Sir Richard Branson, founder of the Virgin Group, has one of the most committed groups of employees in business for these reasons, as well as many others. He has created a culture wherein he personally asks employees for their input, writes their ideas down, and incorporates them when relevant. He is a very visible and approachable authority and inspires a "passion of commitment" for customer service. Virgin Airlines is ranked as the highest in quality for domestic airlines. In the end, empowered employees keep customers happy and coming back for more.[70] For instance, service quality is positively related to employee loyalty. This, in turn, leads to higher customer satisfaction and customer loyalty.[71]

Evidence also suggests that CSR initiatives are a good way to retain and attract employees.[72]

When companies fail to provide value for their employees, loyalty and commitment suffer. One survey by Gallup found relatively low levels of employee loyalty and commitment worldwide. The study, which surveyed thousands of employees in 142 countries, found that only 13 percent of workers indicated feeling engaged in their jobs.[73] Employees spend many of their waking hours at work; thus, an organization's commitment to goodwill and respect of its employees usually results in increased employee loyalty and support of the company's objectives. Academic research on employee commitment

has highlighted the importance of communicating and implementing CSR from a values perspective, not a compliance mandate. Employee commitment is also enhanced when social responsibility principles are integrated into business processes and practices and not just viewed as window dressing or a simple add-on to corporate strategy.[74]

Shareholder Support

Investors look at a corporation's bottom line for profits or the potential for increased stock prices. To be successful, relationships with stockholders and other investors must rest on dependability, trust, and commitment. But investors also look for potential cracks or flaws in a company's performance. Companies perceived by their employees as having a high degree of honesty and integrity had an average three-year total return to shareholders of 101 percent, whereas companies perceived as having a low degree of honesty and integrity had a three-year total return to shareholders of just 69 percent.[75] After hackers broke into Target's databases and stole customers' credit card numbers and other information, the company's stock fell 46 percent.[76] Target has been criticized for its lack of sufficient internal controls.

Many shareholders are also concerned about the reputation of companies in which they invest. Investors have even been known to avoid buying the stock of firms they view as irresponsible. For example, Warren Buffett sold 25 percent of his holdings in General Motors (GM) after a series of recalls was initiated following a federal investigation. The investigation concluded that the company was responsible for several injuries and deaths resulting from negligence of a faulty ignition switch.[77] Many socially responsible mutual funds and asset management firms are available to help concerned investors purchase stock in responsible companies. These investors recognize that corporate responsibility is the foundation for efficiency, productivity, and profits. In contrast, investors know that fines or negative publicity can decrease a company's stock price, customer loyalty, and long-term viability. Consequently, many chief executives spend a great deal of time communicating with investors about their firms' reputations and financial performance and trying to attract them to their stock.

The issue of drawing and retaining investors is critical for CEOs, as roughly 50 percent of investors sell their stock in companies within one year, and the average household replaces 80 percent of its common stock portfolio each year.[78] This focus on short-term gains subjects corporate managers to tremendous pressure to boost short-term earnings, often at the expense of long-term strategic plans, including those needed to fulfill strategic social responsibility goals. The resulting pressure for short-term gains deprives corporations of stable capital and forces decision-makers into a "quarterly" mentality.

Conversely, those shareholders willing to hold onto their investments for lengthy periods are more willing to sacrifice short-term gains for long-term income. Attracting these long-term investors shields companies from the vagaries of the stock market and gives them flexibility and stability in long-term strategic planning. In the aftermath of the Enron scandal and other significant scandals, as listed in Table 1.6, public trust and confidence in financial audits and published financial statements were severely shaken.

Membership in grassroots investment clubs declined, retail stock investments declined, and investors called for increased transparency in company operations and reports.[79] Gaining and retaining investors' trust and confidence are vital for sustaining a firm's financial stability, as well as the stability of entire market economies.

The Bottom Line: Profits

Social responsibility is positively associated with return on investment, return on assets, and sales growth.[80] A company cannot be socially responsible and nurture and develop an ethical organizational culture continuously unless it has achieved financial performance in terms of profits.

Businesses with greater resources—regardless of their staff size—have the ability to promote their social responsibility along with serving their customers, valuing their employees, and establishing trust with the public. As mentioned before, the stock returns of the world's most ethical companies are often higher than that of companies listed on the S&P 500. Many studies have identified a positive relationship between social responsibility and financial performance.[81] For example, a survey of the 500 largest public corporations in the United States found that those that commit to responsible behavior and emphasize compliance with codes of conduct show better financial performance.[82] A managerial focus on stakeholder interests can affect financial performance, although the relationships between stakeholders and financial performance vary and are very complex.[83] A meta-analysis of 25 years of research identified 33 studies (63 percent)

Table 1.6 Top 10 Corporate Scandals

Rank	Company Name	Year	Type of Scandal
1	Enron	2001	Fraudulent financial reporting
2	Volkswagen	2015	Emissions scandal
3	Lehman Brothers	2008	Subprime mortgage crisis
4	Uber	2017	Culture crisis
5	Apple	2017	Batterygate
6	BP	2010	*Deepwater Horizon* oil spill
7	Facebook	2013–2016	Privacy breach and dubious targeted ad campaigns
8	Valeant Pharmaceuticals	2015	Drug price inflation
9	Kobe Steel	2017	Falsified data on product quality
10	Equifax	2017	Security breach

Source: Will Hall-Smith, "Top 10 Biggest Corporate Scandals and How They Affected Share Prices," *IG*, https://www. ig.com/no/tradingstrategier/top-10-biggest-corporate-scandals-and-how-they-affected-share-pr-181031 (accessed July 31, 2019).

demonstrating a positive relationship between corporate social performance and corporate financial performance, 5 studies (about 10 percent) indicating a negative relationship, and 14 studies (27 percent) yielding an inconclusive result or no relationship.[84] Research on the effects of legal infractions suggests that the negative effect of misconduct does not appear until the third year following a conviction, with multiple convictions being more harmful than a single one.[85]

In summary, a company with strong efforts and results in social responsibility is generally not penalized by market forces, including the intention of consumers to purchase the firm's products. Social responsibility efforts and performance serve as a reputational lever and resource advantage that managers may use to influence and cultivate stakeholders as partners. A high-performing company may also receive endorsements from governmental officials or other influential groups, and these are more believable than company messages. A company with a strong social responsibility orientation often becomes quite proactive in managing and changing conditions that yield economic benefits, including avoiding litigation and increased regulation. Finally, corporate social performance and corporate financial performance are positively correlated. These findings subjugate the belief that social responsibility is just a "cost factor" for business and has no real benefits to the firm.[86]

National Economy

An often-asked question is whether business conduct has any bearing on a nation's overall economic performance. Many economists have wondered why some market-based economies are productive and provide a high standard of living for their citizens, whereas other market-based economies lack the kinds of social institutions that foster productivity and economic growth. Perhaps a society's economic problems can be explained by a lack of social responsibility. Trust stems from principles of morality and serves as an important "lubricant of the social system."[87] Many descriptions of market economies fail to take into account the role of such institutions as family, education, and social systems in explaining standards of living and economic success. Perhaps some countries do a better job than others of developing economically and socially because of the social structure of their economic relationships.

Social institutions, particularly those that promote trust, are important for the economic well-being of a society.[88] Society has become economically successful over time "because of the underlying institutional framework persistently reinforcing incentives for organizations to engage in productive activity."[89] In some developing countries, opportunities for political and economic development have been stifled by activities that promote monopolies, graft, and corruption and by restrictions on opportunities to advance individual, as well as collective, well-being. As found in Table 1.7, L. E. Harrison offers four fundamental factors that promote economic well-being: "(1) The degree of identification with others in a

Table 1.7 Fundamental Factors That Promote Economic Well-Being

Four Fundamental Factors That Promote Economic Well-Being
Factor 1   The degree of identification with others in a society—the radius of trust or the sense of community
Factor 2   The rigor of the ethical system
Factor 3   The way that authority is exercised within the society
Factor 4   Attitudes about work, innovation, saving, and profit

Source: Lawrence E. Harrison, *Who Prospers? How Cultural Values Shape Economic and Political Success* (New York: Basic Books, 1992).

society—the radius of trust, or the sense of community; (2) the rigor of the ethical system; (3) the way authority is exercised within the society; and (4) attitudes about work, innovation, saving, and profit."[90]

Countries with institutions based on strong trust foster a productivity-enhancing environment because they have ethical systems in place that reduce transaction costs and make competitive processes more efficient and effective. In market-based systems with a great degree of trust, such as Australia, Canada, Germany, the Netherlands, and the United Kingdom, highly successful enterprises can develop through a spirit of cooperation and ease in conducting business.[91]

Superior financial performance at the firm level within a society is measured as profits, earnings per share, return on investment, and capital appreciation. Businesses must achieve a certain level of financial performance to survive and reinvest in the various institutions in society that provide support. However, at the institutional or societal level, a key factor distinguishing societies with high standards of living from those with lower standards of living is whether the institutions within the society are generally trustworthy. The challenge is to articulate the process by which institutions that support social responsibility can contribute to superior, firm-level financial performance.[92]

A comparison of countries that have high levels of corruption and underdeveloped social institutions with countries that have low levels of corruption reveals differences in the economic well-being of the country's citizens. Transparency International, an organization discussed earlier, publishes an annual report on global corruption that emphasizes the effects of corruption on the business and social sectors. Table 1.8 lists the countries with the most- and least-corrupt public sectors, as perceived by Transparency International. As stated several times in this chapter, conducting business in an ethical and responsible manner generates trust and leads to relationships that promote higher productivity and a positive cycle of effects.[93]

Framework for Studying Social Responsibility

The framework that we have developed for this text is designed to help you understand how businesses fulfill social expectations. It begins with the social responsibility philosophy, includes the four levels of social responsibilities, involves many types of stakeholders, and ultimately results in both short- and long-term performance benefits. As discussed earlier, social responsibility must have the support of top management—both in words and deeds—before it can become

Table 1.8 Perceptions of Countries as Least/Most Corrupt

Least Corrupt Countries			Most Corrupt Countries		
Rank	Country	CPI Score	Rank	Country	CPI Score
1	Denmark	88	180	Somalia	10
2	New Zealand	87	179	Syria	13
3	Finland	85	178	South Sudan	13
3	Singapore	85	177	Yemen	14
3	Sweden	85	176	North Korea	14
3	Switzerland	85	172	Sudan	16

Note: Corruption Perceptions Index (CPI) score relates to perceptions of the degree of public-sector corruption as seen by businesspeople and country analysts and ranges between 10 (highly clear) and 0 (highly corrupt).

Source: Transparency International, *Corruption Perceptions Index 2018,* https://www.transparency.org/cpi2018 (accessed August 14, 2019).

an organizational reality. Like many organizations, Cummins Engine Company has faced a number of challenges over the past several decades. Cummins is currently the world leader in the design and manufacture of diesel engines and was the largest employer in Columbus, Indiana, for many years. Cummins's drive to build positive relationships with employees, customers, and community led *Business Ethics* to rank the firm on its list of the "100 Best Corporate Citizens." The company received the highest possible rating for their corporate governance practices from Governance Metrics International (GMI), even during the global recession of 2009. In addition, *Ethisphere* magazine has named the company as one of the "World's Most Ethical Companies" for 12 years in a row.[94]

Once the social responsibility philosophy is accepted, the four aspects of CSR are defined, implemented, and refined through programs that incorporate stakeholder input and feedback. Cummins, like other companies, is aware of the potential costs associated with addressing social responsibility issues and stakeholder requirements. For example, as part of its ethics and compliance program, Cummins discloses its tax strategy, which is to fully comply with tax law in all jurisdictions in which it operates. The strategy also includes the deliberate avoidance of transactions that are primarily designed to reap a tax advantage.[95] When social responsibility programs are put into action, they have both immediate and delayed outcomes.

Figure 1.4 depicts how the chapters of this book fit into our framework. This framework begins with a look at the importance of working with stakeholders to achieve social responsibility objectives. It also includes an examination of the influence on business decisions and actions of the legal, regulatory, and political environment; business ethics; and corporate governance. The remaining chapters of the book explore the responsibilities associated with specific stakeholders and

Figure 1.4 An Overview of This Book

issues that confront business decision-makers today, including the process of implementing a social responsibility audit.

Strategic Management of Stakeholder Relationships

Social responsibility is grounded in effective and mutually beneficial relationships with customers, employees, investors, competitors, government, the community, and others who have a stake in the company. Increasingly, companies are recognizing that these constituents both affect and are affected by their actions. For this reason, many companies attempt to address the concerns of stakeholder groups, recognizing that failure to do so can have serious long-term consequences. For example, the Better Business Bureau of the Alaska, Oregon, and Western Washington region revoked the membership of 12 businesses in a period of three months for not meeting the organization's standards.[96] Chapter 2 examines the types of stakeholders and their attributes, how stakeholders become influential, and the processes for integrating and managing stakeholders' influence on a firm. It also examines the impact of corporate reputation and crisis situations on stakeholder relationships.

Corporate Governance

Because both daily and strategic decisions affect a variety of stakeholders, companies must maintain a governance structure to ensure proper control of their actions and assign responsibility for those actions. In Chapter 3, we define corporate governance and discuss its role in achieving strategic social responsibility. Key governance issues addressed include the rights of shareholders, the accountability of top management for corporate actions, executive compensation, and strategic-level processes for ensuring that financial, legal, ethical, and philanthropic responsibilities are satisfied.

Legal, Regulatory, and Political Issues

In Chapters 4 and 5, we explore the complex relationship between business and government. Every business must be aware of and abide by the laws and regulations that dictate acceptable business conduct. These chapters also examine how business can influence government by participating in the public policy process. A strategic approach for legal compliance is also provided.

Business Ethics and Strategic Approaches to Improving Ethical Behavior

Because individual values are a component of organizational conduct, these findings raise concerns about the ethics of future business leaders. Chapters 6 and 7 are devoted to exploring the role of ethics in business decision-making. These chapters explore business responsibilities that go beyond the conduct that is legally prescribed. We examine the factors that influence ethical decision-making and consider how companies can apply this understanding to increase their ethical conduct. We also examine ethical leadership and how it contributes to an ethical corporate culture.

Employee Relations

In today's business environment, most organizations want to build long-term relationships with a variety of stakeholders, but particularly with employees—the focus of Chapter 8. Employees today want fair treatment, excellent compensation and benefits, and assistance in balancing work and family obligations. This is increasingly important, as employee privacy issues have become a major concern in recent years. Raytheon developed a computer program called SilentRunner that can detect patterns of data activity that may reflect employee fraud, insider trading, espionage, or other unauthorized activity.[97] Critics, however, question whether the use of such software contributes to an environment of trust and commitment. Research has shown that committed and satisfied employees are more productive, serve customers better, and are less likely to leave their employers. These benefits are important to successful business performance, but organizations must be proactive in their human resources programs if they are to receive them.

Consumer Relations

Chapter 9 explores companies' relationships with consumers or consumer relations. This constituency is part of a firm's primary stakeholder group, and there are a number of financial, legal, ethical, and philanthropic responsibilities that companies must address. This chapter, therefore, considers the obligations that companies have toward their customers, including health and safety issues, honesty in marketing, consumer rights, and related responsibilities.

Community and Philanthropy

Chapter 10 examines community relations and strategic philanthropy, which is the synergistic use of organizational core competencies and resources to address key stakeholders' interests and to achieve both organizational and social benefits. Whereas traditional benevolent philanthropy involves donating a percentage of sales to social causes, a strategic approach aligns employees and organizational resources and expertise with the needs and concerns of stakeholders, especially the community. Strategic philanthropy involves both financial and nonfinancial contributions (employee time, goods and services, technology and equipment, and facilities) to stakeholders and reaps benefits for the community and company.

Technology Issues

In Chapter 11, we examine the issues that arise as a result of enhanced technology in the business environment, including the effects of new technology on privacy, intellectual property, and health. We also discuss the rise of artificial intelligence and its enablers, such as big data, blockchain, drones, and robotics. The strategic direction for technology depends on government, as well as on a business's ability to plan the implementation of new technology and to assess the influence of that technology on society.

Thanks to the internet and other technological advances, we can communicate faster than ever before, find information about just about anything, and live longer, healthier lives. However, not all of the changes that occur as a result of new technologies are positive. For example, because shopping via the internet does not require a signature to verify transactions, online credit card fraud is significantly greater than fraud through mail-order catalogs and traditional storefront retailers. A major identity theft ring in New York affected thousands of people. Members of the theft ring illegally obtained the credit records of consumers and then sold them to criminals for about $60 per record. The criminals used the credit records to obtain loans, drain bank accounts, and perform other fraudulent activities.[98]

Sustainability Issues

In Chapter 12, we dedicate the entire content to issues of sustainability, including the interdependent nature of economic development, social development, and environmental impact. "Sustainability" has become a watchword in business and community circles, and this chapter explores the ways in which companies define and develop goals, implement programs, and contribute to sustainability concerns. The Dow Jones Sustainability Index (DJSI) makes an annual assessment of companies' economic, environmental, and social performance based on more than 50 general and industry-specific criteria. The DJSI includes 2,500 companies from 20 countries and is used by investors who prefer to make financial investments in companies engaged in socially responsible and sustainable practices.[99]

Global Social Responsibility

Finally, for many businesses to remain competitive, they must evolve continually to reach global markets and anticipate emerging world trends. Chapter 13 delves into the complex and intriguing nature of social responsibility in a global economy. Building on key concepts discussed throughout this book, we examine the forces that make overseas business plans and activities of paramount concern to host countries, local and national governments, NGOs, and other members of society. The chapter covers a wide range of challenges and opportunities, such as outsourcing, environmental protection, living wages, labor standards, and trade restrictions.

We hope that this framework provides you with a way of understanding the range of concepts, ideas, and practices that are involved in an effective social responsibility initiative. So that you can learn more about the practices of specific companies, a number of cases are provided at the end of the book. In addition, every chapter includes an opening vignette and other examples that shed more light on how social responsibility works in today's businesses. Every chapter also includes a real-life scenario entitled "What Would You Do?" a contemporary debate issue, and another exercise to help you apply concepts and examine your own decision-making process. As you will soon see, the concept of social responsibility is both exciting and controversial; it is in a constant state of development—just like all important business concepts and practices. A recent survey of thought leaders in the area of social responsibility found that a majority believes that social responsibility has made steady progress into conventional business thinking. Much like the social responsibility continuum introduced in this chapter, the thought leaders described several stages of commitment to CSR. These stages range from shallow, where companies are concerned about responding to complaints, to deep, where companies are founded on a business model of improving social or environmental circumstances. Many companies fall somewhere in between, with a focus on complying with new standards and surviving in a climate of increasing social responsibility expectations.[100] We encourage you to draw on current news events and your own experiences to understand social responsibility and the challenges and opportunities that it poses for your career, profession, role as a consumer, and leadership approach, as well as the business world.

Earth in the Balance

Sustainable Fashion Is the Dress Code at Evrnu

The apparel industry is one of the worst polluters of our environment. According to Evrnu, an organization that has invested in regenerative fiber technology, "the clothing we wear is contributing to some of the world's worst environmental health issues." The cofounder and CEO of Evrnu, Stacy Flynn, realized that she was playing a role in the pollution of our environment when she and a coworker were on a business trip to China. She stepped out of the car and could barely see through the smog that was being generated by the country's local textile industry. Instead of doing nothing, Flynn started working on producing recycled fibers and collaborating with apparel makers to turn textile waste into sustainable pieces. Not only is the creation of clothing creating problems for the health of our environment, what our clothing is made of is affecting the world we live in.

According to the World Wildlife Fund, it takes about 2,700 liters of water—equal to more than 700 gallons—to produce the cotton that is needed to make one T-shirt. Evrnu is stepping up to change these numbers. More global organizations like IKEA also have plans to switch to 100% Better Cotton. Another problem with human clothing is the amount of plastic that it contains. Polyester, acrylic, nylon, and Spandex are all plastics that are used to make clothing. Even cotton isn't totally free from harmful products and contains insecticides a lot of the time. It just takes one person to notice the impact people have on the environment and make changes to the way we go about creating our products.

When looking at textile waste, the U.S. Environmental Protection Agency (EPA) found that from the year 2003 to the year 2013, the generation of textile and apparel waste increased by 43 percent, which is more than double the growth of other waste categories. There are two reasons why this is happening. The apparel industry is rapidly producing more styles of clothing at faster rates and cheaper prices. This is called "fast fashion," and in turn, this is driving the high clothing disposal rate. While the rate of growth is increasing, the rate of recycling and reuse is staying stagnant. This is what creates enormous amounts of textile waste and why the percentage of waste increase is so exorbitant. Textile-sorting technologies and recycling convenience for consumers are projected to improve recycling rates. The Council for Textile Recycling states that the average US citizen throws away 70 pounds of clothing a year, while donating or recycling only 12 pounds. If recycling textiles were more convenient, this number could be dramatically lowered. After clothing is donated or recycled, 45 percent is reused and recycled, 30 percent is recycled and converted into cleaning rags, and 20 percent is recycled into fiber.

The answer to the textile waste problem is more recycling. There are a couple of companies that have answers as to what should be done with clothes that thrown away or donated. Retailers like American Eagle Outfitters and H&M offer in-store clothing recycling bins to collect clothing and accessories from any brand. Patagonia, another retailer that encourages recycling, asks its loyal customer base to buy less, not more. It encourages its customers to bring their clothes in for repair rather than replacing them immediately.

Reducing consumption creates the most positive impact of all. Patagonia has a website called Worn Wear, which is where customers can trade in their used Patagonia gear at any retail location and receive a credit toward another new or used Patagonia garment. If the gear is not in good enough condition for resale, the company recycles the textiles for other uses. Patagonia urges its customers to make recycling less of a hassle by doing it when they are already running errands. This company is doing everything it can to curb the growth of textile waste. If more organizations were to take on efforts like this, it would be fascinating to see the impact.

Sources: Heather Green, "Patagonia's Ongoing Recycling Program," *Bloomberg*, November 5, 2018, www.bloomberg.com/news/articles/2008-11-05/patagonias-ongoing-recycling-programbusinessweek-business-news-stock-market-and-financial-advice (accessed October 2, 2018); Anne Johnson and Marisa Adler, "Textile Waste," *Recycle.com*, February 23, 2017, recycle.com/textile-recycling/ (accessed October 2, 2018); Valerie Vande Panne, "Want Sustainable Clothing? It's Time to Meet Regenerative Fiber," *EcoWatch*, March 4, 2018, www.ecowatch.com/fast-fashion-environmental-impact-2541799617.html (accessed October 2, 2018); "How to Recycle Clothing & Accessories," *Earth911.com*, earth911.com/recycling-guide/how-to-recycle-clothing-accessories/ (accessed October 2, 2018); World Wildlife Fund, "The Impact of a Cotton T-Shirt," January 16, 2013, www.worldwildlife.org/stories/the-impact-of-a-cotton-t-shirt (accessed October 2, 2019); Evrnu, "The Problem: Textile Waste," https://www.evrnu.com/ (accessed October 2, 2018); "The Lifecycle of Secondhand Clothing," Council for Textile Recycling, weardonaterecycle.org/about/clothing-life-cycle.html (accessed October 2, 2018); "Why Recycle Shoes and Clothing?" World Wear Project, worldwearproject.com/about-us/global-responsibility (accessed October 2, 2018).

Summary

The term *social responsibility* came into widespread use during the last several decades, but there remains some confusion over the term's exact meaning. This text defines social responsibility as the adoption by a business of a strategic focus for fulfilling the economic, legal, ethical, and philanthropic responsibilities expected of it by its stakeholders.

All types of businesses can implement social responsibility initiatives to further their relationships with their customers, their employees, and the community at large. Although the efforts of large corporations usually receive the most attention, the actions of small businesses may have a greater impact on local communities.

The definition of social responsibility involves the extent to which a firm embraces the social responsibility philosophy and follows through with the implementation of initiatives. Seven main areas of social responsibility include social issues, consumer protection, sustainability, corporate governance, philanthropy, legal responsibilities, and employee well-being. Social responsibility must be fully valued and championed by top managers and given the same planning time, priority, and management attention as is given to any other company initiative.

Many people believe that businesses should accept and abide by four types of responsibilities: financial, legal, ethical, and philanthropic. Companies have a responsibility to be financially or economically viable so that they can provide a return on investment for their owners, create jobs for the community, and contribute goods and services to the economy. They are also expected to obey laws and regulations that specify what is responsible business conduct. "Business ethics" refers to the principles and standards that guide behavior in the world of business. Philanthropic activities promote human welfare or goodwill. These responsibilities can be viewed holistically, with all four related and integrated into a comprehensive approach. Social responsibility can also be expressed as a continuum. Because customers, employees, investors and shareholders, suppliers, governments, communities, and others have a stake in or claim on some aspect of a company's products, operations, markets, industry, and outcomes, they are known as "stakeholders." Adopting a stakeholder orientation is part of the social responsibility philosophy.

The influence of business has led many people to conclude that corporations should benefit their employees, their customers, their business partners, and their community as well as their shareholders. However, these responsibilities and expectations have changed over time. After World War II, many large U.S. firms dominated the global economy. Their power was largely mirrored by the autonomy of their top managers. Because of the relative lack of global competition and stockholder input during the 1950s and 1960s, there were few formal governance procedures to restrain management's actions. The stability experienced by midcentury firms dissolved in the economic turmoil of the 1970s and 1980s, leading companies to focus more on their core competencies and reduce their product diversity. The 1980s and 1990s brought a new focus on efficiency and productivity, which fostered a wave of downsizing and restructuring. Concern for corporate responsibilities was renewed in the 1990s. In the 1990s and beyond, the balance between the global market economy and an interest in social justice and cohesion best characterizes the intent and need for social responsibility. Despite major advances in the 1990s, the sheer number of corporate scandals at the beginning of the twenty-first century prompted a new era of social responsibility.

The increasing globalization of business has made social responsibility an international concern. In most developed countries, social responsibility involves economic, legal, ethical, and philanthropic responsibilities to a variety of stakeholders. Global social responsibility also involves responsibilities to a confluence of governments, businesses, trade associations, and other groups. Progressive global businesses recognize the shared bottom line that results from the partnership among businesses, communities, governments, and other stakeholders.

The importance of social responsibility initiatives in enhancing stakeholder relationships, improving performance, and creating other benefits has been debated from many perspectives. Many business managers view such programs as costly activities that provide rewards only to society, at the expense of their bottom line. Others hold that some costs of social responsibility can be recovered through improved performance. Although it is true that some aspects of social responsibility may not accrue directly to the bottom line, we believe that organizations benefit indirectly over the long run from these activities. Moreover, ample research and anecdotal evidence demonstrate that there are many rewards for companies that implement such programs.

The process of social responsibility begins with the social responsibility philosophy, includes the four responsibilities, involves many types of stakeholders, and ultimately results in both short- and long-term performance benefits. Once the social responsibility philosophy is accepted, the four types of responsibility are defined and implemented through programs that incorporate stakeholder input and feedback.

Responsible Business Debate

The Brand Name You Won't Forget: Brandless

Issue: *Can a company compete without a brand?*

When Tina Sharkey set out to build an online marketplace, she knew that it would be difficult to gain traction with consumers, especially in the early stages of the business. The majority of people go to their favorite grocery store, visit a big-box retailer, or simply use a website like Amazon to buy food, as well as household and personal items. Despite this, she recognized an opportunity to enter the "better for you" (BFY) market, targeting conscious millennials who wish to take care of their bodies with healthy, safe foods and products. It's been estimated that 77 percent of millennials don't want to use the same products their parents use. Sharkey recognized this point and built a clean, easy-to-use website called Brandless that sells all products at the same price. Brandless quickly drew in customers of all ages, selling the idea that people can buy high-quality products for low prices. The strategy was based on integrity and sustainability.

Tina Sharkey and her cofounder, Ido Leffler, began working on their idea for a BFY marketplace in 2014. They decided to differentiate themselves in a few key ways. First and most important, all their products had to be healthy. All Brandless foods are from non-genetically modified organisms and over 70 percent are organic. For beauty and personal care products, the company ensures that over 400 toxic ingredients are banned, including phthalates, sulfates, or anything artificial. Second, all

products are promoted as being free of any branding, as the name of the company would suggest. Sharkey estimates that customers are saving about 70 percent compared to national brands by shopping at Brandless, and the majority of those savings simply come from eliminating the manufacturers' branding and marketing expenses. Sharkey wanted to make shopping as simple as possible, so her third focus was to sell all the company's products for $3. When customers shop at Brandless, they don't have to consider prices because everything sells for a simple, low price. This strategy has allowed Sharkey and the Brandless brand name to differentiate themselves and attain positive media attention since the site launched in July 2017.

The Brandless website emphasizes the idea of community. In an interview with Medha Agarwal at Redpoint Ventures, Sharkey stated that Brandless is not an e-commerce company, but instead a community. She desires that her customers have trust in the "brand." She believes that brands should be about community, about "living more and branding less." The Brandless philosophy is that people should transact kindness and be transparent. Through this community lifestyle, Sharkey and her team at Brandless believe that people everywhere deserve better without it having to cost more. A visit to Whole Foods can be an expensive trip, and Sharkey understands that average Americans don't have the resources to shop at upscale grocery stores. As an entrepreneur, Sharkey is taking the initiative to be available to everyone. Instead of focusing on the strategy of serving only a certain type of customer or target market, Brandless is treating all people the same by doing what they do best—serving.

Sharkey and the team at Brandless want to live out the ideals that they are trying to create around the world. In her words, they want to "model the behavior that [they] want to see in the world." People come first for the community at Brandless. The company wants to have a relationship with their consumers by staying in constant contact with those that are a part of their community. Sharkey recently said, "We pay attention to what people buy and listen closely to what matters to them, and use that feedback to plan our collection." The Brandless organization is built around their customers, customers' feedback, and the interests of society in general.

There Are Two Sides to Every Issue

1. Brandless has become an antidote to an overcommercialized and expensive retail marketplace and has a great opportunity to set itself apart from other competitors.

2. In reality, Brandless is a brand name. Despite the company's intentions and core values, Brandless is still competing with traditional and popular retailers.

Sources: Agarwal, Medha, 2018, "A Conversation with Tina Sharkey, Co-founder and CEO of Brandless," *Medium*, https://medium.com/redpoint-ventures/a-conversation-with-tina-sharkey-co-founder-and-ceo-of-brandless-88efdb0abe2b (accessed September 19, 2018); Brandless, "Better Stuff, Fewer Dollars. It's That Simple." https://brandless.com/about, accessed September 27, 2018); Grisworld, Allison, 2017, "Hot New E-commerce Startup Brandless Is Totally Obsessed with Its Own Brand," *Quartz*, https://qz.com/1032202/tina-sharkeys-e-commerce-startup-brandless-is-totally-obsessed-with-its-own-brand/ (accessed August 20, 2019); McBride, Sarah, 2018, "This No-Brand Startup Won $240 Million to Fight Amazon on Price and Quality," *Bloomberg*, https://www.bloomberg.com/news/articles/2018-07-31/brandless-is-battling-amazon-with-240-million-from-softbank (accessed August 20, 2019); Zarya, Valentina, 2018, "Female Founders Got 2% of Venture Capital Dollars in 2017," *Fortune*, January 31, http://fortune.com/2018/01/31/female-founders-venture-capital-2017/ (accessed August 20, 2019).

Key Terms

artificial intelligence (p. 16)
blockchain (p. 17)
business ethics (p. 10)
code of conduct (p. 10)
common good (p. 5)
consumer protection laws (p. 5)
core competencies (p. 14)
corporate culture (p. 9)

corporate governance (p. 6)
employee well-being (p. 6)
interorganizational networks (p. 12)
legal responsibility (p. 6)
license to operate (p. 4)
mission statement (p. 8)
philanthropic activities (p. 11)

philanthropy (p. 6)
resource advantage theory (p. 11)
social responsibility (p. 7)
stakeholders (p. 12)
stakeholder orientation (p. 11)
sustainability (p. 6)
vision statement (p. 8)

Discussion Questions

1. Define social responsibility. How does this view of the role of business differ from your previous perceptions? How is it consistent with your attitudes and beliefs about business?

2. If a company is named to one of the "best in social responsibility" lists, what positive effects can they potentially reap? What are the possible costs or negative outcomes that may be associated with being named to one of these lists?

3. What historical trends have affected the social responsibilities of business? How have recent scandals affected the business climate, including any changes in responsibilities and expectations?

4. How would you respond to the statement that this chapter presents only the positive side of the argument that social responsibility results in improved organizational performance?

5. On the basis of the social responsibility model presented in this chapter, describe the philosophy, responsibilities, and stakeholders that make up a company's approach to social responsibility. What are the short- and long-term outcomes of this effort?

6. Consider the role that various business disciplines, including marketing, finance, accounting, and human resources, play in social responsibility. What specific views and philosophies do these disciplines bring to the implementation of social responsibility?

Experiential Exercise

Evaluate *Fortune* magazine's annual list of the most admired companies found on the magazine's website (fortune.com). These companies as a group have superior financial performance compared to other firms. Go to each company's website and try to assess its management commitment to the welfare of stakeholders. If any of the companies have experienced legal or ethical misconduct, explain how this may affect specific stakeholders. Rank the companies on the basis of the information available and your opinion on their fulfillment of social responsibility.

Two Sides to Tobacco: What Would You Do?

Jamie Ramos looked out her window at the early morning sky and gazed at the small crowd below. The words and pictures on their posters were pretty tame this time, she thought. The last protest group used pictures of tarred lungs, corpses, and other graphic photos to show the effects of smoking on a person's internal organs. Their words were also hateful—so much so that employees at the Unified Tobacco headquarters were afraid to walk in and out of the main building. Those who normally took smoking breaks on the back patio decided to skip them and eat something at the company-subsidized cafeteria instead.

By midday, Unified hired extra security to escort employees in and out of the building and to ensure that protestors followed the state guideline of staying at least 15 feet from the company's entrance. The media picked up on the story—and the photos—and it caused quite a stir in the national press. At least this protest group seemed fairly reasonable. Late yesterday, a state court had provided a reduced judgment to the family of a lifelong smoker, now deceased. This meant that Unified was going to owe millions less than originally expected. The length and stress of the lawsuit had taken its toll, especially on top management, although all employees were certainly affected. After two years of being battered in the media, learning of a huge settlement, and then continuing on with the appeals process, emotions were wearing thin under the brunt of the continued criticism.

Jamie wondered what this day would bring. As the manager of community relations, her job was to represent Unified in the community, manage the employee volunteer program, create a quarterly newsletter, serve as a liaison to the company's philanthropic foundation, develop solid relationships, and serve on various boards related to social welfare and community needs. The company's foundation donated nearly $1.5 million a year to charities and causes. Over one-quarter of its employees volunteered 10 hours a month in their communities.

Jamie reported to a vice president and was pleased with the career progress that she had made since graduating from college eight years earlier. Although some of her friends wondered out loud how she could work for a tobacco company, Jamie was steadfast in her belief that even a tobacco firm could contribute something meaningful to society. She had the chance to affect some of those contributions in her community relations role.

Jamie's phone rang and she took a call from her vice president. The vice president indicated that, although the protestors seemed relatively calm this time, he was not comfortable with their presence. Several employees had taped signs in office windows telling the protestors to "Go away." Other vice presidents had dropped by his office to discuss the protest and thought that the responsibility for handling these issues fell to his group. He went on to say that he needed Jamie's help, and the assistance of a few others, in formulating a plan to (1) deal with the protest today and (2) strengthen the strategy for communicating the company's message and goodwill in the future. Their meeting was slated to begin in one hour, so Jamie had some time to sketch out her recommendations on both issues. What would you do?

Strategic Management of Stakeholder Relationships

Whole Foods: Challenging the "Whole Paycheck" Reputation

In 1978, two entrepreneurs, John Mackey and Rene Hardy, began a challenging venture to create a company that incorporated the values of healthy living and conscious capitalism, all with a $45,000 loan. Their efforts led them to open a small natural foods store named SaferWay, founded in Austin, Texas, in 1980. The two founders had a difficult time beginning the company, and later they merged it with Clarksville Natural Grocery. Together, the two companies became Whole Foods, the world's largest retailer of organic and natural food and personal care products. Whole Foods has grown not only domestically, but also internationally, since its initial expansion in 1984.

The company's values involve meeting customer needs and demonstrating its commitment toward selling the highest-quality natural and organic products. Whole Foods also aims to create positive and ethical ongoing partnerships with suppliers, while simultaneously creating wealth through profits and growth and caring about the community and environment. In addition, the company aims to delight customers by promoting the health of all stakeholders through healthy eating education. Along with management striving to implement these core values, employees help to create this environment through daily interactions with customers. Employees are highly valued at Whole Foods and are labeled "team members" as a symbol of their empowerment through their everyday contributions.

Despite its success, the company has struggled to get rid of its "whole paycheck" reputation in recent years, such that many consumers viewed Whole Foods products as unaffordable. Even their 365 Everyday Value brand, which was the supposedly "generic" brand, failed to shake off this image. Due to the grocer's financial struggles, Amazon acquired Whole Foods in 2017 for $13.7 billion. Stakeholder hopes were high that Amazon would decrease prices on Whole Foods goods and effectively compete with stores like Sprouts Farmer's Market. Shortly after Amazon acquired Whole Foods, chief executive officer (CEO) John Mackey stated in an interview with Food Business News that he felt the "whole paycheck" reputation had "disappeared."

According to Gordon Haskett Research Advisors, prices on over 100 Whole Foods items have dropped less than 1.5 percent within the first year. Amazon has implemented discounts and deals on Whole Foods products for Amazon Prime members to continue to improve their reputation with stakeholders. Whole Foods dropped off of the Fortune 100 "Best Companies to Work For" list for the first time in 20 years, immediately after Amazon's acquisition, an indicator that the company has a lot of work ahead of it before it finishes improving its reputation. Whole Foods will continue to focus on all their important stakeholders, including consumers, employees, suppliers, and responsibility to investors. Now that the company is part of Amazon, it can play an important role in advancing online food retailing under the Amazon business model.[1]

Shutterstock/Y Photo Studio

Chapter Objectives

- Define stakeholders and understand their importance
- Distinguish between primary and secondary stakeholders
- Discuss the global nature of stakeholder relationships
- Consider the impact of reputation and crisis situations on social responsibility performance
- Examine the development of stakeholder relationships
- Explore how stakeholder relationships are integral to social responsibility

A s this example illustrates, most organizations have a number of constituents and a web of relationships that interface with society.

In this case, Amazon, the new owner of Whole Foods, faces the complex task of balancing the concerns of consumers, the public, environmental groups, and corporate culture. These stakeholders are increasingly expressing opinions and taking actions that have an effect on the industry's reputation, relationships, and products. Today, many organizations are learning to anticipate such issues and to address them in their strategies long before they become the subject of negative media stories.

In this chapter, we examine the concept of stakeholders and explore why these groups are important for today's businesses. First, we define stakeholders and examine primary, secondary, and global stakeholders. Then, we examine the concept of a stakeholder orientation to enhance social responsibility. Next, we consider the impact of corporate reputation and crisis situations on stakeholder relationships. Finally, we examine the development of stakeholder relationships implementing a stakeholder perspective and the link between stakeholder relationships and social responsibility.

Stakeholders Defined

In Chapter 1, we defined "stakeholders" as those people and groups to whom an organization is responsible—including customers, shareholders, employees, suppliers, governments, communities, and many others—because they have a "stake," or claim, in some aspect of a company's products, operations, markets, industry, or outcomes. These groups not only are influenced by businesses, but they also have the ability to influence businesses in return.

Responsibility issues, conflicts, and successes revolve around stakeholder relationships. Building effective relationships is considered one of the more important areas of business today. The stakeholder framework is recognized as a management theory that attempts to balance stakeholder interests. Issues related to indivisible resources and unequal levels of stakeholder influence and importance constrain managers' efforts to balance stakeholder interests.[2] A business exists because of relationships among employees, customers, shareholders or investors, suppliers, and managers that help them develop strategies to attain success. In addition, an organization usually has a governing authority, often called a "board of directors," which provides oversight and direction to make sure that the organization stays focused on objectives in an ethical, legal, and socially responsible manner. Corporate governance is discussed in Chapter 3. When misconduct is discovered in organizations, it is often found that in most instances, there is knowing cooperation or compliance that facilitates the acceptance and perpetuation of unethical conduct.[3] Therefore, relationships are associated not only with organizational success, but also with organizational failure to assume responsibility.

These perspectives take into account both market and nonmarket constituencies that may interact with a business and have some effect on the firm's policies and strategy.[4] Market constituencies are those that are directly involved and affected by the business purpose, including investors, employees, customers, and other business partners. Nonmarket constituencies include the general community, media, government, special-interest groups, and others who are not always directly tied to issues of profitability and performance.

The historical assumption that the foremost objective of business is profit maximization led to the belief that business is accountable primarily to shareholders and others involved in the market and economic aspects of an organization. Because shareholders and other investors provide the financial foundation for business and expect something in return, managers and executives naturally strive to maintain positive relationships with them.[5] In the latter half of the twentieth century, however, perceptions of business accountability evolved toward an expanded model of the role and responsibilities of business in society. The expansion included questions about the normative role of business, including: "What is the appropriate role for business to play in society?" and "Should profit be the sole objective of business?"[6]

Many businesspeople and scholars have questioned the role of social responsibility in business. Legal and economic responsibilities are generally accepted as the most important determinants of performance: "If this is well done," say classical economic theorists, "profits are maximized more or less continuously and firms carry out their major responsibilities to society."[7] Some economists believe that if companies address economic and legal issues, they are satisfying the demands of society and trying to anticipate and meet additional needs would be almost impossible. Milton Friedman has been quoted as saying that "the basic mission of business [is] thus to produce goods and services at a profit, and in doing this, business [is] making its maximum contribution to society and, in fact, being socially responsible."[8] Even with the business ethics scandals of the twenty-first century, Friedman suggests that, although individuals guilty of wrongdoing should be held accountable, the market is a better deterrent than new laws and regulations that discourage firms from wrongdoing and punish them for it.[9] Thus, he would diminish the role of stakeholders such as the government and employees in requiring that businesses demonstrate responsible and ethical behavior.

This form of capitalism has unfortunately been exported to many less-developed and developing countries without the appropriate concerns for ethics and social responsibility. Friedman's capitalism is a far cry from that of Adam Smith, one of the founders of capitalism. Smith created the concept of the invisible hand and spoke about self-interest; however, he went on to explain that this common good is associated with psychological motives and that each individual has to produce for the common good with values such as propriety, prudence, reason, sentiment, and "promoting the happiness of mankind."[10] These values could be associated with the needs and concerns of stakeholders.

In the twenty-first century, Friedman's form of capitalism is being replaced by Smith's original concept (what is now called **enlightened capitalism**), a notion of capitalism that reemphasizes stakeholder concerns and issues. The acceptance of enlightened capitalism may be occurring faster in developed countries than in those that are still developing. Theodore Levitt, a renowned business professor, once wrote that although profit is required for business, just as food is required for living, profit is not the purpose of business any more than food is the purpose of life.[11] Norman Bowie, a well-known philosopher, extended Levitt's sentiment by noting that focusing on profit alone can create an unfavorable paradox that causes a firm to fail to achieve its objectives. Bowie contends that when a business also cares about the well-being of stakeholders, it earns trust and cooperation that ultimately reduce costs and increase productivity.[12] This in turn results in the organization's increased profits and success.

Some critics of business believe there is a trade-off between profits and social responsibility. They believe that to increase profits, a firm must view social responsibility as a cost that reduces profits. However, there is much evidence that social responsibility is associated with increased profits. For example, 55 percent of adults worldwide are willing to pay more for goods from companies demonstrating social responsibility. Younger generations are more likely to factor social responsibility into purchases than older generations, which indicates that social responsibility will become even more important as time goes on. There is a trade-off for the costs of social responsibility, but the benefits could attract more customers and increase customer retention.[13] As mentioned in Chapter 1, the Ethisphere Institute has found that the world's most ethical companies outperform the companies on the Standard & Poor's (S&P) index. This clearly demonstrates that social responsibility decisions are good for business.

enlightened capitalism
a theory of capitalism originally proposed by Adam Smith as "promoting the happiness of mankind" that emphasizes stakeholder concerns and issues

Stakeholder Issues and Interaction

Stakeholders provide resources that are more or less critical to a firm's long-term success. These resources may be both tangible and intangible. Shareholders, for example, supply capital; suppliers offer material resources or intangible knowledge; employees and managers grant expertise, leadership, and commitment; customers generate revenue and provide loyalty and positive or negative word-of-mouth promotion; local communities provide infrastructure; and the media transmits positive or negative corporate images. When individual stakeholders share similar expectations about desirable business conduct, they may choose to establish or join formal communities that are dedicated to better defining and advocating these values and expectations. Stakeholders' ability to withdraw—or threaten to withdraw—these needed resources gives them power over businesses.[14]

New reforms to improve corporate accountability and transparency also suggest that stakeholders such as suppliers—including banks, law firms, and public accounting firms—can play a major role in fostering responsible decision-making. Stakeholders apply their values and standards to many diverse issues, such as working conditions, consumer rights, environmental conservation, product safety, and proper information disclosure. These are issues that may or may not directly affect an individual stakeholder's own welfare. We can assess the level of social responsibility that an organization bears by scrutinizing its efforts and communication on the issues of concern to its stakeholders. **Stakeholder engagement** refers to the process of involving stakeholders who may be affected by an organization's decisions or that may influence the content or implementation of the organization's decisions. Engagement with stakeholders takes place over a broad range of concerns and issues. Table 2.1 provides examples of common stakeholder issues, along with indicators of businesses' impacts on these issues.[15]

stakeholder engagement
the organizational process of involving stakeholders who may be affected by the decisions it makes or may influence the content and implementation of its decisions

Identifying Stakeholders

We can identify two types of stakeholders: primary and secondary. **Primary stakeholders** are those whose continued association is absolutely necessary for a firm's survival; these include employees, customers, suppliers, and shareholders, as well as the governments and communities that provide necessary infrastructure. After a tax reform bill passed in 2017, many large companies decided to reward stakeholders with bonuses or raises. For example, the cable company Cox Enterprises gave bonuses of $1,000 to $2,000 to most of their 60,000 employees to give back some of the savings that the 2017 tax reform provided. Initiatives that reward primary stakeholders can enhance employer-employee relationships, which we discuss in a later chapter.[16] Other primary stakeholders, such as customers, are directly affected by the quality of products and the integrity of communication and relationships. Shareholders depend on transparency regarding financial information, as well as forward-looking statements about sales and profits.

primary stakeholders
people or groups who are fundamental to a company's operations and survival; these include shareholders and investors, employees, customers, suppliers, and public stakeholders, such as government and the community

Secondary stakeholders do not typically engage in direct transactions with a company and thus are not essential for its survival; these include the media, trade associations, and special-interest groups. For example, the American Association of Retired People (AARP), a special-interest group, works to support the rights of retirees in areas such as healthcare benefits. Both primary and secondary stakeholders embrace specific values and standards that dictate what constitutes acceptable or unacceptable corporate behaviors. It is important for managers to recognize that primary groups may present more day-to-day concerns, but secondary groups cannot be ignored or given less consideration. Sometimes a secondary stakeholder, such as the media, can have more of an impact than a primary stakeholder.

secondary stakeholders
people or groups who do not typically engage in direct transactions with a company and thus are not essential for its survival; these include the media, trade associations, and special-interest groups

Table 2.1 Examples of Stakeholder Issues and Associated Measures of Corporate Impacts

Stakeholder Groups and Issues	Potential Indicators of Corporate Impact on These Issues
Employees	
1. Compensation and benefits	1. Average wage paid versus industry averages
2. Training and development	2. Changes in average training dollars spent per year per employee; resources for ethics training versus industry averages
3. Employee diversity	3. Percentages of employees from different genders and races, especially in leadership roles
4. Occupational health and safety	4. Standard injury rates and absentee rates
5. Communications with management	5. Availability of open-door policies or ombudsmen management
Customers	
1. Product safety and quality	1. Number of product recalls over time
2. Management of customers	2. Number of customer complaints and availability of complaint procedures to address them
3. Services to customers with disabilities	3. Availability and nature of measures taken to ensure services to customers with disabilities
Investors	
1. Transparency of shareholders	1. Availability of procedures to inform shareholders about corporate activities
2. Shareholder rights	2. Frequency and type of litigation involving violations of shareholder rights
Suppliers	
1. Encouraging suppliers in developing countries	1. Prices offered to suppliers in developed countries and developing countries in comparison to other suppliers
2. Encouraging minority suppliers	2. Percentage of minority suppliers
Community	
1. Public health and safety	1. Availability of emergency response plan protection
2. Conservation of energy and materials	2. Data on reduction of waste produced and materials comparison to industry
3. Donations and support of local organizations	3. Annual employee time spent in community service organizations
Environmental Groups	
1. Minimizing the use of energy	1. Amount of electricity purchased; percentage of "green" electricity
2. Minimizing emissions and waste	2. Type, amount, and designation of waste generated
3. Minimizing adverse environmental effect of products	3. Percentage of product weight reclaimed after the product has been used

Ethical Responsibilities in HUMAN RESOURCES

Walmart's Investment in Employees Beyond Wages

Raising the minimum wage for retail employees has been a hot topic in the last few years. Many believe that retail chains should pay their employees a living wage (i.e., the minimum income needed to meet a worker's basic needs). Facing pressure from politicians and the general public, some retailers such as Target have promised to raise their minimum wage to $15 an hour in the near future. Walmart, however, has taken a different approach.

Rather than provide $15 at the start, Walmart has gradually increased its employees' hourly wages since 2015 and has promoted employees to higher-paid positions. The company proudly points out that it pays greater than minimum wage in 47 states and that 75 percent of its managers are promoted from within. The average Walmart employee makes $14.26 per hour, nearly twice the current federal minimum wage of $7.25.

Beyond wages, Walmart rewards employee loyalty by offering bonuses based on years of employment. For example, Walmart employees who have been with the company for more than 20 years are eligible for a $1,000 bonus. Additional bonuses range from $200 to $750, depending on years of service. In addition to bonuses, Walmart extended its maternity and parental leave to a combined 16 weeks for full-time hourly workers.

With the increases in pay, bonuses, and parental leave, Walmart is actively competing with other retailers. These changes are made possible by the recent corporate tax cut. Walmart is showing that their employees are important stakeholders and are using their tax cut to benefit their workers. Time will tell if these changes are enough to compete with other retailers that are also using their tax cut to improve the lives of their employees.

Sources: Lauren Thomas and Courtney Reagan, "Walmart to Raise Its Starting Wage to $11, Give Some Employees Bonuses Following Tax Bill Passage," *CNBC*, January 11, 2018, https://www.cnbc.com/2018/01/11/walmart-to-boost-starting-wage-give-employees-bonus-after-tax-bill.html (accessed March 21, 2019); Daniel B. Kline, "How Much Does Walmart Pay Its Workers?" *Motley Fool*, April 30, 2018, https://www.fool.com/careers/2018/04/30/how-much-does-walmart-pay-its-workers.aspx (accessed March 21, 2019); Dan Monk, "Kroger, Walmart in No Hurry to Match Amazon's $15 Starting Pay," *WCPO Insider*, November 26, 2018, https://www.wcpo.com/news/insider/kroger-walmart-in-no-hurry-to-match-amazon-s-15-starting-pay (accessed March 21, 2019); Cameron Albert-Deitch, "Time for That Pay Raise? Walmart Employees Now Make More Than Minimum Wage," *Inc.*, May 9, 2019, https://www.inc.com/cameron-albert-deitch/walmart-employee-compensation-report-minimum-wage.html (accessed August 19, 2019).

stakeholder interaction model
a model that conceptualizes the two-way relationships between a firm and a host of stakeholders

Figure 2.1 offers a conceptualization of the relationship between businesses and stakeholders. In this **stakeholder interaction model**, there are two-way relationships between a firm and a host of stakeholders. In addition to the fundamental input of investors, employees, and suppliers, this approach recognizes other stakeholders and explicitly acknowledges the dialogue and interaction that exist between a firm's internal and external environments. The stakeholder interaction model is a conceptual tool that a company may use to create a company-specific

stakeholder map
a company-specific map that names its primary and secondary stakeholders, identifies key issues, and examines relationships and networks between the organization and stakeholders

stakeholder map that names the primary and secondary stakeholders, identifies salient issues, and illuminates relationships and networks. Through its process of stakeholder engagement and mapping, BSR (which stands for "Business for Social Responsibility") assisted Twin Metals Minnesota as the company planned to develop the world's largest underground copper mine near an area widely used for recreation and outdoor activities. Twin Metals continues to face criticism and relies on its stakeholder map, as well as updates and changes to it, to engage with stakeholders more effectively.[17]

A Stakeholder Orientation

stakeholder orientation
the degree to which a firm understands and addresses stakeholder demands

The degree to which a firm understands and addresses stakeholder demands can be referred to as a **stakeholder orientation**. This orientation comprises three sets of activities: (1) the organizationwide generation of data about stakeholder groups and assessment of the firm's effects on these groups, (2) the distribution of this information throughout the firm, and (3) the organization's responsiveness

Figure 2.1 Stakeholder Model for Implementing Social Responsibilities

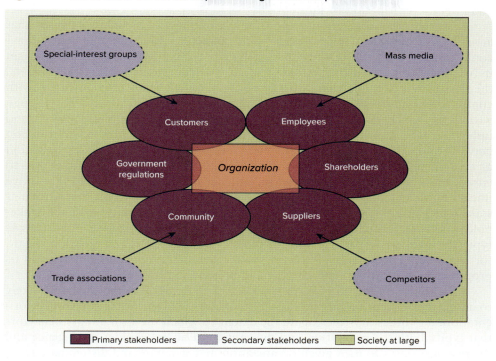

Primary stakeholders · Secondary stakeholders · Society at large

Source: Adapted from Isabelle Maignan, O. C. Ferrell, and Linda Ferrell, "A Stakeholder Model for Implementing Social Responsibility in Marketing," *European Journal of Marketing* 39 (September/October 2005): 956–977.

as a whole to this intelligence. Generating data about stakeholders begins with identifying the stakeholders that are relevant to the firm. Relevant stakeholder communities should be analyzed on the basis of the power that each enjoys, as well as by the ties among its parts. Next, the firm should characterize the concerns about the business's conduct that each relevant stakeholder group shares. This information can be derived from formal research, including surveys, focus groups, internet searches, or press reviews. For example, Ford Motor Company obtains input on social and environmental responsibility issues from company representatives, suppliers, customers, and community leaders. Shell has an online discussion forum where website visitors are invited to express their opinions on the company's activities and their implications. Employees and managers can also generate this information informally as they carry out their daily activities. For example, purchasing managers know about suppliers' demands, public relations executives about the media, legal counselors about the regulatory environment, financial executives about investors, sales representatives about customers, and human resources advisors about employees. Finally, the company should evaluate its impact on the issues that are important to the various stakeholders that it has identified.[18] To develop effective stakeholder dialogue, management needs to appreciate how others perceive the risks of a specific decision. A multiple stakeholder perspective must take into account communication content and transparency when communicating with specific stakeholders.[19]

Given the variety of the employees involved in the generation of information about stakeholders, it is essential that this intelligence be circulated throughout the firm. This requires that the firm facilitate the communication of information about the nature of relevant stakeholder communities, stakeholder issues, the stakeholder map, and the current impact of the firm on these issues to all members of the organization. The dissemination of stakeholder intelligence can be organized formally through activities such as newsletters, internal databases and repositories, and internal information forums.[20]

A stakeholder orientation is not complete unless it includes activities that actually address stakeholder issues. For example, Cloetta, an international confectionary company, has taken stakeholder orientation seriously. A page on its website is dedicated to the topic and clearly identifies all of its stakeholders, the issues that are important to them, and how the company interacts with consumers to address these issues. Cloetta engages with all stakeholders through various media: social media, face-to-face meetings, virtual meetings, surveys, and influential leaders in the community. This allows for a free flow of information between stakeholders and the company.[21] The responsiveness of the organization as a whole to stakeholder intelligence consists of the initiatives the firm adopts to ensure that they abide by or exceed stakeholder expectations and have a positive impact on stakeholder issues. Such activities are likely to be specific to a particular stakeholder group (e.g., family-friendly work schedules) or to a particular stakeholder issue (e.g., pollution-reduction programs). These responsiveness processes typically involve the participation of the stakeholder groups in question. Kraft, for example, includes special-interest groups and university representatives in its programs in order to become sensitized to present and future ethical issues.

Stakeholder orientation can be viewed as a continuum, in that firms are likely to adopt the concept to varying degrees. To gauge a given firm's stakeholder orientation, it is necessary to evaluate the extent to which the firm adopts behaviors that typify both the generation and dissemination of stakeholder intelligence and the responsiveness to it. A given organization may generate and disseminate more intelligence about certain stakeholder communities than about others and, as a result, may respond to that intelligence differently.[22]

Stakeholder Attributes

Traditionally, companies have had an easier time understanding the issues that stakeholders raise than their attributes and the tactics they use to affect organizational decision-making. It is, therefore, necessary to understand both the content (specific issues) and process (actions, tactics) of each stakeholder relationship.[23] For example, animal rights activists sometimes use an unreasonable process to communicate their beliefs. Some members of Direct Action Everywhere, an animal rights group in California, recently faced felony charges for trespassing on farms and stealing chickens they felt were being mistreated. Although animal rights protests such as these are controversial, animal rights issues do have solid support from a number of citizens.[24] One mechanism for understanding stakeholders and their potential salience to a firm involves assessing three stakeholder attributes: power, legitimacy, and urgency. Table 2.2 describes these three attributes. This assessment provides one analytical tool to help managers uncover the motivations and needs of stakeholders and how they relate to the company and its interests. In

Table 2.2 Stakeholder Attributes

Attribute	Examples
Power	A well-established employee in a specialized field has power if replacing the employee would require extensive training and resources.
Legitimacy	Special-interest groups that are against genetically modified foods encourage protests after legislation favorable to biotechnology companies is passed.
Urgency	A company that has discovered a serious product defect that can cause injury must immediately implement a product recall.

addition, stakeholder actions may sensitize the firm to issues and viewpoints not previously considered.[25]

Power, legitimacy, and urgency are not constant, meaning that stakeholder attributes can change over time and context. For example, there was a very strong "Buy American" sentiment in the United States in the 1980s, a time when Japanese manufacturers were making steady market share gains. As globalization increased and overseas manufacturing became the norm, consumer activism or retailer strategy on activism toward this nationalistic buying criterion waned. In the late 1990s and the first decade of the twenty-first century, there was increased urgency concerning Chinese manufacturers and legitimate claims concerning market share gains. However, nationalism, as it relates to retail purchasing, seems to contribute to the intensity of the power gained in the stakeholder environment. This was largely because the U.S. economy was strong, so products from other countries were not seen as threatening. The "Buy American" sentiment rose again after the advent of the Great Recession in 2008–2009, as Americans felt the sting of job losses. American manufacturing came to the forefront of consumer consciousness through organizations and movements promoting American-made products and activists pressuring companies to bring manufacturing back to the United States. More recently, although controversial, the use of hydraulic fracturing (fracking) of shale, a method of extracting natural gas from the earth by means of fluid and other substances, has significantly increased American gas and oil production, making the country more energy independent. The signing of the American Recovery and Investment Act also put pressure on domestic sourcing, investment, and reinvestment in the United States. Some companies have taken this sentiment to heart and are investing in American manufacturing.[26]

Power   A stakeholder has **power** to the extent that it can gain access to coercive, utilitarian, or symbolic means to impose or communicate its views to an organization.[27] *Coercive power* involves the use of fear, suppression, punishment, or some type of restraint. *Utilitarian power* involves financial or material control based on a decision's utility or usefulness. Finally, *symbolic power* relies on the use of symbols that connote social acceptance, prestige, or some other attribute.

power
the extent to which a stakeholder can gain access to coercive, utilitarian, or symbolic means to impose or communicate its views to an organization

Symbolism contained in letter-writing campaigns, advertising messages, and websites can be used to generate awareness and enthusiasm for more responsible business actions. In fact, the internet has conferred tremendous power on stakeholder groups in recent years. Disgruntled stakeholders, especially customers and former employees, may share their concerns or dissatisfaction on social media sites. Even current employees are increasingly expressing their job frustrations over the internet. But symbolic power is the least threatening of the three types.

Utilitarian measures, including boycotts and lawsuits, are also fairly prevalent, although they often come about after symbolic strategies fail to yield the desired response. For example, the government, an important stakeholder for most firms, banned the importation of goods made by children under the age of 15 through indentured or forced labor.[28] This action came about after the media and activist groups exposed widespread abuses in the apparel industry. This law carries financial—utilitarian—repercussions for firms that purchase products manufactured under unacceptable labor conditions. Utilitarian power also can be exerted over the fear that profits will fall if the company spends too much on managing labor or sustainability.

Finally, some stakeholders use coercive power to communicate their message, especially when the issue is emotionally charged and somewhat controversial. For example, a protest in Denton, Texas, resulted in several fracking protesters being arrested by police for trespassing. Protesting of this nature is not exclusive to the United States. In 2018, antifracking protestors in England were jailed for impeding equipment and workers from engaging in fracking.[29]

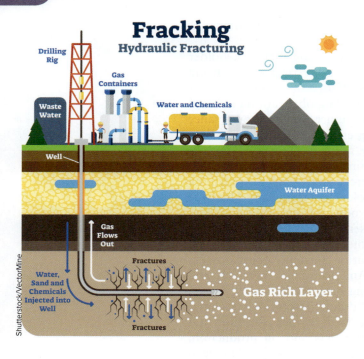

Fracking
Hydraulic Fracturing

Drilling Rig

Gas Containers

Waste Water

Water and Chemicals

Well

Water Aquifer

Gas Flows Out

Fractures

Water, Sand and Chemicals Injected into Well

Gas Rich Layer

Fractures

Shutterstock/VectorMine

legitimacy

the perception or belief that a stakeholder's actions are proper, desirable, or appropriate in a given context

urgency

the time sensitivity and the importance of the claim to the stakeholder

Legitimacy   The second stakeholder attribute is **legitimacy**, which is the perception or belief that a stakeholder's actions are proper, desirable, or appropriate in a given context.[30] This definition suggests that stakeholder actions are considered legitimate when claims are judged to be reasonable by other stakeholders and by society in general. Legitimacy is gained through the stakeholder's ability and willingness to explore the issue from a variety of perspectives, and then to communicate in an effective and respectful manner on the desire for change. Legitimacy is also linked to compliance with regulations, values, and norms that support ethical conduct.

Thus, extremist views are less likely to be considered legitimate because these groups often use covert and inflammatory measures that overshadow the issues and create animosity. Over the years, extreme groups have destroyed property, threatened customers, and committed other acts of violence that ultimately discredit their legitimacy. Opponents of fracking are at risk of delegitimizing their efforts if the main theme of their communication is violent. It is important to remember that this issue is highly controversial, and it is in the best interest of companies engaged in this activity to be sensitive to the requests of stakeholders. After many years of stakeholders requesting acknowledgment and measurement of the risks of fracking from various oil and energy companies, ExxonMobil agreed to become the first to disclose such information. Its report addressed fracking's effects on air and water quality, roads, and potential effects of the chemicals used in the process. While some stakeholders were not completely satisfied with the details of this report, as they think many more issues need to be addressed, ExxonMobil has taken a step in the right direction toward becoming more transparent in addressing stakeholder concerns. The pressure that stakeholders in this example have exerted on the industry was seen as a legitimate concern to ExxonMobil. This report may spur other energy companies to follow their lead. Although an issue may be legitimate, such as environmental sensitivity, it is difficult for the claim to be evaluated independent of the way the stakeholder group communicates on it.[31]

Urgency   Stakeholders exercise greater pressures on managers and organizations when they stress the urgency of their claims. **Urgency** is based on two characteristics: time sensitivity and the importance of the claim to the stakeholder. Time sensitivity usually heightens the stakeholder's effort and may compress an organization's ability to research and react to a claim. For example, hundreds of protesters in Bangladesh took to the streets after a major garment factory fire in 2012 killed over 100 workers. This fire came after a string of similar incidents in the region, which caused the death of more than 600 workers in a period of six years. The aim of the protest was to obtain justice for the death of the workers. Factory owners and managers had known that the factory was deemed an unsafe workplace, but they allowed work to continue despite this knowledge. The urgency of the protestors resulted in the arrest of factory managers, investigations into the safety practices for factories in the region, and a refocusing of multinational companies that used the factories in their operations.[32]

In another example, labor and human rights are widely recognized as critical issues because they are fundamental to the well-being of people around the world.

These rights have become a focal point for college student associations that criticized Nike, the world's leading shoe company, for its failure to improve the working conditions of employees of suppliers and in not making information available to interested stakeholders. Nike experienced a public backlash from its use of offshore subcontractors to manufacture its shoes and clothing. When Nike claimed no responsibility for the subcontractors' poor working conditions and extremely low wages, some consumers demanded greater accountability and responsibility by engaging in boycotts, letter-writing campaigns, public-service announcements, and so forth. Nike ultimately responded to the growing negative publicity by changing its practices and becoming a model company in managing offshore manufacturing.

Overall, stakeholders are considered more important to an organization when their issues are legitimate, their claims are urgent, and they can make use of their power on the organization. These attributes assist the firm and employees in determining the relative importance of specific stakeholders and making resource allocations for developing and managing the stakeholder relationship.

Performance with Stakeholders

Effectively managing stakeholder relationships requires careful attention to a firm's reputation and the effective handling of crisis situations. Boeing's release of the acclaimed 787 Dreamliner was grounded when the plane's lithium ion battery began to overheat. The company had outsourced production of many components of the aircraft, one of which was the battery to Japanese manufacturer GS Yuasa. Although the 787 Dreamliner had undergone many tests, the company learned that excessive outsourcing could cause coordination issues, as well as some unforeseen quality issues. CVS made the strategic decision to drop tobacco products from its offerings, forgoing $2 billion in tobacco sales. The pharmacy, which was the first national chain to do so, believes selling a harmful and addictive substance is contrary to its goal of becoming a healthcare firm. Despite its short-term losses, CVS believed that it would gain long-term stakeholder relationships. Not all pharmacies have followed CVS's lead, although cities and states have enacted regulations that prevent pharmacies from selling tobacco products.[33]

Reputation Management

There are short- and long-term outcomes associated with positive stakeholder relationships. One of the most significant of these is a positive reputation. Because a company's reputation has the power to attract or repel stakeholders, it can be either an asset or a liability in developing and implementing strategic plans and social responsibility initiatives.[34] Reputations take a long time to build or change, and it is far more important to monitor reputation than many companies believe. Whereas a strong reputation may take years to build, it can be destroyed seemingly overnight if a company does not handle crisis situations to the satisfaction of the various stakeholders involved.

Corporate reputation, image, and brands are more important than ever and are among the most critical aspects of sustaining relationships with constituents, including investors, customers, financial analysts, media, and government watchdogs. It takes companies decades to build a great reputation, yet just one slip can cost a company dearly. Although an organization does not control its reputation in a direct sense, its actions, choices, behaviors, and consequences do influence the reputation that exists in perceptions of stakeholders. A corporate reputation poll showed that quality is typically the biggest driver of corporate reputation, but company purpose and vision play a big role. While consumers are primarily concerned about the quality of their goods and services, consumers also want companies to maintain strong values through their vision and purpose.[35]

reputation management
the process of building and sustaining a company's good name and generating positive feedback from stakeholders

Reputation management is the process of building and sustaining a company's good name and generating positive feedback from stakeholders. A company's reputation is affected by every contact with a stakeholder.[36] Various trends may affect how companies manage their reputations. These trends include market factors, such as increased consumer knowledge, the emergence of instantaneous communication, stakeholder activism, and community access to information, and workplace factors, including technological advances, closer vendor relationships, and more inquisitive employees. These factors make companies more cautious about their actions and words because increased scrutiny in this area requires more attention from management. A company needs to understand these factors and how to properly address them to build a strong reputation. These factors have also helped companies recognize the link between reputation and competitive advantage. If these trends are dealt with wisely and if internal and external communication strategies are used effectively, a firm can position itself positively in stakeholders' minds and thus create a competitive advantage. Intangible factors related to reputation can account for as much as 50 percent of a firm's market valuation.[37]

The importance of corporate reputation has created a need for accurate reputation measures. As indicated in Table 2.3, business publications, research firms, consultants, and public relations agencies have established a foothold in the new field of reputation management through research and lists of "the most reputable" firms. However, some

Table 2.3 Reputation Measures

Reputation List	Conducted By	Groups Surveyed	Primary Purpose
100 Best Companies to Work for in America	*Fortune* magazine, Great Place to Work Institute	Companies that are at least five years old and employ at least 1,000 employees; employees and top managers are surveyed	Publication
100 Best Corporate Citizens	*Corporate Responsibility* magazine, Corporate Responsibility Officers Association (CROA)	Russell 1000 companies	Publication
America's Most Admired Companies	*Fortune* magazine, Hay Group	Fortune 1000 companies and Fortune's Global 500 with revenues at or over $10 billion; company executives, directors, and analysts are surveyed	Publication
Best and Worst: Social Responsibility	*Fortune* magazine, Hay Group	Fortune 1000 companies and Fortune's Global 500 with revenues at or over $10 billion; company executives, directors, and analysts are surveyed	Publication
Corporate Branding Index	CoreBrand, LLC	Business executives responsible for purchasing and strategic relationship decisions from the top brands with over $50 million as well as high-level customers	Customized for clients
Global Reputation Pulse	Reputation Institute	All of the company's stakeholders	Customized for clients
Reputation Quotient	Reputation Institute and Harris Interactive	General public	Customized for Clients
World's Most Respected Companies	Barron's	Professional money managers	Publication

questions have arisen as to who can best determine corporate reputation. For example, some measures survey only chief executives, whereas others also elicit perceptions from the general public. Although executives may be biased toward a firm's financial performance, the general public may lack experience or data on which to evaluate a company's reputation. Regardless of how it is measured, reputation is the result of a process involving an organization and various constituents.[38]

The process of reputation management involves four components that work together: organizational identity, image, performance, and ultimately, reputation.[39] Organizational performance involves the actual interaction between the company and its stakeholders.

To build and manage a good reputation, these four areas must be aligned. Companies must manage identity and culture by pinpointing those standards and responsibilities that will allow them to achieve their objectives, work with stakeholders effectively, and continuously monitor and change for effectiveness.[40]

For example, Microsoft, which is recognized for its outstanding performance in corporate responsibility, has the mission to "empower every person and every organization on the planet to achieve more." It accomplishes this mission through its focus on technology, diversity, and corporate social responsibility (CSR). For example, in keeping in line with their mission, Microsoft has been carbon neutral since 2012. The company is not solely focused on its own sustainability efforts; it also contributes to environmental projects around the world. For instance, Microsoft has aided Taiwan in increasing renewable energy for the country by over 15 percent by 2025. Leading by example, Microsoft invested in hydrorenewable energy credits to power their businesses in Taiwan. One of Microsoft's most innovative services has been its Airband Initiative, which allows populations in rural and hard-to-reach geographic locations around the world to gain access to broadband internet. In addition, Microsoft has partnered with places in Colombia, South Africa, Kenya, and India to bring this technology to farmers and communities where internet connectivity was previously impossible or impractical. This technology has had a dramatic effect on improving the educational needs of children in rural areas of the United States, as well as businesses in places all over the world. Given these helpful initiatives, it appears that Microsoft has been successful in balancing its goals and objectives with the desires and demands of its stakeholders.[41] Table 2.4 lists 10 socially responsible companies known for their CSR initiatives. Salesforce. com, for instance, has developed a model called the 1-1-1 model, which contributes 1 percent of the company's time, 1 percent of equity, and 1 percent of company products to worthy causes, such as significantly discounting its products for nonprofit organizations.

Thus, all these elements must be continually implemented to ensure that the company's reputation is maximized through community relations. However, most firms will, at one time or another, experience crisis situations that threaten or harm this reputation. How a company reacts, responds, and learns from the situation is indicative of its commitment and implementation of social responsibility. The acceptance and implementation of reputation management strategies, concurrent with widespread use of the internet and social media, also may bring challenges to the **marketplace of ideas**. Unlike the traditional economic marketplace, where competition determines superior products and services, an ideas marketplace assumes that ideas compete against one another for truth and acceptability. Although the marketplace of ideas was initially conceptualized with respect to free speech, it also applies to the dual responsibility of executives and managers with respect to reputation management: advocating for the company while simultaneously ensuring transparency and full disclosure with stakeholders.[42]

Reputation management is a key consideration for corporations around the world. An annual poll by Edelman revealed an increase

marketplace of ideas
the assumption that ideas compete against one another for truth and acceptability

Table 2.4 Ten Socially Responsible Companies

AT&T	Patagonia
Bueno Foods	Salesforce.com
Cummins	SC Johnson
Eaton	Starbucks
Marriott	Whole Foods

in trust of businesses for both the informed public and the general population. According to The Reputation Institute, the 10 businesses with the best reputations in the world are Rolex, LEGO, Walt Disney Company, Adidas Group, Microsoft, Sony, Canon, Michelin, Netflix, and Bosch. Netflix has increased its reputation so much that it went from number 24 to number 9 in just one year. The Reputation Institute speculates that part of the reason for this jump from 24 to 9 could be tied to its termination of Kevin Spacey from *House of Cards* shortly after sexual harassment accusations against him.[43]

Crisis Management

Organizational crises are far-reaching events that can have dramatic effects on both the organization and its stakeholders. Along with the industrialization of society, companies and their products have become ever more complex, and therefore more susceptible to crisis. As a result, disasters and crisis situations are increasingly common events from which few organizations are exempt.[44] In April 2018, an engine that blew out on a Southwest Airlines flight caused the death of one passenger who was partially sucked out of the broken window of the airplane. Linda Rutherford, chief communications officer, started by quickly communicating all known facts shortly after the incident and updating information as new facts emerged, with a sympathetic tone toward the victims. For airlines, most flights are uneventful and go unnoticed. But when a high-profile accident like this occurs, it receives enormous media coverage. Proper crisis management is necessary, and companies must be ready at any moment to adapt to challenges.[45]

ethical misconduct disaster (EMD)
an unexpected organizational crisis that results from employee misconduct, illegal activities such as fraud, or unethical decisions and that significantly disrupts operations and threatens or is perceived to threaten the firm's continuity of operations

An **ethical misconduct disaster (EMD)** can be an unexpected organizational crisis that results from employee misconduct, illegal activities such as fraud, or unethical decisions and that significantly disrupts operations and threatens or is perceived to threaten the firm's continuity of operations. An EMD can even be more devastating than natural disasters such as a hurricane or technology disruptions.[46] Table 2.5 discusses some recent EMDs that happened due to lapses in leadership and the failure to manage risks properly.

As organizations plan for natural disasters and insure against traditional risks, so too should they prepare for ethical crises. An EMD can be managed by organizational initiatives to recognize, avoid, discover, address, and recover from the misconduct. The potential damage of an ethical disaster can affect both business and society. The costs of an EMD from both financial and reputation

Table 2.5 Ethical Misconduct Disasters

Company	Disaster
FIFA	Engaged in widespread corruption by top officials, including bribery, racketeering, and fraud
Credit Suisse	Pleaded guilty to helping Americans evade taxes and agreed to pay $2.5 billion in penalties
Target	Appeared to ignore warnings of potential hacking activity, resulting in the theft of the personal information of millions of customers
U.S. Air Force	Discovered a massive cheating scandal at its base in Montana among officers involved in the launching of intercontinental ballistic missiles
GlaxoSmithKline	Paid $3 billion to settle allegations that it had marketed various medications for uses that were unapproved by the Food and Drug Administration (FDA)
Volkswagen	Purposefully installed defeat devices in diesel vehicles to fool regulators during emissions testing
Barclay's Bank	Rigged the Libor rate—used as the benchmark for trillions of dollars of loans—to benefit the company

perspectives can be assessed, as well as the need for planning to avoid an EMD in the first place. The role of leadership in preventing a crisis relates to a contingency plan to develop effective crisis management programs.

The risks facing organizations today are significant, and the reputational damage caused can be far greater for companies that find themselves unprepared. The key is to recognize that the risks associated with misconduct are real and that, if insufficient controls are in place, the company can suddenly find itself the subject of an EMD. Although it is hard to predict an ethical disaster, companies can and must prepare for one.

Data protection is a major issue in the modern era, and companies now have more responsibility to protect consumer data. In 2017, Equifax leaked the data for more than 143 million American consumers. Data included social security numbers, driver's license numbers, and other identifying information. Hackers were able to access the information due to weak data protection policies implemented by the agency. Public outcry for this incident sparked a national debate about data protection and privacy issues for consumers. As a response, Equifax reported the breach to law enforcement and hired a cybersecurity firm to help determine the scale of the breach. Additionally, Equifax created a website to help consumers see if they were affected by the breach. Still, there is no way for the agency to fix this issue, as the data had already been leaked. Consumer outrage was enormous, and Equifax has struggled to reestablish a good corporate reputation since the incident.[47]

Of course, not every unethical decision relates to negligence. Many often begin as a marketing effort, and only in retrospect is it revealed to be unethical. And clearly not every decision becomes a crisis. Lord & Taylor, for instance, settled charges that it deceived consumers when it paid for a native advertisement in the online publication *Nylon* without including a disclosure that the article was paid content. It also paid 50 fashion influencers to wear one of its dresses without disclosing that it had done so. This was found to be deceptive because consumers were not aware of the company's direct connections to these promotions.[48]

It is critical for companies to manage crises effectively because research suggests that these events are a leading cause of organizational mortality. What follows are some key issues to consider in **crisis management**, the process of handling a high-impact event characterized by ambiguity and the need for swift action. In most cases, the crisis situation will not be handled in a completely effective or ineffective manner. Thus, a crisis usually leads to both success and failure outcomes for a business and its stakeholders and provides information that can be used to make improvements to future crisis management and social responsibility efforts.[49]

Organizational crises are characterized by a threat to a company's high-priority goals, surprise to its membership, and stakeholder demands for a short response time. The nature of crises requires a firm's leadership to communicate in an often stressful, emotional, uncertain, and demanding context. Crises are very difficult on a company's stakeholders as well. For this reason, the firm's stakeholders, especially its employees, shareholders, customers, government regulators, competitors, creditors, and the media, will scrutinize communication after a crisis. Hence, a crisis has widespread implications not only for the organization, but also for each group affected by the crisis. To better understand how crises develop and move toward resolution, some researchers use a medical analogy. Using that analogy, the organization proceeds through chronological stages, similar to a person with an illness. The *prodromal stage* is a precrisis period, during which warning signs may exist. Next is the *acute stage*, in which the actual crisis occurs. During the *chronic stage*, the business is required to explain their actions sufficiently for them to move to the final stage, *crisis resolution*. Figure 2.2 illustrates these stages. Although the stages are conceptually distinct, some crises happen so quickly, and without warning, that the organization may move from the prodromal to the acute stage

crisis management
the process of handling a high-impact event characterized by ambiguity and the need for swift action

Figure 2.2 The Crisis Management Process

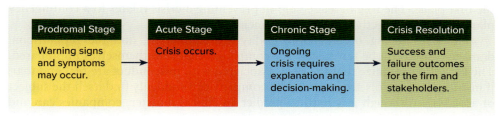

within minutes. Many organizations faced this situation after Hurricane Katrina crashed into New Orleans and the Mississippi Gulf Coast in 2005, disrupting all business and social activity for years. More recent natural disasters, such as Hurricane Harvey in Texas in 2017, have also modified the economic landscape, especially for small and medium-sized businesses.

One of the fundamental difficulties that a company faces is how to communicate effectively to stakeholders during and after a disaster. Once a crisis strikes, the firm's stakeholders need a quick response in the midst of the duress and confusion. They need information about how the company plans to resolve the crisis, as well as what each constituent can do to mitigate its own negative effects. If a company is slow to respond, stakeholders may feel that the company does not care about their needs or is not concerned or remorseful (if the company is at fault) about the crisis. Furthermore, a delayed response may in fact increase the suffering of particular stakeholder groups. For instance, some stakeholders may take on considerable debt due to medical expenses as a result of the crisis. Therefore, a rapid response to stakeholders is central to any crisis resolution strategy so that these various groups can plan their recovery.

Ironically, crisis events are often so chaotic that a company's leadership may not be certain of the cause of the situation before the media and other relevant groups demand a statement. Thus, it is not surprising for organizations to begin their crisis responses with some degree of ambiguity in their statements. In fact, some crisis theorists advise companies to avoid too much detail in their initial responses due to the embarrassment that results from changing positions later in the crisis, when more information is available. Still, stakeholder groups want or, as a matter of safety in some cases, need access to whatever information the firm can share. Although tensions between the public's needs and the organization's fear of litigation can hamper the willingness to communicate, the demand for information in such situations is unyielding.

Not only should the firm's leadership make a public statement quickly, but it is also necessary for the organization to communicate about specific issues to stakeholder groups. First, leadership should express concern and/or remorse for the event. Second, the organization should delineate guidelines regarding how they intend to address the crisis so that stakeholders can be confident that the situation will not escalate or reoccur. Finally, the company should provide explicit criteria to stakeholders regarding how each group will be compensated for any negative effects it experiences as a result of the crisis. Many companies, however, overlook these three essential conditions of crisis management. More often, they focus on minimizing harm to the organization's image, denying responsibility for the crisis, and shifting blame away from the organization and toward other stakeholder groups. Although this may be an appropriate strategy when firms are not actually responsible, too often they choose this course of action under the stress of the crisis when they are responsible (or partially responsible) for the crisis without expressing sufficient remorse for their involvement or concern for their stakeholders.

The varying communication needs and levels of concern of stakeholders during and after a crisis often hamper effective communication. The firm's leadership should try to communicate as much accurate information to these groups as possible to minimize their uncertainty. When a firm fails to do so, their credibility, legitimacy, and reputation in the eyes of stakeholders often suffer. Adding to the complexity of communication challenges, the needs of various stakeholder groups may conflict. For instance, the needs of customers who become ill as a result of a contaminated product and their desire to have medical bills paid may be at odds with the company's ability to bolster their stock price to satisfy shareholders. Some stakeholders will obviously have more opportunities than others to voice their concerns after a crisis. Victims and the general public rarely have an opportunity to meet with the organization's leadership after a crisis. Conversely, the organization's stockholders and employees will likely have a greater opportunity to express their views about the crisis and therefore may have their ideas accepted by management. Some researchers suggest that, due to this ability to communicate directly with leadership, internal stakeholder needs often take precedence over those of external stakeholders.

Organizations have a responsibility to manage the competing interests of stakeholders to ensure that all stakeholder groups are treated fairly in the aftermath of a crisis. Responsible companies try to balance the needs of their stakeholders rather than favoring some groups over others. The Walt Disney Corporation experienced a major crisis in 2016, when an alligator killed a two-year-old boy who was wading in a lake at one of Disney's resorts. Although Disney had posted "Do not swim" signs around the lake and had worked with Florida wildlife officials to remove alligators from the lake in the past, it did not have signs posted warning about alligators, despite the fact that they were likely to be present. While Disney may face legal repercussions for not warning consumers about the possibility of alligators, crisis-communication experts praised the response of Disney's CEO, George Kalogridis, who personally contacted the parents from Shanghai to offer condolences. Other experts, however, thought that the company could have done a better job of placing a public statement of regret on their websites. Disney has since put up signs warning about the possibility of dangerous wildlife.[50]

Organizations that fail to accomplish effective crisis communication alienate stakeholder groups and intensify the negative media attention toward the company. For many reasons, including effective crisis management, organizations need to understand and pursue solid and mutually beneficial relationships with stakeholders.

Development of Stakeholder Relationships

Relationships of any type, whether they involve family, friends, coworkers, or companies, are founded on principles of trust, commitment, and transparent communication. They also are associated with a certain degree of time, interaction, and shared expectations. For instance, we do not normally speak of "having a relationship" with someone we have just met. We even differentiate between casual acquaintances, work colleagues, and close friends.

In business, the concept of relationships has gained much acceptance. Instead of just pursuing one-time transactions, companies are now searching for ways to develop long-term and collaborative relationships with their customers and business partners.[51] Many companies focus on relationships with suppliers, buyers, employees, and others directly involved in economic exchange. These relationships involve investments of several types. Some investments are tangible, such as buildings, equipment, new tools, and other elements dedicated to a particular relationship. Apple made an unprecedented move in this regard when it launched an iPhone trade-in day in select retail locations. Some owners of older iPhones were sent an email invitation to upgrade to a new device.[52] Other investments are less tangible, such as the time, effort, trust, and commitment required to develop a relationship with customers. Southwest Airlines develops the intangible aspect of relationships through the level of customer service they provide, as well as the enjoyable experience they offer.[53]

Whereas tangible investments are often customized for a specific business relationship, intangible efforts have a more lucid and permeable quality. Although social responsibility involves tangible activities and other communication signals, the key to good stakeholder relationships resides in trust, communication quality, and mutual respect. As a company strives to develop a dialogue and a solid relationship with one stakeholder, investments and lessons learned through the process should add value to other stakeholder relationships. For example, Starbucks provides excellent benefits, including healthcare for part-time employees, and supports fair trade or a fair income for the farmers who grow the coffee they sell.

social capital
an asset that resides in relationships and is characterized by mutual goals and trust

These efforts result in **social capital**, an asset that resides in relationships and is characterized by mutual goals and trust.[54] Social capital include the social connections that can provide economic benefits that are mutually advantageous. Social capital provides social networks that have value. Like financial and intellectual capital, social capital facilitates internal and external transactions and processes. This is especially true as more businesses become part of the sharing economy. Companies such as Airbnb, a home rental sharing company, and Uber, a car reservation company, are prime examples of businesses whose level of social capital is necessary for their success. These business models depend upon building and reinforcing transparency and accountability among users, as well as between users and the company.[55]

Unlike financial and intellectual capital, however, social capital is not tangible or the obvious property of one organization. In this same regard, social responsibility is not compartmentalized or reserved for a few issues or stakeholders but should have the companywide strategic focus discussed in Chapter 1.

Implementing a Stakeholder Perspective in Social Responsibility

An organization that develops effective corporate governance and understands the importance of business ethics and social responsibility in achieving success should develop some processes for managing these important concerns. Although there are many approaches, we provide some steps that have been found effective to utilize the stakeholder framework in managing responsibility and business ethics, including (1) assessing the corporate culture, (2) identifying stakeholder groups, (3) identifying stakeholder issues, (4) assessing the organization's commitment to social responsibility, (5) identifying resources and determining urgency, and (6) gaining stakeholder feedback. The importance of these steps is to include feedback from relevant stakeholders in formulating organizational strategy and implementation.[56] Table 2.6 summarizes these six steps.

Step 1: Assessing the Corporate Culture

To enhance organizational fit, a social responsibility program must align with the corporate culture of the organization. The purpose of this first step is to identify the organizational mission, values, and norms that are likely to have implications for social responsibility. In particular, relevant existing values and norms are those that specify the stakeholder groups and stakeholder issues that are deemed most important by the organization. Very often, relevant organizational values and

Table 2.6 Six Steps for Utilizing a Stakeholder Framework

Steps	Example
Assess the corporate culture.	New Belgium Brewing decides to invest in wind power because doing so aligns with its mission of environmental responsibility.
Identify stakeholder groups.	Whole Foods recognizes the importance of working with animal activist organizations to ensure that the animals supplying its meat products are treated humanely.
Identify stakeholder issues.	Chevron identifies sustainability and the increasing concern over greenhouse gas emissions as important stakeholder considerations affecting the industry.
Assess the organization's commitment to social responsibility.	CVS determines that eliminating cigarette sales will reinforce its commitment toward becoming a health services company.
Identify resources and determine urgency.	Home Depot provides emergency supplies in areas that are struck by natural disasters.
Gain stakeholder feedback.	Best Buy asked consumers for feedback and realized that the recycling of electronic waste was a major concern.

norms can be found in corporate documents such as the mission statement, annual reports, sales brochures, or websites. For example, REI crafts its corporate culture around love of the outdoors. Because of this, the company puts a heavy emphasis on protecting the environment. REI has initiatives to reduce packaging waste, to increase recycling, and to increase green building practices. The REI Foundation was created to help the environment, encourage outdoor activities, and help communities recover from natural disasters.[57]

Step 2: Identifying Stakeholder Groups

In managing this stage, it is important to recognize stakeholder needs, wants, and desires. There are many important issues that gain visibility because key constituencies such as consumer groups, regulators, and the media express an interest. When agreement, collaboration, or even confrontation exists around an issue, there is a need for a decision-making process. A model of collaboration to overcome the adversarial approaches to problem-solving has been suggested. Managers can identify relevant stakeholders that may be affected by or may influence the development of organizational policy, which is an important element of stakeholder engagement.

Stakeholders have some level of power over a business because they are in the position to withhold, or at least threaten to withhold, organizational resources. Stakeholders have most power when their own survival is not really affected by the success of the organization, and when they have access to vital organizational resources. For example, most consumers of shoes do not have a specific need to buy Nike shoes. Therefore, if they decide to boycott Nike, they have to endure only minor inconvenience. Nevertheless, their loyalty to Nike is vital to the continued success of the sport apparel giant. The proper assessment of the power held by a given stakeholder community also requires an evaluation of the extent to which that community can collaborate with others to pressure the firm.

Step 3: Identifying Stakeholder Issues

Together, Steps 1 and 2 lead to the identification of the stakeholders who are both the most powerful and legitimate. The level of power and legitimacy determines the degree of urgency in addressing their needs. Step 3, then, consists of understanding the nature of the main issues of concern to these stakeholders. A stakeholder map

Shutterstock/mariakray

may be especially useful at this stage. Conditions for collaboration exist when problems are so complex that multiple stakeholders are required to resolve the issue and the weaknesses of adversarial approaches are understood.

For example, environmental issues have become a huge issue for stakeholders. Companies now must focus on their environmental impact and how their productions affect the environment and their stakeholders. Many companies have begun to reduce their emissions and focus on using recyclable material and renewable energy as a response to environmental concerns.

Step 4: Assessing the Organization's Commitment to Social Responsibility

Steps 1 through 3 consist of generating information about social responsibility among a variety of influencers in and around the organization. Step 4 brings these three first stages together to arrive at an understanding of social responsibility that specifically matches the organization of interest. This general definition will then be used to evaluate current practices and to select concrete social responsibility initiatives. Firms such as Starbucks have selected activities that address stakeholder concerns. Starbucks has formalized its initiatives in official documents such as annual reports, webpages, and company brochures. They also have a website devoted to social responsibility. Starbucks is concerned with the environment and integrates policies and programs throughout all aspects of operations to minimize their environmental impact. They also have many community-building programs that help them be good neighbors and contribute positively to the communities where their partners and customers live, work, and play.[58]

Step 5: Identifying Resources and Determining Urgency

The prioritization of stakeholders and issues, along with the assessment of past performance, provide for allocating resources. Two main criteria can be considered. First, the levels of financial and organizational investments required by various actions should be determined. A second criterion when prioritizing social responsibility challenges is urgency. When the challenge under consideration is viewed as significant, and when stakeholder pressures on the issue could be expected, then the challenge can be treated as urgent. For example, environmental issues have become a huge concern across groups and stakeholders. Companies now must focus on their environmental impact and how their productions affect the environment and their stakeholders. Many companies have begun to reduce their emissions and focus on using recyclable material and renewable energy as a response.[59]

Step 6: Gaining Stakeholder Feedback

Stakeholders' feedback can be generated through a variety of means. First, their general assessment of the firm and its practices can be obtained through satisfaction or reputation surveys. Second, to gauge stakeholders' perceptions of the firm's contributions to specific issues, stakeholder-generated media such as blogs, websites, podcasts, and newsletters can be assessed. Third, more formal research may be conducted using focus groups, observation, and surveys. Websites can be both positive and negative; for example, user review sites such as Yelp have both generated and decreased sales of business establishments based on reviews left on the site. Because so many consumers refer to these websites before visiting a business, many companies are focusing on good customer service to ensure good reviews. However, these reviews can be misleading and do harm to a business. For example, the owner of a small salon expressed concern over the effect of one negative review left by a customer who never set foot in her place. The customer perceived the salon owner as rude and rushed in a telephone call and wrote about it. The owner has seen a decrease in business that she attributes to the review.[60]

In the process of developing stakeholder relationships, most strategies are focused on increasing the trust that a stakeholder has in a particular company. Of course, there is no "one size fits all" approach for building and sustaining trusting relationships with stakeholders. As discussed earlier in the chapter, not all stakeholders engage with a company with the same level of intensity or locus of control, whether internal or external. For example, employees are highly engaged internal stakeholders, while suppliers may be considered low-intensity external stakeholders. Depending on the specific issues at hand, historical interactions, relationship intensity, and other factors, managers must understand the relative importance of transparency, competence, benevolence, integrity, values, and other factors.[61]

Link Between Stakeholder Relationships and Social Responsibility

You may be wondering what motivations companies have for pursuing stakeholder relationships. As the previous section indicates, a great deal of time, effort, and commitment goes into the process of developing and implementing a stakeholder perspective. Sometimes, however, these efforts do not have the desired effect. Coca-Cola and PepsiCo have received criticism regarding the messages of their social responsibility initiatives compared with their perceived role in the obesity issue. For example, Coca-Cola partnered with the Rwandan government and other organizations to open EKOCENTER, a site that will provide internet services, the company's products, clean water, and other basic goods for people in the local community. Despite Coca-Cola's impact on communities, some critics accuse the firm of promoting soft drinks in low-income areas that would benefit more from nutritious items rather than sugary, unhealthy drinks.[62] As discussed in Chapter 1, social responsibility is a relational approach that involves the views and stakes of a number of groups. Stakeholders are engaged in the relationships that both challenge and support a company's efforts. Thus, without a solid understanding of stakeholders and their interests, a firm may miss important trends and changes in its environment and not achieve strategic social responsibility.

Rather than holding all companies to one standard, our approach to evaluating performance and effectiveness resides in the specific expectations and actual results that develop between each organization and its stakeholders. Max Clarkson, an influential contributor to our understanding of stakeholders, sums up this view:

Performance is what counts. Performance can be measured and evaluated. Whether a corporation and its management are motivated by enlightened self-interest, common sense or high standards of ethical behavior cannot be determined by empirical methodologies available today. These are not questions that can be answered by economists, sociologists, psychologists, or any other kind of social scientist. They are interesting questions, but they are not relevant when it comes to evaluating a company's performance in managing its relationships with its stakeholder groups.[63]

Although critics and some researchers may seek answers and evidence as to the motivations of business for social responsibility, we are interested in what companies are actually doing that is positive, negative, or neutral for their stakeholders and their stakeholders' interests. The Reactive–Defensive–Accommodative–Proactive Scale (see Table 2.7) provides a method for assessing a company's strategy and performance for each stakeholder. This scale is based on a continuum of strategy options and performance outcomes with respect to stakeholders.[64] This evaluation can take place as stakeholder issues arise or are identified. Therefore, it is possible for one company to be rated at several different levels because of varying performance and transitions over time. For example, a poorly handled crisis may provide feedback for continuous improvement that creates more satisfactory performance in the future. Or a company may demonstrate a proactive stance toward employees, and yet be defensive with consumer activists.

The reactive approach involves denying responsibility and doing less than is required. This approach can be characterized as "fighting it all the way." A firm that fails to invest in safety and health measures for employees is denying its responsibilities. An organization with a defensive strategy acknowledges reluctantly and partially the responsibility issues that may be raised by its stakeholders. A firm in this category fulfills basic legal obligations and demonstrates the minimal responsibility discussed in Chapter 1. With an accommodative strategy, a company attempts to satisfy stakeholder demands by doing all that is required and may be seen as progressive because it is obviously open to this expanded model of business relationships. Today, many organizations are giving money and other resources to community organizations as a way of demonstrating social responsibility. Finally, the proactive approach not only accepts, but also anticipates stakeholder interests. In this case, a company sincerely aligns legitimate stakeholder views with its responsibilities and will do more than is required to meet them.[65] Hoechst, a German life sciences company that is now part of Aventis, gradually assumed the proactive orientation with communities in which it operates. The initiation of a community discussion group led to information sharing and trust building and helped transform Hoechst into a society-driven company.[66]

The Reactive–Defensive–Accommodative–Proactive Scale is useful because it evaluates real-life practices and allows an organization to see its strengths and weaknesses within each stakeholder relationship. SABMiller, the second-largest brewer in the world, uses a risk assessment program to understand the stakeholders and issues that may pose a potential risk to its reputation. These risks are prioritized, planned for, monitored, and if necessary, responded to if SABMiller

Table 2.7 The Reactive–Defensive–Accommodative–Proactive Scale

Rating	Strategy	Performance	Example
Reactive	Deny responsibility	Doing less than required	Exxon refuses to continue oil spill cleanup after a certain date.
Defensive	Admit responsibility, but "fight it all the way"	Doing the least that is required	Valero Energy claims that it meets federal regulation; therefore, community complaints are not legitimate.
Accommodative	Accept responsibility	Doing all that is required	General Motors (GM) promises job security if productivity gains are realized.
Proactive	Anticipate responsibility	Doing more than is required	Xerox shares product blueprints with suppliers and takes suggestions before production.

Source: Adapted from Max B. E. Clarkson, "A Stakeholder Framework for Analyzing and Evaluating Corporate Social Performance," *Academy of Management Review* 20 (January 1995): 92–117; I. M. Jawahar and Gary McLaughlin, "Toward a Descriptive Stakeholder Theory: An Organizational Life Cycle Approach," *Academy of Management Review* 26 (July 2001): 397–414.

cannot predict, preempt, or avoid the concern.[67] Results from a stakeholder assessment like the one at SABMiller should be included in the **social audit**, the process of assessing and reporting a firm's performance in adopting a strategic focus for fulfilling the economic, legal, ethical, and philanthropic social responsibilities expected of it by its stakeholders. Because stakeholders are so important to the concept of social responsibility, as well as to business success, Chapters 3–13 are devoted to exploring significant stakeholder relationships and issues.

social audit
the process of assessing and reporting a firm's performance in adopting a strategic focus for fulfilling the economic, legal, ethical, and philanthropic social responsibilities expected of it by its stakeholders

Summary

Stakeholders refer to those people and groups who have a stake in some aspect of a company's products, operations, markets, industry, or outcomes. The relationship between organizations and their stakeholders is a two-way street.

The historical assumption that the key objective of business is profit maximization led to the belief that business is accountable primarily to investors and others involved in the market and economic aspects of the organization. In the latter half of the twentieth century, perceptions of business accountability evolved to include both market constituencies that are directly involved and affected by the business purpose (e.g., investors, employees, customers, and other business partners) and nonmarket constituencies that are not always directly tied to issues of profitability and performance (e.g., the general community, media, government, and special-interest groups).

In the stakeholder model, relationships, investors, employees, and suppliers provide inputs for a company to benefit stakeholders. The stakeholder model assumes a two-way relationship between the firm and a host of stakeholders. This approach recognizes additional stakeholders and acknowledges the two-way dialogue and effects that exist with a firm's internal and external environment.

Primary stakeholders are fundamental to a company's operations and survival and include shareholders and investors, employees, customers, suppliers, and public stakeholders, such as governments and communities. Secondary stakeholders influence and/or are affected by a company but are neither engaged in transactions with the firm nor essential for their survival.

As more firms conduct business overseas, they encounter the complexity of stakeholder issues and relationships in tandem with other business operations and decisions. Although general awareness of the concept of stakeholders is relatively high around the world, the importance of stakeholders varies from country to country. All types of organizations must understand the stakeholder interaction model, as well as the utility of developing a stakeholder map.

A stakeholder has power to the extent that it can gain access to coercive, utilitarian, or symbolic means to impose or communicate its views to the organization. Legitimacy is the perception or belief that a stakeholder's actions are proper, desirable, or appropriate within a given context. Stakeholders exercise greater pressures on managers and organizations when they stress the urgency of their claims. These attributes can change over time and context.

The degree to which a firm understands and addresses stakeholder demands can be referred to as a "stakeholder orientation." This orientation comprises three sets of activities: (1) the organizationwide generation of data about stakeholder groups and assessment of the firm's effects on these groups, (2) the distribution of this information throughout the firm, and (3) the organization's responsiveness to this intelligence as a whole.

Reputation management is the process of building and sustaining a company's good name and generating positive feedback from stakeholders. The process of reputation management involves the interaction of organizational identity (how the firm wants to be viewed), organizational image (how stakeholders initially perceive the firm), organizational performance (actual interaction between the company and stakeholders), and organizational reputation (the collective view of stakeholders after interactions with the company). Stakeholders will reassess their views of the company on the basis of how the company has actually performed. The widespread use of reputation management strategies, along with instantaneous communication via social media and the internet, means that companies must also understand the marketplace of ideas.

Crisis management is the process of handling a high-impact event characterized by ambiguity and the need for swift action. Some researchers describe an organization's progress through a prodromal, or precrisis, stage to the acute stage, chronic stage, and finally, crisis resolution. Stakeholders need a quick response from the company, with information about how the company plans to resolve the crisis, as well as what the stakeholders can do to mitigate any negative effects on themselves. It is also necessary to communicate specific issues to stakeholder groups, including remorse for the event, guidelines as to how the organization is going to address the crisis, and criteria regarding how stakeholder groups will be compensated for negative effects.

Companies are searching for ways to develop long-term, collaborative relationships with their stakeholders. These relationships involve both tangible and intangible investments. Investments and lessons learned through the process of developing a dialogue and relationship with one stakeholder should add value to other stakeholder relationships. These efforts result in social capital, an asset that resides in relationships and is characterized by mutual goals and trust.

The first step in developing stakeholder relationships is to acknowledge and actively monitor the concerns of all legitimate stakeholders. A firm should adopt processes and modes of behavior that are sensitive to the concerns and capabilities of each stakeholder. Information should be communicated consistently across all stakeholders. A firm should be willing to acknowledge and openly address potential conflicts. Investments in education, training, and information will improve employees' understanding of and relationships with stakeholders. Relationships with stakeholders need to be periodically assessed through both formal and informal means. Sharing feedback with stakeholders helps establish the two-way dialogue that characterizes the stakeholder model.

An organization that develops effective corporate governance and understands the importance of business ethics and social responsibility in achieving success should develop some processes for managing these important concerns. Although there are many approaches, we provide some steps that have been found effective to utilize the stakeholder framework in managing responsibility and business ethics. The steps include (1) assessing the corporate culture, (2) identifying stakeholder groups, (3) identifying stakeholder issues, (4) assessing the organization's commitment to social responsibility, (5) identifying resources and determining urgency, and (6) gaining stakeholder feedback. The importance of these steps is to include feedback from relevant stakeholders in formulating organizational strategy and implementation.

The Reactive–Defensive–Accommodative–Proactive Scale provides a method for assessing a company's strategy and performance with one stakeholder. The Reactive approach involves denying responsibility and doing less than is required. The Defensive approach acknowledges only reluctantly and partially the responsibility issues that may be raised by the firm's stakeholders. The Accommodative strategy attempts to satisfy stakeholder demands. The Proactive approach accepts and anticipates stakeholder interests. Results from this stakeholder assessment should be included in the social audit, which assesses and reports a firm's performance in fulfilling the economic, legal, ethical, and philanthropic social responsibilities expected by the stakeholders.

Responsible Business Debate

Best Buy Excels in Stakeholder Communication

Issue: *Is communication the key to stakeholder satisfaction?*

Best Buy was founded in 1966 by Richard Schulze. Ranking 72 on the Fortune 500 list, it is known for its discounted, high-quality products, customer-centered approach, sustainable outreach, and extensive recycling program. The success of Best Buy over the years can be attributed to a variety of factors, including savvy business decisions and services to increase employee and customer satisfaction.

As primary stakeholders, customers and employees have a major impact on the continued existence and profit of Best Buy; therefore, their satisfaction is a high priority. To meet stakeholders' interests, Best Buy has implemented methods to foster communication with both customers and employees. The company uses its website to learn more about its customers' needs and preferences, and customers can use that website to rate every product purchased. It was this type of communication that led Best Buy to develop its first *Corporate Social Responsibility Report* in 2007. The report was a response to its customers' repeated concerns over sustainability, particularly in the area of electronics. It showed customers that the company had received and understood their concerns. Electronic waste was filling landfills, and customers wanted to see this problem addressed. In response, Best Buy implemented a wide-scale electronics recycling program. The company has set a goal to cut carbon emissions by 60 percent in the next year and to be carbon neutral by 2050.

After a period of stagnant growth, Best Buy hired a new CEO, Hubert Joly, in 2012. Under Joly, Best Buy once again became a growth company. Research has shown that Best Buy's advertisements tend to have more of an impact when they highlight products, which is prompting the company to engage in more product-oriented advertising campaigns. For example, the company introduced a service called "Assured Living" in 2017, which uses smart home technology to allow millennials/caregivers to look in on their aging parents while permitting the seniors to live independently. To communicate this new service to consumers, Best Buy has developed a website and has advisors that can offer more detailed information to customers about the technology. Best Buy's current CEO, Corie Barry, will work to continue this growth.

Best Buy invests in different platforms to foster its communication with employees. For example, Geek Squad forums provide a way for all Best Buy employees to exchange information and share ideas. In addition, Best Buy has conducted a multitude of interviews with employees to determine issues with usability of the store's products. In response to these interviews, according to vice president of retail operations, Shari Rossow, Best Buy has invested in everyday products familiar to employees to cut back on necessary training, make employee duties easier, and help employees focus more on customer service than learning arduous programs. This not only benefits the employees, but also benefits customers and Best Buy as a company.

Stakeholder satisfaction is crucial to the success of any business, and communication with stakeholders is the key to that satisfaction. Best Buy has proved that it can listen to its stakeholders and will implement initiatives based upon their feedback. This communication has been integral in allowing Best Buy to develop strong stakeholder relationships, allowing the company to compete against online rivals and adapt to an increasingly digital world.

There Are Two Sides to Every Issue

1. Communication is the most important factor in stakeholder satisfaction.
2. Though communication is critical, it is one of many factors in stakeholder satisfaction.

Sources: Courtney Reagan, "Best Buy CEO Sees 'Growth Opportunities' Ahead, Wall Street Isn't Buying It," *CNBC*, September 19, 2017, https://www.cnbc.com/2017/09/19/best-buy-ceo-weve-fixed-what-was-broken-now-focus-is-on-growth.html (accessed January 6, 2019); Adrianne Pasquarelli, "Why Best Buy Is Reorganizing Its Marketing Team," *AdAge*, April 21, 2017, http://adage.com/article/cmo-strategy/buy-reorganizes-marketing-team/308756/ (accessed January 6, 2019); Jeff Bullas, "How Best Buy Energized 170,000 Employees with Social Media," *jeffbullas.com*, http://www.jeffbullas.com/how-best-buy-energized-170000-employees-with-social-media/ (accessed January 6, 2019); Best Buy, "Corporate Responsibility and Sustainability," 2018, https://corporate.bestbuy.com/sustainability/ (accessed January 6, 2019); Corinne Ruff, "Why Best Buy Is Investing in Employees," *Retail Dive*, February 7, 2018, https://www.retaildive.com/news/why-best-buy-is-investing-in-employees/516497/ (accessed January 6, 2019); "Fortune 500," *Fortune*, 2018, http://fortune.com/fortune500/list/ (accessed January 6, 2019).

Key Terms

crisis management (p. 51)
enlightened capitalism (p. 39)
ethical misconduct disaster (EMD)
     (p. 50)
legitimacy (p. 46)
marketplace of ideas (p. 49)

power (p. 45)
primary stakeholders (p. 40)
reputation management (p. 48)
secondary stakeholders (p. 40)
social audit (p. 59)
social capital (p. 54)

stakeholder engagement (p. 40)
stakeholder interaction model
     (p. 42)
stakeholder map (p. 42)
stakeholder orientation (p. 42)
urgency (p. 46)

Discussion Questions

1. Define "stakeholder" in your own terms. Compare your definition with the definition used in this chapter.
2. What is the difference between primary and secondary stakeholders? Why is it important for companies to make this distinction?
3. How do legitimacy, urgency, and power attributes positively and negatively affect a stakeholder's ability to develop relationships with organizations?
4. What is reputation management? Explain why companies are concerned about their reputation and its effects on stakeholders. What are the four elements of reputation management? How has the marketplace of ideas affected reputation management strategies in companies?

5. Define "crisis management." What should a company facing a crisis do to satisfy its stakeholders and protect its reputation?
6. Describe the process of developing stakeholder relationships. What parts of the process seem most important? What parts seem most difficult?
7. How can a stakeholder orientation and stakeholder map be implemented to improve social responsibility?
8. What are the differences between the reactive, defensive, accommodative, and proactive approaches to stakeholder relationships?

Experiential Exercise

Choose two companies in different industries and visit their respective websites. Peruse these sites for information that is directed at three company stakeholders: employees, customers, and the general public. For example, a company that places its annual reports online may be appealing primarily to the interests of investors. Make a list of the types of information that are on the site and indicate how the information might be used and perceived by these three stakeholder groups. What differences and similarities did you find between the two companies?

Thai Die…Environmental Exploitation or Economic Development: What Would You Do?

Literally hundreds of buildings dotted the ground below, and the thousands of cars on highways looked like ants on a mission. The jet airliner made its way to the Bangkok International Airport and eased into the humid afternoon. The group of four passed through customs control and looked for the limousine provided by Suvar Corporation, their Thai liaison in this new business venture. Representing Global Amusements were the vice president of corporate development, director of Asian operations, vice president of global relations, and director of governmental relations for Southeast Asia.

Global Amusements, headquartered in London, was considering the development of a Thai cultural amusement center on the island of Phuket. Phuket is a tourist destination known for its stunning beaches, fine resorts, and famous Thai hospitality. Both Global Amusements and Suvar Corporation believed that Phuket was a great candidate for a new project. The amusement center would focus on the history of Thailand and include a variety of live performances, rides, exhibits, and restaurants. Domestic and international tourists who visited Phuket would be the primary target market.

Global Amusements had been in business for nearly 20 years and currently used a joint venture approach in establishing new properties. Suvar was its Thai partner, and the two firms had been successful two years ago in developing a water amusement park outside Bangkok. Phuket could hold much promise, but there were likely to be questions about the potential destruction of its beauty and the exploitation of this well-preserved island and cultural reserve. These concerns were heightened as the island slowly recovered from the 2004 tsunami and set a course for managing future development.

Following a day to adjust to the time zone and refine the strategy for the visit, the next three days would be spent in Bangkok, meeting with various company and governmental officials who had a stake in the proposed amusement facility. After a short flight to Phuket, the group would be the guest of the Southern Office of the Tourism Authority of Thailand for nearly a week. This part of the trip would involve visits to possible sites, as well as meetings with island government officials and local interest groups.

After arriving at the hotel, the four employees of Global Amusement agreed to meet later that evening to discuss their strategy for the visit. One of their main concerns was the development of an effective stakeholder analysis. Each member of the group was asked to bring a list of primary and secondary stakeholders and indicate the various concerns, or stakes, that each might have with the proposed project. What would you do?

Corporate Governance

Bored with Male Dominance: California Requires Women on Corporate Boards

The number of women on public company boards is growing but still small compared to the number of men. In the United States, only 19 percent of board members of S&P 500 companies are women. While women are as qualified as men to serve on boards, there has been a failure in developing diversity. This is highly limiting for corporations, given the many benefits of having women on boards of directors.

According to one study, having three or more female board members has been linked to more innovation and limits the chance that women's views will be sidelined. Another study by the European Corporate Governance Institute revealed that of the 1,691 corporate boards studied, firms with a larger female presence had larger dividend payouts. Tere Blanca, founder and chair of the commercial real estate firm Blanca, says that studies back the idea that better financial performance is linked to higher representation of women.

Women are also becoming more educated than men. According to data released by the National Center for Education Statistics, during the 2016–2017 academic year, women earned 57 percent of bachelor's degrees, over 62 percent of master's degrees, and 53 percent of PhDs, medical degrees, and law degrees in the United States. This means that there are more women educated at each level each year than men. Therefore, women are just as qualified as men to serve at the highest levels in business.

Given these benefits, there has been a push for women to be included on corporate boards. Jerry Brown, former governor of California, signed a bill requiring all California public companies to have at least one female board member by 2019. That number will increase by the end of 2021 to a minimum of two to three women board members depending on the size of the board. If companies fail to comply with these requirements, they will face large fines. This push is not limited to the United States. Recently, Germany passed a regulation stating that at least 30 percent of board members must be women.

Although the California bill faces skepticism, and many call it unconstitutional, it has received overwhelming support. In addition to legal requirements, the 2020 Women on Boards campaign was dedicated to increasing the percentage of women on corporate boards by 20 percent by 2020, a goal which was achieved. According to research done by the campaign, 60 percent of female board seats were added in 2019 instead of taking seats from men.

Connecticut, Michigan, Minnesota, and Washington are the leading states when it comes to female representation, according to the 2020 Women on Boards campaign. As statistics show, women are starting to accomplish a lot more than men in all aspects of education. This could translate into more and more women leading the business world in the near future.[1]

Chapter Objectives

- Define corporate governance
- Describe the history and practice of corporate governance
- Examine key issues to consider in designing corporate governance systems
- Describe the application of corporate governance principles around the world
- Provide information on the future of corporate governance

Business decisions today are increasingly placed under a microscope by stakeholders and the media, especially those made by high-level personnel in publicly held corporations. Stakeholders are demanding greater transparency in business, meaning that company motives and actions must be clear, open for discussion, and subject to scrutiny. Recent scandals and the associated focus on the role of business in society have highlighted a need for systems that take into account the goals and expectations of various stakeholders. Additionally, boards need to be representative of the larger population, as the push for more female involvement on boards illustrates. To respond to these pressures, businesses must effectively implement policies that provide strategic guidance on appropriate courses of action. This focus is part of *corporate governance*, the system of checks and balances that ensures that organizations are fulfilling the goals of social responsibility.

Governance procedures and policies are typically discussed in the context of publicly traded firms, especially as they relate to corporations' responsibilities to investors.[2] However, the trend is toward discussing governance within many industry sectors, including nonprofits, small businesses, and family-owned enterprises. Corporate governance deserves broader consideration because there is evidence of a link between good governance and strong social responsibility, which is the adoption by a business of a strategic focus for fulfilling the economic, legal, ethical, and philanthropic responsibilities that their stakeholders expect. Corporate governance and accountability are key drivers of change for business in the twenty-first century. The corporate misconduct at firms such as Wells Fargo, Intel, and Volkswagen (VW) represent fundamental failures in corporate governance systems that provide oversight. Investors and other stakeholders must be able to trust management while boards of directors oversee managerial decisions. During the Great Recession in 2008–2009, some of the nation's oldest and most respected financial institutions teetered on the brink of failure and were either bailed out or acquired by other firms. Many problems in the financial sector come from boards of directors allowing excessive risk taking.

In this chapter, we define corporate governance and integrate the concept with the other elements of social responsibility. Then, we examine the corporate governance framework used in this book. Next, we trace the evolution of corporate governance and provide information on the status of corporate governance systems in several countries. We look at the history of corporate governance and the relationship of corporate governance to social responsibility. We also examine primary issues that should be considered in the development and improvement of corporate governance systems, including the roles of boards of directors, shareholder activism, internal control and risk management, and executive compensation. Finally, we consider the future of corporate governance and indicate how strong governance is tied to corporate performance and economic growth. Our approach in this chapter is to demonstrate that corporate governance is a fundamental aspect of social responsibility.

Corporate Governance Defined

In a general sense, the term *governance* relates to the exercise of oversight, control, and authority. For example, most institutions, governments, and businesses are organized so that oversight, control, and authority are clearly delineated. These organizations usually have an owner, president, and chief executive officer (CEO), as well as a board of directors that serves as the ultimate authority on decisions and actions. The **board of directors** is made up of members who represent shareholders and oversee the firm's operations and legal and ethical compliance. A

board of directors
a group of members who represent shareholders and oversee the firm's operations and legal and ethical compliance

board of directors should have final authority on decisions, including the ability to approve corporate strategy, provide financial oversight, and even remove the CEO. Nonprofit organizations, such as homeowners' associations, have a president and a board of directors to make decisions in the interest of a specific community (such as homeowners, in this example). A clear delineation of power and account-ability helps stakeholders understand why and how the organization chooses and achieves its goals. This delineation also demonstrates who bears the ultimate risk for organizational decisions. Legally, Sarbanes-Oxley and the Federal Sentencing Guidelines for Organizations (FGSO) place responsibility and accountability on top officers and the board of directors. Although many companies have adopted decentralized decision-making, empowerment, team projects, and less hierarchical structures, governance remains a required mechanism for ensuring accountability to regulatory authorities. Even if a company has adopted a consensus approach for its operations, there has to be authority for delegating tasks, making tough and controversial decisions, and balancing power throughout the organization. Governance also provides oversight to uncover and address mistakes, risks, and ethical and legal misconduct. More recently, boards at Wells Fargo and Nissan have been criticized for issues such as failing to implement the division of leader-ship, thereby giving certain members of their boards excessive power, and failing to consider stakeholders such as employees in the governance decisions. On the other hand, Hasbro and Estée Lauder have been celebrated for their innovation, strong leaders who have capitalized on advances in technology, and executive compensation that is dependent upon return on investment.[3]

We define **corporate governance** as the formal system of oversight of, account-ability for, and control over organizational decisions and resources. *Oversight* relates to a system of checks and balances that limit employees' and managers' opportunities to deviate from policies and codes of conduct. *Accountability* relates to how well the content of workplace decisions is aligned with a firm's stated strategic direction. *Control* involves the process of auditing and improving organizational decisions and actions. The philosophy that is embraced by a board or firm regarding oversight, accountability, and control directly affects how corporate governance works. Table 3.1 describes some examples of important corporate governance decisions.

corporate governance
formal system of oversight of, accountability for, and control over organizational decisions and resources

Corporate Governance Framework

The majority of businesses and many courses taught in colleges of business operate under the belief that the purpose of business is to maximize profits for shareholders. A **shareholder** is any person or entity that owns at least one share of a company's stock. Shareholders are not liable for a company's financial

shareholder
any person or entity that owns at least one share of a company's stock

Table 3.1 Corporate Governance Decisions

Decision Area	Example
Ethical and legal risks	The board approve ethics and compliance programs
Regulatory financial reporting	Audit committee oversees financial reporting
Compensation	Committee approves compensation for top officers
Strategy	The board approves decisions related to strategies, mergers, and acquisitions
Finance	Major decisions related to the use of financial assets, including issuing stocks and bonds
Stakeholders	Decisions regarding employee benefits, shareholder rights, and contributions to society

obligations. The Michigan Supreme Court, in the 1919 case of *Dodge v. Ford Motor Co.*, ruled that a business exists for the profit of shareholders and the board of directors should focus on that objective.[4] On the other hand, the stakeholder model places the board of directors in the central position in order to balance the interests and conflicts of the various constituencies. As we will see, there should be no conflict between maximizing profits and maintaining a stakeholder orientation. External control of the corporation includes not only government regulations, but also key stakeholders such as employees, consumers, and communities, who exert pressure favoring responsible conduct. Many of the obligations to balance stakeholder interest have been institutionalized in legislation that provides incentives for responsible conduct. It is not correct to assume that it is necessary to take advantage of or ignore stakeholders to maximize profits. There is much evidence that a stakeholder orientation maximizes profits in the long run. By taking preventive action against misconduct, a company may avoid onerous penalties should a violation occur. Top officers and the board of directors are legally responsible for accurate financial reporting, as well as providing oversight to manage ethical decision-making. Today, most companies understand that ethical decision-making supports their reputation and encourages the cooperation of their stakeholders.

Therefore, the failure to balance stakeholder interests can result in a failure to maximize shareholders' wealth. Sometimes the issue is so major that fines and serious penalties occur as a result. For example, Tyson Foods pleaded guilty to criminal charges for violating the Clean Water Act by improperly dumping waste. Tyson Foods agreed to pay a $2 million criminal fine and a $500,000 fine to help clean up the waste it dumped. Tyson chose to favor its shareholders over its stakeholders by saving money through improper waste-dumping, but they ended up harming stakeholders, many of which were also shareholders.[5] Most firms are moving more toward a balanced stakeholder model, as they see that this approach will sustain the relationships necessary for long-run success.

Both directors and officers of corporations are fiduciaries for the shareholders. **Fiduciaries** are persons placed in positions of trust who use due care and loyalty in acting on behalf of the best interests of the organization. There is a **duty of care**, also called a *duty of diligence*, to make informed and prudent decisions.[6] Directors have an obligation to avoid ethical misconduct in their role and to provide leadership in decisions to prevent ethical misconduct in the organization. Directors are not held responsible for negative outcomes if they are informed and diligent in their decision-making. For example, the directors of General Motors (GM) must be diligent in ensuring that financial reporting is accurate to the best of their knowledge. Manufacturing cars that lose market share is a serious concern, although it is not a legal issue. On the other hand, if the directors know that the firm is covering up a safety concern, then they can be held responsible. This means directors have an obligation to request information, do research, use accountants and attorneys, and obtain the services of consultants in matters where they need assistance or advice.

The **duty of loyalty** means that all decisions should be in the interests of the corporation and its stakeholders. **Conflicts of interest** exist when a director uses the position to obtain personal gain, usually at the expense of the organization. For example, Nissan's former CEO Carlos Ghosn may have experienced a conflict of interest when he served as the CEO and chairman of Nissan, the CEO and chairman of Renault, and chairman of Mitsubishi. Following the termination and arrest of Ghosn, the Nissan board of directors approved the establishment of a Special Committee for Improving Governance, which recommended that Nissan senior executives refrain from working for either Renault or Mitsubishi. As they are Nissan's alliance partners, working for Renault or Mitsubishi poses a conflict of interest for Nissan executives. Many corporate governance experts have criticized appointing the same person as both CEO and chairman, although it has been a

fiduciaries
persons placed in positions of trust who use due care and loyalty in acting on behalf of the best interests of the organization

duty of care
(also known as duty of diligence) the obligation of directors and officers to avoid ethical misconduct and provide leadership to prevent ethical misconduct in the organization

duty of loyalty
the obligation of directors and officers to make decisions in the interests of the corporation and its stakeholders

conflicts of interest
using one's position within an organization to obtain personal gain, at the expense of the organization

common occurrence in U.S. companies. Recently, however, this has been changing. The percentage of S&P 500 businesses with CEOs who also serve as chairman has decreased by 3 percent from previous years.[7]

Officer compensation packages are a challenge for directors, especially those on the board who are not independent of the company. Directors have an opportunity to vote for others' compensation in return for their own increased compensation. Opportunities to know about the investments, business ventures, and stock market information create issues that could violate the duty of loyalty. Insider trading of a firm's stock is illegal, and violations can result in serious punishment. **Insider trading** is the act of purchasing or selling a public company's security with access to nonpublic information about the company. A probe of Samsung involving several employees, including president-level executives, was launched to investigate whether the employees used insider trading tips to profit from an upcoming purchase. The employees allegedly purchased $43 million in a Samsung de facto holding company before it disclosed plans to purchase an affiliate firm. This knowledge would have provided them with an unfair advantage that other shareholders did not have. If found guilty, employees could face fines and jail time.[8] The ethical and legal obligations of directors and officers are intertwined with their fiduciary relationships to the company. Ethical values should guide decisions and protect against the possibility of illegal conduct. With increased pressure on directors to provide oversight for organizational ethics and compliance, there is a trend toward director training to increase their competence in ethics program development, as well as other areas, such as accounting.

Corporate governance establishes fundamental systems and processes for oversight, accountability, and control. This requires investigating, disciplining, and planning for recovery and continuous improvement. Effective corporate governance creates compliance and values so that employees feel that integrity lies at the core of competitiveness.[9] Even if a company has adopted a consensus approach to decision-making, there should be oversight and authority for delegating tasks, making difficult and sometimes controversial decisions, balancing power throughout the firm, and maintaining social responsibility. Governance also provides mechanisms for identifying risks and planning for recovery when mistakes or problems occur.

The development of a stakeholder orientation should work with the corporation's governance structure. Corporate governance is also the part of a firm's corporate culture that establishes the integrity of all relationships. A governance system that does not provide checks and balances creates opportunities for top managers to put their own self-interests before those of important stakeholders. Medical products distributor McKesson Corp. announced changes in corporate governance at the behest of stakeholders. CEO John H. Hammergren's compensation has been called into question for reaching unprecedented levels, and the restructuring addressed these issues. The company reevaluated other aspects of governance and plans to implement more changes in phases. McKesson Corp. has demonstrated transparency on their website by listing all of the members of the board and various committees, including an independent chair of the board of directors.[10] Concerns about the need for greater corporate governance are not limited to the United States. Reforms in governance structures and issues are occurring all over the world.[11] In many nations, companies are being pressured to implement stronger corporate governance mechanisms by international investors; by the process of becoming privatized after years of unaccountability as state companies; or by the desire to imitate successful governance movements in the United States, Japan, and the European Union.[12] As the business world becomes more global, standardization of governance becomes important in order for multinational and international companies to maintain standards and a level of control.

insider trading
the act of purchasing or selling a public company's security with access to nonpublic information about the company

Table 3.2 lists examples of major corporate governance issues. These issues normally involve strategic-level decisions and actions taken by boards of directors, business owners, top executives, and other managers with high levels of authority and accountability. Although these people have often been relatively free from scrutiny, changes in technology, consumer activism, government attention, recent ethical scandals, and other factors have brought new attention to such issues as transparency, executive pay, risk and control, resource accountability, strategic direction, stockholder rights, and other decisions made for the organization.

History of Corporate Governance

In the United States, a discussion of corporate governance draws on many parallels with the goals and values held by the U.S. founders.[13] As mentioned earlier in the chapter, governance involves a system of checks and balances, a concept associated with the distribution of power within the executive, judiciary, and legislative branches of the U.S. government. The U.S. Constitution and other documents have a strong focus on accountability, individual rights, and the representation of broad interests in decision-making and resource allocation.

In the late 1800s and early 1900s, corporations were headed by such familiar names as Andrew Carnegie, E.I. DuPont, and John D. Rockefeller. These so-called captains of industry had ownership investment and managerial control over their businesses. Thus, there was less reason to talk about corporate governance because the owner of the firm was the same individual who made strategic decisions about the business. The owner primarily bore the consequences—positive or negative—of decisions. During the twentieth century, however, an increasing number of public companies and investors brought about a shift in the separation of ownership and control. By the 1930s, corporate ownership was dispersed across a large number of individuals. This raised new questions about control and accountability for organizational resources and decisions.

One of the first known anecdotes that helped shape our current understanding of accountability and control in business occurred in the 1930s. In 1932, Lewis Gilbert, a stockholder in New York's Consolidated Gas Company, found his questions repeatedly ignored at the firm's annual shareholders' meeting. Gilbert and his brother took the problem to the federal government and pushed for reform, which led to the creation of the **U.S. Securities and Exchange Commission (SEC)**. The SEC is the government agency that oversees the operations and protection of securities markets and investors. Because of the Gilbert brothers' activism, the SEC

U.S. Securities and Exchange Commission (SEC)
the government agency that oversees the operations and protection of securities markets and investors

Table 3.2 Corporate Governance Issues

Shareholder rights
Executive compensation
Composition and structure of the board of directors
Auditing and control
Risk management
CEO selection and termination decisions
Integrity of financial reporting
Stakeholder participation and input into decisions
Compliance with corporate governance reform
Role of the CEO in board decisions
Organizational ethics programs

formalized the process by which executives and boards of directors respond to the concerns and questions of investors.[14]

Since the mid-1900s, the approach to corporate governance has involved a legal discussion of principals and agents to the business relationship. Essentially, owners are "principals" who hire "agents," the executives, to run the business. A key goal of businesses is to align the interests of principals and agents so that organizational value and viability are maintained. Achieving this balance has been difficult, as evidenced by these business terms coined by the media—*junk bonds*, *empire building*, *golden parachute*, and *merger madness*—all of which have negative connotations. In these cases, the long-term value and competitive stance of organizations were traded for short-term financial gains or rewards. The results of this short-term view included workforce reduction, closed manufacturing plants, struggling communities, and a generally negative perception of corporate leadership. In our philosophy of social responsibility, these long-term effects should be considered alongside decisions designed to generate short-run gains in financial performance.

The Sarbanes-Oxley Act was the most significant piece of corporate governance reform at the time since the 1930s. Under these rules, both CEOs and chief financial officers (CFOs) are required to certify that their quarterly and annual reports accurately reflect performance and comply with the requirements of the SEC. Among other changes, the act also required more independence of boards of directors, protected whistleblowers, and established the Public Company Accounting Oversight Board (PCAOB). The New York Stock Exchange (NYSE) and NASDAQ also overhauled the governance standards required for listed firms. Business ethics, director qualifications, unique concerns of foreign firms, loans to officers and directors, internal auditing, and many other issues were part of the NYSE and NASDAQ reforms.[15]

Despite the implementation of Sarbanes-Oxley, corporate misconduct and the quest for short-term profits led the U.S. financial system to a near-collapse during the last recession. The cause was a pervasive use of instruments like credit default swaps, risky debt like subprime lending, and corruption in major corporations. The government was forced to step in and bail out many financial companies. Later, because of the weak financial system and reduced consumption, the government also had to step in to help the major automotive companies GM and Chrysler. The U.S. government became a majority shareholder in GM, an unprecedented move (it has since divested itself of its final shares). Not since the Great Depression and President Franklin Delano Roosevelt has the United States seen such widespread government intervention and regulation—something that most deem necessary but is nevertheless worrisome to free market capitalists. The basic assumptions of capitalism are under debate as countries around the world work to stabilize markets and question those that managed the money of individual corporations and nonprofits. The latest recession caused many to question government institutions that provide oversight and regulation. As changes are made, there is a need to address issues related to law, ethics, and the required level of compliance necessary for government and business to serve the public interest.

In recent years, diversity has become an important issue in corporate governance. Corporate boards are traditionally comprised only of men, which can lead to a lack of perspective. In response, some countries have passed laws mandating a certain number of women on corporate boards. For example, Germany passed a law requiring boards to be comprised of at least 30 percent women. In the United States, there is no federal mandate to include women in corporate boards; however, California recently passed a law requiring that at least one woman be included on a corporate board for a publicly traded company. Critics argue that this practice could lead to more unqualified board members, but proponents argue that without such quotas, companies won't diversify their boards.[16]

Finance Reforms

The lack of effective control and accountability mechanisms prompted a strong interest in corporate governance. In 2010, the Dodd-Frank Wall Street Reform and Consumer Protection Act was passed to protect consumers from overly complex financial instruments, better regulate the financial industry, and prevent too-big-to-fail financial institutions. (One of the reasons why the government had to intervene during the financial meltdown was that allowing large institutions such as Bank of America or AIG to fail would devastate the economy at a much higher rate.) The Dodd-Frank Wall Street Reform and Consumer Protection Act established a Consumer Financial Protection Bureau (CFPB), among other agencies. The CFPB is similar to the Bureau of Consumer Protection of the Federal Trade Commission (FTC), in that its purpose is to protect consumers from being deceived by institutions selling high-risk financial products. The Dodd-Frank Act will be discussed in detail in the following chapter. Boards of directors have the responsibility to provide oversight and compliance with regulations.

Beyond the legal issues associated with governance, there has also been interest in the board's role in social responsibility and stakeholder engagement. Table 3.3 provides a list of companies with good corporate governance. The board of directors should provide leadership for social responsibility initiatives. It is apparent that some boards have been assuming greater responsibility for strategic decisions and have decided to focus on building more effective social responsibility.

Table 3.3 Companies with Good Corporate Governance

AT&T
Coeur Mining
Comscore
General Motors Company
Guardian Life
IBM
NorthWestern Energy
Royal Bank of Canada
Salesforce.com
VF Corporation

Source: IR Media Group Ltd., "Corporate Governance Awards 2019," *Corporate Secretary*, 2019, https://events.irmagazine.com/cga/wp-content/uploads/sites/122/2019/11/CGA19-short-lists-FINAL-WINNERS.pdf.

Corporate Governance and Social Responsibility

Corporate social responsibility (CSR) can be a difficult concept to define. While there is broad agreement among professionals, academics, and policymakers that being socially responsible does pay, CSR always involves trade-offs, and most businesses have yet to formulate an idea of what social responsibility really entails for their organizations.[17] Interpreted narrowly, a company can consider itself socially responsible if it generates returns for shareholders and provides jobs for employees (called the *shareholder model*). A broad definition of social responsibility interprets the corporation as a vehicle for stakeholders and for public policy (called the *stakeholder model*). A company that takes the latter view would be more concerned with the public good, as well as with profitability and shareholder return. Because most firms have so many potential stakeholders, a key to developing a socially responsible agenda involves determining which of these groups are most important for your business. Social responsibility should seek to help a firm's principal stakeholders. For example, a line of high-end organic soaps might seek to source its ingredients from sustainable sources, avoid products that have been tested on animals, and hire workers at living wages.

To understand the role of corporate governance in business today, it is also important to consider how it relates to fundamental beliefs about the purpose of business organizations. Some people believe that so long as a company is maximizing shareholder wealth and profitability, it is fulfilling its core responsibility. Although this must be accomplished in accordance with legal and ethical standards, the primary focus is on the economic dimension of social responsibility. Thus, this belief places the philanthropic dimension beyond the scope of business. Other people, however, take the view that a business is an important member, or citizen, of society and must assume broad responsibilities. This view assumes that business performance is reflexive, meaning it both affects and is influenced by internal and external factors. In this case, performance is often considered from a financial, social, and ethical perspective. From these assumptions, we can derive two major conceptualizations of corporate governance: the shareholder model and the stakeholder model.

The **shareholder model of corporate governance** is founded in classic economic precepts, including the maximization of wealth for investors and owners. For publicly traded firms, corporate governance focuses on developing and improving the formal system of performance accountability between top management and the firms' shareholders.[18] Thus, the shareholder model should drive management decisions toward what is in the best interests of investors. Underlying these decisions is a classic agency problem, where ownership (i.e., investors) and control (i.e., managers) are separate. Managers act as agents for investors, and their primary goal is to generate value for shareholders. However, investors and managers are distinct parties with unique insights, goals, and values with respect to the business. Managers, for example, may have motivations beyond shareholder value, such as market share, personal compensation, or attachment to particular products and projects. Because of these potential differences, corporate governance mechanisms are needed to ensure an alignment between investor and management interests.

For example, Deutsche Bank was investigated for a number of questionable practices, including possible manipulation of worldwide benchmark interest rates and legality of payment processing in various countries. These activities generated profits and raised the company's stock price. As a result of alleged misconduct, numerous employees were fired, at least $6.9 billion were paid in fines and penalties, and former senior executive William Broeksmit died by suicide in 2014 after displaying anxiety toward potential investigations of Deutsche Bank. This caused harm to investors, as these costs drove down the stock price.[19] The shareholder model has been criticized for its somewhat singular purpose and focus because there are other ways of investing in a business. Suppliers, creditors, customers, employees, business partners, the community, and others also "invest" their resources in the success of the firm.

In the **stakeholder model of corporate governance**, the purpose of business is conceived in a broader fashion. Although a company has a responsibility for economic success and viability, it must also answer to other parties, including employees, suppliers, government agencies, communities, and groups with which it interacts. This model presumes a collaborative and relational approach to business and its constituents. Because management time and resources are limited, a key decision within the stakeholder model is to determine which stakeholders are primary. Once primary groups have been identified, appropriate corporate governance mechanisms are implemented to promote the development of long-term relationships.[20] As discussed in Chapter 2, primary stakeholders include shareholders, suppliers, customers, employees, the government, and the community. Governance systems that consider stakeholder welfare in tandem with corporate needs and interests characterize this approach. For instance, several companies, including ASOS, Marks & Spencer, and Uniqlo, have been accused of using child labor in their supply chains in order to produce their products.

Questionable market channels can damage a firm's reputation and social responsibility agenda. For example, students of Georgetown University staged several protests over the university's licensing agreement with Nike. Students were concerned over labor conditions for Nike employees in foreign countries like Vietnam. The company barred third-party monitors from investigating working conditions in Vietnam and engaged in labor abuses like wage theft, forced overtime, and dangerous working

shareholder model of corporate governance
founded in classic economic precepts, a model that focuses on making decisions toward what is in the best interest of investors

stakeholder model of corporate governance
a model where the business is accountable to all its stakeholders, not just shareholders

Shutterstock/Leonard Zhukovsky

conditions. These protests damaged Nike's reputation and pressured the company into agreeing to better monitor labor conditions in their foreign factories.[21]

Although these two approaches seem to represent opposite ends of a continuum, the reality is that the shareholder model is often a precursor to the stakeholder model. Many businesses have evolved into the stakeholder model as a result of government initiatives, consumer activism, industry activity, and other external forces. In the aftermath of corporate scandals, it became clear how the economic accountability of corporations could not be detached from other responsibilities and stakeholder concerns. Although this trend began with large, publicly held firms, its aftereffects are being felt in other types of organizations and industries as well. Figure 3.1 illustrates a continuum of stakeholder concerns. One end demonstrates the shareholder model. The other end demonstrates a stakeholder model, with concern for various company stakeholders.

The shareholder model focuses on a primary stakeholder—the investor— whereas the stakeholder model incorporates a broader philosophy toward internal and external constituents. According to the World Bank, a development institution whose goal is to reduce poverty by promoting sustainable economic growth around the world, corporate governance is defined by both internal (i.e., long-term value and efficient operations) and external (i.e., public policy and economic development) factors.[22] We are concerned with the broader conceptualization of corporate governance in this chapter.

In the social responsibility model that we propose, governance is the organizing dimension for keeping a firm focused on continuous improvement, accountability, and engagement with stakeholders. Although financial return, or economic viability, is an important measure of success for all firms, the legal dimension of social responsibility is also a compulsory consideration. The ethical and philanthropic dimensions, however, have not been traditionally mandated through regulation or contracts. This represents a critical divide in our social responsibility model and associated governance goals and systems because there are some critics who challenge the use of organizational resources for concerns beyond financial performance and legalities. This view was summarized in an editorial in *National Journal*, a nonpartisan magazine on politics and government: "Corporations are not governments. In the everyday course of their business, they are not accountable to society or to the citizenry at large.... Corporations are bound by the law, and by the rules of what you might call ordinary decency. Beyond this, however, they have no duty to pursue the collective goals of society."[23] This type of philosophy, long associated with the shareholder model of corporate governance, prevailed throughout the twentieth century. However, as the consequences of neglecting the stakeholder model of CSR have become clearer, fewer firms persist in adhering to such a narrow view.

Figure 3.1 The Stakeholder Continuum

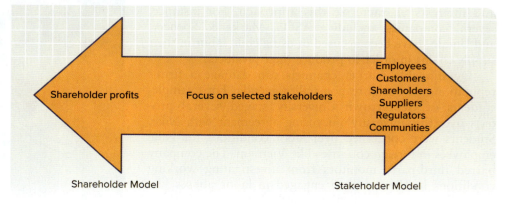

Ethical Responsibilities in **MANAGEMENT**

Home Depot Levels Out Its Management System

When Home Depot was founded by Bernie Marcus and Arthur Blank in 1979, the two men built a strong culture that placed customers and employees at the top and executives at the bottom. Home Depot's store-centric culture put emphasis on the satisfaction of the customer and the associate, leading to many years of success. However, after Robert Nardelli, a high-level executive at General Electric (GE), took over as CEO in December 2000, the style of leadership at Home Depot abruptly changed. Nardelli took a top-down approach to running the company: executives at the top and customers and employees at the bottom.

The new Home Depot culture created a hostile work environment for employees and executives, as Nardelli ran the store more like a military work environment than the laid-back climate workers were accustomed to. While sales doubled under Nardelli and many successful technology initiatives were implemented, the board of directors faced negative feedback from stakeholders.

Nardelli was replaced by Frank Blake as CEO in 2007. Blake quickly refocused on the inverted pyramid and began to restore the customer experience. When Blake took over as CEO, customer satisfaction was at an all-time low. He admitted that there were customer service problems, and each of the complaints was addressed.

After seven years with the company, Blake stepped down as CEO and was replaced by Craig Menear, who continues to hold the position. The succession was smooth—so well planned, in fact, that it had a minimal effect on Home Depot's stock price. Much like Blake, Menear proved that he would continue to focus on the core culture of the company. The 12-member board includes 3 women, and it regularly engages in board refreshment practices where board members from different backgrounds and genders are included in executive roles.

The firm has focused on employees and customers over the last five years, with a 135 percent increase in value for investors who bought shares. Executives are at the bottom of the pyramid, with employees being well compensated. They are given opportunities for learning and career development and provide excellent service to customers. Home Depot believes having managers at the bottom of the pyramid makes them take on the most responsibility in the business in order to provide employees with the resources that they need to focus on customers. The board of directors continues to provide leadership to support executives in developing and implementing the employee- and market-focused culture. Home Depot has overcome many issues in its culture, and the future is bright.

Sources: Julie Creswell and Michael Barbaro, "Home Depot Ousts Highly Paid Chief," *The New York Times,* January 4, 2007, http://www.nytimes.com/2007/01/04/business/04home.html?mcubz=3 (accessed April 25, 2019); Nathan Owen Rosenberg, "The Key to Home Depot's Success is Transformational Leadership," Insigniam, http://insigniam.com/blog/the-key-to-home-depots-success-is-transformational-leadership/ (accessed April 25, 2019); Rachel Tobin, "Frank Blake Is Home Depot's 'Calmer-in-Chief'," *Seattle Times,* September 4, 2010, https://www.seattletimes.com/business/frank-blake-is-home-depots-calmer-in-chief/ (accessed April 25, 2019); Home Depot, "Proxy Statement and Notice of 2019 Annual Meeting of Shareholders," April 8, 2019, https://ir.homedepot.com/~/media/Files/H/HomeDepot-IR/2019_Proxy_Updates/Final%202019%20Proxy%20Statement_vF.PDF (accessed April 25, 2019); Joseph McAdory, "Student Center for Public Trust: Carol Tome," Center for Ethical Organizational Cultures, September 27, 2018, http://harbert.auburn.edu/research-and-centers/center-for-ethical-organizational-cultures/student-center-for-public-trust.php (accessed April 25, 2019).

Issues in Corporate Governance Systems

Organizations that strive to develop effective corporate governance systems consider a number of internal and external issues. In this section, we look at four areas that need to be addressed in the design and improvement of governance mechanisms. We begin with boards of directors, which have the ultimate responsibility for ensuring governance. Then, we discuss shareholder activism, internal control and risk management, and executive compensation within the governance system. These issues affect most organizations, although individual businesses may face unique factors that create additional governance questions. For example, a company operating in several countries will need to resolve issues related to international governance policy. Table 3.4 discusses major areas of risk in corporate governance that organizational leaders are facing across various corporations.

Boards of Directors

A company's board of directors assumes responsibility for their resources and legal and ethical compliance. The board appoints top executive officers and is responsible for overseeing their performance. This is also true of a university's board of trustees, and there are similar arrangements in the nonprofit sector. In each of these cases, board members have a fiduciary duty, as discussed earlier in this chapter. These responsibilities include acting in the best interests of those they serve. Thus, board membership is not designed as a vehicle for personal financial gain; rather, it provides the intangible benefit of ensuring the success of the organization and the stakeholders affected and involved in the fiduciary arrangement.

In the case of public corporations, boards of directors hold the ultimate responsibility for their firms' ethical culture and legal compliance. This governing authority is held responsible by the 2004 and 2007 amendments to the Federal Sentencing Guidelines for Organizations (FGSO), for creating an ethical culture that provides leadership, values, and compliance. The members of a company's board of directors assume legal responsibility for the firm's resources and decisions, and they appoint its top executive officers. For example, Citigroup's board of directors decided that it was best to avoid conflicts of interest in corporate governance by separating the role of CEO from that of chairman.[24]

The traditional approach to directorship assumed that board members managed the corporation's business. Research and practical observation have shown that boards of directors rarely, if ever, perform the management function.[25] Because boards usually meet four to six times a year, there is no way that time allocation would allow effective management. In small nonprofit organizations, the board may manage most resources and decisions. The complexity of large organizations requires full attention on a daily basis. Today, boards of directors are concerned primarily with monitoring the decisions made by managers on behalf of the company. This includes choosing top executives, assessing their performances, helping to set strategic direction, evaluating company performance, developing CEO succession plans, communicating with stakeholders, maintaining legal and ethical practices, ensuring that control and accountability mechanisms are in place, choosing and communicating with auditors, and evaluating the board's own performance.

Table 3.4 Challenges in Corporate Governance

Challenge	Example
Independence	Increasing the percentage of independent directors who do not own shares or otherwise have a material interest in the company
Quality	Tracking quality control issues and ensuring that the organization meets benchmarks for product quality
Performance	Ensuring that performance meets shareholder expectations
Shareholder activism	Dealing with shareholder demands, such as calls for limiting executive compensation
Internal controls	Appointing an ethics officer to oversee the company's ethics and compliance program
Audits	Auditing different areas of the company periodically to determine areas of improvement
Risk management	Understanding major risks that the company faces and developing controls to limit these risks

Independence Just as social responsibility objectives require more employees and executives, boards of directors are also experiencing increasing accountability and disclosure mandates. The desire for independence is one reason that a few firms have chosen to split the powerful roles of chair of the board and CEO. Although the practice is common in the United Kingdom and activists have called for this move for years, the idea is newer to the United States and is sometimes met with resistance.

For instance, pressure has been repeatedly placed on JPMorgan Chase chairman and CEO James Dimon. After a number of regulatory hearings concerning the London Whale fiasco in which a trader lost billions for the bank, lack of oversight in the Bernard Madoff Ponzi scheme, and risky loans before the Great Recession, shareholders at JPMorgan requested that the chairman and CEO roles be divided. The request was met with resistance and did not pass a board vote, but Dimon did relinquish his role as chairman of the banking business. Some think this is an acknowledgment of responsibility and a step in the right direction concerning better corporate governance.[26]

Traditionally, board members were retired company executives or friends of current executives, but the trend since the corporate scandals associated with Enron, WorldCom, and more recently Countrywide Financial and JPMorgan has been toward independent directors who have valuable expertise, but little vested interest in the firm before assuming the director role. According to Rule 303A.01 of the NYSE corporate governance guidelines, the boards of listed companies must be comprised of a majority of independent directors.[27] However, a listed company in which more than 50 percent of the voting power for the election of directors is held by a group or individual does not have to abide by Rule 303A.01.[28]

Thus, directors today are more likely chosen for their competence, motivation, and ability to bring enlightened and diverse perspectives to strategic discussions. Outside directors are thought to bring more independence to the monitoring function because they are not bound by past allegiances, friendships, current roles in the company, or some other matter that may create a conflict of interest. However, independent directors who sit on a board for a long time may eventually lose some of their outsider perspective. Also, while they are more likely to be impartial, independent directors are not always guaranteed to avoid conflict of interest issues. For example, the Galleon Group, a hedge fund management firm, had independent directors on its board, but this did not stop massive misconduct. Founder Raj Rajaratnam was convicted of insider trading and was sentenced to 11 years in prison, one of the longest sentences to date for this crime. Directors have to avoid "groupthink" and be competent enough to understand risks. They must also be willing to ask for information relevant to avoiding organizational misconduct.

Quality Finding board members who have some expertise in the firm's industry or who have served as chief executives at similar-sized organizations is a good strategy for improving the board's overall quality. Directors with competence and experiences that reflect some of the firm's core issues should bring valuable insights to bear on discussions and decisions. Directors without direct industry or comparable executive experience may bring expertise on important issues, such as auditing, executive compensation, succession planning, and risk management,

Shutterstock/fizkes

to improve decision-making. Board members must understand the company's strategy and operations; this suggests that members should limit the number of boards on which they serve. Directors need time to read reports, attend board and committee meetings, and participate in continuing education that promotes strong understanding and quality guidance. For example, directors on the board's audit committee may need to be educated on new accounting and auditing standards. Experts recommend that fully employed board members sit on no more than four boards, whereas retired members should limit their memberships to seven boards. Directors should be able to attend at least 75 percent of the meetings. Thus, many of the factors that promote board quality are within the control of directors.[29]

Performance An effective board of directors can serve as a type of insurance against the business cycle and the natural highs and lows of the economy. A company with a strong board free from conflicts of interest and clearly stated corporate governance rules will be more likely to weather a storm if something bad does happen.[30] As federal regulations increase and the latitude afforded boards of directors shrinks, boards are going to be faced with greater responsibility and transparency.

Board independence, along with board quality, stock ownership, and corporate performance, is often used to assess the quality of corporate boards of directors. Many CEOs have lost their jobs because the board of directors have concerns about performance, ethics, and social responsibility. The main reason for this is the boards' fear of losing their personal assets, which stems from shareholders who have sued the directors of financial firms over their roles in the collapse on Wall Street. **Shareholder lawsuits** are lawsuits brought against a key member of a company, like a director or executive, where a shareholder or group of shareholders is suing on behalf of the corporation. If the lawsuit is won, the proceeds go back to the corporation, not the shareholder who brought the suit. These events make it clear that board members are accountable for oversight.

Just as improved ethical decision-making requires more of employees and executives, so too are boards of directors feeling greater demands for ethics and transparency. Directors today are increasingly chosen for their proficiency and ability to bring different perspectives to strategic discussions. As mentioned earlier, outside directors are thought to bring more independence to the monitoring function because they are not bound by past allegiances and other issues that may create a conflict of interest. The chair of the board audit committee must be an outside independent director with financial expertise.

Many of the corporate scandals uncovered in recent years might have been prevented if the companies' boards of directors had been better qualified, more knowledgeable, and less biased. The institution of the Volcker Rule, one component of the Dodd-Frank Act, provides stricter rules on financial management and controls on hedge funds and money-market mutual funds. The aim is to ensure that banks will have more liquid assets than before. It also aims to provide increased openness and transparency, greater oversight and enforcement, and clearer, more common-sense language in the financial system.[31] Board members are being asked to understand changes in regulations and participate in providing better oversight on risk-taking in their firms.

Rules promulgated by the Sarbanes-Oxley Act and various stock exchanges now require a majority of independent directors on the board that have no material relationship to the firm; regular meetings between nonmanagement board members; audit, compensation, governance, and nominating committees either fully made up of or with a majority of independent directors; no more than $120,000 in compensation for independent directors per year; and a financial expert on the audit committee. The governance area will continue to evolve as corporate scandals are resolved and the government and companies begin to implement and test new policies and practices. Regardless of the size and type of business for

shareholder lawsuits lawsuits brought against a key member of a company by a shareholder or group of shareholders suing on behalf of the corporation

which boards are responsible, a system of governance is needed to ensure effective control and accountability. As a corporation grows, matures, enters international markets, and takes other strategic directions, it is likely that the board of directors will evolve to meet its new demands. Sir Adrian Cadbury, former president of the Centre for Board Effectiveness at the Henley Business School in Reading, England, and an architect of corporate governance changes around the world, outlined the following responsibilities of strong boards:

- Boards are responsible for developing company purpose statements that cover a range of aims and stakeholder concerns.
- Annual reports and other documents must include more nonfinancial information.
- Boards are required to define their role and implement self-assessment processes better.
- Selection of board members must be increasingly formalized, with less emphasis on personal networks and word of mouth.
- Boards need to work effectively as teams.
- Serving on boards will require more time and commitment than in the past.[32]

These trends are consistent with our previous discussion of social responsibility. In all facets of organizational life, greater demands are being placed on business decisions and businesspeople. Many of these expectations emanate from those who provide substantial resources in the organization—namely, shareholders and other investors.

Shareholder Activism

Shareholders, including large institutional ones, have become more active in articulating their positions with respect to company strategy and executive decision-making. *Activism* is a broad term that can encompass engaging in dialogue with management, attending annual meetings, submitting shareholder resolutions, bringing lawsuits, and other mechanisms designed to communicate shareholder interests to the corporation. Table 3.5 lists characteristics of effective shareholder activism campaigns.

Shareholder resolutions are nonbinding, yet important, statements about shareholder concerns. A shareholder that meets certain guidelines may bring one resolution per year to a proxy vote of all shareholders at a corporation's annual meeting. A **proxy** is an agent who is legally authorized to act on behalf of another person/party. It is commonly used as a voting mechanism when a shareholder is

shareholder resolutions
nonbinding, yet important, statements about shareholder concerns

proxy
an agent legally authorized to act on behalf of another person/party. Used as a voting mechanism when a shareholder is not present at a shareholder's meeting

Table 3.5 Characteristics of Successful Shareholder Activism Campaigns

Characteristics	Description
Alliances	Partnerships with public interest groups with shared goals.
Grass-roots pressure	Encouraging the general public to contact government officials and legislators to generate support for a cause.
Public Relations	Proactive media outreach, media monitoring, and analysis of public sentiment.
Senior decision-makers	High-level negotiations and discussions with company executives and directors.
Adjusting the climate	A compelling financial argument, that makes it difficult for company management and other shareholders to say no.
Persistence	Commitment to the campaign, no matter how long it takes.

not able to physically attend a shareholder's meeting. Recent resolutions brought forth relate to auditor independence, executive compensation, independent directors, environmental impact, human rights, and other social responsibility issues. In some cases, the company will modify its policies or practices before the resolution is ever brought to a vote. In other situations, a resolution will receive less than a majority vote, but the media attention, educational value, and other stakeholder effects will cause a firm to reconsider, if not change, its original position to meet the resolution's proposal. For example, shareholders of Procter & Gamble (P&G) engaged in one of the biggest and most expensive proxy battles in the United States. Nearly 2 billion votes were cast to appoint Nelson Peltz to the P&G board of directors. While the proxy vote narrowly failed, Peltz was still appointed to the board after a recount. The proxy battle was estimated to cost more than $100 million.

Although labor and public pension fund activists have waged hundreds of proxy battles in recent years, they rarely have much effect on the target companies. Now shareholder activists are attacking the process by which directors themselves are elected. This includes **proxy access**, where a long-term shareholder, or a group of long-term shareholders, has the ability to nominate alternative candidates for the board of directors on the company's annual shareholder meeting ballot. After a poor performance leading up to the latest recession, Bank of America shareholders voted to oust six board members. The move got rid of entrenched directors with possible conflicts of interest and replaced them with qualified financial experts.[34] Although shareholders and investors want their resources used efficiently and effectively, they are increasingly willing to take a stand to encourage companies to make changes for reasons beyond financial return.

proxy access
the ability of long-term shareholders to nominate alternative candidates for the board of directors on the company's annual shareholder meeting ballot

Investor Confidence

Shareholders and other investors must have assurance that their money is being placed in the care of capable and trustworthy organizations. These primary stakeholders are expecting a solid return for their investment, but as illustrated earlier, they have additional concerns about social responsibility. When these fundamental expectations are not met, the confidence that investors and shareholders have in corporations, market analysts, investment houses, stockbrokers, mutual fund managers, financial planners, and other economic players and institutions can be severely tested. In Chapter 1, we discussed the importance of investor trust and loyalty to organizational and societal performance. Part of this trust relates to the perceived efficacy of corporate governance. Table 3.6 shows the characteristics of a well-governed board of directors.

Internal Control and Risk Management

Controls and a strong risk management system are fundamental to effective operations, as they allow comparisons between the actual performance and the planned performance and goals of the organization. Controls are used to safeguard corporate assets and resources, protect the reliability of organizational information, and ensure compliance with regulations, laws, and contracts. **Risk management** involves hedging uncertainty through quantitative plans and models and is the process used to anticipate and shield the organization from unnecessary or overwhelming circumstances, while ensuring that executive leadership is taking the appropriate steps to move the organization and its strategy forward.

risk management
hedging uncertainty while ensuring that leadership is taking the appropriate steps to move the organization and its strategy forward

Internal and External Audits   Auditing, both internal and external, is the linchpin between risk and controls and corporate governance. Boards of directors must ensure that the internal auditing function of the company is provided with

Table 3.6 Attributes of a Highly Functioning Board

Attribute	Description
Skills and knowledge	The board understands the attributes of successful leaders and how to apply them to the organization and its strategic plans; has experience developing leadership pipelines in organizations of similar size and scale; understands the mechanics of the company's compensation plans and the risks inherent in those plans.
Process	• Appoints the CEO and oversees the CEO's development, goal-setting, and compensation • Approves and monitors compensation performance metrics for the CEO • Oversees CEO compensation and transparent disclosure of executive compensation to stakeholders • Ensures the development of executive succession plans that contemplate various scenarios • Collaborates with management to develop and adopt a compensation philosophy for the organization • Meets periodically with executive leadership, including risk management and human resources, to understand organizational compensation plans, talent pipeline, and underlying risks • Monitors external stakeholder considerations related to executive management and compensation
Information	Obtains independent views and peer-company benchmarks of compensation plans proposed by management; has access to and receives periodic reports related to compensation plans, including internal audit and other reports; and monitors marketplace developments.
Behavior	Board leadership takes responsibility for the development of the CEO; appropriately supports and mentors the CEO; develops and maintains relationships with other key executives, especially those with potential to succeed the CEO.

Source: "Framing the Future of Corporate Governance," *Deloitte*, 2016, http://www2.deloitte.com/content/dam/Deloitte/us/Documents/risk/us-aers-framing-the-future-of-corporate-governance-09262014.pdf (accessed August 14, 2019).

adequate funding, up-to-date technology, unrestricted access, independence, and the authority to carry out its audit plan. To ensure these characteristics, the internal audit executive should report to the board's audit committee and, in most cases, the CEO.[35]

The external auditor should be chosen by the board and must clearly identify its client as the board, not the company's CFO. Under Sarbanes-Oxley, the board's audit committee should be directly responsible for the selection, payment, and supervision of the company's external auditor. Auditors are required to report directly to the board's audit committee rather than management. The act also prohibits an external auditing firm from performing some nonauditing work for the same public company, including bookkeeping, human resources, actuarial services, valuation services, legal services, and investment banking. However, even with regulations in place, many auditors failed to do their jobs properly. For example, trustees of New Century Financial Corporation sued its auditor, KPMG LLP, for "reckless and grossly negligent audits" that hid the company's financial problems and sped its collapse. New Century was one of the early casualties of the subprime mortgage crisis, but it was once one of the country's largest mortgage lenders to those with poor credit histories. After it disclosed accounting errors not discovered by KPMG, New Century collapsed.[36] Part of the problem relates to the sheer size and complexity of organizations, but these factors do not negate the tremendous responsibility that external auditors assume.

Control Systems   The area of internal control covers a wide range of company decisions and actions, not just the accuracy of financial statements and accounting records. Controls also foster understanding when discrepancies exist between corporate expectations and stakeholder interests and issues. Internal controls effectively limit employee or management opportunism or the use of corporate assets for individualistic or nonstrategic purposes. Controls also ensure the board of directors has access to timely and quality information that can be used to determine strategic options and effectiveness. For these reasons, the board should have ultimate oversight of the integrity of the internal control system.[37] Although board members do not develop or administer the control system, they are responsible for ensuring that an effective system exists. The need for internal controls is rarely disputed, but implementation can vary. The CEO or chair appears to be the key decision-maker relating to public and political debates that have an impact on shareholder value. Thus, internal control represents a set of tasks and resource commitments that require high-level attention. See Table 3.7 for an integrated framework for implementing internal controls.

Although most large publicly traded corporations have designed internal controls, smaller private companies and nonprofit organizations are less likely to have invested in a complete system. For example, the electric car company Green Tech Automotive came under investigation by the SEC for questionable practices in recruiting foreign investors. The claims that the company overstated guaranteed returns on investment and accepted investment from investors that may compromise national security are highlighted in the investigation. This investigation contributed to the company eventually declaring bankruptcy. While not the main reason for the bankruptcy, the investigation did not help improve public opinion of the company.[38] Such questionable behaviors are common in private businesses because they often lack effective internal controls. The framework in Table 3.7, while developed for large corporations, can be used in all types of organizations. These techniques are not always costly, and they conform to best practices in the prevention of ethical and legal problems that threaten the efficacy of governance mechanisms.

Amendments to the FGSO make it clear that a corporation's governing authority must be well informed about its control systems with respect to implementation and effectiveness. This places the responsibility squarely on the shoulders of the firm's leadership (usually the board of directors). The board must ensure that there is a high-ranking officer accountable for the day-to-day operational responsibility of the control systems. The board must also have adequate authority and resources and offer access to the board or an appropriate subcommittee of the board. The guidelines further call for confidential mechanisms whereby the organization's employees and agents may report or seek guidance about potential or actual misconduct without fear of retaliation. Finally, the board is required to oversee the discovery of risks and to design, implement, and modify approaches to deal with those risks. Thus, the board of directors is clearly accountable for discovering risks associated with a firm's specific industry and assessing their ethics program to ensure that it is capable of uncovering misconduct.[39]

Risk Management   A strong internal control system should alert decision-makers to possible problems, or risks, that may threaten business operations, including worker safety, company solvency, vendor relationships, proprietary information, environmental impact, and other concerns. As discussed in Chapter 2, having a strong crisis management plan is part of the process for managing risk. The term risk management is normally used in a narrow sense to indicate responsibilities associated with insurance, liability, financial decisions, and related issues. Kraft General Foods, for example, has a risk management policy for understanding how prices of commodities, such as coffee, sugar, wheat, and cocoa, will affect their relationships throughout the supply chain.[40]

Table 3.7 An Integrated Framework for Internal Control

Components of Internal Control	Description
Control environment	• The organization demonstrates a commitment to integrity and ethical values. • The board of directors demonstrates independence from management and exercises oversight of the development and performance of internal control. • Management establishes, with board oversight, structures, reporting lines, and appropriate authorities and responsibilities in the pursuit of objectives. • The organization demonstrates a commitment to attract, develop, and retain competent individuals in alignment with objectives. • The organization holds individuals accountable for their internal control responsibilities in the pursuit of objectives.
Risk assessment	• The organization specifies objectives with sufficient clarity to enable the identification and assessment of risks relating to objectives. • The organization identifies risks to the achievement of its objectives across the entity and analyzes risks as a basis for determining how they should be managed. • The organization considers the potential for fraud in assessing risks to the achievement of objectives. • The organization identifies and assesses changes that could significantly impact the system of internal control.
Control activities	• The organization selects and develops control activities that contribute to the mitigation of risks to the achievement of objectives to acceptable levels. • The organization selects and develops general control activities over technology to support the achievement of objectives. • The organization deploys control activities through policies that establish what is expected and procedures that put policies into action.
Information and communication	• The organization obtains or generates and uses relevant, high-quality information to support the functioning of internal control. • The organization internally communicates information, including objectives and responsibility for internal control, necessary to support the functioning of internal control. • The organization communicates with external parties regarding matters affecting the functioning of internal control.
Monitoring activities	• The organization selects, develops, and performs ongoing and/or separate evaluations to ascertain whether the components of internal control are present and functioning. • The organization evaluates and communicates internal control deficiencies in a timely manner to those parties responsible for taking corrective action, including senior management and the board of directors, as appropriate.

Source: "Internal Control—Integrated Framework Executive Summary," Committee of Sponsoring Organizations of the Treadway Commission, May 2013, https://www.coso.org/Documents/990025P-Executive-Summary-final-may20.pdf (accessed August 14, 2019).

Most corporate leaders' greatest fear is discovering serious misconduct or illegal activity somewhere in their organization. The fear is that a public discovery can immediately be used by critics in the mass media, competitors, and skeptical stakeholders to undermine a firm's reputation. Corporate leaders worry that something outside their control will be uncovered that will jeopardize their careers and their organizations. Fear is a paralyzing emotion. Of course, maybe even organizational leaders such as the Galleon Group's Raj Rajaratnam experienced fear as they participated in misconduct. The former chairman of Satyam Computer

Services, Ramalinga Raju, said that it was a terrifying experience to watch a small act of fudging some numbers snowball out of control. He compared knowingly engaging in misconduct for years to "riding a tiger, not knowing how to get off without being eaten."[41] These leaders were the captains of their respective ships, and they made a conscious decision to steer their firms into treacherous waters with a high probability of striking an iceberg.[42]

Corporate leaders do fear the possibility of damage to reputation, financial loss, or a regulatory event that could potentially end their careers, and even threaten their personal lives through fines or prison sentences. Indeed, the whole concept of risk management involves recognizing the possibility of a misfortune that could jeopardize or even destroy the corporation.[43] Organizations face significant risks and threats from financial misconduct. There is a need to identify potential risks that relate to misconduct that could devastate the organization. If risks and misconduct are discovered and disclosed, they are more likely to be resolved before they become front-page news.

Risk is always present within organizations, so executives must develop processes for remedying or managing its effects. A board of directors will expect the top management team to have risk management skills and plans in place. There are at least three ways to consider how risk could pose either a negative or positive concern for organizations.[44] First, risk can be categorized as a hazard. In this view, risk management is focused on minimizing negative situations, such as fraud, injury, or financial loss. Second, risk may be considered an uncertainty that needs to be hedged through quantitative plans and models. This type of risk is best associated with the term risk management, which is used in financial and business literature. Third, risk also creates the opportunity for innovation and entrepreneurship. Just as management can be criticized for taking too much risk, it can also be subject to concerns about not taking enough risk.

All three types of risk are implicitly covered by our definition of corporate governance because there are risks for both control (i.e., preventing fraud and ensuring accuracy of financial statements) and accountability (i.e., innovation to develop new products and markets). For example, the internet and electronic commerce capabilities have introduced new risks of all types for organizations. Privacy, as discussed in Chapter 10, is a major concern for many stakeholders and has created the need for policies and certification procedures. A board of directors may ensure that its company has established privacy policies that are not only effective, but also can be properly monitored and improved as new technology risks and opportunities emerge in the business environment.[45]

Executive Compensation

Executive compensation has been a topic rife with controversy. In the midst of government bailouts of corporations and financial institutions and loss of jobs and life savings, top executives continued to receive incredibly high bonuses and golden parachutes. This brought attention to the manner in which executives are paid, which had largely been left uninvestigated up to this point. The Dodd-Frank Act included a number of measures to rein in overcompensation, including a "say-on-pay" mandate, requiring shareholders to vote on their company's compensation policies; and "compensation committee independence," requiring board members in charge of determining compensation to be independent from the company's management. Other mandates that have been proposed by the SEC include requiring companies to disclose the ratio between CEO and employee pay, the disclosure of pay as it relates to performance, the process of recovering compensation that was wrongly awarded, and disclosure of any hedging activities conducted by directors or employees. While these measures have been controversial, the SEC has passed the mandate for businesses to disclose CEO-to-employee pay ratios.[46]

Executive compensation is such an important matter that many boards spend more time deciding how much to compensate top executives than they might do with ensuring the integrity of the company's financial reporting systems. Because of the large government bailouts during the last recession, many people became enraged because they felt that the government was sponsoring corporate excess with taxpayer money. This was a major contributor to the Occupy Wall Street protests of 2011. Even many boards of directors—which are responsible for setting executive pay—believe that the United States has a problem in that executive pay is not in line with performance or demonstration of stewardship to the company.[47] According to the AFL-CIO, average executive pay is $14.5 million, which is 287 times the pay of the average U.S. worker.[48]

Executive pay can be controversial, especially for companies struggling to make a profit. For example, Uber paid its top five executives a total of $143 million in cash and stock options. For Uber, executive pay was under much scrutiny, especially as Uber's drivers have complained about low pay. The average Uber driver earns $783 a month.[49]

An increasing number of corporate boards are imposing performance targets on the stock and stock options they include in their CEOs' pay packages. A **stock option** gives a shareholder the right to buy or sell a stock at a set price for a certain amount of time. Stock options are not considered obligations to the option buyer and often have an expiration date. The SEC proposed that companies disclose how they compensate lower-ranking employees, as well as top executives. This was part of a review of executive pay policies that addresses the belief that many financial corporations have historically taken on too much risk. The SEC believes that compensation may be linked to excessive risk-taking.[50] Another issue is whether performance-linked compensation encourages executives to focus on short-term performance at the expense of long-term growth.[51] Shareholders today, however, may be growing more concerned about transparency than short-term performance and executive compensation.

stock option
a financial tool that gives a shareholder the right to buy or sell a stock at a set price for a certain amount of time

Some people argue that executives deserve the rewards that follow from strong company performance because they assume so much risk on behalf of the company. In addition, many executives' personal and professional lives meld to the point that they are "on call" 24 hours a day. Because not everyone has the skill, experience, and desire to become an executive, with the accompanying pressure and responsibility, market forces dictate a high level of compensation. When the pool of qualified individuals is limited, many corporate board members feel that offering large compensation packages is the only way to attract and retain top executives and thereby ensure that their firms are not left without strong leadership. In an era when top executives are increasingly willing to "jump ship" to other firms that offer higher pay, potentially lucrative stock options, bonuses, and other benefits, such thinking is not without merit.[52]

Executive compensation is a difficult but important issue for boards of directors and other stakeholders to consider because it receives much attention in the media, sparks shareholder concern, and is hotly debated in discussions of corporate governance. One area for board members to consider is the extent to which executive compensation is linked to company performance. Corporate plans that base compensation on the achievement of several performance goals, including profits and revenues, are intended to align the interests of owners with management. For example, GE CEO Jeff Immelt missed his five-year performance target and lost out on a stock award that was valued at more than $3 million.[53]

Table 3.8 shows CEO compensation at some of the world's largest companies. While still hundreds of times higher than what the average worker makes, CEO compensation is decreasing overall, indicating a possible change in the way that executives are compensated. But critics still believe that there is a mismatch between the compensation of Wall Street CEOs and company performance. In 2015, Wall Street CEOs saw their pay rise about 10 percent, even though shares

Table 3.8 Examples of CEO Compensation

Company	Executive	Pay
Discovery Inc.	David M. Zaslav	$129,499,005
Walt Disney Company	Robert A. Iger	$ 65,645,214
Jefferies Group	Richard B. Handler	$ 44,674,213
Hologic	Stephen P. MacMillan	$ 42,040,142
Align Technology	Joseph M. Hogan	$ 41,758,338
PayPal	Daniel H. Schulman	$ 37,764,588
Netflix	Reed Hastings	$ 36,080,417
Comcast	Brian L. Roberts	$ 35,026,207
Activision Blizzard	Robert A. Kotick	$ 30,841,004
JPMorgan Chase	James Dimon	$ 30,019,840

Source: "Equilar/Associated Press CEO Pay Study 2019," Equilar, May 24, 2019, https://www.equilar.com/reports/65-equilar-associated-press-ceo-pay-study-2019.html (accessed August 14, 2019).

of major banks fell. In addition, an analysis of over 100 S&P 500 CEO salaries showed an increase in pay from $11.7 million to $12.4 million in 2018.[54]

Corporate Governance Around the World

Increased globalization, enhanced electronic communications, economic agreements and zones, and the reduction of trade barriers have created opportunities for firms around the world to conduct business with both international consumers and industrial partners. These factors propel the need for greater homogenization in corporate governance principles. Standard & Poor's (S&P) has a service called Corporate Governance Scores, which analyzes four macroforces that affect the general governance climate of a country, including legal infrastructure, regulation, information infrastructure, and market infrastructure. On the basis of these factors, a country can be categorized as having strong, moderate, or weak support for effective governance practices at the company level. Institutional investors are very interested in this measure, as it helps determine possible risk.[55] As financial, human, and intellectual capital crosses borders, a number of business, social, and cultural concerns arise. Institutional investors in companies based in emerging markets claim to be willing to pay more for shares in companies that are well governed. Global shareholders also would like companies in their countries to disclose more financial data, to adopt CEO pay plans that reward only strong performance, and to use independent boards, with no ties to management.

In response to this business climate, the Organisation for Economic Co-operation and Development (OECD), a forum for governments to discuss, develop, and enhance economic and social policy, issued a set of principles intended to serve as a global model for corporate governance.[56] The purpose of the OECD Principles of Corporate Governance (see Table 3.9) is to formulate minimum standards of fairness, transparency, accountability, disclosure, and responsibility for business practice. The principles focus on the board of directors, which the OECD says should recognize the impact of governance on the firm's competitiveness. In addition, the OECD charges boards, executives, and corporations with maximizing shareholder value, while responding to the demands and expectations of their key stakeholders. After years of discussion and debate among institutional investors, business executives, government representatives, trade unions, and nongovernmental organizations, 30 OECD member-governments signaled their agreement with the principles by signing a declaration to integrate them within their countries' economic systems and institutions.

Table 3.9 OECD Principles of Corporate Governance

Principle	Explanation
1. Ensuring the basis for an effective corporate governance framework	The corporate governance framework should promote transparent and efficient markets, be consistent with the rule of law and clearly articulate the division of responsibilities among different supervisory, regulatory and enforcement authorities.
2. The rights of shareholders and key ownership functions	The corporate governance framework should protect facilitate the exercise of shareholders' rights.
3. The equitable treatment of shareholders	The corporate governance framework should ensure the equitable treatment of all shareholders, including minority and foreign shareholders. All shareholders should have the opportunity to obtain effective redress for violation of their rights.
4. The role of stakeholders in corporate governance	The corporate governance framework should recognize the rights of stakeholders as established by law and encourage active cooperation between corporations and stakeholders in creating wealth, jobs, and the sustainability of financially sound enterprises.
5. Disclosure and transparency	The corporate governance framework should ensure that timely and accurate disclosure is made on all material matters regarding the corporation, including the financial situation, performance, ownership, and governance of the company.
6. The responsibilities of the board	The corporate governance framework should ensure the strategic guidance of the company, the effective monitoring of management by the board, and the board's accountability to the company and the shareholders.

Source: ComplianceOnline.com, "OECD Principles of Corporate Governance," http://www.complianceonline.com/dictionary/OECD_Principles_of_Corporate_Governance.html (accessed August 14, 2019).

The OECD Principles of Corporate Governance cover many specific best practices, including (1) ensuring the basis for an effective corporate governance framework; (2) guaranteeing the rights of shareholders to vote and influence corporate strategy; (3) having greater numbers of skilled, independent members on boards of directors; (4) implementing fewer techniques to protect failing management and strategy; (5) having wider use of international accounting standards; and (6) improving disclosure of executive pay and remuneration. Although member-governments of the OECD are expected to uphold the governance principles, there is some room for cultural adaptation.

Best practices may vary slightly from country to country because of unique factors such as market structure, government control, role of banks and lending institutions, labor unions, and other economic, legal, and historical factors. Both industry groups and government regulators moved quickly in the United Kingdom after the Enron crisis. Because some British bankers were indicted in the scandal, corporate governance concerns increased. Several British reforms resulted, including annual shareholders' votes on board compensation policies and greater supervision of investment analysts and the accounting profession.

Corporate governance, or lack of it, was one of the reasons for the financial crisis that occurred in Southeast Asia in the late 1990s. For example, the government structure of some Asian countries created greater opportunities for corruption and nepotism. Banks were encouraged to extend credit to companies favored by the government. In many cases, these companies were in the export business, which created an imbalance in financing for other types of businesses. The concentration of business power within a few families and tycoons reduced overall competitiveness and transparency. Many of these businesses were more focused on size and expanded operations than profitability. Foreign investors recognized the weakening economies and pulled their money out of investments. India has experienced a decrease in foreign investment for this reason. Despite the government's maneuvers to improve the economy, by easing restrictions on joint ventures in certain sectors, foreign firms decided against investing, as this was not enough incentive in light of the nation's weakening currency.[57]

To encourage greater transparency and corporate governance practices that foreign investors would approve of, businesses in India have made dramatic changes since the 1990s. For example, family-owned businesses began shifting executive power to outside parties, the internal actions of the businesses became known to people outside the family system, and boards of directors were subject to higher scrutiny than before. These changes, while difficult for executives, have proved successful for businesses such as the Mahindra group and the Aditya Birla group.[58]

Future of Corporate Governance

As the issues discussed in the previous sections demonstrate, corporate governance is primarily focused on strategic-level concerns for accountability and control. Although many discussions of corporate governance still revolve around responsibility in investor-owned companies, good governance is fundamental to effective performance in all types of organizations. As you have gleaned from history and government classes, a system of checks and balances is important for ensuring a focus on multiple perspectives and constituencies; proper distribution of resources, power, and decision authority; and the responsibility for making changes and setting directions.

To pursue social responsibility successfully, organizations must consider issues of control and accountability. As we learned earlier, the concept of corporate governance is in transition from the shareholder model to one that considers broader stakeholder concerns and inputs to financial performance. A number of market and environmental forces, such as the OECD and shareholder activism, have created pressures in this direction. This evolution is consistent with our view of social responsibility. Although some critics deride this expanded focus, a number of external and internal forces are driving businesses toward the stakeholder orientation and the formalization of governance mechanisms. One concern centers on the cost of governance. Companies like Nike have had problems in the past and have implemented strong ethics and compliance systems. However, many of the largest firms on Wall Street, which were overleveraged and did not have strong ethics and compliance programs in place, either failed or had to be bailed out to prevent failure.[59]

Most businesspeople and academicians agree that the benefits of a strong approach to corporate governance outweigh the costs. However, the positive return on governance goes beyond organizational performance to benefit the industrial competitiveness of entire nations, something that was discussed in Chapter 1. For example, corrupt organizations often fail to develop competitiveness on a global scale and can leave behind financial ruin, thus negating the overall economic growth of the entire region or nation. At the same time, corrupt governments usually have difficulty sustaining and supporting the types of organizations that can succeed in global markets. Thus, lack of good governance can lead to insular and selfish motives because no effective system of checks and balances is in place. In today's interactive and interdependent business environment, most organizations are learning the benefits of a more cooperative approach to commerce. It is possible for a company to retain its competitive nature while seeking a "win-win" solution for all parties to the exchange.[60] Furthermore, as nations with large economies embrace responsible governance principles, it becomes even more difficult for nations and organizations that do not abide by such principles to compete in these lucrative and rich markets. There is a contagion effect toward corporate governance among members of the global economy, much as peer pressure influences the actions and decisions of individuals.

Because governance is concerned with the decisions made by boards of directors and executives, it has the potential for far-reaching positive—and negative—effects. A recent study by the OECD found that stronger financial performance is the result of several governance factors and practices, including (1) large institutional shareholders that are active monitors of company decisions and boards; (2) owner-controlled firms; (3) fewer mergers, especially between firms with disparate corporate values and business lines; and (4) decisions by shareholders, not board of directors, on executive remuneration.[61] The authors of the study note that these practices may not hold true for strong performance in all countries and economic systems. However, they also point out that a consensus view is emerging, with fewer differences among OECD countries than among all other nations. Similarities in organizational-level accountability and control should lead to smoother operations between various companies and countries, thereby bolstering competitiveness on many levels.

The future of corporate governance is directly linked to the future of social responsibility. Because governance is the control and accountability process for achieving social responsibility, it is important to consider who should be involved in the future. First and most obviously, business leaders and managers will need to embrace governance as an essential part of effective performance. Some of the elements of corporate governance, particularly executive pay, board composition, and shareholder rights, are likely to stir debate for many years. However, business leaders must recognize the forces that have brought governance to the forefront as a precondition of management responsibility. Thus, they may need to accept the "creative tension" that exists among managers, owners, and other primary stakeholders as the preferable route to mutual success.[62]

Second, governments have a key role to play in corporate governance. National competitiveness depends on the strength of various institutions, with primacy on the effective performance of business and capital markets. Strong corporate governance is essential to this performance, and thus governments will need to be actively engaged in affording both protection and accountability for corporate power and decisions. Just like the corporate crises in the United States, the Asian economic crisis discussed earlier prompted companies and governments around the world to consider tighter governance procedures. Finally, other stakeholders may become more willing to use governance mechanisms to influence corporate strategy or decision-making. Investors—whether shareholders, employees, or business partners—have a stake in decisions and should be willing to take steps to align various interests for long-term benefits. There are many investors and stakeholders willing to exert great influence on underperforming companies.

Until recently, governance was one area in the business literature that had not received the same level of attention as other issues, such as environmental impact, diversity, and sexual harassment. Over the next few years, however, corporate governance will emerge as the operational centerpiece to the social responsibility effort. The future will require that business leaders have a different set of skills and attitudes, including the ability to balance multiple interests, handle ambiguity, manage complex systems and networks, create trust among stakeholders, and improve processes so that leadership is pervasive throughout the organization.[63]

In the past, the primary emphasis of governance systems and theory was on conflicts of interest between management and investors.[64] Governance today holds people at the highest organizational levels accountable and responsible to a broad and diverse set of stakeholders. Although top managers and boards of directors have always assumed responsibility, their actions are now subject to greater accountability and transparency. A writer for *The Wall Street Journal* put the shift succinctly: "Boards of directors have been put on notice." A key issue going forward will be a board's ability to align corporate decisions with various stakeholder interests.[65] Robert Monks, the activist money manager and leader in corporate governance issues, wrote that effective corporate governance requires understanding that the "indispensable link between the corporate constituents is the creation of a credible structure (with incentives and disincentives) that enables people with overlapping but not entirely congruent interests to have a sufficient level of confidence in each other and the viability of the enterprise as a whole."[66] We will take a closer look at some of these constituents and their concerns in the next few chapters.

Summary

To respond to stakeholder pressures for companies to be more accountable for organizational decisions and policies, organizations must implement policies that provide strategic guidance on appropriate courses of action. Such policies are often known as corporate governance, the formal system of accountability and control for organizational decisions and resources. Accountability relates to how well the content of workplace decisions is aligned with the firm's stated strategic direction, whereas control involves the process of auditing and improving organizational decisions and actions. Both directors and officers of corporations are fiduciaries for the shareholders. Fiduciaries are persons placed in positions of trust who are loyal and take due care in acting on behalf of the best interests of the organization. There is a duty of care, also called a duty of diligence, to make informed and prudent decisions. As directors, they too have a duty to avoid ethical misconduct and to provide leadership in decisions to prevent ethical misconduct in the organization. Directors are not held responsible for negative outcomes if they are informed and diligent in their decision-making. The duty of loyalty means that all decisions should be in the interests of the corporation and its stakeholders. Conflicts of interest exist when a director uses the position to obtain personal gain, usually at the expense of the organization.

There are two major conceptualizations of corporate governance. The shareholder model of corporate governance focuses on developing and improving the formal system of performance accountability between the top management and the firm's shareholders. The stakeholder model of corporate governance views the purpose of business in a broader fashion, in which the organization not only has a responsibility for economic success and viability, but also must answer to other stakeholders. The shareholder model focuses on a primary stakeholder—the investor—whereas the stakeholder model incorporates a broader philosophy that focuses on internal and external constituents.

Governance is the organizing dimension that keeps a firm focused on continuous improvement, accountability, and engagement with stakeholders. Although financial return, or economic viability, is an important measure of success for all firms, the legal dimension of social responsibility is also a compulsory consideration. The ethical and philanthropic dimensions, however, traditionally have not been mandated through regulation or contracts. This represents a critical divide in our social responsibility model and associated governance goals and systems because there are some critics who challenge the use of organizational resources for concerns beyond financial performance and legalities.

In the late 1800s and early 1900s, corporate governance was not a major issue because company owners made strategic decisions about their businesses. By the 1930s, ownership was dispersed across many individuals, raising questions about control and accountability. In response to shareholder activism, the SEC required corporations to allow shareholder resolutions to be brought to a vote of all shareholders. Since the mid-1900s, the approach to corporate governance has involved a legal discussion of principals (owners) and agents (managers) in the business relationship.

The lack of effective control and accountability mechanisms in years past has prompted a current trend toward boards of directors playing a greater role in strategy formulation than they did in the early 1990s. The board of directors assumes legal responsibility and a fiduciary duty for organizational resources and decisions. Boards today are concerned primarily with monitoring the decisions made by managers on behalf of the company. The trend today is toward boards being composed of external directors who have little vested interest in the firm. Shareholder activism is helping to propel this trend, as they seek better representation from boards that are less likely to have conflicts of interest.

Another significant governance issue is internal control and risk management. Controls allow comparisons between actual performance and the planned performance and goals of the organization. They are used to safeguard corporate assets and resources, protect the reliability of organizational information, and ensure compliance with regulations, laws, and contracts. Controls foster understanding when discrepancies exist between corporate expectations and stakeholder interests and issues. A strong internal control system should alert decision-makers to possible problems or risks that may threaten business operations. Risk can be categorized (1) as a hazard, in which case risk management focuses on minimizing negative situations, such as fraud, injury, or financial loss; (2) as an uncertainty that needs to be hedged through quantitative plans and models; or (3) as an opportunity for innovation and entrepreneurship.

How executives are compensated for their leadership, service, and performance is another governance issue. Many people believe the ratio between the highest-paid executives and median employee wages in the company should be reasonable. Others argue that because executives assume so much risk on behalf of the organization, they deserve the rewards that follow from strong company performance. One area for board members to consider is the extent to which executive compensation is linked to company performance.

The Organisation for Economic Co-operation and Development (OECD) has issued a set of principles from which to formulate minimum standards of fairness, transparency, accountability, disclosure, and responsibility for business practices. These principles help guide companies around the world and are part of the convergence that is occurring with respect to corporate governance.

Most businesspeople and academicians agree that the benefits of a strong approach to corporate governance outweigh its costs. Because governance is concerned with the decisions taken by boards of directors and executives, it has the potential for far-reaching positive (and negative) effects. The future of corporate governance is directly linked to the future of social responsibility. Business leaders and managers will need to embrace governance as an essential part of effective performance. Governments also have a role to play in corporate governance. National competitiveness depends on the strength of various institutions, with primacy on the effective performance of business and capital markets. Other stakeholders may become more willing to use governance mechanisms to affect corporate strategy or decision-making.

Responsible Business Debate

Does Aligning Pay to Performance Make Cents?

Issue: *Should businesses align pay with performance?*

Corporate governance is the formal system of oversight, accountability, and control for organizational decisions. During the financial recession of 2007–2009, many respected companies showed a failure in corporate oversight and decision-making, even as they required massive government bailouts to stay afloat. When AIG announced it was awarding $165 million to executives after accepting $170 billion in taxpayer money, the resulting outcry prompted demands for executive pay to be tied more to performance.

More than 10 years later, the debate rages on. With the two CEOs of Oracle receiving $108.3 million in one year, the discrepancy between the pay of executives and the average employee can be great indeed. At one large company, the CEO made nearly 5,000 times the median pay of employees.

On the other hand, more companies are making efforts to align executive compensation more closely to company performance. Mondelez International, for instance, announced that it was increasing the amount of executive compensation tied to business performance. Under this system, executives earn large salaries if the company does well but earn less if the company does not meet expectations. Shareholders are now allowed to vote on executive pay. Although these votes are nonbinding, negative votes provide clear indicators of shareholder discontent.

Yet not everyone is in favor of aligning executive compensation closely to company performance. Critics claim that while performance-based compensation works well for jobs that perform routine day-to-day activities, the challenges of running a company and a quickly changing business environment make this an unfeasible solution for executives. They argue that it can hinder executives from coming up with creative solutions to company problems because a misstep could easily lead to negative consequences. Another argument is that performance-based pay tends to look more at earnings in the short term than the long term. With no clear consensus in sight, the debate is likely to continue into the foreseeable future.

There Are Two Sides to Every Issue

1. Businesses should align pay with performance to best compensate employees.
2. Aligning pay with performance isn't the best way to compensate employees.

Source: "Highest-Paid CEOs at America's Largest Companies," *USA Today*, May 3, 2019, https://www.usatoday.com/picture-gallery/money/2019/04/24/highest-paid-ceos-at-americas-largest-companies/39390367/ (accessed May 3, 2019); Emily Stewart, "How Does a Company's CEO Pay Compare to Its Workers? Now You Can Find Out," *Vox*, April 8, 2018, https://www.vox.com/policy-and-politics/2018/4/8/17212796/ceo-pay-ratio-corporate-governance-wealth-inequality (accessed May 3, 2019); Alexia Elejalde-Ruiz, "After CEO Got $42.4 Million in 2017, Oreo-maker Vows to Link Executive Pay to Business Performance," *Chicago Tribune*, April 30, 2019, https://www.bizjournals.com/philadelphia/news/2019/05/03/proxy-advisors-and-executive-compensation-watchers.html (accessed May 3, 2019); Dan Cable and Freek Vermeulen, "Stop Paying Executives for Performance," *Harvard Business Review*, February 23, 2016, https://hbr.org/2016/02/stop-paying-executives-for-performance (accessed May 3, 2019); Daniel R. Kinel, "The Impact of the Dodd-Frank Act on Executive Compensation and Corporate Governance," *The Marcum Advisor*, October 2010, http://www.marcumllp.com/insights-news/the-impact-of-the-dodd-frank-act-on-executive-compensation-and-corporate-governance (accessed May 3, 2019); Joshua Zumbrun, "AIG's Bonus Distraction," *Forbes*, March 16, 2009, https://www.forbes.com/2009/03/16/bailout-bonus-aig-business-washington-aig.html#39eb1e9e4e92 (accessed May 3, 2019).

Key Terms

board of directors (p. 66)
conflicts of interest (p. 68)
corporate governance (p. 67)
duty of care (p. 68)
duty of loyalty (p. 68)
fiduciaries (p. 68)
insider trading (p. 69)

proxy (p. 79)
proxy access (p. 80)
risk management (p. 80)
shareholder (p. 67)
shareholder lawsuits (p. 78)
shareholder model of
     corporate governance (p. 73)

shareholder resolutions (p. 79)
stakeholder model of
     corporate governance (p. 73)
stock option (p. 85)
U.S. Securities and Exchange
     Commission (SEC) (p. 70)

Discussion Questions

1. What is corporate governance? Why is it an important concern for companies pursuing the social responsibility approach? How does it improve or change the nature of executive and managerial decision-making?
2. Compare the shareholder and stakeholder models of corporate governance. Which one seems to predominate today? What implications does this have for businesses in today's complex environment?
3. What role does executive compensation play in risk-taking and accountability? Why do some people partially blame compensation for the failures of the subprime mortgage and financial industries in 2008–2009?
4. What is the role of the board of directors in corporate governance? What responsibilities does the board have?
5. What role do shareholders and other investors play in corporate governance? How can investors effect change?
6. Why are internal control and risk management important in corporate governance? Describe three approaches that organizations may take to manage risk.
7. Why is the issue of executive compensation controversial? Are today's corporate executives worth the compensation packages they receive?
8. In what ways are corporate governance practices becoming standardized around the world? What differences exist?
9. As corporate governance becomes a significant aspect of social responsibility, what new skills and characteristics will managers and executives need to possess? Consider how pressures for governance require managers and executives to relate and interact with stakeholders in new ways.

Experiential Exercise

Visit the website of the Organisation for Economic Co-operation and Development (http://www.oecd.org). Examine the origins of the organization and its unique role in the global economy. After visiting the site, answer the following questions:

1. What are the primary reasons that OECD exists?

2. How would you describe OECD's current areas of concern and focus?
3. What role do you think OECD will play in the future with respect to corporate governance and related issues?

Core-Tex Creates a Vortex Around Aggressive Accounting: What Would You Do?

The statewide news carried a story about Core-Tex that evening. There were rumors swirling that one of the largest manufacturers in the state was facing serious questions about its social responsibility. A former accountant for Core-Tex, whose identity was not revealed, made allegations about aggressive accounting methods and practices that overstated company earnings. He said he left Core-Tex after his supervisor and colleagues did not take his concerns seriously. The former accountant hinted that the company's relationship with its external auditor was quite close, since Core-Tex's new CFO had once been on the external auditing team. Core-Tex had recently laid off 270 employees—a move that was not unexpected given the turbulent financial times. However, the layoffs hit some parts of the site's community pretty hard. Finally, inspectors from the state environmental protection agency had just issued a series of citations to Core-Tex for improper disposal methods and high emissions at one of its larger manufacturing plants. A television station had run an exposé on the environmental citations a week ago.

CEO Kelly Buscio clicked off the television set and thought about the company's next steps. Core-Tex's attorney had cautioned the executive group earlier that week about communicating too much to the media and other constituents. The firm's vice president for marketing countered the attorney by insisting that Core-Tex needed to stay ahead of the rumors and assumptions that were being made about the company. He said that suppliers and business partners were starting to question Core-Tex's financial viability. The vice president of information technology and the vice president of operations were undecided on the next step, while the vice president of manufacturing had not attended the meeting. Buscio wondered what tomorrow could bring.

To her surprise, the newspapers had gone easy on Core-Tex the next day, owing to a shift in the media attention on a major oil spill, the retirement of a *Fortune* 500 CEO, and a major league baseball championship game the night before. The company's stock price, which averaged around $11.15, was down $0.35 by midmorning. The vice-president of marketing suggested that employees needed to hear from the CEO and be reassured about Core-Tex's strong future. Her first call after lunch came from a member of the board asking Buscio what the board could do to help the situation. What would you do?

Business, Government, and Regulation

Regulating Trade for Global Business

Responsible, transparent, and ethical leadership is needed in order for companies to develop and maintain a long-term commitment to social responsibility for the benefit of multiple stakeholders. This is especially true of multinational corporations (MNCs) because of the power and influence that these businesses and their executives represent. MNCs operate in multiple environments and contexts in which laws, rules, expectations, and social mores are divergent. In addition, the enforcement and monitoring mechanisms to oversee these expectations range from barely existent entities to well-resourced government agencies.

The failure to have a global legal and regulatory scheme has resulted in environmental disasters, child labor, financial fraud, antitrust violations, tainted food products, and other problems. For example, Google was charged more than €1 billion (nearly $1.2 billion) in fines for antitrust violations in Europe. The European Union (EU) fined the company for preventing competitors from advertising on certain websites. Google was able to do this mainly because of contractual clauses that restricted competition, as well as its search engine control. The company's third violation in the EU has brought up other concerns about the regulation of large businesses.

Multilateral trade agreements are made to help regulate business trade among several countries. The North American Free Trade Agreement (NAFTA) was created in 1994 to establish regulations and assist with business among the United States, Canada, and Mexico, mainly by removing trade tariffs among the countries. In 2018, a new agreement was signed by the leaders of the three countries and renamed the United States-Mexico-Canada Agreement (USMCA). This agreement, which is intended to replace NAFTA, changes the requirements for certain industries. For example, car companies must use parts primarily made in North America or pay tariffs for noncompliance. Under NAFTA, the requirement was that 62.5 percent of parts had to be made in North America, while under USMCA, the number has increased to 75 percent. Higher worker wages, increased intellectual property protections, and the growth of certain agricultural products such as dairy are addressed in the latter agreement.

Economists debate how the USMCA will affect the financial situation of Mexico, Canada, and the United States. The U.S. International Trade Commission believes that the impact will be positive but only minimal, predicting that the gross domestic product (GDP) in the United States would increase by 0.35 percent and jobs would increase by 0.12 percent. Technology, data requirements, and concerns that were not as prevalent in 1994 are addressed in USMCA, which economists see as a benefit. However, the restrictions on automotive parts are expected to raise the prices of vehicles and lower the number of purchases. Companies may view the tariffs for noncompliance to be more bearable than the cost of compliance. Additionally, tariffs imposed on Canada and Mexico for aluminum and steel products are a source of debate among the countries.

Trade wars result from imposing tariffs to accomplish a trade objective, such as creating a fair balance of trade. Most recently, a trade war has developed between the United States and China over protection of intellectual property, laws that protected Chinese firms, and a trade imbalance.[1]

Shutterstock/Angel Soler Collonet

Chapter Objectives

- Understand the rationale for government regulation of business
- Analyze the role of regulatory agencies in the enforcement of public policy
- Examine the costs and benefits of regulation
- Analyze global regulation
- Assess the nonregulatory influence of governments on business
- Provide an overview of government deregulation

T he government has the power, through laws and regulations, to structure how businesses and individuals achieve their goals. The purpose of regulating firms is to create a fair competitive environment for businesses, consumers, and society. All stakeholders need to demonstrate a commitment to social responsibility through compliance with relevant laws and proactive consideration of social needs. The law is one of the most important business subjects, in terms of its effect on organizational practices and activities. Thus, compliance with the law is a fundamental expectation of social responsibility. Because the law is based on principles, norms, and values found within society, the law is the foundation of responsible decision-making.

This chapter explores the complex relationship between business and government. First, we discuss some of the laws that structure the environment for the regulation of business. **Regulation** refers to the act of creating and enforcing rules for a specific purpose. For businesses, the government typically provides this oversight to ensure ethical and legal practices among corporations. The costs and benefits of regulation are reviewed, as well as the unique issues that occur in global regulation. We discuss the nonregulatory influence of governments on business and conclude with a consideration of deregulation.[2]

regulation
the act of creating and enforcing rules for a specific purpose

Government's Regulatory Influence on Business

The government has a profound influence on business. Most Western countries have a history of elected representatives working through democratic institutions to provide a structure for the regulation of business conduct. For example, one of the differences that have long characterized the two major parties in U.S. politics involves the government's role with respect to business. In general, the Republican Party tends to favor smaller, central government, with less regulation of business, while the Democratic Party is more open to government oversight, federal aid programs, and sometimes higher taxes. From the start, President Barack Obama worried some businesspeople, as he favored more oversight of many areas of the economy. For example, he promised to be tough on antitrust violations and followed through by reversing a policy from the George W. Bush administration that made it more difficult for the government to pursue such violations.[3]

Over the past 10 years, there have been major conflicts between the Democrats and Republicans over regulation of business. While President Obama wanted more regulation and social programs, including healthcare coverage for all Americans, his successor, President Donald Trump, reversed rules that regulated businesses and was able to reduce corporate taxes. President Obama brought U.S. policy regarding antitrust cases more in line with Europe's model. This trend continued with the Trump administration. While it was unsuccessful in defeating the merger between AT&T and Time Warner in 2019, cracking down on antitrust violations and breaking up monopolies was a stated goal of the Trump administration.[4] Third-party and independent candidates typically focus on specific business issues or proclaim their distance from the two major political parties. However, the power and freedom of big business have resulted in conflicts among private businesses, governments, private interest groups, and even individuals as businesses try to influence policymakers.

In the United States, the roles that society delegates to government are to provide laws that are logically deduced from the U.S. Constitution and the Bill of Rights and to enforce these laws through the judicial system. Individuals and businesses, therefore, live under a rule of law designed to protect society and support an acceptable quality of life. Ideally, by limiting the influence and force exerted by some parties, the overall welfare and freedom of all participants in the social system will be protected.

The provision of a court system to settle disputes and punish criminals, both organizational and individual, provides justice and order in society. Both Google (now a subsidiary of Alphabet, Inc.) and Microsoft have come under numerous ongoing investigations for alleged antitrust activity in Europe, where the companies have been accused of engaging in behavior that prevents smaller companies from competing. In just over a year, the EU's antitrust regulator filed four charges against Alphabet alleging that, among other actions, Google favored its search functions over rival sites, it restricted how a website could show advertisements from other companies, and it forced smartphone makers into preinstalling its search engine as the default on their mobile devices.[5] The EU is famous for being tough on companies suspected of antitrust violations, igniting the ire of many multinational corporations that feel as if they are being punished for being successful. Being aware of antitrust laws is important for all large corporations around the world because judicial systems can punish businesses that fail to comply with laws and regulatory requirements.

The legal system is not always accepted in some countries as insurance that business will be conducted in a legitimate way. For example, after generations of being known for its top-secret bank accounts, Swiss banks were ordered by the U.S. Internal Revenue Service (IRS) to disclose information about some of their clients because of concerns over illegal activities. In many places around the world, the business climate has become less tolerant of illegal and immoral actions, and countries like Switzerland, Liechtenstein, and Luxembourg now are being pressured to share information on potential tax dodgers with government agencies like the IRS. Credit Suisse pleaded guilty to aiding wealthy Americans in tax evasion. The company was ordered to give the U.S. Department of Justice all records concerning American clients and was charged a fine of $2.6 billion for criminal misconduct.[6] This case illustrates the complexity of complying with international business laws.

While many businesses may object to regulations aimed at maintaining ethical cultures and preserving stakeholder welfare, the very existence of businesses is based on laws permitting their creation, organization, and dissolution. From a social perspective, it is significant that a corporation has the same legal status as a "person" who can sue, be sued, and be held liable for debts. Laws may protect managers and stockholders from being personally liable for a company's debts, but both individuals and organizations remain responsible for their conduct. Because corporations have a perpetual life, larger companies like ExxonMobil, Ford, and Sony take on an organizational culture, including social responsibility values, that extends beyond a specific time period, management team, or geographical region. Organizational culture plays an important role in the ability of corporations to outlive individual executives—it sets the tone for businesses and allows continuity even during times of leadership turnover.

Most, generally smaller, companies are owned by individual proprietors or operated as partnerships. However, large incorporated firms like those just mentioned often receive more attention because of their size, visibility, and impact on so many aspects of the economy and society. In a pluralistic society, diverse stakeholder groups such as businesses, workers, consumers, environmentalists, privacy advocates, and others attempt to influence public officials who legislate, interpret laws, and regulate business. The public interest is served through open participation and debate that result in effective policy. Because no system of government is perfect, legal and regulatory systems are constantly evolving in response to changes in the business environment and social institutions. For example, increasing use of the internet for information and business has created a need for legislation and regulations to protect the owners of creative materials from unauthorized use and consumers from fraud and invasions of privacy. The line between acceptable and illegal activity on the internet is increasingly difficult

Shutterstock/Andrey_Popov

to discern and is often determined by judges and juries and discussed widely in the media.

New **disruptive technology** is changing both the business and the regulatory environment. Artificial intelligence (AI) enabled by big data drones, facial recognition, and other technology provides more opportunity to create business models that current regulation does not adequately address. Humans are being replaced by robots in some cases, and the work environment is changing to address more technology and digital communication. AI will provide more information and oversight of employees, and both government and investors will have access to operations, accounting, and financial results. The amount of data about a firm's activities is exploding. This will cause a review and update of existing regulations.

In the next section, we take a closer look at why and how the government affects businesses through regulation, the costs and benefits of regulation, and how regulation may affect companies doing business in foreign countries.

disruptive technology
new technology that displaces an established technology and changes an industry or a unique new product that creates a completely new industry

The Rationale for Regulation

The United States was established as a capitalist system, but the prevailing capitalistic theory has changed over time. Adam Smith published his critical economic ideas in *The Theory of Moral Sentiments* and *Inquiry into the Nature and Causes of the Wealth of Nations* (often abbreviated to *The Wealth of Nations*) during the late 1700s, which are still considered important today. Smith observed the supply and demand, contractual efficiency, and division of labor of various companies within England. His writings formed the basis of modern economics. Smith's idea of *laissez faire*, otherwise known as "the invisible hand," is critical to capitalism, in that it assumes that the market, through its own inherent mechanisms, will keep commerce in equilibrium.

A second form of capitalism gained support at the beginning of the Great Depression. During the 1930s, John Maynard Keynes argued that the state could stimulate economic growth and improve stability in the private sector—through, for example, controlling interest rates, taxation, and public projects.[7]

Keynes argued that government policies could be used to increase aggregate demand, thus increasing economic activity and reducing unemployment and deflation. He argued that the solution to depression was to stimulate the economy through some combination of a reduction in interest rates or government investment in infrastructure. President Franklin D. Roosevelt employed Keynesian economic theories to pull the United States out of the Great Depression.

The third form of capitalism was developed by Milton Friedman and represented a swing to the right on the political spectrum. Friedman had lived through the Great Depression, but he rejected the Keynesian conclusion that the market sometimes needs some intervention to function most efficiently. Friedman instead believed in deregulation because he thought that the system could reach equilibrium without government intervention.[8] Friedman's ideas were the guiding principles for government policymaking in the United States, and increasingly throughout the world, starting in the second half of the twentieth century, especially during the presidencies of Ronald Reagan, George H. W. Bush, Bill Clinton, and George W. Bush. However, President Obama's policies moved back in the direction of Keynesian capitalism, with higher taxes and more spending on healthcare, as well as other public projects related to stabilizing the economy after the financial crisis. When Trump took over from Obama, a transition back to Friedman capitalism was expected. However, while Trump did institute major tax cuts, he also increased government spending on infrastructure. Thus, some claimed that he took a more Keynesian economic stance than his Republican predecessors.[9]

Many communist countries also are adopting components of capitalism. *State capitalism* occurs when the government runs commercial activity in a capitalist manner. In China, for instance, many of the largest for-profit firms are owned in some capacity by the government. Despite this ownership, the day-to-day workings of the companies operate in a capitalist manner. This gives them the ability to compete against global firms. Table 4.1 gives a brief overview of the forms of capitalism.

Although the opinions about which form of capitalism is the better option have changed over time, the federal and state governments in the United States have always stepped in to enact legislation and create regulations to address particular issues and restrict the behavior of business in accordance with society's wishes. Many of the issues used to justify business regulation can be categorized as economic or social.

Economic Regulation A great number of regulations have been passed by legislatures over the last 100 years in an effort to level the playing field on which businesses operate. Economic regulation has the goal of providing a fair and open market to encourage a balance in supply and demand in the economic system. Economic regulation addresses the power of monopolies or firms that use their size to create undesirable results.[10]

Antitrust legislation attempts to provide fair competition to protect competitors and the public. The Federal Trade Commission (FTC) exists to protect consumers and prevent anticompetitive activities. The FTC stops unfair, deceptive, or fraudulent practices from happening. It also enforces antitrust laws to make sure that the economic market continues to be open and free. The agency is able to do this through tools developed to help better stop the unfair practices. We discuss the FTC in more detail in Chapter 5.

The Securities and Exchange Commission (SEC) protects investors and attempts to promote a transparent system for investment markets to function. The SEC requires that public companies disclose any financial and other information that may be meaningful to an investor. It believes that investors should be privy to basic facts before they decide whether they want to invest. When the United States became an independent nation in the eighteenth century, the business environment consisted of many small farms, manufacturers, and cottage industries operating on a primarily local scale. With the increasing industrialization of the United States after the Civil War, so-called captains of industry like John D. Rockefeller (oil), Andrew

Table 4.1 Forms of Capitalism

Type of Capitalism	Description	Example
Adam Smith's *laissez-faire* approach	The market, through its own inherent mechanisms, will keep commerce in equilibrium.	Popular in the United States during the nineteenth century
Keynesian capitalism	Government policies can be used to stimulate growth.	Popular in the United States after the Great Depression
Friedman capitalism	This approach emphasizes deregulation and significantly less government intervention.	Popular in the second half of the twentieth century
State capitalism	Major organizations are owned by the government, but are run in a capitalist manner.	China's economic system

Carnegie (railroads and steel), Andrew Mellon (aluminum), and J. P. Morgan (banking) began to consolidate their business holdings into large national trusts.

trusts
organizations established to gain control of a product market or industry by eliminating competition

Trusts are organizations generally established to gain control of a product market or industry by eliminating competition. Such organizations are often considered detrimental because, without serious competition, they can potentially charge higher prices and provide lower-quality products to consumers. Thus, as these firms grew in size and power, public distrust of them likewise grew because of often-legitimate concerns about unfair competition. This suspicion and the public's desire to require these increasingly powerful companies to act responsibly spurred the first antitrust legislation. If trusts are successful in eliminating competition, a monopoly can result.

monopoly
a market type in which just one business provides a good or service in a given market

A **monopoly** occurs when just one business provides a good or service in a given market. Natural monopolies are monopolies that occur because of the unique nature of the product or components of the product such as technology. They can also occur when one corporation is able to engage in the business while competitors are unable to engage due to costs and other entry barriers.[11] Utility companies that supply electricity, natural gas, water, or cable television are examples of monopolies, but that is starting to change. The government tolerates these monopolies because the cost of supplying the good or providing the service is so great that few companies would be willing to invest in new markets without some protection from competition. Monopolies may also be allowed by **patent laws** that grant the developer of a new technology a period of time (usually 20 years), during which no other firm can use the same technology without the patent holder's consent. Patent protections are permitted to encourage businesses to engage in riskier research and development by allowing them time to recoup their research, development, and production expenses and to earn a reasonable profit.

patent laws
laws that grant the developer a period of time (usually 20 years) during which no other firm can use the same technology without the patent holder's consent

Because trusts and monopolies lack serious competition, there are concerns that they may either exploit their market dominance to restrict their output and raise prices or reduce quality to gain greater profits. This concern is the primary rationalization for their regulation by the government. Public utilities, for example, are regulated by state public utility commissions and, where they involve interstate commerce, are subject to federal regulation as well. Some of these industries have been deregulated with the idea that greater competition will police the behavior of individual firms. However, in areas like utilities, it is difficult to develop perfect competition because of the large sunk costs required. Often, deregulation has led to increased costs to stakeholders. For example, Maryland deregulated the state's residential energy market in the late 1990s, and when rate caps came off in 2004, residences were hit with skyrocketing utility costs. The problem has been market prices—when petroleum costs are high, so are the costs to generate energy. In a deregulated privatized market, these costs are passed on to consumers. The governor has tried numerous tactics to relieve the burden, including a one-time handout, but stakeholders remain concerned.[12]

Related to the issue of regulation of trusts and monopolies is the society's desire to restrict destructive or unfair competition. What is considered unfair varies with the standard practice of the industry, the impact of specific conduct, and the individual case. When one company dominates a particular industry, it may engage in destructive competition or employ anticompetitive tactics. For example, it may slash prices in an effort to drive competitors out of the market and then raise prices later. It may conspire with other competitors to set, or "fix," prices so that each firm can ensure a certain level of profit. Other examples of unfair competitive trade practices are stealing trade secrets or obtaining confidential information from a competitor's employees, trademark and copyright infringement, false advertising, and deceptive selling methods such as "bait and switch" and false representation of products.

Regulation is also intended to protect consumers from unethical business practices. For instance, the government has been scrutinizing large-scale increases in the price of pharmaceuticals. Although businesses generally have freedom to determine their pricing strategies, pharmaceuticals are a hot-button issue because of their impact on people's health. The nation was outraged, for instance, when Turing Pharmaceuticals and their cofounder and CEO Martin Skreli raised the price of an old generic drug 5,000 percent in 2015. Even though most pharmaceutical firms do not implement such massive price increases, many are increasing their prices. There is some concern among drug makers that Congress might implement controls on the amount that pharmaceutical companies can raise the prices of their drugs.[13]

Real-world customers often lack complete information about products they might buy, or they may have difficulty understanding technical terms describing goods like cars, pharmaceutical drugs, and mortgages. Consumer protection regulations help by requiring companies to spell out the features and risks of their products. In the real world, markets are often dominated by a small number of sellers—sometimes only one—who can limit production and force customers to pay artificially high prices. Antimonopoly regulations can ensure greater competition and fairer prices.

Social Regulation Regulation may also occur when marketing activities result in undesirable consequences for society. **Social regulation** is concerned with the overall welfare of citizens. Protecting and supporting consumers and providing the work environment with safe work conditions, equal opportunity, and healthcare are the focus of social regulation. On the other hand, **economic regulation** focuses on creating a strong economy and the protection of competition to provide an opportunity for organizations and individuals to be financially successful. This success supports employment, as well as the tax base to support most government services. Therefore, social and economic regulation work together to promote the health, welfare, and a standard of living to support society.

An example of social regulation is the Affordable Health Care Act (ACA) passed in 2009. The ACA, also known as "Obamacare," had three primary goals when it was formed. The first was to allow more people to have affordable health insurance; the second was to expand the Medicaid program to cover more adults; and the third was to support innovative healthcare delivery methods. All of these goals were directed to lowering the cost of healthcare. Social regulation focuses are not limited to one industry and can address issues such as consumer protection, pollution, job safety, discrimination, and the right of employees and consumers to seek remedy for damages.

Many manufacturing processes, for example, create air, water, or land pollution. Such consequences create uncounted "costs" in the form of contamination of natural resources, illness, and so on that neither the manufacturer nor the consumer "pays" for directly, although consumers may end up paying for these costs nevertheless. Because few companies are willing to shoulder these costs voluntarily, regulation is necessary to ensure that all firms within an industry do their part to minimize damages and pay their fair share. Likewise, regulations have proved necessary to protect natural (e.g., forests, fishing grounds, and other habitats) and social resources (e.g., historical and architecturally or archeologically significant structures). We will take a closer look at some of these environmental protection regulations and related issues in Chapter 12, on sustainability.

Other regulations have come about in response to social demands for equality in the workplace, especially after the 1960s. Such laws and regulations require that companies ignore race, ethnicity, gender, religion, and disabilities in favor of qualifications that more accurately reflect an individual's capacity for performing a particular job.

Likewise, deaths and injuries because of employer negligence resulted in regulations designed to ensure that people can enjoy a safe working environment. The airline industry has become a prime example of how tough economic times

social regulation
protection and support for consumers providing safe work conditions, equal opportunity, and healthcare

economic regulation
protection of competition to provide opportunity for organizations and individuals to be financially successful in order to create a strong economy

result in overworked, undertrained employees. Many pilots receive low compensation, poor health benefits, and are forced to work long hours—all factors that contribute to challenging organizational culture. For example, the crash of the Boeing 737 MAX 8 aircraft in Indonesia in October 2018 and a subsequent crash in Ethiopia may have been the result of flaws in a new antistall system and lack of pilot training. There is evidence that Boeing did not properly prepare the pilots in Indonesia to work with the new system. The Ethiopian pilots had been trained; however, it is uncertain if their training was sufficient. Furthermore, flaws in the system made it difficult to maintain control of the plane in both crashes. A major issue that has surfaced in the aftermath of the crashes is Boeing's lack of intervention when pilots reported problems with the new aircraft. Prior to the Ethiopian crash, American Airlines pilots suggested grounding the plane until the system was fixed, but upper management did not agree. The Boeing 737 MAX 8 were grounded until investigations could be completed and improvements could be made. The grounding of these planes has cost Boeing in both reputation and finances. Regulators also are being investigated for suspicions about the certification process for the MAX 8. As the reaction from the crashes shows, consumers are holding businesses and regulatory bodies accountable for their behavior.[14]

Still other regulations have resulted from special-interest group crusades for safer products. For example, special-interest groups such as the Center for Food Safety (CFS), Consumers Union, and U.S. Right to Know have spoken out against genetically modified (GM) organisms in American foods. These groups have argued that GM foods are dangerous to health and that stricter regulations need to be made to inform the public about GM products. In response to this outcry, the U.S. government passed the National Bioengineered Food Disclosure Law in 2016. The law required the development of regulations around bioengineered food labeling. This led to the National Bioengineered Food Disclosure Standard, which requires GM ingredients to be disclosed on food products. Companies have several options for how to display the label, one of which is via QR codes. The CFS has argued that the QR code option is discriminatory towards low-income consumers who may not have the means to scan QR codes. According to the Non-GMO Project, 64 countries in the world require labeling of genetically modified (GM) foods. The specifics of each law vary from country to country. The debate continues on the safety of GM goods as well as the best way to inform the public of foods containing GM organisms.[15]

Cannabis and hemp legalization and regulation have also attracted public interest, and regulations differ at both the state and federal levels. Medical marijuana has been legalized by 33 states, and recreational marijuana has been legalized by 10 states. At the federal level, both medical and recreational marijuana are illegal. Hemp, a product of the cannabis plant that contains 0.3 percent or less of the chemical tetrahydrocannabinol (THC), was legalized federally by the 2018 Farm Bill. Cannabidiol (CBD), a substance from the cannabis plant that has been shown to have medicinal qualities, was also legalized federally, with restrictions. Only CBD derived from hemp is legal federally under the Farm Bill; CBD derived from marijuana is still illegal. This subtle distinction has confused consumers, and many hope that all CBD and marijuana products will soon be fully legalized in

Shutterstock/kostrez

the United States. Regulation of hemp growth will occur at both the federal and the state level.[16] As we will see in Chapter 9, consumer activists also helped secure passage of several other consumer protection laws, such as the Wholesome Meat Act of 1967, the Clean Water Act of 1972, and the Toxic Substance Act of 1976.

Issues arising from the increasing use of the internet have led to demands for new laws protecting consumers and business. Laws such as the Stop Online Piracy Act (SOPA) and the Protect Intellectual Property Act (PIPA) were proposed to prevent copyright infringement over the internet. Under these provisions companies could be penalized for posting pirated content over the internet. However, Google, Yahoo, and other internet companies protested the bills, saying that it gave the government too much power to shut down websites and infringe on freedom of speech.[17] Wikipedia, Google, and other websites underwent a service blackout for an entire day to protest the bills. The proposed laws were defeated, much to the frustration of content providers who hoped the bills would help protect their intellectual property. Intellectual property protection versus freedom of speech is a tricky balance that requires legislators to research solutions that respect both of these rights.

As we shall see in Chapter 11, the technology associated with the internet has generated a number of issues related to privacy, fraud, and copyright law. For instance, creators of copyrighted works such as movies, books, and music are calling for new laws and regulations to safeguard their ownership of these works. In response to these concerns, Congress enacted the Digital Millennium Copyright Act in 1998, which extended existing copyright laws to better protect digital recordings of music, movies, and the like. While other countries have implemented similar measures, copyright violations continue to plague many global industries, which to some critics calls into question the effectiveness of legal action. A team of security specialists recommends technological, not legal, solutions as being most effective in the fight against piracy and copyright infringement.[18]

Concerns about the collection and use of personal information, especially regarding children, resulted in the passage of the Children's Online Privacy Protection Act of 2000 (COPPA). The Act was revised in 2012 and is enforced by the FTC levying fines against noncompliant website operators. For example, in 2016 the Singapore-based mobile advertising firm InMobi paid $950,000 in civil penalties for tracking the locations of hundreds of millions of consumers (many of them children) for the purpose of geotargeting ads.[19]

Internet safety among children is a major topic of concern. This is true for children of all ages. Studies have shown that approximately 50 percent of children between the ages of six and nine use social media, and over 90 percent of children under the age of two have accessible information online, including photos and other personal information. A study showed that children aged three to four increased their internet use by 20 percent in five years. While there are many contributing factors to the access and amount of time spent online among children, online safety is a concern for all children. Many are urging parents to encourage their children to practice safe online behavior, such as using privacy restrictions and not posting information or photos that contain too much personal information.[20]

New technology continues to challenge the legal system. AI involving machine learning can simulate human cognitive functions, while predictive analytics can make decisions that relate to human resource management and relationships with customers. This can create ethical and legal conflicts because machines may not understand bias in hiring or discrimination in interactions with different types of people. Early use of AI found that there could be racial or gender bias. Therefore, going forward, consideration of these legal implications will be required. Law schools are already offering classes in AI regulatory issues.

Over the last several years, data privacy issues have become a significant public interest issue as large, notable companies like Google, Facebook, Target, and Marriott have been breached, allowing millions of users' personal data to fall into

Ethical Responsibilities in **MARKETING**

Dieselgate: Volkswagen Fools Regulators

Volkswagen (VW) was founded in 1937 in Nazi Germany as a pet project of Adolf Hitler, who desired to develop what he termed the "people's car" (which is what "Volkswagen" literally means in German). After the war, VW sales were slower in the United States than in other areas because of its questionable origins, but the introduction of the VW Beetle to the U.S. market in 1947 caused sales to skyrocket. VW was highly valued for its sustainability goals. For instance, it became the first car manufacturer to adopt ISO 14001 principles, international environmental principles that act as standards for global firms. When VW introduced the VW XL1, it claimed that the vehicle was the most fuel-efficient car in the world at the time. The company's reputation for sustainability worsened the blow to its reputation when it all came crashing down years later.

It was discovered that VW had purposefully fooled regulators and consumers with its emissions claims. The company used a so-called defeat device in its software that changed the vehicle's performance depending upon the environment. For instance, the software was able to detect when vehicles were undergoing emissions testing. During this testing, the software made the vehicles run below performance, which released fewer emissions and met the requirements. However, on the road, the cars ran at maximum performance and gave off up to 40 times the allowable limit for emissions in the United States. VW estimated that 11 million vehicles in the United States and Europe were affected by this defeat device.

The automaker pled guilty to three criminal felony charges that included defrauding the U.S. government, violating environmental regulations, obstructing justice, engaging in wire fraud, and violating import regulations. Such fraud not only violates ethical standards, but also laws and regulations in Europe and the United States.

Perhaps the worst impact the scandal caused was to VW's reputation. Many VW customers claimed they purchased the cars because they believed them to be better for the environment and felt utterly betrayed by the company. Consumer rights were violated because buyers did not have accurate information, so they were not able to make informed purchasing decisions. As a global firm, VW lost the trust of regulators—a major obstacle in future global relationships. To restore consumer trust, the CEO, Martin Winterkorn, resigned and VW offered a $1,000 goodwill package to its American car owners. The cars affected by the scandal were also recalled.

While these steps helped rehabilitate VW's reputation, another scandal threatens to damage it once again. VW is accused of selling preproduction vehicles under the title "Certified Pre-Owned." Preproduction vehicles cannot be sold to consumers legally because they do not meet U.S. safety regulations. VW again used technology to deceive consumers. Referred to as "odometer fraud," the automaker provided secret data to CARFAX, a website with information on vehicles' history, to create the illusion that a car had a driving history similar to a preowned vehicle. In addition, the vehicles were sold as "CARFAX 1-Owner vehicles," when in reality, they were press cars driven by journalists or corporate pool-fleet cars. To attract publicity for new vehicles, companies often have automotive journalists drive the cars. These press vehicles often include features desirable to the journalist, rather than the standard features. In addition, journalists do not always take the best care of these cars while test-driving them, according to a *Jalopnik* journalist. The cars are often destroyed after testing.

The fact that VW sold these cars under false labeling and violated safety regulations resulted in a lawsuit. Recalls had been made on the vehicles, but the lawsuit claims that VW delayed acting on the recalls and did not recall all the vehicles in the scandal. Additionally, the company will have to contend with its growing scandalous reputation and mistrust from consumers as the lawsuit continues. The company's exploits present an example of how the failure to not only follow laws and regulations of a country, but also to make amends and remain transparent with customers after a scandal, can severely hurt a business.

Sources: A&E Television News Networks, LLC, "This Day in History," History.com, 2017, http://www.history.com/this-day-in-history/volkswagen-is-founded (accessed May 9, 2019); Sam Abuelsamid, "Does VW Diesel Cheating Threaten Consumer Trust of Automotive Software?" *Forbes*, October 21, 2015, http://www.forbes.com/sites/pikeresearch/2015/10/21/vw-diesel/ (accessed May 9, 2019); Sarah Griffiths, "The Most Fuel-Efficient Car in the World: Volkswagen XL1 Does 300 MILES to the Gallon (And It Looks Cool Too)," *Daily Mail*, January 16, 2014, http://www.dailymail.co.uk/sciencetech/article-2540618/The-fuel-efficient-car-world-Volkswagen-XL1-does-300-MILES-gallon-looks-cool-too.html (accessed May 10, 2019); Russell Hotten, "Volkswagen: The Scandal Explained," *BBC News*, November 4, 2015, http://www.bbc.com/news/business-34324772 (accessed May 10, 2019); Mike Spector and Mike Colias, "Volkswagen Faces up to Penalties," *The Wall Street Journal*, March 1–12, 2017, B1–B2; William Wilkes, "Volkswagen Adds to Scandal Cost," *The Wall Street Journal*, February 2, 2017, B3; EHS Today Staff, "Lawsuit: Volkswagen Sold Cars in Violation of Safety Standards: Automobile Manufacturer Allegedly Misrepresented Prior Use of Vehicles," *EHS Today*, April 15, 2019, https://www.ehstoday.com/safety/lawsuit-volkswagen-sold-cars-violation-safety-standards (accessed May 9, 2019); Matt Hardigree, "The Truth About Press Cars," *Jalopnik*, June 29, 2015, https://jalopnik.com/the-truth-about-press-cars-1714460086 (accessed May 13, 2019); Sean Szymkowski, "Another Scandal at VW: Automaker Sold Pre-production Vehicles as Used Cars," *MotorAuthority*, December 11, 2018, https://www.motorauthority.com/news/1120404_another-scandal-at-vw-automaker-sold-pre-production-vehicles-as-used-cars (accessed May 13, 2019).

the wrong hands. Questions have been raised as to why these companies are not doing more to protect users, and as a result, regulators are lobbying for legislation that would hold corporate executives criminally liable for negligence that relates to data and privacy breaches. As it stands now, there is little accountability for executives when these breaches occur. Some corporations suffer short-term financial losses and receive negative publicity, while others walk away completely unscathed. For instance, 1 in 10 Facebook users have quit the popular social media platform due to privacy issues. Facebook stock dipped after their scandal but is back on the rise again. But although they were plagued by several data and privacy issues, Google beat analysts' expected sales and earnings numbers and, as a result, the company still has a healthy stock price. Passing regulation takes time, but companies can take quick, low-cost steps to improve their cybersecurity by properly training their employees and installing oversight frameworks in the hope of regaining public trust.[21]

Another major concern is online fraud. Online fraudsters use more than 70 types of scams, some of which are directed toward specific populations, like the elderly. The Internet Crime Complaint Center reported that between 2014 and 2018, online crimes caused $7.45 billion in losses.[22] The EU has introduced many new regulations that pertain to policies on data privacy and protection. While these changes have not yet occurred in the United States, many people suggest that changes are coming, and businesses should be prepared to adhere to a more stringent policy. Also, if there is a company in the United States with an international presence, then these changes will certainly affect them. The costs of noncompliance can be potentially devastating for a small business—fines of 4 percent of annual global turnover or up to 20 million euros, whichever is greater.

Costs and Benefits of Regulation

Regulation results in numerous costs for businesses, consumers, and society at large. Although many experts have attempted to quantify these costs, it is quite difficult to find an accurate measurement tool. To generate such measurements, economists often classify regulations as economic or social. One yardstick for the direct costs of regulation is the administrative spending patterns of federal regulatory agencies. The 2018 estimated cost of regulatory activities was $70 billion, which was up by approximately 4.7 percent from the previous year. Many people in the business world and beyond are concerned about the upward trajectory of regulatory costs. Another way to measure the direct cost of regulation is to look at the staffing levels of federal regulatory agencies. The expenditures and staffing of state and local regulatory agencies also generate direct costs to society. Federal regulatory agency jobs have been on the rise, growing to 280,872 jobs in recent years. However, 2019 saw a decline in federal agency staffing by 604 jobs. More cuts were made in social regulation programs than economic regulation programs. The one exception was that jobs with the U.S. Department of Homeland Security, part of social regulation programs, did increase.[23]

Still another way to approach the measurement of the costs of regulation is to consider the burden that businesses incur in complying with them. Various federal regulations, for example, may require companies to change their manufacturing processes or facilities (e.g., smokestack "scrubbers," to clean the air, and wheelchair ramps, to make facilities accessible to people with disabilities). Companies also must keep records to document their compliance and obtain permits to implement plans that fall under the scope of specific regulatory agencies. Again, state regulatory agencies often add costs to this burden. Regulated firms may also spend large amounts of money and other resources to prevent additional legislation and to appear responsible. Of course, businesses generally pass these regulatory costs on to consumers in the form of higher prices, a cost that some label a "hidden tax" of government. Additionally, some businesses contend that the financial and time costs of complying with regulations stifle their ability to develop new products and make investments in facilities and equipment. Moreover, society must pay for the cost of staffing and operating regulatory agencies, and these costs may be reflected in federal income taxes. Table 4.2 describes the primary drivers of the costs of regulation, including those associated with administering, enforcing, and complying with regulations.

Despite business complaints about the costs of regulation, it provides many benefits to business, consumers, and society as a whole. These benefits include greater equality in the workplace, safer workplaces, resources for disadvantaged members of society, safer products, more information about and greater choices among products, cleaner air and water, and the preservation of wildlife habitats to ensure that future generations can enjoy their beauty and diversity.

Companies that fail to respond to consumer desires or that employ inefficient processes are often forced out of the marketplace by more efficient and effective firms. Truly competitive markets also spur companies to invest in researching and developing product innovations, as well as new, more efficient methods of production. These innovations benefit consumers through lower prices and improved goods and services. For example, companies such as Apple, Samsung, and Lenovo continue to engineer smaller, faster, and more powerful computers and mobile devices that help individuals and businesses to be more productive.

Regulatory Reform   Many businesses and individuals believe that the costs of regulation outweigh its benefits. They argue that removing regulation will allow Adam Smith's "invisible hand of competition" to dictate business conduct more effectively and efficiently. Some people desire complete deregulation—the removal of all regulatory authority. Proponents of deregulation believe that less government intervention allows business markets to work more effectively. For example, many companies want their industries deregulated to decrease their costs of doing business. Many industries have been deregulated to a certain extent since the 1980s, including trucking, airlines, telecommunications (long-distance telephone and cable television), and electric utilities. In many cases, this deregulation has resulted in lower prices for consumers, as well as greater product choice.

However, the onset of the 2008–2009 financial crisis, now known as the Great Recession, slowed the call for deregulation. After the economy plummeted, the United States and other countries around the world saw the need for greater regulation, particularly of the financial industry, and began to reverse the deregulatory trend of the previous two or three decades. Although the economic crisis stemmed from a variety of factors, many perceived that much of it stemmed from a lack of appropriate governmental oversight and a lack of ethical leadership

Table 4.2 The Costs of Regulation

Type of Cost	Description
Administration and enforcement	Expenditures by government to develop and administer regulatory requirements, including the salaries of government workers, hiring inspectors, purchasing office supplies, and other overhead expenses
Compliance	Expenditures by organizations, both private and public, to meet regulatory requirements, such as reporting activities and establishing an ethics and compliance program
Costs of legal consultants	Expenditures by organizations to hire companies or legal consultants to deal with legal accusations or issues associated with regulations
Additional costs to operations	Additional costs to the operations of an organization related to improved safety, sustainability, communication, product requirements, and other elements

in businesses. However, governments' reactions and plans have many worrying that governments will take too much control. There has always been considerable debate on the relative merits and costs of regulation, and these new changes resulting from the worst financial crisis since the Great Depression are not likely to lessen this controversy.

According to an article by the Pew Charitable Trusts, reporting of compliance costs is often misleading and inaccurate. Compliance costs are often predicted to be higher than they actually are, leading many to believe that deregulation is better for the economy. However, the article argues that regulations have been very helpful to environmental causes, as well as automobile safety. For example, without regulations, cars might not have seat belts or airbags in them. Proponents of regulation argue that even when costs to comply with regulations are high for consumers, the benefits far outweigh the monetary sacrifices.

Another benefit of regulation is preventing market entry for competitors. Governmental regulation can help domestic businesses by placing restrictions on foreign companies. This lack of competition helps local businesses seize market opportunities.[24]

Self-Regulation

Self-regulation, is when an industry-level organization, such as a trade association or professional society, creates a set of rules and enforces regulations within its industry without outside prodding. Many companies join industry groups in an effort to demonstrate legal compliance and social responsibility, to signal responsibility to stakeholders, and to preclude further regulation by federal or state government. Many firms choose to join trade associations that have self-regulatory programs, often established as a preventative measure to stop or delay the development of laws and regulations that would restrict the business practices of association members. Some trade associations establish codes of conduct by which their members must abide or else risk discipline or expulsion from the association. Trade associations will be further discussed in Chapter 5.

Perhaps the best-known self-regulatory association is the **Better Business Bureau (BBB)**. Founded in 1912, the BBB is a self-regulatory association supported by businesses. It offers an Online Accredited Business certification to retailers, which certifies their high ethical standards and safety for online shoppers. The BBB lists the companies on its website and directs consumers to approved businesses' websites. Over 14,000 BBB Business Reviews are viewed by consumers daily. Today there are more than 128 bureaus in the United States, Canada, and Puerto Rico. The bureaus have accredited almost 400,000 local and national businesses and charities and resolve problems for millions of consumers and businesses each year.[25]

Each bureau also works to champion good business practices within a community, although it usually does not have strong tools for enforcing its business conduct rules. When a company violates what the BBB believes to be good business practices, the bureau warns consumers through local newspapers or broadcast media. If the offending organization is a member of the BBB, it may be expelled from the local chapter. For example, the BBB revoked accreditation for two Texas businesses for not adhering to its standards. One firm agreed to arbitration with the customer but failed to honor the arbitrator's decision.[26]

The **National Advertising Division (NAD)**, a program of the BBB, was created in 1971 as an investigatory branch of the National Advertising Review Council (NARC). NAD provides reviews of advertisements to check for accuracy and truthfulness, as well as to resolve disputes. The NAD is generally more cost-effective than legal counsel when a claim is filed. By taking on this role, NAD helps the FTC focus on other more pressing matters.[27]

The **Data and Marketing Association (DMA)**, formerly known as the Direct Marketing Association, is another major self-regulatory resource for businesses.

self-regulation
when an industry-level organization, such as a trade association or professional society, creates a set of rules and enforces regulations within its industry

Better Business Bureau (BBB)
a self-regulatory association supported by businesses

National Advertising Division (NAD)
an investigatory branch of the National Advertising Review Council (NARC) that provides reviews of advertisements for accuracy and truthfulness and resolves disputes

Data and Marketing Association (DMA)
a self-regulatory resource that assists its business members in becoming more efficient and up to date in marketing by relying on accurate consumer data and adjusting to new technology

The focus of the DMA is direct marketing businesses, and it offers membership to companies as diverse as technology companies, service providers, and media businesses. The association assists businesses in becoming more efficient and up to date in their marketing endeavors by relying on accurate consumer data and adjusting to new technology. It also provides training and workshops for businesses to learn more about new features in marketing, as well as how to ethically implement marketing changes. The DMA has outlined several regulations for their members in a formal document called "the Code." The Code highlights different rules on how members are to treat customers, as well as each other. It emphasizes the following core values: Respect privacy, be honest and fair, be diligent with data, and take responsibility. It also discusses benefits to members' businesses, while emphasizing that the customer comes first. Transparency is a huge regulatory practice with DMA. For example, members are required to be honest and open about exactly who they are and what the data they collect will be used for. They must also provide a way for consumers to end future communication if the consumer so chooses.[28]

Self-regulatory programs like the BBB and DMA have a number of advantages over government regulation. The establishment and implementation of such programs are usually less costly, and their guidelines or codes of conduct are generally more practical and realistic. Furthermore, effective self-regulatory programs reduce the need to expand government bureaucracy. However, self-regulation has several limitations. Nonmember firms are under no obligation to abide by a trade association's industry guidelines or codes. Moreover, most associations lack the tools or authority to enforce their guidelines. Finally, these guidelines are often less strict than the regulations established by government agencies.

Global Regulation

The twentieth century brought a number of regional trade agreements that decreased the barriers to international trade. NAFTA and the EU are two such alliances that were formed with the intention of enhancing regional competitiveness and decreasing inequalities. NAFTA, which eliminates virtually all tariffs on goods produced and traded between the United States, Canada, and Mexico, makes it easier for businesses of each country to invest in the other member-countries. The agreement also provides some coordination of legal standards governing business transactions among the three countries. NAFTA promotes cooperation among various regulatory agencies to encourage effective law enforcement in the free trade area. Within the framework of NAFTA, the United States and Canada have developed many agreements to enforce each other's antitrust laws. The agreement provides for cooperation in investigations, including requests for information and the opportunity to visit the territory of the other nation in the course of conducting investigations. The pending United States-Mexico-Canada Agreement (USMCA), which is intended to modernize and replace NAFTA, also supports trade in North America.

The EU was established in 1958 to promote free trade among its members and now includes 28 European nations, with more expected to join in the coming years.[29] However, in 2016, the United Kingdom (UK) voted to leave the EU. If the separation takes place, it will take some years for it to occur. As shown in Table 4.3, these changes will likely have a profound impact on both the UK and the EU economy.

To facilitate trade among its members, the EU standardized business laws and trade barriers, eliminated customs checks among its members, and introduced the euro as a standard currency. Moreover, the Commission of the European Communities entered into an agreement with the United States, similar to NAFTA, regarding joint antitrust laws. The EU is in favor of tighter financial-market regulation in the wake of the most recent financial crisis. Proposals discussed by the European Commission include laws restricting proprietary trading at large

Table 4.3 Projected Impact of Brexit on the UK

Annual Impact of Leaving the EU on the UK after 15 Years (Difference from Being in the EU)			
	European Economic Area	Negotiated Bilateral Agreement	World Trade Organization
GDP level – central	–3.8%	–6.2%	–7.5%
GDP level	–3.4% to –4.3%	–4.6% to –7.8%	–5.4% to –9.5%
GDP per capita – central*	–£1,100	–£1,800	–£2,100
GDP per capita*	–£1,000 to –£1,200	–£1,300 to –£2,200	–£1,500 to –£2,700
GDP per household – central*	–£2,600	–£4,300	–£5,200
GDP per household*	–£2,400 to –£2,900	–£3,200 to –£5,400	–£3,700 to –£6,600
Net impact on receipts	–£20 billion	–£36 billion	–£45 billion

Adapted from HM Treasury Analysis: The Long-Term Economic Impact of EU Membership and the Alternatives, April 2016; *Expressed in terms of 2015 GDP in 2015 prices, rounded to the nearest £100

Source: Will Kenton, "Brexit," *Investopedia*, May 24, 2019, https://www.investopedia.com/terms/b/brexit.asp (accessed June 10, 2019).

banks, revisions on rules regulating occupational pension funds, and improving benchmarks used as reference prices for financial instruments.[30] However, not all countries in the EU agree on which reforms to adopt. Citizens in the United Kingdom disagreed on certain policies such as immigration and disliked the impact the EU's financial struggles were having on the economy. This likely contributed to the Brexit vote to leave the EU. It is noteworthy that the vote won by only a slim margin—less than 4 percent.[31]

A company that engages in commerce beyond its own country's borders must contend with the potentially complex relationship among the laws of its own nation, international laws, and the laws of the nation in which it will be trading, as well as restrictions imposed on international trade. International business activities are affected to varying degrees by each nation's laws, regulatory agencies, courts, political environment, and special-interest groups. The EU, for example, has been tough on large businesses, leaving some critics in the United States to call the EU anticompetitive and anti-innovative. However, as regulations in the United States and the EU continue to be modified as a result of the 2008–2009 financial crisis, incongruences from each side can be seen. For example, as part of the Dodd-Frank Wall Street Reform and Consumer Protection Act, the United States mandated that large banks rely more on liquid capital than on debt for financing. While this mandate seems to reduce risks in the financial industry, those banks in the EU see this mandate as creating a competitive disadvantage. Financial firms have historically been held to the local standards of the country where business is conducted. EU regulators fear that this new capital requirement will restrict economic growth and give U.S. firms an advantage over those in the EU. They also cite potential issues regarding international trade.[32]

This example demonstrates how companies can experience major barriers when doing business in foreign countries. In addition to stricter regulations, countries can establish import barriers, including tariffs, quotas, minimum price levels, and port-of-entry taxes that affect the importation of products. Other laws govern product quality and safety, distribution methods, and sales and advertising practices.

Although there is considerable variation in focus among different nations' laws, many countries have laws that are quite similar to those in the United States. Indeed, the Sherman Antitrust Act has been copied throughout the world as the basis for regulating fair competition. Antitrust issues, such as price fixing and

Table 4.4 Signs of Possible Antitrust Violations

- Any evidence that two or more competing sellers of similar products have agreed to price their products a certain way, to sell only a certain amount of their product, or to sell only in certain areas or to certain customers.

- Large price changes involving more than one seller of very similar products of different brands, particularly if the price changes are of an equal amount and occur at about the same time.

- Suspicious statements from a seller suggesting that only one firm can sell to a particular customer or type of customer.

- Fewer competitors than normal submit bids on a project.

- Competitors submit identical bids.

- The same company repeatedly has been the low bidder on contracts for a certain product or service or in a particular area.

- Bidders seem to win bids on a fixed rotation.

- There is an unusual and unexplainable large dollar difference between the winning bid and all other bids.

- The same bidder bids substantially higher on some bids than on others, and there is no logical cost reason to explain the difference.

Source: U.S. Department of Justice, "Antitrust Enforcement and the Consumer," http://www.justice.gov/atr/public/div_stats/antitrust-enfor-consumer.pdf (accessed June 17, 2016).

market allocation, have become a major arena of international cooperation in the regulation of business.[33] Table 4.4 provides a list of situations and signs indicating that antitrust violations may become a concern.

Government's Nonregulatory Influence on Business

Governments can have influence on business through nonregulatory actions without enforcement. Government can encourage industries to engage in self-regulation. The growth of voluntary civil regulations has advanced in the global economy. **Civil regulations** include pressures exerted in society to encourage and persuade organizations to address issues in the social and physical environments. For example, pressure is placed on firms to address sustainability. The widespread acceptance of fair trade, which addresses economic, social, and environmental inequalities, is an example of a nongovernment global initiative. Government often supports these types of global initiatives. Civil regulations include multishareholder codes and the involvement of **nongovernmental organizations (NGOs)**.

Industry agreements include product certifications that can persuade government to decrease or avoid regulations. The key to avoiding formal regulations is to achieve assurance that businesses understand the formal regulatory environment and are addressing legal and ethical challenges. The government often provides resources and works with NGOs and businesses to reach standards and information to achieve best practices of appropriate conduct. As mentioned previously, the NAD independently evaluates the truth and accuracy of advertising. If an advertiser disagrees, they can appeal the decision. If not resolved, the FTC may evaluate and take action on the case. Therefore, the agency supports and cooperates with the NAD. National conferences include advertisers, NAD staff, and FTC staff. The **Ethics & Compliance Initiative (ECI)** educates and guides organizations on regulatory compliance, as well as best ethical practices. Government officials from regulatory agencies, such as the U.S. Department of Justice, often speak at their conferences.

civil regulations
pressures exerted in society to encourage and persuade organizations to address issues in the social and physical environment

nongovernmental organizations (NGOs)
nonprofit, citizen-based groups that function independent of government

Ethics & Compliance Initiative (ECI)
a community of organizations that educates about regulatory compliance and best ethical practices

An important way that government can have a nonregulatory influence on business is through the issuance of resources for businesses to use as guidelines. The Department of Justice has a page on its website that is dedicated to Compliance Assistance Resources, including sections on "Statutory Provisions" and "Guidelines and Policy Statements." The latter section has information on merger enforcement and criminal enforcement, as well as other guidelines. The Department of Justice also provides guidance on intellectual property. This is a great resource for any start-up or established business that wants to learn more about the application of general principles or to understand more about markets that are affected by licensing arrangements.

Another example of government's nonregulatory influence on business is the Public Company Accounting Oversight Board (PCAOB), a private, nonprofit company that oversees the audits of public companies. Its goal is to protect the integrity of the financial information that is published by public companies and used by investors and others. In addition to the PCAOB's standards and rules, it also provides guidance that is used by many public companies. For example, it provides staff audit practice alerts to call attention to new or noteworthy matters that have the potential to impact how auditors conduct audits. All this information is easily accessible and improves the quality and effectiveness of accounting audits. It also can have the potential to decrease misconduct. The PCAOB will be discussed further in Chapter 5.

Along with ethical auditing, online security is a growing interest in both the private and public sectors. The Federal Communications Commission (FCC), for instance, has a section on its website that provides guidance on cybersecurity for small businesses. This guidance provides tips to help protect businesses, customers, and data that may be under attack by a cybersecurity threat. Some of these include helping secure Wi-Fi networks, limiting employees' access to data and information, and making backup copies of that important data and information. The website also provides resources from the U.S. government on cybersecurity.

Government's Focus on Deregulation

Thus far, we have seen that, although legal and regulatory forces have a strong influence on business operations, businesses can also affect these forces through the political process. In addition, socially responsible firms strive to comply with society's wishes for responsible conduct via legal and ethical behavior. Indeed, the most effective way for businesses to manage the legal and regulatory environment is to establish values and policies that communicate and reward appropriate conduct. Most employees will try to comply with an organization's leadership and directions for responsible conduct. Therefore, top management must develop and implement a highly visible strategy for effective compliance. This means that top managers must take responsibility and be accountable for assessing legal risks and developing corporate programs that promote acceptable conduct.

Deregulation

Deregulation, introduced earlier in the chapter, involves changing or deleting existing laws or regulations to provide less oversight of business activities, operation, and outcomes. The amount of regulation seems to be cyclical with change in political control of Congress and the executive branch of government. President Ronald Reagan, for example, is known for scaling down regulation to let the free market work better. His philosophy was, "Government is not the solution to our problem; it is the problem." Reagan cut taxes, eliminated price controls, and reduced regulations that restricted free market trade.

deregulation
changing or deleting existing laws or regulations to provide less oversight of business activities, operation, and outcomes

George H. W. Bush took a slightly different approach to regulation and deregulation. He encouraged increased regulation when it came to certain environmental goals. For example, he pushed for changes to the Clean Air Act, and passed the Clean Air Act Amendments of 1990 with support from both Democrats and Republicans. President Bush also passed the Global Change Research Act to study global changes in the environment. Due to the growing recession, the president allowed regulations over savings and loans companies in the bank bailout of 1989. However, one of President Bush's main regulatory accomplishments was the creation of the Americans with Disabilities Act (ADA). Signed in 1990, the ADA provided regulations on employees and changes in accessibility for those with disabilities. In contrast to his regulatory acts, President Bush was instrumental in the deregulation of tariffs in North American countries, culminating in the passage of NAFTA in 1994, which greatly reduced tariffs on trade between the United States, Mexico, and Canada.[34] Though NAFTA began as a Republican initiative, its passage is often viewed as one of Bill Clinton's first major victories, as it created the largest free trade area in the world.[35] The policies under Clinton resulted in strong economic growth, low unemployment, and a surplus in the federal budget. In fact, by the final year of his presidency, unemployment was as low as 3.8 percent.[36]

Despite these victories, many suggest that Clinton's deregulation of finance, particularly the repeal of the Glass-Steagall Act in 1999, greatly contributed to the Great Recession. The Act, which kept investment and retail banking separate, was implemented in 1933 during the Great Depression to end bank runs and irresponsible banking practices Deregulating allowed banks to become "too big to fail" once more and later resulted in the bank bailout of 2008.[37]

George W. Bush continued the deregulatory approach but made an exception with the Sarbanes-Oxley Act in 2002, which will be discussed further in Chapter 5. This was a government regulation that required auditors to be more independent of the firms that they were auditing and required corporations to improve their financial reporting controls. This act was the result of major corporations not having proper regulation of their financial reporting. But Bush was a supporter of free trade and tried to push bilateral trade agreements with multiple countries. With the effects of the Great Recession that began in 2007, investment bank Bear Stearns began to collapse. The federal government stepped in and bailed out banks, industrial firms, and passed the Troubled Asset Relief Program (TARP) under the Emergency Economic Stabilization Act of 2008.

TARP attempted to improve the recession by obtaining ownership of stocks and assets of banks and financial companies that were devastated by the financial crisis. The government then provided loans from these funds to support struggling businesses. The program provided money to the auto industry, citizens facing foreclosure, banks, and financial institutions. It also set up a system to encourage banks to pay back the money they were loaned as the economy improved. This was successful, and the government actually made a profit from TARP.[38]

Obama's presidency took place immediately following the financial recession, and he promised his efforts to deregulate would be "more sensibly targeted."

He sought to bring more order to regulations that "had become a patchwork of overlapping rules." His intention was to increase input from experts, businesses, and ordinary citizens.[39] The first goal was to reestablish the government's relations with corporate America, which had been strained during the financial crisis. He increased federal spending by pushing a $787 billion stimulus package to restore the financial market. He was successful in raising the GDP by the end of his first year as president. He also established federal regulations within the Federal Reserve that allowed the government to shut down and take over large, struggling financial firms. This legislation enabled increased monitoring of the financial system and government control over derivatives.[40] By the end of his first term, Obama had signed three significant bills to stimulate the economy, increase access and affordability of healthcare, and reform U.S. financial institutions. He signed an executive order as "a government-wide review of the rules already on the books to remove outdated regulations that stifle job creation and make our economy less competitive."[41] Overall, Obama issued 101 regulations that reduced compliance costs. On an annualized basis, he was able to reduce $7.9 billion in costs through deregulation.[42]

The next president, Donald Trump, embarked on a major deregulation philosophy in an effort to reduce redundancy. This resulted in federal agencies issuing 22 deregulatory actions for every new regulatory action.[43] On the other hand, he started a trade war with China by placing 25 percent tariffs on a majority of their products at one point. China retaliated by placing a tariff on many U.S. products, but exports from China far exceed U.S. imports to China.[44] In addition, Trump lowered taxes for individuals and corporations and reduced some healthcare services. He supported legislation related to economic development, such as the Farm Act of 2018.[45]

Overall, deregulation has been a popular theme for Republicans, with Democrats being more receptive to the idea of government oversight of business; however, over the last 40 years, all presidents have engaged in some level of deregulation. Deregulation is a very popular issue with voters based on the belief that it will lower the costs of business, which will subsequently stimulate the economy, create jobs, and reduce oversight activities that provide no benefit. The proponents of deregulation, on the other hand, see government as blocking free markets and efficient operations in business. Globally, deregulation is also popular, with legislation such as the Deregulation Act in the UK, which addressed housing controls, insurance, energy, and urban development.

Role of Deregulation   While regulatory measures taken by the government do have some benefits, some argue that the market would function better with deregulation than it would with regulation. Some believe if there is a strong judicial system in place, then there is no need for regulating bodies to stop businesses from creating faulty products because any business that creates poor goods will not stay in business. In addition, a strong judicial system would ensure that anyone who does anything to recklessly put consumers at risk would be prosecuted.

Beyond safety regulations, banking regulations are also seen as unnecessary by those who call for deregulation. The argument is that governmental regulations of banks do not benefit the economy and cost the United States a great deal of money. Regulating product prices does not lead to market fairness either; rather, competition among businesses does. Therefore, some believe that regulations harm more than they help.

A major area of contention among businesses is financial regulations. With the passing of the Dodd-Frank Act in 2010, financial institutions such as banks were required to adhere to a multitude of new regulations. For example, various councils and bureaus were set up under the Act with the power to liquidate large financial companies that could result in devastating economic consequences if they fail. While the Dodd-Frank Act was meant to help prevent another recession, many do not feel that it is beneficial to a free market. A new bill called the Economic Growth, Regulatory Relief and Consumer Protection Act passed during the Trump administration revised several parts of the Act for this reason. The Dodd-Frank Act will be discussed in more detail in Chapter 5.[46]

Benefits of Deregulation

As shown in Table 4.5, there are arguments against regulations. Complying with government regulations costs Americans a lot of money and time that could be spent elsewhere. For example, it cost businesses approximately $1.96 trillion in 2017 to comply with governmental regulations. Many believe that saving this money is just as vital to the health of the U.S. economy as tax cuts. Another argument concerns worker benefits. Regulatory costs can take away from certain benefits that employees would have gotten without the regulations.

The amount of regulations that occur every year at both the state and federal levels is staggering. These regulations often are not self-explanatory and can be very difficult to enforce within a business due to their complexity. Additionally, the benefits of regulation to consumers are not always readily seen, thus begging the question of who actually benefits from governmental regulation.[47]

An important area of regulation and potential benefit of deregulation can be found in energy. As sustainable and ecofriendly options become more readily available, businesses are not limited to one source of energy. They have the option, in a deregulated market, to purchase energy from alternative, competitive sources such as American Power and Gas. Switching to a different energy company is also easier under deregulation than if energy were highly regulated.

Beyond the practical benefits, deregulation of energy, as well as other business necessities, can provide a better working environment. When companies are competing to obtain customers, there is more focus on positive customer service. Companies that do not treat their customers with the utmost respect and attention to service could lose their customers to competitors. With deregulation and more of a free market, customers can choose where and when to go for their needs, and businesses are held to a higher standard, knowing that slip-ups can result in loss of revenue.[48]

In the aviation industry, deregulation has resulted in lower prices to travel and increased productivity for airlines. These improvements came in the wake of the Airline Deregulation Act of 1978 in the United States. With less regulation, airliners are able to make more decisions about how to include more people on flights, what routes to take, and what to charge for flights. Freedom in route navigation, in particular, has led to more competition between airlines. Airlines also installed hub-and-spoke systems, which helped planes engage in more

Table 4.5 Arguments Against Regulations

- Government regulations are a hidden tax on the market.
- Government regulations hinder competitive market forces by erecting barriers to entry.
- Government regulations are a form of special-interest protection and rent-seeking by the business community.
- Government regulations are redundant because the free market is self-regulating.
- Government regulations threaten the rule of law and violate property rights, often subverting market forces to the arbitrary whims of bureaucratic decision-makers.
- Government regulations are rarely subject to thorough cost-benefit analysis.

Source: Tom Lehman, "Six Arguments Against Government Regulations," *Capitalism.com*, May 19, 2017, https://www.capitalism.com/six-arguments-government-regulations/ (accessed June 10, 2019).

resourceful flights with more appropriate and individualized equipment for each flight.

Costs of Deregulation

While deregulation has brought about noticeable benefits, problems have occurred as a result of the lack of regulation. While a competitive market is beneficial in driving prices down and allowing consumers more options, it can also weed out smaller businesses. For example, 85 percent of the airline industry is controlled by United, Delta, American, and Southwest, effectively excluding smaller airlines.

Monopolies and mergers between large companies have resulted in unfair pricing for passengers, who cannot enjoy discounts or deals when paying fares. To help with unfair pricing, the government could increase competition in the market by further removing regulations from the airline industry. It could also be more diligent about penalizing antitrust law violators. As a last resort for a deregulated airline industry, the government could reinstate price ceilings. Some argue that deregulation of the airline industry has led to an increasingly miserable flying experience, with overcrowded planes and airports.[49] However, this can be seen as a consequence of the industry itself, rather than deregulation per se. As competition increases, airports offer more and more deals to passengers and encourage more and more passengers to fly. This can create congestion and too many people for the resources that are available to airports to handle. Ironically, airports rely on the government to provide resources, so a shortage of resources based on demand can be seen as a governmental distribution issue rather than a cost of deregulation.[50]

From an economic perspective, regulation and deregulation can be beneficial, but it depends on the area of the market. The Council of Economic Advisors argues that some regulations are helpful and necessary for a stable market. However, it also argues for deregulation in certain sectors, such as healthcare and rental housing. Therefore, the debate for whether deregulation is best for the economy and American citizens continues.[51]

Summary

The government has a profound influence on business. There has been conflict over the regulation of business. The legal system is not always accepted in some countries as insurance that business will be conducted in a legitimate way. While many businesses may object to regulations aimed at maintaining ethical cultures and preserving stakeholder welfare, the very existence of businesses is based on laws permitting their creation, organization, and dissolution. Large, incorporated firms often receive more attention than small businesses because of their size, visibility, and impact on so many aspects of the economy and society. Many diverse stakeholder groups attempt to influence the public officials who legislate, interpret laws, and regulate business. Additionally, new disruptive technology is changing both the business and the regulatory environment.

Economic reasons for regulation often relate to efforts to level the playing field on which businesses operate. These efforts include regulating trusts, which are generally established to gain control of a product market or industry by eliminating competition, and eliminating monopolies, which occur when just one business provides a good or service in a given market. Another rationale for regulation is society's desire to restrict destructive or unfair competition. Social regulation is concerned with the overall welfare of citizens. Protecting and supporting consumers and providing the work environment with safe work conditions, equal opportunity, and healthcare are the focus of social regulations.

Regulation creates numerous costs for businesses, consumers, and society at large. Some measures of these costs include administrative spending patterns, staffing levels of federal regulatory agencies, and costs businesses incur in complying with regulations. The cost of regulation is passed on to consumers in the form of higher prices and may stifle product innovation and investments in new facilities and equipment. Regulation also provides many benefits, including greater equality in the workplace, safer workplaces, resources for disadvantaged members of society, safer products, more information about and greater choices among products, cleaner air and water, and the preservation of wildlife habitats. Antitrust laws and regulations strengthen competition and spur companies to invest in research and development. Many businesses and individuals believe that the costs of regulation outweigh its benefits. Some people desire complete deregulation, or removal of regulatory authority.

There are many benefits of deregulation. These include a more competitive, free market, more control and choice for consumers over goods and services, and less regulatory costs to businesses. Deregulation has occurred in many areas, often depending on the political stance of the government. One of the main ones is an increase in money for the economy. Deregulation can also provide a better working environment. In the aviation industry, deregulation has resulted in lower prices to travel and increased productivity for airlines.

Because government is a stakeholder of business (and vice versa), businesses and government can work together as both legitimately participate in the political process. Business participation can act in society's interests either positively or negatively, based not only on the outcome, but also on the perspective of the stakeholders.

Responsible Business Debate

Uber Puts It in Reverse on International Expansion

Issue: *Should businesses proactively adapt to local laws and regulations?*

Uber Technologies, Inc. first began doing business in the United States utilizing the sharing economy. It quickly expanded internationally, setting up in countries such as China, India, Germany, and France. While this expansion has been beneficial for Uber, international markets involve unique challenges in the realms of regulation and law. Regulatory requirements differ from country to country. The company has run into problems because it has attempted to apply the same practices in other countries as it does in the United States.

A wide-reaching problem that has occurred for Uber is the failure to obtain taxi licenses, even though Uber drivers offer many of the same services as taxis. Governments have responded by banning Uber or certain Uber services due to the lack of professional licenses for drivers. For instance, in Germany, a court banned Uber services if they used unlicensed drivers. Uber challenged this decision, but the Federal Court of Justice ruled that the firm's business model clearly infringes on the Personal Transportation Law because drivers are transporting riders without a personal transportation license.

Regulatory issues such as these forced Uber to temporarily pull out of most German cities. Rather than insisting on its own business methods that align with U.S. regulations, Uber reentered Germany with the mindset that it will adapt its business to the laws and regulations of the country it is in. For example, transportation drivers are legally required in Germany to report to a garage or home base between rides. While this is less cost effective for the drivers, Uber is attempting to follow that rule. At the same time, management is working with the government to alter some of the regulatory requirements and is using already-licensed drivers in order to reinstate Uber's business in various German towns.

Although Uber defines itself as an "agent" of its "individual contractors," many courts do not view its services in the same way. They are forcing Uber to comply with licensing laws or stop doing business in certain areas. Working with governments, knowing the laws of each country that the company expands into, and changing the business to fit the local laws and regulations are important lessons that Uber is learning. Time will tell whether Uber's changes will be enough to restore trust in the company in some of the countries that have banned its services in the past.

There Are Two Sides to Every Issue

1. It's more beneficial for businesses to adapt to local laws and regulations prior to entering new countries.
2. It's more beneficial for businesses to expand and adapt to local laws and regulations as needed after entering new countries.

Sources: Eric Auchard and Christoph Steitz, "German Court Bans Uber's Unlicensed Taxi Services," *Reuters*, March 18, 2015, http://www.reuters.com/article/2015/03/18/us-uber-germany-ban-idUSKBN0ME1L820150318 (accessed May 8, 2019); Rob Davies, "Uber Suffers Legal Setbacks in France and Germany," *The Guardian*, June 9, 2016, https://www.theguardian.com/technology/2016/jun/09/uber-suffers-legal-setbacks-in-france-and-germany (accessed May 8, 2019); *Economist* staff, "Uberworld," *The Economist*, September 3, 2016, p. 9; Jefferson Graham, "App Greases the Wheels," *USA Today*, May 27, 2015, p. 5B; Felicitas Hackmann, "UberPOP, Uber's Ride-Sharing Service, Pops up in More EU Cities," *VentureBeat*, April 15, 2014, http://venturebeat.com/2014/04/15/uberpop-ubers-peer-to-peer-service-pops-up-in-more-eu-cities/ (accessed May 8, 2019); Sam Schechner and Tom Fairless, "Europe Steps up Pressure on Tech Giants," *The Wall Street Journal*, April 2, 2015, http://www.wsj.com/articles/europe-steps-up-pressure-on-technology-giants-1428020273 (accessed May 8, 2019); Spiegel, "Vermittlung Privater Fahrer: Gericht Verbietet Uber deutschlandweit," http://www.spiegel.de/wirtschaft/unternehmen/uber-urteil-gericht-verbietet-uber-deutschlandweit-a-1024214.html (accessed May 8, 2019); Uber, Home Page, https://www.uber.com/ (accessed May 8, 2019); UNM Daniels Fund Ethics Initiative, "Truth, Transparency, and Trust: Uber Important in the Sharing Economy," slide presentation, https://danielsethics.mgt.unm.edu/teaching-resources/presentations.asp (accessed May 8, 2019); Adam Satariano, "Needing Growth, Uber Returns to Germany. This Time on Best Behavior," *The New York Times*, November 19, 2018, https://www.nytimes.com/2018/11/19/technology/uber-growth-ipo-germany.html (accessed May 8, 2019).

Key Terms

Better Business Bureau (BBB) (p. 107)
civil regulations (p. 110)
Data and Marketing Association (DMA) (p. 107)
deregulation (p. 111)
disruptive technology (p. 98)
economic regulation (p. 101)

Ethics & Compliance Initiative (ECI) (p. 110)
monopoly (p. 100)
National Advertising Division (NAD) (p. 107)
nongovernmental organizations (NGOs) (p. 110)

patent laws (p. 100)
regulation (p. 96)
self-regulation (p. 107)
social regulation (p. 101)
trusts (p. 100)

Discussion Questions

1. Discuss the existence of both cooperation and conflict between government and businesses concerning the regulation of business.
2. What is the rationale for government to regulate the activities of businesses? How is our economic and social existence shaped by government regulations?
3. What is the role and function of the FTC in the regulation of business? How does the FTC engage in proactive activities to avoid government regulation?
4. How do global regulations influence U.S. businesses operating internationally? What are the major obstacles to global regulation?
5. In what ways is disruptive technology changing the regulatory environment?
6. How are social regulation and economic regulation different? How do they work together?
7. What are the benefits of joining trade associations with self-regulatory programs?
8. Why are civil regulations effective? What are possible limitations to their influence?
9. Compare the costs and benefits of regulation. In your opinion, do the benefits outweigh the costs or vice versa? What are the advantages and disadvantages of deregulation?

Experiential Exercise

Visit the Better Business Bureau website (https://www.bbb.org/). What is the BBB's current vision? What is the BBB's current mission? Review the news updates on the site. On the basis of these posts, how does the BBB help businesses? How does the BBB help consumers?

The Taxing Role of Being a Politician: What Would You Do?

The election of a new governor brings many changes to any state capital, including the shuffling of a variety of appointed positions. In most cases, political appointees have contributed a great deal to the governor's election bid and have expertise in a specific area related to the appointed post. Joe Barritz was in that position when he became assistant agricultural commissioner in January 2020. He was instrumental in getting the governor elected, especially through his fundraising efforts. Joe's family owned thousands of acres in the state and had been farming and ranching since the 1930s. Joe earned a bachelor's degree in agricultural economics and policy and a law degree from one of the state's top institutions. He worked as an attorney in the state's capital city for over 18 years and represented a range of clients, most of whom were involved in agriculture. Thus, he possessed many characteristics that made him a strong candidate for assistant commissioner.

In June, after about six months on the job, Joe had lunch with a couple of friends he had known for many years. During that lunch, they had a casual conversation about the fact that Joe never did have a true "celebration" after being named assistant agricultural commissioner. His friends decided to discuss with others and plan such a celebration in a few months. Before long, eight of Joe's friends were busy planning to hold a reception in his honor on October 5. Two of these friends were currently employed as lobbyists. One represented the beef industry association, and the other worked for the cotton industry council. They asked Joe if they could hold the celebration at his lake home in the capital. Joe talked with the commission's ethics officer about the party and learned that these types of parties, between close friends, were common for newly appointed and elected officials. The ethics officer told Joe that the reception and location were fine, but only if his lobbyist friends paid for the reception with personal funds. The state's ethics rules did not allow a standing government official to take any type of gift, including corporate dollars, that might influence his or her decision-making. Joe communicated this information to his friends.

During the next few months, Joe was involved in a number of issues that could potentially help or harm agriculture-based industries. Various reports and policy statements within the Agricultural Commission were being used to tailor state legislation and regulatory proposals. The beef and cotton councils were actively supporting a proposal that would provide tax breaks to farmers and ranchers. The staff on the Agricultural Commission were mixed on the proposal, but Joe was expected to deliver a report to a legislative committee on the commission's preferences. His presentation was scheduled for October 17.

On October 5, nearly 60 of Joe's friends gathered at the catered reception to reminisce and congratulate him on his success. Most were good friends and acquaintances, so the mood and conversation were relatively light that evening. A college football game between two big rivals drew most people to the big-screen TV. By midnight, the guests were gone. Back at the office the following week, Joe began working on his presentation for the legislative committee. Through a series of economic analyses, long meetings, and electronic discussions, he decided to support the tax benefits for farmers and ranchers. News reports carried information from his presentation.

It was not long before some reporters made a connection between the reception in Joe's honor and his stand on the tax breaks for agriculture industries. An investigation quickly ensued, including reports that the beef and cotton industry associations had not only been present, but also financially supported the reception. The small company used to plan and cater the party indicated that checks from the cotton industry council and beef industry association were used to cover some of the expenses. A relationship between the gift of the reception and Joe's presentation to the legislative committee would be a breach of his oath of office, as well as state ethics rules. If you were Joe, what would you do?

The Impact of Business on Government and the Political Environment

NFL's Headaches over Concussion Responsibility

Playing professional football, almost by definition, is not one of the safest jobs in the world, especially at the level of the National Football League (NFL), where players get injured almost every week of play. Sprained ankles, torn ligaments, concussions, and broken bones are pretty much par for the course. More than 200 concussions are reported during a typical football season. It is possible that if the NFL does not resolve the issue, regulatory and administrative agencies could get involved.

Over the past few decades, retired NFL players in particular, have raised concerns about how repetitive head injuries and concussions that they sustained while playing in the NFL have negatively affected them later in life. Evidence began to mount that many retired NFL players faced considerable neurological problems, including permanent brain damage, dementia, and much higher than average incidents of Alzheimer's disease and clinical depression. Some NFL players have arguably even died by suicide due to their degenerative brain disease. Players have argued that the NFL knew or should have known the risks that they were incurring due to concussions and traumatic repetitive brain injuries suffered during games, and that the NFL did not do enough to prevent these injuries.

In 2013 the league announced that a neurologist would be present on the field of every NFL game as a new concussion safety measure. Additionally, the league introduced new penalties for crown of the helmet hits where players lower their helmet before a tackle. Soon after, the league agreed to settle a series of lawsuits by paying nearly $1 billion to retired football players who suffered these types of injury. Moreover, it gave $10 million to fund brain injury research and various education and safety programs. Considering that in one year, the NFL's total revenues amounted to about $14 billion, many felt that $1 billion was insufficient—only a drop in the bucket. In addition, there were concerns that the agreement did not really reach the more systemic issue of making the game safer. The class-action lawsuit was officially settled by the NFL giving each player a maximum of $5 million each.

Just one year after the settlement, the NFL contributed $100 million for brain research and development and instituted a new policy for handling concussions in players. Though the league is taking measures to improve safety, some fans as well as athletes have criticized the new rules for softening the sport of football, saying defenses have become less effective at stopping offense players.

Later, the league was dealt another blow. Researchers discovered after examining the post-mortem brains of 202 men who had played football sometime during their lives from pre–high school to the NFL—that 177 showed evidence of chronic traumatic encephalopathy (CTE), a degenerative brain disease and one of the most common long-term injuries linked to concussion among football players. These brains were donated rather than selected at random, though, and so the results could be skewed. However, the findings suggest that concussion trauma among NFL players is much more prevalent than originally thought.

The risks of suffering from permanent brain damage and other injuries have already convinced some NFL players (such as Indianapolis Colts quarterback Andrew Luck in 2019) to retire early. One poll found that parents are 44 percent less likely to allow their children to play football.

Addressing these issues is vital to the continued existence of the NFL. The league has said that they are pushing for players to wear helmets that are more impact-resistant and shock-absorbent, and the use of these helmets may be a factor in fewer concussions. Recently, concussions decreased by 30 percent during the regular season, according to the NFL. Along with improved helmets, the NFL continues to do research on the impact of injuries on the brain and how to better protect football players.[1]

Shutterstock/Billion Photos

Chapter Objectives

- Understand changes in the contemporary political environment
- Examine how business participates in and influences public policy
- Describe the government's approach to ensuring legal and ethical compliance

The government has the power, through laws and regulations, to structure how businesses and individuals achieve their goals. The purpose of regulating firms is to create a fair competitive environment for businesses, consumers, and society. All stakeholders need to demonstrate a commitment to corporate social responsibility through compliance with relevant laws and proactive consideration of social needs. The law is one of the most important business subjects in terms of its effect on organizational practices and activities. Thus, compliance with the law is a fundamental expectation of social responsibility. Because the law is based on principles, norms, and values found within society, the law is the foundation of responsible decision-making.

This chapter explores the complex relationship between business and government. First, we discuss the contemporary political environment. We examine the historical context related to major social and economic events and political and regulatory initiatives. This includes sustainability, technology, social issues, and the reaction of the U.S. Congress to address issues. The role of special-interest groups is involved in influencing political decisions.

The Contemporary Political Environment

During the 1960s, a significant "antiestablishment" movement manifested in the form of hostile protests toward businesses. These efforts spurred a 15-year wave of legislation and regulation to address a number of issues of the day, including product safety, employment discrimination, human rights, energy shortages, environmental degradation, and scandals related to bribery and payoffs. During the 1980s, the pendulum swung back in favor of business, and the economic prosperity of the 1990s was driven by technological advances and the self-regulation of business. In addition, businesses' priorities were beginning to be focused on protecting competition and the natural environment. These policies continued through 2008, with continued self-regulation of industries and the rolling back of environmental laws that businesses deemed detrimental. However, the regulatory climate changed again in 2009 toward more regulation of environmental and health issues, resulting in higher taxes and increased social services. The onset of the financial crisis created an even greater need for stricter legislation, such as the **Troubled Assets Recovery Program (TARP)** that authorized the U.S. Treasury to purchase up to $700 billion of troubled assets like mortgage-backed securities. It has also resulted in support for entirely new regulation and regulatory agencies such as the Consumer Financial Protection Bureau (CFPB). These new regulations have had wide-sweeping effects on the financial industry. Other organizations, such as the Environmental Protection Agency (EPA) and the Food and Drug Administration (FDA) in the United States, also began to regulate with renewed vigor, with the aim of protecting stakeholders. Recent years have seen a swing toward deregulation. For example, the Affordable Care Act (ACA), passed during the administration of President Barack Obama, has been dialed back. Previously, there was a penalty (which the Supreme Court ruled was a tax) that uninsured individuals were required to pay. But this was eliminated from the ACA after the White House Council of Economic Advisers argued that deregulating health insurance by removing the mandate and easing requirements on health insurers would not destabilize the insurance market.[2]

Such changes in the political environment over the last 60 years shaped the political environment in which businesses operate and created new avenues for businesses to participate in the political process. Among the most significant factors shaping the political environment were changes in Congress and the rise of special-interest groups. As the Obama administration sought to revive and even

Troubled Assets Recovery Program (TARP)
a law authorizing the U.S. Treasury to purchase up to $700 billion of troubled assets such as mortgage-based securities

increase oversight of the finance industry, more companies became interested in hiring lobbyists to campaign on behalf of their interests in Washington. The administration of Obama's successor, Donald Trump, saw an increase in regulatory lobbying. According to a Brookings report, while lobbying increased, the administration did not necessarily give lobbying groups increased priority. Both big business and industry trade association lobbying increased in both the Obama and Trump administrations.[3]

Changes in Congress

Among the calls for social reform in the 1960s were pressures for changes within the federal legislative process itself. Bowing to this pressure, Congress enacted an amendment to the Legislative Reorganization Act in 1970, which ushered in a new era of change for the political process. This legislation significantly revamped the procedures of congressional committees, most notably stripping committee chairpersons of many of their powers, equalizing committee and chair assignments, and requiring committees to record and publish all roll-call votes taken in the committee. By opening up the committee process to public scrutiny and reducing the power of senior members and committee leaders, the act reduced the level of secrecy surrounding the legislative process and effectively brought an end to an era of autonomous committee chairs and senior members.[4]

Another significant change occurred in 1974, when Congress amended the Federal Election Campaign Act to limit contributions from individuals, political parties, and special-interest groups organized to get specific candidates elected or policies enacted.[5] Around the same time, many states began to shift their electoral processes from the traditional party caucus to primary elections, further eroding the influence of the party in the political process. These changes ultimately had the effect of reducing the importance of political parties by decreasing members' dependence on their parties. Many candidates for elected offices began to turn to special-interest groups to raise enough funds to mount serious campaigns and reelection bids.

In 2002, Congress passed the Bipartisan Campaign Reform Act (BRCA), sponsored by senators John McCain and Russell Feingold. This new legislation limited the amount of contributions that parties could make to political campaigns, and it implemented rules for how corporate and labor funds could be used in federal elections. The Act also forbade national party committees from raising or spending unregulated funds. Though it outraged certain legislators, who appealed to the Supreme Court over its constitutionality, the Supreme Court upheld it.[6] However, the decision, popularly referred to as *Citizens United*, also granted more powers to organizations regarding corporate contributions. The decision gave corporations the right to spend as much as they want in independent political expenditures to support governmental candidates. These independent political expenditures are provided through **political action committees (PACs)**, organizations that solicit donations from individuals and then contribute these funds to candidates running for political office. Companies can organize PACs to which their executives, employees, and stockholders can make significant donations as individuals. PACs operate independently of business and are usually incorporated. Labor unions and other special-interest groups, such as teachers and medical doctors, can also establish PACs to promote their goals.

political action committees (PACs)
organizations that solicit donations from individuals and then contribute these funds to candidates running for political office

The *Citizens United* decision enabled the creation of what has been termed "super PACs," because of what is seen as their unlimited ability to receive political donations.[7] Before *Citizens United*, individuals were able to contribute no more than $2,500 to PACs, and unions and corporations were not allowed to contribute at all. The Supreme Court ruled that these prohibitions violated the First Amendment. The Federal Election Committee has rules to restrict PAC donations to $5,000 per candidate for each election. However, many PACs exploit loopholes in these regulations by donating so-called soft money to political parties, which is money that does not support a specific candidate for federal office. Under the current rules, these contributors can make unlimited donations to political parties for general activities. Donors can donate through a company they own without disclosing their name.

gerrymandering
the practice of manipulating district boundaries for partisan political advantage which ultimately has the power to greatly influence legislation

Congressional maps have been in the spotlight since the Supreme Court ruled in 2019 that the Constitution doesn't bar **gerrymandering**, the practice of manipulating district boundaries for partisan political advantage. The court decided that the question of gerrymandering must be resolved by the elected branches of government, not the courts. In 2018, the Pennsylvania Supreme Court declared the state's Republican-drawn congressional map was unconstitutional based on the state constitution. Partisan gerrymandering has the power to greatly influence legislation.[8]

Rise of Special-Interest Groups

The success of activists' efforts in the 1960s and 1970s marked the rise of special-interest groups. The movements to promote African American and women's rights and to protest the Vietnam War and environmental degradation evolved into well-organized groups working to educate the public about significant social issues and to crusade for legislation and regulation of business conduct that they deemed irresponsible. These progressive groups were soon joined on Capitol Hill by more conservative groups working to further their agenda on issues such as business deregulation, restriction of abortion and gun control, and promotion of prayer in schools. Businesses joined in by forming industry and trade associations.

Common Cause
a nonprofit, nonpartisan organization that fights corrupt government and special interests

These increasingly powerful special-interest groups now focused on getting candidates elected who could further the groups' political agendas. **Common Cause**, for example, is a nonprofit, nonpartisan organization working to fight corrupt government and special interests backed by large sums of money. Since 1970, Common Cause, with over 1 million members, has campaigned for greater openness and accountability in government. Some of its self-proclaimed victories include reform of presidential campaign finances, tax systems, congressional ethics, open meeting standards, and disclosure requirements for lobbyists. Table 5.1 lists the dates and areas of Common Cause's major accomplishments over the past three decades.[9] Today, the organization is trying to modernize the election process by allowing automatic voter registration, election-day registration at polling stations, online registration, and preregistration for high school students. At least partly due to their efforts, automatic voter registration has been adopted in 17 states. Also, Common Cause is promoting increased voting security by lobbying for eliminating online voting, which is subject to hacking; ensuring that paper backups of votes are created; retiring old voting machines; and requiring risk-limiting audits of voting. Common Cause promotes the integrity of the voting process through these solutions so that citizens can have confidence in the results of elections and feel that their votes have been protected from potential threats.[10]

Influencing Government

The political environment has a strong impact on a company's economic value, and new regulations can affect how businesses operate. To influence government, many businesses and private interest groups proactively participate in the political process.

Table 5.1 Accomplishments of Common Cause

1971: Helps pass the Twenty-Sixth Amendment, giving 18-year-olds the right to vote

1974: Leads efforts to pass presidential public financing, contribution limits, and disclosure requirements

1974–1975: Helps pass Freedom of Information Act (FOIA) and open meetings laws at federal, state, and local levels

1978: Leads efforts to pass the historic Ethics in Government Act of 1978, requiring financial disclosure for government officials and restricting the "revolving door" between business and government

1982: Works to pass extension of the Voting Rights Act

1990: Works to help pass the Americans with Disabilities Act (ADA), guaranteeing civil rights for the disabled

1995: Lobbies for limits on gifts in the House and Senate and for passage of the Lobby Reform Act, providing disclosure of lobbyists' activity and spending

2000: Successfully works for legislation to unmask and require disclosure of "527" political groups which are tax-exempt organizations created primarily to get candidates elected or appointed to local, state, or federal office

2001: Lobbies successfully with a coalition for the Help America Vote Act, which provided funding to states for improvement of the nation's system of voting

2002: Leads successful multiyear campaign to enact the Bipartisan Campaign Reform Act, banning soft money in federal campaigns. In 2003, in a landmark decision, the U.S. Supreme Court upheld the law

2004: Launches major voter mobilization and election monitoring programs for presidential election

2005: Wins the fight against efforts to cut federal funding for the Corporation for Public Broadcasting, and gathers 150,000 petition signatures calling for the resignation of CPB chairman Ken Tomlinson for partisan and unethical behavior

2005/2006: Leads the charge against disgraced Majority Leader Tom DeLay and fights for major ethics reform

2007: Fights successfully for passage of the Honest Leadership and Open Government Act of 2007, making major improvements in ethics and lobby laws and rules

2008: Leads successful campaign to create the first-ever independent ethics commission in the U.S. House of Representatives

2010: Spurred by the U.S. Supreme Court's Citizens United decision that lifted the decades-old ban on corporate and union spending around elections, Common Cause redoubles efforts to pass the Fair Elections Now Act, which would allow candidates to run competitive campaigns on small donations and fair elections funds

2011: Successfully helps pass Online Voter Registration Senate Bill 397, resulting in thousands of people in California registering online to vote

2012: Pushes for the Assembly Bill 1436 in California, which give voters more opportunity to vote closer to the election

2016: Voter's Choice Act passes; meant to take effect in 2018, allows voters in California to have different options in voting methods

2017: Works with the California Clean Money Campaign to pass the California DISCLOSE Act, requiring transparency regarding funding for voting advertisements

2018: Helps pass the Legislative Employee Whistleblower Protection Act for legislative employee protection in California

Sources: California Common Cause, "Our Successes," Common Cause, https://www.commoncause.org/california/about-us/our-impact/ (accessed June 19, 2019); Assembly Bill No. 1436, Chapter 497, California Legislative Information, https://www.commoncause.org/california/about-us/our-impact/ (accessed June 19, 2019); Assembly Bill No. 403, Chapter 2, California Legislative Information, https://leginfo.legislature.ca.gov/faces/billTextClient.xhtml?bill_id=201720180AB403 (accessed June 19, 2019).

Ethical Responsibilities in SOCIETY

High Society: Marijuana on the Slow Road to Legalization

Marijuana can be dated back as far as 6000 BC, when its seeds were used for food in China. During the time of Napoleon, it was used for its pain-relieving mechanisms and sedative effects. Marijuana is made from the flowering top of the *Cannabis sativa* plant and contains tetrahydro cannabinol (THC), which is what causes a mind-altering state in marijuana users. About $2.3 million is spent annually on lobbying in the marijuana industry.

Marijuana is also used for its psychoactive effects. For instance, it has been used to induce changes in mood and consciousness, as well as to relax and calm down. Studies indicate that the use of marijuana can have both positive and negative effects on overall health. For example, research has shown that using marijuana reduces the nausea and vomiting of cancer patients receiving chemotherapy. Negative short-term effects of marijuana use include inability to concentrate and distortion of sense and time. The long-term effects can include respiratory issues, fatigue, decreases in libido, impaired fertility, and unfavorable changes in fat and muscle mass.

One ethical concern is the lack of extensive testing. Testing is expensive, and there aren't enough approved testing laboratories. Because marijuana is still illegal at the federal level, insufficient funds are set aside for cannabis research. Additionally, there are no federal standards or procedures in place for testing labs, meaning that two labs can follow different procedures and thus produce different results running the same test. This has led to inconsistent and inconclusive results. Additionally, conflicting federal and state laws create an ethical gray area for many individuals and businesses. For example, providing legal services to clients in the marijuana industry could still be considered a violation of federal law, even if marijuana use is legal in the state.

The majority of states have legalized marijuana for medicinal purposes because of the potential positive effects of its use, while attempting to mitigate the potential negative effects via medical oversight of its administration.

The group spending the most on lobbying to defend and expand the cannabis industry is the National Cannabis Industry Association, a nonprofit representing about 2,000 businesses. While medical marijuana has been increasingly accepted by Americans, recreational marijuana has been strongly debated. In 2012, Colorado and Washington became the first states to legalize the use of recreational marijuana for adults over 21. Colorado's marijuana industry has surpassed $6 billion in total sales since its legalization. Many states have followed suit, creating a multibillion-dollar industry.

Along with marijuana, other products from the cannabis plant have attracted interest. For example, the 2018 Farm Bill addressed hemp production. Hemp is defined as a substance containing 0.3 percent or less of tetrahydrocannabinol (THC). Because of the limited amount of THC, hemp is thought to be safer than marijuana. The 2018 Farm Bill legalized hemp production and sale at the federal level. In addition, hemp can now be sold across state lines without federal penalties. Marijuana, on the other hand, has not been legalized at the federal level, even under the new bill.

Hemp is used in a variety of items, from household goods to medicinal products. Cannabidiol (CBD) has increased in popularity over the years as a medicinal agent. Under the 2018 Farm Bill, CBD products cultivated from hemp plants are now legal federally, but CBD cultivated from marijuana continues to be illegal. The process of growing hemp will be regulated by the federal government under the bill, as well as state legislature. Those growing hemp must have a license in order to operate legally.

Continual research into the benefits and possible pitfalls of hemp products is also encouraged under the new bill. Hemp farmers are now considered to be controlled by the Federal Crop Insurance Act, giving them equal rights with other farmers. The bill is a success for those who are hoping to move closer to marijuana legalization. The political environment and government regulation will determine further actions for or against marijuana legalization, at both the medicinal and recreational levels.

Sources: Aaron Cadena, "Hemp vs. Marijuana: The Difference Explained (2019 Update)," *Medium*, September 10, 2018, https://medium.com/cbd-origin/hemp-vs-marijuana-the-difference-explained-a837c51aa8f7; John Hudak, "The Farm Bill, Hemp Legalization, and the Status of CBD: An Explainer," Brookings Institution, December 14, 2018, https://www.brookings.edu/blog/fixgov/2018/12/14/the-farm-bill-hemp-and-cbd-explainer/; Michael Nepveux, "2018 Farm Bill Provides a Path Forward for Industrial Hemp," American Farm Bureau Federation, February 28, 2019, https://www.fb.org/market-intel/2018-farm-bill-provides-a-path-forward-for-industrial-hemp; National Commission of Marijuana and Drug Abuse, "History of Medical Marijuana Use," Erowid, 1972, http://www.erowid.org/plants/cannabis/cannabis_medical_info3.shtml; "Cannabis in the Clinic? The Medical Marijuana Debate," Learn Genetics Utah Education, January 24, 2011, https://learn.genetics.utah.edu/content/addiction/cannabis/; Thomas J. Bouril, "Marijuana and Hemp: The Untold Story," 1997, http://azinelibrary.org/trash/Marijuana_and_Hemp-_The_Untold_Story.pdf; T. T. Brown and A. S. Dobs, "Endocrine Effects of Marijuana," *Journal of Clinical Pharmacology*, 42(2002), 90–96; Maia Szalavitz, "Study: Marijuana Not Linked with Long-Term Cognitive Development," *TIME*, July 19, 2011, http://healthland.time.com/2011/07/19/study-marijuana-not-linked-with-long-term-cognitive-impairment/; Aaron Smith, "Marijuana legalization Passes in Colorado, Washington," *CNNMoney*, November 8, 2012, http://money.cnn.com/2012/11/07/news/economy/marijuana-legalization-washington-colorado/index.html; Matt Ferner, "Marijuana Legalization: What Everyone Needs to Know: Authors Discuss Risks and Rewards of Legal Weed," *Huffington Post*, September 4, 2012, http://www.huffingtonpost.com/2012/09/04/marijuana-legalization-research_n_1850470.html; Open Secrets, "Lobbying Spending in Marijuana, 2019," https://www.opensecrets.org/lobby/indusclient.php?id=N09; Sandra Fish, "Cannabis Lobby Gains New Clout in Colorado as Its Spending Tripled in the Past Five Years," *Colorado Sun*, March 13, 2019, https://coloradosun.com/2019/03/13/colorado-cannabis-lobby-clout-legislature/.

Corporate Approaches to Influencing Government

Although some businesses view regulatory and legal forces as beyond their control and simply react to conditions arising from those forces, other firms actively seek to influence the political process to achieve their goals. In some cases, companies publicly protest the actions of legislative bodies. More often, companies work for the election of political candidates who look upon them positively. Lobbying, PACs, and campaign contributions are some of the tools that businesses employ to influence the political process.

Lobbying

Among the most powerful tactics a business can employ to participate in public policy decisions is direct representation through full-time staff who communicate with elected officials. **Lobbying** is the process of working to persuade public and/or government officials to favor a particular position in decision-making. Organizations may lobby officials either directly or by combining their efforts with other organizations.

lobbying
the process of working to persuade public and/or government officials to favor a particular position in decision-making

Many companies concerned about the threat of legislation or regulation that may affect their operations negatively will employ lobbyists to communicate their concerns to officials on their behalf. For example, 1,300 clients lobbied on issues related to tariffs and trade in response to the trade war between the United States and China in 2018. Also, General Motors (GM), which manufactures many vehicles in Mexico, has lobbied in an attempt to block new tariffs on imported cars.[11] Table 5.2 lists the organizations that spend the most money on lobbying.

Table 5.2 Top Spenders in Lobbying

Lobbying Client	Total
U.S. Chamber of Commerce	$ 1,528,450,680
National Association of Realtors	$ 557,674,732
American Medical Association	$ 400,154,500
American Hospital Association	$ 378,868,630
Pharmaceutical Research and Manufacturers of America	$ 374,388,550
GE	$ 359,742,000
Blue Cross/Blue Shield	$ 353,789,086
Business Roundtable	$ 287,680,000
AARP	$ 284,461,064
Boeing Company	$ 278,133,310
Northrop Grumman	$ 277,852,213
Lockheed Martin	$ 259,162,792
ExxonMobil	$ 257,572,742
AT&T Inc.	$ 251,474,644
Verizon Communications	$ 247,836,109
National Association of Broadcasters	$ 233,188,000
Edison Electric Institute	$ 227,185,085
Southern Company	$ 226,280,694
Comcast Corporation	$ 201,034,323
Altria Group	$ 200,265,200

Source: Center for Responsive Politics, "Top Spenders," *Open Secrets*, 2019, https://www.opensecrets.org/lobby/top. php?indexType=s (accessed June 18, 2019).

The financial industry has long employed lobbyists to push for increased deregulation so that it can pursue more profitable (but riskier) avenues. However, changes in regulation and compensation practices in the financial sector are making this a more difficult task. In the past, bank officials have often been rewarded for the quantity of business they do, rather than the quality, which encouraged employees to engage in riskier business practices to increase their compensation packages. Some changes in bank compensation packages include adjusting pay to account for any risks taken in the process of generating profits and changing the system of awarding bonuses from a more individualistic focus to one that is more encompassing of the entire organization. Additionally, Treasury rules mandate banks to better inform borrowers about the costs of certain loans, create greater supervision of bank practices, and even establish a capital surcharge for certain banks. Banks and other financial organizations voiced their opinions on these financial reforms through discreet lobbying and industry groups.[12]

Corporations can influence shareholders to become lobbyists. If the government is proposing a bill that could have a negative impact on a corporation, then that corporation can send a message to its shareholders detailing the impact. If there is a large enough public impact made by the shareholders of that corporation, then they have come together as lobbyists for the corporation. A lobbyist doesn't have to be a professional. It can be any people or entities that use their voice to make sure that the government understands their position. Corporate lobbying can affect many aspects of the economy. Most of the time, lobbying will focus on controversial topics. In 2018, more than $3.4 billion was spent on federal lobbying—the most that has been spent in eight years. Another more than $1 billion was spent by corporations at the state level.[13]

Companies may attempt to influence the legislative or regulatory process more indirectly as well, through trade associations and umbrella organizations that represent the collective business interests of many firms. Virtually every industry has one or more trade associations that represent the interests of their members to federal officials and provide public education and other services for their members. Examples of such trade associations include the National Association of Home Builders, the American Booksellers Association, and the Pet Food Institute. Additionally, there are often state trade associations, such as the Hawaii Coffee Association and the Michigan Beer and Wine Wholesalers Association, which work on state and regional-level issues.

Umbrella organizations such as the National Federation of Independent Businesses and the U.S. Chamber of Commerce also help promote business interests to government officials. The Chamber of Commerce takes positions on many political, regulatory, and economic questions. With more than 3 million member-companies, its goal is to promote its members' views of the ideal free enterprise marketplace. The cozy relationship between corporations and the government has been a growing concern for years, and was a topic of serious discussion after the 2008–2009 financial crisis. For example, 48 members of the Energy and Commerce Committee of the House of Representatives, which was at the forefront of climate change legislation, owned stock in energy, oil, and natural gas companies. This was a concern to some citizens, as these investments could create a conflict of interest among legislators. However, House and Senate ethics do not forbid members of Congress from having a stake in companies unless they pass a law that benefits only their own interests.[14]

In 2012, the Stop Trading on Congressional Knowledge (STOCK) Act banned Congress from insider trading and stock trades using information obtained in the government. The STOCK Act was designed to prevent conflict of interest when information was not yet publicly available. Additionally, the legislation requires congressmen to report trading within 45 days.[15]

Congressional rules allow members of the House and Senate to own companies (or shares in companies), as well as sit on corporate boards, so long as they do not draw a salary. The concept behind this allowance is that executive branch officials do not want to deny congresspeople the opportunity to accept positions on the boards of charities or other philanthropic organizations. However, it does create a conflict of interest when members of Congress feel loyalty to a business and share information that they obtained in the government with the business. Even nonprofits have an interest in seeing certain legislation passed. Additionally, serving on a board can become a distraction with the full-time responsibilities of being in Congress.[16]

Campaign Contributions   Corporate money can also be channeled into candidates' campaign coffers as corporate executives' or stockholders' personal contributions. A sizable contribution to a candidate may carry with it an implied understanding that the elected official will perform some favor, such as voting on a particular law in accordance with the contributor's wishes. Occasionally, some businesses find it so important to ensure favorable treatment that they make illegal corporate contributions to campaign funds. As mentioned earlier, it is also common for businesses and other organizations to make donations to political parties through PACs. As previously discussed, critics are concerned that decisions such as *Citizens United* will give organizations unfettered power and allow large corporations to effectively "buy" elections.[17]

Private Interest Group Influence

Similar to businesses, private interest groups actively work to influence the government. **Private interest groups** are people with a shared interest who work to influence public policy in their favor in various ways, including lobbying.

private interest groups
people with a shared interest who work to influence public policy in their favor

Trade Associations   In the business world, members of certain industries sometimes form groups to promote the interests of their industry. These groups are called **trade associations**. Trade associations serve the function of promoting the interest of their industry through lobbying, publishing, advertising, and more. One trade association, the American Medical Association (AMA), publishes its own journal, the *Journal of the American Medical Association*, to educate its members. Other trade associations, like the American Institute of Certified Public Accountants, help with rule-making and standard setting in the certified public accountant (CPA) profession.

trade associations
groups formed by members of industries to promote the interests of their industry through means such as lobbying, publishing, and advertising

Trade associations represent the voice of their industry and act as the main point of contact in communication with the industry. They bring value to their stakeholders through the knowledge and expertise that they pass to regulators and policymakers. Trade associations have membership criteria ensuring their members have sufficient credibility in the industry. Trade associations are able to support multiple stakeholders' platforms, organize forums and conferences, and develop joint positions on questions submitted by authorities. Trade associations are allies that work to reach consensus and unity among the industry and do not intend to create division.

Medical Nutrition International Industry (MNI) is a trade association that serves the public interest by forming effective evidence-based and future-proof policies in the healthcare industry. They represent companies seeking solutions for nutritional therapy, including oral supplements and intravenous feeding. MNI enforces detailed criteria for membership to ensure that its members are reputable businesses committed to achieving better patient care across all demographics. The group promotes awareness of the prevalence of malnutrition and recognizes that their primary responsibility is to educate regulators and the general public to address this public health issue. In 2014, MNI launched a campaign to promote malnutrition screening in Europe. The experts involved worked together to enhance policies to provide equal nutritional care for patients.[18]

Self-Regulatory Community

Self-regulation, previously discussed in Chapter 4, is when an industry-level organization, such as a trade association or professional society, creates a set of rules and enforces regulations within its industry. Examples of self-regulatory organizations include the New York Stock Exchange (NYSE) and the Chicago Board of Trade. Businesses can often be wary of using questionable practices when they are unsure of whether their competition is using these practices as well. Self-regulation helps the industry agree on acceptable practices. The government encourages self-regulation and often helps industries have internal regulators to develop self-regulatory programs. Most people have shied away from following these guidelines because there is a history of repeated failures in the programs that have been put forth. Businesses could take it upon themselves to have a fair self-regulation and work with the government to help tailor the rules and regulations accordingly for each industry.[19]

The American College of Physicians (ACP), a national professional organization for physicians who practice internal medicine, created new guidelines in 2019 that establish the professional obligation of healthcare organizations to address the issue of impaired physicians. A physician is impaired when she or he is unable to provide patient care safely and effectively. This may be due to mental illness, substance abuse, or deterioration of skills due to aging or illness. The Ethics, Professionalism, and Human Rights Committee of the ACP published five positions detailing the expectations of the profession to respond to these situations and the profession's commitment to public safety. Position 1 states, "The professional duties of competence and self-regulation require physicians to recognize and address physician illness and impairment."[20]

Corporate Public Affairs Activities

corporate public affairs activities
actions that build a relationship between a corporation and a governmental body or politician to mold and influence the decisions that the government makes to be in the best interest of corporations

Public affairs can be any issue that concerns building a relationship between an organization and a governmental body or group of politicians. The government is responsible for making decisions that can affect public and private businesses. The objective of **corporate public affairs activities** is to mold and influence the decisions that the government makes to be in the best interest of corporations. Public relations (PR) departments try to present information and statistics to help persuade what laws and regulations get passed. If a corporation can bring enough attention to a situation via the media, then the government will be more likely to respond to the attention that is being raised.[21]

General Electric (GE) owns the NBC network and has used this major media outlet to influence government to legislate in their favor. For example, the GE vice president and the NBC president lobbied the New York City Council against a pending resolution to support the EPA's proposal to clean up the Hudson River. GE was able to gain political influence through the use of media.[22]

Corporations have more ability to engage in the media today, thanks to various social media platforms and the universality of the internet. Companies can easily share and "like" content, or leave comments on matters they wish to engage in. The online presence of a company indicates their values and the issues that they would like resolved. The ability to influence through involvement in the media is much easier in today's technological era.[23]

Laws and Regulations

As a result of business abuses and social demands for reform, the federal government began to pass legislation to regulate business conduct in the late nineteenth century. In this section, we will look at a few of the most significant of these laws. Table 5.3 summarizes many of the laws that affect business operations.

Sherman Antitrust Act

The **Sherman Antitrust Act**, passed in 1890, is the principal tool employed by the federal government to prevent businesses from restraining trade and monopolizing markets. Congress passed the law, almost unanimously, in response to public demands to curtail the growing power and abuses of trusts in the late nineteenth century. The law outlaws "every contract, combination in the form of trust or otherwise, or conspiracy, in restraint of trade or commerce." It also makes a violation a felony, punishable by a fine of up to $100 million for corporate violators and $1 million and/or 10 years in prison for individual offenders.[24]

Sherman Antitrust Act
the principal tool used to prevent businesses from restraining trade and monopolizing markets

The Sherman Antitrust Act applies to all firms operating in interstate commerce, as well as to U.S. firms engaged in foreign commerce. The law has been used to break up some of the most powerful companies in the United States, including the Standard Oil Company (1911), the American Tobacco Company (1911), and AT&T (1984). Google was placed under investigation by the U.S. Department of Justice to determine whether they violated fair competition laws. That company is dominant in the search engine industry and controls the technology used to buy online advertisements. Complaints were made by other web companies, such as Yelp and TripAdvisor, that Google uses its market dominance to unfairly promote its own services through skewing search results. Most of Google's revenue comes from advertisements tied to search results. Google was required to make mild changes to its business practices and was allowed to continue to promote its own services in search results.[25]

The Federal Trade Commission (FTC) launched a special task force to monitor the tech industry including Google, Amazon, Apple, and Facebook. With current public concern about data privacy on the rise, Google and Facebook have been under scrutiny because they collect the personal data of their users to better target advertising to them. Many people believe that these companies have too much power over the economy, society in general, and democracy.[26] The Sherman Act remains the primary source of antitrust law in the United States, although it has been supplemented by several amendments and additional legislation.

Clayton Antitrust Act
created to clarify the Sherman Antitrust Act and limit mergers and acquisitions, prohibit price discrimination, tying agreements, exclusive agreements, and the acquisition of stock in another corporation where the effect may be to hinder competition or create a monopoly

Clayton Antitrust Act

Because the provisions of the Sherman Antitrust Act were vague, the courts have interpreted the law in various ways. To rectify this situation, Congress enacted the **Clayton Antitrust Act** in 1914 to limit mergers and acquisitions that have the potential to stifle competition.[27] The Clayton Antitrust Act also specifically prohibits price discrimination, tying agreements (when a supplier furnishes a

Table 5.3 Major Federal Legislation Regulating Business

Sherman Antitrust Act, 1890	Prohibits monopolies
Clayton Act, 1914	Prohibits price discrimination, exclusive dealing, and other efforts to restrict competition
Federal Trade Commission Act, 1914	Created the FTC to help enforce antitrust laws
Robinson-Patman Act, 1936	Prohibits price discrimination between retailers and wholesalers
Wheeler-Lea Act, 1938	Prohibits unfair and deceptive acts, regardless of whether competition is injured
Lanham Act, 1946	Protects and regulates brand names, brand marks, trade names, and trademarks
Celler-Kefauver Act, 1950	Prohibits one corporation from controlling another when the effect substantially lessens competition
Consumer Goods Pricing Act, 1975	Prohibits price maintenance agreements among manufacturers and resellers in interstate commerce
Antitrust Improvements Act, 1976	Strengthens earlier antitrust laws; gives Department of Justice more investigative authority
Federal Corrupt Practices Act, 1977	Makes it illegal to pay foreign government officials to facilitate business or to use third parties such as agents and consultants to provide bribes to such officials
Trademark Counterfeiting Act, 1984	Provides penalties for individuals dealing in counterfeit goods
Trademark Law Revision Act, 1988	Amends the Lanham Act to allow brands not yet introduced to be protected through patent and trademark registration
Federal Trademark Dilution Act, 1995	Provides trademark owners the right to protect trademarks and requires them to relinquish those that match or parallel existing trademarks
Digital Millennium Copyright Act, 1998	Refines copyright laws to protect digital versions of copyrighted materials, including music and movies
Sarbanes-Oxley Act, 2002	Made securities fraud a criminal offense; stiffened penalties for corporate fraud; created an accounting oversight board; and instituted numerous other provisions designed to increase corporate transparency and compliance
Controlling the Assault of Non-solicited Pornography and Marketing Act (CAN-SPAM), 2003	Bans fraudulent or deceptive unsolicited commercial email and requires senders to provide information on how recipients can opt out of receiving additional messages
Fraud Enforcement and Recovery Act, 2009	Strengthens provisions to improve the criminal enforcement of fraud laws, including mortgage fraud, securities fraud, financial institutions fraud, and fraud related to the federal assistance relief program
Dodd-Frank Wall Street Reform and Consumer Protection Act (2010)	Increases accountability and transparency in the financial industry, protects consumers from deceptive financial practices, and establishes the CFPB

product to a buyer with the stipulation that the buyer must purchase other products as well), exclusive agreements (when a supplier forbids an intermediary to carry products of competing manufacturers), and the acquisition of stock in another corporation where the effect may be to substantially lessen competition or to tend to create a monopoly. In addition, the Clayton Antitrust Act prohibits members of one company's board of directors from holding seats on the boards of competing corporations, and exempts farm corporations and labor organizations from antitrust laws.

Federal Trade Commission Act

In the same year that the Clayton Act was passed, Congress also enacted the Federal Trade Commission Act to further strengthen the antitrust provisions of the Sherman Act. Unlike the Clayton Act, which prohibits specific practices, the **Federal Trade Commission Act** more broadly prohibits unfair methods of competition. Of all the federal regulatory agencies, the FTC has the greatest influence on business activities.

When the FTC receives a complaint about a business or finds reason to believe that a company is engaging in illegal conduct, it issues a formal complaint stating that the company is in violation of the law. If the company continues the unlawful practice, the agency can issue a cease-and-desist order, which requires the offender to stop the specified behavior. Many complaints have been waged against the weight loss industry. Tachht, Inc., and Teqqi, LLC, were required to pay a fee of $500,000 to customers who bought their weight loss products. The FTC took the companies to court for using illegal email techniques, publishing fake celebrity endorsements, and making unsubstantiated health benefits of using its products.[28]

Although a firm can appeal to the federal courts to have the order rescinded, the FTC can seek civil penalties in court, up to a maximum penalty of $10,000 a day for each infraction, if a cease-and-desist order is ignored. The commission can also require businesses to air corrective ads to counter previous advertising that the commission considers misleading. For example, LASIK surgery providers were required by the FTC to run corrective advertising to inform consumers about the risks of undergoing the irreversible surgery, along with the benefits.[29]

In addition, the FTC helps to resolve disputes and makes rulings on business decisions. The mattress company Moonlight Slumber, LLC, was charged with misleading advertising claiming organic materials were being used in their baby mattresses. The company claimed that "natural" and "organic" materials made up the majority of two of their mattress brands, while in reality inorganic and synthetic materials were mainly used. The result was that the FTC implemented several restrictions on Moonlight Slumber's ecofriendly advertising.[30]

Federal Trade Commission Act a law enacted to further strengthen the antitrust provisions of the Sherman Antitrust Act and broadly prohibit unfair methods of competition

Proposed Financial Reforms

In response to the 2008–2009 financial crisis, government leaders proposed sweeping reforms to increase consumer protection. This proposed legislation was a step away from the deregulation practices of the last several decades. Instead, it gave government a freer hand in regulating the financial industry, in some instances engaging in reregulation. The Obama administration, for example, gave the Federal Reserve more power over the financial industry and established the Consumer Financial Protection Bureau (CFPB), which aids in regulating banks, credit card companies, and other financial institutions. More specifically, the agency monitors financial instruments like subprime mortgages and other high-risk lending practices. The problems leading up to the financial crisis included inaction on the part of federal regulators to protect consumers from fraud and predatory lending practices, lack of responsibility on the part of mortgage brokers, taking large risks, conflicts of interest among credit rating industries, and complex financial instruments that investors did not understand.

To prevent these problems from leading to future financial crises, the Obama administration removed some of the FTC's powers, created the CFPB, created the Financial Stability Oversight Council to identify and address key risks to the financial industry, required loan bundlers to retain a percentage of what they sell (a proposal also being considered by the European Union); provided new powers for the Securities and Exchange Commission (SEC) to monitor credit rating industries for objectivity; and required complex financial instruments to be traded on a regulated exchange.

The FTC has remained in place, though it has not filed as many actions against financial institutions as it did during the Obama administration. While some are concerned that this indicates less government protection for consumers, others feel that the numbers do not necessarily show the effectiveness of the current administration.[31]

Federal Sentencing Guidelines for Organizations

Federal Sentencing Guidelines for Organizations (FSGO)

a set of standards developed by the U.S. Sentencing Commission and approved by Congress in November 1991 to streamline sentencing and punishment for organizational crimes and holds companies and employees responsible for misconduct

Companies are increasingly establishing organizational compliance programs to ensure that they operate legally and responsibly, as well as to generate a competitive advantage based on a reputation for responsible citizenship. There are also strong legal incentives to establish such programs. The **Federal Sentencing Guidelines for Organizations (FSGO)** were developed by the U.S. Sentencing Commission and approved by Congress in November 1991. These guidelines streamline sentencing and punishment for organizational crimes and holds companies, as well as their employees, responsible for misconduct. The guidelines codified into law incentives to reward organizations for implementing controls to prevent misconduct, such as developing effective internal legal and ethical compliance programs.[32] The commission describes seven steps that companies must implement to demonstrate due diligence. These steps are discussed in Table 5.4.

The assumption underlying the FSGO is that good, socially responsible organizations maintain compliance systems and internal governance controls that deter misconduct by their employees. Thus, these guidelines provide guidance for both organizations and courts regarding program effectiveness. Organizations have flexibility about the type of program they develop; the seven steps are not a checklist requiring that legal procedures be followed to gain certification of an effective program. Organizations implement the guidelines through effective core practices that are appropriate for their firms. The programs they put into effect must be capable of reducing the opportunity for organizational misconduct.

The guidelines pertain to all felonies and class A misdemeanors committed by employees regarding their work. Organizations demonstrating due diligence in developing effective compliance programs can avoid or reduce organizational penalties if an employee commits a crime.[33] The number of cases per year involving organizational offenders is declining. In recent years, the number of reported cases is the lowest since 1996.[34] As seen in Figure 5.1, the most common offenses are fraud (such as mail or wire fraud, healthcare fraud, and false statements) and environmental crimes (such as water, air, wildlife, and hazardous material–related offenses). A breakdown of types of fraud offenses can be seen in Figure 5.2.

Pacific Gas and Electric Company (PG&E) faced a $3 million fine, 10,000 hours of community service, and five years of probation after a pipeline explosion killed eight people. During its probationary period, a federal judge barred PG&E from paying dividends to shareholders after the company's equipment was linked to California wildfires. The judge's order could set a precedent for repeat corporate

Table 5.4 Seven Steps to Effective Compliance and Ethics Programs

1. Establish codes of conduct (identify key risk areas).
2. Appoint or hire a high-level compliance manager (e.g., an ethics and compliance officer).
3. Take care in delegating authority (background checks on employees).
4. Institute a training program and communication system (e.g., ethics training).
5. Monitor and audit for misconduct (e.g., institute reporting mechanisms).
6. Enforce and discipline (e.g., management implementation of policy).
7. Revise the programs as needed (e.g., feedback and action).

Source: U.S. Federal Sentencing Guidelines for Organizations.

Figure 5.1 Organizational Cases by Primary Offense

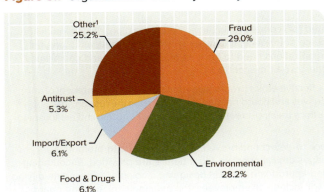

Figure 5.2 Types of Fraud Offenses

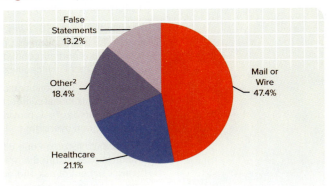

Source: U.S. Sentencing Commission, "Quick Facts on Organizational Offenders," 2013–2017, https://www.ussc.gov/sites/default/files/pdf/research-and-publications/quick-facts/Organizational-Offenders_FY17.pdf (accessed July 25, 2019).

Note: Only organizations convicted of a federal offense are included in Commission data. It does not collect data on other dispositions, including nonprosecution or deferred prosecution agreements.

[1]The "Other" primary offense category includes drugs, bribery, immigration, obstruction of justice, money laundering, administration of justice, copyright/trademark infringement, firearms, gambling, larceny/embezzlement, racketeering, and tax offenses, among others.
[2]The "Other" fraud offense category includes bank fraud and false claims offenses, as well as others.

offenders.[35] Overall, the spirit behind the FSGO is that legal violations can be prevented through organizational values and a commitment to ethical conduct. The law develops new amendments frequently. Table 5.5 shows a selection of the amendments made to date.

In 2004, an amendment to the FSGO placed responsibility on the business's governing authority, requiring them to be knowledgeable about the company's ethics program regarding content, implementation, and effectiveness. Usually the governing authority in an organization is the board of directors, which must make certain there is a high-ranking manager responsible for the daily oversight of the ethics program; provide for sufficient authority, resources, and access to the board or an appropriate board subcommittee; and ensure that there are confidential mechanisms so the organization's employees and agents may ask questions or report concerns without fear of retaliation. The board is also required to oversee the discovery of risks and to design, apply, and modify approaches to deal with those risks. If board members do not understand how to execute an ethics program, the organization risks insufficient oversight and misconduct that can snowball into a crisis.[36]

In 2005, the Supreme Court held that the FSGO were not mandatory but would act as recommendations for judges to use in their decisions. Some legal experts thought that this might weaken the effectiveness of the FSGO, but the majority of federal sentences have remained similar to what they had been before the Supreme Court decision. Thus, the guidelines are important in developing a successful ethics and compliance program.[37]

The 2007–2008 amendments to the FSGO extend the necessary ethics training to board members or the governing authority, managers, employees, and the organizations' agents. This change pertains to mandatory training at all organizational levels. Simply disseminating a code of ethics is not enough to meet training requirements. The new amendments compelled most governmental contractors to implement ethics and compliance training.

In 2010, the FSGO adopted four new amendments. The first simplified reporting relationships by recommending that ethics and compliance officers report misconduct directly to the board or to a board committee, rather than simply to the general counsel. The second encouraged organizations to strengthen

Table 5.5 Institutionalization of Ethics Through the Federal Sentencing Guidelines for Organizations (FSGO)

Laws: In 1991, the FSGO was created for federal prosecutions of organizations. These guidelines provide for just punishment, adequate deterrence, and incentives for organizations to prevent, detect, and report misconduct. Organizations need to have an effective ethics and compliance program to receive incentives in the case of misconduct.

Amendments: The definition of an effective ethics program now includes the development of an ethical organizational culture. Executives and board members must assume the responsibility of identifying areas of risk, providing ethics training, creating reporting mechanisms, and establishing ethics program oversight.

Firms should focus on due diligence to detect and prevent misconduct and to promote an organizational culture that encourages ethical conduct. More details are provided, encouraging the assessment of risk and outlining appropriate steps in designing, implementing, and modifying ethics programs and training that will include all employees, top management, and the board or governing authority. These modifications continue to reinforce the importance of an ethical culture in preventing misconduct.

Chief compliance officers are directed to make their reports to their firm's board rather than to the general counsel. Companies are encouraged to create hotlines, perform self-audit programs, and adopt controls to detect misconduct internally. More specific language has been added to the word *prompt* with regard to what it means to promptly report misconduct. The amendment also extends operational responsibility to all personnel within a company's ethics and compliance program.

Sources: "U.S. Sentencing Guidelines Changes Become Effective November 1," *FCPA Compliance & Ethics*, November 2, 2010, http://fcpacompliancereport.com/2010/11/us-sentencing-guidelines-changes-become-effective-november-1/ (accessed July 25, 2019). U.S. Sentencing Commission, "Amendments to the Sentencing Guidelines," April 30, 2012, http://www.ussc.gov/Legal/Amendments/Reader-Friendly/20120430_RF_Amendments.pdf (accessed July 25, 2019); Paula Desio, Deputy General Counsel, *An Overview of the Organizational Guidelines*, http://www.ussc.gov/sites/default/files/pdf/training/organizational-guidelines/ORGOVERVIEW.pdf (accessed July 9, 2019).

internal controls through hotlines, self-auditing programs, and other mechanisms to increase the chances that misconduct will be detected internally instead of externally. The third adopted more specific wording to clarify what it means to report an ethical violation promptly. Finally, a fourth amendment extended operational responsibility to all personnel within a company's ethics and compliance program. This means that everyone in an organization has a responsibility to ensure ethical conduct.[38]

In 2014, the Federal Sentencing Commission reiterated the importance of best practices in organizations. The commission advocated the sharing of best practices among regulatory and law enforcement agencies. Agencies such as the Department of Justice's Antitrust Division are using the FSGO's seven steps for ethics programs to develop their own compliance programs. The Commission also encourages the sharing of best practices among industry associations. The FSGO does not believe this sharing of best practices should be limited to for-profit organizations, however. It also assessed the success of nonprofit organizations, businesses, regulators, and other organizations in creating effective organizational cultures that will work toward preventing misconduct. The emphasis of the FSGO is increasingly geared toward stressing best practices, principles, and values over formal regulations in which organizations would do the bare minimum to comply with the law.[39]

The Department of Justice also recommended general principles to apply in cases of corporate misconduct. Ethics and compliance programs are essential in discovering the types of misconduct common in a particular organization's industry. If an organization does not have an effective ethics and compliance program in place, a firm convicted of misconduct will likely not be treated lightly, particularly as the prosecutor has a large amount of freedom in determining when, whom, and whether to prosecute illegal conduct. Even minor misconduct could result in significant penalties if committed by a large number of employees or approved by upper management. Without an effective ethics and compliance program to identify misconduct, a firm can face severe consequences from legal issues, enforcement, and sentencing.[40] Legal and administrative policies mostly agree that an effective ethics and compliance program is required to prevent misconduct and reduce legal repercussions should it occur.

Sarbanes-Oxley Act

The **Sarbanes-Oxley (SOX) Act** was enacted to restore stakeholder confidence and provide a new standard of ethical behavior for U.S. businesses in the wake of Enron and WorldCom in the early 2000s. During probes into financial reporting fraud at many of the world's largest companies, investigators learned that hundreds of public corporations were not reporting their financial results accurately. Accounting firms, lawyers, top corporate officers, and boards of directors had developed a culture of deception in an attempt to gain investor approval and competitive advantage. The downfall of many of these companies resulted in huge losses to thousands of investors, and employees even lost much of their savings from 401ks.

The SOX Act legislation protects investors by improving the accuracy and reliability of corporate disclosures. The act had almost unanimous support by Congress, government regulatory agencies, and the general public. When President George W. Bush signed the bill into law, he emphasized the need for the standards it provides, especially for top management and boards of directors responsible for company oversight. Table 5.6 details the requirements of the Act.

The section of SOX that initially caused the most concern for companies was compliance with section 404. Section 404 comprises three central issues: (1) it requires that management create reliable internal financial controls; (2) it requires that management attest to the reliability of those controls and the accuracy of financial statements that result from those controls; and (3) it requires an independent

Sarbanes-Oxley (SOX) Act legislation created to protect investors by improving the accuracy and reliability of corporate disclosures

Table 5.6 Major Provisions of the Sarbanes-Oxley Act

Requires the establishment of an Independent Accounting Oversight Board, in charge of regulations administered by the SEC.
Requires CEOs and CFOs to certify that their companies' financial statements are true and include no misleading statements.
Requires that corporate board of directors' audit committees consist of independent members with no material interests in the company.
Prohibits corporations from making or offering loans to officers and board members.
Requires codes of ethics for senior financial officers; code must be registered with the SEC.
Prohibits accounting firms from providing both auditing and consulting services to the same client.
Requires company attorneys to report wrongdoing to top managers and, if necessary, to the board of directors; if managers and directors fail to respond to reports of wrongdoing, the attorneys should stop representing the company.
Mandates "whistleblower protection" for persons who disclose wrongdoing to authorities.
Requires financial securities analysts to certify that their recommendations are based on objective reports.
Requires mutual fund managers to disclose how they vote shareholder proxies, giving investors information about how their shares influence decisions.
Establishes a 10-year penalty for mail or wire fraud.
Prohibits the two senior auditors from working on a corporation's account for more than 5 years; other auditors are prohibited from working on an account for more than 7 years; in other words, accounting firms must rotate individual auditors from one account to another from time to time.

auditor to further attest to the statements made by management. Because the cost of compliance was so high for many companies, some publicly traded companies considered delisting themselves from the NYSE. Compliance costs have varied over the years since Sarbanes-Oxley was passed. Although compliance costs dropped by 50 percent in recent years, costs rose for many companies. The study showed that compliance costs ranged from between $750,000 to $1,501,300. Many factors are involved in the rise and fall of compliance costs, and researchers have stated that the Sarbanes-Oxley costs seem to be normalizing.[41]

Public Company Accounting Oversight Board (PCAOB)
required by the Sarbanes-Oxley Act, a private, nonprofit company that provides oversight of the accounting firms that audit public companies and sets standards for the auditors in these firms

To address fraudulent occurrences, SOX required the creation of the **Public Company Accounting Oversight Board (PCAOB)**, which provides oversight of the accounting firms that audit public companies and sets standards for the auditors in these firms. The board has investigatory and disciplinary power over accounting firm auditors and securities analysts who issue reports about companies. Specific duties include (1) registration of public accounting firms; (2) establishment of auditing, quality control, ethics, independence, and other standards relating to preparation of audit reports; (3) inspection of accounting firms; (4) investigations, disciplinary proceedings, and imposition of sanctions; and (5) enforcement of compliance with accounting rules of the board, professional standards, and securities laws relating to the preparation and issuance of audit reports and obligations and liabilities of accountants.

SOX also requires corporations to take more responsibility and to provide principles-based ethical leadership. Enhanced financial disclosures are required, including certification by top officers that audit reports are complete and nothing has been withheld from auditors. For example, registered public accounting firms are now required to identify all material correcting adjustments to reflect accurate financial statements. Also, all material off-balance sheet transactions and other relationships with unconsolidated entities that affect current or future financial conditions of a public company must be disclosed in each annual and quarterly financial report. In addition, public companies must report "on a rapid and current basis" material changes in the financial condition or operations. Section 201 of SOX prohibits registered public accounting firms from providing both audit and nonaudit services to a public company, a major issue with the now-defunct accounting firm Arthur Andersen in its relationship with Enron.

whistleblower
a person who exposes an employer's wrongdoing to outsiders, such as the media or government regulatory agencies

Other provisions of the Act include **whistleblower** protections, which prohibit an employer from taking certain actions against employees who lawfully disclose private employer information to, among others, parties in a judicial proceeding involving a fraud claim, and which change the attorney-client relationship so that attorneys are now required to report wrongdoing to top managers or to the board of directors, even if it violates client confidentiality. Employees of public companies and accounting firms, in general, are also accountable to report unethical behavior. SOX is designed to motivate employees by offering to shield whistleblowers. Whistleblowers are also granted a remedy of special damages and attorney's fees. This protection is designed to encourage whistleblowers to come forward when detecting business misconduct, as much of the fraud that eludes audits or other controls may be detected by employees. According to a 2018 report published by the Association of Certified Fraud Examiners, data compiled on 2,690

Shutterstock/wutzkohphoto

cases of occupational fraud showed that 40 percent of the cases were detected by tipsters and 53 percent of those tips were provided by employees.[42] Acts of retaliation that harm informants, including interference with the lawful employment or livelihood of any person, shall result in fines and/or imprisonment for 10 years.

Dodd-Frank Wall Street Reform and Consumer Protection Act

In 2010, the **Dodd-Frank Wall Street Reform and Consumer Protection Act** was passed. The Act was hailed as "a sweeping overhaul of the financial regulatory system...on a scale not seen since the reforms that followed the Great Depression." Dodd-Frank seeks to prevent financial crisis through improved financial regulation, additional oversight of the industry, and preventative measures to reduce the types of risk-taking, deceptive practices, and lack of oversight that led to the financial crisis in 2007–2008.[43] Its provisions include increasing the transparency of financial institutions, creating a bureau to educate consumers about financial products and protect them from deceptive financial practices, implementing added incentives for whistleblowers, increasing oversight of the financial industry, and regulating the use of derivatives. In 2019, the SEC and the Commodity Futures Trading Commission announced an agreement on how much capital and margin firms need to hold when trading swaps based on securities.[44]

> **Dodd–Frank Wall Street Reform and Consumer Protection Act** legislation created to prevent financial crisis by increased financial deregulation, additional oversight of the industry, and preventative measures against unhealthy risk-taking and deceptive practices

Unlike Sarbanes-Oxley, there was not a clear consensus on the Dodd-Frank Act. Opponents of the Act expressed many concerns, asserting that the rules on derivatives would be too difficult to follow, the changes would create chaos in the financial system, and the government could gain too much power.[45] J. P. Morgan claimed that they supported the law but were against certain provisions.[46] Included in these provisions was the creation of new financial regulatory agencies that would increase government oversight of the financial system. Eight years after passing Dodd-Frank, some rules were loosened. The regulatory rollback freed banks with less than $250 billion in assets from regulatory burdens. Supporters of the rollback said that the purpose of the move was to stop overregulation.[47]

The Office of Financial Research was developed, with the responsibility to improve the quality of financial data accessible to government officials and construct an improved system of analysis for the finance industry.[48] The Financial Stability Oversight Council (FSOC) was also created, with the responsibility to keep the financial system stabilized through market monitoring, threat identification, the promotion of market discipline among public constituents, and responses to risks that threaten stability.[49] FSOC can limit or supervise financial risks, create more stringent rules for banking and nonbanking financial organizations, and break up financial organizations that present major risks to market stability.[50] The purpose of these two agencies is to eliminate loopholes that allowed financial companies to commit the types of risky and deceptive actions that led up to the financial crisis.

The Dodd-Frank Act also developed the **Consumer Financial Protection Bureau (CFPB)**. The CFPB is an independent agency within the Federal Reserve System that "regulate[s] the offering and provision of consumer financial products or services under the Federal consumer financial laws."[51] A major problem leading up to the Great Recession of 2008–2009 was that average investors usually did not understand the complex financial products that they were trading. The federal government has granted the CFPB supervisory power over credit markets and the ability to monitor lenders to ensure that they are in legal compliance. The CFPB also has the authority to restrict unfair lending and credit card practices, enforce consumer financial protection laws, and ensure the safety of financial products before their release onto the market.[52]

> **Consumer Financial Protection Bureau (CFPB)** an independent agency within the Federal Reserve System that was established by the Dodd-Frank Act to regulate banks and other financial institutions by monitoring consumer financial products and services

Some have major concerns about the extent of the agency's powers. For instance, critics are concerned that this increased power could lead to severe sanctions or overly heavy regulations.[53] Goldman Sachs was one financial organization affected by the regulations. To comply with part of the Dodd-Frank Act, it was forced to limit investing in its own private-equity funds. This provision restricts financial organizations from using their own money to make large bets.[54] The CFPB has oversight powers over organizations that tend to be accused of questionable conduct, such as payday lenders and debt collectors.[55] The bureau's goal is to maintain a more transparent financial environment for consumers.

In addition to overseeing large financial institutions like Goldman Sachs, the CFPB provides financial information to students, retirees, and consumers who are interested in learning more about home ownership. While the CFPB continues to receive mixed views on its relevance, the agency has several accomplishments. It is credited with discovering expensive fraudulent activities and penalizing the companies responsible for them. For example, the CFPB was instrumental in holding Wells Fargo accountable for millions of fake accounts that the bank created in customers' names. It charged the bank millions of dollars in restitution, so it would serve as an example of the cost of fraud. The agency also listens to consumer complaints and helps facilitate conversation between companies and consumers. From a political standpoint, studies have shown that the CFPB is regarded favorably by the majority of both Democrats and Republicans.[56]

Finally, the Dodd-Frank law created a whistleblower bounty program. Whistleblowers who report financial fraud to government agencies are eligible to receive 10–30 percent of fines and settlements if their reports result in convictions of more than $1 million in penalties.[57] In 2012, the government awarded its first payout, $50,000 to a whistleblower who assisted regulators in convicting a company of fraud.[58]

Enforcement of the Laws Because violations of the Sherman Act are felonies, the Antitrust Division of the Department of Justice enforces it. The FTC enforces antitrust regulations of a civil, rather than criminal, nature. There are many additional federal regulatory agencies (see Table 5.7) that oversee the enforcement of other laws and regulations. Most states also have regulatory agencies that make and enforce laws for individuals and businesses. Over the years, cooperation among state attorneys general, regulatory agencies, and the federal government has increased, particularly in efforts related to the control of drugs, organized crime, and pollution.

The 2008–2009 financial crisis revealed the need for better enforcement of the financial industry. Institutions took advantage of loopholes in the regulation system to make quick profits. For example, some adjustable mortgage rates offered low "teaser" rates that did not even cover the monthly interest on the loans. This ended up increasing the principal balances on mortgages, resulting in debt that many consumers could not pay off. Unethical actions such as these led to the financial crisis. However, because these institutions were not as carefully monitored as other institutions, such as banks, regulators did not catch them until it was too late.[59]

New enforcement aims to require brokers to show a greater fiduciary duty to their clients, requiring them to put their clients' interests above their own and eliminate any conflicts of interest. This could cause them to offer products that are less costly and more tax-efficient for consumers rather than promoting products that would benefit their companies at consumers' expense.[60]

In addition to enforcing stricter regulations for financial institutions, the Obama administration took steps to protect consumers. This included encouraging consumers to manage credit cards, savings, and mortgages more carefully; providing cardholders with warnings about how long it will take to pay off their debt

Table 5.7 Federal Regulatory Agencies

Food and Drug Administration (FDA), 1906	Enforces laws and regulations to prevent the distribution of adulterated or misbranded foods, drugs, medical devices, cosmetics, veterinary products, and potentially hazardous consumer products
Federal Reserve Board, 1913	Regulates banking institutions; protects the credit rights of consumers; maintains the stability of the financial system; conducts the nation's monetary policy; and serves as the nation's central bank
Federal Trade Commission (FTC), 1914	Enforces laws and guidelines regarding business practices; takes action to stop false and deceptive advertising and labeling
Federal Deposit Insurance Corporation, 1933	Insures deposits in banks and thrift institutions for at least $250,000; identifies and monitors risks related to deposit insurance funds; and limits the economic effects when banks or thrift institutions fail
Federal Communications Commission (FCC), 1934	Regulates communication by wire, radio, and television in interstate and foreign commerce
Securities and Exchange Commission (SEC), 1934	Regulates the offering and trading of securities, including stocks and bonds
National Labor Relations Board, 1935	Enforces the National Labor Relations Act; investigates and rectifies unfair labor practices by employers and unions
Equal Employment Opportunity Commission, 1970	Promotes equal opportunity in employment through administrative and judicial enforcement of civil rights laws and through education and technical assistance
Environmental Protection Agency (EPA), 1970	Develops and enforces environmental protection standards and conducts research into the adverse effects of pollution
Occupational Safety and Health Administration, 1971	Enforces the Occupational Safety and Health Act and other workplace health and safety laws and regulations; makes surprise inspections of facilities to ensure safe workplaces
Consumer Product Safety Commission, 1972	Ensures compliance with the Consumer Product Safety Act; protects the public from unreasonable risk of injury from any consumer product not covered by other regulatory agencies
Commodity Futures Trading Commission, 1974	Regulates commodity futures and options markets; protects market users from fraud and abusive trading practices
Federal Housing Finance Industry, 2008	Combined the agencies of the Office of the Federal Housing Enterprise Oversight, the Federal Housing Finance Board, and the GSE mission office of the Department of Housing and Urban Development to oversee the country's secondary mortgage markets
Consumer Financial Protection Bureau (CFPB), 2010	Created as part of the Dodd-Frank Act to educate consumers and protect them from deceptive financial products and services

if they pay only the minimum on their credit cards each month; and preventing certain credit card issuers from offering credit cards to people under the age of 21.

In addition to enforcement by state and federal authorities, lawsuits by private citizens, competitors, and special-interest groups are used to enforce legal and regulatory policy. Through private civil action, an individual or organization can file a lawsuit related to issues such as antitrust, price fixing, or unfair advertising. An organization can even ask for assistance from a federal agency to address a concern. For example, broadcasting companies gained the assistance of the Department of Justice in fighting the start-up service Aereo, which used equipment to stream local television content to consumers for a fee. The case was eventually taken to the Supreme Court, where it was ruled that Aereo needed to secure permission from content providers.[61]

Apple was under an antitrust investigation for fixing prices on electronic books as a means to block competition with Amazon. A U.S. District Court judge ruled that the computer company colluded with five e-book publishers on pricing. Apple denied any wrongdoing and claimed that their pricing was due to natural competitive pressures that resulted as they entered the market. The company filed an appeal to the ruling, which was denied. Apple was forced to pay $400 million in compensation. Consumers who purchased e-books from *The New York Times* bestseller lists received a $6.93 credit for every purchase.[62]

Summary

While regulations are highly influential to businesses, as was seen in Chapter 4, businesses have a great impact on the government and the political environment as well. Changes over the last 60 years have shaped the political environment in which businesses operate. Among the most significant of these changes were amendments to the Legislative Reorganization Act and the Federal Election Campaign Act, which had the effect of reducing the importance of political parties. Many candidates for elected office turned to increasingly powerful special-interest groups to raise funds to campaign for elected office. Until the Supreme Court's *Citizens United* decision, corporations were restricted in giving contributions to PACs. However, the decision gives corporations the right to spend as much as they want in political independent expenditures to support governmental candidates.

Some organizations view regulatory and legal forces as beyond their control and simply react to conditions arising from those forces; other firms seek to influence the political process to achieve their goals. One way that they can do this is through lobbying, the process of working to persuade public and/or government officials to favor a particular position in decision-making. Companies can also influence the political process through PACs, organizations that solicit donations from individuals and then contribute these funds to candidates running for political office. Corporate funds may also be channeled into candidates' campaign coffers as corporate executives' or stockholders' personal contributions, although such donations can violate the spirit of corporate campaign laws. It is also common for businesses and other organizations to make donations to political parties. The creation of trade associations, self-regulatory communities, and mutual marketing and advertising communications between business and the government are all examples of the interrelationship between business and the government. Business participation can be a positive or negative force in society's interest, depending not only on the outcome, but also on the perspective of various stakeholders.

The federal government passed legislation to regulate business conduct in the late nineteenth century. The Sherman Antitrust Act is the principal tool used to prevent businesses from restraining trade and monopolizing markets. The Clayton Antitrust Act limits mergers and acquisitions that could stifle competition and prohibits specific activities that could substantially lessen competition or tend to create a monopoly. The Federal Trade Commission Act prohibits unfair methods of competition and created the FTC. Legal and regulatory policy is also enforced through lawsuits by private citizens, competing companies, and special-interest groups. A company that engages in commerce beyond its own country must contend with the complex relationship among the laws of its own nation, international law, and the laws of the nation in which it will be trading. There is considerable variation and focus among different nations' laws, but many countries' antitrust laws are quite similar to those of the United States.

More companies are establishing organizational compliance programs to ensure that they operate legally and responsibly, as well as to generate a competitive advantage based on a reputation for good citizenship. Under the Federal Sentencing Guidelines for Organizations (FSGO), a company that wants to avoid or limit fines and other penalties as a result of an employee's crime must be able to demonstrate that it has implemented a reasonable program for deterring and preventing misconduct. To implement an effective compliance program, an organization should develop a code of conduct that communicates expected standards, assign oversight of the program to high-ranking personnel who abide by legal and ethical standards, communicate standards through training and other mechanisms, monitor and audit to detect wrongdoing, punish individuals responsible for misconduct, and take steps to continuously improve the program. A strong compliance program acts as a buffer to keep employees from committing crimes and to protect a company's reputation should wrongdoing occur despite its best efforts.

Enacted after many corporate financial fraud scandals, the Sarbanes-Oxley Act created the Public Company Accounting Oversight Board (PCAOB) to provide oversight and set standards for the accounting firms that audit public companies. The board has investigatory and disciplinary power over accounting firm auditors and securities analysts. The act requires corporations to take responsibility to provide principles-based ethical leadership and holds chief executive officers (CEOs) and chief financial officers (CFOs) personally accountable for the credibility and accuracy of their company's financial statements.

However, the 2008–2009 recession, which included the collapse of the subprime mortgage market, and troubles on Wall Street all pointed to systemic flaws and gaps in the regulatory system. In 2010, the Obama administration passed the Dodd-Frank Wall Street Reform and Consumer Protection Act. Dodd-Frank seeks to prevent financial crisis through the improvement of financial regulation, increase in oversight of the industry, and preventative measures to reduce types of risk-taking, deceptive practices, and lack of oversight. It established several agencies, including the Consumer Financial Protection Bureau (CFPB), to protect consumers from deceptive financial products and services. It also established a whistleblower bounty program, in which whistleblowers are eligible to receive 10–30 percent of fines and settlements if their reports result in convictions of more than $1 million in penalties.

Responsible Business Debate

Good, Better, Best: The Better Business Bureau Fights for Good Business

Issue: *How do trade associations protect businesses?*

The Better Business Bureau (BBB) is one of the best-known self-regulatory trade associations in the United States. Trade associations such as the BBB create self-regulatory programs for their members. Self-regulation expresses a commitment on a company's part to adhere to certain rules that demonstrate best practices and social responsibility. Although their standards do not have the force of law, companies that engage in self-regulation agree to go beyond what is legally required. The BBB uses its website, newspapers, and the media to inform consumers of businesses that violate these standards. These bad actors may also receive low ratings in BBB reliability reports, and accredited members can be expelled from the association.

The mission of the BBB is "to be the leader in advancing marketplace trust" by creating a community of trustworthy businesses, setting standards for marketplace trust, encouraging and supporting best practices, celebrating marketplace roles, and denouncing substandard marketplace behavior. The BBB has accredited about 400,000 businesses based on BBB standards and provides a BBB Accredited Business Seal for approved businesses to place on their websites.

The BBB developed a formula of 17 metrics used to arrive at a business's rating, which currently uses an alphabetic system of A–F. Companies that get low ratings can change their scores by addressing customer complaints, and many companies do so because they do not want to lose their client base. Investigations by the BBB are an important tool in self-regulation.

In addition to the BBB, the National Advertising Division (NAD) is very helpful to consumers. In 1971 the NAD was created as the investigatory arm of the National Advertising Review Council (NARC). The division provides services to companies that run national advertising campaigns, typically involving advertisement reviews completed by professional counsel and usually released within 60 days. The services have a low cost compared to the cost of legal proceedings. NAD's procedures give advertisers an automatic right to appeal to the self-regulatory system's peer review body, the National Advertising Review Board. The NAD's secondary purpose is to aid the FTC. If the NAD did not investigate the accuracy of advertisements, this responsibility would fall solely upon the FTC. Therefore, the NAD saves resources and time for the FTC so that it can focus on more significant issues.

As a nongovernment agency, the NAD is restricted in the actions it can take. The division does not have the authority to issue subpoenas, hold hearings, or levy damages. The NAD's lack of authority makes the voluntary self-regulation from companies a challenging issue. The Advertising Self-Regulatory Council (ASRC) was created to help companies self-regulate and avoid unnecessary investigations by creating policies and procedures when developing advertisements. The idea is to get all companies to self-regulate their advertisements voluntarily, before the NAD has to step in and provide guidance for an organization. Despite the many challenges of self-regulation, both the BBB and the NAD are highly important entities and are used by millions of people worldwide.

There Are Two Sides to Every Issue

1. The BBB mostly benefits businesses.
2. The BBB mostly benefits consumers.

Sources: "About BBB," Better Business Bureau, https://www.bbb.org/about-bbb (accessed May 17, 2019); "What Is a BBB?" Better Business Bureau, https://www.bbb.org/iowa/get-to-know-us/about-us/what-is-a-bbb/ (accessed May 17, 2019); "Get Accredited," Better Business Bureau, https://www.bbb.org/lexington/for-businesses/about-bbb-accreditation/ (accessed May 17, 2019). "BBB Dynamic Seal," Better Business Bureau, https://www.bbb.org/lexington/for-businesses/about-bbb-accreditation/for-accredited-businesses/bbb-dynamic-seal/ (accessed May 17, 2019). "BBB Standards for Trust," Better Business Bureau, https://www.bbb.org/standards-for-trust (accessed May 17, 2019). "Council of Better Business Bureaus," Better Business Bureau, https://www.bbb.org/council/about/council-of-better-business-bureaus/ (accessed May 17, 2019); "FAQs," Better Business Bureau, https://www.bbb.org/council/about/frequently-asked-questions/ (accessed May 17, 2019); Give.org, Home Page, http://www.give.org/ (accessed May 17, 2019); "History and Traditions," Better Business Bureau, https://www.bbb.org/atlanta/get-to-know-us/history-and-traditions (accessed May 17, 2019); "Mission & Vision," Better Business Bureau, https://www.bbb.org/council/about/vision-mission-and-values/ (accessed May 17, 2019); ASRC, "About NAD," http://www.asrcreviews.org/ (accessed May 17, 2019); Better Business Bureau, "National Advertising Division (NAD)," https://bbbprograms.org/programs/nad/ (accessed May 17, 2019); "Overview of BBB Rating," Better Business Bureau, https://www.bbb.org/council/overview-of-bbb-grade/ (accessed May 17, 2019); "The Complaint Form: The Complaint Process," Better Business Bureau, http://odrcomplaint.bbb.org/odrweb/public/ourbbbcomplaintprocess.aspx?bbbid=3 (accessed May 17, 2019); Council of Better Business Bureaus, "Self-Regulation: Leadership and Support," Advertising Self-Regulatory Council, 2019, http://www.asrcreviews.org/supporting-advertising-industry-self-regulation/ (accessed May 17, 2019); D. McPherson, "NAD: Testimonials on Pinterest Need Disclaimers," Response, 2012, 10; C. Lee Peeler, "Four Decades Later, Ad Industry's Self-Regulation Remains the Gold Standard, Yet the Program Does Not Enjoy Broad-Based Financial Support," *Advertising Age*, March 13, 2013, http://adage.com/article/guestcolumnists/40-years-adland-s-regulation-remains-gold-standard/240245/ (accessed May 17, 2019); David Roos, "How Better Business Bureaus Work," *How Stuff Works*, https://money.howstuffworks.com/better-business-bureau4.htm (accessed May 17, 2019); John E. VillaFranco and Katherine E. Riley, "So You Want to Self-Regulate? The National Advertising Division as Standard Bearer," *Antitrust* 27(2), 2013, 79–84.

Key Terms

Clayton Antitrust Act (p. 131)
Common Cause (p. 124)
Consumer Financial Protection Bureau (CFPB) (p. 139)
corporate public affairs activities (p. 130)
Dodd–Frank Wall Street Reform and Consumer Protection Act (p. 139)

Federal Sentencing Guidelines for Organizations (FSGO) (p. 134)
Federal Trade Commission Act (p. 133)
gerrymandering (p. 124)
lobbying (p. 127)
political action committees (PACs) (p. 123)
private interest groups (p. 129)

Public Company Accounting Oversight Board (PCAOB) (p. 138)
Sarbanes-Oxley (SOX) Act (p. 137)
Sherman Antitrust Act (p. 131)
trade associations (p. 129)
Troubled Assets Recovery Program (TARP) (p. 122)
whistleblower (p. 138)

Discussion Questions

1. What was the historical background that encouraged the government to enact legislation such as the Sherman Antitrust Act and the Clayton Antitrust Act? Do these same conditions exist today?
2. What is the role and function of the FTC? How does it engage in proactive activities to avoid government regulation?
3. Name three tools that businesses can employ to influence government and public policy. Evaluate the strengths and weaknesses of each of these approaches.
4. How do PACs influence society, and what is their appropriate role in a democratic society?
5. Why should an organization implement the FSGO as a strategic approach for legal compliance?
6. What is the significance of Sarbanes-Oxley and the Dodd-Frank Act to business operations in the United States?

Experiential Exercise

Visit the website of the FTC (http://www.ftc.gov/). What is the agency's current mission? What are the primary areas for which the FTC is responsible?

Review the press releases of the last two months: On the basis of these releases, what appear to be major issues of concern at this time?

The Case of the Weight-Loss Radio Ads: What Would You Do?

A company based in Salt Lake City manufacturers and markets some products that are comprised of acai berries and other antioxidants. Natural Oxidant Relief (NOR) markets these nutritional supplements in support of weight loss. The company recently began advertising these products nationally through radio ads (on broadcast and subscription media). Nutritional supplements are unregulated, and their safety is of particular concern to pregnant women, nursing mothers, children, and those with medical conditions, compromised immune systems, or take other medications.

NOR hired M&M Advertising, out of New York, to create their advertising. The agency met extensively with the company to determine the target market, the salient advertising claims that would drive awareness of the NOR products, and sales. In addition, subscriptions (involving automated shipment of products for ease and convenience, as well as to achieve the best prices for customers) were being promoted.

M&M quickly grasped these claims and created messages that touted that the products were so effective that they worked day and night (even during sleep). The products were also believed to "boost metabollic rate," resulting in greater calorie burning. NOR supplements were believed to allow people to live a normal lifestyle, eating the foods they enjoy, and to support dramatic weight loss, with testimonials of users who claimed to "lose up to 30 pounds in 6 months."

In addition to the radio advertising, M&M provided interactive voice-response telemarketing support for sales. They used a proprietary automated computer system that let consumers place orders through bots, without human interaction. The FTC and Utah's attorney general began investigating the support for NOR's dramatic weight-loss claims, looking for scientifically supported clinical trials to validate the product claims. The investigation led to the conclusion that the dramatic weight-loss claims were unsubstantiated or downright false.

The FTC maintains ongoing concerns about companies who market weight-loss products without sound science in support of their claims. In addition, there were concerns about the "framing" of the radio ads. One ad sounded like a health news report, another was like a public service announcement, and a third claimed that the message "was not a radio commercial."

NOR continues to deny responsibility for not having performed the proper testing to validate the advertised claims. What do you do if you work for M&M Advertising? The agency was the one that created the advertising campaigns; so, are they responsible for potential damage to consumers? What is M&M's liability or potential liability? What would you do if you were the account supervisor of the NOR account?

*Note: This scenario was based on actual FTC cases.

Business Ethics and Ethical Decision-Making

A Tough Pill to Swallow: The Ethics of Raising Drug Prices

It is no surprise that drug pricing has become a hot topic in the last decade. With healthcare reform being a huge issue during both the Obama and the Trump administrations, drug cost debates have become prominent. Many stakeholders have decried the high cost of certain pharmaceuticals. Even those with insurance often pay a significant percentage of the cost. Other times, insurers will restrict access to drugs that are highly expensive, which could result in the patient not getting as much of the medicine as he or she needs. And while the state healthcare systems of many other countries cap drug prices and work directly with pharmaceutical companies to manage prices, this is not the case for the United States.

Another issue is the fact that many pharmaceutical companies have artificial monopolies on new drugs because of patents. Under a patent, competitors cannot copy or sell a drug for 20 years. With patents, companies can use innovation to develop new products and earn enough revenue to recoup their investment and make a profit. Unfortunately, this also can lead companies to overprice products. As the only seller of a product, a company can charge whatever it wants.

Critics feel that lack of competition has led to pharmaceutical firms setting exorbitant prices that most consumers cannot afford. Another reason that pharmaceutical companies are thought to charge such high prices is that in the United States, they work mostly with insurance companies and healthcare systems. Therefore, they are pricing their drugs at whatever they believe the insurance companies are willing to cover, rather than at a price point the average consumer can afford to pay.

A more recent development in the pharmaceutical realm is drugs that can effectively treat an ailment in a single treatment. Insurance companies are concerned about what they would have to pay upfront, given the expensive nature of these drugs. For example, a drug called Zolgensma was developed to treat spinal muscular atrophy (SMA). The drug could cost between $1.5 to $5 million, and there are multiple issues regarding who would pay and how. One major issue, as with other pharmaceutical drugs, is whether or not the pricing of the drug is ethical and reasonable as new drugs are developed. The drug pricing issue is complex, and several suggestions have been made to address it.

One of these is to restructure the rebate system to benefit both patients and research and development of new drugs. Another suggestion is government intervention to restrict drug pricing. Additionally, according to the American Medical Association, pricing methods are kept hidden from consumers, so transparency could be a first step in lowering drug prescription prices. The Trump administration ruled that drug ads that specifically target consumers must include the list price of the drug if it costs $35 or more a month. Pharmaceutical companies have argued that the ruling violates free speech and could confuse consumers about the actual price that they will pay. Others have argued that doing this will lead to greater transparency, and thus more ability for consumers to choose which companies they do business with. In addition, some argue that although list prices are not typically paid by consumers due to rebates and health insurance, many people have high deductibles or no health insurance at all, thus requiring them to pay the list price of the medications. The debate continues and will be influenced by the political environment of the United States in the coming years.[1]

Chapter Objectives

- Define and describe the importance of business ethics
- Understand the diverse and complex nature of existing and emerging ethical issues
- Discuss the individual factors that influence ethical or unethical decisions
- Explore the effects of organizational relationships on ethical decision-making
- Evaluate how opportunity influences ethical or unethical decisions
- Understand how to implement an ethical culture

Shutterstock/i viewfinder

Key business ethics concerns relate to questions about whether various stakeholders consider specific business practices acceptable. A reputation as an ethical firm takes a long time to earn, but just minutes to lose. Once lost, it can take considerable time to restore goodwill with stakeholders. For example, banks and financial institutions have had major reputational damage. The financial services industry ranks the lowest in consumer and investor trust. About 57 percent of the general population claim they trust the financial services industry. The informed public far exceeds the mass population on trust of the financial services industry, however.[2] Business ethics is important to build trust and create an organizational culture that establishes a good reputation.

By its very nature, the field of business ethics is complex because organizational issues often require subject matter knowledge. For example, accounting ethics is embedded with principles, rules, and regulatory requirements. Most businesses are establishing initiatives that include the development and implementation of ethics programs designed to deter misconduct. Raytheon Company, a long-established defense and security company employing more than 75,000 people worldwide, has a comprehensive ethics and compliance program. The company has a strong ethics education program to help employees make ethical decisions. The strength of the program has contributed to a strong organizational culture of integrity. Employees engage in annual "Ethics Checkpoint" peer meetings, where everyone has an opportunity to reflect on and provide solutions to real-life ethical dilemmas. Thousands of employees have utilized these sessions, lending support to its effectiveness. Video vignettes and other online educational materials on supplier relations, product integrity, and labor issues are also utilized. The company displays an outward focus on ethics by supporting education and proper conduct in defense and university programs. In addition, more than 100,000 modules in compliance have been held to train employees. When ethical issues do occur, employees are encouraged to report them. Raytheon clearly expresses how to go about making an ethics complaint on its website. Employees and consumers can choose to call or use the online reporting system, but both use anonymous communication technology. Raytheon has a ranking of 92 percent on the Corporate Social Responsibility and Environment, Social, Governance (CSR/ESG) Metrics scale. This indicates a high score on social and corporate responsibility.[3]

The definition of social responsibility that appears in Chapter 1 incorporates society's expectations and includes four levels of concern: economic, legal, ethical, and philanthropic. Because ethics is becoming an increasingly important issue in business today, this chapter and Chapter 7 are devoted to exploring this dimension of corporate social responsibility (CSR). First, we define business ethics, examine its importance from an organizational perspective, and review its foundations. Next, we define ethical issues in business to help understand areas of risk. We then look at the individual, organizational, and opportunity factors that influence ethical decision-making in the workplace. We conclude by examining requirements for developing an ethical organizational culture.

The Nature of Business Ethics

Business decisions can be both acceptable and beneficial to society. It is necessary to examine business ethics to understand decisions made in the context of an organizational culture. The term *ethics* relates to choices and judgments about acceptable standards of conduct that guide the behavior of individuals and groups. These standards require both organizations and individuals to accept responsibility for their actions and to comply with established principles, values, and norms. Without a shared view of which values and norms are appropriate and acceptable, companies will not have consistency in decisions, with individuals differing in how they resolve issues. Building an ethical culture results in shareholder loyalty and can contribute to success that supports even broader social causes and concerns. The director of sustainability at the Verdigris Group, Garratt Hasenstab, has stated regarding its CSR initiatives that "the true value we receive from our ongoing initiatives is that of social goodwill—we believe that setting a good example is the greatest benefit."[4] Society has developed rules—both legal and implied—to guide companies in their efforts to earn profits through means that do not cause harm to individuals or to society at large.

Business ethics comprises the principles and standards that guide the behavior of individuals and groups when carrying out tasks to meet business objectives. Most definitions of business ethics relate to rules, standards, and principles regarding what is right or wrong in specific situations. **Principles** are specific and pervasive boundaries for behavior that are universal and absolute, and that often become the basis for rules. Some examples of principles include freedom of speech, principles of justice, and equal rights to civil liberties. **Values** are used to develop norms that are socially enforced. Integrity, accountability, and trust are examples of values. Investors, employees, customers, interest groups, the legal system, and the community often determine whether a specific action is right or wrong, ethical or unethical. Although these groups are not necessarily right, their judgments influence society's acceptance or rejection of a business and its activities.

Managers, employees, consumers, industry associations, government regulators, business partners, and special interest groups all contribute to these conventions, and they may change over time. The most basic of these standards have been codified as laws and regulations to encourage companies to conform to society's expectations of business conduct. As stated in Chapter 5, public concerns about accounting fraud and conflicts of interest in the securities industry led to the passage of the Sarbanes-Oxley Act to restore the public's trust in the stock market.

It is vital to recognize that business ethics goes beyond legal issues. Ethical business decisions foster trust in business relationships, and as discussed in Chapter 1, trust is a key factor in improving productivity and achieving success in most organizations. When companies deviate from the prevailing standards of industry and society, the result is customer dissatisfaction, lack of trust, and lawsuits. In the case of Yahoo's former chief executive officer (CEO), Scott Thompson, failure to tell the truth resulted in major consequences. Thompson lied about having a degree in computing and falsely placed the degree on his resume. Not only did he lose his job, but the incident raised suspicion about the duties of the board members to thoroughly investigate those they hire.[5]

Some businesspeople choose to behave ethically because of enlightened self-interest, or the expectation that "ethics pays." They want to act responsibly and assume that the public and customers will reward a company for their ethical actions. For example, Patagonia's founder, Yvon Chouinard, helped start the 1% for the Planet movement. Patagonia donates 1 percent of their sales to environmental causes and encourages customers not to buy their products if they do not need them. While these activities have the potential to negatively affect the company's sales, consumers value Patagonia's responsible message and opt to

business ethics
the principles and standards that guide the behavior of individuals and groups when carrying out tasks to meet business objectives

principles
specific and pervasive boundaries for behavior that are universal and absolute and often form the basis for rules

values
norms that are socially enforced, such as integrity, accountability, and trust

support them over other outdoor retailers, which could increase long-run profitability. The 1% for the Planet movement has over 1,800 members and is popular worldwide, demonstrating that consumers will reward ethical behavior.[6]

Foundations of Business Ethics

ethical conflict
a situation where individuals and groups within a company do not embrace the same set of values

Because all individuals and groups within a company may not embrace the same set of values, there is always the possibility of **ethical conflict**. Most ethical issues in an organizational context are addressed openly whenever a policy, code, or rule is questioned. Even then, it may be hard to distinguish between the ethical issue and the legal means used to resolve it. Because it is difficult to draw a boundary between legal and ethical issues, all questionable issues need an organizational mechanism for resolution.

The legal ramifications of some issues and situations may be obvious, but questionable decisions and actions more often result in disputes that must be resolved through some type of negotiation or even litigation. Companies that sell e-cigarettes, for instance, may be subject to such risks, similar to traditional tobacco firms. The Food and Drug Administration (FDA) issued tough new rules for e-cigarettes that ban selling to minors, require warning labels on packaging, and have all e-cigarette products undergo government approval. While it was federally illegal to sell e-cigarettes to minors under these rules, the sales continued. Failure to uphold legal controls can lead to increased regulations and laws. E-cigarette businesses face greater restrictions on flavored products due to noncompliance among retailers.[7] Such highly publicized issues strengthen the perception that ethical standards in business need to be raised.

When ethical disputes wind up in court, the costs and distractions associated with litigation can be devastating to a business. In addition to the compensatory or nominal damages actually incurred, punitive damages may be imposed on a company that is judged to have acted improperly to punish the firm and to send an intimidating message to others. The legal system, therefore, provides a formal venue for businesspeople to resolve both ethical and legal disputes; in fact, many of the examples cited in this chapter had to be resolved through the courts. To avoid the costs of litigation, companies should develop systems to monitor complaints, suggestions, and other feedback from stakeholders. In many cases, issues can be negotiated or resolved without legal intervention. Strategic responsibility entails systems for listening to, understanding, and effectively managing stakeholder concerns.[8]

A high level of personal morality may not be sufficient to prevent an individual from violating the law in an organizational context in which even experienced attorneys sometimes debate the exact meaning of a law. Because it is impossible to train all the members of an organization as lawyers, the identification of ethical issues and the implementation of standards of conduct that incorporate both legal and ethical concerns are the best approaches to preventing crime and avoiding civil litigation. Codifying ethical standards into meaningful policies that spell out what is and is not acceptable gives businesspeople an opportunity to reduce the probability of behavior that could create legal problems. Without proper ethical training and guidance, it is impossible for the average business manager to understand the exact boundaries for illegal behavior in the areas of product safety, price fixing, fraud, collusion, copyright violations, and so on. For example, 20 drug companies were sued in a class-action lawsuit for price fixing. Teva Pharmaceuticals, the main drug company accused in the suit, was charged with leading a conspiracy to increase generic drug prices over several years. The drug companies colluded to increase prices and prevent competition for their drugs, thus hurting the American people and the drug industry. The lawsuit included 44 U.S. states and argued that the inflation rate of the drugs was as high as 1,000 percent.[9]

Although the values of honesty, respect, and trust are often assumed to be self-evident and universally accepted, business decisions involve complex and detailed discussions in which correctness may not be so clear-cut. Both employees and managers need experience within their specific industry to understand how to operate in gray areas or to handle close calls in evolving areas. Warren Buffett and his company, Berkshire Hathaway, command significant respect from investors because of their track record of financial returns and the integrity of their organizations. Buffett says, "I want employees to ask themselves whether they are willing to have any contemplated act appear the next day on the front page of their local paper—to be read by their spouses, children and friends—with the reporting done by an informed and critical reporter." The high level of accountability and trust that Buffett places in employees translates into investor trust and confidence.[10]

Many people with limited business experience suddenly find themselves required to make decisions about product quality, advertising, pricing, sales techniques, hiring practices, privacy, and pollution control. For example, how do advertisers know when they are making misleading statements in advertising, as opposed to **puffery**, exaggerated statements that no reasonable person would believe to be fact? Bayer is "the world's best aspirin," Snapple "made from the best stuff on Earth," and Firestone (before recalling 6.5 million tires) promised "quality you can trust."[11] The personal values learned through nonwork socialization from family, religion, and school may not provide specific guidelines for these complex business decisions. In other words, a person's experiences and decisions at home, in school, and in the community may be quite different from the experiences and the decisions that he or she has to make at work. Moreover, the interests and values of individual employees may differ from those of the company in which they work, from industry standards, and from society in general. When personal values are inconsistent with the configuration of values held by the work group, ethical conflict may ensue. Conflict that is dealt with openly and effectively can be a positive growth opportunity. However, when employees' personal values clash with those of the organization and the conflict is not dealt with appropriately or is ignored, it can lead to lower worker productivity, higher turnover rates, and increased unethical behavior.[12]

It is important that a shared vision of acceptable behavior develop from an organizational perspective to cultivate consistent and reliable relationships with all concerned stakeholders. A shared vision of ethics that is part of an organization's culture can be questioned, analyzed, and modified as new issues develop. However, business ethics should relate to work environment decisions and should not control or influence personal ethical issues.

puffery
exaggerated statements that no reasonable person would believe to be fact

Recognizing an Ethical Issue

Although we have described a number of relationships and situations that may generate ethical issues, it can be difficult to recognize specific ethical issues in practice. Failure to acknowledge ethical issues is a great danger in any organization, particularly if business is treated as a game in which ordinary rules of fairness do not apply. Sometimes people who take this view do things that are not only unethical, but also illegal, to maximize their own position or boost the profits or goals of the organization.

Figure 6.1 provides the reasons why observed misconduct is not reported. It was found that 74 percent fear that the report would not be confidential, and 69 percent are concerned that there would be no action taken. This demonstrates the need for a confidential reporting system associated with comprehensive ethics and compliance standards. According to a study by the Institute of Business Ethics, 30 percent of workers across Europe have observed misconduct in the workplace.

Figure 6.1 Why Observed Misconduct Is Not Reported

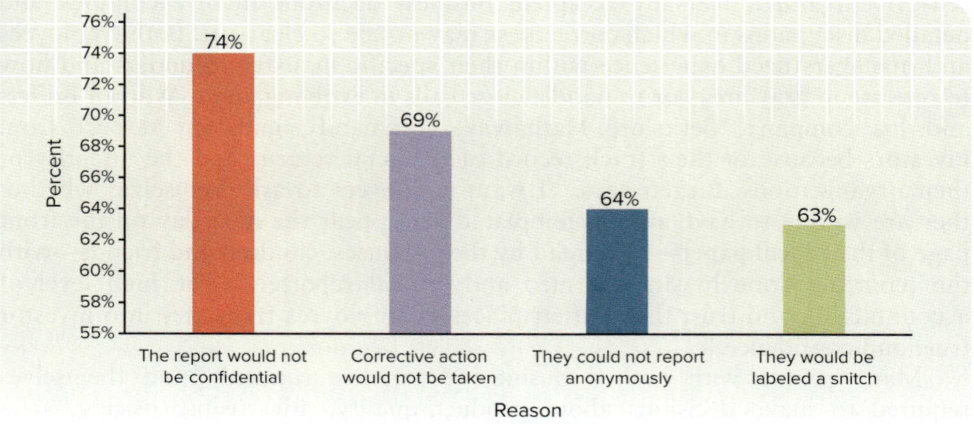

Source: Ethics and Compliance Initiative, "Interactive Maps: 2018 Global Benchmark on Workplace Ethics," https://www.ethics.org/knowledge-center/interactive-maps/ (accessed July 15, 2019).

The study found that the United Kingdom is the most likely to notify others of the misconduct at 67 percent, and Portugal is the least likely, at 49 percent.[13]

However, just because an unsettled situation or activity is an ethical issue does not mean that the behavior is necessarily unethical. An ethical issue may relate to a situation, a problem, or even an opportunity that requires thought, discussion, or investigation to determine the potential impact of the decision. Because the business world is dynamic, new ethical issues are emerging all the time.

One way to determine whether a specific behavior or situation has an ethical component is to ask other individuals in the business for feedback and guidance, or approval/disapproval of your decision. Another way is to determine whether the organization has adopted specific policies or whether there are legal ramifications. An activity approved of by most members of an organization, if it is also customary in the industry, is probably ethical. An issue, activity, or situation that can withstand open discussion between many stakeholders, both inside and outside the organization, and survive untarnished probably does not pose a threat. For instance, it is a common legal practice for medical device manufacturers to have close relationships with medical practitioners, which often include monetary transactions. However, the nature of these relationships may concern outside stakeholders, especially when devices are found to malfunction and cause patients harm. For instance, Medtronic was targeted by a lawsuit that resulted in a settlement of $2.8 million when it was found that sales representatives of the company were directed to promise thousands of dollars in profit for doctors who would market Medtronic products using specific billing codes. The neurostimulation products sold by Medtronic were not adequately tested and were not approved by the FDA; but the billing codes that the doctors were instructed to use indicated that the devices had been FDA-approved. It is estimated that doctors in at least 20 states were misled by Medtronic.[14]

Ethical Issues in Business

ethical issue
a problem, situation, or opportunity requiring an individual, group, or organization to choose among several actions that must be evaluated as right or wrong, ethical or unethical

An **ethical issue** is a problem, situation, or opportunity requiring an individual, group, or organization to choose among several actions that must be evaluated as right or wrong, ethical or unethical. Surveys can render a useful overview of the many unsettled ethical issues in business. A constructive step toward identifying and resolving ethical issues is to classify the issues relevant to most business organizations. In this section, we examine ethical issues related to abusive behavior, misuse of company resources, conflict of interest, bribery, discrimination and sexual harassment, fraud, and privacy issues.

Although not all-inclusive or mutually exclusive, these classifications provide an overview of some major ethical issues that business decision-makers face. Table 6.1 provides statistics on organizational misconduct in the United States. Putting one's own interests ahead of those of the organization, displaying abusive behavior, and lying to employees are all personal in nature and present three major issues that directly relate to the firm's agenda.

Although Table 6.1 documents some ethical issues that exist in global organizations, due to the almost infinite number of ways that misconduct can occur, we cover only the major organizational ethical issues. Any type of manipulation, deceit, or the absence of transparency in decision-making can cause harm to others.

Abusive or Intimidating Behavior

Abusive or intimidating behavior is the most common ethical problem for employees, but what does it mean to be abusive or intimidating? The concepts can mean anything from physical threats, false accusations, annoying a coworker, profanity, insults, yelling, harshness, and ignoring someone to the point of being unreasonable, and the meaning of these words are subjective and can vary from person to person. It is important to understand that each term falls on a continuum. For example, what one person may define as yelling might be another's definition of normal speech. A lack of civility in our society has been a concern, and the workplace is no exception. The productivity level of many organizations has declined on account of the time spent unraveling abusive relationships.

Table 6.1 Organizational Misconduct in the U.S. Workplace

Types of Interpersonal Misconduct	Observation Rate
Abusive or Intimidating Behavior	
Verbal	88%
Physical	24%
Online	21%
Sexual Harassment	
Unwelcome sexual comments	70%
Intentional physical contact	56%
Unwelcome sexual advances or propositions	55%
Pressure to engage in sexual activity	32%
Preferential treatment for submitting to sexual conduct	28%
Discrimination	
Race	58%
Gender	49%
Ethnicity	47%
Age	42%
Sexual orientation	34%
Disability	29%
Religion	26%

Source: Ethics and Compliance Initiative, *Interpersonal Misconduct in the Workplace*, December 2018 (Vienna, VA: Ethics and Compliance Initiative 2018), 7.

Collection agencies and finance companies often use abusive approaches to collect debts. As discussed in Chapter 5, the Consumer Financial Protection Bureau (CFPB) prohibits abusive acts or practices. Its newest standard provides broader protection against "unfair, deceptive, or abusive acts or practices." A business should know what constitutes abusive behavior and avoid engaging in it.[15]

Abusive behavior from supervisors is a problem that has been studied for decades. Researcher Bennett Tepper has found that about 10 percent of bosses in various fields can be considered abusive. Among college sports, the percentage increases to about 30 percent. Studies also show that abusive behavior from supervisors causes stress and loss of productivity in employees, greater turnover of hard-working and highly productive employees, and negative health effects for both employees and the bosses who treat them badly. There are some companies that are trying to curb the causes of abusive behavior in the workplace. For example, Netflix has voiced a desire for employees to speak candidly about how business is going, whether positive or negative. Because many supervisors become upset at bad news because they fear they will be blamed for it, by creating a safe place for honest communication, Netflix is making a positive move away from abusive behavior.[16]

Within the concept of abusive behavior, intent should be a consideration. If the employee was trying to give someone a compliment but that person considers the comment abusive, then it was probably a mistake. The way that a word is spoken (voice inflection) can be important. Add to this the fact that we now live in a multicultural environment, doing business and working with many cultural groups, and the businessperson soon realizes the depth of the ethical and legal issues that may arise. There are problems of word meanings across various age groups and cultures. For example, an expression such as, "Did you guys hook up last night?" can have a number of meanings, including some that could be considered offensive in a work environment.

Misuse of Company Time and Resources

time theft
a major form of observed misconduct including late arrivals, long lunch breaks, leaving early, day dreaming, excessive socializing, and use of social media that costs companies billions annually

The "theft" of time is estimated to cost companies hundreds of billions of dollars annually. It is estimated that the average employee steals more than 10 hours per week by arriving late to work, taking long lunch breaks, leaving early, daydreaming, excessive socializing, engaging in personal activities, and using social networking sites such as Facebook.[17] The misuse of time and resources has been identified by the Ethics Resource Center as a major form of observed misconduct. In one survey, 43 percent of respondents stated that they participated in **time theft** through exaggerating their hours worked, and 23 percent admitted to punching in for employees who were absent from work or coming in late, also known as buddy punching.[18]

According to a survey by International Data Corp., nearly 38 percent of information technology (IT) managers were aware that employees installed personal software on company computers, and 57 percent of employees admitted to this practice. The personal software downloaded enables the employees to use company time to complete personal work. When enforcement is lax or nonexistent, employees may get the impression that they are entitled to certain company resources.

Shutterstock/GeorgeJmclittle

Using company computer equipment for personal business is a common way employees engage in time theft. While employees might recognize that spending the workday talking with friends and relatives is unacceptable, they might not hesitate to go online and do the same thing. Typical examples of misusing company computers include sending personal emails, socializing on Facebook, shopping on Amazon or eBay, downloading music, doing personal banking, or watching sporting events online. Many employees, for instance, engage in time theft during "March Madness" (the annual college basketball tournament). As a result, many organizations block websites on which employees could watch sports events. Some also block sites such as Netflix and Pandora to prevent employees from watching video clips or streaming music.[19]

To deter this type of misconduct, many organizations implement policies describing the acceptable use of such resources. For example, Boeing's code of ethics states that limited resource use is acceptable with the consent of management, and only if it has no negative consequences for the company. In addition, the code states that such activity must not conflict with Boeing's policies, disrupt productivity, or reduce the security of company resources. Boeing also has guidelines for how employees are to use company information on social media and outside internet platforms.[20]

Conflict of Interest

A **conflict of interest** exists when an individual has competing interests and must choose whether to advance his or her own interests, those of his or her organization, or those of some other group. For example, the Transportation Demand Management Program in Sunnyvale, California, required businesses to encourage carpooling systems for employees to reduce traffic. Google agreed to pay $1.23 million for the city of Sunnyvale to hire a traffic engineer and a transportation manager to help with the traffic. However, it was discovered that the traffic engineer helped review Google's vehicle reduction plan for the offices in Sunnyvale, creating a conflict of interest. Because the employee's wages were paid by a private corporation, it raised concerns that Google may receive preferential treatment.[21]

To avoid conflicts of interest, employees must be able to separate their private interests from their work roles. Organizations, too, must avoid potential conflicts of interest in providing goods or services. The Sierra Club, an environmental organization, requested documents from the U.S. State Department regarding the hiring of Environmental Resources Management, a contractor set to work on the Keystone XL pipeline. The documents revealed several conflicts of interest, as many of its consultants also worked for companies that benefited greatly from the completion of the pipeline. It was found that the company did not disclose these issues, nor did it appear that the U.S. government investigated them.[22]

conflict of interest
an issue that arises when an individual has competing interests and must choose whether to advance his or her own interests, those of his or her organization, or those of some other group

Bribery

Bribery is the practice of offering something, such as money, entertainment, travel, or other gifts to gain an illicit advantage from someone in authority. The definition of bribery depends upon whether the illicit payment or favor is used to gain an advantage in a relationship. In many developed countries, society generally recognizes that employees should not accept bribes or special favors from people who could influence the outcome of a decision. For example, the IT consulting firm Computech Corporation and its former CEO are banned from doing business in Detroit after bribing a city department head. The company is banned for 10 years while the CEO is banned for 20. The former IT head of Detroit pled guilty to accepting bribes from Computech, which provided IT services and personnel to the city. The bribes included cash payments, trips, and other incentives.[23] The U.S. Securities and Exchange

bribery
the practice of offering something, such as money, entertainment, travel, or other gifts to gain an illicit advantage from someone in authority

Commission (SEC) has cracked down on cases of bribery involving hundreds of companies. For example, Cognizant Technology Solutions Corporation paid a $25 million settlement after two former corporate executives were found to have bribed a government official in India to obtain a building permit for the company.[24]

Bribery is considered an unlawful act in the United States and other Western countries, but in some cultures, bribing business or government officials with fees is considered standard practice. In this case, this becomes a business ethics issue. According to the United Nations, global corruption, which includes bribery, incurs a cost of $3.6 trillion each year. Not only have bribes led to the downfall of many managers, legislators, and government officials, but it has also contributed to poverty. In a survey by Transparency International, 25 percent of respondents stated that paying bribes was necessary for them to access public services like healthcare. Often, it is the poor who are forced to pay bribes, and this creates an ethical issue for international business.[25]

In the United States, where bribery is strongly discouraged and punished when discovered, there are still those who utilize corruption to get ahead. While bribery may not be as widespread in the United States as it is in other countries, it can and does often result in unsafe business practices and fallout for consumers. For example, Philip Esformes, owner of nursing homes and assisted living facilities in Miami, was convicted of money laundering, defrauding the United States, and other charges. He was accused of giving patients unnecessary treatments in his facilities and then billing these charges to Medicare and Medicaid. He also bribed doctors and healthcare regulators involved in the scheme. In addition to this money laundering, it was discovered that Esformes bribed the University of Pennsylvania's basketball coach to get his son admitted to the university. This college admissions scandal was part of a large conspiracy by more than 50 parents across the United States who paid money to William Rick Singer, the organizer of the scheme. Parents included celebrities Felicity Huffman and Lori Loughlin. Singer used money to fraudulently inflate college entrance exam scores and bribe college officials.[26]

When a government official accepts a bribe, it is usually from a business that seeks some advantage, perhaps to obtain business or the opportunity to avoid regulation. Giving bribes to legislators or public officials, then, is both a legal and a business ethics issue. It is a legal issue in the United States under the **Foreign Corrupt Practices Act (FCPA)**. This Act maintains that it is illegal for individuals, firms, or third parties doing business in U.S. markets to "make payments to foreign government officials to assist in obtaining or retaining business."[27] Companies have paid billions of dollars in fines to the U.S. Department of Justice for bribery violations. The law applies not only to American firms, but to all firms transacting business with operations in the United States. This also means that firms do not necessarily have to commit bribery in the United States to be held accountable.

The Bribery Act, passed in 2010 in the United Kingdom, is similar to the FCPA but is more encompassing. For instance, while the FCPA applies to bribing foreign government officials, the Bribery Act holds people or businesses responsible for commercial bribery as well. The first cases convicted under the Bribery Act were acts committed largely by individuals, such as a student who tried to bribe a professor to let him pass her course. The Act also does not allow facilitation payments or small payments to get normal services performed. Like the FCPA, any organization is subject to the Bribery Act if it does business in the United Kingdom, no matter where the bribery occurred.

Foreign Corrupt Practices Act (FCPA)

maintains that it is illegal for individuals, firms, or third parties doing business in U.S. markets to, in the words of the law, "make payments to foreign government officials to assist in obtaining or retaining business"

Discrimination and Sexual Harassment

Discrimination remains a significant ethical issue in business despite nearly 60 years of legislation outlawing it. Once dominated by white middle-aged men, today's U.S. workforce includes significantly more women, African Americans, Hispanics, LGBTQ, and other minorities, as well as workers with disabilities and older workers. These groups have traditionally faced discrimination and higher unemployment rates and have been denied opportunities to assume leadership roles in corporate America. Experts project that within the next 25–30 years, Hispanic Americans will represent 24.6 percent of the population, African Americans and Asian Americans will represent 13.1 percent and 7.9 percent of the population, respectively, and European Americans will be the minority.[28]

The most significant piece of legislation against discrimination is **Title VII of the Civil Rights Act of 1964**, which prohibits employment discrimination on the basis of race, national origin, color, religion, and gender, and applies to employers with 15 or more employees, including state and local governments. This law is fundamental to employees' right to join and advance in an organization according to merit, rather than one of the characteristics just mentioned.[29] As a result of racial discrimination class-action settlements, some companies, such as Coca-Cola, were required to establish an independent task force to monitor and modify company practices to combat racial discrimination.

Title VII of the Civil Rights Act of 1964
prohibits employment discrimination on the basis of race, national origin, color, religion, and gender, and applies to employers with 15 or more employees, including state and local governments

Additional laws passed in the 1970s, 1980s, and 1990s were designed to prohibit discrimination related to pregnancy, disabilities, age, and other factors. The Americans with Disabilities Act (ADA), for example, prohibits companies from discriminating on the basis of physical or mental disability in all employment practices and requires them to make facilities accessible to and usable by persons with disabilities. The Age Discrimination in Employment Act specifically outlaws hiring practices that discriminate against people ages 40 or older, but it also bans policies that require employees to retire before the age of 70.

Despite this legislation, charges of age discrimination persist in the workplace. Currently, about half of the United States workforce is 40 or older. This is a large segment of the workplace, and naturally age discrimination lawsuits are prevalent. In a 5–4 decision, the U.S. Supreme Court ruled to make it more difficult for workers to claim age discrimination in lawsuits. Now employees must be able to prove that their employers terminated them for age-related reasons which is a difficult thing to prove. The ruling was part of a case brought to trial by Jack Gross, who at 54 was demoted from a director position by his employer, FBL Financial Group.[31] However, a bipartisan proposal called the Protecting Older Workers Against Discrimination (POWAD) Act would overturn the *Gross v. FBL Financial Services* decision. Under the Act, workers would only have to prove that age discrimination was *part* of the reason they received negative treatment such as termination rather than the only reason. Given that more than 30 percent of the nation's workers will be 50 years old or older by 2022, the new legislation would help change companies' approach toward older workers.[30]

Along with racial and age discrimination, gender discrimination also occurs in the workplace. The women's rights movement, first begun in 1848 and resulting in the 19th Amendment, increased awareness of gender equality disparities. Voting was initially the right that was won for women, but as the years have progressed, new challenges have surfaced. Gender discrimination, particularly in the form of pay, has been subject to legal action. For example, the U.S. Women's National Soccer Team filed a lawsuit against the U.S. Soccer Federation just months after the kickoff of the World Cup in 2019. The women alleged gender discrimination due to female players earning less than their male counterparts on the U.S. National Soccer Team. The women stated that they have the same job responsibilities and have even had more success on the field than the men. They pointed out that the men's team has never won the World Cup and did not even qualify for the tournament in 2018, whereas the women's teams won the World Cup three times (in 1991, 1999, and 2015); they would go on to win again in 2019. A comparison showed that if each team played and won 20 tournament games a year, a top-tier women's player would earn 38 percent of what a men's player could make.[32]

Sexual harassment is a form of sex discrimination that violates Title VII of the Civil Rights Act of 1964. **Sexual harassment** can be defined as any repeated, unwanted behavior of a sexual nature perpetrated upon one individual by another. It may be verbal, visual, written, or physical and can occur between people of different genders or those of the same gender. Displaying sexually explicit materials "may create a hostile work environment or constitute harassment, even though the private possession, reading, and consensual sharing of such materials is protected under the Constitution."[33] Title VII applies to employers with 15 or more employees, including state and local governments. It also applies to employment agencies, labor organizations, and the federal government.

When investigating sexual harassment allegations, the U.S. Equal Employment Opportunity Commission (EEOC) looks at the circumstances of each case, including the nature of the alleged acts and the context of the situation. The EEOC determines the course of action based on each individual case. The commission contacts the employer to notify them of the sexual harassment complaint and the investigation. If the EEOC cannot settle the issue, it dismisses the case and issues a "right-to-sue" letter to the person who filed the complaint. In sexual harassment cases, as with other claims of discrimination, the employer is prohibited by law from retaliating against the employee who filed the complaint. Along with the EEOC, many states also have agencies that enforce state laws regarding sexual harassment in the workplace.[34] The EEOC received 7,609 charges of sexual harassment in one year, of which men filed almost 16 percent. In the same year, the commission resolved 7,986 sexual harassment charges and recovered $56.6 million in penalties.[35]

To establish sexual harassment, an employee must understand the definition of a **hostile work environment**, for which three criteria must be met: (1) the conduct was unwelcome; (2) the conduct was severe, pervasive, and regarded by the claimant as so hostile or offensive as to alter his or her conditions of employment; and (3) the conduct was such that a reasonable person would find it hostile or offensive. To assert a hostile work environment, an employee need not prove that it seriously affected his or her psychological well-being or that it caused an injury; the decisive issue is whether the conduct interfered with the claimant's work performance.[36]

Fraud

When an individual engages in deceptive practices to advance his or her own interests over those of the organization or some other group, charges of illegal fraud may result. In general, **fraud** is any false communication that deceives, manipulates, or conceals facts to create a false impression when others are damaged or denied a benefit. It is considered a crime, and convictions may result in fines, imprisonment, or both. For example, Elizabeth Holmes, founder of Theranos, was indicted on charges of defrauding investors. The company misled doctors and patients with promises of revolutionizing healthcare through quick and painless finger pricking; however, the company never produced a working product. The U.S. attorney's office in San Francisco filed the indictment after the SEC settled civil fraud charges against Holmes. Holmes, through Theranos, scammed many people out of hundreds of millions of dollars.[37]

Employee expense fraud is estimated to cost businesses more than $7 billion annually. The Association of Certified Fraud Examiners found that asset misappropriation such as larceny and fraudulent disbursements was the most common type of fraud, followed by corruption and financial statement fraud. Financial statement fraud, though the least likely to occur, costs companies the most.[38]

sexual harassment
any repeated, unwanted behavior of a sexual nature perpetrated upon one individual by another; it may be verbal, visual, written, or physical and can occur between people of different genders or those of the same gender

hostile work environment
a kind of workplace environment where the conduct is unwelcome; severe, pervasive, and hostile such as to affect conditions of employment; and offensive to a reasonable person

fraud
any false communication that deceives, manipulates, or conceals facts to create a false impression when others are damaged or denied a benefit

Table 6.2 indicates how occupational fraud is committed by employees. Misappropriation of assets represents the greatest source of fraud.[39]

Privacy

The final category of ethical issues relates to privacy, especially within the healthcare and internet industries. Some **privacy issues** that businesses must address include the monitoring of employees' use of available technology, consumer privacy, and online marketing. Companies often use cookies or other devices to engage in online tracking, and many websites use consumer information to improve services. Although this can benefit consumers in the form of better marketing and tailored searches, it is also controversial because many consumers do not want their information being tracked. Others are still willing to provide personal information despite the potential risks.[40] The challenge for today's firms is balancing their need for consumer or employee information with the desire for privacy. In terms of employees, there are few legal protections for their right to privacy, giving businesses flexibility in establishing policies regarding employee privacy while using company equipment on company property. Some common ways that an employer might track employee use of equipment is through computer monitoring, telephone monitoring, video surveillance, and global positioning system (GPS) satellite tracking. Although employers have the right to make sure that their resources are being used for appropriate purposes, the ability to gather and use data about employee behavior creates the need for trust and responsibility.

The use of **biometric data**, including fingerprints and facial scans, is creating ethical issues. It is used as a common method for companies with warehouses to verify employee hours and check workers in and out of their facilities. Lawsuits have been filed by employees regarding how firms use and store their personal biometric data. Illinois is regarded as having stringent privacy protection laws. According to their Biometric Information Privacy Act, companies that collect this data must first obtain user consent and notify the individuals about why, how, and how long their data will be used and stored. The risks involved with biometric data is that privacy could be compromised and ultimately lead to identity theft. This could occur if the data were subject to data breaches or if access was incorrectly given to a third party.[41]

There are two issues involving consumer privacy: consumer awareness of information collection and growing lack of consumer control with respect to how organizations use personal information. For example, many are not aware that Google reserves the right to track each time they click on a link from one of their searches.[42] Data tracking of information about consumers without their knowledge or consent occurs daily. Cookies are a common way for websites to track users, but third-party trackers use more sophisticated tracking methods to collect personal data on visitors. This nonconsensual collection of personal data has led to such regulatory measures as the passage of the General Data Protection Regulation (GDPR) in Europe. The GDPR will be discussed in more detail in Chapter 11.[43]

Consumer information is valuable not only to businesses, but also to criminals. An identity is stolen approximately once every two to three seconds in the United States.[44] Criminals may try to steal personal consumer information and sell it online. Some of this information comes from publicly accessible sources, such as social networking profiles, but poorly protected corporate files are another major source for criminals. Recently, Marriott International had a privacy breach that

Table 6.2 How Is Occupational Fraud Committed?

Corruption 38%
Conflicts of interest
Purchasing schemes
Sales schemes
Bribery
Invoice kickbacks
Bid rigging
Illegal gratuities
Economic extortion
Asset Misappropriation 89%
Theft of cash on hand
Theft of cash receipts
Skimming
Cash larceny
Fraudulent disbursements
Billing schemes
Payroll schemes
Expense reimbursement schemes
Check tampering
Register disbursements
Inventory and all other assets
Misuse
Larceny
Financial Statement Fraud 10%
Net worth/net income overstatements
Net worth/net income understatements

Source: Association of Certified Fraud Examiners, *Report to the Nations 2018 Global Study on Occupational Fraud and Abuse,* 2018 https://www.acfe.com/report-to-the-nations/2018/ (accessed July 15, 2019).

privacy issues

issues that businesses must address that include the monitoring of employees' use of available technology, consumer privacy, and online marketing

biometric data

digital data used for personal verification or identification that includes fingerprints, facial scans, retina scans, voice, and DNA

resulted in the exposure of the personal information of 500 million people. The hackers who accessed the information stole a great deal of data, including people's full names, addresses, passport numbers, and date of birth.[45]

To reassure consumers that their information will be protected, an increasing number of companies are displaying an online seal from the Better Business Bureau (BBB), which is available to websites that subscribe to certain standards. A similar seal is provided through the TRUSTe certification program from TrustArc. These seals assure customers that the websites adhere to certain policies meant to protect their privacy.

AI and Ethics: An Emerging Issue

Emerging technologies are disrupting the workplace and creating new challenges to ethical decision-making. Transformative technology such as three-dimensional (3D) printing, the Internet of Things (IoT), drones, and robotics are enabled by artificial intelligence (AI). All of these developments need oversight to monitor, audit, and ensure accountability for ethical decisions.[46]

AI involves machine learning that can simulate some aspects of human behavior. AI can exhibit cognitive functions associated with humans, as well as problem solving and learning at a complexity beyond what a human being can process. The ability of AI to incorporate ethical decision-making has been challenged. The important question is how AI should make ethical decisions. What is a responsible role for AI in our society? Big data enables AI to engage in advanced analytics combined with cloud computing to create "smart" systems to interact and provide information and solutions in business. There is the potential for AI to disrupt and change all aspects of business.

Introducing AI requires public safety, security, and privacy, as well as building trust and understanding. Values, norms, and behavior relate to social and cultural human decisions. As AI systems become more complex, there is a need to explore the ethics-related impact and develop ethics components to machine learning. Ethical concerns exist because of the ability to make autonomous decisions. AI can make decisions and implement actions based on the algorithms or rules provided by the programmers. In addition, an AI program will need oversight to monitor and access outcomes that result from decisions or directions from machine learning.[47]

There is evidence that AI systems have been involved in accidental or in some cases intentional ethical dilemmas that could have major consequences. Targeting markets based on demographics could even result in discrimination. Predictive analytics can target market segments, but it can also involve data privacy issues.

For example, Facebook is facing backlash for allowing companies to target consumers via sharing private data without consumers' permission. A code of ethics has become increasingly important as data breaches and unauthorized data sharing have grown. This will require the design of AI systems that are programmed with an ethical decision-making component, as well as transparency with the public on the algorithms used to ensure ethical decision-making. AI machines will require complex algorithms that are similar to the ethical decision-making of their human partners. In the future, humans will be working alongside AI-enabled robots, drones, and other devices and will depend on these machines to help maintain ethical organizational cultures.

Another ethical consideration is the organization of the workforce. Companies will have to make ethical decisions about how to retain employees as jobs become more automated. They will also have to decide how to redistribute work tasks between AI devices and human workers to encourage efficient human-machine partnerships.

The development of an independent code of ethics for specific AI applications will be needed to address risk areas. General value statements used in organizational codes of ethics may be too broad to provide directions. AI initially will rely more on compliance algorithms, such as directions on privacy. Should AI-enabled drones scan to identify individuals and their behavior? Methodologies will need to be developed to render decisions in the same way that humans make ethical decisions. AI will not only be concerned about ethical decisions, but also legal compliance must be built into machine learning. Mandated boundaries will need to be imposed to address laws, regulations, and other requirements. Ethics will be a buffer that develops areas such as industry self-regulation and core practices that meet societal expectations.

As AI advances, there may be new laws to protect consumers and employees. Laws promoting equity and safety as well as competitive relations may be needed. Microsoft was the first tech company to call for regulation of facial-recognition technology. A key challenge will be transparency about how algorithms work to make ethical decisions. Already, some systems have been found to discriminate against African Americans and Hispanics, and safeguards need to be put in place to prevent future discrimination. Additionally, AI is used to observe cities in China.

Developing AI for the common good of society should be the objective. From diagnosing cancer to performing high-risk jobs, this technology has the potential to make the business world more responsible and accountable. AI for the common good should be focused beyond individual and business interests. In a way, it may change relationships with many stakeholders who have an interest in the company. Therefore, AI must operate to understand the impact on a firm's social responsibility. There will be a need to look beyond just the impact on internal organizational, legal, and ethical concerns, but also issues such as sustainability, consumer protection, employee welfare, social issues, and even corporate governance.

AI enabled by blockchain has the potential to improve ethics. Blockchain, as discussed in detail in Chapter 11, is a series of blocks of information that record ordered transactions and data. This information system is decentralized and distributed on a peer-to-peer network. No one can change the history or data to take advantage of others. This immutable audit trail means financial transactions will be less susceptible to fraud.[48] In accounting and financial reporting, there will be a permanent record and identification of who made the entries. Carrefour SA and Walmart are already using blockchain to improve food safety. Through blockchain, suppliers have the ability to quickly trace food that can cause health dangers such as norovirus or listeria, which can save lives.[49]

Finally, there is concern that AI will result in unemployment because it will displace workers. However, employment has remained high over the last 100 years despite drastic changes in technology. New technology requires new types of jobs. This means that the labor force will need education and training to fill these new high-tech jobs. These "new-collar" jobs, as compared to white- and blue-collar jobs, will be needed to build, maintain, and operate the AI-driven replacements for some existing occupations. Society is in the early stage of identifying the issues and solutions related to incorporating AI into business and society. But the benefits of AI are so great that the ethical challenges need to be resolved to create integrity in this powerful technology.[50]

Understanding the Ethical Decision-Making Process

To grasp the significance of ethics in business decision-making, it is important to understand how ethical decisions are made within the context of an organization. Understanding the ethical decision-making process can help individuals and businesses design strategies to deter misconduct. Our descriptive approach to understanding ethical decision-making does not prescribe what to do; rather, it provides a framework for managing ethical behavior in the workplace. Figure 6.2 depicts this framework, which shows how individual factors, organizational relationships, and opportunities interact when making ethical decisions in business.

Individual Factors

Individuals make ethical choices on the basis of their own concepts of right or wrong, and they act accordingly in their daily lives. Studies suggest that individual ethics are reaching a new low, but also that individual ethics are increasingly important to new generations. A survey by Bloomberg News and Morning Consult found that individual values are very important to today's youth. To capitalize on this, companies have to market their products to a younger, more sustainability-minded public. For example, the Kellogg Company has used teenagers to help create new flavors of cereal, and Ulta Beauty has marketed makeup that is environmentally friendly.[51] If today's students are tomorrow's leaders, there is likely to be a correlation between acceptable behavior today and tomorrow.

Significant factors that affect the ethical decision-making process include an individual's personal moral philosophy, motivation, and other personal factors such as gender, age, and experience.

Ethical Theories   Many people have justified difficult decisions by citing the golden rule ("Do unto others as you would have them do unto you") or some other principle. Such principles, or rules, which individuals apply in deciding what is right or wrong, are often referred to as **moral philosophies**. *Morals* refer to the individuals' philosophies about what is right or wrong. It is important to understand the distinction between moral philosophies and business ethics. A *moral philosophy* is a person's principles and values that are used to define what is moral or immoral. Moral philosophies are person-specific, whereas *business ethics*

moral philosophies
principles, or rules, which individuals apply in deciding what is right or wrong; *morals* refers to individuals' philosophies about what is right or wrong

Figure 6.2 Factors That Influence the Ethical Decision-Making Process

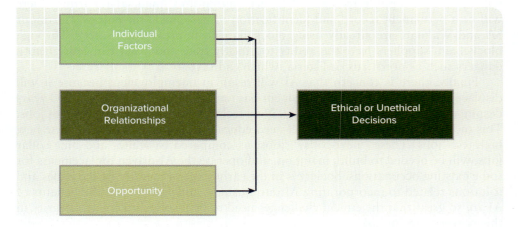

is based on decisions in groups or those made when carrying out tasks to meet business objectives. Socialization by family members, social groups, religion, and formal education teaches moral philosophies. This idea is particularly important to the concept of **social exchange theory**, which states that social behavior is determined by social exchanges between different parties. Most moral philosophies can be classified as consequentialism, ethical formalism, or deontology, or justice.

Consequentialism is a class of moral philosophy that considers a decision right or acceptable if it accomplishes a desired result, such as career growth, the realization of self-interest, or utility in a decision. This looks at the moral outcome based on the consequences associated with decision-making. Egoism and utilitarianism are two important consequentialist philosophies that often guide decision-making in business. **Egoism** is a philosophy that defines right or acceptable conduct in terms of the consequences for the individual. Egoists believe that they should make decisions that maximize their own self-interest, which, depending on the individual, may be defined as career success, power, fame, a satisfying career, a good family life, wealth, and so forth. In a decision-making situation, the egoist will probably choose the alternative that most benefits his or her self-interest. Many people feel that egoists are inherently unethical, that they focus on the short term, and that they will take advantage of any opportunity to exploit consumers or employees. **Utilitarianism** is another consequentialist philosophy that is concerned with seeking the greatest good for the greatest number of people. Using a cost-benefit analysis, a utilitarian decision-maker calculates the utility of the consequences of all possible alternatives and then chooses the one that achieves the greatest utility.

In contrast with consequentialism, **ethical formalism**, or deontology, is a class of moral philosophy that focuses on the rights of individuals and on the intentions associated with a particular behavior rather than on its consequences. This theory falls under what is known as *rights-based ethics*. Deontologists regard certain behaviors as inherently right, and their determination of rightness focuses on the individual actor, not on society. Thus, these perspectives are sometimes referred to as *nonconsequentialism* and the ethics of respect for persons. Contemporary ethical formalism has been greatly influenced by the German philosopher Immanuel Kant, who developed the so-called categorical imperative: "Act as if the maxim of thy action were to become by thy will a universal law of nature."[52] Unlike utilitarians, ethical formalists contend that there are some things that people should not do, even to maximize utility. For example, an ethical formalist would consider it unacceptable to allow a coal mine to continue to operate, even if it made a profit, if some workers became ill and died of black lung disease. A utilitarian, however, might consider some disease or death an acceptable consequence of a decision that resulted in large-scale employment and economic prosperity.

Justice theory is a class of moral philosophy that relates to evaluations of fairness, or the disposition to deal with the perceived injustices of others. Justice demands fair treatment and due reward in accordance with ethical or legal standards. A similar concept is the **Principle of Equal Freedom**, which asserts that all persons must have equality under the law. In business, this requires that the rules an individual uses to determine justice be based on the perceived rights of individuals and on the intentions associated with a business interaction. Justice, therefore, is more likely to be based on nonconsequentialist moral philosophies than on consequentialist philosophies. Justice primarily addresses the issue of what individuals feel they are due based on their rights and performance in the workplace. For example, the EEOC exists to help employees who suspect the injustice of discrimination in the workplace.

There are three types of justice that can be used to assess fairness in different situations. *Distributive justice* evaluates the outcomes or results of a business relationship. For example, if an employee feels that she is paid less than her coworkers for the same work, she has concerns about distributive justice. *Procedural justice*

---

social exchange theory
a theory stating that social behavior is determined by social exchanges between different parties

consequentialism
a class of moral philosophy that considers a decision right or acceptable if it accomplishes a desired result, such as career growth, the realization of self-interest, or utility in a decision

egoism
a philosophy that defines right or acceptable conduct in terms of the consequences for the individual

utilitarianism
a consequentialist philosophy that is concerned with seeking the greatest good for the greatest number of people

ethical formalism
also known as *deontology*, class of moral philosophy that focuses on the rights of individuals and on the intentions associated with a particular behavior rather than on its consequences

justice theory
a class of moral philosophy that relates to evaluations of fairness, or the disposition to deal with the perceived injustices of others

Principle of Equal Freedom
asserts that all persons must have equality under the law

assesses the processes and activities employed to produce an outcome or results and is associated with group cohesiveness and helping behaviors. Such concerns about compensation would relate to the perception that salary and benefit decisions are consistent and fair to all categories of employees.[53] *Interactional justice* evaluates the communication processes used in the business relationship. Being untruthful about the reasons for missing work is an example of an interactional justice issue.[54]

It is important to recognize that there is no one "correct" moral philosophy to apply in resolving ethical and legal issues in the workplace. It is also important to acknowledge that each philosophy presents an ideal perspective and that most people seem to adapt a number of moral philosophies as they interpret the context of different decision-making situations. Each philosophy could result in a different decision in a situation requiring an ethical judgment. And depending on the situation, people may even change their value structure or moral philosophy when making decisions.[55]

Strong evidence shows that individuals use different moral philosophies depending on whether they are making a personal decision outside the work environment or a work-related decision.[56] Two possible reasons may explain this. First, in the business arena, some goals and pressures for success differ from the goals and pressures in a person's life outside of work. As a result, an employee might view a specific action as "good" in the business sector but "unacceptable" in the nonwork environment. Business has two variables that are absent from other situations: the profit motive and the influence of managers and coworkers (corporate culture). The weights on the various factors that make up a person's moral philosophy are shifted in a business (profit) situation. The statement "it's not personal, it's just business" demonstrates the conflict businesspeople can have when their personal values do not align with utilitarian or profit-oriented decisions. In extreme cases, this mentality could become Machiavellian in nature. **Machiavellianism** in business is the use of duplicity or cunning to achieve business goals. The second reason people change moral philosophies could be the corporate culture where they work. When a child enters school, for example, he or she learns certain rules, such as raising your hand to speak or asking permission to use the restroom. So it is with a new employee. Rules, personalities, and historical precedence exert pressure on the employee to conform to the new firm's culture. As this occurs, the individual's moral philosophy may change to be compatible with the work environment. Employees may alter some or all of the values within their moral philosophy as they shift into the firm's different moral philosophy. There are many examples of people who are known for their goodness at home or in their communities making unethical decisions in the workplace.

Ethical Diversity   It is obvious that not everyone holds the same ethical values. One person may have values that another person does not have, or that person might value a certain trait more highly than another. Additionally, individuals can have significantly different values than those of the organization.[57] This concept is referred to as **ethical diversity**, the fact that employee values often differ from person to person. Every employee has developed his or her personal values over a lifetime, and these values are not likely to disappear just because they differ from others or the organization. However, it also means that employees cannot be allowed to bring their individual values to the workplace as they see fit. Imagine the chaos that would happen if each employee acted in a way that was appropriate in his or her eyes. Instead, members need to accept that some values are superior to others and handle the organizational need to develop consensus among employees. This may result in possible tensions and conflicts that must be figured out between individual and organizational values.[58] However, it is best to follow a consensus approach, rather than just having managers assign and enforce their own individual

Machiavellianism
the use of duplicity or cunning to achieve business goals

ethical diversity
refers to the fact that employee values often differ from person to person

values to the organization. There should be group discussions, negotiations, and modifications to determine how organizational values are implemented.[59]

Organizational Relationships

Although individuals can and do make ethical decisions, they do not operate in a vacuum.[60] Ethical choices in business are most often made jointly in committees and work groups, or in conversations with coworkers. Moreover, people learn to settle ethical issues not only from their individual backgrounds, but also from others with whom they associate in the business environment. The outcome of this learning process depends on the strength of each individual's personal values, opportunity for unethical behavior, and exposure to others who behave ethically or unethically. Consequently, the culture of the organization, as well as superiors, peers, and subordinates, can have a significant impact on the ethical decision-making process.

Organizational Culture   **Organizational, (corporate) culture** can be defined as a set of values, norms, and artifacts shared by members or employees of an organization. It answers questions such as "What is important?" "How do we treat each other?" and "How do we do things around here?" Culture may be conveyed formally in employee handbooks, codes of conduct, memos, and ceremonies, but it is also expressed informally through dress codes, extracurricular activities, and anecdotes. A firm's culture gives its members meaning and offers direction as to how to behave and deal with problems within the organization. The corporate culture at American Express, for example, includes numerous anecdotes about employees who have gone beyond the call of duty to help customers out of difficult situations. This strong tradition of customer service might encourage an American Express employee to take extra steps to help a customer who encounters a problem while traveling overseas.

> **organizational, (corporate) culture**
> a set of values, beliefs, and artifacts shared by members or employees of an organization

Organizational culture depends on company strategy because it prioritizes stakeholders. For example, Marriott prioritizes employees to provide exceptional service for customers. Therefore, its strategic priority is keeping Marriott as one of the best companies to work for. Walmart, on the other hand, values customers and therefore places a priority on a low-cost, efficient operating environment. Amazon has developed a culture that focuses on their competitors and is making extreme inroads into traditional markets for durable goods sold in stores. Therefore, the company's strategy will help shape stakeholder relationships and the ethical culture.

On the other hand, an organization's culture can also encourage employees to make decisions that others may judge as unethical, or it can encourage actions that may be viewed as socially irresponsible. Some misconduct comes from employees trying to attain the performance objectives of the firm, whatever they have to do to accomplish it. While high performance objectives are not a bad thing, it is important for managers to ensure that these objectives can be reached without cutting corners or engaging in questionable conduct. For example, bankers who worked for Wells Fargo felt downward pressure from upper management to open more accounts at their banks. Wells Fargo's intention when it started requesting more accounts from its bankers was to generate more revenue by having more customers do business with them. The senior leadership of Wells Fargo, however, put extensive pressure on its employees, which created an unethical environment for its retail banks. Many employees created fake accounts for customers who didn't exist, despite knowing that it was unethical. The drive to meet their sales goals superseded their sense of right and wrong, and the scandal has had a lasting effect on the company.[61]

Derivatives used in financial markets to transfer risk are so complex, difficult to value, poorly regulated, and have been so widely used that they can bring down a company. They also contributed a great deal to the severity of the U.S. recession, challenging the entire country's financial systems. To make ethical decisions when using derivatives, one requires a great deal of transparency, financial expertise and competence, and responsibility.[62] Because of their complexity, derivatives provide openings for manipulation and misconduct. When a corporation uses certain compensation systems, employees striving for financial success could be inadvertently rewarded for their sales of dangerous derivatives. The corporate culture may drive decisions on developing and selling derivatives because of the difficulty in applying moral reasoning.

Earth in the Balance

Dressed for Success: Ethical Business Practices at Patagonia

The popular outdoor apparel store Patagonia was founded upon environmental principles with a three-part mission: sell quality products, cause no unnecessary harm, and find business solutions to environmental issues. One of Patagonia's most infamous promotions featured its popular R2 coat with the counterintuitive headline: "Don't Buy This Jacket." The advertisement explained that although the R2 used recycled materials, it was still harmful to the environment. Because excessive consumption generates waste, encouraging consumers to purchase less demonstrates Patagonia's environmental commitment. The company wants consumers to purchase their apparel, but only as needed.

The company serves as an example of the concept "ethics pay," meaning that society will reward Patagonia for its high standards, even though its finances may initially take a hit. For example, to be more environmentally friendly, in 1996 the company switched to the more expensive organic cotton. This increased the firm's supply costs, but it also made its products more durable. It would be logical to think that the more durable the product, the less customers need to purchase from the company, and sales would go down. However, the exact opposite occurred. Consumers were more willing to do business with Patagonia due to its environmental consciousness and the fact that they could trust Patagonia's products to last a long time. As the change to organic cotton shows, Patagonia puts the values of integrity, accountability, and trust into practice in its business by backing its mission with action. The company is moving toward using recycled or renewable materials for 70 percent of its clothing.

Patagonia has spoken out about sustainability practices in areas besides its clothing. For example, the company has produced films about the environmental impacts of common business practices. One of these films, called *Artifishal*, discusses the need for more natural salmon fishing rather than relying on the controversial practices of fish hatcheries.

Patagonia's commitment to the environment extends so far that they even urge their customers to return worn-out merchandise so that the company can recycle it into something else. By 2025, Patagonia plans to be carbon neutral, and even to be carbon positive projecting into the future. Customer and shareholder loyalty continue to be strong for the company due to its ethical values and actions.

Sources: Tessa Byars, "Patagonia Releases a Documentary About The High Cost of Fish Hatcheries, Fish Farms, and Human Ignorance," *Patagonia Works*, April 12, 2019, http://www.patagoniaworks.com/press/2019/4/18/patagonia-releases-a-documentary-about-the-high-cost-of-fish-hatcheries-fish-farms-and-human-ignorance (accessed May 28, 2019); Daniel Bentley, "Doing Good and Making a Profit: These Apparel Companies Are Proving They Aren't Mutually Exclusive," *Fortune*, January 23, 2019, http://fortune.com/2019/01/23/patagonia-art-eden-sustainability/ (accessed May 28, 2019); Tim Nudd, "Ad of the Day: Patagonia," *Ad Week*, November 28, 2011, http://www.adweek.com/news/advertising-branding/ad-day-patagonia-136745 (accessed May 28, 2019); Kyle Stock, "Patagonia's Confusing and Effective Campaign to Grudgingly Sell Stuff," *Bloomberg*, November 25, 2013, https://www.bloomberg.com/news/articles/2013-11-25/patagonias-confusing-and-effective-campaign-to-grudgingly-sell-stuff (accessed May 28, 2019); Andrew Cave, "'Don't Buy This Racket': Patagonia to Give Away All Retail Revenues on Black Friday," *Forbes*, November 21, 2016, http://www.forbes.com/sites/andrewcave/2016/11/21/dont-buy-this-racket-patagonia-to-give-away-all-retail-revenues-on-black-friday/#1ea56050230c (accessed May 28, 2019); J. B. MacKinnon, "Patagonia's Anti-Growth Strategy," *The New Yorker*, May 21, 2017, https://www.newyorker.com/business/currency/patagonias-anti-growth-strategy (accessed June 1, 2019); Nick Paumgarten, "Patagonia's Philosopher-King," *The New Yorker*, September 19, 2017, https://www.newyorker.com/magazine/2016/09/19/patagonias-philosopher-king (accessed June 1, 2019); Daniela Sirtori-Cortin, "From Climber to Billionaire: How Yvon Chouinard Built Patagonia into a Powerhouse His Own Way," *Forbes*, March 20, 2017, https://www.forbes.com/sites/danielasirtori/2017/03/20/from-climber-to-billionaire-how-yvon-chouinard-built-patagonia-into-a-powerhouse-his-own-way/#651643b2480c (accessed June 1, 2019); Patagonia, "20 Years of Organic Cotton," *The Footprint Chronicles*, https://eu.patagonia.com/cz/en/20-years-of-organic-cotton.html (accessed June 1, 2019).

Whereas a firm's overall culture establishes ideals that guide a wide range of behaviors for members of the organization, its **ethical climate** focuses specifically on issues of right and wrong. We think of ethical climate as the part of a corporate culture that relates to an organization's expectations about appropriate conduct. To some extent, ethical climate is the character component of an organization. Corporate policies and codes, the conduct of top managers, the values and moral philosophies of coworkers, and opportunity for misconduct all contribute to a firm's ethical climate. When top managers strive to establish an ethical climate based on responsibility and citizenship, they set the tone for ethical decisions.

New Belgium Brewing (NBB) is an example of a company in which their leaders set the tone for the rest of the organization. Former CEO and current executive chair Kim Jordan helped cofound the company with her former husband, Jeff Lebesch. Before starting NBB, the two carefully considered the values they wanted to use as the foundation for the company, including sustainability and employee empowerment. Under Jordan's leadership, NBB's ethical climate placed a great deal of emphasis on these two values.[63] Among a number of sustainability initiatives, the company became the first brewery to use 100 percent wind power.[64] Over the years, NBB has become a 100 percent employee-owned company, giving employees the ability to make crucial decisions regarding operations.[65] Ethical climate also determines whether an individual perceives an issue as having an ethical component. Recognizing ethical issues and generating alternatives to address them are manifestations of ethical climate.

ethical climate
the part of a firm's culture that focuses specifically on issues of appropriate conduct and right and wrong

Significant Others   Although people outside the firm, such as family members and friends, also influence decision-makers, organizational structure and culture operate through significant others to influence ethical decisions. **Significant others** include superiors, peers, subordinates, and others in an organization who influence the ethical decision-making process.[66] Reporting misconduct is most likely to come from upper levels of management compared to lower-level supervisors and nonmanagement employees. Employees in lower-level positions have a greater tendency to not recognize misconduct or to be complacent about the misconduct they observe. Having ethics and compliance officers is an option to allow employees to report misconduct when they are unable or unwilling to report to upper management. Ethics and compliance officers are high-ranking employees known to respect and understand legal and ethical standards. They help a company resolve ethical dilemmas and uphold regulatory responsibilities.[67] While ethics officers and ethics hotlines exist, however, the vast majority of employees surveyed prefer to report to supervisors and other higher management.

significant others
superiors, peers, subordinates, and others in an organization who influence the ethical decision-making process

Most experts agree that the CEO establishes the ethical tone for the entire firm. This can be problematic when managers are more likely to engage in certain forms of misconduct. Table 6.3 shows that the type of misconduct, such as abusive or intimidating behavior, sexual harassment, and discrimination, varies by management level. Nonmanagement employees are the most likely to engage in abusive or intimidating behavior and sexual harassment. Lower-level managers pick up their cues from top managers, and they in turn impose some of their personal values on the company. This interaction between corporate culture and

Table 6.3 Observed Misconduct by Perpetrator Level

Abusive or Intimidating Behavior	
Nonmanagement employee	34%
Senior leader	25%
Middle manager	22%
First-line supervisor	16%
Other	2%
Someone you work with outside the company	1%
Sexual Harassment	
Nonmanagement employee	32%
Middle manager	24%
Senior leader	23%
First-line supervisor	16%
Someone you work with outside the company	3%
Other	2%
Discrimination	
Middle manager	29%
Senior leader	28%
Nonmanagement employee	22%
First-line supervisor	18%
Someone you work with outside the company	3%
Other	1%

Source: Ethics and Compliance Initiative, *2018 Global Business Ethics Survey: Interpersonal Misconduct in the Workplace*, December 2018; https://www.ethics.org/download-the-2018-global-business-ethics-survey/ (accessed July 15, 2019).

executive leadership helps determine the ethical value system of a firm. However, obedience to authority can also explain why many people resolve workplace issues by following the directives of a superior. An employee may feel obligated to carry out the orders of a superior, even if those orders conflict with the employee's values of right and wrong. If that decision is later judged to have been wrong, the employee may justify it by saying, "I was only following orders" or "My boss told me to do it this way."

Coworkers' influence on ethical decision-making depends on each person's exposure to unethical behavior when making ethical decisions. The more a person is exposed to unethical activity by others in the organization, the more likely it is that he or she will behave unethically, especially in (ethically) gray areas. Thus, a decision-maker who associates with others who act unethically is more likely to behave unethically as well. Within work groups, employees may be subject to the phenomenon of **groupthink**, which means going along with group decisions even when those decisions run counter to their own values. They may rationalize the decision with "safety in numbers" when everyone else appears to back a particular decision. Most businesspeople take their cues or learn from coworkers how to solve problems—including ethical dilemmas.[68] Close friends at work exert the most influence on ethical decisions that relate to roles associated with a particular job.

Superiors and coworkers can create organizational pressure, which plays a key role in creating ethical issues. Although power differences exist between supervisors and their employees, ethical leaders attempt to reduce these differences when communicating with employees. It is not uncommon for leaders within the organization to adopt the habit of viewing employee information as unimportant.[69]

groupthink
a phenomenon whereby individuals go along with group decisions even when those decisions run counter to one's own values

However, employees who feel that they are not being heard are less likely to report concerns and more likely to ignore questionable conduct in the workplace. Ethical leaders can help to reduce these perceived power differences through frequent employee communication. This interaction creates more beneficial relationships with employees, making them more comfortable in bringing up issues of concern to their supervisors. Leader–follower congruence occurs when leaders and followers share the same organizational vision, ethical expectations, and objectives. A crucial way to communicate ethical values to employees is through codes of ethics and training to familiarize employees with the ethical decision-making process.

Nearly all businesspeople face difficult issues where solutions are not obvious or where organizational objectives and personal ethical values may conflict. For example, a salesperson for a web-based retailer may be asked by a superior to lie to a customer over the telephone about a late product shipment. A study by the Ethics Resource Center found that 22 percent of U.S. employees said they felt pressure from other employees or managers to compromise their standards. In addition, 76 percent of employees reported misconduct after they observed it, and 53 percent of these instances were met with some type of retaliation.[70]

Opportunity

Together, organizational culture and the influence of coworkers may foster conditions that either hinder or permit misconduct. **Opportunity** is a set of conditions that limits barriers or provides rewards. When these conditions provide rewards—be it financial gain, recognition, promotion, or simply the good feeling from a job well done—the opportunity for unethical conduct may be encouraged or discouraged. For example, a company policy that fails to specify the punishment for employees who violate the rules provides an opportunity for unethical behavior because it allows individuals to engage in such behavior without fear of consequences. Thus, company policies, processes, and other factors may create opportunities to act unethically. Advancing technology associated with the internet is challenging companies working to limit opportunities to engage in unethical and illegal behavior. Individual factors as well as organizational relationships may influence whether an individual becomes opportunistic and takes advantage of situations in an unethical (or even illegal) manner.

opportunity
a set of conditions that limits barriers or provides rewards

Opportunity usually relates to employees' immediate job context—where they work, with whom they work, and the nature of the work. This context includes the motivational "carrots and sticks," or rewards and punishments, that superiors can use to influence employee behavior. Rewards, or positive reinforcers, include pay raises, bonuses, and public recognition, whereas reprimands, pay penalties, demotions, and even firings act as negative reinforcers. For example, a manager who decides to sell customers' personal data may be confident that such behavior is an easy way to boost revenue because other companies sell customer account information. Even if this activity violates the employee's personal value system, it may be viewed as acceptable within the organization's culture. This manager may also be motivated by opportunities to improve his or her performance standing within the organization by taking such actions. A survey by Kessler International indicates that 52 percent of employees take office supplies for personal use. As Table 6.4 shows, many employees pilfer office supplies for matters unrelated to the job. It is possible that the opportunity is provided for small-scale theft in the company; in some cases, no concern is shown about whether employees take pens, sticky notes, envelopes, notepads, and paper. Printing large documents at work for their own or their spouse's use, or even for their children's school assignments, is a common form of misconduct. Additionally, some indicated that they

Table 6.4 Most Common Items Stolen by Employees

1	Pens and pencils
2	Notepads
3	Printer paper
4	Staplers
5	Food

Source: Kelly Meyers, "5 Things People Steal from Work," Radio.com, November 30, 2018, https://1079thelink.radio.com/blogs/kelly-meyers/5-things-people-steal-work (accessed July 2, 2019).

take more expensive items such as universal serial bus (USB) drives and computer accessories.[71] If there is no policy against this practice, employees will not learn where to draw the line and will get into the habit of taking even more expensive items for personal use.

Stealing office supplies and inflating business expenditure reports is prevalent in businesses. While these acts do not seem serious, they build up over time and establish norms. Studies show that employees have "blind spots" that cause them to be unaware of the ethical and legal meanings behind their actions. The opportunity to act unethically often arises in situations when employees are unsure about the company standards, when the victims are not identified or are invisible (such as public shareholders), or when performance goals are unrealistic.[72]

Often, opportunity can arise from someone whose job is to create opportunities for others. Barbara Toffler, an ethics consultant and professor, learned firsthand how difficult it can be to follow one's own moral compass when she worked as a consultant at Arthur Andersen, creating ethics programs for Andersen clients (the firm itself had no internal ethics program). After charging a client $1 million for developing an ethics program that should have cost $500,000, the praise Toffler earned from Andersen "was the only day in four years that I felt truly valued by Arthur Andersen." Despite her expertise, she learned that "unethical or illegal behavior happens when decent people are put under the unbearable pressure to do their jobs and meet ambitious goals without the resources to get the job done right."[73]

General Electric (GE) has taken steps to place itself at the head of the ethical pack. Its Ecomagination campaign is designed to "build innovative solutions for today's environmental challenges while driving economic growth." It also has an initiative called Healthymagination, which aims to improve the quality of healthcare. As part of its investment, GE focuses on investigating clean-tech research, releasing products that are ecofriendlier, partnering with community health organizations, and continuing employee healthcare programs.[74]

If an employee takes advantage of an opportunity to act unethically and is rewarded or at least suffers no penalty, he or she may repeat such acts as other opportunities arise. Dov Charney, founder and former CEO of American Apparel, was pushed out of his position by the board after allegations concerning sexual misconduct and sexual harassment. These allegations had persisted for more than a decade before he was eventually terminated.[75] His removal as CEO demonstrates the effectiveness of good corporate governance and the duty of the board of directors to maintain an ethical organizational culture. When company managers get away with unethical conduct, their behavior is reinforced, and a culture of manipulation and misconduct can develop. Indeed, the opportunity to engage in unethical conduct is often a better predictor of unethical activities than personal values.[76]

In addition to rewards and the absence of punishment, other elements in the business environment tend to create opportunities. Professional codes of conduct and ethics-related corporate policies also influence opportunity by prescribing what behaviors are acceptable. Compliance programs are necessary to provide internal controls to prevent situations just discussed. The larger the rewards and the milder the punishment for unethical behavior, the greater is the probability that unethical behavior will be practiced.

ethical culture
refers to the character of the decision-making process that employees use to determine if their responses to ethical issues are right or wrong

Developing an Ethical Culture

Organizational ethics and compliance initiatives are developed to establish appropriate conduct and core values. The term **ethical culture** refers to the character of the decision-making process that employees use to determine if their responses to ethical issues are right or wrong. Ethical culture is that part of corporate culture that encompasses the values and norms an organization defines as appropriate conduct. The goal of an ethical culture is to curtail the need for enforced compliance of rules and amplify the use of principles that contribute to ethical reasoning in complex or new situations. Ethical culture is positively related to organizations with hotlines and with employees who confront ethics issues in the workplace and/or report observed misconduct to management.[77] Developing an ethical culture involves communicating organizational values and norms to employees throughout the organization, developing effective ethics programs, and appointing ethics officers to run them. An ethical culture creates shared values and managerial commitment for ethical decisions.

Organizational Values

Organizational values are abstract ideals distinct from individual values. Values can evolve over time. They are more subjective and are viewed by societal members as ethical or unethical. Values-based practices become the end results and are separate from organizational practices based on technical or efficiency considerations.[78]

    Both stakeholders and the organizational culture affect the development of organizational values. Because values are more subjective, they are influenced by firm, industry, country, and global specific factors.[79] For instance, firms from countries that stress individualism might encourage the ability to work independently, whereas firms from more collectivist nations might place more value on teamwork. Additionally, core values might differ depending upon the industry. Although safety is a core value of many firms, it is more likely to be emphasized in a factory environment than in an office environment. For instance, organizations from countries that value risk may value innovative risk taking, while organizations from countries more averse to risk may take a different position. Table 6.5 provides an example of the organizational values of Marriott. From these values, one can determine that the hotel group tries to deliver exceptional customer service and operate with high ethical standards. Marriott's values reinforce its vision "to be the #1 hospitality company in the world."[80] These types of organizational values are critical to organizational ethical decision-making. Organizations that have ethics programs based upon values tend to make a greater contribution than those based simply on compliance, or obeying rules.[81]

Normative Considerations of Ethical Decision-Making

Earlier in this chapter, we described how ethical decision-making occurs in an organization. Understanding what affects the ethical decision-making process is necessary for developing and managing an ethical culture within an organization. However, understanding how ethical decisions are made is different from determining what ought to guide ethical decisions. **Normative approaches** are concerned with how organizational decision-makers *should* approach an ethical issue. It is concerned with providing a vision and recommendations for improving ethical decision-making. Concepts like fairness, justice, and moral philosophies such as deontology and utilitarianism are important to a normative approach. Strong normative approaches in organizations have a positive relationship to ethical decision-making. Besides values, norms provide more specific beliefs about expected behaviors in a specific context. Norms may exist about expected behavior in work groups and teams throughout the organization. Examples of norms could relate to expected professionalism and how to resolve a reoccurring ethical issue.

organizational values
abstract ideals distinct from individual values

normative approaches
provide a vision and recommendations for improving ethical decision-making; are concerned with how organizational decision-makers *should* approach an ethical issue

Table 6.5 Organizational Values of Marriott

Put people first
Pursue excellence
Embrace change
Act with integrity
Serve our world

Source: Marriott, "Core Values and Heritage," https://www.marriott.com/culture-and-values/core-values.mi (accessed August 24, 2019).

virtue ethics
adhering to general ideas, social values, and good character for appropriate ethical behavior

Virtue ethics involves adhering to general ideals, social values, and good character for appropriate ethical behavior. A virtue represents an acquired disposition valued as a part of an individual's character. As individuals develop socially, they come to behave in ways they consider to be moral. A person with the virtue of honesty, for example, will be predisposed to tell the truth because it is considered to be the right approach in terms of human communication. Examples of business virtues include trust, self-control, empathy, fairness, truthfulness, learning, gratitude, civility, and moral leadership.[82]

Managing the Ethical Culture: Variations of Employee Conduct

Despite the creation and implementation of shared organizational values, organizations must recognize that employee behavior will still vary. Overall, it is up to the organization to take responsibility for an ethical culture and implementation. However, research indicates that there are major differences in the values and philosophies that influence how individuals that comprise organizations make ethical decisions.[83] Due to their ethical diversity, employees will often interpret situations differently and vary in their responses to an ethical issue.

Table 6.6 reflects a study that measures variation in employee conduct. It demonstrates that approximately 10 percent of employees will take advantage of situations to further their own personal interests. These employees are often referred to as "bad apples" and are more likely to manipulate, cheat, or be self-serving when the benefits gained from misconduct are greater than the penalties. They are more likely to steal office supplies or engage in other forms of misconduct. The lower the risk of penalties, the higher the likelihood that this 10 percent of employees will commit unethical activities.

Approximately 40 percent of workers go along with their work group on most decisions. These employees are most concerned about the social implications of their actions and desire to be accepted in the organization. They have their own personal opinions but are easily affected by other employees around them. For instance, they might be well aware that using office supplies for personal use is improper. However, if it is common for other employees to take office supplies for personal use, then these employees are likely to do the same just to fit in. These employees tend to rationalize, claiming that the use of office supplies is just one of the benefits of their jobs, and because there is no company policy prohibiting it, then it must be acceptable. Coupled with this is the belief of safety in numbers. These employees feel that they will not get into trouble because everybody is doing it (groupthink, as discussed earlier in this chapter).

On the other hand, approximately 40 percent of a company's employees always try to follow company policies and rules. These workers have a strong understanding of how their corporate culture defines acceptable behavior and try to comply with organizational codes of ethics, ethics training, and other communications

Table 6.6 Variation in Employee Conduct

10 Percent	40 Percent	40 Percent	10 Percent
Follow their own values and beliefs; believe that their values are superior to those of others in the company	Always try to follow company policies	Go along with their work group	Take advantage of situations if the penalty is less than the benefit—the risk of being caught is low

Source: These percentages are based on a number of studies in the popular press and data gathered by the authors. The percentages are not exact and represent a general typology that may vary by organization. The 10 percent that will take advantage is adapted from John Fraedrich and O. C. Ferrell, "Cognitive Consistency of Marketing Managers in Ethical Situations," *Journal of the Academy of Marketing Science* 20 (Summer 1992): 243–252.

about ethical conduct. In the office supply example, if the company has a policy that prohibits taking office supplies from work for personal use, these employees would most likely obey the policy. However, they probably would not tell anyone about the 40 percent who go along with the work group, for these employees prefer to focus on their jobs and avoid any conflicts or organizational misconduct. These employees rely heavily on organizational communication and expectations. If the organization fails to communicate standards for ethical conduct, then members of this group will devise their own.

The final 10 percent of employees attempt to uphold formal ethical standards focusing on rights, duties, and rules. They adopt values that support certain inalienable rights and actions. From their perspective, these actions are always ethically correct if they protect inalienable rights. Overall, these employees believe that their values are correct and superior to the values of other employees in the organization, or even to the organization's own value system, when an ethical issue arises. These employees tend to report observed misconduct or report when they view activities within the organization that they believe are unethical. As a result, these employees would most likely report coworkers who steal office supplies.

It should be clear by now that employees use different approaches when making ethical decisions. Because of the probability that a large percentage of employees will take advantage of a situation or go along with the rest of employees, it is important that companies provide communication and internal controls to support an ethical culture. Organizations that do not monitor activities and enforce ethical policies provide a low-risk environment for employees inclined to take advantage of situations to accomplish their own personal objectives.

Although the percentages in Table 6.6 are only estimates, the specific percentages are less important than the fact that research has identified these employee variations as existing within most organizations. Organizations should pay particular attention to managers who monitor the daily operations of employees. They should also provide ethics training and communication to make certain that the business operates in an ethical manner, misconduct is caught before it becomes a major issue, and risk to stakeholders is eliminated or minimized.

Maintaining ethical conduct is a business goal that should be no different from increasing profits. If progress in maintaining an ethical culture stalls, then the organization must determine the reason and take corrective action by enforcing existing standards or setting higher standards. If the code of ethics is strongly enforced and becomes part of the corporate culture, it can lead to strong improvements in the ethical conduct within the organization. On the other hand, if the code of ethics and managerial commitment are merely window-dressing and not truly a part of the corporate culture, they will not be effective.

Summary

Business ethics comprises principles and standards that guide individual and work-group behavior in the world of business. Principles are specific and pervasive boundaries that are absolute, while values are used to develop norms that are socially enforced. Stakeholders determine these conventions, and they may change over time. The most basic of these standards have been codified as laws and regulations. Business ethics goes beyond legal issues.

Because individuals and groups within a company may not have embraced the same set of values, ethical conflict may occur. An ethical issue is a problem, situation, or opportunity that requires an individual, group, or organization to choose among several actions that must be evaluated as right or wrong, ethical or unethical. Questionable decisions and actions may result in disputes that must be resolved through some type of negotiation or even litigation. Codifying ethical standards into meaningful policies that spell out what is and is not acceptable gives businesspeople an opportunity to reduce the possibility of behavior that could create legal problems. Business decisions involve complex and detailed discussions in which correctness may not be clear-cut. It is important that a shared vision of acceptable behavior develops from an organizational perspective to create consistent and reliable relationships with all concerned stakeholders. Common ethical issues faced by businesses include abusive or intimidating behavior, misuse of company time and resources, conflicts of interest, bribery, discrimination and sexual harassment, fraud, and privacy issues. An emerging issue involves AI and ethical decision-making.

Understanding the ethical decision-making process can help individuals and businesses design strategies to prevent misconduct. Three of the important components of ethical decision-making are individual factors, organizational relationships, and opportunity.

Significant individual factors that affect the ethical decision-making process include personal moral philosophy, stage of moral development, motivation, and other personal factors such as gender, age, and experience. Moral philosophies are the principles or rules that individuals apply in deciding what is right or wrong. Most moral philosophies can be classified as consequentialism, ethical formalism, or justice. Consequentialist philosophies consider a decision to be right or acceptable if it accomplishes a desired result such as pleasure, knowledge, career growth, the realization of self-interest, or utility. Consequentialism may be further classified as egoism and utilitarianism. Ethical formalism focuses on the rights of individuals and on the intentions associated with a particular behavior rather than on its consequences. Justice theory relates to evaluations of fairness or the disposition to deal with perceived injustices of others.

The culture of the organization, as well as superiors, peers, and subordinates, can have a significant impact on the ethical decision-making process. Organizational, or corporate, culture can be defined as a set of values, beliefs, goals, norms, and rituals shared by members or employees of an organization. Whereas a firm's overall culture establishes ideals that guide a wide range of behaviors for members of the organization, its ethical climate focuses specifically on issues of right and wrong. Significant others include superiors, peers, subordinates, and others in the organization who influence the ethical decision-making process. Interaction between corporate culture and executive leadership helps determine the ethical value system of the firm, but obedience to authority can also explain why many people resolve workplace issues by following the directives of a superior. The more exposed a person is to unethical activity in the organization, the more likely it is that he or she will behave unethically. Superiors and coworkers can create organizational pressure, which plays a key role in creating ethical issues.

Opportunity is a set of conditions that limit barriers or provide rewards. If an individual takes advantage of an opportunity to act unethically and escapes punishment or gains a reward, that person may repeat such acts when circumstances favor it.

To develop an ethical culture, it is crucial for the organization to develop strong organizational values to guide the organization. The values often form the basis of a normative structure. A normative approach is concerned with how organizational decision-makers *should* approach an ethical issue. Finally, studies have shown that employee ethical behavior in the workplace tends to vary. While 10 percent are bad apples who will take advantage of the organization, 40 percent of employees are estimated to go along with the majority in ethical decision-making. Another 40 percent are likely to obey policies and procedures themselves but will not often report the misconduct of others. The final 10 percent view their values as superior to others. They adhere to their high ethical values and will report those employees whom they consider to be unethical. Organizations should pay particular attention to managers who monitor the daily operations of employees.

Responsible Business Debate

Sherwin-Williams Painted into a Corner

Issue: *Should Sherwin-Williams Be Liable for the Lead Paint Debacle?*

Most would agree that companies advertising a dangerous product should be held accountable. However, what if the advertisement was more than a century old? This is the dilemma that paint makers like Sherwin-Williams, NL Industries, and ConAgra faced from a California lawsuit seeking damages for such firms' marketing of lead paint in homes. For instance, Sherwin-Williams made advertisements for paint that was lead-based in the early 1900s. In 1943, the company stopped selling white lead paint for inside use. However, the California court argued that although lead paint wasn't illegal until 1978, Sherwin-Williams and these other companies knew about some of the dangers of this product and continued marketing it to homeowners anyway.

In 2013, the California court ruled that Sherwin-Williams, NL Industries, and ConAgra were liable for the cleanup. Later, the damages were limited to paint used in houses prior to 1950 because at this time, paint manufacturers began publicly acknowledging the dangers of lead paint.

NL Industries agreed to a $60 million settlement. But Sherwin-Williams and ConAgra appealed to the U.S. Supreme Court, who in 2018 refused to hear the case. The lawsuit was a public-nuisance suit, and the two companies argued that the suit violated their free speech and due process, and allowed businesses to be held accountable for decades-old advertising. Sherwin-Williams and ConAgra were required to pay a $400 million settlement after the Court decided not to hear the case.

It is unclear how this lawsuit will affect the world of advertising. Social responsibility and ethical presentation of safe products are major concerns among businesses. Advertisers may be called on to utilize more discretion, apply ethical guidelines, and consider the impact of their advertisements (past, present, and future), when doing business with consumers. Although ethics guidelines do not hold the same weight as laws, the lawsuit against Sherwin-Williams demonstrates how important ethical practices are to a business's reputation and success.

There Are Two Sides to Every Issue

1. Despite the time that has passed, Sherwin-Williams should be held accountable.
2. Because of the time that has passed, Sherwin-Williams should not be held accountable.

Source: Alexander Bruell, "Sherwin-Williams Lands in Trouble over 114-Year-Old Paint Ad," *Wall Street Journal*, September 2, 2018, https://www.wsj.com/articles/sherwin-williams-lands-in-trouble-over-114-year-old-paint-ad-1535886000?mod=searchresults&page=1&pos=1 (accessed March 8, 2019); Jon Bilyk, "Lead Paint Makers Lose Another Round in Long-Running, $1.1 Billion California Lawsuit," *Forbes*, November 14, 2017, https://www.forbes.com/sites/legalnewsline/2017/11/14/lead-paint-makers-lose-another-round-in-long-running-1-1-billion-california-lawsuit/#e4d5c343b398 (accessed March 8, 2019); "$60 Million Settlement Reached in Lead Paint Lawsuit; Companies Fight to Overturn Court Ruling," *Silicon Valley Newsroom*, May 18, 2018, https://www.sanjoseinside.com/2018/05/18/60-million-settlement-reached-in-lead-paint-lawsuit-companies-fight-to-overturn-ruling/ (accessed March 8, 2019); Liam Dillon, "Paint Companies Pull Lead Cleanup Measure from California's November Ballot," *Los Angeles Times*, June 28, 2018, http://www.latimes.com/politics/essential/la-pol-ca-essential-politics-may-2018-paint-companies-pull-lead-cleanup-1530233556-htmlstory.html (accessed March 8, 2019); John O'Brien, "Attack on Paint Industry Spreads to Pennsylvania; Sherwin-Williams Asks Judge for Help," *Forbes*, October 31, 2018, https://www.forbes.com/sites/legalnewsline/2018/10/31/attack-on-paint-industry-spreads-to-pennsylvania-sherwin-williams-asks-judge-for-help/#43c739a1400c (accessed March 8, 2019); William Sassani, "Delaware County Fights for Its Right to Sue; Sherwin-Williams Wants to Block Pa. Lead Paint Litigation Pushed by Private Lawyers," *PennRecord*, January 23, 2019, https://pennrecord.com/stories/511719277-delaware-county-fights-for-its-right-to-sue-sherwin-williams-wants-to-block-pa-lead-paint-litigation-pushed-by-private-lawyers (accessed March 8, 2019); Sam Allard, "Sherwin-Williams, ConAgra Must Pay $400 Million for Lead Paint Remediation in California, Supreme Court Says," *Cleveland Scene*, October 16, 2018, https://www.clevescene.com/scene-and-heard/archives/2018/10/16/sherwin-williams-conagra-must-pay-400-million-for-lead-paint-remediation-in-california-supreme-court-says (accessed March 8, 2019).

Key Terms

biometric data (p. 159)
bribery (p. 155)
business ethics (p. 149)
conflict of interest (p. 155)
consequentialism (p. 163)
egoism (p. 163)
ethical climate (p. 167)
ethical conflict (p. 150)

ethical culture (p. 170)
ethical diversity (p. 164)
ethical formalism (p. 163)
ethical issue (p. 152)
Foreign Corrupt Practices Act (FCPA) (p. 156)
fraud (p. 158)
groupthink (p. 168)

hostile work environment (p. 158)
justice theory (p. 163)
Machiavellianism (p. 164)
moral philosophies (p. 162)
normative approaches (p. 171)
opportunity (p. 169)
organizational values (p. 171)

continued

Discussion Questions

1. Why is business ethics a strategic consideration in organizational decisions?
2. How do individual, organizational, and opportunity factors interact to influence ethical or unethical decisions?
3. How do moral philosophies influence the individual factor in organizational ethical decision-making?
4. How can ethical formalism be used in organizational ethics programs and still respect diversity and the right for individual values?
5. What are the potential benefits of an emphasis on procedural justice?
6. Describe the importance of normative approaches to ethical decision-making.
7. How do organizations create an ethical climate?
8. Why are we seeing more evidence of widespread ethical dilemmas within organizations?
9. Describe the importance of organizational values to the development of an ethical culture.
10. Why is it important for managers to take ethical diversity into account?

Experiential Exercise

Visit www.bbb.org, the home page for the Better Business Bureau (BBB), and locate the International Marketplace Ethics award criteria (https://www.bbb.org/council/international-torch-awards/how-to-apply/award-criteria/). Find recent winners of the award and summarize what they did to achieve this recognition. Describe the role of the BBB in supporting self-regulatory activities and business ethics.

Moonlighting Monica: What Would You Do?

On Sunday, Armando went to work to pick up a report he needed to review before an early Monday meeting. While at work, he noticed a colleague's light on and went over to her cubicle for a short visit. Monica was one of the newest systems designers on the department's staff. She was hired six weeks ago to assist with a series of human resources (HR) projects for the company. Before joining the firm, she had worked as an independent consultant to organizations trying to upgrade their HR systems that track payroll, benefits, compliance, and other issues. Monica was very well qualified, detail oriented, and hardworking. She was the only female on the systems staff.

In his brief conversation with Monica, Armando felt that he was not getting the full story of her reason for being at work on a Sunday. After all, the systems team completed the first HR systems proposal on Thursday and was prepared to present its report and recommendations on Monday. Monica said she was "working on a few parts" of the project but did not get more specific. Her face turned red when Armando joked, "With the beautiful weather outside, only someone hoping to earn a little extra money would be at work today."

Armando and another coworker, David, presented the systems team's report to the HR staff on Monday. The HR team was generally pleased with the recommendations but wanted a number of changes in specifications. This was normal and the systems designers were prepared for the changes. Everyone on the team met that afternoon and Tuesday morning to develop a plan for revamping the HR system. By Tuesday afternoon, each member was working on his or her part of the project again.

On Friday afternoon, David went up and down the hall, encouraging everyone to go to happy hour at the pub down the street. About 10 people, including Monica and Armando, went to the pub. The conversation was mainly about work and the new HR project. On several occasions, Monica offered ideas about other systems and companies with which she was familiar. Most of the systems designers listened, but a few were quick to question her suggestions. Armando assumed her suggestions were the result of work with previous clients. Over the weekend, however, Armando began to wonder whether Monica was talking about her current clients. He remembered their conversation on Sunday and decided to look into the matter.

On Monday, Armando asked Monica directly whether she still had clients. Monica said yes and that she was finishing up on projects with two of them. She went on to say that she worked late hours and on the weekends and was not skimping on her company responsibilities. Armando agreed that she was a good colleague but was not comfortable with her use of company resources on personal, moneymaking projects. He was also concerned that the team's intellectual capital was being used. What would you do?

Strategic Approaches to Improving Ethical Behavior

Deep in Fraud in Dixon, Illinois

The Rita Crundwell case in Dixon, Illinois, is a good example of the need for financial controls. Crundwell was the treasurer of the small city of Dixon, Illinois. In 2011, while she was out of the office, a city clerk filled in for Crundwell and came across a strange-looking bank account in the city's name. Money from the account was being used to purchase items such as jewelry and vehicles. The suspicious account was reported to the mayor and the Federal Bureau of Investigation (FBI). The FBI arrested Crundwell for municipal fraud. She was found guilty of stealing $53 million from the city of Dixon over more than two decades. Kathe Swanson, the clerk who reported the fraud, is known today for her whistleblowing that brought down Crundwell's corruption.

The most notable aspect of this case is how easy it would have been to detect the fraud if proper controls had been in place. For instance, Crundwell had accumulated hundreds of prize horses and various vehicles costing hundreds of thousands of dollars. On her tax returns, there were no documents to explain how she was making so much money—a fact that the city's accounting firm, CliftonLarsonAllen, should have questioned.

According to *All the Queen's Horses*, a documentary about the fraud, CliftonLarsonAllen had potential conflicts of interests in their dealings with Crundwell. The accounting firm wrote the financial statements for the city and then audited those statements. In addition, the firm handled Crundwell's personal taxes. Despite the fact that Crundwell had unexplainable cash inflow, the accounting firm never questioned her about the inconsistencies. Crundwell also provided fraudulent invoices for city projects that did not look legitimate (and weren't, it turned out). It should also have been relatively simple to check whether these projects were actually taking place.

The Fifth Third Bank and the city of Dixon also share part of the blame for the fraud. The bank allowed Crundwell to open an account without formal documentation, such as a corporate resolution. Checks were deposited under Crundwell's name rather than "City of Dixon." Furthermore, Dixon officials did not have the training in finances and accounting to understand city documents. When faced with a question about accounts they would just ask Crundwell. Therefore, she was considered to have expert power to run the city's finances in their entirety.

Dixon has since put in place several controls to prevent future fraud. After Crundwell was arrested, the city hired a new finance director who reorganized the city's finances and restructured the department. Internal controls were implemented so that no one person could complete an entire process alone. This included signing checks and approving payments.

The city council's role was changed into a managerial role, with the City Manager serving executively. New council members were elected, and a new mayor. The city hired more clerks that specialize in specific areas, such as payroll and billing. Mail, which had been picked up almost exclusively by Crundwell, is now sent directly to City Hall.

This case shows that massive fraud does not always have to involve an elaborate, hard-to-detect scheme. In fact, many instances of fraud would have been obvious if the right questions were asked and suspicions were investigated. Controls must always be adopted to ensure that financial gatekeepers are held accountable for the money in their charge.[1]

Shutterstock/Zuzule

Chapter Objectives

- Provide an overview of the need for an organizational ethics program
- Consider crucial keys to the development of an effective ethics program
- Demonstrate the elements of a corporate culture
- Examine leadership and its importance to an ethical corporate culture
- Discuss the requirements for ethical leadership

A strategic approach to ethical decisions will contribute to both business and society. This chapter provides a framework that is consistent with research, best practices, and regulatory requirements for improving ethical conduct within the organization. Some companies have not implemented effective business ethics programs, but they should because ethics and compliance programs create good systems to manage organizational misconduct. Our framework for developing effective ethics programs is consistent with the ethical decision-making process described in Chapter 6. In addition, the strategic approach to an ethics program presented here is consistent with the Federal Sentencing Guidelines for Organizations (FSGO), the Sarbanes-Oxley Act, and the Dodd-Frank Wall Street Reform and Consumer Protection Act described in Chapter 5. These legislative reforms require managers to assume responsibility and ensure that ethical standards are implemented properly on a daily basis. Ethics programs include not only the need for top executive leadership, but also responsibility by boards of directors for corporate governance. Unethical and illegal business conduct occurs, even in organizations that have ethics programs. For example, although Facebook has a code of conduct and is a member of the Better Business Bureau (BBB), the company continues to have issues with ethical treatment of users' information.[2]

Many business leaders believe that personal moral development and character are all that is needed for corporate responsibility. There are those who feel that ethics initiatives should arise inherently from a company's culture, and hiring good employees will limit unethical behavior within the organization. Many executives and board members do not understand how organizational ethical decisions are made, nor how to develop an ethical corporate culture. Customized ethics programs may help many organizations provide guidance for employees from diverse backgrounds to gain an understanding of acceptable behavior within the organization. Many ethical issues in business are complex and include considerations that require organizational agreement regarding appropriate action. Top executives and boards of directors must provide leadership, a system to resolve these issues, and support for an ethical corporate culture.

In this chapter, we provide an overview of why businesses need to develop organizational ethics and compliance programs. Next, we consider the factors that are crucial for the development of such programs: a code of conduct, an ethics officer and appropriate delegation of authority, effective ethics training, a system to monitor and support ethical compliance, and continual efforts to improve the ethics program. Next we discuss the institutionalization of business ethics through mandated and voluntary programs. We discuss the importance of ethical leadership to a company's ethics program. Finally, we examine the requirements of ethical leadership and its impact on organizational culture, including the different forms of communication that an ethical leader must master.

Scope and Purpose of Organizational Ethics Programs

Usually, an organization is held accountable for the conduct of its employees. Companies must assess their ethical risks and develop values and compliance systems to avoid legal and ethical mistakes that could damage the organization. The FSGO holds corporations responsible for conduct engaged in as an entity. Some corporate outcomes cannot be tied to one individual (or even a group), and misconduct can result from a collective pattern of decisions supported by a corporate culture. Therefore, corporations can be held accountable, fined, and even ordered to close their doors when they are operating in a manner inconsistent with major legal requirements. Organizations are typically careful to avoid infringing on employees' personal freedoms and ethical beliefs. In cases where an individual's personal beliefs and activities are inconsistent with company policies on ethics, conflict may develop. If the individual feels that ethics systems in the organization are deficient or directed in an inappropriate manner, some type of open conflict resolution may be needed to deal with the differences.

Understanding the factors that influence how individuals make decisions to resolve ethical issues, as discussed in Chapter 6, can help companies encourage ethical behavior and discourage undesirable conduct. Fostering ethical decisions within an organization requires eliminating unethical behavior and improving the firm's ethical standards. Some people will always do things in their own self-interest, regardless of organizational goals or accepted standards of conduct. For example, professional athletes know that using performance-enhancing drugs is prohibited, yet some players still choose to use them to gain an edge. Not only do athletes continue to use illegal substances like steroids to boost their performance, but doping using legal substances is becoming more and more common. For instance, Olympic swimmer Ryan Lochte was banned from the sport for 14 months after it was found that he had engaged in doping using an intravenous (IV) infusion that was over the limit and violated U.S. Anti-Doping Agency rules.[3] Eliminating inappropriate or abnormal behavior through screening techniques and enforcement of the firm's ethical standards can help improve the firm's overall ethical conduct.

Organizations can foster unethical corporate cultures not because individuals within them are bad, but because the pressures to succeed create opportunities that reward unethical decisions. A study by the Reboot Digital Agency found that 34 percent of respondents engaged in unethical behavior to meet deadlines. It also found that 33 percent of workers have witnessed management rewarding employees who engaged in unethical behavior to accomplish assignments. This not only adds incentives for unethical business practices, but also can demoralize employees who participate in ethical practices.[4]

In the case of an unethical corporate culture, the organization must redesign its ethical standards to conform to industry and stakeholder standards of acceptable behavior. Most businesses attempt to improve ethical decision-making by establishing and implementing a strategic approach to improving organizational ethics. Companies such as Texas Instruments (TI), Starbucks, and Levi's take a strategic approach to organizational ethics but monitor their programs on a continuous basis and make improvements when problems occur.[5]

To be socially responsible and promote legal and ethical conduct, an organization should develop **organizational ethics and compliance programs** by establishing, communicating, and monitoring ethical values and legal requirements that characterize its history, culture, industry, and operating environment. While some companies treat ethics and compliance initiatives separately, the trend is to combine ethics and compliance programs. Without such programs and uniform standards and policies of conduct, it is difficult for employees to determine what behaviors are acceptable within a company. As discussed earlier, in the absence of such programs and standards, employees generally will make decisions based on their observations of how their coworkers and managers behave. A strong ethics and compliance program includes a written code of conduct, an officer to oversee the program, careful delegation of authority, formal ethics training, auditing, monitoring, enforcement, and periodic revision of program standards. Without a strong customized program, problems are much more likely to arise. Figure 7.1 outlines the effectiveness of various types of misconduct training.

Trust in top management and business is low. According to the Grossman Group, there are seven traits that can aid in building trust within corporations. These traits include open communication with employees, transparency, and clear explanation of company values and expectations.[6] This is a recurring theme

organizational ethics and compliance programs programs developed by an organization to establish, communicate, and monitor ethical values and legal requirements that characterize its history, culture, industry, and operating environment

Figure 7.1 Effectiveness of Types of Misconduct Training

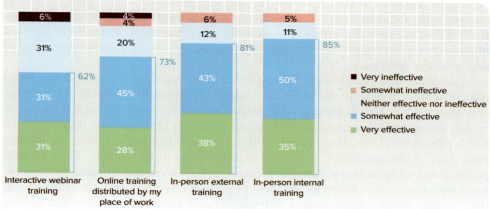

Source: Brunswick Insight, "Workplace Conduct: A U.S. Benchmark Study," October 29, 2018, https://www.brunswickgroup.com/media/4973/workplace-conduct_national-benchmark-study.pdf (accessed August 9, 2019).

among primary stakeholders. Employees are looking for clear, creative, and constructive leadership from chief executive officers (CEOs) that demonstrates trust is a priority.

No universal standards exist that can be applied to ethics programs in all organizations, but most companies develop codes, values, or policies for guidance about business conduct. The majority of companies that have been in ethical or legal trouble usually do have stated ethics codes and programs. **Ethics codes** are guidelines that businesses create to maintain their company's values and hold employees and employers accountable to ethical standards. Certain ethics codes are similar across businesses, such as intolerance of discrimination in the workplace, while other codes are specific to the company.[7] Often, the problem is that top management, as well as the overall corporate culture, has not integrated these codes, values, and standards into daily decision-making. For example, Justin Caldbeck, cofounder of Binary Capital, resigned after allegations were made against him for sexual harassment. These allegations included using his position to grant promotions in exchange for engaging in romantic relations with him, an act clearly against the company's ethics and values.[8] If a company's leadership fails to provide the vision and support needed for ethical conduct, then an ethics program will not be effective. Ethics is not something to be delegated to lower-level employees, while top managers break the rules. Excellent leaders must lead by example and reinforce the integrity of the organizational culture. Ethical leadership is so important that the Ethisphere Institute awards companies for their ethical practices. The institute named 128 companies as the World's Most Ethical Companies, including Best Buy, Canon, Hasbro, and Sony. To be included as one of the World's Most Ethical Companies, businesses must score high on the following five criteria: governance, corporate citizenship and responsibility, leadership and reputation, ethics and compliance program, and culture of ethics. In an era where business scandals can severely hurt an enterprise, being considered one of the most ethical companies is a major advantage when doing business.[9]

No matter what their specific goals, ethics programs are developed as organizational control systems, the aim of which is to create predictability and consistency in employee behavior. There are two types of organizational control systems. A compliance orientation creates order by requiring that employees identify with and commit to specific required conduct. It uses legal terms and statutes that teach employees the rules and penalties for noncompliance. The other type of system is a values orientation, which strives to develop shared values. Although penalties are

ethics codes
guidelines that businesses create to maintain their company's values and hold employees and employers accountable to ethical standards

attached, the focus is more on an abstract core of principles such as respect and responsibility. The goal is to create an environment where employees are compelled and willing to support an ethical organizational culture. More than half of employees in the KPMG Forensic Ethics Survey stated that they had observed misconduct that could cause "a significant loss of public trust if discovered." The industries in which this type of misconduct increased the most include electronics, chemicals and diversified industrials, consumer markets, and aerospace and defense.[10] The goal of an effective ethics program is to get employees to report wrongdoing when they become aware of it and seek guidance when they are uncertain as to how to respond in ambiguous circumstances.

Research into compliance and values-based approaches reveals that both types of programs can interact or work toward the same end, but a values orientation tends to have a stronger influence on employees. Values-based programs increase employees' awareness of ethics at work, their integrity, their willingness to deliver bad news to supervisors, and the perception that better decisions are made. Compliance-based programs are linked to employees' awareness of ethical issues at work and their perception that decision-making is better because of the expectations of its employees.

To meet the public's escalating demands for ethical decision-making, companies need to develop plans and structures for addressing ethical considerations. Some directions for the improvement of ethics have been mandated through regulations, but companies must be willing to have a values and ethics implementation system in place that exceeds the minimum regulatory requirements. By implementing values and ethics into corporate culture, businesses can encourage employees to take a personal interest in the company, thus creating more incentive to uphold ethical guidelines and report unethical behavior. Interestingly, companies that have experienced reputational damage in the past are much further along than their peers in establishing ethics and compliance programs.[11]

Codes of Conduct

Because people come from diverse family, educational, and business backgrounds, it cannot be assumed that they know how to behave appropriately when they enter a new organization or job. Most companies begin the process of establishing organizational ethics programs by developing **codes of conduct** (also called codes of ethics), which are formal statements that describe what an organization expects of its employees. Table 7.1 depicts elements of an effective ethics and compliance program (such as codes and training). Codes of ethics address risk areas that organizations face and that employees may experience in the workplace.

A code of ethics has to reflect the board of directors' and senior management's desire for organizational compliance with the values and principles, mission, rules, and policies that support a climate of high ethics. The development of a code of ethics should involve the board of directors, CEO, president, ethics and compliance officer(s), and senior managers who will be implementing the code. Legal staff should be called on to ensure that the code has correctly assessed key areas of risk and that potential legal problems are buffered by standards in the code. A code of ethics that does not address specific high-risk activities within the scope of daily operations is inadequate for maintaining standards that can prevent misconduct. Table 7.2 lists considerations in developing and implementing a code of ethics.

Texas Instruments (TI) is a large, multinational firm that manufactures computers, calculators, and other high-technology products. Its code of ethics has some of the elements listed in Table 7.2 as its base. It addresses issues relating to policies and procedures, government laws and regulations, acceptance of gifts,

codes of conduct
formal statements that describe what an organization expects of its employees; also called codes of ethics

Table 7.1 Elements of an Effective Ethics Program

1	Standards and codes	Used to prevent and detect criminal conduct by expressing what the right thing is, how it can be accomplished, and the expectations to which the employee is held. They should be communicated and written in a concise, clear language in codes of ethics.
2	Leadership and the ethics and compliance officer(s)	The company's board of directors usually oversees the implementation of the program, and a senior executive or committee of executives should be given overall responsibility for its compliance. Many ethics and compliance officers report to the CEO and interact with the board of directors on a regular basis.
3	Communication and effective training	The company must effectively implement the program through education and training. Training should be focused on industry-specific areas of risk and should not merely recite the law, but explicitly explain the company's policies and ask employees to think through complex "gray areas" that they may encounter in their day-to-day tasks.
4	Monitoring and disclosure	The ethics and compliance program should be implemented. Employees should be asked about the "unwritten rules" within the company to determine whether the program's goals match its actual operations. Employees must be provided with effective mechanisms through which they can anonymously or confidentially report potential misconduct or seek guidance on compliance issues, be protected against retaliation if they do make a report, and adequately follow up.
5	Observation and reinforcement	Appropriate incentives must be provided to encourage employees to comply with the program and impose appropriate disciplinary measures if audits reveal that employees fail to do so. It is important for the company to enforce these rules consistently to maintain the credibility of the program.
6	Corrective action	Misconduct must be addressed after it occurs, including self-reporting to the authorities at times. Reasonable steps must be taken to prevent similar misconduct in the future. In addition, the company's board or audit committee must receive regular and meaningful reports on audit results and the status of corrective action.

Source: Adapted from U.S. Federal Sentencing Guidelines, Chapter 8; 2012 Amendments to the U.S. Federal Sentencing Guidelines; Kristin Graham Koehler and Brian P. Morrissey, "Seven Steps for Developing an Effective Compliance and Ethics Program," *Chain Store Age*, January 3, 2013, http://chainstoreage.com/article/seven-steps-developing-effective-compliance-and-ethics-program (accessed August 9, 2019).

travel and entertainment, handling of proprietary information and trade secrets, and more.[12] To ensure that its employees understand the nature of business ethics and the ethical standards they are expected to follow, TI provides an "Ethics Quick Test" to help employees when they have doubts about the ethics of specific situations and behaviors. It urges employees to reflect upon the following questions and statements:

- Is the action legal?
- Does it comply with our values?
- If you do it, will you feel bad?
- How will it look in a news story?
- If you know it's wrong, don't do it! If you're not sure, ask.
- Keep asking until you get an answer.[13]

TI explicitly states what it expects of its employees and what behaviors are unacceptable. When such standards of behavior are not made explicit, employees sometimes base ethical decisions on their observations of the behavior of peers and management. The use of rewards and punishments to enforce codes and policies

Table 7.2 Developing and Implementing a Code of Ethics

Consider areas of risk and state the values as well as the conduct necessary to comply with laws and regulations. Values and principles are an important buffer in preventing serious misconduct.
Identify values and principles that specifically address current ethical issues.
Consider values and principles that link the organization to a stakeholder orientation. Attempt to find overlaps in organizational and stakeholder values.
Make the code understandable by providing examples that reflect values.
Communicate the code frequently, and in language that employees can understand.
Revise the code every year with input from organizational members and stakeholders.

limits the opportunity to behave unethically and increases employees' acceptance of ethical standards.

As we stated, codes of conduct may address a variety of situations, from internal operations to sales presentations and financial disclosure practices. For example, Coca-Cola has been recognized for having an excellent code of conduct for its employees. It covers topics such as the use of company assets, use of information, conflicts of interest, and dealing with external stakeholders. The code of conduct has great situational examples to educate employees in a practical way. Additionally, it provides in-depth definitions and disciplinary action standards in an easy-to-understand, visually appealing format for its readers.[14]

Research has found that corporate codes of ethics often have five to seven core values or principles, in addition to more detailed descriptions and examples of appropriate conduct.[15] The six values that have been suggested as desirable to appearing in the codes of ethics include (1) trustworthiness, (2) respect, (3) responsibility, (4) fairness, (5) caring, and (6) citizenship. These values will not be effective without distribution, training, and the support of top management in making the values a part of the corporate culture. Employees need specific examples of how the values can be implemented and guide ethical decision-making.

Codes of conduct will not resolve every ethical issue encountered in daily operations, but they help employees and managers deal with ethical dilemmas by prescribing or limiting specific actions. Many companies have a code of ethics, but is it communicated effectively? According to the Ethics Resource Center, the number of companies developing and implementing effective ethics and compliance programs is increasing each year.[16] A code that is placed on a website or in a training manual is useless if it is not reinforced on a daily basis. By communicating to employees both what is expected of them and what punishments they face if they violate the rules, codes of conduct curtail opportunities for unethical behavior and thereby improve ethical decision-making. For instance, Lockheed Martin has a comprehensive code of ethics available online to employees and the general public. The code specifies the company's values, employee rights, and how to report misconduct. Employees, including leadership, are required to engage in ethics awareness training every year, and business conduct compliance training is also provided to help workers understand and implement the code of ethics.[17] Codes of conduct do not have to be so detailed that they take into account every situation, but they should provide guidelines and principles that are capable of helping employees achieve the organization's ethical objectives and address risks in an accepted manner.

Ethics and Compliance Officers

As mentioned in Chapter 6, organizational ethics and compliance programs also must have oversight by a high-ranking person known to respect and understand

ethics officer
a high-ranking person known to
respect and understand legal and
ethical standards

compliance officer
one who develops and oversees
corporate compliance programs to
ensure compliance with state and
federal regulations

legal and ethical standards. This person is often referred to as an **ethics officer**, but can also be the general counsel, the vice president of human resource (HR) management, or any other officer. Corporate wrongdoings and scandal-grabbing headlines have a profound negative impact on public trust. To ensure compliance with state and federal regulations, many corporations are now appointing **compliance officers** and ethics and business conduct professionals to develop and oversee corporate compliance programs. Many firms combine these two roles.

Consistent enforcement and necessary disciplinary action are essential to a functional ethics and compliance program. The ethics or compliance officer is usually responsible for companywide disciplinary systems and for implementing all disciplinary actions the company takes in response to violations of its ethical standards. Many companies are including ethics and compliance in employee performance appraisals. During performance appraisals, employees may be asked to sign an acknowledgment that they have read the company's current guidelines on its ethics policies. The company must also promptly investigate any known or suspected misconduct. The appropriate official, often the ethics officer, needs to make a recommendation to senior management on how to deal with a particular ethics infraction. The Ethics & Compliance Initiative (ECI), discussed in Chapter 4, is a nonprofit organization that helps individuals and businesses understand the best practices for keeping their company at the highest level of integrity and shares strategies to maintain integrity and develop an in-house ethics program. ECI is the leading organization in providing independent research on workplace integrity and compliance practices.[18]

Ethics and compliance officers are instrumental in managing ethics programs and have the ear of top managers and boards of directors.[19] The ethics officer position has existed for decades, but its importance increased tremendously when the FSGO passed in 1991. The guidelines gave companies that faced federal charges for misconduct the incentive of fine reductions of up to 95 percent if they had an effective comprehensive ethics program in place. The financial reporting requirements of the Sarbanes-Oxley Act put more pressure on ethics officers to monitor financial reporting, as well as reporting of sales and inventory movements to prevent fraud in reporting revenue and profits. While not always deemed to be the most effective approach, it is recommended that ethics officers report directly to the board of directors. Building an ethics program and hiring an ethics officer to avoid fines will not be effective by themselves. Only with the involvement of top management and the board can an ethics officer earn the trust and cooperation of all key decision-makers. Ethics and compliance officers should be knowledgeable about the industry's laws and regulations, as well as adept at communicating and reinforcing values that build an ethical corporate culture. For example, Paula Goldman, the chief ethical and humane use officer for Salesforce.com, is responsible for knowing the ethical implications of new technology and to "develop a strategic framework for the ethical and humane use of technology" by the company.[20]

Ethics Training and Communication

Instituting a training program and a system of communication to disseminate the firm's ethical standards is a major step in developing an effective ethics program. Such training can educate employees about the firm's policies and expectations, relevant laws and regulations, and general social standards. Training programs can make employees aware of available resources, support systems, and designated personnel who can assist them with ethical and legal advice. Training also can help empower employees to ask tough questions and make ethical decisions.

Ethics officers provide the oversight and management of most ethics training. Although training and communication should reinforce values and provide learning opportunities about rules, risks, and acceptable behavior, it is only one part of an effective ethics program. The employee's capacity to exercise judgments that result in ethical decisions must be reinforced and developed. Ethics training should be customized to the specific risk areas they face. If ethical evaluations are not a part of regular performance appraisals, the message that employees will receive is that ethics is not an important component of decision-making. For ethics training to make a difference, employees must understand why it is conducted, how it fits into the organization, and their role in its implementation.

Top corporate executives must communicate with managers at the operations level (e.g., in production, sales, and finance) and enforce overall ethical standards within the organization. Table 7.3 lists the actions that are crucial to successful ethics training. It is most important to help employees identify ethical issues and give them the means to address and resolve such issues in ambiguous situations. In addition, employees must be offered direction on seeking assistance from managers or other designated personnel in resolving ethical problems. An effective ethics program can reduce criminal, civil, and administrative consequences, including fines, penalties, judgments, debarment from government contracts, and court control of the organization. An ineffective ethics program that does not ward off unethical acts may cause negative publicity, a decrease in organizational financial performance, and lowered stakeholder trust. An ethical disaster can be more damaging to an organization than a natural disaster because of the damage that occurs to organizational reputation.

Companies can implement ethical principles in their organizations through training programs. Discussions conducted in ethics training programs sometimes break down into personal opinions about what should or should not be done in particular situations. For example, Deluxe Corp. launched an ethics-compliance course that required employees to respond to multiple-choice questions. The course included scenarios including transgender harassment training. One employee felt that the response options did not support his religious beliefs and requested to be excused from the training course. Deluxe denied his request and suggested he take a 1 percent salary reduction for failing to complete the course. The employee went on to sue in the federal court under charges of discrimination. His charge was dismissed in court.[21]

To be successful, business ethics programs need to educate employees about how to identify and deal with business ethics issues. Employees are then able to

Table 7.3 Actions Crucial to Ethics Training

Identify the key ethical risk areas.
Relate ethical decisions to the organization's values, principles, and culture.
Communicate company codes, policies, and procedures regarding ethical business conduct.
Provide leadership training to model desired behavior.
Provide directions for internal questions and nonretaliatory reporting mechanisms.
Engage in regular training events using a variety of educational tools.
Establish manuals, websites, social media, and other communication to reinforce ethics training.
Evaluate and use feedback to improve training.

Source: © O. C Ferrell 2019.

Shutterstock/BlueBarronPhoto

base ethical decisions on their knowledge of appropriate actions, from an organizational perspective, rather than on emotions.

Training and communication initiatives should reflect the unique characteristics of an organization: its size, culture, values, management style, and employee base. It is important for the ethics program to differentiate between personal and organizational ethics. If ethics training is to be effective, it must start with a foundation, a code of ethics, commitment from all levels of the organization, and executive priorities on ethics that are communicated to employees. Managers from every department must be involved in the development of an ethics training program.

Most experts agree that one of the most effective methods of ethics training involves resolving ethical dilemmas that relate to actual situations employees may encounter while performing their jobs. For example, Lockheed Martin developed a training game called "Gray Matters." This training device includes dilemmas that can be resolved by teams. Each member of the team can offer his or her perspective and understand the ramifications of a decision for coworkers and the organization.[22]

Another training device is the behavioral simulation or role-play exercise, in which participants are given a short hypothetical ethical issue scenario to review. The participants are assigned roles within the hypothetical organization and are provided with varying levels of information about the issue. They then must interact to provide recommended courses of action representing short-term, mid-range, and long-term considerations. The simulation re-creates the complexities of organizational relationships and of having to address a situation without complete information. Learning objectives of the simulation exercise include (1) increased awareness by participants of the ethical, legal, and social dimensions of business decision-making; (2) development of analytical skills for resolving ethical issues; and (3) exposure to the complexity of ethical decision-making in organizations. Simulations help teach students about why ethics is important, as well as how to handle ethical conflict situations.[23]

A growing number of small businesses deliver learning-management systems software and content to train and certify employees on a variety of topics. In addition to streamlined training, the systems provide real-time records of instruction that increasingly are the first line of defense for companies facing litigation or questions about whether they are accountable for an employee's actions. The e-learning market is growing very rapidly, both in education and business. For multinational companies, the computerized training elements of such systems provide consistency of content and delivery to all locations and allow for customization of languages and to cultures.

Navex Global offers various ethics and compliance training programs that are trusted by 13,000 customers worldwide, including Toyota and Equifax. Its software platform provides custom-made training plans that are adaptable to a specific business's needs. They also published a first-of-its kind ethics and compliance benchmark report that gives insight about ethics and compliance research. Their report analyzes the elements of the most effective ethics and compliance programs. One identified element was risk-based training. They advise that ethics training should support various languages and take culturally sensitive approaches, as opposed to a one-size-fits-all training program. More advanced programs result in better performance and effectiveness and are ultimately a worthwhile investment for companies.[24]

Some of the goals of an ethics training program might be to improve employee understanding of ethical issues and the ability to identify them, to inform employees of related procedures and rules, as well as to identify the contact person who could help in resolving ethical problems. In keeping with these goals, the purpose of Boeing's Code of Ethics and Business Conduct program is to:

- Communicate the Boeing Values and standards of ethical business conduct to employees.
- Inform employees of company policies and procedures regarding ethical business conduct.
- Establish companywide processes to assist employees in obtaining guidance and resolving questions regarding compliance with the company's standards of conduct and the Boeing Values.
- Establish companywide criteria for ethics education and awareness programs.[25]

Ethical decision-making is influenced by organizational culture, by coworkers and supervisors, and by the opportunity to engage in unethical behavior. All three types of influence can be affected by ethics training. Full awareness of the philosophy of management, rules, and procedures can strengthen both the organizational culture and the ethical stance of peers and supervisors. Such awareness also arms employees against opportunities for unethical behavior and reduces the likelihood of misconduct. Thus, the existence and enforcement of company rules and procedures limit unethical practices in the organization. The primary goals of ethics training are to make employees aware of the risks associated with their jobs, industry, and stakeholders; provide an understanding of the culture and expectations within the organization; create accountability for individual actions; and inform employees not only of the behavior that is unacceptable, but also that which is acceptable and supported in the organization.

Establishing Systems to Monitor and Enforce Ethical Standards

Ethics and compliance programs also involve comparing employee ethical performance with the organization's ethical standards. Ethics programs can be measured through employee observation, internal audits, surveys, reporting systems, and investigations. An effective ethics program uses a variety of resources to effectively monitor ethical conduct. Sometimes external auditing and review of company activities are helpful in developing benchmarks of compliance and identifying areas for improvement.

Systems to Monitor and Enforce Ethical Standards

Many companies set up ethics assistance lines, also known as *hotlines*, to provide support and give employees the opportunity to ask questions or report concerns. The most effective ethics hotlines operate on an anonymous basis and are supported 24 hours a day, 365 days a year. Approximately 38 percent of the employees who report concerns indicated using their company's hotline to do so. In addition, 23 percent use the company's website to report misconduct, and 39 percent use other traditional methods such as face-to-face communication with supervisors or managers, email, fax, and direct mail.[26]

It is interesting that most of the issues reported do not relate to serious ethical and legal issues. More than 70 percent of the issues raised on hotlines relate to HR, diversity, and respectful treatment in the workplace. Other top issues reported include business integrity, at 17 percent; environment, health, and safety, at 7 percent; misuse or misappropriation of assets, at 5 percent; and accounting, auditing, and financial reporting, at 3 percent.[27]

A help line or desk is characterized by ease of accessibility and simple procedures, and it serves as a safety net that facilitates monitoring and reporting. Companies such as Global Compliance provide automated case management systems that collect, categorize, and communicate alerts to the appropriate managers for dealing with ethics issues in the organization. Companies are increasingly using case management services and software to track employees and issues throughout their entire organization. These programs provide reports of employee concerns, complaints, or observations of misconduct. Systems such as these allow the company to track investigations, analysis, resolutions, documentation, emerging/declining issues, and the time required for resolution.

In addition to hotlines, ethical counsel and education can be implemented as a system monitor. For example, Airbnb general counsel Robert Chesnut helps educate and promote ethics in the company in an extensive way. He helped the executives write the code of ethics and posed questions that encouraged them to think about how to best inform their employees on real-world scenarios, not just a copy-and-paste general code of ethics. He also has a goal to embed ethics into the office culture. He does this through training the company's new hires, saying it shows them in person how serious Airbnb is about ethics. He continues to enforce ethics among existing employees by sending a monthly video series to keep ethics at the top of everyone's minds. Airbnb has a reporting email and ethical advisers who are company employees that also serve as part-time volunteers for those struggling with an ethical dilemma.[28]

Observation and Feedback

To determine whether a person is performing his or her job adequately and ethically, observation might focus on how the person handles an ethically charged situation. For example, during role-plays in the training sessions of salespeople and managers, ethical issues can be introduced into the discussion, and the decisions can be videotaped and outcomes evaluated by managers.

Questionnaires that survey employees' ethical perceptions of their company, their superiors, their coworkers, and themselves, as well as ratings of ethical or unethical practices within the firm and industry, can serve as benchmarks in an ongoing assessment of ethical performance. Then, if unethical behavior is perceived to increase, management will have a better understanding of what types of unethical practices may be occurring and why. A change in the ethics training within the company may be necessary. In addition, organization-wide risk management systems identify new and emerging risks employees face and to which management must respond.

Appropriate action involves rewarding employees who comply with company policies and standards and punishing those who do not. When employees comply with organizational standards, their efforts may be acknowledged and rewarded through public recognition, bonuses, raises, or some other means. Conversely, when employees deviate from organizational standards, they may be reprimanded, transferred, docked of pay, suspended, or even fired.

Whistleblowing

Interpersonal conflict ensues when employees think that they know the right course of action in a situation, and yet their work group or company promotes or requires a different, possibly unethical decision. In such cases, employees usually follow their organization's values. If they conclude that they cannot discuss what they are doing or what should be done with their coworkers or immediate supervisors, these employees may go outside the organization to publicize and correct the unethical situation. Whistleblowing, as defined in Chapter 5, means exposing an employer's wrongdoing to outsiders, such as the media or government regulatory agencies.

Whistleblowers have provided pivotal evidence documenting wrongdoing at a number of companies. Since the institution of the Whistleblower Protection Act, many employees have come forward to reveal company misdeeds to government authorities. The Securities and Exchange Commission (SEC) awarded two people a total of $50 million when they provided evidence related to a settlement involving JPMorgan Chase. These whistleblowers were former employees of the bank, and one was an executive at the time that the misconduct took place. The tips provided led to the pursuit of JPMorgan because they were not disclosing to clients that they preferred to invest in their own mutual and hedge funds. The employee received $37 million, while the executive received $13 million. The SEC would not release any information regarding the two whistleblowers, including whether they still worked for JPMorgan.[29]

Despite these large monetary rewards, the fortunes of whistleblowers are peppered with negative pushback. Most are labeled traitors, many lose their jobs, and some find it difficult to gain new employment afterward. For example, associate medical examiner Dr. Megan Quinn of Pierce County, Washington was suspended from her job and accused of insubordination and sexual harassment after filing a whistleblower complaint against medical examiner Dr. Thomas Clark. Quinn had accused Clark of mishandling investigations into the deaths of children. Though she received a settlement of $450,000, and an independent investigation cleared Quinn of wrongdoing, she faced damage to her reputation and ultimately agreed to resign from her job.[30]

Critics have stated that the potential for large monetary sums related to whistleblowing encourage employees to come forward, regardless of whether their claims are valid. However, a survey by the Ethics Resource Center showed that only 14 percent of employees are motivated by such incentives. Rather, the majority of external reporting is a result of other factors, such as lack of trust in company authorities, experience of retaliation from prior internal reporting, and the fear of losing one's job.[31] Although the SEC has given many whistleblowers monetary rewards, whistleblowing is risky and involves a complex process. The threat of retaliation has decreased over the years, but it still occurs. Risking retaliation makes whistleblowing less desirable to many people, despite the potential monetary gains. The SEC has proposed new regulations for whistleblowing. For example, whistleblowers have to participate in external reporting, not just internal, to be considered a whistleblower. This may help mitigate any employees trying to gain money by reporting false events, while also helping those who are genuinely reporting misconduct in the workplace.[32] Because of the risks involved in becoming a whistleblower, an employee should ask questions before doing so. Table 7.4 provides a checklist of these possible questions.

Table 7.4 Questions to Ask Before Engaging in External Whistleblowing

Have I exhausted internal anonymous reporting opportunities within the organization?
Have I examined company policies and codes that outline acceptable behavior and violations of standards?
Is this a personal issue that should be resolved through other means?
Can I manage the stress that may evolve from exposing potential wrongdoing in my organization?
Can I deal with the consequences of resolving an ethical or legal conflict within my organization?

Source: © O. C. Ferrell 2019.

Continuous Improvement of the Ethics Program

Improving the system that encourages employees to make more ethical decisions is not very different from implementing other types of business strategies. *Implementation* means putting strategies into action. In the context of ethics and compliance, the term means the design of activities to achieve organizational objectives using available resources and given existing constraints. Implementation translates a plan for action into operational terms and establishes a means by which organizational ethical performance will be monitored, controlled, and improved.

A firm's ability to plan and implement ethical business standards depends in part on the organization's structuring of resources and activities to achieve its ethical objectives in an effective and efficient manner. Some U.S. companies are setting up computer systems that encourage whistleblowing. For instance, Marvin Windows (one of the world's largest custom manufacturers of wooden windows and doors) was concerned about employees feeling comfortable reporting violations of safety conditions, bad management, fraud, or theft. It established an anonymous system that allows reporting in native-country languages. This system is used to alert management to potential problems in the organization and to facilitate an investigation.[33] Systems such as these help alleviate employee concerns when reporting observed misconduct.

Once a company determines that its ethical performance has been unsatisfactory, the company's management may want to reorganize the way that certain ethical decisions are made. For example, a decentralized organization may need to centralize key decisions, if only for a time, so that top-level managers can ensure improved organizational decision-making. Centralization may reduce the opportunity for lower-level managers and employees to make unethical decisions. Top management can then focus on improving the corporate culture and infusing more ethical values throughout the organization. Dell Computer is an example of a centralized organization, possibly because of its focus on manufacturing processes. In other companies, decentralization of important decisions may be a better way to attack ethical problems so that lower-level managers, familiar with the forces of the local business environment and local culture and values, can make more decisions. Coca-Cola is a more decentralized company due to its use of independent distributors and unique localized cultures. Whether the ethics function is centralized or decentralized, the key need is to delegate authority in such a way that the organization can achieve ethical performance. For example, the former CEO of Samsung, Lee Jae-yong, was arrested on allegations of bribery. After his arrest and resignation, the company needed corrective action and improvement to establish standards in its ethics program. As a result, the corporate legal office of Samsung developed a compliance team and a Privacy Steering Committee to help advance their compliance management and decision-making within top management.[34]

Institutionalization of Business Ethics

To successfully implement ethics and compliance programs, managers should be aware of the core, legally mandated, and voluntary elements of organizational business practices. All three should be incorporated into an organization's ethics program. This generates an ethical culture that successfully controls and manages ethical risks. Institutionalization involves the legal and social forces that provide organizational rewards and punishments based upon stakeholder assessments of an organization's behavior. In business ethics, institutionalization is associated with the establishment of laws, regulations, norms, and organizational programs. A refusal to conform to what is believed to be ethical conduct is often perceived to be an ethical issue and a concern to stakeholders. Institutions involve obligations, structures, and social expectations that reward and limit ethical decisions. Federal agencies, for instance, are institutions that mandate laws for appropriate conduct. They may even recommend core practices for developing an ethical organizational culture.[35]

Voluntary, Core Practices, and Mandatory Boundaries of Ethics Programs

Table 7.5 describes the three elements of institutionalization. **Voluntary practices** are the beliefs, values, and voluntary responsibilities of an organization. All organizations engage in some level of voluntary activities to help different stakeholders.[36] These responsibilities often manifest themselves through philanthropy, which occurs when businesses give back to communities and causes. For instance, Home Depot strongly supports the nonprofit organization Habitat for Humanity and encourages employees to volunteer. Evidence suggests that a sense of the law and ethical behavior increases voluntary responsibility activities. Research has also confirmed that when a company's core practices support ethical and legal responsibilities, they enhance economic performance.[37]

voluntary practices
the beliefs, values, and voluntary responsibilities of an organization

Core practices are recognized best practices that are often encouraged by regulatory forces and industry trade associations. As mentioned in the previous chapter, the Better Business Bureau (BBB) provides guidance for managing customer conflicts and reviewing advertising disputes. Core practices are appropriate practices often common to the industry. They guarantee compliance with legal requirements and social expectations. Core practices align the expectations of consumers with a business in order to create satisfying exchanges.[38]

core practices
recognized best practices that are often encouraged by regulatory forces and industry trade associations

Although core practices are not enforced on a legal basis, businesses can face consequences for not engaging in them when misconduct occurs. For example, the FSGO provides incentives for firms that effectively implement core practices.

Table 7.5 Voluntary Boundary, Core Practices, and Mandated Boundaries of Ethical Decisions

Voluntary boundary	A management-initiated boundary of conduct (beliefs, values, voluntary policies, and voluntary responsibilities)
Core practices	Highly appropriate and common practices, often common to an industry, that help ensure compliance with legal requirements, industry self-regulation, and societal expectations
Mandated boundary	An externally imposed boundary of conduct (laws, rules, regulations, and other requirements)

Source: Adapted from the "Open Compliance Ethics Group (OCEG) Foundation Guidelines," v1.0, Steering Committee Update, December 2005, Phoenix; Open Compliance Ethics Group (OCEG), "Compliance Officers, Compliance Professionals Are Part of GRC," https://www.oceg.org/about/people-like-you-compliance/ (accessed November 20, 2019).

mandated boundaries
externally imposed boundaries
of conduct, such as laws,
rules, regulations, and other
requirements

If misconduct occurs, firms that have demonstrated best practices may be able to avoid serious penalties. However, if the board took no initiative to oversee ethics and compliance in the organization, its failure could increase the level of punishment the company experiences. In institutionalizing core practices, the government allows organizations to structure their own methods and takes action only if violations occur. **Mandated boundaries** are externally imposed boundaries of conduct, such as laws, rules, regulations, and other requirements. Laws regulating business competition are examples of mandated boundaries.

Organizations manage stakeholder expectations for ethical conduct through corporate governance mechanisms, compliance, risk management, and voluntary activities. Government initiatives and stakeholder demands have helped to institutionalize these drivers of an ethical organizational culture. For instance, the governing authority of an organization structures corporate governance to provide oversight, checks, and balances to ensure that the organization meets its ethical objectives. Compliance represents areas that must follow laws and regulations. Risk management examines the chance that misconduct may occur based on the type of business and the risk areas it commonly faces. Voluntary activities often involve the values and responsibilities organizations adopt in contributing to stakeholder expectations. For example, Novo Nordisk is a healthcare company that specializes in diabetes treatment. The business provides employees opportunities to volunteer up to 80 paid hours with various organizations.[39] According to their website, this allows the company to implement their Triple Bottom Line framework by honoring their values while keeping return on investment in mind.[40]

Ethical Leadership

A company's leaders provide the blueprint for an organization's corporate culture.[41] If organizational leaders do not display ethical conduct, the corporate culture will evolve on its own to exhibit the organization's norms and values. Consider the infamous accounting firm Arthur Andersen, once one of the "Big Five" accounting firms (they were reduced to the "Big Four" after Arthur Andersen's demise). Arthur Andersen, who founded the company, valued ethical behavior. In one situation, he refused to improperly record an accounting entry for a major client.[42] Contrast this to the firm named for him a few years before their demise, and you can see what can happen when an organization strays from ethical leadership. Without ethical leadership, an organizational culture cannot be maintained for long periods of time. Organizational leaders are important to ethical decision-making because they have the ability to motivate employees and enforce the organization's norms, policies, and procedures. Ethical leaders make certain that operational goals are achieved in an ethical manner. They do not simply allow employees to follow their individual moral codes, but enforce shared organizational values to support an ethical organizational culture. Ethical leaders also take the responsibility to model acceptable conduct for employees.[43] Ethical leadership is positively related to employee organizational citizenship; conversely, it is negatively related to employee misconduct. In other words, ethical leaders are more likely to have employees that support the organization's ethical culture and less likely to have employees that deviate from organizational values.[44]

One great example of an ethical leader is Bill Gates. He is one of the richest and most powerful people in business, but it doesn't seem like that has changed his character. In fact, it has amplified his ability to be able to contribute to causes he believes in and work harder to give to others. He and his wife, Melinda, have vowed to give away 95 percent of their wealth in their lifetime. The greatest example

Ethical Responsibilities in **BANKING**

Wells Fargo Pays the Price for Cultural Bankruptcy

In 2016, Wells Fargo announced the firing of thousands of employees for creating fake bank accounts. This has been followed by millions of dollars in settlements and a cap of Wells Fargo's assets by the Federal Reserve. No company wants negative publicity, and Wells Fargo has had plenty in recent years. To this day, the company is still trying to repair its reputation in the eyes of the public.

During the investigation of the fake accounts scandal, it was discovered that the employees who created the accounts were put under immense pressure to meet certain sales goals. According to one former branch manager, Susan Fischer, upper management informed her that the employees had to make the sales goals "no matter what." Another former branch manager, Rasheeda Kamar, stated in an interview that her district manager expected employees to convince customers to open accounts whether the customers needed them or not.

In addition to the pressures placed on the employees, branch managers were micromanaged and deluged with constant requests to report on the progress of their employees. If the employees did not make their numbers, the branch managers could be fired. Branch managers were not the only ones at risk of being fired for refusing to act unethically. Whistleblowers were also at risk. Some employees utilized the ethics hotline of the bank to report the unethical behavior, but there is evidence that these employees were fired in retaliation. As this is a violation of the Sarbanes-Oxley Act, the bank had to make restitution to these employees.

As a result of these actions, Wells Fargo lost the trust of customers and the general public. The irony of this scandal is that the bank offers a comprehensive code of conduct that specifies: "If you violate any provision of the Code or fail to cooperate fully with any inquiries or investigations, you will be subject to corrective action, which may include termination of your employment." While codes of conduct are necessary for businesses, they are ineffective if leadership does not follow them along with their employees.

In the aftermath of the scandal, Wells Fargo has been attempting to repair its reputation. In 2018, they launched an ad campaign called Re-Established. The first commercial released was titled "Trust" and featured a background on Wells Fargo's roots as a trusted carrier of gold in the 1800s. The commercial stated that "'we always found the way—until we lost it.'" The commercial went on to note that Wells Fargo planned on making things right for their customers by focusing on a recommitment to them. Reviews on the campaign were mixed, with some approving of Wells Fargo taking responsibility and others wanting more involvement from the CEO.

Wells Fargo launched another ad campaign called "This Is Wells Fargo." Its focus was on demonstrating positive customer service by showing employees helping customers in need of banking advice. The bank has also made visual changes to its promotional material (namely, changing the stagecoach and changing the yellow letters to white on its logo). Considering that the Wells Fargo logo was iconic and had endured for over 100 years, these changes were a big step in the bank's quest to recover from the 2016 scandal.

Sources: BusinessWire, "Wells Fargo Launches New Brand Campaign, 'This Is Wells Fargo,' Focused on Customer Experience," *AP News*, January 24, 2019, https://www.apnews.com/b4c9232e491940079183626835060086a (accessed June 3, 2019); Steve Cocheo and Bill Streeter, "Wells Fargo Unveils New Logo to Rebuild Its Battered Brand," *The Financial Brand*, 2019, https://thefinancialbrand.com/80290/wells-fargo-logo-rebrand/ (accessed June 3, 2019); Jackie Wattles, Ben Geier, Matt Egan, and Danielle Wiener-Bronner, "Well Fargo's 20-Month Nightmare," CNN Business, April 24, 2018, https://money.cnn.com/2018/04/24/news/companies/wells-fargo-timeline-shareholders/index.html (accessed June 3, 2019); Matt Egan, "The Two-Year Wells Fargo Horror Story Just Won't End," CNN Business, September 7, 2018, https://money.cnn.com/2018/09/07/news/companies/wells-fargo-scandal-two-years/index.html (accessed June 3, 2019); Erika Fry, "How Wells Fargo Is Dealing with Its Fake Accounts Scandal," *Fortune*, October 3, 2018, http://fortune.com/2018/10/02/wells-fargo-fake-phony-accounts-scandal/ (accessed June 3, 2019); James F. Peltz, "Wells Fargo Launches Ad Campaign to Leave Accounts Scandal Behind. Not Everyone is Buying It," *Los Angeles Times*, May 9, 2018, https://www.latimes.com/business/la-fi-wells-fargo-ad-campaign-20180509-story.html (accessed June 3, 2019); Matt Egan, "Wells Fargo Admits to Signs of Worker Retaliation," *CNN Business*, January 24, 2017, https://money.cnn.com/2017/01/23/investing/wells-fargo-retaliation-ethics-line/index.html?iid=EL (accessed June 3, 2019); "Wells Fargo Team Member Code of Ethics and Business Conduct," https://www.sec.gov/Archives/edgar/data/72971/000119312509127827/dex991.htm (accessed June 3, 2019); Jason Zuckerman, "OSHA Orders Wells Fargo to Pay $5.4M to Whistleblower," *Zuckerman Law: Whistleblower Protection Law Blog*, January 1, 2019, https://www.zuckermanlaw.com/osha-orders-wells-fargo-pay-5-4m-whistleblower/ (accessed June 3, 2019); Alan R. Kabat, "Retaliation Against Whistleblowers—The Wells Fargo Lesson," Bernabei & Kabat, PLLC, 2019, https://www.bernabeipllc.com/Articles/Retaliation-Against-Whistleblowers-The-Wells-Fargo-Lesson.shtml (accessed June 3, 2019).

Shutterstock/VDB Photos

of his ethical leadership is the Bill and Melinda Gates Foundation, which has donated billions of dollars to help research causes of all kinds, including healthcare for the poor in developing countries and education for youth in the United States. The foundation's goals show the character, ethical responsibility, and commitment of Gates and his wife.[45]

In addition to CEOs and managers, the board of directors is important in whether the organization displays ethical leadership. Legally, the board has a fiduciary duty to stakeholders to manage in the best interests of the organization. However, it is not always easy to determine what is in the best interests of the organization. A good example would be whether to engage in a risky activity that would result in short-term gains, but could cost the organization significantly in the long run. To determine the appropriate course of action, board members must consider the impact that a decision will have on different stakeholders.[46]

So far, we have discussed individuals in a position of authority within an organization. However, ethical leadership is not limited to authority figures. It should also be practiced by employees at all levels of the organization. Often, the actions of fellow employees significantly influence the ethical decision-making of an individual.[47] Thus, both leaders and regular employees within an organization have the responsibility to demonstrate ethical leadership when making decisions.

If stakeholders are dissatisfied with an organizational leader, that leader will not remain in that position. Ethical leaders must have the trust and respect of their followers. For instance, Martin Winterkorn, the former CEO of Volkswagen, stepped down after it was discovered that Volkswagen had installed defeat devices into its diesel vehicles to fool regulators. Although initially is was unclear whether Winterkorn knew about the misconduct, as the leader of the company, the misconduct occurred during his watch—hence, he was responsible.[48]

Just as strong ethical leadership plays a key role in guiding employee behavior, so does a strong corporate culture of support. A KPMG Forensic Integrity Survey asked employees whether the leaders of their companies displayed personal integrity and ethical leadership traits. Approximately 68 percent of employees indicated that leaders emphasized ethics and integrity in the organization.[49] These types of responses are becoming more common as organizations continue strengthening their ethics programs. The results of having an ethical focus are proving to be beneficial toward business operations. Challenges persist, however, and ethical leaders must be vigilant in nurturing the corporate culture of their organizations.

Leadership Power

As we have shown, organizational leaders use their power and influence to shape corporate culture. *Power* refers to the influence that leaders and managers have over the behavior and decisions of subordinates. An individual has power over others when his or her presence causes them to behave differently. Exerting power is one way to influence the ethical decision-making framework described in Chapter 6 (especially significant others and opportunity).

The status and power of leaders are directly related to the amount of pressure that they can exert on employees to conform to their expectations. A superior in a position of authority can put strong pressure on employees to comply, even when their personal ethical values conflict with the superior's wishes. For example, a manager might say to a subordinate, "I want the confidential data about our competitor's sales on my desk by Monday morning, and I don't care how you get it." A subordinate who values his or her job or who does not realize the ethical questions involved may feel pressured to do something unethical to obtain the data. Unfortunately, there has been an increase in pressure from employers toward employees. One study found that 16 percent of employees surveyed had experienced pressure to comply with unethical requests, which is higher than it was just a few years ago. In addition to placing employees in a difficult position, pressure to engage in unethical behavior by employers can lead to an increase in misconduct when the unethical behavior is rewarded by the boss.[50]

There are five power bases from which one person may influence another: (1) reward power, (2) coercive power, (3) legitimate power, (4) expert power, and (5) referent power.[51] These five bases of power can be used to motivate individuals to behave either ethically or unethically.

Reward Power   *Reward power* refers to using incentives to get people to change their behavior. Sometimes employee incentives can result in goal-fixation, which can lead to unethical behavior. It can increase dishonesty in managers' reporting when hitting certain targets results in bonuses. While incentives are not intentionally negative, they can lead to increased risk-taking, escalation of commitment, and lack of self-control. For example, service professionals such as auditors or lawyers bill hours against a target budget based on a fixed price. The incentive to overreport hours in order to make more money presents an ethical dilemma that would negatively affect the firm. Incentives at Wells Fargo encouraged sales staff to open new accounts. This resulted in opening millions of accounts for customers without their knowledge, damaging their credit rating.[52] This "carrot dangling" and incentives have been shown to be very effective in getting people to change their behavior in the long run. In the short run, however, it is not as effective as coercive power.

Coercive Power   Coercive power is essentially the opposite of reward power. Instead of rewarding a person for doing something, *coercive power* penalizes actions or behavior. As an example, suppose that a valuable client asks an industrial salesperson for a bribe and insinuates that he will take his business elsewhere if his demands are not met. Although the salesperson believes that bribery is unethical, her boss has told her that she must keep the client happy or lose her chance at promotion. The boss is also imposing a negative sanction if certain actions are not performed. Every year, 20 percent of Enron's workforce was asked to leave because they were ranked as "needs improvement," or because of other issues. Employees not wanting to fall into the bottom 20 percent engaged in corruption or showed complacency toward corruption.[53]

Coercive power relies on fear to change behavior. For this reason, it has been found to be more effective in changing behavior in the short run than in the long run. Coercion is often employed in situations where there is an extreme imbalance in power. However, people who are continually subjected to coercion may seek a counterbalance by aligning themselves with other more powerful persons or simply by leaving the organization. In firms that use coercive power, relationships usually break down in the long run. Power is an ethical issue not only for individuals, but also for work groups that establish policy for large corporations.

Legitimate Power   *Legitimate power* stems from the belief that a certain person has the right to exert influence and certain others have an obligation to accept it. The titles and positions of authority that organizations bestow on individuals appeal to this traditional view of power. Many people readily acquiesce to those who wield legitimate power, sometimes committing acts that are contrary to their beliefs and values. Betty Vinson, an accountant at WorldCom, objected to her supervisor's requests to produce improper accounting entries in an effort to conceal WorldCom's deteriorating financial condition. She finally gave in to their requests, however, after being told that this was the only way to save the company. She and other WorldCom accountants eventually pleaded guilty to conspiracy and fraud charges.[54]

Such loyalty to authority figures can also be seen in corporations that have strong charismatic leaders and centralized structures. In business, if a superior tells an employee to increase sales "no matter what it takes," and that employee has a strong affiliation to legitimate power, she may try anything to fulfill that order.

Expert Power   *Expert power* is derived from a person's knowledge (or at least the perception that the person possesses knowledge). Expert power usually stems from a superior's credibility with subordinates. Credibility, and thus expert power, is positively related to the number of years that a person has worked in a firm or industry, the person's education, or the honors that he or she has received for performance. Expert power can also be conferred on a person by others who perceive him or her as an expert on a specific topic. A relatively low-level secretary may have expert power because he or she knows specific details about how the business operates and can even make suggestions on how to inflate revenue through expense reimbursements.

Expert power may cause ethical problems when it is used to manipulate others or to gain an unfair advantage. Physicians, lawyers, or consultants can take unfair advantage of uninformed clients, for example. Accounting firms may gain extra income by ignoring concerns about the accuracy of financial data they are provided in an audit.

Referent Power   *Referent power* may exist when one person perceives that his or her goals or objectives are similar to another's. The second person may attempt to influence the first to take actions that will lead both to achieve their objectives. Because they share the same objectives, the person influenced by the other will perceive the other's use of referent power as beneficial. For this power relationship to be effective, however, some sort of empathy must exist between the individuals. Identification with others helps to boost the decision-maker's confidence when making a decision, thus increasing his or her referent power.

Consider the following situation: Lisa Jones, a manager in the accounting department of a manufacturing firm, has asked Michael Wong, a salesperson, to speed up the delivery of sales contracts so that the revenue could be reported in the current quarter. Michael protests that he is not to blame for the slow process. In this case, Lisa is using referent power. She invites Michael to lunch, and they discuss some of their work concerns. They agree to speed up document processing, and Lisa suggests that Michael start asking for contracts that he expects in the next quarter. He agrees to give it a try, and within several weeks, the contracts are moving faster and revenue has increased in the current quarter. Lisa's job is made easier, and Michael gets his commission checks a little sooner. The one issue that they would need to be aware of and prevent is channel stuffing in order to remain ethical with their referent power relationship.

The five bases of power are not mutually exclusive. People typically use several power bases to effect change in others. Although power in itself is neither ethical nor unethical, its use can raise ethical issues. Sometimes a leader uses power to manipulate a situation or a person's values in a way that creates a conflict with the person's value structure. For example, a manager who forces an employee to choose between staying home with his sick child and keeping his job is using coercive power, which creates a direct conflict with the employee's values.

The Role of an Ethical Corporate Culture

Top management sets the tone for the ethical culture of an organization. If executives and CEOs do not explicitly address ethics issues, a culture may emerge where unethical behavior is sanctioned and rewarded. To be most successful, ethical standards and expected behaviors should be integrated throughout every organizational process, from hiring, training, compensating, and rewarding to firing. This requires ethical leadership. An ethical organizational culture is important to employees. A fair, open, and trusting organizational climate supports an ethical culture and can be attributed to lower turnover and higher employee satisfaction. Southwest Airlines has a very strong organizational culture that has remained consistent from the days of its key founder, Herb Kelleher. All Southwest employees have heard the stories of Kelleher engaging employees and emphasizing loyalty, teamwork, and the creation of a fun environment. By placing importance on employees first, customers next, and shareholders last, while maintaining care for all three stakeholders, Kelleher built a unique culture that has succeeded for almost 50 years. He strove to treat employees like family. Today, Southwest continues that legacy and culture. Pilots willingly support the Adopt-A-Pilot program, which allows students countrywide to adopt a Southwest pilot to mentor their classroom for a four-week educational program.[55]

Some leaders assume that hiring or promoting good, ethical managers will automatically produce an ethical organizational climate. This ignores the fact that an individual may have limited opportunity to enforce his or her own personal ethics on management systems and informal decision-making that occurs in the organization. The greatest influence on employee behavior is peers and coworkers.[56] Many times, workers do not know what constitutes specific ethical violations such as price fixing, deceptive advertising, consumer fraud, and copyright violations. The more ethical the culture of the organization is perceived to be, the less likely it is that unethical decision-making will occur. For example, FedEx maintains a strong ethical culture and has woven its values and expectations throughout the company. FedEx's open-door policy specifies that employees may bring up any work issue or problem with any manager in the organization.[57]

In the event that unethical decision-making does occur, businesses should address it and seek to resolve the problem quickly. When this action does not occur, businesses are vulnerable to misconduct. Over time, an organization's failure to monitor or manage its culture may foster questionable behavior.

Requirements of Ethical Leadership

Ethical leaders develop their skills through years of training, experience, and learning.[58] In identifying what makes an effective leader, there is no clear consensus of the exact skills needed. However, there are certain skills that seem to be common to ethical organizational leaders. To be ethical organizational leaders, individuals should model corporate values, place the organization's own interests above their own, understand their employees, develop tools for reporting, and recognize the limitations of organizational rules and values.[59] Additionally, ethical leaders should never ignore issues of misconduct.

Ethical leaders do not live in a vacuum; they are constantly interacting with others to encourage them to develop ethical leadership skills. Perhaps the best ethical leaders recognize their own limitations and establish strong support networks within the organization to help them in the decision-making process. In so doing, they motivate employees toward reaching their full potential and emphasize their importance to the organization.[60] They also establish incentives for those in the organization who train new leaders.[61] Developing effective ethical leaders should be a never-ending process within an organization.

Archie Carroll developed a list of characteristics called the "7 Habits of Highly Moral Leaders," based on Stephen Covey's *The 7 Habits of Highly Effective People*.[62] We have adapted Carroll's work to develop "The 7 Habits of Strong Ethical Leaders."[63] These characteristics include (1) having a strong personal character, (2) having a passion to do what is right, (3) being proactive, (4) considering stakeholder interests, (5) modeling the organization's values, (6) being transparent and actively involved in organizational decision-making, and (7) being a competent manager who takes a holistic view of the firm's ethical culture. Ethical leadership requires holistic thinking that is willing to take on the challenging issues that organizations face every day. Strong ethical leaders have the knowledge and courage to put together important information in order to make the most ethical decision. Various stakeholder demands and conflicts make this a major challenge, but ethical leaders are up to the task. Above all, ethical leaders abide by their principles. This might even require the leader to leave the organization if he or she feels that the culture is too unethical to change.

Additionally, effective ethical leaders are so passionate about the organization and its success that they place the organizations' interests above their own.[64] It also requires them to align employees behind a shared vision.[65] Ethical leaders are concerned with the legacy of their companies, desiring for the company's success to continue long after they are gone. For example, actor Paul Newman's legacy in the retail industry has continued more than a decade after his death. Newman committed to and succeeded at giving all of the revenue from his company, Newman's Own, to charity. While companies cannot give away all of their revenue as he did, placing importance on ethical allocation of funds and corporate social responsibility (CSR) is vital for businesses. Newman's company serves as a guide for philanthropic and ethical business today.[66]

Ethical leaders must be proactive in anticipating, planning, and acting to avoid potential ethical crises.[67] They shoulder the important responsibility of developing effective ethics programs to guide employees in their ethical decision-making. Ethical leaders understand social needs and develop core practices of ethical leadership. Former vice chairman Tom Mendoza of NetApp told managers to let him know when employees were "doing something right." Mendoza then called the employees to thank them. He averaged approximately 10–20 personal "thank you" calls per day.[68] Recognizing employee accomplishments in promoting ethical conduct is a great way to make employees feel appreciated and reinforce an ethical organizational culture.

Finally, ethical leaders should be role models. If leaders do not model the values that they advocate, then those values become little more than window dressing. Behavioral scientist Brent Smith claims that leaders acting as role models are the primary influence on individual ethical behavior. On the other hand, leaders whose decisions go against the organization's values signal to employees that their ethical values are meaningless.[69] Whole Foods is an example of a company that strongly supports its core values. In addition to providing quality products, Whole Foods establishes employee well-being through the creation of a transparent workplace. To reduce the power gap between executives and employees, a salary cap has been placed on executive compensation. Each Whole Foods store donates at least 5 percent of profits to its communities.[70] Table 7.6 displays the core values of Whole Foods.

Table 7.6 The Core Values of Whole Foods

Sell the highest-quality natural and organic products.
Satisfy, delight, and nourish our customers.
Support team member happiness and excellence.
Create wealth through profits and growth.
Serve and support our global and local communities.
Practice and advance environmental stewardship.
Create ongoing win-win partnerships with our suppliers.
Promote the health of our stakeholders through healthy eating education.

Source: "Our Core Values," Whole Foods Markets, https://www.wholefoodsmarket.com/mission-values/core-values (accessed July 12, 2019).

Benefits of Ethical Leadership

Perhaps the most important influence of ethical leadership is its impact on organizational culture.[71] Because ethical leaders communicate and oversee the implementation of an organization's values, they make certain that employees are familiar with core beliefs.[72] Some may provide incentives for ethical conduct, such as rewards for making ethical decisions. These incentives have a positive impact on ethical conduct among employees.[73] Teaching employees to value integrity is a key component in creating an ethical organization.

Research has shown that ethical leadership tends to favor higher employee satisfaction and commitment.[74] Employees seem to like working for ethical companies and are more likely to stay with ethical organizations.[75] This saves the firm money and leads to higher productivity. Employees at The Container Store are provided with 263 hours of training, receive higher pay than at competing stores, and are shown appreciation through events like We Love Our Employees Day. This strong organizational culture has resulted in a turnover rate of 10 percent—compared to 100 percent for other retailers in the industry.[76]

In addition to employee satisfaction and productivity, ethical leadership creates strong connections with stakeholders external to the organization. Studies have revealed that customers are willing to pay higher prices for products from companies they consider to be ethical.[77] More than 90 percent of Millennials buy more products from ethical companies than they do from companies perceived to be unethical.[78] A major factor in this purchasing pattern is trust. If consumers do not trust the business, they are much less likely to buy products from that business. Fortunately the Edelman Trust Barometer found that trust has increased toward nongovernmental organizations (NGOs) and businesses among the informed public and has remained neutral for the general population.[79] Consumer trust for businesses still has a long way to go after the latest recession, and organizations that can establish trust are likely to receive a large and loyal customer following.

Ethical leadership also affects an organization's long-term value. Evidence shows that the ethical commitment of organizational members is positively associated with the organization's value on the stock market.[80] This is because reputation has a profound influence on whether an investor will even give money to a company. Investors consider risk a major factor in their funding decisions, and because corporate social responsibility (CSR) programs are negatively related to long-term risks, ethical conduct is likely to improve reputation and consequently lower the risks of investment.[81] As already discussed in the previous chapters, from a regulatory standpoint, organizations demonstrated as having strong ethics programs are more likely to see reduced penalties if misconduct should happen.[82] By creating strong relationships with a variety of stakeholders, ethical leaders are able to develop major competitive advantages for their organizations. For example, Coca-Cola engages with various stakeholders, including bottling partners, customers, the community, trade groups, and shareholders. In addition, the company is active in the World Economic Forum and the United Nations Global Compact.[83]

Leadership Styles

Leadership styles affect not only how a leader leads but also how employees accept and/or adhere to organizational norms and values.[84] Clearly, leadership styles that reinforce the development of organizational values are beneficial. These styles of leadership affect the organization's communication and oversight of values, norms, and ethics codes.[85] The challenge that leaders face is earning employee trust. This trust is imperative if a leader hopes to guide employees into ethical decision-making. Trustworthy leaders tend to be seen as ethical stewards.[86] Employees often look to their organizational leaders to determine how to respond to a situation, even when that response may be ethically questionable.

Shutterstock/fizkes

Effective ethical leadership requires the leader to understand the organization's vision and values, ethical challenges, and risks involved in accomplishing their objectives. One of the biggest assumptions is that those who fail in ethical leadership do not have an ethical character. This is a fallacy. In reality, there are a number of examples of people implicated in misconduct who appeared to have good character. For instance, Rajat Gupta, who was convicted for passing on insider trading tips, has been recognized for his strong philanthropic endeavors and exceptional kindness.[87]

Ethical leaders must learn from their experiences and gain knowledge about appropriate practices. They display transparency in their leadership and have the ability to both understand current ethical issues and anticipate future issues. These leaders often adopt a stakeholder orientation approach to management. Peter Lynch, the former Fidelity manager, was so successful with the company that he was able to retire at age 46, just 13 years after taking over the Magellan Fund. He encouraged investors to become knowledgeable about their investments, and his leadership benefited stakeholders immensely, with an annual 29 percent return on investment.[88] It is also important to note that even the most ethical leaders are human; they will make ethical mistakes, but how they acknowledge these mistakes is often what separates them from other leaders.

One important characteristic that many ethical leaders appear to possess is **emotional intelligence**, or the skills to manage themselves and their relationships with others effectively. Emotionally intelligent leaders are characterized by self-awareness, self-control, and relationship building. They see their efforts as achieving "something greater than themselves."[89] Warren Buffett and Howard Schultz are examples of emotionally intelligent leaders. These leaders are able to motivate employees to support a common vision, making them feel that their efforts matter in the successful operation of the organization.[90] Because emotionally intelligent leaders exhibit self-control and self-awareness, they are more proficient in tackling stressful and challenging situations. Because of the impact of emotional intelligence on the success of the organization, some employers have begun viewing emotional intelligence as more important than IQ.[91]

Daniel Goleman examined leadership styles based upon emotional intelligence. He came up with the following six styles:[92]

emotional intelligence
an important characteristic possessed by ethical leaders, referring to the skills to manage themselves and their relationships with others effectively

1. The coercive leader requires complete obedience and focuses on achievement, initiative, and self-control. This style can be highly effective during times of crisis but tends to be detrimental to long-term performance.
2. The authoritative leader motivates employees to follow a shared vision, embraces change, and creates a strongly positive performance climate.
3. The affiliative leader values people and their needs. This leader depends upon friendship and trust to encourage flexibility and innovation.
4. The democratic leader values participation and teamwork to develop collaborative decisions. This style focuses heavily on communication and creating a positive work climate.
5. The pacesetting leader sets high standards of performance. This style works well for achieving quick results from motivated, achievement-oriented employees but can have negative results due to its stringent performance standards.

6. The coaching leader creates a positive work climate by developing skills to promote long-term success, delegating responsibility, and assigning challenging assignments.

Using Goleman's research, Richard Boyatzis and Annie McKee came up with the idea of a resonant leader. *Resonant leaders* are mindful of their emotions, believe that goals can be achieved, and display a caring attitude toward other employees. This leads to resonance within the organization, enhancing collaboration and the ability of employees to work toward shared goals.[93] Resonant leaders are highly effective in creating an ethical corporate culture, as well as strong relationships with employees.

The most successful leaders tend to adapt their styles based upon the situation. Leadership style relies heavily on how the leader measures risks as well as his or her desire to attain a positive corporate culture. Like other leadership characteristics, many emotional intelligence skills can be learned. Starbucks places great importance on emotional intelligence. New employees at the company undergo a training program called the "Latte Method" to learn how to detect negative emotions from their customers and the best ways of responding to them.[94]

Two dominant leadership styles in an organization are transactional and transformational. **Transactional leadership** attempts to create employee satisfaction through negotiating for levels of performance or "bartering" for desired behaviors. **Transformational leadership**, in contrast, tries to raise the level of commitment of employees and creates greater trust and motivation.[95] Transformational leaders attempt to promote activities and behavior through a shared vision and common learning experiences. Both transformational and transactional leaders can positively influence an organizational climate.

Transformational leaders communicate a sense of mission, stimulate new ways of thinking, and enhance as well as generate new learning experiences. Transformational leadership considers the employees' needs and aspirations in conjunction with organizational needs. Therefore, transformational leaders have a stronger influence on coworker support and the building of an ethical culture than transactional leaders. Transformational leaders also build a commitment to and respect for values that provide agreement on how to deal with ethical issues. Transformational ethical leadership is best suited for higher levels of ethical commitment among employees and strong stakeholder support for an ethical climate.

A number of industry trade associations, such as the American Institute of Certified Public Accountants, Defense Industry Initiative on Business Ethics and Conduct, and the Ethics and Compliance Officer Association, are assisting companies in providing transformational leadership.[96] Research suggests that organizations with transformational leadership are more likely to be involved in CSR activities.[97]

Transactional leadership focuses on ensuring that the required conduct and procedures are implemented. The "barter" aspects of negotiations to achieve the desired outcomes result in a dynamic relationship between lenders and employees where reactions, conflicts, and crises influence the relationship more than ethical concerns. Transactional leaders produce employees who achieve a negotiated level of required ethical performance or compliance. So long as employees and leaders find the exchange mutually rewarding, the compliance relationship is likely to be successful. However, transactional leadership is best suited to quickly changing ethical climates or ethical problems or issues. After a major leadership scandal at Tyco resulted in the conviction of CEO Dennis Kozlowski and the removal of its board members, the need for quick action to pull up the struggling company was apparent. Without a quick turnaround—both in leadership and in the company's ethical conduct—Tyco may not have survived. Eric Pillmore was hired to be the senior vice president of corporate governance at Tyco. Pillmore had to institute ethics and corporate governance decisions quickly to aid in the turnaround. He

transactional leadership
a leadership style that attempts to create employee satisfaction through negotiating for levels of performance or "bartering" for desired behaviors

transformational leadership
a leadership style that tries to raise the level of commitment of employees and creates greater trust and motivation

helmed a new ethics program that changed leadership policies and gave him direct communications with the board of directors.[98]

Other leadership experts are classifying leaders into a new category based on how they model organizational values. Authentic leadership includes individuals who are passionate about the organization, display corporate values in their daily behavior at work, and establish enduring relationships with stakeholders. Kim Jordan, the former CEO of craft brewery New Belgium Brewing (NBB), is an example of an authentic leader. She constantly attempts to embody NBB's purpose statement, to "manifest our love and talent by crafting our customers' favorite brands and proving business can be a force for good."[99] Jordan has also successfully aligned employees at NBB toward a shared goal of providing high-quality products, improving sustainability, and embracing a stakeholder orientation.

Authentic leadership can also be learned. In fact, authentic leaders often learn by observing the successful leadership habits of other strong leaders.[100] Authentic leaders possess principle-centered power, meaning that they can handle difficult situations and are extremely dedicated to their organizations.[101] They also exhibit organizational core values and incorporate these values into daily operations. This type of leadership should be the aim for all ethical leaders in an organization.

Leader-Follower Relationships

leader–follower congruence
when leaders and their followers (i.e., employees) share the same organizational vision, ethical expectations, and objectives

Communication is the key to establishing strong relationships between organizational leaders and employees. **Leader–follower congruence** takes place when leaders and their followers (i.e., employees) share the same organizational vision, ethical expectations, and objectives. It is important for ethical leaders to get employees to adopt shared organizational goals and values. If employees feel that the organizational leaders are unapproachable, this will create a major obstacle to the achievement of the organization's vision and objectives.[102]

On the other hand, leaders may take the opposite approach by micromanaging employees. Managing employees too closely will make them feel stifled and give them the feeling that the management does not trust them. Micromanagement in organizations is associated with lower morale, decreased productivity, and greater tendency to leave the company.[103] These disadvantages can be avoided when ethical leaders use communication to develop respectful relationships with employees. These more positive relationships tend to increase job satisfaction and employee commitment.[104]

Because organizational leaders are often managers or executives, they may not work very much with lower-level employees. This could create a sense of isolation in which the leader feels cut off from other employees. The more isolated organizational leaders are, the less connected they will be with employees—and the less likely they will be to detect organizational misconduct. Instead, ethical leaders must interact frequently with employees. This takes the form of not only speaking with them, but also listening to them and encouraging them to provide feedback. Often employees tend to want to avoid discussing ethical issues in the workplace. To get past this hesitation, ethical leaders must proactively communicate the firm's ethical values and develop a transparent workplace, in which employees can feel comfortable expressing concerns.[105] We discuss communication in more detail in the next section. When organizational leaders and employees are on the same page, they are able to advance the organization's goals and culture more effectively.

Ethical Leadership Communication

The development of an ethical culture is impossible without strong communication in the organization. If an organizational leader communicates through highly controlling speech that tolerates little criticism, employees will be reluctant to

Table 7.7 Communication Skills for Becoming an Ethical Leader

Tell employees the truth about the leader's conduct.
Listen to employee concerns about ethical issues they observe.
Engage in direct personal communication about appropriate conduct.
Use coaching to provide expectations about behavior.
Include performance feedback on ethical evaluations.
Be sure that your feedback on ethical conduct is correct.
Always ask for feedback from employees.
Continue to develop your leadership skills.

bring up any ethical issues or problems.[106] However, ethical leaders understand the importance of frequent communication and interaction with employees. Table 7.7 lists the communication skills needed to become better leaders.

An ethical culture must contain both transparency and strong mechanisms for reporting. Ethical leaders in the organization must create a transparent environment where ethics is frequently discussed. This helps remove the idea that discussing issues is a taboo topic. Reporting occurs when organizational leaders and their employees communicate. Most of the time, employees report to the leaders. However, ethical leaders should also be responsible for reporting crucial information to employees to promote an ethical workplace and advance organizational goals.

Reporting can be either formal or informal. Formal reports occur in contexts such as conferences and meetings. An important tool for formal reporting is an anonymous ethics hotline that employees can use to report concerns, as discussed previously. Informal reporting is no less important. It happens when ethical leaders interact with their employees to keep them apprised of organizational policies, expectations, and decisions.[107] Informal discussions are incredibly important in identifying ethical risk areas, as concerns are frequently expressed through casual conversations. Ethical leaders must recognize the importance of both formal and informal communication mechanisms.

Just as individuals can learn leadership skills, they can learn how to communicate effectively. Effective communication skills are often developed and honed through training and experience. Organizational communication necessary for the establishment of an ethical culture includes the following: interpersonal communication, small group communication, nonverbal communication, and listening. Table 7.8 summarizes the four categories of communication.

Interpersonal Communication   Interpersonal communication is the most common form of communication. It occurs when two or more people communicate with one other.[108] A meeting between an employee and her supervisor is an example of interpersonal communication. Interpersonal communication (versus small group

Table 7.8 Four Categories of Communication

Communication	Description
Interpersonal	When two or more people communicate with one another
Small group	Communication that occurs in small groups
Nonverbal	Expressed through body language, actions, expressions, tone of voice, proximity, volume, rhythm, or any other way that is not oral or written
Listening	Actively paying attention to another person's verbal or nonverbal behavior

communication) is more intimate because fewer people are involved. This type of communication should occur often within an organization because it gives ethical leaders a greater chance to uncover ethical risk areas, create better employee relationships, and encourage feedback about the organization's ethical climate. For interpersonal communication to be effective, ethical leaders must show the employee respect and dignity in order to maintain a positive relationship—even during disciplinary procedures. Respecting an employee means that the leader cares about what the employee has to say. On the other hand, this does not mean that ethical leaders should ignore or compromise on unethical employee conduct. It is less about placating an employee and more about showing him or her dignity as a person.

It is not uncommon for employees to feel intimidated by their superiors due to power differences.[109] An ethical leader can use communication to reassure employees, as well as balance the interests of all relevant stakeholders.[110] A good way to reduce perceived power distances is for the ethical leader to be open and respectful to the employee instead of being judgmental. This approach helps make employees feel more comfortable about bringing up ethical concerns.[111]

Communication is not always black-and-white. Like many ethical issues, there are times when an ethical leader will have different options on what to communicate, with some being more or less ethical than others. For instance, lying to a customer is clearly unacceptable, but white lies that do not damage stakeholders (such as complimenting an employee on a haircut despite the fact that it looks awful) may be permissible in some instances. Additionally, as the Rajat Gupta example from earlier demonstrates, communication that is not thought out carefully can have serious consequences. For Gupta, giving his friend Raj Rajaratnam from the Galleon Group nonpublic information directly violated the law. Ethical leaders will encounter numerous situations in which they must consider the ethical consequences of communication with stakeholders. Leaders who strongly support ethical interpersonal communication can empower employees while promoting the organization's ethical objectives.

Small Group Communication   Small group communication is becoming increasingly important to ethical decision-making.[112] Because ethical decision-making does not occur in a silo, small group communication is often necessary in order for people to investigate and select the most ethical course of action. Small group communication has an advantage over interpersonal communication because it increases collaboration, explores more options, and allows employees to participate more in ethical decision-making. Small groups generate a variety of perspectives on a particular issue, enabling ethical leaders to look at an issue from a number of different angles. This diversity of perspectives can lead to better solutions than if the leader had tried to arrive at the outcome individually.

Small groups also help to create checks and balances through accountability. An effective team holds individual members accountable for their contributions. For effective small group communication to take place, all small group members should feel comfortable with contributing input, understand the organization's ethical values, be trained in ethical communication, know how to listen to the input of other members, try to understand the other person's point of view, demonstrate a readiness to seek common agreement, investigate different alternatives, and commit to choosing the most ethical solution.[113]

However, ethical leaders should also recognize the limitations of small group communication. Sometimes routine group decision-making can cause the group to overlook possibilities. It is also not uncommon for teams to experience groupthink or group polarization. **Group polarization** is the tendency to decide on a more extreme solution than an individual might choose on his or her own. A small group, for instance, might choose to pursue a riskier decision than normal.[114] Groupthink is when group members feel pressured to conform to the consensus, even if they personally disagree with it. This could result in a less-than-optimal ethical decision.

group polarization
the tendency for a team to decide on a more extreme solution than an individual might choose on their own

Nonverbal Communication Nonverbal communication is a dimension of ethical communication that is just as important as spoken forms. It is expressed through body language, actions, expressions, tone of voice, proximity, volume, rhythm, or any other way that is not oral or written. Nonverbal communication is important because it provides clues to an individual's emotional state.[115] Paralanguage, which includes the way we talk, can indicate whether a person is angry, sad, happy, or feeling other emotions. Often nonverbal communication is more trustworthy than spoken communication. For instance, although a person might say one thing, if his or her body language communicates something else, then the nonverbal communication is often a better indicator of what the person really means. This is because nonverbal communication is harder to control than the spoken word, as much of it occurs in the subconscious. One study found that up to 70 percent of communication is nonverbal. This is seen mostly with emotional content and works in tandem with verbal communication.[116]

Nonverbal communication helps to clarify ambiguous or confusing language, alerting the communicator about whether the recipient understands the message. Because nonverbal communication provides important insights into a person's feelings, ethical leaders should pay careful attention to their employees' nonverbal cues. Sometimes permission to engage in unethical activities is granted by an expression or nodding of the head. They should also be careful to monitor their own nonverbal cues so that they do not give the wrong impression to employees.

Listening Ethical communication is not limited to speaking or communicating nonverbally. It also involves actively listening to the other person's verbal or non-verbal behavior.[117] Communication between stakeholders cannot occur without listening. Organizational leaders who fail to listen can overlook ethical issues and fail to stop them before they snowball into a crisis. In fact, many employees have cited the failure to listen as one of their top complaints in the workplace, so listening to employee concerns is crucial in advancing an ethical organizational culture.[118] Without listening, ethical leaders cannot learn important information from employee reports necessary in understanding the ethical climate of the firm.

On the other hand, listening to employees increases morale, as well as their willingness to participate in the ethical decision-making process. Effective listening skills create a sense of credibility and trustworthiness.[119] This supports a transparent organizational culture in which ethical concerns can be discussed freely. Because ethical leaders act as role models, their ability to listen encourages employees to do the same, further promoting the acceptance of the organization's ethical values.

Summary

A strategic approach to ethical decisions will contribute to both business and society. To be socially responsible and promote legal and ethical conduct, an organization should develop an organizational ethics program by establishing, communicating, and monitoring ethical values and legal requirements that characterize its history, culture, industry, and operating environment. Most companies begin the process of establishing an organizational ethics program by developing a code of conduct, a formal statement that describes what the organization expects of its employees. A code should reflect senior management's desire for organizational compliance with values, rules, and policies that support an ethical climate. Codes of conduct help employees and managers address ethical dilemmas by prescribing or limiting specific activities.

Organizational ethics programs must be overseen by high-ranking people reputed for their legal and ethical standards. Ethics and compliance officers are responsible for assessing the needs and risks to be addressed in an organization-wide ethics program, developing and distributing a code of conduct, conducting training programs for employees, establishing and maintaining a confidential service to answer questions about ethical issues, making sure that the company is in compliance with government regulations, monitoring and auditing ethical conduct, taking action on possible violations of the organization's code, and reviewing and updating the code. Instituting a training program and a system to communicate and educate employees about the firm's ethical standards is a major step in developing an effective ethics program. The Ethics & Compliance Initiative (ECI) is a nonprofit organization that helps individuals with their businesses and understanding the best practices for keeping their company at the highest level of integrity. It also helps organizations by sharing strategies to maintain integrity and develop an in-house ethics program, and it performs independent research on workplace integrity and compliance practices.

Compliance involves comparing each employee's ethical performance with the organization's ethical standards. Ethics programs can be measured through employee observation, internal audits, reporting systems, and investigations. An internal system for reporting misconduct is especially useful. Many companies set up ethics assistance lines, also known as hotlines, to provide support and give employees the opportunity to ask questions or report concerns. Employees who conclude that they cannot discuss current or potential unethical activities with coworkers or superiors and hence go outside the organization for help are known as whistleblowers.

Consistent enforcement and necessary disciplinary action are essential to a functional ethics and compliance program. Continuous improvement of the ethics program is necessary. Ethical leadership and a strong corporate culture in support of ethical behavior are required to implement an effective organizational ethics program.

Having ethical leadership is particularly important to the organization's ethical culture. There are five power bases from which one person may influence another: (1) reward power, (2) coercive power, (3) legitimate power, (4) expert power, and (5) referent power. These five bases of power can be used to motivate individuals to behave either ethically or unethically. The most effective leaders are able to adapt their leadership styles—reward, coercive, legitimate, expert, and referent—to the type of situation. These styles also have a major impact on the organization's corporate culture. Emotional intelligence is also an important component of ethical leadership.

There are many requirements for ethical leadership, including a passion for doing good, being competent and proactive, taking a holistic view of the ethics program, considering stakeholder interests, and acting as a role model. Ethical leadership leads to several benefits for the organization, including higher employee satisfaction and productivity as well as the promotion of ethical values. Leaders have different methods of leading. These methods, including transactional, transformational, and authentic, have different impacts on the organization's ethical culture. To promote an ethical culture, it is necessary for leaders to have strong positive relationships with the employees.

It is important for ethical leaders to get employees to adopt shared organizational goals and values (a concept known as leader-follower congruence). A major way of maintaining these relationships is through communication. Ethical leaders should master interpersonal, small group, and nonverbal communication, as well as listening. Being an effective communicator helps the ethical leader to develop positive employee relationships, uncover ethical issues, address employee concerns, and include employees in the ethical decision-making process.

Trust Us…Good Ethics is Good Business

Issue: *Are companies responsible for creating a strong ethical culture?*

Trust, a word that is thrown around quite a bit, is often coupled in opinion data with its opposite, *distrust*. Trust is the foundation of ethics and the glue that holds relationships together, both personal and with employers. That fact emerged loud and clear in the latest Edelman Trust Barometer, with 75 percent of employees indicating that their employer is their most trusted institution (above NGOs, business, government, and media). The Edelman Trust Barometer is an annual survey of more than 33,000 respondents evaluating trust toward various institutions. Increasingly, the data shows that companies need to take control and manage both their profitability and their support of economic and social causes in the communities where they operate.

When there is increased alignment of values between employers and employees, employees become bigger advocates, are more loyal, operate with greater engagement, and maintain a stronger level of commitment. This can manifest itself in organizational outcomes that go toward the bottom line, including lower turnover, greater productivity, and increased customer satisfaction. This is not an unconditional relationship, however. Employees expect that their trust is earned and that their employers recognize and then address societal problems. Finally, the benefits of trust should help create a strong ethical culture.

Other interesting findings from the Edelman Trust Barometer include the fact that women are less trusting than men, with women's trust of business institutions 7 points lower globally and 15 points lower in the United States. Speculation includes the fallout of the sexual harassment cases that have been so visible in recent years. In addition, pay inequity and glass ceilings with less leadership roles and opportunities may contribute to women being less trusting of business institutions. There is also a prevailing fear of the change that is coming from

so many directions. The greatest fear in this year's study is the fear of automation, with two-thirds of workers afraid of being replaced by machines. With artificial intelligence (AI)–enhanced robotics and AI affecting many organizational processes and procedures, the uncertainty and fear of change is looming. By 2025, AI will perform or assist in half of the jobs in the workplace, versus 30 percent today.

Back to the original premise that "good ethics is good business," the Edelman study showed that highly trusted companies (those with ability, integrity, dependability, and purpose) outperformed their sector's stock performance by 5 percent. This supports *Ethisphere Magazine*'s assessment of the performance of the World's Most Ethical Companies, showing that over three years, the companies outperformed the U.S. Large Cap Index by nearly 5 percent. One reason for this is that consumers want to purchase from firms that they trust. If trust is broken, then they may stop purchasing and find another firm they do trust. Research indicates that the evaluation of a firm's business ethics has a direct impact on brand attitudes. Corporate social responsibility also has a positive impact on brand attitudes, but unethical conduct can erode trust in the brand, even if a company takes part in positive CSR activities. With so much more information available on company behavior, a good reputation may get a customer to buy a product, but, as the Edelman study shows, it will take ongoing trust to maintain the relationship (67 percent of the respondents agreed with that sentiment). The mistrust that employees have of the wider society has created a real opportunity for companies, their leaders, and impassioned employees to take control of their community and societal impact and "do good while doing well."

There Are Two Sides to Every Issue

1. Companies are responsible for creating a strong ethical culture for their employees.
2. More important than culture is the alignment of individual values between employees and managers.

Sources: Edelman, "2019 Edelman Trust Barometer," January 20, 2019, https://www.edelman.com/trust-barometer (accessed June 22, 2019); Patrick Watson, "Machines Will Do Half Our Work by 2025," *Forbes*, September 27, 2018; "Leading Practices and Trends from the 2018 World's Most Ethical Companies," *An Ethisphere Research Report*, 2018. https://bela.ethisphere.com/wp-content/uploads/leading-practices-and-trends-from-the-2018-wmec.pdf (accessed February 14, 2019); O. C. Ferrell, Dana Harrison, Linda Ferrell, and Joe Hair, "Business Ethics, Corporate Social Responsibility, and Brand Attitudes: An Exploratory Study," *Journal of Business Research*, 95 (February 2019): 491–501.

Key Terms

codes of conduct (p. 183)
compliance officers (p. 186)
core practices (p. 193)
emotional intelligence (p. 202)
ethics codes (p. 182)

ethics officer (p. 186)
group polarization (p. 206)
leader–follower congruence
    (p. 204)
mandated boundaries (p. 194)

organizational ethics and
    compliance programs (p. 181)
transactional leadership (p. 203)
transformational leadership (p. 203)
voluntary practices (p. 193)

Discussion Questions

1. How can an organization be socially responsible and promote legal and ethical conduct?
2. What are the elements that should be included in a strong ethics program?
3. What is a code of conduct, and how can a code be communicated effectively to employees?
4. How and why are a training program and a communications system important in developing an effective ethics program?
5. What does ethical compliance involve, and how can it be measured?

6. What role does leadership play in influencing organizational behavior?
7. Describe some of the skills needed to be an ethical leader.
8. List some of the benefits of ethical leadership.
9. Compare transformational leadership and transactional leadership.
10. Describe the four types of communication.

Experiential Exercise

Visit the website of the Ethics and Compliance Officer Association (ECOA; http://www.theecoa.org). What is the association's current mission and membership composition? Review the website to determine the issues and concerns that comprise the ECOA's most recent programs, publications, and research. What trends do you find? What topics seem most important to ethics officers today?

Upcharging the Government: What Would You Do?

Robert Rubine flipped through his messages and wondered which call he should return first. It was only 3:30 p.m., but he felt as though he had been through a week's worth of decisions and worries. Mondays were normally busy, but this one was anything but normal. Robert's employer, Medic-All, is in the business of selling a wide array of medical supplies and equipment. The company's products range from relatively inexpensive items, like bandages, gloves, and syringes, to more costly items, such as microscopes, incubators, and examination tables. Although the product line is broad, it represents the "basics" required in most healthcare settings. Medic-All utilizes an inside sales force to market its products to private hospitals, elder care facilities, government healthcare institutions, and other similar organizations. The company employs 275 people and is considered a small business under government rules.

The inside sales force has the authority to negotiate on price, which works well in the highly competitive market of medical supplies and equipment. The salespeople are compensated primarily on a commission basis. The sales force and other employees receive legal training annually.

All employees are required to sign Medic-All's code of ethics each year and attend an ethics training session. Despite the importance of the inside sales force, Medic-All has experienced a good deal of turnover in its sales management team. A new lead manager was hired about four months ago. Robert oversees the sales division in his role as vice president of marketing and operations.

Late Friday afternoon last week, Robert received word that two employees in the company's headquarters were selling products to the government at a higher price than they were selling them to other organizations. Both employees have been on the job for over two years and seem to be good performers. A few of their sales colleagues have complained to the lead sales manager about the high quarterly commissions that the two employees recently received. They insinuated that these commissions were earned unfairly, by charging government-run hospitals artificially high prices. A cursory review of their accounts showed that, in many instances, the government was paying more than other organizations. Under procurement rules, the government is supposed to pay a fair price—one that other cost-conscious customers would pay. When asked about the situation, the two employees said that the price offered was based on volume, so the pricing always varied from customer to customer.

Robert took the information to his boss, the president. The two of them discussed how these employees received legal and ethics training, signed the company code of ethics, and should have been knowledgeable about the rules related to government procurement. The president said that these two salespeople sounded like "rogue employees," who committed acts without the approval of the management to increase their commissions. They also discussed many issues and scenarios, such as how to deal with the two salespeople, whether to continue the investigation and inform the government, what strategies to put in place for preventing similar problems in the future, how to protect the firm's good name, whether the company could face suspension from lucrative government business, and others. What would you do?

CHAPTER

8

Employee Relations

The Container Store: An Employee-Centric Retailer

To early skeptics, The Container Store seemed like an odd retail concept. Who would choose to specialize in selling containers, shelving, and home storage items, let alone make a profit from it? Yet with $800 million in annual sales, The Container Store manages to do both. The Container Store is a storage and organization retailer that sells over 10,000 products to meet consumers' needs, from desktop organizers to laundry racks and closet solutions.

When cofounders Kip Tindell and Garrett Boone started The Container Store in 1978, their vision was to take a "solutions-based approach to retail" by selling products that would save consumers time and space. Throughout the years, The Container Store gained widespread notoriety, not only for its eclectic assortment of goods, but also for its unique and compelling corporate culture. Perhaps most strikingly, the retailer views shareholders as less important stakeholders than customers and employees. Such a strong emphasis on corporate culture over profits might appear risky, as every business requires profits—and the goodwill of shareholders and investors—to survive. However, rather than damaging The Container Store's bottom line, its culture has caused the company to thrive. Six principles serve as the foundation of the retailer's approach:

- *One great person equals three good people.* In terms of business productivity, one great person is equal to three good people.
- *Communication IS leadership.* Simply put, we want every single employee in our company to know absolutely everything.
- *Fill the other guy's basket to the brim. Making money then becomes an easy proposition.* Business is not a zero-sum game. Someone doesn't have to lose for someone else to win.

- *The best selection, service, and price.* We work to offer a well-edited, carefully curated collection of 10,000 products, expert advice and service that customers delight in, and competitive prices.
- *Intuition does not come to an unprepared mind. You need to train it before it happens.* Our extensive training, coupled with our employees' life experiences, allows them to intuitively solve all of our customers' storage and organization challenges.
- *Serve the man in the desert.* Imagine a man lost in the desert. He stumbles across an oasis where he's offered a glass of water because he must be thirsty. But if you stop to think about what he's just been through and what his needs really are, you know that he needs more than just water. He needs food, a comfortable place to sleep, and much, much more.
- *Air of excitement.* Three steps in the door and you can tell whether or not a store has it.

These principles demonstrate the importance of both customer service and employee engagement at The Container Store. The retailer's founders were determined to create a work environment where employees can feel valued and appreciated. And their efforts have met with success. The Container Store has been on *Fortune*'s "100 Best Companies to Work For" for more than nineteen consecutive years. Like most retailers, the company has experienced ups and downs in its 40-year history; recently, The Container Store slipped out of the list of top places to work. Is this a temporary glitch in their "culture of care," or have other companies simply made more strides toward improving employee relations, thus increasing the standard?[1]

Chapter Objectives

- Discuss employees as stakeholders
- Examine the economic, legal, ethical, and philanthropic responsibilities related to employees
- Describe an employer of choice and that employer's relationship to social responsibility

Shutterstock/Anakumka

T he Container Store illustrates the extent to which some firms consider the needs, wants, and characteristics of employees and other stakeholders in designing various business processes and practices. Although it is widely understood that employees are of great importance, beliefs about the extent and types of responsibilities that organizations should assume toward employees are likely to vary. For example, some managers are primarily concerned with economic and legal responsibilities, whereas proponents of the stakeholder interaction model discussed in Chapter 2 advocate for a broader perspective. As this chapter will show, a delicate balance of power, responsibility, and accountability exists in the relationships a company develops with its employees.

Because employee stakeholders are so important to the success of any company, this chapter is devoted to the employer-employee relationship. We explore the many issues related to the social responsibilities that employers have to their employees, including the employee-employer contract, workforce reduction, wages and benefits, labor unions, health and safety, equal opportunity, sexual harassment, whistleblowing, diversity, and work/life balance. Along the way, we discuss a number of significant laws that affect companies' human resources (HR) programs. Finally, we look at the concept of employer of choice and what it takes to earn that reputation and distinction.

Employee Stakeholders

Think for a minute about the first job or volunteer position you held. What information were you given about the organization's strategic direction? How were you managed and treated by supervisors? Did you feel empowered to make decisions? How much training did you receive? The answers to these questions may reveal the types of responsibilities that employers have toward employees. If you worked in a restaurant, for example, training should have covered safety, cleanliness, and other health issues mandated by law. If you volunteered at a hospital, you may have learned about the ethical and economic considerations in providing healthcare for the uninsured or poor and the philanthropic efforts used to support the hospital financially. Although such issues may have seemed subtle, or even unimportant, at the time, they are related to the responsibilities that employees, government, and other stakeholders expect of employers.

Responsibilities to Employees

In her book *The Working Life: The Promise and Betrayal of Modern Work*, business professor Joanne B. Ciulla writes about the different types of work, the history of work, the value of work to a person's self-concept, the relationship between work and freedom, and as the title implies, the rewards and pitfalls that exist in the employee-employer relationship. Ciulla contends that two common phrases—"Get a job!" and "Get a life!"—are antithetical in today's society, meaning they seem diametrically opposed goals or values.[2] For the ancient Greeks, work was seen as the gods' way of punishing humans. Centuries later, Benedictine monks, who built farms, church abbeys, and villages, were considered the lowest order of monks because they labored. By the eighteenth century, the Protestant work ethic had emerged to imply that work was a method for discovering and creating a person.[3] Today, psychologists, families, and friends lament how work has become the primary source of many individuals' status, fulfillment, and happiness. Critics point to the ways in which business influences the personal choices that individuals make, not only as consumers, but as employees. As with the complicated history of work, the responsibilities, obligations, and expectations between employees and employers are also fraught with challenges, debates, and opportunities. In this section, we review the four levels of corporate social responsibility (CSR) as they relate to employees. Although we focus primarily on the responsibilities of employers to employees, we also acknowledge the role that employees have in achieving strategic social responsibility.

Economic Issues

The significance of the economic realm of employment is evident in the story of Malden Mills Industries, a company established in 1906 and credited with inventing synthetic fleece in 1981. In 1995, just a few weeks before the winter holidays, the factory and office space at Malden Mills burned to the ground, injuring many workers. In an unusual move, the company's CEO, Aaron Feuerstein, paid full wages, year-end bonuses, and benefits to employees while the buildings were reconstructed. HR managers set up a temporary job-training center, collected holiday gifts for employees' children, and worked with community agencies to support employees and their families.[4] When economic factors forced Malden Mills through several employee layoffs in the late 1990s, employees were offered jobs at another plant and received career transition assistance. Feuerstein believed in an unwritten contract that considers the economic prospects of both employer and employees.

Several years later, Malden Mills filed for bankruptcy protection. The company's assets were sold and the company name was changed to Polartec, LLC. Polartec started with the original synthetic fleece developed by Malden and today offers 300 different fabrics. Customers include the U.S. military, L. L. Bean, Patagonia, Jack Wolfskin, and other apparel brands around the world. While Feuerstein is no longer at the company, his product inventions and commitment to social responsibility continue to exist at Polartec, now a leader in sustainable engineering and manufacturing.[5]

Employee-Employer Contract As discussed in Chapter 1, the recent history of social responsibility has brought many changes to bear on stakeholder relationships. One of the more dramatic shifts has been in the "contract" and mutual understanding that exist between employee and employer. By the beginning of the twenty-first century, many companies had to learn and accept new rules for recruiting, retaining, and compensating employees. For example, although employers held the position of power for many years, the new century brought record employment rates and the tightest job market in years. Huge salaries, signing bonuses, multiple offers, and flexible, not seniority-based, compensation plans became commonplace throughout the late 1990s. However, the first decade of the 2000s reversed this trend. Business scandals in the early 2000s, the World Trade Center attacks on September 11, 2001, and the Great Recession of 2008–2009 brought a decline in lucrative employment opportunities and forced many firms to implement layoffs and other cost-cutting measures. At one point, the **unemployment rate**, which is the percentage of the available labor force that is currently unemployed, in the United States reached 10 percent. Pay raises, healthcare benefits, mental health coverage, retirement funding, paid maternity leave, and other benefits were reduced, or costs were shifted to employees.[6]

Bolstered by job growth, the U.S. economy rebounded, and by 2019, the U.S. unemployment rate was less than 4 percent. From a statistical perspective, a very low unemployment rate in a growing economy is sometimes considered full employment because of sampling error and related concerns. **Full employment** occurs when the available labor force is fully utilized and employers have difficulty finding employees to fill available positions. From a psychological perspective,

unemployment rate
the percentage of the available labor force that is currently unemployed

full employment
occurs when the available labor force is fully utilized and employers have difficulty finding employees to fill available positions

low unemployment rates generally make it easier for employees to change jobs and employers, seek higher wages and new benefits, and otherwise exert more stakeholder power in the employment relationship.

Regardless of the economy, employing organization, or salary and perks of a specific position, a **psychological contract** exists between an employee and employer. This contract is largely unwritten and includes the beliefs, perceptions, expectations, and obligations that make up the agreement between individuals and the organizations that employ them.[7] Details of the contract develop through communications, via interactions with managers and coworkers, and through perceptions of the corporate culture often formed by watching management and leadership. These interactions are especially important for new employees, who are trying to make sense of their new roles within the context of their prior beliefs and experiences.[8] New employee orientation, along with ongoing training, performance evaluation discussions, internal newsletters, and company-sponsored social events, are important mechanisms for introducing and communicating the psychological contract.

This contract, though informal, has a significant influence on the way employees act. When promises and expectations are not met, a psychological contract breach occurs, and employees may become less loyal, less trusting, inattentive to work, or otherwise dissatisfied with their employment situation.[9] On the other hand, when employers present information in a credible, competent, and trustworthy manner, employees are more likely to be supportive of and committed to the organization. Therefore, employers and employees are the two groups that contribute to the development, maintenance, and evolution of the psychological contract at work. Table 8.1 provides an overview of what is needed for employee commitment to the firm and employer promises to the employee.

An employee's perception of how well employer promises are kept provides an ongoing psychological assessment of the employment relationship, including whether the employee will choose to leave the organization, recommend it to others, or increase commitment to the employer. Recent research has revealed that the psychological contract is dynamic over the lifetime of an employment relationship. Steps in the dynamic process include creation, maintenance, renegotiation, and repair. Like other relationships, intentional maintenance is important, and there may be times when perceived violations of trust, miscommunication, goal incongruency, and other disruptive situations create the need for reconciliation and repair. In the latter cases, the employer's timeliness and responsiveness to employee concerns is one of the main predictors of the relationship's health in the future. Experienced managers maintain open and transparent communication, so that issues are discussed and resolved before a serious breach in the psychological contract occurs.[10] The promises, or inducements, made by the organization are valuable to nearly all employees, but one study of over 5,000 employees indicates this rank order for their importance to employees: (1) social atmosphere, (2) career development opportunities, (3) job content, (4) work/life balance, and (5) financial rewards. This same sample ranked the organizational fulfillment of these promises as: (1) job content, (2) social atmosphere, (3) work/life balance, (4) career development opportunities, and (5) financial rewards. Based on these results, it is clear that career development opportunities deserve more attention from managers to strengthen the psychological contract and provide incentives for employee retention. Organizations that are able to implement their key promises so that employees view them as fulfilled reap rewards in terms of increased employee loyalty and decreased intentions to leave and/or search for a

psychological contract
largely unwritten, it includes beliefs, perceptions, expectations, and obligations that make up the agreement between individuals and the organizations that employ them

Table 8.1 The Psychological Contract Between Employee and Employer

Employee Commitment	Employer Promises
Loyalty to the company	Respect from management
Teamwork and cooperation	Training opportunities
Compliance with policies	Opportunity to advance
Ethical leadership and behavior	Adequate benefits
Protection of company resources	Fairness in work assignments
Volunteering to address challenges	Ethical culture
Solving problems independently	Financial rewards
Trust and confidentiality	Work/life balance

Table 8.2 Measuring Employee Engagement: Say, Stay, Strive

If they *Say* positive things about their organization and act as advocates
If they intend to *Stay* at their organization for a long time
If they are motivated to *Strive* to give their best efforts to help the organization succeed

Source: AON, "2018 Trends in Global Employee Engagement," http://images.transcontinentalmedia.com/LAF/lacom/Aon_2018_Trends_In_Global_Employee_Engagement.pdf (accessed November 19, 2019).

new employer.[11] **Employee engagement** is the connection that employees have with their employers that influences behavior, effort, and commitment. Strong employee engagement is revealed through positive interactions with key stakeholders, especially customers, and ultimately has a positive influence on organizational success, as discussed in Chapter 1.[12]

Employee engagement is an international phenomenon that has caught the attention of leaders, managers, and researchers. Recently, more than 8 million employees in 1,000 companies around the world participated in a study of employee engagement. The study used the "Say, Stay, Strive" model for measuring engagement found in Table 8.2.

The annual survey results indicated that while engagement is increasing in many parts of the world, some areas are experiencing declining employee engagement. Declines were found in several Latin American countries, including Argentina, Brazil, and Mexico. Even with these declines, employees in the region maintain a relatively high level of engagement (75 percent) compared to the global average (65 percent). In contrast, results for employees in Algeria, South Africa, Nigeria, and other African nations has improved dramatically since 2011, when 52 percent of survey respondents indicated strong engagement. By 2017, this engagement was at 66 percent, even though some of these nations have experienced economic and social instability. In all likelihood, business leaders in Africa recognized the disruptive effects of instability and implemented methods to strengthen employee recruiting and retention efforts and fortify corporate cultures to withstand external pressures.[13]

Just as in other stakeholder relationships, expectations in the employment psychological contract are subject to a variety of influences. This section discusses how the contract has generally ebbed and flowed over the last 100 years. Even with these overarching trends, employers should be mindful of differences that may exist in particular industries, geographic regions, job types, and employee characteristics. Table 8.3 provides examples of the methods and programs that companies prioritize and implement to fulfill aspects of the psychological contract. These examples demonstrate that there is not a "one-size-fits-all" approach for meeting the needs and expectations of employees.

Until the early 1900s, the relationship between employer and employee was best characterized as a master-servant relationship.[14] In this view, there was a natural imbalance in power that meant employment was viewed as a privilege that included few rights and many obligations. Employees were expected to work for the best interests of the organization, even at the expense of personal and family welfare. At this time, most psychologists and management scholars believed that good leadership required aggressive and domineering behavior.[15] Images from Upton Sinclair's novel *The Jungle*, which we discuss briefly in the next chapter, characterized the extreme negative effects of this employment contract.[16]

In the 1920s and 1930s, employees assumed a relationship with an employer that was more balanced in terms of power, responsibilities, and obligations. This shift meant that employees and employers were coequals, and in legal terms, employees had many more rights than under the master-servant model.[17] Much of the employment law in the United States was enacted in the 1930s, when legislators passed laws related to child labor, wages, working hours, and labor unions.[18] Throughout the twentieth century, the employee-employer contract evolved along

employee engagement
the connection that employees have with their employers that influences behavior, effort, and commitment

Table 8.3 Methods That Companies Use to Fulfill Psychological Contracts

Company	Employee Promise
Google	Child care
Starbucks	Two years of college tuition
The Container Store	Extensive employee training and higher pay
SAS	Free on-site healthcare clinic
REI	Provides annual surveys to employees to get feedback on employee engagement
Salesforce.com	Employee recognition and reward programs for the company's salespeople
Wegman's Market	Strong growth opportunities in the company
W. L. Gore and Associates	Flat nonhierarchical business structure
Nvidia	Reimbursement for student loan debt
Baird	Reverse mentoring program pairs senior leaders with junior employees
Pinterest	Fertility benefits and coverage of in vitro fertilization treatments

the coequals model, although social critics began to question the influence that large companies had on employees and the rest of society.

In the mid-twentieth century, companies exerted a more patriarchal approach to employees, which emphasized job security along with generous benefits, retirement income, and continuing professional development and growth. The concept of the "company man" was born out of this time frame, with television and movies depicting white-collar men working in stable and generous middle-class jobs in exchange for company loyalty.[19] In 1951, the political commentator and sociologist C. Wright Mills criticized white-collar work as draining on employees' time, energy, and even personalities. He also believed that individuals with business power were apt to keep employees happy in an attempt to ward off the development of stronger labor unions and unfavorable government regulations.[20] A few years later, the classic book *The Organization Man* by William H. Whyte was published. This book examined the social nature of work, including the inherent conflict between belonging and contributing to a group on the job while maintaining a sense of independence and identity.[21]

Organizational researchers and managers in the 1960s began to question authoritarian behavior and consider participatory management styles that assumed that employees were motivated and eager to take responsibility for their work. A study by the U.S. Department of Health, Education, and Welfare in the early 1970s confirmed that employees wanted interesting work and a chance to demonstrate their skills. The report also recommended job redesign and managerial approaches that increased participation, freedom, and democracy at work.[22] By the 1980s, a family analogy was being used to describe the workplace. This implied strong attention to employee welfare and prompted the focus on business ethics that have been explored in previous chapters of this book. At the same time, corporate mission statements touted the importance of customers and employees, and *In Search of Excellence*, a best-selling book by Thomas J. Peters and business consultant Robert H. Waterman Jr., profiled companies with strong corporate cultures that inspired employees toward better work, products, and customer satisfaction.[23] The total quality management (TQM) movement increased empowerment and teamwork on the job throughout the 1990s and led the charge toward workplaces simultaneously devoted to employee achievement at work and home.[24]

Although there were many positive initiatives for employees in the 1990s, the confluence of economic progress with demands for global competitiveness convinced many executives of the need for cost cutting. A common method for cost reduction came in the form of **outsourcing**, which occurs when a company hires external parties to perform tasks and functions that had been previously performed by company employees. This practice has long been associated with plans to increase efficiencies, In the late 1930s and early 1940s, business writers exalted the practice of subcontracting as a way to ensure that the U.S. government had armament and other provisions to compete in World War II. **Subcontracting** takes place when one company hires external parties to perform specific tasks or functions in partial fulfillment of a larger contract. During World War II, subcontracting created an economic ripple effect, as small businesses became part of the supply chain and offered jobs when the country was in a state of austerity.[25] Unlike subcontracting, outsourcing is used for traditional business functions, like payroll, information technology (IT), accounting, auditing, and other services that are largely independent of a company's core business and mission. Outsourcing is positioned as a way for companies to reduce distractions as well as costs.[26]

For individuals accustomed to messages about the importance of employees to organizational success, workforce reduction was both unexpected and traumatic. These experiences effectively ended the loyalty- and commitment-based contract that employees had developed with employers. A study of young employees showed that their greatest psychological need in the workplace was security, but that they viewed many employers as "terminators."[27] By the time Barack Obama became president of the United States in 2009, his administration was facing an economy in terrible condition. By mid-2009, over 8 million employees had been laid off and recessionary effects loomed large. The Conference Board, which publishes the Employment Trend Index (ETI) monthly, announced the index was declining faster than at any other time in the 35-year history of the ETI. Eight indicators contribute to the index, including claims for unemployment insurance, number of part-time workers due to economic reasons, consumer confidence, industrial production, and manufacturing and trade sales, among others.

Although unemployment went as high as 10 percent during the Great Recession, the economy slowly began to recover. In 2015, unemployment had decreased to 5.3 percent, and the number of long-term unemployed individuals had been reduced. According to economists, it had been the slowest recovery in 55 years.[28] By 2019, unemployment in the United States was below 5 percent, and some states, including Hawaii, reached unprecedented unemployment rates of 2 percent.[29] For a state that depends heavily on tourism, low unemployment could mean that jobs in the retail, hospitality, and travel sectors go unfilled and the overall tourist experience diminishes. However, this particular unemployment rate in Hawaii was precipitated by a decline in tourism spending that resulted in job losses.[30] This is a cautionary tale on the importance of assessing the overall health of the economy by multiple indicators. Unfortunately, recovery is often slower for minorities and individuals under the age of 30. In 2019, unemployment for younger adults aged 16 to 24 was 8 percent, double the national average.[31] There are concerns that the opportunities for employment based on education and skills has diminished. For example, many college graduates experience **underemployment** in their first jobs. Underemployment occurs when employees are engaged in work that require skills or education below the qualifications of the employee. It also occurs when an employee wishes to work on a full-time basis but can find only a part-time position. Like unemployment, time-based underemployment leads to "enforced leisure," a situation linked to increasing levels of stress, depression, and polarization in society.[32]

Workforce Reduction   At different points in a company's history, there are likely to be factors that beg the question, "How can we decrease our overall costs?"[33] In a highly competitive business environment, where new companies, customers, and products emerge and disappear every day, there is a continuous push for greater organizational efficiency and effectiveness. This pressure often leads to difficult

outsourcing
the practice of hiring an outside individual or organization to perform tasks and functions traditionally performed by company employees

subcontracting
the practice of hiring an outside individual or organization to perform specific tasks and functions in partial fulfillment of a larger company contract

underemployment
occurs when employees engage in work that requires skills or education below their qualifications, or when employees want to work on a full-time basis but can find only part-time positions

Shutterstock/fizkes

decisions, including ones that require careful balance and consideration for the short-run survival and long-term vision of the company. This situation can create the need for **workforce reduction**, the process of eliminating employment positions. This places considerable pressure on top management, causes speculation and tension among employees, and raises public ire about the role of business in society.[34]

There are several strategies that companies use to reduce overall costs and expenditures. For example, organizations may choose to reduce the number of employees, simplify products and processes, decrease quality and promises in service delivery, or develop some other mechanism for eliminating resources or nonperforming assets. Managers may find it difficult to communicate about cost reductions, as this message carries both emotional and social risk. Employees may wonder, "What value do I bring to the company?" and "Does anyone really care about my years of service?" Customers may inquire, "Can we expect the same level of service and product quality?" Governments and the community may ask, "Is this really necessary? How will it affect our economy?" For all of these questions, company leadership must have a clear answer that should be based on a thorough analysis of costs within the organizational system and how any changes are likely to affect business processes and outcomes. In 2016, Intel reduced its global workforce by 11 percent. This is a decision that many large technology companies are facing as newcomers in the industry gain more market share.[35]

In the last two decades, many firms chose to adopt the strategy that also creates the most anxiety and criticism—the reduction of the workforce. Throughout the 1990s, the numbers were staggering, as Sears eliminated 50,000 jobs and Kodak terminated nearly 17,000 people. Economic decline and financial scandals in the first decade of the twenty-first century also created a wave of layoffs. General Motors (GM) cut thousands of jobs and needed government assistance just to stay afloat. These actions effectively signaled the "end of the old contract" that employees had with employers.[36] These strategies, sometimes called **downsizing** or **rightsizing**, may entail employee layoffs, reorganizations, and related measures. In other cases, a company freezes new hiring, hopes for natural workforce attrition, offers incentives for early retirement, brings in consultants to analyze workloads, or encourages job sharing among existing employees.

There are three tactics for downsizing. We have already discussed workforce reduction through layoffs, retirement incentives, buyout packages, and transfers. Another tactic is organization redesign to eliminate organizational layers or functions and/or merge units. The third tactic is systemic redesign, which necessitates a major culture change, the simplification of processes, an emphasis on continuous improvement, and changes in employee responsibilities.[37] The reality is that some employees will lose their current positions in one way or another. Thus, although workforce reduction may be the strategy chosen to control and reduce costs, it may have profound implications for the welfare of employees, their families, and the economic prospects of a geographical region and other constituents, as well as for the company itself.

As with other aspects of business, it is difficult to separate financial considerations for costs from other obligations and expectations that develop between a company and its stakeholders. Depending on a firm's resource base and current financial situation, the psychological contract that exists between an employer and

workforce reduction
the process of eliminating employment positions

downsizing
the process of making permanent reductions in an organization's labor force

rightsizing
the process of reorganizing or restructuring an organization's labor force

employee is likely to be broken through layoffs, and the **social contract** between employers, communities, and other groups may also be threatened. Downsizing makes the private relationship between employee and employer a public issue that affects many stakeholders and subsequently draws heavy criticism.[38] Fundamentally, top managers must recognize the many types of costs that occur through workforce reduction. These include costs associated with future talent and leadership, company morale, shareholder and analyst perceptions on Wall Street, and rehiring needs.[39]

The impact of the workforce reduction process depends on a host of factors, including corporate culture, long-term plans, and creative calculations on both quantitative and qualitative aspects of the workplace. Because few HR directors and other managers have extensive experience in restructuring the workforce, there are several issues to consider before embarking on the process.[40] First, a comprehensive plan must be developed that takes into account the financial implications and the qualitative and emotional toll of the reduction strategy. This plan may include a systematic analysis of workflow so that management understands how tasks are currently completed and how they will be completed after restructuring. Second, the organization should commit to assisting employees who must make a career transition as a result of the reduction process. To make the transition productive for employees, this assistance should begin as soon as management is aware of possible reductions. Through the **Worker Adjustment and Retraining Notification (WARN) Act**, U.S. employers are required to give at least 60 days' advance notice if a layoff will affect 500 or more employees or more than one-third of the workforce.[41] Offering career assistance and other services is beneficial over the long term, as it demonstrates a firm's commitment to social responsibility.

External factors also play a role in how quickly employees find new work and affect perceptions of a firm's decision to downsize. Michigan launched an initiative called Community Ventures to connect the long-term unemployed with jobs. The public-private partnership provides support and resources to participants, including a success coach who offers assistance from job placement through at least one year of employment and services such as literacy training, networking connections, and transportation. Since its beginning, the initiative has put 6,600 hard-core unemployed into new jobs.[42] Those unemployed for long periods of time are likely to experience feelings of discouragement and low morale. On the other hand, individuals who are reemployed quickly, whether through company efforts or market circumstances, experience fewer negative economic and emotional repercussions. In addition, employees who are kept well informed about the downsizing process are more likely to retain a positive attitude toward the company, even if they experience job loss.[43]

Companies must be willing to accept the consequences of terminating employees. Although workforce reduction can improve a firm's financial performance, especially in the short run, there are costs to consider, including the loss of intellectual capital.[44] The years of knowledge, skills, relationships, and commitment that employees develop cannot be easily replaced, and the loss of one employee can cost a firm between $50,000 and $100,000.[45] So although workforce reduction lowers costs, it often results in lost knowledge and experience, strained customer relationships, negative media attention, and other issues that drain company resources. Employees who retain their jobs may suffer guilt, depression, or stress as a result of the reduction in the workforce. Thus, a long-term understanding of the qualitative and quantitative costs and benefits should guide downsizing decisions. Some researchers point to the lack of empirical evidence that workforce reduction actually leads to sustainable financial gains and performance. Investors' reactions to downsizing announcements is critical because their immediate actions could drastically reduce a corporation's stock value and trigger other negative outcomes. A recent study recommended that in order to hedge against the devastating effects,

social contract
an implicit agreement between members of society that establishes the rights and duties of each party to the agreement

Worker Adjustment and Retraining Notification (WARN) Act
a federal law requiring that U.S. employers give at least 60 days' advance notice if a layoff will affect 500 or more employees or more than one-third of the workforce

companies introduce workforce reduction while firm performance is still strong, concurrent with the downsizing plans of other industry players, and when the macroeconomic outlook is improving.[46]

Although workforce reduction is a corporate decision, it is also important to recognize the potential role of employees in these decisions. Whereas hiring and job growth reached a frantic pace by the late 1990s, a wave of downsizings in the early 1990s and 2000s meant that some individuals had embraced the reality of having little job security. Instead of becoming cynical or angry, employees may have reversed roles and began asking, "What is this company doing for me?" and "Am I getting what I need from my employer?" Employees of all types began taking more responsibility for career growth, demanding balance in work and personal responsibilities, and seeking opportunities in start-up firms and emerging industries. Thus, although workforce reduction has negative effects, it has also shifted the psychological contract and power between employee and employer. The following suggestions examine how individuals can potentially mitigate the onset and effects of downsizing.

First, all employees should understand how their skills and competencies affect business performance. Not recognizing and documenting this relationship makes it more difficult to prove their worth to managers faced with workforce reduction decisions. Second, employees should strive for cost-cutting and conservation strategies, regardless of the employer's current financial condition. This is a workforce's first line of defense against layoffs—assisting the organization in reducing its costs before drastic measures are necessary. Third, today's work environment requires that most employees fulfill diverse and varying roles. For example, manufacturing managers must understand the whole product development and introduction process, ranging from engineering to marketing and distribution activities. Thus, another way of ensuring worth to the company, and to potential employers, is through an employee's ability to navigate different customer environments and organizational systems. It is now necessary to participate in **cross-training**, show flexibility, and learn the entire business, even if a company does not offer a formal program for gaining this type of experience and exposure to a variety of job duties. In particular, cross-training expands an employee's ability to contribute in multiple roles. Although this advice may not prevent workforce reduction, it does empower employees against some of its harmful effects. Through laws and regulations, the government has also created a system for ensuring that employees are treated properly on the job. The next section covers the myriad of laws that all employers and employees should consider when making both daily and long-term strategic decisions.

cross-training
the process of ensuring that employees have the knowledge and skills to perform more than a single set of job duties

Legal Issues

Employment law is a very complex and evolving area. Most large companies and organizations employ HR managers and legal specialists who are trained in the detail and implementation of specific statutes related to employee hiring, compensation, benefits, safety, and other areas. Smaller organizations often send HR managers to workshops and conferences to keep abreast of legal imperatives in the workplace. Table 8.4 lists the major federal laws that cover employer responsibilities with respect to wages, labor unions, benefits, health and safety, equal opportunity, and other areas. Most of these laws are overseen and enforced by the **Department of Labor**, the federal agency charged with, among other things, promoting the welfare of wage earners, job seekers, and retirees and improving working conditions and opportunities for employment. Until the early 1900s, employment was primarily governed by the concept of **employment at will**, a common-law doctrine that allows either the employer or the employee to terminate the relationship at any time, so long as it does not violate an employment contract or law. Today, many states still use the employment-at-will philosophy, but laws and statutes may limit

Department of Labor
the U.S. federal agency charged with fostering, promoting, and developing the welfare of wage earners, job seekers, and retirees in the United States; improving working conditions; advancing opportunities for profitable employment; and assuring work-related benefits and rights

employment at will
a common-law doctrine that allows either the employer or the employee to terminate the relationship at any time, so long as it does not violate an employment contract so long as it does not violate an employment contract or law

Table 8.4 Major Employment Laws

Act (Date Enacted)	Purpose
National Labor Relations Act (1935)	Established the rights of employees to engage in collective bargaining and to strike.
Fair Labor Standards Act (1938)	Established minimum wage and overtime pay standards, recordkeeping, and child labor standards for most private and public employers.
Equal Pay Act (1963)	Protects women and men who perform substantially equal work in the same establishment from gender-based wage discrimination.
Civil Rights Act, Title VII (1964)	Prohibits employment discrimination on the basis of race, national origin, color, religion, and gender.
Age Discrimination in Employment Act (1967)	Protects individuals aged 40 or older from age-based discrimination.
Occupational Safety and Health Act (1970)	Ensures safe and healthy working conditions for all employees by providing specific standards that employers must meet.
Employee Retirement Income Security Act (1974)	Sets uniform minimum standards to ensure that employee benefit plans are established and maintained in a fair and financially sound manner.
Americans with Disabilities Act (1990)	Prohibits discrimination on the basis of physical or mental disability in all employment practices and requires employers to make reasonable accommodation to make facilities accessible to and usable by persons with disabilities.
Family and Medical Leave Act (1993)	Requires certain employers to provide up to 12 weeks of unpaid, job-protected leave to eligible employees for certain family and medical reasons.
Uniformed Services Employment and Reemployment Rights Act (1994)	The preservice employer must reemploy service members returning from a period of service in the uniformed services if those service members meet five criteria.
Patient Protection and Affordable Care Act (2010)	Among other provisions, makes healthcare affordable and universal so that all employees and Americans have access to it.

Source: U.S. Department of Labor, *Employment Law Guide,* https://webapps.dol.gov/elaws/elg/ (accessed June 15, 2019).

total discretion in this regard.[47] The following discussion highlights employment laws and their fundamental contribution to social responsibility.[48]

Wages and Benefits   After the Great Depression in the 1920s, the U.S. Congress enacted a number of laws to protect employee rights and extend employer responsibilities. The Fair Labor Standards Act (FLSA) of 1938 prescribed minimum wage and overtime pay, recordkeeping, and child labor standards for most private and public employers. The federal **minimum wage** is set by the U.S. government and is periodically revised, although states have the option to adopt a higher standard. For example, the federal minimum wage was raised from $6.55 per hour to $7.25 per hour in 2009. The minimum wage has been changed over 30 times since it was first introduced in the 1930s. Table 8.5 documents many of the changes that have been authorized in the minimum wage since that time.

In 2013, the Fair Minimum Wage Act was introduced. It proposed that the federal minimum wage be raised to $10.10 per hour, but it did not pass. Various members of Congress, including the U.S. Chamber of Commerce, have proposed a $15 per hour minimum wage. Conversely, other members of the U.S. Congress and aligned opponents are worried that a substantial minimum wage increase would lead to job losses or higher prices for consumers. The nonprofit Empire

minimum wage
the lowest hourly wage that may be legally paid to employees

Table 8.5 History of the Minimum Wage

Year	Hourly Wage
1938	$0.25
1939	$0.30
1950	$0.75
1961	$ 1.15
1968	$ 1.60
1977	$2.30
1981	$3.35
1997	$5.15
2007	$5.85
2009	$ 7.25

Source: U.S. Department of Labor, "History of Federal Minimum Wage Rates Under the Fair Labor Standards Act, 1938–2009," https://www.dol.gov/whd/minwage/chart.htm (accessed June 15, 2019).

living wage
an hourly wage on which it is possible to live according to minimum standards

vesting
the legal right to pension plan benefits

Center for New York State Policy has concerns that increasing the minimum wage too much will lead to increased costs for businesses, leading to a major detrimental impact on smaller businesses.[49]

As demonstrated, the minimum wage remains a highly debated topic, especially since it roughly corresponds to federal poverty guidelines and not the actual cost of living. According to the Department of Labor, a two-person household with a combined annual income of less than $16,910 is at the poverty level. Employees in full-time jobs being paid at minimum wage earn just over $15,000 a year. Many workers are not earning enough to make ends meet and, along with activist groups, are calling for a **living wage** approach to worker compensation. Living wages take into account the costs associated with basic necessities such as food, clothing, housing, transportation, and healthcare. Living wage calculators, like the one found at http://livingwage.mit.edu/, incorporate actual costs, which vary dramatically from state to state and city to city. Advocates for a living wage point to the ethical obligations associated with employees and society.[50] While many states abide by the federal standard, others, including Alaska, Arkansas, California, Florida, Massachusetts, Oregon, Vermont, and Washington have adopted a higher minimum wage. Most employees who work more than 40 hours per week are entitled to overtime pay, amounting to one and a half times their regular pay. There are exemptions to the overtime pay provisions for four classes of employees: executives, outside salespeople, administrators, and professionals.[51]

The FLSA also affected child labor, including the provision that individuals under the age of 14 are allowed to do only certain types of work, such as delivering newspapers and working in their parents' businesses. Children under age 16 are often required to get a work permit, and their work hours are restricted so that they can attend school. Persons between the ages of 16 and 18 are not restricted in terms of number of work hours, but they cannot be employed in hazardous or dangerous positions. Although passage of the FLSA was necessary to eliminate abusive child labor practices, its restrictions may become somewhat problematic when unemployment rates are extremely low. Some business owners may have even considered lobbying for relaxed standards in very restrictive states so that they could hire more teens. In addition, general FLSA restrictions have created problems in implementing job-sharing and flextime arrangements with employees who are paid on an hourly basis.[52]

Two other pieces of legislation relate to employer responsibilities for benefits and job security. The Employee Retirement Income Security Act (ERISA) of 1974 set uniform minimum standards to ensure that employee benefit plans are established and maintained in a fair and financially sound manner. ERISA does not require companies to establish retirement pension plans; instead, it developed standards for the administration of plans that management chooses to offer employees. A key provision relates to **vesting**, the legal right to pension plan benefits. In general, contributions an employee makes to the plan are vested immediately, whereas company contributions are vested after five years of employment. ERISA is a very complicated aspect of employer responsibilities because it involves tax law, financial investments, and plan participants and beneficiaries.[53]

The Family and Medical Leave Act (FMLA) of 1993 requires certain

Shutterstock/Ternavskaia Olga Alibec

employers to provide up to 12 weeks of unpaid, job-protected leave to eligible employees for certain family and medical reasons. Typical reasons for this type of leave include the birth or adoption of a child, personal illness, or the serious health condition of a close relative. However, if the employee is paid in the top 10 percent of the entire workforce, the employer does not have to reinstate him or her in the same or a comparable position.[54] The FMLA applies to employers with 50 or more employees, which means that its provisions do not cover a large number of U.S. employees. In addition, employees must have worked at least one year for the firm and at least 25 hours per week during the past year before the FMLA applies.

Labor Unions   In one of the earliest pieces of employment legislation, the National Labor Relations Act (NLRA) of 1935 legitimized the rights of employees to engage in collective bargaining and to strike. **Collective bargaining** allows a group of employees, through their unions, to negotiate employment contracts and conditions with their employers. This law was originally passed to protect employee rights, but subsequent legislation gave more rights to employers and restricted the power of unions. Before the NLRA, many companies attempted to prohibit their employees from creating or joining labor organizations altogether. Employees who were members of unions were often discriminated against in terms of hiring and retention decisions. This act sought to eliminate the perceived imbalance of power between employers and employees. Through unions, employees gained a collective bargaining mechanism that enabled greater power on several fronts, including wages and safety.[55] For example, in a series of strikes against Walmart, members of the Organization for United Respect at Walmart (OUR Walmart), founded by the United Food and Commercial Workers (UFCW) union, called for the retailer to offer employees a minimum of $25,000 per year and enough hours for workers to support their families, ensure no more retaliation against those making these requests, and provide fair treatment to pregnant workers. When the strikes were ongoing, they had the following results: Walmart agreed to a $21 million settlement regarding wages in one of its warehouses, the U.S. government initiated prosecutions regarding illegal firing of workers, and the city of Portland cut ties with the retailer.

collective bargaining
a negotiating process where employees work through their unions to establish employment contracts and conditions with their employers

Health and Safety   In 1970, the Occupational Safety and Health Act (OSHA) sought to ensure safe and healthy working conditions for all employees by providing specific standards that employers must meet. This act led to the development of the **Occupational Safety and Health Administration (OSHA)**, the agency that oversees the regulations intended to make U.S. workplaces the safest in the world. In its more than 50 years of existence, OSHA has made great strides to improve and maintain the health and safety of employees. For example, since the 1970s, the workplace death rate in the United States has been reduced by more than 60 percent, and the agency's initiatives in cotton dust and lead standards have reduced disease in several industries. The agency continues to innovate and uses feedback systems for improving its services and standards. As more Spanish-speaking workers entered the workforce, officials were concerned about their understanding of the agency and their rights in the workplace. In response, OSHA translated a variety of its documents into Spanish and posted them onto a prominent place on its website.[56] OSHA has the authority to enter and make inspections of most employers.

Occupational Safety and Health Administration (OSHA)
the U.S. government agency charged with ensuring safe and healthful working conditions for working men and women by setting and enforcing standards and by providing training, outreach, education, and assistance

Because of its far-reaching power and unwarranted inspections made in the 1970s, the agency's relationship with business has not always been positive. For example, OSHA proposed rules to increase employer responsibility for **ergonomics**, the design, arrangement, and use of equipment to maximize productivity and minimize fatigue and physical discomfort. Without proper attention to ergonomics, employees may suffer injuries and long-term health issues as a result of work motion and tasks. Many business and industry associations initially opposed the proposal, citing enormous costs and unsubstantiated claims. A federal ergonomics

ergonomics
the design, arrangement, and use of equipment to maximize productivity and minimize fatigue and physical discomfort

rule was established during Bill Clinton's presidency in the 1990s but was repealed by his successor, President George W. Bush. However, the issue continues to be raised on the regulatory agenda. OSHA has focused its ergonomics efforts on developing guidelines for specific industries, including poultry processing, beverage distribution, nursing homes, and retail grocery stores. Individual states, such as Alaska, Washington, and California, have implemented their own ergonomics rules.[57] Despite differences between this federal agency and some states and companies on a number of regulations, most employers are required to display the poster shown in Figure 8.1, or one required by their state safety and health agency. Gildan Activewear Inc., a manufacturer and marketer of clothing, developed a program to improve ergonomic practices and reduce injuries. The program includes access to in-house clinics, stretching and exercise sessions, and opportunities for consultation on back and shoulder health. This is particularly important because repetitive actions in the sewing industry are common and prolonged repetitive actions can lead to injury over time.[58]

Figure 8.1 Job Safety and Health Protection Poster

Source: Occupational Safety and Health Administration, "OSHA's Free Workplace Poster," https://www.osha.gov/Publications/poster.html (accessed June 15, 2019).

An emerging issue in the area of health and safety is the increasing rate of violence in the workplace. According to OSHA, 2 million workers are assaulted, and over 450 are the victim of homicide in the workplace every year.[59] A 2019 survey of Fortune 1000 companies indicated that workplace violence is one of the most important security issues they face, costs up to $36 billion annually, and results in three deaths daily and thousands of injuries each year. Organizations in particular industries, including public service, law enforcement, healthcare, and transportation and delivery, are particularly susceptible to conditions associated with violence in the workplace.[60]

The Society for Human Resource Management (SHRM) has identified four types of workplace violence: (1) crimes committed by strangers and intruders in the workplace; (2) acts committed by nonemployees, such as customers, patients, students, and clients; (3) violence committed by coworkers; and (4) incidents involving those with a personal relationship with an employee.[61] Taxi drivers, ride-share drivers, and clerks working late-night shifts at convenience stores are often subject to the first type of violence. Airline attendants are increasingly experiencing the second category of workplace violence when passengers become unruly, drunk, or otherwise violent during a flight. Nurses and customer service associates also experience verbal and sometimes physical violence from angry patients and customers.

Many instances abound of employee-related workplace violence. A worker at a lawn care company in Kansas opened fire, killing three people and injuring an additional 16. The shooter himself was shot by a police officer. In a similar incident, an engineer for the city of Virginia Beach opened fire and killed 12 people in a city building. The shooter worked for the public utilities department.[62] Today, many organizations are developing emergency response plans and conducting workplace shooter training in order to decrease the number of fatalities in these types of violent situations. Although crimes reflect general problems in society, employers have a responsibility to assess risks and provide security, training, and safeguards to protect employees and other stakeholders from such acts. Companies often purchase insurance policies to cover the costs of workplace violence, including business interruption, psychological counseling, informant rewards, and medical claims related to injuries. Experts recommend that all organizations publish and communicate an antiviolence policy and make employees and managers aware of warning signs of possible workplace violence by current employees, such as alcohol and drug use, visible signs of stress, disciplinary and termination proceedings, isolation, and others.[63]

Equal Opportunity Title VII of the Civil Rights Act of 1964 prohibits employment discrimination on the basis of race, national origin, color, religion, and gender. This law is fundamental to employees' rights to join and advance in an organization according to merit rather than one of the characteristics just mentioned. For example, employers are not permitted to categorize a job as only for men or women unless there is a reason that gender is fundamental to the job's tasks and responsibilities. For example, a men's fashion company is able to hire male models exclusively. Additional laws passed in the 1970s, 1980s, and 1990s were designed to prohibit discrimination related to pregnancy, disabilities, age, and other factors. The Americans with Disabilities Act (ADA) prohibits companies from discriminating on the basis of physical or mental disability in all employment practices and requires them to make facilities accessible to and usable by persons with disabilities. The Pregnancy Discrimination Act, now more than 30 years old, was created to help protect the rights of mothers and mothers-to-be in the workplace. The act has been modified many times since its inception. As a result, the number of pregnancy discrimination complaints filed with the Equal Employment Opportunity Commission (EEOC), discussed in earlier chapters, has

Figure 8.2 Growth in Filings and Resolutions of Pregnancy Discrimination Act Complaints to the EEOC

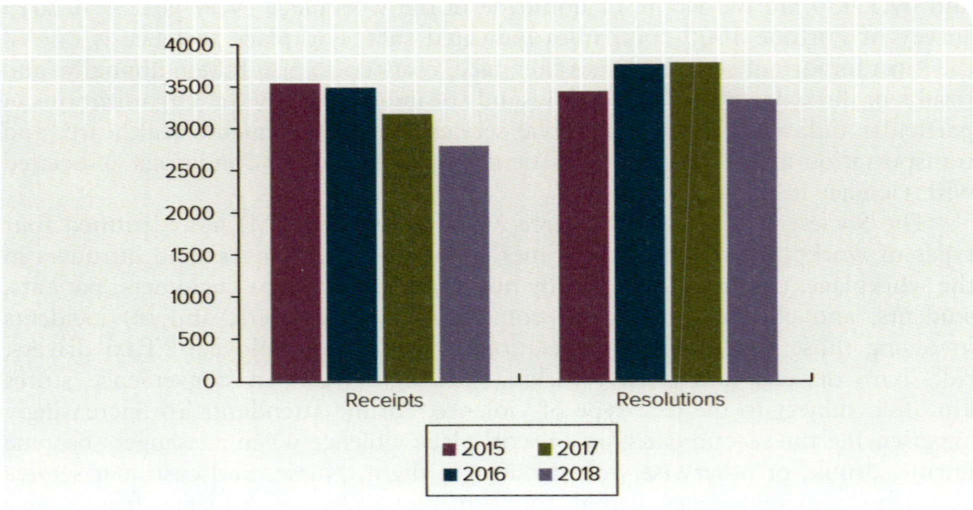

Source: U.S. Equal Employment Opportunity Commission, "Pregnancy Discrimination Charges," https://www.eeoc.gov/eeoc/statistics/enforcement/pregnancy_new.cfm (accessed June 19, 2019).

continually decreased over the years.[64] Figure 8.2 depicts the number of complaints and resolutions of pregnancy discrimination cases from 2015 through 2018.

These legal imperatives require that companies formalize employment practices to ensure that no discrimination is occurring. Thus, managers must be fully aware of the types of practices that constitute discrimination and work to ensure that hiring, promotion, annual evaluation, and other procedures are fair and based on merit. The spread of HIV and AIDS has prompted multinational firms with operations in Africa to distribute educational literature and launch prevention programs. Some companies work with internal and external stakeholders and even fund medical facilities that help prevent the disease and treat HIV/AIDS patients. Another component to their initiatives involves education on fair treatment of employees with the disease. Multinational companies in Mexico, for instance, produced a written commitment to eliminate the stigma and discrimination that often surrounds HIV/AIDS in the workplace.[65]

To ensure that they build balanced workforces, many companies have initiated affirmative action programs, which involve efforts to recruit, hire, train, and promote qualified individuals from groups that have traditionally been discriminated against on the basis of race, sex, or other characteristics. Coca-Cola established a program to create a level foundation so that all employees have access to the same information and development opportunities.[66] A key goal of these programs is to reduce any bias that may exist in hiring, evaluating, and promoting employees. A special type of discrimination, sexual harassment, is also prohibited through Title VII.

Sexual Harassment The flood of women into the workplace during the last half of the twentieth century brought new challenges and opportunities for organizations. Although harassment has probably always existed in the workplace, the presence of both genders in roughly equal numbers changed norms and expectations of behavior. When men dominated the workplace, photos of partially nude women or sexually suggestive materials may have been posted on walls or in lockers. Today, such materials could be viewed as illegal if they contribute to a work environment that is intimidating, offensive, or otherwise interfering with an employee's work performance. The U.S. government indicates the nature of this illegal activity: unwelcome sexual advances, requests for sexual favors, and other verbal or physical conduct of a sexual nature constitutes **sexual harassment** when submission to or rejection of this conduct explicitly or implicitly affects an individual's employment, unreasonably interferes with an individual's work performance, or creates an intimidating, hostile, or offensive work environment.[67]

Prior to 1986, sexual harassment was not a specific violation of federal law in the United States. In *Meritor Savings Bank v. Vinson*, the U.S. Supreme Court ruled that sexual harassment creates a "hostile environment" that violates Title VII of the Civil Rights Act, even in the absence of economic harm or demand for sexual favors in exchange for promotions, raises, or related work incentives.[68] In other countries, sexual harassment in the workplace is considered an illegal act, although the specific conditions may vary by legal and social culture. Until recently, Mexican sexual harassment law protected public-sector employees only if their jobs were jeopardized on the basis of the exchange of sexual favors or relations. In the European Union (EU), sexual harassment legislation focuses on the liability that employers carry when they fail to create a workplace culture free of harassment and other forms of discrimination. The EU has strengthened its rules on sexual harassment, including definitions of direct and indirect harassment, the removal of an upper limit on victim compensation, and the requirement that businesses develop and make "equality reports" available to employees.[69]

There are two general categories of sexual harassment: quid pro quo and hostile work environment.[70] **Quid pro quo sexual harassment** is a type of sexual extortion where there is a proposed or explicit exchange of job benefits for sexual favors. For example, telling an employee, "You will get the promotion if you spend the weekend with me in Las Vegas," is a direct form of sexual harassment. Usually, the person making such a statement is in a position of authority over the harassed employee, and thus, the threat of job loss is real. One incident of quid pro quo harassment may create a justifiable legal claim. **Hostile work environment sexual harassment** is less direct than quid pro quo harassment and can involve epithets, slurs, negative stereotyping, intimidating acts, graphic materials that show hostility toward an individual or group, and other types of conduct that affect the employment situation. For example, at one automobile manufacturing plant, male employees drew inappropriate sexually explicit pictures on cars before they were painted. This was found to be sexual harassment. An email containing sexually explicit jokes that is sent out to employees could be viewed as contributing to a hostile work environment. Some hostile work environment harassment is nonsexual, meaning the harassing conduct is based on gender without explicit reference to sexual acts. For example, in *Campbell v. Kansas State University* (1991), the U.S. District Court for the District of Kansas found repeated remarks about women "being intellectually inferior to men" to be part of a hostile environment. Unlike quid pro quo cases, one incident may not justify a legal claim. Instead, the courts will examine a range of acts and circumstances to determine if the work environment was intolerable and the victim's job performance was impaired.[71]

From a social responsibility perspective, a key issue in both types of sexual harassment is the employing organization's knowledge and tolerance of these types of behaviors. A number of court cases have shed more light on the issues that constitute sexual harassment and organizations' responsibility in this regard.

In *Harris v. Forklift Systems* (1993), Teresa Harris claimed that her boss at Forklift Systems made suggestive sexual remarks, asked her to retrieve coins from his pants pocket, and joked that they should go to a motel to "negotiate her raise." Courts at the state level threw out her case because she did not suffer major psychological injury. The U.S. Supreme Court overturned these decisions, though, ruling that employers can be forced to pay damages even if the worker suffered no proven psychological harm. This case brought about the "reasonable person" standard in evaluating what conduct constitutes sexual harassment. From this case, juries now evaluate the alleged conduct with respect to commonly held beliefs and expectations.[72]

---

sexual harassment
unwelcome sexual advances, requests for sexual favors, and other verbal or physical conduct of a sexual nature which, when submitted to or rejected, explicitly or implicitly affects an individual's employment, unreasonably interferes with an individual's work performance, or creates an intimidating, hostile, or offensive work environment

quid pro quo sexual harassment
a type of sexual extortion where there is a proposed or explicit exchange of job benefits for sexual favors

hostile work environment sexual harassment
a type of sexual harassment that involves epithets, slurs, negative stereotyping, intimidating acts, graphic materials that show hostility toward an individual or group, and other types of conduct that affect the employment situation

Several firms have been embroiled in sexual harassment suits. For example, Sterling Jewelers, the parent company of Kay Jewelers and Jared the Galleria of Jewelry, is accused of discrimination against women for a period of over ten years. The class-action suit, which at one point involved about 70,000 women, could result in substantial punitive damages and fines.[73] In another case, a jury awarded the victim $95 million in damages due to years of experiencing severe sexual harassment by a manager at the furniture rent-to-own store, Aarons Inc. The manager's behavior encouraged other male employees to harass the victim as well, creating a hostile workplace. To make matters worse, the company neglected to respond to the victim when she left a message on their hotline.[74]

U.S. Supreme Court decisions on sexual harassment cases indicate that (1) employers are liable for the acts of supervisors; (2) employers are liable for sexual harassment by supervisors that culminates in a tangible employment action (loss of job, demotion, etc.); (3) employers are liable for a hostile environment created by a supervisor but may escape liability if they demonstrate that they exercised reasonable care to prevent and promptly correct any sexually harassing behavior and that the plaintiff employee unreasonably failed to take advantage of any preventive or corrective measures offered by the employer; and (4) claims of hostile environment sexual harassment must be severe and pervasive to be viewed as actionable by the courts.[75]

Much like the underlying philosophy of the Federal Sentencing Guidelines for Organizations (FSGO) that we discussed in earlier chapters, these decisions require top managers in organizations to take the detection and prevention of sexual harassment seriously. To this end, many firms have implemented programs on sexual harassment. To satisfy current legal standards and set a higher standard for social responsibility, employees, supervisors, and other close business partners should be educated on the company's **zero tolerance** policy against harassment. Employees must also be educated on the policy prohibiting harassment, including the types of behaviors that constitute harassment, how offenders will be punished, and what employees should do if they experience harassment. Just like an organizational compliance program, employees must be assured of confidentiality and no retaliation for reporting harassment.

zero tolerance
the practice of applying penalties to even minor infractions of policy

Training on sexual harassment should be balanced in terms of legal definitions and practical tips and tools. Although employees need to be aware of the legal issues and ramifications, they also may need assistance in learning to recognize and avoid behaviors that may constitute quid pro quo harassment, create a hostile environment, or appear to be retaliatory in nature. In fact, retaliation claims have more than doubled since the early 1990s, prompting many companies to incorporate this element into sexual harassment training. Finally, employees should be aware that same-sex conduct may also constitute sexual harassment.[76] Sexual harassment from women to their male subordinates is yet another issue. One law enforcement officer in Texas won a lawsuit against his female boss after claiming that she frequently wanted sexual favors and touched him inappropriately.[77] Table 8.6 lists facts about sexual harassment that should be used in company communication and training on this workplace issue.

Whistleblowing   An employee who reports individual or company wrong- doing to either internal or external sources is considered a whistleblower.[78] Whistleblowers usually focus on issues or behaviors that need corrective action, although managers and other employees may not appreciate reports that expose company weaknesses, raise embarrassing questions, or otherwise detract from organizational tasks. Although not all whistleblowing activity leads to an extreme reaction, whistleblowers have been retaliated against, demoted, fired, and subject to even worse consequences as a result of their actions.[79] For example, Eddie Garcia, an energy specialist working for Santa Fe County in New Mexico, was accused of grand larceny and was fired from his job after pointing out improper conduct on the part of an exclusive

Table 8.6 Sexual Harassment in the Workplace

Sexual harassment is a form of sex discrimination that violates Title VII of the Civil Rights Act of 1964.

Unwelcome sexual advances, requests for sexual favors, and other verbal or physical conduct of a sexual nature constitute sexual harassment when submission to or rejection of this conduct explicitly or implicitly affects an individual's employment, unreasonably interferes with an individual's work performance, or creates an intimidating, hostile, or offensive work environment.

Sexual harassment can occur in a variety of circumstances, including but not limited to the following:

- The victim as well as the harasser may be a woman or a man. The victim does not have to be of the opposite sex.
- The harasser can be the victim's supervisor, an agent of the employer, a supervisor in another area, a coworker, or a nonemployee.
- The victim does not have to be the person harassed, but could be anyone affected by the offensive conduct.
- Unlawful sexual harassment may occur without economic injury to or discharge of the victim.
- The harasser's conduct must be unwelcome.

It is helpful for the victim to inform the harasser directly that the conduct is unwelcome and must stop. The victim should use any employer complaint mechanism or grievance system available.

When investigating allegations of sexual harassment, the EEOC looks at the whole record: the circumstances, such as the nature of the sexual advances, and the context in which the alleged incidents occurred. A determination of the allegations is made from the facts on a case-by-case basis.

Source: U.S. Equal Employment Opportunity Commission, "Facts About Sexual Harassment," http://www.eeoc.gov/eeoc/publications/fs-sex.cfm (accessed June 15, 2019).

government contractor. Garcia revealed to his supervisors that the contractor had double-billed the county and was failing to obtain the required permits for work. When they did not respond, he expressed his concerns to the media, which spurred retaliation from his employer. In the end, the charges against Garcia were dropped and he was awarded $180,000 in settlement fees, but he suffered personal and professional hardship for five years as a result.[80]

Whistleblowers do have legal protections. The federal government and most state governments in the United States have enacted a number of measures to protect whistleblowers from retaliation. The Whistleblower Protection Act of 1986 shields federal employees from retaliatory behavior; the Sarbanes-Oxley Act provides solid protection to whistleblowers and strong penalties for those who retaliate against them; and other legislation such as the Dodd-Frank Wall Street Reform and Consumer Protection Act has provisions to reward whistleblowers for revealing illegal behavior. Even with this protection, most reported misconduct to the government does not result in an investigation. Most internal and external whistleblowers are not legal experts and use their own judgment about an issue. Therefore, it is important to know the facts and conduct research before reporting.

Ethical Issues

Laws are imperative for social responsibility. The ethical climate of the workplace, however, is values-driven and dependent on top management leadership and corporate culture. In this section, we examine several trends in employment practices that have not fully reached the legal realm. Company initiatives in these areas indicate a corporate philosophy or culture that respects and promotes certain ethical values.

Training and Development As discussed in Chapter 6, "Business Ethics and Ethical Decision-Making," organizational culture and the associated values, beliefs, and norms operate on many levels and affect a number of workplace practices. Organizations should value employees as individuals, not just as functional units to do work. Firms with this ethical stance fund initiatives to develop employees' skills, knowledge, and other personal characteristics. Although this development is linked to business strategy and aids the employer, it also demonstrates a commitment to the future of the employee and his or her interests. Jiffy Lube has been listed as number one for *Training Magazine's* list of top 125 employee training programs. It was selected for focused approach on training on topics including customer service, leadership, and new services. Its training program is credited with helping the organization increase approval ratings by 93 percent.[81]

Professionals also appreciate and respect a training and development focus from their employers. For example, the University of California, Berkeley incorporates an Individual Development Plan (IDP) component into their professional employee training program. The IDP is a one-on-one mentoring process between the employee and supervisor, in which they discuss setting specific goals, how to reach them, and overcoming obstacles.[82] These organizations are enjoying many benefits from employee training and development, including stronger employee recruitment and retention strategies. Indeed, there is a link between investments in employees and the amount of commitment, job satisfaction, and productivity demonstrated by them. Happier employees tend to stay with their employer and to better serve coworkers, customers, and other constituents, which has a direct bearing on the quality of relationships and financial prospects of a firm. Leadership training is also critical, as the main reason that employees leave a company is poor or unskilled management and leadership, not salary, benefits, or related factors. In exit interviews, departing employees often mention their desire for more meaningful feedback and steady communication with managers.[83]

Employees recognize when a company is diligently investing in programs that not only improve operations, but also increase their empowerment and provide new opportunities to improve their knowledge and grow professionally. Through formal training and development classes, workers get a better sense of where they fit and how they contribute to the overall organization. This understanding empowers them to become more responsive, accurate, and confident in workplace decisions. Training also increases ethical decision-making skills, accountability, and responsibility, reducing micromanaging or "hand-holding." All these effects contribute to the financial and cultural health of an organization.[84] Thus, a commitment to training enables a firm to enhance its organizational capacity to fulfill stakeholder expectations.

Training and development activities require sufficient resources and the commitment of all managers to be successful. For example, a departmental manager must be supportive of an employee using part of the workday to attend a training session on a new software package. At the same time, the organization must pay for the training, regardless of whether it uses inside or outside trainers and develops in-house materials or purchases them from educational providers. A study by the Association for Talent Development indicates that, on average, employers in the U.S. spend about $1,296 per employee on training every year, and employees engaged in approximately 34.1 hours of annual learning. The survey also tracked the major topics offered to employees. Over 45 percent of material fell into the following main topics: managerial and supervisory; mandatory and compliance; processes, procedures, and business practices; and interpersonal skills.[85] Another area that has received much attention in the United States involves support for outside education. For example, Starbucks partnered with Arizona State University to offer tuition coverage for eligible employees to earn their bachelor's degrees.[86]

workplace diversity
recruiting and retaining individuals regardless of age, gender, ethnicity, physical or mental ability, or other characteristics

Diversity and Inclusion Whereas Title VII of the Civil Rights Act grants legal protection to different types of employees, initiatives in **workplace diversity** focus on recruiting and retaining a diverse workforce as a business imperative.[87] With diversity programs, companies assume an ethical obligation to employ and empower individuals regardless of age, gender, ethnicity, physical or mental ability, or other characteristics. These firms go beyond compliance with government guidelines to develop cultures that respect and embrace the unique skills, backgrounds, and contributions of all types of people. Thus, legal statutes focus on removing discrimination, whereas diversity represents a leadership approach for cultivating and appreciating employee talent.[88]

Firms with an effective diversity effort link their diversity mission statement with the corporate strategic plan, implement plans to recruit and retain a diverse talent pool, support community programs of diverse groups, hold management accountable for various types of diversity performance, and have tangible outcomes of their diversity strategy. Each firm must tailor their diversity initiative to meet unique employee, market, and industry conditions. To ensure effectiveness, many large corporations have hired **chief diversity officers (CDOs)** to move diversity to the forefront of decision-making, outcomes assessment, and resource allocation. By having CDOs in high-ranking positions, these firms are signaling their commitment to core values associated with tolerance, respect, and transparency. Several studies have found that companies led by women are more likely to employ CDOs than those led by men. This may be explained by the fact that women are underrepresented in corporate executive roles, and thus may have been outsiders on their way up the leadership ranks. Andrea Jung, the former CEO of Avon, reflected that she was often the only woman and the only person of Asian origin in meetings with other senior leaders.[89] Jung expressed the theory of **intersectionality**, which considers the multidimensional nature of identity and resulting effects on social dynamics. Catalyst, a nonprofit organization, recently surveyed 1,600 people who identify as Asian, African-American, and Latino about intersectionality in the workplace, specifically as a form of emotional tax. More than half of the respondents indicated that they felt "on guard," with women more likely to report greater stress about racial bias than gender bias at work.[90]

chief diversity officer (CDO) the corporate executive responsible for diversity and inclusion initiatives and results

intersectionality theory a theory which focuses on the multidimensional nature of identity, including class, gender, and race, and its effects on social dimensions of differences

Many firms embrace employee diversity to deal with supplier and customer diversity. Their assumption is that to effectively design, market, and support products for different target groups, a company must employ individuals who reflect its customers' characteristics.[91] Organizations and industries with a populationwide customer base may use national demographics for assessing their diversity effort. Kaiser Permanente uses a dashboard to assess the links between its senior-executive compensation and diversity. It is mandatory for company recruiters to present diverse slates of candidates for open positions.[92] As demographics in the United States continue to shift, companies are faced with reconsidering their marketing and hiring strategies, including the link between employee and customer characteristics. The sharp growth in the Hispanic population is one of the most important demographic shifts recorded. This has prompted firms to hire Hispanic employees and consultants and tailor their offerings to this demographic. Clorox and General Mills, for instance, are appealing to Hispanics with bilingual advertisements via mobile apps.[93]

As discussed in Chapter 1, there are opportunities to link social responsibility objectives with business performance, and many firms are learning the benefits of employing individuals with different backgrounds and perspectives. For example, at New York Life, diversity is treated like all other business goals. The company employs a CDO to create accountability and inclusion strategies with employees, suppliers, community members, and other stakeholders.[94] Hewlett-Packard (HP), a multinational IT company, is committed to including people with disabilities in their workplace. The company was named Private-Sector Employer of the Year by *CAREERS & the disABLED Magazine*, a publication that provides career advice for people with disabilities. HP was recognized by the magazine's readers for providing a positive environment in which to work. The company values diversity and believes that this component of their culture allows them to innovate in ways

workplace inclusion
organizational (corporate) culture that ensures that policies, procedures, and practices are fair, transparent, supportive, and empowering for all employees

that less diverse companies cannot do. In addition, HP designs goods and services that are informed by its diverse workforce.[95] Organizations with an intentional commitment and sustainable outcomes with diversity management progress toward **workplace inclusion**, a culture that ensures that policies, procedures, and practices are fair, transparent, supportive, and empowering for all employees.[96]

Conflicting views and voices of different generations abound in the workplace, and this is the first time in history that the workforce has been composed of so many generations at one time. Generations have worked together in the past, but these groups were usually divided by organizational stratification. Many workplaces now include members of multiple generations working shoulder to shoulder. The result may be greater dissension among the age groups than when they were stratified by the organizational hierarchy. Because employees serve an important role in the social responsibility framework, managers need to be aware of generational differences and their potential effects on teamwork, conflict, and other workplace behaviors. Table 8.7 lists the four generations present in today's workplace, as well as their key characteristics.

Baby boomers are service oriented, good team players, and want to please. However, they are also known for being self-centered, overly sensitive to feedback, and not budget-minded. People in Generation X are adaptable, technologically literate, independent, and unintimidated by authority. However, their liabilities include impatience, cynicism, and inexperience. Generation Y, whose members are also called *Millennials*, is a technologically savvy group. In addition, they bring the assets of collective action, optimism, multitasking ability, and tenacity to the workplace. However, they also have the liabilities of inexperience, especially with difficult people issues, and a need for supervision and structure. Members of Generation Z are relatively new to the workplace, with many still in high school and college. This generation is very diverse, aware of social justice issues, and on track to becoming the most highly educated group in the workplace.

Although generational issues have always existed in the workforce, there are some new twists today. The older generations no longer have all the money and power. Times of anxiety and uncertainty can aggravate differences and generational conflict, and these conflicts need to be handled correctly when they occur. Understanding the different generations and how they see things is a crucial part of handling this conflict. The book *Generations at Work: Managing the Clash of Veterans, Boomers, Xers, and Nexters in Your Workplace* developed the ACORN acronym (detailed in Table 8.8) to describe five principles that managers can use to deal with generational issues.

Accommodating employee differences entails treating employees as customers and giving them the best service that the company can give. Creating workplace choices as to what and how employees work can allow change and satisfaction. Operating from a sophisticated management style requires that management be

Table 8.7 Profiles of Generations at Work

Generation Name	Birth Years	Key Characteristics
Baby boomers	1946–1964	Rejection of traditional values, optimistic, achievement-oriented
Generation X	1965–1980	Family-oriented, impatient, individualistic
Generation Y (Millennials)	1981–1996	Technologically savvy, greater expectations for workplace, optimistic
Generation Z	After 1996	Ethically and racially diverse, aware of social justice, entrepreneurial, digital natives

Source: Michael Dimock, "Defining Generations: Where Millennials End and Generation Z Begins," Pew Research Center, https://www.pewresearch.org/fact-tank/2019/01/17/where-millennials-end-and-generation-z-begins/ (accessed June 18, 2019).

direct, but tactful. Respecting competence and initiative assumes the best of the different generations and responds accordingly. Nourishing retention means keeping the best employees. When combined with effective communication skills, the ACORN principles can help managers mend generational conflicts for the benefit of everyone in the company.[97] As noted in Table 8.3 earlier in this chapter, Baird, a private financial services firm, implemented a **reverse mentoring** program so that senior leaders had the opportunity to learn from junior employees. This intergenerational program paired Millennials with executives born during the baby boom and generation X time frame. GM, Microsoft, Sodexo, UnitedHealth, and Procter & Gamble have also employed this approach, which is recommended when employees would benefit from getting to know and learning from other employees with different personal and professional characteristics. Lately, companies are investing in reverse mentoring as a way to cross the digital divide, where younger employees teach and inspire older employees to use technology for achieving daily tasks, as well as strategic goals. These programs may also reveal opportunities and problems that, to date, have not been communicated to those in the executive suite.[98]

Although workplace diversity reaps benefits for both employees and employers, it also brings challenges that must be addressed. Diverse employees may have more difficulty communicating and working with each other. Although differences can breed innovation and creativity, they can also create an atmosphere of distrust, dissatisfaction, or lack of cooperation.[99] For example, growth in the number of children and adults with autism spectrum disorders (ASD) has prompted companies to consider the ways in which this diagnosis affects the workplace, as well as consumer interactions. Although high-functioning individuals with ASD and similar neurodiverse diagnoses are capable of productive work and contributions, they often face stigmas associated with mental health, fear, and accommodations. Recognizing the value that these individuals bring to the workplace, Ernst & Young, SAP, and other companies have instituted programs that provide an environment and job structure that supports the special talents of employees with ASD.[100] As this example demonstrates, many organizations are seizing the opportunity to discuss diversity and create stronger bonds among employees with different ethnicities, religious backgrounds, beliefs, health conditions, sexual orientations, generations, gender identities, and experiences. Coupled with a commitment to authenticity in the workplace, firms engage employees in training programs, community service projects, and similar initiatives that promote teamwork, relationship-building, and cohesion, and ultimately help to maximize the positive effects and minimize the difficulties associated with diversity.

Finally, the diversity message will not be taken seriously unless top management and organizational systems fully support a diverse workforce. After Home Depot settled a gender-discrimination lawsuit, it developed an automated hiring and promotion computer program. Although the Job Preference Program (JPP) system was originally intended as insurance against discrimination, the system opens all jobs and applicants to the companywide network, eliminates unqualified applicants, and enables managers to learn about employee aspirations and skills in a more effective manner. JPP has also brought a positive change to the number of female and minority managers at Home Depot.[101] On the other hand, Silicon Valley has been highly criticized for its apparent lack of diversity. Although many tech firms are setting more diversity goals, companies like Facebook have made only minimal gains. Facebook has often claimed that there is simply not enough available talent.[102]

In addition, some employees of companies with diversity training programs have viewed such training as intended to blame or change white men only. Other training has focused on the reasons that diversity should be important, though not

Table 8.8 ACORN: Principles for Managing Generations at Work

| **A**ccommodate employee differences |
| **C**reate choices in the workplace |
| **O**perate from a sophisticated management style |
| **R**espect competence and initiative |
| **N**ourish employee retention |

Source: Ron Zemke, Claire Ranes, and Bob Filipczak, *Generations at Work: Managing the Clash of Veterans, Boomers, Xers, and Nexters in Your Workplace* (New York: ACACOM, 2000).

reverse mentoring
organizational mentoring program where less experienced employees mentor more experienced employees

the actual changes in attitudes, work styles, expectations, and business processes that are needed for diversity to work.[103] Professional development initiatives to reveal **unconscious bias** are particularly useful for employees, including those with a deep commitment to inclusion and diversity, who may be unaware of how unconscious attitudes and associations affect both daily and long-term aspects of work, including hiring practices, job promotions, networking, and mentoring relationships. This lack of cognition about one's own biases has led some researchers to conclude that effective diversity training includes educating employees about implicit bias, teaching strategies to reduce bias, and motivating employees to act in more egalitarian ways.[104]

unconscious bias
a lack of awareness of one's own unconscious attitudes and associations

Work/Life Balance   Just as increasing numbers of women in the workplace have changed the norms of behavior at work and prompted attention to sexual harassment, they have also brought challenges in work/life balance. This balance is not just an issue for women, as men also have multiple roles that can create the same types of stress and conflict.[105] The work/life balance may be described otherwise, such as people who are torn between work and home on a regular basis. An employee thinking about work (or actually working) when he is at home and vice versa is ultimately struggling with multiple responsibilities.[106]

Because employees have roles within and outside the organization, there is increasing corporate focus on the types of support that employees have in balancing these obligations. Deloitte & Touche (now part of Deloitte Touche Tohmatsu), an international professional services firm, was forced to address issues of work/life balance when it discovered the alarming rate at which women were leaving the firm. In the early 1990s, only 4 of the 50 employees being considered for partner status were women, despite the company's heavy recruitment of women from business schools. The company convened the Initiative for the Retention and Advancement of Women task force and soon uncovered cultural beliefs and practices that needed modification. The task force found that younger employees—both male and female—wanted a balanced life, were willing to forgo some pay for more time with family and less stress, and had similar career goals. Therefore, Deloitte & Touche developed a major work/life balance initiative that included reduced travel schedules and flexible work arrangements to benefit both men and women employed at the firm. According to a survey, issues related to work/life balance, such as telecommuting, flexible scheduling, and assistance with child care and elder care, are almost equally important to male and female employees. Whereas men rarely utilized these benefits in the past, this is no longer the case. Many midlevel executives, both male and female, are part of dual-earner couples "sandwiched" between raising children and caring for aging parents.[107]

work/life programs
programs that assist employees in balancing work responsibilities with personal and family responsibilities

Such **work/life programs** assist employees in balancing work responsibilities with personal and family responsibilities. A central feature of these programs is flexibility, such that employees of all types are able to achieve their own definition of balance. For example, a single parent may want child care and consistent work hours, whereas another employee may need assistance in finding elder care for a parent with Alzheimer's disease. A working mother may need access to "just-in-time" care when a child is sick or school is out of session. Employees of

Shutterstock/Elizaveta Galitckaia

all types appreciate flextime arrangements, which allow them to work 40 hours per week on a schedule that they develop within a range of hours specified by the company. Other employees work some hours at home or in a location more conducive to their personal obligations. SAS Institute, the world's largest private software company, has been recognized by Glassdoor.com for its exceptional work/life balance program. The company offers employees and their families many perks supporting a balanced life, such as free access to a gymnasium, a healthcare clinic on company grounds, discounted child care, free "work-life" counseling, and more.[108] Work/life balance not only enhances employee productivity, but it is also an imperative to attracting and maintaining a healthy workforce.

More than 80 million Americans suffer from symptoms of stress at work, including headaches, sleeplessness, and other physical ailments.[109] To address these concerns, Americans spend more than $20 billion per year on stress-reducing goods, services, and strategies.[110] Compared to Japanese and Chinese workers, however, the U.S. figures are moderate. The term *karoshi*, which means, "death from overwork," became widely used in Japan. Thousands of deaths per year are attributed to overwork, such as brain hemorrhages, heart attacks, and suicides. The Japanese government passed legislations to establish support centers, assist businesses in reducing the number of deaths, and conduct more research into the phenomenon. China, as its economy continues to grow, is beginning to experience the same issue. The death toll was estimated at 600,000 employees per year, or 1,600 per day.[111]

Managers must become sensitive to cues that employees need to create a stronger work/life balance. Frustration, anger, moodiness, a myopic focus, and physiological symptoms are often present when an employee needs to take a vacation, work fewer hours, utilize flexible scheduling, or simply reduce his or her workload. One manager of a telecommunications firm in California returned to the workplace around 11:30 p.m. every night to send people home. Otherwise, she knew that many of them would sleep on the floor in the office.

Not only do some employees work too many hours, but they may largely ignore nutrition and fitness, friendships, community involvement, and other aspects of work/life balance.[112] For this reason, many organizations offer an **employee assistance program (EAP)** that includes a range of services typically associated with counseling and mental health. EAPs began in the United States in response to increasing rates of alcoholism and its effects in the workplace. Today, EAPs focus on broader issues that affect employees' stress levels, well-being, and productivity. The majority of companies with EAPs outsource them to other firms that specialize in meeting the personal needs of employees. EAPs are becoming part of an organization's ability to be globally competitive. A shift in beliefs about work/life balance and mental health, along with changing regulations and employee demand, is prompting more and more organizations to develop these programs. Technology advancements have also spurred the online delivery of EAP services.[113] These programs may also be needed when a community is faced with a crisis, such as natural disasters or violence. With the increase of mass shootings in schools, EAPs continue to be needed to assist employees and first responders dealing with significant trauma.[114]

employee assistance program (EAP)

workplace program that provides employees with services to improve mental health and well-being

There is no generic work/life program. Instead, companies need to consider their employee base and the types of support that their employees are likely to need and appreciate. James Goodnight, SAS's founder, believes that dinnertime should be spent with family and friends, not in the office. Most employees leave by 5:00 p.m., and others participate in flextime or job-sharing arrangements. This, among other characteristics listed earlier, has resulted in the company receiving honors such as its high ranking on *Fortune* magazine's annual list of the 100 Best Companies to Work For and one of *Computer World* magazine's 100 Best Places to Work in IT.[115]

Ethical Issues in **HUMAN RESOURCES**

The Sharing Economy: Fueled by Independent Contractors

The sharing economy is a relatively new phenomenon, largely propelled by innovative and disruptive approaches to traditional business models, advances in technology, and consumer use of the internet for all types of activities, including purchasing. For example, the founders of Uber wondered if there was a better and easier way for customers to find a taxi ride. They also hoped that they could hire drivers who were willing to use their personal vehicles to pick up and drive people to their destinations. The founders of Airbnb hoped that consumers would take a risk by staying in a stranger's spare bedroom or second home instead of an expensive hotel. They started the home-sharing company when they were struggling to pay their rent in San Francisco and offered to rent air mattresses in their apartment to attendees coming to a large conference. While their initial offering only attracted three conference-goers, the founders persevered and built a company with over $900 million in annual revenues.

Currently, the cornerstone of the sharing economy is the independent, nonemployee status of service providers, suppliers, and partners of firms such as Airbnb, Lyft, HomeAway, and Uber. These firms are often referred to as *digital matching firms* because they utilize technology to link service or product providers to customers. Digital matching firms have challenged the status quo in many industries where companies have traditionally relied on employees to deliver their services.

The Human Resources (HR) model of the sharing economy relies on brief and electronically facilitated exchanges between the digital matching firm, customers, and suppliers, rather than extensive hiring and training protocols associated with best practices in HR management. Unlike traditional employees, owners and partners in the sharing economy may not be subject to thorough background and reference checks and, given a technology-mediated platform, do not have lengthy interactions with company representatives to learn the organization's values, ethical standards, and culture. Reviews posted by customers help to assess service providers but are often limited in number and subject to credibility questions.

Current U.S. law takes a binary approach to worker classification: Either a worker depends on an organization or is self-employed as an independent contractor. New business practices by digital matching firms and others call into question this two-pronged approach. To some observers, the current classification system reflects the country's agrarian and manufacturing roots, not the service and technology economy of today.

Uber drivers complained about their worker classification after Uber implemented penalties for drivers who failed to accept a high percentage of rides offered them. Although such penalties may be effective in eliminating drivers who are not committed to timely customer service, they may also ensure that drivers cannot effectively represent multiple transportation services. These Uber drivers perceived the tactic as a way of increasing their dependency on Uber and decreasing their choices and independence.

In response to a multitude of questions and complaints, the U.S. Department of Labor recently took action to answer worker complaints about misclassification. This is a significant issue for the Department of Labor because employees improperly classified as independent contractors may not be provided workplace protections such as the minimum wage, payment of overtime, and availability of unemployment and workers' compensation insurance coverage. These independent relationships are deemed beneficial by workers who appreciate flexibility and personal control. However, regulators are concerned that some employees may be purposefully misclassified in an attempt to substantially reduce costs and evade U.S. labor laws.

The Department of Labor recently reminded employers that the classification of workers should be based on the *suffer or permit to work* standard pertaining to an individual's degree of economic dependence on the employer. Cases and decisions made by the U.S. Supreme Court and U.S. Circuit Courts of Appeals have yielded the economic realities test, which guides employers and the Department of Labor in making this determination:

- Is the work performed by the worker essential or fundamental to the business?
- Does the worker's managerial ability affect their prospects for financial gain or loss?
- How does the worker's financial investment compare with the employer's investment?
- Is the worker required to exercise special skills and initiative?
- To what extent does the employer control the work?

In the absence of a new worker classification approach, critics worry that the sharing economy creates a business-sided economic model that mirrors the labor market long before there were laws affecting wages, hours worked, safety, and other conditions. Traditional competitors of digital matching firms also question the independent worker status because these firms are not required to provide or pay for overtime, sick leave, vacation leave, retirement plans, health insurance, or other benefits. Legal scholars point to privacy concerns around the data and monitoring that occurs within the sharing economy and how this ultimately affects power and fairness for both workers and competitors. As the sharing economy continues to expand, more research is needed to understand labor markets, worker classification, competition laws, and other ramifications for stakeholders.

Sources: Ryan Calo and Alex Rosenblat, "The Taking Economy: Uber, Information, and Power," *Columbia Law Review* 117 (October 2017): 1623–1690; Juliet Schor, "Debating the Sharing Economy," *Journal of Self-Governance and Management Economics*, 4 (2016): 7–22; Arun Sundararajan, *The Sharing Economy: The End of Employment and the Rise of Crowd-Based Capitalism* (Cambridge, MA: MIT Press, 2017); Rudy Telles, Jr., "Digital Matching Firms: A New Definition in the Sharing Economy Space," U.S. Department of Commerce, Economics, and Statistics Administration, https://www. commerce.gov/sites/default/files/migrated/reports/digital-matching-firms-new-definition-sharing-economy-space.pdf (accessed June 25, 2019); Debbie M. Thorne and Floyd F. Quinn, "Supplier Resources in the Sharing Economy: Three Regulatory Concerns," *Journal of Marketing Channels* 24 (2017): 73–83; U.S. Department of Labor, "Fair Labor Standards Act Advisor," https://webapps.dol.gov/elaws/whd/flsa/scope/ee14.asp (accessed June 25, 2019); U.S. Department of Labor, "The Application of the Fair Labor Standards Act's "Suffer or Permit" Standard in the Identification of Employees Who Are Misclassified as Independent Contractors," https://casetext.com/analysis/the-application-of-the-fair-labor-standards-acts-suffer-or-permit-standard-in-the-identification-of-employees-who-are-misclassified-as-independent-contractors-1 (accessed October 8, 2019).

Successful work/life programs, like that developed by the SAS Institute, are an extension of the diversity philosophy such that employees are respected as individuals in the process of contributing to company goals. Thus, connecting employees' personal needs, lives, and goals to strategic business issues can be fruitful for both parties. This perspective is in contrast to the "employee goals versus business goals" trade-off mentality that has been pervasive. IBM implemented a work/life strategy over two decades ago and periodically conducts employee surveys to see if changes or additions are needed.[116]

The Silk Road Survey found that 55 percent of all applicants consider work/life balance the most important consideration in identifying potential employers and considering job offers.[117] For this reason, companies have become quite innovative in their approach to work/life balance. Agilent Technologies, for example, not only offers flexible work schedules and employee discounts, but also has organized sports teams, massages on site, and yoga sessions.[118] Nokia is known for making employees feel cared for. Employees have noted that beyond flexible work schedules and the ability to work from home, the company encourages them to take time off and recharge.[119] Such efforts demonstrate the company's willingness to accommodate employee needs and concerns beyond the workplace.

Philanthropic Issues

In later chapters of this book, we examine the philanthropic efforts of companies and the important role that employees play in the process of selecting and implementing projects that contribute time, resources, and human activity to worthy causes. In social responsibility, philanthropic responsibilities are primarily directed outside the organization, so they are not directly focused on employees. However, employees benefit from participating in volunteerism and other philanthropic projects. Employee volunteerism increases the level of engagement the employee feels, which contributes not only to their performance, but also to the company's performance. The engagement is a result of many factors, including gaining a sense of purpose through volunteering, having the ability to work in positions of leadership, and gaining new skills. In addition, engaged employees are more likely to stay with the company for longer periods of time.[120]

Many employers help organize employees to participate in walkathons, marathons, bikeathons, and similar events. For example, Blue Cross Blue Shield companies hold an annual event called National Walk@Lunch Day. The event challenges employees and community members to put on their sneakers and walk at least 30 minutes at lunch. Over a six-week period, participants log their steps on the company's Facebook page. At the end of the event, Blue Cross Blue Shield donates up to $1 per mile reported to the American Diabetes Association.[121] Thus, the benefits of corporate philanthropy in the community reflect positively on the organization. There are many strategies for demonstrating community involvement and care. CA Technologies holds a monthlong volunteer program in which employees from all over the world spend time volunteering at nonprofits in their local communities.[122]

Strategic Implementation of Responsibilities to Employees

As this chapter has demonstrated, a company's responsibilities toward their employees are varied and complex. The legal issues alone require full-time attention from lawyers and HR specialists. These issues are also emotional because corporate decisions have ramifications on families and communities, as well as on employees. In light of this complexity, many companies have chosen to embrace these obligations to benefit both employee and organizational goals. This philosophy stands in stark contrast to the master-servant model popular more than 100 years ago. Today, companies are using distinctive programs and initiatives to set themselves apart and to become known as desirable employers. Low unemployment levels before the last recession, along with diversity, work/life balance, outsourcing, and generational differences, prompted companies to use marketing strategy and business insights normally applied to customer development in the employee recruitment and retention realm. Even in a time of economic downturn, employers will need to be mindful of keeping top talent and maintaining employee satisfaction. For example, Patagonia encourages its employees to stay physically fit. It places so much emphasis on employee satisfaction and physical fitness, in fact, that employees are allowed to go surfing in the middle of the workday.[123]

employer of choice
an organization of any size in any industry that is able to attract, optimize, and retain the best employee talent over the long term

An **employer of choice** is an organization of any size in any industry that is able to attract, optimize, and retain the best employee talent over the long term. AECOM, a global infrastructure firm, recently received a perfect score on the Corporate Equality Index, measured and reported by the Human Rights Campaign Foundation. The roots of AECOM's commitment to being an employer of choice are deep and emanate from a cross-functional and geographically diverse committee that focused on ways in which AECOM's top management can ensure that integrity, respect, open communication, flexibility, and balance are the key values and defining qualities of every employee's career.[124] Advertising, websites, and other company communications often use the term to describe and market the organization to current and potential employees. These messages center on the various practices that companies have implemented to create employee satisfaction. Firms with this distinction value the human component of business, not just financial considerations, ensure that employees are engaged in meaningful work, and stimulate the intellectual curiosity of employees. These businesses have strong training practices, delegate authority, and recognize the link between employee morale, customer satisfaction, and other performance measures.[125] Thus, becoming an employer of choice is an important manifestation of strategic social responsibility. Potential employees may look for signs that social responsibility is a top concern. College graduates may evaluate a potential employer's socially responsible and ethical behavior when deciding on a career path. Table 8.9 shows the percentage of college students who indicated the job characteristics they considered to be the most important. The table demonstrates the kind of culture and messages companies should cultivate to attract employees.

Despite the negative effects that certain actions may have on perceptions of a company's social responsibility, there are strategies and programs that demonstrate a proactive approach to employee relations. One traditional way to strengthen trust is through **employee stock ownership plans (ESOPs)**, which provide the opportunity both to contribute to and benefit from organizational success. Under these plans, employees must take on an ownership perspective, work as a team in an environment that forges trust, and provide excellent interactions and service to customers. Such programs confer not only ownership, but also opportunities for employees to participate in management planning, which foster an environment that many organizations believe increases profits.

Several studies of companies with ESOPs cast a positive light on these plans. ESOPs appear to increase sales by about 2.3–2.4 percent over what would have been expected otherwise. ESOP companies were also found to pay better benefits, higher wages, and provide nearly twice the retirement income for employees than their non-ESOP counterparts. Some of the 7,000 "employee-owned" firms include Dunn-Edwards Paints, Publix Supermarkets, and Round Table Pizza.[126] Of *Fortune* magazine's "100 Best Companies to Work For", more than half are employee-owned.[127] Research has shown that the decision to become an employee-owned company enhances company performance and provides higher wealth accumulation for employee-owners. Despite the advantages of ESOPs, however, experts warn that some are potentially risky for employees, as in the case of Enron.[128] Just like any other company initiative, management must take responsibility for managing an ESOP well.

Becoming an employer of choice has many benefits, including an enhanced ability to hire and retain the best people, who in turn offer a strong commitment to the company's mission and stakeholders. The expectations of such businesses are very high because employee stakeholders often have specific criteria in mind when assessing the attractiveness of a particular employer. Some people may be focused on specific environmental issues, whereas others may be searching for a company that markets healthy and helpful products. Although top managers must decide on how the firm will achieve strategic social responsibility with employees, Table 8.10 provides guidance on eight key principles that are typically exhibited and managed by employers of choice. Although most companies have long understood the importance of attracting and keeping customers through strong branding efforts, many are relatively new to the implementation of strategies to create an employer brand.[129]

Finally, the global dimensions of today's workplace shape an organization's ability to effectively work with employee stakeholders and to become an employer of choice. Firms with offices and sites around the world must deal with a complexity of norms, laws, and expectations, all of which can affect its reputation at home. For example, when Nike was first accused of dealing with suppliers that used child labor in the mid-1990s, the company claimed that it was not in the business of manufacturing shoes (only selling them), and that therefore it could not be blamed for the practices of Asian manufacturers. Following media criticism, Nike publicized a report claiming that the employees of its Indonesian and Vietnamese suppliers were living quite well. The veracity of this report was tarnished by contradictory evidence produced by activists. Next, Nike started introducing workers' rights and environmental guidelines for its suppliers. Yet some company representatives explained that any additional social responsibility initiatives would damage the competitive position of the firm.

In the late 1990s, Nike designed a suppliers' auditing process that invited student representatives, along with other activists, to visit manufacturing plants

Table 8.9 What College Students Consider the Most Important Characteristics of a Job

Characteristic	Percentage
1. Job security	82.9
2. Opportunity to develop job-specific skills	82.5
3. Opportunity to develop applied skills	79.7
4. Friendly coworkers	78.8
5. Good insurance/benefits package	76.5

Source: National Association of Colleges and Employers, "Job Security Tops Students' Wish List," https://www.naceweb.org/talent-acquisition/student-attitudes/job-security-tops-students-wish-list/ (accessed June 21, 2019).

employee stock ownership plans (ESOPs)

employment benefits programs that confer stock ownership to employees providing the opportunity to contribute to and benefit from organizational success

Table 8.10 Key Principles of Employers of Choice

Principle	Explanation
1. Organizational reputation	Employees desire to work in an organization that maintains a good reputation among stakeholders.
2. Organizational culture	Employees want to work in an ethical organizational culture that maintains integrity and encourages employee contributions.
3. Strong leadership	Employees want to work in an environment that has strong ethical leaders who care passionately about the company.
4. Interesting work	Employees want their jobs to be challenging and rewarding, not either mundane or too difficult.
5. Opportunities for growth	Employees want to work in a job or industry where there are significant opportunities for career advancement.
6. Employee recognition	Employees appreciate being recognized for their contributions to the company and are encouraged to continue serving.
7. Employee well-being	Employees expect fair compensation, appropriate benefits, and an adequate work/life balance from their employers.
8. Social responsibility	Studies have demonstrated that employees enjoy working for a company that considers the needs of stakeholders and contributes toward improving society.

Sources: Roger E. Herman and Joyce L. Gioia, *How to Become an Employer of Choice* (Winchester, VA: Oakhill Press, 2000); Amy Hirsh Robinson, "Are You an 'Employer of Choice'? 3 Ways to Attract the Best," *HR Specialist* 17 (March 2019): 7; Jody Ordioni, "How to Become an Employee of Choice," ere.net, July 15, 2013, http://www.eremedia.com/ere/how-to-become-an-employer-of-choice/ (accessed June 21, 2019); Karnica Tanwar and Amresh Kumar, "Employer Brand, Person-Organisation Fit and Employer of Choice," *Personnel Review* 48 (2019): 799–823.

and provide recommendations for improving practices. Before the company's shift, many media reports discussed their manufacturing practices, and it is likely that some consumers and potential employees were rejecting Nike. Nike actually settled the legal case after losing a Supreme Court appeal. Nike agreed to pay $1.5 million to the Fair Labor Association to help fund worker development programs. In this case, Nike's relationships with its manufacturing suppliers and their employees affected its ability to achieve strategic social responsibility.[130] Today, Nike's supply chain practices have improved considerably. The company has been awarded the Corporate Register Reporting Award for excellence in global reporting, demonstrating that its auditing and ethical programs for supply chains have significantly increased the transparency and accountability of the company.[131]

Summary

Throughout history, people's perceptions of work and employment have evolved from a necessary evil to a source of fulfillment. The relationship between employer and employee involves responsibilities, obligations, and expectations as well as challenges.

On an economic level, many believe there is an unwritten, informal psychological contract that includes the beliefs, perceptions, expectations, and obligations that make up the agreement between individuals and their employers. This contract has evolved from a primarily master-servant relationship, in which employers held the power, to one in which employees assume a more balanced relationship with employers. Workforce reduction, the process of eliminating employment positions, breaches the psychological contract that exists between an employer and employee and threatens the social contract among employers, communities, and other groups. Although workforce reduction lowers costs, it often results in lost intellectual capital, strained customer relationships, negative media attention, and other issues that drain company resources.

Employment law is a complex and ever-evolving area. In the past, employment was primarily governed by employment at will, a common-law doctrine that allows either the employer or employee to terminate the relationship at any time, so long as it does not violate an employment contract. Many laws have been enacted to regulate business conduct with regard to wages and benefits, labor unions, health and safety, equal employment opportunity, sexual harassment, and whistle blowing. Title VII of the Civil Rights Act, which prohibits employment discrimination on the basis of race, national origin, color, religion, and gender, is fundamental to employees' rights to join and advance in an organization according to merit. Sexual harassment is defined as unwelcome sexual advances, requests for sexual favors, and other verbal or physical conduct of a sexual nature when submission to or rejection of this conduct explicitly or implicitly affects an individual's employment, unreasonably interferes with an individual's work performance, or creates an intimidating, hostile, or offensive work environment. Sexual harassment may take the form of either quid pro quo harassment or hostile work environment harassment. An employee who reports individual or corporate wrongdoing to either internal or external sources is considered a whistleblower and hence may have certain protections. Although legal compliance is imperative for social responsibility, the ethical climate of the workplace is more subjective and dependent on top management support and corporate culture. Companies with strong ethical standards are more likely to fund initiatives to develop employees' skills, knowledge, and other personal characteristics. With diversity programs, companies assume an ethical obligation to employ and empower individuals regardless of age, gender, physical and mental ability, and other characteristics. Inclusion efforts take diversity management one step further, by ensuring that organizational policies, procedures, and practices are fair, transparent, supportive, and empowering for all employees. Many companies are training employees to recognize their unconscious biases that affect both daily and long-term aspects of work. Work/life programs assist employees in balancing work responsibilities with personal and family responsibilities.

Employees may play an important role in a firm's philanthropic efforts. Employees benefit from such initiatives through participation in volunteerism and other projects.

In light of the complexity of and emotions involved with responsibilities toward employees, many companies have chosen to embrace these obligations to benefit both employee and organizational goals. An employer of choice is an organization of any size in any industry that is able to attract, optimize, and retain the best employee talent over the long term. One traditional way to strengthen trust is through Employee Stock Ownership Plans (ESOPs), which provide the opportunity both to contribute to and gain from organizational success. Finally, the global dimensions of today's workplace shape an organization's ability to effectively work with employee stakeholders and to become an employer of choice.

Responsible Business Debate

The Pros and Cons of Hiring Convicted Criminals

Issue: *Should companies hire applicants with criminal backgrounds?*

At age 23, Darrell Jobe, who spent his teenage years in and out of juvenile detention, decided to turn his life around. He was determined to become a better father than his own father had been. He was also committed to becoming a productive citizen. Like most criminal offenders, however, he had a very difficult time finding an employer to take a chance on him. Eventually with the help of a friend's father, Jobe found a job in the packaging industry. By age 35, he had launched his own business, Vericool, specializing in sustainable and environmentally friendly packaging. Vericool's products are designed to replace Styrofoam and other foam packaging for shipments that need to stay cold, like food, flowers, and fish. In recognition of the power of second chances, Vericool employs a number of former prisoners. Not only do these individuals have a chance at employment, they also have the opportunity to become owners through the company's stock-option plan.

Each year in the United States, more than 600,000 people are released from prison. Most of these people reenter a society that has changed, sometimes significantly, since the time they were first incarcerated. Along with adjusting to freedom and new living arrangements, repairing relationships, and dealing with other changes, many individuals begin looking for employment. While research has shown that employment is a key factor for reducing recidivism, experts estimate that formerly incarcerated individuals experience unemployment at a much higher rate than other citizens. Even after five years of release from prison, 65 percent of these individuals remain unemployed or underemployed. Poor employment prospects often have long-lasting negative effects on individuals, families, and communities.

Legal and regulatory frameworks may prevent the previously incarcerated from obtaining professional licensure. This means employment in nursing, education, and other high-demand fields is off-limits. Regulations may also disqualify the previously incarcerated from securing employment in fields that deal with vulnerable populations and law enforcement. Private employers use background checks on a routine basis, and applicants with criminal convictions are often disqualified from employment. Although federal statutes do not prohibit discrimination on the basis of criminal history, the EEOC has advised that a criminal background should not be used the sole determinant of a prospective employee's qualifications. Instead, employers are expected to conduct an individual assessment of the criminal convictions for severity, job-relatedness, and recency.

Beyond the regulatory environment, hiring managers may have an unconscious or conscious bias toward ex-offenders. Research has shown that employers often view the previously incarcerated as untrustworthy, lacking in social skills, and more likely to steal. Some hiring managers may not believe that criminals can be rehabilitated. Concerns about safety, liability, security, and reputation also come into play, especially for firms with strict policies prohibiting any criminal conduct by current employees. This apprehension is especially strong for individuals with criminal pasts that include violent and sexual acts.

To deter bias, a number of states have initiated "Ban the Box" programs that revise how and when an applicant's criminal history is revealed in the hiring process. These programs require employers to remove all questions about criminal history from job applications and to ensure that applications are reviewed for qualifications, skills, and other job-specific factors. Ban the Box allows potential employers to assess and get to know applicants before a criminal history is introduced. Background checks are typically performed once an applicant has been chosen as the finalist.

Recently, leaders in the business community launched an initiative to change attitudes about hiring people with criminal records. Well-known organizations, including Butterball Farms, Georgia-Pacific, Koch Industries, the National Restaurant Association, Uber, and the U.S. Chamber of Commerce, have signed the "Getting Talent Back to Work" pledge to give job opportunities to qualified people with a criminal background who are deserving of a second chance. The pledge is designed to end outdated and noninclusive hiring practices and to enhance the labor pool.

The pledge comes on the heels of the FIRST STEP Act passed by the U.S. Congress. The legislation emphasizes rehabilitation, education, work-release, and other programs to support the successful reintegration of former prisoners. In the state of Wisconsin, the Department of Corrections already offers employers the opportunity to hire work-release participants who are nearing the end of their prison sentences. The Oneida Airport Hotel Corporation in Green Bay, Wisconsin, was an early adopter of the work-release program. The company is now an advocate, citing the business, social, and intrinsic benefits of helping ex-offenders resume healthy, stable, and productive roles.

There Are Two Sides to Every Issue

1. Because of discrimination and bias against individuals with criminal backgrounds, employers are missing a significant opportunity to enhance their workforces as well as benefit society.
2. Because there are risks in hiring employees with criminal backgrounds, employers are understandably hesitant to consider individuals with criminal backgrounds.

Sources: Ifeoma Ajunwa and Angela Onwuachi-Willig, "Combating Discrimination Against the Formerly Incarcerated in the Labor Market," Northwestern University Law Review 112 (2018): 1385–1415; Barry Goldman, Dylan Cooper, and Tamar Kugler "Crime and Punishment," International Journal of Conflict Management 30 (January 2019): 2–23; Amy Feldman, "An Entrepreneur and His Ex-Cons: Meet the Former Gang Member Who Created a $10 Million Packaging Startup That Hires Former Inmates," Forbes.com, March 27, 2019, https://www.forbes.com/sites/amyfeldman/2019/03/27/from-bullets-to-boxes-meet-the-former-gang-member-who-created-a-15m-packaging-startup-that-hires-ex-cons/#770ce6361895 (accessed June 24, 2019); Jakari N. Griffith and Nicole C. Jones Young, "Hiring Ex-Offenders? The Case of Ban the Box," Equality, Diversity, and Inclusion: An International Journal 36 (2017): 501–518; Society for Human Resource Management, "Getting Talent Back to Work," https://www.gettingtalentbacktowork.org/ (accessed June 24, 2019); Margaret Waldo, "Second Chances: Employing Convicted Felons." HR Magazine 57 (March 2012): 36–40.

Key Terms

chief diversity officer (CDO) (p. 233)	hostile work environment sexual harassment (p. 229)	social contract (p. 221)
collective bargaining (p. 225)		subcontracting (p. 219)
cross-training (p. 222)	intersectionality theory (p. 233)	unconscious bias (p. 236)
Department of Labor (p. 222)	living wage (p. 224)	underemployment (p. 219)
downsizing (p. 220)	minimum wage (p. 223)	unemployment rate (p. 215)
employee assistance program (EAP) (p. 237)	Occupational Safety and Health Administration (OSHA) (p. 225)	vesting (p. 224)
		work/life programs (p. 236)
employee engagement (p. 217)	outsourcing (p. 219)	Worker Adjustment and Retraining Notification (WARN) Act (p. 221)
employee stock ownership plans (ESOPs) (p. 241)	psychological contract (p. 216)	
	quid pro quo sexual harassment (p. 229)	workforce reduction (p. 220)
employer of choice (p. 240)		workplace diversity (p. 232)
employment at will (p. 222)	reverse mentoring (p. 235)	workplace inclusion (p. 234)
ergonomics (p. 225)	rightsizing (p. 220)	zero tolerance (p. 230)
full employment (p. 215)	sexual harassment (p. 229)	

Discussion Questions

1. Review Table 8.1 and indicate the positive effects associated with the psychological contract's characteristics. For example, what is positive about an employee's ability to solve problems independently?

2. What is workforce reduction? How does it affect employees, consumers, and the local community? What steps should a company take to address these effects?

3. What responsibilities do companies have with respect to workplace violence? Using the categories of violence presented in the chapter, describe the responsibilities and actions that you believe are necessary for an organization to demonstrate social responsibility in this area.

4. Describe the differences between workplace diversity and equal employment opportunity. How do these differences affect managerial responsibilities and the development of social responsibility programs?

5. Why is it important to understand the profiles of different generations at work? How can managers use the ACORN principles to develop a strong sense of community and solidarity among all employee groups?

6. What trends have contributed to work/life programs? How do work/life programs help employees and organizations?

7. What is an employer of choice? Describe how a firm could use traditional marketing concepts and strategies to appeal to current and potential employees.

8. Review the best practices in Table 8.10 for becoming an employer of choice. What are some potential drawbacks to each practice? Rank the eight practices in terms of their importance to you.

Experiential Exercise

Develop a list of five criteria that describe your employer of choice. Then, visit the websites of three companies in which you have some employment interest. Peruse each firm's website to find evidence on how it fulfills your criteria. On the basis of this evidence, develop a chart to show how well each firm meets your description and criteria of your employer of choice. Finally, provide three recommendations on how these companies can better communicate their commitment to employees and the employer of choice criteria.

X, Y, & Millennial: What Would You Do?

Dawn Burke, director of employee relations, glanced at her online calendar and remembered her appointment at 3:00 p.m. today. She quickly found the file labeled "McCullen and Aranda" and started preparing for the meeting. She recalled that this was essentially an employee-supervisor case where the employee had been unwilling or unable to meet the supervisor's requests. The employee claimed that the supervisor was too demanding and impatient. Their conflict had escalated to the point that both were unhappy and uncomfortable in the work environment. Other employees had noticed, and overheard, some of the negative interactions between them.

In her role, Dawn was responsible for many programs, including a new mediation initiative to resolve workplace conflicts. The program was designed to help employees develop stronger communication and conflict resolution skills. In this case, the program was also providing an intermediary step between informal and formal discipline. Today, she was meeting with both parties to discuss mediation guidelines, a timeline, their goal, and their general points of conflict.

John McCullen, 51, a buyer in the facilities department, and Terry Aranda, the director of facilities procurement, arrived separately. John had been with the company for 32 years and had started his career with the company right out of high school. Terry, 31, was hired from another firm to oversee the procurement area a year ago and had recently graduated from a prestigious MBA program. Dawn started the meeting by reviewing the mediation guidelines and timeline. She reminded John and Terry that their goal was to develop a workable and agreeable solution to the current situation. Dawn then asked for each party to explain his or her position on the conflict.

John began, "Ms. Aranda is a very smart lady. She seems to know the buying and procurement area, but she knows less about the company and its history. I am not sure she has taken the time to learn our ways and values. Ms. Aranda is impatient with our use of the new software and computer system. Some of us don't have college degrees, and we haven't been using computers since we were young. I started working at this company about the time she was born, and I am not sure that her management style is good for our department. Everything was going pretty well until we started changing our systems."

Terry commented, "John is a valuable member of the department, as he knows everyone at this company. I appreciate his knowledge and loyalty. On the other hand, he has not completed several tasks in a timely manner, nor has he asked for an extension. I feel that I must check up on his schedule and proof all of his work. John has attended several training classes, and I asked that he use an electronic calendar so that projects are completed on time. He continues to ignore my advice and deadlines. We've had several conversations, but John's work has not substantially improved. We have many goals to achieve in the department, and I need everyone's best work in order to make that happen."

Dawn thanked them for their candor and told them she would meet with them next week to start the mediation process. As she contemplated what each had said, she remembered an article that discussed how people born in different generations often have contrasting perceptions about work. Dawn started to jot a few notes about the next steps in resolving their conflict. What would you do?

Consumer Relations

The Power of Positive Consumer Reviews

When consumers begin planning their vacations, they are focused on finding the best location and lodging to fulfill their desire for fun and relaxation. Increasingly, these would-be vacationers are opting for private home rentals instead of hotels and resorts. Driven by advances in technology and consumer demand for spacious, private, and unique accommodations, companies like Airbnb, HomeAway, and others are thriving. While home rentals have been popular in Europe for years, tourists in the United States have more recently discovered the joys and opportunities of "living like a local." The annual global vacation rental market is estimated at $24 billion and seems to be growing each year.

Many of the same technologies and consumer attitudes that bolstered vacation rentals have given rise to a culture of consumer ratings. Websites like Yelp, TripAdvisor, Rotten Tomatoes, and others empower consumers to rate restaurants, movies, television shows, retailers, and other providers of experience-based goods and services. Customer satisfaction is a significant concern for all companies, as ratings provide a mechanism for recognizing, rewarding and even disciplining employees. For example, the Net Promoter Score (NPS) has become very important for many businesses. The NPS was developed by Fred Reichheld and uses only one question: "How likely are you to recommend Company XX to a friend or colleague?" Even though statisticians and other experts warn against the use of a single indicator to measure customer loyalty, business leaders have wholeheartedly embraced NPS. While critics of NPS call it a "dubious management fad," and even Reichheld was puzzled at the way that NPS was being used to determine employee bonuses, corporate leaders are embedding the scores in annual reports and earnings conference calls with Wall Street analysts.

The ratings culture primarily persists because business owners and managers believe that new and continuing customers are driven by other consumers' opinions. This was certainly the case for Shore to Please Vacations and Staffordshire Property Management. Both vacation rental companies inserted nondisparagement clauses into the lengthy contracts that consumers signed to rent properties. These clauses sought to prevent consumers from leaving negative or less-than-perfect reviews, but they are in violation of the Consumer Review Fairness Act (CRFA), administered by the Federal Trade Commission (FTC). These companies also threatened consumers with significant penalties for violating the clause—a minimum of $25,000 in the case of Shore to Please. After consumers left honest reviews, Shore to Please levied lawsuits against them for damages. The FTC said these clauses violated the CRFA, and Shore to Please dismissed its pending lawsuits. Beyond the vacation rental industry, the FTC found that companies in the flooring, recreational, and air conditioning and heating industries have used nondisparagement provisions in contracts.

Consumers are clearly a pivotal stakeholder group and driver of business success. The far-reaching nature of the internet means that product and service ratings are becoming more important as direct sources of information for consumer decision-making. Consumer influencers who review and write about products attract millions to their blogs and websites. Many have become so instrumental that companies now compensate them for their opinions. Consumers around the world are connected in real time and enjoy sharing their experiences and opinions as the electronic equivalent of word of mouth, even while shopping in physical stores.[1]

Chapter Objectives

- Describe customers as stakeholders
- Investigate consumer protection laws
- Examine six consumer rights
- Discuss the implementation of responsibilities to consumers

consumer relations
a firm's process for creating and maintaining a positive relationship with consumers by meeting customer needs

This case illustrates the complexities associated **consumer relations**, a firm's process for creating and maintaining a positive relationship with consumers by meeting customer needs. From a social responsibility perspective, the key challenge is how an organization assesses its stakeholders' needs, integrates them with company strategy, reconciles differences between stakeholders' needs, strives for better relationships with stakeholders, achieves mutual understandings with them, and finds solutions for problems. In this chapter, we explore relationships with consumers and the expectations of the economic, legal, ethical, and philanthropic responsibilities that must be addressed by business.

Consumer Stakeholders

For the past 20 years, "green marketing," the promotion of more environmentally friendly products, has become a much-discussed strategy in the packaged goods industry. Procter & Gamble (P&G), the venerable manufacturer of soap, paper goods, and other household products, feared that increasing environmental consciousness among consumers would lead to a resurgence in the use of cloth diapers, which would have had a negative effect on its disposable diaper business. P&G launched a marketing campaign touting the benefits of disposables, including the fact that their use does not require hot water for laundering or fuel for diaper service trucks. The company also initiated a pilot project for composting disposable diapers. Today, the debate over cloth versus disposables has largely faded, and the P&G marketing campaign has disappeared.

The dawn of the twenty-first century brought many new products, including disposable tableware, food containers that can be used repeatedly or thrown away, and electrostatic mops with cloths that are disposed of after one use. Although these product introductions suggest a decline in environmental consciousness among consumers, other initiatives counter this assumption. Whole Foods Markets, a grocery chain that specializes in organic and environmentally friendly items, reports $940 of sales per square foot, as opposed to the $496 per square foot earned by Kroger.[2] Today, the company utilizes a wide variety of approaches to reinforce its green philosophy, including blogs, store projects, loans for local producers, selling organic foods, and the use of biodiesel for its trucks.[3] Indeed, environmental and related social initiatives have become a global concern. One goal of the annual International Buy Nothing Day, sponsored by consumer associations around the world, is to encourage consumers to consider the environmental consequences of their buying habits. The 24-hour period occurs on the same day that many Americans are launching the holiday shopping season, the day after Thanksgiving, known as "Black Friday." Another goal is to remind consumers about the power of retail and the fact that the richest 20 percent of people consume 80 percent of the world's resources. The idea has spawned other initiatives, including Buy Nothing community groups that aim to build trust and reduce waste through a gift-giving and sharing economy.[4]

Although the future of different marketing strategies can be debated, the real test of effectiveness lies in the expectations, attitudes, and ultimate buying patterns of consumers. The preceding examples illustrate that there is no true consensus around issues such as environmental responsibility; therefore, companies face complex decisions about how to respond to them. This is true for all types of expectations, including the ones explored in this chapter. In the sections that follow, we examine the economic, legal, ethical, and philanthropic responsibilities that businesses have to **consumers**, individuals who purchase, use, and dispose of products for themselves and their households.

consumers
individuals who purchase, use, and dispose of products for themselves and their households

Responsibilities to Consumers

Not too long ago, the emphasis of marketing was on investors and competitors. However, as marketers began to develop a stakeholder orientation, the importance of consumers as a primary stakeholder became apparent. Consumers are necessary for the success of a business; any company that does not consider the impact that its operations have on consumers will likely not be in business very long. As such, organizations must consider their responsibility to meet consumer needs. The following sections illustrate how the various components of social responsibility are applied to consumers.

Economic Issues

As discussed in earlier chapters, consumers are primary stakeholders because their awareness, purchase, use, and repurchase of products are vital to a company's existence. Fundamentally, therefore, consumers and businesses are connected by an economic relationship. This relationship begins with an exchange, usually of a good or service for money, which often leads to a deeper attachment or affiliation. In addition to its well-known advertising slogan, "Delivering Happiness," Zappos launched an advertising campaign focused on real customer stories. These marketing approaches typify the close relationship that customers develop with the shoes they purchase from Zappos.[5] Other consumers may choose to shun particular brands or opt for the environmentally sensitive products described earlier. In all of these cases, however, consumers expect the products they purchase to perform as guaranteed by their sellers. Thus, a firm's economic responsibilities include following through on promises made in the exchange process.

Although this responsibility may seem basic today, business practices have not always been directed in this way. In the early part of the 1900s, the caveat "Let the buyer beware" typified the power that business—not consumers—wielded in most exchange relationships.[6] In some parts of the world, this phrase often accurately describes the consumer marketplace. For example, although Indonesia has consumer protection laws, consumers often feel like they have to test products in stores before purchasing them. It is not uncommon for them to take electronics out of the packaging and plug them in to see if they work. Many Indonesian consumers may not be fully aware of their rights in the exchange process.[7] In a more nefarious example, mothers in China continue to be concerned about the quality of infant formula and milk produced by Chinese manufacturers. Fear was rampant in 2008 when thousands of infants were poisoned by Chinese milk formula, and the Chinese government eventually prosecuted business owners for contaminating milk with melamine. Melamine is commonly used to manufacture plastics, paper board, and industrial coatings. Consumer distrust continues over a decade later, despite advances in safety protocols, inspections, and public relations efforts.[8]

Companies' fulfillment of economic responsibilities depends on their interactions with consumers. However, there are situations in which the consumer does not act as a fair participant in the exchange.[9] **Consumer fraud** involves intentional deception to derive an unfair economic advantage over an organization. Examples of fraudulent activities include shoplifting, collusion or duplicity, and guile. Collusion typically involves an employee who assists the consumer in fraud. For example, a cashier may not scan all merchandise or may give a customer an unwarranted discount. Duplicity may involve a consumer staging a fake accident in a grocery store and then seeking damages against the store for its lack of attention to safety. A consumer may purchase, wear, and then return an item of clothing for a full refund. In other situations, the consumer may ask for a refund by claiming a defect that either is nonexistent or was caused by consumer misuse.[10] Although

consumer fraud
intentional deception to derive an unfair economic advantage over an organization

Table 9.1 Types of Consumer Fraud

Type	Example
Shoplifting	A teenager steals a flash drive from an office supply store.
Collusion	An employee provides a consumer with substantial company discounts because of their friendship.
Duplicity	A consumer stages a fake accident with the intent to file false claims against a retailer.
Tag switching	A customer switches the tags of a higher-priced item with that of a lower-priced item.
Credit card fraud	A consumer uses a credit card that he or she got through fraudulent means.

some of these acts warrant legal prosecution, they can be very difficult to prove, and many companies are reluctant to accuse patrons of a crime when there is no way that it can be verified. Businesses that operate with the "customer is always right" philosophy have found that some consumers will take advantage of this promise and have therefore modified their return policies to curb unfair use. REI, for instance, modified its 100 percent satisfaction guarantee; now, consumers have a year to return defective or unwanted products (whereas previously there was no limit). Other companies, especially electronic firms, charge a "restocking fee" if goods are not returned within a specified time period.[11] Table 9.1 describes types of consumer fraud.

Because of the vague nature of some types of consumer fraud, its full financial toll is somewhat difficult to tally. However, rough estimates indicate that the average inventory shrinkage—which occurs when inventory is lost through shoplifting, vendor fraud, employee error, or other means—costs U.S. businesses more than $46 billion per year.[12] While shrinkage is most often considered in the context of brick-and-mortar establishments, companies in many industries have problems with fraud and related issues that raise costs and lower profitability. The internet has complicated matters, as it can be harder for consumers to determine which online retailers are legitimate. Table 9.2 shows some effective tools that individuals can use to combat credit card fraud over the internet.

Many consumers, of course, do not engage in such activities. However, there are cases when buyers and sellers disagree on whether or how well companies have satisfied their economic responsibilities. Thus, a consumer may believe that a product is not worth the price paid, perhaps because he or she believes that the product's benefits have been exaggerated by the seller. For example, although some

Table 9.2 Ways to Avoid Credit Card Fraud on the Internet

Don't give out your credit card number unless the site is secure and reputable.
Before using the site, check out security software/encryption software that it uses.
Obtain a physical address and phone number, rather than settling for a post office box number. Call the telephone number to ensure that the company is legitimate.
Check out the email address to make sure that it is active.
Check out the Better Business Bureau (BBB) from the seller's area.
Check out other websites about this person/company.
When possible, purchase items with your credit card because you can dispute the charges if something goes wrong.
Keep a list of all your credit cards, as well as the seller's information. If anything looks suspicious, immediately contact your credit card issuer.

Source: Federal Bureau of Investigations, "Credit Card Fraud," https://www.fbi.gov/scams-and-safety/common-fraud-schemes/credit-card-fraud (accessed June 4, 2019).

marketers claim that their creams, pills, special massages, and other techniques can reduce or even eliminate cellulite, most medical experts and dermatologists believe that only exercise and weight loss can reduce the appearance of this undesirable condition. Products for reducing cellulite remain on the market, but many consumers have returned these products and complained about the lack of results. In the United Kingdom, a number of cosmetics companies have been reprimanded by the Advertising Standards Authority for making misleading claims in advertising and packaging.[13] If a consumer believes that a firm has not fulfilled its basic economic responsibilities, he or she may ask for a refund, tell others about the bad experience, discontinue patronage, post a complaint to a website, contact a consumer agency, and even seek legal redress.

A variety of consumer and government agencies keep track of consumer complaints. For example, the **Federal Trade Commission (FTC)** reports the top consumer complaints across the nation every year. Problems related to identity theft, debt collection, fraud involving bankers and lenders, imposter scams, and scams involving telephone and mobile services have been at the top of the list in recent years.[14] To protect consumers and provide businesses with guidance, a number of laws and regulations have been enacted to ensure that economic responsibility is met in accordance with institutionalized standards.

Legal and Regulatory Issues

As discussed earlier, legal issues with respect to consumers in the United States primarily fall under the domain of the FTC, which enforces federal antitrust and consumer protection laws. Within this agency, the **Bureau of Consumer Protection** works to protect consumers against unfair, deceptive, and fraudulent practices. The bureau is further organized into eight divisions, including those focused on marketing practices, privacy and identity protection, advertising practices, and international consumer protection.[15] For example, the FTC charged Lumosity for claiming that their brain-training devices could help with brain trauma and cognitive decline. The FTC claims that the firm does not have sufficient evidence to back this up. The agency is cracking down on firms that claim they can improve cognitive ability without substantiation, especially because many ads for these products tend to be geared toward elderly people more likely to suffer from dementia or other cognitive issues.[16]

In addition to the FTC, several other federal agencies regulate specific goods, services, or business practices to protect consumers. The **Food and Drug Administration (FDA)**, for example, enforces laws and regulations enacted to prevent distribution of adulterated or misbranded foods, drugs, medical devices, cosmetics, veterinary products, and potentially hazardous consumer products. The **Consumer Product Safety Commission** enforces laws and regulations designed to protect the public from unreasonable risk of injury from consumer products. This commission is well known to many consumers because it works with manufacturers to widely communicate product recalls, warnings, and recommendations for future product use. Many states also have regulatory agencies that enforce laws and regulations regarding business practices within their states. This means a U.S.-based company that only sells in the U.S. must comply with 51 sets of laws and regulations. Further, state and local laws can be more stringent than federal statutes, so it is important that businesses fully investigate the laws applicable to all markets in which they operate. In Texas, for example, the Deceptive Trade Practices Act prohibits a business from selling anything to a consumer that he or she does not need or cannot afford.[17] The Colorado Consumer Protection Law is a broad regulation protecting consumers from damages associated with fraud. As noted in earlier chapters, laws in other countries are often quite different from U.S. law, so companies operating in international markets must consider the

Federal Trade Commission (FTC)
the U.S. government agency charged with protecting consumers and competition by preventing anticompetitive, deceptive, and unfair business practices through law enforcement, advocacy, and education about unduly burdening legitimate business activities

Bureau of Consumer Protection
a bureau within the Federal Trade Commission (FTC) charged with protecting consumers against unfair, deceptive, or fraudulent practices

Food and Drug Administration (FDA)
the U.S. government agency charged with protecting the public health by ensuring the safety, efficacy, and security of foods, drugs, cosmetics, biological products, medical devices, tobacco, veterinary products, and electronic products that give off radiation

Consumer Product Safety Commission
the U.S. government commission charged with protecting the public from unreasonable risks of injury or death associated with the use of thousands of types of consumer products under the agency's jurisdiction

complex relationships among local, state, national, and international regulation and laws.

Most federal agencies and states have consumer affairs or information offices to help consumers remain informed about agency activities and alerts. The Consumer Affairs and Outreach Division of the **Federal Communications Commission (FCC)** educates consumers on issues related to cable and satellite service, telecommunications, wireless technology, and other areas under the FCC's domain.[18] The Montana Department of Justice's Consumer Protection Division publishes information on their website to assist consumers in complaining effectively, recognizing scams, and avoiding identity theft. They also post information specific to the region, such as farming and oil and gas industry concerns.[19] In this section, we focus on U.S. laws related to exchanges and relationships with consumers. Table 9.3 summarizes some of the laws that are likely to affect a wide range of companies and consumers.

Health and Safety   One of the first consumer protection laws in the United States came about in response to public outrage over a novel. In *The Jungle*, Upton Sinclair exposed atrocities, including unsanitary conditions and inhumane labor practices, by the meat-packing industry in Chicago at the turn of the twentieth century. Appalled by the unwholesome practices described in the book, the public demanded reform. Congress responded by passing the Pure Food and Drug Act in 1906, just six months after *The Jungle* was published.[20] In addition to prohibiting the adulteration and mislabeling of food and drug products, the new law also established one of the nation's first federal regulatory agencies, the Food and Drug Administration.

Since the passage of the Pure Food and Drug Act, public health and safety have been major targets of federal and state regulation. For example, the Consumer Product Safety Act established the Consumer Product Safety Commission to enforce rules relating to product safety. For example, IKEA recalled 36 million dressers after three children were killed after the dressers fell on them. A second recall for the dressers was issued after an eighth child died.[21] Companies that provide defective or faulty products resulting in customer harm must respond quickly to avoid government penalties. They will still probably face civil litigation from those who were harmed or killed by the defective products. Other laws attempt to protect children from harm, including the Child Protection and Toy Safety Act and the Children's Online Privacy Protection Act (COPPA).

Credit and Ownership   Abuses and inequities associated with loans and credit have resulted in the passage of laws designed to protect consumers' rights and public interests. The most significant of these laws prohibits discrimination in the extension of credit, requires creditors to disclose all finance charges and related aspects of credit transactions, gives consumers the right to dispute and correct inaccurate information on their credit reports, and regulates the activities of debt collectors. For example, the Home Ownership and Equity Protection Act requires home equity lenders to disclose, in writing, the borrower's rights, payment amounts, and the consequences of defaulting on the loan. Together, the Department of Justice and the U.S. Department of Housing and Urban Development (HUD) enforce laws that ensure equal access to sale and rental housing. Every April, the government sponsors Fair Housing Month to educate property owners, agents, and consumers on their rights with respect to housing.

While home ownership is often considered part of the American Dream, specific business practices in the banking and finance industry have been questioned. Between 2007 and 2009, the alarming number of mortgage foreclosures arose from a combustible situation involving risky lending practices, subprime mortgage disasters, and a general economic downturn. Many Americans assumed

Federal Communications Commission (FCC)
the U.S. government commission charged with regulating interstate and international communications by radio, television, wire, satellite, and cable in all 50 states, the District of Columbia and U.S. territories

Table 9.3 Major Consumer Laws

Act (Date Enacted)	Purpose
Pure Food and Drug Act (1906)	Established the FDA; outlaws the adulteration or mislabeling of food and drug products sold in interstate commerce.
Cigarette Labeling and Advertising Act (1965)	Requires manufacturers to add to package labels warnings about the possible health hazards associated with smoking cigarettes.
Fair Packaging and Labeling Act (1966)	Outlaws unfair or deceptive packaging or labeling of consumer products.
Truth in Lending Act (1968)	Requires creditors to disclose in writing all finance charges and related aspects of credit transactions.
Child Protection and Toy Safety Act (1969)	Requires childproof devices and special labeling.
Fair Credit Reporting Act (1970)	Promotes accuracy, fairness, and privacy of credit information; gives consumers the right to see their personal credit reports and to dispute any inaccurate information contained therein.
Consumer Product Safety Act (1972)	Established the Consumer Product Safety Commission to regulate potentially hazardous consumer products.
Equal Credit Opportunity Act (1974)	Outlaws the denial of credit on the basis of race, color, religion, national origin, sex, marital status, age, or receipt of public assistance and requires creditors to provide applicants, on request, with the reasons for credit denial.
Magnuson-Moss Warranty (FTC) Act (1975)	Establishes rules for consumer product warranties, including minimum content and disclosure standards; allows the FTC to prescribe interpretive rules in policy statements regarding unfair or deceptive practices.
Consumer Goods Pricing Act (1975)	Prohibits the use of price maintenance agreements among manufacturers and resellers in interstate commerce.
Fair Debt Collection Practices Act (1977)	Prohibits third-party debt collectors from engaging in deceptive or abusive conduct when collecting consumer debts incurred for personal, family, or household purposes.
Toy Safety Act (1984)	Authorizes the Consumer Product Safety Commission to recall products intended for use by children when they present substantial risk of injury.
Nutrition Labeling and Education Act (1990)	Prohibits exaggerated health claims and requires all processed foods to contain standardized labels with nutritional information.
Home Ownership and Equity Protection Act (1994)	Requires home equity lenders to disclose to borrowers in writing the payment amounts, the consequences of default, and the borrowers' right to cancel the loan within a certain time period.
Telemarketing and Consumer Fraud and Abuse Prevention Act (1994)	Authorizes the FTC to establish regulations for telemarketing, including prohibiting deceptive, coercive, or privacy-invading telemarketing practices; restricting the time during which unsolicited telephone calls may be made to consumers; and requiring telemarketers to disclose the nature of the call at the beginning of an unsolicited sales call.
Identity Theft Assumption and Deterrence Act (1998)	Makes the FTC a central clearinghouse for identity theft complaints and requires the FTC to log and acknowledge such complaints, provide victims with relevant information, and refer their complaints to appropriate entities (e.g., the major national consumer reporting agencies and other law enforcement agencies).
Children's Online Privacy Protection Act (COPPA) (1998)	Protects children's privacy by giving parents the tools to control what information is collected from their children online.
Do-Not-Call Registry Act (2003)	Allows the FTC to implement and enforce a do-not-call registry.

(continued on next page)

Table 9.3 (*Continued*)

Fair and Accurate Credit Transactions Act (2003)	Amends the Fair Credit Reporting Act (FCRA), gives consumers the right to one free credit report a year from the credit reporting agencies, adds provisions designed to prevent and mitigate identity theft, and grants consumers additional rights with respect to how information is used.
Bankruptcy Abuse Prevention and Consumer Protection Act (2005)	Amends the Truth in Lending Act to include requiring certain creditors to disclose on the front of billing statements a minimum monthly payment warning for consumers and a toll-free telephone number, established and maintained by the FTC, for consumers seeking information on the time required to repay specific credit balances.
Credit Card Accountability Responsibility and Disclosure Act (2009)	Amends the Truth in Lending Act to prescribe fair practices regarding the extension of credit under an open-end consumer credit plan.
Dodd-Frank Wall Street Reform and Consumer Protection Act, Titles X and XIV (2010)	Established the Consumer Financial Protection Bureau (CFPB) to protect consumers from complex and deceptive financial products.
Economic Growth, Regulatory Relief, and Consumer Protection Act (2018)	Consumers are able to contact each of the three major credit-reporting agencies and direct them to place a free freeze on the consumer's credit file. A credit freeze makes it harder for identity thieves to open new accounts in consumers' names.

Sources: Federal Trade Commission, "Statutes Enforced or Administered by the Commission," https://www.ftc.gov/enforcement/statutes (accessed June 4, 2019).

high-interest-rate loans or bought a house that they could not really afford and eventually could no longer make mortgage payments. In many cases, individuals or institutions bought or sold financial products that they did not fully understand. The response included Titles X and XIV of the Dodd-Frank Act, which established the Consumer Financial Protection Bureau (CFPB) to oversee the finance industry and help prevent financial practices that could deceive consumers. Concurrently, the attorneys general of all 50 states launched investigations of industry players, while the federal government pursued charges that ended in settlements of $26 billion dollars.[22]

Marketing, Advertising, and Packaging Legal issues in marketing often relate to sales and advertising communications and information about product content and safety. One of the more subtle regulatory concerns with marketing involves **product placement**, which is a type of advertising in which a company pays for its product to be viewed in a movie, television show, or other form of media. The FCC requires all sponsors to be identified so that consumers recognize the layers and types of advertising strategies employed within the media production. Use of product placement has been common for media produced in the United States, but other countries, including Great Britain, have only recently allowed these placements. After a 2011 change in British law, a British soap opera, *Coronation Street*, began product placement relationships with Costa Coffee and Co-op. Not only are these two stores re-created on the set, the stores' products are seen throughout the show. Actors drink coffee from Costa Coffee at their workplaces and carry grocery bags that read "Co-op" into their houses. While the producers of British soap operas may entertain product placement relationships, placements are not allowed in children's programs, news shows, and current affairs programs. Certain types of products may never be placed, including alcohol and foods that are high in fat, salt, or sugar.[23] While product placement is easily recognized by some consumers as a promotional tool, ethical concerns have been raised about

product placement
a type of advertising in which a company pays for its product to be viewed in a movie, television show, or other form of media

product placement in video games, movies, and other outlets targeted to young children. In 250 children's movies that debuted between 1991 and 2005, over 64 percent of them included some form of product placement. Vehicles, clothing and shoes, technical equipment, drinks, and media outlets were the most common product categories represented. Surprisingly, toys were only present in about 3 percent of the movies.[24]

Abuses in promotion can range from exaggerated claims, concealed facts, and deception to outright lying. Such misleading information creates legal and ethical issues because these messages do not include all the information that consumers need to make sound purchasing decisions. Skechers paid consumers $40 million after they were found to have engaged in deceptive advertising. The company claimed that its Shape-Up shoes, as well as other shoe lines, would help women lose weight and shape their posteriors. This settlement came a year after Reebok was forced to pay $25 million to settle deceptive advertising claims stating that its EasyTone and RunTone shoes would help to tone glutes, thighs, and calves better than regular walking shoes. The FTC determined that there was no evidence to support either of these claims.[25]

Although a certain amount of exaggeration and puffery is tolerated, deceptive claims or claims that cannot be substantiated are likely to invite legal action from the FTC. For example, the FTC levied a $26.5 million fine against the marketers of Sensa, a supposed weight loss company, for marketing campaigns that used unsupported claims and misleading endorsements. The FTC also sued L'Occitane over claims that their skin cream had slimming properties. Cases such as these prompted the FTC to develop a list of phrases that should alert both consumers and marketers to unsubstantiated or false claims about weight loss products (see Figure 9.1).[26]

Since the FTC Act of 1914 outlawed all deceptive and unfair trade practices, additional legislation has further delineated which activities are permissible as opposed to illegal. For example, the Telemarketing and Consumer Fraud and Abuse Prevention Act requires telemarketers to disclose the nature of the call at the beginning of an unsolicited sales call and restricts the times during which such calls may be made to consumers. Another legal issue in marketing has to do with the promotion of products that may negatively affect health or safety. Numerous laws regulate the promotion of alcohol and tobacco products, including the Public Health Cigarette Smoking Act (1970) and the Cigarette Labeling and Advertising Act (1965). The 18th Amendment to the U.S. Constitution prohibited the manufacture and sale of alcoholic beverages in 1919. Prohibition was repealed in 1933 by the 21st Amendment, but the new amendment gave states the power to regulate the transportation of alcoholic beverages across state lines. Today, each state has unique regulations, some of which require the use of wholesalers and retailers to limit direct sales of alcoholic beverages to final consumers in other states. In this

Figure 9.1 Red Flags: Likely Inaccurate Claims About a Weight-Loss Product

- Cause weight loss of 2 pounds or more a week for a month or more without dieting or exercise
- Cause substantial weight loss no matter what or how much the consumer eats
- Cause permanent weight loss (even when the consumer stops using the product)
- Block the absorption of fat or calories to enable consumers to lose substantial weight
- Cause substantial weight loss for all users
- Cause substantial weight loss by wearing it on the body or rubbing it into the skin

Source: Federal Trade Commission, "Gut Check: A Reference Guide for Media on Spotting False Weight Loss Claims," https://www.ftc.gov/tips-advice/business-center/guidance/gut-check-reference-guide-media-spotting-false-weight-loss (accessed June 5, 2019).

case, a law aimed at protecting consumers by promoting temperance in alcohol consumption now affects wine sellers' ability to implement e-commerce and subsequent interstate sales. Currently, roughly 37 states prohibit interstate shipping from retail wine shops. The U.S. Supreme Court struck down a Tennessee law that permitted the granting of retail or wholesale liquor licenses only to individuals or entities that have resided in the state for a specified time. While not directly related to interstate sales, arguments in the case raised questions about the patchwork of regulations that now govern liquor sales both within and between states.[27]

Sales and Warranties   Another area of law that affects business relationships with consumers has to do with warranties. Many consumers consider the **warranty** behind a product when making a purchase decision, especially for expensive durable goods such as automobiles, computers and other technical equipment, and appliances. One of the most significant laws affecting warranties is the Magnuson-Moss Warranty (FTC) Act of 1975, which established rules for consumer product warranties, including minimum content and standards for disclosure. All 50 states have enacted "lemon laws" to ensure that automobile sales are accompanied by appropriate warranties and remedies for defects that impair the safety, use, or value of the vehicle. Courts have ruled that consumers who lease instead of purchase automobiles are also entitled to warranty protection under Magnuson-Moss.[28] The consumer market for used electronics and other products has created new challenges and opportunities with respect to warranties. Understandably, consumers want assurance that a secondhand product is worth the advertised price. Automobile companies provide these assurances on their branded cars through "certified preowned" programs, which signal that the automaker has evaluated the used car, made necessary repairs, and guarantees its quality. Other products, such as secondhand electronics, may be sold through a variety of retailers unaffiliated with the electronics brands. For used computers, mobile phones, and televisions, retailers often rely on third-party warranty providers to assess, repair, and guarantee the products, including providing service after the sale. SquareTrade is a well-known third-party warranty provider that has partnerships with Amazon, eBay, and other retailers to package product sales with warranty sales.[29]

warranty
a written guarantee issued at the time of purchase that promises to repair or replace the purchased product within a certain time frame

Product Liability   One area of law that has a profound effect on business and its relations with consumers is **product liability,** which refers to a business's legal responsibility for the performance of its products. This responsibility, which has evolved through both legislation and court interpretation (common law), may include a legal obligation to provide financial compensation to a consumer who has been harmed by a defective product. To receive compensation, a consumer who files suit in the United States must prove that the product was defective, that the defect caused an injury, and that the defect made the product unreasonably dangerous. Under the concept of *strict liability*, an injured consumer can apply this legal responsibility to any firm in the supply chain of a defective product, including contractors, suppliers of component parts, wholesalers, and retailers. Companies with operations in other countries must understand the various forms of product liability law that exist. For example, China passed a new law providing parameters for product liability. The law, which was passed as a result of many consumer injuries and deaths, covers medical devices, environmental pollution, and automobiles. Prior to this legislation, victims could file civil suits, but many claimed that doing so was insufficient. Now, consumers have a more effective means of retribution through the courts and a chance to receive monetary compensation for their distress.[30]

product liability
a business's legal responsibility for the performance of its products

Because the law typically holds businesses liable for their products' performance, many companies choose to recall potentially harmful products; such recalls may be required by legal or regulatory authorities as well. However, critics believe that the FTC's recall process is too slow. For instance, it took 165 days for a nut butter manufacturer to recall its products after salmonella was detected. Part of the delay may come from the firm's chance to issue a voluntary recall. The FDA would prefer the firm to recall a dangerous product voluntarily rather than having it be mandatory.[31]

Product liability lawsuits have increased dramatically in recent years, and many suits have resulted in huge damage awards to injured consumers or their families. In a much-publicized case, a jury awarded a McDonald's customer $2.9 million after she was scalded when she spilled hot coffee on her lap. Although that award was eventually reduced on appeal, McDonald's and other fast-food restaurants now display warning signs that their coffee is hot to eliminate both

further injury and liability. Most companies have taken steps to minimize their liability, and some firms—such as medical technology company C. R. Bard—have stopped making products or withdrawn completely from problematic markets because of the high risk of expensive liability lawsuits. Johnson & Johnson discontinued its power morcellator, used to remove uterine fibroids in women, because it could spread undetected cancers. Multiple wrongful death and product liability lawsuits were filed against the company, which spent millions to resolve these cases.[32] Although some states have limited damage awards and legislative reform is often on the agenda, the issue of product liability remains politically sensitive.

Technology Issues　Widespread use of the internet and social media has created new opportunities, as well as potential problems related to consumer protection. Many technology issues center on the collection and sale of consumer data, including the ways in which consumers are informed about these practices. In particular, social media creates business opportunities in dual markets, including the ability of retailers to market products to consumers on social media sites and the ability of social media sites to sell information gained about consumers back to retailers. Given the number of consumers around the world using Facebook, Instagram, and Twitter, the latter market has been subject to significant scrutiny, including legal challenges.[33]

Privacy and technology also intersect in the Telephone Consumer Protection Act, administered by the FCC. Many smartphone users are inundated with automated phone calls that lead to recorded messages or worse, faintly veiled attempts to scam or confuse consumers. These phone calls have left many consumers without a desire to answer their phones. Sophisticated programming is used so that incoming calls appear with the same area code as the phone being contacted, creating more difficulty for legitimate callers to get wary consumers to answer their phones. Each year, Americans receive more than 50 million robocalls, which are dependent on Voice Over Internet Protocol (VOIP) infrastructure and U.S. regulations that require the receiving party of a call to pay for any charges. Other parts of the world, including the European Union (EU), require the calling party to pay the charges. This regulatory environment has created a large number of telecommunications firms in the United States. To answer consumer complaints, the FCC recently launched an aggressive plan to curb illegal robocalling, especially those individual and companies that have placed over 1 billion unsolicited calls to promote financial schemes and scams.[34]

Beyond concerns about privacy and nuisance, technology facilitates new methods for reaching consumers and engaging them in exchange relationships. The founder of iBackPack, a new company dedicated to the development of technology-enhanced backpacks and other products, used a **crowdfunding** approach to generate start-up capital. Consumers donated over $800,000 to iBackPack on two crowdfunding sites, including Kickstarter and Indiegogo. Unlike strictly charitable donations, consumers were promised delivery of a specific product in exchange for their donations. For example, consumers who donated $169 were promised one of the start-up's first products, the iBackPack 1.0 Power Pack. When no products materialized, hundreds of consumers complained. In 2019, the FTC filed a complaint against the company and its founder, alleging most of the donations were used for personal expenses or other expenses unrelated to the development of new products.[35]

International Issues   Concerns about protecting consumers' legal rights are not limited to the United States. Most developed nations have laws and offices devoted to this goal. For example, the Chinese government enacted tougher safety standards for automobiles, bringing Chinese expectations in line with safety standards in the United States and Europe.[36] In the EU, the health and consumer protection directorate general oversees efforts to increase consumer confidence in the unified market. Its initiatives center on health, safety, economic, and public-health interests. One EU directive establishes minimum levels of consumer protection in member-states. For example, EU consumers now have a legal guarantee of two years on all consumer goods. If they find a defective product, they may choose repair or replacement or, in special circumstances, ask for a price reduction or rescind the contract altogether.[37]

In Japan, unlike in the United States, product liability lawsuits are much less common. In the early 1990s, Chikara Minami filed one of the first such lawsuits, against the Japanese automaker Mitsubishi. Minami's suit alleged a defect in the Mitsubishi Pajero. Although the court sided with the automaker in this case, 10 years later, Mitsubishi was accused of deliberately covering up consumer complaints. Despite this revelation and an enhanced product liability law in 1995, consumer rights are often subverted to preserve the power and structure of big business in Japan.[38] Much like Japan, China's consumer rights movement is relatively new; it resulted from economic policy changes away from isolationism and central economic planning. The China Consumers' Association was established in 1984 and has helped create consumer expectations and company responses that are starting to resemble those found in Western economies. Despite this action, however, there have been numerous consumer scares surrounding products manufactured in China and other countries. Table 9.4 lists a number of cases globally involving product recalls for food products, furniture, medicine, automotive products, and toys.[39]

As discussed in this section, there are many laws that influence business practices with respect to consumers all over the world. Every year, new laws are enacted, and existing rules are modified in response to the changing business environment, including the incidence of consumer product concerns. Although companies must monitor and obey all laws and regulations, they also need to keep abreast of the ethical obligations and standards that exist in the marketplace.

crowdfunding
the practice of funding a project or by securing relatively small donations from a large number of people

Consumer Bill of Rights
a group of four consumers rights (to choose, to safety, to be informed, and to be heard) first introduced by U.S. President John F. Kennedy in 1962

Ethical Issues

In 1962, U.S. president John F. Kennedy proclaimed a **Consumer Bill of Rights** that includes the rights to choose, to safety, to be informed, and to be heard.

Table 9.4 Product Recalls

Year	Recall	Description
2007	Lead-painted toys	It was discovered that many Mattel toys were painted using lead paint, which is poisonous if ingested.
2007	Pet food	Contaminated pet food from China resulted in the sickness and death of many pets.
2010	Children's medicines	Johnson & Johnson issued a massive recall on children's medicines such as Tylenol due to product contamination.
2012	Peanut products	Salmonella bacteria were detected in many peanut products, including peanut butter.
2013	Yogurt	Mold was detected in some Chobani yogurt products.
2014	General Motors (GM)	GM issued a recall on several car models because of faulty ignition switches.
2016	Samsung	Samsung recalled its Galaxy Note 7 due to overheating and fire risk.
2015	Takata	Takata, the maker of airbags for automobiles, began a lengthy recall of defective airbags.
2019	Knape & Vogt	Sit-stand workstations manufactured by Knape & Vogt were recalled due to problems with hydraulic gas pressure that enables the workstations to be raised or lowered.

Kennedy also established the Consumer Advisory Council to integrate consumer concerns into government regulations and processes. These four rights established a philosophical basis on which state and local consumer protection rules were later developed, with a clear emphasis on how regulation may serve the public interest.[40] Around the same time, Ralph Nader's investigations of auto safety and his publication of *Unsafe at Any Speed* in 1965 alerted citizens to the dangers of a common consumer product. Nader's activism and Kennedy's speech provided support for **consumerism**, the movement to protect consumers from an imbalance of power on the side of business and to maximize consumer welfare in the marketplace.[41] The consumer movement is a global phenomenon, as is indicated by the annual celebration of World Consumer Rights Day.

consumerism
the movement to protect consumers from an imbalance of power on the side of business and to maximize consumer welfare in the marketplace

Over the last five decades, consumerism has affected public policy through a variety of mechanisms. Early efforts were aimed primarily at advocating for legislation and regulation, whereas more recent efforts have shifted to education and protection programs directed at consumers.[42] For years, the Consumers Union, for example, worked with regional and federal legislators and international groups to protect consumer interests, sponsored conferences and research projects, tested consumer products, and published the results in *Consumer Reports* magazine. The magazine details business practices that are deemed to be unfair to consumers, such as predatory lending, the poor value of some life insurance products, product quality concerns, and advertisements aimed at vulnerable groups, like children and senior citizens.[43] Consumers Union has been absorbed into the Consumer Reports organization, but consumer advocacy efforts are still on their agenda. Over the past few years, Consumer Reports has advocated for a bipartisan bill in the U.S. House of Representatives aimed at curbing robocalls, which are often associated with scams. The organization also alerted consumers that many smart televisions have built-in automatic content recognition (ACR), which tracks what programs are watched on the television. ACR data are sent back to the television manufacturer and its business partners, often resulting in recommendations for other shows and the development of targeted marketing messages.

Consumer Reports has also dedicated their efforts toward many consumer product categories, including automobiles, energy, health, food, and other areas

ambient advertising
a form of advertising where unconventional or unexpected messages are placed in a target market's social environment

that permeate daily life. **Ambient advertising**, which places unconventional or unexpected messages in a target market's social environment, is considered "ad creep" by critics who lament the number of advertisements that consumers are exposed to each day. Thus, in addition to the content of advertising and unseen data collection, consumer groups may express concerns about the timing and placement of advertising. Many ambient advertisements appear in outdoor locations, restroom stalls, taxis, or other places where consumers are not necessarily expecting to see them. In other cases, technology is used to personalize promotional messages and offers. Today, it is possible for companies to send marketing messages to potential consumers based on location data sent from these consumers' smartphones. While some consumers appreciate marketing based on physical proximity, others view the approach as a clear invasion of privacy, even if they are able to refuse the wireless signal and communications.[44]

The internet and electronic communication have become main vehicles for consumer advocacy, education, and protection. Visitors to the National Consumers League (NCL) website at nclnet.org or consumerworld.org easily find publications on many consumer issues, research and campaign reports, product reviews, updates on legal matters, and many other types of services. Thus, consumer groups and information services have shifted the balance of power between consumer and business because consumers are able to compare prices, read independent rankings, communicate with other buyers, and have greater knowledge about products, companies, and competitors.[45] Recently, the NCL launched information resources about coding boot camps, which are technical training opportunities that teach students how to develop computer code. While many boot camps are legitimate, NCL recommends that potential students independently investigate the job placement rates, tuition costs, and state authorizations for these schools.[46]

Despite the opportunities to exert more power, some researchers question whether most consumers take the time and energy to do so. For example, although the internet provides a great deal of information and choices, access to the internet partly depends on educational level and income. In addition, the volume of information available online may actually make it more difficult to analyze and assimilate. Even with these issues, consumer groups have developed a legion of e-activists who email legislators and regulators and work to get consumer protection legislation passed. These consumer activists hope to use their campaigns to spur policy changes in the area of consumer protection. Some major accomplishments include lower credit card rates, improved card services, and higher security of financial information.[47] Consumer Reports provides a number of consumer advocacy tools on its website, such as the opportunity to sign petitions, read letters written by Consumer Reports and other groups to government agencies and corporations, report safety concerns, and submit stories and ideas for the organization to investigate.

U.S. presidents since Kennedy have confirmed the four basic consumer rights and added new ones in response to changing business conditions. President Bill Clinton, for example, appointed a commission to study the changing healthcare environment and its implications for consumer rights. The result was the proposal of a Patient's Bill of Rights and Responsibilities to ensure rights to confidentiality of patient information, to participate in healthcare decisions, to access emergency services, and other needs.[48] During the same period, a Financial Consumer's Bill of Rights Act was proposed in the U.S. House of Representatives to curb high bank fees, automated teller machine (ATM) surcharges, and other practices that have angered consumers.[49]

Consumer rights were first formalized through a presidential speech and subsequent affirmations, resulting in the legal establishment of specific elements of these rights. However, the relatively broad nature of the rights means they must be interpreted and implemented on a company-by-company basis. Table 9.5 lists six consumer rights that have become part of the ethical expectations of business.

Table 9.5 Basic Consumer Rights

Right	General Description
To choose	Consumers have the opportunity to select from a variety of products at reasonable prices.
To safety	All products should be safe for their intended use, include instructions for proper and safe use, and have been sufficiently tested to ensure reliability.
To be informed	Information is accurate, adequate, and free of deception so that consumers can make a sound decision.
To be heard	Consumers have the opportunity to communicate or voice their concerns in the public policy process.
To redress	Consumers have the right to express dissatisfaction and seek restitution from a business when a product does not meet their expectations.
To privacy	This right is related to consumers' awareness of how their personal data are collected and used and places a burden on firms to protect this information.

Although these rights are not necessarily provided by all organizations, our social responsibility philosophy requires their attention and implementation.

Right to Choose   The right to choose implies that, to the extent possible, consumers have the opportunity to select from a variety of products at competitive prices. This right is based on the philosophy of the competitive nature of markets, which should lead to high-quality products at reasonable prices. Antitrust activities that reduce competition may jeopardize this right, and it has been called into question with respect to safety in some parts of the United States. The right has manifested itself differently in recent times. Google, for example, was ordered by an EU ruling to erase consumers' information in search results. The ruling, dubbed the "right to be forgotten," gives consumers in the EU more power to choose how their information will be used. While the rule currently applies only in the EU, the effects of this mandate are potentially far-reaching.[50]

Right to Safety   The right to safety also implies that all products should be safe for their intended use, include instructions for proper and safe use, and have been sufficiently tested to ensure reliability. Companies must take great care in designing warning messages about products with potentially dangerous or unsafe effects. These messages should take into account consumers' ability to understand and respond to the information. Warnings should be relevant and meaningful to every potential user of the product. Some warnings use symbols or pictures to communicate no matter what languages consumers speak. Companies that fail to honor the right to safety risk expensive product liability lawsuits and damages to their reputations.

McDonald's announced its response to media allegations of serving unsafe food items in China soon before World Consumer Rights Day. Claims involved the serving of chicken an hour past the suggested time period after being cooked and the serving of unsanitary beef. The incident damaged the company's reputation and came at a most unfortunate time, as the fast food giant had launched a marketing campaign highlighting their commitment to food quality and safety only weeks before. Kentucky Fried Chicken (KFC) was embroiled in a chicken-related scandal in China around the same time, and both companies used social media to manage the crises. McDonald's apologized within 24 hours of news reports, which is very uncommon in a collectivist society like China that strives to maintain "face." On the other hand, KFC did not issue an apology until its role in the scandal was verified over one month later. Researchers concluded that McDonald's approach both surprised and delighted consumers and other stakeholders.[51]

Shutterstock/Ekaterina_Minaeva

Right to Be Informed   Consumers also have the right to be informed. Any information, whether communicated in written or verbal format, should be accurate, adequate, and free of deception so that consumers can make a sound decision. This general assertion has also led to specific legislation, such as the Nutrition Labeling and Education Act of 1990, which requires certain nutrition facts on food labels. This right can be associated with safety issues if consumers do not have sufficient information to purchase or use a product effectively. Other types of violations include companies charging customers for unrequested products or not providing them with enough information. The FCC fined AT&T $100 million because it did not inform customers with unlimited plans that after using 5 GB of data per month, the carrier would reduce transmission speeds. This slower speed interfered with the functionality of mobile apps and appeared to contradict the network speeds that AT&T advertised. The FCC believed this lack of disclosure violated consumer rights.[52]

In an age of rapid technological advances and globalization, the degree of complexity in product marketing is another concern related to consumers' right to information. This complexity may relate to the ways in which product features and benefits are discussed in advertising, how effective salespeople are in answering consumer questions, the expertise needed to operate or use the product, and the ease of returning or exchanging the product. To help consumers make decisions based on adequate and timely information, some organizations sponsor consumer education programs. For example, pharmaceutical companies and health maintenance organizations sponsor free seminars, health screenings, websites, and other programs to educate consumers about their health and treatment options. The nonprofit organization URAC (which stands for their original name, "Utilization Review Accreditation Commission") is committed to promoting healthcare quality through a series of accreditations that companies and organizations may pursue. The approval process is extensive, and applicants must provide evidence of meeting national standards for healthcare quality, consumer protection, and health outcomes. URAC is an independent, third-party quality validator that provides a seal of approval to let consumers know which healthcare providers have met rigorous standards in dentistry, telehealth, pharmacy, and other fields.[53]

Right to Be Heard   The right to be heard relates to opportunities for consumers to communicate or voice their concerns in the public policy process. This also implies that governments have the responsibility to listen and take consumer issues and concerns into account. One mechanism for fulfilling this responsibility is through the FTC and state consumer affairs offices. Another vehicle includes congressional hearings held to educate elected officials about specific issues of concern to consumers. At the same time, consumers are expected to be full participants in the process, meaning they must be informed and willing to take action against misconduct in the marketplace.

Right to Seek Redress   In addition to the rights described by Kennedy, consumers have the right to express dissatisfaction and seek restitution from a business when a good or service does not meet their expectations. However, consumers

Table 9.6 Dispute Resolution Services of the BBB

Mediation—BBB provides a professionally trained mediator to talk with the parties and guide them in working out their own mutually agreeable solution.

Informal dispute resolution—BBB provides a professionally trained hearing officer who will listen to both sides and make a nonbinding decision on how to resolve the dispute.

Conditionally binding arbitration—BBB provides a professionally trained arbitrator who will listen to both sides and make a decision on how to resolve the dispute that is binding on the parties only if the customer accepts the decision.

Binding arbitration—BBB provides a professionally trained arbitrator who will listen to both sides, weigh the evidence presented, and make a decision on how to resolve the dispute that is binding on all parties.

Source: Better Business Bureau, "Dispute Resolution Processes and Guides," https://www.bbb.org/bbb-dispute-handling-and-resolution/dispute-resolution-rules-and-brochures/dispute-resolution-processes-and-guides/ (access June 20, 2019).

need to be educated in the process for seeking redress and to recognize that the first course of action in such cases should be with the seller. At the same time, companies need to have explicit and formal processes for dealing with customer dissatisfaction. Although some product problems lead to third-party intervention or legal recourse, the majority of issues should be resolvable between the consumer and the business. One third party that consumers may consult in such cases is the Better Business Bureau (BBB), which promotes the self-regulation of business. To gain and maintain membership, a firm must agree to abide by the ethical standards established by the BBB. This organization collects complaints on businesses and makes this information, along with other reports, available for consumer decision-making. The BBB also operates the dispute resolution division to assist in out-of-court settlements between consumers and businesses. These settlements are less costly than litigation in terms of money, time, and stress. Specific dispute resolution services fall into one of four categories, which are listed in Table 9.6.

Mediation offers the opportunity for a trained mediator to guide the customer and company toward their own mutually acceptable solution, whereas informal dispute resolution includes a more central role for a hearing officer, who makes a nonbinding decision. A trained arbitrator is used in both conditionally binding arbitration and binding arbitration, with the latter approach resulting in a decision that is binding on all parties.[54] This self-regulatory approach not only provides differentiation in the market, but can also minimize or even prevent new laws and regulations from being passed and imposed on businesses.

Right to Privacy Information technology and the use of the internet prompted increasing concerns about consumer privacy. This right relates to consumers' awareness of how personal data are collected and used, and it places a burden on firms to protect this information. How information is used can create concerns for consumers. Although some e-commerce firms have joined together to develop privacy standards for the internet, many websites do not meet the FTC's criteria for fair information practices, including notice, choice, access, and security. Recent action by the FTC resulted in a $235,000 settlement with Explore Talent, an online talent search company. The firm violated provisions of the COPPA because it collected personal information from children without gaining parental consent.[55] We will take a closer look at the debate surrounding privacy rights in Chapter 10.

A firm's ability to address these consumer rights can serve as a competitive advantage. Service Line Warranties of America (SLWA), a utility service company and a past recipient of the National Torch Award for Marketplace Ethics given by the BBB, is highly regarded for their ethical approach to consumers. They help consumers understand their responsibilities with respect to utility maintenance so that they are not charged extra fees by their utility companies. The company's mission is to take care of the complexities of home ownership so that consumers can enjoy more free time.[56]

Consumer Action When consumers believe that a firm is operating outside ethical or legal standards, they may be motivated to take some type of action. As discussed earlier, there are a number of strategies that consumers can employ to communicate their dissatisfaction, such as complaining or discontinuing the relationship. For example, some people believe that Walmart's presence has contributed to the demise of locally owned pharmacies and variety stores in many small towns. The chain's buying power ensures lower prices and wider product variety for consumers, but it also makes it difficult for some smaller retailers to compete. Other consumers and community leaders worry about the traffic congestion and urban sprawl that accompany new retail sites. Some Walmart critics have taken their discontent with the retailer to the internet. Disgruntled customers and others share complaints about the retail chain, provide updates about legal action, and promote campaigns against the retailer on changewalmart.org. The website is managed by the United Food and Commercial Workers (UFCW) union, although consumers are active participants in the effort. Walmart has sought legal relief so that members of UFCW are permitted to shop there but may not picket, protest, demonstrate, or otherwise disrupt customers, management, and store operations.[57]

Stakeholders may use the three types of power—symbolic, utilitarian, and coercive—discussed in earlier chapters to create organizational awareness of important issues. For example, wealthy Thai consumers who support military rule asked consumers to avoid purchasing European brands after the EU criticized a Thai government coup. In particular, the EU criticized government decisions to make it harder to express dissent, as well as delays in elections. Brussels announced that it was suspending official visits to Thailand and would not sign an agreement with the country. Wealthy Thai consumers felt betrayed by a region with which they extensively trade.[58] While this response is not a result of a company's action, the situation highlights the lingering contention between Thailand and the EU. These consumers are engaging in another form of consumer action, a **boycott**, by abstaining from using, purchasing, or dealing with a company or other organization.

Many groups choose to boycott certain businesses or products because of disagreements over an owner's beliefs or a government's policies. Famous celebrities and organizations boycotted the Beverly Hills Hotel because of the actions of its owner, Sultan Hassanal Bolkiah of Brunei, a country located on the north coast of the island of Borneo. The boycott occurred after the sultan stated that he was enforcing sharia law in his country. Boycotters protested against some of the harsher punishments levied against certain people and groups convicted of crimes under sharia law.[59]

Protests are also a common consumer method of showing displeasure with an organization's policies and are often used in tandem with boycotts. **Consumer protests** are a form of consumer action that involves the organized and public display of consumers' disapproval of a firm's actions. Protests have been used around the world for years, including high-profile events in the United States that were largely organized by women. In 1935, women in Chicago led a national campaign to protest the high cost of meat. In the 1960s, women in Denver, Colorado, and other large cities boycotted supermarkets to bring attention to the increasing cost of consumer goods.[60] More recently, oil and gas companies have been alarmed by the number and actions of protestors who are against the development of underground pipelines to transport oil and gas throughout parts of the United States. Beyond crowds numbering over 4,000 people, protesters tried to close pipeline valves manually in facilities near the Canadian border in October 2016.[61] Today, consumer protests are often implemented online via social media channels,

boycott
a form of consumer action in which consumers abstain from using, purchasing, or dealing with a company or other organization

consumer protest
a form of consumer action that involves the organized and public display of consumers' disapproval of a firm's actions

Ethical Responsibilities in **MARKETING**

The Rise of Femtech

When health expert Tania Boler became pregnant, she wondered why all of the options for breast pumps were loud, bulky, and looked like were designed in the 1980s. Armed with degrees from Oxford University (BA) and Stanford University (MA), Boler set out to design the perfect breast pump for her—one that was discreet, quiet, and wearable.

In the United States, approximately 80 percent of women breastfeed their newborns. However, many of them stop earlier than physicians recommend because of complications in the workplace and a lack of options that integrate with today's fast-paced lifestyles. By using modern technologies, like Wi-Fi, that most now take for granted, Boler created a wireless, silent breast pump. Marketed as the Elvie Pump, Boler's invention allows mothers to take care of their children without the struggle of using outdated technology. Mothers use a smartphone app to remotely control the device and monitor the volume of milk output. The Elvie has been worn on fashion runways, sold out in five minutes when it debuted in the United States, and recently raised over $40 million in investment funding, providing evidence that a new industry called *femtech* is emerging and much needed.

The term refers to an array of companies and technology that have been or will be created to help women better track, monitor, and understand the individual female body. Like Boler, Dr. Piraye Yurttas Beim realized an unmet need in the fertility business. In the United States alone, nearly 7 million women have trouble conceiving a baby, and no two cases of infertility are alike. Yet fertility services are often designed using generic or broad factors, such as age. Dr. Beim's company, Celmatix, allows women and their partners to be more proactive and informed about the specific factors leading to their infertility. Using a database of millions of women, Celmatix analyzes a patient's personal health profile against the profiles of other women with similar health factors who have overcome fertility problems. Complex algorithms result in patient-specific recommendations, on the likelihood that a particular fertility treatment will be successful. This big data approach helps doctors create treatment plans and ensures that women and their partners understand potential genetic difficulties on the pathway to conception. Celmatix has raised over $70 million in investments.

These female entrepreneurs are not alone. Other companies have emerged to tackle issues related to menopause, breastfeeding, fertility, postpregnancy needs, birth control, and feminine hygiene. Beyond the knowledge and understanding that these products bring to women, they also instill a sense of agency and power. Based on the recent growth in femtech, some observers have asked, "Why did it take so long for these solutions to emerge?" One answer may be that business leaders have simply not been comfortable talking about—much less developing products for—the female body, reproduction, and other facets of women's health.

Another answer may lie in how venture capitalists, those individuals and companies who invest millions in start-up ideas and firms, have traditionally viewed opportunities led by female entrepreneurs, as well as new products that cater to women. According to recent estimates, less than 5 percent of venture capital funding goes to female-led start-ups. This is beginning to change, though, and femtech is leading the way, with over $390 million in venture capital committed in 2018 alone. As the Elvie website proudly proclaims, "It's time for female-first innovation."

Sources: Anna Altman, "Mommy and Data." *New Republic* 250 (January/February 2019): 28–35; Elvie, https://www.elvie.com/ (accessed June 25, 2019); Tanya Klich, "Elvie, A FemTech Startup That Developed a Wireless and Wearable Breast Pump, Raises $42 Million in VC," *Forbes*, April 2, 2019, https://www.forbes.com/sites/tanyaklich/2019/04/02/elvie-a-femtech-startup-that-developed-a-wireless-and-wearable-breast-pump-raises-42-million-in-vc/#2bef7ca32753 (accessed June 27, 2019); Dana Olsen, "The Top 13 VC Investors in Femtech Startups," *Pitchbook*, https://pitchbook.com/news/articles/the-top-13-vc-investors-in-femtech-startups (accessed June 27, 2019); Leena Rao, "This Entrepreneur Is Using Big Data to Help More Women Get Pregnant," *Fortune*, February 18, 2016, http://fortune.com/2016/02/18/piraye-yurtess-beim-entrepreneur-celmatix-fertility/ (accessed June 26, 2019).

blogs, message boards, closed group platforms, and other methods. In contrast to protests that take place at specific locations and times, online protests often surprise companies. Protests have the potential to negatively affect a company's reputation, sales, and stakeholder relationships. The effects of protests, however, may be mitigated by crisis management plans and the effective implementation of a stakeholder perspective discussed in Chapter 2.

Philanthropic Issues

Although relationships with consumers are fundamentally grounded in economic exchanges, the previous sections demonstrate that additional levels of expectations exist. Research continues to show that the majority of consumers would be likely to switch to brands associated with a good cause, so long as price and quality were equal. These results suggest that today's consumers take for granted that they can obtain high-quality products at reasonable prices, so businesses need to do something to differentiate themselves from the competition. More firms, therefore, are investigating ways to link their philanthropic efforts with consumer interests. Starbucks, for example, has contributed to environmental programs, sustainable farming initiatives, and investment in employee well-being and happiness. These programs not only form a link between the company's possible effects and its interest in the natural environment, but also provide a service to its customers and other stakeholders.

From a strategic perspective, a firm's ability to link consumer interests to philanthropy should lead to stronger economic relationships. As we shall see in Chapter 10, philanthropic responsibilities to consumers usually entail broader benefits, including those that affect the community. For example, large pharmaceutical and health insurance firms provided financial support to the Foundation for Accountability (FACCT), a nonprofit organization that assisted healthcare consumers in making better decisions from 1995 to 2004. FACCT initiated an online system for patients to evaluate their physician on several quality indicators. Although FACCT ceased its operations, the Markle Foundation continues to host the nonprofit's legacy with documents and white papers. The foundation partners with other organizations to improve the role of technology in addressing critical public health needs.[62]

A company will have more successful philanthropic efforts when the cause is a good fit with their product category, industry, customer concerns, and/or location. This alignment is an important contributor to the long-term relationships that often develop between specific companies and cause-related organizations. Many firms involved in medicine and pharmaceuticals will contribute to causes that improve access to proper healthcare and medication, provide stronger patient support and outcomes, decrease accidents and injuries, and respond to emergency or critical needs of a community. Table 9.7 describes the philanthropic contribution levels of the top 10 corporate foundations in the United States in terms of annual giving. These companies have established corporate foundations with large endowments,

Table 9.7 Top 10 Corporate Foundations in the United States

Corporate Foundation	Annual Giving
Novartis Patient Assistance Foundation, Inc.	$ 542,136,898
Wells Fargo Foundation	$226,902,237
Wal-Mart Foundation, Inc.	$ 166,403,573
JPMorgan Chase Foundation	$ 159,401,094
Bank of America Charitable Foundation, Inc.	$ 149,183,853
GE Foundation	$ 106,397,515
Coca-Cola Foundation, Inc	$ 84,831,796
Citi Foundation	$ 78,094,000
ExxonMobil Foundation	$ 74,264,738
Johnson & Johnson Family of Companies Contribution Fund	$ 66,469,618

Source: Foundation Center, "The 50 Largest Corporate Foundations by Total Giving," http://data.foundationcenter.org/#/foundations/corporate/nationwide/top:giving/list/2015 (accessed August 13, 2019).

which means that annual contributions are relatively unaffected by corporate profitability and the economic cycle. Nonprofits prefer consistent donations rather than wide variance from year to year.

Strategic Implementation of Responsibilities to Consumers

As this chapter has demonstrated, social responsibility involves relationships with many stakeholders—including consumers—and many firms are finding creative ways to meet these responsibilities. Just as in other aspects of social responsibility, these relationships must be managed, nurtured, and continuously assessed. Resources devoted to this effort may include programs for educating and listening to consumers, surveys to discover strengths and weaknesses in stakeholder relationships, the hiring of consumer affairs professionals, the development of a community relations office, and other initiatives. Business in the Community, a coalition of companies in the United Kingdom (UK), developed principles to guide its members and other businesses in dealing with consumers and the supply chain. Guided by a "Responsible Business Map," the coalition offers training, tracking mechanisms, and best practices for effectively putting principles into action. Each year, the coalition honors companies with a variety of awards, including "Responsible Small Business of the Year." Salary Finance was recognized for its innovative business purpose and outcomes, which center on the development of employer-sponsored programs to provide employees with financial wellbeing benefits such as debt consolidation, refinancing, and other measures. The small firm, which was established in the UK, recently began operations in the United States.[63] Table 9.8 provides an overview of the Responsible Business program, along with four key goals for a responsible business leader.

Understanding consumer and stakeholder issues can be especially complex in the global environment. For example, PUMA intended to honor the United Arab Emirates (UAE) in November 2011, as it celebrated its 40th National Day, by developing a limited-edition shoe with the colors of the nation's flag. However, when the product was released, UAE consumers were outraged. They viewed it as putting a respected symbol on shoes, something perceived to be unclean in Middle

Table 9.8 Responsible Business Principles According to Business in the Community

Business in the Community defines a responsible business as one that puts creating healthy communities and a healthy environment at the center of its strategy to achieve long-term financial value. A responsible business demands purposeful leaders to drive leadership at every level in order to do the following:

- Understand where a business is able to have the most impact by identifying those material issues that are of greatest importance to both commercial success and key stakeholders and the long-term benefit to society.
- Understand how to take advantage of the opportunities brought by digital innovation (e.g., more efficient use of resources, access to new markets), as well as manage the unintended consequences (e.g., cybersecurity, access to jobs, inequality).
- Support and empower customers, embrace the changing nature of work, deliver products and services that serve society and drive a transparent, inclusive and productive value chain.
- Move from a "do less harm" approach to one where they are a genuine force for positive change, creating competitive advantages, meeting changing customer needs, and attracting, retaining, and developing the best talent.

Source: Business in the Community, "What Is Responsible Business?" https://www.bitc.org.uk/what-responsible-business (accessed June 10, 2019).

Eastern culture. PUMA had to apologize and recall all the shoes.[64] Organizations must understand the importance of integrating all stakeholders into their social responsibility efforts, including employees, as we explored in Chapter 8, and the general community, which we examine in Chapter 10.

Summary

Companies face complex decisions about how to respond to the expectations, attitudes, and buying patterns of consumers—those individuals who purchase, use, and dispose of products for personal and household use. Consumers are primary stakeholders because their awareness, purchase, use, and repurchase of products are vital to a company's existence.

Consumers and businesses are fundamentally connected by an economic relationship. Economic responsibilities include following through on promises made in the exchange process. Consumer fraud involves intentional deception to derive an unfair economic advantage over an organization. If consumers believe that a firm has not fulfilled its economic responsibility, they may ask for a refund, tell others about the bad experience, discontinue their patronage, contact a consumer agency, or seek legal redress.

In the United States, legal issues with respect to consumers fall under the jurisdiction of the FTC, which enforces federal antitrust and consumer protection laws. Other federal and state agencies regulate specific goods, services, or business practices. Among the issues that may have been addressed through specific state or federal laws and regulations are consumer health and safety, credit and ownership, marketing and advertising, sales and warranties, and product liability. Product liability refers to a business's legal responsibility for the performance of its products. Concerns about protecting consumers' legal rights are not limited to the United States.

Ethical issues related to consumers include the Consumer Bill of Rights enumerated by President Kennedy. Consumerism refers to the movement to protect consumers from an imbalance of power with business and to maximize consumer welfare in the marketplace. Some specific elements of consumer rights have been mandated by law, but the relatively broad nature of the rights means they must be interpreted and implemented on a company-by-company basis. Consumer rights have evolved to include the right to choose, the right to safety, the right to be informed, the right to be heard, the right to seek redress, and the right to privacy. When consumers believe that a firm is operating outside ethical or legal standards, they may be motivated to take action, including boycotting—abstaining from using, purchasing, or dealing with an organization.

More firms are investigating ways to link their philanthropic efforts with consumer interests. From a strategic perspective, a firm's ability to link consumer interests to philanthropy should lead to stronger economic relationships.

Many companies are finding creative ways to satisfy their responsibilities to consumers. Much like employee relationships, these responsibilities must be managed, nurtured, and continuously assessed. Resources devoted to this effort may include programs for educating and listening to consumers, surveys to discover strengths and weaknesses in stakeholder relationships, hiring consumer affairs professionals, working with industry groups, and the development of other initiatives that engage consumers.

Responsible Business Debate

Clearance Pricing: Business Communication in Practice

Issue: *Should the use of clearance pricing be regulated?*

Sales are price discounts that are designed to encourage purchase of a particular item. Sometimes the term *clearance* is used, but not together with the term *sale* because the use of the latter term is regulated in most states. According to the American Marketing Association, clearance is "an end-of-season sale to make room for more goods." While retailers can offer sales for temporary time periods, items on clearance do not return to their original prices. Rather, the product is discounted until it is sold. Clearance events are often short in duration, and items under clearance are not always advertised.

Studies have demonstrated that many consumers view the word *clearance* as a signal indicating substantial discounts. Yet unlike other forms of sales promotion, clearance events are less regulated. Many retailers, including Macy's and other clothing stores, use the word *clearance* extensively. Experts estimate that more than 30 percent of merchandise is now sold at clearance. Consumers may be attracted to clearance pricing due to the following factors: (1) fear that the product will be discontinued before they purchase it, (2) belief that others will get to the item first and another is not available, (3) perceived value of the product, (4) the belief that they are saving money, and (5) an escalation of commitment due to time spent searching for sales.

It has generally been ruled that the term *clearance* is an example of *puffery*, an exaggerated promotional claim that should not be taken seriously by a reasonable person. For example, the state of Wisconsin filed a lawsuit against American TV & Appliance alleging that the retailer's claims of offering "a clearance sale on the finest washers and dryers you can buy" was deceptive due to the following factors: (1) the products were not actually of the finest quality, (2) the store was using the advertisement to get people in the store and then tried to upsell them higher-priced products, and (3) the products were purchased exclusively for the event and therefore, it did not qualify as clearance. Although at first the courts ruled against the retailer, the ruling was overturned, confirming that the term *clearance* in the ad was an example of puffery.

However, do consumers themselves view the term *clearance* as an exaggerated claim that they should not accept at face value? Critics argue no. It has been generally accepted that *clearance* indicates substantial price discounts, so using that term inappropriately can be deceptive. Without regulation, they argue, retailers can use the term to make consumers think that they are receiving a substantial deal. In fact, research has shown that less than 15 percent of consumers know the amount of the associated price discount. Because inventory levels are not typically visible in online shopping websites, consumers may be further disadvantaged in assessing the relative scarcity of an item.

On the other hand, regulating how the term *clearance* is used could have negative repercussions. Like any form of business regulation, regulation of the word *clearance* would limit what a business can and cannot do. Placing limits on how clearance sales can be used will likely mean that retailers will display the term *clearance sale* less due to the fear of violating FTC regulations. Yet clearance sales can be important strategies for retailers, particularly for firms that face demand uncertainty for products, sell perishable items, and sell demonstration models. Clearance sales are common in the fast fashion industry, where clothing is targeted to younger consumers who are interested in the latest fashions at low prices. In contrast to traditional clothing retailers, fast fashion companies like H&M and Zara turn over inventory at a very quick pace and need to make room for new inventory on a regular basis.

There Are Two Sides to Every Issue
1. Retailers should be able to use the term *clearance* without having to qualify or justify the amount of the discount.
2. Because the term *clearance* is potentially misleading, use of it should be regulated, and it should not be used unless there are documented and substantial price discounts.

Sources: State of Wisconsin v. American TV & Appliance of Madison, Inc., 430 N.W.2d 709 (Wisc. App. Ct. 1988); Cullen Goretzke, "The Resurgence of Caveat Emptor: Puffery Undermines the Pro-Consumer Trend in Wisconsin's Misrepresentation Doctrine," 2003 *Wis. L. Rev.* 171, 222; Kit Yarrow, "Why Shoppers Just Can't Resist Clearance Sales," *Time,* http://business.time.com/2013/01/07/why-shoppers-just-cant-resist-clearance-sales/ (accessed June 5, 2019); Volker Nocke and Martie Peitz, "A Theory of Clearance Sales, *Economic Journal* 117, no. 522 (July 2007): 964; American Marketing Association, "Clearance Sale," *Common Use Marketing Dictionary,* https://marketing-dictionary.org/c/clearance-sale/ (accessed June 5, 2019); Kenneth C. Manning, O. C. Ferrell, and Linda K. Ferrell, "Toward Understanding 'Clearance' Promotions," Working paper; J. Jeffrey Inman, Leigh McAlister, and Wayne D. Hoyer, "Promotion Signal: Proxy for a Price Cut?" *Journal of Consumer Research* 17 (June 1990): 74–81; Balram Avittathur and Indranil Biswas, "A Note on Limited Clearance Sale Inventory Model," *International Journal of Production Economics,* 193 (2017): 647–653.

Key Terms

ambient advertising (p. 262)
boycott (p. 266)
Bureau of Consumer Protection (p. 253)
Consumer Bill of Rights (p. 260)
consumer fraud (p. 251)
Consumer Product Safety Commission (p. 253)

consumer protest (p. 266)
consumer relations (p. 250)
consumerism (p. 261)
consumers (p. 250)
crowdfunding (p. 260)
Federal Communications Commission (FCC) (p. 254)

Federal Trade Commission (FTC) (p. 253)
Food and Drug Administration (FDA) (p. 253)
product liability (p. 258)
product placement (p. 256)
warranty (p. 258)

Discussion Questions

1. List and describe the consumer rights that have become social expectations of business. Why have some of these rights been formalized through legislation? Should these rights be considered ethical standards?

2. Look at Southwest Airline's Customer Service Commitment at https://www.southwest.com/assets/pdfs/corporate-commitments/customer-service-commitment.pdf. Describe how different elements of its commitment relate to specific economic, legal, ethical, or philanthropic responsibilities that the airline has to its customers.

3. What is the purpose of a boycott? Describe the characteristics of companies and consumers that are likely to be involved in a boycott situation. What circumstances would cause you to consider participating in a boycott?

4. How can companies strive for successful relationships with consumers, including meeting their economic, legal, ethical, and philanthropic expectations?

5. How will consumer rights and activism change over the next decade? Will the movement strengthen or decline? Why?

Experiential Exercise

Visit the website of Consumers International (http://www.consumersinternational.org). What is the purpose of this website? Select a current issue and read the information provided by the consumers' groups organization on that issue. How useful is this information to you? With what information do you agree and/or disagree? How could a business manager use this site to understand and improve a company's relationship and reputation with consumers?

There's a Ringing in My Ears: What Would You Do?

Justin Thompson was excited. He really enjoyed his job at the Kingston's department store downtown. This location housed Kingston's first store and still had many of its original features. As he rode the subway into the city center, Justin thought about the money he would earn this summer and the great car that he hoped to buy before school started. He was lucky to have secured this type of job—many of his friends were working early or late hours at fast-food chains or out in the summer heat. The management team at Kingston's had initiated a program with his high school counselors, hoping to attract top high school seniors into retail management throughout their college career and beyond. Justin was a strong student from a single-parent background, and his counselor was highly complementary of his work ethic and prospects for professional employment. Justin's first week was consumed with various training sessions. There were eight students in

the special high school program. They watched a company video that discussed Kingston's history, ethics policy, current operations, and customer service philosophy. They met with staff from HR to fill out paperwork. They learned how to scan merchandise and operate the computer software and cash register. They toured the store's three levels and visited with each department manager. Justin was especially excited about working in the electronics department, but he was assigned to men's clothing.

Justin worked alongside several employees during the first few weeks on the store floor. He watched the experienced employees approach customers, help them, and ring up the sale. He noticed that some employees took personal telephone calls, and others did not clean up the dressing rooms or restock items very quickly. On slower days, he eventually worked alone in the department. Several times when he came to work in the afternoon, he had to clean up a mess left behind by the morning shift. When he spoke to various colleagues about it in the break room, they told him it was best to keep quiet. After all, he was a high school student earning money for a car, not a "real employee," with kids to feed and bills to pay. Justin assumed that retail work was much like team projects in school—not everyone pulled their weight, but it was hard to be the tattletale.

One Saturday morning was extremely busy, as Kingston's was running a big sale. People were swarming to the sales racks, and Justin was amazed at how fast the time was passing. In the late afternoon, several friends of one of his coworkers dropped by the men's section. Before long, their hands were full of merchandise. The crowd was starting to wane, so Justin took a few minutes to clean up the dressing room. When he came out, his coworker was ringing up his friends' merchandise. Justin saw two ties go into one of the bags, but only one was scanned into the system. He saw an extra discount given on an expensive shirt. Justin was shocked to see that not every item was scanned and that improper discounts were being applied, and his mind was racing. Should he stop his coworker? Should he "take a break" and get security? Was there another alternative? What would you do?

CHAPTER 10

Community Relations and Strategic Philanthropy

Google Employee Volunteers Target Dark Side of the Web

The philanthropic arm of Google, Google.org, recently launched a fellowship program for employees to take up to six months to do pro bono work for a nonprofit or charitable organization. Google.org's goal is to deploy 50,000 employee volunteer hours each year through the program. With its vast resources of technical know-how and expert employees, Google.org is setting its sights on how technology can help nonprofits solve emerging and ongoing social challenges.

The program is an extension of Google.org's philanthropy and community partnership efforts and aids the technology giant in achieving two goals: (1) support the community with the company's expertise and (2) motivate employees and help them improve their skills. Google.org has five areas of interest: economic opportunity, education, inclusion, crisis response, and the impact challenge, where leaders and social entrepreneurs pitch ideas for how they would make their community an even better place. Google.org communicates their approach as "data-driven, human-focused philanthropy—driven by Google."

The fellowship program is the result of a six-month pilot initiative that placed Google employees with Thorn, a nonprofit organization dedicated to fighting the exploitation of children on the internet. Thorn, established by celebrities Ashton Kutcher and Demi Moore, focuses on finding technology solutions that protect children from sexual abuse. Five Google employees spent six months at the organization to assist with using artificial intelligence (AI) to track down victims of child trafficking, unearth the origins of child pornography, and enable law enforcement to identify and apprehend perpetrators. Text, phone numbers, and photos on the darkest reaches of the internet create millions of pieces of data that can be mined for patterns and revelations.

Like many organizations, Thorn grew out of innovation in technology. Despite its many positive ramifications, technology has also made it easier to exploit children. Based on its own research, Thorn acknowledges that more than 60 percent of exploited children are advertised on the internet or found on the dark web, parts of the internet that require specific software or authorization to access. The organization is recognized for employing the first, or only, engineering and data analytics team fully dedicated to combating online child abuse.

The pilot program at Thorn was successful on many fronts, including employee engagement, community relations, and strategic philanthropy. Six months at Thorn convinced one engineer that her technology skills could make a huge difference, especially in the lives of exploited children. She admits that she became a better software designer as a result of seeing how the nonprofit organization operates with both efficiency and elegance. Because of the sensitive and troubling nature of its work, Thorn has developed a culture of self-care, empathy, and emotional awareness. Ultimately, the experience at Thorn taught the entire Google volunteer team how to be better colleagues and leaders. One member of the team remarked, "My work with Thorn reminded me that our mission as engineers is not to simply build the newest and fastest technologies: our mission is to seek solutions to pressing problems no matter how daunting."[1]

Chapter Objectives

- Describe the community as a stakeholder
- Discuss the community relations function
- Distinguish between strategic philanthropy and cause-related marketing
- Examine how social entrepreneurship relates to social responsibility
- Identify the benefits of strategic philanthropy
- Explain the key factors in implementing strategic philanthropy

Google, like most organizations with operational expertise and other core competencies, can also focus on implementing social responsibility and satisfying stakeholder groups. From a social responsibility perspective, the key challenge is how an organization assesses its stakeholders' needs, integrates them with company strategy, reconciles differences between stakeholders' needs, strives for better relationships with stakeholders, achieves mutual understandings with them, and finds solutions for problems. In this chapter, we explore community stakeholders and how organizations deal with stakeholder needs through philanthropic initiatives. We explore the relationship with communities and the economic, legal, ethical, and philanthropic responsibilities that must be addressed by business. We define strategic philanthropy and integrate this concept with other elements of social responsibility. Next, we trace the evolution of corporate philanthropy and distinguish the concept from cause-related marketing. We also provide examples of best practices of addressing stakeholders' interests that meet our definition of strategic philanthropy. From there, we define social entrepreneurship and explain how it relates to strategic philanthropy and social responsibility. Then we consider the benefits of investing in strategic philanthropy to satisfy both stakeholders and corporate objectives. Finally, we examine the process of implementing strategic philanthropy in business. Our approach in this chapter is to demonstrate how companies can link strategic philanthropy with economic, legal, and ethical concerns for the benefit of all stakeholders.

Community Stakeholders

The concept of *community* has many varying characteristics that make it a challenge to define. The community does not always receive the same level of acceptance as other stakeholders. Some people even wonder how a company determines who is in the community. Is a community defined by city or county boundaries? What if the firm operates in multiple locations? Or is a community prescribed by the interactions a firm has with various constituents who do not fit neatly into other stakeholder categories? For a small restaurant in a large city, the owner may define the community as the immediate neighborhood where most patrons live. The restaurant may demonstrate social responsibility by hiring people from the neighborhood, participating in the neighborhood crime watch program, donating food to the elementary school's annual parent-teacher meetings, or sponsoring a neighborhood Little League team. For example, JPMorgan Chase & Co. has instituted a program called Corporate Challenge, a global initiative that invites employees and others to participate in running events for charity. Today, participants in the Corporate Challenge include teams from many other organizations although employees of JPMorgan Chase still produce the largest participation from a single company. One of the events, which took place in Syracuse, New York, hosted over 28,000 runners and walkers from more than 350 companies. The proceeds supported the local nonprofit Hillside Work-Scholarship Connection. Now in its 43rd year, the challenge recently included 9,000 JP Morgan Chase employees in seven countries and provided donations to causes around the world. In the last few years, causes included support for indigenous Australians, a youth foundation in China, sports in South Africa, and veterans.[2] For a corporation with facilities in North and South America, Europe, and Africa, the community may be viewed as virtually the entire world. To focus its social responsibility efforts, the multinational corporation might employ a community relations officer in each facility who reports to and coordinates with the company's head office.

Under our social responsibility philosophy, the term *community* should be viewed from a global perspective, beyond the immediate town, city, or state where a business is located. Thus, we define **community** as those members of society who are aware of, concerned with, or in some way affected by the operations and output of an organization. With information technology, high-speed travel, and the emergence of global business interests, the community as a constituency can be geographically, culturally, and attitudinally quite diverse. Issues that could become important include pollution of the environment, land use, economic advantages to the region, and discrimination within the community, as well as exploitation of workers, natural resources, or consumers.

From a positive perspective, an organization can significantly improve the **quality of life** for people in a community through employment opportunities, economic development, and financial contributions for educational, health, cultural, and recreational activities. Quality of life is a broad concept, typically associated with the social, physical, economic, and environmental health conditions that affect an individual or group. *U.S. News and World Report* conducts an annual survey of 20,000 citizens of 80 countries to determine its Best Country rankings. Part of the survey relates to quality of life, which considers the quality of healthcare and public education, political and economic stability, and other factors. Table 10.1 lists the highest- and lowest-rated countries for quality of life.[3]

Countries with the highest ratings are known for their social safety nets, progressive policies, and commitment to public health and education. Countries at the bottom of the list have experienced years of strife, often brought on by war, corruption, and unemployment. As discussed in earlier chapters, business both affects society and is affected by it. The intersection of business and society, as well as managerial attention and actions toward the intersection, lie at the heart of the social responsibility orientation discussed in this book. Even a company with a past reputation for damaging the quality of life in its community may be able to overcome criticism and begin to forge a healthier relationship with its stakeholders.

The story of Asia Pulp & Paper (APP) demonstrates the power that stakeholders have in changing corporate perspectives. Based in Indonesia, APP is one of the largest producers of pulp and paper products in the world, with operations in 120 countries spread over six continents. For many years, critics of the company pointed to its supply-chain practices and lack of consideration for the environment and communities in which it operated. The Indonesian company was named in a scathing report issued by Greenpeace about illegal logging activity in Indonesia and its devastating effects on rainforests. The report, *Partners in Crime*, also took aim at the companies that purchased from APP. When Greenpeace activists learned that Mattel was using APP paperboard generated from rainforests to package its popular Barbie doll, they draped a banner of Ken, Barbie's love interest, from the roof of Mattel's headquarters in California. Ken wore a disapproving look amid the phrases, "Barbie, it's over. I don't date girls that are into deforestation." These efforts, and many more, led hundreds of companies to stop doing business with APP. Before long, company executives committed to a host of sustainability policies and action plans, including the involvement of the local community. Today, APP has a full-fledged management approach to social responsibility. While some critics still question the company's motives and outcomes, other observers point to evidence of APP's turnaround. For example, APP has established schools in several towns and cities to serve

Table 10.1 Highest- and Lowest-Rated Countries for Quality of Life

1. Canada	76. Angola
2. Sweden	77. Jordan
3. Denmark	78. Lebanon
4. Norway	79. Iran
5. Switzerland	80. Iraq

community
members of society who are aware of, concerned with, or in some way affected by the operations and output of an organization

quality of life
a measure of social, physical, economic, and environmental health conditions affecting an individual or group

local children, many of whom would have gone without much formal education. The school curriculum includes science, engineering, forestry, and computing. While the APP schools certainly change lives through education, they also ensure the company is developing a strong future workforce.[4]

neighbor of choice
an organization that builds and sustains trust with the community through employment opportunities, economic development, and financial contribution to education, health, artistic, and recreational activities of the community

Through long-term efforts, a firm may become a **neighbor of choice,** an organization that builds and sustains trust with the community.[5] To become a neighbor of choice, a company should strive for positive and sustainable relationships with key individuals, groups, and organizations; demonstrate sensitivity to community concerns and issues; and design and implement programs that improve the quality of community life, while promoting the company's long-term business strategies and goals.[6] Merck's Neighbor of Choice program interacts with organizations and initiatives that are in line with the company's mission on well-being. The program is dedicated to finding solutions to health and social issues where the company is located, improving healthcare quality, and increasing access to care for underserved populations in the areas of Alzheimer's disease, cancer, diabetes, heart disease, hepatitis C, HIV/AIDS, and maternal health. The company awards grants to local nonprofit organizations in health, education, social services, and international issues. In one year alone, 130 grants infused $3.1 million, along with a cadre of employee volunteers, into communities around the world.[7]

Similar to other areas of life, the relationship between a business and the community should be symbiotic. A business may support educational opportunities in the community because the owners feel it is the right thing to do, but it also helps develop the human resources (HR) and consumer skills necessary to operate the business. Customers and employees are also community members who benefit from contributions supporting recreational activities, environmental initiatives, safety, and education. Many firms rely on universities and community colleges to provide support for ongoing education of their employees, as well as advances in research. The Dow Chemical Company, for example, committed to an annual investment of $250 million over the course of 10 years to universities for research purposes. For example, Dow partnered with University of California, Santa Barbara, to design a laboratory safety program that applies to both university settings and corporate laboratories. Beyond that, the company has working relationships with faculty, students, and other academicians to apply the research and create useful solutions to pressing issues, including renewable energy.[8]

community relations
the organizational function dedicated to building and maintaining relationships and trust with the community

To build and support these initiatives, companies may invest in **community relations,** the organizational function dedicated to building and maintaining relationships and trust with the community. In the past, most businesses have not viewed community relations as strategically important or associated them with the firm's ultimate performance. Although the community relations department interacted with the community and often doled out large sums of money to charities, it essentially served as a buffer between the organization and its immediate community. Today, community relations activities have achieved greater prominence and responsibility within most companies, especially due to the rise of stakeholder power and global business interests. The function has gained strategic importance through linking to overall business goals, professionalizing its staff and their knowledge of business and community issues, assessing its performance in quantitative and qualitative terms, and recognizing the breadth of stakeholders to which the organization is accountable.[9] Community relations also assist in short-term crisis situations, such as disaster relief. The humanitarian aid organization Direct Relief was given an Excellence Award by the Committee Encouraging Corporate Philanthropy (CECP) for its collaboration with FedEx to bring health services to people and places stricken by disaster. When a typhoon hit the Philippines, more than 250,000 people received needed medical supplies. Direct Relief and FedEx brought medications and other relief to Paraguay after flooding left 70,000 people without shelter, food, and water. Additionally, the partnership

Table 10.2 Community Mission Statements

Organization	Community Mission Statement
Capital One	At Capital One, we have always believed that as business leaders, we have a unique opportunity to create value in the communities where we live and work. Applying the same principles we use in our business of innovation, collaboration, and empowerment to our investments in the community helps leverage our investment of time and money to fuel new ideas and inspire others to act.
Education Advisory Board (EAB)	EAB's mission to make education smarter and our communities stronger infuses everything we do—especially our active, intentional approach to corporate social responsibility. It's by design that our work with our members and our communities intertwine: it allows us to have an outsized, positive impact. This service orientation strengthens our own organization, too—by ensuring we hire staff attuned to our members' missions, by creating skill-development opportunities beyond our office walls, and by giving employees the fulfillment of serving communities where they live and work.
Eli Lilly and Company	We have a long, proud heritage of strengthening the communities where we work and live. We do this through giving, volunteering, and focusing on key issues that affect our business, such as education. At the heart of our efforts to strengthen communities are our employees, who donate their time, talent and treasure in countless ways. As a company, we actively encourage our employees to volunteer and give, and we develop programs that allow them to help improve communities at home and around the world. We view this as an important investment that connects us more deeply with the people we serve, which helps make us a better company.
Pinnacol Assurance	We have a policy of serving people. It's pretty simple. We love our community. For more than 100 years, our job has been all about protecting the health and safety of people on their jobs. And that sense of caring extends to the communities where we live and work. We donate time, money and support through grants, sponsorships, our employee volunteer program and the Pinnacol Foundation's scholarship program.
UnitedHealth Group	The people of UnitedHealth Group are working together in support of local communities. UnitedHealth Group's year-round giving program supports employees' desires and efforts to give back to the communities where they live and work, across the nation and around the world. Through charitable contributions and volunteering, our people are deeply and personally involved in improving the health and welfare of their neighbors. The United Health Foundation matches employee contributions, dollar for dollar, to nearly all nonprofit organizations, doubling their impact. Employees have the ability to give whenever, wherever and however they choose.
Volvo Group	For the Volvo Group, creating shared value involves moving both our business and society forward. We enhance our competitiveness while simultaneously advancing the economic, environmental and social conditions of the societies in which we operate. The highest potential for mutual benefit is where our business significantly interacts with society. Therefore, our selected focus areas are: • Education and skills development • Traffic and worksite safety • Environmental sustainability

Sources: Capital One, "Capital One Community Involvement Report," https://www.capitalone.com/media/doc/about/capitalone-sustainability-report.pdf (accessed June 30, 2019); EAB, "Corporate Citizenship," https://www.eab.com/careers/corporate-citizenship (accessed June 30, 2019); Lilly, "Strengthening Communities," https://www.lilly.com/caring/strengthening-communities (accessed June 19, 2019); Pinnacol, "Community Relations," https://www.pinnacol.com/community-relations (accessed June 29, 2019); UnitedHealth Group, "Our People," https://www.unitedhealthgroup.com/social-responsibility/giving.html (accessed June 15, 2019); Volvo Group, "Societal Engagement," https://www.volvogroup.com/en-en/about-us/csr-and-sustainability/moving-business-and-society-forward.html (accessed June 29, 2019).

has provided over 10 million Americans with approximately $400 million in necessary medications.[10] Progressive companies manage community relations with partnership in mind. They seek out community partners for a range of interests and activities—philanthropy, volunteerism, creating a quality educational system and a qualified workforce, appropriate roads and infrastructure, affordable housing, and other community assets.

Over the past two decades, corporate support for philanthropy has been steadily growing. According to Giving USA Foundation, corporate giving totaled more than $20 billion in 2018. This number increased by 5.4 percent from the year before. The sluggish recovery of the economy since the Great Recession had an effect on corporate giving, but as the economy recovers corporate giving has begun to increase once more. PepsiCo, for instance, has a matching gifts program and is involved in a number of sustainability initiatives. The company donated a $1 million grant to Kiva, a nonprofit organization that provides small loans to entrepreneurs in developing countries to start their own businesses.[11] Even before the economic downtown, corporate giving was becoming more effective and strategic. Companies are working to align their stakeholder interests and develop partnerships that are more closely aligned to business goals, community interests, and sustainable activities.[12]

In a diverse society, however, there is no general agreement as to what constitutes the ideal model of business responsibility to the community. Businesses are likely to experience conflicts among stakeholders as to what constitutes a real commitment to the community. Therefore, the community relations function should cooperate with various internal and external constituents to develop community mission statements and assess opportunities and develop priorities for the types of contributions it will make to the community. Table 10.2 provides several examples of company missions and programs with respect to community involvement. As you can see, these missions are specific to the needs of the

Table 10.3 Community Needs Assessment

Community Issues	Exceptional	Adequate	Inadequate	Don't Know
Parks	3	2	1	0
Culinary water system	3	2	1	0
Street maintenance	3	2	1	0
Garbage collection	3	2	1	0
Snow removal	3	2	1	0
Fire protection	3	2	1	0
Police protection	3	2	1	0
Ambulance service	3	2	1	0
Building inspection	3	2	1	0
Animal control	3	2	1	0
Other code enforcement (weeds, junk cars, etc.)	3	2	1	0
Arts	3	2	1	0
Street lighting	3	2	1	0

Other issues that can be evaluated: grocery stores, pharmacies, clothing stores, fast-food restaurants, entertainment, hardware/lumber stores, auto services, banking/financial services, affordable housing, business offices, warehouses, convenience stores, community colleges, higher education satellite campuses.

Source: Community Tool Box, "Community Needs Assessment Survey Guide," https://ctb.ku.edu/en/table-of-contents/assessment/assessing-community-needs-and-resources/conducting-needs-assessment-surveys/main (accessed June 27, 2019).

people and areas in which the companies operate and are usually aligned with the competencies of the organizations involved and their employees.

Community mission statements are likely to change as needs are met and new issues emerge. For example, as the Japan-based Takeda Pharmaceutical Company Ltd. continues to expand operations throughout the world, their community involvement also expands to meet the needs of each community. In Brazil, the company focuses on renovating orphanages, while in South Africa, they have initiatives teaching children to make blankets. When global communities experience unexpected disasters, such as flooding in Australia, Takeda has been there to assist with the recovery. On its website, Takeda proudly displays recognition as a top employer in most countries where it operates, including awards granted in Ecuador, Spain, Russia, Ukraine, and the United States.[13] Thus, as stakeholder needs and concerns change, the organization will need to adapt its community relations efforts. To determine key areas that require support and to refine the mission statement, a company should periodically conduct a community needs assessment, like the one presented in Table 10.3.[14]

Responsibilities to the Community

It is important for a company to view community stakeholders in a trusting manner, recognizing the potential mutual benefit to each party. In a networked world, much about a company can be learned with a few clicks of a mouse. Activists and disgruntled individuals have used websites to publicize the questionable activities of some companies. Target and Ryanair have been the focus of "hate" websites that broadcast concerns about the company's treatment of employees, pricing strategies, and marketing and advertising tactics.[15] Because of the visibility of business activities and the desire for strategic social responsibility, successful companies strive to build long-term mutually beneficial relationships with relevant communities. Achieving these relationships may involve some trial and error. Table 10.4 illustrates some of the common myths about community relations. A positive example, on the other hand, is Lilly Pharmaceuticals' strong support for the Indianapolis Symphony Orchestra. In return, the orchestra stages private concerts for Eli Lilly employees. Dell Computer has a similar relationship with the Round Rock Express, a minor-league baseball team. A community focus can be integrated with concerns for employees and consumers. Chapter 1 provided evidence that satisfied customers and employees are correlated with improved organizational performance.

Table 10.4 Common Myths About Community Relations

Support of political and regulatory officials is not needed.
We will cause a problem for our company if we engage in community relations.
The community has no expertise on our decisions and actions.
Engaging the community will delay us in finding the right solution.
Community officials have no concern for the cost of solutions to issues.
We serve the community simply through employment opportunities and paying taxes.
Our only focus is national and global relationships.
Community relationships involve only public relations.
The local community does not impact our success.
Spending time with the community distracts from the economic success of the firm.

Economic Issues

From an economic perspective, business is absolutely vital to a community. Companies play a major role in community economic development by bringing jobs to the community and allowing employees to support themselves and their families. These companies also buy supplies, raw materials, utilities, advertising services, and other goods and services from area firms; this in turn produces more economic effects. In communities with few employers, an organization that expands in or moves to the area can reduce some of the burden on community services and other subsidized support. Even in large cities with many employers, some companies choose to address social problems that tax the community. In countries with developing economies, a business or industry can also provide many benefits. A new company brings not only jobs, but also new technology, related businesses, improvements to infrastructure, and other positive factors. Conversely, globalization has incited criticism regarding the effects of U.S. businesses on other parts of the world, namely developing countries. For example, Sig Sauer, a New Hampshire-based manufacturer of a full range of firearms and ammunition, has been condemned in the media for continuing to sell weapons in Mexico. The company is the largest seller of firearms in Mexico and its customers include federal, state, and local police. Given the rate of violence, organized crime, and police corruption in the country, critics question why neither the U.S. government nor Sig Sauer have put an end to shipping thousands of weapons across America's southern border. Similarly, Nestlé has been criticized for marketing baby formula to nursing mothers in Turkey, claiming that their offspring will receive more nutrition from the formula than from their mothers; aggressive selling of bottled water in developing parts of the world, which is said to be expensive for consumers and works as a deterrent to governments to solve water sanitation issues; and for child labor accusations in African cocoa farms. The company has committed to "The Nestlé Cocoa Plan," which involves building schools and providing cocoa trees to farmers with the aim of contributing to the betterment of the local community.[16]

Interactions with suppliers and other vendors also stimulate the economy. Some companies are even dedicated to finding local or regional business partners in an effort to enhance their economic responsibility. For example, Starbucks, in an unprecedented move for the company, began franchising locations in Europe. By having locals run the coffee chains' stores, the company hopes to further its influence in the region.[17] Furthermore, there is often a contagion effect when one business moves into an area: By virtue of its prestige or business relationships, such a move can signal to other firms that the area is a viable and attractive place for others to locate. There are parts of the United States that are highly concentrated with automotive manufacturing, financial services, or technology. Local chambers of commerce and economic development organizations often entice new firms to a region because of the positive reputation and economic contagion it brings. Finally, business contributions to local health, education, and recreation projects not only benefit local residents and employees, but also may bring additional revenue into the community from tourism and other businesses that appreciate the region's quality of life. AT&T, for example, has hosted the Pebble Beach National Pro-Am golf tournament for more than 30 years. The annual event honors influential groups each year and has raised more than $110 million that the Monterey Peninsula Foundation provides to local charities in the counties that surround Monterey, California. After the event, tournament banners are upcycled into backpacks, then stuffed with school supplies for area schoolchildren in need.[18]

Just as a business brings positive economic effects by expanding in or relocating to an area, it can also cause financial repercussions when it exits a particular market or geographical location. Thus, workforce reduction, or downsizing—a topic discussed in Chapter 8—is a key issue with respect to economic responsibility. The impact of layoffs due to plant closings and corporate restructuring often extends well beyond the financial well-being of affected employees. Laid-off employees typically limit their spending to basic necessities while they look for new employment, and many may ultimately leave the area altogether. Even employees who retain their jobs in such a downsizing may suffer from poor morale, distrust, guilt, and continued anxiety over their own job security, further stifling spending in a community.

Because companies have such a profound impact on the economic viability of the communities in which they operate, firms that value social responsibility consider both the short- and long-term effects on the community of changes in their workforce. Today, many companies that must reduce their workforce—regardless of the reasons—strive to give both employees and the community advance notice and offer placement services to help the community absorb employees who lose their jobs. Quad/Graphics, one of the largest printers in the United States, closed plants in Illinois and Minnesota. The company offered to transfer affected employees to other plants in the nation. However, for those who did not want to transfer, Quad/Graphics agreed to offer a severance package including pay, career placement assistance, and extension of benefits.[19] Depending on economic circumstances and business profitability, companies may choose to offer extra compensation commensurate with an employee's length of employment that gives laid-off employees a financial cushion while they find new work. However, the realities of economic turmoil mean that many employees receive little compensation.

Legal Issues

To conduct business, a company must be granted a "license to operate." For many firms, a series of legal and regulatory matters must be resolved before the first employee is hired or the first customer is served. If you open a restaurant, for example, most states require a business license and sales tax number. These documents require basic information, such as business type, ownership structure, owner information, number of expected employees, and other data.

On a fundamental level, society has the ability to dictate what types of organizations are allowed to operate. In exchange for the license to operate, organizations are expected to uphold all legal obligations and standards. We have discussed many of these laws throughout this book, although individual cities, counties, and municipalities will have additional laws and regulations that firms must obey. For example, a construction company in Destin, Florida, was charged with repeated safety violations that have endangered employees. The leading cause of fatality in the construction industry is falling, and the company was found liable for neglecting to provide employees with protections against this well-known danger. Despite widespread news stories and regulatory education about fatal falls, engineering and construction companies continue to receive penalties. Two contractors were assessed penalties of over $150,000 after two workers were killed when scaffolding collapsed on an Orlando hotel project.[20]

Other communities have concerns about whether and how businesses fit into existing communities, especially those threatened by urban sprawl and small towns working to

Shutterstock/Cassionhabib

preserve a traditional way of life. Some states, cities, and counties have enacted legislation that limits the square footage of stores in an effort to deter "big-box stores," such as Walmart and Home Depot, unless local voters specifically approve their being allowed to build. In most cases, these communities have called for such legislation to combat the noise and traffic congestion that may be associated with such stores, to protect neighborhoods, and to preserve the viability of local small businesses.[21] Beyond big-box stores, online competition is another threat to local businesses. In New York City, the owner of Gold Leaf Stationers realized the power of community relations when a decrease in annual sales meant that his store could no longer afford rent of $12,500 per month. The store is housed in a co-op building controlled by a board of directors. The board, which included many customers of Gold Leaf, voted to reduce the monthly rent to $9,500 and capped the store's share of annual real estate taxes due on the co-op property. In this case, New York law allows the co-op board to make such significant decisions. After the decision, the co-op president remarked, "This type of store adds value to the fabric of the community."[22] Although the importance of preserving small business, paying living wages, which we discussed in Chapter 8, and restricting store locations may be ethical issues for some communities, consumers, and businesses, the legal environment may facilitate or restrict these issues, as well.

Ethical Issues

As more companies view themselves as responsible to the community, they will contemplate their role and the impact of their decisions on communities as they make managerial ethical decisions. Many companies have opted to be proactive on important issues, such as minimum wages and benefits for employees. While legislative bills have been proposed on raising the minimum wage, it may take time before any changes to federal law are made in this respect. Amazon, Target, and Cox Communications, however, raised the minimum wage for employees in all U.S. locations to $15 per hour because they believe it is the right thing to do. Employees of Disney's theme parks are also offered a starting wage of $15 per hour. Other companies such as Costco have followed suit, raising its minimum wage to $14 per hour.[23] In 2018, Walmart raised wages so that new employees will receive $11 per hour. The retail giant had been paying $9 to $10 per hour to new hires, although long-term employees often make more than $14 per hour. According to a recent social responsibility report, Walmart store managers in the U.S. earn an average of $175,000 per year.[24]

Business leaders are increasingly recognizing the significance of the role their firms play in the community and the need for their leadership in tackling community problems. Bill Daniels, founder of Cablevision, was an extremely successful entrepreneur. His approach to ethical decision-making in Cablevision had a positive impact on the communities. He established the Daniels Fund, which has a significant impact on business ethics education and other social concerns in the states of Wyoming, Colorado, New Mexico, and Utah. Millions of dollars have been donated to causes such as ethics and integrity, education, youth development, and amateur sports.[25]

These examples demonstrate that the ethical dimension of community responsibility can be multifaceted. This dimension and related programs are not legally mandated but emanate from the particular philosophy of a company and its top managers. Because many cities have not mandated a living wage, the actions of Target, Amazon, and Costco are based on an ethical obligation felt toward employees and the community as well as competition for the best employees. There are many ways that a company can demonstrate its ethical commitment to the community. As Bill Daniels's commitment to business ethics illustrates, a common extension of "doing the right thing" ethically provides a role model for all political and civic leaders.

Philanthropic Issues

The community relations function has always been associated with philanthropy, as one of the main historical roles of community relations was to provide gifts, grants, and other resources to worthy causes. Today, that thinking has shifted. Although businesses have the potential to help solve social issues, the success of a business can be enhanced from the publicity generated by and through stakeholder acceptance of community activities. For example, Colorado-based New Belgium Brewing Company donates $1 for every barrel of beer brewed the prior year to charities within the markets it serves. The brewery divides the funds among states in proportion to interests and needs, considering environmental, social, drug and alcohol awareness, and cultural issues. Donation decisions are made by the firm's coworker grants committee that, since 1995, has been the backbone of the philanthropic program. The committee is open to all coworkers and takes on the task of researching, reviewing and allocating funds to worthy organizations. To date, the company has provided over $10.5 million in grants to support efforts in climate change, social equity, smart growth, and sustainable agriculture.[26] However, New Belgium belongs to an industry that some members of society believe contributes to social problems. Thus, regardless of the positive contributions such a firm makes to the community, some members will always have a negative view of the business.

One of the most significant ways that organizations are exercising their philanthropic responsibilities is through volunteer programs. **Volunteerism** in the workplace, when employees spend company-supported time in support of social causes, has become a routine expectation in companies of all sizes. Each year, approximately 77.4 million Americans spend nearly 6.9 billion hours supporting formal volunteer activities. The estimated value of these volunteer efforts is over $166 billion. The four main activities that volunteers perform are fundraising, collecting and distributing food, helping with general labor needs, and tutoring or teaching. These activities are performed for a variety of organizations, with religious, education, and social service agencies topping the list. Recent research has examined the factors that either promote or inhibit volunteerism, with shorter commute times, home ownership, and higher educational levels associated with higher rates of volunteerism.[27] Figure 10.1 shows the states with the

volunteerism
when employees spend company-supported time in support of social causes

Figure 10.1 States with Highest Volunteerism Rates

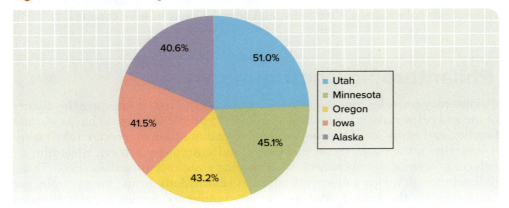

Source: Corporation for National and Community Service, "Volunteering in America: States," https://www.nationalservice.gov/serve/via/states (accessed June 25, 2019).

highest percentage of their populations who are actively engaged in volunteer activities.

People who volunteer feel more connected to other people and society and ultimately have lower mortality rates, greater functional ability, and lower rates of depression later in life than those who do not volunteer. When volunteering is a result of employment, benefits of volunteering accrue to both the individual, in terms of greater motivation, enjoyment, and satisfaction, and to the organization through employee retention and productivity increases.[28] Communities benefit from the application of new skills and initiatives toward problems, better relations with business, a greater supply of volunteers, assistance to stretch limited resources, and social and economic regeneration.[29] Philanthropic issues are just another dimension of voluntary social responsibility and relate to business's contributions to stakeholders.

Chicago-based Exelon Energy, for example, instituted their Powering Communities volunteer engagement program that offers incentives to encourage employees to volunteer. One of the incentives is the Dollars for Doers program in which an employee can volunteer either 10, 20, or 40 hours per year at an organization of his or her choice, and Exelon awards a corresponding grant to the organization. In 2018, Exelon provided $1.1 million to recognize the volunteer efforts of its employees. Employees who volunteer more than 50 hours per year are nominated for the Exelon Employee Volunteer Award, and the recipients are then recognized during National Volunteer Week. In the most recent year, employees volunteered for over 240,000 hours, including 5,200 employees who participated in National Volunteer Week and topped 18,000 hours of service.[30]

There are several considerations in deciding how to structure a volunteer program. Attention must be paid to employee values and beliefs; therefore, political or religious organizations should be supported on the basis of individual employee initiative and interest. Some companies will partner with nonprofit organizations as a means to give their employees more options for volunteerism. For example, World Vision humanitarian organization partners with corporations for financial, volunteer, and product donations, as well as opportunities for cause-related marketing. Volunteer opportunities exist in education, sanitation, economic development, and related areas all over the globe. World Vision even provides guidance to corporate partners on how to integrate volunteerism and philanthropy with their business goals.[31]

Another issue is what to do when some employees do not wish to volunteer. If the company is not paying for the employees' time to volunteer and volunteering is not a condition of employment or an aspect of the job description, it may be difficult to convince a certain percentage of the workforce to participate. On the other hand, if the organization is paying for one day a month to allow the employee exposure to volunteering, then individual compliance is usually expected.

Philanthropic Contributions

philanthropy

acts such as donations to charitable organizations to improve quality of life, reduce government involvement, develop employee leadership skills, and create an ethical culture to act as buffer to organizational misconduct

Philanthropy provides four major benefits to society. First, it improves the quality of life and helps make communities places where people want to do business, raise families, and enjoy life. Thus, improving the quality of life in a community makes it easier to attract and retain employees and customers. Second, philanthropy reduces government involvement by providing assistance to stakeholders. Third, philanthropy develops employee leadership skills. Many firms, for example, use campaigns by the United Way and other community service organizations as leadership- and skill-building exercises for their employees. Philanthropy helps create an ethical culture and promotes the values that can act as a buffer to

Figure 10.2 Sources of Charitable Giving

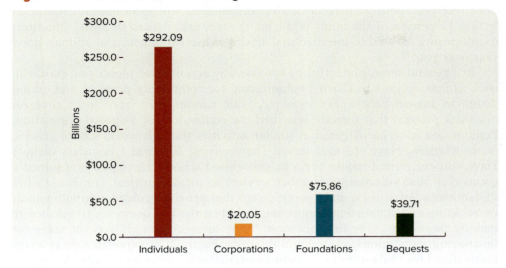

Source: "Giving USA 2019," Giving USA, https://givingusa.org/giving-usa-2019-americans-gave-427-71-billion-to-charity-in-2018-amid-complex-year-for-charitable-giving/ (accessed June 27, 2019).

organizational misconduct.[32] In the United States, charitable giving has stagnated at 2.1 percent of gross domestic product (GDP) annually.[33]

The most common way that businesses demonstrate philanthropy is through donations to local and national charitable organizations. Corporations gave more than $20.5 billion to environmental, educational, and social causes in a recent year. Individual giving, which is always the largest component of charitable contributions, was an estimated $292.09 billion, or 71 percent of the total. Figure 10.2 displays the sources of charitable giving. Figure 10.3 displays the major recipients

Figure 10.3 Recipients of Charitable Giving

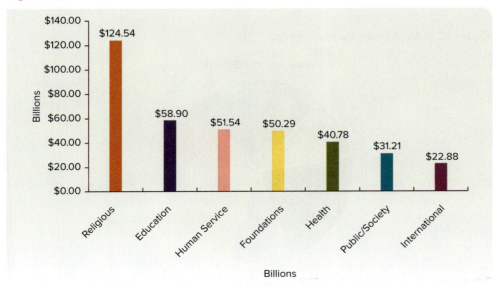

Source: "Giving USA 2019," Giving USA, https://givingusa.org/giving-usa-2019-americans-gave-427-71-billion-to-charity-in-2018-amid-complex-year-for-charitable-giving/ (accessed June 27, 2019).

of the $427 billion in philanthropic donations made in 2018. Religious organizations received about 30 percent of all contributions, with educational causes collecting 13 percent of the funds While many areas experienced declines, donations to nonprofits devoted to international affairs, the environment, and animals grew year over year.[34]

In a general sense, philanthropy involves any acts of benevolence and goodwill, such as making gifts to charity, volunteering for community projects, and taking action to benefit others. For example, your parents may have spent time on nonwork projects that directly benefited the community or a special population. Perhaps you have participated in similar activities through work, school groups, or associations. Have you ever served Thanksgiving dinner at a homeless shelter? Have you ever raised money for a neighborhood school? Have you ever joined a social club that volunteered member services to local charities? The Rockefeller Philanthropy Advisors is a nonprofit group that provides guidance to individuals on selecting and supporting nonprofits, including the key questions to ask before making these plans. The first question, "Why are you giving?" sets the stage for uncovering motivations, values, and interests. Figure 10.4 explores nine primary motivations for philanthropy. In most cases, philanthropists have multiple reasons for giving, including those driven by both **intrinsic motivation** and **extrinsic motivation**.

According to the Rockefeller group, individuals within families are increasingly interested in giving as a collective group. Often, the family is motivated by an ancestor or core values and beliefs. In other cases, philanthropists may be motivated by recognition and the rewards of being associated with specific efforts and good works. Still others are looking for ways to minimize taxes and enable future generations to benefit from estate planning.

Most religious organizations, educational institutions, and arts programs rely heavily on philanthropic donations from both individuals and organizations. Philanthropy is a major driver of the nonprofit sector of the economy, as these organizations rely on the time, money, and talents of both individuals and organizations to operate and fund their programs. Consider the partnership between Pampers and UNICEF. These two organizations have had a successful decade-long partnership, in which Pampers donated a portion of their profits to UNICEF to

intrinsic motivation
wanting to take action based on internal factors

extrinsic motivation
wanting to take action based on external factors

Figure 10.4 Motivations for Philanthropy

Why Are You Giving?

■ Family ■ Legacy ■ Experience ■ Faith ■ Values
■ Heritage ■ Analysis ■ Financial ■ Recognition

provide tetanus shots for babies around the world. This partnership fits well with the company's core product and target market.[35]

Strategic Philanthropy Defined

Our concept of corporate philanthropy extends beyond financial contributions and explicitly links company missions, organizational competencies, and various stakeholders. Thus, we define **strategic philanthropy** as the synergistic use of an organization's core competencies and resources to address key stakeholders' interests and to achieve both organizational and social benefits. Strategic philanthropy goes well beyond the traditional benevolent philanthropy of donating a percentage of sales to social causes by involving employees (utilizing their core skills), organizational resources and expertise (equipment, knowledge, and money), and the ability to link employees, customers, suppliers, and social needs with these key assets. Strategic philanthropy involves both financial and nonfinancial contributions to stakeholders (employee time, goods and services, and company technology and equipment as well as facilities), but it also benefits the company.

Organizations are best suited to deal with social or stakeholder issues in areas with which they have some experience, knowledge, or expertise. From a business perspective, companies want to refine their intellectual capital, reinforce their core competencies, and develop synergies between business and philanthropic activities. The process of addressing stakeholder concerns through philanthropy should be strategic to a company's ongoing development and improvement. For example, SAP, a global software company, has made financial and product investments in developing economies such as Mexico and Swaziland. These investments are beneficial to both parties, as the technology aids economic, educational, and health advancements for the communities. However, it also allows the company to identify emerging talent and become established in these economies for their own growth.[36]

Some critics would argue that this is not true philanthropy because SAP will receive business benefits. However, social responsibility takes place on many levels, and effective philanthropy depends on the synergy between stakeholder needs and business competencies and goals. Thus, the fact that each partner receives unique benefits does not diminish the overall good that results from a project. As global competition escalates, companies are increasingly responsible to stakeholders in justifying their philanthropic endeavors. This ultimately requires greater planning and alignment of philanthropic efforts with overall strategic goals. Table 10.5 provides additional examples of philanthropic activities.

strategic philanthropy
the synergistic use of an organization's core competencies and resources to address key stakeholders' interests and to achieve both organizational and social benefits

Table 10.5 Examples of Strategic Philanthropy

Target donates 5 percent of its pretax income to charity.
Patagonia donates 1 percent of profits to 1 Percent for the Planet, a global movement that donates the proceeds to environmental organizations.
Salesforce.com donates 1 percent of its technology, 1 percent of its resources, and 1 percent of its people (employees can take off six days a year to volunteer) to nonprofits and to their communities.
Home Depot has a strong partnership with the nonprofit Habitat for Humanity, spending significant time and resources in its mission to build homes for those in need.
New Belgium Brewing engages in extensive philanthropy grants, product donations, and sponsorships to support the community.
Whole Foods holds a number of community giving days in which 5 percent of the day's net revenue goes toward nonprofits or education.

Strategic Philanthropy and Social Responsibility

It is important to place strategic philanthropy in the context of organizational responsibilities at the economic, legal, ethical, and philanthropic levels. Most companies understand the need to be economically successful for the benefit of all stakeholders and to comply with the laws required within our society and others in which they do business. Additionally, through the establishment of core values and ethical cultures, most firms are recognizing the many benefits of good ethics. As we saw in Chapter 1, evidence is accumulating that there is a positive relationship between social responsibility and performance, especially with regard to customer satisfaction, investor loyalty, and employee commitment. Strategic social responsibility can reduce the cost of business transactions, establish trust among stakeholders, improve teamwork, and preserve the social capital necessary for an infrastructure for doing business. In sum, these efforts improve the context and environment for corporate operations and performance.[37]

When Daniel Lubetzky founded KIND Healthy Snacks, he had transparency and kindness in mind. Transparency is demonstrated in the fact that the company's bars and snacks contain ingredients that are easily pronounced (meaning that they are natural) and come in clear packaging where those ingredients can be seen. The company initiated a charitable campaign in which it donated $10,000 per month to a different charity through a program called "Do the Kind Thing." Each charity was crowdsourced, meaning that people would visit the company's website to vote for the charity they thought should get that month's donation. The self-described "not-only-for-profit" company has become the fastest-growing energy and nutrition bar in the United States.[38] In this way, KIND Healthy Snacks has linked philanthropic contributions to revenue generation.

Many companies consider philanthropy only after they have met their financial, legal, and ethical obligations. As companies strive for social responsibility, their ability to meet each obligation lays the foundation for success with other responsibilities. In addition, there is synergy in corporate efforts directed at the four levels of responsibility. As one of the most voluntary dimensions of social responsibility, philanthropy has not always been linked to profits or business ethics. In fact, the traditional approach to philanthropy disconnects giving from business performance and its impact on stakeholders. Before the evolution of strategic philanthropy, most corporate gift programs separated the company from the organizations, causes, and individuals that its donations most benefited.[39]

Research has begun to highlight organizations' formalization of philanthropic activities and their efforts to integrate philanthropic goals with other business strategies and implementation. U.S. companies are adopting a more businesslike approach to philanthropy and experiencing a better image, increased employee loyalty, and improved customer ties.[40] Philanthropy involves using organizational resources, and specific methods are used to measure its impact on key stakeholders. In this case, philanthropy is an investment from which a company can gain some type of value. For instance, JPMorgan Chase and other wealthy entities and individuals engage in impact investing. **Impact investing** is the investment of a significant amount of money toward finding solutions for a social problem, with the promise of financial returns that depend upon the achievement of a stated goal. This measured activity is becoming increasingly popular because not only is it drawing in millions of dollars to be invested, but many hurdles are being overcome in environmental and social issues. The Esmée Fairbairn Foundation (EFF) is one of the largest grant-making organizations in the United Kingdom. Founded in 1961, EFF works to improve quality of life and has traditionally made grants to support the arts, education and learning, environment, social change, and sustainable food initiatives. Recently, EFF provided a £12 million impact investment in the Bridges

impact investing
investments made with the intention of generating positive and measurable social and environmental impact, as well as financial returns

Social Entrepreneurs Fund, which was developed to provide bridge funding for fast-growing social enterprises ready to scale their operations. Other examples of initiatives include sustainable farming in East Africa and banking options to low-income communities in Mexico. J. P. Morgan has spent $68 million in impact investing across 11 funds.[41] Indeed, there are numerous examples of companies supporting community involvement. Although these actions are noble, they are not always considered in tandem with organizational goals and strengths.

In some cases, corporate contributions may be made to nonprofit organizations in which top managers have a personal interest. When Unilever acquired the Ben and Jerry's Homemade ice cream company, they agreed to support the causes and initiatives that are extremely important to founders Ben Cohen and Jerry Greenfield. Unilever agreed to maintain the Vermont-based employment and manufacturing, pay workers a livable wage with complete benefits, buy milk from Vermont dairy farmers who do not use bovine growth hormones, contribute over $1.1 million annually to the Ben and Jerry's Foundation, open more Partner Shops owned by nonprofit organizations providing employment opportunities for disadvantaged persons, and maintain relationships with alternative suppliers.[42] Finally, many companies will match employees' personal gifts to educational institutions. Although gift-matching programs instill employee pride and assist education, they are rarely linked to company operations and competencies.[43] In the traditional approach to corporate philanthropy, then, companies have good intentions, but there is no solid integration with organizational resources and objectives.

In the social responsibility model that we propose, philanthropy is only one focal point for a corporate vision that includes both the welfare of the firm and benefits to stakeholders. This requires support from top management, as well as a strategic planning structure that incorporates stakeholder concerns and benefits. Corporate giving, volunteer efforts, and other contributions should be considered and aligned not only with corporate strategy, but also with financial, legal, and ethical obligations. The shift from traditional benevolent philanthropy to strategic philanthropy has come about as companies struggled to redefine their missions, alliances, and scope, while becoming increasingly accountable to stakeholders and society.

Strategic Philanthropy Versus Cause-Related Marketing

The first attempts by organizations to coordinate organizational goals with philanthropic giving emerged with cause-related marketing in the early 1980s. Whereas strategic philanthropy links corporate resources and knowledge to address broader social, customer, employee, and supplier problems and needs, **cause-related marketing** ties an organization's products directly to a social concern. Table 10.6 compares cause-related marketing and strategic philanthropy.

cause-related marketing
ties an organization's products directly to a social concern

Table 10.6 Strategic Philanthropy Contrasted with Cause-Related Marketing

Attribute	Strategic Philanthropy	Cause-Related Marketing
Focus	Organizational	A company's product or product line
Goals	Improvement of organizational competence or tying organizational competence to a social need or charitable cause; builds brand equity	Increase of product sales
Time frame	Ongoing	Traditionally of limited duration
Organizational members involved	Potentially all organizational employees	Marketing department and related personnel
Cost	Moderate—alignment with organizational strategies and mission	Minimal—alliance development and promotion expenditures

Cause-related marketing donates a percentage of a product's sales to a cause appealing to the relevant target market. The Avon Breast Cancer Crusade, for example, generates proceeds for the breast cancer cause through several fundraising efforts, including the sale of special "pink ribbon" products by Avon independent sales representatives nationwide. Gifts are awarded by the Avon Products Foundation, Inc., a nonprofit 501(c)(3) accredited public charity, to support six vital areas of the breast cancer cause. Both the cause and Avon Crusade "pink ribbon" products appeal to Avon's primary target market: women. The Avon Breast Cancer Crusade generated more than $800 million net in total funds raised worldwide to fund access to care and in finding a cure for breast cancer.[44]

American Express was the first company to use cause-related marketing widely, when it began advertising in 1983 that it would give a percentage of credit card charges to the Statue of Liberty and Ellis Island Restoration Fund.[45] As is the case with Avon, American Express companies generally prefer to support causes that are of interest to their target markets. In a single year, organizations raised roughly $1.92 billion for causes through marketing efforts.[46] Thus, a key feature of cause-related marketing is the promise of donations to a particular social cause based on customer sales or involvement. Whereas strategic philanthropy is tied to the entire organization, cause-related marketing is linked to a specific product and marketing program. The program may involve in-store promotions, messages on packages and labels, and other marketing communications.[47]

Although cause-related marketing has its roots in the United States, the marketing tool is gaining widespread usage in other parts of the world. Population Services International (PSI) was created with marketing for social issues as its base strategy. After traveling to Africa and witnessing the devastating effects of HIV/AIDS on the population, founder Kate Roberts decided to use her marketing expertise to address the problem. She established YouthAIDS as an education and prevention program for young people using media, celebrity partnerships, and music to relay messages to the target group. YouthAIDS has partnered with many well-known global brands, including ALDO, H&M, Roberto Coin, Levi-Strauss, and Cartier. Over the years, YouthAIDS became a recognizable brand. This success led to the organization's involvement with other social issues such as malaria, sanitary water, and tuberculosis in over 50 countries. In a recent annual report, PSI estimated that its programs prevented 5 million unintended pregnancies, 135,800 deaths due malaria and pneumonia, and 278,000 HIV infections in one year.[48]

Cause-related marketing activities have real potential to affect buying patterns. For cause-related marketing to be successful, consumers must have awareness and affinity for the cause, the brand and cause must be associated and perceived as a good fit, and consumers should be able to transfer feelings toward the cause to their brand perceptions and purchase intentions. Studies have found that a majority of consumers said that, given equal price and product quality, they would be more likely to buy the product associated with a charitable cause. More than 80 percent of customers say they have more positive perceptions of firms that support causes about which they personally care. These surveys have also noted that most marketing directors felt that cause-related marketing would increase in importance over the coming years.[49] Through cause-related marketing, companies first become aware that supporting social causes, such as environmental awareness, health and human services, education, and the arts, can support business goals and help bolster a firm's reputation, especially if the firm has an ethically neutral image. However, firms that are perceived as unethical may be suspected of ulterior motives in developing cause-related campaigns.[50]

One of the main weaknesses of cause-related marketing is that some consumers cannot link specific philanthropic efforts with companies.[51] Consumers may have difficulty recalling exact philanthropic relationships because many cause-related marketing campaigns have tended to be of short duration and have not always had a direct correlation to the sponsoring firm's core business. Because strategic philanthropy is more pervasive and relates to company attributes, values, and skills, such alliances should have greater stakeholder recognition and appreciation.

Social Entrepreneurship and Social Responsibility

While social philanthropy and cause-related marketing are important ways for businesses to demonstrate social responsibility, some entrepreneurs are taking this a step further by designing their entire business model for creating positive social change. Traditionally, organizations that structured themselves around the creation of social value chose to become nonprofit organizations. Nonprofits are organizations that are formed to meet some public purpose rather than making profits. Unlike for-profit companies, nonprofits must reinvest any additional earnings into their operations.[52] While some nonprofits sell their goods or perform services to raise funds, many depend upon stakeholder donations to support their causes.

However, a new type of organizational structure is emerging that spans across or within nonprofit, business, and government industries. The social enterprise is an organization that uses entrepreneurial principles to create positive social change. Because it is an emerging field, researchers have not yet come up with a consensus on how to define it. For our purposes, we define **social entrepreneurship** as an entrepreneur creating a business with the purpose of creating social value rather than making money. This means that unlike a traditional for-profit business, the primary goal of a social entrepreneur is not to earn profits but to provide a solution to a social problem.[53]

As mentioned earlier, because the overarching purpose of social entrepreneurship is creating social value, social enterprises can be organized as a nonprofit, business, or government form of an organization—as well as a combination of any of these. Many social enterprises are set up with a nonprofit organizational structure. However, social enterprises differ from more traditional nonprofits as they pursue business-led strategies to achieve social objectives.[54] While a social enterprise might be a nonprofit, it operates more like an entrepreneurial business venture in its strategy, structure, norms, values, and its approach to finding innovative solutions to social problems.[55] Like a business entrepreneur, social entrepreneurs seek to be change agents by seizing upon opportunities and finding solutions that others missed to solve challenges in society. Because a social entrepreneur needs funds to support the venture, economic considerations and the social mission go hand-in-hand. Strong leadership is fundamental for these hybrid organizations, as they differ from a strictly for-profit or nonprofit orientation. More case studies and research are needed to ensure that social entrepreneurship is understood as something more than a tradeoff between economic and social priorities.[56] We go into further detail about nonprofit and for-profit types of social enterprises in the following sections.

social entrepreneurship
when an entrepreneur founds a business with the purpose of creating social value rather than making money

History and Development of Social Entrepreneurship

Social entrepreneurship as a term and concept is relatively new, but its precursors go back hundreds of years. Examples of using entrepreneurial practices as a means to support a social mission are found in history. For instance, monasteries sold surplus wine and cheese and used the money to further their mission. The York Female Friendly Society (YFFS), established in England in 1788, prospered and survived until the late twentieth century. Among other successful projects, YFFS operated the Grey Coat School for Girls until 1984. Donations from families and religious groups were a key source of funds while women in the YFFS provided extensive administrative and management support the school and other projects. Because women were not legally allowed to sign contracts during the society's early history, they relied on supportive male friends and family members to learn how to operate.[57] Early social entrepreneurs included historical figures such as Florence Nightingale, John Muir, Susan B. Anthony, and Maria Montessori.[58] The concept itself was first widely used in the 1960s and 1970s. In 1980, entrepreneur Bill Drayton made major inroads in popularizing the concept when he founded Ashoka as an enterprise to encourage and support social entrepreneurs throughout the world.[59]

microlending
small loans provided to individuals and businesses, typically in impoverished areas, that are unable to obtain loans from traditional lending institutions

Probably the most famous social entrepreneurship success story is the establishment of the microlending organization Grameen Bank in Bangladesh by Muhammad Yunus. **Microlending** occurs when investors provide small loans to local entrepreneurs to start their own businesses, cutting out intermediaries and avoiding the predatory lending rates that are often common in developing countries. The inspiration for Grameen Bank occurred in 1974 during a famine, when Yunus lent $27 to a woman and her neighbors to help them earn a living. After he was paid back in full, Yunus realized the difference that these small amounts of money could have in the lives of poor people. The Grameen Bank Project was founded in 1976, and in 1983, a government ordinance allowed Yunus to turn his microlending project into an independent bank.[60]

Grameen Bank adopted an innovative approach to lending. It would have borrowers take out loans in groups of five, and each borrower would guarantee the other's debts.[61] Interest rates are around 16 percent, which is lower than bank rates in many other countries. Grameen's model places pressure upon the borrowers to repay their loans or risk being shamed in front of their community members. Grameen Bank has had a high repayment rate, with 95 percent of borrowers paying back their loans.[62]

Grameen Bank has successfully changed the business environment in Bangladesh. Not only did it develop an innovative model to help villagers get out of poverty, but because 97 percent of loans are made to women, its microlending model promoted respect for women entrepreneurs.[63] Grameen also established training programs to replicate its microlending model in other countries.

Approximately 95 percent of the bank is owned by the borrowers themselves, giving them the incentive to see the bank succeed.[64] In 2006, Yunus and Grameen Bank won the Nobel Peace Prize.[65] The bank's emphasis on joint accountability and ownership has led to a successful lending model to address a major economic problem. Grameen Bank has also been sustainable; with the exception of a couple of years, the bank has earned a profit. Unlike traditional banks in Bangladesh, Grameen has developed a compliance program to shield itself from corruption, which is considered acceptable to many citizens.[66] Today, similar microfinance organizations include Kiva, BRAC (whose acronym stands for "Building Resources Across Communities"), Accion, and FINCA International.

Social entrepreneurs typically follow a four-stage process. In the first stage of envisioning, a clear need, gap, and opportunity are identified. The second stage involves engaging in the opportunity and doing something about it. Enabling something to happen is the third stage. The final stage includes enacting and leading the project to completion. Today, social entrepreneurs are present all over the world. One example is SEKEM, located just north of Cairo, SEKEM was founded in 1977 by Dr. Ibrahim Abouleish. Since 1977, the organization has grown from one person to several business firms. SEKEM produces organic products on its farms, ships organic textiles from Egypt around the world, and manufactures natural food, medicines, and spices. SEKEM's activities are grounded in the following principles:

- Sustained commitment to the benefits of biodynamic agriculture
- Commitment to the highest product quality and its continuous improvement

- Provision of required capital and its optimal use
- Assurance of continuous measures in organizational development
- Investment in education and training for all employees
- Dedication toward customers' real needs
- A marketing strategy sensitive to human values, truthfulness, sensibility, and in alignment with SEKEM's long-standing vision and values
- The promotion of the principles of associative economics

SEKEM developed an alternative method for using pesticides to protect cotton crops. This new system led to a ban on crop dusting in Egypt. Among numerous awards, SEKEM won the IMPACT Business Award in recognition of innovative contributions to preventing climate change. In 2013, Dr. Abouleish won the Award for Excellence in Positive Change by the Global Thinker Forum. Even after the death of Dr. Aboulesih in 2017, SEKEM continues in its mission.[67]

Types of Social Entrepreneurship

Many social enterprises tend to organize themselves as nonprofits. For instance, the Delancey Street Foundation is a nonprofit based in San Francisco. Founded by Mimi Silbert in 1971, the Delancey Foundation was created to help homeless people, drug addicts, felons, and others change their lives. The Delancey Street Foundation acts as a residential education center that trains people in skills and expertise so they can become productive members of society. Approximately 65 percent of the foundation's operating costs are paid for by operating more than 20 small businesses, including the Delancey Street Restaurant, which are staffed by the people using Delancey's services. Thus far, Delancey Street has helped more than 18,000 people change their lives.[68]

Other social entrepreneurs decide to organize as a for-profit organization or as a hybrid of for-profit and nonprofit. Blake Mycoskie's TOMS, for instance, was created with the mission to provide a pair of shoes to children in need throughout the world. However, the model was incorporated into a for-profit business that builds the cost of the free pair of shoes into their shoe sales. After distributing its 1-millionth pair of shoes in 2010, TOMS began to consider other products that could be used in the one-to-one model. Because 80 percent of vision impairment in developing countries is preventable or curable, TOMS decided that for every pair of sunglasses it sold, the company would provide treatment or prescription glasses for those in need.[69] Another for-profit firm, Sseko Designs, provides internships to women in Uganda. The women make leather bags and ribbon sandals to sell in the United States. The intention of the internships is to help these Ugandan women save enough to go to college. A certain amount of the women's earnings go toward a college fund. Sseko Designs matches the savings at the end of the women's internships so that the women will have enough to attend college.[70]

It is clear that social entrepreneurship does not encompass any particular type of business structure. Rather, it is distinguished from traditional organizations—both for-profit and nonprofit—by its emphasis on innovative solutions and entrepreneurial principles to solve social problems.

Social Entrepreneurship and Strategic Philanthropy

There are many distinct similarities among social entrepreneurship, cause-related marketing, and strategic philanthropy. All of these concepts emphasize social responsibility and a desire to support positive change. The delineation occurs more in how they achieve their goals. Businesses with cause-related marketing

Shutterstock/MindStorm

initiatives have not incorporated philanthropy into their business models. Rather, they use programs to strongly support initiatives to benefit society, such as Yoplait's support of the Susan G. Komen Foundation or Avon's support for breast cancer research. Strategic philanthropy uses organizational core competencies to achieve both organizational and social benefits. Strategic philanthropy in business occurs when organizations incorporate these causes into their overall strategies. As part of its strategy to support environmental awareness, Patagonia donates 1 percent of its profits to a global movement of companies called 1 Percent for the Planet, which in turn donates to environmental organizations.

Like social entrepreneurship, strategic philanthropy implements strategies to support solutions for societal challenges. Companies incorporating strategic philanthropy, however, usually outsource the execution of their program and its goals to other organizations, often nonprofits. Home Depot, for instance, strongly supports Habitat for Humanity, but its operations are not centered around building houses for people in need. In contrast, the social entrepreneur executes the organization's program for change directly.[71] The business objectives of these organizations are to create social value; Grameen is in the business of microlending, while Sseko Designs was founded to increase Ugandan women's access to a college education. Cause-related marketing, strategic philanthropy, and social entrepreneurship are all innovative and socially responsible ways to meet the organization's obligations to society.

Benefits of Strategic Philanthropy

To pursue strategic philanthropy successfully, organizations must weigh both the costs and benefits associated with planning and implementing it as a corporate priority. Companies that assume a strategic approach to philanthropy are using an investment model with respect to their charitable acts and donations. In other words, these firms are not just writing checks; they are investing in solutions to stakeholder problems and corporate needs. Such an investment requires the commitment of company time, money, and human talent to succeed. Companies often need to hire staff to manage projects, communicate goals and opportunities throughout the firm, develop long-term priorities and programs, handle requests for funds, and represent the firm on other aspects of philanthropy. In addition, philanthropy consumes the time and energy of all types of employees within the organization. Thus, strategic philanthropy involves real corporate costs that must be justified and managed.

Most scholars and practitioners agree that the benefits of strategic philanthropy ultimately outweigh its costs. The positive return on strategic philanthropy is closely aligned with benefits obtained from strong social responsibility. First, in the United States, businesses can declare up to 10 percent of pretax profits as tax-deductible contributions. Most firms do not take full advantage of this benefit, as 10 percent

Earth in the Balance

Where There's Beer, There's Smoke?

Years of research has illuminated the environmental toll of the tobacco industry. Beyond the clear health concerns about smoking and inhaling secondhand smoke, the World Health Organization asserts that tobacco farming and use lead to deforestation, dump chemicals into water sources, damage air quality, and result in postconsumption waste via discarded cigarette butts, lighters, and packaging. The European Union (EU) has enacted strict laws and regulations in a long-term campaign to create a smoke-free EU. Powered by statistics and a profound interest in public health, the EU leadership made earlier and more significant strides regarding tobacco and smoking than most other developed nation-states.

Anti-smoking regulations have been in force in the Netherlands since 2002, when a general ban on smoking in workplaces and public transportation went into effect. Special provisions of the regulations focused on the hospitality industry, which includes bars that serve as community hubs for socializing, networking, and relaxing after work. Due to extensive lobbying efforts by the hospitality industry, the regulations were phased in over time. In 2008, the Dutch government enacted rules that meant that all industries, including hospitality, were smoke-free.

The Dutch equivalent of a food and consumer product safety administration enforced the law and made regular inspections to ensure compliance. Fines of up to 2,400 euros were levied against bar owners, with repeat violations met by criminal prosecution and the potential for a business to lose its license to operate. In response, many owner-operators of small bars in the Netherlands developed a coalition to fight the strict nonsmoking laws. In a resistance campaign called "Save the Small Bars," these owners asserted that a ban on smoking would directly and negatively affect their ability to attract and retain customers, who largely come from the immediate neighborhood. In effect, the bar owners believed that smoking and drinking beer go hand-in-hand and that their livelihoods would be destroyed by the government's attempt to decouple these two activities.

In resisting the new law, bars typically had the support of their customers and local communities. Customers of bars created and donated to "smoke pots," which helped business owners pay fines after government inspections. One bar owner asked each customer to donate 1 euro toward such a fund. Other bar owners took part in protests and quit their industry trade association because it did not do enough to protect their small businesses and their community's way of life. As one owner concluded, "[T]he bar should be an extension of your living room." Two years after the total ban, the government reported that approximately 60 percent of small bars were complying with the nonsmoking law. A recent research study concluded that community relations and the cohesive nature of small bars and their customers provided the power to resist the government.

Meanwhile, supporters of stricter tobacco control policies are framing the debate as a measure of child protection, which is another concern for communities. Arguments include the need to prevent youth access to tobacco products, as well as the need to prevent their exposure to tobacco smoke and other by-products. A recent survey of Dutch citizens age 18 and older indicated that beliefs about child protection were positively associated with support for tobacco control. This approach is even palatable to some pro-tobacco citizens because it does not restrict the free will of adults or infringe their civil liberties. Taken one step further, some citizens are concerned with any government encroachment on adult liberties, regardless of whether it involves tobacco, firearms, or seatbelt protection. Child protection is viewed quite differently and, as the opening vignette of this chapter described, is also a fervent theme in community relations.

The fight for smokers' rights is not over in the EU. Despite a ban on smoking indoors, bar owners in Greece continue to insist that their livelihoods would be destroyed if they turned smokers away. Coupled with the fears evoked by the country's recent economic crisis, critics wonder if the Greek government will ever begin to enforce its laws. Like their Dutch counterparts, Greek bar owners are bolstered by customers and communities that want to smoke and drink at the same time in the same place. One bar owner in Athens believes that for many smokers, "the habit is part of their DNA," and "If they are not allowed to light up while having a drink, they'll stay at home."

Sources: Joanna E. Cohen, Nancy Milio, R. Gary Rozier, Roberta Ferrence, Mary Jane Ashley, and Adam O. Goldstein, "Political Ideology and Tobacco Control," *Tobacco Control* 9 (September 2000): 263–267; "Tobacco," European Commission, https://ec.europa.eu/health/tobacco/overview_en (accessed June 29, 2019); Filipppos T. Filippidis, "Tobacco Control: A Victim of Political Instability in Greece." *Lancet* 387 (January 23, 2016): 338–339; Thomas G. Kuijpers, Marc C. Willemsen, and Anton E. Kunst, "Public Support for Tobacco Control Policies: The Role of the Protection of Children Against Tobacco," *Health Policy* 122 (August 2018): 929–935; Tal Simons, Patrick A. M. Vermeulen, and Joris Knoben, "There's No Beer Without a Smoke: Community Cohesion and Neighboring Communities' Effects on Organizational Resistance to Antismoking Regulations in the Dutch Hospitality Industry," *Academy of Management Journal* 59 (April 2016): 545–578; Nektaria Stamouli, "Greece's Anti-Smoking Effort Has One Major Problem: Greeks," *Wall Street Journal,* July 11, 2018, https://www.wsj.com/articles/greeces-anti-smoking-effort-has-one-major-problem-greeks-1499714738 (accessed July 1, 2019), "Tobacco-Free Initiative," World Health Organization, https://www.who.int/tobacco/research/economics/rationale/environment/en/ (accessed June 15, 2019).

is viewed as a very generous contribution level. In fact, corporate giving has dipped as low as 0.7 percent of pretax profits in 2013 but typically has hovered close to 1 percent of pretax profits over the past 15 years.[72] Second, companies with a strategic approach to philanthropy experience rewards in the workplace. Employees involved in volunteer projects and related ventures not only have the opportunity to refine their professional skills but also develop a stronger sense of loyalty and commitment to their employer. A national survey of employees demonstrated that corporate philanthropy is an important driver in employee engagement, a key term discussed in Chapter 8. Those who perceive their employer as strong in philanthropy were four times as likely to be very loyal as those who believed their employer was less philanthropic. Employees in firms with favorable ratings on philanthropy are also more likely to recommend the company and its products to others and have intentions to stay with the employer. Positive impressions of the executives' role in corporate philanthropy also influenced employees' affirmative attitudes toward their employer.[73] Results such as these lead to improved productivity, enhanced employee recruitment practices, and reduced employee turnover, each contributing to the overall effectiveness and efficiency of the company. When philanthropy is combined with employee volunteerism, companies may experience enhanced hiring pools for job openings. While hiring is often the result of contacts with the LinkedIn and Glassdoor websites, a company's active community engagement makes a positive impression on a broader group of people, some of whom may become employees in the future.[74]

As a third benefit, companies should experience enhanced customer loyalty as a result of their strategic philanthropy. By choosing projects and causes with links to its core business, a firm can create synergies with its core competencies and customers. Consider the Pampers partnership with UNICEF described earlier. Pampers has developed a partnership to donate a portion of proceeds to help improve the health of babies throughout the world. This resonates well with the target market for Pampers: parents of infants and newborns. Another example is Home Depot's partnership with Habitat for Humanity. Research has revealed that consumer perceptions of corporate philanthropy are also influenced by the relative cost of a donation. Large companies like Netflix are expected to make large donations, so a small donation may be viewed as disingenuous. This research also shows that small and midsize companies, who may be afraid that modest donations will seem inconsequential, may be pleasantly surprised by consumers' favorable reactions.[75]

Finally, strategic philanthropy should improve a company's overall reputation in the community and ease government and community relations. Research indicates a strong negative relationship between illegal activity and reputation, whereas firms that contribute to charitable causes enjoy enhanced reputations. Moreover, companies that contribute to social causes, especially to problems that arise as a result of their actions, may be able to improve their reputations, even after committing a crime.[76] If a business is engaged in a strategic approach to contributions, volunteerism, and related activities, a clear purpose is to enhance and benefit the community. By properly implementing and communicating these achievements, the company will "do well by doing good." Essentially, community members and others use cues from a strategic philanthropy initiative, along with other social responsibility programs, to form a lasting impression—or reputation—of the firm. These benefits, together with others discussed in this section, are consistent with research conducted on European firms. Table 10.7 highlights the perceived benefits of corporate philanthropy, which suggests that companies believe that their charitable activities generally have a positive effect on goodwill, public relations, community relations, employee motivation, and customer loyalty.[77]

Table 10.7 Benefits of Socially Responsible Strategic Corporate Philanthropy

- Consumer trust
- Stakeholder loyalty
- Employee engagement
- Reputation
- Enhanced brand image
- Increased share value
- Positive publicity

Implementation of Strategic Philanthropy

Attaining the benefits of strategic philanthropy depends on the integration of corporate competencies, business stakeholders, and social responsibility objectives to be fully effective. However, fruitfully implementing a strategic philanthropy approach is not simple; it requires organizational resources and strategic attention. In this section, we examine some of the key factors associated with implementing strategic philanthropy.

Although some organizations and leaders see beyond economic concerns, other firms are far less progressive and collaborative in nature. To the extent that corporate leaders and others advocate for strategic philanthropy, planning and evaluation practices must be developed, just as with any other business process. Almost all effective actions taken by a company are well-thought-out business plans. However, although most large organizations have solid plans for philanthropy and other community involvement, these activities typically do not receive the same attention that other business forays garner. A study by the American Productivity & Quality Center found that many organizations are not yet taking a systematic or comprehensive approach in evaluating the impact of philanthropy on their business and their stakeholders.[78]

Top Management Support

The implementation of strategic philanthropy would be impossible without the endorsement and support of the chief executive officer (CEO) and other members of top management. Although most executives care about their communities and social issues, there may be debate or confusion over how their firms should meet stakeholder concerns and social responsibility. Under CEO Jean-Laurent Bonnafé, BNP Paribas has partnered with the Chair of Philanthropy at ESSEC Business School in order to collaborate and contribute to the development of philanthropy itself. This is in addition to the Individual Philanthropy Offering program and the social activities of the BNP Paribas Foundation.[79]

Top managers often have unique concerns with respect to strategic philanthropy. For example, CEOs may worry about having to defend the company's commitment to charity. Some investors may see these contributions as damaging to their portfolios. A related concern involves the resources required to manage a philanthropy effort. Top managers must be well versed in the performance benefits of social responsibility discussed in Chapter 1. Additionally, some executives may believe that less philanthropic-minded competitors have a profit advantage. If these competitors have any advantage at all, it is probably just a short-term situation. The tax benefits and other gains that philanthropy provides should prevail over the long run.[80] In today's environment, there are many positive incentives for strategic philanthropy and social responsibility and reasons that they make good business sense.

Planning and Evaluating Strategic Philanthropy

As with any initiative, strategic philanthropy must prove its relevance and importance. For philanthropy and other stakeholder collaborations to be fully diffused and accepted within the business community, a performance benefit must be evident. In addition, philanthropy should be treated as a corporate program that deserves the same professionalism and resources as other strategic initiatives. Thus, the process for planning and evaluating strategic philanthropy is integral to its success.

To make the best decisions when dealing with stakeholder concerns and issues, there should be a defensible, workable strategy to ensure that every donation is wisely spent. Curt Weeden, president of Business and Nonprofit Strategies, Inc., has developed a multistep process for ensuring effective planning and implementation of strategic philanthropy:

1. **Research.** If a company has too little or inaccurate information, it will suffer when making philanthropic decisions. Research should cover the internal organization and programs, organizations, sponsorship options, and events that might intersect with the interests and competencies of the corporation.

2. **Organize and design.** The information collected by research should be classified into relevant categories. For example, funding opportunities can be categorized according to the level of need and alignment with organizational competencies. The process of organizing and designing is probably the most crucial step in which management should be thoroughly involved.

3. **Engage.** This step consists of engaging management early on so as to ease the approval process in the future. Top managers need to be co-owners of the corporate philanthropy plan. They will have interest in seeing the plan receive authorization, and they will enrich the program by sharing their ideas and thoughts.

4. **Spend.** Deciding what resources and dollars should be spent and where is a very important task. A skilled manager who has spent some time with the philanthropy program should preferably handle this. If the previous steps were handled appropriately, this step should go rather smoothly.[81]

Evaluating corporate philanthropy should begin with a clear understanding of how these efforts are linked to the company's vision, mission, and resources. As our definition suggests, philanthropy can be strategic only if it is fully aligned with the values, core competencies, and long-term plans of an organization. Thus, the development of philanthropic programs should be part of the strategic planning process.

Assuming that key stakeholders have been identified, organizations need to conduct research to understand stakeholder expectations and their willingness to collaborate for mutual benefit. Although many companies have invested time and resources to understand the needs of employees, customers, and investors, fewer have examined other stakeholders or the potential for aligning stakeholders and company resources for philanthropic reasons. Philanthropic efforts should be evaluated for their effects on and benefits to various constituents.[82] Philanthropists have always been concerned with results, which includes maintaining trust within the communities they support. The aftermath of the terrorist attacks in the United States on September 11, 2001, brought not only widespread contributions, but also a heightened sensitivity to accountability. For example, the American Red Cross suffered intense scrutiny after its leaders initially decided to set aside a portion of donations received in response to the terrorist attacks. The rationale for setting aside $200 million was that a long-term program on terrorism response needed to be developed and funded. Many donors rejected this plan, though, and the Red Cross reversed its decision. A survey in late 2002 indicated that 42 percent of Americans had less confidence in charities than they did before the September 11, 2001, attacks. Unfortunately, technological advances have also resulted in fake charities, many developed in the aftermath of a disaster, significant news, or a community event. While these scams are often short lived and regional in scope, ongoing fraud or misrepresentation is occurring on an international scale. In some cases, the names of fraudulent charities are easily confused with the names of well-known and respected charities. Experts advise companies and individuals to use Charity Navigator, Guide Star, and other services to research charitable entities, including the percentage of revenue that supports direct services. Give. org, a service of the Better Business Bureau (BBB), provides evaluations of charities. The 20 Standards for Charity Accountability include an assessment of tax status, governance, complaints, financial stability, and other elements.[83] Major philanthropists are also stepping up their expectations for accountability, widespread impact, strategic thinking, global implications, and results. A recent report by the Panel on the Nonprofit Sector discusses four major areas that all nonprofit organizations need to address in order to demonstrate solid governance and ethical practices. Those areas are legal, governance, finance, and fundraising. Table 10.8 lists specific recommendations on how charitable organizations can go about preserving the soundness and integrity of the nonprofit community.[84] Table 10.9 lists A Donor Bill of Rights which offers 10 guidelines that potential donors should use in evaluating and choosing organizations with which to partner or provide funding. Both types of input are important to individuals and companies in the process of deciding where to donate time and money.

Methods to evaluate strategic philanthropy should include an assessment of how these initiatives are communicated to stakeholders. It is recommended that organizations develop an overall evaluation framework to be used to measure the initiative's success. This evaluation framework provides guidelines for how the organization will view the evaluation, as well as descriptions of the evaluation type, standards to demonstrate successful implementation, and methods for communicating results.[85] Such reporting mechanisms not only improve stakeholder knowledge, but also lead to improvements and refinements. Although critics may deride organizations for communicating their philanthropic efforts, the strategic philanthropy model depends on feedback and learning to create greater value for the organization and its stakeholders.

Table 10.8 Principles for Sound Practice for Charities and Foundations

1. Legal compliance and public disclosure
2. Effective governance
3. Strong financial oversight
4. Responsible fundraising

Source: "Principles for Good Governance and Ethical Practice: A Guide for Charities and Foundations," Independent Sector, https://www.independentsector.org/principles (accessed July 1, 2019).

Table 10.9 A Donor Bill of Rights

Philanthropy is based on voluntary action for the common good. It is a tradition of giving and sharing that is primary to the quality of life. To assure that philanthropy merits the respect and trust of the general public and that donors and prospective donors can have full confidence in the not-for-profit organizations and causes they are asked to support, we declare that all donors have these rights:

1. To be informed of the organization's mission, of the way the organization intends to use donated resources, and of its capacity to use donations effectively for their intended purposes

2. To be informed of the identity of those serving on the organization's governing board, and to expect the board to exercise prudent judgment in its stewardship responsibilities

3. To have access to the organization's most recent financial statements

4. To be assured their gifts will be used for the purposes for which they were given

5. To receive appropriate acknowledgment and recognition

6. To be assured that information about their donations is handled with respect and with confidentiality to the extent provided by law

7. To expect that all relationships with individuals representing organizations of interest to the donor will be professional in nature

8. To be informed whether those seeking donations are volunteers, employees of the organization, or hired solicitors

9. To have the opportunity for their names to be deleted from mailing lists that an organization may intend to share

10. To feel free to ask questions when making a donation and to receive prompt, truthful, and forthright answers

Source: Association of Fundraising Professionals (AFP), all rights reserved. Reprinted with permission from the Association of Fundraising Professionals.

Summary

More firms are investigating ways to link their philanthropic efforts with consumer interests. From a strategic perspective, a firm's ability to link consumer interests to philanthropy should lead to stronger economic relationships. Community relations are the organizational functions dedicated to building and maintaining relationships and trust with the community. To determine the key areas that require support and to refine the mission statement, a company should periodically conduct a community needs assessment.

Companies play a major role in a community's quality of life and economic development by bringing jobs to the community, interacting with other businesses, and making contributions to local health, education, and recreation projects that benefit residents and employees. When a company leaves an area, the financial repercussions may be devastating. Because they have such a profound impact on the economic viability of their communities, firms that value social responsibility consider both the short- and long-term effects of changes in their workforce on the community.

For many firms, a series of legal and regulatory matters must be resolved before launching a business. On a basic level, society has the ability to dictate what types of organizations are allowed to operate. As more companies view themselves as responsible to the community, they consider their role and the impact of their decisions on communities from an ethical perspective.

The success of a business can be enhanced by the publicity generated from and through stakeholder acceptance of community activities. One way that organizations are exercising their philanthropic responsibilities is through volunteerism, the donation of employee time by companies in support of social causes. In structuring volunteer programs, attention must be paid to employee values and beliefs.

Generally, philanthropy involves any acts of benevolence and goodwill. Strategic philanthropy is defined as the synergistic use of organizational core competencies and resources to address key stakeholders' interests and to achieve organizational and social benefits. Strategic philanthropy involves both financial and nonfinancial contributions to stakeholders, but it also benefits the company. As such, strategic philanthropy is part of a broader philosophy that recognizes how social responsibility can help an organization improve its overall performance. Research suggests that companies that adopt a more businesslike approach to philanthropy will experience a better image, increased employee loyalty, and improved customer ties.

Corporate giving, volunteer efforts, and other philanthropic activities should be considered and aligned with corporate strategy and financial, legal, and ethical obligations. The concept of strategic philanthropy has evolved since the middle of the twentieth century, when contributions were prohibited by law, to emerge as a management practice to support social responsibility beginning in the 1990s. Whereas strategic philanthropy links corporate resources and knowledge to address broader social, customer, employee, and supplier problems and needs, cause-related marketing ties an organization's product(s) directly to a social concern. By linking products with charities and social causes, organizations acknowledge the opportunity to align philanthropy to economic goals and to recognize stakeholder interests in organizational benevolence.

Social entrepreneurship occurs when an entrepreneur founds a business with the purpose of creating social value. There are many distinct similarities among social entrepreneurship, cause-related marketing, and strategic philanthropy. All of these concepts emphasize social responsibility and a desire to support positive change. The delineation occurs more in how they achieve their goals. Like social entrepreneurship, strategic philanthropy implements strategies to support solutions for societal challenges. Companies incorporating strategic philanthropy, however, usually outsource the execution of their program and its goals to other organizations, often nonprofits. The social entrepreneur executes the organization's program for change directly. The business objectives of these organizations are to create social value.

Many organizations have skillfully used their resources and core competencies to address the needs of employees, customers, business partners, the community and society, and the natural environment. To pursue strategic philanthropy successfully, organizations must weigh the costs and benefits associated with planning and implementing it as a corporate priority. The benefits of strategic philanthropy are closely aligned with benefits obtained from social responsibility. Businesses that engage in strategic philanthropy often gain a tax advantage. Research suggests that they may also enjoy improved productivity, stronger employee commitment and morale, reduced turnover, and greater customer loyalty and satisfaction. In the future, many companies will devote more resources to understanding how strategic philanthropy can be developed and integrated to support their core competencies.

The implementation of strategic philanthropy is impossible without the support of top management. To integrate strategic philanthropy into the organization successfully, the efforts must fit with the company's mission, values, and resources. Organizations must also understand stakeholder expectations and the propensity to support such activities for mutual benefit. This process relies on the feedback of stakeholders in improving and learning how to better integrate the strategic philanthropy objectives with other organizational goals. Finally, companies will need to evaluate philanthropic efforts and assess how these results should be communicated to stakeholders.

Responsible Business Debate

The Giving Pledge

Issue: *Should billionaires be expected to give away some of their fortunes?*

In 2010, 40 billionaires from the United States decided to commit more than half of their wealth to charitable or philanthropic causes. Led by Warren Buffett and Bill and Melinda Gates, Michael Bloomberg, Mark Zuckerberg, and executives and entrepreneurs from Microsoft, eBay, Intel, Citigroup, and Cisco Systems signed the Giving Pledge. At the time, news reports heralded the approach as a catalyst to increase rates of giving, create more significant monetary donations, and tackle some of the world's most pressing challenges and needs. Today, more than 200 billionaires from 23 countries have signed the pledge, including the founders of WhatsApp, Airbnb, Spanx, Home Depot, and the Virgin Group. Pledgers range in age from their 30s to their 90s and are devoted to all kinds of charitable causes, including poverty alleviation, autism, disaster relief, global health, homelessness, education, medical research, and much more.

In making the pledge, individuals and couples pen a personal letter explaining their values, goals, and reasons for joining the effort. Phrases from these letters provide a glimpse into the hearts and minds of these billionaires:

- There is a saying that a great trip can set you down a path that doesn't end when you return. With this pledge, I want to help more kids realize the kind of journey I have had. (Brian Chesky, CEO of Airbnb)
- Cancer terrifies us and often takes our lives, irrespective of age, gender, or walk of life. As I have publicly stated countless times, my duty is to make sure cancer is vanquished. (Jon and Karen Huntsman, Jon and Karen Huntsman Foundation)
- I will never forget that my path was paved by my parents, grandparents, and generations of African Americans whose names I will never know. My story would only be possible in America, and it is incumbent

on all of us to pay this inheritance forward. (Robert Frederick Smith, CEO of Vista Equity Partners)

Recently, media reports have surfaced about the number of billionaires who have yet to sign the Giving Pledge. While the initial results of the initiative were strong, only 1 in 6 billionaires in the United States have committed to it. That means that well-known businesspeople such as Oprah Winfrey, Jeff Bezos, Michael Dell, and the families of Walmart are not part of the effort. Of course, uncovering their reasons is difficult.

Some critics of the initiative point to the fact that there is no formal accountability built into the pledge. One journalist wondered if the pledgers were more focused on feeling good or gaining publicity. In other words, are some billionaires pledging without real plans or timely actions to meet the promise? Others may be signing on as a result of peer pressure, even if it's subtle. The Gateses and Buffett have hosted intimate dinner parties aimed at bringing together billionaires, including pledgers and would-be pledgers. When another journalist at *Fortune* magazine suggested that Bezos, one of the wealthiest people in the world, should sign the Giving Pledge, readers shot back. One proclaimed, "Wanting to take you to task a little for the criticisms of Jeff's philanthropy." While few people doubt the noble intentions of its founding and current members, the Giving Pledge may not be the salve for soothing world problems after all.

There Are Two Sides to Every Issue

1. The wealth of billionaires is largely the result of business success and the work of countless others. They should be expected to make significant philanthropic contributions.

2. Like other people, billionaires are entitled to spend their wealth as they wish. Neither their peers nor society should expect them make significant philanthropic contributions.

Sources: Marc Gunther, "5 in 6 U.S. Billionaires Haven't Signed the Giving Pledge. Why Not?" *Chronicle of Philanthropy* 31 (June 2019): 9–16; the Giving Pledge, https://givingpledge.org/#enter (accessed June 30, 2019); Nicole Lewis and Maria Di Mento, "Giving Pledge Signers Gave Big in 2013 but Not Much for Today's Needs," *Chronicle of Philanthropy* 26 (February 2014): 6; Alan Murray and David Meyer, "Call for Jeff Bezos to Join Giving Pledge Causes a Stir: CEO Daily." *Fortune.com*, May 31, 2019, https://fortune.com/2019/05/31/jeff-bezos-ceo-daily-may-31/ (accessed July 2, 2019); Scott Walter, "Gates and Buffett Take the Pledge," *Philanthropy Daily*, June 22, 2010, https://www.philanthropydaily.com/gates-and-buffett-take-the-pledge/ (accessed July 2, 2019); Christopher Zara, "Mackenzie Bezos Joins the Giving Pledge. Still No Sign of Jeff," *Fast Company*, May 28, 2019, https://www.fastcompany.com/90355929/mackenzie-bezos-joins-the-giving-pledge-still-no-sign-of-jeff (accessed July 2, 2019).

Key Terms

cause-related marketing (p. 291)
community (p. 277)
community relations (p. 278)
extrinsic motivation (p. 288)
impact investing (p. 290)

intrinsic motivation (p. 288)
microlending (p. 294)
neighbor of choice (p. 278)
philanthropy (p. 286)
quality of life (p. 277)

social entrepreneurship (p. 293)
strategic philanthropy (p. 289)
volunteerism (p. 285)

Discussion Questions

1. What are some of the issues that you might include in a defense of strategic philanthropy to company stockholders?

2. Describe your personal experiences with philanthropy. In what types of activities have you participated? Which companies that you do business with have a philanthropic focus? How did this focus influence your decision to buy from those companies?

3. How have changes in the business environment contributed to the growing trend of strategic philanthropy?

4. Compare and contrast cause-related marketing with strategic philanthropy. What are the unique benefits of each approach?

5. Compare social entrepreneurship to cause-related marketing and strategic philanthropy.

6. What role does top management play in developing and implementing a strategic philanthropy approach?

7. Describe the four-stage process for planning and implementing strategic philanthropy.

Experiential Exercise

Choose one major corporation and investigate how closely their philanthropic efforts are strategically aligned with their core competencies. Visit the company's website, read their annual reports, and use other sources to justify your conclusions. Develop a chart or table to depict how the company's core competencies are linked to various philanthropic projects and stakeholder groups. Finally, provide an analysis of how these efforts have affected the company's performance.

Creating "Buy-in" for Volunteerism: What Would You Do?

As a new vice president of corporate philanthropy, Jack Birke was looking forward to the great initiatives and partnerships that the company could create through his office. During his 18-year career, Jack worked for several large nonprofit organizations and earned an excellent reputation for his ability to raise funds, develop advisory boards, and in general, work well with the business community.

About a year ago, Jack decided to investigate other opportunities within the fundraising industry and started looking at companies that were formalizing their philanthropy efforts. He was hired as vice president less than a month ago and was in the process of developing an office structure, getting to know the organization, and creating a strategic plan. His charge over the next year was to develop a stronger reputation for philanthropy and social responsibility with the company's stakeholders, including employees, customers, and the community. An executive assistant, director of volunteerism, and director of community relations were already on board, and Jack was looking for additional staff.

The position and office were new to the company, and Jack had already heard dissent from other employees, who openly questioned how important philanthropy was to the business. After all, the economy was slowing, and it seemed that customers were more concerned about price and value than any "touchy-feely" program. About half of the company's employees worked on the manufacturing line, and the other half was employed in administrative or professional positions. Both groups seemed to be equally suspicious of Jack and his office. The company developed an employee volunteer program two years ago, but it was never very successful. A program to gather food, gifts, and money to support needy families at Christmas, however, drew strong support. The firm had fairly good relationships in the community, but these were primarily the top executives' connections through the chamber of commerce, industry associations, nonprofit boards, and so forth. In sum, while Jack had the support of top management, many employees were unsure about philanthropy and its importance to the company. Jack was starting to think about short-term policies and long-term strategy for marketing his office and its goals to the rest of the organization. What would you do?

Technology Issues

Sustainability Goes High-Tech

Businesses have great influence on the environment, as waste, pollution, and the use of resources contribute to the changing climate. Modern technology is improving how businesses contribute to the sustainability of the environment. In the past, consumers and businesses often had a throwaway mentality when creating and using products. In some cases, it was lack of information about the condition of the planet and the effects of consumerism that led to subpar sustainability efforts. Technology can be used to reduce waste and pollution, encourage recycling, and save energy by providing data regarding the impact of consumer and business practices.

For example, Amazon is known for shipping items in a way that uses less packaging. This cuts down on resource use and waste production, and promotes more mindful supply chain management. Technology has allowed the collection of digital data on the use of materials, and it has helped businesses and consumers adopt more ecofriendly practices in their day-to-day lives. For instance, drones are used to snapshot areas of pollution in the Los Angeles River to see where trash is entering the marine ecosystem. Cities can use this data to detect areas where intervention is needed, whether the solution is more frequent trash pickup or adding more trash cans in the surrounding areas.

Along with water pollution, air pollution is a major issue in cities today. Air quality can vary in different parts of a city. Continued research into this phenomenon could provide sustainable solutions. The Environmental Defense Fund (EDF) is working in tandem with Geotab and cities such as Houston to monitor pollution through the use of telematics. *Telematics* is a method of monitoring that uses global positioning system (GPS) and onboard diagnostics. The EDF is using Geotab's telematics technology on cars to locate high levels of pollution in the city. With this data, policies and plans can be developed to reduce air pollution and improve both the environment and the local community.

Deforestation, water availability, and catastrophic natural event predictions are all areas where technology is used to benefit society. Cartographers and geologists create custom maps—even in three dimensions—that aid experts in managing water supplies, finding oil, and pinpointing future earthquakes. Planet, a firm that takes daily snapshots of the Earth using satellites, offers their data to services like Global Forest Watch, which monitors deforestation and makes their findings available to the public. These snapshots help bust illegal loggers or discover areas susceptible to forest fires. Additionally, businesses in the financial and insurance industries value this information because it helps them become aware of weather and climate risks that could affect their businesses. Google is another firm that plays a role in the use of technology for sustainability endeavors. Google gathered 30 years of measurements from ancient magnetic tapes around the globe and created a digital tool to help developing countries identify areas that need additional water protection.

Values and accountability are paramount in the use of technology for sustainability. It has been seen that technology can be used to help both the human population and the environment. However, without ethical controls and social responsibility, machines could be relied on more than human beings, jobs could be lost, and sensitivity to the planet could be overlooked in the race to innovate. Therefore, ethical guidelines and programs need to be developed among businesses to meet these new advances. Technology has been and will continue to be a major force that can continue to improve society.[1]

Chapter Objectives

- Examine the nature and characteristics of technology
- Explore the economic impact of technology
- Examine technology's influence on society
- Provide a framework for the strategic management of technology issues

Shutterstock/Sergei_Kazmiruk

I n this chapter, we explore the nature of technology and its positive and negative effects on society. Technology's influence on the economy is very powerful, especially with regard to growth, employment, and working environments. This influence on society includes issues related to the internet, privacy, intellectual property, artificial intelligence (AI), health, and the general quality of life. The strategic direction for technology depends on government, as well as on business's ability to plan, implement, and audit the influence of technology on society.

The Nature of Technology

technology

the application of knowledge, including the processes and applications to solve problems, perform tasks, and create new methods to obtain desired outcomes

Technology relates to the application of knowledge, including the processes and applications to solve problems, perform tasks, and create new methods to obtain desired outcomes. It includes intellectual knowledge, as well as the physical systems devised to achieve business and personal objectives. The evolution of civilization is tied to developments in technology. Through technological advances, humans have moved from a hunter-gatherer existence to a stable agricultural economy to the Industrial Revolution. Today, our economy is based more on IT and services than on manufacturing. This technology is changing the way we take vacations, shop for groceries, do homework, track criminals, navigate to places, and maintain friendships. Technology has made it possible to go to work or attend meetings without leaving home. Our new economy is based on these dynamic technological changes in our society.

Characteristics of Technology

Some of the characteristics of technology include the dynamics, reach, and self-sustaining nature of technological progress. The dynamics of technology relate to the constant change that often challenges the structure of social institutions. The automobile, airplane, and personal computer all created major changes and influenced government, the family, social relationships, education, the military, and leisure. These changes can happen so fast that they require significant adjustments in the political, religious, and economic structures of society. Some societies have difficulty adjusting to this rate of change to the point that they even attempt to legislate against new technologies to isolate themselves. China tried to isolate its citizens from the internet and the social trends resulting from the application of new technology to music, movies, and other carriers of culture. But eventually they eased restrictions, allowing for limited and monitored use. Since then, internet use in China has grown, with the number of regular users totaling more than 800 million, usually on mobile devices. However, the government still utilizes a number of strategies for reminding Chinese citizens that their internet activity is being monitored. Often, the Chinese government will completely shut down the use of instant messaging or social media applications to limit the potential of groups to organize protests or other antigovernment activities.[2]

The *dynamics* of technology are not only changing many traditional products, such as books and music, but also the way in which we conduct everyday activities. **Smart devices** are connected to other devices on networks and are capable of communication and computation for different wireless protocols, such as Wi-Fi and Bluetooth, operating interactively. According to Amazon, more than 100 million devices with its Alexa virtual assistant have been sold to date.[3] These devices changed the way that people accomplish both work-related

smart devices

devices connected to other devices on networks that are capable of communication and computation for different wireless protocols, such as Wi-Fi and Bluetooth, operating interactively

and personal tasks, as well as the way we store data. As the capacity for cloud storage of data increases, other storage devices such as universal serial bus (USB) drives will likely become a thing of the past. Today, we can conduct banking transactions without going to a bank, draft a document while riding the bus to work and save it to the cloud, and share information with others with a tap of a screen.

Each advance in technology seems to lead to new developments across industries, sometimes making things more convenient, while at other times raising serious concerns about privacy, protection of digital property, and other issues. *Reach* relates to the broad nature of technology as it moves through society. For instance, every community in both developed and developing countries has been influenced by cellular phones and smartphones. The ability to make a call from almost any location has many positive effects, but negative side effects include increases in traffic accidents and noise pollution as well as fears about potential health risks. Through telecommunications, businesses, families, and governments have been linked from far distances. Satellites allow instant visual and voice electronic connections almost anywhere in the world. These technologies have reduced the need for in-person meetings via business travel. Web conferencing and video conferencing are becoming more popular alternatives, although it may be difficult for technology to fully replace the nature of face-to-face encounters. Even though collaboration technology continues to grow in lieu of business travel, companies recognize that some occasions demand face-to-face interaction, such as meeting a new client for the first time, dealing with certain cultures, and discussing significant financial and legal transactions.

The *self-sustaining nature* of technology relates to the fact that technology acts as a catalyst to spur even faster development. As innovations are introduced, they stimulate the need for more technology to facilitate further development. For example, the internet created the need for broadband transmission of electric signals through digital subscriber lines (DSL), satellites, and cable. Broadband allows connections to the internet to be 50 times faster than through a traditional telephone modem. It also allows users to download large files and creates the opportunity for a rich multimedia experience. Today, most people refer to it as Wi-Fi, and many restaurants and coffee shops offer it as a feature to attract customers. The latest discussion in the advancement of internet transmission is through fiber-optic cables. Many developed countries are heavily investing in building and utilizing fiber-optic infrastructure for faster internet connections, and we are seeing adoption among consumers rapidly increase.[4]

Effects of Technology

Civilizations must harness and adapt to changes in technology to maintain a desired quality of life. The mobile phone, for example, has dramatically altered communication patterns, particularly in developing countries where there are few telephone lines. Innovations can also change entire industries. Companies and governments are creating supercomputers that are millions of times more powerful than personal computers. The computers are making use of **big data**, which consists of large structured and unstructured sets of data that can be analyzed to reveal information and associations. The concept of big data is a result of the continual use of the internet via computers and mobile devices.[5] Big data is complex and calls for advanced software that can glean insights from these massive amounts of data. These insights can inform knowledge of the impact of business strategies on society. For example, Instagram uses big data to fuel its explore and search functions, while Johnson & Johnson uses it to evaluate the likelihood of success for new drugs.[6] Such examples illustrate how technology can provide new methods to accomplish tasks that were once thought impossible. These advancements

big data
large structured and unstructured sets of data that can be analyzed to reveal information and associations

create new processes, new products, and economic progress and ultimately have profound effects on society.

The global economy experienced the greatest acceleration of technological advancement that ever occurred, propelling increased productivity, output, corporate profits, and stock prices, over the last decade.[7] Among the positive contributions of these advances were reductions in the number of worker-hours required to generate the nation's output. At the same time, the economic conditions that accompanied this period of technical innovation resulted in increased job opportunities. But in the early 2000s, with the fall of the dot-coms and the integrity meltdown of major U.S. corporations, the economy had taken a downturn, along with the falling stock market. Many IT firms expanded too rapidly and misreported revenue and earnings to hold onto stock prices and please executives and investors. The result was incidences of massive accounting fraud that damaged confidence and the economy. Earlier chapters dealt with many of these cases and their effect on social responsibility expectations. The traditional work environment has changed because telecommunications (e.g., email and video conferencing) reduce the need for face-to-face interaction. GoToMeeting, a video conference software, facilitates 80 million online meetings per year.[8] Through online shopping, the internet can also reduce the need for trips to a shopping center and has increased the amount of business done by the U.S. Postal Service (USPS), UPS, and FedEx. In addition, the ease and number of business-to-business transactions have expanded.

However, there are concerns that dramatic shifts in the acceleration and innovations derived from technology may be spurring imbalances not only in the economy but also in our social existence. The flow of technology into developing countries can serve as a method to jump-start economic development. In Kenya, many residents use the mobile phone payment service M-Pesa to quickly and securely transfer funds to merchants and family members, reducing the need to travel long distances to banks. The service has also allowed many to start their own businesses, contributing to the growth of the local economy.[9] However, a failure to share technology or provide methods to disseminate technology could cause a major divide in the quality of life. Limited resources in underdeveloped countries and the lack of a technology infrastructure may lead to many social, political, and economic problems in the future.

In the United States, the federal government implemented plans to subsidize computers, mobile phones, and internet access for low-income households and individuals across the nation. Although this initiative was somewhat controversial, proponents argued that it had the potential to raise the standard of living for low-income families.[10] Some companies are also trying to help bridge the technology gap that exists between those who can afford technology and those who are on the other side of the so-called digital divide. For instance, Comcast established a program called Internet Essentials, where people can sign up to see if they qualify for low-cost internet service, computers for $150, and free internet training.[11] Other internet providers offer programs similar to Comcast's and serve as examples of a corporate attempt to keep the positive effects of the reach of technology available to all segments of society.

There are concerns about the way that information technology (IT) can improve the quality of life for society. In addition, there are concerns about the negative consequences of the reduction of privacy and the emergence of cybercrime. It is becoming common for hackers to install malware into company and government computer systems to steal secrets or consumer data. If higher-security measures are not taken, significant changes in our economy and individual lifestyles could occur, causing the roles of business, government, and technology to be questioned. Public advocacy organizations are helping by participating in charting the future of computer networks to integrate these technological innovations into the way we live.[12]

Technology's Influence on the Economy

Technology has had an enormous influence on the global economy. In many ways, technology has contributed to significant economic growth through new business opportunities, better ways to connect across long distances, and more efficient processes. For example, the growing gig economy has flourished with advancements in technology. In the burgeoning **gig economy** independent contractors offer their services to large and small companies or individuals for an agreed level of compensation. Typical freelance work includes writing and editing, consulting, accounting, and creative work. Additionally, the widespread growth of companies like Uber and Airbnb have led to an economic system called the **sharing economy,** in which independent contractors can "rent out" underutilized resources such as their cars or lodging to earn extra income. Companies like Uber act as agents. Their technology links the buyer and seller, but they do not engage in the distribution process directly. These economies have led to a number of opportunities.

However, technology has also given rise to concerns as well. The following sections document technology's overall impact on the economy.

gig economy
a labor market in which independent contractors offer their services to large and small companies or individuals for an agreed level of compensation

sharing economy
a labor market in which independent contractors "rent out" underutilized resources such as their cars or lodging to earn extra income

Economic Growth and Employment

Technological advancements have had a profound impact on economic growth and employment. Over the past several decades, technology has been a major factor in the economic growth of the United States. Investments in educational technologies, increased support for basic government research, and continued commitment to the mission of research and development (R&D) in both the public and private sectors have become major drivers of economic growth. Through lower interest rates, tax credits, and liberalization of export controls, the government established the economic infrastructure for using technology to drive economic development. The expansion of industry-led technology partnerships among corporations, governments, and nonprofit organizations has also been a key component of growth. Table 11.1 shows some leading technology firms and their number of employees.

Investments in R&D are among the highest return investments a nation can make. Technological innovation has been a key contributor to the nation's growth in productivity.[13] For example, the ability to access information in real time through the electronic data interface among retailers, wholesalers, and manufacturers has reduced the time that it takes to produce and deliver products. Likewise, product design times and costs have declined because computer modeling has minimized the need for architectural drafters and some engineers required for building projects. New software can provide multiple iterations of a design based on inputs and parameters set by an architect. Medical diagnoses have become faster, more thorough, and more accurate thanks to the accessibility of information and records over the internet, which has hastened treatment and eliminated unnecessary procedures.[14]

The relationship between businesses and consumers has been transformed through e-commerce, as more people turn to the internet to make all type of purchases from one-time purchases to everyday purchases. The sharing of information has led to greater transparency, and social media has facilitated closer communication and greater customer loyalty. Business-to-business (B2B) e-commerce involving companies buying from and selling to each other online is also growing in popularity, as it is the preferred method of purchase for more than half of all businesses. Certain aspects of internet transactions are particularly important in B2B relationships, where the improved quantity, reliability, and timeliness of information have reduced uncertainties.

Table 11.1 Leading Technology Firms

Company	Number of Employees
Alphabet	100,000
Amazon	647,500
Apple Inc.	132,000
IBM	350,600
Intel	107,400
Microsoft	134,944
Samsung	320,671
Sony	117,300

supply chain management
the coordination of all the activities involved with the flow of supplies and products from raw materials through to the end customer

It has also facilitated **supply chain management** as more companies outsource purchasing over the internet.[15]

Walmart and Amazon are two companies that have not only mastered the management and integration of their supply chains over the years, but have also used the internet to establish further efficiencies within the supply chain. Walmart's technology infrastructure is among the largest in the world and informs operations regarding accurate forecasting of demand and inventory, the most efficient transportation routes, and management of customer relationships and service response logistics. Amazon has fulfillment centers strategically located in areas where customers can be reached quickly. In some markets, Amazon even offers same-day delivery. A technology known as sortation allows Amazon to determine how different items can be combined to efficiently fit into boxes. The software instructs employees on where to store the item in the warehouse and how large a package will be needed when it comes time to ship. Amazon's expertise at supply chain management has earned it strong accolades and saved it billions of dollars in costs.[16] Amazon is becoming a growing competitor to USPS, UPS, and FedEx as it increases delivery of its own packages.

Science and technology are powerful drivers of economic growth and improvements in the quality of life in the United States. Advancements in technology have created millions of new jobs, better health and longer lives, new opportunities, and more. Public and private investment in R&D contributes to these advancements and continues to produce more jobs and improve living standards. Industries that have grown as a result of innovations in technology include biotechnology, computers, communications, software, aerospace, and semiconductors. Retailing, wholesaling, and other commercial institutions have also been transformed by technology.

Economic Concerns about the Use of Technology

Despite the staggering economic growth fostered by technological advancements, there are some economic downsides to technology. For instance, some people have lost their jobs because of technology.

AI has created many new jobs. However, there are also concerns that AI used in business will lead to widespread unemployment. As this technology is used for routine, manual, or cognitive tasks, some traditional jobs will be eliminated. These ethical and social responsibility issues require the attention of businesses. There will be tremendous demand for workers skilled in developing and implementing AI technologies. Business has a responsibility to help reskill workers to fit into this new AI work environment. Workers may need to develop more soft skills in the application of AI technologies. Educational institutions and business need to work together to keep employment dynamic.[17] Although technology also creates numerous job opportunities, this is little consolation for those who lose their jobs and do not have the technological skills to get new jobs in the growing technological field.

Small businesses in particular may have difficulty taking advantage of certain opportunities, such as digital supply chain management systems or other large-scale IT applications. The ability to purchase technology may affect the nature of competition and the success of various types of businesses. Limited resources and tough economic times may cause small businesses to cancel, modify, or delay IT projects, decrease IT budgets, and reduce staffing and training levels. Experts recommend several solutions to IT problems in small business:

- Focus on core competencies while seeking to explore outsourcing options.
- Take advantage of free software and other offerings.
- Explore the benefits of "cloud computing" where applications are utilized and maintained on a subscription basis.
- Consider IT infrastructure alternatives to capital expenditures through hosted hardware, software, and services.[18]

As mentioned earlier, a key concern today with advancing technology is the digital divide that occurs when certain groups have limited access to the latest technology. Also, part of the debate involves access issues for certain populations, such as persons with disabilities, people who are barely literate, the distribution of technology among low- and high-income households, and accommodations for senior citizens.[19]

There are several ways to address these inevitable consequences of accelerating change in the technology drivers of the new economy. One way to address the negative consequences of accelerating new technology is to assess problems related to its impact on competition. Restraining competition (whether domestic or international) to suppress competitive turmoil is a major concern of governments. Allowing anticompetitive practices, price fixing, or other unfair methods of competition would be counterproductive to rising standards of living.[20]

Technology's Influence on Society

IT and telecommunications technology minimize the borders between countries, businesses, and people and allow people to overcome the physical limitations of time and space. Technological advances also enable people to acquire customized goods and services that cost less and are of higher quality than ever imagined.[21]

For example, airline passengers can purchase tickets online and either print out boarding passes on their home or office printers or download them to their mobile devices so that they can go straight to their plane on arrival at the airport after clearing security.[22] Cartographers and geologists can create custom maps—even in three dimensions—that aid experts in managing water supplies, finding oil, and pinpointing future earthquakes.[23] In this section, we explore five broad issues related to technology and its impact on society, including the internet, privacy, intellectual property, AI, and health and biotechnology. Although there are many other pressing issues related to technology, these seem to be the most widely debated at this time.

The Internet

The internet, the global information system that links many computer networks, has profoundly altered the way that people communicate, learn, do business, and find entertainment. Although many people believe the internet began in the early 1990s, its origins can be traced to the late 1950s (see Table 11.2). Over five decades, the network evolved from a system for government and university researchers into an information and entertainment tool used by billions around the globe. With the development of the World Wide Web, which organizes the information on the internet into interconnected "pages" of text, graphics, audio, and video, use of the internet exploded in the 1990s.

Today, more than 4.3 billion people around the world utilize the internet. In the United States alone, nearly 292 million access the internet via computers or mobile devices. Internet use by consumers

Shutterstock/Rido

Table 11.2 History of the Internet

Year	Event
1969	The first node is connected to Advanced Research Projects Agency Network (ARPANET), the initial version of the internet. ARPANET was a government project created to serve as a communications network during the Cold War.
1972	Email is invented by adapting an internal messaging program and extending it to use the ARPANET to send messages between sites. Within a year, three-quarters of ARPANET traffic is email.
1989	The World Wide Web is invented to make information easier to publish and access on the internet.
1993	The first web-browser, Mosaic, is launched. It introduced proprietary Hypertext Markup Language (HTML) tags and more sophisticated image capabilities. The browser is a massive success and businesses start to notice the web's potential.
1994	*Internet Magazine* launches, reporting on London's first internet café and reviewing 100 websites. It was known as the "most extensive" list of websites ever to appear in a magazine. A 28.8-Kbps modem costs £399 (plus value-added tax). Jerry and David's Guide to the World Wide Web is renamed Yahoo! and receives 100,000 visitors. In 1995, it begins displaying advertisements.
1995	The search engine Alta Vista is introduced, which can store and index the HTML from every internet page. It also introduces the first multilingual search. Amazon, an online bookseller that pioneers ecommerce, is launched. eBay is launched to enable internet users to trade with each other.
1998	Google launches and pioneers a ranking system that uses links to assess a website's popularity. The site's simple design is soothing, while existing search engines cram their pages with animated advertisements.
2000	The infamous dotcom bust occurs, after several years of venture capitalists investing in internet business proposals that do not have a viable business model.
2004	Media companies start selling music and video online. Napster and iTunes are the major players. Facebook launches at Harvard University. The social networking site gained 30 million members by 2007 and over 200 million active users in 2009. The photo-sharing website Flickr begins, coinciding with the rise in digital photography. (Kodak discontinues selling reloadable film cameras in western Europe and North America later this year.)
2005	YouTube and Reddit are launched.
2006	Twitter is introduced.
2010	The industry of big data is estimated to be worth more than $100 billion.
2013	Media reports reveal the extent to which national security agencies monitor the online activities of citizens without search warrants.
2014	Google pushes for a safer internet by boosting the rankings of Hypertext Transfer Protocol Secure (HTTPS) and Secure Sockets Layer (SSL) sites. Amazon introduces the Echo virtual assistant.
2015	The Internet of Things (IoT), in which consumer or industrial devices are connected to the internet for management and monitoring, became a popular concept in our connected environment. The Federal Communications Commission (FCC) passed net neutrality rules preventing the blocking, throttling, or prioritizing of any internet traffic. (In 2017, the FCC votes to remove these rules.)
2017	By 2017, ICANN releases more than 1,200 new TLDs for domains including .chat, .cloud, .jewelry, and .tours.
2019	Facebook reaches 2.3 billion active users, YouTube reaches 1.9 billion active users, Instagram reaches 1 billion active users, and Twitter reaches 335 million active users.

Sources: Adapted from "A Short History of the Internet," http://www.sean.co.uk/a/science/history_of_the_internet.shtm (accessed June 22, 2015); *Economist* staff, "Data, Data Everywhere," *The Economist,* February 25, 2010, http://www.economist.com/node/15557443 (accessed June 22, 2016); Irfan Ahmad, "A Timeline of the Internet: 1969–2018 (Infographic)," *Digital Information World,* August 29, 2018, https://www.digitalinformationworld.com/2018/08/history-of-the-internet-infographic.html (accessed June 25, 2019); Alfred Lua, "21 Top Social Media Sites to Consider for Your Brand," *Buffer,* January 24, 2019, https://buffer.com/library/social-media-sites (accessed June 25, 2019).

Figure 11.1 Internet Users in the World

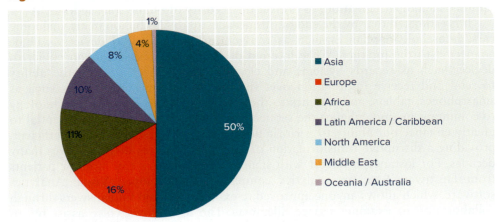

■ Asia	
■ Europe	
■ Africa	
■ Latin America / Caribbean	
■ North America	
■ Middle East	
■ Oceania / Australia	

Source: "World Internet User Statistics and 2019 World Population Stats," Internet World Stats, https://www. internetworldstats.com/stats.htm (accessed June 25, 2019).

in other countries, especially Japan (118 million users), the United Kingdom (63 million), Germany (79 million), Brazil (149 million), and France (60 million), has escalated rapidly.[24] Figure 11.1 shows the pattern of active internet usage around the world. To keep up with the growing demand for new email and website addresses, the **Internet Corporation for Assigned Names and Numbers (ICANN)** now has more than 1,500 top-level domains (TLDs), such as .com, .org, .info, or .chat to allow for the creation of millions of new addresses.[25]

The interactive nature of the internet has created tremendous opportunities for businesses to forge relationships with consumers and business customers, target markets more precisely, and even reach previously inaccessible markets. The internet also facilitates supply chain management, allowing companies to network with manufacturers, wholesalers, retailers, suppliers, and outsource firms to serve customers more efficiently.[26] However, widespread use of the internet has also led to the storing of mass amounts of information and hackers and other cybercriminals can take advantage.

Online fraud has become a major issue for businesses and consumers, with U.S. business losing more than $57 billion each year.[27] Interestingly, the rate of online fraud targeting businesses is decreasing, while the rate for consumer online fraud is increasing. This is largely because companies are using more sophisticated methods of tracking abnormal credit and debit transactions. Many are using data by analyzing trends such as the average amount spent per month and locations where the money is spent. Automated systems quickly keep track of these behaviors and notify customers when there are any abnormalities from the trends.[28] However, the methods by which cybercriminals and other hackers infiltrate payment and information systems all across the internet are also becoming increasingly sophisticated. It is often hard for the average consumer to spot malware or other viruses created by hackers, which can lead to unknowing participation in scams and significant monetary losses. As detailed in the media almost daily, consumers, companies, and governments alike are having difficulty keeping up with the fast pace of cybercriminal technology. Sometimes consumers and companies can become victims of online fraud without making a purchase from a personal computer or mobile device. Credit card transactions occur by means of the internet, even when a purchase is made in a physical location. Online fraud can include information as well as money. A flaw in the popular online video game Fortnite put its 200 million users at risk. Personal account information could be accessed, in-game currency could be purchased, and game chatter could be listened to by hackers because of

Internet Corporation for Assigned Names and Numbers (ICANN)
a nonprofit organization overseen by the U.S. Department of Commerce and charged with overseeing basic technical matters related to addresses on the internet

the data breach.[29] Consumers, government agencies, and merchants are exploring options, including regulation, to protect the security of online transactions.[30]

It is estimated that by the end of this decade, up to 500 billion items, including cars, household appliances such as refrigerators, and medical devices, will be connected to the internet.[31] The **Internet of Things (IoT)** extends connectivity to devices such as security systems and electric appliances to provide the ability to send and receive information over the internet. Connecting devices such as smartphones, tablets, and watches to the internet provides embedded technology to communicate and enhance the service experience. The IoT has the potential to greatly enhance our ability to perform activities and make devices more efficient, providing a disruptive transformation of how services were delivered over many decades. For instance, a doctor with smart medical devices can monitor patients from far away. SAS, an analytics company, has developed Visual Analytics software, which allows anyone approved to explore data and find answers through collaboration to examine service dilemmas. The IoT allows voice assistants to answer questions and perform tasks and services. Wi-Fi providing connections to a variety of devices, including wearables, will have a tremendous impact on business.[32]

On the other hand, with cybersecurity risks increasing, many are worried that criminals will use these connections to sabotage or hack into devices. Just as a hacker hacks into a computer. For example, a criminal might be able to hack into a smart car. The risks are even worse than accessing personal information (as bad as that is) because hacking into a smart car or smart medical device could endanger lives. Technology firms such as Cisco and IBM are setting up consortiums to identify innovative ways to prevent these attacks. They believe that the sharing of information will help alert both people and companies to risks, prompting them to take action to prevent cybercrimes before they strike.[33]

Internet of Things (IoT)
the connectivity of devices such as security systems and electric appliances to provide the ability to send and receive information over the internet

Privacy

The extraordinary growth of the internet has generated issues related to privacy. As instances of hacking become more commonplace and severe, consumers are realizing the responsibility that they have to protect their own privacy. However, while a large percentage of online shoppers are concerned about their privacy, many are not taking appropriate measures to protect their information. This is largely a result of consumers feeling like the problem is beyond their control. Figure 11.2 illustrates the top privacy concerns for consumers.

Figure 11.2 Top Privacy Concerns for Consumers

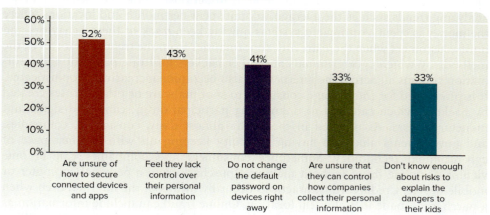

Source: Adapted from Gary Davis, "Key Findings from Our Survey on Identity Theft, Family Safety, and Home Network Security," McAfee, January 2, 2018, https://securingtomorrow.mcafee.com/consumer/key-findings-from-our-survey-on-identity-theft-family-safety-and-home-network-security/ (accessed June 28, 2019).

Because of the ease of access to personal information, however, unauthorized use of this information may occur.[34] Information can be collected on the internet with or without a person's knowledge. Many websites track users' actions by storing "cookies," or identifying strings of text, on their computers, which permit website operators to track how often a user visits the site, what he or she looks at while there, and in what sequence. Cookies also allow website visitors to customize services, such as virtual shopping carts, as well as the particular content they see when they log on to a webpage. There are benefits to cookies, such as making shopping more convenient and customizable. However, if a website operator can exploit cookies to link a visitor's interests to a name and address, that information could be sold to advertisers and other parties without the visitor's consent or knowledge. The potential for misuse has left many consumers uncomfortable with this technology.[35]

Identity theft, the access and theft of personal information, is a top crime in the nation, with more than 400,000 identity theft complaints submitted to the Federal Trade Commission (FTC) annually. Fraud is another major type of misconduct. The most common types of theft include credit card fraud, tax fraud, phone or utility fraud, and bank fraud.[36] **Identity fraud** is defined as the use of someone's personal information to access money online. More than 16 million individuals are affected by identity theft, resulting in more than $16 billion stolen each year. Nearly 60 million Americans have been affected.[37] Data breaches, like the one that Fortnite experienced, are the most common source of identity theft and identity fraud. Internal data breaches are also becoming a problem. It is estimated that 28 percent of attacks on organizations come from within the organization.[38] New tools are being developed that can be used to analyze the language in employee emails and flag anything that seems suspicious or indicates that the employee is unhappy. However, this too generates privacy concerns, as employees may not realize that the language in their emails is being examined.

Nearly all internet websites and services require users to register and provide information about themselves to access some or all of their content. How this information is used is generating concern. The Chinese telecommunications company Huawei, which holds 16 percent of the smartphone market, has been a target of growing concern around privacy. Many countries worry that Huawei's products and services could be used to spy on their citizens and enable cyberattacks. Its smartphones were banned by networks including AT&T and Verizon, and the United States and Australia have blacklisted the company from providing equipment for 5G networks. The ban has negatively affected U.S. companies (like Intel) that are suppliers for Huawei.[39] A variety of organizations have been collecting and storing information on consumers for years and are now able to see trends and behaviors. This information is valuable to companies that want to better target people's buying behaviors and interests, and it is becoming a multibillion-dollar industry. For example, Facebook generates revenue by selling access to its users by using data to better target advertising efforts, while Barclays sells anonymized customer data to third parties. Because there are no current regulations regarding the selling of customer information, many people are concerned about the practice.[40]

Privacy issues related to children are generating even more debate, as well as laws to protect children's interests. The **Children's Online Privacy Protection Act (COPPA)** in the United States prohibits websites and internet providers from seeking personal information from children under age 13 without parental consent.[41] The law was recently amended to protect children's privacy in using social media sites and mobile devices. However, issues still exist. Instagram received criticism for not verifying the age of its users, effectively allowing children under the age of 13 to join the site. Facebook and Instagram announced they would more proactively lock the accounts of users suspected to be under the age requirement. They will require users to provide proof of age to regain access, though they still do not require proof of age up front.[42] Instagram is an incredibly popular app among

identity theft
the access and theft of personal information, leading to identity fraud

identity fraud
the use of someone's personal information to access money online

Children's Online Privacy and Protection Act (COPPA)
a U.S. law which prohibits websites and internet providers from seeking personal information from children under the age of 13 without parental consent

Table 11.3 Six Tips to Improve Child Safety on the Internet

1. Know what your children are doing online.
2. Get to know the technologies that your children are using.
3. Discuss the risks with your children and agree on rules for internet use.
4. Install an internet content filter.
5. Make sure that your children know not to share personal information or photos online.
6. Report inappropriate, harmful, or criminal activities that occur online or on a mobile device.

Source: "Protect Your Children," *Stay Smart Online,* http://www.staysmartonline.gov.au/home_users/protect_your_children (accessed July 14, 2014).

teens, and this concerns parents because their children are posting pictures of themselves and their friends, along with the locations they frequent. This can make them vulnerable to predators or create other dangerous situations. Parents are calling for tighter company controls and monitoring of user ages.[43] Table 11.3 provides recommendations for improving child safety on the internet.

Some measure of protection for personal privacy is already provided by the U.S. Constitution, as well as Supreme Court rulings and federal laws (see Table 11.4). The FTC also regulates, enforces privacy standards, and monitors websites to ensure compliance. Similar laws are coming into existence to address privacy issues resulting from mobile device use. The Location Privacy Protection Act addresses the use of GPS devices in the following areas: Companies are required to obtain users' permission before collecting location information, mobile apps created explicitly for stalking are prohibited, and companies that collect location information of more than 1,000 devices must post on their company website, the details of what is collected and how the data are used. These are just a few provisions of the law.[44]

Unsurprisingly, many other issues regarding mobile and internet privacy exist. For example, company privacy statements are often lengthy and filled with legal jargon that average consumers will not understand even if they take the time to read them (which they often don't). The FTC has set out some best practices for mobile companies to be more transparent. Some of these principles include creating "just-in-time" permission requests for the company to collect location, personal information, photos, and other information, and instituting a "Do Not Track" feature on devices and websites so the user has a choice as to the data being collected.[45] The commission has also addressed best practices for mobile payment security and children's use of mobile applications.[46] These best practices are important guidelines for companies to follow to avoid litigation and protect the privacy of customers.

General Data Protection Regulation (GDPR)
a European Union (EU) law that requires businesses to protect the personal data of EU citizens by standardizing laws and increasing privacy; U.S. organizations processing the data of individuals in the EU must comply with the regulation

International Initiatives on Privacy The European Union (EU) has made great strides in protecting the privacy of its citizens. The EU adopted the **General Data Protection Regulation (GDPR)**, a law that requires businesses to protect personal data of EU citizens. Its goal is to standardize data protection laws and increase privacy. The regulations require companies to ask consumers for permission to collect data and respond to consumer inquiries about data usage within 72 hours, placing the burden on companies to protect information about their users. This widely affected sites worldwide that service European consumers, causing companies to revise privacy policies and clean up cookie tracking. News sites decreased their third-party cookies by 22 percent, and consent banners increased by 16 percent. Fines for noncompliance could reach up to 4 percent of a company's revenue.[46] Google was fined €50 million by France for failure to comply. France's data protection regulator said that Google did not provide users with sufficient information regarding data consent policies, nor did it give users enough control over the company's use of their information.[47] Holding companies accountable will be critical in enforcing GDPR. Microsoft, a critic of U.S. privacy legislation, says that the United States should follow in the EU's footsteps. Many countries, including Brazil, China, India, Japan, South Korea, and Thailand, already have.[48]

In Canada, private industry has taken the lead in creating and developing privacy policies through the Direct Marketing Association of Canada (DMAC). The DMAC's policies resulted in the proposal of legislation to protect personal privacy. The Personal Information Protection and Electronic Documents Act (PIPEDA) established a right of personal privacy for information collected by Canadian

Table 11.4 Privacy Laws

Act (Date Enacted)	Purpose
Privacy Act (1974)	Requires federal agencies to adopt minimum standards for collecting and processing personal information; limits the disclosure of such records to other public or private parties; requires agencies to make records on individuals available to them on request, subject to certain conditions.
Right to Financial Privacy Act (1978)	Protects the rights of financial institution customers to keep their financial records private and free from unjust government investigation.
Computer Security Act (1987)	Brought greater confidentiality and integrity to the regulation of information in the public realm by assigning responsibility for the standardization of communication protocols, data structures, and interfaces in telecommunications and computer systems to the National Institute of Standards and Technology (NIST), which also announced security and privacy guidelines for federal computer systems.
Computer Matching and Privacy Protection Act (1988)	Amended the Privacy Act by adding provisions regulating the use of computer matching, the computerized comparison of individual information for purposes of determining eligibility for federal benefits programs.
Video Privacy Protection Act (1988)	Specifies the circumstances under which a business that rents or sells videos can disclose personally identifiable information about a consumer or reveal an individual's video rental or sales records.
Telephone Consumer Protection Act (1991)	Regulates the activities of telemarketers by limiting the hours during which they can solicit residential subscribers, outlawing the use of artificial or prerecorded voice messages to residences without prior consent, prohibiting unsolicited advertisements by telephone facsimile machines, and requiring telemarketers to maintain a "do not call list" of any consumers who request not to receive further solicitations from them.
Driver Privacy Protection Act (1993)	Restricts the circumstances under which state departments of motor vehicles may disclose personal information about any individual obtained by the department in connection with a motor vehicle record.
Fair Credit Reporting Act (amended in 1997)	Promotes accuracy, fairness, and privacy of information in the files of consumer reporting agencies (e.g., credit bureaus); grants consumers the right to see their personal credit reports, to find out who has requested access to their reports, to dispute any inaccurate information with the consumer reporting agency, and to have inaccurate information corrected or deleted.
Children's Online Privacy Protection Act (COPPA) (amended in 2013)	Regulates the online collection of personally identifiable information (name, address, email address, hobbies, interests, or information collected through cookies) from children under age 13 by specifying what a website operator must include in a privacy policy, when and how to seek consent from a parent, and what responsibilities an operator has to protect children's privacy and safety online.
General Data Protection Regulation (GDPR)* (2016)	Regulates the collection and use of private data of individuals in the EU regardless of a company's location; provides guidelines around how companies can process, store, and protect personal data; requires companies to report data breaches to affected individuals within 72 hours of detection and obtain consent of subjects of data processing.

Note: Though GDPR is a European regulation, U.S. organizations processing data of individuals in the EU must comply.
Sources: "Computer Matching and Privacy Protection Act," Internal Revenue Service, http://www.irs.gov/irm/part11/irm_11-003-039.html (accessed July 1, 2019); "United States Privacy Laws," *Information Shield*, http://www.informationshield.com/usprivacylaws.html (accessed July 14, 2014).

Ethical Responsibilities in **TECHNOLOGY**

Block Party: Blockchain Technology Expands

Advances in technology lead to new developments across industries. While some developments create convenience for businesses and consumers, others raise serious concerns about privacy and protection of digital property. Technology has made it possible to collect, share, and sell vast quantities of personal information, often without consumers' knowledge, leading to major privacy concerns. Blockchain has been proposed as a solution to digital fraud and privacy breaches in various industries.

The innovative uses of blockchain are becoming so significant to society that Congress has received a bill, the Blockchain Promotion Act of 2018, requesting the development of a federal definition of what constitutes blockchain and its technology. While this is still in progress, a working definition of blockchain could be that it is a decentralized technology that stores an immutable record of data blocks over time. The storage of information allows for record keeping while respecting the privacy of the individual users. No personally identifying data are recorded. Instead, a "digital signature" is used for each participant in the blockchain. The fact that the system is not centralized affords less chance of cyberattacks and more equitable treatment of users involved in the blockchain. This is important as society works together to increase technological innovation and create responsible boundaries for its use.

One industry using blockchain is the medical field. Medical fraud is costly and highly detrimental to society. The source of medical fraud stems from individuals who destroy or manipulate medical records. With blockchain, that manipulation of data cannot easily occur due to the inability of hackers to alter data after they have been recorded. Medical records, therefore, remain in their original form. Although there is a slight chance that hacking of the documents could still occur, it would be a very labor-intensive cyberattack, which companies believe will strongly deter fraudsters. Blockchain also tracks when data is recorded, who recorded the data, and each place that the medical record has gone. This information allows investigators to target the source of fraud.

Another area where blockchain could be beneficial is voting. The data that blockchain stores are not kept in one place, but rather many places, which all support each other. This allows any transaction to be virtually free of corruption or alteration. This new technology could benefit the voting process by providing more security. The process could be transitioned online, and officials would be able to identify each vote, effectively cutting down on lost votes or fake votes. Along with increasing the privacy and security of votes, blockchain would reduce corruption and errors. It would streamline the voting process, helping increase voter turnout and providing a faster way to do a recount when fraud is suspected. All of these aspects of blockchain would benefit society and corporate social responsibility (CSR) by increasing the transparency, accountability, and productivity of the voting process. In the highly charged political environment in the United States and worldwide, particularly on election days, the use of blockchain could provide greater unity of the citizenry.

Another popular area to use blockchain is in food safety. For example, Walmart has said that it will use blockchain to track lettuce and spinach products from farm to store in order to assist in disease detection during food contamination incidents. The Walmart China Traceability Platform uses blockchain to provide product information relating to food safety to customers. The goal is to have half of the packaged meats and vegetables sold by Walmart on the platform within a year.

Blockchain offers many opportunities for businesses and society to utilize technology in improving consumer goods and services. According to Michael Casey, coauthor of *The Truth Machine*, blockchain is significant because "record keeping is at the heart of how societies go through the process of figuring out how to trust each other to enter into economic exchange." As trust and transparency continue to be major issues in society, incorporating blockchain into business transactions could benefit all stakeholders.

Sources: Tyler Wetzel, "What Is a Blockchain? A Consensus-Based Definition of 'Blockchain' to Be Used by the U.S. Congress," *Medium*, October 10, 2018, https://medium.com/@twwetzel76/a-blockchain-is-a-digital-mechanism-capable-of-not-only-storing-data-and-information-but-also-2458403252a5 (accessed July 22, 2019); Adrian Zmudzinski, "US Senate Committee Approves the Blockchain Promotion Act," *Cointelegraph*, https://cointelegraph.com/news/us-senate-committee-approves-the-blockchain-promotion-act (accessed July 22, 2019); Kayla Matthews, "How Blockchain Technology Could Help Prevent Medical Fraud," *HIT Consultant*, July 10, 2018, https://hitconsultant.net/2018/07/10/blockchain-technology-medical-fraud/#.XRp0MOhKiUk (accessed July 23, 2019); Joe Liebkind, "How Blockchain Technology Can Prevent Voter Fraud," *Investopedia*, June 25, 2019 (updated), https://www.investopedia.com/news/how-blockchain-technology-can-prevent-voter-fraud/ (accessed July 23, 2019); Blockgeeks, "What Is Blockchain Technology?" YouTube, November 5, 2018, https://www.youtube.com/watch?v=27nS3p2i_3g (accessed July 22, 2019); Luke Fortney, "Blockchain Explained," *Investopedia*, June 25, 2019 (updated), https://www.investopedia.com/terms/b/blockchain.asp (accessed July 22, 2019); Michael Corkery and Nathaniel Popper, "From Farm to Blockchain: Walmart Tracks Its Lettuce," *The New York Times*, September 24, 2018, https://www.nytimes.com/2018/09/24/business/walmart-blockchain-lettuce.html (accessed July 22, 2019); Chris Duckett, "Walmart China Turns to Blockchain for Food Safety," CBS Interactive, June 26, 2019, https://www.zdnet.com/article/walmart-china-turns-to-blockchain-for-food-safety/ (accessed July 23, 2019).

businesses and organizations. The law instituted rules governing the collection, use, and disclosure of personal information in the private sector. It also works in conjunction with other legislation that protects personal information collected by federal and/or provincial governments. The Canadian Standards Association (CSA) was also instrumental in bringing about privacy protection guidelines in Canada. The CSA Model Code for the Protection of Personal Information requires organizations to protect personal information and to allow individuals access to their own personal information, allowing for correction if necessary.[49]

In Japan, the Ministry of International Trade and Industry established the Electronic Network Consortium (ENC) to resolve issues associated with the internet. The ENC (which comprises 93 organizations) has prepared guidelines for protecting personal data gathered by Japanese online service providers. These guidelines require websites to obtain an individual's consent before collecting personal data or using or transferring such data to a third party. The guidelines also call for organizations to appoint managers who understand the ENC guidelines to oversee the collection and use of personal data and to utilize privacy information management systems.[50] In 2003, Japan adopted the **Act on the Protection of Personal Information (APPI)**, one of Asia's first data protection regulations, which is still in place today. APPI applies to all businesses that service individuals in Japan, whether the company is based in Japan or not. Businesses are required to disclose how personal data is being used and correct, suspend, or delete personal data if requested to do so by a user.[51] The act is reviewed every three years to ensure that the rules are sufficient as technology evolves. In the wake of the EU's GDPR regulations, Japan put additional safeguards in place to protect data transferred from the EU. The EU and Japan officially and publicly recognized each other's systems as adequate, allowing personal data to be shared between the two.[52]

Protection of citizens' privacy on the internet is not a major public concern in Russia. For many years, internet activity was largely left unmonitored, and citizens and companies were able to do what they wanted with data. However, the Russian parliament passed legislation requiring internet companies to store Russian users' data within the country's borders. The country will put restrictions on how the companies can use the data if they do not comply with these storage measures, and will most likely ask them to stop doing business in the country. In addition, the government granted itself the authority to block websites. In conjunction with this law, another one, deemed the "bloggers law," requires influential bloggers (defined as those whose sites are visited more than 3,000 times per day) to register with the state. This limits the number of outspoken writers who previously were able to voice their opinions anonymously, without fear. While the government claims to be doing this for the sake of protecting people's privacy, ensuring national security, and protecting against piracy, many conclude that it is for the purpose of controlling and censoring free speech.[53] Russia implemented what is widely called the "Big Brother" data law, which requires telecom providers to store details of text messages, phone calls, and chat activity on behalf of Russian intelligence services for at least six months. The law greatly limits the privacy of Russian citizens and places a financial burden on the companies which have to foot the bill to house these large amounts of data.[54]

Privacy Officers and Certification Businesses are beginning to recognize that the only way to circumvent further government regulation with respect to privacy is to develop systems and policies to protect consumers' interests.

In addition to creating and posting policies regarding the gathering and use of personal information, more companies—including American Express, AT&T, and Citigroup—employ a **chief privacy officer (CPO)**. The **International Association of Privacy Professionals (IAPP)** was established as a result of this movement and is responsible for developing and launching the first broad-based credentialing

Act on the Protection of Personal Information (APPI) Japanese data regulation stipulating that all businesses servicing individuals in Japan, whether based in Japan or not, are required to disclose how personal data is being used and correct, suspend, or delete data if requested by a user

chief privacy officer (CPO) high-level executives who are given broad powers to establish policies to protect consumer privacy and, in so doing, protect their companies from negative publicity and legal scrutiny

International Association of Privacy Professionals (IAPP) U.S. group responsible for developing and launching the first broad-based credentialing program in information privacy

Certified Information Privacy Professional (CIPP)

an information privacy credential from the International Association of Privacy Professionals (IAPP)

program in information privacy. This program is known as the **Certified Information Privacy Professional (CIPP)**. Most healthcare-related businesses must appoint a privacy official to safeguard patient data. High-level executives are typically given broad powers to establish policies to protect consumer privacy and, in so doing, to protect their companies from negative publicity and legal scrutiny. Table 11.5 lists the major provisions of the FTC's Fair Information Practices, which can be used as a starting point in developing a corporate privacy policy.

Data privacy management platforms, like TrustArc, have stepped in to help companies develop privacy policies. TrustArc is a for-profit organization devoted to promoting global trust in internet technology by providing a standardized, third-party oversight program that addresses the privacy concerns of consumers, website operators, and government regulators. Companies that agree to abide by TrustArc's privacy standards may display a TRUSTe certification badge on their websites. These firms must disclose their personal information collection and privacy policies in a straightforward privacy statement. TrustArc is supported by a network of corporate, industry, and nonprofit sponsors.[55]

Intellectual Property

intellectual property

the ideas and creative materials developed to solve problems, carry out applications, educate, and entertain others

In addition to protecting personal privacy, many are concerned about protecting their rights to property they create, including songs, movies, books, and software. Such **intellectual property** consists of the ideas and creative materials developed to solve problems, carry out applications, educate, and entertain others. It is the result, or end product, of the creative process. Intellectual property is most commonly protected by patents and copyrights; however, technological advancements are increasingly challenging the ownership of such property. Online advertising is one of these challenging areas, as Google has experienced. The company has been sued by several companies regarding the selling of trademarked keywords in Google AdWords. For instance, Rosetta Stone filed a lawsuit against Google for allowing other companies—including competitors—to purchase Rosetta Stone's trademarked names to use as key search words. These keyword searches would generate "sponsored links" advertisements on search results webpages. The two companies eventually reached a settlement.[56] While this may be considered a general competitive practice, intellectual property protections complicate the matter and require clear guidelines that internet firms can follow when dealing with this issue.

Intellectual property losses in the United States total more than $300 billion a year in lost revenue from the illegal copying of computer programs, movies,

Table 11.5 Fair Information Practice Principles

Notice	Websites would be required to provide consumers clear and conspicuous notice of their information practices, including what information they collect, how they collect it, how they use it, how they provide Choice, Access, and Security to consumers, whether they disclose the information collected to other entities, and whether other entities are collecting information through the site.
Choice	Websites would be required to offer consumers choices as to how their personal identifying information is used beyond the purpose for which the information was provided. Such choice would encompass both internal secondary uses and external secondary uses.
Access	Websites would be required to offer consumers reasonable access to the information that a Web site has collected about them, including a reasonable opportunity to review information and to correct inaccuracies or delete information.
Security	Websites would be required to take reasonable steps to protect the security of the information they collect from consumers.

Source: Federal Trade Commission, "Privacy Online: Fair Information Practices in the Electronic Marketplace," May 2000, https://www.ftc.gov/reports/privacy-online-fair-information-practices-electronic-marketplace-federal-trade-commission (accessed June 30, 2019).

TV shows, and books. Such losses also relate to stolen business plans, customer-related information, basic research reports, manufacturing process plans, product specifications, and many other proprietary documents. Intellectual property and other intangible assets typically represent about 70 percent of a company's value and source of revenue creation. Some experts estimate that companies lose several billions of dollars in proprietary information and intellectual property each year through a variety of channels. Most cases involve one of the following scenarios:

1. **Inadvertent actions by current or former employees,** such as oral seminar presentations, discussions at an exhibit booth, and electronically misdirected fax and/or email.
2. **Deliberate actions by current or former employees,** such as unauthorized physical access to information and deliberate disclosure to unauthorized parties.
3. **Deliberate actions by individuals/entities in trusted relationships other than employee relationships,** such as the exploitation of vendor-client relationships, subcontractor knowledge, joint ventures, and other relationships.
4. **Deliberate actions or activities by outsiders—those without a trusted relationship,** such as data mining of open-source data and public information and the practice of hiring away employees and placing them in a position where they must use trade secrets from a former employer.[57]

This issue has become a global concern because of disparities in enforcement of laws throughout the world. For example, a report by the Commission on the Theft of American Intellectual Property (IP Commission) revealed an instance wherein an American software company's software was downloaded illegally onto 30 million Chinese computers—a multibillion-dollar infraction.[58] The Business Software Alliance says that 37 percent of software installed on computers worldwide is unlicensed. This is particularly concerning because malware attacks occur more frequently with unlicensed software. It is estimated that malware from unlicensed software cost companies $359 million annually.[59] Russia and China are the two worst countries in terms of piracy violations. It is predicted that the trade-related aspects of intellectual property rights disputes will make countries more accountable for adhering to copyright standards.[60]

Microsoft has been particularly aggressive in battling software piracy. In one year alone, the company settled 3,265 cases related to copyright infringement worldwide. Only 35 of these cases took place in the United States, while 3,230 were international cases encompassing 42 other countries. The company's efforts to stamp out piracy have been facilitated by customers reporting the illegal activity. Microsoft is working to transform the economics of the software business, allowing cheaper, more innovative software to be available for legitimate, paying customers, as well as some free online software options. Microsoft has even opened up a howtotell.com website for people to consult when loading software onto their computers. The website helps educate customers on how to tell if their software is genuine.[61]

U.S. copyright laws protect original works in text form, pictures, movies, computer software, musical multimedia, and audiovisual works. Owners of copyrights have the right to reproduce, derive from, distribute, and publicly display and perform the copyrighted works. **Copyright infringement** is the unauthorized execution of the rights reserved by a copyright holder. Congress passed the Digital Millennium Copyright Act (DMCA) in 1998 to protect copyrighted materials on the internet and to limit the liability of online service providers. The DMCA provides a "safe harbor" provision that limits judgments that can be levied against these providers for copyright infringement by their customers. To limit their liability, service providers must pay a nominal fee and comply with the Act's reporting requirements.[62]

copyright infringement
the unauthorized execution of the rights reserved by a copyright holder

cybersquatter
an individual who deliberately registers web addresses that match or relate to other firms' trademarks and then attempts to sell the registration to the trademark owners

Digital copyright violations are not always clear cut and often involve lengthy lawsuits that can progress all the way to the higher courts. A Supreme Court ruling declared that copyright holders can file a lawsuit only when the U.S. Copyright Office registers a copyright, which could make it more difficult to fight piracy. On average it takes the office six to nine months to process a copyright claim.[63] Table 11.6 provides additional facts about copyrights.

The internet has created other copyright issues for some organizations that have found that the web addresses or Uniform Resource Locators (URLs) of other online firms either match or are very similar to their own trademarks. In some cases, **cybersquatters** have deliberately registered domain names that match or relate to other firms' trademarks and then have attempted to sell the registration to the trademark owners. A number of companies, including Taco Bell, Management and Training Corporation, and KFC, have paid thousands of dollars to gain control of names that match or parallel company trademarks.[64] Registering a domain name involves filling out an online form to automatically reserve a domain name. This process makes it easy for cybersquatters or other scammers to defraud businesses and consumers. The Federal Trademark Dilution Act of 1995 and the Anti-Cybersquatting Consumer Protection Act of 1999 were enacted to help companies resolve this conflict. The laws give trademark owners the right to protect their trademarks, prevent the use of trademark-protected entities by others, and require cybersquatters to relinquish trademarked names.[65] However, this does not always hold up in foreign countries that do not have strict intellectual property laws. More than 3,400 cases of cybersquatting are reported annually from 109 countries.[66]

ICANN, the nonprofit organization charged with overseeing basic technical matters related to addresses on the internet, has had success, including the introduction of a competitive domain registrar and registration market and the Uniform Dispute Resolution Policy (UDRP).[67] Many trademark holders immediately turn to the UDRP as a vehicle for combatting cybersquatters. However, remedies available in federal court under the Anti-Cybersquatting Consumer Protection Act may better protect the rights of trademark holders. All ICANN-authorized registrars of TLDs must agree to abide by the UDRP. Under the terms of the UDRP, a domain

Table 11.6 Facts About Copyrights

- No registration is required to acquire copyright ownership of original works. No registration is required to place copyright notice on works (i.e., © Year Name of Owner). (No "innocent infringers" if there is notice on the work.) Copyright registration is required before a lawsuit may be brought.

- Works in public domain are free to use. The copyright duration may have expired, the creator of works may have relinquished his or her rights, or it may not be copyright protectable.

- An exception for seeking copyright permission to use a work, called the "fair use doctrine," involves weighing four factors (see US Copyright Office Publication) and the use of a work for criticism, comment, news reporting, teaching, scholarship, research, or parody.

- The "right of first sale" occurs when an owner of a copyrighted work sells a copy of it; the new owner does not now possess the copyright but can sell the copy or give it away without the copyright owner's permission.

- Derivative works are works that are derived from other copyrighted sources or works. With the exception of works that fall under the "fair use doctrine," derivative works cannot be sold without permission from the original copyright holders.

- Courts consider remedies for copyright infringement of one work in the range of $750 (for innocent infringers) up to $150,000 for intentional, willful violations. Remedies can go up or down, depending upon whether the copyright violation was intentional or not.

Source: Derived and paraphrased with permission from Willow Misty Parks, © Copyrights and Businesses, Microsoft PowerPoint presentation on UNM Daniels Fund Ethics Initiative website, http://danielsethics.mgt.unm.edu/teaching-resources/presentations.asp (accessed June 22, 2016); "U.S. Copyright Office," http://copyright.gov.

name will be transferred between parties only by agreement between them or by order of a court of competent jurisdiction or a UDRP-authorized dispute resolution provider.[68]

Because ICANN is overseen by the U.S. Department of Commerce, leaders in other countries have begun to question whether the United States has too much control over the internet. Under the philosophy that the internet is out of the domain of any one government, these leaders present several concerns. First, ICANN controls the master root file that provides users with access to the internet. Some countries have threatened to develop a competing master root file, which would create parallel internets. China has already developed a competing file and is encouraging other countries to join its effort. Second, ICANN has the power to affect selective parts of the internet. For example, the organization temporarily delayed the adoption of the .xxx TLD for adult content because of pressure from U.S. government agencies.[69] Third, because ICANN is a private corporation performing a significant public service, critics point to lack of transparency and effectiveness in its operations and decisions. Finally, some leaders worry that ICANN will serve as a social and cultural gatekeeper because all new TLD names and other requests must be approved by ICANN. The debate over governance of the internet is related to a number of significant issues, including intellectual property, privacy, security, and other top-level concerns of the public and government.[70]

Artificial Intelligence

Artificial Intelligence (AI) is a rapidly changing area. As discussed in Chapter 1, AI is the concept of machines learning and performing tasks that typically require human intelligence by using algorithms. An **algorithm** is a set of rules providing a procedure or formula for problem solving. For example, algorithms are behind search engines like Google, which take inputs of information and provide an output for a task or decision. In computing, it is step-by-step directions for an outcome. AI's enablers include blockchain, drones, robotics, and other technology. Big data enabled by AI provides massive files of structured and unstructured data that can be used with sophisticated software for decision-making. See Figure 11.3 to understand AI's relationship to its enablers.

algorithm
a set of rules providing a procedure or formula for problem solving

While AI offers many benefits, there are many ethical concerns about how the technology is used. *Ethics* relates to decisions about challenging issues in any organization. AI must be programmed with ethical decision-making abilities and parameters. Ethics in AI is different because machines cannot internalize human principles and values at this point of development. For example, there is growing concerns about the accuracy of facial recognition software. Axion Enterprise, which supplies body cameras to law enforcement agencies, announced that it would not use that type of software on its devices. Many fear the technology could falsely identify minorities and women and be used for the intrusive surveillance of citizens.[71] Businesses must consider public safety, security, and cultural

Figure 11.3 Distinguishing AI from Its Associated Enablers

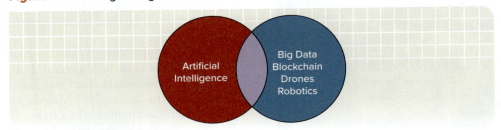

Source: © O. C. Ferrell 2019.

human decisions and be careful not to cause harm to society by using technology inappropriately.[72]

machine learning
a subset of AI that explains the application of AI using algorithms and data in order to allow the computer to learn without being programmed for a specific task

Machine learning, a subset of AI, explains the application of AI using algorithms and data in order to allow the computer to learn without being programmed for a specific task. For example, Spotify uses machine learning to curate a user's music discovery experience based on music the user has listened to on the site. **Deep learning**, a subset of machine learning, simulates how humans learn from experience by using algorithms that relate to the structure and function of the brain. While machine learning models require guidance, deep learning models can determine the accuracy of its work. For example, Google's AlphaGo computer program learned to play an abstract board game called Go by playing against professional players without being told what moves to make.[73] Exploring the ethical impact becomes increasingly important as AI systems become more complex.

deep learning
a subset of AI that simulates how humans learn from experience by using algorithms that relate to the structure and function of the brain

Big Data   Big data, introduced earlier in this chapter, refers to massive amounts of data transmitted at fast speeds. It includes consumer shopping behavior, preferences, liked content on social media, web browsing history, and much more. It is estimated that each person generates 1.7 MB of data every second. Businesses must use advanced software to interpret the data and effectively respond to the insights. Parsing data can be a difficult, labor-intensive task that requires highly skilled workers, creating a burden for companies with limited resources. AI algorithms can rapidly and efficiently process data in a way that humans cannot, enabling businesses to analyze larger data sets in a more meaningful way and make better, more informed decisions.[74] Instagram uses big data and AI to power its explore page and search function, improve targeted advertising, filter spam, and more.[75]

Blockchain   Blockchain is an important enabler for AI because blockchain information systems can overcome biased or inaccurate data. Blockchain is a decentralized record-keeping technology that stores an immutable record of data "blocks" (or ledgers) over time. The distinguishing feature is a limited block of ordered transactions with rules about how the data goes into the database. Most important, the data is locked into the system without a central control. Businesses are looking to this technology to create information that is open yet secure, protecting the interest of both businesses and consumers. There is almost no opportunity for biased, inaccurate, or altered data to get into the systems. Blockchain enables AI to access high-integrity data, improving business systems.[76]

Shutterstock/Sunday Photography

Walmart is using blockchain to trace products from their source to the retail store. Produce from farms can be accurately traced through the supply chain to consumers.[77] For example, if a food safety issue occurred with a produce item, blockchain could potentially track individual items not only to specific farms, but also the exact location where the item was planted. This quality and speed of traceability should be used for the benefit of society.

Blockchain information systems that provide an audit trail will protect both consumers and businesses from fraud and provide accurate, accessible records of transactions. Blockchain works extremely well for medical records because healthcare providers have a low risk tolerance when it comes to the management of electronic medical records. It could potentially be the best solution to help make sure that healthcare providers' medical records are accurate, tamperproof, and anonymous. The result is that healthcare service providers can trust data used for medical treatment.[78] Blockchain technology should be used for the common good. Congress is seeking to define blockchain in order to guide government regulations on the technology. Corporate governance will be critical as blockchain applications becomes more complex.[79] By addressing concerns about the impact of technology on society, firms positively contribute to society through socially responsible activities, as well as increase its financial performance.

Drones Drones, unmanned aerial devices that can be programmed with AI, can be used to observe physical conditions, as well as human or even wildlife activities. From a societal perspective, drones can observe conditions that pose risks such as traffic patterns, wildfires, flooding conditions, and environmental conditions related to sustainability. For example, Miami-Dade Fire Rescue uses drone technology to help first responders during hurricanes.[80] In a retail environment, knowing in advance how many customers are in the store, when they entered the store, and the items being purchased could alert store management to the number of employees needed to assist in checkout to provide a smooth guest experience. Providing inspections in processing insurance claims could take a fraction of the time that it did in the past.[81] Any service that involves obtaining visual information to carry out service tasks can be enabled by drones. Caution will be needed to protect consumers' privacy in making visual observation of their behavior.

AI-enabled drones can reduce delivery time and costs by providing quick on-site delivery of products, saving businesses both time and money. Drone use will advance rapidly in areas like insurance, delivery services, outdoor entertainment events, and retail. Drones are also assisting in work that is being done in maritime and offshore services. In the United Kingdom, the Royal Navy uses drones to help identify any defects that its ships may have, allowing them to diagnose and repair these issues while at sea. This service is much faster and safer than if someone had to move around the ship to try and find any problems manually. Other examples include a drone checking an aircraft warning light tower for potential repairs or maintenance that must be completed. Currently, drones cannot do any of the repairs necessary, but the routine checkup portion is finished more quickly and safely. A great example of this is a drone called the Naviator. This drone was specifically designed to be able to fly or swim in all kinds of rough weather conditions. If a boat is experiencing a terrible storm but needs to gather critical information on its status, the Naviator can provide a safer alternative to sending a person to make a check.[82] As drone technology combined with AI develops, there will be many more applications.

Robotics Robots that carry out actions, movements, or tasks can perform human-like activities. They can be taught to perform custom tasks, to have interactive communication, and to provide interactions with customers.[83] In Canada, robots are used to help off-site doctors assess patients in remote northern communities to deliver care to vulnerable populations who lack access to robust medical facilities.[84] This could also be a sustainable and efficient way to support developing countries. AI-enabled robotics offer elements of intellectual ability and advance the creation of the human thought process with the ability to learn, reason, use language, and formulate original ideas through machine learning.

Retailers are developing robots to provide a personal experience. For example, Lowes has been developing a customer service robot, OSHbot, that can speak multiple languages and help customers locate items that they are looking for in their stores. Additionally, Best Buy has launched Chloe, a robot that will replace store workers by retrieving a requested item for customers. These "social robots" can provide consistent and higher-quality engagement.[85] While robots will undoubtedly eliminate jobs, they will also increase the need for workers skilled in the application of AI technologies. For example, Walmart uses autonomous robots to clean the floors using employee-created maps. Robotic automation used in this capacity also protects employee well-being by limiting exposure to dangerous chemicals. Employees are needed to set up the machines and perform basic maintenance tasks.[86]

AI has the ability to make decisions and take action. It is important to consider the values and decision parameters that go into drones, robots, and driverless cars. Does a driverless Uber vehicle prioritize the safety of the driver and passengers over a pedestrian? Businesses will need to implement processes to monitor and audit the technology in order to create accountability for decision-making.[87] Additional considerations include accidental or intentional discrimination, corporate intelligence, privacy, and intellectual property. Data used in AI should be unbiased.[88] For example, Facebook uses predictive analytics to predict the future browsing and shopping behavior of its users in its advertising program. Concerns around data privacy are high. This will require ethics components to be established both internally (i.e., programmed into the AI) and externally to guide decision-making and create checks and balances.[89] All of the risk areas associated with AI decisions have to be monitored and compared to the ethical expectations of the organization. This will require custom ethics codes that identify the risks associated with AI. Most organizations are governed by ethical values, codes, and compliance. The same will be required by AI and its enablers.

Health and Biotechnology

bioethics

the study of ethical issues in the fields of medical treatment and research, including medicine, nursing, law, philosophy, and theology

The advance of life-supporting technologies has raised a number of medical and health issues related to technology. **Bioethics** refers to the study of ethical issues in the fields of medical treatment and research, including medicine, nursing, law, philosophy, and theology, though medical ethics is also recognized today as a separate discipline.[90] All these fields have been influenced by rapid changes in technology that require new approaches to solving issues. Genetic technologies have shown promise in giving medical ethics an even greater role in social decision-making. For example, the Human Genome Project, a program to decode the entire human genetic map, identified a number of genes that may contribute to particular diseases or traits.

Because so many of our resources are spent on healthcare, the role of the private sector in determining the quality of healthcare is an important consideration to society. The pharmaceutical industry, for example, has been sharply criticized by politicians, healthcare organizations, and consumers because of escalating drug costs. Investigators from federal and state agencies all over the nation have initiated legal action over allegations that Medicare and Medicaid overpaid for drugs by $1 billion or more a year.[91] On the other hand, pharmaceutical companies claim that the development of new lifesaving drugs and tests requires huge expenditures in R&D. It is projected that the annual cost for popular name-brand bioethics drugs will double every seven to eight years.[92] The pharmaceutical industry is among the most profitable in the United States; it spends billions each year in marketing, including drug samples provided to doctors, advertising in medical journals, and other strategies. More than $6 billion is spent by the pharmaceutical industry on direct-to-consumer (DTC) advertising.[93] The visibility of pharmaceutical advertising and promotion prompted the Pharmaceutical Research and Manufacturers of America (PhRMA), an industry association, to develop its Guiding Principles on Direct-to-Consumer Advertising. The voluntary guidelines are designed to ensure that DTC advertising is accurate, accessible, and useful. Table 11.7 shows the preamble that accompanies the association's booklet on the guiding principles.

Table 11.7 Preamble to PhRMA Guiding Principles for Direct-to-Consumer Advertisements

Given the progress that continues to be made in society's battle against disease, patients are seeking more information about medical problems and potential treatments so they can better understand their healthcare options and communicate effectively with their physicians. An important benefit of direct-to-consumer (DTC) advertising is that it fosters an informed conversation about health, disease and treatments between patients and their healthcare practitioners.

A strong empirical record demonstrates that DTC communications about prescription medicines serve the public health by:

Increasing awareness about diseases;

Educating patients about treatment options;

Motivating patients to contact their physicians and engage in a dialogue about health concerns;

Increasing the likelihood that patients will receive appropriate care for conditions that are frequently under-diagnosed and under-treated; and

Encouraging compliance with prescription drug treatment regimens.

Source: Pharmaceutical Research and Manufacturers of America, "PhRMA Guiding Principles: Direct to Consumer Advertisements About Prescription Medicines," http://phrma-docs.phrma.org/files/dmfile/PhRMA_Guiding_Principles_2018.pdf (accessed June 30, 2019).

Biotechnology The biotechnology industry emerged over 40 years ago when Stanley Cohen and Herbert Boyer published a new recombinant deoxyribonucleic acid (DNA) technique, a method of making proteins, such as human insulin, in cultured cells under controlled manufacturing conditions. Boyer went on to cofound Genentech, which is one of the best-known biotechnology companies. From these insights, other scientists set out to map the human genome, a 13-year project to discover all of the estimated 20,000–25,000 human genes and make them accessible for further biological study. The ability to map the human genome has spurred over 250 new vaccines and medicines, and many more are being tested in product trials. These innovations are changing the way that cancer, diabetes, AIDS, arthritis, and multiple sclerosis are treated. Biotech innovations in other fields, such as manufacturing, have led to cleaner processes that produce less waste and use less energy and water. Most laundry detergents marketed in the United States contain biotechnology-based enzymes that combine better with bleach, are biodegradable, and reduce the need for hot water. Law enforcement officials use DNA fingerprinting, a biotech process, to catch criminals, increase conviction rates, and perform stronger investigations and forensic science.[94] There are over 1,300 biotechnology companies in the United States in a variety of sectors including health, agriculture, and industrial.[95] Finally, the biotechnology industry invests approximately $70 billion per year in R&D activities.[96]

The government and the private sector often partner with academic researchers and nonprofit institutes to develop new technologies in health and biotechnology. Research ranges from mapping the human genetic code to finding drugs that cure cancer to genetically modifying food products. Many of these collaborative efforts to improve health involve scientists, funded globally by a variety of sources. For example, the nonprofit Oro Valley Innovation Labs operates an incubator to support biotech start-ups by providing equipment and a sterile working environment. Using cell-engineering techniques, scientists may have found a way to generate unlimited supplies of brain cells for transplanting into patients with amyotrophic lateral sclerosis (ALS), Parkinson's disease, epilepsy, and stroke. Other advances have revealed ways to slow the progression of Alzheimer's disease and provide treatments for blindness.[97] These examples illustrate technology advances that could result in commercially viable products that save and/or prolong life.

Cloning, the replication of organisms that are genetically identical to the parent, has become a highly controversial topic in biotechnology and bioethics.

Human cloning has raised unanswered questions about the future of human reproduction. Since Scottish scientists first cloned Dolly the sheep, scientists have also successfully cloned mice, cows, pigs, goats, and cats but with mixed reports about the health of the cloned progeny. ViaGen Pets, which began as a livestock cloning company, now clones household pets for clients such as Barbra Streisand.[98] While cloning humans would appear to be the final step of scientific reproduction, indisputable proof of the first human clone will actually serve as a starting point for many years of research. Like in vitro fertilization, human clones will need to grow up before scientists know the effects that this process will have on a person's physical, mental, and emotional states.[99] Cloning has the potential to revolutionize the treatment of diseases and conditions such as Parkinson's disease and cancer. Stem cell technology has allowed doctors to create replacement organs, thereby restoring infected organs and lengthening human lives.[100] The ability to create and modify life processes is often generated through collaborative research involving businesses, universities, and government. The results of such research have already contributed to life-altering products of the future, and more progress is expected for years to come.

Despite the potential of this technology, many people have negative views about cloning. Some contend that it is unethical to "meddle with nature," whereas others believe that cloning is wrong because every time it is used to treat a patient, a cloned human embryo is destroyed. New processes in cloning and stem cell research have reduced the need for embryos because cells can be taken from consenting adults without invasive procedures. Nevertheless, ethical concerns continue.[101] The cloning of a miniature pig, Goldie, lacking both copies of a gene involved in immediate immune rejection has brought the prospect of transplanting pig organs into people a little closer. The small pig's organs are similar in size to those of humans, and the missing genes make the organs less likely to be rejected. But although Goldie's creation may have solved the problem of immediate transplant rejection, a slower rejection is still possible, in which the transplant is attacked by the recipient's white blood cells.[102] Some people argue that cloning of human beings should be banned, and several bills have been introduced in Congress and various state legislatures to do just that. Additionally, 19 European nations have signed an agreement prohibiting the genetic replication of humans. Harvesting stem cells from surplus in vitro fertilization (IVF) embryos is allowed by the Australian government, and the United Kingdom allows researchers to harvest stem cells from surplus IVF embryos and to conduct therapeutic cloning. In the past, the United States restricted federally funded researchers from pursuing therapeutic cloning or harvesting stem cells from discarded embryos. However, today the ban is lifted, allowing both public and private entities to conduct research.[103]

Genetic research holds the promise to revolutionize how many diseases are diagnosed and treated. However, consumer advocates urged the World Trade Organization (WTO) to place limits on gene patents, which they claim are tantamount to "ownership of life." As patents dealing with human DNA increased, worries about the limitations on ownership also increased. These worries came to the forefront of a Supreme Court decision that stated natural DNA cannot be patented as it does not fit within the characteristics of things that can be patented ("novel, useful, and non-obvious"), but complementary DNA (a copy of the original), also known as cDNA, can be patented. While this may seem a straightforward solution to the advocates' concerns, these definitions are not as distinct as they sound. There are times when cDNA contains components that are both natural and synthetic. Many other issues arise from patents relating to genetics, whether the genes in question belong to humans, animals, or even plants. For example, Monsanto has been involved in many lawsuits regarding the patents of their genetically modified (GM) seeds. As more discoveries are made in the field, more complexities in the realm of laws and ethics will be made manifest.[104]

A final concern with genetics is the increasing availability of DTC testing kits. With these kits, consumers can proactively manage their health, including gaining access to knowledge about predispositions to cancer, diseases, and illnesses. Most specialists agree that the results of such tests are best delivered in a professional medical setting, not via the internet or mail. A consumer could receive a positive finding on a DNA-based prostate cancer screening test through a mail-order kit and take measures to self-treat rather than consult a doctor. Other dangerous situations may ensue, as receiving the news of potentially having cancer is hard to hear. In addition, the result of the test may not be straightforward. For instance, the consumer may have cancerous growths that can be removed, cancer that has spread, or neither because the test is a false positive. Medical advice is warranted at this point because the consumer has no way of determining the appropriate course of action.

Genetically Modified Organisms   More than 800 million people around the world don't have enough to eat. Increasing food production to satisfy the growing demand for food without increasing land use will require farmers to achieve significant increases in productivity. **Genetically modified (GM) organisms** offer a way to quickly improve crop characteristics such as yield, pest resistance, or herbicide tolerance, often to a degree not possible with traditional methods. GM crops can be manipulated to produce completely artificial substances, from the precursors of plastics to consumable vaccines.[105] GM, or transgenic, crops are created when scientists introduce a gene from one organism to another. Scientists believe that GM crops could raise overall crop production in developing countries by as much as 25 percent.[106]

genetically modified (GM) organisms
organisms created through manipulating plant and animal DNA so as to produce a desired effect like resistance to pests and viruses, drought resistance, or high crop yield

But the idea that GM crops can significantly reduce world hunger is hotly debated. Some say it will make all the difference, while others point out issues with these claims. For example, a large population of the developing world suffers from hunger and malnourishment. A new development called "golden rice" is said to be high in vitamin A and can serve as a food source for these people. However, it has been noted that the "golden rice" will require fertilizer, pesticides, significant amounts of water, and corresponding irrigation systems that are too expensive for these areas. Further, because of the severe state of the populations' malnutrition, the vitamin A cannot be absorbed into their bodies.[107]

Others are concerned about potential health and environmental risks of GM foods. The European public has been known to call GM products "Frankenfood" out of the fear that it could pose a health threat or create an environmental disaster. It is presumed that genes may jump from GM crops to wild plants and reduce biodiversity or create superweeds. For a time, Europe held up approvals of U.S. exports of GM foods, until the European Parliament voted to require extensive labeling and traceability of food containing GM organisms. Only those foods that meet these standards are accepted into the EU. However, regulations still restrict the growing of GM crops. Over 20 years have passed since countries have begun growing GM crops all over the world, and there has not been significant evidence showing that these foods or the presence of crops are actually harmful. For this reason, many advocates, scientists, and others in the EU are pressing the regulatory agencies to rethink and update the GM crop and food laws to better reflect evidence-based research.[108]

Many people do not realize that some of the foods they eat are made from GM crops. Consumer groups are increasingly concerned that these foods could be unhealthy and harmful to the environment. The power of genetic modification techniques raises the possibility of human health, environmental, and economic problems, including unanticipated allergic responses to novel substances in foods, the spread of pest resistance or herbicide tolerance to wild plants, inadvertent toxicity to benign wildlife, and increasing control of agriculture by biotechnology

Table 11.8 Commercial Cultivation of GM Crops

Year	Hectares (Million)	Acres (Million)
1998	27.8	69.5
1999	39.9	98.6
2000	44.2	109.2
2001	52.6	130.0
2002	58.7	145.0
2003	67.7	167.2
2004	81.0	200.0
2005	90.0	222.0
2006	102.0	250.0
2007	114.3	282.0
2008	125.0	308.8
2009	134.0	335.0
2010	148.0	365.0
2011	160.0	395.0
2012	170.3	420.8
2013	175.2	433.2
2014	181.5	448.0
2015	179.7	444.0
2016	185.1	457.4
2017	189.8	469.0
TOTAL	**2,339.5**	**5,780.0**

Source: "Pocket K No. 16: Biotech Crop Highlights in 2017," *International Service for the Acquisition of Agri-Biotech Applications*, October 2018, http:// www.isaaa.org/resources/publications/pocketk/16/ (accessed June 30, 2019).

corporations.[109] Many consumers are boycotting products made from GM materials, and several countries have opposed trade in GM foods through the WTO. In addition, Japan has asked U.S. corn producers not to include GM corn in animal feed exported to Japan.[110] Insects and birds transport seeds from one field to the next, allowing cross-pollination that geneticists never intended. Unlike chemical or nuclear contamination, gene pollution can never be cleaned up. Advocates in the United States are urging regulators to mandate that GM foods be labeled. Vermont had already signed such a law into action. Under pressure from states, Congress passed a requirement for labeling products containing GM ingredients. However, in a blow to Vermont the new requirement, which supersedes its law, gives manufacturers years to comply and allows them the option to use straightforward language, digital codes, or symbols to indicate the presence of GM ingredients.[111] Table 11.8 demonstrates the millions of hectares that are being used to cultivate GM crops across the world.[112]

A number of companies have responded to public concerns about GM food products by limiting or avoiding their use altogether, while others have responded on the basis of transparency. Unilever and General Mills, for example, state on their websites that they are committed to following regulations regarding GM labeling, while at the same time maintaining their belief in the benefits of GM products to alleviate hunger and reduce the amounts of energy and water needed to maintain traditional crops. They also state that their organic product lines will be packaged with non-GM labels as appropriate. Whole Foods Market and Allegro Coffee, on the other hand, are committed to mandatory GM labeling. Whole Foods ensures all GM products are labeled in their Canada and U.S. stores, while Allegro Coffee has many products approved by the Non-GMO Project, and several others in the process of being approved.[113]

Ethical questions about the use of some types of GM products have also been raised. For example, Monsanto and other companies had begun developing so-called terminator technology to create plants that are genetically engineered to produce sterile seeds. Other plants in development will require spraying with chemicals supplied by the seed companies to produce desired traits, such as resistance to certain pests or disease. Farmers say the issue isn't the technology itself but, rather, who controls the technology—in most cases, the multinational seed companies. In response to global concerns about this issue, Monsanto halted their commercial development of the terminator technology.[114]

Control over who owns the seeds after purchase continues to be an issue with GM crops. In one case, Indiana soybean farmer Vernon Hugh Bowman purchased seeds from Monsanto and continued to use them for eight seasons. When Monsanto discovered this, they sued Bowman for patent infringement. The court ruled in favor of Monsanto, and some worry that the incident would renew interest in terminator technology so companies can further protect their patents.[115]

Defenders of biotechnology say consumer health fears about GM foods have not been substantiated by research.[116] As the U.S. agriculture industry is eager to point out, the technology has been a big success: it has reduced the amount of pesticides that farmers have had to spray on their cornfields, with happy consequences for the environment and human health. U.S. health regulators have not been able to find anything wrong with eating *Bacillus thuringiensis (Bwt)* corn. It is now found in roughly 90 percent of all corn, beet, and soybean products on U.S. store shelves.[117] One disturbing trend that is occurring, however, is growing resistance to certain GM crops. Rootworms once vulnerable to GM crops containing a gene called *Bt* are now developing a resistance against it, making the gene ineffective. As resistance grows, some farmers are beginning to turn to older pesticides.[118] The issue of resistance to herbicides and pesticides is a significant issue that Monsanto and other biotechnology companies are working to address.

Strategic Implementation of Responsibility for Technology

To accrue the maximum benefits from the technologies driving the new economy, many parties within society have important roles to play. While many continue to debate the issues associated with technology, the government must take steps to provide support for continued technological advancements and to ensure the benefits of technology apply to as many people as possible. The challenge is to establish regulations as needed in order to minimize any potential for harm to competition, the environment, and human welfare while not stifling innovation. Stakeholders, including employees, customers, special-interest groups, and the general public, can influence the use and control of technology through the public policy process. Businesses also have a significant role to play in supporting technology. New technologies are developed, refined, and introduced to the market through the R&D and marketing activities of business. Businesses that aspire to be socially responsible must monitor the impact of technology and harness it for the good of all.

The Role of Government

An economy that is increasingly driven by technology requires a government that maintains the basic infrastructure and support for technology in our society. The U.S. Department of Defense, for example, explores ways that technology can improve the quality of life. The government also serves as a watchdog to ensure that technology benefits society, not criminals. However, as the pace of technology continues to escalate, law enforcement agencies ranging from the Federal Bureau of Investigation (FBI) to local police forces are struggling to recruit and retain officers and prosecutors who are knowledgeable about the latest technology and the ways that criminals can exploit it. High-caliber forensic computer experts are often lured away to technology firms and private security outfits by salaries more than twice their government paychecks.[119] Computer crimes currently share sentencing guidelines with larceny, embezzlement, and theft, where the most significant sentencing factor is the amount of financial loss inflicted, and additional points are awarded for using false IDs or ripping off more than ten victims.

"Cyberterrorism," in which a foreign power sabotages another country's computer system, has been declared a potential act of war by the U.S. government. The government believes that cyberattacks represent a significant threat toward U.S. security and therefore requires serious action in response. This decision came after a major cyberattack was launched against Google and its computer servers—which included the accounts of some government officials.[120] More recently, the Russian government interfered with the U.S. election system during the 2016 presidential election. This type of cyberterrorism is a significant, ongoing challenge for federal and state government because it cannot be prevented entirely.[121]

Digital copyright lawsuits illustrate a significant difference in opinion in the interpretation of existing laws when exploiting the evolving multimedia potential of the internet. Although the government's strategy thus far has been not to interfere with the commercial use of technology, disputes and differing interpretations of current laws increasingly bring technology into the domain of the legal system. New laws related to breakthrough technologies that change the nature of competition are constantly being considered. Usually, the issues of privacy, ownership of intellectual property, health and safety, environmental impact, competition, or consumer welfare are the legislative platforms for changing the legal and regulatory system.

The Role of Business

Business, like government, is involved in both reactive and proactive attempts to market and make effective use of technology. Reactive concerns relate to issues that have legal and/or ethical implications, as well as issues of productivity, customer welfare, and other stakeholder concerns. Many large firms have suffered public embarrassment, legal bills, compensation claims, and clean-up costs when employees seek inappropriate material online, send email to people they shouldn't, accidentally circulate confidential information outside a business, or spread a computer virus. As a result, some companies are purchasing software that assists employees in managing the internet time they spend on personal activities.

On the other hand, a strategic, proactive approach to technology will consider its impact on social responsibility. Proactive management of technology requires developing a plan for utilizing resources to take advantage of competitive opportunities. For instance, many companies address the proper use of computers and other technology in their codes of ethics. Addressing these risk areas beforehand allows employees to understand what is and is not acceptable. These policies inform employees about corporate expectations regarding company technology and the potential penalties for misuse.

With competition increasing, companies are spending more time and resources to establish technology-based competitive advantages. The strategic approach to technology requires an overall mission, strategy, and coordination of all functional activities, including a concern for social responsibility, in order to have an effective program. To promote the responsible use of technology, a firm's policies, rules, and standards must be integrated into its corporate culture. Reducing undesirable behavior in this area must be a goal that is no different from reducing costs, increasing profits, or improving quality; it must be aggressively enforced and integrated into the corporate culture to be effective in improving behavior within the organization.

Top managers must consider the social consequences of technology in the strategic planning process. When all stakeholders are involved in the process, everyone can better understand the need for and requirements of responsible development and use of technology. There will always be conflicts in making the right choices, but through participation in decision-making, the best solutions can be found. Individual participants in this process should not abdicate their personal responsibility as concerned members of society. Organizations that are concerned about the consequences of their decisions create an environment for different opinions on important issues.

technology assessment
a procedure used by companies to calculate the effects of new technologies by foreseeing the effects new products and processes will have on their firm's operations, on other business organizations, and on society in general

Strategic Technology Assessment

To calculate the effects of new technologies, companies can employ a procedure known as a **technology assessment** to foresee the effects new products and processes will have on their firm's operations, on other business organizations, and on society in general. This assessment is a tool that managers can use to evaluate their firm's performance and to chart strategic courses of action to respond to new technologies. With information obtained through a technology assessment or audit, managers can estimate whether the benefits of adopting a specific technology outweigh costs to the firm and to society at large. The assessment process can also help companies ensure compliance with government regulations related to technology. Remember that one of the four components of social responsibility is legal compliance. A strategic technology assessment or audit can help organizations understand these issues and develop appropriate and responsible responses to them (see Table 11.9).[122]

If the assessment process indicates that the company has not been effective at utilizing technologies or is using them in a way that raises questions, changes may be necessary. Companies may need to consider setting higher standards, improving reporting processes, and improving communication of standards and training programs, as well as participating in aboveboard discussions with other organizations. If performance has not been satisfactory, management may want to reorganize the way certain kinds of decisions are made. Table 11.9 includes some issues to assess for proactive and reactive technology responsibility issues. Some social concerns might relate to a technology's impact on the environment, employee health and working conditions, consumer safety, and community values.

Finally, the organization should focus on the positive aspects of technology to determine how it can be used to improve the work environment, its products, and the general welfare of society. Technology can be used to reduce pollution, encourage recycling, and save energy. Also, information can be made available to customers to help them maximize the benefits of products. Technology has been and will continue to be a major force that can improve society.

Table 11.9 Strategic Technology Assessment Issues

Yes	No	Checklist
O	O	Are top managers in your organization aware of the federal, state, and local laws related to technology decisions?
O	O	Does your organization have an effective system for monitoring changes in the federal, state, and local laws related to technology?
O	O	Is there an individual, committee, or department in your organization responsible for overseeing government technology issues?
O	O	Does your organization do checks on technology brought into the organization by employees?
O	O	Are there communications and training programs in your organization to create an effective culture to protect employees and organizational interests related to technology?
O	O	Does your organization have monitoring and auditing systems to determine the impact of technology on key stakeholders?
O	O	Does your organization have a method for reporting concerns about the use or impact of technology?
O	O	Is there a system to determine ethical risks and appropriate ethical conduct to deal with technology issues?
O	O	Do top managers in your organization understand the ramifications of using technology to communicate with employees and customers?
O	O	Is there an individual or department in your organization responsible for maintaining compliance standards to protect the organization in the areas of privacy and intellectual property?

Summary

Technology relates to the application of knowledge, including the processes and applications to solve problems, perform tasks, and create new methods to obtain desired outcomes. The dynamics of technology relate to the constant change that requires significant adjustments in the political, religious, and economic structures of society. Reach relates to the far-reaching nature of technology as it moves through society. The self-sustaining nature of technology relates to the fact that technology acts as a catalyst to spur even faster development. Civilizations must harness and adapt to changes in technology to maintain a desired quality of life. Although technological advances have improved our quality of life, they have also raised ethical, legal, and social concerns.

Advances in technology have created millions of new jobs, better health and longer lives, new opportunities, and the enrichment of lives. Without greater access to the latest technology, however, economic development could suffer in underserved areas. The ability to purchase technology may affect the nature of competition and business success. Information and telecommunications technology minimizes borders, allows people to overcome the physical limitations of time and space, and enables people to acquire customized goods and services that cost less and are of higher quality.

The internet, a global information system that links many computer networks together, has altered the way people communicate, learn, do business, and find entertainment. The growth of the internet has generated issues never before encountered and that social institutions, including the legal system, have been slow to address.

Because current technology has made it possible to collect, share, and sell vast quantities of personal information, often without consumers' knowledge, privacy has become a major concern associated with technology. Many websites follow users' tracks through their site by storing a cookie, or identifying string of text, on the users' computers. What companies do with the information about consumers they collect through cookies and other technologies is generating concern. Privacy issues related to children are generating even more debate and laws to protect children's interests. Identity theft and fraud occur when criminals obtain personal information that allows them to impersonate someone else to use that individual's credit to obtain financial accounts and to make purchases. Some measure of protection of personal privacy is provided by the U.S. Constitution, as well as by Supreme Court rulings and federal laws. Europe and other regions of the world are also addressing privacy concerns. In addition to creating and posting policies regarding the gathering and use of personal information, more companies are beginning to hire chief privacy officers (CPOs). Intellectual property consists of the ideas and creative materials developed to solve problems, carry out applications, educate, and entertain others. Copyright infringement is the unauthorized execution of the rights reserved by a copyright holder. Technological advancements are challenging the ownership of intellectual property. Other issues relate to "cybersquatters" who deliberately register Web addresses that match or relate to other firms' trademarks and then attempt to sell the registration to the trademark owners.

Artificial intelligence (AI) and its enablers, including blockchain, drones, and robotics, are rapidly changing the business environment as we know it. Machines that perform tasks that previously required human intelligence have created efficiencies for business and improved the customer experience. However, AI-enabled technology has also raised ethical concerns as AI systems become more complex.

Bioethics refers to the study of ethical issues in the fields of medical treatment and research, including medicine, nursing, law, philosophy, and theology. Genetic research, including cloning, may revolutionize how diseases are diagnosed and treated. Genetically modified (GM) crops are created when scientists introduce a gene from one organism to another. However, these technologies are controversial because some people believe they are immoral, unsafe, or harmful to the environment.

To accrue the maximum benefits from the technology driving the new economy, many parties within society have important roles to play. With an economy that is increasingly driven by technology, the government must maintain the basic infrastructure and support for technology in our society. The government also serves as a watchdog to ensure that technology benefits society, not criminals.

Business is involved in both reactive and proactive attempts to make effective use of technology. Reactive concerns relate to issues that have legal or ethical implications as well as to productivity, customer welfare, or other stakeholder issues. Proactive management of technology requires developing a plan for utilizing resources to take advantage of competitive opportunities. The strategic approach to technology requires an overall mission, strategy, and coordination of all functional activities, including a concern for social responsibility, to produce an effective program. To calculate the effects of new technologies, companies can employ a procedure known as technology assessment to foresee the effects of new products and processes on their firm's operation, on other business organizations, and on society in general.

Responsible Business Debate

Ctrl-Alt-Delete: Exploring the Downside of Technology

Issue: *What are the benefits and drawbacks of technology to social interaction?*

While technology has brought advancements, conveniences, and efficiencies to our lives, some critics wonder if the costs outweigh the benefits, especially those that are transforming the ways we communicate, connect with other people, solve problems, and generally interact as human beings. In other words, are we losing the relationships that have made the United States a great place to live and work?

In 1831, Alexis de Tocqueville visited the United States on behalf of the French government. He wrote a grand treatise, *Democracy in America*, noting how Americans were dedicated to social cohesion, equality, common purpose, and concern for both individuals and the community. Now, recent studies indicate civic engagement is declining. Is technology part of the problem? Consider these daily occurrences: Students text on their phones instead of interacting with classmates; people rely on autocorrect features rather than their own knowledge; people on public transportation rarely acknowledge other riders because they are busy checking their smartphones; many children spend more time on the internet or playing video games than they do playing outside with other children; coworkers send each other emails and instant messages, rather than walk 30 steps to the next office

for a brief conversation; and handwriting has become so passé that a handwritten envelope will be opened much sooner than any other piece of mail.

Nonverbal communication is crucial to positive human relationships and building social skills. In the business world, not having face-to-face communication can hurt the relationship by creating misunderstandings and preventing empathic exchanges between colleagues. Additionally, research has shown that when someone asks for something in a face-to-face interaction, it is 34 times more likely to be well received than if the request came in an email.

On the other hand, technology has opened up new avenues for daily responsibilities, research, and business activities. Ordering groceries, buying clothing, and refilling medications are as easy and convenient as pushing a few buttons. This frees up more time for busy adults to engage in other activities. Because of the internet, researchers literally have libraries of knowledge at their fingertips. E-commerce and global reach are possible in the modern age in contrast to a few decades ago. Marketers use social media and other digital channels to connect more on a one-on-one basis with customers. Many companies, including Southwest Airlines, have social media teams to answer customer concerns quickly, creating a smoother customer service process. Small business owners now have the ability to use technology to sell their products across the world without the infrastructure that is required to set up a large company. Online chat forums can help people connect from different parts of the country who never would have met otherwise. Many people have used social networks like Facebook to reconnect with friends they knew long ago. Additionally, video chats enable long-distance friends and family to connect, while also providing some of the nonverbal communication that is missing from other media like email.

There Are Two Sides to Every Issue

1. Defend the changes that technology has brought to society's communication patterns, such as the expediency of email and texting, reduced costs, and access to people around the world.
2. Defend the need for society to rely less on technology and more on traditional communication patterns, such as face-to-face meetings, verbal conversations, and hand-written correspondence.

Sources: Carol Kinsey Goman, "Has Technology Killed Face-to-Face Communication?" *Forbes,* November 14, 2018, https://www.forbes.com/sites/carolkinseygoman/2018/11/14/has-technology-killed-face-to-face-communication/#4aee7be4a8cc (accessed July 29, 2019); Molly Schleisinger and Kathy Hirsh-Pasek, "The Power of Human: Re-inventing Technology to Prompt More Social Connection," Centers for Scholars and Storytellers, https://www.scholarsandstorytellers.com/character-blogs-technology/2018/12/29/the-power-of-human-re-inventing-technology-to-prompt-more-social-connection (accessed July 29, 2019).

Key Terms

Act on the Protection of Personal Information (APPI) (p. 321)
algorithm (p. 325)
big data (p. 309)
bioethics (p. 328)
Certified Information Privacy Professional (CIPP) (p. 322)
chief privacy officer (CPO) (p. 321)
Children's Online Privacy and Protection Act (COPPA) (p. 317)
copyright infringement (p. 323)

cybersquatter (p. 324)
deep learning (p. 326)
General Data Protection Regulation (GDPR) (p. 318)
genetically modified (GM) organisms (p. 331)
gig economy (p. 311)
identity fraud (p. 317)
identity theft (p. 317)
intellectual property (p. 322)
International Association of Privacy Professionals (IAPP) (p. 321)

Internet Corporation for Assigned Names and Numbers (ICANN) (p. 315)
Internet of Things (IoT) (p. 316)
machine learning (p. 326)
sharing economy (p. 311)
smart devices (p. 308)
supply chain management (p. 312)
technology (p. 308)
technology assessment (p. 334)

Discussion Questions

1. Define technology and describe three characteristics that can be used to assess it.
2. What effect has technology had on the United States and global economies? Have these effects been positive or negative?
3. Many people believe that the government should regulate business with respect to privacy online, but companies say self-regulation is more appropriate. Which approach would benefit consumers most? Businesses?
4. What is intellectual property? How can owners of intellectual property protect their rights?
5. What is AI? What are some ethical concerns about AI-enabled technology?
6. What is bioethics? What are some of the consequences of biomedical research?
7. Should GM foods be labeled as such? Why or why not?
8. How can a strategic technology assessment help a company?

Experiential Exercise

Visit three websites that are primarily designed for children or that focus on products of interest to children under age 13. For example, visit the websites for new movies, games, action figures, candy, cereal, or beverages. While visiting these sites, put yourself in the role and mindset of a child. What type of language and persuasion is used? Is there a privacy statement on the site that can be understood by children? Are there any parts of the site that might be offensive or worrisome to parents? Provide a brief evaluation of how well these sites attend to the provisions of the COPPA.

The Email Police: What Would You Do?

James Kitling thought about his conversation with Ira Romero earlier that day. He was not really surprised that the human resources (HR) department was concerned about the time that employees were spending on personal issues during the workday. Several departments were known for their rather loose management approach. Internet access for personal tasks, like shopping, using Instant Messaging services, and answering nonwork emails, had been a concern for several months. Recent news reports indicated that over 50 percent of large companies now filter or monitor email. Companies are also monitoring Web browsing, file downloads, chat-room use, and group postings. A survey published in the media reported that workers spend an average of eight hours a week looking at nonwork internet sites.

As the director of IT, James was very dedicated to the effective use of technology to enhance business productivity. Although he was knowledgeable about technology, James was equally attuned to the ways in which technology can be abused in a work setting. He knew that some employees were probably using too much internet time on personal tasks.

On the other hand, his company mainly employed professionals, administrative staff, and customer service personnel. All 310 employees were expected to use the computer a great deal throughout the day. At present, the company had a skeleton code of ethics and policy on the use of company resources, including the internet. A couple of managers, and now HR, had spoken with James about the prospects of monitoring employee computer and internet use. Ira's inquiry about the software, however, was a bit more serious. An employee had recently been formally reprimanded for downloading and printing nonwork documents from the internet. These documents were designed to help the employee's spouse in a new business venture. Although the employee did most of the searching and downloading during lunch, the supervisor felt that this was an improper use of company resources. Other employees had been informally spoken with about their use of the internet for personal matters. Ira believed that this was a growing problem that definitely affected productivity. He had read the news reports and believed that monitoring software was becoming a necessary tool in today's workplace.

So far, James had been hesitant to purchase and implement one of these systems. The employee internet management software was somewhat expensive, running approximately $25 per computer. He felt that the software could cause employee trust to decline sharply, resulting in even greater problems than currently existed. After all, most (if not all) employees engage in some personal tasks during work hours, including making personal telephone calls, getting coffee, chatting with coworkers, and so forth. James wondered if the internet was that much different from these other personal activities. He recalled a discussion in a management class in his master's of business administration (MBA) program, where it was revealed that employees in the early 1900s were allowed to use the telephone only to call the police. Thus, the telephone was once thought of as a great distracter, much as the internet is today.

Ira and a few other managers were pretty firm in their beliefs about the internet monitoring system. James was still not convinced that it was the best route to curbing the problem. In his role, however, he was expected to provide leadership in developing a solution. What would you do?

CHAPTER
12

Sustainability Issues

Purpose and Profit: The Rise of the B Corporation

Sustainability in business has become increasingly important as society becomes more aware of the detrimental impacts of pollution, water shortages, and climate change. One company that exemplifies care and concern for the environment is Cascade Engineering. Cascade Engineering's leaders and managers make decisions that differentiate the company from the competition. One major decision was to become a B corporation. The *B* stands for *beneficial,* and it is a certification awarded by the nonprofit B Lab to signal that member-companies will conform to a set of transparent and comprehensive social and environmental performance standards. These businesses are purpose-driven and are designed to give back to communities, the environment, and employees.

Cascade Engineering makes an unlikely B corporation, in that it manufactures plastic products, operating in an industry that tends to be seen as environmentally unfriendly. It has made the proactive decision to make sustainability the focus of its strategy in product and business development. To further this goal, the company produces its own alternative energy products. By using thermoplastics and multiple types of molding that cut down on waste, the company is able to produce goods that do not negatively affect the environment.

Most manufacturers would feel constrained by the performance standards of a B corporation. Fred Keller, Cascade Engineering's founder, welcomed regulation, using it as a motivation to improve processes. Cascade Engineering looks at decisions based on how they can benefit the community, which often requires managers to make nonprogrammed decisions to develop unique solutions. Rather than waiting for legislation and ethical guidelines to be imposed by the government, Cascade Engineering has taken it upon themselves to adopt ecofriendly business practices.

The company has adopted the triple-bottom line approach of people, planet, and profits. This approach views success based not only on financial standards like profit, but also on how the firm positively affects society and the environment. For instance, the .firm started its "Welfare to Career" program as a way to reach out to their community. Keller hired low-income individuals on welfare within his community to help them get out of poverty. This training and career program has helped hundreds of people get off of welfare. Interestingly, the program has also helped Cascade financially; the company has saved an estimated half-million dollars over a five-year period through tax credits, wage subsidies, and lower contracting costs.

Not only has Cascade made decisions to benefit the community, but it also has benefited other stakeholders. The company has spent more than a decade helping customers reduce oil use and eliminate waste. It has developed a cradle-to-cradle certified product line based on a design concept that stresses reusable and safe materials, renewable energy, water quality, social fairness, and continuous improvement. Unlike many manufacturers, Cascade supports a switch to renewable energy. While this might be perceived as a risky move, Cascade is aware that this type of energy is at the forefront of innovation.

Cascade Engineering has worked to develop a culture of positive decision-making when addressing the impact of the industry. Keller believes that businesses should be analyzed not only by how much money they make, but also by how they benefit society. His efforts have netted him multiple awards, respect, and the business of like-minded companies.[1]

Shutterstock/Bannafarsai_Stock

Chapter Objectives

- Define sustainability
- Examine the nature of sustainability as it relates to social responsibility
- Explore a variety of global environmental issues faced by business and society
- Examine the impact of environmental policy and regulations
- Gain an understanding of different types of alternative energy
- Examine business responses to sustainability
- Discuss a strategic approach to respond to environmental responsibility

As concerns over fracking, global warming, erratic weather patterns, and diminished quality of life continue to rise, public and business support for environmental causes has increased a great deal since the first Earth Day was held in 1970. Most Americans claim that they have made changes in their lifestyles, like switching to energy-efficient light bulbs or recycling, to help the environment. One survey indicated that 68 percent of consumers consider sustainability to be an important factor when making a purchase, regardless of age or gender, with Gen Z shoppers more likely to pay more for green products than other age groups.[2] Many businesses have adopted environmental policies in their operations, and 74 Fortune 500 corporations are using nearly 32 billion kilowatt-hours of green power each year.[3]

In this chapter, we explore the concept of sustainability in the context of corporate social responsibility in today's complex business environment. First, we define sustainability and explore some of the significant environmental issues that businesses and society face. Next, we consider the impact of government environmental policy and regulation on business and examine how some companies are going beyond the scope of these laws to address environmental issues and act in an environmentally responsible manner. We also examine different types of alternative energy. Finally, we highlight a strategic approach to environmental issues, including risk management and strategic audits.

Defining Sustainability

Most people probably associate the term *environment* with nature, including wildlife, trees, oceans, rivers, mountains, and prairies. Until the twentieth century, people generally thought of the environment solely in terms of how these resources could be harnessed to satisfy their needs for food, shelter, transportation, and recreation. As Earth's population swelled and technology advanced, however, humans began to use more of these resources with greater efficiency. Although these conditions have resulted in an improved standard of living, they come at a cost. Plant and animal species, along with wildlife habitats, are disappearing at an accelerated rate; water use has become a critical issue in many parts of the globe; and pollution has rendered the skies of some cities a gloomy haze. How to deal with these issues has become a major concern for business and society in the twenty-first century. Although the scope of the word *sustainability* is broad—including plants, animals, human beings, oceans and other waterways, land, and the atmosphere—in this book, we discuss the term from a strategic business perspective. Thus, we define **sustainability** as the potential for long-term well-being of the natural environment, including all biological entities, as well as the interaction among nature and individuals, organizations, and business strategies. Sustainability includes the assessment and improvement of business strategies, economic sectors, work practices, technologies, and lifestyles while maintaining the natural environment. It meets the needs of the present without compromising the ability of future generations to meet their own needs.[4]

However, it is important to realize that sustainability means different things to different cultures. Europeans use both environmental and economic variables when considering the sustainability of an organization. In the United States, the term *sustainability* is used more often in relation to environmental concerns. Others still believe that the term is too broad; some researchers want the term *sustainability* in business to only emphasize human sustainability with a customer focus.[5] This lack of a clear consensus complicates the matter for businesses, especially when trying to evaluate ways to broaden the sustainable footprint of their operations.[6] For the purposes of this chapter, we use the U.S. concept of sustainability to describe how organizations interact with the natural environment.

sustainability
the potential for long-term well-being of the natural environment, including all biological entities, as well as the interaction among nature and individuals, organizations, and business strategies

How Sustainability Relates to Social Responsibility

Sustainability does not mean the same thing as social responsibility.[7] Rather, it is a domain of social responsibility. Social responsibility is an attempt to maximize an organization's positive impact and minimize its negative impact on stakeholders. Sustainability, according to our definition, seeks to minimize a business's negative impact on the natural environment while maximizing its positive impact. Like any social concern, organizations should respond to consumer concerns over sustainability by addressing the issue in their strategies, policies, and objectives. This involves the process of assessing risks, monitoring ethical and legal compliance, and developing policies to minimize unethical conduct.

Although social responsibility and sustainability are not the same, many socially responsible organizations display sustainable behaviors. Social responsibility meets the needs of stakeholders, including both environmental stakeholders and consumers concerned about the impact of business operations on the Earth. Sustainability requires the organization to make ethical decisions on how it will implement, monitor, and improve upon sustainability initiatives. Figure 12.1 reillustrates the major emphases of social responsibility featured in Chapter 1 to demonstrate sustainability's role.

Stakeholders are demanding that businesses become more sustainable. At the very least, organizations are expected to minimize their negative effects on the environment through such activities as the proper disposal of chemicals, recycling, or keeping greenhouse gas emissions to a minimum. Organizations such as Kimberly-Clark have been responding by including sustainability as a key factor in annual corporate social responsibility (CSR) reports. While this is a new practice for many organizations, companies such as Ford Motor Company have published annual sustainability reports for more than 20 years.[8] These reports are mandatory for publicly held corporations in Europe.

Sustainability has become a major issue for organizations for different reasons. First, **sustainable business practices** can result in competitive advantages. Sustainable practices are beneficial to stakeholder relationships and even can lower costs in areas such as energy in the long term. Second, as consumers become more aware of environmental issues, their power over organizations in this area is increasing.[9] For example, as consumers became increasingly aware of the environment impact of **single-use plastics**, plastic straws rapidly fell out of favor, and bans became widespread. As a result, the soda giants Coca-Cola and PepsiCo are

sustainable business practices
actions a company takes to reduce their environmental impact and that may lower costs and improve competitive advantage, stakeholder relationships, and the company's reputation and branding

single-use plastics
also known as *disposable plastics*, these materials are used only once before they are discarded or recycled

Figure 12.1 Major Emphases of Social Responsibility

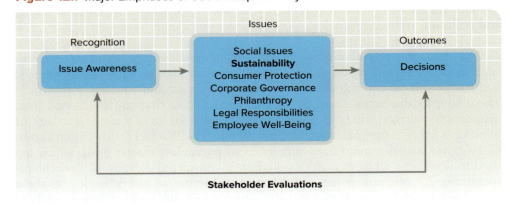

Source: © O.C. and Linda Ferrell, 2019.

preparing for potential bans on single-use plastic bottles by testing new dispensers that require customers to supply their own bottles.[10] Third, sustainable organizations are more likely to have their brand associated with positive concepts such as social value and product quality. Fourth, organizations are using sustainability to differentiate themselves from competitors and to market their goods and services. Patagonia has adopted the unique campaign of encouraging consumers not to buy products from the company that they do not need. They also want customers to return used products that the customer no longer wants so that the organization can reuse them. This positions Patagonia as a sustainable company, truly desiring to live its mission.

Sustainability not only involves best practices, but is also increasingly becoming an issue of concern to lawmakers. Many firms are becoming proactive in addressing sustainability. For example, as many states roll out aggressive climate strategies, AB InBev, the maker of Budweiser, is tackling its energy usage proactively with plans to use only renewable sources for electricity by 2025.[11] Many stakeholders respond positively to these changes.

Global Environmental Issues

biodiversity
the variety of living organisms found in a given area on Earth or on Earth as a whole and the ecological systems in which they live

The protection of air, water, land, **biodiversity**, and renewable natural resources emerged as a major issue in the twentieth century in the face of increasing evidence that pollution, uncontrolled use of natural resources, and population growth were putting increasing pressure on the long-term sustainability of these resources. As the environmental movement sounded the alarm over these issues, governments around the globe responded with environmental protection laws during the 1970s. In recent years, companies have been increasingly incorporating these issues into their overall business strategies. Most have been the focus of concerned citizens, as well as government and corporate efforts. Some nonprofit organizations have stepped forward to provide leadership in gaining the cooperation of diverse groups in responsible environmental activities. For example, the **Coalition for Environmentally Responsible Economies (CERES)**, a union of businesses, consumer groups, environmentalists, and other stakeholders, has established a set of goals for environmental performance.

Coalition for Environmentally Responsible Economies (CERES)
a union of businesses, consumer groups, environmentalists, and other stakeholders, who have established a set of goals for environmental performance

In the following section, we examine some of the most significant environmental issues facing business and society today, including air pollution, acid rain, global warming, water pollution and water quantity, land pollution, waste management, deforestation, urban sprawl, biodiversity, and genetically modified (GM) foods.

Atmospheric Issues

Among the most far-reaching and controversial environmental issues are those that relate to the air we breathe. These include air pollution, acid rain, global warming, and pollution emitted by coal.

particulate matter (PM)
a mixture of solid particles and liquid droplets found in the air; also known as particle pollution

Air Pollution   Air pollution typically arises from three sources: stationary sources such as factories and power plants; mobile sources such as cars, trucks, planes, and trains; and natural sources such as windblown dust and volcanic eruptions.[12] These sources discharge gases, as well as particulates, that can be carried long distances by surface winds or linger on the surface for days if there is a lack of wind or if other geographical conditions permit. The World Health Organization (WHO) has issued standardized safe levels of **particulate matter (PM)**, which are used to determine whether a city's pollution is considered dangerous. Particulates measuring 2.5 microns or less are the most dangerous to public health, as these particles are small enough to enter the bloodstream and cause ailments such as cancer and emphysema. It is estimated that 91 percent of the world's population lives in a place where air quality exceeds WHO guideline limits, with China and India having the most air-polluted cities.[13] It is estimated that 1.2 million people in India die premature deaths annually as a result of pollution.[14] Such conditions can cause markedly shorter life spans, along with chronic respiratory problems (e.g., asthma, bronchitis, and allergies) in humans and animals, especially in the elderly and the very young. Projections show the market for asthma products and services will reach $31.4 billion by 2026.[15] Additionally, some of the chemicals associated with air pollution may contribute to birth defects, cancer, and brain, nerve, and respiratory system damage. Air pollution can also harm plants, animals, and water bodies. Haze caused by air pollution can reduce visibility, interfering with aviation, driving, and recreation.[16] As a result of experiencing the detrimental effects of pollution on the population and the economy, China declared war on pollution by reducing energy levels, closing factories, and minimizing the number of cars on the roads. Between 2013–2017, China made significant progress, reducing particulates measuring 2.5 microns or less by 32 percent. China has continued its war on air pollution by introducing the Three-Year Action Plan for Winning the Blue Sky Defense Battle in 2018.[17]

Acid Rain   In addition to the health risks posed by air pollution, when nitrous oxides and sulfur dioxides emitted from manufacturing facilities react with air and rain, the result is **acid rain**. This phenomenon has contributed to the deaths of many valuable forests and lakes in North America and Europe. It also corrodes paint and deteriorates stone, leaving automobiles, buildings, and cultural resources such as architecture and outside art vulnerable unless they are protected from its effects.[18] While we have made great strides since the passing of the Clean Air Act in 1963, some of our forests and lakes are still recovering from the damage caused by acid rain.[19] In addition, we have not yet been able to eliminate this phenomenon, although implementing more environmentally conscious practices has been successful in reducing emissions that cause acid rain. In the United States, the concentration of sulfur dioxide in the air has decreased by 68 percent and emissions of sulfur dioxide have decreased by 65 percent over the past eight years.[20] Cleaning up emissions from factories and cars is one way to help reduce acid rain.

Global Warming   When carbon dioxide and other gases collect in the Earth's atmosphere, they trap the Sun's heat like a greenhouse and prevent Earth's surface from cooling. Without this natural process, the planet becomes too cold to sustain life. However, during the twentieth century, the burning of fossil fuels—gasoline, natural gas, oil, and coal—accelerated dramatically, increasing the concentration of so-called greenhouse gases like carbon dioxide and methane in the Earth's atmosphere to levels that are too high, which disrupted Earth's natural temperate regulation. This is known as the **greenhouse effect**. Chlorofluorocarbons—from refrigerants, coolants, and aerosol cans—also harm the Earth's **ozone** layer. A hole, measuring nine miles high and several hundred miles wide, was discovered in the lowest layer of the atmosphere and is believed to be caused by the presence of chlorofluorocarbons. The protective layer of the ozone, which protects the Earth from the Sun's harmful ultraviolet rays, is said to be stripped away. These harmful rays not only damage the environment but also humans' eyesight and skin health.[21]

World carbon dioxide emissions are currently around 37.1 billion metric tons and are expected to rise to 45 billion metric tons by 2040.[22] Figure 12.2 shows that world carbon dioxide emissions are on the rise. The United States and China are the two largest greenhouse gas emitters in the world.[23] Developing countries, are going to make up an increasing percentage of overall emissions because they are most likely to use coal—the dirtiest of all fossil fuels in terms of emissions. After years of decline, coal generation has now increased by 3 percent in recent years.[24] To cut

acid rain
a phenomenon when nitrous oxides and sulfur dioxides emitted from manufacturing facilities react with air and rain

greenhouse effect
when Earth's atmosphere becomes thick with carbon dioxide, other gasses, and substances which trap the Sun's heat making Earth's surface warmer

ozone
a highly reactive form of oxygen that is a critical component of the stratosphere where it encircles the Earth in a deep layer that protects the planet from the Sun's ultraviolet radiation

Figure 12.2 World Carbon Dioxide Emissions

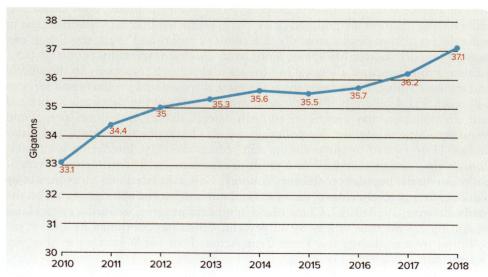

Source: Kelly Levin, "New Global CO2 Emissions Numbers Are In. They're Not Good," World Resources Institute, December 5, 2018, https://www.wri.org/blog/2018/12/new-global-co2-emissions-numbers-are-they-re-not-good (accessed August 2, 2019).

greenhouse gas emissions, the Environmental Protection Agency (EPA) has written rules providing stricter standards for new cars to cut the amount of greenhouse gases emitted from new cars by 25 percent. According to the rule, the standards would increase every year.[25] The EPA has considered freezing its escalating standards to avoid scaring off consumers with more expensive vehicles.[26]

Most scientists believe that concentrations of greenhouse gases like methane and carbon dioxide in the atmosphere are accelerating a warming of the planet. The past five years have been the hottest on record.[27] If no changes are made to curb global warming, many cities will experience an entire month each year with heat index temperatures above 100 degrees by 2050.[28] Accumulations of greenhouse gases have increased dramatically in the past century. The accumulation of gases appears to have increased average temperatures by 1.4°F over the last century. Although this does not sound like much of a change, it is enough to increase the rate of polar ice sheet melting, which is occurring at unprecedented rates.[29] **Climate change** has caused such dramatic melting of glaciers along the Italian/Swiss border in the Alps that mapmakers were forced to redraw the border between the two countries to follow the new glacial boundaries.[30] Climate change has also affected weather in this region—making Switzerland to the north more prone to flooding and Italy to the south more drought-ridden.

As the polar ice caps melt, scientists fear that rising sea levels will flood many coastal areas and even submerge low-lying island nations. With less snow and ice cover to reflect the Sun's rays, the Earth absorbs even more of the Sun's heat, accelerating the warming process. Global warming has caused more than 3 trillion tons of ice melt over the last 25 years.[31] Some scientists also think that global warming may alter long-term weather patterns, causing drought in some parts of the world, while bringing floods to others—something that many believe we are already witnessing in the form of extreme weather patterns. Insurers are building models to better estimate the impact of climate change and expanding in-house resources by hiring climatologists. These new models consider the effect of global warming on wildfires, flooding, hurricanes, and hailstorms.[32] Additionally, record-breaking

climate change
the alteration of weather patterns and temperature in an area or across the entire Earth due to global warming

heat waves, droughts, and winter storms are also said to be a result of the changing atmospheric conditions caused by global warming.[33]

The concept of global warming has been controversial among some groups, especially in the United States. Critics of global warming argue that apparent temperature increases are part of a natural cycle of temperature variation that the planet has experienced over millions of years. Some people even like the sound of global warming, as it brings to mind warmer temperatures and longer growing seasons. Many companies and organizations have also maligned the theory because reducing emissions and tightening environmental laws means greater expenses at the outset. Nevertheless, most nations, scientists, and businesses now agree that something must be done about climate change. Failure to act may create extreme climate conditions that could have negative consequences.

Hydraulic fracturing (fracking) is controversial due to its effects on global warming. While supporters claim that fracking is better for the environment and is leading to energy independence for the United States, critics disagree. They claim the burning of natural gas releases harmful methane into the atmosphere. They estimate methane to be 21 times more potent than carbon dioxide over a period of 100 years. The Intergovernmental Panel on Climate Change claims that the estimate is closer to 34 times. Since the rise of fracking, the EPA has issued rules for production and consumption and will continue to do so as more information on its effects on the climate become known.[34] Several states such as Maryland, Washington, and New York have banned fracking outright.[35]

The **Kyoto Protocol** is a treaty among industrialized nations aimed at slowing global warming. The United States did not ratify the treaty and therefore was not bound to it. Since its creation in 1997, the protocol has been highly unpopular among global corporations that engage in operations that damage the environment. At the time, signing the treaty required a commitment to reducing levels of greenhouse gas emissions by 5 percent that of 1990 levels. However, only 37 countries, as well as the European Union (EU), signed the protocol, leaving out the largest polluters such as Canada, the United States, Australia, and developing countries including China and India. The United States has adopted a voluntary **U.S. Global Climate Change Initiative** for reporting greenhouse gases, as outlined in Table 12.1. Many leaders

Kyoto Protocol
a treaty among industrialized nations aimed at slowing global warming

U.S. Global Climate Change Initiative
a voluntary protocol for reporting greenhouse gases

Table 12.1 Elements of the U.S. Global Climate Change Initiative

Enhancement of the 1605(b) Voluntary Reporting of Greenhouse Gases Program
Significantly expanded funding for basic scientific research and advanced technology development
Tax incentives, such as credits for renewable energy, cogeneration, and new technology
Challenges for business to undertake voluntary initiatives and commit to greenhouse gas intensity goals, such as through recent agreements with the semiconductor and aluminum industries
Transportation programs, including technology research and development and fuel economy standards
Carbon sequestration programs, which include increased funding for U.S. Department of Agriculture conservation programs in the Farm Bill
Investments in climate observation systems in developing countries
Funding for "debt-for-nature" forest conservation programs
Use of economic incentives to encourage developing countries to participate in climate change initiatives
Expanding technology transfer and capacity building in the developing world
Joint research with Japan, Italy, and Central America

Sources: Energy Information Administration, U.S. Department of Energy, "Voluntary Reporting of Greenhouse Gases—Summary," http://www.eia.doe.gov/oiaf/1605/vrrpt/summary/special_topic.html (accessed June 22, 2016); USAID, "U.S. Global Climate Change Initiative," https://www.usaid.gov/ climate (accessed July 17, 2019).

worried that compliance would jeopardize businesses and the economy.[36] The Kyoto Protocol, which went into effect in 2005, now has 192 signatory nations.[37] In 2012, another attempt to develop a legally binding international agreement to reduce greenhouse gas emissions was discussed. The Doha Gateway Agreement calls for both developed and developing countries to decrease greenhouse gas emissions. As of 2019, 134 countries have signed the amendment.[38]

Many U.S. businesses are responding to stakeholder pressure and are committing to self-regulatory standards with respect to global warming and related areas, even in the absence of federal mandates. States such as California have worked hard to gain the right to issue their own environmental legislation. After many years of making arguments to the federal government, the EPA granted California the right to impose tough emissions standards on cars and trucks. For example, California signed an emissions reduction deal with Canada in 2019 that sidestepped the U.S. federal government as it was discussing relaxing emissions standards.[39] This change in ruling opened the door for other states to pass similar emissions legislation and demonstrated a willingness on the part of the EPA to let states decide how strict they want to be on polluters.[40] A host of energy-efficient designations now exist to help consumers make more environmentally friendly choices. For example, Energy Star, a joint program between the EPA and the U.S. Department of Energy, helped Americans and businesses reduce greenhouse gas emissions by 3 billion metric tons—all while saving them more than $400 billion on utility bills.[41] Table 12.2 describes some ways that companies and governments are adopting climate change strategies.

Coal and Carbon Emissions   As already mentioned, coal is an area of debate among different countries and is considered to be one of the dirtiest forms of energy.[42] The consumption of coal pollutes the air by releasing large amounts of gaseous and PM into the atmosphere. Many governments believe that their intervention is needed to bring down levels of greenhouse gas emissions. Some countries are intervening with **cap-and-trade programs**, which set emissions limits (caps) for businesses, countries, or individuals. A company is given a certain amount of carbon that they are allowed to emit, and to legally emit anything beyond that limit, they must purchase carbon credits from another company that did not pollute as much. The EU has been at the forefront of mandated emissions reductions and has implemented a cap-and-trade program on carbon emissions known as the European Union Emission Trading Scheme.

When the EU signed the Kyoto Protocol, it committed to collectively reduce its greenhouse gas emissions by 8 percent. The EU does this by issuing a fixed

cap and trade programs
programs that set carbon emissions limits (caps) for businesses, countries, or individuals. To legally emit beyond that limit, carbon credits must be purchased from another entity that did not pollute to its own limit

Table 12.2 Climate Change Strategy

Climate Change Strategy	Description	Example
Greenhouse gas reduction	A commitment to reduce carbon emissions by a certain percentage	To reduce greenhouse gas emissions, the U.S. government required cars and light trucks to get 36.9 miles per gallon by 2020
Cap-and-trade program	Set emissions limits (caps) for businesses, countries, or individuals	The United States used a cap-and-trade program for acid rain, requiring fossil-fueled power plants to reduce levels of sulfur oxide and nitrogen oxide emissions
Proactive business practices	Occurs when businesses proactively adopt business practices to address sustainability before they need to do so	Walmart has worked on adopting a sustainability index that will allow customers to determine how ecofriendly a product is

number of permits to businesses and other parties that limits the amount of emissions their companies can give off. A carbon emissions cap can strain many businesses, especially manufacturing companies, which emit large amounts of carbon in the process of operating. Opponents of this scheme argue that a single cap puts certain companies at a financial disadvantage, as they can only reduce their carbon footprint by so much before they begin sacrificing productivity. To solve this problem, a cap-and-trade system allows for businesses to sell the carbon permits they do not use. In other words, companies that do not release as much carbon emissions can sell their permits to companies that do. Companies that pollute less are therefore rewarded with extra income, while companies that produce more are allowed to continue working. To give companies time to adapt more efficient technologies, governments impose progressively smaller caps over the years.[43]

The cap-and-trade program has gained some support in the United States. Twenty-three states have actively been involved in three regional cap-and-trade programs to reduce emissions: the Regional Greenhouse Gas Initiative (RGGI), the Midwestern Greenhouse Gas Reduction Accord (Midwestern Accord), and the Western Climate Initiative (WCI).[44] Cap-and-trade has also been used to reduce acid rain by restricting the amount of sulfur dioxide and nitrogen oxides released by fossil-fueled power plants.[45] However, opposition has been fierce, and federal legislation has not focused on mandating cap-and-trade programs. Instead, the government is more concerned with providing collective goals that must be met. The EPA works with companies and states on implementing rules to meet these goals. The EPA has suggested market-based programs, investment in existing or new energy efficiency programs, or expansion of renewable energy initiatives to state legislators, who will decide what methods work best for their states.[46] The Clean Power Plan (CPP), first proposed by the EPA in 2014, was the first time that the United States set mandatory guidelines on power plant emissions. Though it was projected to reduce emissions from the power sector by 32 percent by 2030, opposition to this proposed rule was high, particularly as it would have significantly affected the nation's 600 coal-fired plants. In 2019, CPP was replaced by the **Affordable Clean Energy (ACE) rule** after it was decided that the CPP exceeded the EPA's statutory authority. ACE, which gives more power at the state level, is projected to have an annual net benefit of $120 to $730 million.[47]

New companies are emerging with smaller carbon footprints than their predecessors. As the meat industry is increasingly criticized for its negative environmental impact, new alternative protein products have become available. For example, Impossible Foods, the company behind the Impossible Burger, positions its plant-based product as being more ethical and more sustainable than traditional beef products. According to one study, the Impossible Burger results in use of 87 percent less water, 96 percent less land, and 89 percent fewer greenhouse gas emissions than burgers made from beef.[48] Many existing businesses are partnering with these new companies to improve emissions. For example, start-ups are working to address the carbon dioxide emissions created by concrete production, one of the world's biggest sources of emissions. CarbonCure uses liquefied carbon dioxide captured from industry sites in the concrete-mixing process to eliminate it, while making the concrete stronger. This technology could have a widespread impact across the construction industry.[49]

Proactive businesses do not have to wait for legislation to be passed to reduce their carbon footprint. Many companies have created best practices programs that utilize cleaner energy over dirty forms of energy like gasoline or coal, as well as more efficient building codes. These codes have been shown to cut energy consumption by a significant amount. As these codes are implemented and reevaluated, drafters are able to revise the codes, making them all the more effective.[50] However, most companies have a long way to go. According to a report compiled by the EPA, nearly half of all U.S. emissions are produced by businesses across all industries.[51]

Affordable Clean Energy (ACE) rule
a rule (replacing the EPA's Clean Power Plan that set mandatory guidelines on power plant emissions) giving more power at the state level to reduce emissions

Figure 12.3 U.S. Carbon Dioxide Emissions by Source

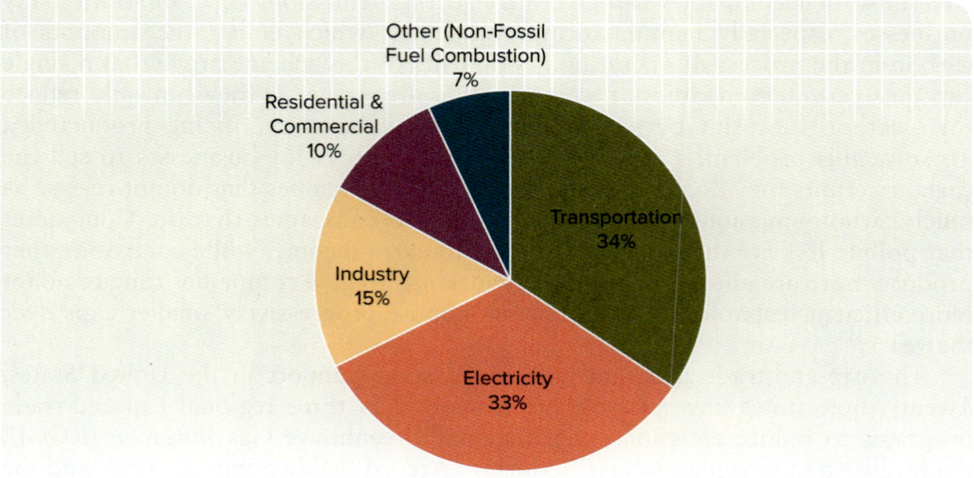

Source: U.S. Environmental Protection Agency, "Overview of Greenhouse Gases," https://www.epa.gov/ghgemissions/overview-greenhouse-gases (accessed July 17, 2019).

Figure 12.3 breaks down carbon dioxide emissions by source. A business needs to know the size of its carbon footprint before it can effectively reduce emissions and other environmental pollutants. Companies including Walmart, Coca-Cola, and 3M have actively monitored their carbon output and have set ambitious goals, such as eventually becoming net zero when it comes to emissions.

Water Issues

Water is emerging as the most important and contested resource of the twenty-first century. Nothing is more important to human survival, yet water is being polluted and consumed at an unprecedented rate. According to the United Nations, more than 2 billion people currently live in countries with high water stress, and 1.8 billion people will be living in conditions of absolute water scarcity by 2025. There are many reasons for this—including industrial waste, 70 percent of which pollutes water supplies in developing countries; human waste, which accounts for 2 million tons per day; and agricultural waste, which pollutes 40 percent of water in high income areas and 54 percent in low income areas.[52] In order to remain viable, all businesses must think about water conservation, purification, and allocation.

Water Pollution   Water pollution results from the dumping of sewage and toxic chemicals from manufacturing into rivers and oceans; from oil and gasoline spills; and from the burial of trash and industrial waste in the ground where it can contaminate underground water supplies. Fertilizers and pesticides used in farming and grounds maintenance also drain into water supplies with each rainfall. These chemicals are harmful to all life that depends on oceans and streams. Fertilizers upset algae balances in rivers causing fish to die. Mercury contaminates the oceans, and therefore human food supplies. Overuse of water can lead to shortages; deforestation and climate change are contributing to the desertification of sections of China and even the United States; and various chemical and methane leaks associated with fracking are seeping into water supplies.[53] Additionally, one in nine people lack access to safe water, and every two minutes, a child dies from water-related disease.[54]

From the passage of the Clean Water Act in 1972 to 2001 the United States made significant strides to clean up and protect water sources. However, the water preservation movement lost federal backing in the early 2000s. According to the Natural Resources Defense Council (NRDC), 10 percent of U.S. beaches are highly polluted, causing them to be closed or on advisory for most of the year.[55] A large percentage of streams, lakes, and other American waterways are not fit for fishing or swimming, and pollution from agriculture and organic decomposition is significant enough to have created **dead zones** in large bodies of water that have a reduced level of oxygen. The Gulf of Mexico is known to have a dead zone the size of the state of New Jersey, the second-largest dead zone in the world.[56] In recent years, the United States has considered changes to the Clean Water Act that would cut back on important water protections, creating a narrower regulatory scope.[57]

While the United States has one of the safest drinking water supplies in the world, pollution remains a problem. The city of Flint, Michigan, experienced a state of emergency after it switched its water supply from Lake Huron to the Flint River, which was known for being filthy. Soon iron and lead was leaking into the water, creating a toxic water supply that could cause long-term effects to residents who drank from it. However, the problem of lead is not limited to Flint. Reports show that only 15 states and Washington, D.C., have laws for testing lead in school drinking water, and less than half of districts regularly test. The Government Accountability Office reported 37 percent of the school districts who did test have detected elevated lead levels in students.[58]

Many of the side effects on people and wildlife are unknown. The EPA released a study on the quality of water coming from 50 wastewater treatment plants all over the nation and found 56 active pharmaceutical ingredients present in the water supply. Pharmaceutical companies have released the drugs into the water supply, but consumers who take the drugs are the largest contributor to the problem. Pharmaceuticals have also been found in water sources in Europe, Asia, and Australia. Although the concentrations found have been small, scientists worry about the long-term health effects that they could have upon humans. Effects have already been found in male frogs that have ingested small amounts of estrogen and developed eggs.[59] A chemical plant manager in Georgia was sentenced to house arrest and a $2,000 fine for violating the Clean Water Act by telling his employees to wash a toxic chemical into the Chattahoochee River.[60] Tougher regulations are needed globally to address pollution from activities such as dumping waste into the ocean, large animal-feeding operations, logging sites, public roads, parking lots, and industrial waste created by production operations.

dead zone
an area in a large body of water that has a reduced level of oxygen and increased algae blooms due to excessive nutrient pollution from human activities, which negatively affects marine life and can be toxic to humans as well

Water Quantity In addition to concerns about the quality of water, some parts of the globe are increasingly worried about its quantity. Over the last two decades, water use has soared, resulting in serious consequences for the global water supply. This creates issues for businesses in various industries that consume large amounts of water in their operations. For example, it takes approximately 20 gallons of water to brew a pint of beer, 132 gallons to make a two-liter bottle of soda, and 500 gallons to make a pair of jeans. In light of the decreasing amount of water on the planet, companies are taking a responsible approach by measuring their water footprints. Levi Strauss & Co. partnered with several organizations to develop assessments for the lifecycle impact of their jeans. As a result, the company has been able to determine ways to use up to 96 percent less water to make their jeans without compromising the quality, a process called Water<Less. Additionally, the company has invested in designing products made from 100 percent recyclable materials.[61] New technology has made it possible to reduce the use of water and wasteful chemicals in jean production, and companies are taking advantage. For example, AYR sells a sustainable jean made from recycled materials at a facility that recycles 90 percent of its water.[62]

Record-breaking years of heat and below-average precipitation result in costly and dangerous droughts across the nation. Drought has affected many parts of the United States. Droughts are predicted to become hotter and longer due to climate change.[63] These conditions put added pressure on facility managers to conserve water. The nation's supply of accessible fresh water is decreasing drastically, in no small part because of consumption rates. The average American uses 100 gallons of water per day, and it is estimated that up to 10 percent of American homes are fitted with leaking water pipes, faucets, and toilets that waste 90 gallons of water each day. As a result, at least 40 states expect to see water shortages within the next decade. There are many small things that companies and individuals can do to slow down water consumption rates. For example, switching to low-flow toilets could save as much as 520 billion gallons of water each year.[64]

Land Issues

Land sustainability is diverse and encompasses some of the issues already discussed, such as pollution and waste, as well as loss of biodiversity and GM foods. Experts also believe climate change is driven by land-use changes such as cutting down trees and paving over the Earth. Unchecked, global climate change could cause hundreds of billions of dollars in loss in the U.S. alone by the end of the century.[65] Our land is becoming less viable for human and animal habitation due to the impact of these activities. Because businesses generate waste and require natural resources, stakeholders believe that they have the responsibility to minimize their harmful impact on the environment.[66]

Land Pollution   Land pollution results from the dumping of residential and industrial waste, strip mining, and poor forest conservation. Such pollution causes health problems in humans, jeopardizes wildlife habitats, causes erosion, alters watercourses (leading to flooding), and can eventually poison groundwater supplies. China is at the epicenter of a debate over pollution. The country's rapid development as manufacturer to the world has exposed hundreds of millions of people to the ill effects of pollution. After a report indicated 16 percent of China's land was polluted with heavy metals, including cadmium, nickel, and arsenic, China ramped up cleanup efforts. The government announced an investment of $4.8 billion to clean polluted land and prevent these levels from recurring. Continued efforts will take time and significant damage has already been done. To date, only 20 percent of the polluted land has been cleaned.[67] In order to reduce pollution around the planet, businesses are all going to have to be aware of and accept responsibility for the problem of pollution.

Determining responsibility for environmental degradation is not always easy, especially on a global scale involving different countries. China introduced its first soil pollution law to create new standards for pollution control and increase monitoring of soil pollution and polluters. Under the new law, businesses are required to monitor their own soil pollution and report incidents as they occur to increase transparency and accountability.[68] Ecuador sued Chevron for environmental damage that occurred years earlier with oil and gas firm Texaco. Chevron later acquired Texaco, and the country claimed that Chevron was responsible for the environmental damage. After many court battles, a U.S. court ruled in favor of Chevron, citing an agreement that Texaco had signed with Ecuador, absolving Chevron of liability.[69]

Fracking has also led to concerns over land pollution. Fracking often occurs in rural areas where trees are cut down to make way for roads, well pads, and other infrastructure specific to fracking. Wyoming, for example, has experienced habitat fragmentation, a reduction in hunting, and a depopulation of wildlife; sections of forests in Pennsylvania have been cut down; and Alberta, Canada, has reported serious detrimental effects to land and other natural resources in the area believed to be caused by fracking. Studies have shown that fracking in Texas has resulted in habitat fragmentation, but because 95 percent of land in Texas is privately owned, it's extremely difficult to determine the full impact of fracking on vegetative resources, agriculture, and wildlife.[70]

Waste Management Improper or irresponsible disposal of waste is another aspect of the land pollution problem. American consumers are by far the world's biggest wasters. In one year, they contributed more than 262 million tons of waste, which strains declining landfill space. The United States has over 3,000 active landfills and more than 10,000 abandoned landfills. Often left untreated, these abandoned landfills result in hazardous leakage. Methane gas makes up the largest emissions given off from landfills, which is 20 times more powerful than carbon dioxide in terms of atmospheric heating. Some organizations have learned to convert that gas into power.[71] The EPA established the Landfill Methane Outreach Program (LMOP), with partners consisting of landfill owners and operators, industry organizations, energy providers and marketers, state agencies, communities, end users, and other stakeholders to convert landfill methane gas into power. Waste-to-energy, also called **bioenergy**, is used in many European plants

Shutterstock/Kwangmoozaa

bioenergy
renewable energy made from biological waste

to treat household waste and create energy from it. Approximately 28 percent of municipal waste is treated at these plants, resulting in 50 million tons of carbon dioxide emissions being avoided annually.[72]

Plastics in landfills are a major concern, as they can take up to 1,000 years to biodegrade. A large contributor is plastic bags, of which Americans use 100 billion per year. Many cities, such as Boston and Chicago, and several states, such as California and Hawaii, have passed legislation either prohibiting the use of plastic bags in stores or charging a fee for their use. Many countries have passed similar legislation in various regions.[73] Stores like Whole Foods ban plastic bags voluntarily and offer incentives for consumers to use more recyclable materials, such as canvas grocery bags. Whole Foods became the first national grocery store in the United States to eliminate plastic straws. The United States recycles less than 26 percent of waste produced, while other countries such as Germany, Austria, and Belgium recycle at least half of their waste.[74]

Electronic waste (e-waste) in landfills has been proven to release harmful toxins into the air and water. It is estimated that the United States generates more than 11 million tons of e-waste annually, and only 16 percent of the world's e-waste is recycled.[75] Increasingly, electronics firms are pressured to take back used electronics for recycling. Large chains such as Best Buy offer electronics and appliances recycling. Many computer companies such as Apple offer trade-in or buyback programs. Dell partnered with Goodwill to offer a free recycling program.[76] The EPA established its own electronics recycling program, and a host of state governments have passed laws to encourage the recycling of electronic devices. Many stakeholders, including environmental groups and some politicians, believe that companies that produce the goods should be responsible for their proper disposal and recycling.[77]

Improper waste practices greatly affect countries with insufficient waste facilities. In India, for example, trash that would be sent to controlled landfills in countries such as the United States is instead sent to open dumps or buried underground. This poses a significant health risk, particularly to India's network of waste pickers who search trash for recyclables. Procter & Gamble (P&G) has been urged by the waste pickers and the government in India to address waste created by its diapers and sanitary pads. With sanitary pad sales projected to double in the next five years, India is among P&G's fastest-growing markets. P&G is being held accountable for the growth because its Whisper brand is the dominant disposable pad brand in India. Sanitary waste disposal facilities will need to be established to make this business sustainable.[78]

Deforestation   Rainforests serve to regulate temperatures and weather patterns, absorb carbon dioxide, and maintain water supplies. Before deforestation became a common occurrence, there was approximately 6 million square miles of rainforest, whereas today rainforest covers a little over 2 million square miles. It is estimated that the global tree count has fallen to 46 percent of what it was at the dawn of human civilization.[79] Although tree cover has increased in recent years, many new areas of tree growth were previously considered too cold to support trees, suggesting that global warming has affected these landscapes.[80] The reasons for deforestation are varied. The boom in biofuels in Southeast Asia and the Pacific regions have resulted in the cutting down of trees to make room for palm oil plantations. Brazil cuts down the Amazon rainforests for farming or for raising sugarcane. Its deforestation rate is the highest it has been in 10 years. The amount of deforestation that occurred in Brazil's rain forests last year covered an area approximately five times the size of London.[81]

A competitive global economy drives the need for money in economically challenged tropical countries. In the short term, logging and converting forestlands to other uses seem to be the profitable thing to do. However, the profits from deforestation are generally short lived due to the poor quality of rainforest soil. While initially, it can create a boom of prosperity, farming and other activities are only sustainable by moving and cutting down more trees.[82] Deforestation began largely out of need that sprang from poverty in these areas. However, those involved in the activity are more commonly large corporations. Many see this as an advantage because it is easier to put pressure on these entities to be more responsible. In addition, this pressure can come from many stakeholder groups, which can increase the response time.[83]

Companies are obtaining certifications like the one granted by the Forest Stewardship Council (FSC), a nonprofit organization comprised of loggers, environmentalists, and sociologists. The FSC seeks to coordinate forest management around the world and to develop a uniform set of standards. FSC-certification helps companies indicate to consumers and stakeholders that they are committed to preserving forest resources, are focused on social responsibility, and hold a long-term perspective of environmental management. Table 12.3 lists some facts about global deforestation.

Table 12.3 Global Deforestation Facts

Since people began cutting down trees, approximately 46 percent of trees have been felled.
In the past 50 years, approximately 17 percent of the Amazon has been destroyed.
A total of 80 percent of Earth's land mammals and plants live in forests.
If tropical deforestation were a country, it would be the third highest in carbon dioxide–equivalent emissions.
Approximately 6–12 percent of forests fall annually.
About 15 percent of greenhouse gas emissions come from deforestation.
It takes 27,000 trees each day to manufacture toilet paper.

Source: Christina Nunez, "Deforestation Explained," National Geographic, February 7, 2019, https://www.nationalgeographic.com/environment/global-warming/deforestation/ (accessed July 19, 2019); Kiri Rowan, "Interesting Deforestation Facts and Impact on Human Health," *Monq*, April 9, 2019, https://monq.com/eo/forest-bathing/interesting-deforestation-facts/ (accessed July 19, 2019); "10 Facts About Deforestation," *Pure Planet*, November 11, 2018, https://pureplanetclub.com/blogs/roll-with-us/10-facts-about-deforestation (accessed July 19, 2019).

Urban Sprawl Urban sprawl began in the United States with the post–World War II building boom that transformed the nation from primarily low-density communities designed to accommodate one-car households, bicyclists, and pedestrians to large-scale suburban developments at the edges of established towns and cities. Downtowns and inner cities deteriorated as shopping malls, office parks, corporate campuses, and residential developments sprang up on what was once forest, prairie, or farmland. As the places where people live, work, and shop grew further apart, people began spending more time in automobiles, driving ever-greater distances. Urban sprawl consumed wildlife habitat, wetlands, and farmland, and has also contributed to land, water, and air pollution. Land that is paved over contributes to flash flooding, making big storms more deadly. Lack of urban planning means that these places grow without reason, contributing to uneven development of services. In an age of erratic gas prices, traffic congestion, and obesity, it has become increasingly expensive, in both dollars and health, to live in sprawling cities. Large companies with many locations, such as Walmart and Starbucks, have been criticized for contributing to urban sprawl.

Some urban areas fight to limit sprawl. Portland, Oregon, for example, established an urban growth boundary to restrict growth and preserve open space and rural land around the city. The California legislature passed a bill that limits urban sprawl through better transportation and more efficient land use. Adding to the appeal of returning to cities is a movement to increase urban parks. Rather than allowing loggers to profit from forests, more cities are buying forested land to convert to park space. Stemming sprawl also preserves natural spaces outside of the city. Additionally, people realize that living near their place of employment is more convenient, cheaper, and better for their health. Although limiting urban sprawl creates disadvantages for car and oil companies, many businesses can benefit from urban renewal movements that reduce sprawl.

Biodiversity

Deforestation, pollution, development, and urban sprawl put increasing pressure on wildlife, plants, and their habitats. Many plants and animals have become extinct, and thousands more are threatened. It is estimated that 200 to 2,000 animal species become extinct each year.[84] Experts' fears that overutilization of natural resources will cause catastrophic imbalance to the environment are becoming realized. Because each biological species plays a unique role in its ecosystem and is part of a complex chain of events, the loss of any one of them may threaten the entire ecosystem.

Decrease in Bees, Bats, and Frogs An alarming rate of decline in the populations of bees, bats, and frogs are at the forefront of this issue. Pollinators play a significant role in that they help fruits and vegetables grow by spreading pollen from plant to plant. Increasing development and widespread use of pesticides have reduced populations of bees, insects, and bats needed for plant reproduction. The population of domestic honeybees, the primary pollinators of food-producing plants, has declined by at least one-third, and many wild honeybees have become virtually extinct in many places around the world. This decline has become so widespread that the phenomenon has been termed *Colony Collapse Disorder (CCD)*, and organizations are working to stop the decline before complete extinction occurs. Declines in pollinating species not only threaten the success of their relevant ecosystems but also may harm long-term global food production because significant portions of all food products require pollinators to reproduce.[85]

Bat populations are also on the decline, due mainly to a fungus disease called White Nose Syndrome. More than 6 million bats have died as a result of the outbreak. Many believe that this epidemic is due to environmental and habitat changes resulting from human-related activities. Bats aid the environment in a number of ways, such as feeding on insects, which reduces the need for pesticide use.[86] The same is true for amphibians such as toads, salamanders, and frogs, which are declining at an annual rate of 3.7 percent. Scientists found the root of the decline was a fungus that was inadvertently spread by humans. Frogs are especially vulnerable to environmental changes including habitat modification, urban sprawl, pollution, and depletion of the ozone layer because their skin is made to absorb the water wherein they live. Any changes in frog populations immediately inform us of negative changes in the environment.[87]

Genetically Modified Organisms

Depending on whom you ask, genetically modified (GM) foods are either going to save impoverished areas from starvation and revolutionize agriculture, or they will destroy biodiversity and make us all sick. Genetically modified (GM) organisms are created through manipulating plant and animal DNA so as to produce a desired effect like resistance to pests and viruses, drought resistance, or high crop yield. This process generally involves transferring genes from one organism to another in a way that would never occur naturally, in order to create a new life form that has unique traits. Companies like Monsanto and DuPont develop GM corn, soybeans, potatoes, canola oil seeds, and cotton plants they claim are more resistant to weeds and insects, sometimes require fewer chemicals to produce, and produce higher yields. However, studies show that certain GM crops are losing their effectiveness as insects become increasingly resistant. More farmers have reverted to using pesticides, which also damages the environment.[88]

Many people also fear that these unnatural genes will have negative effects on nature, somewhat like how invader species of plants and animals can wipe out native ones, or even have negative effects on humans. Other concerns result from the fact that these seeds are patented, restricting farmers from keeping and replanting the seeds and requiring them to purchase new seeds each year. Nevertheless, considerable interest in GM products remains. In countries where malnutrition is a problem, the prospect of higher yields is very appealing, even if the seed itself is more expensive. Monsanto, the world's largest agricultural biotechnology company, has released GM seeds that can withstand drought, which could make a major difference in many regions.[89]

GM foods may be controversial, but some researchers and scientists see the technology as a valuable way to develop drugs in the future. The U.S. Food and Drug Administration (FDA) approved the first drug made from genetically engineered animals, ATryn, created to treat people who suffer from the blood-clotting condition antithrombin deficiency. The drug comes from goats that were genetically engineered to produce human antithrombin in their milk.[90] As with GM plants, the problem with the genetic engineering of animals or animal products is that the long-run effects are unknown. Large numbers of genetically altered animals could upset the balance in relationships among various species with undetermined effects, such as the ability to reproduce or fight diseases and pests. Additionally, if GM plant seeds are carried by wind or pollinators to areas with native plants, it is possible that genetic contamination could take place among native plants, thus reducing biological diversity. Further research is needed to address public concerns about the safety and long-term environmental effects of these technologies.

The long-term impact of this genetic tinkering is a question that concerns many, despite the fact that the FDA has deemed GM food safe to consume and many scientific research studies have shown no dangers to human health. Today, more than 75 percent of all processed food contains GM ingredients.[91] The United States does not require labeling. Because many consumers demand to know what is in their food, organic and all-natural grocery chains like Whole Foods have

Earth in the Balance

Drones Take Sustainability Sky-High

The applications of unmanned aerial vehicles (UAVs), also known as *drones,* have multiplied dramatically. Although the use of drones is controversial due to privacy and air-traffic concerns, they are a growing resource for some of society's most important challenges. For example, drones can be used to assist police departments and first responders by providing the exact location of car accidents, decreasing response times. They also can be used to deter poaching of wildlife, lessen food shortages, and more effectively prevent and contain forest fires.

As sustainability and social responsibility become higher priorities to businesses and the general public, the protection of natural resources and endangered species becomes more important, and UAVs can be useful. To help prevent poaching, for instance, drones can be dispatched to cover large areas of land with limited lighting by utilizing infrared cameras, which is highly beneficial at night. These cameras then can be used by conservationists to spot groups of poachers before they are able to cause any harm. This has the potential to help in the preservation of at-risk species, thus contributing to a more socially conscious society.

Additionally, crop health is significant to the rising human population. Many areas of the world experience food shortages, and with the population growing to an estimated 9 billion by 2050, smarter and more cost-effective farming is necessary. Drones help farmers increase plant health by analyzing soil and fields, leading to greater awareness about the most productive areas in which to plant. When crops are planted, drones assist with watering them, which frees up time for farmers. Drones also monitor plants for disease. When disease is found, farmers are able to act quickly and may be able to avoid significant crop failure by preventing the disease from passing to other plants.

Drones are used to study air quality and pollen count. This data could be used to inform the public or for scientific research. Solar-power businesses and wind farms are using drones to check on technical problems involving material loss or malfunctioning equipment without having to move staff to each area of the business. Wind turbine maintenance is one of the most dangerous jobs in the energy sector. The use of drones in this application greatly improves efficiency, productivity, and safety.

While environmental preservation is vital to a socially responsible society, the aftermath of natural disasters has largely been outside of society's control. Natural disasters can result in loss of life and severe damages to industry. Each year, California experiences severe wildfires. Knowing that this happens annually, technology can be used to reduce the injury wildfires cause. The White House has asked federal organizations to utilize UAVs in conjunction with the Federal Aviation Administration (FAA) to help increase the effectiveness of dealing with wildfires. Drones can locate "hot spots" and transport water to those areas to put out fires. This decreases the number of firefighters needed and improves the ability to fight fires at night.

Traditionally, ground and air control has been used to combat natural disasters. However, unlike ground and air control, using UAVs reduces energy use and greenhouse gas emissions. The advantages of drones to society are strong and increasing every year. Drone technology has proven itself to be a viable, ecofriendly alternative in many applications. The abilities of drones will continue to develop with technological advancements and discoveries.

Sources: Frances Beldia, "Impact of Drones on Society—Business, Connections, Privacy," *Bold Business,* 2019, https://www.boldbusiness.com/society/impact-of-drones-on-society/ (accessed July 25, 2019); Sebastien Long, "Drones and Precision Agriculture: The Future of Farming," *Microdrones,* November 16, 2017, https://www.microdrones.com/en/content/drones-and-precision-agriculture-the-future-of-farming/ (accessed July 25, 2019); Michal Mazur, "Six Ways Drones Are Revolutionizing Agriculture," *MIT Technology Review,* July 20, 2016, https://www.technologyreview.com/s/601935/six-ways-drones-are-revolutionizing-agriculture/ (accessed July 25, 2019); Dee Ann Divis, "Feds Directed to Use Drones to Fight Wildfires," *Autonomous Media,* February 5, 2019, http://insideunmannedsystems.com/feds-directed-to-use-drones-to-fight-wildfires/ (accessed July 25, 2019); "What Are the Most Dangerous Jobs in the Energy Sector?" *Power Technology,* September 6, 2018, https://www.power-technology.com/features/most-dangerous-jobs-in-the-energy-sector/ (accessed August 2, 2019).

taken advantage of this marketing opportunity by implementing their own policies regarding labeling or the elimination of GM ingredients.

Another example of the backlash against GM organisms is in the dairy industry. Many large dairy producers use hormones, called *recombinant bovine growth hormone (rBGH)* to increase milk production in cows. Many cows get sick from the hormones and are also given antibiotics. Even in the United States, where government bans are not in place and GM food is more accepted, many Americans refuse to buy milk that has come from cows given these drugs because it is perceived as less healthy. Companies such as Walmart, Starbucks, Kroger, and Safeway grocery store chains stopped carrying rBGH milk after strong consumer backlash.[92] This has also created great opportunities for organic milk and producers of milk alternatives such as almond milk and oat milk.[93]

Countries Against GM Food All of these concerns have prompted consumers around the world, particularly in Europe and Japan, to boycott products made from GM crops. Moreover, 64 countries—including all of the members of the EU, Australia, and Japan—have imposed bans or restrictions on GM products.[94] Farmers in France and Germany destroyed crops after traces of GM seeds were discovered by suppliers. The cultivation of GM crops is outlawed in France.[95] However, as more GM crops are grown and more GM foods are consumed without detrimental effects, some countries are becoming open to the technology. However slowly it may be occurring, countries in Africa are adopting the crops in order to combat hunger and ecological changes. Additionally, Nigeria approved its first GM food crop, pest-resistant cowpeas.[96]

GM Fish and Other Living Organisms Researchers have created GM rainbow trout with up to 20 percent more muscle mass that non-GM trout. By injecting 20,000 eggs with a protein that controls muscle growth, 300 eggs were found to carry the gene, resulting in muscular trout. These fish carry the potential benefit of increasing food supply, although concerns about them being released into water streams are high. The effects of them breeding with native fish are unknown, as their new genes will be transferred to offspring. In addition, their size will require them to consume more food, which may cause shortages, and birds that typically feed on small fish may eventually find their food supply lacking. In effect, releasing these muscular fish into the wild could upset the entire ecosystem.[97]

There are many types of GM animals under development for the purpose of selling commercially as food. AquaBounty Technologies is the leading company that has fully developed GM Atlantic salmon for the dinner table. These salmon require less feed to grow to the same size as conventional Atlantic salmon because they grow twice as fast. After new labeling regulations were published, the FDA cleared AquaBounty to begin selling food derived from its AquAdvantage salmon. Despite this progress, the company will undoubtedly continue to face criticism and pushback from fishing and environmental groups, and it will be an uphill battle for AquaBounty to convince retailers, many of which have indicated they have no plans to carry GM salmon, to stock AquAdvantage.[98]

Seed Contamination Seed contamination is described as the cross-pollination of natural seeds with GM seeds. The crops of farmers who are committed to producing natural and/or organic foods have been compromised when GM seeds are blown into their fields. Because the GM seeds are patent protected, there is little recourse farmers can take in this regard. In fact, they are likely to be charged with patent infringement if GM seeds are found in their fields without them purchasing them. Monsanto has been known for enforcing their patents on farmers whose fields are found with their seeds, as well as farmers who have purchased their seeds and reused them in succeeding years. In a Supreme Court ruling regarding seed contamination, the verdict was in favor of Monsanto, mainly because of the patented nature of the seeds. Monsanto has said that it will not sue farmers whose fields end up with the protected seeds by accidental means, but farmers whose livelihood depends on the organic or all-natural quality of food could be compromised by the presence of these seeds. On the other hand, the Oregon legislature may pass a bill that would allow farmers to sue companies such as Monsanto that hold patents on GM seeds if GM crops contaminate other crops. Contamination can cause certain crops to be unsellable.[99]

Environmental Policy and Regulation

The United States, like most other nations, has passed numerous laws and established regulatory agencies to address environmental issues. Most of these efforts have focused on the activities of businesses, government agencies, and other organizations that use natural resources in providing goods and services.

Environmental Protection Agency

The most influential regulatory agency that deals with environmental issues and enforces environmental legislation in the United States is the **Environmental Protection Agency (EPA).** The agency's founding in 1970 was the culmination of a decade of growing protests over the deterioration of environmental quality. This movement reached a significant climax with the publication of Rachel Carson's *Silent Spring*, an attack on the indiscriminate use of pesticides, which rallied scientists, activists, and citizens from around the country to crusade to protect the environment from abuses of the time. Twenty million Americans joined together on April 22, 1970, for the first Earth Day, a nationwide demonstration for environmental reforms. The EPA was formed in response to these events. The EPA is an independent agency that establishes and enforces environmental protection standards, conducts environmental research, provides assistance in fighting pollution, and assists in developing and recommending new policies for environmental protection. The agency is also charged with the following:

Environmental Protection Agency (EPA)
the most influential regulatory agency that deals with environmental issues and enforces environmental legislation in the United States

- Protecting Americans from significant risks to their health and to the environment.
- Managing environmental risks based on the best scientific information available.
- Enforcing federal laws protecting human health and the environment fairly and effectively.
- Ensuring environmental protection is an integral consideration in U.S. policies.
- Ensuring access to accurate information sufficient to all parts of society.
- Ensuring environmental protection contributes to diverse, sustainable, and economically productive communities and ecosystems.[100]

To fulfill its primary mission to protect human health and sustainability into the twenty-second century, the EPA established six priority goals to define its planning, budgeting, analysis, and accountability processes (see Table 12.4). To support its efforts, the Office of Inspector General conducts investigations to protect "the integrity of programs and operations" within these goals.[101] The EPA is empowered to file civil charges against companies that violate the law. For years, many companies involved in the mining and extraction industries were not

Table 12.4 Priority Goals of the Environmental Protection Agency

1. Improve air quality by implementing pollution control measures to reduce the number of nonattainment areas.
2. Empower communities to leverage EPA water infrastructure investments.
3. Accelerate the pace of cleanups and return sites to beneficial use in their communities.
4. Meet new statutory requirements to improve the safety of chemicals in commerce.
5. Increase environmental law compliance rate.
6. Accelerate permitting-related decisions.

Source: Environmental Protection Agency, "Strategic Plan 2019–2023," https://www.epa.gov/sites/production/files/2019-03/documents/_epaoig_epaoig_strategicplan2019-2023_3-12-2019.pdf (accessed July 19, 2019).

forced to pay for cleanup of environmental damage. However, the EPA has taken steps to ensure that companies are financially responsible for future environmental damage, rather than taxpayers and other stakeholders.[102]

Environmental Legislation

A number of laws have been passed to address both general and specific environmental issues, including public health, threatened species, toxic substances, clean air and water, and natural resources. For instance, leaded gasoline was phased out during the 1990s because catalytic converters, which are used to reduce pollution and required by law on most vehicles, do not work properly with leaded gasoline. In addition, lead exposure is harmful to people. The automobile industry is responding to increased Corporate Average Fuel Economy (CAFE) standards by determining methods to increase gas mileage. Federal regulation required automobiles to get 35.5 miles per gallon (mpg) by 2016 and 54.5 mpg by 2025, and car makers have devised alternative ways of building their cars to achieve these goals.[103] Strategies include incorporating lighter materials like aluminum, increased production and sales of hybrid vehicles, and improving electric cars and hydrogen fuel-cell technology.[104] Table 12.5 summarizes some significant laws related to environmental protection.

Clean Air Act   The Clean Air Act (CAA) is a comprehensive federal law that regulates atmospheric emissions from a variety of sources.[105] The law established national air quality standards as well as standards for significant new pollution sources emitting hazardous substances. These maximum pollutant standards, called National Ambient Air Quality Standards (NAAQS), are federally mandated to protect public health and the environment. States have the responsibility of developing implementation plans to meet the NAAQS by restricting emissions of criteria pollutants from stationary sources (industries) within the state.

The Clean Air Act mandates that states are responsible for their air quality. The majority of people appear to overwhelmingly agree with the purpose of the CAA. For instance, a survey conducted by the American Lung Association indicated that 75 percent of respondents view clean air as very or extremely important.[106] This means that clean air should be a primary concern for businesses in order to maintain good relationships with stakeholders.[107] Though air quality has improved significantly since the passage of the CAA, the rollback of CAA rules, such as greenhouse gas standards for cars and light trucks, has been a focus in recent years.[108]

Endangered Species Act   The Endangered Species Act established a program to protect threatened and endangered species, as well as the habitats in which they live.[109] An endangered species is one that is in danger of extinction, whereas a threatened species is one that may become endangered without protection. The U.S. Fish and Wildlife Service of the Department of the Interior maintains the list of endangered and threatened species, which currently includes 1,275 endangered species (772 are plants) and 388 threatened species (172 are plants).[110] The Endangered Species Act prohibits any action that results in the harm to or death of a listed species or that adversely affects endangered species habitat. It also makes the import, export, and interstate and foreign commerce of listed species illegal. For example, a man was charged $6,800 for purchasing a tiger-skin rug.[111] Protected species may include birds, insects, fish, reptiles, mammals, crustaceans, flowers, grasses, cacti, and trees. Approximately 2 percent of endangered animals, including the bald eagle, have recovered.[112]

The Endangered Species Act is highly controversial because some threatened or endangered species are a nuisance to ranchers and farmers and have been harmed or killed by landowners seeking to avoid the hassle or expense of

Table 12.5 Major Environmental Laws

Act (Date Enacted)	Purpose
National Environmental Policy Act (1969)	Established a national environmental policy and a Council on Environmental Quality, set goals, and provided a means for implementing the policy; promotes efforts to prevent damage to the biosphere and to stimulate human health and welfare.
Occupational Safety and Health Act (1970)	Ensures worker and workplace safety by requiring employers to provide a place of employment free from health and safety hazards.
Clean Air Act (1970)	Regulates emissions from natural, stationary, and mobile sources; authorized the EPA to establish National Ambient Air Quality Standards (NAAQS) to protect public health and the environment.
Federal Insecticide, Fungicide, and Rodenticide Act (1972)	Provides for federal control of pesticide distribution, sale, and use; requires users to register when purchasing pesticides.
Endangered Species Act (1973)	Established a conservation program for threatened and endangered plants and animals and their habitats; prohibits any import, export, interstate, and foreign commerce/action that results in a "taking" of a listed species or that adversely affects habitat.
Safe Drinking Water Act (1974)	Protects the quality of drinking water in the United States; authorized the EPA to establish water purity standards and required public water systems to comply with health-related standards.
Toxic Substances Control Act (1976)	Empowered the EPA to track industrial chemicals currently produced or imported into the United States; authorized the EPA to require reporting or testing of chemicals and to ban the manufacture and import of chemicals that pose an unreasonable risk.
Resource Conservation Recovery Act (1976)	Empowered the EPA to control the generation, transportation, treatment, storage, and disposal of hazardous waste.
Clean Water Act (1977)	Authorized the EPA to set effluent standards on an industry-wide basis and to continue to set water quality standards for all contaminants in surface waters; made it unlawful for any person to discharge any pollutant from a point source into navigable waters without a permit.
Comprehensive Environmental Response, Compensation, and Liability Act (1980)	Established prohibitions and requirements concerning closed and abandoned hazardous waste sites; authorized a tax on the chemical and petroleum industries to establish a "superfund" to provide for cleanup when no responsible party could be identified.
Superfund Amendments Reauthorization Act (1986)	Amended the Comprehensive Environmental Response, Compensation, and Liability Act to increase the size of the superfund; required superfund actions to consider the standards and requirements found in other state and federal environmental laws and regulations; provided new enforcement authorities and tools.
Emergency Planning and Community Right-to-Know Act (1986)	Enacted to help local communities protect public health and safety and the environment from chemical hazards; requires each state to appoint a State Emergency Response Commission (SERC) and to establish Emergency Planning Districts.
Oil Pollution Act (1990)	Requires oil storage facilities and vessels to submit plans detailing how they will respond to large spills; requires the development of area contingency plans to prepare and plan for responses to oil spills on a regional scale.
Pollution Prevention Act (1990)	Promotes pollution reduction through cost-effective changes in production, operation, and use of raw materials and practices that increase efficiency and conserve natural resources, such as recycling, source reduction, and sustainable agriculture.
Food Quality Protection Act (1996)	Amended the Federal Insecticide, Fungicide, and Rodenticide Act and the Federal Food, Drug, and Cosmetic Act to change the way the EPA regulates pesticides; applies a new safety standard—reasonable certainty of no harm—to all pesticides used on foods.

(continued on next page)

Table 12.5 (*Continued*)

Beaches Environmental Assessment and Coastal Health Act (2000)	Amended the Clean Water Act to include provisions decreasing the risks of illness due to using the nation's recreational waters.
Energy Policy Act (2005)	Addresses the way energy is produced in the United States in terms of energy efficiency, renewable energy, oil and gas, coal, Tribal energy, nuclear matters and security, vehicles and motor fuels, hydrogen, electricity, energy tax incentives, hydropower and geothermal energy, and climate change technology.
Energy Independence and Security Act (2007)	Established corporate average fuel economy standards, renewable fuel standards, and the appliance/lighting efficiency standards.
American Clean Energy Act (2009)	Seeks to create clean energy jobs; more energy independence; reduce greenhouse gas emissions; and lay the groundwork for a clean energy economy.

Sources: Environmental Protection Agency, "Major Environmental Laws," http://www.epa.gov/pahome/laws.htm (accessed June 22, 2016); Environmental Protection Agency, "Summary of the Energy Policy Act," http://www2.epa.gov/laws-regulations/summary-energy-policy-act (accessed June 22, 2016); Environmental Protection Agency, "About the BEACH Act," beach-act (accessed June 22, 2016); Environmental Protection Agency, "Laws and Executive Orders," https://www.epa.gov/laws-regulations/laws-and-executive-orders (accessed July 22, 2019).

complying with the law. Concerns about the restrictions and costs associated with the law are not entirely unfounded. For example, a man was charged with unlawfully killing a mama grizzly bear (a species listed as threatened under the Endangered Species Act) when she and her two cubs showed up on his property. Several of the man's children were playing outside when the bears appeared, and he shot at them in order to protect his family. At the time of trial, the man was facing two years in prison, a $50,000 fine, and one-year probation. In the end, the man was not convicted, but this example shows the kind of issues that can arise from this law.[113]

Toxic Substances Control Act   Congress passed the Toxic Substances Control Act to empower the EPA with the ability to track the 75,000 industrial chemicals currently produced in or imported into the United States. The agency repeatedly screens these chemicals and requires reporting or testing of those that may pose an environmental or human health hazard. It can also ban the manufacture and import of chemicals that pose an unreasonable risk. The EPA tracks the thousands of new chemicals developed by industry each year with either unknown or dangerous characteristics. It also controls these chemicals as necessary to protect human health and the environment.[114] Ten states and the District of Columbia have sued the EPA for failure to create sufficient rules over the use of asbestos, a carcinogen that kills tens of thousands of people each year. Though it is known to cause cancer, federal law allows limited use of the substance.[115]

Clean Water Act   The Federal Water Pollution Control Act was renamed as the Clean Water Act in 1977. The law grants the EPA the authority to establish effluent standards on an industry basis and continue the earlier law's requirements to set water quality limits for all contaminants in surface waters. The Clean Water Act makes it illegal for anyone to discharge any pollutant from a point source into navigable waters without a permit.[116] This includes the pouring of contaminates down the drain. Formosa Plastics will pay a $50 million settlement after violating the Clean Water Act. For years, the company illegally discharged plastic pellets and other pollutants into Lavaca Bay in Texas.[117]

Food Quality Protection Act   The Food Quality Protection Act amended the Federal Insecticide, Fungicide, and Rodenticide Act and the Federal Food, Drug, and Cosmetic Act to fundamentally change the way the EPA regulates pesticides. The law included a new safety standard—reasonable certainty of no harm—that must be applied to all pesticides used on foods.[118] The legislation establishes a more consistent, science-based regulatory environment and mandates a single health-based standard for all pesticides in all foods. The law also provides special protections for infants and children, expedites approval of safer pesticides, provides incentives for the development and maintenance of effective crop protection tools for farmers, and requires periodic reevaluation of pesticide registrations and tolerances to ensure that they are up-to-date and based on good science.

Energy Policy Act The Energy Policy Act focuses the nation's priorities on alternative forms of energy in the hopes to lessen U.S. dependence on foreign oil. The bill offered tax breaks and loan guarantees to alternative energy companies, like nuclear power plants, solar companies, and wind energy farms, and also requires utilities to comply with federal reliability standards for the electricity grid. Consumers who purchased hybrid gasoline-electric cars and other energy-saving measures were rewarded with tax benefits. Tax credits were also provided for plug-in electric drive conversion kits.[119] The bill also extended daylight savings time by one month to save energy.[120]

Alternative Energy

Ongoing plans to reduce global carbon emissions are spurring countries and companies alike toward alternative energy sources. Traditional fossil fuels are problematic because of their contribution to climate change and global warming, as well as because of the increasing depletion of resources. Foreign fossil fuels are often imported from politically and economically unstable regions, often making it unsafe or unseemly to conduct business there. About 11 percent of petroleum consumed in the United States came from foreign sources. This is the lowest level since 1957.[121] This decrease is largely due to the recognition by the U.S. government of the need to look toward alternative forms of energy as a source of fuel and electricity. These sources include wind power, solar power, nuclear power, biofuels, and hydro and geothermal power. Table 12.6 provides some examples of companies and/or countries that use these alternative power sources.

Table 12.6 Alternative Energy

Energy Source	Examples
Wind	SC Johnson uses wind power to power its largest manufacturing facility
Geothermal	The largest complex of geothermal plants In the world, known as the Geysers in Northern California, produces 60 percent of the average electricity demand in the North Coast region of California
Solar	IKEA uses solar power at 90 percent of its U.S. stores
Nuclear	75 percent of France's electricity comes from nuclear power
Biofuels	BP is partnering with Bunge Ltd. to produce ethanol and electricity from sugar cane
Hydropower	Yahoo! uses hydropower at its New York facilities

Sources: Calpine Corporation, "About Geyser Energy," http://www.geysers.com/geothermal.aspx (accessed July 22, 2019); Yevgeniy Sverdlik, "Yahoo Launches Second 'Computing Coop' Data Center in New York State," *Data Center Knowledge*, April 27, 2015, in-new-york-state/ (accessed June 22, 2016); SC Johnson, "SC Johnson Powers Up Wind Energy at Company's Largest Manufacturing Facility," December 18, 2012, http://www.scjohnson.com/en/press-room/press-releases/12-18-2012/sc-johnson-powers-up-wind-energy-at-largest-mfg-facility.aspx (accessed June 22, 2016); Alexa Chianis, "5 Major Retailers Utilizing Solar Power in the U.S. Right Now," Solar Power Authority, https://www.solarpowerauthority.com/major-retailers-utilizing-solar-power-right-now/ (accessed July 22, 2019); World Nuclear Association, "Nuclear Power in France," June 2019, https://www.world-nuclear.org/information-library/country-profiles/countries-a-f/france.aspx (accessed July 22, 2019).

Wind Power

The Great Plains of the United States is one of the greatest sources of wind energy in the world, and many people believe that harnessing this energy will go a long way toward providing the United States' energy needs in the future. In fact, wind power is the fastest-growing form of renewable energy worldwide, and the amount of electricity generated by wind is set to surpass hydropower generation. It consists of nearly 7 percent of total electricity generation capacity in the United States.[122] However, there are a number of roadblocks standing between taking abundant wind and turning it into affordable energy. First of all, restructuring the nation's power grids to efficiently transmit wind, solar, and other forms of renewable energy will require a large investment. Widespread adoption of wind power has been slowed by the high cost of the turbines and limitations on an outdated national power grid. The technology is more expensive and less efficient than fossil fuels currently, but advances are being made continously. Many people believe that the United States will be a wind power hot spot in the future, and more Americans than ever are supporting the movement. The United States is a close second to China, the largest producer of wind power.[123]

Wind energy has long been popular in other countries such as the Netherlands and Denmark and is becoming a lucrative business for many companies. The Danish company Vestas Wind Systems is the world's largest producer of wind turbines, with 35 percent of the U.S. wind energy market. It has even expanded production to the United States in order to take advantage of the growing interest in wind energy.[124] Wind power is not without its faults. A Harvard study indicates that expansion of wind power could warm the United States because of the way the spinning blades affect the atmosphere. The researchers said that although wind energy has this negative environmental impact, the climate change from greenhouse gas emissions is a much greater threat.[125]

Geothermal Power

Geothermal energy comes from the natural heat inside the Earth, which is extracted by drilling into steam beds. Procter & Gamble, Mars, General Motors (GM), and Cargill have called for cost-effective, market-ready geothermal energy.[126] Although initial costs to build geothermal plants are high, savings in the long-term are well worth the investment. Carbon dioxide emissions are less than those produced by efficient natural gas power plants, and geothermal plants use less water than coal power plants. Geothermal power also provides a steady flow of electricity every day of the year, unlike wind or solar energy.

Despite these advantages, the extraction of fluids from the ground causes pollution and can sometimes cause the land to subside if careful environmental measures are not implemented. Additionally, geothermal drilling sites are not readily available everywhere because of certain factors such as the permeability of rock. This—along with the high cost—has resulted in slow adoption, as geothermal power represents less than five percent of global energy. The United States, Indonesia, and the Philippines, are the countries with the greatest capacity for geothermal power generation.[127] Research has shown that geothermal energy could become cheaper than fossil fuels as research and development receive more investment.

Solar Power

Solar power is a 100 percent renewable, passive energy source that can be converted into electricity through the use of either photovoltaic cells (solar cells) on homes and other structures or solar power plants. The major disadvantages of solar power are that the technology remains expensive and inefficient compared to traditional fossil fuel-generated energy and that the infrastructure for mass production of solar panels is not in place in many locations. Cloudy days, a seeming disadvantage, are not necessarily a problem as the ultraviolet rays required to generate power filter through clouds. Germany, a country not exactly known for its abundant sunshine, is number one in the world for solar power implementation.[128]

Given the strong sunshine in places like the U.S. Southwest and California, solar power has gained a lot of support in the United States. California, which is a decade ahead of its energy goals, produced so much solar energy that it was forced to cut back.[129] Additionally, the United States is adopting solar power at a record-breaking rate. More than 1 percent of U.S. electricity demand is supplied by solar power.[130] Solar energy is becoming an increasingly viable alternative for businesses to cut their pollution and emissions. Many Walmart facilities, with their huge flat roofs perfect for solar panels, now use solar power to generate the electricity of some stores. Walmart also subscribes to community solar gardens to power its locations.[131]

Nuclear Power

Countries throughout Europe have managed to greatly reduce their emissions through the implementation of nuclear power plants, yet this form of power remains controversial. Because of the danger associated with nuclear meltdowns and radioactive waste disposal, nuclear power has some significant disadvantages. On the one hand, nuclear power is pollution-free and cost-competitive. Uranium is abundant enough that generating as much as 60 times more energy than what is produced today would not be a problem. The United States is the leader in nuclear power generation. The nuclear power industry invests approximately $7.5 billion each year in maintenance and upgrades.[132]

On the other hand, concerns over the safety of nuclear power plants and the disposal of waste are prevalent. Radiation output of nuclear power can be harmful to workers and the areas where transport of nuclear waste occurs. The Chernobyl accident in Ukraine resulted in deaths, sickness, and birth defects. The crisis that occurred in Fukushima, Japan, after nuclear reactors were damaged in the 2011 earthquake and tsunami was disturbing to many people as Japan is a developed country that has significant infrastructure. The fact that a natural disaster could lead to a nuclear emergency has led some to question our abilities to ensure the complete safety of nuclear power.

Biofuels

Biofuels are derived from organic materials like corn, sugarcane, vegetable oil, and even trash. Ethanol made from sugarcane has been widely used in Brazil for decades, and the United States has adopted the use of ethanol made mostly from corn. This has become especially popular with those who want to reduce their car's carbon output or who are concerned with the nation's addiction to foreign oil. Automobile makers have responded by creating flex fuel and hybrid vehicles that can run on biofuels or gasoline. The Chevy Cruze, Audi A8, and Jeep Grand Cherokee can all run on B20, the most common biodiesel blend (20 percent biodiesel and 80 percent petroleum diesel). Panalpina Singapore launched new biodiesel trucks to support L'Oréal's sustainability program, Sharing Beauty with All. The company collects waste cooking oil from restaurants across Singapore to convert to biodiesel fuel.[133]

Legal mandates to incorporate biofuels have been passed in some countries. This is a major reason for Brazil's widespread use, as they made it a requirement to blend gasoline with ethanol. There is some controversy over the use of biofuels in the United States, however, because it is made from corn, which is highly energy intensive to produce. Another point of criticism is that they currently use food crops, which with widespread adoption, could lead to food shortages.

Researchers have been hard at work developing new technologies that could produce biofuels without deforestation of land or compromising food supplies. Cellulosic ethanol would be made from nonedible plants like grasses, sugarcane waste, algae, and wood waste. All Nippon Airways, Japan's top airline, will test biofuel made from rabbit droppings which contain enzymes that are helpful in ethanol production.[134]

Hydropower

Throughout history, people have used water as a power source and a means of transportation. From the water-powered mills of centuries past to modern hydroelectric dams, water is a powerful renewable energy source. Although in the United States, hydroelectric power only provides 2.8 percent of total output, hydropower provides 17 percent of total electricity production worldwide, making it the largest form of renewable energy. As with all other forms of energy production, hydropower has benefits and downsides. One of the major downsides is the destruction of wildlife habitats and sometimes even human habitations, when valleys are flooded due to dams. Hydroelectricity also disrupts the life cycles of aquatic life. Damming the Columbia River between Washington and Oregon states decimated the region's salmon industry, for example. Benefits of hydroelectric energy include little pollution and inexpensive maintenance costs once the infrastructure is in place.[135]

Business Response to Sustainability Issues

Many businesses have adopted a triple-bottom line approach that takes into consideration social and environmental performance in addition to economic performance. Firms are learning that being environmentally friendly and sustainable has numerous benefits—including increased goodwill from stakeholders and even money savings from being more efficient and less wasteful. Positions such as vice president of environmental affairs have been created to help companies achieve their business goals in an environmentally responsible manner. Additionally, companies such as Mars Inc. and Royal Dutch Shell are tying executive pay to sustainability goals to give managers more incentive to hit company targets.[136] Businesses such as Procter & Gamble have also developed environmental scorecards for their suppliers. Corporate efforts to respond to environmental issues focus on green marketing, recycling, emissions reductions, and socially responsible buying.

Yet despite the importance of the environment, companies are in business to make a profit. Economic performance is still a necessary bottom line for most businesses. For example, LEGO committed to converting its building blocks to sustainable materials by 2030. Although the company invested $150 million in research and development, LEGO has struggled to find a plant-based plastic that works as well as its existing materials.[137] This begs the question: Is going green cost-effective for companies? Studies suggest that improving a company's environmental performance can in fact increase revenues and reduce costs. Table 12.7

Table 12.7 Sustainability Opportunities for Economic Performance

Sustainability Opportunity	Example
Differentiation of products	Method, a company that makes cleaning products, successfully uses sustainability to differentiate its products from the competition.
Cost of energy	Walmart lowers its energy costs through the use of solar power.
Relationship with customers	Customers that purchase a Preserve Products recycled toothbrush are given a mailer that they can use to mail the toothbrush back to the company for recycling at the end of their use.
Employee loyalty	New Belgium Brewing motivates employees to be sustainable by providing them with a mountain bike after they have worked there for one year.
Community relations	Patagonia has a Common Threads Initiative that encourages people to reduce their consumption and help the environment by refraining from buying items they do not need.

provides examples of how companies have used sustainability opportunities to affect performance.

Better environmental performance can increase revenue in three ways: through better access to certain markets, differentiation of products, and the sale of pollution-control technology. A firm's innovation in sustainability can be based on applying existing knowledge and technology or creating a completely new approach. Improving a firm's reputation for environmental stewardship may help companies capture this growing market niche.

Supply Chain Issues

An important aspect of building a corporate reputation is ensuring the sustainability of the supply chain. Walmart, for instance, is requiring its green marketing suppliers to be more environmentally friendly. Walmart has developed a Sustainability Index that it uses to track the environmental impact of its products. Walmart purchases more than 70 percent of its U.S. products from suppliers that participate in the program. So far, the index has been applied to 125 product categories and 1,800 suppliers.[138] These kinds of activities should go a long way toward helping consumers make "greener" choices.[139] Improving a supply chain's environmental performance may be key to attracting more business from the retail industry. Better environmental performance can also reduce costs by improving risk management and stakeholder relationships, reducing the amount of materials and energy used, and reducing capital and labor costs. Improved environmental standards should help prevent some major environmental disasters in the future. For those disasters that cannot be avoided, the firm can at least show that it applied due diligence with its environmental performance, which may reduce the company's culpability in the public's eye. Companies can also decrease the costs of compliance with governmental regulations and reduce fines if they become more energy efficient.

Green Marketing

Green marketing is a strategic process involving stakeholder assessment to create meaningful, long-term relationships with customers, while maintaining, supporting, and enhancing the natural environment. One company that is known for its commitment to being green is New Belgium Brewing in Fort Collins, Colorado. From its conception, New Belgium has been a company committed to sustainability. Its facilities use natural lighting and evaporative coolers to save on energy costs, and the buildings themselves were constructed of pine trees that were killed by invasive beetles (a growing problem in the Rockies). The brewery has been

green marketing
a strategic process involving stakeholder assessment to create meaningful, long-term relationships with customers while maintaining, supporting, and enhancing the natural environment

Figure 12.4 The European Ecolabel

Source: "European Union Ecolabel Logo," *Europa*, European Union, http://ec.europa.eu/environment/ecolabel/ (accessed July 18, 2019).

greenwashing
misleading a consumer into thinking that a product is more environmentally friendly than it is

wind-powered for over a decade and also uses waste from the brewing process to produce on-site methane gas for energy. The company encourages its employees to bike to work and actively engages in benchmarking and setting ambitious goals for reducing energy and waste even further.[140]

Many products are certified as "green" by environmental organizations such as Green Seal and carry a special logo identifying them as such. In Europe, companies can voluntarily apply for an Ecolabel (see Figure 12.4) to indicate that their product is less harmful to the environment than competing products based on scientifically determined criteria. The EU supports the Ecolabel program, which has been utilized in product categories as diverse as refrigerators, mattresses, vacuum cleaners, footwear, and televisions. Certification does not include food and medicine.[141]

Greenwashing

Businesses must approach their green marketing tactics with caution so as not to mislead consumers.[142] **Greenwashing** involves misleading a consumer into thinking that a good or service is more environmentally friendly than it is. It occurs when companies want to attract environmentally conscious consumers and can range from making environmental claims that are required by law and are therefore irrelevant (like "CFC-free") to puffery (exaggerating environmental claims) to outright fraud. Researchers compared claims on products sold in 10 countries, including the United States, to labeling guidelines established by the International Organization for Standardization (ISO), which prohibit vague and misleading claims, as well as unverifiable ones such as "environmentally friendly" and "nonpolluting." The study found that many products' claims are too vague or misleading to meet ISO standards.[143] For example, some products will be labeled as "chemical-free" when in fact everything contains chemicals, including plants and animals. Products with the highest number of misleading or unverifiable claims were laundry detergents, household cleaners, and paints. Advocates agree there is still a long way to go to ensure that shoppers are adequately informed about the environmental impact of the products they buy.[144]

Often, consumers do not find out about these false claims until after the purchase.[145] So while greenwashing may increase sales in the short-term and build the appearance of a company's sustainability reputation, it will cause serious repercussions when consumers learn they have been misled. This leads to poor long-term financial performance, which negatively affects all stakeholders of the company.[146] The retailer Zara has been accused of greenwashing after publicly committing to its sustainability efforts, promising sustainable fabrics over the next few years. Zara and other fast fashion retailers such as H&M and Forever 21 produce billions of new clothing items annually and greatly contribute to fashion industry waste.[147] At the same time, the terms *green* and *sustainability* can be hard to define, resulting in unintentional greenwashing. The FTC issued green guidelines to help marketers determine the truthfulness of "green" claims in order to reduce this confusion.[148]

Strategic Implementation of Environmental Responsibility

Businesses have responded to the opportunities and threats created by environmental issues with varying levels of commitment. Some companies, like New Belgium Brewing, consider sustainability a core component of the business. Other companies engage in greenwashing and do not actively seek to be more sustainable at all. As Figure 12.5 indicates, a low-commitment business attempts to avoid

Figure 12.5 Strategic Approaches to Environmental Issues

Low Commitment	Medium Commitment	High Commitment
Deals only with existing problems	Attempts to comply with environmental laws	Has strategic programs to address environmental issues
Makes only limited plans for anticipated problems	Deals with issues that could cause public relations problems	Views environment as an opportunity to advance the business strategy
Fails to consider stakeholder environmental issues	Views environmental issues from a tactical, not a strategic, perspective	Consults with stakeholders about their environmental concerns
Operates without concern for long-term environmental impact	Views environment as more of a threat than an opportunity	Conducts an environmental audit to assess performance and adopts international standards

dealing with environmental issues and hopes that nothing bad will happen or that no one will ever find out about an environmental accident or abuse. Such firms may try to protect themselves against lawsuits. Other firms are more proactive in anticipating risks and environmental issues. Such firms develop strategic management programs, which view the environment as an opportunity for advancing organizational interests. These companies respond to stakeholder interests, assess risks, and develop a comprehensive environmental strategy. Home Depot, for example, has established a set of environmental principles that include selling responsibly marketed products, eliminating unnecessary packaging, recycling and encouraging the use of products with recycled content, and conserving natural resources by using them wisely. The company also makes contributions to many environmental organizations.

Recycling Initiatives

Many organizations engage in **recycling**, the reprocessing of materials, especially steel, aluminum, paper, glass, rubber, and some plastics, for reuse. In fact, recycling is one of the country's greatest sustainability success stories. Today, 67 percent of all newspaper and mechanical paper used in the United States is recycled. About 68 percent of paper and paperboard is recovered.[149] Paper is not the only thing that is recyclable, however. For example, MillerCoors reuses or recycles nearly 100 percent of its waste, including residual brewer's grain and spent yeast.[150]

Sometimes companies join partnerships and become members of organizations like WasteWise, which aims to reduce municipal solid waste and industrial waste.[151] These collaborations help companies save money through reducing waste, receiving positive publicity, and tracking how they reduce waste over time. Local and regional governments are also finding ways to recycle water to avoid discharging chemicals into rivers and streams and to preserve diminishing water supplies. After decades of siphoning water from surrounding regions, the city of Dallas, Texas, had to change its behaviors due to dwindling resources. Many conservationists see city-dwellers' love of green lawns and golf courses in a drought-prone region as simply wasteful and irresponsible. Part of the plan to address this thirst for water is the installation of more and larger water-recycling facilities.[152]

recycling
the reprocessing of materials, especially steel, aluminum, paper, glass, rubber, and some plastics, for reuse

Stakeholder Assessment

Stakeholder assessment is an important part of a high-commitment approach to environmental issues. This process requires acknowledging and actively monitoring the environmental concerns of all legitimate stakeholders. Thus, a company must have a process in place for identifying and prioritizing the many claims and stakes on its business and for dealing with trade-offs related to the impact on different stakeholders. Although no company can satisfy every claim, all risk-related claims should be evaluated before a firm decides to take action on or ignore a particular issue. To make accurate assumptions about stakeholder interests, managers need to conduct research, assess risks, and communicate with stakeholders about their respective concerns.

However, not all stakeholders are equal. There are specific regulations and legal requirements that govern some aspects of stakeholder relationships, such as air and water quality. A business cannot knowingly harm the water quality of other stakeholders in order to generate a profit. Additionally, some special-interest groups take extreme positions that, if adopted, would undermine the economic base of many other stakeholders (e.g., fishing rights, logging, and hunting). Regardless of the final decision a company makes with regard to particular environmental issues, information should be communicated consistently across all stakeholders. This is especially important when a company faces a crisis or negative publicity about a decision. Another aspect of strong relationships is the willingness to acknowledge and openly address potential conflicts. Some degree of negotiation and conciliation will be necessary to align a company's decisions and strategies with stakeholder interests.

Risk Analysis

The next step in a high-commitment response to environmental concerns is assessing risk. Through industry and government research, an organization can usually identify environmental issues that relate to manufacturing, marketing, consumption, and use patterns associated with its products. Through risk analysis, it is possible to assess the environmental risks associated with business decisions. The difficulty is measuring the costs and benefits of environmental decisions, especially in the eyes of interested stakeholders. Research often conflicts, adding to the confusion and controversy over sustainability.

Debate surrounding environmental issues will force corporate decision-makers to weigh the evidence and take some risks in final decisions. The important point for high-commitment organizations is to continue to evaluate the latest information and to maintain communication with all stakeholders. For example, if the millions of sport utility vehicles (SUVs) on U.S. roads today were replaced with fuel-efficient electric-powered cars and trucks, there would be a tremendous reduction of greenhouse gas emissions. However, the cooperation and commitment needed to gain the support of government, manufacturers, consumers, and other stakeholders to accomplish this would be impossible to achieve. Although SUVs may contribute to the detriment of the environment, many of their owners prefer them because they provide greater protection in an accident than smaller vehicles.

The issue of environmental responsibility versus safety in SUVs illustrates that many environmental decisions involve tradeoffs for various stakeholders' risks. Through risk management, it is possible to quantify these tradeoffs in determining whether to accept or reject environmentally related activities and programs. Usually, the key decision is between the amount of investment required to reduce the risk of damage and the amount of risk acceptable in stakeholder relationships. A company should assess these relationships on an ongoing basis. Both formal and informal methods are needed to get feedback from stakeholders. For example, the employees of a firm can use formal methods such as exit interviews, an open-door policy, and toll-free telephone hotlines. Conversations among employees could provide informal feedback. But it is ultimately the responsibility of the business to make the best decisions possible after processing all available research and information. Then, if it is later discovered that a mistake has been made, change is still possible through open disclosure and thoughtful reasoning. Finally, a high-commitment organization will incorporate new information and insights into the strategic planning process.

The Strategic Environmental Audit

Organizations that are highly committed to environmental responsibility may conduct an audit of their efforts and report the results to all interested stakeholders. Table 12.8 provides a starting point for examining environmental sensitivity. Such organizations may also wish to use globally accepted standards, such as ISO 14000, as benchmarks in a strategic environmental audit. The International Organization for Standardization developed **ISO 14000** as a comprehensive set of environmental standards that encourage a cleaner, safer, and healthier world. There is considerable variation among the environmental laws and regulations of nations and regions, making it difficult for high-commitment organizations to find acceptable solutions on a global scale. The goal of the ISO 14000 standards is to promote a common approach to environmental management and to help companies attain and measure improvements in environmental performance. Companies that choose to abide by the ISO standards must review their environmental management systems periodically and identify all aspects of their operations that could affect the environment.[153] Other performance benchmarks available for use in environmental audits come from nonprofit organizations such as CERES, which has also developed standards for reporting information about environmental performance to interested stakeholders. The Green Globe program also offers environmental auditing and benchmarking services along with worldwide environmental certification for businesses.[154]

ISO 14000
a comprehensive set of environmental standards that encourage a cleaner, safer, and healthier world developed by the International Organization for Standardization

Table 12.8 Strategic Sustainability Audit

Yes	No	Checklist
O	O	Does the organization show a high commitment to a strategic environmental policy?
O	O	Do employees know the environmental compliance policies of the organization?
O	O	Do suppliers and customers recognize the organization's stand on environmental issues?
O	O	Are managers familiar with the environmental strategies of other organizations in the industry?
O	O	Has the organization compared its environmental initiatives with those of other firms?
O	O	Is the company aware of the best practices in environmental management regardless of industry?
O	O	Has the organization developed measurable performance standards for environmental compliance?
O	O	Does the firm reconcile the need for consistent responsible values with the needs of various stakeholders?
O	O	Do the organization's philanthropic efforts consider environmental issues?
O	O	Does the organization comply with all laws and regulations that relate to environmental impact?

As this chapter has demonstrated, social responsibility entails responding to stakeholder concerns about the environment, and many firms are finding creative ways to address environmental challenges. Although many of the companies mentioned in this chapter have chosen to implement strategic environmental initiatives to capitalize on opportunities and achieve greater efficiency and cost savings, most also believe that responding to stakeholders' concerns about environmental issues will both improve relationships with stakeholders and make the world a better place.

Summary

Although the scope of sustainability is quite broad, we define it as the potential for long-term well-being of the natural environment, including all biological entities, as well as the interaction among nature and individuals, organizations, and business strategies. Sustainability includes the assessment and improvement of business strategies, economic sectors, work practices, technologies, and lifestyles while maintaining the natural environment. Sustainability does not mean the same thing as social responsibility. Rather, it is a domain of social responsibility.

A major part of achieving sustainability is reducing sources of pollution. Air pollution arises from stationary sources such as factories and power plants; mobile sources such as cars, trucks, planes, and trains; and natural sources such as windblown dust and volcanic eruptions. Acid rain results when nitrous oxides and sulfur dioxides emitted from manufacturing facilities react with air and rain. Scientists believe that increasing concentrations of greenhouse gases in the atmosphere are warming the planet, although this theory is still controversial. The Kyoto Protocol is a treaty among industrialized nations to slow global warming. However, major polluters such as the United States and China were not signatories of the Kyoto Protocol. The second commitment phase is currently in place. Europe has instituted a cap-and-trade program, which places a limit (cap) on carbon emissions but allows businesses to purchase carbon permits from other companies. The United States is avoiding a wide-scale cap-and-trade program but is placing limits on carbon emissions that will affect coal plants.

Water pollution results from the dumping of raw sewage and toxic chemicals into rivers and oceans; from oil and gasoline spills; from the burial of industrial waste in the ground where it can reach underground water supplies; and from the runoff of fertilizers and pesticides used in farming and grounds maintenance. The amount of clean water available is also a concern and the topic of political disputes.

Land pollution results from the dumping of residential and industrial waste, strip mining, and poor forest conservation. How to dispose of waste in an environmentally responsible manner is an important issue. Deforestation to make way for agriculture and development threatens animal and plant species, as well as humans. Urban sprawl, the result of changing human development patterns, consumes wildlife habitat, wetlands, and farmland.

Deforestation, pollution, and urban sprawl threaten wildlife, plants, and their habitats and have caused many species to become endangered or even extinct. Biodiversity is threatened by all these activities and should be an important topic of consideration for organizations and businesses.

GM organisms are created through manipulating plant and animal genes so as to produce a desired effect like resistance to pests and viruses, drought resistance, or high crop yield. Many farmers now plant GM crops that are more pest and insecticide resistant, require fewer chemicals to produce, and have higher yields. The long-term consequences of these scientific innovations are unknown. Some fear that, because GM food is not naturally occurring, it could harm biodiversity or cause health problems in humans. Even so, there is a continued interest in GM products as a way to solve problems such as world hunger, drought, and pest invasions.

The EPA is an independent regulatory agency that establishes and enforces environmental protection standards, conducts environmental research, provides assistance in fighting pollution, and assists in developing and recommending new policies for environmental protection.

To reduce greenhouse gas emissions and dependence on fossil fuels, many countries and businesses are investigating in alternative forms of renewable energy. Wind power utilizes large turbines to convert wind into electricity. It has long been popular in windy regions such as northern Europe and is catching on in places like the United States and Mexico. Geothermal power harnesses the heat trapped inside the Earth to generate power. While not feasible everywhere, it is an attractive option because geothermal energy is available all of the time, unlike wind or solar power. Solar power can also be converted to electricity. Sunny places like the American Southwest are the sites of intensive solar power research. Nuclear power is another possible, albeit controversial, form of alternative energy. Countries in Europe and Asia continue to use nuclear power a great deal, but concerns remain over possible meltdowns and how to dispose of the waste. Biofuels have gained in popularity as a way to reduce the consumption of gasoline. However, adopting corn ethanol in the United States has been more problematic as it involves using a key food source. Hydropower is the most common alternative fuel used in the world, but it is expensive to set up initially and can have detrimental effects on river systems and surrounding areas.

Businesses are applying creativity, technology, and business resources to respond to environmental issues. Some firms have a vice president of environmental affairs to help them achieve their business goals in an environmentally responsible manner. Green marketing is a strategic process involving stakeholder assessment to create meaningful long-term relationships with customers, while maintaining, supporting, and enhancing the natural environment. While green marketing has become more popular, companies must be careful not to engage in greenwashing. Greenwashing involves misleading a consumer into thinking that a product is more environmentally friendly than it really is.

There is growing agreement among environmentalists and businesses that companies should work to protect and preserve sustainability. Many organizations engage in recycling, the reprocessing of materials—especially steel, aluminum, paper, glass, rubber, and some plastics—for reuse. Businesses have responded to the opportunities and threats created by environmental issues with varying levels of commitment. A high-commitment business develops strategic management programs, which view the environment as an opportunity for advancing organizational interests. Stakeholder assessment requires a process for identifying and prioritizing the many claims and stakes on its business and for dealing with trade-offs related to the impact on different stakeholders. Risk analysis tries to assess the environmental risks and trade-offs associated with business decisions. Organizations that are highly committed to environmental responsibility may conduct an audit of their efforts and report the results to all interested stakeholders. Such organizations may use globally accepted standards, such as ISO 14000, as benchmarks in a strategic environmental audit.

Responsible Business Debate

The Powers That Be: How Sustainable Is Nuclear Energy?

Issue: *Is nuclear power worth the risk?*

When it comes to energy sources, businesses and society can hold opposing views. Nuclear power has been beneficial to businesses because it is abundant and cost-effective. However, it also has traditionally been frowned upon by social groups due to the potential danger of nuclear meltdowns and radioactive waste disposal. In light of both the advantages and disadvantages of this energy source, government regulations have been created to encourage greener energy. The Energy Policy Act offers incentives in the form of reduced taxes and loan guarantees to companies who invested in alternative energy. The Nuclear Regulatory Commission provides oversight for nuclear power plants to ensure safety precautions are taken by plants in the production of nuclear power.

While nuclear energy is highly regulated in the United States, there is still controversy around the danger of using fission in the production of nuclear power. Supporters of nuclear energy point out that nuclear power has the lowest number of direct fatalities per kilowatt of energy produced compared to other major energy sources. Additionally, nuclear accidents, though widely feared and publicized, are actually quite rare. Nuclear power plants also keep the air clean, unlike gas or coal.

Fission is the separation of a nucleus into two nuclei. By contrast, *fusion* is the unification of two nuclei. Fusion produces a greater energy output than fission, with much less radioactive waste. The by-products of fission are environmentally detrimental, and although the actual nuclear reactors do not emit carbon dioxide, utilizing fossil fuels for the production of uranium ore does produce it. Another key difference between fission and fusion is that fusion does not leak outward, but rather inward. With fusion, reactors cannot undergo a meltdown, thus creating a safer, more stable energy source. From a sustainability perspective, nuclear energy is one of the few scalable, zero-carbon energy sources. While fusion is more stable than fission, it is less easily controlled. Companies are studying ways to use fusion over fission and continue to make strides.

One company that is pioneering fusion energy is TAE Technologies. TAE's goal has been to make a reactor that will fuse hydrogen and boron atoms at intense temperatures. Its mission started more than 20 years ago. Michl Binderbauer, chief executive officer (CEO) of TAE, stated that this technology will be commercialized in the near future. As a privately held company, TAE is able to do more research more quickly than its competitors. In addition, the company has backing from wealthy investors such as Charles Schwab, the Rockefeller family, and actor Harry Hamlin. TAE is also in the process of funding and developing a project with the U.S. government. Binderbauer said that TAE has been in talks with the Department of Energy and that the department will contribute to a public-private relationship. The partnership between the two could drastically move along the research process toward a safer solution.

There Are Two Sides to Every Issue

1. Nuclear power is affordable and cost effective, and therefore worth the risk.
2. The risks associated with nuclear power make it too risky, despite its benefits.

Sources: Christopher Helman, "The New Nuclear: How A $600 Million Fusion Energy Unicorn Plans to Beat Solar," *Forbes*, May 21, 2019, https://www.forbes.com/sites/christopherhelman/2019/05/21/the-new-nuclear-how-a-600-million-fusion-energy-unicorn-plans-to-beat-solar/#15aa0a0a629e (accessed July 28, 2019); Jeff McMahon, "Energy from Fusion in 'a Couple Years,' CEO Says, Commercialization in Five," *Forbes*, January 14, 2019, https://www.forbes.com/sites/jeffmcmahon/2019/01/14/private-firm-will-bring-fusion-reactor-to-market-within-five-years-ceo-says/#183007731d4a (accessed July 28, 2019); U.S. Energy Information Administration, "Nuclear Explained: Nuclear Power and the Environment," January 16, 2019, https://www.eia.gov/energyexplained/index.php?page=nuclear_environment (accessed July 28, 2019); Duke Energy, "Fission vs. Fusion—What's the Difference?" January 30, 2013, https://nuclear.duke-energy.com/2013/01/30/fission-vs-fusion-whats-the-difference (accessed July 28, 2019); U.S. Environmental Protection Agency, "Summary of the Energy Policy Act," 2005, https://www.epa.gov/laws-regulations/summary-energy-policy-act (accessed July 28, 2019); U.S. Environmental Protection Agency, "Radiation Protection: How Is the EPA Involved with the Regulation and Safety of Nuclear Power Plants?" https://www.epa.gov/radiation/how-epa-involved-regulation-and-safety-nuclear-power-plants (accessed July 28, 2019); World Nuclear Association, "The Nuclear Debate," April 2018, https://www.world-nuclear.org/information-library/current-and-future-generation/the-nuclear-debate.aspx (accessed July 29, 2019).

Key Terms

acid rain (p. 345)
Affordable Clean Energy (ACE) rule
    (p. 349)
biodiversity (p. 344)
bioenergy (p. 353)
cap and trade programs (p. 348)
climate change (p. 346)
Coalition for Environmentally
    Responsible Economies
    (CERES) (p. 344)

dead zone (p. 351)
Environmental Protection Agency
    (EPA) (p. 359)
green marketing (p. 367)
greenhouse effect (p. 345)
greenwashing (p. 368)
ISO 14000 (p. 371)
Kyoto Protocol (p. 347)
ozone (p. 345)
particulate matter (PM) (p. 344)

recycling (p. 369)
single-use plastics (p. 343)
sustainability (p. 342)
sustainable business practices
    (p. 343)
U.S. Global Climate Change
    Initiative (p. 347)

Discussion Questions

1. Define sustainability in the context of social responsibility. How does adopting this concept affect the way businesses operate?
2. Describe the controversy surrounding GM foods.
3. Discuss renewable energy initiatives such as wind, solar, and geothermal. Which do you think are most feasible and most important for businesses to focus on?
4. Think of instances of greenwashing that you have encountered. What is the harm of greenwashing?
5. What is the role of the EPA in U.S. environmental policy? What impact does this agency have on businesses?
6. What federal laws seem to have the greatest impact on business efforts to be environmentally responsible?

7. What role do stakeholders play in a strategic approach to environmental issues? How can businesses satisfy the interests of diverse stakeholders?
8. What is environmental risk analysis? Why is it important for an environmentally conscious company?
9. What is ISO 14000? What is its potential impact on key stakeholders, community, businesses, and global organizations concerned about environmental issues?
10. How can businesses become more sustainable? What are the advantages and disadvantages of striving to become more sustainable?

Experiential Exercise

Visit the website of the EPA (http://www.epa.gov/newsroom/). What topics and issues fall under the agency's authority? Peruse its most recent news releases. What themes, issues, regulations, and other areas is the EPA most concerned with today? How can this site be useful to consumers and businesses?

The "Sustainability" of Sustainability: What Would You Do?

The Sustainability Committee's first meeting was scheduled for Thursday afternoon. Although it was only Tuesday, several people had already dropped by committee members' offices to express their opinions and concerns about the company's new focus on sustainability. Some colleagues had trouble with the broad definition of sustainability—"to balance the economic, environmental, and social needs of today's world while planning for future generations." Others worried that the sustainability project was just another passing fad. A small group of colleagues believed that the company should be most concerned with performance and should forget about trying to become a leader in the social responsibility movement. In general, however, most employees were either supportive or neutral on the initiative.

As the committee's meeting started, the chair reminded the group that the company's CEO was very committed to sustainability, for several reasons. First, the company was engaged in product development and manufacturing processes that had environmental effects. Second, most companies in their industry were starting initiatives on sustainable development. Third, recent scandals had negatively affected public opinion about business in general. Finally, the company was exploring markets in Europe where environmental activism and rules were often more stringent. With these reasons in mind, the committee set out to develop plans for the next year.

For an hour, the committee discussed the general scope of sustainability in the company. They agreed that sustainability was concerned with increasing positive results while reducing negative effects on a variety of stakeholders. They also agreed that sustainability focused on the "triple bottom line" of financial, social, and environmental performance. For example, a company dedicated to sustainability could design and build a new facility that used alternative energy sources, minimized the impact on environmentally sensitive surrounding areas, and encouraged recycling and composting. Another firm might implement its sustainability objectives by requiring suppliers to meet certain standards for environmental impact, business ethics, economic efficiency, community involvement, and others.

After this discussion, the committee made a list of current and potential projects that were likely to be affected by the company's new sustainability focus. These projects included the following:

- Energy consumption
- Manufacturing emissions and waste
- Workplace diversity
- Community relations
- Corporate governance
- Regulations and compliance
- Philanthropy
- Product development
- Technology
- Supplier selection
- Employee health and safety
- Volunteerism

After much discussion, the committee agreed that each member would take one of the projects and prepare a brief report on its link to the environmental component of sustainability. This report should review the ways that environmental issues can be discussed, changed, improved, or implemented within that area to demonstrate a commitment to sustainability. What would you do?

CHAPTER

13

Social Responsibility in a Global Environment

Alibaba: The Gateway to Chinese Consumers

When Jack Ma founded Alibaba as an e-commerce business in 1999, he had never run a company and had no technology experience. After working as an English teacher, Ma took a trip to California's Silicon Valley and saw firsthand how the internet was transforming the business world. He quickly realized the commercial potential of pioneering an online marketing channel in China where small businesses could connect with local and international buyers of business goods and services.

While Ma had a desire to increase the development of China's commerce, he faced a major hurdle when it came to trust. China has a high level of uncertainty avoidance, meaning that Chinese consumers tend to avoid risk if possible. This makes establishing trust highly important. Entrepreneurs like Ma needed to find ways to establish trust between buyers and sellers in order for e-commerce channels to work. He possessed a high level of cultural intelligence and used this information to create culturally sensitive devices to build trust. For example, Alibaba uses rating systems as well as real-time chatting to allow buyers and sellers to learn about one another before they engage in transactions. These technologies helped alleviate trust issues, and Alibaba became a business-to-business e-commerce powerhouse. The initial business-to-business website did so well that Alibaba opened a second online marketplace for selling to consumers called Taobao. Today, the company's many marketplaces and supporting businesses, such as electronic payment systems, serve more than 600 million customers in over 200 nations.

Alibaba has held tightly onto its top spot in China, where non-Chinese e-commerce sites have struggled. For instance, eBay's move into the country lasted only two years and ultimately concluded in the closure of its China web unit. Similarly, Amazon has found little success in China, even with the launch of its Prime membership. As a result of its failure to adapt to the preferences of Chinese consumers, the company shut down its Chinese domestic e-commerce businesses. And Alibaba, with over 58 percent share in China's online retail market, made it difficult for Amazon to compete on price, preventing the U.S. online retail giant from gaining traction. China, with approximately 610 million online shoppers, is overtaking the United States as the largest e-commerce market, and the opportunities are too good for many investors to pass up. Alibaba has expanded into India, Australia, and Russia as well. As one of the largest e-commerce businesses in the world, Alibaba has few competitors other than Amazon. Alibaba opened its platform to welcome U.S. companies to list and sell products. The company said it is not concerned with the competition it faces in the United States and are focused on building a platform to support small businesses and entrepreneurs.

However, with growth comes ethical issues, and Alibaba is no exception. The company has faced bribery allegations and charges related to counterfeit goods in China, as well as a probe into its accounting practices by the U.S. Securities and Exchange Commission (SEC). As the company expands, it has begun removing products that have been flagged as counterfeit. The enormous number of counterfeit products available worldwide makes the pursuit of counterfeiters challenging. Despite concerns of political risk and the sale of counterfeit goods, investors have not been deterred.

Today, Alibaba is one of the top 10 companies in the world based on market value, and Ma, with a net worth of over $40 billion, is the richest man in China. Alibaba's success comes from understanding the global business environment. Managing with an understanding of the economic, legal, sociocultural, and political forces in the environment has been essential to gaining a global competitive advantage.[1]

Chapter Objectives

- Define cultural intelligence and its importance
- Discuss the global nature of stakeholder relationships
- Examine the importance of national competitiveness
- Describe the role of business in global development
- Explore global standards for social responsibility reporting

The expanding global marketplace requires that executives and managers develop the ability to conduct business effectively and in a socially responsible manner in different regions of the world. Values and expectations can differ from country to country. In this chapter, we elaborate on key topics and concepts that have been discussed in Chapters 1 through 12 by examining the unique nature of issues in the global environment and trends around the world. We also discuss the importance of cultural intelligence, delve into the complexities of working with stakeholders, provide emerging trends with primary stakeholders, and point to global standards of social reporting.

Cultural Intelligence

The movement of people across cities and continents means that ideas, values, traditions, languages, and customs have also migrated. While managers in different parts of the world may have unique (and even contrasting) perspectives, they also identify with a number of similar problems and opportunities, such as employee turnover, new business development, environmental protocols, and product innovation plans. Therefore, any culturally diverse work group will have a set of common experiences and another set of differences that must be recognized and managed. The potential for the group to achieve positive outcomes is largely based on each member's level of cultural intelligence. **Cultural intelligence** (sometimes called CQ) is the ability to interpret and adapt successfully to different national, organizational, and professional cultures.[2] There are three components to the development and use of cultural intelligence:

1. Cognitive—Knowledge of economic, legal, ethical, and social systems prevalent in different cultures and subcultures
2. Motivational—The intrinsic desire to learn about different cultures and subcultures and the confidence to function effectively in situations where differences are present
3. Behavioral—The ability to use appropriate verbal and nonverbal actions when interacting with people from different cultures and subcultures[3]

Cultural intelligence is desired of all employees, but it is necessary for those who work in different countries, manage diverse groups, and generally have responsibilities that require the ability to interpret unfamiliar gestures, behaviors, and situations. A start-up called Impact Route provides cultural intelligence training to professionals in Rwanda who work with multicultural organizations.[4] Employees must be comfortable suspending the impulse to make immediate judgments and practice thinking before acting. For example, when an American businesswoman made multiple presentations to potential partners in Bangkok, she was surprised there were so many side discussions while she talked. Because she did not speak Thai, she did not know the content of the audience's discussions and wondered if they were bored, uninterested, or even disrespectful. She decided to relax, continue, and accept the chatter. It occurred to her that these side discussions were likely a cultural norm, or perhaps they were simply the act of translating key points to a colleague with less familiarity with English. In this example, this businesswoman demonstrated strong cultural intelligence, and in so doing ensured that her company established a strong market presence in Thailand and Southeast Asia. If she had shown anger or frustration, the potential partners may have decided to take their business elsewhere. Figure 13.1 provides a short self-assessment of your CQ.

The effective practice of cultural intelligence requires a manager to parcel out what actions are true of all people, those that are unique to a particular group or culture, or whether the action lies somewhere along this continuum.[5] A person with high CQ will be skilled at recognizing how one individual or group is influenced by

cultural intelligence (CQ)
the ability to interpret and adapt successfully to different national, organizational, and professional cultures

Figure 13.1 Quick CQ Self-Assessment Tool

Think about your cultural intelligence in each of the following areas.

Select the answer (1–5) that BEST describes you as you really are.
1 – None of the description fits me.
2 – Only some of this fits me.
3 – Half of the description fits me.
4 – Most of the description fits me.
5 – The statements describe me perfectly.

CQ-Strategy	1	2	3	4	5

I plan carefully before I meet with someone who is from a different cultural background. After one of these experiences, I reflect carefully and try to make sense of the interaction.

CQ-Knowledge	1	2	3	4	5

I generally understand other cultures and cultural values. I know about the basic ways in which cultural are similar and the ways they are different.

CQ-Motivation	1	2	3	4	5

I am very interested in other cultures, and I enjoy meeting people who have different cultural backgrounds. I am confident that I can live in different cultures and that I can adapt to different parts of the world.

CQ-Behavior	1	2	3	4	5

I modify my behavior to make others more comfortable when I interact with people who are from different cultural backgrounds. I change the way I speak and act when I am in cross-cultural settings. I mimic others to make sure that I follow local conventions so that my speech patterns and body language are not offensive.

Interpreting Your Quick CQ Self-Assessment Responses

Sum your answers to the four questions in the Quick CQ Assessment Tool. Your score can range from 4 to 20.

4–7 points You see yourself as low in Cultural Intelligence. A CQ personal development plan could help you to become more capable of functioning effectively in culturally diverse situations.

8–16 points You see yourself as moderate in Cultural Intelligence. A CQ personal development plan could help you to enhance your capabilities in areas where you see yourself as less capable of functioning effectively in culturally diverse situations.

17–20 points You see yourself as high in Cultural Intelligence. A CQ personal development plan could help you to build on your impressive CQ strengths and become even more capable of functioning effectively in culturally diverse situations.

Copyright © 2006 Van Dyne and Ang

Source: Cultural Intelligence Center, "Self-Assessment of Your CQ," http://www.culturalq.com/selfassess.html (accessed July 28, 2014).

national, professional, and organizational cultures. For example, there are multiple layers of cultural effects to manage when an Irish manufacturing process expert from a consulting firm works with a Croatian engineer for a government agency in Croatia. The Irish expert would have to interpret and act according to Croatia's national culture, laws and governmental system, the agency's role and scope, the engineering profession's code of ethics, and the engineer's personality and values. Therefore, to achieve social responsibility in a global context, CQ is integral.

Cognitively, employees are obliged to learn the rules, values, and standards of different cultures. This entails studying the history, laws, symbols, customs, and related facets of a new culture. They should be willing and confident enough to adapt to these standards, but also strong enough to resist adapting when a legal, ethical, or other social responsibility expectation is in jeopardy. Opportunities to travel abroad provided by many universities teach students how people of different cultures work. For example, people in Japan don't use first names, and business cards need to be given and received with both hands. Germans tend to be direct and say what they mean. Mexican businesspeople prefer to not discuss business in front of family. Ethical cultures in firms vary globally.[6] Finally, employees must develop a keen capacity to mirror gestures, words, and other behaviors that demonstrate they have "entered the world" of their cultural counterparts.[7]

Finally, it is important to remember that even one country is not entirely homogeneous. The extent to which a country has experienced immigration, supported and encouraged diversity, and realized the "melting pot" effect determines the internal homogeneity or heterogeneity of the country. For example, Japan, Norway, Saudi Arabia, and Poland are relatively homogeneous compared to India, Australia, Britain, the United States, and Canada. The world's 195 countries contain 5,000 different ethnic groups. Approximately two-thirds of all countries have at least one minority group that comprises 10 percent of the total population and therefore represents a distinct subculture.[8] In more heterogeneous countries, astute managers will need to recognize and respond to subcultures. This, of course, requires a higher commitment to the cognitive, motivational, and behavioral aspects of CQ amid an array of stakeholder interests and influences.

Global Stakeholders

In Chapter 1, we defined *stakeholders* as those people and groups to whom an organization is responsible—including customers, investors, and shareholders, employees, suppliers, governments, communities, and many others—because they have a "stake" in (or a claim to) some aspect of a company's products, operations, markets, industry, or outcomes. These groups not only are influenced by businesses, but they also have the ability to affect businesses. Table 13.1 describes stakeholder issues that are likely to exist when planning and conducting business outside a company's home country. Note that these issues include economic, legal, ethical, and philanthropic considerations of other cultures and countries.

From an economic perspective, differences in the development of countries can easily pose new challenges with stakeholders. As more companies move manufacturing and customer service operations to less-developed nations, critics speak out about job loss in the home country and the pay and working conditions in the offshore operations. While overseas outsourcing adds another layer of complexity for management, economic considerations for cost cutting typically trump social and political concerns. Some firms report significant savings in salary costs due to the eagerness and productivity of workers, allowing salaries to go further in developing nations.[9]

Clearly, the legal and regulatory environment varies from country to country. Managers need to understand not only the written code, but also the nuances of implementation and enforcement. One of the most widely discussed stakeholder issues in the global economy is the extent to which bribery is a common and expected practice. Some American multinational corporations claim that the passage of the **Foreign Corrupt Practices Act** severely reduces their ability to compete in the global marketplace. Walmart paid $138 million to settle claims that it had violated the Foreign Corrupt Practices Act. Walmart's subsidiary in Brazil intentionally led its parent corporation to falsify company records and paid more than $500,000 in bribes to help stores open faster. Executives at Walmart that were responsible for internal accounting and anticorruption practices knew of this for years, and this corruption ultimately allowed unethical practices at Walmart to flourish in other countries, such as Mexico, China, and India. This shows how tolerance of unethical practices has a global impact for firms. The primary elements

Foreign Corrupt Practices Act prohibits bribery of foreign officials and requires accounting transparency

Table 13.1 Examples of Stakeholder Issues in a Global Environment

Stakeholder Groups	Potential Issues
Employees	• Wages and benefits relative to the home country's standards • Attitudes toward employees from different genders and ethnicities, especially in executive positions • Existence of collective bargaining efforts • Laws and regulations for employee rights, health, and safety • Norms of employee volunteering • Availability of and comfort with open-door policies and other management practices
Customers	• Laws and regulations on product safety and liability • Presence and power of consumer rights groups • Respect for the product needs of subcultures and minority groups • Attitudes and accommodations for customers with disabilities
Shareholders	• Laws and regulations regarding ownership and corporate governance • Stability and governance of stock exchanges • Willingness and ability to participate in shareholder meetings
Suppliers	• Ethical and social considerations in the supply chain • Prices offered to suppliers in developed countries and developing countries in comparison to other suppliers • Availability and attitudes toward minority suppliers
Community	• Norms of community relations and dialogue • Expectations of community service and/or philanthropy • Rights of indigenous people • Availability and quality of infrastructure (such as roads, utilities, and schools)
Environmental groups	• Environmental law and regulations • Availability of "green" electricity, recycled materials, and other environmentally friendly inputs • Environmental expectations relative to those in the home country • Use of natural resources to achieve business goals

of the Foreign Corrupt Practices Act are prohibiting bribery of foreign officials and addressing accounting transparency, which relates to accurately and fairly representing the books.[10]

Beyond the complexities of the law lay the ethical standards of stakeholders around the world. As discussed in earlier chapters, there are several factors that influence the ethical decision-making process, with top management setting the tone and communicating their expectations for all employees, suppliers, and business partners. For companies with operations in several countries, the code of conduct originating from the home office may not provide sufficient guidance. For example, UPS realized that an international version of its ethics code was needed. Instead of imposing the American version, the company established advisory panels in different regions and conducted 35 focus groups around the world. Using the domestic code as a starting point, UPS ultimately produced 28 codes of conduct for its overseas operations. The codes incorporated cultural differences that did not override key corporate values. For example, UPS managers in France knew that a policy prohibiting alcohol consumption during working hours would not work; in France, it is customary to have a glass of wine at lunch. When language experts started to translate antitrust law into other languages, the word *antitrust* translated as "against trust" and needed to be revised. UPS understood that the culturally intelligent approach is most effective.[11]

Finally, the philanthropic expectations of stakeholders are also widely varied. The United States has a strong focus on building a culture of business philanthropy and employee volunteerism. However, this is not true around the world. In Latin America, for example, the roots of philanthropy extend to the Catholic Church, which provided education, healthcare, and social services. Later, wealthy families provided funds to "secular societies of social benefit" that implemented welfare and social projects. Corporate interest in philanthropy is more recent, but it has grown significantly as a way for business to become socially engaged. For more than 60 years, the Inter-American Development Bank (IDB) has hosted an annual meeting for Latin American business leaders to learn more about social responsibility and philanthropy. Attendance has increased over the years, and activities in corporate social investing, social reporting activities, and membership associations for philanthropy executives are being implemented.[12]

Shareholder Relations and Corporate Governance

While the prospect for global agreement on economic, legal, ethical, and philanthropic standards for business may seem beyond reach, existing efforts hold great promise. Whatever form it takes, a successful initiative must begin and end with the role of corporate governance and shareholder power in corporate decision-making. The board of directors must be committed to a system of oversight, accountability, and control that incorporates a social responsibility perspective. Without this commitment, checks and balances are not in place to limit opportunism and self-interest, advocate for stakeholder rights, or ensure that a firm's corporate culture establishes integrity in all relationships. As discussed in Chapter 3, corporate governance reflects fundamental beliefs about the purpose of business organizations—ranging from maximizing shareholder value to a more collaborative and relational approach with multiple stakeholders.

The movement to write and implement widely accepted codes of conduct is several decades old. It began with social activists who derided apartheid in South Africa and urged companies to withdraw their investments and business interests from the country. Led by Reverend Leon Sullivan, who sat on the board of General Motors (GM), interested citizens and other groups developed requirements that any company should demand for its employees and workplace conditions. These standards covered nonsegregation, equal and fair compensation, programs to move minorities into management ranks, and other measures that clearly conflicted with South African law permitting racial segregation and unequal rights. Eventually, the Sullivan Principles were adopted by over 100 companies in the United States that also withdrew existing operations and investments out of South Africa.[13]

The influence of the Sullivan Principles prompted several groups to develop codes of conduct or similar documents in an effort to build multicultural consensus on acceptable corporate governance and business practices. Perhaps the most successful initiative resulted in the **Caux Round Table Principles for Business**, which was created by a group of business leaders from all regions of the world who have a strong desire and interest in promoting socially responsible capitalism. Frederick Phillips, former president of Phillips Electronics, and Olivier Giscard d'Estaing, former vice-chairman of INSEAD, a preeminent business school, founded the group in 1986. Although the original intent was to reduce trade tensions, the round table quickly turned to global corporate social responsibility and established its principles. Today, the group's governing board includes executives from multinational corporations and governments.[14]

In addition to this fundamental guidance, the Caux Round Table publishes periodic opinions on a range of social responsibility issues, including executive compensation, environmental protection, and corruption. Table 13.2 provides an example of the type of principles often found in foundational statements such as the Caux Round Table Principles.

Caux Round Table Principles for Business
principles for moral capitalism created by business leaders from all regions of the world who have a strong desire and interest in promoting socially responsible capitalism

Table 13.2 Global Principles for Ethical Business Conduct

Global principles are integrity statements about foundational beliefs that should remain constant as businesses operate globally. These principles address issues such as accountability, transparency, trust, natural environment, safety, treatment of employees, human rights, importance of property rights, and adherence to all legal requirements. The principles are designed to focus on areas that may present challenges to the ethical conduct of global business.

1. **Require accountability and transparency in all relationships.** Accountability requires accurate reporting to stakeholders, and transparency requires openness and truthfulness in all transactions and operations.

2. **Comply with the spirit and intent of all laws.** Laws, standards, and regulations must be respected in all countries, as well as global conventions and agreements developed among nations.

3. **Build trust in all stakeholder relationships through a commitment to ethical conduct.** Trust is required to build the foundation for high-integrity relationships. This requires organizational members to avoid major international risks such as bribery and conflicts of interest. Laws supporting this principle include the U.S. Foreign Corrupt Practices Act, the U.K. Bribery Act, the OECD Convention, and the UN Convention Against Corruption.

4. **Be mindful and responsible in relating to communities where there are operations.** The communities where businesses operate should be supported and improved as much as possible to benefit employees, suppliers, customers, and the community overall.

5. **Engage in sustainable practices to protect the natural environment.** This requires the protection of the long-term well-being of the natural environment including all biological entities, as well as the interaction among nature, individuals, organizations, and business strategies.

6. **Provide equal opportunity, safety, and fair compensation for employees.** Employees should be treated fairly, not exploited or taken advantage of, especially in developing countries. Laws supporting this principle include equal opportunity legislation throughout the world.

7. **Provide safe products and create value for customers.** Product safety is a global issue as various governments and legal systems sometimes provide opportunities for firms to cut corners on safety. All products should provide their represented value and performance.

8. **Respect human rights, as defined in the UN Global Compact.** Human rights are a major concern of the UN Global Compact and most other respected principles statements of international business.

9. **Support the economic viability of all stakeholders.** Economic viability supports all participants in business operations. Concerns such as fair trade and payment of a living wage are embedded in this principle.

10. **Respect the property of others.** Respect for property and those who own it is a broad concept that is an ethical foundation for the operation of economic systems. Property includes physical assets, as well as intellectual property.

Source: © O. C. Ferrell 2019.

Employee Relations

A critical consideration for companies conducting business around the world is how to manage differences that exist in employment standards and expectations. Modern corporations recognize the importance of tapping into global markets and talent pools in order to remain competitive.

Even in the best cases, building a dedicated, engaged, and satisfied workforce takes strategic planning and daily oversight by management. Executing this process in a new culture or across cultures takes more than merely transferring the policies and practices from the home country and home office. It must include consideration of the economic, legal, ethical, and philanthropic expectations of employee stakeholders in different countries. For example, Table 13.3 outlines key differences between employment law in Canada and the United States. There are important differences between these cultures, even though we often consider them to be similar.

Table 13.3 Differences in Employment Law: United States and Canada

Legal Issue	Canada	United States
Termination of employment	Employers must give statutory notice of termination.	Employment is "at will," and notice depends upon employment contracts or policies.
Severance	Severance plans are uncommon and do not overrule statutory rights.	Most severance plans require the employee to agree to a release of claims before receiving severance pay.
Employment litigation	Lawsuits against employers are generally settled quickly, and damage awards are predictable.	Lawsuits against employers usually involve claims of discrimination, and damage awards are unpredictable.
Compensation disclosure	Despite new rules on disclosure, companies are not required to disclose the amounts of compensation actually received by executive officers from their exercise of options.	Public companies must fully disclose the compensation of executives and board members in plain English, including the objectives and implementation of executive compensation programs.
Healthcare benefits	Single-payer universal healthcare system.	Usually tied to employment as part of a benefits package; coverage is not guaranteed.
Unions	No "right-to-work" laws that prohibit unions or for requiring employees covered by union contracts to pay; many provinces have bans on temporary or permanent striker replacement.	Harder to get a union started; states beginning to pass "right-to-work" legislation, which mandates that workers do not have to support a union even though they benefit from collective bargaining.
Changes to postretirement benefits	Very difficult to decrease post-retirement benefits without providing notice; almost impossible to reduce benefits for existing retirees.	More flexibility in making changes to postretirement benefits.

Sources: Adapted from "10 Key Differences Between Canadian and U.S. Employment Laws," Torys LLP, August 20, 2018, https://www.torys.com/insights/publications/2018/08/10-key-differences-between-canadian-and-us-employment-laws (accessed August 5, 2019); St. George's University, "Comparing the U.S. and Canadian Health Care Systems: 4 Differences You Need to Know," April 9, 2019, https://www.sgu.edu/blog/medical/comparing-us-and-canadian-health-care-systems/ (accessed August 5, 2019); Stephen Shores, "What Manufacturers Need to Know About Employment Law in Canada," SHRM, March 7, 2019, https://www.shrm.org/resourcesandtools/legal-and-compliance/employment-law/pages/global-canada-what-manufacturers-need-to-know.aspx (accessed August 5, 2019).

employee engagement
the psychological state in which employees feel a vested interest in the company's success and are motivated to perform at levels that exceed job requirements

Longitudinal research has affirmed what many global managers already know: employee attitudes and perceptions about work vary from country to country. As discussed in Chapter 8, employees typically value high ethical standards and volunteer activities and become more loyal and satisfied with their employer as a result. Thus, variations in employee attitudes and perceptions are integral to the successful implementation of social responsibility programs. For example, workers in France value a work-life balance more than any other national group. Japanese employees are often pleased with incentive compensation but lament relatively low base pay. Australians want a manager who acts as a coach and Chinese employees yearn for more training opportunities. In its annual survey, Mercer, an international research firm, identifies the factors most important for **employee engagement**, the psychological state in which employees feel a vested interest in the company's success and are motivated to perform at levels that exceed job requirements. Table 13.4 depicts the results of Mercer's 2019 study of employees in different countries. Despite national differences, employees in different parts of the world are fairly consistent in noting the importance of work/life balance, recognition, and the work itself. This information is valuable to managers, as it improves the cognitive nature of cultural intelligence and provides direction on motivational and behavioral competencies that should be impactful

Table 13.4 Top Employee Engagement Factors in Six Countries

Brazil	Canada
1. Recognition for contributions	1. Recognition for contributions
2. Opportunities to learn new skills and technologies	2. Ability to manage work/life balance
3. Being empowered to make decisions	3. Feeling a sense of belonging
China	**United States**
1. Ability to manage work/life balance	1. Ability to manage work/life balance
2. Opportunities to learn new skills and technologies	2. Recognition for contributions
3. A fun work environment	3. Feeling a sense of belonging
Hong Kong	**Germany**
1. Ability to manage work/life balance	1. Working on meaningful projects
2. Leaders who set a clear direction	2. A fun work environment
3. Opportunities to learn new skills and technologies	3. Ability to manage work/life balance

Source: Mercer, "Global Talent Trends 2019," https://www.mercer.com/content/dam/mercer/attachments/private/gl-2019-global-talent-trends-study.pdf (accessed August 5, 2019).

across nations. Understanding these drivers enables human resource (HR) professionals to instill consistency across policies in a multinational firm.[15]

Employees in the United States, especially young professionals, have increased expectations for the companies that they work for to reflect their moral, cultural, and political values and are more vocal about their demands when an employer falls short. A survey found nearly 50 percent of millennials said that they recently spoke out in support or in criticism of their employer's actions over a controversial issue. The majority of outspoken employees of all ages stated the reason that they spoke up was to raise concern about their employer's reputation. College students desire to work in the name of a greater purpose or cause. This demand on employers will bring challenges to satisfy employees and uphold company reputation. These attitudes may not apply to all cultures and nations. In some countries, socially active attitudes are not accepted in the workplace.[16]

As discussed earlier in this chapter, cultural intelligence is an integral part of employees' ability to manage and succeed in a global economy. In the context of business ethics, CQ is especially vital. Applying the legal requirements of the host or home country to the problem may be a starting point. However, as we discussed in earlier chapters, legal standards are not sufficient for a firm dedicated to ethical business practices. Some industries operate under a set of values or principles, which may also serve a purpose in the international arena. For example, the tourism industry established a global code of ethics that enumerates the industry's obligation to build respect between societies, assist in sustainable development, maintain cultural heritage, treat employees well, and promote individual fulfillment.[17] In other cases, guidance from a broad set of guidelines, such as the Caux Round Table Principles for Business, could be utilized. However, broad principles are often less useful in day-to-day situations.

The ethical decision-making framework discussed in Chapter 6 is fully effective in the global environment, but cultural differences introduce new complexities to the process. For this reason, companies know that training rubrics are pivotal to an employee's ability to assess an ethical issue and determine the most appropriate decision and action. Organizations develop a fixed set of principles and values globally. While decisions have to comply with national and local laws, codes of conduct for the firm are implemented globally. There are usually adjustments in training approaches, as well as certain ethical risks that may be more important to address in a particular country.

Consumer Relations

International trade leaves some members of the economy, whether independent or corporate, marginalized and vulnerable to economic exploitation. From some consumer perspectives, conventional trade interferes with the ability of many people, particularly those in poor nations, to secure basic, sustainable livelihoods. By contrast, **fair trade** is a trading partnership based on dialogue, transparency, and respect that seeks greater equity in international trade and contributes to sustainable development. Fair trade benefits those who have limited opportunities to begin with and are further stunted by market forces that identify them as negligible. Table 13.5 describes the five principles of fair trade organizations, including the rights and responsibilities of producers, intermediaries, business partners, resellers, and consumers.

As previously discussed, consumers are increasingly concerned with the origins of products they purchase, including the working conditions, ethical standards, and related social responsibility practices of manufacturers. For example, low wages and substandard working conditions have marked the reputation of clothing manufacturers. In an effort to minimize these costs, Fair Trade USA began certifying apparel and other products. Products that meet fair trade standards are licensed to display the Fair Trade Certified label, signifying a producer's

fair trade
a trading partnership based on dialogue, transparency, and respect that seeks greater equity in international trade and contributes to sustainable development

Table 13.5 Charter of Fair Trade Principles

Principle	Description
Market access for marginalized producers	Fair Trade helps producers realize the social benefits of traditional forms of production. It enables buyers to trade with producers who otherwise would be excluded from the markets. It helps shorten trade chains so that producers receive more from the final selling price of their goods than is the norm in conventional trade via multiple intermediaries.
Sustainable and equitable trading relationships	The economic basis of transactions within Fair Trade relationships takes account of all costs of production, both direct and indirect. Fair Trade buyers offer trading terms that enable producers and workers to maintain a sustainable livelihood. Prices and payment terms are determined by assessment of economic, social, and environmental factors, rather than just referring to current market conditions. The commitment to long-term trading partnership found in Fair Trade enables both sides to cooperate through information sharing and planning.
Capacity building and empowerment	Fair Trade relationships assist producer organizations to understand more about market conditions and trends and to develop knowledge, skills, and resources to exert more control and influence over their lives.
Consumer awareness raising and advocacy	Fair Trade relationships provide the basis for connecting producers with consumers and for informing consumers about the need for social justice and the opportunities for change. Consumer support enables Fair Trade organizations to be advocates and campaigners for wider reform of international trading rules and to achieve the ultimate goal of a just and equitable global trading system.
Fair trade as a "social contract"	Fair Trade transactions exist within an implicit "social contract," in which buyers agree to do more than is expected by the conventional market. In return, producers use the benefits of Fair Trade to improve their social and economic conditions, especially among the most disadvantaged members of the organization. Fair Trade is not charity but a partnership for change and development through trade.

Source: World Fair Trade Organization and Fairtrade Labelling Organizations International, *A Charter of Fair Trade Principles*, January 2009, https://wfto.com/sites/default/files/Charter-of-Fair-Trade-Principles-Final%20(EN).PDF (accessed August 2, 2019).

adherence to fair economic, social, and environmental practices in producing and selling products. There are nearly 30,000 Fair Trade Certified products, coming from approximately 1.6 million farmers and workers in 75 countries. Fair Trade Certified products are available in most grocery stores, restaurants, and cafés all over the United States, contributing to the record volume growth year after year.[18] J. Crew launched its first Fair Trade Certified collection for its J. Crew and Madewell brands. The collection includes jeans made in a certified factory in Vietnam.[19]

Rice farming is practiced all over the world and is responsible for billions of jobs, making it an important aspect in the social well-being of numerous communities. Pesticides and chemicals used in rice farming initially increase production, but they eventually reduce production and negatively affect workers' health. A decline in global rice prices puts farmers in difficult situations. When prices fall, some farmers apply for loans that may carry high interest rates, while others might lose their livelihood altogether. Areas particularly dense with rice farms are reported to have high rates of suicide and child sex trafficking. Fair Trade rice seeks to improve these conditions by providing stability in the market, seeking organic methods, and regulating the use of chemicals in production.[20]

The Fair Trade Certified label is not only recognized by 63 percent of American consumers, but it is also a trusted symbol among this group. There is a high level of durability among fair trade certified products even during times of economic downturn. This is due in large part to the system of standards of the Fair Trade organization. In order to continue to remain relevant, they are committed to revising these standards every five years. For example, Fair Trade USA announced that it would revise the previously separate standards for farmers and independent growers by combining them to apply to both groups. Such a move reduces complexity and allows for consistency and relevance in the certification process. Table 13.6 shows some of the Fair Trade Certified brands currently on the market.[21]

Global Development

Companies are increasing their efforts to enhance the infrastructure, human rights, and educational systems of a particular country, state, or city in order to further global development. Experts have concluded that political, social, and economic freedoms are fundamental to national competitiveness and development. Without widespread trust and the effective operations of different institutions, a given society will not be able to enhance and enrich the lives of its people. Political freedoms, such as free speech and elections, lead to economic security, and social freedoms such as education and healthcare lead to stronger economic participation. Finally, economic security frees people to participate in social and political activities.[22] Multinational corporations are increasingly interested in mechanisms for promoting freedom and development.

Economic conflicts can have a negative effect on economic development. An extended trade war between the United States and China has resulted in U.S. manufacturers shifting production out of China to avoid tariffs that were as high as 25 percent. With $300 billion in U.S. imports from China per year, many businesses adjusted their strategy. Apple began shifting assembly of some of its products out of China to countries like Vietnam.[23] With the middle class in China growing and U.S. consumers enjoying lower-priced products, such as furniture, clothing, and electronics, many U.S. firms are moving their operations from China while other firms may keep their operations in other countries because of the cost of investing in new facilities and supply chain arrangements. These changing trade relations can have

Table 13.6 Fair Trade Certified Brands

Nespresso	Endangered Species Chocolate
Conscious Step	Ben & Jerry's
Divine Chocolate	Stonedance Wines
Starbucks	Travel Whyte
Eco Bananas	Belvas Chocolate
Red Diamond Coffee	Looma Home
Reflective Jewelry	London Tea Company

Source: Fair Trade America, "Explore Fair Trade Brands" http://fairtradeamerica.org/Fairtrade-Products/All (accessed August 2, 2019).

an economic boost to some Asian countries, but they change quality of life and employment opportunities in other countries.

Development refers to improvement in the economic, environmental, educational, and health conditions of a country. Common issues in development include poverty, quality of healthcare, access to education, voting rights, water quality, governance and rule of law, domestic finance systems, and climate change. A major goal of the United Nations (UN) is to realize improvements in the development of countries around the world. While these improvements may be grounded in ethical concerns, they are critical to the stability of the global economy. The UN operates on the philosophy that it is in the world's best interest to tackle problems that limit the capacity of some people to live healthy and prosperous lives. The UN's 2030 Agenda for Sustainable Development was designed to meet these challenges and has established the goals related to the following: zero poverty, zero hunger, good health, quality education, gender equality, clean water and sanitation, and affordable clean energy, rights to decent work and economic growth, innovation, reduced inequalities, sustainable cities, responsible consumption, climate action, unpolluted oceans and land, and partnerships to achieve all these goals.[24] Meeting these goals and finding solutions to these problems advance the economy and improve the lives of individuals in areas heavily affected by these issues.

The UN also established the **Global Compact**, which encourages organizations to commit to common principles whereby effective and responsible business can be conducted on a global scale. The Global Compact is a set of 10 universally accepted principles (see Table 13.7) in the areas of human rights, labor, environment, and anti-corruption, to which approximately 13,000 organizations have officially declared their commitment. Corporate signatories attest to their willingness to integrate these principles into everyday business practices, publish examples of their commitment and projects on an annual basis, and commit to a stronger alignment between the objectives of the international community and those of the business world.[25]

Although the UN has been most progressive in gaining corporate support for global development and popularizing business partnerships, corporations have aligned themselves with nonbusiness organizations to advance development for a number of years.[26] For example, a company interested in building an offshore call center may realize that roadways and utilities need to be improved in the area. In another situation, a firm may know that a natural resource is abundant in a developing country, yet the people and government of the country do not have

development
improvement in the economic, environmental, educational, and health conditions of a country

Global Compact
an agreement which encourages organizations to commit to 10 common principles regarding human rights, labor, environment, and anticorruption, whereby effective and responsible business can be conducted on a global scale

Table 13.7 The 10 Principles of the Global Compact

Human Rights

1. Support and respect the protection of internationally proclaimed human rights.
2. Ensure nonparticipation in human rights abuses.

Labor

3. Uphold the freedom of association and the effective recognition of the right to collective bargaining.
4. Eliminate all forms of forced and compulsory labour.
5. Abolition of child labor.
6. Eliminate discrimination with respect to employment and occupation.

Environment

7. Support a precautionary approach to environmental challenges.
8. Undertake initiatives to promote greater environmental responsibility.
9. Encourage the development and diffusion of environmentally friendly technologies.

Anticorruption

10. Work against corruption in all its forms, including extortion and bribery.

Source: "Ten Principles," United Nations Global Compact, https://www.unglobalcompact.org/what-is-gc/mission/principles (accessed August 2, 2019).

Table 13.8 Partnerships for Development of Social Responsibility

Conventional business partnerships

These partnerships focus on efficient and effective decisions to carry out a business objective when there is limited competition. Social responsibility is not a strategic concern. Example: Tennessee Valley Authority, a federal corporation, provides flood control, electricity generation, and more to the Tennessee Valley in partnership with more than 150 local power companies.

Corporate social responsibility partnerships

Businesses make a profit but also serve the public interest. Through voluntary cooperative relationships, businesses and their partners arrive at a win-win authentic partnership. They thrive and prosper for their stakeholders. Example: Starbucks supports coffee growers in receiving a fair wage.

Corporate accountability partnerships

These partnerships focus on rules and structure with an emphasis on ethics, compliance, and social responsibility. Example: ISO 19600, based on the Australian standard for compliance management, is being adopted as an international benchmark. ISO 19600 standards provide an accountability audit to social responsibility.

Social economy partnerships

These are based on partnerships between nonprofit organizations and businesses. Both parties help to develop and institutionalize objectives to benefit society. Example: Home Depot partners with Habitat for Humanity.

Sources: Ananya Mukherjee Reed and Darryl Reed, "Partnerships for Development: Four Models of Business Development," *Journal of Business Ethics* 90, supplement 1 (May 2009): 3–37; Maria May Seitanidi and Andrew Crane, "Implementing CSR Through Partnerships: Understanding the Selection, Design, and Institutionalisation of Nonprofit-Business Partnerships," *Journal of Business Ethics* 85, supplement 2 (April 2008): 413–429; Scott James, "CSR Means True Partnerships," *Forbes*, July 30, 2011, http://www.forbes.com/sites/csr/2011/07/30/csr-means-true-partnerships/ (accessed August 2, 2019); "A New Global Standard for Compliance: ISO 19600," CompliSpace, September 15, 2014, http://complispace.wordpress.com/2014/09/15/a-new-global-standard-for-compliance-iso-19600/ (accessed August 2, 2019).

the economic and educational resources to market it worldwide. In both cases, the company may choose to invest resources by partnering with the local government, nonprofit agencies, and other nongovernmental organizations (NGOs). Critics muse that while this approach certainly has a social component, the business case for making a profit is the overriding concern. An extensive review of the outcomes of development partnerships between large oil companies and local governments in the Nigerian Delta region revealed that (1) the linkage between improvement in social infrastructures and economic growth is nonexistent, (2) it is almost impossible for business investments to make significant gains because these communities have long been neglected, and (3) business-driven investment in social infrastructure has been unevenly distributed and failed to prioritize community needs.[27]

There are many diverse types of partnerships for development. While the partnership consists of at least one public entity and one private entity, the specific kinds of public and private entities involved include a wide range of social and economic players. However, each partnership must confront two elements: (1) the level of social control via stakeholder influence they maintain and (2) the challenges they pose to conventional business management and goals. In lieu of these two points, partnerships for development may be categorized into four types: conventional business partnerships (CBPs), corporate social responsibility partnerships (CSRPs), corporate accountability partnerships (CAPs), and social economy partnerships (SEPs). Table 13.8 provides a brief description of these four types.

Conventional Business Partnerships

Conventional business partnerships (CBPs) for development may seem unlikely. However, in the case of some public services, such as utilities, they do sometimes emerge. The goal of these partnerships is to promote efficiency in markets where competition does not exist. This assumes that states are inefficient and that a

conventional business partnerships (CBPs) partnerships that promote efficiency in markets where competition does not exist; assumes government is inefficient and that a business organization provides the best solution business organization provides the best solution. The role of business is to increase efficiency, while the role of government is to make sure that the benefits of increased efficiency are delivered to consumers. Government also monitors access to and affordability of the public service. CBPs do not have to prove a specific effort toward social responsibility, but they are commonly recognized and supported by the United Nations, World Bank, and other supraregional organizations. Specifically, these organizations have sought privatization through conventional business partnerships.

privatization

a process that occurs when public operations are sold to private entities. Public-private partnerships count as partial privatization

Privatization occurs when public operations are sold to private entities. Public-private partnerships count as partial privatization. Full privatization further reduces the public element of the equation. Social services often attract privatization interest, particularly in developing nations, because privatization provides a point of entry into new markets for investors. But long-standing public provision of goods and services carries deeply embedded interests in keeping the goods and services public.[28]

The World Bank began advocating the privatization of public utilities in the early 1990s, and eventually this became a requirement for some countries seeking substantial loans. While there have been successes, water privatization in El Salvador has contributed to the country's water crisis. Approximately 95 percent of El Salvador's surface water is contaminated, making it one of Latin America's most water-stressed countries.[29] The World Bank eventually softened its position by becoming open to other options besides privatization, but the idea that poor governments need to increase their reliance on private agents for political and economic risks remains.

Corporate Social Responsibility Partnerships

corporate social responsibility partnerships (CSRPs)

voluntary and business-centered partnership providing resources for social initiatives, such as job training and entrepreneurial development, that contribute to a citizen's livelihood and therefore a stronger workforce and economic contagion

Corporate social responsibility partnerships (CSRPs) are voluntary and business centered. Potential benefits compel individual businesses to enter into these partnerships, and success rests in the motivation causing corporate engagement. Such motivation may be philosophical or ethical, though it may be that pragmatic concerns are the major sources of motivation. CSRPs provide resources for social initiatives, such as job training and entrepreneurial development, that contribute to a citizen's livelihood. While these initiatives benefit members of society, they also provide for a stronger workforce and economic contagion. For example, microcredit programs are part of CSRP activity in resource provision, with the largest such partnership being the Microcredit Summit Campaign, a nonprofit organization dedicated to improving access to credit and financial self-sufficiency for the poorest people in the world.[30]

Microcredit activity began in Bangladesh. The initiative enjoyed remarkable success, to the extent that two prominent participants in the endeavor, Grameen Bank and its founder Muhammad Yunus, received the Nobel Peace Prize. Microcredit works toward moving large populations out of poverty through financial assistance. To further its impact, the Microcredit Summit Campaign partnered with the nonprofit Freedom from Hunger to benefit 3.7 million people by combining microfinancing and health.[31] Grameen Bank remains an influential model for microcredit institutions and partnerships all over the world. While microcredit allows borrowers to take action that directly improves their income, indirect improvements such as quality of life also result. Borrowers have access to better housing, food, sanitation, and education and are better able to take advantage of the improved options.[32]

Corporate Accountability Partnerships

The final two categories of partnerships for development take a distrust of CSR models as a starting point for defining their framework. Corporate accountability partnerships (CAPs) spring from the idea that CSRPs are neither accountable nor effective and are only really interested in public relations. As the name implies, **corporate accountability partnerships (CAPs)** focus on accountability and the setting of requirements and standards based on what society expects.

For CAPs to be successful, they must gain and direct public support, maximize the limited resources they tend to have, plan for the long term, and convince public institutions of the necessity and importance of enforcing socially demanded standards. CAPs use legal and social means, ranging from policy and certification initiatives to protests and activism. Certification CAPs focus mainly on labor rights and the environment and try to achieve answerability, enforcement, and universality. CAPs seek to achieve corporate recognition of standards deemed appropriate by society and utilize third-party audits and checks on the partnership.

A widely known certification CAP is the **Fair Labor Association (FLA)**, which was organized after numerous media reports exposed child labor, poor working conditions, and low wages. Today, the FLA works to end sweatshop conditions for factory workers and organizes universities, social groups, and socially responsible organizations to protect workers' rights and insist on better working conditions all over the globe. FLA-affiliated companies source from factories and farms in 84 countries, representing more than 4.6 million workers. Participating companies include PUMA, Hugo Boss, PopSockets, and others.[33]

The accreditation given by the FLA has become increasingly important as investors use environmental, social, and governance (ESG) metrics to determine which companies to invest in.[34] Nestlé is an example of a corporation working with the FLA to ensure fair labor conditions. The cocoa industry is notorious for forced and child labor conditions, and as one of the world's largest food companies, Nestlé allowed the FLA to conduct a review of labor conditions throughout the entire supply chain. The findings concluded that, despite implementation of industry standards, many violations were still occurring. In the Ivory Coast, especially, both child and forced labor are culturally normal behaviors. Nestlé is able to trace only 49 percent of its global cocoa supply, making it difficult for the company to remove the risk of child labor from its supply chain. Nestlé knows that better communication of labor practices and stronger oversight are needed in order to come closer to eliminating these undesirable labor practices.[35]

Social Economy Partnerships

Social economy partnerships (SEPs) pursue alternatives to conventional corporations and profit maximization. SEPs have a distinctly social purpose, use democratic governance, and cooperate with other social economy partnerships. Social economy organizations include nonprofits, community economic development corporations, cooperatives, and cooperative development organizations.

The SEP philosophy emphasizes cooperation and assistance rather than traditional business logic. These partnerships provide resources and support mostly for informal sectors of the urban poor. SEPs bring people together for recycling, street vending, and other work that many other citizens will not perform. Entrepreneurship is viewed collectively, and the group stays connected to social

corporate accountability partnerships (CAPs) focus on accountability and the setting of requirements and standards based on what society expects

Fair Labor Association (FLA) works to end sweatshop conditions for factory workers; organizes universities, social groups, and socially responsible organizations to protect workers' rights

social economy partnerships (SEPs) partnerships that pursue alternatives to conventional corporations and profit maximization and have a distinctly social purpose, use democratic governance, and cooperate with other social economy partnerships and political movements. Social economy partnerships in these informal sectors provide economic profits, as well as social benefits that are usually reserved for those with full-time jobs in the formal sector. The Self-Employed Women's Association (SEWA) is a trade union in India for poor, self-employed women. These women compose the majority of the labor force but they are part of the unorganized sector and are not provided with regular salaries and benefits. SEWA organizes cooperative arrangements to help women find regular employment, increase their incomes, become literate, access better healthcare, obtain child care, and increase their financial assets. Through various cooperatives, women obtain insurance, get assistance in marketing their goods worldwide, participate in leadership training, and access significant loans and banking products. Without SEWA and its extended partnerships, these women would be destined for a life of poverty.[36]

Ethical Responsibilities in **TECHNOLOGY**

Privacy in the Age of Transparency: GDPR Goes Global

When engaging in global business, it is the responsibility of corporate executives and governing parties to know the written code of laws and regulations of the countries with which they do business, as well as to work to implement and enforce these laws satisfactorily. Although Facebook and Google have headquarters in the United States, they engage in international business with Europe and therefore must comply with the laws of the European Union (EU). General Data Protection Regulation (GDPR), discussed in Chapter 11, protects the personal data of EU citizens. The law affects sites worldwide that service European consumers. The regulations require companies to ask consumers for permission to collect their personal data and inform consumers of a data breach within 72 hours of the occurrence. If companies do not comply with this regulation, they could face hefty fines.

Not only has this regulation had a major impact on companies doing business in Europe, but Brazil, Japan, and South Korea are in the process of creating similar laws for internet privacy. The EU is encouraging other countries to develop tougher online privacy regulations by making data protection a part of trade deals. Companies based outside the EU are subject to fines if they do business that involves the personal data of EU citizens. For example, Google was fined €50 million by France for failure to comply with GDPR. These requirements are making privacy protection a globalized issue.

The regulatory barriers from GDPR could have a profound impact on large companies like Facebook, which collect data on consumer internet use to engage in targeted advertising to their users. In light of GDPR, there is concern about the type of data collection required for companies like Facebook and Google to do business with consumers. While Facebook has complied with GDPR in allowing users to refuse targeted advertising, it is continuing to collect data. The company requires EU consumers to accept its privacy terms or forgo using the service. Mark Zuckerberg has expressed his support for greater privacy laws in the United States, while also pointing out that GDPR is ambiguous.

The United States has traditionally opposed strict privacy regulations on internet data collection. With the passage of GDPR, however, that may change. Even CEOs from companies like Apple and Google are encouraging the federal government to implement similar privacy restrictions as the EU. Meanwhile, the state of California passed a law with some similarities to GDPR. The battle between business data collection and consumer privacy will continue as countries implement and fine-tune their regulations, both for their nations and globally.

Sources: Sam Schechner, "Agree to Facebook's Terms or Don't Use It," *Wall Street Journal,* May 11, 2018, https://www.wsj.com/articles/stage-is-set-for-battle-over-data-privacy-in-europe-1526031104 (accessed July 29, 2019); Adam Santariano, "G.D.P.R., a New Privacy Law, Makes Europe World's Leading Tech Watchdog," *The New York Times,* May 24, 2018, https://www.nytimes.com/2018/05/24/technology/europe-gdpr-privacy.html (accessed July 29, 2019); Elizabeth Schulze, "The US Wants to Copy Europe's Strict Data Privacy Law—But Only Some of It," CNBC, May 23, 2019, https://www.cnbc.com/2019/05/23/gdpr-one-year-on-ceos-politicians-push-for-us-federal-privacy-law.html (accessed July 29, 2019); "GDPR Key Changes," EUGDPR. org, https://www.eugdpr.org/the-regulation.html (accessed July 29, 2019); Deepa Seetharaman, "Facebook Provides a Preview of Its Privacy Makeover," *Wall Street Journal,* April 18, 2018, https://www.wsj.com/articles/facebook-provides-a-preview-of-its-privacy-makeover-1524027600?mod=article_inline (accessed July 29, 2019); Jon Porter, "Google Fined €50 Million for GDPR Violations in France," *The Verge,* January 21, 2019, https://www.theverge. com/2019/1/21/18191591/google-gdpr-fine-50-million-euros-data-consent-cnil (accessed July 2, 2019).

The four models of business involvement in development allow almost any firm the opportunity to engage in partnerships that improve health, education, economic, and other prospects for people around the world. In addition to corporate efforts, individual countries are engaged in development efforts. The **Center for Global Development** produces a **Commitment to Development Index (CDI)** that ranks 27 developed nations by their contributions to and support of development in poorer, developing countries. At the top of the rankings are Sweden, Denmark, Finland, and Germany.

While these contributions are considered the right thing to do and usually reflect national ideals and values, there are also benefits to global security and economic health. Countries included in the index are assessed based on governmental policy efforts in areas including aid, trade, investment, migration, the environment, security, and technology. Policy efforts are used as indicators, partly to control for the varying sizes of economies among the countries ranked. For the CDI, policies of rich countries, particularly the coherence of those policies, are important to development. The index also shows evidence that development involves more than monetary aid and that partnerships can provide greater benefits than the individual partners can produce alone.[37]

Center for Global Development
a nonprofit think tank in Washington, D.C., and London that works to reduce global poverty and improve lives through innovative economic research that drives better policy and practice by the world's top decision-makers

Commitment to Development Index (CDI)
a ranking, produced by the Center for Global Development, of 27 developed nations by their contributions to and support of development in poorer, developing countries

Global Reporting Initiative

Regardless of the social responsibility activities that a company pursues, it must also consider the best mechanisms for communicating its values and plans, highlighting successes, and gaining feedback for the future. In some cases, a firm may be a signatory to a set of standards, a member of a particular association, or an entity otherwise obligated to formally assess and document social responsibility outcomes. As stated earlier, companies that commit to the Global Compact are required to present an annual account of how they implement the 10 principles and support the UN's development goals. This document, entitled the **Communication on Progress**, may be part of the company's annual report, sustainability report, or some other social reporting mechanism.

The **Global Reporting Initiative (GRI)**, an independent international organization headquartered in Amsterdam, provides standards for businesses and other organizations to assess their performance across an array of social responsibility indicators. Of the world's largest 250 corporations, 74 percent use GRI's framework to report on their sustainability performance.[38] More than 600 U.S. companies voluntarily use these standards.[39] A firm may use this as a self-audit, but others choose to share the audit results formally with stakeholders. One of the greatest benefits of the GRI is that it makes comparisons possible because it uses a globally applicable and well-vetted framework. The GRI emphasizes consensus and continuous improvement in developing and maintaining the GRI Standards, which seek to provide transparency and accountability in sustainability reporting akin to that found in financial reporting. Diverse representatives contribute business, civil, academic, labor, and other professional perspectives in deciding which areas of sustainability are to be included in the framework and the appropriate measures to be used for determining performance in those areas. The framework is in perpetual draft form, with innovation in technologies and shifts in cultural attitudes accommodated by the GRI's continuous improvement approach.

The GRI Standards includes three categories of core indicators: economic, environmental, and social performance. The social category of core indicators is further divided into labor practice, human rights, product responsibility, and society. Quantitative or qualitative performance indicators are used to evaluate various aspects of each category.

The economic category examines an organization's interaction with the economic system in which it operates by measuring economic performance, market

Communication on Progress
a required annual report of how a company that has committed to the Global Compact implements the 10 principles and supports the UN's developmental goals

Global Reporting Initiative (GRI)
an independent international organization that provides standards for businesses and other organizations to assess their performance across an array of social responsibility indicators and seeks to provide transparency and accountability in sustainability reporting akin to that found in financial reporting

presence, and indirect economic impact indicators. The environmental category covers an organization's energy use, both direct and indirect, as well as pollution. The category assumes a link between energy consumption and emissions that contribute to climate change, and thus emphasizes efficient energy use and an increasing reliance on renewable energy sources over fossil fuel.

The society category examines the organization as it functions in relation to market structures and social institutions. Measures include the impact on local communities, bribery and corruption, and public policymaking. The human rights indicators consider the operation of an organization as it provides for basic human rights. Measures include incidents regarding human rights and provisions made for such rights in an organization's internal and external business relationships. The labor practices category is an extension of the human rights category that focuses specifically on the environment and practices to which workers are subject. An examination of workforce demographics, communications between the organization and its employees, and opportunities extended to workers for personal development comprise the category's measurements. Finally, the product responsibility category focuses on the products of an organization as they affect consumers. Considerations such as safety, product information, and privacy rights of customers are evaluated. Indicators appear in pairs, with one addressing the relevant processes of the organization and the other addressing the compliance of the organization.[40]

Summary

In this chapter, we discussed a variety of social responsibility issues and stakeholders from a global perspective. The expanding global marketplace requires that executives and managers develop the ability to conduct business effectively and in a socially responsible way the world over. The movement of people across cities and continents means that ideas, values, traditions, languages, and customs have also migrated, and global employees need many skills. Cultural intelligence (CQ) is the ability to interpret and adapt successfully to different national, organizational, and professional cultures. There are three components to the development and use of cultural intelligence, including cognitive, motivational and behavioral. Cultural intelligence is desired of all employees but is mandatory for those who work in different countries, manage diverse groups, and have responsibilities that require them to interpret unfamiliar behaviors and situations.

Cultural intelligence is critical for dealing effectively with stakeholders, including customers, investors and shareholders, employees, suppliers, governments, and communities. Stakeholders in other countries and cultures will bring unique insights and attitudes to bear on the business relationship, including differences in economic, legal, ethical, and philanthropic expectations. In addition, we delved into a few trends related to stakeholders in the global economy, including the Caux Round Table Principles for Business, fair trade, employee engagement, and others.

The reflexive nature of the global economy means that the success of a particular company is a function of many factors, including the extent to which the firm's home country is comprised of trust-based institutions. Some nations have well-developed systems for ensuring economic, legal, and ethical standards in business activities. In other cases, corporations are interested in a particular market but know that fundamental institutions and standards are sorely underdeveloped and negatively affect market potential. The four models of business involvement in development allow almost any firm the opportunity to engage in partnerships that improve health, education, economic, and other prospects for people around the world. In addition to corporate efforts, individual countries are engaged in development efforts.

Finally, the GRI provides standards for businesses and other organizations to assess their performance across an array of social responsibility indicators. A firm may use this as a self-audit, but others choose to share the audit results formally with stakeholders. One of the greatest benefits of the GRI is that it makes comparisons possible because it uses a globally applicable and well-vetted framework.

Responsible Business Debate

The Gloves Are Off: The U.S.-China Trade War Escalates

Issue: *What are the benefits and drawbacks to the global economy of the trade war between the United States and China?*

When two powerhouse nations are heavily engaged in trade, there are bound to be some things that don't go smoothly. Trade between the United States and China is a major factor in the world economy. The United States accounts for about 24 percent of the global economy (the highest in the world), followed by China, at 15 percent. Given that these countries make up such a large part of the economic system, their relationship with each other is vital to the world economy. The United States has experienced an increasing demand for cheaper goods, and China has been able to provide these discount prices. In one year, about $700 billion was transferred between the two nations.

The trade war officially began when the United States placed tariffs on products from China. According to U.S. government sources, China backtracked on its pledges to rewrite laws dealing with everything from competition policy to intellectual property. China, by contrast, believed that the United States was becoming inflexible, which contributed to the breakdown of talks between the two nations. This impasse led to increases in tariffs on both sides. China requested that the United States remove a ban on the Chinese telecommunications giant Huawei prior to resuming talks. The ban on Huawei was due to suspicions that the company was using its technology to

spy on the United States, as well as other countries, and it has affected Huawei suppliers such as Google and Intel.

The trade war has had a major influence on the global market because of the amount of control that the United States and China have over the economy. Tariffs can be beneficial to the country that imposes them. By imposing tariffs on Chinese goods, U.S. businesses are more likely to use American sources, and consumers are more likely to buy American products. This increases domestic business while deterring business outside the country (in theory, at least). Tariffs can also be used as a tactic to pressure the other country into meeting demands. On the other hand, trade wars can be negative for business, investors, and consumers. China depends on American exports for much of their business, while the United States imports hundreds of billions of dollars worth of Chinese products each year. The trade war resulted in auto companies and agricultural commodities like soybeans losing sales. Sellers also raised the prices of goods to offset the costs of doing business with countries with high tariffs, thus making goods more expensive for consumers to buy.

There Are Two Sides to Every Issue

1. Trade wars tend to be more beneficial than they are detrimental to the country that imposes them, so they are worth the risk.
2. Trade wars tend to be more detrimental than they are beneficial to the country that imposes them, so they are not worth the risk.

Sources: Jeff Desjardins, "The World's $80 Trillion Economy—in One Chart," World Economic Forum, October 15, 2018, www.weforum.org/agenda/2018/10/the-80-trillion-world-economy-in-one-chart/ (accessed July 30, 2019); Matt Egan, "Why the US-China Trade War Won't Last," *CNN,* May 14, 2019, https://www.cnn.com/2019/05/14/business/china-united-states-economy-trade-war/index.html (accessed July 30, 2019); "A Quick Guide to the US-China Trade War," *BBC News,* June 29, 2019, https://www.bbc.com/news/business-45899310 (accessed July 30, 2019); Ana Nicolaci da Costa, "The Early Victims of Trump's Trade War," *BBC News,* August 5, 2018, https://www.bbc.com/news/business-45028014 (accessed July 30, 2019); Sean Keane, "Huawei Ban: Full Timeline on How and Why Its Phones Are Under Fire," *CNET,* July 30, 2019, www.cnet.com/news/huawei-ban-full-timeline-on-how-and-why-its-phones-are-under-fire/ (accessed July 30, 2019).

Key Terms

Caux Round Table Principles for
    Business (p. 384)
Center for Global Development
    (p. 395)
Commitment to Development Index
    (CDI) (p. 395)
Communication on Progress
    (p. 395)
conventional business partnerships
    (CBPs) (p. 391)

corporate accountability
    partnerships (CAPs) (p. 393)
corporate social responsibility
    partnerships (CSRPs) (p. 392)
cultural intelligence (CQ) (p. 380)
development (p. 390)
employee engagement (p. 386)
Fair Labor Association (FLA)
    (p. 393)
fair trade (p. 388)

Foreign Corrupt Practices Act
    (p. 382)
Global Compact (p. 390)
Global Reporting Initiative (GRI)
    (p. 395)
privatization (p. 392)
social economy partnerships (SEPs)
    (p. 393)

Discussion Questions

1. Define *cultural intelligence (CQ)* in your own terms. Compare your definition with the definition used in this chapter.
2. How are stakeholder relationships in a global context different from those in a domestic context? In what ways are they alike?
3. What is the likelihood that corporate leaders agree on a global set of social responsibility standards? What evidence do you have?
4. How can organizations create stronger engagement with employees? What would be the effects on social responsibility? How would social responsibility affect engagement?

5. Define *fair trade* in your own terms. In what ways should consumers consider fair trade issues when making purchases and investments?
6. Review the Global Compact principles presented in Table 13.7. In what ways are these principles and issues related to a successful global economy? What benefits and/or challenges do they present to multinational corporations?
7. What are some ways that a company can measure its progress to comply with global reporting initiative guidelines? Propose both quantitative and qualitative measures.

Experiential Exercise

Choose two multinational companies, each based in a different home country, and visit their respective websites. Peruse these sites for information that is directed at three company stakeholders: employees, customers, and the community. Make a list of the types of information on the site and indicate how the information might be used and perceived by these three groups. What differences and similarities did you find between the two companies? How are the differences attributable to cultural nuances?

Manufacturing Misconduct: What Would You Do?

Jaime and Catherine looked at each other. Each was thinking, "How do we handle this?" but offered no immediate suggestions. Both were midlevel executives with a multinational corporation that manufactured clothing, handbags, and accessories in developing countries, including Guatemala and Honduras. The company is a member of the FLA and takes pride in its commitment to a safe, healthy, and equitable work environment for all employees. Jaime, a native of Mexico, had professional experience in Peru, Chile, and Mexico. Catherine, a native of the United States, spoke fluent Spanish and was being groomed to take international assignments. Two weeks ago, the vice president of Latin American operations called Jaime and Catherine, asking them to take on an internal consulting project.

The vice president was concerned about rumors surrounding the company's largest manufacturing site in Honduras. This site employed over 1,000 people, the majority of whom worked in low-skilled manufacturing roles. Although no employee had come forward, or used the firm's ethics hotline, the site's regional manager (RM) was concerned about management practices and workplace conditions. Each time the RM visited the site, he sensed that he was not experiencing the daily reality of the manufacturing site. So far, he had little proof, but he decided to share his concerns with other executives. Specifically, he was worried about (1) possible intimidation of union members and leaders, (2) discriminatory management tactics, and (3) forced overtime that was not properly compensated.

Two weeks later, Jaime and Catherine arrived at the site, tasked with determining whether management practices and workplace conditions were compatible with corporate standards and FLA principles. First, they need to develop a plan for gathering information from employees, including those who were either scared of retaliation or generally mistrusting of corporate management. What would you do?

CASE 1

Uber Fuels Controversy

Introduction

Uber Technologies Inc. is a multinational transportation company that provides ride-sharing services, food delivery, freight shipping, and electric bike rentals. Uber was founded in San Francisco in 2009 and has since expanded their operations to more than 700 cities in 85 countries around the world. The company has become a key player in the sharing economy, a new economic model in which independent contractors rent out their underutilized resources, such as vehicles or lodging, to other consumers. The company has experienced resounding success and is looking to expand both within the United States and internationally.

Due to their utilization of technology, Uber does not have as many constraints as taxi cab companies do. A major reason Uber is so popular is because their app allows users to request a ride from drivers in the near vicinity. Uber's business model, which is based on independent contractors instead of employees, takes advantage of smartphone technology by linking consumers with independent drivers as their cabs, but they do not employ drivers or own the vehicles. Drivers receive a commission from Uber, but they do not report to Uber and are their own boss. This provides a potentially more efficient and less expensive way for consumers to purchase transportation. This business model has contributed to the rise of the sharing economy in which independent contractors, drivers in this case, can rent out underutilized resources to earn money.

Global Expansion Challenges

International expansion is a major part of Uber's marketing strategy. Adopting the motto "think local to expand global," Uber believes that consumers from other countries will appreciate their low cost, convenience, and freedom. As it expands into different countries, Uber is engaging in strategic partnerships with local companies. These alliances with local firms are especially important because they allow Uber to utilize the resources and knowledge of domestic firms familiar with the country's culture.

Despite Uber's international success, many countries have regulatory hurdles that have caused trouble for the company. Perhaps the biggest hurdle is Uber's failure to mandate that their drivers obtain the same license types as professional taxi drivers even though Uber drivers offer many of the same services as professionally licensed taxi drivers. Governments have responded by banning Uber—and the services provided via Uber—due to the company's nonenforcement of professional licenses for their drivers. For instance, in Spain, Uber was forced to shut down ride-sharing services after a judge ruled that Uber drivers were not legally authorized to transport passengers, claiming that Uber created unfair competition for professionally licensed taxi drivers. Because the taxi industry is important in many cities, governments like Spain's are not looking favorably at what they view as an unfair competitive advantage that could potentially bankrupt the industry. Uber returned to Spain in March 2018 with UberX, a tier of Uber service that uses professionally licensed drivers, placing it more on par with licensed taxi drivers. However, in 2019, Uber and their Spanish competitor Cabify announced that they were suspending services in Barcelona after a new law was passed requiring all vehicles to be booked with at least 15 minutes advance notice.

Uber faced similar problems in France. In 2011, Paris became the first city outside of the United States where Uber set up operations. However, local authorities attempted to ban one of Uber's services because drivers did not need to be professionally licensed. French police even raided Uber's Paris office. French law mandates that operating a service that connects passengers to nonprofessional drivers is punishable with fines of over $300,000 and up to two years in prison. Hundreds of Uber drivers in France were issued fines for operating illegally, which Uber paid.

Uber challenged that law, claiming that it was unconstitutional because it hindered free enterprise. A French court decided against banning Uber's service and sent the case to a higher court. This generated strong criticism from taxicab officials in France as they maintained that they had to have professionally licensed drivers while Uber was free from this restriction. French courts later ruled against Uber, and the company is no longer allowed to use nonprofessional drivers in the country. However, their past use of nonprofessional drivers continues to haunt Uber. The European Union determined that France could file criminal charges against Uber for their UberPOP service as it had used nonprofessional drivers to operate an illegal taxi service. In another landmark ruling, French courts sided with an Uber driver who claimed he should be recognized as an employee, not

This case was prepared by Jennifer Sawayda for and under the direction of O.C. Ferrell and Linda Ferrell © 2019. It was prepared for classroom discussion rather than to illustrate either effective or ineffective handling of an administrative, ethical, or legal decision by management. All sources used for this case were obtained through publicly available material and the Uber website.

an independent contractor. A similar ruling had been made in the United Kingdom. Uber has stated they will challenge these rulings.

India is Uber's second largest market after the United States. In New Delhi, a woman's rape allegation led to a ban against app-based services without radio-taxi permits in the capital. In response to the alleged rape, Uber began updating their app to include panic button and tracking features. Uber also began offering their service in New Delhi without charging booking or service fees. The company came under fire for how they compensate Indian drivers. As Uber came closer to releasing their initial public offering (IPO), which was filed in May 2019, they began to reduce driver incentives to build up financial performance. As a result, reduced incentives and higher diesel prices negatively impacted Indian drivers' financial earnings, causing growing discontent. Uber must tread carefully to seize upon opportunities in India without violating regulatory requirements or damaging relationships with their drivers.

In 2015, a German court banned Uber services if they used nonprofessional drivers. Uber argued that the company itself is only an agent to connect driver and rider. Rules that apply to taxi services do not apply, and all services are deemed to be legal, according to Uber. The court ruled that Uber's business model clearly infringes the Personal Transportation Law, because drivers transport riders without a personal transportation license. The injunction includes a fine of more than $260,000 per ride for non-compliance. If the injunction is breached, drivers could go to jail for up to half a year, in addition to an imposition of fines. The German Taxi Association (Taxi Deutschland) was pleased with the outcome and claimed that taxi services will remain in the hands of qualified people and keep everyone safer. Uber can operate UberX, Uber Green, and UberTaxi in Germany, but drivers need a professional chauffeur's license to do so.

Uber faces many regulatory and legal issues outside of the United States. The company attempted to take a global approach to expansion by applying the same practices in other countries as they do in the United States. However, they are quickly realizing that they must take a more customized approach. Laws differ from country to country. Although Uber defines themselves as an "agent" of their "individual contractors," many courts do not view their services in the same way. They are forcing Uber to comply with licensing laws or stop business in certain areas.

Threats to the Sharing Economy

There is an ongoing threat to the sharing economy in which Uber operates: worker classification. Under current U.S. law, a worker either depends on an organization as an employee or is self-employed as an independent contractor. The rise of Uber and other digital matching apps has called worker classification into question. This has been a widespread concern because employees receive workplace protections such as minimum wage and overtime pay that independent contractors do not.

Some consider the independent relationships between Uber and their drivers to be beneficial because of the flexibility and personal control for the drivers. However, lawmakers fear companies are evading U.S. labor laws to the detriment of the contractors. California legislators passed Assembly Bill 5 in 2019 which classifies contract workers for companies such as Uber as employees. The bill expands the 2018 California Supreme Court decision known as Dynamex. Together, they established a three-point test, often referred to as the ABC test, to determine if a worker is an employee: (1) the company controls the employee's work; (2) the employee's work is a core part of the company's business; (3) the workers don't typically engage in providing their service to other companies. This poses a major threat to Uber who relies on low-cost, flexible labor. Not only will labor costs increase, but Uber is also concerned they may have to limit the number of drivers or schedule drivers in advance in the long term, eliminating the ability for drivers to work as often or as little as they desire.

This landmark California bill has the potential to influence legislation in other states. Labor groups in states such as New York support similar legislation. Uber unsuccessfully lobbied to be exempt from the bill in exchange for establishing minimum pay rates for drivers, paid time off, and an association to protect the interests of drivers. Uber, Lyft, and DoorDash pledged $90 million to support lobbying efforts to support exemption. It is estimated by officials in the industry that switching to an employee model could increase costs 20 to 30 percent, which would have a significant impact on Uber's bottom line.

Ongoing Controversies

While the company continues to be widely successful, the year 2017 was a hard one for Uber. Multiple controversies cast a negative light on the organization. To start off the year, Uber had to pay over $20 million in a settlement for misleading drivers on how much they would earn. In February, a former Uber female engineer published a blog post alleging that there was widespread sexual harassment and gender discrimination at the company, which prompted an investigation into Uber's corporate culture. This investigation later resulted in 20 employees being fired for various sexual harassment and discrimination violations. In March, five executives left the company, including the senior vice president of engineering.

In April, Uber faced controversy with Apple, Inc. Uber had been secretly identifying and tagging iPhones even after the app and their data had been deleted from the iPhones. Uber tagged these phones to see if users were using the same phone to download the app and then repeatedly wiping it so they could use promo codes multiple times. Although Uber was trying to detect fraud and prevent customer abuse, this action violated Apple's privacy policy. Tim Cook confronted the chief executive of Uber, threatening to remove the app from Apple's app store if Uber did not stop breaking the policy. The impact would have caused millions of iPhone consumers to lose access to the Uber app. The CEO at the time, Travis Kalanick, had developed a reputation for bending or sometimes breaking the rules in order to drive the company toward desired goals. Since their founding in 2009, Uber has gained a negative reputation for challenging the rules and causing disruption.

In May, the U.S. Department of Justice launched a criminal investigation for the company's use of "Greyball." This secret software identified users who were violating the terms of services and denied ride requests to them. The users simply never got paired with a driver on the app. This software even targeted government officials who were using the app to investigate Uber and their drivers. There was controversy over the use of this software as to whether it was in violation of the Foreign Corrupt Practices Act, which bans the use of bribes to foreign officials to get or keep business.

In June, Uber fired top executive Eric Alexander for obtaining medical records of an Uber passenger who was raped by her driver for the purpose of casting doubt upon her case. Uber held an all-staff meeting to discuss reforming company culture, which was immediately followed by CEO Travis Kalanick taking a leave of absence. This ultimately led to Dara Khosrowshahi becoming his successor as CEO in August.

In September, the FBI investigated Uber's software for allegedly illegally interfering with competitors. The internal program, known by Uber as "Hell," could track drivers working for the competitor Lyft. The investigation revealed that Uber created fake Lyft customer accounts to "request" rides around different cities in order to see how many Lyft drivers were nearby and what prices they were being offered for various routes around the cities. The program was also able to identify drivers who worked for both Lyft and Uber in order to give these drivers incentives to leave Lyft. The program was presumably used from 2014 to 2016. The ability to recruit and maintain drivers is a critical component of how these ride-share companies operate. Every major city has users who engage with both apps to determine the most cost-effective option for their trips. Having inside knowledge of the competition and being able to dominate the market in this way was invaluable toward gaining more customers on a more consistent basis. On the other hand, these activities can also violate laws on fair competition.

In September, Uber lost their license to operate in London due to a lack of corporate responsibility. There were questions about Uber's approach to reporting serious driver offenses, driver medical and safety checks, and the use of previously mentioned "Greyball" software. The mayor of London stated that all companies must play by the rules and adhere to standards that involve customer safety—innovation should not come at the expense of customer safety and security. Uber appealed the decision soon after. Several months later, Uber was given a 15-month probationary license to operate in London. Uber acknowledged the past events and made changes to address them. The firm said they changed their senior leadership, updated and improved various policies, strengthened their corporate governance, and was taking initiatives to transform their corporate culture overall.

In November, it was revealed that Uber faced a data breach in 2016. During the breach, email addresses, names, and phone numbers of 50 million global Uber riders were stolen. The personal information of drivers was also compromised, including driver's license numbers. Uber had an obligation to report hacking incidents to regulators and drivers whose information was taken. However, at the time Uber kept the data breach quiet by paying the hackers to delete the data. They were in the process of negotiating with the Federal Trade Commission about the proper handling of consumer data. Uber reported that they believed none of the data was used by the hackers and offered free identity theft protection and monitoring to victims of the hacking. The data breach was not made public until almost a year after it occurred. As a result of this incident, the chief security officer and the legal director of security and law enforcement were fired.

Uber also faced difficulties with accidents and tragedies outside the inner-company operations. In 2018, a self-driving Uber car struck and killed a pedestrian in one of the first video recorded accidents involving the death of a pedestrian. It was found that the vehicle feature that carries out emergency brakes for dangerous situations was disabled by Uber to prevent erratic vehicle behavior. Uber settled a civil case with the pedestrian's family, and Arizona prosecutors decided not to criminally charge Uber. It seemed unclear whether the car or the victim was at fault. Uber responded by suspending their self-driving program for a few months and resuming the program after changing their approach to self-driving vehicles.

Another tragedy brought Uber attention in 2019 when University of South Carolina student Samantha Josephson was murdered after getting into a car she mistook for an Uber. Following her death Uber promoted awareness, reminding riders to verify their drivers through notifications and ads. The university encouraged students and riders everywhere to ask their driver "What is my name?" to confirm they were in the correct vehicle. Uber stated they had been working with college campuses since 2017 to educate students on detecting fake ride-share drivers and will continue to do so to help prevent future incidents. Additionally, the South Carolina House of Representatives passed a bill requiring ride-sharing drivers to display illuminated company signs in their vehicle to further prove their validity to riders.

Other Business Segments

Rather than a ride-sharing company, Uber views itself as a technology and transportation company. Uber has greatly expanded their offerings by exploring food delivery, bike rentals, business transportation solutions, and more.

Food Delivery

In 2014, Uber launched Uber Eats. The app gives users the ability to order food from participating local restaurants. Now, Uber had partnered with more than 100,000 restaurants around the globe. While Uber Eats does not hold the highest market share in the industry, falling behind Grubhub and DoorDash, it still provides Uber with a large revenue source and holds 25 percent of the market for on-demand food delivery services. Uber has also invested at least $2 billion to research autonomous vehicles and test different fleets of these vehicles. Uber entered the autonomous vehicle field in 2015 by partnering with Carnegie Mellon University.

Freight

In 2017, Uber launched Uber Freight, a service that connects shipping companies with drivers. The service, which operates similarly to Uber's core ride-sharing app, has seen triple-digit revenue growth, expanding both nationally and internationally. Freight transportation represents a huge opportunity for Uber, especially as the United States faces a shortage of truck drivers. Now that Uber has established themselves as a pillar of the sharing economy, Uber stands to be a big player in this segment.

Bike Rentals

Uber expanded their offerings by introducing JUMP, an electric bike rental system through their app. The bikes, first introduced in 2018, create an easy solution for commuters in highly populated cities. Many fear for the long-term success of e-bike and scooter rentals. In the beginning, scooter rentals hit the streets at incredibly low prices due to subsidized pricing. This resulted in many rental services such as Bird operating at a financial loss. Now, services like Uber and Lyft have increased prices at the risk of turning off customers.

The Future

As Uber looks to the future, they are investing in advanced transportation technology to stay ahead of the curve. Despite setbacks with their autonomous vehicles,

Uber is working with teams in Detroit, Pittsburgh, San Francisco, Tempe, and Toronto on both self-driving cars and self-driving freight trucks. Even in the face of safety concerns, Uber believes self-driving vehicles to be safer and more sustainable than traditional vehicles. Additionally, Uber has a team called Uber Elevate that is working to develop aerial ridesharing by 2023 in Dallas, Los Angeles, and Melbourne. Uber will face many regulation challenges and ethical concerns with this uncharted territory. They will need to work closely with local and national governments to establish safety standards for urban aviation.

Uber Becomes a Public Company

Uber filed for an initial public offering in 2019 soon after competitor Lyft was listed on NASDAQ in March 2019. The Uber IPO was one of the biggest of all time with a value of $82.2 billion, just behind Facebook at a valuation of $115 billion and Alibaba at $179 billion at the date of their IPOs. All 180 million shares of Uber stock were sold out within three days of the IPO. Uber's initial stock price was $45 a share, raising a total of $8.1 billion at a valuation of $82.2 billion in total. The valuation makes it the largest U.S.-listed IPO since Alibaba Group Holding Ltd. went public in 2014.

Uber took a conservative pricing approach for their stock after observing that their competitor Lyft experienced a 20 percent decrease in stock prices in the weeks following the Lyft IPO. Although there was demand for the shares at higher prices, Uber put them in the hands of as many institutional investors as possible, aiming for more long-term-oriented investments rather than hedge-fund and retail investors. Though the stock price at the time of this writing was down to $31 per share, Uber believes they hold a promising future and that their business will become increasingly necessary as people around the world move toward hiring self-driving vehicles and using electric bikes and scooters instead of owning cars.

Conclusion

Despite Uber's challenges, the company has become widely popular among consumers and independent contractors. Supporters claim that Uber is revolutionizing the transportation service industry. Investors clearly believe Uber is going to be strong in the market in the long run. One lesson that Uber will hopefully take to heart is the need to ensure that independent contractors using their app obey relevant country laws. The company also must revamp their corporate culture to prevent more legal repercussions. Uber has to address these issues to uphold the trust of customers and achieve long-term market success in different countries.

Questions for Discussion

1. What are the ethical challenges that Uber faces in using app-based peer-to-peer sharing technology?
2. Since Uber is using a disruptive business model and marketing strategy, what are the risks that the company will have to overcome to be successful?
3. Because Uber is so popular and the business model is being expanded to other industries, should there be regulation to develop compliance with standards to protect competitors and consumers?

Sources

"Uberworld," *The Economist,* September 3, 2016, 9.

Akiko Fujita, "Uber's Trucking Chief Says Triple Digit Growth is 'Very Sustainable'," *Yahoo! Finance*, August 22, 2019, https://finance.yahoo.com/news/head-of-uber-freight-triple-digit-growth-very-sustainable-145242968.html (accessed August 22, 2019).

Alana Semuels, "'I'm Back to Riding My Own Bike.' Higher Prices Threaten Silicon Valley's Mobility Revolution," *TIME*, August 9, 2019, https://time.com/5648510/uber-lyft-bike-scooter-subsidies/ (accessed August 22, 2019).

Angie Schmitt, "Uber Got Off the Hook for Killing a Pedestrian with its Self-Driving Car," *Streets Blog USA,* https://usa.streetsblog.org/2019/03/08/uber-got-off-the-hook-for-killing-a-pedestrian-with-its-self-driving-car/ (accessed June 25, 2019).

Anna Gallegos, "The Four Biggest Legal Problems Facing Uber, Lyft and Other Ridesharing Services," *LXBN,* June 4, 2014, http://www.lxbn.com/2014/06/04/top-legal-problems-facing-uber-lyft-ridesharing-services/ (accessed July 20, 2019).

Anne Stych, "Uber Eats Abandons Flat Fees for Distance-Based Pricing," *Bizwomen*, August 10, 2018, https://www.bizjournals.com/bizwomen/news/latest-news/2018/08/uber-eats-abandons-flat-fee-for-distance-based.html?page=all (accessed October 16, 2019).

Caitlin Morrison, "Uber Wins Court Appeal over London Ban," *Independent,* June 27, 2018, https://www.independent.co.uk/news/business/news/uber-london-ban-wins-court-appeal-overturn-tfl-revoke-licence-a8418106.html (accessed July 20, 2019).

Christopher Mims, "At Startups, People Are 'New Infrastructure'," *The Wall Street Journal,* March 8, 2015, http://www.wsj.com/articles/at-startups-people-are-new-infrastructure-1425858978 (accessed July 20, 2019).

Corrie Driebusch and Maureen Farrell, "Uber Prices IPO at $45 a Share," *The Wall Street Journal,* May 9, 2019, https://www.wsj.com/articles/uber-prepares-for-ipo-at-midpoint-of-target-range-or-lower-11557422774 (accessed July 20, 2019).

Danielle Abril, "DoorDash Has Pulled Ahead of GrubHub, Uber Eats in the On-Demand Food Delivery Race," *Fortune,* March 11, 2019, https://fortune.com/2019/03/11/doordash-tops-grubhub-on-demand-food/ (accessed July 20, 2019).

Eric Auchard and Christoph Steitz, "German Court Bans Uber's Unlicensed Taxi Services," *Reuters,* March 18, 2015, http://www.reuters.com/article/2015/03/18/us-uber-germany-ban-idUSKBN0ME1L820150318 (accessed July 20, 2019).

Eric Newcomer, "Uber Paid Hackers to Delete Stolen Data on 57 Million People," *Bloomberg,* November 21, 2017, https://www.bloomberg.com/news/articles/2017-11-21/uber-concealed-cyberattack-that-exposed-57-million-people-s-data (accessed June 25, 2019).

George Harrison, "What is Greyball and Why Is the Uber Software So Controversial?" *The Sun,* October 3, 2017, https://www.thesun.co.uk/tech/4523408/greyball-uber-software-enforcement-controversial/ (accessed June 29, 2019).

Henry Grabar, "Uber Reveals One of Its Big Vulnerabilities," *Slate*, April 12, 2019, https://slate.com/business/2019/04/uber-ipo-nyc-london-risks.html (accessed July 20, 2019).

Je Seung Lee, "French Court Follows UK in Ruling against Uber in 'Employment Contract' Case," *The Telegraph,* January 11, 2019, https://www.telegraph.co.uk/news/2019/01/11/french-court-follows-uk-ruling-against-uber-employment-contract/ (accessed July 20, 2019).

Jefferson Graham, "App Greases the Wheels," *USA Today*, May 27, 2015, 5B.

Joana Sugden and Aditi Malhotra, "Indian Officials Drafting National Rules for Uber, Other Taxi Apps," *The Wall Street Journal,* April 7, 2015, http://www.wsj.com/articles/indian-officials-drafting-national-rules-for-uber-other-taxi-apps-1428427528 (accessed July 20, 2019).

Julia Carrie Wong and Sam Morris, "Collision Course: Uber's Terrible 2017," *The Guardian,* https://www.theguardian.com/technology/ng-interactive/2017/dec/27/uber-2017-scandals-investigation (accessed July 20, 2019).

Kate Conger and Noam Scheiber, "California Bill Makes App-Based Companies Treat Workers as Employees," *The New York Times*, September 11, 2019, https://www.nytimes.com/2019/09/11/technology/california-gig-economy-bill.html (accessed October 18, 2019).

Kate Taylor and Benjamin Goggin, "49 of the Biggest Scandals in Uber's History," *Business Insider,* May 10, 2019, https://www.businessinsider.com/uber-company-scandals-and-controversies-2017-11#april-2019-uber-announces-new-safety-initiative-after-student-killed-in-fake-uber-pick-up-48 (accessed June 26, 2019).

Kaylee Hultgren, "At Uber Elevate, Innovations and Experiential Make Flying Cars a Reality," *Event Marketer*, August 7, 2019, https://www.eventmarketer.com/article/uber-elevate-tech-innovations-flying-cars/ (accessed August 22, 2019).

Mansoor Iqbal, "Uber Revenue and Usage Statistics," *Business of Apps,* May 10, 2019, https://www.businessofapps.com/data/uber-statistics/#5 (accessed June 29, 2019).

Maria Vega Paul, "Uber Returns to Spanish Streets in Search of Regulatory U-Turn," *Reuters,* March 30, 2016, http://www.reuters.com/article/us-spain-uber-tech-idUSKCN0WW0AO (accessed July 20, 2019).

Michael Carney, "Playing Favorites: Uber Adds New Security Features, but Only in Select Crisis-Riddled Markets," *PandoDaily,* January 2, 2015, http://pando.com/2015/01/02/playing-favorites-uber-adds-new-security-features-but-only-in-select-crisis-riddled-markets/ (accessed July 20, 2019).

Mihir Zaveri, "Prosecutors Don't Plan to Charge Uber in Self-Driving Car's Fatal Accident," *The New York Times*, March 6, 2019, https://www.nytimes.com/2019/03/05/technology/uber-self-driving-car-arizona.html (accessed July 21, 2019).

Mike Isaac, "Uber's C.E.O. Plays With Fire," *The New York Times,* April 23, 2017, https://www.nytimes.com/2017/04/23/technology/travis-kalanick-pushes-uber-and-himself-to-the-precipice.html?_r=1 (accessed June 29, 2019).

Nick Bilton, "Disruptions: Taxi Supply and Demand, Priced by the Mile," *The New York Times,* January 8, 2012, http://bits.blogs.nytimes.com/2012/01/08/disruptions-taxi-supply-and-demand-priced-by-the-mile/ (accessed July 20, 2019).

Noam Scheiber, "New Lawsuit Against Uber Is Set to Test Its Classification of Workers," *The New York Times*, September 12, 2019, https://www.nytimes.com/2019/09/12/technology/uber-drivers-california.html?searchResultPosition=8 (accessed October 18, 2019).

R. Jai Krishna and Joanna Sugden, "India Asks Internet Service Providers to Block Uber Website in Delhi," *The Wall Street Journal*, May 14, 2015, http://www.wsj.com/articles/india-asks-internet-service-providers-to-block-uber-website-in-delhi-1431606032 (accessed July 20, 2019).

Rebecca Davis O'Brien and Greg Bensinger, "Uber Faces FBI Probe Over Program Targeting Rival Lyft," *The Wall Street Journal*, September 8, 2017, https://www.wsj.com/articles/uber-faces-fbi-probe-overprogram-targeting-rival-lyft-1504872001 (accessed June 29, 2019).

Rob Davies, "Uber Suffers Legal Setbacks in France and Germany," *The Guardian*, June 9, 2016, https://www.theguardian.com/technology/2016/jun/09/uber-suffers-legal-setbacks-in-france-and-germany (accessed July 20, 2019).

Roman Dillet, "Uber Fined $900,000 in France for Running Illegal Transportation Operations with UberPOP," *TechCrunch*, June 9, 2016, https://techcrunch.com/2016/06/09/uber-fined-900000-in-france-for-running-illegal-transportation-operations-with-uberpop/ (accessed October 16, 2019).

Sai Sachin Ravikumar, Aditi Shah, and Aditya Kalra, "As Uber Gears up for IPO, Many Indian Drivers Talk of Shattered Dreams," *Reuters*, May 8, 2019, https://www.reuters.com/article/us-uber-ipo-india-drivers/as-uber-gears-up-for-ipo-many-indian-drivers-talk-of-shattered-dreams-idUSKCN1SE0OP (accessed July 20, 2019).

Sam Jones, "Uber and Cabify to Suspend Operations in Barcelona," *The Guardian*, January 31, 2019, https://www.theguardian.com/world/2019/jan/31/uber-cabify-suspended-operations-barcelona (accessed July 20, 2019).

Sam Schechner and Tom Fairless, "Europe Steps Up Pressure on Tech Giants," *The Wall Street Journal*, April 2, 2015, http://www.wsj.com/articles/europe-steps-up-pressure-on-technology-giants-1428020273 (accessed July 20, 2019).

Sam Schechner, "Uber Wins French Court Reprieve Over Legality of Low-Cost Service," *The Wall Street Journal*, March 31, 2015, http://www.wsj.com/articles/uber-wins-french-court-reprieve-over-legality-of-low-cost-service-1427794312 (accessed July 20, 2019).

Samantha Shankman, "Uber Gets into Ride-Sharing Game in Paris," *Skift*, February 4, 2014, http://skift.com/2014/02/04/uber-gets-into-the-ride-sharing-game-in-paris/ (accessed July 20, 2019).

Saritha Rai, "Uber Gets Serious About Passenger Safety in India, Introduces Panic Button," *Forbes*, February 12, 2015, http://www.forbes.com/sites/saritharai/2015/02/12/uber-gets-serious-about-passenger-safety-in-india-introduces-panic-button/ (accessed July 20, 2019).

Sasha Ingber, "France Can Bring Criminal Charges against Uber, Judges Rule," *NPR*, April 10, 2018, https://www.npr.org/sections/thetwo-way/2018/04/10/601317786/france-can-bring-criminal-charges-against-uber-judges-rule (accessed July 20, 2019).

Spiegel, "Vermittlung Privater Fahrer: Gericht Verbietet Uber Deutschlandweit," http://www.spiegel.de/wirtschaft/unternehmen/uber-urteil-gericht-verbietet-uber-deutschlandweit-a-1024214.html (accessed July 20, 2019).

Suhas Manangi, "Uber's Global Expansion Strategy - "Think Local to Expand Global" - Will It Work for Startups?" LinkedIn, July 31, 2017, https://www.linkedin.com/pulse/ubers-global-expansion-strategy-think-local-expand-work-manangi/ (accessed October 16, 2019).

Uber, "Uber Offerings, Products, and Transportation Innovations," https://www.uber.com/us/en/about/uber-offerings/ (accessed August 22, 2019).

Uber, https://www.uber.com/ (accessed July 20, 2019).

Uber Estimator, "Uber Cities," 2019, https://uberestimator.com/cities (accessed July 20, 2019).

UNM Daniels Fund Ethics Initiative, "Truth, Transparency, and Trust: Uber Important in the Sharing Economy," https://danielsethics.mgt.unm.edu/teaching-resources/presentations.asp (accessed July 20, 2019).

Fixer Upper: Home Depot Works on Stakeholder Relationships

Introduction

When Bernie Marcus and Arthur Blank opened the first Home Depot store in Atlanta in 1979, they forever changed the hardware and home improvement retailing industry. Marcus and Blank envisioned huge warehouse-style stores stocked with an extensive selection of products offered at the lowest prices. Today, this vision defines the business model of the popular home improvement chain. Do-it-yourselfers and building contractors can browse tens of thousands of products for the home and yard, from kitchen and bathroom fixtures to carpeting, lumber, paint, tools, and plant and landscaping items. If a product is not provided in one of the stores, Home Depot offers customers the option to have it special ordered. Some Home Depot stores are open 24 hours a day, and customers can also order products online. Additionally, the company offers free home improvement clinics to teach customers how to tackle everyday projects like tiling a bathroom. For those customers who don't prefer the "do it yourself" method, most stores offer installation services. Knowledgeable employees, recognizable by their orange aprons, are on hand to help customers find items or to demonstrate the proper use of a particular tool.

Home Depot employs 400,000 associates and operates more than 2,200 stores in the United States, Mexico, and Canada. Home Depot is the largest home improvement retailer in the world, with more than $108 billion in revenue. Home Depot continues to do things on a grand scale, including putting their corporate muscle behind a tightly focused social responsibility agenda.

Managing Customer Relationships

Home Depot's former chief marketing officer, John Costello, consolidated marketing and merchandising functions to help consumers achieve their home improvement goals more effectively and efficiently. According to Costello, "Above all else, a brand is a promise. It says here's what you can expect if you do business with us. Our mission is to empower our customers to achieve the home or condo of their dreams." When Costello arrived in 2002 Home Depot's reputation was faltering. His plan called for overhauling the company's website as well as integrating mass marketing and direct marketing with in-store experience. The new philosophy was expressed by the new Home Depot mantra: "You can do it. We can help." Teams from merchandising, marketing, visual merchandising, and operations attempted to provide the very best shopping experience. The idea was simple. Home Depot believed that customers should be able to read and understand how one ceiling fan is different from another, and associates (employees) should be able to offer installation and design advice.

In 2008, Frank Bifulco took over as new chief marketing officer and senior vice president. It was a tough time for Home Depot. Because of the Great Recession, consumers were spending less on their homes. Home Depot's new marketing strategy was to emphasize the store's everyday low prices, high product value, and quality energy-saving products. At the same time, the company cut back on special offers like discounts and promotions. Now, Home Depot's chief marketing officer, Adolfo Villagomez, is also the senior vice president of the company's online business, showing how e-commerce has become a big focus for Home Depot. Home Depot does an impressive amount of sales online, earning nearly $8 billion annually.

Despite Home Depot's proactive approach to customer issues, the company has dealt with negative publicity related to poor customer satisfaction. Some former managers at Home Depot have blamed the company's service issues on a culture that operated under principles reminiscent of the military. Under former CEO Robert Nardelli, some employees feared being terminated unless they followed directions to a T. Harris Interactive's 2005 Reputation Quotient Survey ranked Home Depot number 12 among major companies and said that customers appreciated Home Depot's quality services. However, shortly after the company slipped in the rankings, and Nardelli was ousted and replaced by Frank Blake in January 2007. The start of 2008 seemed more auspicious for Home Depot as it was listed as number six on *Fortune*'s Most Admired Companies (still trailing behind Lowe's), up from 13 in 2006. Home Depot also bounced back up on the American Customer Satisfaction Index.

The increase of customer satisfaction was due to several efforts on the part of Frank Blake. The company's

This case was developed by Jennifer Sawayda, Michelle Urban, and Melanie Drever for and under the direction of O. C. Ferrell and Linda Ferrell © 2019. We appreciate the previous editorial assistance of Jennifer Jackson. This case was prepared for classroom discussion rather than to illustrate either effective or ineffective handling of an administrative, ethical, or legal decision by management. All sources used for this case were obtained through publicly available material.

Twitter feed was inundated with comments from dissatisfied customers about the customer service they encountered in the stores. Blake quickly admitted to the customer service problems the company was facing, apologized for the inconvenience it caused the customers, and encouraged them to continue to leave their feedback so that they could make improvements. Each one of the complaints was addressed; some angry followers were appeased by phone calls from store managers and personal emails responding to their specific issues. The responsiveness of Blake and his Senior Manager of Social Media, Sarah Molinari, not only transformed angry protesters into enthusiastic fans but also resulted in a strategic advantage for the company in terms of how they deal with customer feedback.

Inside the stores, self-checkout lanes were installed so that customers could spend less time waiting in line. However, at peak hours, waiting in line cannot be avoided. During such situations, Home Depot associates can scan items in customers' baskets while they are in line and hand them a card that holds all their purchases. When the customer reaches the cashier, they simply scan the card and pay the total they owe. Home Depot was also the first company to partner with PayPal, making it easier for customers who do not want to carry their wallet or cash with them to be able to pay more conveniently. Many of the Home Depot associates are given devices called "First Phone," which is a phone/walkie-talkie/scanner. This device allows associates to quickly help customers by being able to call or page fellow associates who can answer customers' questions and have immediate access to the price of an item by scanning it right where they stand.

Another way in which Home Depot attempts to practice good customer service and simultaneously act in a socially responsible manner is through their program designed to teach children basic carpentry skills. Home Depot provides a free program called the Kids Workshop available at all of their stores. During the workshops, children learn to create objects that can be used around their homes or neighborhoods. Projects include toolboxes, mail organizers, and window birdhouses and bughouses. Home Depot also offers free workshops specifically designed for women, do-it-yourselfers, and new homeowners.

These efforts have paid off for Home Depot. Boosted by the rising housing market, Home Depot is outperforming the retail market at a time when retail sales are slipping. Home Depot has successfully transformed itself into a firm with strong service, offering great value to consumers.

Environmental Initiatives

Cofounders Marcus and Blank nurtured a corporate culture that emphasizes social responsibility, especially regarding the company's impact on the natural environment. Home Depot began their environmental program on the twentieth anniversary of Earth Day in 1990 by adopting a set of Environmental Principles (see Table 1).

Guided by these principles, Home Depot has initiated several programs to minimize the firm's—and their customers'—impact on the environment. In 1991, the retailer began using store and office supplies, advertising, signs, and shopping bags made with recycled content. They also established a process for evaluating the environmental claims made by suppliers. The following year, the firm launched a program to recycle wallboard shipping packaging, which became the industry's first "reverse distribution" program. In addition, they were the first retailer in the world to combine a drive-through recycling center with one of their Georgia stores in 1993. One year later Home Depot became the first home improvement retailer to offer wood products from tropical and temperate forests that were certified as "well-managed" by the Scientific Certification System's Forest Conservation Program. The company also began to replace their hardwood wooden shipping pallets with reusable "slip sheets" to minimize waste and energy usage and to decrease pressure on hardwood resources.

In 1999, Home Depot joined the Certified Forest Products Council, a nonprofit organization that promotes responsible forest product buying practices and the sale of wood from Certified Well-Managed Forests. Yet, the company continued to sell products made from wood harvested from old growth forests. Protesters led by the Rainforest Action Network, an environmental group, had picketed Home Depot and other home center stores for years in an effort to stop the destruction of old growth forests, of which less than 20 percent still survive. Later that year, during Home Depot's twentieth

Table 1 Home Depot's Environmental Principles

Conserve natural resources by using energy and water wisely, and seek further opportunities to reduce resource consumption and improve the efficiency of our stores, offices and distribution network.

Minimize environmental health and safety risks for our associates and our customers.

Continue our journey to reward suppliers that manufacture, package and label in an environmentally responsible manner to minimize impact to the workers who manufacture them and the consumers who use them, and to preserve raw materials and eliminate unnecessary waste.

Recycle and encourage the use of materials and products with recycled content.

Encourage our customers to become environmentally conscious shoppers.

Source: Home Depot, "The Home Depot and the Environment," http://corporate.homedepot.com/sites/default/files/image_gallery/The%20Home%20Depot%20and%20the%20Environment%202018.pdf (accessed August 2, 2019).

anniversary celebration, Arthur Blank announced that Home Depot would stop selling products made from wood harvested in environmentally sensitive areas.

To be certified by the Forest Stewardship Council (FSC), a supplier's wood products must be tracked from the forest, through manufacturing and distribution, to the customer. Harvesting, manufacturing, and distribution practices must ensure a balance of social, economic, and environmental factors. Blank challenged competitors to follow Home Depot's lead, and within two years several had met that challenge, including Lowe's, the number two home improvement retailer; Wickes, a lumber company; and Andersen Corporation, a window manufacturer. By 2003, Home Depot reported that they had reduced their purchases of Indonesian lauan, a tropical rainforest hardwood used in door components, by 70 percent, and they continued to increase their purchases of certified sustainable wood products.

In 2007, Home Depot adopted the Eco Options program to help customers identify more sustainable product offerings. In order for their products to qualify as Eco Option, suppliers must show that their products meet certain criteria that demonstrate less of an environmental impact than comparable products. In 2017, Home Depot released their Chemical Strategy. This strategy describes how the company will work with suppliers to decrease the negative impact of chemicals in the store's product offerings on indoor air quality. They have also committed to a 2020 goal of reducing customers' water usage by 250 billion gallons with their sale of more water-efficient WaterSense products.

These efforts have yielded many rewards in addition to improved relations with environmental stakeholders. Between 2010 and 2019, Home Depot's stores in the United States decreased energy usage by 26 percent. The company set a goal in 2019 to reduce emissions by 50 percent by 2035. Home Depot's environmental programs have earned the company an A on the Council on Economic Priorities Corporate Report Card, a Vision of America Award from Keep America Beautiful, and a President's Council for Sustainable Development Award. The company has also been recognized by the U.S. Environmental Protection Agency with its Energy Star Award for Excellence.

Corporate Philanthropy

In addition to their environmental initiatives, Home Depot focuses corporate social responsibility efforts on affordable housing and disaster relief. For instance, Home Depot believes that it has a philanthropic responsibility to improve the communities in which they operate. In 2002, the company founded the Home Depot Foundation, which provides additional resources to assist nonprofits in the United States and Canada. The foundation awards grants to eligible nonprofits and partners with innovative nonprofits across the country

that are working to increase awareness and successfully demonstrate the connection between housing, the urban forest, and the overall health and economic success of their communities. The nonprofit is a strong supporter of Habitat for Humanity International and the American Red Cross. Another group The Home Depot Foundation focuses on is veterans. They have improved 14,000 facilities for veterans since 2011. The company is also taking an active stance to ensure the industry has skilled workers for the future. The Home Depot Foundation announced they were investing $50 million to train 20,000 tradespeople for job skills in the home improvement industry.

Additionally, Home Depot addresses the growing needs for relief from disasters such as hurricanes, tornadoes, and earthquakes. After the 9/11 terrorist attacks in 2001, the company set up three command centers with more than 200 associates to help coordinate relief supplies such as dust masks, gloves, batteries, and tools to victims and rescue workers. After the 2010 Haitian earthquake, Home Depot Mexico donated $30,000 to Habitat for Humanity to assist in Haiti's recovery efforts, in addition to launching a fundraising program for their Mexican associates. Home Depot pledged to double the resources that their Mexican associates raised to aid in the relief effort. When Hurricane Sandy hit the American East Coast in 2012, Home Depot responded with $1 million in donations in gift cards, supplies, and contributions to organizations that provided food, clothing, shelter, and volunteer efforts. Members of their own volunteer team, Team Depot, helped with rebuilding efforts. In 2018, Home Depot increased their financial disaster relief contributions to $4 million in the wake of Hurricane Michael and other natural disasters.

Employee and Supplier Relations

Home Depot encourages employees to become involved in the community through volunteer and civic activities. Home Depot also strives to apply social responsibility to their employment practices, with the goal of assembling a diverse workforce that reflects the population of the markets they serve. However, in 1997 the company settled a class-action lawsuit brought by female employees who alleged that they were paid less than male employees, awarded fewer pay raises, and promoted less often. The $87.5 million settlement represented one of the largest settlements in a gender discrimination lawsuit in U.S. history at the time. In announcing the settlement, the company emphasized that they were not admitting to wrongdoing and defended their record, saying that they provide equal opportunities for all and have a reputation of supporting women in professional positions.

Since the lawsuit, Home Depot has worked to show that they appreciate workforce diversity and seeks to give all their associates an equal chance to be employed and advance. In 2005, Home Depot formed partnerships with the ASPIRA Association, Inc., the Hispanic Association of Colleges and Universities, and the National Council of La Raza to recruit Hispanic candidates for part-time and full-time positions. Also in 2005, Home Depot became a major member of the American Association of Retired Persons' (AARP) Featured Retirement Program, which helps connect employees 50 years or older with companies that value their experience. Diversity is also incorporated into Home Depot's board. The 14-member board includes three women members and regularly engages in board refreshment practices where board members from different backgrounds and genders are included in executive roles.

Home Depot also has a strong diversity supplier program. As a member of the Women's Business Enterprise National Council and the National Minority Suppliers Development Council, Home Depot has come into contact and done business with a diverse range of suppliers, including many minority- and women-owned businesses. In 2005, the company became a founding member of The Resource Institute, whose mission is to help small minority- and women-owned businesses by providing them with resources and training. Home Depot's supplier diversity program has won them numerous recognitions. They ranked number 27 for the Top 50 American Organizations for Multicultural Business Opportunities in 2018.

New Technology Initiatives

Home Depot is turning toward technology to improve customer service and become more efficient. Compared to their rivals, Home Depot has traditionally lagged behind technologically. For a time, employees were using computers powered by motorboard batteries and stocking shelves in the same way as they had done for the past 15 years. Unlike their rival Lowe's, Home Depot was slow to allow customers to order products online and then pick them up at the stores. As more and more consumers chose to complete their transactions on the internet, this represented a weakness for Home Depot. In 2010, Home Depot's online sales constituted only 1.5 percent of overall sales. Although rapid expansion had increased their reach, Home Depot was not adapting as quickly to the fast-paced world of technology.

After recognizing their limitations in this field, Home Depot embarked upon several technology initiatives. These initiatives were intended to improve customer service and daily operations. One small victory that Home Depot achieved was beating Lowe's in releasing a mobile app that enables consumers to order Home Depot products. In addition, Home Depot distributed 30,000 of their First Phone devices in more than 1,900 of their stores to replace old computers in associates' carts. The device allows associates to communicate with other associates, print labels, process credit and debit card transactions, and manage inventory, among other functions. According to then-CEO Frank Blake, the purpose of First Phone is to help associates spend less time on routine tasks and more on customer service. Home Depot also redesigned their website to improve navigation and communication channels. The company provided upgrades such as live chat and developed a buy online pickup option. Home Depot has managed to reduce response time to customer emails from 24 hours to one hour or less.

In 2011, a special component of the Home Depot website was launched for "Pros" (Professional and Contractor Services). This website is intended to decrease the time it takes for professionals and contractors to get in and out of the store, allow them to order online and pick up their goods within a couple of hours, and enable delivery for certain products when ordered in bulk. Home Depot recognizes that professionals should spend less time in the store and more on the job. After this website was implemented, the speed with which this target market was able to get in and out of the store was increased by 27 percent from the previous year. Three percent of the customers identified as Pros make up 30 percent of Home Depot's annual revenue, making this a very important market for the retailer. Home Depot has also improved their logistics. Whereas before the company had their suppliers send trucks of merchandise directly to the stores, where associates would then unload them, Home Depot has created distribution centers to make operations run more smoothly. This change also enables their associates to devote more time to customer service.

These are just a few of the steps that Home Depot is taking to adopt a more proactive stance toward technological innovation. By concentrating on innovations that will increase customer service, the retailer is attempting to advance their stakeholder orientation into all aspects of their operations. Home Depot's focus on growing ecommerce has driven the company's growth. Nearly half of Home Depot's online orders are for in-store pickup, an integration that helps the stores to operate more efficiently. These efforts to integrate channels have improved their revenue per square foot.

As competition from online retailers like Amazon grows, Home Depot executives continue to focus on ways the company can compete technologically. After seven years with the company, Blake stepped down as CEO and was replaced by Craig Menear. The succession was smooth, so well planned that it had a minimal effect on Home Depot's stock price. Much like Blake, Menear proved that he would continue to focus on Home Depot's core culture. This is being put to the test as brick-and-mortar retailers like Home Depot are experiencing huge changes in how they do business. Executives have accepted the challenge to lead Home Depot through the "Amazon-era." While many companies have struggled because of online retailing, Home Depot has continued to be successful with increases in revenue, profits, and customer spending, partly because of their strong e-commerce strategy. With online sales increasing 21.5 percent since Menear became CEO, Home Depot seems to be surviving the "Amazon-era" with the help of their committed managers.

A Strategic Commitment to Social Responsibility

Home Depot strives to secure a socially responsible reputation with stakeholders. Although they have received low scores in the past on customer surveys and the American Customer Satisfaction Index, the firm has worked hard to bring those scores back up. They have responded to concerns about their environmental impact by creating new standards and principles to govern their relationship with suppliers.

In the past few years, the firm has taken their strategic commitment to stakeholders to a new level. Home Depot places their stakeholders into a pyramid shape with executives at the bottom of the pyramid, and with customers at the top. Front-line associates are on the second tier. Home Depot strives to treat their associates well through compensation, coupled with opportunities for learning and career development. Carol Tome, Home Depot's CFO, explained in an interview how management at the bottom of the pyramid takes on the most responsibility in the business to provide employees with the resources they need to focus on the customers. The board of directors continues to provide leadership to support executives in developing and implementing the employee- and market-focused culture.

Knowing that all stakeholders, especially customers, feel good about a company that actively commits their resources to environmental and social issues, Home Depot executives have made social responsibility a strategic component of the company's business operations. The company should remain committed to their focused strategy of philanthropy, volunteerism, and environmental initiatives. Customers' concerns over social responsibility and green products are not likely to abate in the future, and Home Depot's sales of green products remain strong. Their commitment to social responsibility extends throughout the company, fueled by top-level support from their cofounders and reinforced by a corporate culture that places customers and their concerns above all else.

Conclusion

Home Depot's strategic commitment to customer service and social responsibility is paying off for all stakeholders. Sales, revenues, and dividends have increased. Within a five-year period, Home Depot's focus on stakeholders, technological growth, and improved business operations had resulted in a 135 percent increase in value for investors who bought shares. In 2018, the stock hit an all-time high at more than $200 per share. To maintain their strategic advantage, the company is investing heavily in their employee training and success.

Home Depot continues to engage their employees and communities in volunteer efforts. The company responds quickly to aid employees and consumers in disaster situations such as floods, earthquakes, and hurricanes. Team Depot, Home Depot's associate-led volunteer force, takes great strides to meet the needs of the communities in need. Home Depot has approximately 400,000 dedicated Team Depot volunteers to improve the communities where they operate. Veterans and those in the military are also crucial stakeholders in Home Depot's corporate social responsibility program.

While any large company faces ethical challenges, Home Depot has established strong principles and values to be a responsible corporate citizen. Home Depot has rebounded from having low customer satisfaction into a company that is respected because of their strong performance and commitment to employees, customers, and communities.

Questions for Discussion

1. Assess the company's strategy and performance with environmental and employee stakeholders.
2. As a publicly traded corporation, how can Home Depot justify budgeting so much money for philanthropy? What areas other than the environment, disaster relief, and affordable housing might be appropriate for strategic philanthropy by Home Depot?
3. How does Home Depot's desire to be passionate about customer service relate to their social responsibility?

Sources

"2005 Reputation Quotient Rankings," *The Wall Street Journal*, December 6, 2005, https://www.wsj.com/articles/SB113388414609415172 (accessed August 21, 2019).

"Here's How Home Depot's E-Commerce Strategy Is Driving Growth," *Forbes*, February 15, 2017, https://www.forbes.com/sites/greatspeculations/2017/02/15/heres-how-home-depots-e-commerce-strategy-is-driving-growth/#b5577319b624 (accessed August 23, 2019).

"Home Depot Announces Commitment to Stop Selling Old Growth Wood. Announcement Validates Two- Year Grassroots Environmental Campaign," *Common Dreams*, August 26, 1999, http://www.commondreams.org/pressreleases/august99/082699c.htm (accessed August 17, 2016).

"Home Depot Builds out Its Online Customer Service," *Internet Retailer*, June 4, 2010, https://www.digitalcommerce360.com/2010/06/04/home-depot-builds-out-its-online-customer-service/ (accessed August 2, 2019).

"Home Depot Retools Timber Policy," *Memphis Business Journal*, January 2, 2003, www.bizjournals.com/memphis/stories/2002/12/30/daily12.html (accessed August 2, 2019).

"Home Depot: A Customer Success Story," *Social Link Media*, August 30, 2011, http://www.socialinkmedia.com/2011/08/the-home-depot-a-customer-service-success-story/ (accessed January 29, 2013).

"The Annual RQ 2007: The Reputations of the Most Visible Companies," Marketing Charts, http://www.marketingcharts.com/direct/corporate-reputation-in-decline-but-top-companies-buck-trend5129/harris-corporate-reputation-2007-most-visible-companiesjpg/ (accessed December 2, 2015).

"World's Most Admired Companies: Home Depot," *Fortune*, https://archive.fortune.com/magazines/fortune/globalmostadmired/2008/snapshots/2968.html (accessed August 2, 2019).

Adam Blair, "Home Depot's $64 Million Mobile Investment Rolls Out to 1,970 Stores," *Retail Info Systems*, December 7, 2010, https://risnews.com/home-depots-64-million-mobile-investment-rolls-out-1970-stores (accessed August 2, 2019).

Ashley M. Heher, "Home Depot Reports Loss of $54M, but Beats Estimates," *USA Today*, February 24, 2009, http://www.usatoday.com/money/companies/earnings/2009-02-24-home-depot_N.htm (accessed August 2, 2019).

Associated Press, "Home Depot CEO Nardelli Quits," *NBC*, January 3, 2007, http://www.nbcnews.com/id/16451112/ns/business-us_business/t/home-depot-ceo-nardelli-quits/ (accessed August 2, 2019).

Brad Tuttle, "Why Home Depot Is Immune to the 'Amazon Effect'," *Time: Money*, August 16, 2016, http://time.com/money/4453962/home-depot-amazon-effect-sales/ (accessed September August 2, 2019).

Brian Grow, Diane Brady, and Michael Arndt, "Renovating Home Depot," *Businessweek*, March 6, 2006, https://www.bloomberg.com/news/articles/2006-03-05/renovating-home-depot (accessed August 2, 2019).

Chris Burritt, "Home Depot's Fix-It Lady," *Bloomberg Business Week*, January 17–23, 2011, 65–67

Cora Daniels, "To Hire a Lumber Expert, Click Here," *Fortune*, April 3, 2000, 267–270.

Craig Webb, "Home Depot Exec Reveals New Initiatives to Serve Pros," *ProSales*, August 21, 2012, http://www.prosalesmagazine.com/business/sales/home-depot-exec-reveals-new-initiatives-to-serve-pros_o (accessed August 2, 2019).

DiversityBusiness.com, America's Top Organizations for Multicultural Business Opportunities, 2015, http://www.diversitybusiness.com/Resources/DivLists/2015/DivTop50/2015Div50C.htm (accessed August 2, 2019).

Energy Star, "Congratulations to the 2017 ENERGY STAR Award Winners!" 2017, https://www.energystar.gov/index.cfm?fuseaction=pt_awards.showawardlist&year=2017 (accessed August 2, 2019).

Greenleaf, "How Home Depot Overcame a Difficult Cultural Shift: A Q&A with CFO Carol Tome," *Greenleaf Center for Servant Leadership*, July 10, 2015, https://www.greenleaf.org/how-home-depot-overcame-a-difficult-cultural-shift-a-qa-with-cfo-carol-tome/ (accessed August 2, 2019).

Habitat for Humanity, "Habitat for Humanity and The Home Depot Foundation Partner to Repair Homes with U.S. Military Veterans and Families," September 26, 2011, https://www.habitat.org/newsroom/09-26-2011-hfh-and-home-depot-partner (accessed August 21, 2019).

Heidi N. Moore, "Chrysler: The End of Bob Nardelli. Again." *The Wall Street Journal*, April 21, 2009, https://blogs.wsj.com/deals/2009/04/21/chrysler-the-end-of-bob-nardelli-again/ (accessed August 2, 2019).

Home Depot, "Through the Years: Doing the Right Thing for Our Environment," March 3, 2016, https://corporate.homedepot.com/newsroom/home-depot-environmental-milestones-2015 (accessed August 17, 2016).

Home Depot, "A Commitment to Community," https://corporate.homedepot.com/community (accessed August 2, 2019).

Home Depot, "About Us," https://corporate.homedepot.com/about (accessed August 2, 2019).

Home Depot, "CEO Craig Menear Talks Innovation: Follow The Consumer," *Home Depot*, October 19, 2016, https://corporate.homedepot.com/newsroom/ceo-craig-menear-talks-innovation-aspen-institute (accessed August 2, 2019).

Home Depot, "Chemical Strategy," April 2018, http://corporate.homedepot.com/sites/default/files/Chemical%20Strategy%20-%2004%202018.pdf (accessed August 2, 2019).

Home Depot, "National Partnerships," https://corporate.homedepot.com/community/The-Home-Depot-Foundation-partnerships (accessed August 2, 2019).

Home Depot, "Proxy Statement and Notice of 2019 Annual Meeting of Shareholders," April 8, 2019, https://ir.homedepot.com/~/media/Files/H/HomeDepot-IR/2019_Proxy_Updates/Final%202019%20Proxy%20Statement_vF.PDF (accessed August 2, 2019).

Home Depot, "Reducing Environmental Impact," https://corporate.homedepot.com/responsibility/reducing-environmental-impact (accessed August 2, 2019).

Home Depot, "Responding to Natural Disasters," 2016, https://corporate.homedepot.com/community/disaster-relief (accessed August 17, 2016).

Home Depot, "Supplier Diversity," https://corporate.homedepot.com/responsibility/people/supplier-diversity (accessed August 2, 2019).

Home Depot, "The Home Depot Foundation Responds to Superstorm Sandy," 2012, http://homedepotfoundation.org/page/the-home-depot-foundation-responds-to-superstorm-sandy (accessed September 15, 2014).

Jena McGregor, "Home Depot Sheds Units," *Bloomberg*, January 26, 2009, http://www.bloomberg.com/news/articles/2009-01-26/home-depot-sheds-units (accessed August 2, 2019).

Jim Carlton, "How Home Depot and Activists Joined to Cut Logging Abuse," *The Wall Street Journal*, September 26, 2000, A1.

Joann Lublin, Matt Murray, and Rick Brooks, "Home Depot Names GE's Nardelli as New CEO in a Surprise Move," *The Wall Street Journal*, December 6, 2000, https://www.wsj.com/articles/SB976051062408860254 (accessed August 2, 2019).

John Kell, "Home Depot's Former CEO Frank Blake to Retire as Chairman," *Fortune*, January 16, 2015, http://fortune.com/2015/01/16/home-depot-former-ceo-retires-as-chairman/ (accessed August 2, 2019).

Joseph McAdory, "Student Center for Public Trust: Carol Tome," *Center for Ethical Organizational Cultures*, September 27, 2018, http://harbert.auburn.edu/research-and-centers/center-for-ethical-organizational-cultures/student-center-for-public-trust.php (accessed April 25, 2019).

Josh Arnold, "Near All-Time Highs, Home Depot Is Still a Buy," *Seeking Alpha,* June 27, 2019, https://seekingalpha.com/article/4272423-near-time-highs-home-depot-still-buy (accessed August 2, 2019).

Julie Creswell and Michael Barbaro, "Home Depot Ousts Highly Paid Chief," *The New York Times,* January 4, 2007, http://www.nytimes.com/2007/01/04/business/04home.html?mcubz=3 (accessed August 2, 2019).

Julie Scelfo, "The Meltdown in Home Furnishings," *The New York Times*, January 28, 2009, http://www.nytimes.

com/2009/01/29/garden/29industry.html (accessed August 2, 2019).

Karen Jacobs, "Home Depot Pushes Low Prices, Energy Savings," *Reuters*, September 10, 2008, http://www.reuters.com/article/ousiv/idUSN1051947020080910 (accessed August 2, 2019).

Kirsten Downey Grimsley, "Home Depot Settles Gender Bias Lawsuit," *The Washington Post*, September 20, 1997, D1.

Louis Uchitelle, "Home Depot Girds for Continued Weakness," *The New York Times*, May 18, 2009, http://www.nytimes.com/2009/05/19/business/19depot.html (accessed August 2, 2019).

Marianne Wilson, "Report: Home Depot to Spend $1.3 Billion on Technology and $700 Million on New Stores," *Chain Store Age*, June 20, 2012, http://www.chainstoreage.com/article/report-home-depot-spend-13-billion-technology-and-700-million-new-stores (accessed August 2, 2019).

Mary Ellen Lloyd, "Home Improvement Spending Remains Tight," *The Wall Street Journal*, May 6, 2009, http://online.wsj.com/article/SB124162405957992133.html (accessed August 2, 2019).

Miguel Bustillo, "For Lowe's, Landscape Begins to Shift," *The Wall Street Journal*, February 24, 2011, B3.

Nathan Owen Rosenberg, "The Key to Home Depot's Success Is Transformational Leadership," *Insigniam*, http://insigniam.com/blog/the-key-to-home-depots-success-is-transformational-leadership/ (accessed August 2, 2019).

Neil Janowitz, "Rolling in the Depot," *Fast Company*, May 2012, 38.

Parija B. Kavilanz, "Nardelli Out at Home Depot," *CNN Money*, January 3, 2007, http://money.cnn.com/2007/01/03/news/companies/home_depot/ (accessed September 27, 2017).

Paul Ziobro, "Home Depot, TJX Cos. Buck Retail Trends," *The Wall Street Journal*, August 16, 2016, http://www.wsj.com/articles/home-depot-t-j-maxx-buck-retail-trends-1471379637 (accessed August 2, 2019).

PR Newswire, "The Home Depot Forms Unprecedented Partnership with Four Leading National Hispanic Organizations," *Puerto Rico Herald*, February 15, 2005, http://www.puertorico-herald.org/issues2/2005/vol09n24/HomeDepo.html (accessed August 2, 2019).

PR Newswire, "The Home Depot Launches Environmental Wood Purchasing Policy," August 26, 1999, http://www.prnewswire.com/cgi-bin/stories.pl?ACCT=104&STORY=/www/story/08-261999/0001010227&EDATE= (accessed August 17, 2016).

Rachel Tobin, "Frank Blake Is Home Depot's 'Calmer-in-Chief'," *Seattle Times*, September, 4, 2010, https://www.seattletimes.com/business/frank-blake-is-home-depots-calmer-in-chief/ (accessed August 2, 2019).

Rebecca Ungarino, "Dow Stock Home Depot Just Hit an All-Time High as It Trains in a 'Sweet Spot'," *CNBC*, September 10, 2018, https://www.cnbc.com/2018/09/10/dow-stock-home-depot-hits-all-time-high-as-it-trades-in-a-sweet-spot.html (accessed August 2, 2019).

Reuters and Fortune, "Home Depot Just Made Its Biggest Acquisition in Nearly a Decade," *Fortune*, July 22, 2015, https://fortune.com/2015/07/22/home-depot-interline-brands-deal/ (accessed August 2, 2019).

Sarah Demaster, "Use Proper Lumber, Demand Protesters," *BNet*, April 5, 1999, http://findarticles.com/p/articles/mi_m0VCW/is_7_25/ai_54373184/ (accessed September 8, 2009).

Shelly DuBois, "Home Depot Knows When to Call It Quits," *Fortune*, October 26, 2012, https://fortune.com/2012/10/26/home-depot-knows-when-to-call-it-quits/ (accessed August 2, 2019).

Susan Jackson and Tim Smart, "Mom and Pop Fight Back," *Business Week*, April 14, 1997, 46.

Tom Brennan, "Home Depot vs. Lowe's," *CNBC*, August 26, 2008, http://www.cnbc.com/id/26406040/?=aol|headline|quote|text|&par=aol (accessed August 17, 2016).

Wharton School, "Home Unimprovement: Was Nardelli's Tenure at Home Depot a Blueprint for Failure?" *Knowledge@Wharton*, http://knowledge.wharton.upenn.edu/article/home-unimprovement-was-nardellis-tenure-at-home-depot-a-blueprint-for-failure/ (accessed August 2, 2019).

Big-Box Retailer Walmart Manages Big Responsibility

Introduction

Walmart is an icon of American business. With annual revenue of more than $514 billion and more than 2.2 million employees, the world's largest retailer must carefully manage many stakeholder relationships. The company's stated mission is to help people save money and live better. Despite past controversies, Walmart has attempted to restore their image with an emphasis on diversity, charitable giving, support for nutrition, and sustainability. The company, along with the Walmart Foundation, has donated more than $1.4 billion in cash and in-kind contributions. Walmart often tops the list of U.S. donors to charities. In 2019, for example, the company spent $42 million on charitable grants to help with community projects and organizations. Walmart also makes use of in-store cause marketing, such as the "Fight Hunger. Spark Change." campaign, which has successfully given millions of dollars to Americans struggling with hunger. However, issues such as bribery accusations in Mexico, Brazil, China, and India have created significant ethics and compliance challenges that Walmart is addressing in their quest to become a socially responsible retailer.

This analysis begins by briefly examining the growth of Walmart. Next, it discusses the company's various relationships with stakeholders, including competitors, suppliers, and employees. The ethical issues concerning these stakeholders include accusations of discrimination, leadership misconduct, bribery, and unsafe working conditions. We discuss how Walmart has dealt with these concerns, as well as some of the company's endeavors in sustainability and social responsibility. The analysis concludes by examining what Walmart is doing to increase their competitive advantage and repair their reputation.

History: The Growth of Walmart

The story of Walmart begins in 1962 when founder Sam Walton opened the first Walmart Discount Store in Rogers, Arkansas. Although their growth was initially slow, the company now serves almost 265 million customers weekly at more than 10,000 locations in 27 countries. Much of Walmart's success can be attributed to the company's founder. A shrewd businessman, Walton believed in customer satisfaction and hard work. He convinced many of his associates to abide by the "10-foot rule," whereby employees pledged that whenever a customer came within 10 feet of them, they would look the customer in the eye, greet him or her, and ask if he or she needed assistance. Walton's famous mantra, known as the "sundown rule," was: "Why put off until tomorrow what you can do today?" Due to this staunch work ethic and dedication to customer care, Walmart claimed early on that a formal ethics program was unnecessary because the company had Mr. Walton's ethics to follow.

In 2002, Walmart officially became the largest grocery chain, topping the *Fortune* 500 list. *Fortune* named Walmart the "most admired company in America" in 2003 and 2004. Since 2002, Walmart has maintained their position as the largest retailer in the world. In addition to being the largest, the company is the only brick-and-mortar store of the three top retailers. Amazon and Alibaba are the second and third largest retailers, respectively, and are predominantly online stores.

While customers still flock to the physical Walmart locations to buy groceries, clothing, and a variety of household items, establishing a greater online presence to compete with digital retailers has been a major goal for Walmart over the past several years. Walmart and Amazon compete not only on online shopping but also on same-day delivery. To become more competitive with the online retailers, Walmart bought Jet.com in 2016. Walmart is using Jet to expanded grocery delivery into New York City, the company's first venture in the city. In addition to Jet, Walmart also has their home site, Walmart.com. Both websites have achieved some success, particularly with online grocery shopping. Walmart has partnered with Microsoft to boost their digital transformation, using a range of Microsoft cloud solutions and collaborating on innovative projects. However, Walmart's current financial losses from digital investments are estimated to be as high as $1 billion. Walmart has achieved so much success as a brick-and-mortar retail chain that it will take time to adjust to the increasingly digital shopping experience that consumers have come to expect. To prevent future losses and continue to hold the number one spot in global retail, Walmart will have to make sound business decisions regarding their online retail.

Competitive Stakeholders

Possibly the greatest complaint against Walmart is that they put other companies out of business. With their low prices, Walmart makes it harder for local stores to compete. Walmart is often accused of being responsible for the downward pressure on wages and benefits in

This case was prepared by Kelsey Reddick, Jennifer Sawayda, Sarah Sawayda, and Michelle Urban under the direction of O.C. Ferrell and Linda Ferrell, © 2019. It was prepared for classroom discussion rather than to illustrate either effective or ineffective handling of an administrative, ethical, or legal decision by management. All sources used for this case were obtained through publicly available material and the Walmart website.

towns where the company locates. Some businesses have filed lawsuits against Walmart, claiming the company uses unfair predatory pricing to put competing stores out of business. Walmart has countered by defending their pricing, asserting that they are competing fairly and that the company's purpose is to provide quality, low-cost products to the average consumer. Yet, while Walmart has saved consumers millions of dollars and is a popular shopping spot for many, there is no denying that many competing stores go out of business once Walmart comes to town.

To compete against the retail giant, other stores must reduce wages. Studies show that overall payroll wages, including Walmart wages, decline by 5 percent after Walmart enters a new market. The impact of Walmart moving into the neighborhood has been coined the "Walmart Effect," a negative connotation that represents all the hardship incurred on smaller businesses. As a result, some activist groups and citizens have refused to allow Walmart to take up residence in their areas. This, in turn, brings up another social responsibility issue: What methods of protest may stakeholders reasonably use, and how should Walmart respond to such actions?

While it is acceptable for stakeholder activists to protest the building of a Walmart store in their area, other actions may be questionable, especially when the government gets involved. When Walmart announced plans to open stores in Washington, D.C., for instance, a chairman of the D.C. City Council introduced a law that required non-unionized retail companies with more than $1 billion in total sales and stores that occupy more than 75,000 square feet to pay their employees a minimum of $12.50 per hour—in contrast to the city's $8.25 an hour minimum wage at the time. The terms of the law made it essentially apply only to Walmart and a few other large chains such as Home Depot and Costco. While supporters of the law argued that it is difficult to live on a wage of $8.25 an hour, critics stated that the proposal gave employees at large retailers an unjustified benefit over those working comparable jobs at small retailers. Perhaps the most scathing criticism was that Walmart and other big-box retailers were being unfairly targeted by a governmental entity. Walmart also responded directly, threatening to cancel their expansion into D.C. if the law passed and emphasizing the economic and development benefits the city would lose out on. The D.C. City Council eventually passed the law, but it was vetoed by the city mayor, and there are now several Walmart stores in D.C. As with most issues, determining the most socially responsible decision that benefits the most stakeholders is a complex issue not easily resolved.

Relationships with Suppliers

Walmart achieves their "everyday low prices" (also called EDLPs) by streamlining the company. Well known for operational excellence in their ability to handle, move, and track merchandise, Walmart expects suppliers to continually improve their systems as well. Walmart typically works with suppliers to reduce packaging and shipping costs, which lowers prices for consumers. The company employs thousands of Walmart trucks to go to the suppliers rather than the suppliers coming to the store, cutting down on cost. Walmart takes supply chain management very seriously, as evidenced by their constant evaluation of how suppliers' products are doing in stores.

Walmart holds suppliers to high standards, especially when it comes to the delivery of products customers order online. In 2019, Walmart revamped their rules to require suppliers to obtain an 87 percent success rate of delivering full trucks of products over two days. For partially full trucks, the success rate of on-time delivery went from 50 percent to 70 percent in 2019, indicating the more stringent standards for suppliers are working.

Since 2009 the company has worked with The Sustainability Consortium, an association of businesses that helps its members achieve sustainability goals, to develop a measurement and reporting system known as the Walmart Sustainability Index (discussed in further detail later in this case). Among their many goals, Walmart desires to use the Sustainability Index to increase the sustainability of their products and create a more efficient, sustainable supply chain. In 2008, Walmart introduced their "Global Responsible Sourcing Initiative," a list providing details of the policies and requirements included in new supplier agreements. In 2017, Walmart and the Sustainability Consortium created Project Gigaton, a sustainability effort to eliminate 1 billion tons of greenhouse gas from Walmart's global supply chain before 2030. With the help of vendors, Walmart has made great progress toward their goal. Suppliers also receive better ratings from Walmart for providing environmentally-friendly products, an incentive that has paid off so far.

Some critics of Walmart's approach note that pressure to achieve their standards will shift more of the cost burden onto suppliers. When a supplier does not meet Walmart's demands, the company may cease to carry that supplier's product or, often, will be able to find another willing supplier of the product at the desired price.

Walmart's power over their suppliers stems from their size and the volume of products they require. Many companies depend on Walmart for much of their business. This type of relationship allows Walmart to significantly influence terms with their vendors. For example, Walmart generally refuses to sign long-term supply contracts, giving them the power to easily and quickly change suppliers at their own discretion. Despite this, suppliers will invest significantly in long-term strategic and business commitments to meet Walmart demands, even without any guarantee that Walmart will continue to buy from them.

There are corresponding benefits to being a Walmart supplier; by having to become more efficient and streamlined for Walmart, companies develop competitive advantages and are able to serve their other customers better as well. For example, as Walmart worked with IBM to develop a blockchain solution to food safety, Walmart began requiring all suppliers of green leafy vegetables to use the blockchain database. Though blockchain technology makes Walmart's supply chain more traceable and transparent, this requirement is a financial and technical burden for many companies. However, as these companies adapt with the help of IBM's onboarding system, they will be better prepared to use blockchain technology in their own businesses. However, many others find the amount of power Walmart wields to be disconcerting. Suppliers in Mexico have said that they have been penalized by Walmart for working with Amazon, Walmart's biggest rival. While Walmart denied explicitly telling suppliers to stop partnering with Amazon, there are suspicions that the retailer used coercion to win suppliers' loyalty from Amazon.

The constant drive by Walmart for lower prices can negatively affect suppliers. Many have been forced to move production from the United States to less expensive locations in Asia. In fact, Walmart is considered to have been one of the major driving forces behind the "offshoring" trend of the past several decades. Companies such as Master Lock, Fruit of the Loom, and Levi's, as well as many other Walmart suppliers, moved production overseas at the expense of U.S. jobs. The challenges and ethical issues associated with managing a vast network of overseas suppliers will be discussed later in this case.

This offshoring trend was not founder Sam Walton's original intention. In the 1980s, after learning his stores were putting other American companies out of business, Walton started his "Buy American" campaign. In 2013, Walmart launched a "Made in America" initiative, pledging to increase the number of U.S.-made goods they buy by $50 billion over 10 years and developing agreements with many suppliers to move their production back to the states. Critics argue that Walmart is merely putting a public relations spin on the fact that rising wages in Asian countries and other international economic changes have actually made local production more cost-efficient than outsourcing for many industries. They also point out that $50 billion is a veritable "drop in the bucket" considering Walmart's size. Still, the symbolic effect of Walmart throwing their considerable influence behind "Made in America" is likely to spur many suppliers to freshly consider or speed up plans to bring production back to the United States.

Ethical Issues Involving Employee Stakeholders

Much of the Walmart controversy over the years has focused on the way the company treats their employees or "associates" as Walmart refers to them. Although Walmart is the largest retail employer in the world, they have been roundly criticized for paying low wages and offering minimal benefits. For example, Walmart has been accused of failing to provide health insurance for more than 60 percent of their employees.

Employee Benefits

A 2014 Walmart policy eliminated healthcare coverage for new hires working less than 30 hours a week. Walmart also stated that they reserve the right to cut healthcare coverage of workers whose workweek falls below 30 hours. Some analysts claim that Walmart might be attempting to shift the burden of healthcare coverage onto the federal government, as some employees make so little that they qualify for Medicaid under the Affordable Care Act. It is important to note that Walmart is not alone in this practice; many firms are moving more of their workforces to part time, and cutting benefits to part-time workers, to avoid having to pay healthcare costs. However, as such a large employer, Walmart's actions are expected to have more of a ripple effect on the economy.

Another criticism levied against Walmart is that they are decreasing their workforce. For example, Walmart is testing staffing fewer midlevel, in-store managers to improve labor costs, increase wages, and attract higher quality employees. Walmart has insisted this is not a cost-saving measure but rather another way to compete with online retailers. Arguably, with fewer employees, it is harder to provide quality customer service. In the 2018 American Customer Satisfaction Index, Walmart was one of the lowest among department and discount stores, ranked only above Sears. Walmart claims the dissatisfaction expressed by some customers is not reflective of the shopping experience of customers as a whole. Additionally, many fear robots and artificial intelligence (AI) will eliminate jobs. Walmart has invested in robots to clean the store and scan inventory, among other functions. Despite this move toward robotics, Walmart says their employees are the key to their success and that they will work to re-skill associates to work alongside new technology.

Though the company has received criticism over their employee wages, Walmart pays greater than minimum wage in 47 states, and 75 percent of their managers are promoted from within. In addition to fair wages, Walmart incentivizes employees to stay with the company longer by rewarding them based on years of employment. Bonuses range from $200 to $1,000 depending on how long the employee has worked for Walmart. Also, Walmart extended their maternity and parental leave to a combined 16 weeks for full-time hourly workers.

Walmart's Stance on Unions

Some critics believe Walmart workers' benefits could improve if workers unionized. Unions have been discouraged since Walmart's foundation; Sam Walton believed they were a divisive force and might render the company uncompetitive. Walmart maintains that they are not against unions in general, but they see no need for unions to come between workers and managers. The company says they support an "open-door policy" in which associates can bring problems to managers without resorting to third parties. Walmart associates have voted against unions in the past.

Although the company's official position is that they are not opposed to unions, Walmart often seems to fight against them. Critics claim that when the word "union" surfaces at a Walmart location, the top dogs in Bentonville are called in. For example, in 2000, seven of ten Walmart butchers in Jacksonville, Texas, voted to join the United Food Workers Union. Walmart responded by announcing that they would only sell precut meat in their Supercenters, getting rid of their meat-cutting departments entirely. In 2004, employees at a Canada Walmart location voted to unionize; six months later, Walmart closed the store. In 2014, two internal Walmart PowerPoint presentations were leaked. The slides provided reasons why unions would negatively impact associates and directed managers to call the Labor Relations Hotline if they spot warning signs of union activity. Although Walmart offers justifications for actions such as these, many see the company as aggressively working to prevent unionization in their stores. The U.S. National Labor Relations Board (NLRB) has cited Walmart on multiple occasions for violating labor laws. Past employees of Walmart have said that watching anti-union videos is part of the training.

However, Walmart's stance against unions has not always held up to the practical realities of doing business in some foreign countries. In China, for example, Walmart found it necessary to accept a union in order to grow. Only one union is legally permitted to operate in China, the All-China Federation of Trade Unions (ACFTU), which is run by the ruling Communist Party. The Chinese government promotes the ACFTU (although the union has been criticized as pro-business and not necessarily looking out for the best interests of workers) and especially seeks to have foreign companies unionized. The Chinese Labor Federation pushed Walmart to allow employees to unionize in 2006. Walmart initially resisted, and although they eventually complied, critics claimed the company then began making unionization progressively more difficult in practice for their Chinese workers. The ACFTU was able to establish union branches at five separate China Walmart locations. Walmart reacted by stating they would not renew the contracts of unionized workers. However, the pressure mounted, and later that year Walmart signed a memorandum with the ACFTU, allowing unions in stores. Some analysts believe Walmart fought so hard against unionization in China, despite the clear unlikelihood of prevailing against the Chinese government itself, because they feared workers in other countries would use the precedent to redouble their own unionization demands. Since then, Walmart has permitted or negotiated with unions in several other countries, including Brazil, Chile, Mexico, Argentina, the United Kingdom, and South Africa. When workers in Mexico threatened to strike in 2019, Walmart reached a deal with the union Revolutionary Confederation of Laborers and Farmworkers to improve wages by an average of 5.5 percent.

Workplace Conditions and Discrimination

Walmart remains the largest nongovernment employer in the United States, Mexico, and Canada. The retailer provides jobs to millions of people and has been a mainstay of *Fortune*'s "Most Admired Companies" list since the start of the twenty-first century. However, in 2019, a class-action lawsuit involving nearly 100 women was filed against the company for gender pay discrimination. The women say they were either paid less than their male counterparts or they were pushed into lower paying positions. Along with gender discrimination, Walmart has been accused of disability discrimination. For example, in 2018, the Equal Employment Opportunity Commission (EEOC) sued Walmart when the retailer would not hire an employment candidate based on the fact that she was an amputee. Despite the disability, the candidate was able to perform the job, and, therefore, the EEOC sued Walmart for violation of Americans with Disability Act (ADA) standards. In Illinois, there was suspicion of racial discrimination in one of Walmart's warehouses. More than 100 black workers were refused employment when Walmart took command of a warehouse, which had been previously run by an outside company, and ran background checks on the existing employees, resulting in legal action from the workers.

In 2010, dissatisfied Walmart employees started the nonprofit United for Respect. Although not a labor union, United for Respect receives much of its funding from the United Food and Commercial Workers International Union (UFCW), which has been trying to unionize U.S. Walmart employees for years. Eventually realizing it needed a different approach, UFCW backed the idea of a non-union advocacy group and hired a market research company to develop United for Respect's message and activism strategy. Its demands include lowering the number of hours needed for part-time workers to qualify for benefits, removing caps on the wages of some long-term workers, and ending the practice of using work-scheduling systems to decrease hours for employees so they will not qualify for benefits. In 2011, 100 United for Respect members traveled to Walmart's headquarters and presented a 12-point declaration of their demands to the company's senior vice president for global labor relations. Since then, United for Respect has arranged a variety of protests and pickets. It has especially targeted the busy holiday season, organizing demonstrations and walkouts at many Walmart stores on every Black Friday since 2012. In 2019, Walmart responded to a shooting at a location in El Paso, Texas, by removing violent video game displays. United for Respect released a statement that the decision was "irresponsible and weak."

Walmart's position is that United for Respect is a small, fringe movement that does not represent the views of the average associate, most of whom are satisfied with their jobs. The company has repeatedly complained to the National Labor Relations Board, claiming, among other things, that United for Respect uses illegal methods and that it is actually a union in disguise. Walmart has also accused the UFCW of anti-labor practices and filed at least one lawsuit against the UFCW and others who protested around their stores for illegal trespassing and disrupting customers. Walmart may have made a tactical error by choosing to acknowledge United for Respect as a threat. The number of United for Respect members is very small compared to the number of U.S. Walmart employees as a whole, and not as many Walmart employees have participated in protests as anticipated. Although Walmart claims this demonstrates that the movement is not as popular as it tries to appear, the company may have unintentionally granted it legitimacy and a large amount of free publicity by responding so directly and forcefully.

Ethical Leadership Issues

Walmart has not been immune from scandal at the top. In March 2005, board vice chairman Thomas Coughlin was forced to resign because he stole as much as $500,000 from Walmart in the form of bogus expenses, reimbursements, and the unauthorized use of gift cards. Coughlin, a protégé and hunting buddy of Sam Walton, was a legend at Walmart. He often spent time on the road with Walton expanding the Sam's Club aspect of the business. At one time, he was the second-highest-ranking Walmart executive and a candidate for CEO. In January 2006, Coughlin agreed to plead guilty to federal wire-fraud and tax-evasion charges. Coughlin secretly used Walmart funds to pay for a range of personal expenses, including hunting vacations, a $2,590 dog enclosure at his home, and a pair of handmade alligator boots. Coughlin's deceit was discovered when he asked a subordinate to approve $2,000 in expense payments without receipts. Walmart rescinded Coughlin's retirement agreement, worth more than $10 million. For his crimes, he was sentenced to 27 months of home confinement, $440,000 in fines, and 1,500 hours of community service.

Confidence in Walmart's governance suffered another serious blow in 2012 when a bribery scandal in Walmart's Mexico branch was uncovered that directly implicated much of the company's top management (the scandal is explored in detail later in this case). That same year, a significant percentage of Walmart's non-family shareholders voted against the reelection of then-CEO Mike Duke to the board. They also voted against the reelection of other board members, including former CEO Lee Scott and board chairman Robson Walton—Sam Walton's eldest son. While these board members still received enough support to be reelected, the votes signaled serious investor disappointment and lack of confidence in the leadership for not preventing the misconduct. Since the scandal, Walmart has invested heavily in demonstrating a renewed commitment toward ensuring the company adheres to ethics and compliance standards to reassure investors, governmental investigators, and the public at large. Because of past scandals, Walmart's board of directors is undoubtedly under close scrutiny. The company has filled their board with reputable leaders such as Sarah Friar, CEO of Nextdoor, Carla A. Harris, senior client advisor at Morgan Stanley, and Timothy P. Flynn, retired chairman and CEO of KPMG International.

Bribery Scandal

The biggest blow to Walmart's reputation in recent years has been the uncovering of a large-scale bribery scandal within their Mexican arm, Walmex. Walmex executives allegedly paid millions in bribes to obtain licensing and zoning permits for store locations. The Mexican approval process for zoning licenses often takes longer than it would in the United States; therefore, paying bribes to speed up the process is advantageous for Walmart but places competing retailers who do not offer bribes at a disadvantage. Walmex apparently even used bribes to have zoning maps changed or certain areas re-zoned in order to build stores in more ideal locations, as well as to overcome environmental or other concerns. The Walmex executives covered their tracks with fraudulent reporting methods.

In recent years, bribery has become a hot button issue for the U.S. government, which has levied substantial fines and penalties against firms found guilty of bribery. It is not unusual for large firms with operations in many countries to face bribery allegations at some point considering the size of their operations and the diversity of cultures of the locations in which they do business. However, Walmart's bribery scandal in Mexico was exacerbated by two major considerations. First, the evidence indicated that the top executives at Walmart, not just Walmex, knew about the bribery and turned a blind eye to it. Second, the evidence gave weight to concerns that bribery by Walmart in foreign countries was widespread and acceptable in the company's culture.

Walmart first reported to the U.S. Justice Department that they were launching an internal investigation of suspected bribery at their Mexico stores in December 2011. However, that report to the U.S. Justice Department was not submitted until after Walmart learned *The New York Times* was conducting an independent investigation. *The New York Times'* final report revealed that top leaders at Walmart had been alerted to the possibility of bribery as early as 2005. That year, Walmart received an email warning of the bribery from a former Walmex executive who claimed he had been involved. The email included cold, hard facts, such as names, dates, bribery amounts, and other information. Walmart sent investigators to Mexico City, who corroborated much of the informant's allegations and discovered evidence that approximately $24 million in bribes had been paid to public officials to get necessary building permits. Walmex's top executives, including the subsidiary's CEO and general counsel, were implicated in the scheme. However, when the investigators reported their preliminary findings to Walmart's top executives, including then-CEO Lee Scott, the executives were reluctant to report the bribery because they knew it would be a serious blow to the firm's reputation, which was already suffering due to other issues. The prospect of revealing the scandal was especially bitter because Walmart had been drawing media and investor attention for their explosive growth in Mexico as a shining success story. Admitting that this growth had been significantly fueled by bribery would look very bad for the company.

The scandal's impact on Walmart was significant. Shortly after the *New York Times'* investigation was published, the stock lost $1 billion in value, and shareholders began filing lawsuits against the company and the company's executives. In addition, Walmart had to pay for their own internal probe, not to mention hire a number of lawyers to represent the company and the company's top management as well as advisors and consultants to help restructure their internal ethics and compliance systems. Walmart spent approximately $900 million in legal fees and investigations, plus the company will pay millions in fines. Walmart's internal probe revealed the likelihood of bribery going on in other countries as well. The company, therefore, expanded the investigation to include their operations in China, India, and Brazil. For example, at their Indian branch, Walmart suspended some key executives who were believed to have engaged in bribery. This investigation halted Walmart's expansion in the country. Indian authorities began investigating Walmart and their joint venture partner at the time, Bharti Enterprises, to determine if they attempted to circumvent Indian laws on foreign investment. Foreign retailers like Walmart are allowed to partner with local businesses and open stores in the country so long as they do not own a majority stake in the venture (less than 51 percent ownership). It is alleged that Walmart offered Bharti an interest-free $100 million loan that would later enable them to gain a majority stake in the company. Both companies deny they tried to violate foreign investment rules and have since broken off their partnership. Such accusations not only have serious consequences for Walmart but also for other foreign retailers in India. Many Indian political officials were against allowing foreign retailers to open stores in the country at all. This alleged misconduct has added fuel for their opposition. Hence, the operation of other foreign retailers may be threatened. This situation demonstrates how the misconduct of one or two companies can impact entire industries.

In Brazil, permits were obtained illegally, and land was obtained illegally in China by bribing landlords and officials. An unidentified individual in Brazil charged about $400,000 to facilitate the process of getting building permits. Walmart took minimal action to address employee tips about bribery occurring in new stores. The Securities and Exchange Commission (SEC) charged the retailer with "...[allowing] subsidiaries in Brazil, China, India, and Mexico to employ third-party intermediaries who made payments to foreign government officials without reasonable assurances that they complied with the FCPA [(Foreign Corruption Practices Act)]".

In the wake of the scandals, many Walmart shareholders demanded, among other things, disciplinary action and compensation cuts against those involved. Shareholders are also demanding that the leaders of Walmart continue to improve transparency and compliance standards. As part of their compliance overhaul, Walmart announced they would begin tying some executive compensation to compliance efforts.

Through federal prosecutors and regulators initially sought $600 million in fines, Walmart will pay just $282 million to settle the charges. In addition, Walmart will be monitored and subject to compliance guidelines of both the Department of Justice and the SEC for the next couple of years. One major reason Walmart may have not faced higher fines and more serious consequences is because of the company's attempts to reform, spending nearly $1 billion to improve prior to the settlement.

Safety Issues

Using overseas suppliers has also caused trouble for Walmart. Many of their suppliers, both inside the United States and in other countries, employ subcontractors to manufacture certain products. This makes the supply chain complex, and retailers like Walmart are forced to exert more oversight to ensure their suppliers meet compliance standards. Citing safety concerns or telling a supplier not to work with a certain subcontractor is not enough without enforcement. Walmart learned this the hard way after a Bangladeshi factory fire killed 112 workers.

The factory, Tazreen Fashions Ltd., had several assembly lines devoted to Walmart apparel because at least one of Walmart's suppliers used the factory to subcontract work for Walmart. However, Walmart claims the supplier was unauthorized to do so, as Walmart had removed Tazreen Fashions from their list of approved factories months before the incident. Walmart subsequently terminated their relationship with that supplier. Previous inspections at Tazreen showed many fire hazards, including blocked stairwells and a lack of firefighting equipment. The fire burned down the building and killed 112 employees, some of whom jumped to their deaths.

Many were outraged that Walmart did not do a better job of ensuring the safety of factory workers that produce merchandise for them. While Walmart does have auditing and approval mechanisms for subcontracted facilities, third parties usually perform the audits. Suppliers often pay for the inspection processes as well. This limits the amount of information that actually gets to the parent company. Critics have also accused Walmart of advocating against equipping factories with better fire protection due to the costs involved. Walmart claims they take fire hazards and worker safety seriously.

Walmart has also faced criticism on the home front, with safety violations being a common complaint. Workers at warehouses in the United States that do business with Walmart have complained about harsh working conditions and violations of labor laws. For example, in 2012, a group of delivery packing workers at a warehouse in Mira Loma, California, went on strike and walked for six days to Los Angeles to draw attention to allegedly miserable and unsafe working conditions and to deliver a petition to the Los Angeles Walmart office. The situation is complex because such warehouse workers are hired and employed by staffing agencies or third-party contractors, making it harder for Walmart to assess working conditions. Walmart has argued that these third-party contractors are responsible for working conditions. Yet, as the firm hiring the contractors, Walmart has the responsibility and generally the power to ensure their contractors and subcontractors obey proper labor laws.

The Bangladeshi fire and ongoing worker complaints have increased the pressure on Walmart to improve their oversight and auditing mechanisms. Previously, Walmart employed a three-strike policy for suppliers and subcontractors who violated their ethical standards. However, after the Bangladeshi fire, Walmart changed their policy to adopt a zero-tolerance approach in which Walmart exerts the right to terminate relationships with suppliers immediately after discovering a violation. Walmart also requires all suppliers to have an independent agency assess the electrical and building safety conditions of their factories. To address domestic complaints, Walmart applies the same monitoring system to U.S. suppliers. Walmart, furthermore, has begun sending independent auditors to make unannounced visits to U.S. third-party-operated warehouses to check whether they adhere to the firm's ethical standards. Walmart hopes these stricter measures improve compliance by their suppliers as well as reiterate the company's commitment to ethical sourcing practices. Yet these measures have failed to appease some critics who believe that Walmart cannot truly be held accountable until the results of their factory audits are made public.

The controversy of worker safety in Bangladesh intensified after yet another factory collapsed in 2013, killing 1,127 workers. The tragedy caused Walmart and other retailers to consider new safety plans. A group of European retailers, worker safety groups, and labor unions came together to develop and sign a five-year legally binding workplace safety agreement to improve worker safety in Bangladesh. The agreement required retailers to pay suppliers more so that factories could afford to make safety improvements, and it also pushed for the development of a standardized worker complaint and risk reporting process. Walmart declined to sign the agreement, however, and instead devised their own safety plan. The plan primarily involved hiring an independent auditor to inspect the more than 200 Bangladeshi factories that produced goods for Walmart and publishing the results publicly, including which factories failed the audit and were no longer allowed to produce for Walmart. The plan also required factories that did not fail but still had some unsafe conditions to improve safety standards. Critics argue that Walmart's independent plan was insufficient and much less ambitious than the workplace safety agreement they declined to join. A recent survey revealed more than 36 percent of Walmart employees believe Walmart should improve working conditions.

Another concern that has been raised is gun safety. In 2019, there were multiple shootings in Walmart stores that resulted in more than 24 deaths. CEO Doug McMillon addressed Walmart workers by expressing his condolences at the loss of life, highlighting heroic acts during the shootings, and briefly outlining steps that would be taken, such as providing counseling to employees who need it. While Walmart has engaged employees in computer-based active shooter trainings since 2015, employees have expressed fears about their safety. Walmart's current security efforts are intended to prevent shoplifting, not shootings. Some have even protested Walmart selling guns due to the belief that selling guns is adding to the gun violence in the country. Walmart agreed to limit sales of guns, including discontinuing select types of rifle ammunition. Despite this change, the company may continue to face pressure from concerned employees, as well as the larger public, for stricter policies.

Responding to Stakeholder Concerns

Walmart has suffered significantly from scandals overseas. Consumer interest, customer loyalty, and other factors important to a brand's value have diminished for Walmart's brand among college-educated adults. The brand has struggled in their battle to gain e-commerce business due to increased competition from online retailers like Amazon. Plus, Walmart has saturated many markets at this point. As discussed, being a large multinational corporation brings many global risks, including bribery and supplier issues. In response to the allegations of bribery, Walmart quietly replaced many top-level executives in both Mexico and the United States.

At a pep rally held in May 2012, former CEO Mike Duke emphasized integrity in operations and employee behavior at all levels and rewarded 11 employees for "leading with integrity." In highlighting the actions of these select employees, he reiterated the firm's ethics hotline and open-door policy. He assured employees and other stakeholders that the company was cooperating with the U.S. Department of Justice in order to get to the bottom of the bribery allegations. Mike Duke acknowledged that there were ethical issues in some Walmart stores and stated that he planned to slow expansion so the company could focus on improving these issues.

As a form of damage control, Walmart ran an advertising campaign to frame the company as an "American success story." After market research revealed Walmart's brand image had lost traction among college-educated adults, Walmart developed a multi-million-dollar advertising campaign called "The Real Walmart." The advertisements featured customers, truck drivers, and employees sharing their happy experiences with the company. Walmart particularly wanted to target opinion leaders who could then convince others of the company's value and positive brand image. The ads were first released during the Kentucky Derby and were also featured on Sunday news shows. This advertising campaign was similar to those released by other companies attempting to restore their image, such as Toyota during their recall crisis and BP after the *Deepwater Horizon* disaster.

Sustainability Leadership

Among Walmart's long-term sustainability goals are to be supplied entirely by renewable energy, create no waste, and sell products that sustain people and the environment. In the short term, Walmart aims to be powered by 50 percent renewable energy, reduce emissions by 18 percent, and achieve zero waste to landfill in the United States, U.K., Japan, and Canada all by 2025. In order to achieve these ambitious goals, Walmart has built relationships with influential people in supplier companies, government, NGOs, and academia. Together they have organized Walmart's environmental goals into 14 Sustainable Value Networks (SVN), from "Global Greenhouse Gas Strategy" to "Packaging" to "Forest & Paper," which allow the company to efficiently integrate, implement, and evaluate their sustainability efforts. This approach has served them well. By 2012, Walmart had 115 onsite rooftop solar installations in seven countries providing 71 million annual kilowatt hours of electricity. They had completed 26 fuel cell installations in the United States, providing 65 million kilowatt hours of annual electricity, and were also testing micro-wind and solar water heating projects in various locations. Walmart's company value of everyday low costs translates to their renewable energy endeavors through the signing of long-term contracts with renewable energy providers. These contracts finance utility-scale projects in renewable sources, allowing these options to be offered at lower cost not only to Walmart but also to other clients of these providers.

By late 2014, Walmart had well over 335 renewable energy projects in operation or under development, including micro-wind installations in parking lots and biodiesel generator sets. Their solar installations provided 105 megawatts of solar capacity, the most of any company in the world by far and greater than the total solar capacity of at least 35 U.S. states. Walmart efficiently manages heating and cooling energy consumption by centrally controlling the temperature of Walmart stores worldwide from the Bentonville headquarters. The company is also opening new stores and retrofitting existing ones with high-efficiency LED and low-mercury fluorescent lighting and is in the process of replacing open freezers with secondary loop refrigeration systems. Walmart is furthermore attempting to reduce fossil fuel use and sell more "green" products. The company has doubled their fuel efficiency for their 6,000 trucks that cross the United States. Since 2007, Walmart has been able to deliver more products while reducing mileage by 300 million.

One of the most unique and well-regarded of Walmart's sustainability efforts is their Sustainability Index, which it developed with the help of a nonprofit coalition known as The Sustainability Consortium. The Sustainability Index is essentially an attempt to rate and categorize all of Walmart's products and suppliers on a variety of sustainability-related issues. Between 2009 and 2012, Walmart worked with researchers to develop the basic categories and determine what information would be required for the Index to work. Then, starting in 2012, Walmart began sending out requests for this information to their suppliers. For example, suppliers of products that contain wheat, such as cakes, cookies, and bread, were asked to provide detailed information about the sourcing of that wheat, from fertilizer use tracking to soil fertility monitoring to biodiversity management. Computer and jewelry suppliers were asked about the mining practices used to extract their materials; toy makers about the chemicals used in their manufacturing processes; and so on. Walmart uses this information to rank their suppliers from best to worst on the Sustainability Index, and then gives that information to those in charge of making Walmart purchasing decisions to use in determining which suppliers to buy from. Presumably, the end result is that more sustainable products end up on Walmart shelves, and suppliers are incentivized to improve their practices to better compete with others on the Index. The initiative is exciting because Walmart's industry power is so great that a successful implementation could truly drive change throughout entire supplier industries and chains. By 2018, Walmart met their goal of purchasing at least 70 percent of goods from suppliers participating in their Sustainability Index. The index covers more than 125 categories of products and more than 300 buyers.

Although Walmart's environmental overhaul is a step in the right direction, some are skeptical as to whether it can accomplish their goals. Many claim that Walmart's apparent sustainability gains are overstated, lacking in critical information, or downright misleading;

in other words, "greenwashing" advertising rather than actual change. Some suppliers are worried about the Sustainability Index, including the amount of increased time and expense it will take to provide the required information and the business implications of products that receive higher "sustainability" rankings being given preferential treatment. Also, the concept of "being green" is subjective, since not everyone agrees on how it is defined or whether one environmentally friendly practice is necessarily more beneficial than another. Despite these obstacles, Walmart seems to have achieved some substantial successes in this area through their dedication to their goals and the strength of their partnerships.

Walmart Today

Walmart remains the preferred shopping destination for many consumers. Although Walmart prospered during the recession while other retailers suffered, the company has faced stagnating sales in many established markets. Walmart acknowledged that they strayed from Sam Walton's original vision of "everyday low prices" in order to court higher-income customers. Several initiatives, such as Walmart's adoption of organic food and trendy clothes, did not achieve much success with discount shoppers. Walmart also underwent a renovation effort that cut certain products, such as fishing tackle, from their stores. These actions alienated Walmart's original customer base. Households earning less than $70,000 annually defected to discounters like Dollar Tree and Family Dollar. Analysts believe Walmart's mistake was trying to be everything to everyone, along with copying their more "chic" rivals like Target. Because of these blunders, in addition to external pressures such as market saturation and strong competition from other retail giants, Walmart faced a sales slump. As a result, Walmart is returning to Sam Walton's original vision and their previous "everyday low prices" mantra. Walmart is also investing significantly in e-commerce as an untapped area of growth in the hopes of competing more directly with Amazon and other e-commerce retailers that have drawn away some of their customer base. In fact, Walmart outpaced Amazon's growth in 2019, with shares increasing by 21 percent. Though Amazon has attracted many investors as a fast-growing stock, Walmart surprised many with their growth after years of declining sales.

Walmart is known for their ability to adapt quickly to different environments, but even this large-scale retailer has experienced trouble. For instance, they were forced to withdraw completely from Germany and South Korea after failing to interest the local populations. In addition, Walmart sold 80 percent of their Brazilian operations in an effort to pull away focus from poorly performing markets. Walmart has also struggled in India, one of the world's largest markets, after failing to find a way to navigate the country's complex regulatory environment for foreign retailers in order to sell directly to the public.

Walmart acquired a majority stake in a massive Indian e-commerce company, Flipkart, to better compete in the country. Flipkart is introducing a streaming service to compete with Amazon Prime and Netflix. The more Walmart expands internationally, the more the company must decide what concessions they are willing to make to enter certain markets.

Despite the difficulties of operating globally, Walmart has a significant presence in many countries such as the U.K., Canada, and Mexico. The company's focus on expanding their operations in India and further developing their presence in China could also pay off for the retailer. Though the company will likely experience several bumps in the road, several of their international markets appear to offer strong growth potential.

The Future of Walmart

Walmart can be viewed through two very different lenses. Some think the company represents all that is wrong with America, while others love the retailer. In response to criticism, and in an attempt to initiate goodwill with consumers, the company has continued to improve stakeholder relationships and made efforts to demonstrate that they are an ethically responsible company. Although they have faced controversy regarding competition, suppliers, employees, and global corruption, among other things, they have also demonstrated concern for sustainability initiatives and social responsibility. Walmart's goals of decreasing waste and carbon emissions and their Sustainability Index extend to all facets of their operations, including suppliers. These efforts demonstrate Walmart's desire (whether through genuine concern for the environment or for their own bottom-line profits) to become a more sustainable company.

Similarly, Walmart's creation of a sophisticated global ethics and compliance program shows that they have come a long way since their beginning, when formal ethics programs were deemed unnecessary. However, without strong monitoring systems and a commitment from top management to enforce the company's ethics policies, such efforts will prove fruitless. Overseas bribery scandals and employee discontent have tarnished Walmart's reputation. As a result, the company is working to improve internal control mechanisms and supplier auditing. Both critics and supporters of Walmart alike are waiting to see whether Walmart's efforts will position the company as a large retailer truly dedicated to social responsibility.

Questions for Discussion

1. Do you think Walmart is doing enough to become more sustainable?
2. What are the ethical issues Walmart has faced?
3. How is Walmart attempting to answer concerns regarding misconduct?

Sources

"Small Farmers Aren't Cashing in with Wal-Mart," February 4, 2013, http://www.npr.org/sections/thesalt/2013/02/04/171051906/can-small-farms-benefit-from-wal-mart-s-push-into-local-foods (accessed May 18, 2015).

"Wal-Mart Concedes China Can Make Unions," *China Daily*, November 23, 2004, http://www.chinadaily.com.cn/english/doc/2004-11/23/content_394129.htm (accessed May 15, 2015).

"Wal-Mart's Raise Could Be a Turning Point for the Whole Economy," *The Huffington Post*, February 19, 2015, http://www.huffingtonpost.com/2015/02/19/raises-for-everyone-thanks-walmart_n_6714936.html (accessed May 18, 2015).

"Walmart to Open 115 Stores in China," *BBC News*, April 29, 2015, http://www.bbc.com/news/business-32509077 (accessed May 18, 2015).

"Walmart's Mexican Morass," *The Economist*, April 28, 2012, 71.

Abram Brown, "Mexican Bribery Scandal Could Cost Wal-Mart $4.5 Billion Shares Down 4.7%," *Forbes*, http://www.forbes.com/sites/abrambrown/2012/04/23/spooked-investors-sink-wal-mart-nearly-5-after-bribery-revelations-at-least-4-5b-penalty-likely/ (accessed May 18, 2015).

Abram Brown, "Wal-Mart Bribery Probe Expands Past Mexico to Brazil, China, And India," *Forbes*, November 15, 2012, http://www.forbes.com/sites/abrambrown/2012/11/15/probe-into-wal-mart-bribery-past-mexico-to-brazil-china-and-india/ (accessed May 15, 2015).

Alan Pyke, "Here's Walmart's Internal Guide to Fighting Unions and Monitoring Workers," *Think Progress*, January 16, 2014, http://thinkprogress.org/economy/2014/01/16/3171251/walmart-leaked-powerpoint-unions/ (accessed May 18, 2015).

Alice Hines, "Walmart's New Health Policy Shifts Burden to Medicaid, Obamacare," *The Huffington Post*, December 1, 2012, http://www.huffingtonpost.com/2012/12/01/walmart-health-care-policy-medicaid-obamacare_n_2220152.html (accessed May 15, 2015).

Alisha Staggs, "An Up-Close Assessment of Walmart's Sustainability Index," *GreenBiz*, May 17, 2013, http://www.greenbiz.com/blog/2013/05/17/up-close-assessment-walmarts-sustainability-index (accessed May 18, 2015).

American Customer Satisfaction Index, "Benchmarks by Industry: Department and Discount Stores," https://www.theacsi.org/index.php?option=com_content&view=article&id=149&catid=14&Itemid=212&i=Department+and+Discount+Stores (accessed August 21, 2019).

Andrew Clark, "Wal-Mart, the U.S. retailer, Taking over the World by Stealth," guardian.co.uk, January 12, 2010, http://www.guardian.co.uk/business/2010/jan/12/walmart-companies-to-shape-the-decade (accessed May 15, 2015).

Andy Kroll, "Walmart Workers Get Organized—Just Don't Say the U-Word," *Mother Jones*, March/April 2013, http://www.motherjones.com/politics/2013/02/our-walmart-black-friday-union (accessed May 18, 2015).

Ann Zimmerman, "Federal Officials Asked to Probe Wal-Mart Firing," *The Wall Street Journal*, April 28, 2005, http://www.wsj.com/articles/SB111462458171818501 (accessed May 15, 2015).

Associated Press, "Former Wal-Mart Executive is Resentenced, Avoids Prison," *Los Angeles Times*, February 2, 2008, http://articles.latimes.com/2008/feb/02/business/fi-coughlin2 (accessed May 15, 2015).

Ben W. Heineman, Jr., "Who's Responsible for the Walmart Mexico Scandal?" *Harvard Business Review*, May 15, 2015, https://hbr.org/2014/05/whos-responsible-for-the-walmart-mexico-scandal/ (accessed May 18, 2015).

Bryce Covert, "Walmart Penalized for Closing Store Just after It Unionized," *Think Progress*, June 30, 2014, http://thinkprogress.org/economy/2014/06/30/3454511/walmart-canada-union/ (accessed May 18, 2015).

Charles Fishman, "5 Surprises at the New Big City Walmart in Washington, D.C." *Fast Company*, http://www.fastcompany.com/3023007/5-surprises-at-the-new-big-city-walmart-in-washington-dc (accessed May 18, 2015).

Charles Fishman, "The Wal-Mart You Don't Know: Why Low Prices Have a High Cost," *Fast Company*, December 2003, 68–80.

Daina Beth Solomon, "Walmart Mexico and Union Agree on Wage Hikes, Avert Strike," *Reuters*, March 14, 2019, https://www.reuters.com/article/us-mexico-walmex/walmart-mexico-and-union-agree-on-wage-hikes-avert-strike-idUSKCN1QV2FU (accessed August 21, 2019).

Daniel McGinn, "Wal-Mart Hits the Wall," *Newsweek*, November 14, 2005, 44–46.

Dave Jamieson, "Feds Charge Walmart with Breaking Labor Law in Black Friday Strikes," *The Huffington Post*, January 25, 2014, http://www.huffingtonpost.com/2014/01/15/walmart-complaint_n_4604069.html (accessed May 18, 2015).

David Barstow, "Vast Mexico Bribery Case Hushed up by Wal-Mart after Top-Level Struggle," *The New York Times*, April 21, 2012, http://www.nytimes.com/2012/04/22/business/at-wal-mart-in-mexico-a-bribe-inquiry-silenced.html?pagewanted=all (accessed May 15, 2015).

Elizabeth A. Harris, "After Bribery Scandal, High-Level Departures at Walmart," *New York Times*, June 4, 2014, http://www.nytimes.com/2014/06/05/business/after-walmart-bribery-scandals-a-pattern-of-quiet-departures.html?_r=2 (accessed May 18, 2015).

Elliot Maras, "An Insider's View of Walmart's Digital Transformation," *Retail Customer Experience*, February 21, 2019, https://www.retailcustomerexperience.com/articles/an-insiders-view-of-walmarts-digital-transformation/ (accessed August 21, 2019).

Emily Jane Fox, "Wal-Mart Toughens Regulations After Bangladesh Fire," *CNNMoney*, January 22, 2013, http://money.cnn.com/2013/01/22/news/companies/walmart-supplier-regulations/index.html (accessed May 15, 2015).

Erica L. Plambeck and Lyn Denend, "Case Study: The Greening of Wal-Mart," *Stanford Social Innovation*, Spring 2008, pp. 52–59.

Esther Wang, "As Wal-Mart Swallows China's Economy, Workers Fight Back," *The American Prospect*, April 23, 2013, http://prospect.org/article/wal-mart-swallows-chinas-economy-workers-fight-back (accessed May 18, 2015).

Fortune, "Most Admired 2015," http://fortune.com/worlds-most-admired-companies/wal-mart-stores-38/ (accessed May 18, 2015).

Greg Stohr, "Wal-Mart vs. a Million Angry Women," *Bloomberg Businessweek*, November 22–28, 2010, 39–40.

Gunjan Banerji, "Walmart Set to Outpace Amazon for 2019," *The Wall Street Journal*, August 15, 2019, https://www.wsj.com/articles/walmart-set-to-surge-past-amazon-11565888272 (accessed August 22, 2019).

Hadley Malcolm, "Scraping by at Walmart," *USA Today*, June 7, 2012, http://usatoday30.usatoday.com/MONEY/usaedition/2012-06-08-Walmart-workers-strugglenew--_CV_U.htm (accessed May 15, 2015).

Jack and Suzy Welch, "Whistleblowers: Why You Should Heed Their Warnings," *Fortune*, June 11, 2012, 86.

James Arkin, "D.C. Council Panel Hears Testimony on 'Living Wage' Bill Targeting Large Retailers," *The Washington Post*, March 20, 2013, https://www.washingtonpost.com/local/dc-politics/dc-council-panel-hears-testimony-on-living-wage-bill-targeting-large-retailers/2013/03/20/ccd8bb44-917b-11e2-bdea-e32ad90da239_story.html.

James Bandler and Ann Zimmerman, "A Wal-Mart Legend's Trail of Deceit," *The Wall Street Journal*, April 8, 2005, A10.

James Bandler, "Former No. 2 at Wal-Mart Set to Plead Guilty," *The Wall Street Journal*, January 7, 2006, A1.

Janet Novack, "Walmart Wins Again as Washington D.C. Mayor Vetoes $12.50 Minimum Wage," *Forbes*, September 12, 2013, http://www.forbes.com/sites/janetnovack/2013/09/12/walmart-wins-again-as-washington-d-c-mayor-vetoes-12-50-minimum-wage/ (accessed May 18, 2015).

Jessica Mason Pieklo, "Why It's So Hard to Sue Wal-Mart for Gender Discrimination," *RH Reality Check*, August 7, 2013, http://rhrealitycheck.org/article/2013/08/07/will-corporations-like-wal-mart-ever-be-liable-for-discriminatory-employment-practices/ (accessed May 18, 2015).

Jessica Wohl and James B. Kelleher, "Insight Wal-Mart 'Made to America' Drive Follows Suppliers' Lead," *Reuters*, September 25, 2013, http://www.reuters.com/article/2013/09/25/us-walmart-manufacturing-insight-idUSBRE98O04Q20130925 (accessed May 18, 2015).

Jessica Wohl, "'No' Votes Jump Against Wal-Mart CEO, Directors," *Reuters*, June 4, 2012, http://www.reuters.com/article/2012/06/04/us-walmart-vote-idUSBRE8530IR20120604 (accessed May 15, 2015).

Jessica Wohl, "Walmart Sues Grocery Workers Union, Others Who Have Protested at Florida Stores," *The Huffington Post*, March 25, 2013, http://www.huffingtonpost.com/2013/03/25/walmart-sues-protesters-florida-stores_n_2950992.html (accessed May 15, 2015).

John Jannarone, "Wal-Mart's Tough Work Experience," *The Wall Street Journal*, February 23, 2011, C 14.

Jordan Weissman, "Walmart Is Killing the Rest of Corporate America in Solar Power Adoption," *Slate*, October 21, 2014, http://www.slate.com/blogs/moneybox/2014/10/21/walmart_green_energy_it_can_produce_more_solar_power_than_35_states.html (accessed May 18, 2015).

Julia Conley, "Workers and Shooting Survivors Slam Walmart Plan to Stop Gun Violence by... Wait for It... Displaying Video Games Less Prominently," *Common Dreams*, August 9, 2019, https://www.commondreams.org/news/2019/08/09/workers-and-shooting-survivors-slam-walmart-plan-stop-gun-violence-bywait (accessed August 21, 2019).

Julia Hanna, "Unpacking Walmart's Workforce of the Future," *Forbes*, August 2, 2019, https://www.forbes.com/sites/hbsworkingknowledge/2019/08/02/unpacking-walmarts-workforce-of-the-future/#1fd49ca1667a (accessed August 21, 2019).

Julia Jacobo, "Walmart to Limit Sales of Guns, Ammunition in Wake of 'Horrific' Shootings," *ABC News*, September 3, 2019, https://abcnews.go.com/US/walmart-limit-sales-guns-ammunition-wake-horrific-shootings/story?id=65361629 (accessed October 16, 2019).

Karen Olsson, "Up against Wal-Mart," *Mother Jones*, March/April 2003, http://www.motherjones.com/politics/2003/03/against-wal-mart (accessed May 15, 2015).

Kate Rockwood, "Will Wal-Mart's 'Sustainability Index' Actually Work?" *Fast Company*, February 1, 2010, http://www.fastcompany.com/magazine/142/attention-walmart-shoppers-clean-up-in-aisle-nine.html (accessed May 15, 2015).

Kathleen Miles, "Walmart Warehouse Workers Rally in Downtown LA Ends 6-Day Pilgrimage (PHOTOS)," *Huffington Post*, September 18, 2012, http://www.huffingtonpost.com/2012/09/18/walmart-warehouse-workers-rally-la-pilgrimage_n_1893843.html (accessed May 18, 2015).

Kyle Smith, "You Won't Believe the Stupidity of The Latest Attack on Walmart," *Forbes*, March 21, 2013, http://www.forbes.com/sites/kylesmith/2013/03/21/you-wont-believe-the-stupidity-of-the-latest-attack-on-walmart/ (accessed May 15, 2015).

Lauren Coleman-Lochner, "Independent Look at Wal-Mart Shows Both Good and Bad: With Savings and Jobs Come Falling Wages and Rising Medicaid Costs," *The San Antonio Express-News*, November 5, 2005, 4D.

Lauren Etter, "Gauging the Wal-Mart Effect," *The Wall Street Journal*, December 3–4, 2005, A9.

Lydia DePillis "Wal-Mart's Threatening to Pull out of D.C. If It Has to Pay a Higher Minimum Wage. So What?" *Washington Post*, July 10, 2013, http://www.washingtonpost.com/blogs/wonkblog/wp/2013/07/10/wal-marts-threatening-to-pull-out-of-d-c-if-it-has-to-pay-a-higher-minimum-wage-so-what/ (accessed May 18, 2015).

Marc Gunther, "The Gunther Report: Game On: Why Walmart Is Ranking Suppliers on Sustainability," *GreenBiz*, April 15, 2013, http://www.greenbiz.com/blog/2013/04/15/game-why-walmart-ranking-suppliers-sustainability (accessed May 18, 2015).

Marcus Kabel, "Wal-Mart at War: Retailer Faces Bruised Image, Makes Fixes," *Marketing News*, January 15, 2006, 25.

Matt Krantz, "Walmart's wages get CEOs' attention," *USA Today*, March 2, 20115, 2B.

Mei Fong and Ann Zimmerman, "China's Union Push Leaves Wal-Mart with Hard Choice," *The Wall Street Journal*, May 13–14, 2006, A1, A6.

Michael Barbaro, "Image Effort by Wal-Mart Takes a Turn," *The New York Times*, May 12, 2006, C1, C4.

Michael Corkery, "A 'Sorceress' in Brazil, a 'Wink' in India: Walmart Pleads Guilty After a Decade of Bribes," *The New York Times*, June 20, 2019, https://www.nytimes.com/2019/06/20/business/walmart-bribery-settlement.html (accessed August 22, 2019).

Michael Corkery, "Walmart Finally Makes It to the Big Apple," *The New York Times*, September 16, 2018, https://www.nytimes.com/2018/09/16/business/walmart-jet-nyc.html (accessed August 21, 2019).

Michael Scher, "Walmart is Now the World's Living Laboratory for Compliance," *The FCPA Blog*, http://www.fcpablog.com/blog/2014/5/21/walmart-is-now-the-worlds-living-laboratory-for-compliance.html# (accessed May 18, 2015).

Miguel Bustillo, "Wal-Mart Merchandise Goes Back to Basics," *The Wall Street Journal*, April 11, 2011, B3.

Miguel Bustillo, "Wal-Mart Pledges to Promote Healthier Foods," *The Wall Street Journal*, January 20, 2011, http://online.wsj.com/article/SB10001424052748704881304576093872178374258.html (accessed May 15, 2015).

Miguel Bustillo, "Wal-Mart Tries to Recapture Mr. Sam's Winning Formula," *The Wall Street Journal*, February 22, 2011, A1, A11.

Miguel Bustillo, "With Sales Flabby, Wal-Mart Turns to Its Core," *The Wall Street Journal*, March 21, 2011, B1, B8.

Nandita Bose and Tatiana Bautzer, "Walmart Sells Majority of Brazil Unit, takes $4.5 Billion Charge," *Reuters*, June 4, 2018, https://www.reuters.com/article/us-walmart-brazil/walmart-sells-majority-of-brazil-unit-takes-4-5-billion-charge-idUSKCN1J01L0 (accessed August 22, 2019).

Newser, "Wal-Mart Will Pay $640M to Settle Wage Lawsuits," December 23, 2008, http://www.newser.com/story/46142/wal-mart-will-pay-640m-to-settle-wage-lawsuits.html?utm_source=ssp&utm_medium=cpc&utm_campaign=story (accessed May 15, 2015).

Nina Martin, "The Impact and Echoes of the Wal-Mart Discrimination Case," *ProPublica*, http://www.propublica.org/article/the-impact-and-echoes-of-the-wal-mart-discrimination-case (accessed May 18, 2015).

Occupy Solidarity Network, "Walmart Organizes Against Workers," January 14, 2014, http://occupywallst.org/article/point-of-public-information/ (accessed May 18, 2015).

PR Newswire, "Interbrand Releases the 2014 Best Retail Brands Report," April 8, 2014, http://www.prnewswire.com/news-releases/interbrand-releases-the-2014-best-retail-brands-report-254348521.html (accessed May 18, 2015).

Rani Molla, "Amazon's White-Collar Workforce Says Their Warehouses Need Better Conditions," *Vox*, January 28, 2019, https://www.vox.com/2019/1/28/18200607/amazon-engineers-warehouse-workers-better-conditions-tesla-blind (accessed August 21, 2019).

Renee Dudley, "Customers Flee Wal-Mart Empty Shelves for Target, Costco," *Bloomberg*, March 26, 2013, http://www.bloomberg.com/news/2013-03-26/customers-flee-wal-mart-empty-shelves-for-target-costco.html (accessed May 15, 2015).

Renee Dudley, "Wal-Mart Releases Names of Bangladesh Factories Inspected," *Bloomberg*, November 18, 2013, http://www.bloomberg.com/news/articles/2013-11-18/wal-mart-releases-names-of-bangladesh-factories-inspected (accessed May 18, 2015).

Renee Dudley, "Wal-Mart Won't Sign Bangladesh Building Safety Agreement," *The Washington Post*, May 14, 2013, http://www.washingtonpost.com/business/economy/wal-mart-to-conduct-safety-inspections-at-all-279-bangladesh-supplier-factories/2013/05/14/c90598e2-bce7-11e2-97d4-a479289a31f9_story.html (accessed May 18, 2015).

Renee Dudley, Christiana Sciaudone, and Jessica Brice, "Why Wal-Mart Hasn't Conquered Brazil," May 8, 2014, http://www.bloomberg.com/bw/articles/2014-05-08/why-wal-mart-hasnt-conquered-brazil (accessed May 18, 2015).

Reuters, "Walmart Threatened Workers for Trying to Organize, Judge Rules," *The Huffington Post*, December 10, 2014, http://www.huffingtonpost.com/2014/12/11/walmart-threatened-workers_n_6305972.html (accessed May 18, 2015).

Rick Ungar, "Walmart Pays Workers Poorly and Sinks while Costco Pays Workers Well and Sails—Proof that You Get What You Pay For," *Forbes*, April 17, 2013, http://www.forbes.com/sites/rickungar/2013/04/17/walmart-pays-workers-poorly-and-sinks-while-costco-pays-workers-well-and-sails-proof-that-you-get-what-you-pay-for/ (accessed May 15, 2015).

Rick Wartzman, "Wal-Mart, Starbucks, Aetna's Pay Hikes. Why Now?" *Fortune*, March 4, 2015, http://fortune.com/2015/03/04/walmart-pay-hikes-why-now/ (accessed May 18, 2015).

Rishi Iyengar, "Walmart Is Offering Free Streaming Video in India to Fend off Amazon," *CNN*, August 6, 2019, https://www.cnn.com/2019/08/06/tech/flipkart-walmart-video-streaming-india/index.html (accessed August 21, 2019).

Ron Miller, "Walmart is Betting on the Blockchain to Improve Food Safety," *TechCrunch*, September 24, 2018, https://techcrunch.com/2018/09/24/walmart-is-betting-on-the-blockchain-to-improve-food-safety/ (accessed August 21, 2019).

Sarah Nassauer and Chip Cutter, "Walmart Worker's New Security Threat Is Active Shooters, Not Shoplifters," *The Wall Street Journal*, August 5, 2019, https://www.wsj.com/articles/walmart-workers-new-security-threat-is-active-shooters-not-shoplifters-11564941183 (accessed August 22, 2019).

Shelly Banjo and Ann Zimmerman, "Protestors Wage Campaign against Wal-Mart," *The Wall Street Journal*, November 23, 2012, http://online.wsj.com/article/SB10001424127887327313104578136992890118444.html (accessed May 15, 2015).

Shelly Banjo, "Wal-Mart Ads Tout 'American Success Story'," *The Wall Street Journal*, May 3, 2013, http://online.wsj.com/article/SB10001424127887324582004578460973584445016.html (accessed May 15, 2015).

Shelly Banjo, "Wal-Mart Cheer: I-n-t-e-g-r-i-t-y," *The Wall Street Journal*, May 31, 2012, B3.

Shelly Banjo, "Wal-Mart to Monitor Warehouses," *The Wall Street Journal*, December 28, 2012, B4.

Shelly Banjo, "Wal-Mart Toughens Supplier Policies," *The Wall Street Journal*, February 22, 2013, B1, B7.

Shelly Banjo, "Wal-Mart Will Tie Executive Pay to Compliance Overhaul," *The Wall Street Journal*, April 23, 2013, B8.

Shelly Banjo, Ann Zimmerman, and Suzanne Kapner, "Wal-Mart Crafts Own Bangladesh Safety Plan," *The Wall Street Journal*, May 15, 2013, B1–B2.

Stephanie Clifford, "More Dissent Is Expected Over a Wal-Mart Scandal," *The New York Times*, June 6, 2013, http://www.nytimes.com/2013/06/07/business/more-dissent-is-in-store-over-wal-mart-scandal.html?pagewanted=all&_r=1& (accessed May 15, 2015).

Stephanie Clifford, "Wal-Mart to Buy More Local Produce," *The New York Times*, October 14, 2010, http://www.nytimes.com/2010/10/15/business/15walmart.html (accessed May 15, 2015).

Steve Quinn, "Wal-Mart Green with Energy," *Coloradoan*, July 24, 2005, E1–E2.

Steven Greenhouse and Stephanie Clifford, "Wal-Mart Steps up Efforts to Suppress Strike," *The New York Times*, November 20, 2012, 15.

Steven Greenhouse, "Documents Indicate Wal-Mart Blocked Safety Push," *The New York Times*, December 5, 2012, http://www.nytimes.com/2012/12/06/world/asia/3-walmart-suppliers-made-goods-in-bangladeshi-factory-where-112-died-in-fire.html (accessed May 15, 2015).

Stuart Weinberg and Phred Dvorak, "Wal-Mart's New Hot Spot: Canada," *The Wall Street Journal*, January 27, 2010, B3.

Susan Berfield, "Walmart vs. Union-Backed OUR Walmart," *Bloomberg Businessweek*, December 13, 2012, http://www.bloomberg.com/bw/articles/2012-12-13/walmart-vs-dot-union-backed-our-walmart#p1 (accessed May 18, 2015).

Susan Berfield, "Walmart vs. Walmart," *Bloomberg Businessweek*, December 13, 2012, pp. 53–60.

Syed Zain Al-Mahmood, Tripti Lahiri, and Dana Mattioli, "Fire Warnings Went Unheard," *The Wall Street Journal*, December 11, 2012, B1, B9.

Tom Van Riper, "Wal-Mart Stands Up to Wave of Lawsuits," *Forbes*, November 10, 2005, http://www.forbes.com/2005/11/09/wal-mart-lawsuits-cx_tvr_1109walmart.html (accessed May 18, 2015).

Vikas Bajaj, "India Unit of Wal-Mart Suspends Employees," *The New York Times*, November 23, 2012, http://www.nytimes.com/2012/11/24/business/global/wal-marts-india-venture-suspends-executives-as-part-of-bribery-inquiry.html?_r=0 (accessed May 15, 2015).

Wal-Mart, "Global Ethics Office," https://www.walmartethics.com/ (accessed May 15, 2015).

Walmart Foundation, https://walmart.org (accessed August 21, 2019).

Walmart, "Company Facts," https://corporate.walmart.com/newsroom/company-facts (accessed August 21, 2019).

Walmart, "Leadership," https://corporate.walmart.com/our-story/leadership (accessed August 22, 2019).

Walmart, "Location Facts," https://corporate.walmart.com/our-story/our-locations (accessed August 21, 2019).

Walmart, "Shared Value Priorities and Aspirations for 2025," 2017, https://corporate.walmart.com/2017grr/priorities-and-aspirations-2025 (accessed August 22, 2019).

Walmart, "Walmart's Sustainability Index Program," https://www.walmartsustainabilityhub.com/sustainability-index (accessed August 22, 2019).

Walmart, "Community Giving," http://foundation.walmart.com/ (accessed May 15, 2015).

Walmart, "Environmental Sustainability," http://walmartstores.com/Sustainability/7785.aspx (accessed May 15, 2015).

Walmart, "Frequently Asked Questions," http://corporate.walmart.com/frequently-asked-questions (accessed May 15, 2015).

Walmart, "Global Compliance Program Report on Fiscal Year 2014," http://corporate.walmart.com/global-responsibility/global-compliance-program-report-on-fiscal-year-2014 (accessed May 18, 2015).

Walmart, "Renewable Energy," http://corporate.walmart.com/global-responsibility/environment-sustainability/waste (accessed May 18, 2015).

Walmart, "Truck Fleet," http://corporate.walmart.com/global-responsibility/environment-sustainability/truck-fleet (accessed May 18, 2015).

Walter Loeb, "How Walmart Plans to Bring Manufacturing Back to the United States," *Forbes*, November 12, 2013, http://www.forbes.com/sites/walterloeb/2013/11/12/walmart-taking-steps-to-bring-manufacturing-back-to-the-united-states/ (accessed May 18, 2015).

CASE 4

Google Searches for Solutions to Privacy Issues

Introduction

Google's ease of use and superior search results have propelled the search engine to its number one status, ousting former competitors such as AltaVista and WebCrawler. Even later offerings by other large tech companies using comparable algorithms, such as Bing by Microsoft, have failed to make significant inroads with internet users, with Google retaining an impressive 90 percent of the global market share of mobile, web, and in-app searches. Each day, more than 3.5 billion searches are processed by Google. As the search engine gained popularity, it began expanding into several different ventures, including web analytics, advertising, and digital book publishing. It has spent billions to acquire hundreds of companies in a variety of industries, from robotics to smart home devices to intangibles such as voice recognition technologies.

As may happen with any large company, Google has experienced their share of ethical issues. Their mantra "Don't Be Evil" was called into question after they worked with the Chinese government on a secret project called Dragonfly to censor aspects of some of their sites to enter the market. Though Dragonfly was ultimately terminated, Google's vice president of public policy would not commit to the U.S. Senate to not engage in censorship in China in the future. Google has also been investigated and sued by multiple governments based on concerns that their widespread reach and market power violate antitrust laws.

The hot ethical topic for many internet users, however, is the company's approach to internet privacy and collection of user information. To improve their services—including customized search results, targeted ads, and more precise integration of their various offerings—Google tracks and leverages user information without explicit permission (although Google's privacy statement informs users about the recordkeeping, and Google does allow users to opt out of some forms of tracking). Such tracking is common practice for internet companies, but Google's deep access to so many different types of user information has led people to question whether Google violates user privacy. Considering the increasing amount of cyberattacks and the U.S. government's determination to crack down on these illegal attacks, consumers also worry their private information, tracked and stored by Google's algorithms, might be compromised.

This case analyzes Google's efforts to be a good corporate citizen and the privacy issues the company has faced. The analysis starts by providing background on Google, their technology, and their initiatives. Google's efforts to be a socially responsible company is discussed. We then discuss the criticisms levied against Google, including their initial attempts to break into the censored Chinese market, their tracking of users, and more recent changes to their privacy policies. We examine how Google has sometimes clashed with government authorities. Finally, we review some of the legal methods that have been proposed to regulate internet data collection practices and Google's response to the proposals.

Company Culture

Google adopted a decentralized approach to empower their employees. Their corporate headquarters in Mountain View, California, is known as the "Googleplex" and consists of a campus containing such amenities as on-site gymnasiums, swimming pools, a bowling alley, an outdoor volleyball court, and even high-tech "nap pods" for optimized downtime. When Sergey Brin and Larry Page founded the company, they recognized employees had to put in long hours to make the company not only successful but flexible enough to adapt to the changing environment. Thus, Google employees are provided with fringe benefits to make the campus seem like their second home. They built a sense of community with break-out zones and micro-kitchens around the campus in addition to their peer-to-peer coaching program, Googler to Googler. The company strives to make their corporate culture fun and innovative.

At the same time, Google works to ensure they have top talent. While they reinvent the office experience, they also take different tactics in recruiting to ensure they hires the most creative, talented individuals. For instance, Google recruiters take a bottom-up approach when reading résumés. Recognizing that top items such as education and work experience do not always guarantee the applicant is innovative, some Google recruiters start at the bottom of the résumé where applicants put more creative information. Google's innovative approach to company culture is one of the reasons why they have become successful in so many different market niches.

This material was developed by Kelsey Reddick, Jennifer Sawayda, Michelle Urban, and Isaac Emmanuel under the direction of O.C. Ferrell and Linda Ferrell, © 2019. This case is intended for classroom discussion rather than to illustrate effective or ineffective handling of administrative, ethical, or legal decisions by management. All sources for this case were obtained through publicly available material.

Products

Although Google started out as a search engine, they have since branched out into a variety of fields, including consumer electronics and productivity tools. While it would be too long to list all of Google's products, some of the more popular offerings are described below.

Search Engine

According to Larry Page, a good search engine "understands exactly what you mean and gives you back exactly what you want." This philosophy was the founding principle behind the creation of Google and is a fundamental reason why the Google search engine surpassed competitors.

Google could not have gained such prominence without an in-depth search index of the web's content. The company creates this index using programs called "Googlebots"—automated web crawlers that visit webpages, add their content to the index, and then follow the links on those pages to other parts of the internet. This process is ongoing, with every indexed page periodically revisited to ensure the index contains the most updated material. Google's index is one of the most extensive in the world, with well over 100 million gigabytes worth of information.

A good search engine's index must not only be comprehensive but also easily accessible. To achieve easy access, Google uses algorithms to organize search results according to their perceived relevancy. Google constantly searches for new pages in a process called *crawling*. When a new page is crawled, Google analyzes its contents and catalogs it, a process called *indexing*. When a user types a search term into Google's search box, Google's index matches the term with what is deemed the most relevant materials and creates a list of these materials for the user, a process called *serving*. The order in which the results are served to users is called *ranking*. Factors considered in ranking include user's location, language, device, site load speed, and more. Each search result is followed by a few sentences describing the webpage (called a "snippet"). To maintain a competitive edge, Google responds quickly to their users' queries, with a typical response time of approximately one-fourth of a second.

Advertising

Google's main source of revenue is advertising. The company earns approximately $116 billion in advertising revenue. Google's signature advertising platform is Google AdWords, first introduced in 2000. Google AdWords differs from traditional advertising in that advertisers do not pay Google anything upfront, but only pay when customers take action—either by viewing the ad (pay-per-impression), clicking on the ad (pay-per-click), or performing a certain predefined action such as making an online purchase (pay-per-conversion). This model is attractive to advertisers because they only pay when their ad is effective, as determined by the metric of their choice. The twist, however, is that Google does not set ad prices, but rather puts their limited advertising space up for auction; companies submit "bids" for how much they will pay per customer action, and higher bids generally get more ad time (other factors are also considered, such as how popular an ad has been so far). Since Google makes no money from even a very high bid if customers do not engage with the ad, advertisers are incentivized to bid high, which benefits Google's bottom line. Google promotes the model as a win-win; the company makes a profit and customers get more bang for their advertising buck.

Google leverages their various product offerings to provide a variety of attractive advertising options. Companies can choose to have their ads displayed as "sponsored links" alongside search results for certain keywords, or as banners on any of the more than two million websites that display Google ads in return for a cut of the profits (known as the Google Display Network). Google continuously expands placement options to improve ad performance. YouTube is another option, offering video ads before, during, or after videos, as well as traditional banner space on the site. Mobile is also becoming a critical advertising space, through searches on both mobile devices and apps that allow advertising. Improving the effectiveness of their AdWords service is a key driver of Google's collection of user information—the more they know about their users, the more targeting options they can provide to advertisers and the more precisely they can serve targeted ads to desired consumer segments.

Web Browser

Google Chrome is the most popular web browser in the world with about two-thirds market share. When Google Chrome was released, it was praised for its unparalleled speed, support, and security. The Chrome browser is known for loading within seconds and maintaining a simplistic design to make it easier for users to navigate. Chrome is also updated more frequently than most of the other browsers, allowing Google to quickly push out new features and security improvements. With more than 1 billion monthly active users, the web browser has a vast audience. The Chrome Web Store contains a wide selection of apps and extensions, providing additional flexibility and functionality for users.

Email Account

Google's email account service, called Gmail, has more than 1.5 billion monthly active users and is the world's largest email service provider. Gmail was initially revolutionary for the huge amount of space it offered—1 gigabyte per user when rivals were only offering 100 megabytes or less—and the integration of Google search, which gave users a robust way to search within their stored emails. Since then, Gmail has continued to offer popular features such as snoozing, email "nudge" reminders, email scheduling, clickable attachments, two-factor authentication, predictive Smart Compose, a variety of add-ons, and deep integration with other Google products such as Hangouts, YouTube, Maps, Drive, and Calendar.

YouTube

In 2006, Google acquired video sharing site YouTube for $1.65 billion. YouTube allows users to upload and share original videos and has become the second most visited of all websites (Google.com is the most visited site in the world). Everyone from global corporations to consumers uses YouTube to share videos ranging from video blogs to parodies, to corporate messages to news events. By selling video advertising slots before, during, and after videos, as well as placing banner ads in free space on the site, Google has made billions in advertising revenue. Additionally, YouTube content creators can share in advertising profits from their videos through YouTube's Partner Program, allowing popular "YouTubers" to make careers out of their channels.

Although YouTube opened up new opportunities in marketing and entertainment, it has had its share of controversy. YouTube has been sued by organizations such as Viacom for copyright infringement after finding copyrighted content on YouTube's site. YouTube's Community Guidelines specifically directs users to respect copyright. However, not all users heed the warning. To detect and eliminate copyrighted material, YouTube enables users to "flag" videos for copyright infringement. If, upon review, the flag is found to be valid, the offending video is removed. YouTube has invested $100 million in automated system called Content ID which automatically compares newly uploaded videos to a database of copyrighted material and notifies the copyright holder if a match is found. To date, Content ID has paid more than $3 billion to rights holders. Google believes providing tools to enable self-interested copyright owners to protect their property is the best way to police YouTube, arguing it is simply not feasible for the company to screen the more than 500 hours of video uploaded to the site every minute.

Android

In 2005, Google acquired the startup firm Android Inc., which worked on mobile phone software technology. In 2008, the Android operating system was released by the Open Handset Alliance, a team of organizations led by Google whose mission is to promote development of open standards for mobile devices. The Android operating system is an open source platform, meaning the source code is available for outside users to view and use. However, Google has copyrighted the Android name and logo, as well as some proprietary features of Google's version of the software. Companies that wish to claim they make "Android" devices must enter into a licensing agreement with Google. The Android operating system is most often used in mobile devices and tablets but can also be found on other devices, including full computers, game consoles, and digital cameras.

Android has become the most popular mobile operating system in the world, making up over 86 percent of the market. In many countries, Android has more than 90 percent market share. Apple's iOS, while undeniably a strong competitor with a loyal customer base, trails far behind with 15 percent of the smartphone market. One reason for Android's larger market share is that, unlike Apple and their iPhone and iPad, Google is not the only company that makes Android phones and tablets; Samsung, HTC, Motorola, T-Mobile, Sony, and many other manufacturers develop Android devices. However, there are disadvantages to this approach. For example, Amazon built their mobile offerings, the Fire Phone and Kindle Fire tablets, off the Android open source code, and now competes directly with Google in the mobile sphere. In Europe, Google's partners can now offer Android-powered phones without Google apps pre-installed on the devices. Google is also a direct player in the mobile device market with their Nexus line of phones and tablets, placing them in the uncomfortable position of competing with their business partners. Still, Android has been a great success for Google, vastly increasing the company's reach into electronics. One top Google executive called the initial Android Inc. acquisition the company's "best deal ever."

Web Analytics

In November 2015, shortly after acquiring Urchin Software Corporation, Google released the free web analytics service Google Analytics which has grown to become the most popular web analytics service on the web with approximately 30 million active sites. Google Analytics tracks and freely reports website traffic statistics, giving businesses a market research tool to understand how customers are interacting with their websites. The dashboard is broken out into five reports: Realtime, Audience, Acquisition, Behavior, Conversions. Google Analytics 360, a premium version, is designed to help companies target potential customers with even more in-depth analytics, tying in data from other Google products such as Tag Manager and Data Studio. The tool identifies the habits of individuals from web and television to mobile, competing with companies like Salesforce and Oracle. Services like Google Analytics helps website owners measure and interpret the effectiveness of business activities. Google tracks visits via a user's IP address, raising some privacy concerns.

Expanding the Product Mix

Google offers several other popular products to businesses and consumers. Google Translate and Google Maps offer automated translation and mapping/directional services. Google Flights provides flight information including price data from many airlines. Google Drive allows users to store files in the cloud and share them with others. The service offers 15 gigabytes of free storage per user, and more can be purchased if desired. The company is also investing in artificial intelligence (AI) processing and has developed a new chip called the Tensor Processing Unit. This is a breakthrough in the more sophisticated systems needed to run artificial intelligence applications. Google aims to push AI processing into devices like phones and virtual assistants.

Google is also known for their forays into exciting and cutting-edge technologies, especially through their semi-secretive Google X department, whose mission is to develop "moonshots"—science fiction-like technologies that have a slim chance of succeeding but could change the world if they do. Research projects underway at Google X include using machine learning to teach robots new skills and using space optics to transmit high-speed data. One of their retired initiatives involved developing a real-time heads-up display for the average consumer. The end result was Google Glass, a wearable computer in the form of glasses worn on the face that can display information in front of the wearer's eyes, respond to verbal and movement commands, and more. Google Glass was publicly released in 2014 and has been applied to a wide variety of commercial applications, from providing doctors with hands-free information during surgery to helping autistic children interact with their environment. However, the device never achieved mainstream popularity. The style of the glasses was unappealing and the technology created privacy concerns since wearers could use them to record others without permission or cheat on exams. Though Glass was retired, the product lives on in its enterprise edition for businesses. The technology highlighted the need for rules to protect people from being recorded.

Google's Initiatives

Like all successful major corporations, Google is expected to act with integrity and give back to the communities where they do business. Google has invested in a number of initiatives that support economic development, environmental awareness, and charitable endeavors.

GV

In 2009, Google formed Google Ventures, later shortened to GV, as a separate entity to provide funding for startup firms. The venture capital fund began with $100 million in seed money and now manages more than $4.5 billion in assets of its own. They invest this money in startup companies at the forefront of technological innovation. The money goes not only to firms that market internet-based technologies or consumer electronics, but also to green technology firms, biotechnology and life-sciences companies, and more. Their best-known investments include Uber, Lime, and Slack. GV's goal is to invest in entrepreneurs that can change the world through technology by having "a healthy disregard for the impossible," mirroring what the Google X department is trying to do within Google itself.

Google Sustainability

Google has recognized the business opportunities that come from adopting sustainable operations and technologies. Greener technology not only saves Google money in the long run with decreased energy costs, it also enables the company to create greener products for consumers. Google, which reached their goal of 100 percent renewable energy for their global operations in 2017, claims their data centers use 50 percent less energy than typical data centers. Now, 100 percent of shipments to and from Google are carbon neutral. Google has committed to include recycled materials in every single product they make. For employees, Google offers a shuttle system run on biodiesel, an on-campus car sharing program, company bicycles to commute between buildings and departments, and the largest electric vehicle charging station in the country. Other sustainability successes for Google include a large solar installation on their campus and LEED-certified buildings.

Google.org

Google.org is the charitable arm of the organization. According to their website, the organization provides assistance to "nonprofits using technology and innovation to tackle complex global challenges" by giving more than $100 million in grants and 200,000 volunteer hours each year. Google.org also develops tools for nonprofits and provides disaster relief. Google for Nonprofits provides resources such as discounts on Google products and free AdWords advertising to nonprofit organizations. Google.org has also partnered with nonprofits to offer them use of Google's considerable resources. For example, they provided tools to the National Center for Missing and Exploited Children to help the nonprofit in their fight against global child exploitation. Google extended their community service outreach efforts with the introduction of the Google.org Fellowship that allows their employees to work full-time for their nonprofit partners for up to six months. Collectively, Google aims for 50,000 hours of pro bono work annually through the program.

In addition to the company's work through Google.org, Google contributes hundreds of millions of dollars directly to various charities and socially responsible organizations. Just before the company's initial public offering in 2004, Google's cofounder Larry Page promised Google would continually contribute 1 percent of their profits, 1 percent of their equity, and a significant amount of employee time to philanthropic endeavors. In terms of giving employee time, Google encourages employees to get involved in giving back to their communities. For instance, Google matches up to $6,000 of each employee's contributions to nonprofits annually. They have donated more than $50 million to thousands of nonprofits. Google also encourages employees to take time to volunteer in their communities, especially during their annual GoogleServe event, which sets aside one to two weeks each June for Google staff worldwide to get involved in their communities and donate time to good causes.

Privacy

Being a large company, Google has many risks and ethical issues they must constantly address. In many ways Google has helped advance ethical conduct in the web and technology industries. Google has been named multiple times among Ethisphere Institute's "World's Most Ethical Companies" due to their contributions to the community and the environment. The company also consistently ranks among *Fortune* magazine's "100 Best Companies to Work for" because of their fun and innovative work environment.

One of the greatest risks faced by digital companies involves hacking attacks and online scams. Google is attempting to address these risks head on. For example, Google was hit with a massive phishing attack. Gmail users were sent an email that supposedly came from someone they knew inviting them to open up a document in Google Docs. Those that clicked on the link were directed to a real Google page, where they were asked to input their passwords to download a fraudulent app. Once the fraudsters had the users' credentials, they used them to access the users' contact lists to send out more phishing emails. Google immediately reacted to disable the accounts and notify their Gmail users. Though phishers are becoming more sophisticated, Google successfully blocks approximately 100 million phishing emails per day. In addition to their preventative efforts, when Google can't positively identify a phishing attempt, they display a safety warning above questionable emails in a user's inbox.

Despite their contributions to ethics, Google's actions have been called into question. For instance, when Google created an ethics board to guide "responsible development of AI" at the organization, thousands petitioned for the removal of a board member who made concerning comments about trans people and whose company was skeptical of climate change. Many questioned whether the eight members who would meet only four times per year could possibly understand the full scope of Google's AI development. When debate about their board members continued, it became clear that the board was a liability for Google. Google dissolved the ethics board after just one week and resolved to find better ways to add outside perspective on AI topics.

Google also faces intense antitrust scrutiny from the European community. Competitors in Europe claim Google uses their dominant market position to promote their own offerings and demote rival results in search listings. In 2010, the European Union (EU) investigated Google's practices. Google proposed concessions and business changes it was willing to make to satisfy competitors and investigators, but none were accepted, and the EU announced formal charges against Google in 2015. The initial charge was that Google favors their comparison-shopping service over competitors. The EU later filed another antitrust charge against Google targeting their AdSense advertising platform. These accusations are similar to the EU's investigation into Microsoft, which eventually led to $2.3 billion in fines and significant changes in how Microsoft conducted business worldwide. Google was fined a third time in 2019 for hindering competition. The $1.7 billion fine was in response to Google allegedly blocking their rivals from placing ads on third-party websites. In total, Google has been fined more than $9 billion by the EU in the past few years alone. Additional changes need to be made by Google to avoid further investigations.

For the sake of brevity, this case will focus on one major ethical issue Google has continually wrestled with as they seek to expand their reach: privacy. The advent of the internet and mobile technology provides so many opportunities for stakeholders that many do not realize the cost for this information might be significant portions of their privacy. Many consumers are shocked to find that web companies such as Google and Facebook track their online activity and use this information to tailor advertisements or sell to marketers. Other consumers feel that Google's use of their personal information is a small price to pay in exchange for access to the company's superior services. For Google—which offers so much free content and gets most of their revenue from advertising—this information is extremely valuable to their continued business success. Google's privacy policy details what information they collect and how they use that information. For instance, Google claims they may share non-personal information with their partners.

Despite Google's attempts to be transparent, there are ethical gray areas regarding the collection and use of data. Because there is still little legislation regulating how internet companies gather and employ user information, it is tempting for firms to push the limits on privacy. Going too far, however, creates reputational and legal problems. Google was fined $57 million under the EU's General Data Protection Regulation (GDPR) in France. The French data protection authority claimed

Google did not disclose how data is collected across their services properly. Such concerns are not exclusive to the GDPR. Although Google is the most popular search engine, one recent poll found that 52 percent of Google users have concerns about their privacy when using it. This could be a potential obstacle for Google since consumer trust plays a big role in how they interact with a company. The following sections discuss some of the major privacy issues Google has experienced.

Search Queries

One of the major privacy criticisms levied against Google is that the company keeps track of users' search terms. Keeping a longer history allows Google to create a custom user experience. Consider all the things you have ever searched for using Google's search engine. Now consider how comfortable you feel knowing the company has recorded and stored all those search terms… forever. This tracking cannot be turned off—users can disable their Google web history to remove any external record of searches and prevent the information from being used in certain ways, but Google will continue to record and store search terms for internal purposes. To address privacy concerns, users can automatically set their Google history to be deleted on a 3-month or 18-month schedule, so it's no longer a manual process. To be fair, the practice of retaining search data is not limited to Google—many other internet firms do the same. Because Google is the most popular search engine in the world, they are more heavily scrutinized.

The big question users ask is whether their search terms can be traced back to them personally. Google claims that although they store users' search terms, after 18 months the data becomes "anonymized" and theoretically untraceable. However, critics debate this claim because supposedly anonymized data from other search engines was later matched to specific users. Google claims they treat this information with respect, using it to refine their search engine. Yet under the Third Party Doctrine and the Patriot Act, the U.S. government could subpoena the data if deemed necessary for national security. Needless to say, Google's storage of users' search terms is a controversial topic. In fact, several smaller search engines such as DuckDuckGo use the fact that they do not track user activity as a competitive differentiator from Google.

Tracking Users

Tracking users has become a major issue for Google. A storm of criticism was unleashed when government regulators and consumers learned the company's phones tracked users' locations. It was revealed that Android phones contained location-logging features enabling the firm to collect GPS coordinates of their users as well as the coordinates of nearby Wi-Fi networks. Similar tracking features were found on the Apple iPhone. The revelations spurred legislators to write letters to Google asking for clarification on how they track users and use this information. It was later discovered by an AP investigation that even when users have turned off location history, Google still saves their location.

Google also tracks users on the internet. For Google, offering advertisers the ability to specifically target their ads to desired users based on their interests is invaluable to remaining competitive in the advertising market. Additionally, Google uses this information to customize their services to individual users. For example, users will see different results for the same Google search terms based on what Google believes they most likely want, based on what they know about them. Many privacy advocates do not like this pervasive use of tracking, and there is ongoing concern by regulators and others over how Google uses the information they collect. Google's privacy policy does allow users to opt out of many tracking functions, but users must actively do so—the default is to be tracked. This is especially problematic for the many users that do not realize they are being tracked and/or do not know how to use Google's settings to opt out. All of the popular web browsers, including Google Chrome, now include a "Do Not Track" option, which indicates to websites that the user does not wish to be tracked. However, the designation has no legal or regulatory authority and has so far remained mostly symbolic, with many websites simply ignoring it.

On the other hand, supporters of Google maintain that tracking is necessary to provide the best services to users. These services are often free because Google is able to generate revenue through advertising. Tracking also allows Google to customize their services to individual user needs. Consumers must therefore be proactive in deciding whether they place greater value on their privacy or Google's free services.

Although some people do not appear to mind having their web activity tracked in exchange for Google's free services, Google has repeatedly violated public trust. In 2012, security analysts revealed that Google was using loopholes in Apple's Safari browser to ignore their default privacy settings while simultaneously telling Safari users they were protected. Google eventually paid $22.5 million to settle the FTC charges and an additional $17 million to settle similar charges brought by 37 states and the District of Columbia. Google has also been accused of failing to respect user privacy in the real world. In 2010, Google announced they had accidentally scanned data from some users' personal wireless networks in the United Kingdom with their vans that collect data and photos for their location-based services. The vans scanned wireless networks of nearby residences and collected activity data from unsecured, open networks, including emails, text messages, video and audio files, and more. Though Google promised they would destroy the data collected, a later investigation revealed Google still retained some of this user data. The violation exacerbated their image of being a firm that disregards privacy. Soon after the incident, it was discovered Google had been collecting the same type of information from unsecured residential wireless networks in other countries as well. In the United States, Google was fined $25,000 by the Federal Communications Commission (FCC) for deliberately delaying and impeding its investigation. The investigation led to a $7 million settlement among Google, the FCC, and 38 states and the District of Columbia. At least seven other countries also found Google guilty of similar activity in their jurisdictions.

Yet another privacy-related incident for Google involved the Google Play App Store. A developer who started selling a mobile application through Google's app store was shocked by the amount of information he was given about his customers, including their names, locations, and email addresses, even though nowhere in the app buying process were customers asked to give consent to release that information. The developer argued that this practice violated Google's privacy policy, which at the time stated that identifiable information would never be given to third parties without user consent. Some privacy experts agreed with the developer; others did not, stating that the information shared was minimal and of the type commonly expected to be given out in making any purchase. Still, Google's approach to privacy continues to be a subject of controversy and debate.

As technology evolves, the definition of personally identifiable data changes. In 2019, Google and the University of Chicago were sued in a lawsuit that accused the company and the university of failing to strip identifiable data from medical records in a collaboration designed to use AI to improve diagnosing medical problems. The artificial intelligence that Google is developing reads health records to assist doctors. To learn and produce accurate results, the machines must analyze large quantities of old health records. Though patient data was largely "de-identified," dates of services were left intact, raising concerns. The lawsuit claims the retention of dates violates HIPAA, the legislation that provides data privacy for medical information, because dates could potentially be cross-referenced against other data Google collects, such as location history from Google Maps, to identify individuals.

Privacy Audits

Although Google has faced lawsuits from consumers claiming the company violated their privacy rights, a lack of internet legislation enables Google to continue many of their practices. However, Google found themselves in trouble with governmental authorities after allegedly violating their own privacy policies. In 2010, Google launched the failed social networking platform Google Buzz. Most of those who chose to join were unaware that the identities of their frequent contacts on

Gmail would be made publicly available on the internet through Google Buzz. Although users could opt out of having this information released, they claimed the opt-out features were difficult to locate. Other accusations claimed that even those users who opted out of joining Google Buzz were still enrolled in certain features of the social network, and that those who requested to leave the network were not fully removed. Although Google worked to fix these problems, the FTC's investigation found Google had acted deceptively and violated their own privacy policies. Google agreed to settle with the FTC by agreeing to never again misrepresent their privacy practices and allowing approved third-party firms to conduct privacy audits every other year regarding how the company uses information. These audits will take place for 20 years from the date of the settlement. That same year, Facebook agreed to a similar deal after allegedly violating their users' rights to privacy, and other companies have since become subject to privacy audits as well. If Google's audits reveal problems, the FTC may impose fines of $16,000 for each violation per day.

These audits are a blow to Google's operations. As one of the first internet companies to have this kind of audit imposed on it, the company will have to tread carefully regarding how it collects and uses information. On the other hand, Google might choose to see this as an opportunity to improve their internal controls and privacy practices to ensure user information is respected. Doing so could gain more trust from users and prevent future legislative action against the company. So far, Google's record in honoring the settlement is mixed. Its 2012 privacy audit found no issues, but that same year the FTC found Google's bypassing of the Safari browser's default privacy controls to be a violation of the agreement and fined the company for it. As one of the world's largest internet companies, the actions Google takes in this area will significantly impact the future activities of other companies.

From Many Privacy Policies to One

For most of their history, Google has had separate privacy policies for most of their products, each detailing how Google collects and uses information for that product. Google's rapid growth and expansion from just search into an internet behemoth had resulted in over 70 separate Google privacy policies across their offerings. This was beneficial in one sense, as consumers who took the time to read the policies could understand in great detail how Google was operating each product. On the other hand, the overwhelming amount of policies was confusing, tedious, and time-consuming to sift through, and the average consumer would have been hard-pressed to decipher them.

Google announced they was unifying their myriad privacy policies into just one, which would govern

Google's practices across their entire organization. At first glance, this seemed like an efficient change. However, it had many subtler implications that sparked widespread concern. Could consumers still opt out of specific information-sharing in individual products? Did the new policy adequately explain all the different ways Google gathered and shared information so consumers could be properly informed? Did the new policy expand Google's information-gathering power under the guise of making things simpler?

One especially concerning aspect of Google's new policy was that it allowed the company to take all the information they gathered on their users across all their products and combine them together. Coupled with the new unified login system, the new privacy policy allowed Google to use information on a much larger and more encompassing scale. Users' Google searches might affect the ads they see on their Android phones, YouTube browsing histories could be combined with Gmail activity to better understand user interests, and more. Was this "all-seeing eye" approach acceptable, especially for such a large company with so many widely used services?

Understandably, the announcement of a unified privacy policy led to considerable backlash. Google received letters from Congress members and U.S. attorneys general expressing concern about the new policy. Competitors such as Microsoft took advantage of the situation to run ads drawing consumer attention to Google's potentially unsettling approach to user privacy. The EU asked Google to delay implementation of the policy until it could study and better understand its implications. In defending itself, Google emphasized that they were not gathering any more information than before, nor were they making any changes to existing user ability to opt out of information-sharing or use product-specific privacy settings. They were merely making their existing practices simpler and clearer for customers to understand, as well as improving their own ability to serve users by unifying the information it gathered across offerings. They argued the new policy was in legal compliance and refused to delay the transition. On March 1, 2012, the unified policy took effect.

The new privacy policy was poorly received in Europe. The EU Justice Commissioner questioned the legality of Google's new policy according to EU law. French data regulators launched an investigation concerning the new policy, believing the policy might not adhere to EU Internet transparency and privacy laws. Google maintained their new policy met EU regulations. However, in 2013 six European countries banded together to take legal action against Google for not complying with the requests of the government. Google has since been fined by several European countries for breaking their privacy or data protection laws, including nearly $1 million by Spain and $204,000 by France. The Netherlands threatened a fine of up to $15 million

if Google does not comply with its desired changes. The company narrowly avoided yet another fine in the U.K. by agreeing to change their privacy policy for U.K. users, and there are signs it may make such a change Europe-wide in an attempt to allay the concerns of the EU and its member nations. Google has learned that activities which are legal in one country might not be legal in another.

The public's reaction to Google's unified privacy policy once again brings to light the more general debate over the company's gathering and use of user information. Supporters argue that Google uses this information to create improved services for users. It helps the firm remain competitive with strong rivals such as Apple and Facebook. Critics are concerned that Google is constantly overreaching and seems to have little actual concern for user privacy, only slowing or backtracking when they are forced to by consumer backlash or governmental regulators. Critics are also worried by the ease with which Google appears to change their policies, which could spell trouble for users and their privacy rights. Google keeps a log of changes made to their policies to improve transparency with a comparison tool that allows users to see what changes were made between versions.

"Right to Be Forgotten"

In 2014, the European Union's highest court ruled that EU citizens have a "right to be forgotten." In other words, consumers have the right to prevent certain types of content from showing up in online search results. Such content includes results that are inadequate, irrelevant, no longer relevant, or excessive. The court decision allows individuals to petition search engines to remove such content from search results, and if refused, to take the matter to a local data protection authority for adjudication.

The court decision sent shockwaves through the internet search community. Was this censorship, or the beginning of an acknowledgment that search engines have a duty to at least somewhat curate their results? Was this a victory for privacy, or a defeat for freedom of speech? How will search companies be able to properly decide whether removal requests are legitimate or stretch beyond the boundaries of the court decision?

In response to the ruling, Google set up a process by which they process "right to be forgotten" requests. The claimant fills out an online form, which is reviewed and processed by a team of Google lawyers, paralegals, and engineers. "Easy" cases, where the correct decision is relatively clear, are made by that team. Difficult cases are forwarded to a senior panel of Google experts and executives to decide. For instance, a published U.S. record of the name of a 16-year-old German individual convicted in the United States of a sex crime could be controversial because in Germany the record would not be published due to his minor status. Google also releases periodic "Transparency Reports" providing information on right to be forgotten requests. So far, Google has received over 650,000 requests to remove 2.43 million URLs, mostly from individuals who want to protect their private information. Google removes approximately 43 percent of these URLs.

Google and other internet search companies continue to express their opposition to the "right to be forgotten" concept, and many others agree. Some are opposed to it outright, citing freedom of speech concerns; others believe it may be a good idea but that private companies such as Google should not be the ones deciding which links to keep and which to take down. Simultaneously, EU regulators are dissatisfied with how Google has chosen to interpret the court decision. For example, Google is only removing links from their Europe-specific search engines such as Google.fr or Google.co.uk, meaning anyone can simply move to Google.com to find the hidden content. Simultaneously, other areas of the world are considering the right to be forgotten idea, with varying success. In Mexico courts have ruled for some individuals petitioning Google to remove content, but critics worry the right is being used largely by politically powerful individuals to remove unsightly aspects of their past. California has passed a law requiring websites to provide a mechanism by which minors can have content they post removed, believing children should not be punished for online missteps. Hong Kong's top privacy regulator has embraced the concept wholeheartedly, suggesting Google should apply the EU ruling to their operations globally.

"Right to be forgotten" adds another wrinkle in Google's privacy concerns. Now, at least in some parts of the world, Google must not only worry about the information they collect itself, but also about what information posted by third parties might be showing in its search results.

Google in China

Google has had a tough time in China. When Google decided to enter the world's most populous country, they faced an ethical dilemma. On the one hand, Google did not want to miss the opportunity to tap into a market consisting of more than one billion potential consumers. On the other hand, Google could not enter China without censorship. If it created a Chinese version of Google and hosted it outside of China, it would be subject to China's "Great Firewall," which the government uses to censor foreign sites. Google tried this method first, but their Chinese search engine was intermittently blocked and was otherwise slow and inconsistent for users, causing Google to steadily lose market share to domestic Chinese competitors such as Baidu. Google's other option, to host a search engine from within China, would require agreeing to self-censor their search results

in accordance with Chinese law. Such an agreement went against the essence of what Google stood for—providing free and open access to information. Could Google agree to censor themselves and still hold true to their "Don't Be Evil" mantra?

Despite criticism, Google applied the principles of utilitarianism to the situation and concluded that the benefits of setting up a search engine inside China outweighed the costs. They refused to offer localized email or blogging, finding the Chinese censorship and reporting requirements for these services to be too egregious. However, for search Google decided the greater good would be to provide Chinese citizens with "the greatest amount of information" possible, even if some of that information was censored. In 2006, Google opened their localized, self-censored Chinese search engine. Whenever a search term led to censored results, Google added a message to the results page notifying the user that some entries were missing. They also left up their original, uncensored Chinese search engine hosted outside of China, so users could try to use it if they wanted.

Despite these precautions, Google's plan ran into problems almost from the onset. Google gained significant market share and became a serious competitor to Baidu, but the company's relationship with the Chinese government was continually tense, with Google accusing the government of interfering with the search engine beyond expectations. Google also faced intense backlash in the United States, including their leadership being called to testify at Congressional hearings about how they could justify self-censoring in China considering the principles they claimed to stand for everywhere else in the world. In 2010, Google announced they had been targeted by a sophisticated cyberattack that appeared to originate from China and, among other things, had attempted to access the Gmail accounts of known Chinese human rights activists. Google stated that the implications of the cyberattack required them to reevaluate their approach toward the Chinese market, and they could no longer justify self-censorship. They shut down their China-hosted site and forwarded visitors to their external, uncensored but often-blocked Chinese search engine. As a result, Google saw their market share in China plunge and Baidu retaking its dominant position. The Chinese government was also not happy with Google's handling of the situation and immediately began blocking and/or censoring large portions of Google's services.

Google did not give up on the largest market in the world. Google began a secret project in 2017 with the Chinese government called Dragonfly. The plan was to again launch a censored search engine in China. The project was kept under wraps until it was exposed by *The Intercept*, an online news publication. A previous Google employee called the project disturbing. In 2019, Google officially terminated Dragonfly, and the company stated they had no active plans to launch in

China. The company will have to remember the lessons they learned from both of their failed attempts and the sensitive ethical issues involved with censorship if they make any future moves into the Chinese market.

Government Response to Privacy Issues

Consumer concerns over privacy issues prompted Congress to consider new legislation regulating what information internet companies such as Google can collect and how they can use it. Internet companies, in turn, are attempting to make such legislation unnecessary by developing their own industry standards, such as the "Do Not Track" feature now found on all major web browsers. Such self-regulation is an attempt to ward off federal legislation that could seriously limit the tracking activities of companies like Google.

Some of the ideas that federal regulators have been discussing include a User's Bill of Rights and a mandatory Do Not Track feature. The Bill of Rights would, among other things, require companies to adhere to certain privacy practices. Its intent in this area would be to make internet privacy policies easier for users to understand. A mandatory Do Not Track mechanism would be comparable to Do Not Call legislation, which makes it illegal for companies to sell to consumers over the telephone if those consumers are on the national Do Not Call registry. A similar law regulating internet tracking could seriously impact how internet companies collect information.

Many states are dissatisfied with the lack of federal action on this topic and have passed their own internet privacy laws. California law, for example, provides special privacy protection to minors online and requires websites to disclose whether they are respecting the "Do Not Track" requests they receive from user browsers. However, more recent government decisions have overturned privacy regulations that would have required internet providers to get users' permission before being able to sell their data. Critics claim that the government is failing to address the privacy gap, giving online companies like Google free rein in collecting, storing, and using user information.

Because legislation could be a serious threat to Google, the company spends millions on lobbying and employs lobbyists on their staff. Google hopes to stave off regulation they feel restricts their ability to coordinate targeted advertising or offer customized services to users. However, with privacy issues and internet breaches becoming a growing concern, the chance of increased regulation in the future is high. Although Google might not be able to prevent legislation restricting some of the activities of internet firms, they can work with regulators to push for legislation with less of a negative effect on their operations. Google's lobbyists are having a profound impact on laws safeguarding internet security.

Conclusion

Google's success story is unparalleled among search engine providers. The company started off as a small search engine and ranking system, and has become one of the most profitable internet companies in the world. Today the company is the owner and provider of products that go above and beyond simply a search engine. While there might be a risk of Google overextending itself, the company has a talent for making highly profitable acquisitions that increase its global reach.

As a way to manage its various businesses, in 2015 Google created a new publicly traded holding company called Alphabet run by Google founders Larry Page and Sergey Brin. Google was made a subsidiary of Alphabet with its own CEO. The founders believe that developing a holding company and "slimming down" Google to focus more on its internet businesses will be beneficial for the firm in the long run.

Google has made itself into the epitome of a "best company to work for." The benefits Google offers employees are extensive, and Google empowers them to make decisions to improve the company's operations. The company has taken a strong stand on green initiatives and supports technologies to address global challenges. Google's "Don't Be Evil" mantra became a popular yardstick to guide Google's actions. After Google became part of the holding company Alphabet, their popular motto was modified to "Do the Right Thing."

On the other hand, Google has faced challenges in privacy, many of which continue to this day. Google is forced to draw a fine line between using user information to generate revenue and violating user privacy. Because Google can offer targeted advertising to advertisers through their collection of information, the company can provide quality internet services to their users for free. At the same time, Google has committed questionable actions that seem to infringe on user rights and has encountered resistance from governmental authorities on many privacy-related initiatives.

With the threat of new regulation, Google lobbies to prevent legislation from being passed that proves unfavorable to the company. Because Google depends on tracking and similar activities to maintain profitability, it has a large stake in the privacy issue. However, rather than seeing this solely as a liability, Google might instead choose to improve its privacy practices and increase transparency in its operations. Google has the responsibility to ensure stakeholder rights are respected. Although Google has made great strides in social responsibility, both the company and society know there is room for improvement. Google's size, reputation, and history give them a unique opportunity to positively impact how companies interact on the internet.

Questions for Discussion

1. Has Google implemented a strategy that serves all stakeholders?
2. How can Google respect privacy and still maintain its profitability?
3. How will increasing global regulation of privacy affect Google's operations?

Sources

"Can Google's Advertising Business Cross $200 Billion in 3 Years?" *Forbes,* June 25, 2019, https://www.forbes.com/sites/greatspeculations/2019/06/25/can-googles-advertising-business-cross-200-billion-in-3-years/#793f29b55408 (accessed August 7, 2019).

"Google's Gmail Turns 15, Now Has over 1.5 Billion Monthly Active Users," *The News Minute,* April 1, 2019, https://www.thenewsminute.com/article/googles-gmail-turns-15-now-has-over-15-billion-monthly-active-users-99275 (accessed August 7, 2019).

"Smartphone Market Share," *IDC,* June 18, 2019, https://www.idc.com/promo/smartphone-market-share/os (accessed August 7, 2019).

"Philosophy and Goals," Open Source Project, http://www.webcitation.org/5wiyo36ap (accessed June 1, 2015).

Adam Minter, "Is Google Going Back into China?" *Bloomberg View,* November 24, 2014, https://www.bloomberg.com/view/articles/2014-11-24/is-google-going-back-into-china (accessed May 6, 2017).

Adi Robertson, "Google France Forced to Notify Visitors of €150,000 Privacy Policy Fine," *The Verge,* February 8, 2014, http://www.theverge.com/2014/2/8/5393418/google-france-forced-to-notify-visitors-of-150ooo-privacy-policy-fine/in/2527939 (accessed May 6, 2017).

Alex Johnson, "Massive Phishing Attack Targets Millions of Gmail Users," *CNBC.com,* May 4, 2017, http://www.cnbc.com/2017/05/04/gmail-google-hack-phishing-attack.html (accessed August 12, 2019).

Alexei Oreskovic and Michael Sin, "Google App Store Policy Raises Privacy Concerns," *Reuters,* February 14, 2013, http://www.reuters.com/article/2013/02/14/us-google-privacy-idUSBRE91D1LL20130214 (accessed May 6, 2017).

Anna Meegan, "Our Hardware Sustainability Commitments," *Google Blog,* August 5, 2019, https://www.blog.google/outreach-initiatives/sustainability/hardware-sustainability-commitments/ (accessed August 7, 2019).

Anthony Spadafora, "These Are the Most Popular Google Chrome Extensions," *Tech Radar,* August 6, 2019, https://www.techradar.com/news/most-popular-google-chrome-extensions (accessed August 7, 2019).

Ari Levy, "Meet the 69-Year-Old Professor Who Left Retirement to Help Lead One of Google's Most Crucial Projects," *CNBC,* May 6, 2017, http://www.cnbc.com/2017/05/06/googles-tpu-for-machine-learning-being-evangelized-by-david-patterson.html (accessed May 6, 2017).

Associated Press, "Developments Related to Google's Privacy Concerns," *The Huffington Post,* April 2, 2013, http://www.huffingtonpost.com/huff-wires/20130402/tec-google-privacy-history/?utm_hp_ref=travel&ir=travel (accessed May 6, 2017).

Associated Press, "Google Buys YouTube for $1.65 Billion," *MSNBC,* October 10, 2006, http://www.msnbc.msn.com/id/15196982/ns/business-us_business/t/google-buys-youtube-billion/ (accessed May 6, 2017).

Austin Ramzy "Google Ends Policy of Self-Censorship in China," *TIME,* January 13, 2010, http://content.time.com/time/world/article/0,8599,1953248,00.html (accessed May 6, 2017).

Barry Schwartz, "You Can Now Automatically Set Your Google History to Be Deleted," *Search Engine Land*, May 1, 2019, https://searchengineland.com/you-can-now-automatically-set-your-google-history-to-be-deleted-316266 (accessed August 12, 2019).

BBC, "Google Privacy Changes 'In Breach of EU Law'" *BBC,* March 1, 2012, http://www.bbc.com/news/technology-17205754 (accessed May 6, 2017).

Ben Elgin, "Google Buys Android for Its Mobile Arsenal," *Bloomberg Businessweek,* August 17, 2005, http://www.webcitation.org/5wk7sIvVb (accessed May 6, 2017).

Bianca Bosker, "Google Privacy Policy Changing for Everyone: So What's Really Going to Happen?" *The Huffington Post,* February 29, 2012, http://www.huffingtonpost.com/2012/02/29/google-privacy-policy-changes_n_1310506.html (accessed May 6, 2017).

Brian Naylor, "Congress Overturns Internet Privacy Regulation," *NPR,* March 28, 2017, http://www.npr.org/2017/03/28/521831393/congress-overturns-internet-privacy-regulation (accessed May 6, 2017).

Bryan Bishop, "Google Responds to EU Privacy Policy Questions, Pausing Rollout Would Have 'Proved Confusing'" *The Verge,* April 5, 2012, https://www.theverge.com/2012/4/5/2928619/google-responds-eu-privacy-policy-questions-pausing-rollout-confusing-users (accessed May 6, 2017).

Byron Acohido, "Lawmakers Request Probe of Tracking by Apple and Google" *USA Today,* April 25, 2011, 1B.

Byron Acohido, "Most Google, Facebook Users Fret Over Privacy," *USA Today,* February 9, 2011, lB.

Charles Arthur, "Google Facing Legal Threat from Six European Countries over Privacy," *The Guardian,* April 2, 2013, http://www.guardian.co.uk/technology/2013/apr/02/google-privacy-policy-legal-threat-europe (accessed May 6, 2017).

Charles Riley and Ivana Kottasová, "Europe Hits Google with a Third, $1.7 Billion Antitrust Fine," *CNN,* March 20, 2019, https://www.cnn.com/2019/03/20/tech/google-eu-antitrust/index.html (accessed August 12, 2019).

Chip Brownlee, "Google's New Chrome Makes It Easier to Bypass Newspaper Paywalls," *Slate Magazine,* July 31, 2019, https://slate.com/technology/2019/07/google-chrome-update-incognito-mode-paywall-workaround.html (accessed August 7, 2019).

Christopher Williams, "Google Faces Privacy Investigation over Merging Search, Gmail, and YouTube Data," *The Telegraph,* April 2, 2013. http://www.telegraph.co.uk/technology/google/9966704/Google-faces-privacy-investigation-over-merging-search-Gmail-and-YouTube-data.html (accessed May 6, 2017).

Clive Thompson, "Google's China Problem (and China's Google Problem)," *The New York Times,* April 23, 2006, http://www.nytimes.com/2006/04/23/magazine/23google.html (accessed May 6, 2017).

Daisuke Wakabayashi, "Google and the University of Chicago Are Sued Over Data Sharing," *The New York Times*, June 26, 2019, https://www.nytimes.com/2019/06/26/technology/google-university-chicago-data-sharing-lawsuit.html (accessed August 12, 2019).

Danielle Abril, "Google Is Paying Employees for Six Months of Charity Work," *Fortune*, January 16, 2019, https://fortune.com/2019/01/16/google-employees-charity-work/ (accessed August 12, 2019).

Dave Drummond, "A New Approach to China: An Update," *Google Official Blog*, March 22, 2010, http://googleblog.blogspot.com/2010/03/new-approach-to-china-update.html (accessed May 6, 2017).

David Kravets, "A Dissection of Google's Wi-Fi Sniffing Debacle," *Wired.co.uk*, May 3, 2012, https://www.wired.com/2012/05/google-wifi-fcc-investigation/ (accessed May 6, 2017).

David Streitfeld and Kevin J. O'Brien, "Google Privacy Inquiries Get Little Cooperation," *New York Times*, May 23, 2012, http://www.nytimes.com/2012/05/23/technology/google-privacy-inquiries-get-little-cooperation.html (accessed May 6, 2017).

David Streitfeld, "Google Is Faulted for Impeding U.S. Inquiry on Data Collection," *New York Times*, April 15, 2012, http://www.nytimes.com/2012/04/15/technology/google-is-fined-for-impeding-us-inquiry-on-data-collection.html (accessed May 6, 2017).

Dennis O'Reilly, "How to Prevent Google from Tracking You," *CNET.com*, January 30, 2012, https://www.cnet.com/how-to/how-to-prevent-google-from-tracking-you/ (accessed May 6, 2017).

Don Karp, "Google AdWords: A Brief History of Online Advertising Innovation" *Publishing 2.0*, May 27, 2008, http://publishing2.com/2008/05/27/google-adwords-a-brief-history-of-online-advertising-innovation/ (accessed May 6, 2017).

Don Reisinger, "Google Responds to Congress over Policy Privacy Inquiries," *CNET.com*, January 1, 2012, https://www.cnet.com/news/google-responds-to-congress-over-privacy-policy-inquiries/ (accessed May 6, 2017).

Doug Aamoth, "Google Turns 14, Was Initially Called 'BackRub'," *Time*, September 27, 2012, http://techland.time.com/2012/09/27/google-turns-14-today-was-initially-called-backrub/ (accessed August 12, 2019).

Doug Osborne, "Google Uses High-Tech Nap Pods to Keep Employees Energized," *Geek.com*, June 18, 2010, http://www.geek.com/news/google-uses-high-tech-nap-pods-to-keep-employees-energized-1264430/ (accessed May 6, 2017).

Elise Ackerman, "Google and Facebook Ignore 'Do Not Track' Requests, Claim They Confuse Consumers" *Forbes*, February 27, 2013, http://www.forbes.com/sites/eliseackerman/2013/02/27/big-internet-companies-struggle-over-proper-response-to-consumers-do-not-track-requests/ (accessed May 6, 2017).

Eric Goldman, "Top Ten Internet Law Developments of 2013," *Forbes*, January 9, 2014, https://www.forbes.com/sites/ericgoldman/2014/01/09/top-ten-internet-law-developments-of-2013/#1daa893646ba (accessed May 6, 2017).

Ethisphere Institute, "Ethisphere Announces the 2015 World's Most Ethical Companies'," *Ethisphere*, March 9, 2015, http://worldsmostethicalcompanies.ethisphere.com/honorees/ (accessed May 6, 2017).

Federal Trade Commission, "FTC Charges Deceptive Privacy Practices in Google's Rollout of Its Buzz Social Network," March 30, 2011, http://www.ftc.gov/opa/2011/03/google.shtm (accessed May 6, 2017).

Florian Mueller, "Google's Once-Secret, Restrictive Android License Agreements with Samsung and HTC Published," *Foss Patents*, February 13, 2014, http://www.fosspatents.com/2014/02/googles-once-secret-restrictive-android.html (accessed May 6, 2017).

Francis Robinson, "Sam Schechner, and Amir Mizroch, "EU Orders Google to Let Users Erase Past," *The Wall Street Journal*, May 13, 2014, https://www.wsj.com/articles/eu-says-google-must-sometimes-remove-links-to-personal-material-1399970326 (accessed May 6, 2017).

Fred Campbell, "Only Congress Can Fix the Google Privacy Gap," *Forbes*, March 28, 2017, https://www.forbes.com/sites/fredcampbell/2017/03/28/only-congress-can-fix-the-google-privacy-gap/2/#17398dd15490 (accessed May 6, 2017).

George Anders, "The Rare Find," *Bloomberg Businessweek*, October 17-October 23, 2011, 106–112.

Google Sustainability, "Environment," https://sustainability.google/environment/ (accessed August 7, 2019).

Google, "Google Chrome," https://www.google.com/chrome/ (accessed August 5, 2019).

Google, "How Google Search Works," https://support.google.com/webmasters/answer/70897?hl=en (accessed August 7, 2019).

Google, "Achieve Your Marketing Goals," *Google AdWords*, http://www.google.com/ads/experienced/our-ad-platforms/ (accessed May 6, 2017).

Google, "Frequently Asked Questions," Google Transparency Report, https://www.google.com/transparencyreport/removals/europeprivacy/faq/?hl=en (accessed May 6, 2017).

Google, "Get Your Ad on Google Today," *Google Ad Words*, http://www.google.com/ads/adwords2/ (accessed May 6, 2017).

Google, "Google Environment," https://environment.google/ (accessed May 6, 2017).

Google, "GV," https://www.gv.com/ (accessed May 6, 2017).

Google, "Human Rights Caucus Briefing," Google Blog, February 1, 2006, https://googleblog.blogspot.com/2006/02/human-rights-caucus-briefing.html (accessed May 6, 2017).

Google, "Our Company," https://www.google.com/about/ (accessed May 6, 2017).

Google, "Use Mobile Advertising to Reach Customers While They're on the Go," *Google Ad Words*, http://www.google.com/ads/mobile/ (accessed May 6, 2017).

Google, "Welcome to the Google Privacy Policy," *Google Privacy & Terms*, January 22, 2019, https://www.google.com/policies/privacy/ (accessed August 12, 2019).

Google, Google, "European Privacy Requests for Search Removals," http://www.google.com/transparencyreport/removals/europeprivacy/?hl=en (accessed May 6, 2017).

Google.org, "Our Work," https://www.google.org/our-work/ (accessed August 7, 2019).

GV, "Press," https://www.gv.com/press/ (accessed August 7, 2019).

Heather Leonard, "The Google Investor: Mobile Advertising Is Google's Next Frontier," *Business Insider*, January 26, 2012, http://www.businessinsider.com/the-google-investor-jan-26-2012-1 (accessed May 6, 2017).

Instant Joseph, "Google's New Data-Sharing Privacy Policy Comes under Scrutiny," *The Verge*, January 26, 2012, http://www.theverge.com/2012/1/26/2744683/google-privacy-policy-under-scrutiny/in/2527939 (accessed May 6, 2017).

Jacob Gershman, "California Gives Teens a Do-Over" *The Wall Street Journal*, September 25, 2013, http://blogs.wsj.com/law/2013/09/25/calif-gov-brown-signs-bill-giving-teens-online-eraser/ (accessed May 6, 2017).

Jacob Kastrenakes, "Google Could Finally Face Serious Competition for Android," *The Verge*, October 18, 2018, https://www.theverge.com/2018/10/18/17989052/google-android-fork-competition-europe-antitrust-commission-lawsuit (accessed August 7, 2019).

James Doubek, "Google Has Received 650,000 'Right to Be Forgotten' Requests Since 2014," *NPR*, February 28, 2018, https://www.npr.org/sections/thetwo-way/2018/02/28/589411543/google-received-650-000-right-to-be-forgotten-requests-since-2014 (accessed August 12, 2019).

James Loke Hale, "More Than 500 Hours of Content Are Now Being Uploaded to YouTube Every Minute," *Tubefilter*, May 7, 2019, https://www.tubefilter.com/2019/05/07/number-hours-video-uploaded-to-youtube-per-minute/ (accessed August 7, 2019).

James Temperton, "Google Changes UK Privacy Policy, but Avoids Hefty Fine," *Wired.co.uk*, January 30, 2015, http://www.wired.co.uk/news/archive/2015-01/3o/google-ico-privacy-policy (accessed June 1, 2015).

Jamie Keene, "Google Clarifies That Its New Privacy Policy Won't Change Users' Privacy Settings," *The Verge*, January 31, 2012, http://www.theverge.com/2012/1/31/2761089/google-clarifies-privacy-policy-leaves-privacy-controls-unchanged/in/2527939 (accessed May 6, 2017).

Jeb Su, "Confirmed: Google Terminated Project Dragonfly, Its Censored Chinese Search Engine," *Forbes*, July 19, 2019, https://www.forbes.com/sites/jeanbaptiste/2019/07/19/confirmed-google-terminated-project-dragonfly-its-censored-chinese-search-engine/#1af966bf7e84 (accessed August 6, 2019).

Jeff Blagdon, "Google's Controversial New Privacy Policy Now in Effect," *The Verge*, March 1, 2012, http://www.theverge.com/2012/3/1/2835250/google-unified-privacy-policy-change-take-effect/in/2527939 (accessed May 6, 2017).

Jeff Desjardins, "How Google Retains More Than 90% of Market Share," *Business Insider*, April 23, 2018, https://www.businessinsider.com/how-google-retains-more-than-90-of-market-share-2018-4 (accessed August 7, 2019).

Jemima Kiss, "Google Admits Collecting Wi-Fi Data through Street View Cars," *The Guardian*, May 14, 2010, https://www.theguardian.com/technology/2010/may/15/google-admits-storing-private-data (accessed May 6, 2017).

Jennifer Valentino-DeVries, "What Do Google's Privacy Changes Mean for You?" *The Wall Street Journal*, January 25, 2012, http://blogs.wsj.com/digits/2012/01/25/what-do-googles-privacy-changes-mean-for-you/ (accessed May 6, 2017).

Jessica Guynn, "Google Creates Company Alphabet, Names New CEO," *USA Today*, August 11, 2015, https://www.usatoday.com/story/tech/2015/08/10/google-alphabet-sundar-pichai-larry-page-sergey-brin/31429423/ / (accessed May 6, 2017).

Jillian D'Onfro, "Here's a Reminder of Just How Huge Google Search Truly Is," *Business Insider*, March 27, 2016, http://www.businessinsider.com/google-search-engine-facts-2016-3/#first-a-trip-down-memory-lane-heres-what-googles-search-page-looked-like-back-in-1997-1 (accessed May 6, 2017).

Jim Edwards, "Here's the Gaping Flaw in Microsoft's 'Do Not Track' System for IE10," *Business Insider*, August 29, 2012, http://www.businessinsider.com/heres-the-gaping-flaw-in-microsofts-do-not-track-system-for-ie10-2012-8 (accessed May 6, 2017).

John Battelle, "The Birth of Google," *Wired*, August 2005, https://www.wired.com/2005/08/battelle/ (accessed May 6, 2017).

John Letzing, "Google Acknowledges Still Having Contested User Data," *The Wall Street Journal*, July 27, 2012, http://online.wsj.com/article/SB10000872396390443343704577553142360965420.html (accessed May 6, 2017).

Jordan Kahn, "Google: We Do Not Charge Licensing Fees for Android's Google Mobile Services," *9to5Google*, January 23, 2014, http://9to5google.com/2014/01/23/google-we-do-not-charge-licensing-fees-for-androids-google-mobile-services/ (accessed May 6, 2017).

Josh Dreller, "A Brief History of Paid Search Advertising," *Search Engine Land*, January 21, 2010, http://searchengineland.com/a-brief-history-of-paid-search-advertising-33792 (accessed May 6, 2017).

Josh Halliday, "Google's Dropped Anti-Censorship Warning Marks Quiet Defeat in China," *The Guardian*, January 7, 2013, http://www.guardian.co.uk/technology/2013/jan/04/google-defeat-china-censorship-battle (accessed May 6, 2017).

Julia Angwin and Jennifer Valentino-Devries, "Google's iPhone Tracking," *The Wall Street Journal*, February 17, 2012, https://www.wsj.com/articles/SB10001424052970204880404577225380456599176 (accessed May 6, 2017).

Justin Wm. Moyer, "Alphabet, Now Google's Overlord, Ditches 'Don't Be Evil' for 'Do the Right Thing'," *The Washington Post*, October 5, 2015, https://www.washingtonpost.com/news/morning-mix/wp/2015/10/05/alphabet-now-googles-overlord-ditches-dont-be-evil-in-favor-of-do-the-right-thing/?utm_term=.e78075a94584 (accessed May 6, 2017).

Kashmir Hill, "So, What Are These Privacy Audits That Google and Facebook Have to Do for The Next 20 Years?" *Forbes*, November 30, 2011, http://www.forbes.com/sites/kashmirhill/2011/11/30/so-what-are-these-privacy-audits-that-google-and-facebook-have-to-do-for-the-next-20-years/ (accessed May 6, 2017).

Kelly Fiveash, "Google Bets Biennial Privacy Audit after Buzz Blunder," *The Register*, March 30, 2011, http://www.theregister.co.uk/2011/03/30/googlebuzzftcproposedsettlement/ (accessed June 1, 2015).

Kelsey Piper, "Exclusive: Google Cancels AI Ethics Board in Response to Outcry," *Vox*, April 4, 2019, https://www.vox.com/future-perfect/2019/4/4/18295933/google-cancels-ai-ethics-board (accessed August 12, 2019).

Kent German, "A Brief History of Android Phones," *CNET*, August 2, 2011, https://www.cnet.com/news/a-brief-history-of-android-phones/ (accessed May 6, 2017).

Lisa Fleisher and Sam Schechner, "How Google's Top Minds Decide What to Forget," *The Wall Street Journal*, May 12, 2015, http://www.wsj.com/articles/how-googles-top-minds-decide-what-to-forget-1431462018 (accessed May 6, 2017).

Loretta Chao, "Google Tips Off Users in China," *The Wall Street Journal*, June 3, 2012, https://www.wsj.com/articles/SB10001424052702303552104577439840152584930 (accessed May 6, 2017).

Matt McGee, "As Google Analytics Turns 10, We Ask: How Many Websites Use It?" *Marketing Land*, November 12, 2015, http://marketingland.com/as-google-analytics-turns-10-we-ask-how-many-websites-use-it-151892 (accessed August 7, 2019).

Megan Smith, "An Update on Google.org and Philanthropy @ Google," *Google Official Blog*, March 8, 2010, https://googleblog.blogspot.com/2010/03/update-on-googleorg-and-philanthropy.html (accessed August 7, 2019).

Mia Feldman, "UK Orders Google to Delete Last of Street View Wi-Fi Data," *IEEE Spectrum,* June 24, 2013, http://spectrum. ieee.org/tech-talk/computing/networks/uk-orders-google-to-delete-last-of-street-view-wifi-data (accessed May 6, 2017).

Molly Wood, "Sweeping Away a Search History," *The New York Times,* April 2, 2014, https://www.nytimes.com/2014/04/03/technology/personaltech/sweeping-away-a-search-history.html (accessed May 6, 2017).

Morgan Downs (Producer), *Inside the Mind of Google* [DVD], United States: CNBC Originals, 2010

Natasha Lomas, "Google's Unified Privacy Policy Draws Threat of \$15M Fine in the Netherlands," *TechCrunch,* December 17, 2014, http://techcrunch.com/2014/12/17/google-dutch-dpa-privacy-penalty/ (accessed May 6, 2017).

Nicole Perloth, "Under Scrutiny, Google Spends Record Amount on Lobbying," *The New York Times,* April 23, 2012, http://bits.blogs.nytimes.com/2012/04/23/under-scrutiny-google-spends-record-amount-on-lobbying/ (accessed May 6, 2017).

Paul Sawers, "YouTube: We've Invested \$100 Million in Content ID and Paid over \$3 Billion to Rightsholders," *VentureBeat,* November 7, 2018, https://venturebeat.com/2018/11/07/youtube-weve-invested-100-million-in-content-id-and-paid-over-3-billion-to-rightsholders/ (accessed August 7, 2019).

Paul, "FTC Releases Google Privacy Report—Minus the Juicy Details," *The Security Ledger,* October 4, 2012, https://securityledger.com/2012/10/ftc-releases-google-privacy-report-minus-the-juicy-details/ (accessed May 6, 2017).

Peter Economy, "A Google Executive Reviewed More Than 20,000 Resumes—He Found These 5 Stunning Mistakes Over and Over," *Inc.*, July 31, 2019, https://www.inc.com/peter-economy/this-google-executive-reviewed-more-than-20000-resumes-he-found-these-5-stunning-mistakes-over-over.html (accessed August 7, 2019).

Philip Michaels, "10 Helpful Gmail Features (and How to Use Them)," *Tom's Guide,* April 2, 2019, https://www.tomsguide.com/us/new-gmail-features,news-27070.html (accessed August 7, 2019).

Quentin Hardy, "Google Introduces Products that will Sharpen its Ad Focus," *The New York Times*, March 15, 2016, https://www.nytimes.com/2016/03/16/technology/google-introduces-products-that-will-sharpen-its-ad-focus.html (accessed August 7, 2019).

Reuters, "Google Forms \$100 Million Venture Fund," Reuters, March 31, 2009, http://uk.reuters.com/article/2009/03/31/google-fund-idUKN3135783620090331 (accessed August 7, 2019).

Rob Pegoraro, "We Keep Falling for Phishing Emails, and Google Just Revealed Why," *Fast Company,* August 9, 2019, https://www.fastcompany.com/90387855/we-keep-falling-for-phishing-emails-and-google-just-revealed-why (accessed August 12, 2019).

Rolfe Winkler, Alistair Barr, and Wayne Ma, "Google Looks to Get Back into China," *The Wall Street Journal,* November 20, 2014, http://www.wsj.com/articles/ google-looks-to-get-back-into-china-1416527873 (accessed May 6, 2017).

Rose Eveleth, "Google Glass Wasn't a Failure. It Raised Crucial Concerns," *Wired,* December 12, 2018, https://www.wired.com/story/google-glass-reasonable-expectation-of-privacy/ (accessed August 7, 2019).

Ross Brooks, "Workplace Spotlight: What Google Gets Right about Company Culture," *Peakon,* June 28, 2018, https://peakon.com/us/blog/workplace-culture/google-company-culture (accessed August 7, 2019).

Ryan Nakashima, "AP Exclusive: Google Tracks Your Movements, like It or Not," *AP*, August 13, 2018, https://www.apnews.com/828aefab64d4411bac257a07c1af0ecb (accessed August 12, 2019).

Ryan Singel, "Google Busted with Hand in Safari-Browser Cookie Jar," *Wired,* February 17, 2012, https://www.wired.com/2012/02/google-safari-browser-cookie/ (accessed May 6, 2017).

Samuel Gibbs, "European Commission Files Third Antitrust Charge Against Google," *The Guardian,* July 14, 2016, https://www.theguardian.com/technology/2016/jul/14/european-commission-files-third-antitrust-charge-against-google (accessed August 12, 2019).

Sara Forden, Eric Engleman, Adam Satariano, and Stephanie Bodoni, "Can the U.S. Get Its Act Together on Privacy?" *Bloomberg Businessweek,* May 16–22, 2011, 27–28.

Seth Marbin, "GoogleServe 2014: More Opportunities to Give Back Globally," *Google Official Blog,* July 10, 2014, http://googleblog.blogspot.com/2014/07/googleserve-2014-more-opportunities-to.html (accessed May 6, 2017).

Shane Richmond, "Google Responds to European Antitrust Investigators," *The Telegraph,* July 2, 2013, http://www.telegraph.co.uk/technology/google/9371092/Google-responds-to-Europe-antitrust-investigators.html (accessed May 6, 2017).

Shira Ovide, "The Smartphone Revolution Was the Android Revolution," *Bloomberg,* August 6, 2019, https://www.bloomberg.com/graphics/2019-android-global-smartphone-growth/ (accessed August 7, 2019).

Stephanie Strom and Miguel Helft, "Google Finds It Hard to Reinvent Philanthropy," *The New York Times,* January 29, 2011, http://www.nytimes.com/2011/01/30/business/30charity.html (accessed May 6, 2017).

Stephen Shankland, "Google's AI Chips Now Can Work Together for Faster Learning," *CNET*, May 7, 2019, https://www.cnet.com/news/google-ai-chips-tpu-now-work-together-faster-learning-cloud-computing/ (accessed August 7, 2019).

Suzanne Monyak, "Google Changed a Major Privacy Policy Four Months Ago, and No One Really Noticed," *Slate,* October 21, 2016, http://www.slate.com/blogs/future_tense/2016/10/21/google_changed_a_major_privacy_policy_and_no_one_really_noticed.html (accessed May 6, 2017).

Sylvia Tippmann and Julia Powles, "Google Accidentally Reveals Data on 'Right to Be Forgotten' Requests," *The Guardian,* July 14, 2015, https://www.theguardian.com/technology/2015/jul/14/google-accidentally-reveals-right-to-be-forgotten-requests (accessed May 6, 2017).

Taylor Armerding, "Google Play Shares Too Much Personal Info, App Developer Says," *CSO,* February 15, 2013, http://www.csoonline.com/article/2132939/privacy/google-play-shares-too-much-personal-info--app-developer-says.html (accessed May 6, 2017).

Time Inc., "100 Best Companies to Work for," *Fortune,* http://beta.fortune.com/best-companies/ (accessed May 6, 2017).

Tom Fairless, Rolfe Winkler, and Alistair Barr, "EU Files Formal Antitrust Charges Against Google," *The Wall Street Journal,* April 15, 2015, http://www.wsj.com/articles/eu-files-formal-charges-against-google-1429092584 (accessed August 12, 2019).

Tom Krazit, "Google's Chrome Browser Gets Do-Not-Track Feature," *Cnet,* January 14, 2011, http://news.cnet.com/8301-30684_3-20029348-265.html (accessed May 6, 2017).

X, "Projects," https://x.company/projects/ (accessed August 7, 2019).

YouTube, "Policies," https://www.youtube.com/yt/about/policies/#community-guidelines (accessed August 7, 2019).

CVS Smokes the Competition in Corporate Social Responsibility

Introduction

In 1963, brothers Stanley and Sidney Goldstein founded the first Consumer Value Store (CVS) with partner Ralph Hoagland in Lowell, Massachusetts. The original CVS store sold health and beauty supplies. The company became widely successful and grew to include 17 stores during its second year of business. By 1967, CVS began offering in-store pharmacy departments, and in less than a decade, the company was acquired by the retail holding corporation Melville Corporation. This marked the beginning of CVS's expansion across the East Coast through new store openings or mergers and acquisitions. In 1974, CVS reached a major milestone of exceeding $100 million in sales.

As the company grew, they faced intense competition, which they responded to through a differentiation strategy. CVS focused on their core offerings of health and beauty products and began placing stores in shopping malls to generate more foot traffic. This strategy worked well for the company, allowing them to hit $1 billion in sales by 1985. The company celebrated its 25th anniversary in 1988 with 750 stores and $1.6 billion in sales. The acquisition of Peoples Drug, a chain of drugstores based in Alexandria, Virginia, allowed CVS to establish their presence more widely along the East Coast and spurred the launch of PharmaCare, a pharmacy benefit management (PBM) company providing services to employers and insurers. PBMs aid employers in managing healthcare benefit plans and in processing prescriptions. PBMs also have strong negotiating power with drug companies. In 1996, the Melville Corporation restructured, and CVS became independent as a publicly traded company on the New York Stock Exchange (NYSE).

This new surge of investment allowed the company to expand widely across the nation into regions such as the Midwest and Southeast. CVS acquired 2,500 Revco stores, a drug store chain, in 1997. It became the largest acquisition in U.S. retail pharmacy history. With the rise of the internet, CVS seized upon the opportunity to launch CVS.com in 1999 (and Caremark.com after the 2007 acquisition). This became the first fully integrated online pharmacy in the United States. In another first for the U.S. pharmacy retail industry, the company introduced the ExtraCare Card loyalty program in 2001. The company's 40th anniversary in 2003 was marked with increasing westward expansion, 44 million loyalty card holders, and more than 4,000 stores in approximately 30 states. In the following five years, the company's acquisitions allowed CVS to gain leadership in key markets, begin a mail order business, and open its 7,000th retail location. The company would later be rebranded as CVS Health.

The three most important acquisitions in the history of CVS include MinuteClinic walk-in health clinics (in 2005), Caremark Rx, Inc. (in 2007), a PBM company, and healthcare company Aetna (in 2018). To make refills simpler for customers and to compete more effectively against rivals, CVS began introducing new services such as online prescription refills. The company makes more than $194 billion in revenue and has over 9,900 retail locations.

CVS sells products that meet the highest quality standards as well as their own line of products whose specifications and performance are annually tested and reviewed to ensure compliance with applicable consumer safety laws. In addition, the company has instituted a Cosmetic Safety Policy that applies to all of the cosmetic products they sell. CVS employs 295,000 people across 49 states, the District of Columbia, Puerto Rico, and Brazil, and the corporate headquarters are located in Woonsocket, Rhode Island. In a one year period, CVS filled and managed 1.9 billion prescriptions through their PBM and provided services to 92 million PBM members. The company is proud to note its eighth spot on the Fortune 500 list. Today, CVS is one of the largest pharmacies and pharmacy healthcare providers in the United States and is composed of four business functions: CVS Pharmacy, CVS Caremark, CVS MinuteClinic, and CVS Specialty.

The following case will explain some of the legal and ethical challenges CVS has encountered, including a settlement with the Federal Trade Commission (FTC) and the U.S. Department of Health & Human Services (HHS) regarding violations of the Health Insurance Portability and Accountability Act (HIPAA) Privacy Rule, deceptive business practices, and failure to report missing medications. Our examination will also include how CVS responded to such allegations, and how they have worked to redefine the company as a healthcare provider. We will analyze the company's ethical structure, including its decision to stop selling cigarettes, as well as

This case was prepared by Jennifer Sawayda, Yixing Chen, Christine Shields, and Michelle Urban for and under the direction of O.C. Ferrell and Linda Ferrell © 2019. It was prepared for classroom discussion rather than to illustrate either effective or ineffective handling of an administrative, ethical, or legal decision by management. All sources used for this case were obtained through publicly available material and the CVS website.

provide an overview of some criticisms the company has received during its transition. The conclusion offers some insights into the future challenges CVS will likely experience.

Ethical Challenges

Like most large companies, CVS must frequently address ethical risk areas and maintain socially responsible relationships with stakeholders. Although CVS has at times excelled in social responsibility, they have suffered from ethical lapses in the past. The next section addresses some of CVS's most notable ethical challenges, some of which resulted in legal repercussions.

HIPAA Privacy Case

As a company grows and achieves widespread influence, they also inherit a responsibility to act ethically and within the law. In 2009, CVS was accused of improperly disposing of patients' health information. It was alleged that company employees threw prescription bottle labels and old prescriptions into the trash without destroying sensitive patient information, making it possible for the information to fall into public hands. This is a violation of the HIPAA Privacy Rule, which requires companies operating in the health industry to properly safeguard the information of their patients. The allegations prompted investigations by the Office of Civil Rights (OCR) and the FTC, marking the first such instance of a collaborative investigation into a company's practices. These investigations revealed other issues as well, including a failure of company policies and procedures to completely address the safe handling of sensitive patient information, lack of proper employee training on the disposal of sensitive information, and negligence in establishing repercussions for violations of proper disposal methods. This was in spite of the fact that CVS materials reassured clients that their privacy was a top priority for the pharmacy. This claim, in addition to the investigative findings, prompted the FTC to allege that CVS was making deceptive claims and had unfair security practices, both of which are violations of the FTC Act.

CVS settled the case with the U.S. Department of HHS, which oversees the enforcement of the HIPAA Privacy Rule, for $2.25 million. The settlement also mandated that the company implement a corrective action plan with the following seven guidelines: (1) revise and distribute policies regarding disposal of protected health information; (2) discipline employees who violate them; (3) train its workforce on new requirements; (4) conduct internal monitoring; (5) involve a qualified, independent third party to assess the company's compliance with the new requirements and submit reports to HHS; (6) establish internal reporting procedures requiring employees to report all violations of these new privacy policies; and (7) submit compliance reports to HHS for three years.

The company also settled with the FTC by signing a consent order requiring the company to develop a comprehensive program that would ensure the security and confidentiality of information collected from customers. In so doing, the company agreed to a biennial audit from an independent third party. This audit was meant to ensure that CVS's program continued to meet the FTC's security program standards.

Deceptive Business Practices

In addition to privacy challenges, CVS has been accused of deceptive business practices. A 2008 civil lawsuit involving 28 states was filed against the PBM division of CVS, which acts as the prescription drug claim intermediary between employers and employees. It also maintains relationships with drugstores and manufacturers. One of the main allegations of the lawsuit claimed that doctors were urged to switch patients to name brand prescriptions under the notion that it would save them money. Furthermore, these switches were encouraged without informing doctors of the financial burden it would impose on patients, and employer health care plans were not informed that this activity would benefit CVS. This could be seen as a conflict of interest at the expense of customers. Due to these allegations, the suit called for a revision in how the division gives information to consumers. In the end, CVS signed a consent decree without admitting fault and paid a settlement of $38.5 million to reimburse states for the legal costs and patients overcharged due to the switch in prescriptions. In a similar matter, a multi-year-long FTC investigation concluded in 2009 that the company had misled consumers regarding prices on certain prescriptions in one of its Medicare plans. The switch harmed elderly customers who were billed up to 10 times the amount they anticipated. CVS settled with the FTC for $5 million to reimburse customers for the change in price.

Misuse of Prescription Pills

In 2012, CVS faced challenges with another federal agency—the Drug Enforcement Administration (DEA). The DEA suspended the company's license to sell controlled substances at two Florida locations, only a few miles apart from one another. These locations were found to have ordered a total of three million oxycodone tablets in 2011. The average order for a U.S. pharmacy in the same year was 69,000 pills. Intensifying the matter, abuse of narcotics pain medications, especially oxycodone tablets, was prevalent in the area. In fact, some local clinics had become known as "pill mills" for their liberal distribution of prescriptions for pain pills. This prompted the state of Florida to implement legislation responding and attempting to control the rampant misuse and diversion of pain medications.

CVS responded to the DEA's investigation by notifying some of the area doctors that they would not fill prescriptions written for oxycodone (Schedule II narcotics). However, the company also requested a temporary restraining order against the DEA, which would disable the temporary suspension of selling oxycodone. The DEA suspension decreased the amount of such narcotics being distributed to the two CVS locations by 80 percent in a period of three months, limiting their ability to make a profit. When the matter came before a federal judge, he ruled that the company was at fault for lack of proper oversight in distributing oxycodone and other narcotics. The ruling further implied company negligence since such a large number of dispensed pills should have been noticed as a blatant abnormality.

Later that year, the DEA completely revoked the licenses of the two locations to sell controlled substances—the first time this has occurred with a national retail pharmacy chain. CVS claims that they have improved procedures regarding distribution of controlled substances; however, the DEA's claims explicitly assigned negligence on the part of pharmacists in light of obvious "questionable circumstances." These circumstances included the fact that several customers were coming to Florida from out of state to fill prescriptions. Many lacked insurance and paid in cash, red flags that can suggest drug abuse. This was in addition to the heavy prescription drug abuse problem in the area that had already prompted state legislation.

Testimonies from employees indicated company negligence as many had knowledge of the top prescribing doctors in the area and awareness that daily oxycodone quotas were being depleted—sometimes within 30 minutes of the pharmacy opening. Pharmacists also indicated that they set aside pills for those patients they considered to have a real need for them because they had strong suspicions that most of the people purchasing the pills were abusers. They did not feel at liberty to refuse prescriptions to customers, however, because they are not trained to diagnose illnesses. In 2013, CVS announced a review of their database of healthcare providers to find abnormalities in narcotic prescriptions. They found and notified at least 36 providers to whom they would no longer fill orders due to high prescription rates.

In 2014, another incident involving the disappearance of 37,000 pain pills in four California stores brought the DEA and CVS together again. These four stores had a history of not being able to account for several pain prescription drugs. The investigations into missing pills was prompted after the DEA found that an employee had stolen approximately 20,000 pills a few years earlier. This was not the first or last time that CVS stores would be investigated for missing pills. The company paid $1.5 million in fines after some of its Long Island stores did not report missing painkillers in a timely manner.

Two years later, CVS agreed to settle an $8 million claim with the DEA for violation of the Controlled Substances Act in its Maryland pharmacies. CVS faced allegations of dispensing controlled substances pursuant to prescriptions that did not have a legitimate medical purpose. CVS acknowledged that between 2008 and 2012 they dispensed controlled substances, including oxycodone, fentanyl, and hydrocodone, in a manner not compliant with its obligations or with regulations. The District Attorney in the case emphasized that pharmacies have a duty to ensure prescriptions filled are issued for a legitimate medical purpose. He also reminded doctors and pharmacists of the charge to protect against abuse of pharmaceutical drugs for non-medical purposes.

Moving Toward a Healthcare Company

Despite the ethical challenges CVS has experienced, they are trying to reposition themselves as a socially responsible organization that places priority on consumer health. Being a quality healthcare company not only offers reputational benefits but also financial advantages as well. Changes in both the economic and healthcare landscape are creating new opportunities for CVS to provide different programs and redefine themselves. Trends including the declining number of primary care physicians, the 16 million baby boomers who are becoming eligible for Medicare benefits, and the millions of newly insured Americans under the Affordable Care Act (ACA) offer CVS an attractive market in which to expand. For example, CVS has refocused their efforts on supplying the growing need for chronic disease management that consumes costly resources when patients do not adhere to physician-recommended medications and monitoring methods to maintain health. PBM services are being successfully implemented, including mail order, specialty pharmacy, plan design and administration, formulary management, discounted drug purchase arrangements, and disease management services.

Innovative programs such as Pharmacy Advisor and Maintenance Choice, developed in collaboration with researchers from Harvard University and Brigham and Women's Hospital, help patients stay on their medications. Research shows that regular interaction between patients and pharmacists increases the likelihood that patients will adhere to their medication regimen. Many patients who take regular prescriptions often think that they are well enough to cease taking their medication at a certain point. However, when the symptoms of their ailments reappear, the costs are great, both financially and medically. CVS's programs allow the company to inform patients about the benefits and risks of these effects through education and awareness. The entire industry also benefits from this knowledge so that it can be better prepared to help prevent costly medical procedures due to medication non-adherence, which occurs when patients skip or incorrectly take their dosage requirements. This is estimated to cost between $5 and $10 for every $1 spent on adherence programs. These services are key components of CVS's competitive advantage, allowing the company to provide the best possible patient care. CVS was also proactive in preparing patients for Health Care Reform. For instance, CVS partnered with the Centers for Medicare and Medicaid Services to raise awareness about new services available to Medicare patients under the ACA.

To help people keep up with these and other changes in healthcare, CVS has established their presence on social media and mobile devices. The company introduced a mobile application that allows customers to conveniently refill prescriptions, and the company's Facebook and Twitter pages provide helpful health tips. Customers benefit from using CVS's digital tools through increased savings and easier access to many of CVS's services. For instance, the CVS iPad app allows individuals to have a 3D digital pharmacy experience reminiscent of shopping in-store. Customers who are unable to physically visit the store, or prefer the convenience of shopping from home, are able to partake in the CVS experience through the company's technology. As a result, many are saving money and time filling and refilling prescriptions, as well as having instant access to essential drug information.

MinuteClinics are one of the major contributors to CVS's rebranding efforts. These clinics are the first in healthcare retail history to be accredited by the Joint Commission, the national evaluation and certifying agency for healthcare organizations and programs in the United States. This accreditation signifies the clinics' commitment to and execution in providing safe, quality healthcare that meets nationally set standards. In addition to healthcare services, MinuteClinics provide smoking cessation and weight loss programs that contribute positively to people's health. These clinics are also the first retail clinic provider to launch a partnership with the National Patient Safety Foundation for its health literacy program to help improve patient education and community health.

In 2015, CVS announced that it was purchasing Target's 1,672 in-store pharmacies for $1.9 billion. These pharmacies were branded as CVS/pharmacy and remained located in Target stores. This increased CVS's reach, particularly in areas like the Northwest where the company did not have a strong presence. Another benefit of the purchase is that it will increase convenience for consumers who use CVS for their prescriptions as they can now choose from a CVS drugstore or a CVS/pharmacy within a Target location. Target pharmacies have generally received higher customer satisfaction ratings compared to CVS. If CVS can tap into the same practices that Target pharmacies have used to keep their customers satisfied, CVS could use what it learns to adopt a more customer-centric culture that

would provide it with an advantage over rivals such as Walgreens.

Despite CVS's strides in becoming a healthcare company, competition from Walgreens has been gaining. In 2017, Walgreens obtained an advantage in prescription management contracts after the Tricare plan from the Department of Defense signed a deal with Walgreens. This deal did not include CVS pharmacies. Walgreens Boots Alliance also made a deal with PBM Prime Therapeutics to launch a specialty pharmacy and mail services company called AllianceRx Walgreens Prime, further increasing the competitive threat to CVS. However, CEO Larry Merlo claims that CVS is about to implement new drug management programs. Combined with the acquisition of Target's pharmacies, Merlo believes CVS will gain an advantage over Walgreens and become more attractive to patients and pharmacies.

Additionally, CVS is moving beyond MinuteClinic and entering the territory of home healthcare. The company began a clinical trial for a home dialysis HemoCare device in 2019 following a White House announcement of an initiative that encourages at-home dialysis treatment that is less costly. The goal of the initiative is to decrease end-stage kidney disease by 25 percent before 2030 by improving prevention, detection, and treatment of the disease. If the CVS clinical trial shows the device is safe and effective, CVS hopes to win the approval of the Food and Drug Administration (FDA) and become a healthcare provider for people with chronic conditions. This bold step sets CVS apart from other drugstores. This move has the potential to influence the markets for at-home medical devices and kidney care and goes hand in hand with CVS's acquisition of Aetna in 2018.

Aetna Merger

In November 2018, CVS merged with Aetna, a health insurance company, for nearly $69 billion. The belief behind the merger was that a combined company could provide better patient care and tighten cost controls through cooperation. CVS Health described their intentions stating, "As a combined company, we are working to transform the consumer health experience and build healthier communities by offering care that is local, easier to use, less expensive and puts consumers at the center of their care."

The acquisition had many benefits. It provides CVS with more business as the company gains customers on both an individual level and through employers purchasing plans for their employees. The benefit of this merger also allows Aetna customers with chronic illnesses to be referred to walk-in CVS clinics for check-ups rather than expensive and frequent doctor visits. Others believe CVS went forward with the merger because of Amazon's continual threat to the industry. They believe it was a strategic move to prepare for Amazon's increasing involvement in the pharmaceutical industry, such as the possibility that Amazon could begin shipping medications. Overall, CVS's moves indicate that the company wants to ensure that they continue to remain relevant to consumers and grow market share.

However, not everyone saw the positive benefits of the merger. Critics who openly opposed this decision voiced concern that the merger could limit consumers' options and control of medical care as well as result in higher expenses. Critics worried that since the market was already dominated by a few key players, the additional reduced competition would present consumers with limited choices and quality. An advocacy group, Consumers Union, opposed the merger of the two companies and argued that people enrolled at Aetna health clinics could be forced to seek care at CVS retail clinics. Conversely, they believed CVS consumers not insured by Aetna could pay higher prices for their medications. CVS's stock price steadily declined after it closed the Aetna deal due to skepticism among investors. However, CVS believes the "breadth and depth" of the consumer data they now have will be an important component of its success. The company also believes it will be a driving force for change in the U.S. health care system.

The Justice Department ultimately approved the acquisition on the condition that Aetna sell off its private Medicare drug plans business referred to as "Part D." The premise of the condition was to ensure that the combined companies did not control too much of the market. Some critics still argued that the merger would make it difficult for small competitors to enter the market in either sector. Other concerns were raised that CVS's affiliation with the insurer would reduce the transparency necessary to the industry.

Despite the companies operating and identifying as one since November 2018, U.S. District Judge Richard Leon spent months thoroughly reviewing and scrutinizing the merger beginning in June 2019. He wanted to identify and further explore any potential harm the deal could cause for the public and therefore refused to sign off on the merger until further review. This attention aligns with the scrutiny that has been placed on the PBM market as a whole. Leon wished to determine if the consolidation in the highly concentrated market would raise premiums and negatively impact the market. Finally, in September 2019 Judge Leon signed off on the proposed settlement and said it was "within the reaches of public interest" in his opinion.

Tobacco-Free CVS

In order to be consistent with its transition from pharmacy to healthcare company, CVS has made some landmark decisions aimed toward helping individuals lead healthier lives. In 2014, CVS announced that it would no longer sell tobacco products. The company became the first national retail pharmacy to stop selling tobacco products. The revenues generated from selling tobacco products were about $2 billion annually, so this bold decision sent a strong message to stakeholders regarding the values of the company. A company that is consistent in their actions will gain a good reputation, which will attract more customers and generate revenue. This decision also gave CVS an advantage in terms of the ACA. As the ACA changes the healthcare landscape, companies are racing to get a stronghold in the new system to be listed as a preferred pharmacy. CVS's alignment in defining themselves as a healthcare provider will likely result in stronger relationships with doctors and hospitals, creating an advantage of preference. The goal is that referrals for medication will be done through CVS and serve to boost reputation within all CVS segments. This puts CVS in a competitive position to attract newly insured Americans.

The decision to become tobacco-free spurred 24 state attorneys general to send letters to other pharmacy retailers, including Walmart and Walgreens, highlighting the contradiction of selling deadly products and healthcare services simultaneously. The letter also noted that drug store sales make it easier for younger age groups to begin smoking and more difficult for those trying to quit smoking. Walmart and Walgreens acknowledged the letter, but made no indication that they would stop selling tobacco products. While this letter does not seem to have much of an influence on retailers, some speculate that it increases the pressure on the $100 billion tobacco industry, which is already facing decreasing sales, rising taxes, and smoking bans. For CVS, the decision affected its short-term profits and reduced each share by $0.06 to $0.09 each. One year after the decision, CVS released a report of results from studying states where it had greater than 15 percent of the retail pharmacy market share. In the eight months following the elimination of tobacco products, the stores in these states reported approximately 95 million fewer packs purchased and a 4 percent increase in nicotine patches, indicating that CVS's decision was positively impacting smokers.

Criticism Against CVS

CVS's new programs are encroaching on the medical industry by providing services to patients. As customers increasingly choose to visit local pharmacy clinics for aches, pains, or common illnesses, primary physicians are feeling the losses, especially since this sectors' healthcare professionals are dwindling. Choosing a retail pharmacy clinic over a physician's office benefits the patient with lower costs and savings, which is a threat to traditional doctors' offices. Some groups are publicizing negative feedback on pharmacy care. For instance, the American Academy of Pediatrics issued a statement warning patients not to visit such clinics because they cannot offer the specialized care children need. Some groups argue that programs such as CVS's

MinuteClinics do not offer the same caliber of service and care as a doctor. However, as stated above, CVS holds itself to a very high standard for care in trying to help patients be healthy. They continue to be accredited by the Joint Commission.

CVS's MinuteClinics do recognize their limitations, however. Their website offers information to visitors regarding when they should and should not visit the clinics. For example, the website recommends that patients with severe symptoms such as chest pain, shortness of breath and difficulty breathing, poisoning, temperatures above 103 degrees Fahrenheit (for adults) and 104 (for children), and ailments requiring controlled substances should seek care elsewhere. MinuteClinics' staff nurse practitioners and physician assistants generally provide services for minor wounds, common illnesses, wellness tests, and physicals, etc. Other information regarding insurance and pricing are also available on the website.

Stakeholder Orientation

CVS's mission to be a pharmacy innovation company is guided by five values: innovation, collaboration, caring, integrity, and accountability. CVS uses these values to determine their actions and decisions, which offer a glimpse into their ethical culture. The company's goal is to use their assets to reinvent the pharmacy experience and offer innovative solutions that help people follow a better path toward health. This goal relays to stakeholders that the company cares about healthcare. CVS's business is committed to fostering a culture that encourages creativity and innovation, recognizing that contributions from all members are a high priority. This commitment highlights the value placed on collaboration with partners and stakeholders, which also serves to hold the company accountable for its operating activities—thus strengthening its integrity. Another important factor in the company's ethical culture is to address enhanced access to care while also lowering its cost.

CEO Larry J. Merlo emphasizes the long-term perspective the company is committed to with each decision and how it will affect each stakeholder group. He states that CVS's priorities remain in customer health, the sustainability of healthcare systems, good stewardship, positive contributions to communities, and a meaningful workplace for employees. Such a statement from the top leader of the company sets the tone that fosters the ethical culture behind CVS. The company's Code of Conduct includes ethical behavior expectations: CVS employs a Chief Compliance Officer, offers regular compliance education and training, provides an ethics hotline for confidential reporting, and has developed a response and prevention guideline for addressing violations of CVS's policies or federal, state, or local laws. CVS's corporate governance includes a privacy program, information security, and a corporate framework that focuses on the company's values.

So far we have addressed how CVS meets the needs of its customer stakeholders. However, CVS tries to maintain a stakeholder orientation in which all stakeholder needs are addressed. The following sections will describe how the company meets the needs of other stakeholders.

Employees

CVS implemented the Values in Action program for employees, giving them a chance to recognize colleagues through online reward systems. Peers can nominate each other across the company for leadership traits and other commendable accomplishments. Each nomination grants points, which can be redeemed for merchandise, travel, and more. Programs like these let employees know they are valued and empower them in their commitment to CVS. The Values in Action Breakthrough Awards is an annual company-wide broadcast that honors specific individuals exemplifying the company's values in innovation, collaboration, caring, integrity, and accountability.

CVS focuses strongly on compliance and integrity training for employees. The compliance and integrity training for employees is led by a compliance officer. Regular compliance education and training programs, a confidential 24/7 ethics hotline, and an efficient audit, response, and prevention process are components that make this program comprehensive. The company also supports the development of employees through professional development training sessions. The purpose of such training is not only to keep employees current on new technologies and processes but also to help them advance in their careers within the company.

Shareholders

CVS seeks to protect shareholder interests while maintaining broad stakeholder engagement. As a result, CVS carefully designed a comprehensive corporate governance system ranging from board independence to executive compensation. Following a corporate governance framework, a variety of specialized committees have been established with different functions for shareholders. From an information governance standpoint, the oversight committee makes recommendations to enhance the ability of information security. On behalf of the board of directors, the audit committee is in charge of the risk oversight and is responsible for protecting the reputation and core interests of the company.

In order to balance the interests of different groups, senior management created a reformative executive compensation system. This system is based on financial performance as well as service quality and customer satisfaction. While a pay-for-performance compensation system is still utilized at CVS, a significant portion of annual executive compensation is delivered into long-term equity rather than short-term. In a move to further align the commitment of CVS to link pay with performance, total shareholder return is added on a three-year incentive plan. Each three-year period is known as a cycle that has a predetermined set of goals for the company/executive to accomplish. At the end of each term, performance is evaluated and the executive receives compensation based on these results. For example, if the results surpass the goal by 25 percent, the executive pay will increase by a certain predetermined amount. The details will vary for each cycle, but the purpose of the plan is to pay only when the company and its shareholders are benefited from the performance of the executive.

Communities

CVS has grown its ethical culture not only to include the company's functions but also the communities around them. Community engagement and philanthropic endeavors, for example, are long-standing commitments CVS has devoted time and resources toward developing. Community partnerships have supported veteran hiring, scholarships to future pharmacists, and high school, college, and post-graduate students' interest in science, technology, engineering, and math (STEM) careers. CVS believes that by helping to further advancement in providing the best health outcomes, they are investing in their current and future workforce.

CVS donates millions of dollars to various organizations and builds strategic partnerships with them to create an awareness of healthy behaviors and educate the community on ways to become insured under the ACA. For instance, CVS embarked upon a five-year, $50 million initiative to fight against tobacco use. The company also offers free health screenings and flu shots for the uninsured, prescription discount card programs, and other community programs to supply individuals with the medications they need to maintain health. The discount card program saves customers over 70 percent on medications, resulting in millions of dollars in savings every year. Volunteerism is also supported by CVS, as employees are encouraged to form groups and obtain sponsorship from the company to address needs within the communities.

Suppliers

CVS has developed a commitment called Prescription for a Better World, which encompasses its Code of Conduct, Supplier Ethics Policy, Supplier Diversity, and Supplier Audit Program to promote integrity, accountability, and diversity. These programs work to ensure that human rights are respected throughout the entire supply chain. In developing these policies, CVS used principles initiated by the International Labor Organization and the United Nations' Universal Declaration of Human Rights. The human rights framework guides all suppliers of CVS to avoid unethical and illegal practices such as child labor, human trafficking, discrimination, and dangerous workplace conditions.

The Supplier Audit Program is a risk-based assessment conducted by multiple third parties to evaluate workplace conditions, including labor, wages and hours, health and safety, management system and environment, as well as operational, financial, and legal risks, to ensure that employees' rights are not being violated. This program was fully expanded to factories in countries considered to be at high risk for such violations, and CVS is in the process of implementing full social audits for subcontractors in these areas. In addition, CVS works with globally recognized organizations including Worldwide Responsible Accredited Production and Social Accountability International to ensure its measurements are relevant and effective. Finally, CVS became the first healthcare firm to partner with the Responsible Factory Initiative. The partnership will provide tools for CVS's factories and suppliers in identifying risk areas from audits and implementing better compliance systems.

Environmental Impact

Environmental impact is also important to CVS. The company records their progress on this front in its annual Corporate Social Responsibility Report. For instance, CVS has reduced their carbon intensity by 34 percent based on a baseline set in 2010. CVS has opened Leadership in Energy and Environmental Design (LEED) facilities, including a more-than-760,000-square-foot distribution center. The information CVS gains from these facilities will be used to set best practices before constructing other stores.

CVS expanded its Energy Management System (EMS), which is designed to International Organization for Standardization (ISO) specifications. This digital system tracks and manages energy use, so that each store can be continually monitored and adjusted according to each location's needs. CVS is also in the process of upgrading lighting in the stores by including more energy efficient bulbs. Increasing water use was identified as a significant inefficiency, and CVS has responded by eliminating irrigation at retail locations and opting for less water-intensive landscapes. Finally, CVS offers customers ways to recycle and properly dispose of expired, unused, or unwanted medications, which benefit both human and environmental well-being.

Conclusion

CVS is implementing strategies and allocating resources in the hope of achieving an ethical culture that benefits all stakeholder groups. This helps CVS maximize ethical decision-making and remain sustainable. It seems the company has learned from previous ethical lapses by being aware of addiction problems within their communities. As the first national retail pharmacy chain to eliminate cigarettes and other tobacco products, CVS boosted their transition from a pharmacy to a healthcare company, helping their customers lead healthier lives. Also, the merger with Aetna has the potential to transform the healthcare industry by offering easy-to-use, affordable care options, including home healthcare solutions. The company's impact on the environment is one of the next big challenges they will have to overcome. As one of the largest pharmacies in the United States, CVS has a long way to go to reduce their overall footprint. However, the company is on the right track, having set goals and action steps to achieve these goals. With the mission of helping people live healthier lives and innovating the pharmacy industry, CVS has a great responsibility in developing a business model, allowing the company to remain competitive while acting ethically at the same time.

Questions for Discussion

1. How has CVS handled ethical challenges?
2. Evaluate CVS's decision to no longer sell tobacco products.
3. What is the future of CVS in positioning themselves as a health care company based on their decision to be socially responsible?

Sources

Amy Pavuk, "Rx for Danger: DEA Blasts CVS for Ignoring 'Red Flags' at Sanford Stores," *Orlando Sentinel,* October 28, 2012, https://www.orlandosentinel.com/news/os-xpm-2012-10-28os-cvs-dea-oxycodone-ban-20121028-story.html (accessed July 20, 2019).

Amy Pavuk, "Two Sanford Pharmacies Banned from Selling Oxycodone, Controlled Substances," *Orlando Sentinel,* September 12, 2012, https://www.orlandosentinel.com/news/os-xpm-2012-09-12os-sanford-cvs-caremark-revoke-drugs-20120912-story.html (accessed July 20, 2019).

Anna Wilde Mathews, "CVS Begins Clinical Trial for Home-Dialysis Device," *The Wall Street Journal,* July 17, 2019, https://www.wsj.com/articles/cvs-begins-clinical-trial-for-home-dialysis-device-11563364801 (accessed October 21, 2019).

Bruce Japsen, "Amid 'Rebuilding Year,' CVS Drugstore Sales Drop," *Forbes,* May 2, 2017, https://www.forbes.com/sites/brucejapsen/2017/05/02/amid-rebuilding-year-cvs-drugstore-sales-drop/#7ac007f24bdd (accessed May 27, 2017).

Bruce Japsen, "How Obamacare Helps CVS Kick the Habit," *Forbes,* February 2, 2014, http://www.forbes.com/sites/bruce-japsen/2014/02/15/how-obamacare-helps-cvs-kick-the-habit/ (accessed July 20, 2019).

Bruce Japsen, "Walgreens and Blue-Cross Owned PBM Launch New Company," *Forbes,* April 3, 2017, https://www.forbes.com/sites/brucejapsen/2017/04/03/walgreens-and-blue-cross-owned-pbm-launch-new-company/#61c565391ed8 (accessed July 20, 2019).

Chris Isidore, "States to Pharmacies: Stop Selling Tobacco," *CNN Money,* March 17, 2014, https://money.cnn.com/2014/03/17/news/companies/pharmacies-tobacco-ban/index.html (accessed July 20, 2019).

Chris Morran, "CVS Being Investigated after 37,000 Pain Pills Go Missing," *The Consumerist,* March 11, 2014, https://www.kpparx.com/cvs-being-investigated-after-37000-pain-pills-go-missing/ (accessed July 20, 2019).

CVS Health, "A New Path to Better Health," https://cvshealth.com/aetna (accessed July 14, 2019).

CVS Health, "Colleague Volunteerism and Support," https://www.cvshealth.com/social-responsibility/our-giving/local-community-support/colleague-volunteerism-and-support (accessed July 20, 2019).

CVS Health, "Company History," https://www.cvshealth.com/about/company-history (accessed July 20, 2019).

CVS Health, "CVS Caremark Maintenance Choice Program Improves Medication Adherence for US Airways Employees and Dependents," September 15, 2010, https://cvshealth.com/newsroom/press-releases/cvs-caremark-maintenance-choice-program-improves-medication-adherence-us (accessed July 20, 2019).

CVS Health, "CVS Health at a Glance," 2019, https://cvshealth.com/about/facts-and-company-information (accessed July 20, 2019).

CVS Health, "CVS Health Completes Acquisition of Aetna, Marking the Start of Transforming the Consumer Health Care Experience," November 28, 2018, https://news.aetna.com/news-releases/2018/11/cvs-health-completes-acquisition-of-aetna-marking-the-start-of-transforming-the-consumer-health-experience/ (accessed July 20, 2019).

CVS Health, *Prescription for a Better World,* https://www.cvshealth.com/sites/default/files/2016-csr-report.pdf (accessed July 20, 2019).

CVS Health, "Strengthening our Commitment to Ethical Sourcing across our Supply Chain," March 28, 2019, https://cvshealth.com/social-responsibility/corporate-social-responsibility/strengthening-our-commitment-to-ethical-sourcing-across-our-supply-chain (accessed July 20, 2019).

CVS Health, "We Quit Tobacco, Here's What Happened Next," September 1, 2015, https://cvshealth.com/thought-leadership/cvs-health-research-institute/we-quit-tobacco-heres-what-happened-next (accessed July 14, 2019).

CVS Health, *2018 Annual Report* (Woonsocket, Rhode Island: CVS Health, 2018).

CVS Health, *2018 Corporate Social Responsibility Report,* (Woonsocket, Rhode Island: CVS Health, 2018).

CVS Minute Clinic, "Everybody Loves a Quitter," http://www.cvs.com/minuteclinic/resources/smoking-cessation (accessed July 20, 2019).

CVS MinuteClinic, "Quality," http://www.cvs.com/minuteclinic/visit/about-us/quality (accessed July 20, 2019).

CVS MinuteClinic, "Services," http://www.cvs.com/minuteclinic/services/ (accessed July 20, 2019).

Devlin Barrett, "Judge Rules against CVS in Oxycodone Fight," *The Wall Street Journal,* March 13, 2012, https://www.wsj.com/news/articles/SB10001424052702303717304577279871365405382 (accessed July 20, 2019).

Donna Leinwand Leger, "DEA: Oxycodone Orders by Pharmacies 20 Times Average" *USA Today,* February 7, 2012, http://usatoday30.usatoday.com/money/industries/health/story/2012-02-06/dea-cvs-oxycodone-raid/52994168/l (accessed July 20, 2019).

Elisabeth Leamy "Drug Discount Cards Help You Save on Prescription Meds," *ABC News,* August 20, 2012, http://abcnews.go.com/Business/drug-discount-cards-save-money-prescription-meds/story?id=17029498 (accessed July 20, 2019).

Federal Trade Commission, "CVS Caremark Settles FTC Charges: Failed to Protect Medical and Financial Privacy of Customers and Employees; CVS Pharmacy Also Pays $2.25 Million to Settle Allegations of HIPAA Violations," February 18, 2009, http://www.ftc.gov/news-events/press-releases/2009/02/cvs-caremark-settles-ftc-chargesfailed-protect-medical-financial (accessed July 20, 2019).

Hank Cardello, "CVS and the Rise of Corporate Profitable Morality," *Hudson Institute,* February 27, 2014, http://www.hudson.org/research/10138-cvs-and-the-rise-of-corporate-profitable-morality (accessed July 20, 2019).

Health Information Privacy, "CVS Pays $2.25 Million & Toughens Disposal Practices to Settle HIPAA Privacy Case," https://www.hhs.gov/hipaa/for-professionals/compliance-enforcement/examples/cvs/index.html (accessed July 20, 2019).

James P. Miller, "CVS Caremark Settles Deceptive-practices Complaint for $38.5 Million," *Chicago Tribune,* February 15, 2008, http://articles.chicagotribune.com/2008-02-15/business/0802140788_1_cvs-caremark-caremark-rx-pharmacy-benefits (accessed July 20, 2019).

Jessica Wohl, "CVS Cuts Off Docs Who Prescribe Too Many Narcotics," *NBC News,* August 22, 2013, http://www.nbcnews.com/health/health-news/cvs-cuts-docs-who-prescribe-too-many-narcotics-f6C10975693 (accessed July 20, 2019).

Joe Pinsker, "Why CVS Wants to Buy Aetna," *The Atlantic,* December 4, 2017, https://www.theatlantic.com/business/archive/2017/12/cvs-aetna-merger-deal-why/547442/ (accessed July 14, 2019).

Joseph H. Harmison, "CVS Caremark Abuses Warrant through FTC Investigation and Remedies," *The Hill,* May 25, 2010, http://thehill.com/blogs/congress-blog/healthcare/99759-cvs-caremark-abuses-warrant-through-ftc-investigation-and-remedies (accessed July 20, 2019).

Katie Thomas, Chad Bray, and Hiroko Tabuchi, "CVS to Buy 1,600 Drugstores from Target for $1.9 Billion," *The New York Times,* June 15, 2015, https://www.nytimes.com/2015/06/16/business/dealbook/cvs-agrees-to-buy-targets-pharmacy-business-for-1-9-billion.html (accessed July 20, 2019).

Kris Maher and Sara Germano, "CVS Takes Steps on Meth Abuse in West Virginia," *The Wall Street Journal,* July 8, 2014, A3.

Kyle Stock, "Pediatricians Seek Risk-to Kids and Themselves-in Drugstore Health Clinics," *Bloomberg Businessweek,* February 24, 2014, http://www.businessweek.com/articles/2014-02-24/pediatricians-see-risk-to-kids-and-themselves-in-drug-store-health-clinics (accessed July 20, 2019).

Mark Morelli, "Healthy First: CVS Will Stop Selling Cigarettes," *The Motley Fool,* February 7, 2014, https://www.fool.com/investing/general/2014/02/07/healthy-first-cvs-will-stop-selling-cigarettes.aspx (accessed July 20, 2019).

Mike Estrel, "States Urge Retailers to Drop Tobacco," *The Wall Street Journal,* March 18, 2014, B3.

Nathan Bomey, "CVS Launches Rebranding of Target Pharmacy," *USA Today,* February 3, 2016, https://www.usatoday.com/story/money/2016/02/03/target-cvs-health-pharmacy-store/79701130/ (accessed July 20, 2019).

Paul Edward Parker, "Rite Aid Responds to CVS Decision to Stop Selling Tobacco," *Providence Journal,* February 6, 2014, http://www.providencejournal.com/breaking-news/content/20140206-rite-aid-responds-to-cvs-decision-to-stop-selling-tobacco.ece (accessed July 20, 2019).

PRxN, "Understanding What Is a PBM," October 2009, https://www.prxn.com/docs/PRxN%20Understanding%20PBMs.pdf (accessed July 20, 2019).

Rebecca Ballhaus, "Trump Signs Executive Order on Kidney Disease," *The Wall Street Journal,* July 10, 2019, https://www.wsj.com/articles/trump-signs-executive-order-on-kidney-disease-11562778294?mod=article_inline (accessed October 21, 2019).

Rebecca Borison, "CVS/Pharmacy iPad App Mimics In-Store Experience," *Mobile Commerce Daily,* August 14, 2013, http://www.retaildive.com/ex/mobilecommercedaily/cvspharmacy-exec-offering-virtual-store-experience-via-ipad-app (accessed July 20, 2019).

Reed Abelson and Natasha Singer, "CVS Settles Prescription Price Case," *The New York Times,* January 12, 2012, http://www.nytimes.com/2012/01/13/business/cvs-caremark-settles-charges-over-prescription-prices.html (accessed July 20, 2019).

Reed Abelson, "CVS Health and Aetna $69 Billion Merger Is Approved with Conditions," *The New York Times,* October 10, 2018, https://www.nytimes.com/2018/10/10/health/cvs-aetna-merger.html (accessed July 14, 2019).

Sharon Terlep, "CVS, Under Pressure after Aetna Deal, Sets Long-Term Profit Goals," *The Wall Street Journal,* June 4, 2019, https://www.wsj.com/articles/cvs-under-pressure-after-aetna-deal-sets-long-term-profit-goals-11559648940 (accessed August 22, 2019).

Shelby Livingston, "Federal Judge Signs off on CVS-Aetna Merger after Post-Deal Review," *Modern Healthcare,* September 4, 2019, https://www.modernhealthcare.com/mergers-acquisitions/federal-judge-signs-cvs-aetna-merger-after-post-deal-review (accessed October 16, 2019).

Susannah Luthi, "Judge Signals Broad CVS-Aetna Antitrust Concerns," *Modern Healthcare,* https://www.modernhealthcare.com/legal/judge-signals-broad-cvs-aetna-antitrust-concerns (accessed July 14, 2019).

Susannah Luthi, "What to Watch as CVS-Aetna Merger Goes Back to Court," *Modern Healthcare,* June 1, 2019, https://www.modernhealthcare.com/legal/what-watch-cvs-aetna-merger-goes-back-court (accessed July 14, 2019).

Thomas Gryta, "What Is a 'Pharmacy Benefit Manager?'" *The Wall Street Journal,* July 21, 2011, https://www.wsj.com/articles/SB10001424053111903554904576460322664055328 (accessed July 20, 2019).

Timothy W. Martin, "CVS to Kick Cigarette Habit," *The Wall Street Journal,* February 6, 2014, Bl–B2.

United States Drug Enforcement Administration, "DEA Reaches $8 Million Settlement Agreement with CVS for Unlawful Distribution of Controlled Substances," February 12, 2016, https://www.dea.gov/press-releases/2016/02/12/dea-reaches-8-million-settlement-agreement-cvs-unlawful-distribution (accessed July 14, 2019).

Wikinvest, "A Long-Term Incentive Plan," March 24, 2009, http://www.wikinvest.com/stock/CVS_Caremark_Corporation_(CVS)/Long-term_Incentive_Plan (accessed May 27, 2017).

Zachary F. Vasile, "Aetna-CVS Merger to Go Back Before Judge; 5 States Support Approval," *Journal Inquirer,* July 13, 2019, https://www.journalinquirer.com/business/aetna-cvs-merger-to-go-back-before-judge-states-support/article_aa63c4b0-a4d3-11e9-b730-5b38cd9d007c.html (accessed July 14, 2019).

CASE 6

Volkswagen Charts a New Course: The Road to Sustainability

Introduction

Volkswagen (VW) Group is the world's largest automaker in car production with twelve European brands: Volkswagen Passenger Cars, Audi, SEAT, ŠKODA, Bentley, Bugatti, Lamborghini, Porsche, Ducati, Volkswagen Commercial Vehicles, Scania, and MAN. In 2018, VW set an all-time record of delivering more than 10.8 million vehicles, resulting in €235.8 billion (about $262.7 billion) in sales revenue. This placed VW as the ninth largest company in the world. Nearly 40 percent of deliveries were in China, where VW is steadily increasing their share of the passenger car market. The automaker has continued to grow globally despite the diesel emissions scandal that tarnished their image in the United States.

In early 2017, the automaker pled guilty to three criminal felony charges related to defrauding the U.S. government, violating environmental regulations, obstructing justice, engaging in wire fraud, and violating import regulations. The company agreed to pay $2.8 billion in criminal charges—only a small portion of the total costs they will have to pay to resolve this scheme. Other costs include product fixes, legal fees, buy back costs, and more. Worse still, VW's reputation has been dealt such a blow that it will likely take years to recover. As a global firm, VW has lost the trust of regulators, which will be a major obstacle in building future global relationships.

Volkswagen's History

Volkswagen was founded in 1937 by the German government, which was at the time controlled by Adolf Hitler. As his "pet project," he desired to develop an affordable and practical car. In fact, *Volkswagen* translates to "the people's car." Headquartered in Wolfsburg, Germany, the automaker's existence was precarious after Germany was defeated in the war. However, a British major opted to keep Volkswagen open, and the firm continued to grow.

Sales of Volkswagen Beetles were slower in the United States than in other areas because of the company's origin. However, the vehicle's small size and odd shape, which was originally a turnoff for U.S. consumers, became the main selling points in a 1959 campaign. Volkswagen Beetle sales skyrocketed. Soon the Beetle had become the best-selling car import in the United States. When sales began to decline in the 1970s, VW began introducing new generations of cars. They also started making a series of acquisitions, most notably the Bentley and Lamborghini brands in 1998 and the Porsche brand in 2012. VW would continue to sell versions of its iconic Beetle until it was discontinued in 2019.

In the decades since their founding, Volkswagen became a formidable competitor to global carmakers such as Toyota, Ford, and General Motors (GM). Their cars have been widely successful, winning a number of global awards. In 1999, the Volkswagen Beetle was selected as the fourth runner-up for the "Car of the Century," after the Model T, the Mini, and the Citroen DS. In 2015, VW was elected to 43rd place among *Fortune* magazine's "World's Most Admired Companies." Earlier that year, the VW Golf had been named the "North American Car of the Year."

Until recently, VW was highly valued for their sustainability goals. They became the first car manufacturer to adopt ISO 14001 principles, international environmental principles that act as standards for global firms. The company adopted a number of sustainability goals in 2002—a time before sustainability became a hot topic. VW also began investing in vehicles that would reduce carbon emissions early, including electric and diesel vehicles. In 2014, VW introduced the VW XL1, which they claimed to be the most fuel-efficient car in the world at the time. The company's reputation for sustainability was so great that they won an international sustainability award. However, this reputation would soon be sullied by a scandal of large proportions.

The Emissions Scandal

VW's downfall stemmed from the same thing that enabled them to commit such wide-scale misconduct in the first place: technology. Although the impact of technology has created benefits for businesses and consumers alike, it has also provided a greater opportunity to cheat ethical and legal requirements. Volkswagen, once lauded for their eco-consciousness, saw their reputation crumble after

European testers noticed that VW vehicles did not perform as well on emissions testing on the road as they did in the lab. The testers commissioned a team in West Virginia to conduct research on VW vehicles made for Americans because the United States has some

This case was prepared by Jennifer Sawayda for and under the direction of O.C. Ferrell and Linda Ferrell, © 2019. It was prepared for classroom discussion rather than to illustrate either effective or ineffective handling of an administrative, ethical, or legal decision by management. All sources used for this case were obtained through publicly available material.

of the toughest emissions standards in the world. The team in West Virginia used a portable emission system measurement to measure emissions on the road. They found that the measurements did not match up with what was shown in lab tests. The results were reported to the Environmental Protection Agency, which confronted Volkswagen with the evidence. Volkswagen eventually admitted that they had designed and installed a defeat device that could detect when the vehicle was being tested and modify its performance levels so that it would meet emissions requirements. During testing, the software made the vehicles run below performance, which released fewer emissions and met requirements. However, on the road, the cars ran at maximum performance and gave off up to 40 times the allowable limit for emissions in the United States.

Volkswagen estimates that 11 million vehicles in the United States and Europe were affected by this defeat device. Until the scandal broke, VW had promoted themselves as an eco-friendly company. Their commercials featured Volkswagen rally driver and host of *Top Gear USA* Tanner Foust driving elderly women around town in a TDI Volkswagen to dispel the myth that diesel is slow. As a result of their marketing, Volkswagen made large in-roads in gaining acceptance for their clean diesel vehicles, even though many car buyers had a negative view of diesel previously. This green image, which was highly beneficial for Volkswagen as consumers have started to value greener products, was threatened by the scandal.

The Impact

As a result of the scandal, Volkswagen's CEO resigned and governments demanded answers. Such a fraud not only violates ethical standards but also laws and regulations in Europe and the United States. The company agreed to pay more than $25 billion to compensate consumers affected by their defeat devices, which included retrofitting and buying back impacted vehicles. Those who knew about or were responsible for the defeat device's installation could face jail time. One of the executives arrested was VW's emissions compliance manager. Germany also launched a probe into whether former CEO Martin Winterkorn knew about the misconduct beforehand. Winterkorn claimed he did not become aware of the misconduct until the scandal erupted in September 2015. However, the investigation on Winterkorn proved his knowledge of the scandal was much sooner. In April 2019, Winterkorn, along with four others, were indicted on charges of conspiracy, unfair competition, embezzlement, tax evasion, and giving false witness. If convicted, Winterkorn could face up to 10 years in prison and substantial fines, as well as the obligation to return his salaries and bonuses of nearly $12.5 million. His indictment is the largest of any executive in Germany.

The investigation found that Winterkorn was aware of the conspiracy as early as 2014 and failed to report it to regulators or consumers. Prosecutors believe that he played a substantial role in the scandal. The indictment revealed that, in 2014, engineers at Volkswagen realized their illegal emission levels would be exposed through a study report issued by the International Council on Clean Transport. When senior managers were made aware that the report could uncover their deception, they set up a task force to handle official inquiries. Their objective was to be strategic in their responses by concealing their defeat devices while seemingly cooperating with regulators.

The most incriminating evidence leading to the indictment of Winterkorn was proof of documents given to him before the timeline of his initial statement. In late July 2015, Winterkorn received an internal PowerPoint explaining how the deception was occurring in the U.S. and what consequences VW could face as a result. They held meetings where management would discuss the possibilities of being uncovered and the impact it would have on them—one slide was even titled "Indictment?" The investigation revealed that Winterkorn agreed to continue the concealment plan of action outlined in the documents. This occurred over a month before the deception was publicized, proving Winterkorn's claim of ignorance to be false. The U.S. Securities and Exchange Commission (SEC) also charged him with defrauding investors, but it is unlikely he will be extradited by German authorities because of his German citizenship.

The recent charges aimed at these individuals will likely initiate more allegations against the company as a whole. For example, in 2019, the SEC filed a claim that Volkswagen and Winterkorn defrauded investors specifically through selling corporate bonds and asset-backed securities while knowingly making false and misleading statements to government regulators, underwriters, and consumers about the quality of their automobiles and their environmental compliance. The company made these false and misleading claims about their financial position to sell to investors at inflated prices. Volkswagen's concealment and deceit allowed them to benefit from hundreds of millions of dollars through issuing securities at attractive rates. A Volkswagen spokesman contested the SEC claim, stating that the investments were sold to sophisticated investors who were not harmed and who had received all interest and principal payments in full and on time. On the other hand, this recent attention by the SEC is expected to fuel the fire in the class action lawsuit in Germany where Volkswagen investors are seeking $9.2 billion in damages from the fall in share prices when the U.S. sector went public in 2015.

Perhaps the worst impact the scandal has caused is to VW's reputation. Many VW customers claim they purchased the cars because they believed them to be better for the environment and felt utterly betrayed by the company. Consumer rights were violated because consumers did not have accurate information, meaning they were not able to make informed purchasing decisions. VW's reputation for sustainability has been shattered, and two awards they had been given for "Green Car of the Year" were pulled.

VW is not the only company implicated in the conspiracy. U.S. lawyers accuse German parts supplier Robert Bosch GmbH of designing the defeat devices and knowing that they were being installed in VW vehicles to cheat emissions standards. A 2008 email was used as evidence in which Robert Bosch allegedly demanded that VW indemnify the firm for any future legal repercussions, suggesting that the company knew full well that they were violating laws. Germany fined Robert Bosch $100 billion for its participation in the scandal.

VW agreed to plead guilty and pay a criminal fine of $2.8 billion in the United States, as well as additional fines for breaking civil, environmental, customs, and financial regulations. The penalty could have been as high as $34 billion under U.S. laws but was reduced because of VW's cooperation with the investigation. This included a settlement with the Federal Trade Commission (FTC) to allegations that the company had engaged in false advertising by marketing their automobiles as "clean vehicles."

Even after pleading guilty to U.S. charges, VW's troubles are far from over. The EU is conducting its own criminal investigation, and class action lawsuits have been filed against VW in the United Kingdom and Germany. The problem could be even more serious than in the United States because VW vehicles are more common in Europe.

Rebuilding their Reputation

VW has begun to take steps to restore consumer trust. For instance, they recalled vehicles and offered a $1,000 goodwill package to their American car owners. They agreed to curb executive compensation as a result of the scandal. Yet even with incentives, VW will have to face this loss of goodwill for years to come. VW is also taking a different tactic in Europe. Because of less consumer-friendly laws, VW has not been as willing to compensate European drivers for damages. One major reason is that if the company is forced to pay out to the same extent in Europe as it has in the United States, the company may very well go bankrupt. VW is also claiming that under European definitions, their software does not qualify as an illegal defeat device. How other countries in Europe will approach VW in terms of fines depends largely on the countries' laws as well as how many consumers file lawsuits against the firm.

VW has also begun to rebuild their reputation for sustainability. The company sees their investments in electric vehicles (EVs) as a core strength crucial to restoring their brand image and becoming a market leader in energy-efficient vehicles. VW launched the "Electric for All" campaign and intends to release 70 EVs over the next ten years at affordable prices. These vehicles will be based on the modular electric drive matrix (MEB), VW's technology platform for EVs. VW plans to sell its MEB platform to other automakers and is investing $800 million to build an EV plant next to their current plant in Chattanooga, Tennessee. VW's investment in and promotion of EVs to curb the release of harmful greenhouse gases demonstrates a renewed commitment toward sustainability.

Conclusion

VW hopes their settlement with U.S. regulators will be the first step toward putting the scandal behind them. As part of their plea, VW agreed to a three-year probation, a ban on selling diesel vehicles in the United States, and an independent compliance monitor who will oversee VW's operations over a three-year period. However, truly restoring their reputation will require VW to incorporate ethical practices into the organization from the inside-out—something that was severely lacking in the firm's corporate culture prior to the scandal.

Because VW operates in an oligopoly, other global car companies may benefit from the scandal and gain market share from Volkswagen. At the same time, while they might benefit from a competitive standpoint, VW's conduct has caused problems for the industry as a whole. Consumers are now questioning the environmental claims of other car brands, and automakers will have to work harder to prove that their claims are accurate. Consumer trust is easily lost and is not restored overnight. However, if VW's continued interest in EVs proves successful, the company could be well on their way to rebuilding the trust they had spent years cultivating among customers. VW's efforts to become a market leader in energy-efficient vehicles, particularly their investment in affordable EVs, could transform the passenger car market and create the next generation "people's car."

Questions for Discussion

1. Explain how the culture of Volkswagen created this ethical scandal?
2. Since Volkswagen claimed to support ethics and sustainability, how can they recover from this ethical disaster?
3. Do you believe this scandal will lead to tougher scrutiny of companies' environmental claims in the future? Why or why not?

Sources

"Global 500," *Fortune*, 2019 https://fortune.com/global500/2019/ (accessed October 21, 2019).

"Volkswagen Is Founded," *History.com*, July 28, 2019, http://www.history.com/this-day-in-history/volkswagen-is-founded (accessed August 20, 2019).

"Volkswagen Wins International Sustainability Award," July 9, 2013, *CSR EUROPE,* https://www.csreurope.org/volkswagen-wins-international-sustainability-award#.XTODfpNKi9Y (accessed July 20, 2019).

"World's Most Admired Companies 2015: Volkswagen," *Fortune,* 2015, https://fortune.com/worlds-most-admired-companies/2015/search/ (accessed July 19, 2019).

Associated Press, "Auto Parts and Technology Company Bosch Fined $100 Million for Role in the Diesel Emissions Scandal," *MarketWatch,* May 23, 2019, https://www.marketwatch.com/story/auto-parts-and-technology-company-bosch-fined-100-million-for-role-in-the-diesel-emissions-scandal-2019-05-23 (accessed July 20, 2019).

Bertel Schmitt, "It's Official: Volkswagen Is World's Largest Automaker in 2016. Or Maybe Toyota." *Forbes,* January 30, 2017, https://www.forbes.com/sites/bertelschmitt/2017/01/30/its-official-volkswagen-worlds-largest-automaker-2016-or-maybe-toyota/#409806c976b0 (accessed July 20, 2019).

Bloomberg News with E.J. Schultz, "VW's $14.7 Billion Settlement Resolves False Ad Claims," *Advertising Age,* June 28, 2016, http://adage.com/article/news/volkswagen-15-billion-emissions-settlement-includes-ftc-fals-advertising-claims/304733/ (accessed July 20, 2019).

Bourree Lam, "The Academic Paper that Broke the Volkswagen Scandal," *The Atlantic,* September 25, 2015, http://www.theatlantic.com/business/archive/2015/09/volkswagen-scandal-cheating-emission-virginia-epa/407425/ (accessed July 20, 2019).

Chris Woodyard, "Volkswagen Faces Lawsuits over Emissions Deception," *USA Today,* September 22, 2015, http://www.usatoday.com/story/money/cars/2015/09/22/volkswagen-vw-emissions-lawsuits/72604396/ (accessed July 20, 2019).

Daniel Shane, "The SEC is Accusing Volkswagen and Its Former CEO of Massive Fraud," *CNN,* March 15, 2019, https://www.cnn.com/2019/03/15/business/volkswagen-winterkorn-sec-emissions/index.html (accessed July 13, 2019).

David McHugh, "Former Volkswagen CEO Charged with Fraud in Germany," *AP News,* April 15, 2019, https://www.apnews.com/faeff4b8855c4b0daf538599ae3f9db2 (accessed July 20, 2019).

David McHugh, "From Nazis to Hippies: End of the Road for Volkswagen Beetle," *AP News,* July 9, 2019, https://www.apnews.com/53243665f30f4d97a2a292e3c7e76a41 (accessed July 20, 2019).

David Morgan, "West Virginia Engineer Proves to Be a David to VW's Goliath," *Reuters,* September 23, 2015, http://www.reuters.com/article/us-usa-volkswagen-researchers-idUSKCN0RM2D720150924#Cl2HkHXLgPtmsqeF.97 (accessed July 20, 2019).

Jack Ewing, "Ex-Volkswagen C.E.O. Charged with Fraud over Diesel Emissions," *The New York Times,* May 3, 2018, https://www.nytimes.com/2018/05/03/business/volkswagen-ceo-diesel-fraud.html (accessed July 13, 2019).

Jack Holmes, "Volkswagen Will Let Other Companies Use Its MEB Electric-Car Platform," *CNET,* March 6, 2019, https://www.cnet.com/roadshow/news/volkswagen-share-meb-electric-car-platform/ (accessed July 29, 2019).

Jackie Wattles, "Volkswagen Stripped of Two 'Green Car of the Year' Titles," *CNNMoney,* October 1, 2015, http://money.cnn.com/2015/10/01/news/companies/volkswagen-green-car-of-year-awards-rescinded/ (accessed July 20, 2019).

James G. Cobb, "This Just In: Model T Gets Award," *The New York Times,* December 24, 1999, http://www.nytimes.

com/1999/12/24/automobiles/this-just-in-model-t-gets-award.html (accessed July 20, 2019).

Jeff Plungis and Dana Hull, "VW's Emissions Cheating Found by Curious Clean-Air Group," *Bloomberg Businessweek,* September 19, 2015, http://www.bloomberg.com/news/articles/2015-09-19/volkswagen-emissions-cheating-found-by-curious-clean-air-group (accessed July 20, 2019).

Jon Porter, "Ex-VW CEO Charged over Dieselgate, Faces Millions in Fines and 10 Years in Prison," *The Verge,* April 16, 2019, https://www.theverge.com/2019/4/16/18369528/vw-ceo-martin-winterkorn-dieselgate-germany-volkswagen-emissions-scandal (accessed July 13, 2019).

Larry Vellequette, "VW Will Add $800 Million EV Plant in U.S.," *Automotive News Europe,* January 14, 2019, https://europe.autonews.com/automakers/vw-will-add-800-million-ev-plant-us (accessed July 29, 2019).

Mike Spector and Mike Colias, "Volkswagen Faces Up to Penalties," *The Wall Street Journal,* March 1–12, 2017, B1–B2.

Paul Argenti, "The Biggest Culprit in VW's Emissions Scandals," *Fortune,* October 13, 2015, http://fortune.com/2015/10/13/biggest-culprit-in-volkswagen-emissions-scandal/ (accessed July 20, 2019).

Peter Valdes-Dapena, "VW Is Creating an Electric Future. This Is What It Looks Like," *CNN,* April 30, 2019, https://www.cnn.com/2019/04/30/success/vw-id-electric-cars/index.html (accessed July 29, 2019).

Reuters, "Lawyers Say Robert Bosch Covered Up Volkswagen's Emissions Scheme," *Fortune,* September 7, 2016, http://fortune.com/2016/09/07/robert-bosch-volkswagen-emissions/ (accessed July 20, 2019).

Roger Parloff, "How VW Paid $25 Billion for 'Dieselgate' – and Got Off Easy," *Fortune,* February 6, 2018, https://fortune.com/2018/02/06/volkswagen-vw-emissions-scandal-penalties/ (accessed July 20, 2019).

Russell Hotten, "Volkswagen: The Scandal Explained," *BBC News,* November 4, 2015, http://www.bbc.com/news/business-34324772 (accessed July 20, 2019).

Sam Abuelsamid, "Does VW Diesel Cheating Threaten Consumer Trust of Automotive Software?" *Forbes,* October 21, 2015, http://www.forbes.com/sites/pikeresearch/2015/10/21/vw-diesel/ (accessed July 20, 2019).

Samuel Rubenfeld, "The Morning Risk Report: VW Executive's Arrest Stirs Compliance Liability Concern," *The Wall Street Journal,* January 10, 2017, https://blogs.wsj.com/riskandcompliance/2017/01/10/the-morning-risk-report-vw-executives-arrest-stirs-compliance-liability-concerns/ (accessed July 20, 2019).

Sarah Griffiths, "The Most Fuel-Efficient Car in the World: Volkswagen XL1 Does 300 MILES to the Gallon (And It Looks Cool Too)," *Daily Mail,* January 16, 2014, http://www.dailymail.co.uk/sciencetech/article-2540618/The-fuel-efficient-car-world-Volkswagen-XL1-does-300-MILES-gallon-looks-cool-too.html (accessed July 20, 2019).

Sarah Sloat, "Volkswagen to Offer $1,000 Package to U.S. Customers Hit by Emissions Scandal," *The Wall Street Journal,* November 9, 2015, http://www.wsj.com/articles/volkswagen-to-offer-1-000-package-to-u-s-customers-hit-by-emissions-scandal-1447088254?alg=y (accessed July 20, 2019).

Sonari Glinton, "How a Little Lab in West Virginia Caught Volkswagen's Big Cheat," *NPR,* September 25, 2015, http://www.npr.org/2015/09/24/443053672/how-a-little-lab-in-west-virginia-caught-volkswagens-big-cheat (accessed April 15, 2017).

Steve Innskeep, "The Volkswagen Scandal and Germany's Reputation," *NPR,* October 1, 2015, http://www.npr.org/2015/10/01/444912600/the-volkswagen-scandal-and-germanys-reputation (accessed July 20, 2019).

The U.S. Department of Justice, "Volkswagen AG Agrees to Plead Guilty and Pay $4.3 Billion in Criminal and Civil Penalties; Six Volkswagen Executives and Employees Are Indicted in Connection with Conspiracy to Cheat U.S. Emissions Tests," January 11, 2017, https://www.justice.gov/opa/pr/volkswagen-ag-agrees-plead-guilty-and-pay-43-billion-criminal-and-civil-penalties-six (accessed July 20, 2019).

Theo Leggett, "How VW Tried to Cover up the Emissions Scandal," *BBC,* May 5, 2018, https://www.bbc.com/news/business-44005844 (accessed July 13, 2019).

Tim Bowler, "Volkswagen: From the Third Reich to Emissions Scandal," *BBC,* October 2, 2015, http://www.bbc.com/news/business-34358783 (accessed July 20, 2019).

Volkswagen, "Mobility and Sustainability: Eco Logical," *Internet Archive WayBack Machine,* https://web.archive.org/web/20110226110727/http://www.volkswagen.com/vwcms/master_public/virtualmaster/en2/unternehmen/mobility_and_sustainability0/management___daten/management_und_verantwortung/Umweltziele.html (accessed July 20, 2019).

Volkswagen, "Modular Electric Drive Matrix (MEB)," https://www.volkswagen-newsroom.com/en/modular-electric-drive-matrix-meb-3677 (accessed July 29, 2019).

Volkswagen, "Volkswagen Group Annual Report 2018," https://annualreport2018.volkswagenag.com (accessed October 21, 2019).

Volkswagen, "Volkswagen Group China Achieves Sales Record in 2018," January 11, 2019, https://www.volkswagenag.com/en/news/2019/01/VW_China_deliveries_2018.html (accessed October 21, 2019).

Volkswagen, "World Premiere of the Modular Electric Drive Matrix—Volkswagen Announced ELECTRIC FOR ALL Campaign," September 2018, https://www.volkswagenag.com/en/news/2018/09/Uncompromising_e-mobility.html (accessed July 29, 2019).

William Boston, "Volkswagen Ex-CEO Faces Fresh Fraud Charges Over Emissions Scandal," *The Wall Street Journal,* April 15, 2019, https://www.wsj.com/articles/volkswagen-ex-ceo-faces-fresh-fraud-charges-over-emissions-scandal-11555336463 (accessed July 13, 2019).

William Wilkes, "Volkswagen Adds to Scandal Cost," *The Wall Street Journal,* February 2, 2017, B3.

CASE 7

Wells Fargo Banks on Recovery

Introduction

Until 2016, Wells Fargo was the world's largest bank. In 2015, they surpassed the Industrial and Commercial Bank of China with the highest market capitalization in the world. Wells Fargo topped the list of most valuable banking brands. Their victory was short-lived, however, as JPMorgan Chase overtook Wells Fargo in 2016 in the wake of a large-scale cross-selling scandal that revealed Wells Fargo employees faked 3.5 million customer accounts to meet short-term sales goals. Approximately 5,300 employees were fired, and the bank was slapped with a $185 million fine by the Consumer Financial Protection Bureau (CFPB), which claimed the firm had opened up or applied for 2.1 million customer bank or credit card accounts without permission from customers. The misconduct allegations did not stop there. Less than two years later, the CFPB fined Wells Fargo $1 billion for charging customers for car insurance they did not need and levying unfair mortgage fees on borrowers.

The issue was further compounded by a corporate culture that seemed to know of and even encourage these illicit activities. Wells Fargo quickly became the poster boy for financial misconduct as their stock price dropped. Customer and government trust in the firm hit an all-time low. In addition to the millions of dollars Wells Fargo will pay to clean up the scandal, new customer checking accounts and credit card applications plummeted. Executives were unsure whether the bank would ever achieve the growth they had attained prior to the scandal.

This case breaks down the Wells Fargo scandal to examine the decisions that contributed to the misconduct and the participants in the fraud. It also looks at Wells Fargo's corporate culture and demonstrates how it led to a toxic unethical environment that encouraged illicit behavior. The immediate aftermath of the scandal is also discussed, as well as what alternatives Wells Fargo faces as they strive to restore their reputation. Whatever course they choose, Wells Fargo must integrate ethical practices and principles into their operations to avoid similar misconduct in the future.

The History of Wells Fargo

Wells Fargo has a long and lucrative history spanning over 150 years. In 1852, Henry Wells and William Fargo joined other investors to form the financial services company Wells Fargo & Co. The first two offices were opened in San Francisco and Sacramento, California, later that year. Wells Fargo became emblematic of the American West after they helped finance the Butterfield Line and assumed control of the Pony Express. In 1866, Wells Fargo began acquiring stagecoach routes all across the West. The red-and-yellow stagecoach would become the iconic corporate logo recognizable by consumers worldwide.

One achievement Wells Fargo is particularly proud of is their early emphasis on diversity. Within decades of their founding, Wells Fargo was printing financial information in Spanish and Chinese to reach a diverse customer base. In 1888, the firm adopted rules that advocated for the equal treatment of all customers, no matter their race, social status, or gender. This reputation for diversity would continue into the twenty-first century, with Wells Fargo securing 13th place on *DiversityInc*'s "Top 50" diverse companies in 2019. More than 30 percent of all director nominees are women and 25 percent are racial or ethnic minorities. Wells Fargo was the first large-scale bank to be chaired by a woman in the United States.

Over the next century, Wells Fargo was an early mover in adopting many innovative financial banking tools, including credit cards, bundled checking, ATMs, and access to online account information. Their success and innovative services allowed them to weather the Great Recession while other banks struggled or went out of business. In 2008, Wells Fargo acquired Wachovia Corp. for more than $15 billion, increasing their number of locations to 10,000. Wells Fargo's business, and their reputation, continued to grow. In 2016, Wells Fargo was listed 25th among *Fortune*'s "Most Admired Companies," scoring particularly high on financial soundness, social responsibility, and product quality. However, none of these positive achievements were enough to prevent the massive loss of consumer confidence in Wells Fargo's integrity after the massive fake accounts scandal came to light.

Fake Accounts Scandal

September 2016 marked the unfolding of the Wells Fargo entanglement in a widespread scandal that would implicate several high-level executives and thousands of employees. On September 8, the CFPB, the Los Angeles City Attorney, and the Office of the Comptroller of Currency levied a massive $185 million fine against Wells Fargo, claiming the firm had opened up or

This case was prepared by Kimberly Thuman and Jennifer Sawayda for and under the direction of O.C. Ferrell and Linda Ferrell © 2019. It was prepared for classroom discussion rather than to illustrate either effective or ineffective handling of an administrative, ethical, or legal decision by management. All sources used for this case were obtained through publicly available material and the Wells Fargo website.

applied for more than 2 million customer bank or credit card accounts without permission from the customers. Furthermore, a bank official acknowledged that the company had terminated more than 5,300 employees in relation to the allegations. Wells Fargo released a statement taking responsibility for the debacle.

Five days following the initial outbreak, the bank announced that it would be ending their employee sales goals program, effective January 1, 2017. Subsequent investigations revealed that controversial sales goals most likely encouraged employees to open accounts without customers' permission and knowledge. Employees had continually engaged in fraudulent activities such as opening up fake bank accounts and falsifying signatures to satisfy sales goals and earn financial rewards under the bank's incentive compensation program. The CFPB claimed Wells Fargo imposed such goals on staff to become the leader in "cross-selling" banking products. In other words, employees were given incentives for selling customers additional products. While offering incentives for additional selling is certainly not unusual, evidence shows that Wells Fargo had unrealistic sales goals and did not have systems in place to ensure employees were actually engaging in selling. Many Wells Fargo employees had adopted the teleological perspective that the ends (higher incentives) justified the means (fraudulent activity).

A day after the bank announced they would eliminate its incentive program, the Federal Bureau of Investigation and federal prosecutors in New York and California began probing the bank over the alleged misconduct, which opened the door to possible criminal charges. By September 20, Wells Fargo's Chief Executive, John Stumpf, appeared in front of the Senate Banking Committee, where Senator Elizabeth Warren called on him to resign and said he should face criminal charges. Furthermore, Senator Bob Corker claimed Stumpf would be engaging in "malpractice" if the bank did not "claw back" money that the company had paid to executives during the period the accounts were being opened without customers' permission. The rest of the month would put Wells Fargo through investigations, numerous lawsuits, employee and consumer backlash, and lengthy lectures from both political parties. October 12, over a month following the initial break of the scandal, marked the retirement of the CEO and Chairman Stumpf, effective immediately.

Tim Sloan, an employee of the company for 29 years, took over as CEO in October 2016. Sloan was quoted as saying that Wells Fargo's biggest priority would be reestablishing customer trust in the bank. The bank's attempt to reestablish trust occurred almost immediately. Wells Fargo began running an advertisement campaign on October 24 that was evocative of their long history in serving banking customers. The ads featured the company's signature horse-drawn carriage motif and pledged to address customer concerns. However, investigations continued. By November, Wells Fargo

disclosed in regulatory filings that the U.S. Securities and Exchange Commission (SEC) was investigating their sales practices. Additionally, the U.S. Department of Justice, congressional committees, California state prosecutors, and attorneys general were also making formal inquiries into the bank's practices. At the crux of the investigations was one question that still needed to be answered: what caused such a well-known, popular bank to engage in such blatant misconduct?

Sloan's tenure was rocky, as revelations of additional misconduct led regulators to place restrictions on the bank. Sloan was criticized by many for being an insider. Senator Warren said on Twitter that Sloan "enabled Wells Fargo's massive fake accounts scam" and profited from it. Though Sloan and other Wells Fargo executives, including Mary Mack, head of consumer banking, claimed the company's culture was improved, several employees told *The New York Times* that high performance goals still plagued the bank. Sloan announced his retirement less than three years after assuming the position.

The Decision-Makers

Though Wells Fargo was accused of opening more than 2 million fake customer accounts beginning in 2011, managers at Wells Fargo claim these same practices had occurred long before then. Susan Fischer, a former Wells Fargo branch manager who worked at the bank for five years starting in 2004, joined almost a dozen Wells Fargo workers to confirm that these shocking sales tactics that encouraged employees to open unauthorized accounts had been around much longer than bank executives have acknowledged. A letter to the CEO was recovered from 2007 describing how employees were opening up fake accounts and forging customer signatures. CEO Stumpf claims he never received these letters. However, several employees came forward to claim that they reported the misconduct and had their employment terminated as a result. If true, the misconduct takes on a more sinister turn. Not only were executives aware of the misconduct, but anyone who protested was punished as a result. This would also directly violate laws that protect whistleblowers from retaliation.

Although the employees themselves were the ones who made the ultimate decision to engage in fraudulent behavior, it is worth examining the corporate culture to determine why so many chose to do so. It soon became clear that Wells Fargo had established aggressive cross-selling sales quotas that employees must meet or risk being fired. What started off as a legitimate sales strategy became increasingly coercive as employees began to take shortcuts to meet sales goals and keep their jobs.

To reach their lofty sales goals, Wells Fargo also set up incentives to engage employees, which increased commissions around the product being emphasized. These products were cross-sold to customers with an aggressive sales incentive program tied to employee compensation. This incentive program suggests that Wells Fargo executives, managers, and employees forgot that a bank's reputation is built on a basic cultural value of trust. Rather, they falsely became a leader in the banking industry through the utilization of unrealistic sales goals. With the desire to become a leader in the industry through achieving unrealistic sales goals, management became the relevant decision-maker responsible for setting up a system that encouraged misconduct. Managers at many branches played a large role in the establishment of unauthorized accounts.

Yet, the responsibility for the misconduct stemmed even further up the organization. After all, if the managers' branches did not meet these new goals, not only could employees be terminated, but the managers as well. Although employees opened the accounts and managers implemented procedures to ensure goals were met, it was the high-level executives who initially set the goals that are the most relevant decision-makers in this ethical dilemma. These executives were faced with the challenge of finding new ways to distinguish the bank as the leader in the banking industry. To do so, Wells Fargo executives made the decision to establish the sales of simple-to-understand, simple-to-use products such as credit and debit cards, coupled with traditional banking services such as car and home loans. These products were then cross-sold to customers with an aggressive sales incentive program. Once Wells Fargo branch employees realized they could not reach the high-set goals, many began opening unauthorized accounts so it would look like they were meeting these goals. In so doing, they betrayed the trust of their customers.

Relevant Ethical Values

The scandal had a far-reaching impact on Wells Fargo. The banking and financial services industry depends on a public perception of trustworthiness for its success. Due to public perception and weight on credibility, arguably the scandal could be more destructive to Wells Fargo than a business in a different industry. While, ultimately, the underlining goal for banks is to make a profit, the financial services industry has a duty to manage their clients' assets responsibly. Thus, when a bank puts the company's interests above the interests of its depositors, consumer trust rapidly shatters.

The scandal also cast significant doubt as to whether Wells Fargo believed in the vision and values they claimed to hold so dear. The illicit activities directly conflicted with Wells Fargo's publicly expressed Vision and Values, which states that Wells Fargo strives to set "the standard among the world's great companies for integrity and principled performance," and goes as far to express, "We value what's right for our customers in everything we do." This underlying value of honest business practices comes into direct conflict with the

Wells Fargo scandal. Ultimately, the acts undertaken by Wells Fargo were not only unethical, but they were also highly illegal, opening Wells Fargo up to the possibility of criminal charges. While setting goals is a legitimate business practice, senior management failed to communicate the appropriate sales practices expected. Even worse, their failure to make sure employees were using appropriate practices seems to indicate an attitude of ethical indifference on the part of top leadership. Senior management's lack of communication and their lack of action in making sure sales goals were reasonably achievable led branch employees to deal with company pressures in ways that would save jobs—even if it meant engaging in illegal behavior. These activities clearly compromised Wells Fargo's value of honesty and the importance of their clients' trust.

The facts point to a cultural failing on behalf of Wells Fargo's senior management. It was senior management that fostered a culture in which lying was acceptable. Over a long-term period, Wells Fargo issued credit cards without customers' authorization, misusing the concept of assumed consent. Assumed consent occurs when customers imply consent through their actions or lack of actions, even if they do not consent verbally. There was no such consent in this case. In fact, customer signatures were often forged, making these activities an obvious example of fraudulent behavior.

Bank customers felt deceived. The bank reported that checking account openings had fallen 43 percent and credit card applications 55 percent from the year before. The situation worsened in 2017 when the bank discovered 1.4 million more fake accounts, bringing the total number of fake accounts to 3.5 million. Since the Great Recession, the financial services industry has been struggling to recoup lost trust. The Wells Fargo scandal will likely not only affect their own business but could also impact the level of trust for the entire industry.

Auto Insurance and Home Loan Scandal

Wells Fargo's woes were far from over after the fake accounts scandal. Further investigation revealed misconduct in the firm's auto insurance and mortgage businesses. The company charged many borrowers late fees for not meeting deadlines to lock in interest rates. The problem is that the delays were caused by the bank, not the customer. The company had also charged customers for a type of car insurance called collateral protection insurance without their knowledge. Some of these customers had their cars repossessed for not making their payments. A lawsuit filed against the firm alleged that executives, including those in the general counsel, risk, and auditing areas, had known about the scheme and its negative impact for four years before Wells Fargo ended the program in 2016.

Wells Fargo agreed to refund mortgage customers who paid unfair mortgage fees during the period of September 2013 to February 2017. It also said it would refund 570,000 customers who were charged auto insurance they did not need. The CFPB charged Wells Fargo with a $1 billion fine, the largest penalty levied by the organization to date.

This additional scandal demonstrates that once unethical behavior is deemed acceptable within an organization, misconduct can easily snowball to encompass all areas of the company. In the case of Wells Fargo, the seeming complacency of executives and results-oriented incentives programs provided a culture that rewarded employees for unethical behavior. The system caused the misconduct to propagate until Wells Fargo ended up with more than $1 billion in fines, serious reputational damage, and a massive loss of confidence by regulators, customers, and employees.

The Future for Wells Fargo

For years, Wells Fargo enjoyed a reputation for sound management. Their reputation was so intact that they emerged from the 2008–2009 financial crisis with one of the best reputations of any of the major retail banks. Wells Fargo sidestepped many of the errors of other banks and prospered on meaningful customer relations with a focus on sales. Yet, today, the bank finds their reputation tarnished thanks to unrealistic sales quotas and a coercive corporate environment. Even worse, sources claim that top executives were aware of these practices years ago, but instead of taking action, they retaliated against whistleblowers for speaking up.

Once Wells Fargo's illegal practices had been discovered internally, the company could have worked to amend these practices, re-emphasize their corporate values, and begin restoring trust with customers. Reporting the misconduct early might have actually enhanced Wells Fargo's reputation as it would have shown the bank had no tolerance for unethical behavior whenever it was discovered. Greater senior management involvement and alignment with the values and mission statement of the company would have allowed Wells Fargo to make necessary changes to avoid ensuring scandals. Instead, Wells Fargo embraced short-term gains such as increased revenues and incentives even when it resulted in illegal activity and customer harm. By adopting such stringent and ambitious goals—and punishing employees who were unable to meet them in a legitimate manner—Wells Fargo also destroyed relationships with their employees.

Charles Sharf joined Wells Fargo as CEO in October 2019 to help the bank continue their recovery from the scandal. Sharf, who has experience in the banking industry at Bank of New York Mellon Corp. and Visa Inc., is an outsider, unlike both Stumpf and Sloan who were promoted from within. Sharf plans to get to know the bank's strategies better before implementing changes, though his priority is to address regulatory issues as quickly as possible. He will need to find a way to tackle revenue declines and cut costs with the ultimate goal of regaining market share from rivals such as Bank of America and JPMorgan Chase. Sharf wrote to Wells Fargo employees, "We have the foundation to again be the most respected bank in the U.S. and the world." This foundation will require Sharf to build an ethical culture that avoids the misconduct that continues to damage the reputation of the Wells Fargo brand.

Resolution

With the above considered, it is no surprise that Wells Fargo is struggling to keep customers. Despite taking credit for the scandal, having the CEO step down, and implementing marketing campaigns targeted at rebuilding consumer trust, Wells Fargo's business practices have been compromised in the eyes of both the government and consumers. In 2018, the Federal Reserve barred Wells Fargo from growing their asset size any further than their 2017 level until the company remedies the issues that have plagued them over the past few years.

In addition to government restrictions, former Wells Fargo employees have filed lawsuits against the firm. In one lawsuit, Wells Fargo was forced to rehire an employee and pay $5.4 million. The whistleblower claimed he was fired after calling the company's ethics hotline to report suspected misconduct. Former CEO Stumpf was forced to pay back millions in compensation for allegedly turning a "blind eye" to the misconduct. The level of misconduct was so great that the Federal Reserve Board accused Wells Fargo's board of directors of failing in their duties to ensure effective oversight over the company.

Ultimately, the stakeholders injured in this situation were the individuals who were victims of the creation of fake accounts, the stockholders, and the employees convicted of fraud. Wells Fargo chose to adopt a short-term perspective and abandoned a deontological approach for the temporary gains that came with committing fraud. Deontology focuses on the means used to achieve an end rather than the end itself. According to deontological moral theory, the means of attaining a certain outcome are just as important morally as the outcome itself. If Wells Fargo executives and managers had prioritized *how* employees were making their sales goals, then they would have detected the fraud sooner and taken steps to correct it.

Wells Fargo had a duty to their customers and employees to operate in an ethical manner, but the company allowed lofty sales goals to get in the way of ethical business practices. The company also had a duty to their depositors to manage accounts honestly rather than opening fake accounts without depositors' knowledge. Moreover, Wells Fargo had a duty to their employees to create an environment where sales goals could be met without employees taking matters into their own hands. Instead, whistleblowers are now coming forward to say they were punished for speaking up, which likely created a strong culture of distrust with employees and kept the misconduct hidden. While the company valued their position as a top retail bank in the United States, deontology states that Wells Fargo's duty to their stakeholders carried significantly more weight than meeting sales goals.

Bouncing Back from the Brink

Wells Fargo is determined to restore their reputation. After the scandals, the company went through a massive restructuring program. They reduced management levels and developed a strategic execution and operations unit to work with regulators. Wells Fargo reorganized their commercial banking division by combining their business, government and institutional, and middle-market banking organizations into one group. Wells Fargo believes this newly restructured division will allow the company to focus more on customers and specific target markets.

Wells Fargo also restructured their wholesale banking line (of which the commercial banking division is a part) in the hopes of creating a more simplified, relationship-oriented customer service environment. As part of their customer-centered focus, and to reduce the "silos" that might have contributed toward Wells Fargo's wide-scale misconduct, Wells Fargo is also reducing the number of regions their 12,000 financial advisors work within from 21 to 14. Management hopes this reduction will allow advisors to develop stronger relationships and serve their customers more quickly and efficiently. Although it is too early to tell how successful Wells Fargo will be in their efforts, a renewed focus on customers and cooperation with regulators could be the first steps toward rebuilding the bank's staggering reputation.

Conclusion

Going forward, Wells Fargo must put their duty to stakeholders above the company's aim to make short-term gains. Taking a more long-term, ethical approach would not only benefit the company's stakeholders but also the firm itself. Since the banking industry is built on trust, Wells Fargo has a duty to maintain that trust with depositors and employees even if it means sacrificing some profits in the short-term. Developing a strong ethical culture that is intolerant of misconduct will not only allow Wells Fargo to avoid future scandals, but it will also allow the company to rebuild trust over time. Thoroughly embracing their ethical values will help Wells Fargo regain trust among regulators, consumers, and employees. Until Wells Fargo fully embraces their duties, the company will struggle to put the scandals behind them. Wells Fargo must adopt a renewed focus

on their stakeholders to repair the shattered trust and rebuild their reputation.

Questions for Discussion

1. How did Wells Fargo's focus on short-term gains violate the duties they owed to consumers, regulators, and employees?
2. Describe how the Wells Fargo scandal demonstrates that organizational leaders must not only establish goals but ensure that those goals are being acted upon appropriately.
3. Why are ethical values useless unless they are continually reinforced within the company?

Sources

"Wells Fargo (WFC) to Overhaul Commercial Banking Business," *Yahoo! Finance*, June 6, 2019, https://finance.yahoo.com/news/wells-fargo-wfc-overhaul-commercial-105210513.html (accessed August 1, 2019).

"World's Most Admired Companies," *Fortune*, 2016, https://fortune.com/worlds-most-admired-companies/2016/search/?sector=Financials (accessed August 1, 2019).

Adam Shell, "Wells Fargo Fined $1 Billion by Regulators to Settle Auto-Loan, Mortgage Abuses," *USA Today*, April 20, 2018, https://www.usatoday.com/story/money/2018/04/20/wells-fargo-fined-1-billion-auto-loan-mortgage-abuses/535534002/ (accessed August 2, 2019).

Bill Chappell, "Wells Fargo Hit with $1 Billion in Fines Over Home and Auto Loan Abuses," *NPR*, April 20, 2018, https://www.npr.org/sections/thetwo-way/2018/04/20/604279604/wells-fargo-hit-with-1-billion-in-fines-over-consumer-abuses (accessed August 2, 2019).

Bloomberg News, "Wells Fargo Now Plans to Operate Under Growth Ban through 2019," *American Banker*, January 15, 2019, https://www.americanbanker.com/articles/wells-fargo-now-plans-to-operate-under-growth-ban-through-2019 (accessed August 1, 2019).

Brian Tayan, "The Wells Fargo Cross-Selling Scandal," *Harvard Law School Forum on Corporate Governance and Financial Regulations*, December 19, 2016, https://corpgov.law.harvard.edu/2016/12/19/the-wells-fargo-cross-selling-scandal/ (accessed August 1, 2019).

Bruce Kelly, "Wells Fargo Advisors Looks to Cut Red Tape for Advisors in Reorganization," *Investment News*, May 1, 2019, https://www.investmentnews.com/article/20190501/FREE/190509992/wells-fargo-advisors-looks-to-cut-red-tape-for-advisers-in (accessed August 1, 2019).

Curtis C. Verschoor, "Lessons from the Wells Fargo Scandal," *Strategic Finance*, November 1, 2016, http://sfmagazine.com/post-entry/november-2016-lessons-from-the-wells-fargo-scandal/ (accessed August 1, 2019).

DiversityInc, "No. 13 | Wells Fargo," https://www.diversityinc.com/wells-fargo/ (accessed August 1, 2019).

Donna Borak and Danielle Bronner-Wiener, "Wells Fargo Will Be Fined $1 Billion," *CNN*, April 19, 2018, https://money.cnn.com/2018/04/19/news/companies/wells-fargo-regulators-auto-lending-fine/index.html (accessed August 2, 2019).

Emily Flitter and Stacy Cowley, "Wells Fargo Says Its Culture Has Changed. Some Employees Disagree," *The New York Times*, March 9, 2019, https://www.nytimes.com/2019/03/09/

business/wells-fargo-sales-culture.html?module=inline (accessed October 17, 2019).

Emily Flitter, Binyamin Appelbaum, and Stacy Cowley, "Federal Reserve Shackles Wells Fargo after Fraud Scandal," *The New York Times*, February 2, 2018, https://www.nytimes.com/2018/02/02/business/wells-fargo-federal-reserve.html (accessed August 1, 2019).

Emily Flitter, Stacy Cowley and David Enrich, "Wells Fargo C.E.O. Timothy Sloan Abruptly Steps Down," *The New York Times*, March 28, 2019, https://www.nytimes.com/2019/03/28/business/wells-fargo-timothy-sloan.html (accessed October 17, 2019).

Emily Glazer and Christina Rexrode, "Wells Fargo CEO Testifies Before Senate Banking Committee," *The Wall Street Journal*, September 20, 2016, https://www.wsj.com/articles/wells-fargo-ceo-testifies-before-senate-banking-committee-1474390303 (accessed August 1, 2019).

Emily Glazer, "Wells Fargo to Eliminate Product Sales Goals, Aiming to Rebuild Trust," *The Wall Street Journal*, September 13, 2016, https://www.wsj.com/articles/wells-fargo-cuts-all-sales-goals-as-it-seeks-to-rebuild-trust-1473766077 (accessed August 1, 2019).

Geoff Colvin, "The Wells Fargo Scandal Is Now Reaching VW Proportions," *Fortune*, January 26, 2017, http://fortune.com/2017/01/25/the-wells-fargo-scandal-is-now-reaching-vw-proportions/ (accessed August 1, 2019).

Greg Edwards, "What Wells Fargo & Co.'s Restructuring Means for St. Louis," *St. Louis Business Journal*, June 5, 2019, https://www.bizjournals.com/stlouis/news/2019/06/05/what-wells-fargo-co-s-restructuring-means-for-st.html (accessed August 1, 2019).

Hugh Son and Kate Rooney, "Wells Fargo CEO Tim Sloan Is Retiring, and Shares Jump," *CNBC*, March 28, 2019, https://www.cnbc.com/2019/03/28/wells-fargo-ceo-tim-sloan-retiring.html (accessed August 1, 2019).

Ian Mount, "Wells Fargo's Fake Accounts May Go Back More than 10 Years," *Fortune*, October 12, 2016, http://fortune.com/2016/10/12/wells-fargo-fake-accounts-scandal/ (accessed August 1, 2019).

James Venable, "Wells Fargo: Where Did They Go Wrong?" Working Paper, *Harvard University*, February 9, 2017, https://scholar.harvard.edu/files/jtv/files/wells_fargo_where_did_they_go_wrong_by_james_venable_pdf_02.pdf (accessed August 1, 2019).

John Stout, "Business Forum: Fed's Message to Wells Fargo Board: You're Responsible," *Star Tribune*, February 24, 2018, http://www.startribune.com/business-forum-fed-s-message-to-wells-fargo-board-you-re-responsible/475016873/ (accessed August 1, 2019).

Katy Barnato, "Guess Which Bank Has the Most Valuable Brand," *CNBC*, February 3, 2014, http://www.cnbc.com/2014/02/03/guess-which-bank-has-the-most-valuable-brand.html (accessed August 1, 2019).

Laura J. Keller and Katherine Chiglinsky, "Wells Fargo Eclipsed by JPMorgan as World's Most Valuable Bank," *Bloomberg*, September 13, 2016, https://www.bloomberg.com/news/articles/2016-09-13/wells-fargo-eclipsed-by-jpmorgan-as-world-s-most-valuable-bank (accessed August 1, 2019).

Laura Lorenzetti, "This Is the Most Valuable Bank in the World," *Fortune*, July 23, 2015, http://fortune.com/2015/07/23/wells-fargo-worlds-most-valuable-bank/ (accessed August 1, 2019).

Lisa Cook, "The Wells Fargo Scandal: Is the Profit Model to Blame?" *Knowledge@Warton*, University of Pennsylvania, September 13, 2016, http://knowledge.wharton.upenn.edu/article/how-the-wells-fargo-scandal-will-reverberate/ (accessed August 1, 2019).

Lucinda Shen, "Wells Fargo Sales Scandal Could Hurt Growth Permanently," *Fortune*, April 13, 2017, http://fortune.com/2017/04/13/wells-fargo-report-earnings/ (accessed August 1, 2019).

Mark Snider, "Ex-Wells Fargo Bankers Sue over Firing amid Fraud," *USA Today*, September 25, 2016, http://www.usatoday.com/story/money/2016/09/25/ex-wells-fargo-employees-sue-over-scam/91079158/ (accessed August 1, 2019).

Matt Egan, "5,300 Wells Fargo Employees Fired Over 2 Million Phony Accounts," *CNN*, September 9, 2016, https://money.cnn.com/2016/09/08/investing/wells-fargo-created-phony-accounts-bank-fees/index.html (accessed April 14, 2017).

Matt Egan, "I Called the Wells Fargo Ethics Line and Was Fired," *CNN Money*, September 21, 2016, http://money.cnn.com/2016/09/21/investing/wells-fargo-fired-workers-retaliation-fake-accounts/ (accessed August 1, 2019).

Matt Egan, "Letter warned Wells Fargo of 'Widespread' Fraud in 2007 – Exclusive," *CNN Money*, October 18, 2016, http://money.cnn.com/2016/10/18/investing/wells-fargo-warned-fake-accounts-2007/ (accessed August 1, 2019).

Matt Egan, "More Wells Fargo Workers Allege Retaliation for Whistleblowing," *CNN Business*, November 7, 2017, https://money.cnn.com/2017/11/06/investing/wells-fargo-retaliation-whistleblower/index.html (accessed August 1, 2019).

Matt Egan, "Wells Fargo Knew for Years that Auto Insurance Was Hurting Customers, Lawsuit Says," *CNN*, November 7, 2018, https://www.cnn.com/2018/11/07/business/wells-fargo-auto-insurance-lawsuit/index.html (accessed August 2, 2019).

Matt Egan, "Wells Fargo Uncovers up to 1.4 Million More Fake Accounts," *CNN Money*, August 31, 2017, http://money.cnn.com/2017/08/31/investing/wells-fargo-fake-accounts/index.html (accessed August 1, 2019).

Matt Egan, "Wells Fargo Workers: Fake Accounts Began Years Ago," *CNN Money*, September 26, 2016, http://money.cnn.com/2016/09/26/investing/wells-fargo-fake-accounts-before-2011/ (accessed August 1, 2019).

Michael Corkery, "Wells Fargo Struggling in the Aftermath of Fraud Scandal," *The New York Times*, January 13, 2017, https://www.nytimes.com/2017/01/13/business/dealbook/wells-fargo-earnings-report.html (accessed August 1, 2019).

Paul Blake, "Timeline of the Wells Fargo Accounts Scandal," *ABC News*, November 3, 2016, http://abcnews.go.com/Business/timeline-wells-fargo-accounts-scandal/story?id=42231128 (accessed August 1, 2019).

Rachel Louise Ensign, "Wells Fargo Finally Has a CEO. Here's What He Has to Do," *The Wall Street Journal*, October 21, 2019, https://www.wsj.com/articles/wells-fargo-finally-has-a-ceo-heres-what-he-has-to-do-11571659202 (accessed October 22, 2019).

Sara Lepro and Business Writer, "Wells Fargo Buys Wachovia for $15.1 Billion," *ABC News*, October 3, 2008, https://abcnews.go.com/Business/SmartHome/story?id=5946486&page=1 (accessed August 1, 2019).

Stacy Cowley and Jennifer A. Kingson, "Wells Fargo to Claw Back $75 Million from 2 Former Executives," *The New York Times*, April 10, 2017, https://www.nytimes.com/2017/04/10/

business/wells-fargo-pay-executives-accounts-scandal.html (accessed August 1, 2019).

Stacy Cowley, "At Wells Fargo, Complaints about Fraudulent Accounts Since 2005," *The New York Times,* October 11, 2016, http://www.nytimes.com/2016/10/12/business/dealbook/at-wells-fargo-complaints-about-fraudulent-accounts-since-2005.html (accessed August 1, 2019).

Wells Fargo, "Wells Fargo History," https://www.wellsfargohistory.com/timeline/ (accessed August 1, 2019).

Winston Craver, "Wells Fargo Draws Senators' Ire on Fraud Accounts Response," *Winston-Salem Journal,* December 23, 2016, http://www.journalnow.com/news/local/wells-fargo-draws-senators-ire-on-fraud-accounts-response/article_b2c44587-e2cf-5cb1-966e-6e20c89fa9d8.html (accessed August 1, 2019).

CASE 8

A Brew above the Rest: New Belgium Brewing

Introduction

Although large companies are frequently cited as examples of ethical and socially responsible firms, it is often businesses that start small that stand to have the greatest impact. Craft beer pioneer New Belgium Brewing Company began as a microbrewery in Fort Collins, Colorado. They have created jobs and contributed money, resources, and volunteer time to local causes for 30 years, serving as community leaders. Though New Belgium Brewing Company is no longer considered a craft brewery after its acquisition by Lion Little World Beverages in 2019, the company continues to be a role model in both the world of brewing and the local communities in which they operate.

History of New Belgium Brewing Company

The idea for the New Belgium Brewing Company began with a bicycling trip through Belgium. Belgium is arguably the home of some of the world's finest ales, some of which have been brewed for centuries in monasteries. As Jeff Lebesch, an American electrical engineer, cruised around Belgium on his mountain bike, he wondered whether he could produce such high-quality beers back home in Colorado. After acquiring a special strain of yeast used to brew Belgian-style ales, Lebesch returned home and began to experiment in his Colorado basement. When his beers earned thumbs-up from friends, Lebesch decided to market them.

The New Belgium Brewing Company (NBB) opened for business in 1991 as a tiny basement operation in Lebesch's home in Fort Collins. Lebesch's wife at the time, Kim Jordan, became the firm's marketing director. They named their first brew Fat Tire Amber Ale in honor of Lebesch's bike ride through Belgium. Initially, getting New Belgium beer onto store shelves was not easy. Jordan often delivered the beer to stores in the back of her Toyota station wagon. However, New Belgium beers quickly developed a small but devoted customer base, first in Fort Collins and then throughout Colorado. The brewery soon outgrew the couple's basement and moved into an old railroad depot before settling into their present custom-built facility in 1995. The brewery includes two brew houses, four quality assurance labs, a wastewater treatment facility, a canning and bottling line, and numerous technological innovations for which New Belgium has become nationally recognized as a "paradigm of environmental efficiencies."

NBB currently offers a variety of permanent and seasonal ales and pilsners. The company has their Year Round series, including Citradelic, Dayblazer, and Pilsener; their Voodoo Ranger series of IPAs; their Vintage Sour series La Folie, Transatlantique Kriek, and Le Terroir; their Belgian Collection of Abbey, Trippel, and 1554 ales; and their Fat Tire Collection, still the firm's bestseller. Some customers even refer to the company as the Fat Tire Brewery. The firm also has a line of "Glütiny," or reduced gluten, beers. In 2018, the brewery introduced its Up Next series, unique beer flavors that rotate quarterly throughout the year.

Additionally, New Belgium works in collaboration with other companies to come up with new products. Through this, they hope to create improved efficiency and experimentation as they take collaborative strides toward the future of American craft beer making. One such collaboration resulted in the Grilled Pineapple Golden Ale, brewed in partnership with Red Robin to complement the restaurant's Banzai Burger. The new ale was unveiled at the Great American Beer Festival. NBB also partnered with Ben & Jerry's to develop new flavors of beer such as Chocolate Chip Cookie Dough Ale. Fifty thousand dollars of the proceeds from the beer were used to raise awareness about climate change.

NBB's most effective form of advertising has always been their customers' word of mouth, especially in the early days. Indeed, before New Belgium beers were widely distributed throughout Colorado, one liquor-store owner in Telluride is purported to have offered people gas money if they would stop by and pick up New Belgium beer on their way through Fort Collins. Today, New Belgium is sold in all 50 states, the District of Columbia, Brazil, Finland, Canada, South Korea, Norway, Japan, Australia, and Sweden.

NBB experienced strong growth, which led the firm to build a 76,000 square foot addition to their 100,000 square foot plant in 2005, as well as a second brewery

This case was prepared by Jennifer Sawayda for and under the direction of O.C. Ferrell and Linda Ferrell, © 2019. We appreciate the input and assistance of Greg Owsley, New Belgium Brewing, in developing this case. It was prepared for classroom discussion rather than to illustrate either effective or ineffective handling of an administrative, ethical, or legal decision by management. All sources used for this case were obtained through publicly available material and the New Belgium Brewing website.

in Asheville, North Carolina, in 2016. The organization sold more than 844,000 barrels of beer in 2018. In April 2019, NBB opened a 125-seat restaurant at Denver International Airport (DIA), a strategic move that stands to increase brand awareness as DIA is the fifth busiest airport in the United States. Although NBB is still a small brewery when compared to many beer companies like fellow Coloradan Coors, NBB's place in U.S. brewing history was recognized by the Smithsonian's National Museum of American History in its "FOOD: Transforming the American Table" exhibition in 2019. The travel notebook Lebesch kept that helped inspire the brewery was included in a showcase about the craft brewing revolution.

Beer connoisseurs who appreciate the high quality of NBB's products, as well as the company's environmental and ethical business practices, have driven growth. For example, when the company began distribution in Minnesota, the beers were so popular that a liquor store had to open early and make other accommodations for the large number of customers. The store sold 400 cases of Fat Tire in the first hour it was open. With expanding distribution, however, the brewery recognized a need to increase opportunities for reaching their far-flung customers. They consulted with Dr. Douglas Holt, an Oxford professor and cultural branding expert. After studying the company, Holt, together with former Marketing Director Greg Owsley, drafted a 70-page "manifesto" describing the brand's attributes, character, cultural relevancy, and promise. In particular, Holt identified in New Belgium an ethos of pursuing creative activities simply for the joy of doing them well and harmony with the natural environment.

With the brand thus defined, NBB worked with New York advertising agency Amalgamated to create a $10 million advertising campaign. The campaign would target high-end beer drinkers, men aged from 25 to 44, and highlight the brewery's down-to-earth image. The grainy ads focused on a man, Charles the Tinkerer, rebuilding a cruiser bike out of used parts and then riding it along pastoral country roads. The product appeared in just five seconds of each ad between the tag line, "Follow Your Folly … Ours Is Beer." With nostalgic music playing in the background, the ads helped position the growing brand as whimsical, thoughtful, and reflective. NBB later re-released their Tinkerer commercial during the U.S. Pro Challenge. The re-released commercial featured on NBC had an additional scene with the Tinkerer riding part way next to a professional cyclist contestant, with music from songwriter Sean Hayes.

It would be eight more years before NBB would develop their next television advertising campaign. In 2013, NBB developed a campaign called "Pairs Well with People" that included a 30-second television advertisement. The television ad described the unique qualities of NBB as an organization, including their environmental consciousness and 100 percent employee ownership (see more on this below). The advertisement was launched on four major networks in large cities across the United States. Because the primary purpose of the campaign was to create awareness in areas not as familiar with the brand (such as Raleigh-Durham and Minneapolis), NBB did not air the commercial in Colorado and states where the brand was already well-known. The campaign also featured four 15-second online videos of how the company's beer "pairs well with people." Bar patrons featured in the 15-second digital ads were NBB employees.

In addition to the ad campaign, the company maintains their strategy of promotion through event sponsorships and digital media. To launch their Ranger IPA beer, New Belgium created a microsite and an online video of their NBB sales force dressed as rangers performing a hip-hop dance number to promote the beer. The only difference was that instead of horses, the NBB rangers rode bicycles. The purpose of the video was to create a hip, fun brand image for their new beer, with the campaign theme "To Protect. To Pour. To Partake." The company's Beer Mode mobile app gives users who download it access to exclusive content, preselects messages to post on the users' social media sites when they are spending time enjoying their beers, and provides users with the locations of retailers that sell NBB products. NBB started a free digital loyalty program called Grand Cru that rewards members with exclusive experiences and merchandise for engaging with the company and offering insights for new products. In so doing, NBB not only increases customer loyalty but is able to obtain valuable customer feedback on the firm and their products. NBB is highly active on Facebook, seeing it as an effective way for reaching their customers. After conducting one study, NBB found that their Facebook fans contribute $50.7 million in sales annually.

New Belgium's Ethical Culture

According to New Belgium, the company places great importance on the ethical culture of the brand and their branding strategy is rooted in the core values of the company. They are aware that if NBB embraces citizenship in the communities they serve, they can forge enduring bonds with customers. More than ever before, what a brand says and what a company does must be synchronized. NBB believes that as the mandate for corporate social responsibility gains momentum, business managers must realize that business ethics is not so much about the installation of compliance codes and standards as it is about the spirit in which such codes and standards are integrated. The modern-day brand steward—usually the most externally focused of the business management team—must prepare to be the internal champion of the bottom-line necessity for ethical, values-driven company behavior.

At New Belgium, a synergy of brand and values occurred naturally because the firm's ethical culture (in the form of core values and beliefs) was in place long before NBB had a marketing department. Back in early 1991, when New Belgium was just a fledgling home-brewed business, Jeff Lebesch and Kim Jordan took a hike into Rocky Mountain National Park armed with a pen and a notebook. There they took the first stab at what the company's core purpose would be. If they were going forward with this venture, what were their aspirations beyond profitability? What was at the heart of their dream? What they wrote down that spring day, give or take a little editing, are the core values and beliefs you can read on the NBB website today.

Since their inception, NBB adopted a triple bottom line (TBL) approach to business. Whereas the traditional bottom line approach for measuring business success is economic, TBL incorporates economic, social, and environmental factors. In other words, rather than just looking at financial data to evaluate company success, NBB looks at their impact upon profits, people, and the planet. One way that the company is advancing the TBL approach is through the creation of a high-involvement corporate culture. All employees at NBB are expected to contribute to the company vision, and accountability is spread throughout the organization. Just about any New Belgium worker can list many, if not all, of these shared values.

New Belgium's Purpose and Core Beliefs

New Belgium's dedication to quality, the environment, their employees, and their customers is expressed in its mission statement: "To operate a profitable brewery which makes our love and talent manifest." The company's stated core values and beliefs about their role as an environmentally concerned and socially responsible brewer include the following:

1. Remembering that we are incredibly lucky to create something fine that enhances people's lives while surpassing our consumers' expectations
2. Producing world-class beers
3. Promoting beer culture and the responsible enjoyment of beer
4. Kindling social, environmental, and cultural change as a business role model
5. Environmental stewardship: minimizing resource consumption, maximizing energy efficiency, and recycling
6. Cultivating potential through learning, participative management, and the pursuit of opportunities
7. Balancing the myriad needs of the company, staff, and their families

8. Trusting each other and committing ourselves to authentic relationships, communications, and promises
9. Continuous, innovative quality and efficiency improvements
10. Having fun

Employees believe that these statements help communicate to customers and other stakeholders what New Belgium, as a company, is about. These simple values—developed roughly 30 years ago—are just as meaningful to the company and their customers today, even though there has been much growth.

Employees

Recognizing employees' role in the company's success, New Belgium provides many generous benefits for their employees. In addition to the usual paid health and dental insurance and retirement plans, employees who stay with the company for five years earn an all-expenses paid trip to Belgium to "study beer culture." Employees are also reimbursed for one hour of paid time off for every two hours of volunteer work that they perform. Open book management allows employees to see the financial costs and performance of the company. Employees are provided with financial training so they can understand the books and ask questions about the numbers.

In their decision to open a second brewery, NBB demonstrated how seriously they take their employees' contributions. NBB had chosen 13 possible locations on the East Coast for their new brewery. The company wanted to select an area that met 33 criteria NBB developed as to what they were looking for in a town. NBB owners visited all 13 locations. They returned on a second visit accompanied by employees and other stakeholders. Employees were an integral part of the decision-making process. Although this process took longer because it involved more stakeholders, NBB's actions assured employees that the firm values their feedback and views them more like family than employees.

New Belgium also wishes to get their employees involved not only in the company but in their sustainability efforts as well. To help their own sustainability efforts, employees are given a fat-tired cruiser bike after one year's employment so they can ride to work instead of drive. An on-site recycling center is also provided for employees. In addition, each summer, New Belgium hosts the Tour de Fat, where employees dress in costumes and lead locals on a bike tour. Other company perks include inexpensive yoga classes, free beer at quitting time, and a Prius to run company errands. To ensure that workers' voices are heard, NBB has a democratically elected group of coworkers called POSSE. POSSE acts as a liaison between the board, managers, and employees.

Sustainability

New Belgium's marketing strategy involves linking the quality of their products, as well as their brand, with the company's philosophy of environmental friendliness. As co-chair of the sustainability subcommittee for their trade group the Brewers Association, NBB is at the forefront in advancing eco-friendly business processes among companies in their industry. Co-workers and managers from all areas of the organization meet monthly to discuss sustainability ideas as part of NBB's natural resource management team. From leading-edge environmental gadgets and high-tech industry advancements to a strong belief in giving back to the community, New Belgium demonstrates their desire to create a living, learning community.

NBB strives for cost-efficient energy-saving alternatives for conducting their business and reducing their impact on the environment. In staying true to the company's core values and beliefs, the brewery invested in a wind turbine, making New Belgium the first fully wind-powered brewery in the United States. NBB also charges itself a per-kilowatt-hour internal tax on their purchased energy consumption that they use for energy efficiency projects. NBB has also invested in the following energy-saving technologies:

- A smart grid installation that allows NBB to communicate with their electricity provider to conserve energy. For example, the smart grid will alert NBB to non-essential operational functions, allowing the company to turn them off and save power.
- The installation of 1,235 solar photovoltaics panels on top of the packaging hall. The array produces 4.5 percent of the company's electricity.
- A brew kettle, the second of its kind installed in the nation, which heats wort sheets instead of the whole kettle at once. This kettle heating method conserves energy more than standard kettles do.
- Sun tubes, which provide natural daytime lighting throughout the brew house all year long.
- A system to capture its wastewater and extract methane from it. This can contribute up to 15 percent of the brewery's power needs while reducing the strain on the local municipal water treatment facility.
- A steam condenser that captures and reuses the hot water that boils the barley and hops in the production process to start the next brew. The steam is redirected to heat the floor tiles and de-ice the loading docks in cold weather.

In April 2014, New Belgium was featured in a half-page advertisement supporting the EPA clean water rule that was introduced March 26, 2014. Andrew Lemley, New Belgium's Government Relations Director, was quoted in an EPA news release championing continued support for the Clean Water Act while also associating quality water with quality beer.

In addition to voicing political support for environmental protections, New Belgium also takes pride in reducing waste through recycling and creative reuse strategies. The company strives to recycle as many supplies as possible, including cardboard boxes, keg caps, office materials, and the amber glass used in bottling. For example, NBB partnered with Original Grain in 2019, a sustainable wood and steel watch company, supplying wood foeder barrels for the creation of a collection of limited edition watches. Foeder barrels are used for many decades before they are retired. The brewery also stores spent barley and hop grains in an on-premise silo and invites local farmers to pick up the grains, free of charge, to feed their pigs. Beyond the normal products that are recycled back into the food chain, NBB has also worked with partners to take the same bacteria that creates methane from NBB wastewater and convert it into a harvestable, high-protein fish food. NBB also buys recycled products when they can, and even encourages their employees to reduce air pollution by using alternative transportation. Reduce, Reuse, Recycle—the three Rs of environmental stewardship—are taken seriously at NBB. The company has been a proud member of the environmental group Business for Innovative Climate & Energy Policy (BICEP), and they signed BICEP's Climate Declaration in 2013 which calls for American businesses, stakeholders, and regulators to address climate change.

Additionally, New Belgium has been a long-time participant in green building techniques. With each expansion of their facility, the company has incorporated new technologies and learned a few lessons along the way. In 2002, NBB agreed to participate in the United States Green Building Council's Leadership in Energy and Environment Design for Existing Buildings (LEED-EB) pilot program. From sun tubes and daylighting throughout the facility to reusing heat in the brew house, NBB continues to search for new ways to close loops and conserve resources.

New Belgium has made significant achievements in sustainability, particularly compared to other companies in the industry. For instance, New Belgium uses only 4 gallons of water to make 1 gallon of beer, which is 20 percent less than most other companies. The company is attempting to create a closed-loop wastewater system with its own Process Water Treatment Plant, in which microbes are used to clean the wastewater. NBB keeps 99.9 percent of their waste out of landfills, and today 100 percent of their electricity comes from renewable energy sources. Despite these achievements, they have no intention of halting their sustainability efforts. The company hopes to reduce the amount of water used to make their beer through better production processes as well as decrease their carbon footprint per barrel. To encourage sustainability throughout the supply chain, NBB adopted Sustainable Purchasing Guidelines. The

Guidelines allow the company to pinpoint and work closely with eco-friendly suppliers to create sustainability throughout the entire value chain. For their part, NBB conducts life-cycle analysis on their packaging components while continually seeking more efficient refrigeration and transportation technology that can be incorporated into their supply chain.

In 2013, NBB achieved B corporation certification as a way to further solidify their belief that business can be a "force for good." The B stands for benefit. B corporation certification, awarded by the nonprofit B Lab, is a type of certification for for-profit firms that certifies they meet stringent environmental and social performance goals, as well as practice transparency and accountability. Companies that have received B corporation certification are scored based upon their performance in ethical, social, and environmental areas, including governance, worker relations, community relations, and the environment. NBB scored 143 out of 200, whereas the median B corporation score is 80. NBB demonstrates through certification that they go above and beyond what is expected to try and make the world a better place.

Social Responsibility

Beyond their use of environmentally friendly technologies and innovations, New Belgium also strives to improve communities and enhance people's lives through corporate giving, event sponsorship, and philanthropic involvement. NBB has donated more than $10.5 million through their grants program to philanthropic causes. For every barrel of beer sold the prior year, NBB donates $1 to philanthropic causes within their distribution territories. The donations are divided between states in proportion to their percentage of overall sales. This is the company's way of staying local and giving back to the communities that support and purchase NBB products. NBB also participates in One Percent for the Planet, a philanthropic network to which the company donates one percent of Fat Tire sales.

Funding decisions are made by NBB's Philanthropy Committee, which is composed of employees throughout the brewery, including owners, area leaders, and production workers. NBB looks for nonprofit organizations that demonstrate creativity, diversity, and an innovative approach to their mission and objectives. The Philanthropy Committee also looks for groups that incorporate community involvement in their operations.

In addition, NBB maintains a community bulletin board in their facility and posts an array of community involvement activities and proposals. This community board allows tourists and employees to see the various opportunities to help out in the community, and it gives nonprofit organizations a chance to make their needs known. The NBB website also has a dedicated link where organizations can apply for grants. The company donates to causes with a particular emphasis on water conservation, sensible transportation and bike advocacy, sustainable agriculture, and youth environmental education.

NBB also sponsors a number of events, with a special focus on those that involve "human-powered" sports that cause minimal damage to the natural environment. Through event sponsorships, such as the Tour de Fat, NBB supports various environmental, social, and cycling nonprofit organizations. In the course of one year, New Belgium can be found at anywhere from 150 to 200 festivals and events across the nation.

Organizational Success

New Belgium Brewing's efforts to embody a sustainability-oriented business has paid off with a very loyal following—in fact, the company expanded the number of tours they offer of their facilities due to high demand. The company has also been the recipient of numerous awards. Past awards for NBB include the Business Ethics Magazine's Business Ethics Award for its "dedication to environmental excellence in every part of its innovative brewing process," their inclusion in *The Wall Street Journal*'s 15 best small workplaces, and the award for "best mid-sized brewing company of the year" and "best mid-sized brewmaster" at the Great American Beer Festival. New Belgium has been awarded medals for three different brews: Abbey Belgian Style Ale, Blue Paddle Pilsner, and La Folie specialty ale.

Many applaud New Belgium Brewing Company's sustainability and philanthropic initiatives. According to David Edgar, former director of the Institute for Brewing Studies at the Brewers Association in Boulder, Colorado, "They've created a very positive image for their company in the beer-consuming public with smart decision-making." Although some members of society do not believe that a company whose major product is alcohol can be socially responsible, NBB has set out to prove that for those who make a choice to drink responsibly, the company can do everything possible to contribute to society. NBB also promotes the responsible appreciation of beer through their participation in and support of the culinary arts. For instance, they frequently host New Belgium Beer Dinners, in which every course of the meal is served with a complementary culinary treat.

Although NBB has made great strides in creating a socially responsible brand image, their work is not done. They must continually reexamine their ethical, social, and environmental responsibilities. In 2004, they received the Environmental Protection Agency's regional Environmental Achievement Award. It was both an honor and a motivator for the company to continue their socially responsible goals. After all, there are still many ways for NBB to improve as a corporate citizen. For example, although all electric power comes from renewable sources, the NBB plant is still heated in part by using natural gas. Furthermore, continued expansion requires longer travel distances to distribute their products, which increases the use of fossil fuels. In addition to addressing logistical challenges, NBB is part of an industry where there is always a need for more public dialogue on avoiding alcohol abuse. Practically speaking, the company has a never-ending to-do list.

NBB executives acknowledge that as their annual sales increase, the company will face increasing challenges to remain committed on a human level while also being culturally authentic. Indeed, how to boldly grow the brand while maintaining their perception of a humble feel has always been a challenge. Additionally, reducing waste to an even greater extent will require more effort on behalf of managers and employees, creating the need for a collaborative process that will require the dedication of both parties toward sustainability.

Perhaps as a way to deal with the long transportation distances necessary for national distribution as well as to expand production capacity, NBB opened their second brewery in Asheville, North Carolina in 2015. Its grand opening in 2016 was marked with a celebration that coincided with NBB's 25th anniversary. Like Sierra Nevada, who already operates a brewery in Asheville, NBB is hoping to use its new $175 million facility as a hub for product distribution to eastern states—Asheville has legislation in place that makes regional distribution easier. However, opening their second brewery is more than just about increasing production capacity; NBB, along with hundreds of other craft brewers, are attracted to Asheville for their local culture that values sustainability and locally produced products. Asheville is surrounded by mountains, is near protected water sources, and is inhabited by many outdoor enthusiasts. Indeed, NBB is not the only craft brewery to recognize the potential of positive tourist exposure and local support by operating in the Asheville area. Sierra Nevada added tours of their brewery to emphasize their history and sustainable brewing practices. Additionally, other Asheville breweries have spent millions expanding their current operations in anticipation of NBB's entrance to the area.

NBB also faces increased competition from larger craft breweries. They still remain behind D. G. Yuengling & Son Inc., Boston Beer Co. (maker of Samuel Adams beer), and Sierra Nevada in market share. Like NBB, Boston Beer Co. and Sierra Nevada have plans to expand. NBB must also compete against craft beer alternatives released by traditional breweries, such as MillerCoor's New Moon Belgian White. They must constantly engage in environmental scanning and competitive analysis to compete in this increasingly competitive environment.

Finally, New Belgium is facing a potential slowdown in craft beer consumption. Smaller local competitors, called microbreweries, are increasing and have begun to draw away some of NBB's customers. There is concern that NBB might be getting too big, thereby losing their "niche" feel. With sales slowing, NBB was forced to lay off 28 workers in 2018. Employees received severance packages and the company purchased their shares.

Every six-pack of New Belgium Beer displays the phrase "In this box is our labor of love. We feel incredibly lucky to be creating something fine that enhances people's lives." Although Jeff Lebesch and Kim Jordan are divorced and Lebesch has left the company to focus on other interests, the founders of New Belgium hope this statement continues to capture the spirit of the company. In 2015, Kim Jordan announced she was turning the CEO position over to Chief Operations Officer and President Christine Perich so she could transition into becoming the Executive Chair of NBB's board of directors. This allowed Jordan to focus more on the long-term strategy and vision of the firm. However, after only a year on the job, Christie Perich announced her resignation and was replaced by external hire Steve Fechheimer. In 2019, Fechheimer and Jordan announced the sale of NBB to Australia-based Lion Little World Beverage. NBB, which was previously 100 percent employee-owned, announced its 300 employee-owners would receive $100,000 or more in retirement money from the deal. Current and former employees received nearly $190 million through NBB's employee stock ownership plan (ESOP) over the life of the plan. Jordan will maintain an active role at NBB, and Fechheimer will remain as CEO. Additionally, the company will retain their B corporation certification, and their headquarters will remain in Fort Collins, Colorado.

Despite the challenges the brewery has faced, NBB leaders are optimistic about the future. Jordan indicated the purchase provides the opportunity to expand capacity and continue to grow the company. Not to mention, resources for research and development will be much greater. NBB is the 11th-largest overall brewer in the U.S. and continues to be a role model for ethics and social responsibility for the entire brewing industry.

Questions for Discussion

1. What environmental issues does the New Belgium Brewing Company work to address? How has NBB taken a strategic approach to addressing these issues? Why do you think the company has taken such a strong stance toward sustainability?

2. Do you agree that New Belgium's focus on social responsibility provides a key competitive advantage for the company? Why or why not?

3. Some segments of society contend that companies that sell alcoholic beverages and tobacco products cannot be socially responsible organizations because of the nature of their primary products. Do you believe that New Belgium's actions and initiatives are indicative of a socially responsible corporation? Why or why not?

Sources

"A Tour of the New Belgium Brewery—Act One," LiveGreen Blog, April 9, 2007, http://www.livegreensd.com/2007/04/tour-of-new-belgium-brewery-act-one.html (accessed April 13, 2012).

"How New Belgium Brewing Is Positioning Itself to Remain Independent," *Denver Post*, January 15, 2013, http://blogs.denverpost.com/beer/2013/01/15/new-belgium-positio/7872/ (accessed August 5, 2019).

"Industry Profile: Breweries," *First Research*, October 17, 2011, http://www.firstresearch.com (accessed February 17, 2012).

"New Belgium Brewing Announces Asheville as Site for Second Brewery," *The Denver Post*, April 5, 2012, http://marketwire.denverpost.com/client/denver_post/release.jsp?actionFor=1595119 (accessed April 19, 2012).

"New Belgium Brewing Launches 'Up Next' Rotator Series with Brut IPA," *Brewbound*, December 5, 2018, https://www.brewbound.com/news/new-belgium-brewing-launches-up-next-rotator-series-with-brut-ipa (accessed August 2, 2019).

"New Belgium Brewing Wins Ethics Award," *Denver Business Journal*, January 2, 2003, http://www.bizjournals.com/denver/stories/2002/12/30/daily21.html (accessed August 5, 2019).

"New Belgium Develops Burger-Inspired Beer for Red Robin," *Beverage Industry*, September 26, 2016, http://www.bevindustry.com/articles/89650-new-belgium-develops-burger-inspired-beer-for-red-robin (accessed August 5, 2019).

"The 2011 World's Most Ethical Companies" *Ethisphere*, Q1 2011, 37–43.

Better Business Bureau, "Four Businesses Honored with Prestigious International Award for Outstanding Marketplace Ethics," September 23, 2002, http://www.bbb.org/alerts/2002torchwinners.asp.

Bryan Simpson, "New Belgium Brewing: Brand Building through Advertising and Public Relations," *Coronado Art & Design*, http://www.michaelcoronado.com/michaelcoronado/images/pdf/NBB_research/newbelgiumbrewing.pdf (accessed August 5, 2019).

Certified B Corporation, "About B Corps," https://bcorporation.net/about-b-corps (accessed August 5, 2019).

Chris Furnari, "New Belgium Cuts 4 Percent of Workforce Amid Craft Beer Slowdown," *Brewbound*, February 23, 2018, https://www.brewbound.com/news/new-belgium-cuts-4-percent-work force-amid-craft-beer-slowdown (accessed August 2, 2019).

Chuck Skypeck, "Walker Modic of Bell's Brewery Named Sustainability Subcommittee Co-Chair," *Brewers Association*, November 7, 2018, https://www.brewersassociation.org/association-news/walker-modic-named-sustainability-co-chair/ (accessed August 5, 2019).

Cotton Delo, "New Belgium Toasts to Its Facebook Fans," *Advertising Age*, February 13, 2012, http://adage.com/article/news/belgium-toasts-facebook-fans/232681/ (accessed August 5, 2019).

Darren Dahl, "How New Belgium Brewing Has Found Sustainable Success," *Forbes*, January 27, 2016, https://www.forbes.com/sites/darrendahl/2016/01/27/how-new-belgium-brewing-has-found-sustainable-success/#7f5b960286a6 (accessed August 5, 2019).

Darren Dahl, "Why Did New Belgium Brewing Pick Asheville?" *Forbes*, May 11, 2015, https://www.forbes.com/sites/darrendahl/2015/05/11/why-did-new-belgium-pick-asheville/#146cdb4371f6 (accessed August 5, 2019).

David Kemp, Tour Connoisseur, New Belgium Brewing Company, personal interview by Nikole Haiar, November 21, 2000.

Del I. Hawkins, Roger J. Best, and Kenneth A. Coney, *Consumer Behavior: Building Marketing Strategy*, 8th ed. (Burr Ridge, IL: McGraw-Hill/Irwin, 2001).

Denver International Airport, "Passenger Traffic Reports," https://www.flydenver.com/about/financials/passenger_traffic (accessed October 23, 2019).

Devin Leonard, "New Belgium and the Battle of the Microbrews," *Bloomberg Businessweek*, December 1, 2011, http://www.businessweek.com/magazine/new-belgium-and-the-battle-of-the-microbrews-12012011.html (accessed August 5, 2019).

Dick Kreck, "Strange Brewing Standing Out," *The Denver Post*, June 2, 2010, http://www.denverpost.com/2010/05/31/strange-brewing-standing-out/ (accessed August 5, 2019).

Environmental Protection Agency, "Here's What They're Saying about the Clean Water Act Proposed Rule," March 26, 2014, http://yosemite.epa.gov/opa/admpress.nsf/docf6618525a9efb85257359003fb69d/3f954ci79cfo720985257ca700492ofa!OpenDocument (accessed August 18, 2014).

John Kell, "These Are America's 10 Largest Craft Breweries," April 5, 2016, http://fortune.com/2016/04/05/largest-craft-breweries-us/ (accessed August 5, 2019).

Jonathan Shikes, "New Belgium Airs TV Commercials for the First Time in Eight Years, but Not in Colorado," *Westword*, May 21, 2013, http://www.westword.com/restaurants/new-belgium-airs-tv-commercials-for-the-first-time-in-eight-years-but-not-in-colorado-5728121 (accessed August 5, 2019).

Josie Sexton, "New Belgium Brewing, Colorado's Largest Craft Brewery, Announces Sale to International Beer Conglomerate," *The Denver Post*, November 19, 2019, https://www.denverpost.com/2019/11/19/new-belgium-brewing-sale-kirin/ (accessed November 22, 2019).

Julie Gordon, "Lebesch Balances Interests in Business, Community," *Coloradoan.com*, February 26, 2003.

Karen Crofton, "How New Belgium Brewery Leads Colorado's Craft Brewers in Energy," *GreenBiz*, August 1, 2014, https://www.greenbiz.com/blog/2014/08/01/how-new-belgium-brewery-leads-colorados-craft-brewers-energy (accessed August 5, 2019).

Karlene Lukovitz, "New Belgium Brewing Gets 'Hopped Up'," *Media Post News*, February 3, 2010, https://www.mediapost.com/publications/article/121806/new-belgium-brewing-gets-hopped-up.html (accessed August 5, 2019).

Kelly K. Spors, "Top Small Workplaces 2008," *The Wall Street Journal*, October 13, 2008, http://online.wsj.com/article/SB122347733961315417.html (accessed August 5, 2019).

Leigh Buchanan, "It's All about Ownership," *Inc.*, April 18, 2013, https://www.inc.com/audacious-companies/leigh-buchanan/new-belgium-brewing.html (accessed August 5, 2019).

Megan Braa, "New Belgium Plans $7M Expansion, Launches New Beer and Improves Employee Health Care," *The Rocky Mountain Collegian*, October 20, 2015, https://collegian.com/2015/10/new-belgium-plans-7m-expansion-on-site-healthcare-for-employees/ (accessed August 5, 2019).

Mike Esterl, "Craft Brewers Tap Big Expansion," *The Wall Street Journal*, December 28, 2011, https://www.wsj.com/articles/SB10001424052970203686204577114291721661070 (accessed August 5, 2019).

Mike Snider, "Big Brewers Happy to Go Hoppy," *USA Today*, October 30, 2013, 4B.

Mike Snider, "Sales of Craft Beer Are Still Bubbling Up," *USA Today*, April 3, 2014, 3B.

NBB Films, "NBBspotsonNBC," YouTube, http://wwwyoutube.com/watch?v=KCnzyX-x-WQ (accessed August 18, 2014).

New Belgium Brewing, "Beer Mode: A Brand (Spanking) New Mobile App! For Your Consideration…," April 23, 2013, http://www.newbelgium. com/community/Blog/13-04-23/Beer-Mode-a-brand-spanking-new-mobile-app-For-your-consideration.aspx (accessed May 6, 2015).

New Belgium Brewing, "Benefits," https://www.newbelgium.com/brewery/company/benefits/ (accessed August 5, 2019).

New Belgium Brewing, "Corporate Sustainability Report," http://www.newbelgium.com/culture/alternativelyempowered/sustainable-business-storyaspx (accessed April 13, 2012).

New Belgium Brewing, "Energy," https://www.newbelgium.com/sustainability/environmental-metrics/our-breweries/ (accessed August 4, 2019).

New Belgium Brewing, "Good Water Means Good Beer," https://www.newbelgium.com/sustainability/environmental-metrics/water/ (accessed August 5, 2019).

New Belgium Brewing, "Grand Cru," https://www.newbelgium.com/grandcru (accessed August 5, 2019).

New Belgium Brewing, "Grants Program," https://www.newbelgium.com/sustainability/community/grants/ (accessed August 5, 2019).

New Belgium Brewing, "New Belgium Brewing: Follow Your Folly," May 9, 2007, http://www.newbelgium.com/Files/NBB_student-info-packet.pdf (accessed April 15, 2017).

New Belgium Brewing, "Rankings," https://www.newbelgium.com/brewery/company/craft-beer-rankings-and-financials/ (accessed August 2, 2019).

New Belgium Brewing, "Sustainability in Strategic Alignment," http://www.newbelgium.com/Sustainability/Environmental-Metrics/strategic-alignment (accessed August 5, 2019).

New Belgium Brewing, "Sustainability," https://www.newbelgium.com/sustainability/one-percent-for-the-planet/ (accessed August 5, 2019).

New Belgium Brewing, "Tour de Fat FAQs," https://www.newbelgium.com/events/tour-de-fat/faq/ (accessed August 5, 2019).

New Belgium Brewing, "Waste Reduction," https://www.newbelgium.com/sustainability/environmental-metrics/waste/ (accessed August 5, 2019).

New Belgium Brewing, "We're Brewing Up Another Beer with Ben & Jerry's," June 20, 2016, http://www.newbelgium.com/community/Blog/new-belgium-brewing/2016/06/20/we're-brewing-another-beer-with-ben-jerry's (accessed April 15, 2017).

New Belgium Brewing, https://www.newbelgium.com/ (accessed August 2, 2019).

Peter Asmus, "Goodbye Coal, Hello Wind," *Business Ethics*, 13 (July/August 1999): 10–11.

PR Newswire, "Original Grain Launches Watch Collection Made from New Belgium Brewing Beer Barrels," *Yahoo! Finance*, October 16, 2019, https://finance.yahoo.com/news/original-grain-launches-watch-collection-200300662.html (accessed October 23, 2019).

Robert Baun, "What's in a Name? Ask the Makers of Fat Tire," *Coloradoan*, October 8, 2000, El, E3.

Robert F. Dwyer and John F. Tanner, Jr., *Business Marketing* (Burr Ridge, IL: McGraw-Hill/ Irwin, 1999), 104.

Sheb L. True, Linda Ferrell, O. C. Ferrell, *Fulfilling Our Obligation, Perspectives on Teaching Business Ethics* (Atlanta, GA: Kennesaw State University Press, 2005), 128–132.

Steve Raabe, "Plans Brewing for New Belgium Facility on East Coast," *The Denver Post*, December 22, 2011, http://www.denverpost.com/business/ci_19597528 (accessed April 15, 2017).

Susan Adams, "New Belgium Brewing Hires a New CEO from the Liquor Industry," *Forbes*, July 17 2017, https://www.forbes.com/sites/susanadams/2017/07/17/new-belgium-brewing-hires-a-new-ceo-from-the-liquor-industry/#1353b9a45e7a (accessed August 2, 2019).

Susan Adams, "Once a Craft Beer Darling, New Belgium Brewing Is Struggling to Go from Niche to National," *Forbes*, July 27, 2017 https://www.forbes.com/sites/susanadams/2017/07/17/once-a-craft-beer-darling-new-belgium-brewing-is-struggling-to-go-from-niche-to-national/#be609a83982c (accessed August 2, 2019).

The Egotist Network, "New Belgium Pairs Well with People in New Campaign from Denver's Cultivator," *The Denver Egotist,* May 20, 2013, https://www.thedenveregotist.com/news/new-belgium-pairs-well-with-people-in-new-campaign-from-denvers-cultivator/ (accessed August 5, 2019).

Tyra Sutak, "O.G. New Belgium Brewing Company Is Still Innovating," *5280*, April 23, 2019, https://www.5280.com/2019/04/o-g-new-belgium-brewing-company-is-still-innovating/ (accessed October 23, 2019).

William Bostwick, "Craft Brewers Go High-Tech," *The Wall Street Journal,* June 23, 2016, https://www.wsj.com/articles/bitter-truths-1466715201 (accessed August 5, 2019).

CASE 9

Starbucks Takes on Coffee Culture

Introduction

The first Starbucks store was opened in Seattle's Pike Place Market in 1971. Howard Schultz joined Starbucks in 1982 as director of retail operations and marketing. Returning from a trip to Milan, Italy, with its 1,500 coffee bars, Schultz recognized an opportunity to develop a similar retail coffee bar culture in Seattle.

In 1985, the company tested their first downtown Seattle coffeehouse, served the first Starbucks Caffè Latte, and introduced their Christmas Blend. Since then, Starbucks has expanded across the United States and around the world, now operating over 30,600 stores in 76 countries. Historically, Starbucks grew at a rate of about three stores a day, although the company cut back on expansion in recent years. The company serves approximately 85 million customers per week and has an annual revenue of over $24 billion. The firm is the largest coffeehouse company in the world.

Starbucks locates their retail stores in high-traffic, high-visibility locations. The stores are designed to provide an inviting coffee bar environment that is an important part of the Starbucks product and experience. It was the intention of Howard Schulz to make Starbucks into "the third place" for consumers to frequent, after home and work. Because the company is flexible regarding store size and format, many of their locations are in or near a variety of settings, including office buildings, bookstores, and university campuses. Retail stores are also situated in select rural and off-highway locations to serve a broader array of customers outside major metropolitan markets and to further expand brand awareness.

In addition to selling products through retail outlets, Starbucks sells coffee and tea products and licenses their trademark through other channels and partners. For instance, their Frappuccino coffee drinks, Starbucks Doubleshot espresso drinks, iced espresso drinks, almond milk Frappuccino coffee drinks, and VIA coffees can be purchased in grocery stores and through retailers like Walmart and Target.

A common criticism of Starbucks is their strategy for location and expansion. The company's "clustering" strategy—placing a Starbucks on nearly every corner in some areas of operation—forced many smaller coffee shops out of business. This strategy dominated for most of the 1990s and 2000s, and Starbucks became the source of parodies and pop culture jokes. Many people began to wonder whether two Starbucks directly across the street from each other were really needed. The Great Recession brought a change in policy, however. Starbucks pulled back on expansion, closed hundreds of stores around the United States, and focused more on international markets. In the years following the recession, Starbucks began increasing U.S. expansion once more. However, in response to criticism from consumers about their "clustering" strategy, the company closed stores that were perhaps redundant. In June 2018, Starbucks announced the closing of 150 store locations, which is three times the number of stores the corporation typically closes in a year. The affected stores were in densely populated urban areas that already had multiple Starbucks locations.

At the end of 2014, Starbucks opened a 15,000 square-foot Starbucks Reserve Roastery and Tasting Room in Seattle, a place where coffee is roasted, bagged, sold, and shipped internationally. Equipped with a Coffee Library and Coffee Experience Bar, the roastery is intended to redefine the coffee retail experience for customers. The roastery sells 28 to 30 different coffees and gets 1,000 to 2,000 customers daily. Starbucks has also added local Mora ice cream to the product line at the roastery so consumers can create Affogato-style beverages (espresso poured over ice cream). The Starbucks Reserve Roastery in Shanghai has been called the "biggest Starbucks in the world." Starbucks also has roasteries in Milan, Tokyo, Manhattan, and Chicago. While the roasteries have been extremely successful, CEO Kevin Johnson is slow to continue further expansion due to a desire to perfect the existing roasteries first.

New Product Offerings

Starbucks introduced a number of new products over the years to remain competitive. In 2008, Starbucks decided to return to the essentials with the introduction of their Pike Place Blend. The company hoped that the blend would return Starbucks to their roots of distinctive, expertly blended coffee. In order to perfect the flavor, Starbucks enlisted the inputs of 1,000 customers over 1,500 hours. To kick off the new offering, Starbucks held the largest nationwide coffee tasting in history. To make the brew even more appealing, Starbucks joined forces with Conservation International to ensure the beans were sustainably harvested. After feedback revealed many of their customers desired a lighter blend, Starbucks introduced the Blonde Roast blend in 2011. In 2015, the company commercialized the Flat White based

This case was prepared by Jennifer Sawayda, Michelle Urban, and Sarah Sawayda for and under the direction of O.C. Ferrell and Linda Ferrell, © 2019. It was prepared for classroom discussion rather than to illustrate either effective or ineffective handling of an administrative, ethical, or legal decision by management. All sources used for this case were obtained through publicly available material.

on a latte drink popular in Australia. Unlike previous new offerings, the company did not perform limited-market testing but instead introduced it nationwide in an attempt to remain competitive with rivals. In 2018, Starbucks and Nestlé partnered under a global coffee alliance. This alliance has produced Starbucks Creamer as a new product with a variety of flavors.

Not only does Starbucks have a variety of coffees, bakery items, and breakfast and lunch options, they also have six different sizes of drinks for patrons to choose from: short (8 fl. oz.), tall (12 fl. oz.), grande (16 fl. oz.), venti hot (20 fl. oz.), venti cold (24 fl. oz.), and trenta (31 fl. oz.). Trenta, Starbucks' largest drink size, was first introduced in 2011. Starbucks has developed multiple ways to stay competitive, and in a society that values choice, having six different size options is yet another way the company appeals to consumers.

The Starbucks Reserve Roasteries in Europe, Asia, and the United States also sell alcoholic beverages such as beer and wine. A unique aspect of the alcoholic drinks is that many of them are mixed with the company's famous coffee. Starbucks aims to give customers an experience they cannot get anywhere else, and the roasteries have proven to be valuable in this endeavor.

Additionally, Starbucks fosters brand loyalty by increasing repeat business. One of the ways they accomplish this is through the Starbucks Card, a reloadable card introduced in 2001. For the tech-savvy visitor, Starbucks also introduced the Starbucks Reward Mobile app. With the app, customers are able to order or pre-order their coffee and merely scan their phone for payment. Today, the Starbucks Rewards mobile app has 44 million active users—making it the fourth most popular digital payment app in the country. Howard Schultz believed that the future is digital, and, thus, Starbucks is placing more emphasis on digital marketing strategies.

Starbucks Culture

In 1990, the Starbucks' senior executive team created a mission statement that specified the guiding principles for the company. They hoped the principles included in the mission statement would assist partners in determining the appropriateness of later decisions and actions. After drafting the mission statement, the executive team asked all Starbucks partners to review and comment on the document. Based on their feedback, the final statement put forth the mantra of "people first and profits last." In fact, the number one guiding principle in the Starbucks' mission statement is to create a great and respectable work environment for its employees.

Starbucks has done three things to keep the mission and guiding principles alive over the decades. First, they distribute the mission statement and comment cards for feedback during orientation to all new partners. Second, Starbucks continually relates company decisions back to the guiding principle or principles they support. These principles focus on coffee, partners, customers, stores, neighborhoods, and shareholders. And finally, the company formed a "Mission Review" system so partners can comment on a decision or action relative to its consistency with one of the six principles. These guiding principles and values have become the cornerstone of a strong ethical culture of predominately young and educated workers.

Former Starbucks founder and CEO Howard Schultz has long been a public advocate for increased awareness of ethics in business. In a 2007 speech at Notre Dame, he spoke to students about the importance of balancing "profitability and social consciousness." Schultz is a true believer that ethical companies do better in the long run, something that has been backed by research. According to the Ethisphere Institute, ethical companies perform better and have higher shareholder returns. Schultz maintains that, while it can be difficult to do the right thing at all times, in the long term, it is better for a company to take short-term losses than to lose sight of their core values.

The care a company shows their employees is a large part of what sets them apart from other firms. Starbucks offers all employees who work more than 20 hours per week a comprehensive benefits package that includes stock options as well as medical, dental, and vision benefits. In another effort to benefit employees, Starbucks partners with Arizona State University (ASU) to offer tuition assistance to those who want to earn a degree from the university's online program.

Another key part of the Starbucks image involves their commitment to ethics and sustainability. Social responsibility, transparency, and sustainability are all important values of Starbucks. In an effort to become more transparent about ethical harvesting, as well as to build trust in the company among consumers, Starbucks partnered with Microsoft in 2019 to use blockchain technology to allow customers to trace where and how their coffee came to be.

With an eye toward reducing the company's negative impact on climate change and waste, Starbucks has also created plastic drinkable lids to replace their plastic straws. While the lids are still made of a type of plastic, they are recyclable and, thus, safer for the environment. Considering that about half of Starbucks drink orders are now cold drinks, this change could make a significant impact on the company's sustainability practices. Straws will still be available, particularly for Frappuccinos; however, these will be made out of a material that can be recycled. In addition to helping the environment, Starbucks is hoping that the move from plastic straws to sustainable materials will drive more business from younger generations. According to a Nielsen poll, 73 percent of Millennials are willing to spend more money for sustainable goods. Starbucks, a company already popular with both generations, may be able to increase their sales even more among young people with a simple change to their straws.

Despite these efforts to be more environmentally conscious, there is some controversy among environmental groups about the positive results of the switch. Questions remain about other ecological issues, such as the company's cup waste. In order to stay ahead, Starbucks will have to continue to innovate and meet the demands of sustainability-minded consumers.

Starbucks actively partners with nonprofits around the globe and is one of the largest buyers of Fair Trade Certified as well as certified organic coffee. Conservation International joined with Starbucks in 1998 to promote sustainable agricultural practices, namely shade-grown coffee, and to help prevent deforestation in endangered regions around the globe. The results of the partnership proved to be positive for both the environment and the farmers. For example, in Chiapas, Mexico, shade-grown coffee acreage (that reduces the need to cut down trees for coffee plantations) increased well over 220 percent, while farmers receive a price premium above the market price. Starbucks and Oprah, two of the biggest global brands, also joined forces to create the limited edition Oprah Chai Tea in 2014.

Starbucks works with many other organizations as well, including the African Wildlife Foundation and Business for Social Responsibility. The company's efforts at transparency, the treatment of their workers, and their philanthropic commitments demonstrate how genuine Starbucks is in their mission to be an ethical and socially responsible company.

Corporate Social Mission

Although Starbucks supported responsible business practices virtually since their inception, as the company has grown, so has the importance of defending their image. At the end of 1999, Starbucks created a Corporate Social Responsibility department, now known as the Global Responsibility Department. Global Responsibility releases an annual report in order for shareholders to keep track of the company's performance.

Environment

In 1992, long before it became trendy to be "green," Starbucks developed an environmental mission statement to articulate the company's environmental priorities and goals. This initiative created the Environmental Starbucks Coffee Company Affairs team, the purpose of which was to develop environmentally responsible policies and minimize the company's "footprint." As part of this effort, Starbucks began using environmental purchasing guidelines to reduce waste through recycling,

conserving energy, and educating partners through the company's "Green Team" initiatives. Concerned stakeholders can now track the company's progress through their website where there is a clear outline of Starbucks' environmental goals and how the company fares in living up to those goals. Starbucks also began offering a $1 plastic cup for purchase that is good for a recommended 30 uses. In addition, the company has set a goal to reach 10,000 "greener stores" by 2025.

Employees

Growing up poor with a father whose life was nearly ruined by an unsympathetic employer who did not offer health benefits, Howard Schultz always considered the creation of a good work environment a top priority. He believed companies should value their workers. When forming Starbucks, he decided to build a company that provided opportunities his father did not have. The result is one of the best healthcare programs in the coffee shop industry. Schultz's key to maintaining a strong business was developing a shared vision among employees as well as an environment to which they can actively contribute. Understanding how vital employees are, Schultz is the first to admit his company centers on personal interactions: "We are not in the coffee business serving people, but in the people business serving coffee." Starbucks is known for their diversity, and 46 percent of their baristas are ethnic minorities.

However, being a great employer does take its toll on the company. In 2008, Starbucks closed 10 percent of stores in order to continue to provide employees with health insurance. This decision, based on their guiding principle of "people first, profits last," shows how much the company values their employees.

As a way to improve employee health, Starbucks established a program for employees called "Thrive Wellness" that offers various resources aimed at assisting employees in incorporating wellness into their lives. The program offers resources to assist with smoking cessation, weight loss, and exercise. Starbucks also estimates that 70 percent of employees are either currently in college or desire to earn a degree. The aforementioned partnership with ASU provides this opportunity as students can choose from 80 online programs with no obligation to remain a Starbucks employee while receiving or achieving their degree. More than 2,000 employees applied to the program when it was initially launched. The rising cost of education is an important issue that former CEO Howard Schultz wanted to help alleviate. By 2025, Starbucks hopes to have 25,000 graduates among their employees.

Along with educational opportunities, employees have an opportunity to join Starbuck's stock-sharing program called Bean Stock. Starbucks has generated over $1 billion in financial gains through stock options. After receiving a tax cut in 2018, Starbucks used their saved money to raise employee pay and provide $500 grants to workers.

Suppliers

Even though they are one of the largest coffee brands in the world, Starbucks maintains a good reputation for social responsibility and business ethics throughout the international community of coffee growers. They build positive relationships with small coffee suppliers while also working with governments and nonprofits wherever they operate. Starbucks practices conservation as well as Starbucks Coffee and Farmer Equity Practices (C.A.F.E.), a set of socially responsible coffee buying guidelines that ensure preferential buying status for participants who receive high scores in best practices. Starbucks pays coffee farmers premium prices to help them make profits and support their families. Starbucks is close to their goal of 100 percent of total coffee purchases being C.A.F.E. verified. The company is currently at 99 percent.

The company is also involved in social development programs, investing in programs to build schools and health clinics, as well as other projects that benefit coffee-growing communities. Starbucks collaborates directly with some of its growers through Farmer Support Centers, located in Costa Rica, Rwanda, Tanzania, South America, Ethiopia, Indonesia, Mexico, and China. Farmer Support Centers provide technical support and training to ensure high-quality coffee into the future. The company is a major purchaser of Fair Trade Certified, shade-grown, and certified organic beans that further support environmental and economic efforts. In 2018, Starbucks welcomed the public into the coffee process and experience through their new Visitor Center in Costa Rica. Again, the goal is transparency and educating the public on how coffee beans go from the fields to the stores.

Customers

Starbucks is focused more on quality coffee, the atmosphere of their stores, and the overall Starbucks experience rather than the rapid expansion of stores after the company began missing same-store sales targets in 2016. Additionally, strengthening their brand and customer satisfaction is more important than ever as Starbucks seeks to regroup after the latest recession forced the company to rethink their strategy. Starbucks refocused the brand by upgrading their coffee-brewing machines, introducing new food and drink items for health and budget-conscious consumers, and refocusing on their core product. Recognizing the concern over the obesity epidemic, Starbucks ensures that their grab-and-go lunch items are under 500 calories and is involved in two sodium reduction programs: the National Salt and Sugar Reduction Initiative in New York and the UK Food Standards Agency's salt campaign. Conscious of

dairy allergies, Starbucks also offers milk alternatives such as almond, soy, and coconut milk for the majority of drinks.

Communities

Starbucks coffee shops have long sought to become an "instant gathering spot" and a "place that draws people together." The company established "community stores," which not only serve as a meeting place for community programs and trainings but also as a source of funding to solve issues specific to the local community. There are currently twelve such locations, including one in Thailand.

Schultz used the advance and ongoing royalties from his book, *Pour Your Heart Into It*, to create the Starbucks Foundation, which provides opportunity grants to nonprofit literacy groups, sponsors young writers' programs, and partners with Jumpstart, an organization helping children prepare developmentally for school. The company also announced their intention to hire 10,000 veterans by 2018. In 2018, Starbucks proudly confirmed that they had not only reached that goal but had more than doubled it for a total of 21,000 veteran hires.

Additionally, Starbucks takes a proactive approach to addressing employment opportunities and job training. The company has joined other firms to support the "100,000 Opportunities Initiative," with the goal of creating 100,000 employment and internship opportunities for lower-income youth between 16 and 24 years of age. Former CEO Howard Schultz helped spearhead the initiative and announced plans to hire 10,000 young workers over a three-year period. Achieving this goal early, Starbucks now has 75,000 young workers. Starbucks also announced that they were building 15 new store locations in lower-income, predominately minority neighborhoods in an attempt to improve communities through employment, education, and training. For instance, their location in Ferguson, Missouri, acts as a coffee shop as well as a job training facility for community members. Starbucks also plans to partner with local organizations to sell their products in local stores.

Brand Evolution

Although Starbucks achieved massive success in the last four decades, the company realized they had to modify their brand to appeal to changing consumer tastes. All established companies, no matter how successful, must learn to adapt their products and image to appeal to the shifting demands of their target markets. Starbucks is no exception. The company is associated with premium coffee beverages, an association that has served them well over the years. However, as competition in specialty coffee drinks increased, Starbucks recognized the need to expand their brand in the eyes of consumers.

With brand expansion in mind, the company has begun to adopt more products. In addition to coffee, Starbucks stores sell coffee accessories, teas, muffins, water, grab-and-go products, upscale food items, hand-crafted sodas called Fizzios, as well as wine and beer in select locations. Food sales make up 20 percent of Starbucks' revenue. CEO Kevin Johnson stated that the company plans to double that in the near future. The rise in coffee prices has created an opportunity for expansion into consumer packaged goods that will protect Starbucks against the risks of relying solely on coffee. In order to remain competitive, Starbucks made a series of acquisitions to increase the value of its brand, including Bay Bread (a small artisan bakery), La Boulange (a bakery brand), Evolution Fresh (a juice brand), and Teavana (a tea brand). This allows Starbucks to offer high-quality breakfast sandwiches as well as Paninis and wraps for lunch.

To symbolize this shift into the consumer packaged goods business, Starbucks gave their logo a new look. Previously, the company's circular logo featured a mermaid with the words "Starbucks Coffee" encircling it. In 2011, Starbucks removed the words and enlarged the mermaid to signal to consumers that Starbucks is more than just the average coffee retailer.

Innovation

In September 2018, Starbucks announced their plans for an organizational "shake-up." This shake-up included corporate layoffs at top levels. Starbucks explained the reasoning was to innovate the company as well as to combat stagnant sales and spark investor and customer interest. In the years leading up to 2018, Starbucks faced lagging U.S. sales for several quarters, and sales growth was not up to investors' expectations. Kevin Johnson sent an email to employees stating his plan was "to make significant changes to how we work as leaders in all areas of the company." According to the CEO, approximately 5 percent of the company's global corporate workforce would be cut, including about 350 employees in marketing, creative, product, technology, and store development areas of the company. Johnson said that while the decision was very difficult, the positions affected were related to work that has been eliminated or deprioritized as the company streamlined their business over time.

Starbucks' goal is to speed the arrival of new menu items at their cafes and push innovation. One way they want to push innovation is through the automation of their back-of-store inventory system. They want to implement a waste reduction function which will allow employees to spend more time and energy in customer service. The company began to implement these organizational changes just weeks after they were initially announced. Starbucks even added new menu options, such as a non-dairy, plant-based cold-brew drink, and

implemented a grab-and-go sandwich and salad line to reduce afternoon traffic in stores.

In 2018, Starbucks and Alibaba, one of the world's largest online retailers, formed a partnership to provide an online Starbucks store for customers in China. China is Starbucks' largest growth market. Utilizing Alibaba's technology, Starbucks products are ordered online and delivered to customers directly. While the delivery system benefits Starbucks company, Alibaba will also benefit by carrying Starbucks drinks in their popular supermarkets, called Hema, via "Starbucks Delivery Kitchens." Since partnering with Alibaba in China, Starbucks has formed two additional partnerships in the United States, with Brightloom and Uber Eats, in 2019, with a focus again on virtual deliveries and expansion of the company through technology. The idea behind the partnership with Uber Eats came from the success of the Alibaba delivery program in China, which caters to 2,000 stores in over 30 cities. Starbucks' goal was to reach a quarter of their U.S. stores with delivery through Uber Eats by the end of the second quarter of 2019. Capitalizing on the fact that digital and mobile orders, especially through delivery services, often result in higher checks, Starbucks hopes to lure customers into spending more money via their delivery system.

Additionally, in 2018, Starbucks noticed a 3 percent decline in Frappuccino sales, a signature drink of their brand. Starbucks attributed the decrease to customers becoming more health-conscious and moving away from sugary drinks. As a result, Starbucks will continue to develop more health-conscious drinks, such as low-sugar iced tea, to cater to customers' changing preferences.

In an effort to ramp up innovation, Starbucks created the Tryer Center in 2018 at their headquarters in Seattle, a 20,000-square-foot facility where employees test new beverages using rapid prototyping. Product development can traditionally take companies months, and sometimes years, to perfect an idea, and this is a way that Starbucks is attempting to accelerate the process. At the center, employees can quickly test new concepts. For example, a new single-cup brewing prototype was able to go through 10 versions in a month's time using the lab's 3D printer. Another month later, the final product made it into Starbucks locations. From the more-than 130 projects that have been tested to date, approximately 30 percent are currently in Starbucks cafes. Starbucks partners from every level of the business are invited to submit ideas, helping foster a sense of community among team members. The creation of this innovation lab will make Starbucks more agile in developing, testing, and releasing new products and systems.

Starbucks is also investing in innovation with technology. The company teamed up with Microsoft to enhance the Starbucks app, using reinforcement learning technology to provide users with a personalized ordering experience. This technology uses artificial intelligence (AI) to give users custom food and drink suggestions based on factors such as previous order history, weather, time of day, and inventory at the user's local Starbucks. Starbucks believes this use of machine learning builds on the Starbucks experience of customer connection. Additionally, with the rise of connected internet of things (IoT) devices, Starbucks, with the help of Microsoft, has put the right technology in place to accommodate cloud-connected store equipment. This type of connectivity provides Starbucks with data points on equipment performance such as coffee temperature and water quality, so baristas can focus less on machine maintenance. The company is able to send new coffee recipes directly to the machines instead of having store partners manually loading them from flash drives, saving time and money. The data-driven system allows Starbucks to have a predictive rather than reactive approach.

Success and Challenges

Starbucks is the most prominent brand of high-end coffee in the world but also one of the defining brands of our time. In most large cities, it is impossible to walk more than a few blocks without seeing the familiar mermaid logo. In the past few decades, Starbucks achieved amazing levels of growth, creating financial success for shareholders. Starbucks' reputation is built on product quality, stakeholder concern, and a balanced approach to all of their business activities. Of course, Starbucks does receive criticism for putting other coffee shops out of business and for creating a uniform retail culture in many cities. Yet, the company excels in relationship-building with their employees and is a role model for the fast-food industry in employee benefits. In addition, in an age of shifts in supply chain power, Starbucks is as concerned about their suppliers and meeting their needs as they are about any other primary stakeholder.

In spite of Starbucks' efforts to support sustainability and maintain high ethical standards, the company garnered harsh criticism in the past on issues such as a lack of fair trade coffee, hormone-added milk, and Howard Schultz's alleged financial links to the Israeli government. In an attempt to counter these criticisms, in 2002, Starbucks began offering Fair Trade Certified coffee, a menu item that was quickly made permanent. As of 2015, approximately 99 percent of their coffee in the United States is ethically sourced.

Starting in late 2008, Starbucks had something new to worry about. A global recession caused the market to bottom out for expensive coffee drinks. The company responded by slowing their global growth plans after years of expanding at a nonstop pace and instead refocused on strengthening their brand, satisfying customers, and building consumer loyalty. After Starbucks stock started to plummet, Howard Schultz returned as CEO to bring the company back to their former glory.

Schultz was successful, and Starbucks rebounded from the effects of the recession. The company is once again looking toward possibilities in international markets. This represents both new opportunities and challenges. When attempting to break into the U.K. market, for instance, Starbucks was met with serious resistance. Realizing the homogenization of their stores did not work as well in the United Kingdom, Starbucks began to remodel their stores so they took on a more local feel. At the end of 2012, Starbucks came under public scrutiny for allegedly not paying taxes for the last 14 of the 15 years they were established in the United Kingdom. A protest group called UK Uncut began "sitting in" at the stores, encouraging coffee drinkers to buy their coffee elsewhere. Starbucks claims they did not pay taxes because they did not make a profit. However, the company said they would stop using certain accounting techniques that showed their profits overseas. Starbucks also agreed to pay 20 million pounds over the next two years, whether or not they made a profit.

Starbucks is rapidly expanding in China and is the number one market for the company. When Starbucks first entered the country in 1999, coffee was not nearly as popular as tea. Starbucks positioned themselves in highly trafficked areas to gain awareness and crafted beverages using local ingredients, such as green tea, to create appealing drinks. Additionally, Starbucks strategically partnered with various coffee companies around China that provided local expertise to help Starbucks expand quickly. Starbucks effectively overcame obstacles in tapping into the Chinese market and adapted their strategy to attract Chinese consumers. For example, after the 2007 closure of the retail operation in the Forbidden City, resulting from cultural concerns of the presence of a Western staple in a sacred area, Starbucks became more sensitive to the specific needs and nuances of the country.

Starbucks faced a major setback in customer trust in 2018 after two black men were refused access to the bathroom at a Philadelphia location. A video that was recorded of the incident was shared to Twitter and viewed more than 11.5 million times. After the incident, Starbucks closed all of its stores for a one-day anti-bias training for employees. Starbucks publicly apologized and acknowledged the need to make changes to prevent racial bias. This one-time training was costly due to millions in lost profits but showed the company was willing to right their wrong. Additionally, the two men received an apology along with a financial settlement.

Another challenge Starbucks must address is sustainability. Despite the company's emphasis on becoming more environmentally conscious, billions of disposable Starbucks cups continue to be thrown into landfills each year. Although Starbucks has taken initiatives to make the cups more eco-friendly, such as changing from polyethylene No. 1 to the more eco-friendly polypropylene No. 5, the cup represents a serious waste problem for Starbucks. Starbucks encourages consumers to bring in reusable cups (such as the Starbucks tumblers they sell) for a 10-cent rebate, yet these account for less than 2 percent of drinks served. The company hopes to achieve less cup waste with their $1 reusable cup. It remains to be seen whether Starbucks will achieve their goal of total recyclability in the short term.

Conclusion

Despite the setbacks experienced during the Great Recession, the future looks bright for Starbucks. In 2015, the company underwent a 2-for-1 stock split as their way of addressing record highs in the company's stock history. It is estimated that Starbucks shares have quadrupled four times over the past five years. The company continues to expand globally into markets such as Bangalore, India; San Jose, Costa Rica; Oslo, Norway; and Ho Chi Minh City, Vietnam. With new roasteries, the innovation lab, and implementing IoT, the company hopes that their innovation will continue to spread the brand name and the distribution of their coffee globally. The challenges the company experienced and will continue to experience in the future have convinced the firm to focus on their strengths and emphasize community involvement, outreach work, and their overall image and offerings.

Questions for Discussion

1. What impact do you think recyclable plastic lids and straws will have on the sustainability goals of Starbucks?
2. Is Starbucks unique in being able to provide a high level of benefits and college tuition reimbursement to their employees?
3. Do you think Starbucks has grown because of their mission to put people ahead of profits or because of innovative ideas like online ordering and global roasteries?

Sources

"Coffee Deal Has Stocks Soaring," *USA Today*, March 11, 2011, 5B.

"Number of Starbucks Stores Globally, 1992-2018," *Knoema*, March 12, 2019, https://knoema.com/infographics/kchdsge/number-of-starbucks-stores-globally-1992-2018 (accessed August 1, 2019).

"Starbucks Corporation (SBUX)," *YAHOO! Finance*, http://finance.yahoo.com/q/is?s=SBUX+Income+Statement&annual (accessed August 4, 2019).

"Starbucks Introduces $1 Reusable Cup to Cut Down on Waste," *Eatocracy*, January 3, 2013, https://cnneatocracy.wordpress.com/2013/01/03/starbucks-introduces-1-reusable-cup-to-cut-down-on-waste/comment-page-2/ (accessed August 4, 2019).

"Starbucks Plans 'Significant Changes' to Company's Structure," *Los Angeles Times*, September 24, 2018, https://www.latimes.com/business/la-fi-starbucks-organizational-changes-20180924-story.html (accessed August 4, 2019).

"Starbucks to Enter China's Tea Drinks Market," *China Retail News*, March 11, 2010, www.chinaretailnews.com/2010/03/11/3423-starbucks-to-enter-chinas-tea-drinks-market (accessed August 4, 2019).

"Starbucks Unveils Minimalist New Logo," *USA Today*, January 6, 2011, 11B.

"Starbucks: A Farm of Its Own," *Bloomberg Businessweek*, March 25–31, 2013, 23.

"Statistics and Facts on Starbucks," *Statista*, October 2013, http://www.statista.com/topics/1246/starbucks/ (accessed August 4, 2019).

Aamer Madhani, "Starbucks to Open Stores in Low-Income Areas," *USA Today*, July 16, 2015, http://www.usatoday.com/story/news/2015/07/16/starbucks-to-open-15-locations-in-low-income-minority-communities/30206071/ (accessed August 4, 2019).

Adam Campbell-Schmitt, "Roastery, Reserve Bar, Regular Starbucks: What's the Difference?" *Food & Wine*, December 20, 2018, https://www.foodandwine.com/news/starbucks-roastery-reserve-bar-store-difference (accessed August 4, 2019).

Adam Minter, "Why Starbucks Won't Recycle Your Cup," *Bloomberg View*, April 7, 2014, http://www.bloombergview.com/articles/2014-04-07/why-starbucks-won-t-recycle-your-cup (accessed August 4, 2019).

Alicia Kelso, "Starbucks' Plan To Double Food Offerings Could Further Disrupt Traditional QSRs," *Forbes*, March 27, 2018, https://www.forbes.com/sites/aliciakelso/2018/03/27/starbucks-plans-to-double-food-offerings-could-further-disrupt-traditional-qsrs/#7959d11f4f0f (accessed August 4, 2019).

Amy Elisa Jackson, "Coffee & College: How Starbucks Is Investing in Its Employees' Future," *Glassdoor*, May 8, 2018, https://www.glassdoor.com/blog/starbucks-college-achievement-plan/ (accessed August 4, 2019).

Arwa Mahdawi, "Starbucks Is Banning Straws – But Is It Really a Big Win for the Environment?" *The Guardian*, July 23, 2018, https://www.theguardian.com/business/2018/jul/23/starbucks-straws-ban-2020-environment (accessed August 4, 2019).

Beth Kowitt, "Coffee Shop, Contained," *Fortune*, May 20, 2013, 24.

Bobbie Gossage, "Howard Schultz, on Getting a Second Shot," *Inc.*, April 2011, 52–54.

Brandi Neal, "Starbucks' New Reserve Store Will Sell Alcohol & The Cocktails Sound Amazing," *Bustle*, February 27, 2018, https://www.bustle.com/p/starbucks-new-reserve-store-will-sell-alcohol-the-cocktails-sound-amazing-8335877 (accessed August 4, 2019).

Bruce Horovitz and Howard Schultz, "Starbucks Hits 40 Feeling Perky," *USA Today*, March 7, 2011, 1B, 3B.

Bruce Horovitz, "For Starbucks, a Split and a Jolt," *USA Today*, March 19, 2015, 2B.

Bruce Horovitz, "Handcrafted Sodas to Bubble Up Atat Starbucks," *USA Today*, June 23, 2014, 4B.

Bruce Horovitz, "Starbucks Aims beyond Lattes to Extend Brand to Films, Music and Books," *USA Today*, May 19, 2006, A1–A2.

Bruce Horovitz, "Starbucks Brews Wireless Charging," *USA Today*, June 12, 2014, 2B.

Bruce Horovitz, "Starbucks Remakes Its Future," *USA Today*, October 18, 2010, 1B–2B.

Bruce Horovitz, "Starbucks Sales Pass BK, Wendy's," *USA Today*, April 27, 2011, 1A.

Bruce Horovitz, "Starbucks Serving Alcohol at More Sites," *USA Today*, March 21, 2014, 3B.

Bruce Horovitz, "Starbucks Shells Out Bread for Bakery," *USA Today*, June 5, 2012, 1B.

Bruce Horovitz, "Starbucks Taps into Tasting Room Fad," *USA Today*, December 5, 2014, 1B–2B.

Business Wire, "Starbucks Opens New Community Store in Dallas Oak Cliff Area to Help Support Economic Revitalization and Youth Hiring," *Business Wire*, November 29, 2018, https://www.businesswire.com/news/home/20181129005231/en/Starbucks-Opens-New-Community-Store-Dallas-Oak (accessed August 4, 2019).

CC, "Starbucks Brings Imported Coffee to a Land of Exported Coffee," *Fast Company*, May 2012, 30.

Charlie Rose, "Charlie Rose Talks to Howard Schultz," *Bloomberg Businessweek*, April 7–13, 2014, 32.

Christine Birkner, "Taking Care of Their Own," *Marketing News*, February 2015, 45–49.

Conservation International, "Follow Starbucks' 15 Year Journey to 100% Ethically Sourced Coffee," https://www.conservation.org/partners/starbucks (accessed August 4, 2019).

Craig Smith, "30 Interesting Starbucks Facts and Statistics (2019) By the Numbers," *DMR*, July 27, 2019 (last updated), https://expandedramblings.com/index.php/starbucks-statistics/ (accessed August 1, 2019).

Dan Welch, "Fairtrade Beans Do Not Mean a Cup of Coffee is Entirely Ethical," *guardian.co.uk*, February 28, 2011, http://www.guardian.co.uk/environment/green-living-blog/2011/feb/28/coffee-chains-ethical (accessed August 4, 2019).

Danielle Wiener-Bronner, "Starbucks says it will close 150 stores next year," *CNN Business*, June 19, 2018, https://money.cnn.com/2018/06/19/news/companies/starbucks-store-closures/index.html (accessed August 4, 2019).

David Kesmodel and Ilan Brat, "Why Starbucks Takes On Social Issues," *The Wall Street Journal*, March 24, 2015, B3.

David Schorn, "Howard Schultz: The Star of Starbucks," *60 Minutes*, https://www.cbsnews.com/news/howard-schultz-the-star-of-starbucks/ (accessed August 4, 2019).

David Teather, "Starbucks Legend Delivers Recovery by Thinking Smaller," *The Guardian*, January 21, 2010, https://www.theguardian.com/business/2010/jan/21/starbucks-howard-schultz (accessed August 4, 2019).

Eartheasy.com, "Shade Grown Coffee," http://www.earth-easy.com/eat_shadegrown_coffee.htm (accessed August 4, 2019).

Emily Canal, "Starbucks Is Putting $250 Million into Boosting Employee Pay and Benefits After the Tax Cut," *Inc.*, n.d., https://www.inc.com/emily-canal/starbucks-boosts-workers-pay-corporate-tax-savings.html (accessed August 4, 2019).

Eric Corbett, "These 8 Companies Are Ditching Plastic Straws. Here's How They Are Replacing Them," *Fortune*, July 11, 2018, https://fortune.com/2018/07/11/ditching-plastic-straws-replacements/ (accessed August 4, 2019).

Erica Salmon Byrne, "A Clear Correlation: Ethical Companies Outperform," *Ethisphere Institute*, June 9, 2017, https://insights.ethisphere.com/a-clear-correlation-ethical-companies-outperform/ (accessed October 17, 2019).

Erika Cruz, "It's Coffee Time: Find out How Starbucks Turns to Technology to Brew up a More Personal Connection with Its Customers," Microsoft, June 14, 2019, https://blogs.microsoft.com/latinx/2019/06/14/its-coffee-time-find-out-how-starbucks-turns-to-technology-to-brew-up-a-more-personal-connection-with-its-customers/ (accessed October 25, 2019).

Gary Stern, "Starbucks' Reserve Roastery Is Spacious and Trendy, so Why Is It Slowing down Expansion?" *Forbes*, January 22, 2019, https://www.forbes.com/sites/garystern/2019/01/22/starbucks-reserve-roastery-its-spacious-and-trendy-but-why-is-starbucks-slowing-down-expansion/#6aef24681bc6 (accessed August 4, 2019).

Geoff Colvin, "Questions for Starbucks' Chief Bean Counter," *Fortune*, December 9, 2013, 78–82.

Haley Geffen, "Starbucks: Howard Schultz on the Coffee Chain's Expansion Under His Leadership," *Bloomberg Businessweek*, December 8–14, 2014, 32.

Helen H. Wang, "Five Things Starbucks Did to Get China Right," Forbes, August 10, 2012, https://www.forbes.com/sites/helenwang/2012/08/10/five-things-starbucks-did-to-get-china-right/#3ae6fec53af2 (accessed October 17, 2019).

Ilan Brat, "Starbucks Lines Up Delivery Options," *The Wall Street Journal*, March 19, 2015, B2.

Jason Groves and Peter Campbell, "Starbucks Set to Cave in and Pay More Tax After Threats of Boycott at its 'immoral' Financial Dealings," *dailymail.co.uk*, December 3, 2012, http://www.dailymail.co.uk/news/article-2242596/Starbucks-pay-tax-public-outcry-financial-dealings.html (accessed August 4, 2019).

Jessica Tyler, "Starbucks Just Opened a Reserve Roastery in New York That Has a Full Cocktail Bar and Is Almost 13 Times the Size of the Average Starbucks. Here's How It Compares to a Typical Starbucks," *Business Insider*, December 17, 2018, https://www.businessinsider.com/starbucks-reserve-roastery-compared-regular-starbucks-2018-12 (accessed August 4, 2019).

John Jannarone, "Grounds for Concern at Starbucks," *The Wall Street Journal*, May 3, 2011, C10.

Jonathan Watts, "Starbucks Faces Eviction from the Forbidden City," *www.guardian.co.uk*, January 18, 2007, http://www.guardian.co.uk/world/2007/jan/18/china.jonathanwatts (accessed August 4, 2019).

Julie Jargon and Douglas Belkin, "Starbucks to Subsidize Online Degrees," *The Wall Street Journal*, June 16, 2014, B3.

Julie Jargon, "At Starbucks, Baristas Told No More than Two Drinks," *The Wall Street Journal,* October 13, 2010, http://online.wsj.com/article/SB10001424052748704164004575548403514060736.html (accessed August 4, 2019).

Julie Jargon, "Coffee Talk: Starbucks Chief on Prices, McDonald's Rivalry," *The Wall Street Journal,* March 7, 2011, B6.

Julie Jargon, "Starbucks Brews Plan Catering to Aficionados," *The Wall Street Journal*, September 11, 2014, B7.

Julie Jargon, "Starbucks CEO to Focus on Digital," *The Wall Street Journal*, January 30, 2014, B6.

Julie Jargon, "Starbucks Leads Push to Boost Youth Jobs," *The Wall Street Journal*, July 14, 2015, B3.

Julie Jargon, "Starbucks Logo Loses 'Coffee,' Expands Mermaid as Firm Moves to Build Packaged-Goods Business," *The Wall Street Journal,* January 6, 2011, B4.

Kate McClelland, "Starbucks Founder Speaks on Ethics," *Notre Dame Observer,* March 30, 2007, http://ndsmcobserver.com/2007/03/starbucks-founder-speakson-ethics/ (accessed August 4, 2019).

Kate Rogers, "Starbucks is Speeding up Innovation at Its Seattle Research Hub," *CNBC*, May 2, 2019, https://www.cnbc.com/2019/05/02/starbucks-is-speeding-up-innovation-at-its-seattle-research-hub.html (accessed October 25, 2019).

Kate Rogers and Christine Wang, "Starbucks to Cut 5% of Its Corporate Workforce," *CNBC*, November 13, 2018, https://www.cnbc.com/2018/11/13/starbucks-to-cut-5percent-of-its-corporate-workforce.html (accessed August 4, 2019).

Kate Taylor, "Starbucks Has a New Innovation Lab That Developed More Than 130 Projects in under a Year, Including Tech Updates, Instagram-Worthy Drinks, and Soup-Making Equipment," *Business Insider*, June 13, 2019, https://www.businessinsider.com/starbucks-tryer-center-innovation-lab-tour-2019-6 (accessed October 25, 2019).

Katie Lobosco, "Oprah Chai Tea Comes to Starbucks," *CNN Money*, March 19, 2014, https://money.cnn.com/2014/03/19/news/companies/oprah-starubucks-tea/index.html (accessed August 4, 2019).

Laura Lorenzetti, "Where Innovation Is Always Brewing," *Fortune*, November 17, 2014, 24.

Laurie Burkitt, "Starbuck Menu Expands in China," *The Wall Street Journal,* March 9, 2011, B7.

Lucas Mearian, "From Coffee Bean to Cup: Starbucks Brews a Blockchain-Based Supply Chain with Microsoft," *Computerworld*, May 7, 2019, https://www.computerworld.com/article/3393211/from-coffee-bean-to-cup-starbucks-brews-a-blockchain-based-supply-chain-with-microsoft.html (accessed August 4, 2019).

Mariko Sanchanta, "Starbucks Plans Big Expansion in China," *The Wall Street Journal*, April 14, 2010, B10.

Matt Naham, "Starbucks Hit with Class Action Lawsuit Alleging That Customers Were Exposed to 'Toxic Pesticide'," *Law & Crime*, May 21, 2019, https://lawandcrime.com/high-profile/starbucks-hit-with-class-action-lawsuit-alleging-that-customers-were-exposed-to-toxic-pesticide/ (accessed August 4, 2019).

Micah Solomon, "Starbucks to Open Store, Customer Service Training Center in Ferguson, 14 Other Distressed Locations," *Forbes*, July 16, 2015, http://www.forbes.com/sites/micahsolomon/2015/07/16/starbucks-to-open-store-customer-service-training-center-in-ferguson-14-other-distressed-locations/ (accessed August 4, 2019).

MSNBC.com, "Health Care Takes Its Toll on Starbucks," September 14, 2005, http://www.nbcnews.com/id/9344634/ns/business-us_business/t/health-care-takes-its-toll-starbucks/ (accessed August 4, 2019).

Nestle, "Nestle and Starbucks close deal for the perpetual global license of Starbucks Consumer Packaged Goods and Foodservice products," August 28, 2018, https://www.nestle.com/media/pressreleases/allpressreleases/nestle-starbucks-close-deal-consumer-packaged-goods-foodservice-products (accessed August 4, 2019).

Nielsen, "Consumer-Goods' Brands That Demonstrate Commitment to Sustainability Outperform Those That Don't," October 12, 2015, https://www.nielsen.com/us/en/press-releases/2015/consumer-goods-brands-that-demonstrate-commitment-to-sustainability-outperform/ (accessed October 17, 2019).

Peter Campbell, "Starbucks Caves in to Pressure and Promises to Hand the Taxman £20m after Public Outcry," *dailymail.co.uk*, December 6, 2012, http://www.dailymail.co.uk/news/article-2244100/Starbucks-caves-pressure-promises-pay-20m-corporation-tax-2-years.html (accessed August 4, 2019).

Rachel Abrams, "Starbucks to Close 8,000 U.S. Stores for Racial-Bias Training after Arrests," *The New York Times*, April 17, 2018, https://www.nytimes.com/2018/04/17/business/starbucks-arrests-racial-bias.html (accessed August 23, 2019).

Rana Foroohar, "Starbucks for America," *Time*, February 16, 2015, 18–23.

Reuters, "Starbucks to Open First Outlet in Vietnam in Early February," *Economic Times,* January 3, 2013, http://www.reuters.com/article/2013/01/03/starbucks-vietnam-idUSL4N0A815420130103 (accessed August 4, 2019).

Ron Shevlin, "Walmart Tops Starbucks, Amazon And Uber For Mobile App Adoption Dominance," *Forbes*, May 20, 2019, https://www.forbes.com/sites/ronshevlin/2019/05/20/walmart-tops-starbucks-amazon-and-uber-for-mobile-app-adoption-dominance/#23d540897a1c (accessed August 4, 2019).

Roxanne Escobales and Tracy McVeigh, "Starbucks hit by UK Uncut Protests as Tax Row Boils Over," *guardian. co.uk*, December 8, 2012, http://www.guardian.co.uk/business/2012/dec/08/starbucks-uk-stores-protests-tax (accessed August 4, 2019).

Sarah Jones, "Starbucks Shows that Healthcare isn't a Job Killer by Adding 1,500 Cafes," *PoliticusUSA*, December 6, 2012, http://www.politicususa.com/2012/12/06/healthcare-providing-starbucks-expanding1500-cafes.html (accessed August 4, 2019).

Sarah Whitten and Kate Rogers, "Starbucks Cuts Long-Term Earnings per Share Forecast; Shares Fall," *CNBC*, December 13, 2018, https://www.cnbc.com/2018/12/13/starbucks-partners-with-uber-eats-to-deliver-to-customers.html (accessed August 4, 2019).

Sarah Whitten, "A Look inside Starbucks' Newest Reserve Roastery in New York City," *CNBC*, December 13, 2018, https://www.cnbc.com/2018/12/12/heres-what-starbucks-new-roastery-in-new-york-city-looks-like.html (accessed August 4, 2019).

SCS Global Services, "Starbucks C.A.F.E. Practices," http://www.scsglobalservices.com/starbucks-cafe-practices (accessed August 4, 2019).

Starbucks "Starbucks Opens Community Store in Birmingham to Support Economic Revitalization and Youth Hiring," August 29, 2018, https://stories.starbucks.com/press/2018/starbucks-opens-community-store-in-birmingham/ (accessed August 4, 2019).

Starbucks Reserve, https://www.starbucksreserve.com/en-us/coffee (accessed August 4, 2019).

Starbucks, "Global Social Impact," https://www.starbucks.com/responsibility/global-report (accessed August 4, 2019).

Starbucks, "Affogato Line-up at Starbucks Roastery in Seattle," June 27, 2016, https://news.starbucks.com/news/affogato-line-up-at-starbucks-roastery (accessed August 4, 2019).

Starbucks, "Community Stores," http://www.starbucks.com/responsibility/community/community-stores (accessed August 4, 2019).

Starbucks, "Diversity at Starbucks," https://www.starbucks.com/responsibility/community/diversity-and-inclusion/aspirations (accessed August 4, 2019).

Starbucks, "Explore Our Menu," https://www.starbucks.com/menu/catalog/product?food=bakery#view_control=product (accessed August 4, 2019).

Starbucks, "Farming Communities," http://www.starbucks.com/responsibility/community/farmer-support (accessed August 4, 2019).

Starbucks, "Food," https://www.starbucks.com/promo/food (accessed August 4, 2019).

Starbucks, "Greener Stores," https://www.starbucks.com/responsibility/environment/leed-certified-stores (accessed August 4, 2019).

Starbucks, "Investing in Farmers," http://www.starbucks.com/responsibility/community/farmer-support/farmer-loan-programs (accessed August 4, 2019).

Starbucks, "Mobile Applications," http://www.starbucks.com/coffeehouse/mobile-apps (accessed August 4, 2019).

Starbucks, "On the Ground Support for Farming Communities," https://www.starbucks.com/responsibility/community/farmer-support/farmer-support-centers (accessed August 4, 2019).

Starbucks, "Opportunity for Youth," https://www.starbucks.com/responsibility/community/opportunity-youth (accessed August 4, 2019).

Starbucks, "Recycling & Reducing Waste," http://www.starbucks.com/responsibility/environment/recycling (accessed August 4, 2019).

Starbucks, "Small Changes Add Up to a Big Impact," http://www.starbucks.com/promo/nutrition (accessed August 4, 2019).

Starbucks, "Starbucks and Alibaba Group Announce Partnership to Transform the Coffee Experience in China," August 2, 2018, https://stories.starbucks.com/press/2018/starbucks-and-alibaba-announce-partnership-to-transform-coffee-experience/ (accessed August 4, 2019).

Starbucks, "Starbucks CEO Kevin Johnson Discusses Recent Announcements With Brightloom and Uber Eats," July 23, 2019, https://stories.starbucks.com/stories/2019/starbucks-ceo-kevin-johnson-discusses-recent-announcements-with-brightloom-and-uber-eats/ (accessed August 4, 2019).

Starbucks, "Starbucks Company Timeline," https://www.starbucks.com/about-us/company-information/starbucks-company-timeline (accessed August 4, 2019).

Starbucks, "Starbucks Creamers Launching Nationwide," July 22, 2019, https://stories.starbucks.com/press/2019/starbucks-creamers-launching-nationwide/ (accessed August 1, 2019).

Starbucks, "Starbucks hires twice as many veterans as its 2018 commitment," November 9, 2018, https://stories.starbucks.com/press/2018/starbucks-hires-twice-as-many-veterans-as-its-2018-commitment/ (accessed August 4, 2019).

Starbucks, "Starbucks Reports Q3 Fiscal 2019 Results," July 25, 2019 (updated), https://s22.q4cdn.com/869488222/files/doc_financials/quarterly/2019/q3/FY19-Q3-Earnings-Release-FINAL-7-25-19.pdf (accessed August 1, 2019).

Starbucks, "Starbucks Reserve Roastery Milano Fact Sheet: Overview," September 6, 2018, https://stories.starbucks.com/press/2018/starbucks-reserve-roastery-milano-fact-sheet-overview/ (accessed August 4, 2019).

Starbucks, Starbucks Investor Relations, "Financial Data: Latest Annual Reports," 2019, https://investor.starbucks.com/financial-data/annual-reports/default.aspx (accessed August 1, 2019).

Susan Berfield, "Starbucks' Food Fight," *Businessweek*, June 12, 2012, http://www.businessweek.com/articles/2012-06-12/starbucks-food-fight (accessed August 4, 2019).

Tess Koman, "How Big Is Each Starbucks Drink Size Anyway?" *Delish*, February 7, 2019, https://www.delish.com/food-news/a26238255/starbucks-sizes-guide/ (accessed August 4, 2019).

Tom Brennan, "Starbucks and Alibaba Group Announce Partnership to Transform the Coffee Experience in China," *Starbucks*, August 2, 2018, https://stories.starbucks.com/press/2018/starbucks-and-alibaba-announce-partnership-to-transform-coffee-experience/ (accessed August 4, 2019).

Tonya Garcia, "Starbucks and McDonald's Plastic Straw Removal Will Go Down Well with Millennials," *MarketWatch*, July 11, 2018, https://www.marketwatch.com/story/starbucks-and-mcdonalds-plastic-straw-removal-will-go-down-well-with-millennials-2018-07-09 (accessed August 4, 2019).

Trefis Team, "Starbucks' Profits Surge Despite Sales Slowing Down," *Forbes*, January 30, 2014, http://www.forbes.com/sites/greatspeculations/2014/01/30/starbucks-profits-surge-despite-sales-slowing-down/ (accessed August 4, 2019).

United States Securities and Exchange Commission: Starbucks Corporation, 2019, https://s22.q4cdn.com/869488222/files/doc_financials/quarterly/2018/q4/4afc20cc-2933-41ec-b817-d11bcff947ca.pdf (accessed August 1, 2019).

Venessa Wong, "Starbucks Serves Up 'Flat Whites,' Tries to Prove It Can Still Be Different," *Bloomberg Businessweek*, January 6, 2015, http://www.bloomberg.com/news/articles/2015-01-06/starbucks-serves-up-flat-whites-tries-to-prove-it-can-still-be-different (accessed August 4, 2019).

If the Shoe Fits: TOMS and the One for One Movement

Introduction

TOMS Shoes is a for-profit business with a large philanthropic component. The company was started after entrepreneur Blake Mycoskie witnessed the poverty among villagers in Argentina, poverty so extreme that the villagers could not even afford a pair of shoes. Mycoskie returned to the United States with 200 Argentinian shoes and a mission. He went from one retail store to another with a unique business proposal. He would start an organization that would provide a pair of shoes for an Argentinian child in need for every pair of shoes purchased from his business. After many meetings and discussions, a few Los Angeles boutiques agreed to sell the shoes. Mycoskie's idea was eventually picked up by the *Los Angeles Times*, who ran an article on his extremely unique business idea. To his surprise, the following weekend garnered $88,000 in orders. The orders didn't slow down there, and two years after officially establishing TOMS Shoes, the business had $9.6 million in revenue.

Most firms do not want other companies to copy their successful business model. However, the shoe retailer TOMS is not your typical retailer, and the firm's business model is unusual to say the least. While many organizations try to incorporate social entrepreneurship into their business operations, TOMS took the concept of philanthropy one step further by blending a for-profit business with a philanthropic component in what they termed the One for One model. For every product purchased, TOMS donates products or resources to help those in need. The cost of providing the products to those in need is already built into the products' sales price, turning the customer into the benefactor. The philanthropic component is just as important as the for-profit business for TOMS. TOMS' goal is to be able to turn a profit, support themselves, make the world a better place, and educate consumers, all at the same time.

TOMS has applied the One for One model to its other products as well. For every product purchased, including TOMS Shoes, TOMS Eyewear, and coffee bags from TOMS Roasting Co., TOMS will help a person in need. For every pair of glasses sold, for example, TOMS provides a person in need with a full eye exam and treatment including prescription glasses, sight-saving surgery, or medical treatment to restore their sight. For each bag of TOMS Roasting Co. Coffee purchased, TOMS gives an entire week's supply of safe drinking water to a person in need. When consumers buy a TOMS product, they get the additional value of helping others.

In this case, we discuss Mycoskie's revolutionary business model and how it has achieved such success. We begin by analyzing the background and origins of the TOMS Shoes business concept, and then discuss TOMS' operational approach, including how the organization manages to carry out their central mission. Their unique corporate culture is a necessity for the successful operation of TOMS, which is examined along with the firm's marketing strategy. Next, we analyze how this business model has impacted today's society, as well as other business organizations. Then, we evaluate changing attitudes toward social issues and how TOMS has responded. We discuss various criticisms and risks that TOMS faces on a daily basis, as well as the company's decision to evolve their famous One for One model. Last, we conclude by speculating about the future of TOMS as a business.

The History of TOMS

Blake Mycoskie is the founder and Chief Shoe Giver of TOMS Shoes. Before founding TOMS Shoes, Mycoskie had started five companies that ranged from billboard advertising to laundry services. His foray into the shoe industry, however, was almost accidental. After participating in the 2002 Amazing Race reality television show, Mycoskie decided to return to all the countries he had visited during the show. When Mycoskie returned to Argentina in early 2006, he had no idea that the country's backwoods would be the inspiration for his new company. When interacting with the local villagers, he immediately noticed that many of the families could not afford a pair of shoes for their children. He was shocked and deeply saddened to see the number of children forced to live barefooted every day. This observation stuck with him for the remainder of his trip, and when he discovered the Alpargata (the comfortable and unique farm shoe worn by some of the locals), his initial idea for TOMS was born. He completed his trip in Argentina and left the country determined to take action for all of those children he saw in need.

Upon coming back home, Mycoskie sold his online driver education company for $500,000 and used that money to finance the creation of TOMS Shoes. TOMS was derived from "tomorrow," which was taken from the original company concept: "the shoes for tomorrow project." After a lot of hard work, TOMS Shoes opened for

This case was prepared by Lexie Olszewski, Jennifer Sawayda, and Sarah Sawayda for and under the direction of O.C. Ferrell and Linda Ferrell, © 2019. It was prepared for classroom discussion rather than to illustrate either effective or ineffective handling of an administrative, ethical, or legal decision by management. All sources used for this case were obtained through publicly available material.

business in May of 2006. In addition to their core shoe-selling business, the company also runs the non-profit subsidiary known as Friends of TOMS. The for-profit and non-profit organizations work in conjunction to operate the TOMS enterprise. Since their founding, TOMS has been widely successful across the entire United States, even drawing the attention of well-known celebrities. Scarlett Johansson and Keira Knightley were among the first to publicly endorse TOMS Shoes. Internationally, the non-profit side of the business is also making a huge impact in communities, evidenced by the 88 million shoes that have been distributed to children in need.

The TOMS Movement

TOMS initially made the decision to develop their business model and, therefore, their product line around shoes for several key reasons. Mycoskie knew from his travels that many children in impoverished countries live in areas with unsafe terrains. He saw firsthand the lack of paved roads and other common hazards that could cause injury for children walking around barefoot. In fact, children can contract a range of soil-transmitted diseases from not wearing shoes. For example, soil-transmitted Helminthiasis, an infection developed from intestinal worms, is common in South Africa. Simply wearing shoes can prevent many diseases, and Mycoskie wanted to help. Mycoskie also understood the value of education. In many nations, shoes are required in order to attend school. Owning a pair of shoes provides a child with an opportunity to be educated, leading to higher school attendance. According to TOMS, this combination of education and health provides children the opportunity for a better tomorrow.

As mentioned, Mycoskie's organization consists of two parts: TOMS Shoes and Friends of TOMS. TOMS Shoes is a for-profit company that manages the overall operations and logistics. Friends of TOMS, the company's non-profit subsidiary, is responsible for organizing volunteer activities and all "shoe drops," when shoes are distributed to communities in need. This was critical to the One for One business model that TOMS popularized. The model was simple: for every pair of shoes that TOMS sold, they donated a pair of shoes to a child in need on behalf of the customer. The One for One model enabled Friends of TOMS to remain in operation because the shoes sold covers the cost of the shoes for countries in need. Mycoskie dubbed this business system "Philanthropic Capitalism" because the company makes a profit but incorporates philanthropy into their business strategy. The company's ultimate vision is to demonstrate the effect of how working together as a society can "create a better tomorrow by taking compassionate action today."

The philanthropic component of TOMS contributed to their widespread popularity among consumers. One consumer survey revealed that nearly half of respondents had purchased or would purchase items during a certain time period if part of the revenues supported charitable causes. Cause-related marketing is growing and businesses like TOMS Shoes—where philanthropy is embedded within the business model—are likely to attract the support of consumers who want to make a difference. TOMS has developed successful collaborations with recognizable brands such as Ralph Lauren and Element Skateboard. Ralph Lauren worked with TOMS to develop a co-branded Polo Rugby shoe, which maintained the One for One premise. Element Skateboard joined forces with TOMS to fashion a limited edition TOMS+ Element shoe, donating a pair of shoes to a child in need for each pair sold. To further the One for One movement, Element Skateboard also promised that for every skateboard purchased, one would be donated to a child participating in the Indigo Skate Camp in Durban, South America.

In the beginning, TOMs did not have a marketing budget and relied on word-of-mouth, viral marketing, and social networks to spread their marketing efforts. Word-of-mouth can be one of the most effective forms of marketing because many consumers believe it to be more trustworthy than corporate advertisements. The challenge for any organization is to convince customers to talk about their products. For TOMS Shoes, many customers are excited that their purchase is going toward a good cause and are eager to discuss it with others. TOMS Shoes has taken proactive steps to encourage word-of-mouth communication. Each pair of TOMS Shoes comes with a blue-and-white TOMS flag and a small card asking customers to take pictures of themselves wearing their new shoes and holding up the flag. The customers are then asked to upload those photos to the "HOW WE WEAR THEM" section on the company's website, in addition to social networking websites such as Facebook and Twitter. The photos of customers using TOMS' products increase both product awareness and the credibility of the brand.

TOMS' Supply Chain

Due to their lack of knowledge about the shoe industry, Mycoskie and his team initially faced supply chain management problems. Mycoskie was unaware how fast the demand for TOMS Shoes would escalate. Two weeks after Mycoskie began selling his products to retailers, a fashion reporter wrote an article about Mycoskie's business and mission in the *Los Angeles Times*. The TOMS' website sold 2,200 pairs of shoes that same day—but Mycoskie had only 40 pairs available. The situation required him to hire interns to personally call customers and ask them to wait eight weeks for delivery. Mycoskie then flew back to Argentina where he had 40,000 shoes manufactured. Amazingly, all pairs in the batch were sold within the next few weeks.

Since then, TOMS has improved at managing their increasingly complex supply chain. They have opened up additional manufacturing factories in China, Argentina, and Ethiopia and plan to open another location in Brazil. These factories are audited by third parties to ensure that workers are being treated fairly. TOMS has their factory workers sign a code of conduct stating that they will follow all the stipulations of TOMS Shoes. TOMS' production staff visits each of the factories on a regular basis to verify that the factories are continuing to adhere to the code of conduct and other working standards. TOMS' manufacturing standards are modeled after International Labor Organization compliance standards.

Over 500 retailers around the world now carry TOMS' shoe collections. In their first couple of years in business, TOMS was able to secure distribution deals of their shoes with Nordstrom, Bloomingdale's, Neiman Marcus, Whole Foods, and Urban Outfitters. TOMS has also expanded to retailers that are independently owned small businesses. TOMS continuously seeks retailers that are passionate about their firm's mission. Retailers are able to purchase the bulk of their shoes at cost from TOMS, and thus are able to turn a profit as well as support the One for One movement. All shoes that the retailers purchase are directly shipped to the retailers—TOMS does not operate on a consignment basis. TOMS Shoes are sold in retail stores in the United States, the United Kingdom, Australia, Canada, Germany, and France. Consumers can also purchase TOMS Shoes on their website.

Manufacturing the shoes and selling them to customers is only the first step of the process. Next, TOMS must distribute shoes to the children that need them. TOMS collaborates with nonprofits to identify children in need. These Giving Partners must be actively involved with the children in their communities and objectively evaluate where TOMS Shoes can have the biggest impact on children's lives. The organizations that TOMS chooses are found in the humanitarian, health, and education fields. For instance, TOMS has worked with Partners in Health to distribute shoes to children in Haiti and the health organization SANA Guatemala to distribute shoes to Guatemalan children. In Argentina, TOMS works with an organization that provides Podoconiosis treatment programs, assisting children who are at a high risk of developing the disease. In Rwanda, TOMS is currently partnering with a non-profit business to help with over 100,000 genocide orphans. TOMS also works with a Zimbabwean organization to provide shoes to children who make extensive walks to school in various weather conditions.

In order to become a Giving Partner, organizations must go through audits to ensure that they meet TOMS' specific criteria. These five criteria are detailed in Table 1. Through TOMS' Giving Partnerships, locations are identified to show where providing a pair of shoes to children in need contributes the most toward improving the standard of living for the community. When a customer purchases a pair of TOMS' shoes, a child in the chosen

Table 1 Criteria to Become a Giving Partner

Sustainable: Giving Partners work with communities to address their needs in a way that will enable the community to meet its own needs in the future.
Local: We seek locally staffed and led organizations that have a long-term commitment to the regions where they work.
Need: TOMS' support furthers our Giving Partners' long-term goals and is integrated into their programs.
Evolving: TOMS is committed to improving our Giving by continually evolving. We look for partners who can report back to us on how we can improve.
Neutral: TOMS products and services are provided to help people in need. Our partners do not distribute them with any religious or political affiliations.

Source: "The Qualities We Look For," https://www.toms.com/thoughtful-partners (accessed January 2, 2019).

community will receive a pair of shoes approximately four to six months after the initial date of purchase. Currently, TOMS distributes shoes to children in need in 24 different countries around the world.

Friends of TOMS helps coordinate shoe drops to various communities. Every time a shoe drop occurs, TOMS seeks volunteers and individuals affiliated with TOMS to fly to the area for one week and work with their partners to distribute the shoes. Those involved in the shoe drop personally place the shoe on each child's feet.

Even after the shoes have been delivered, TOMS continues to maintain relationships with their Giving Partners and communities. TOMS constantly monitors their partners for accountability. Additionally, the organization recognizes that one pair of shoes is not going to last for the child's entire lifetime. Therefore, as the children grow out of their shoes—approximately every six months—TOMS provides replacement shoes to these same children on a regular basis. A schedule is set up with the identified community and local Giving Partner to maintain a regular shoe drop for the children. TOMS believes that repeat giving allows them to understand the locale's needs more thoroughly. TOMS also works to adapt their products to account for the region's terrain, weather, and education requirements.

TOMS' Product Line

TOMS' original product lines were derived from the Argentinian Alpargata shoe design worn by farmers in the region. The shoe is made from either canvas or a fabric material with rubber soles. Since their inception, TOMS has introduced different styles of shoes, such as the Bota and the Cordones, along with wrap boots and wedges. The Bota resembles an ankle boot with soft materials, while the Cordones are more of a traditional canvas-style sneaker with laces. In addition, the children's line includes Velcro Alpargatas.

TOMS has also created other varieties of shoes, such as Vegan TOMS and the wedding collection. Vegan

TOMS are comprised of 70 percent recycled plastic bottles and 30 percent hemp. Hemp is an extremely sustainable product that outlasts organic cotton. TOMS is committed to creating more products that are better for the environment. Additionally, TOMS introduced comfortable shoes meant for weddings. Wearing comfortable slip-on shoes to a formal event may seem odd, but some young people have already worn TOMS for prom.

Not all the shoes that are available for purchase are actually donated to children. TOMS does not give the wedge or the wraparound boot to children. Primarily the shoe that is bestowed on children is the canvas Alpargata with modifications to suit local residents. With each new community that TOMS enters, research is conducted to learn about the environment and terrain. TOMS alters their shoes to fit the children's lives. For example, in some of the regions that experience monsoons, the shoes include more of a ridged thicker rubber sole. The shoes are typically black because that is the required shoe color to attend school in several countries. TOMS has also developed a wider shoe due to the fact that children living barefoot for the majority of their lives tend to have wider feet.

Aside from selling shoes, TOMS has expanded into selling apparel, including TOMS t-shirts, sweatshirts, and caps. Any of the apparel purchased also comes with the One for One movement guarantee, meaning that for every t-shirt purchased a pair of shoes will still be given to a child in need. TOMS has also started selling the TOMS flag, stickers, necklaces, and gift cards. After distributing their one-millionth pair of shoes, Toms began to consider other products that could be used in the One for One model. Mycoskie explained, "When I thought about launching another product with the TOMS model, vision seemed the most obvious choice." Because 80 percent of vision impairment in developing countries is preventable or curable, TOMS decided that for every pair of eyewear they sold, the company would provide treatment or prescription glasses for those in need. TOMS chose Nepal as the first country in which to apply their One for One model for eyewear.

In 2011, TOMS launched TOMS Eyewear, which has helped provide prescription eyewear to more than 770,000 people in need. The company works in 13 countries to provide prescription glasses, medical treatments, and even sight-saving surgery with each purchase of eyewear. Along with restoring sight, TOMS Eyewear supports community-based eye care programs, creation of professional jobs, and trainings to local health volunteers and teachers. TOMS Eyewear purchases provide economic opportunities, gender equality, access to education, and restored independence.

In 2014, TOMS made the decision to expand the One for One model into the coffee industry and started TOMS Roasting Co. Each purchase of a bag of TOMS Roasting Co. coffee provides an entire week's supply of safe drinking water to a person in need. More than 780 million people don't have access to safe water systems. TOMS works with Giving Partners that have expertise in water, sanitation, and hygiene to help create sustainable water systems in seven countries, from the same regions where coffee beans are sourced. Since launching in 2014, TOMS has helped provide 335,000 weeks of clean water in 6 countries. By supporting and working to provide sustainable water systems, TOMS is helping provide communities with access to safe water, which has a clear trickle-down effect. With safer water comes improved health, increased economic productivity, job creation, and better access to education.

TOMS has also invested in the health care of mothers and babies in need by distributing birthing kits. TOMS Bag Collection was founded in 2015 with a mission to provide training for skilled birth attendants and to distribute birth kits containing items that help a woman deliver her baby safely. As of 2018, TOMS has supported safe births for over 175,000 mothers. Each purchase supports one delivery of a safe birth kit, two trainings for skilled birth attendants, and three healthy deliveries for newborn babies and mothers. With proper training and materials to deliver babies, mothers are 80 percent less likely to develop an infection, which means communities can prevent almost half of newborn deaths. In 2015, TOMS also first introduced the High Road Backpack, which helps fund the training of school staff and crisis counselors to prevent and respond to the widespread problem of bullying in schools.

TOMS' Corporate Culture

When the business first started, TOMS did not have a lot of money to pay individuals. The company instead focused on hiring individuals who were passionate about their mission instead of being passionate about money. Due to the lack of finances, Mycoskie hired recent college graduates and even high school graduates. Despite their youth and inexperience, the employees consistently rose to the occasion. Because TOMS did not initially engage in traditional advertising, it was important to have enthusiastic employees willing to spread the word about the organization.

TOMS soon realized that full-time employees were not the only ones willing to help the company achieve their mission. The company also relies upon interns to spread the word and support their endeavors. Employees and interns alike know that their work is supporting a good cause, and many even get to participate in their own call-to-action by participating in shoe drops.

Internships

The company started off with Mycoskie and two interns who managed to propel TOMS into a successful business. The success of those two initial interns has prompted the company to hire interns each year through the nine-week, full-time TOMS Internship Program at the TOMS headquarters. TOMS provides their interns with a high degree of responsibility in the individual's chosen discipline, whether it's online marketing, retail marketing, or operations. Intern classes include eight to ten college seniors and recent graduates. The number one criterion that TOMS looks for in the applicants are that the individuals truly believe and are enthusiastic about what TOMS stands for. According to TOMS, the company would not be where they are today if it were not for the hard work of their diverse team of interns. When an internship ends, a TOMS' intern coordinator works with the intern to strengthen his or her resume with an updated work summary of the experience gained at TOMS. The intern coordinator also provides guidance on future development of career goals.

One Day without Shoes

Perhaps the most popular event promoting TOMS is the One Day Without Shoes campaign. This campaign was started in 2008 to raise public awareness about the impact that a pair of shoes can have on a child's life. It asks the average individual to go one day without shoes. Going without shoes engages individuals to see how it feels to be in these children's situations. The premise is to instill a sense of appreciation for what a difference a pair of shoes can make. Furthermore, the sight of a large group of barefoot individuals walking around makes an impression on others. In both cases, TOMS' mission and their brand are spread to those that otherwise may not have known about it. The success of this campaign, which continues to grow every year, is largely due to college students and Campus Clubs nationwide. Participants have included Kristen Bell, Charlize Theron, the Dallas Cowboys Cheerleaders, Nordstrom, and Microsoft.

Social Media

TOMS has effectively used social media to spread the word about the company and their mission, a method that is less costly than traditional advertising and creates a unity among the individuals that promote TOMS. TOMS has used viral videos, blogs, Facebook, and Twitter to spread the message about their cause. Their approach has allowed TOMS to reach a vast audience worldwide. TOMS maintains their own blog to educate the public about current events in the company and their shoe drops. The company has also posted clips on YouTube. In addition, many consumers create their own digital content regarding their experiences with TOMS Shoes. By encouraging events and word-of-mouth communication, TOMS is allowing consumers to do much of the marketing for the company.

TOMS' Impact

During their first year in business, TOMS managed to donate 10,000 shoes to children living in Argentina. Since then, TOMS has expanded to distribute shoes to other regions of the world. Now, TOMS has given more than 100 million pairs of new shoes worldwide. TOMS gives in over 70 nations around the world including Argentina, Peru, Ethiopia, Rwanda, and South Africa.

TOMS was awarded and honored in 2007 with the People's Design Award from the Cooper-Hewitt National Design Museum, Smithsonian Institution. TOMS was also awarded the 2009 ACE award given by Secretary of State Hillary Clinton. The Award for Corporate Excellence recognized TOMS for their "commitment to corporate social responsibility, innovation, exemplary practices, and democratic values worldwide."

Under Mycoskie's inspirational leadership, the company's One for One concept has inspired other firms—such as eyeglass retailer Warby Parker—to adopt similar models as a way to give back to society. Rather than feel threatened, Mycoskie is funding social entrepreneurship firms with similar missions. However, Mycoskie's revolutionary idea might be difficult to replicate in other fields. The One for One concept must be embedded into the business strategy. The business must also be sustainable on its own, which is difficult to achieve for many nonprofits that depend upon fundraising. The product and mission must be something that people will care about. For the movement to work effectively, the product should be tangible and identifiable. Product differentiation is an important component for success, as consumers appear less able to identify with commodity products.

Mycoskie offers additional advice to entrepreneurs who want to create business that will make a difference in the world. He advises businesses to look at their strengths and comprehend how those strengths can be used to help those who need them the most. For instance, TOMS Shoes and their Giving Partners study the communities before dropping off the shoes to ensure that the shoes will make a positive difference in children's lives. They pick out the communities that appear to have the most need for their products. According to Mycoskie, it is important that companies with a philanthropic focus allow their products to speak for themselves. The products should be able to impress consumers, prompting them to spread the word to others without constant marketing from the company.

Not many businesses have attempted to replicate the One for One movement in terms of incorporating it into their business models. Two companies that have created businesses around this concept include a bedding and mattress organization, which donates one bed to those in need for every product bought, and an apparel store, which will match customers' purchases by giving clothes to those in disadvantaged areas. Time will tell whether these companies, and additional organizations, will succeed to the extent of TOMS Shoes.

Evolving the Mission

Social issues such as bullying, gender equality, inclusion, and homelessness have been key area of TOMS' philanthropy. However, in 2018 Mycoskie boldly introduced the End Gun Violence Together initiative as the company's primary focus. To kick off the initiative, consumers could visit the TOMS website to deliver postcards supporting gun safety laws to government representatives. The postcard initiative attracted 700,000 participants. Mycoskie appeared on *The Tonight Show* multiple times to champion the cause and has hosted rallies in Washington, D.C., to support the Bipartisan Background Checks Act of 2019, which was passed in February 2019.

In the face of slowing sales, Mycoskie said he believes that the TOMS business formula only works "if it's fresh, provocative, radical and somewhat newsworthy." Though TOMS has donated more than 100 million pairs of shoes, Mycoskie says their record-breaking growth occurred during the firm's first six years before the brand became mainstream. The brand has struggled with debt over the past five years and growth has stalled.

TOMS attempted to stay relevant by creating new product lines. However, despite the introduction of eyewear, coffee, and bags, footwear is still at the core of TOMS' business, making up 90 percent of sales. Product innovation held the company back instead of moving them forward. Now, instead of evolving their products, the company is evolving their mission. Though gun violence is a divisive issue, Mycoskie chose this social issue as the company's new mission after a mass shooting at a bar in Thousand Oaks, California, hit close to home. By measuring social media sentiment around universal background checks, he discovered that 75 percent of people reacted extremely positively to the concept, regardless of political beliefs. To date, the firm's gun violence platform has resulted in 59 billion media impressions and new account opening growth of 20 percent year over year. Mycoskie hopes this positive growth will continue.

Changing the Business Model

Shortly after introducing the End Gun Violence Together initiative, TOMS made another change that would alter the company's business model forever. In an effort to adapt to changing attitudes toward social issues, TOMS announced a bold decision to disrupt their own One for One business model. Customers now have more control over the causes they support with their purchase of a pair of TOMS shoes. As of May 2019, customers can choose to support campaigns related to shoe giving, safe water, ending gun violence, homelessness, mental health, or equality with their purchase.

The new giving model was introduced under a program called Stand for Tomorrow. This radical shift empowers TOMS customers to make their own decisions about how their dollar is best spent and allows them to pick issues of personal importance. Customers are instructed to "pick your stand" when they shop online. The move allows TOMS to capitalize on hot social issues that resonate with consumers. The company will monitor popular issues and continue to adapt their giving options. The continual evolution of TOMS' giving model stands to keep the brand relevant to existing customers while attracting new ones.

Criticisms and Ethical Issues

Most people might find it hard to understand why anyone would criticize TOMS Shoes. As a successful philanthropic for-profit company, TOMS has been able to help children in need all over the world. However, criticisms about the company's model do exist, many of which come from philanthropists. Probably the biggest criticism is that TOMS Shoes makes people in poor countries dependent upon the goodwill of others rather than creating opportunities for them to better themselves. Though TOMS conducted their own studies that show the company has not had a negative impact on local economies from shoe donation, many social entrepreneurs and philanthropists of today believe that the best way to create sustainable change is through education and job creation. In response, TOMS began manufacturing shoes within some of the communities that they support in order to aid and build up local economies.

Another criticism has been the fact that TOMS has manufacturing locations in China—a country that has received much scrutiny for factory abuse. One could successfully argue that as a business, it is advantageous to manufacture products in countries where labor costs are lower in order to keep prices reasonable. Supporters also point out that TOMS' factories are creating jobs in disadvantaged countries like Ethiopia. As a for-profit business, TOM Shoes will constantly have to balance the financial aspects of their for-profit business with the humanitarian elements of their philanthropic organization.

Since TOMS is for-profit, the company faces the same risks as other for-profit companies. Ethical lapses can occur just as easily in philanthropic organizations as they can in large corporations, particularly as it relates to the supply chain. It is necessary for TOMS to monitor business activities such as factory compliance, sustainability, finances, and even their shoe drop operations in order to maintain appropriate business conduct. TOMS Shoes must never be complacent regarding these risks simply because they have built philanthropy into their business. The company must also innovate constantly. Although consumers tend to like purchasing from a philanthropic organization, they appear to be more financially supportive when they get something in return. In the case of TOMS, it is a pair of unique shoes. However, with consumer tastes constantly changing, TOMS must remain vigilant regarding new designs and products and find ways to stay current with their social missions. TOMS Shoes must remain proactive in managing these risks to maintain their current success rate.

The Future of TOMS Shoes

Mycoskie revolutionized social entrepreneurship by introducing his One for One Movement. An emphasis on social entrepreneurship has been sweeping the nation, supported by high-profile individuals such as former Presidents Barack Obama and Bill Clinton. Many questioned whether or not TOMS' One for One business model was sustainable, so the recent evolution of the firm's giving model indicates that there is an even bigger question at hand: "How can TOMs continue to adapt to be sustainable for the future?"

Moving forward, TOMS will need to keep an eye on risks that affect both for-profit and non-profit organizations. Mycoskie's combination of these two business models has limited certain industry-specific risks. For instance, the for-profit business supports the non-profit component, which means TOMS does not have to rely on donations. On the other hand, the model has also introduced additional risks. Because TOMS sells a tangible product, they require a supply chain that must be constantly monitored for compliance. The company also must manage criticism of their philanthropic endeavors, an issue not as common among corporations where philanthropy is a secondary activity. It's also apparent that continually monitoring and improving the company's giving model could be critical to long-term financial success as TOMS fights to stay relevant.

Despite these challenges, the future of TOMS Shoes looks bright. The excitement over the Stand for Tomorrow demonstrates that consumers remain enthusiastic about the brand. With careful risk management, their strong mission and values, and successful promotional campaigns, TOMS will likely remain a sustainable business for years to come.

Questions for Discussion

1. Why was it necessary for TOMS to evolve their business model?
2. Who are TOMS most important stakeholders, and why?
3. Is the One for One movement business model appropriate for any other businesses?

Sources

"One for One: TOMS + Element Collaboration," Element, http://www.elementeden.com/TOMS/ (accessed June 3, 2011).

"Our Social Action Initiatives," Rugby Ralph Lauren, http://www.rugby.com/social_action/default.aspx (accessed June 3, 2011).

"Don't Be an Intern at TOMS," TOMS, http://www.toms.com/our-movement/intern (accessed June 9, 2011).

"Solid Ground," *APICS eXTRA*, September 14, 2008, http://www.apics.org/APICSXtra/img/sunday_solidground.html (accessed June 3, 2011).

Adele Peters, "Toms Made Buy-One, Give-One Famous. Now It's Updating the Model," *Fast Company*, May 7, 2019, https://www.fastcompany.com/90344987/toms-made-buy-one-give-one-famous-now-its-updating-the-model (accessed October 24, 2019).

Athima Chansanchai, "Happy Feet: Buy a Pair of TOMS Shoes and a Pair Will Be Donated to a Poor Child Abroad," *Seattle Pi*, June 11, 2007, http://www.seattlepi.com/default/article/Happy-feet-Buy-a-pair-of-TOMS-shoes-and-a-pair-1240201.php (accessed June 3, 2011).

Booth Moore, "Toms Shoes' Model Is Sell a Pair, Give a Pair Away," *Los Angeles Times*, April 19, 2009, http://www.latimes.com/features/image/la-ig-greentoms19-2009apr19,0,3694310.story (accessed June 9, 2011).

Cathleen McGuigan, "Designed to Help: A Pair for You, A Pair for the Needy," *Newsweek*, October 19, 2007, http://www.newsweek.com/2007/10/18/toms-shoes-wins-design-award.html (accessed June 3, 2011).

Craig Sharkton, "Toms Shoes – Philanthropy as a Business Model," *sufac.com*, August 23, 2008, http://sufac.com/2008/08/toms-shoesphilanthropy-as-a-business-model/ (accessed June 3, 2011).

Emily Lerman, "PhiLAnthropist Interview: TOMS Shoes Founder Blake Mycoskie Plans to Give Away 300,000 Pairs in 2009," *Laist*, April 15, 2009, http://laist.com/2009/04/15/what_happens_when_you_travel.php (accessed June 3, 2011).

Erin Alberts, "COLUMN: TOMS' Business Model a Self-Sustaining Charity," *The Volante*, April 12, 2011, http://www.volanteonline.com/opinion/column-toms-business-model-a-self-sustaining-charity-1.2540233 (accessed June 3, 2011).

Erin Kutz, "Consumers Like It When Their Purchases Help Charities," *USA Today*, December 23, 2010, http://www.usatoday.com/money/industries/retail/2010-12-23-retailcharity23_ST_N.htm (accessed June 2, 2011).

Gretchen Fogelstrom, "Another Business Giving One for One!" *Global Endeavors*, April 13, 2011, http://globalendeavors.com/2011/04/13/another-business-going-one-for-one/ (accessed June 3, 2011).

Jeff Rosenthal, "Products With Purpose Will Change the World," *Huffington Post*, January 27, 2010, http://www.huffington-post.com/jeffrosenthal/products-with-purpose-wil_b_437917.html (accessed June 3, 2011).

Katie Abel, "Can Blake Mycoskie's Bold New Social Agenda Reboot Toms?" *Footwear News*, March 25, 2019, https://footwearnews.com/2019/business/retail/toms-blake-mycoskie-interview-business-sales-mission-1202764082/ (accessed October 24, 2019).

Kelsey Timmerman, "The Problem with TOMS Shoes and Its Critics," *Where Am I Wearing*, http://whereamiwearing.com/2011/04/06/toms-shoes/ (accessed June 3, 2011).

Linda Miller, "Shoes Offer a Better Tomorrow," *NewsOK*, April 5, 2009, http://newsok.com/shoes-offer-a-bettertomorrow/article/3358735 (accessed June 3, 2011).

M.J. Prest, "The Other Shoe Drops," *Ethical Style*, March 26, 2009, http://ethicalstyle.com/issue-12/the-other-shoe-drops/ (accessed June 3, 2011).

Michelle Prasad, "TOMS Shoes Always Feels Good," *KENTON Magazine*, March 19, 2011, http://kentonmagazine.com/toms-shoesalways-feel-good/ (accessed June 3, 2011).

Mike Zimmerman, "The Business of Giving: TOMS Shoes," *Success Magazine*, September 30, 2009, http://www.successmagazine.com/the-business-of-giving/PARAMS/article/852 (accessed June 3, 2011).

Patricia Sellers, "Power Point: Be the change," *CNNMoney*, October 11, 2008, http://postcards.blogs.fortune.cnn.com/2008/10/11/power-point-be-the-change/ (accessed June 3, 2011).

Patrick Cole, "Toms Free Shoe Plan, Boosted by Clinton, Reaches Million Mark," *Bloomberg*, September 15, 2010, http://www.bloomberg.com/news/2010-09-16/toms-shoe-giveaway-for-kids-boosted-by-bill-clinton-reaches-millionmark.html (accessed June 2, 2011).

Simon Mainwaring, "Purpose at Work: How TOMS Is Evolving Its Brand To Scale Its Impact," *Forbes*, June 12, 2019, https://www.forbes.com/sites/simonmainwaring/2019/06/12/purpose-at-work-how-toms-is-evolving-its-brand-to-scale-its-impact/#6006029a1485 (accessed August 9, 2019).

Stacy Perman, "Making a Do-Gooder's Business Model Work," *Bloomberg Businessweek*, January 23, 2009, http://www.businessweek.com/smallbiz/content/jan2009/sb20090123_264702.htm (accessed June 3, 2011).

TOMS, "How We Give," http://www.toms.com/how-we-give (accessed June 3, 2011).

TOMS, "How We Wear Them," http://www.toms.com/how-we-wear-them/ (accessed June 3, 2011).

TOMS, "One for One," http://www.toms.com/our-movement/movement-one-for-one (accessed June 3, 2011).

TOMS, "Our Movement: Giving Partners," http://www.toms.com/our-movement-giving-partners (accessed June 3, 2011).

TOMS, "Our Movement: Shoe Drops," http://www.toms.com/our-movement-shoe-drops (accessed June 3, 2011).

TOMS, "TOMS Company Overview," http://www.toms.com/corporate-info/ (accessed June 3, 2011).

TOMS, "TOMS Helps Haiti," January 10, 2010, http://www.tomsshoesblog.com/http://www.tomsshoesblog.com/toms-helps-haiti (accessed June 3, 2011).

TOMS, "End Gun Violence Together," https://stories.toms.com/EGV-Giving/index.html (accessed August 9, 2019).

TOMS, "Get to Know Our Giving Partners: Guatemala SANA," http://toms.com/blog/node/901 http://www.toms.com/blog/hqupdates (accessed June 3, 2011).

TOMS, "Have Your Own Style Your Sole Party with TOMS," http://www.toms.com/style-your-sole (accessed June 2, 2011).

TOMS, "One Day Without Shoes," http://www.onedaywithout-shoes.com/ (accessed June 3, 2011).

TOMS, "TOMS Manufacturing Practices," http://www.toms.com/manufacturing-practices (accessed June 3, 2011).

TOMS, One for One Giving Report, http://images.toms.com/media/content/images/giving-report/TOMS-Giving-Report-2010.pdf (accessed June 3, 2011).

World Clothes Line, http://www.worldclothesline.com/ (accessed June 3, 2011).

World Health Organization and UNICE, Prevention and control of schistosomiasis and soil-transmitted helminthiasis, 2004.

CASE 11

Apple Bites into Ethics

Introduction

Headquartered in Cupertino, California, Apple Inc. has experienced many successes throughout their business history. Apple's journey to success has not been without ethical challenges along the way. Apple's success can be seen from their stock price, up 43,000 percent since their IPO in 1980. For the last 12 years, Apple earned first place among *Fortune*'s "World's Most Admired Companies." To millions of consumers, the Apple brand embodies quality, prestige, and innovation. Although companies try to copy the Apple business model, none have been able to discover what it is that makes Apple so unique. Apple is a market leader in the development and sales of mobile devices. As a "tech giant," Apple is monitored extensively due to their extremely large market share and consequently the ability to abuse this power. Consumers and regulators stay alert for instances of abusive power, monopolies, and unfair practices that should be rectified.

Apple's History

Apple's first product, the Apple I, was vastly different from the Apple products most are familiar with today. This first handmade computer kit was constructed by Apple cofounder Steve Wozniak. It lacked a graphic user interface (GUI), and buyers had to add their own keyboard and monitor. Cofounder Steve Jobs convinced Wozniak that it could be sold as a commercial product. In 1976, the Apple I was unveiled at the Home Brew Computer Club and put on sale for $666.66.

Jobs and Wozniak continued to create innovative products. Soon their new company, Apple Computer Inc., surpassed $1 million in sales. However, the mid-1980s brought difficult times for Apple. In 1983, the company introduced the Apple Lisa aimed at business users for $10,000. The product flopped. In 1985, Steve Jobs was ousted after internal conflicts with Apple's then-CEO. The company's products, such as the Mac I and the Newton, an early personal digital assistant (PDA), were not successful, and the company underwent several CEO changes. With declining stock prices, the future of Apple was in jeopardy.

Steve Jobs returned to Apple in 1997 to try and save the struggling company. The return of Jobs introduced a new era for Apple. Jobs immediately began to change the company's corporate culture. Before Jobs's return, employees were more open with the public about Apple projects. After he returned, Jobs instituted a "closed door" policy. Aside from efforts to protect intellectual property internally, Jobs was also a proponent of using litigation against rival companies suspected of patent infringement later in his tenure. As competition in the smart phone category heated up, Apple sued Nokia, HTC, and Samsung in 2009, 2010, and 2011, respectively. Perhaps the most notable lawsuits were made against Samsung, where both companies filed suits against each other across nine countries over a three-year period. In total, Apple and Samsung filed more than 40 patent infringement lawsuits and countersuits related to intellectual property rights. The companies decided to end litigation outside of the United States, choosing to focus instead on cases that are still active in the United States. Today, Apple continues to remain vigilant in protecting their technology and ensuring information remains proprietary.

Jobs also created a flattened organizational structure; rather than go through layers of management to address employees, he addressed them directly. Perhaps one of the most noticeable changes, however, was Apple's expansion into new product lines within the electronics industry. In 2001, Apple launched the iPod—a portable music player that forever changed the music industry. The company also introduced iTunes, an application that allowed users to upload songs from CDs onto their Macs and then organize and manage their personalized song libraries. Two years later, Apple introduced the iTunes Store, where users could download millions of their favorite songs for $0.99 each online. The introduction of the iPhone in 2007 was a turning point for Apple and the beginning of a paradigm shift for the entire world. The iPhone was a revolutionary new smartphone with the music capabilities of an iPod. As of this writing, the iPhone still has about 40 percent of the market share in North America.

The same year that Apple introduced the iPhone, Jobs announced Apple Computer, Inc. would be renamed Apple Inc. This signified that Apple was no longer just a computer manufacturer but also a driver in consumer electronics. Some saw this as a shift away from computers toward consumer electronics such as Apple TV, iPods, iTunes, iPhones, and iPads. However, it may be more accurate to say Apple is reinventing computers, or at least what they look like and how they are used. With the introduction of tablet computers such as the

This case was prepared by Kelsey Reddick, Jennifer Sawayda, Harper Baird, Danielle Jolley, and Julian Mathias for and under the direction of O.C. Ferrell and Linda Ferrell © 2019. It was prepared for classroom discussion rather than to illustrate either effective or ineffective handling of an administrative, ethical, or legal decision by management. All sources used for this case were obtained through publicly available material.

iPad, Apple began to take market share away from their top competitors in the computer industry. However, in the process, sales of their Mac computer line were also cannibalized by consumers opting for a tablet. Sales of desktops, laptops, and netbooks began to decline after tablet computers were introduced.

Although analysts believed tablet sales would continue growing at a rapid rate, the tablet market eventually became saturated with fewer than expected customers upgrading their current tablets to newer versions. Because nearly half of all U.S. households now own at least one tablet, this has translated into stagnating industry growth. Consequently, just as Apple cannibalized their own line of Mac computers with the introduction of the iPad, it appears that their newer iPhones, which feature a larger screen, are eroding the iPad market. The dynamic fluctuation in PC and Mac computer sales and the frequent introduction of new smartphones make it difficult to predict future sales of Apple products. Only time will tell if Apple's devices improve in market share or are overtaken by a rival platform.

In October 2011, Apple Inc. lost its iconic leader with the death of Steve Jobs. Apple's current CEO Tim Cook takes a more traditional approach in his management style by prioritizing project and supply chain management over creative engineering, attending investor meetings, being accessible to the media, and paying out dividends to stockholders. He still maintains the secretive nature of the company but is more approachable than Jobs. Yet, while Cook seems to possess the skills necessary for the CEO position, some fear he lacks the creative skills that made Jobs such a visionary.

Apple is attempting to design products to continue expanding their customer base and remain relevant in the industry. In 2015, the Apple Watch was released, making waves in wearable technology. It is a wearable computing device that functions as an extension of the iPhone. With its easy-to-use interface and broad selection of apps, Apple has dominated the smartwatch category. Though many of Apple's competitors, like Samsung and companies targeting fitness enthusiasts, have extensive lines of wearable devices that sync with various operating systems and mobile platforms, Apple holds 46 percent of the market share. It's next closest competitor, Samsung, only holds 16 percent of the market. Apple followed up this win with the introduction of Airpods, wireless Bluetooth earbuds, in 2016. Cook contends that wearables are a top contributor to the company's growth.

Apple's Corporate Culture

Apple's transition from a computer to a consumer electronics company is unprecedented—and hard to replicate. Although many can only speculate about why Apple succeeded so well, they tend to credit Steve Jobs's leadership abilities, Apple's highly skilled employees, and their strong corporate culture.

The concept of evangelism is an important component of Apple's culture. Corporate evangelists refer to people who extensively promote a corporation's products. Apple even had a chief evangelist whose job was to spread the message about Apple and gain support for their products. However, as the name evangelism implies, the role of evangelist takes on greater meaning. Evangelists believe strongly in the company and will spread that belief to others, who in turn convince other people. Therefore, evangelists are not only employees but loyal customers as well. In this way, Apple was able to form what they refer to as a "Mac cult"—customers who are loyal to Apple's Mac computers and who spread a positive message about Macs to their friends and families.

Successful evangelism only occurs with dedicated, enthusiastic employees who are willing to spread the word. When Jobs returned to Apple, he instituted two cultural changes: he encouraged debate on ideas and he created a vision employees could believe in. By implementing these two changes, employees felt their input was important and they were a part of something bigger than themselves. Such feelings created a sense of loyalty among those working at Apple.

Apple prides themselves on this unique corporate culture. On their job site for corporate employees, Apple markets the company as a "demanding" but rewarding workplace where employees work among "the best of the best." Original thinking, innovation, inventing—all are common daily activities for Apple employees. By offering both challenges and benefits to applicants, Apple hopes to attract those who fit best with their corporate culture.

Apple also looks for retail employees who fit well in their culture. It wants to ensure that their retail employees make each customer feel welcome. Inside Apple retailers are stations where customers can test and experiment with the latest Apple products. Employees are trained to speak with customers within two minutes of entering the store. To ensure their retail employees feel motivated, Apple provides extensive training, greater compensation than employees might receive at similar stores, and opportunities to move up to higher level positions, such as manager, genius (an employee trained to answer the more difficult customer questions), or creative (an employee who trains customers one-on-one or through workshops). Apple also offers young people the chance to intern with the firm, become student representatives at their schools, or work remotely during college as home advisors.

Another benefit Apple offers combines employee concerns with concerns of the environment. In an effort to reduce their overall environmental impact, Apple offers incentives such as transit subsidies for employees who opt to use public transportation. In addition, as part of their long-term commitment to sustainability, Apple is spending $850 million for 25 years of solar power.

Their Cupertino facility runs on 100 percent renewable energy and is equipped with shuttles for employees. Apple's free buses are powered by biodiesel. Apple also opened a new facility, named Apple Campus 2. With a budget of $5 billion, the new facility include a fitness center, underground auditorium, and 300 electric vehicle charging stations. The new buildings at the campus are Leadership in Energy and Environmental Design (LEED) certified and incorporate solar technology. The campus is also conveniently located so that many employees can walk, ride, or carpool to work. These incentives reduce fuel costs for employees while simultaneously lowering emissions released into the environment. Over the last few years, Apple has reduced their carbon emissions by 35 percent, making significant progress toward their goals related to renewable energy, low-carbon design, and energy efficiency.

Apple's Ethics

Apple has tried to ensure their employees and those with whom they work display appropriate conduct in all situations. They base their success on "creating innovative, high-quality products and services and on demonstrating integrity in every business interaction." According to Apple, four main principles contribute to integrity: honesty, respect, confidentiality, and compliance. To thoroughly detail these principles, Apple drafted a code of business conduct that applies to all their operations, including those overseas. They also provide specific policies regarding corporate governance, director conflict of interest, and guidelines on reporting questionable conduct on their website. Apple provides employees with a Business Conduct Helpline they can use to report misconduct to Apple's Audit and Finance Committee.

Many of Apple's product components are manufactured in countries with low labor costs. The potential for misconduct is high because of differing labor standards and less direct oversight. As a result, Apple makes each of their suppliers sign a "Supplier Code of Conduct" and performs factory audits to ensure compliance. Apple may refuse to do additional business with suppliers who refuse to comply with their standards. To emphasize their commitment toward responsible supplier conduct, Apple releases an annual Apple Supplier Responsibility Report that explains their supplier expectations as well as audit conclusions and corrective actions the company takes against factories where violations occur.

Ethical Issues at Apple

Although Apple has consistently won first place as *Fortune's* "World's Most Admired Company," they have experienced several ethical issues in recent years. These issues could have a profound effect on the company's future success. Apple's sterling reputation could easily be damaged by serious misconduct or a failure to address risks appropriately.

Privacy

Consumer tracking is a controversial issue. With the increase in social networking, mobile devices, and internet use, the ability for companies to track customers is greater than ever before. For Apple, more customer information can help the company better understand consumer trends and subsequently market their products more effectively. However, a perceived breach in privacy is likely to result in backlash against the company.

In 2011, Apple experienced just such a backlash. Apple and Google disclosed that certain smartphone apps and software, often utilizing the phones' internal GPS devices, collected data on the phones' locations. Consumers and government officials saw this as an infringement on user privacy. The companies announced that users have the option to disable these features on their phones, yet this was not entirely true for Apple's iPhone. Some smartphones continued to collect location information even after users disabled the "location" feature. Apple attributed this to a glitch they remedied with new software. In subsequent iPhone releases, Apple improved the privacy features of iOS, the mobile operating system found in the iPhone and iPad. The security upgrades have included enhanced Wi-Fi security and a default policy that location features are turned. Once the smartphone is set up, users have the option of turning on the location feature if they desire. Both Google and Apple defend their data-collection mechanisms, but many government officials question whether these tracking techniques are ethical.

Another privacy controversy was related to Apple Pay, software that allows consumers to purchase items both online and in-person through their iPhones. The mobile payment system became a target for hackers, who exploited vulnerabilities in the verification process of adding a credit card to an Apple Pay account. The issue with hackers gaining access to payment information is at least partially the responsibility of the banking institutions, since they approve the addition of credit cards to Apple Pay accounts. Banks did not ask enough security verification questions, making it easier for consumers to add credit cards to their accounts and also leaving the door open for increased fraud. Apple released a credit card in 2019 with advanced security features to make credit card fraud significantly more difficult. The Apple Card, intended to replace a traditional credit card, is built into the iPhone Wallet. Its enhanced security and privacy features mean Apple, unlike regular credit card companies, will not know purchase data for its customers. Additionally, the card uses one-time unique dynamic security codes, replacing the static three-digit CVV.

To improve the security of their devices, Apple launched a bug bounty program designed to reward security researchers who discover and disclose to Apple vulnerabilities in Macs, MacBooks, Apple TV, and Apple Watch. Apple then resolves the security issues and rewards the finder with $1 million. Before the bug bounty existed, security researchers could discover system flaws and abuse them or sell the knowledge to exploit brokers. Additionally, under the new iOS Security Research Device Program, Apple gives development phones to trusted security researchers to discover vulnerabilities in the underlying software and operating system.

In 2016, after a couple opened fire in an office in San Bernardino, California, killing 14 people, Apple faced a privacy issue that pitted them against the FBI. The FBI believed that the husband's encrypted iPhone could reveal important information about the attack. Interestingly, only a few years earlier, Apple had developed encryption systems making it more difficult for forensic investigators to get into the system. The FBI asked for Apple's help, but Apple claimed that providing the government with a way to bypass their own security measures would set a dangerous precedent that could place the privacy of millions of customers who use Apple products at risk. The FBI issued a court order mandating Apple to help the government in this matter. Apple refused, and the FBI dropped the case after they were able to hack into the iPhone without Apple's help. The conflict elicited mixed feelings from the general populace. Some felt that this was a special case that could be used to fight terrorism while others believed it would allow the U.S. government, and possibly other governments, to hack into the phones of private citizens whenever they felt a need. This is just one of several cases where the government has asked for access to secured tech devices in their investigation. Privacy advocates believe the conflict between the government and tech giants like Apple is far from over.

Another large complaint from consumers and developers occurred when Apple removed several screen-time and parental control apps from the App Store. In some cases, Apple asked companies to remove parental control features from their apps, and in other cases the apps were simply removed from the store entirely. One app, Freedom, which allowed users to temporarily block certain sites and apps on their devices, had more than 770,000 downloads before it was removed. Apple stated that the apps they removed violated their rules because they allowed one iPhone to control another. However, these practices had been allowed for years and the apps had approved hundreds of versions of their apps over this time period. Apple responded that they made these changes because of the risk that these apps could gain too much information from the users' devices, particularly a concern because the devices often belonged to children. The threat against privacy and data security is something that Apple does not tolerate, but the timing of the ban on these particular apps brought suspicion. Shortly after the incident, Apple launched their own Screen Time tool, allowing users to limit and monitor their use of apps and overall phone usage. Such timing focused antitrust concern and scrutiny on the issue of Apple's dominance and control over apps in their marketplace. Apple denies that the timing of these changes had to do with the launch of their Screen Time tool. Users have voiced discontent with Apple's Screen Time tool, stating it provides less restrictions and is more complicated than the apps they were previously using. Another issue raised is that the new tool included in Apple's software requires all users within a family to have iPhones, whereas the apps used previously allowed parents with iPhones to control their child's Android devices.

Price Fixing

Another major ethical issue for Apple includes allegations of price fixing. A judge ruled that Apple conspired to fix prices on e-books in conjunction with five major book publishers. A federal judge ruled that Apple was part of a deal that required publishers to give Apple's iTunes store the best deals in the marketplace for e-books. According to allegations, Apple allowed publishers to set the e-book prices for the iPad, and Apple received 30 percent of the proceeds (known as the "agency model"). The agency model is thought to be less competitive than the wholesale model, in which retailers and publishers negotiate on the price. However, if a competitor was found to be selling the e-book for less, Apple was to be offered the same lower price. This scheme is more commonly referred to as a most-favored-nation clause and can be used by companies to dominate the market by keeping competitors out. After striking the deal with Apple, publishers approached Amazon about participating in the contract. In court, Apple faced fines totaling $450 million as part of a settlement agreement.

Price-fixing allegations against Apple are not confined to the United States. Russia's Federal Antimonopoly Service found Apple guilty of forcing 16 retailers to fix prices on the iPhone. Allegedly, Apple even contacted retailers who they felt were not adhering to the agreed-upon price. Apple has denied these charges and claims resellers have always had the right to price their products as they choose.

Antitrust

Just months after the introduction of the iPhone, a class action lawsuit was filed against Apple claiming Apple illegally formed a monopoly with AT&T. The claim was that Apple violated California's antitrust law and the Sherman Antitrust Act. At the time, customers who purchased an Apple iPhone signed a two-year service contract with AT&T, the exclusive carrier of the iPhone. This locked in Apple customers with only one option. The five-year exclusivity agreement between Apple and AT&T was publicly reported. However, many argued that the exclusivity was not disclosed in the contracts customers signed, and customers were not aware they were ultimately locked into five years of AT&T service. This lawsuit resulted in many other similar lawsuits being filed. The case went to the Supreme Court.

The antitrust case against Apple turned its focus to the App Store practices of Apple. Apple charges up to a 30 percent commission to app developers, bans them from selling their apps elsewhere, and ultimately drives the price of apps. The 30 percent commission fee forces app developers to increase the price of their apps in order to maintain profits. App makers have complained for years that the practices are unfair, and that Apple has used monopoly power to raise app prices and become a tech giant. The app store has more than 2 million apps and these apps drive the daily lives of customers. Without the app store, iPhone users could not listen to music (Spotify), catch a ride (Uber), or share photos (Instagram). Some competitors of Apple such as Spotify, Netflix, and Amazon have sought to avoid these fees paid to Apple by encouraging their consumers to subscribe directly to their services, but small app developers do not have this option.

Apple's questionable app store practices resulted in more legal attention. In previous litigation against Apple, the court noted that the 30 percent commission fee is a cost that in the end falls on consumers because consumers pay the premium app price, a price that developers have set to cover their fees. There was much controversy over whether consumers could sue Apple for the practices they use to regulate the app store or not. In *Apple v. Pepper*, Apple argued they were simply re-selling the apps from third-party developers to consumers and therefore had no direct relationship with the consumers. They argued that consumers had no grounds to seek damages from them, as they were a marketplace from which developers could sell their products. They held the position that app developers set their own prices therefore the apps were actually purchased from the developers, not from Apple. Apple's evidence supported that app developers were the only party able to bring antitrust lawsuits against them. The Supreme Court, however, did not agree, and the case ruled that since consumers purchased apps directly from Apple, the consumers did have the ability to seek antitrust charges against Apple. This court case made clear that consumers may sue Apple for allegedly monopolizing the market for the sale of iPhone apps. However, this case did not address whether Apple is guilty of violating antitrust laws. The ruling simply allowed antitrust cases to proceed forward. The lawsuit has raised anti-tech sentiment among the big tech giants

and concerns of their dominance have grown causing a wide-spread antitrust of these large companies.

Sustainability

Apple has taken steps to become a greener company and reduce the environmental impact of their facilities. They also have restrictions addressing the manufacturing, use, and recycling of their products. However, the company admits that most of their emissions come from their products. Since Apple's success hinges on constantly developing and launching new products, the environmental impact of their products is a serious issue.

One practice for which some consumers have criticized Apple is planned obsolescence—pushing people to replace or upgrade their technology whenever Apple comes out with an updated version. Since Apple constantly releases upgraded products, this could result in older technology being tossed aside. Apple has undertaken different approaches to combat this problem. For one, the company strives to build quality, long-lasting products with materials suitable for recycling. The MacBook Air and Mac mini enclosures are made from 100 percent recycled aluminum, one of the many ways Apple is improving their environmental impact. In addition, in the past 10 years the average energy consumption of their latest products has decreased by 70 percent. To encourage recycling, Apple implemented a program at their stores, Apple Trade, so old devices such as iPods, iPhones, and Mac computers can be recycled. Apple securely wipes the data and resells or recycles it. In fact, more than two-thirds of the iPhones Apple receives through Apple Trade are used by new owners. If a phone is not in good enough shape to refurbish, Apple invented a disassembly robot, Daisy, that can take apart iPhones to recover the materials.

Consumers that trade in their old iPods receive a discount on newer versions; those with old Mac computers that still have value can receive gift cards. Apple partners with hundreds of regional recyclers and has established recycling programs in 99 percent of the countries where their products are sold. Despite the recycling programs, many consumers still throw away their old products out of convenience, particularly if they have no value. E-waste remains a significant issue as consumers continue to improperly dispose of their old electronic devices.

Intellectual Property

Intellectual property theft is a key concern at Apple and is an issue the company aggressively pursues. As we've discussed, Apple is serious about keeping their proprietary information a secret to prevent other companies from acquiring their ideas. This has led to many lawsuits between Apple and other technology firms. In 1982, Apple filed a lawsuit against Franklin Computer

Corporation that impacted intellectual property laws. Apple alleged Franklin was illegally formatting copies of Apple II's operating system and ROM so they would run on Franklin computers. Franklin's lawyers argued that portions of computer programs were not subject to copyright law. At first, the courts sided with Franklin, but the verdict was later overturned. The courts eventually determined that codes and programs are protected under copyright law. This law provided technology companies with more extensive intellectual property protections.

Another notable case was Apple's lawsuit against Microsoft after Apple licensed technology to Microsoft. When Microsoft released Windows 2.0, Apple claimed the licensing agreement was only for Windows 1.0 and that Microsoft's Windows had the "look and feel" of Apple's Macintosh GUI. The courts ruled in favor of Microsoft, deciding the license did not cover the "look and feel" of Apple's Macintosh GUI. Although there were similarities between the two, the courts ruled that Windows did not violate copyright law or the licensing agreement simply by resembling Macintosh systems.

Two other lawsuits involved more serious ethical issues on Apple's part. One involved Apple's use of the domain name iTunes.co.uk. The domain name had already been registered by Ben Cohen in 2000, who used the name to redirect users to other sites. Cohen eventually used the domain name to redirect users to the Napster site, a direct competitor of Apple. Apple attempted to purchase the domain name from Cohen, but when negotiations failed the company appealed to U.K. registry Nominet. Usually, whoever registers the domain name first gets the rights to that name. However, the mediator in the case determined that Cohen abused his registration rights and took unfair advantage of Apple. Apple won the right to use the domain name, which led to complaints that Apple was being favored at the expense of smaller companies.

Apple faced another trademark lawsuit from Cisco Systems in 2007. Cisco claimed Apple infringed on their iPhone trademark, a name Cisco had owned since 2000. Apple and Cisco negotiated to determine whether to allow Apple to use the trademark. However, Apple walked away from the discussions. According to Cisco, the company then opened up a front organization, Ocean Telecom Services, and filed for the iPhone trademark in the United States. Some stakeholders saw Apple's actions as a deceptive way to get around negotiation procedures. The lawsuit ended with both parties agreeing to use the iPhone name. Apple's actions in this situation remain controversial. In a twist of events, iOS, the name given to Apple's mobile software, was also a trademark owned by Cisco. This time, Apple avoided controversy by acquiring the iOS trademark from Cisco before publicly using the name.

As was mentioned in the introduction, a more recent case came in the form of a lawsuit between Samsung and Apple. Apple claimed Samsung infringed on multiple intellectual property rights, including patents, trademarks, user interface, style, false designation of origin, unfair competition, and trademark infringement. Specifically, Apple claimed Samsung used key features of their iPhone and iPad, including glass screens and rounded corners, along with many performance features and physical similarities. A jury found Samsung guilty of willfully infringing on Apple's design and utility patents. Apple was initially awarded more than $1 billion in damages, and Samsung's allegations of infringement against Apple were dismissed within the United States. After years of litigation, Apple was ultimately awarded $539 million, only a fraction of the initial damages the company sought against Samsung.

One overarching ethical issue is the question of the legitimacy of Apple's claims. Is Apple pursuing companies they honestly believe infringed on their patents, or are they simply trying to cast their competitors in a bad light to gain market share? Although it might seem Apple is too aggressive, companies that do not adequately protect their intellectual property can easily have it copied by the competition, which uses it to gain a competitive foothold.

Supply Chain Management Issues

Also mentioned earlier, Apple makes each supplier sign a supplier code of conduct and performs factory audits to ensure compliance. In addition, Apple says they have empowered millions of workers by teaching them about their rights, increased the number of suppliers they audit each year, and allowed outside organizations to evaluate their labor practices. These audits appear to be an important component of controlling the supply chain. Apple discovered a correlation between improved compliance and the number of audits—facilities audited twice, instead of once, showed a 25 percent gain in compliance rating, while three audits resulted in an even greater 31 percent compliance score improvement. Serious supply chain issues have threatened to undermine Apple's status as a highly admired and ethical company. This threat is likely the catalyst to Apple's continuous supply chain improvements.

To meet the repeated demands of Apple consumers, products from the company must be readily available. Most of Apple's products are manufactured throughout Asia, with a majority produced within Foxconn and Pegatron factories in China. In the past, multiple accusations pertaining to improper working conditions, underage labor disputes, and worker abuse have come into question. Apple has been labeled as an unfair sweatshop, and critics have launched multiple campaigns against the company. This has resulted in negative publicity from protestors, who asked current Apple consumers not to support Apple's unlawful practices by purchasing their products. A report by China Labor Watch, a New York-based non-profit, in September 2019 said that more than

50 percent of Apple's workforce at Foxconn in August were temporary workers, violating China's labor laws which set a limit at 10 percent. Even as student workers returned to school, the number of temporary workers still exceeded China's labor laws. Other issues included violations related to overtime work, failed bonuses, internship laws, and safety. Some workers had more than 100 overtime hours in one month, though Chinese law sets a limit at 36 overtime hours. Some dispatch workers were not paid their bonuses. Additionally, student employees worked overtime which violates internship laws. Lastly, the safety of the workers was put at risk due to the lack of protective equipment and occupational health and safety training. The report also revealed that the factory in question does not report work injuries. Though Apple denied most of the allegations and said workers are all receiving the appropriate compensation, Apple would not disclose which allegations were true. Apple should work to be as transparent as possible in the face of negative publicity.

In addition to being scrutinized over improper working conditions, Apple has been criticized for its tight profit margins. Suppliers claim Apple's manufacturing standards are hard to achieve because of the slim profit margins afforded to suppliers. In contrast, competitors like Hewlett-Packard allow suppliers to keep more profits if they improve worker conditions. According to suppliers, Apple's focus on the bottom line forced them to find other ways to cut costs, usually by requiring employees to work longer hours and using less expensive but more dangerous chemicals.

In this environment, mistakes and safety issues become more common. According to the company's own audits, 96 percent of Apple's suppliers are in compliance of working-hour limits (60 hours per week). Apple won the "Stop Slavery Award" from The Thomas Reuters Foundation for their efforts to create a more transparent supply chain. In addition, audits in 2018 discovered only one underage worker. Apple acknowledges that the problem of underage workers needs to be totally eliminated from the supply chain, and each year the audits uncover fewer facilities out of compliance. Apple's policy requires suppliers to continue to pay wages to underage workers, even after they are sent home, and provide educational opportunity. After the worker reaches legal age, the supplier is required to offer the individual employment once again. Apple claims suppliers who violate company policies are re-audited every 30, 60, and 90 days or until the problem has been rectified. If a core violation is discovered, such as employing underage labor, employee retaliation, and falsified documents, the supplier is put on immediate probation while senior officials from both companies address the problem. Apple will drop suppliers who do not improve.

In spite of these audits, several high-profile events at factories have generated criticism of Apple's supply chain practices. In January 2010, over 135 workers

fell ill after using a poisonous chemical to clean iPhone screens. In 2010, more than a dozen workers died by suicide at Apple supplier factories. In 2011, aluminum dust and improper ventilation caused two explosions that killed four people and injured 77. Much of the media attention focused on the conditions at Foxconn, one of Apple's largest suppliers with a background of labor violations, but Foxconn asserts it is in compliance with all regulations. The death of an employee at a Chinese iPhone factory in 2018 renewed concerns over working conditions.

Some blame factory conditions on Apple's culture of innovation—more specifically, the need to release new and improved products each year—which requires suppliers to work quickly at the expense of safety standards. Because the Foxconn and Pegatron factories are some of only a handful of facilities in the world with the capacity to build iPads and iPhones, it is difficult for Apple to change suppliers. Inconsistent international labor standards and fierce competition mean that virtually every major electronics producer faces similar manufacturing issues. As media and consumer scrutiny increase, Apple must continue to address their supply chain management issues. As one current Apple executive told *The New York Times*, customer expectations could also be part of the problem since customers seem to care more about the newest product than the labor conditions of those who made it.

Apple has worked to improve supplier conditions and transparency about their labor processes. CEO Tim Cook personally visited Foxconn to see the labor conditions firsthand. Apple has worked with Foxconn to improve worker safety, including testing more equipment and setting limits on workers' hours. The Fair Labor Association (FLA) confirms that Apple has dramatically improved the accountability of Foxconn. However, continual monitoring of their suppliers and enforcement of ethical standards are necessary to assure stakeholders that Apple takes the well-being of workers seriously.

Taxes

Tax issues have become a substantial burden for Apple on an international scale. In 2016, the European Union ruled that Apple owed $13.9 billion in back taxes due to their business dealings with Ireland. The decision created conflict among Apple, the EU, Ireland, and the United States. Before this controversial EU decision, the U.S. government had questioned Apple over their tax practices. In what is known as a tax inversion, Apple moved their headquarters to Ireland. According to some regulators, Apple funnels non-U.S. income through two Ireland businesses to avoid paying the higher U.S. corporate tax. The United States has one of the world's highest corporate tax rates at 35 percent, while Ireland has one of the lowest corporate tax rates at 12.5 percent. By law, Apple's profits that are kept offshore are not taxable in the United States. Many multinational companies that started in the United States, including Caterpillar and McDonald's, have chosen to incorporate in countries that have lower tax rates.

This has generated criticism that Apple and other firms are using loopholes in tax law to avoid paying the taxes they would normally owe. Many stakeholders have decried these tax arrangements as unfair, claiming that the business Apple does in the United States incurs significant profits, and therefore Apple should reinvest in the U.S. economy by paying their fair share of taxes. Countries like Ireland have received serious pressure to close loopholes that allowed large tax breaks. In 2013, the U.S. Senate led a special probe to determine whether Apple was using tax strategies simply to avoid paying U.S. taxes. As part of their findings, the Senate claimed Apple was using special loopholes to pay less than a 2 percent tax rate in Ireland.

Much like the U.S. government, the EU believes multinational firms are using European countries with lower tax rates and higher tax breaks to avoid taxes. In 2013, a special task force was created to investigate whether the tax breaks these companies received were illegal according to European law. If Ireland provided Apple with special tax breaks it did not provide to similar companies, it could constitute as illegal favoritism. CEO Tim Cook questioned the fairness of the proceedings. Nevertheless, in 2016, the EU claimed Apple's tax agreements with Ireland that provided them with special tax breaks were illegal, and the firm owed Ireland $13.9 billion in back taxes. With interest, Apple paid more than $16.7 billion to the Irish government in 2018. Ireland was not pleased with the ruling, claiming the EU overstepped their bounds by prescribing Irish tax law. Apple claims the EU does not understand how Apple operates and that the taxes they pay in Ireland adhere to all applicable laws. However, the EU continues to maintain that Ireland provided Apple with favorable treatment, which clearly violates European law.

In another push from Europe, Apple agreed to pay more than 10 years in back taxes to France, totaling approximately $558 million in 2019. Many believe the EU is unfairly targeting Apple. France, in particular, has its eye on U.S. tech giants. It became the first country to introduce a digital tax targeting Google, Apple, Facebook, and Amazon, earning the tax the acronym GAFA. The GAFA tax law is a 3 percent tax on digital advertising and other revenues of tech firms with total revenue of more than $842 million. Only time will tell if other countries will follow suit.

Batterygate

In December 2017, Apple admitted that it had been intentionally throttling the performance of old iPhone models in order to prevent issues with older batteries. While many people were upset to hear Apple was knowingly slowing their devices, much of the criticism stemmed from Apple's lack of transparency. The company's admission followed consumer speculation and data from an iPhone benchmark developer. Apple defended its decision, saying that slowing the devices helped to prolong the life of the products. The throttling mechanism was designed to prevent phones from unexpectedly shutting down when old iPhones tried to draw too much power. Regardless of Apple's intent, many declared the company was not trustworthy. Consumers also speculated if Apple was bogging down old phones to push new iPhone sales.

In an attempt to win over the critics, Apple discounted iPhone battery replacements for select models in 2018 and released educational content about how to maximize battery performance and preventing unexpected shutdowns. Apple iOS 11.3, released in March 2018, included a new Battery Health feature that provides data on charge level over time, average screen on and off times, battery usage by app, and maximum battery capacity. Despite Apple's efforts to save face, the company faces more than 60 class-action lawsuits. Without a doubt, Apple could have protected its reputation by proactively disclosing to consumers the intention to slow down old phones. Instead, Apple risked damaging consumer trust by failing to speak up.

The Future of Apple Inc.

In recent times, the headlines have more frequently cast a negative light on Apple, some of which undoubtedly has been caused by their practices. The U.S. and international governments face unprecedented challenges in determining how to control the tech giants in the right way. These challenges have been a significant topic in politics, as governments debate how to manage the power of these large companies that are continually undermining fair competition in their markets. The government must decide where to draw the line to provide fair practices for both consumers and the competing companies.

Despite continued conflicts with the EU government over their tax arrangements, Apple appears optimistic about their future. The company has created a cult following of consumers who are intensely loyal to Apple products. Notable acquisitions include Shazam, Emagic, Siri, Beats Electronics, NeXT, Inc., Anobit Technologies, and PrimeSense. Apple has made strategic acquisitions to improve their products and stay ahead of the pack. For example, Apple acquired a British artist-services startup called Platoon in 2018. The service allows music artists to distribute music without a record label. Many theorize Platoon could be a key component in Apple becoming a music-rights owner, giving Apple Music exclusive recordings.

Apple has their share of threats. They constantly face lawsuits from competitors over alleged intellectual property violations. In addition, although Apple's aggressive stance helped protect their intellectual property, their tight hold over their products and secrets could ultimately be disadvantageous. Google, for instance, has a more open-source approach. Google has shown great support for the open-source movement, which advocates opening software and software codes in order to secure more input from outside sources. Although this openness increases the risks of intellectual property theft, it allows for innovation to occur more rapidly because of additional collaboration. This software strategy has helped Google compete with Apple; Android phones greatly outnumber Apple iPhones in many countries. Apple may eventually need to reexamine whether their closed system is the best way to compete.

In the last decade, Apple has excelled at keeping pace with the quickly evolving computer and consumer electronics industries. Although skeptics have raised questions on whether Apple is still the driving force behind innovation, many believe new products are on the horizon. Their diversification, collaborative corporate culture, and product evangelism propelled them to heights that could not have been envisioned when Jobs and Wozniak sold their first computer kit in 1976. Although Apple has experienced many challenges along the way, the company has clearly showcased their ability to understand consumers and create products that have been implemented and used in customers' everyday lives.

Questions for Discussion

1. Explain how Apple's philosophy and organizational culture have impacted how they handle ethical decisions.
2. Why is Apple's industry so competitive and how could this affect the ethical risks in Apple's operations?
3. How do you think Apple has handled the various ethical issues that they have faced in the past?

Sources

"Smartphone Market Share," *IDC*, June 18, 2019, https://www.idc.com/promo/smartphone-market-share/os (accessed August 7, 2019).

"Former Apple Evangelist on Company's History," *ZDNet*, March 29, 2006, http://www.zdnet.com/article/former-apple-evangelist-on-companys-history/ (accessed April 22, 2017).

"Inside the Minds of Most Hard-Charging CEOs," Inc., September 2012, 142–146.

"The Evangelist's Evangelist," *Academia*, http://www.academia.edu/4182207/The_Evangelist_s_Evangelist_Developing_a_Customer_Evangelism_Scale_using_Faith-Based_Volunteer_Tourism_Data (accessed May 4, 2015).

Adam Lashinsky, "How Tim Cook Is Changing Apple," *Fortune*, June 11, 2012.

Adam Lashinsky, "The Secrets Apple Keeps," *Fortune*, February 6, 2012, 85–94.

Adam Liptak and Jack Nicas, "Supreme Court Allows Antitrust Lawsuit Against Apple to Proceed," *The New York Times*, May 13, 2019, https://www.nytimes.com/2019/05/13/us/politics/supreme-court-antitrust-apple.html (accessed August 4, 2019).

Alan Deutschman, "The Once and Future Steve Jobs," *Salon*, October 11, 2000, http://www.salon.com/technology/books/2000/10/11/jobs_excerpt/ (accessed April 22, 2017).

Alberto Zanco, "Apple Inc: A Success Built on Distribution & Design," http://www.slideshare.net/Nanor/distribution-policy-apple-presentation (accessed May 4, 2015).

Alex Heath, "How Steve Jobs Steamrolled Cisco on the Name 'iPhone,'" *Cult of Mac*, January 27, 2012, http://www.cultofmac.com/143006/how-steve-jobs-steamrolled-cisco-on-the-name-iphone/ (accessed April 22, 2017).

Amanda Cantrell, "Apple's Remarkable Comeback Story," *CNN Money*, March 29, 2006, http://money.cnn.com/2006/03/29/technology/apple_anniversary/ (accessed April 22, 2017).

Amit Chowdhry, "Apple and Samsung Drop Patent Disputes Against Each Other Outside of U.S." *Forbes*, August 6, 2014, https://www.forbes.com/sites/amitchowdhry/2014/08/06/apple-and-samsung-drop-patent-disputes-against-each-other-outside-of-the-u-s/#1a535085418c (accessed April 22, 2017).

Amy Moore, "Complete Guide to Apple's Campus 2, Everything We Know about the New Spaceship HQ, Plus: 4k Drone Flyover Video," *Mac World*, April 2, 2015, http://www.macworld.co.uk/feature/apple/apple-spaceship-campus-facts-pictures-video-info-3489704/ (accessed April 22, 2017).

Andrew Griffin, "Apple Given Stop Slavery Award as It Opens up about Trying to Stop Abuses in Its Supply Chain," *Independent*, November 15, 2018, https://www.independent.co.uk/life-style/gadgets-and-tech/news/apple-slavery-modern-stop-award-supply-chain-thomson-reuters-foundation-latest-a8634376.html (accessed August 13, 2019).

Annie Gaus, "Apple Is Dominating the Watch Game—Here's Why That's Good News for Investors," *TheStreet*, August 12, 2019, https://www.thestreet.com/investing/apple-is-dominating-the-watch-game-here-s-why-that-s-great-news-for-investors-15053914 (accessed August 13, 2019).

Apple History, http://www.apple-history.com/ (accessed May 4, 2015).

Apple Inc. v. Pepper. (July 1, 2019). Retrieved from https://en.wikipedia.org/wiki/Apple_Inc._v._Pepper (accessed August 4, 2019).

Apple Inc., "Apple Introduces iTunes—World's Best and Easiest to Use Jukebox Software," January 9, 2001, https://www.apple.com/pr/library/2001/01/09Apple-Introduces-iTunes-Worlds-Best-and-Easiest-To-Use-Jukebox-Software.html (accessed April 22, 2017).

Apple Inc., "Apple Recycling," Apple, https://www.apple.com/recycling/ (accessed April 22, 2017).

Apple Inc., "Jobs at Apple," https://www.apple.com/jobs/us/index.html?&cid=us_paid_search_agnostic_google_US_B_Jobs_Exact_139685460 (accessed April 22, 2017).

Apple Inc., "Policy on Reporting Questionable Accounting or Auditing Matters," November 16, 2010, http://files.shareholder.com/downloads/AAPL/1281913948x0x443017/68a6df9d-b0ef-4870-ba8e-accc695b39e2/reporting_accounting_auditing_matters.pdf (accessed April 22, 2017).

Apple Inc., Business Conduct: The Way We Do Business Worldwide, October 2015, http://files.shareholder.com/downloads/AAPL/0x0x443008/5f38b1e6-2f9c-4518-b691-13a29ac90501/business_conduct_policy.pdf (accessed April 22, 2017).

Apple Insider, "Apple Begins Counting Down to 25 Billion App Store Downloads," February 17, 2012, http://appleinsider.com/articles/12/02/17/apple_begins_counting_down_to_25_billion_app_store_downloads (accessed April 22, 2017).

Apple, "Environment," https://www.apple.com/environment/ (accessed August 13, 2019).

Apple, "Supplier Responsibility: 2019 Progress Report," 2019, https://www.apple.com/supplier-responsibility/pdf/Apple_SR_2019_Progress_Report.pdf (accessed August 13, 2019).

Arthur Shi, "Batterygate: A Complete History of Apple Throttling iPhones," iFixit, September 8, 2018, https://www.ifixit.com/News/batterygate-timeline (accessed October 24, 2019).

Ashby Jones, "So What's up with This Apple/Google Lawsuit?" *The Wall Street Journal*, March 30, 2010, https://blogs.wsj.com/law/2010/03/03/so-whats-up-with-this-applegoogle-lawsuit/ (accessed April 22, 2017).

Ashkan Soltani and Hayley Tsukayama, "Apple's New Feature to Curb Phone Tracking Won't Work If You're Actually Using Your Phone," *The Washington Post*, September 25, 2014, http://www.washingtonpost.com/blogs/the-switch/wp/2014/09/25/apples-new-feature-to-curb-phone-tracking-wont-work-if-youre-actually-using-your-phone/ (accessed April 22, 2017).

BBC, "Building the Digital Age," *BBC News*, http://news.bbc.co.uk/2/hi/technology/7091190.stm (accessed April 22, 2017).

Ben Lovejoy, "Apple Hits a Dozen Years as the World's Most Admired Company," *9to5Mac*, January 22, 2019, https://9to5mac.com/2019/01/22/the-worlds-most-admired-company/ (accessed August 12, 2019).

Brian X. Chen, "Lawsuit Advances Claiming AT&T iPhone Monopoly," *Wired*, https://www.wired.com/2010/07/iphone-class-action/ (accessed August 3, 2019).

Bryan Gardiner, "Learning from Failure: Apple's Most Notorious Flops," *Wired*, January 24, 2008, https://www.wired.com/2008/02/gallery-apple-flops/ (accessed April 22, 2017).

Cable News Network, "Apple Chronology," *CNN Money*, January 6, 1998, http://money.cnn.com/1998/01/06/technology/apple_chrono/ (accessed April 22, 2017).

Cable News Network, "Apple Unveils Two New iPhones, Apple Watch and Apple Pay," *CNN Money*, September 9, 2014, http://money.cnn.com/2014/09/09/technology/mobile/apple-iphone-iwatch-event/ (accessed April 22, 2017).

Chance Miller, "Canalys: Apple Shipped 14.6M iPhones in North America During Q1, Securing 40% Marketshare," *9to5Mac*, May 9, 2019, https://9to5mac.com/2019/05/09/iphone-north-america-marketshare/ (accessed August 13, 2019).

Charles Duhigg, "In China, Human Costs Are Built Into an iPad," *The New York Times*, January 25, 2012, http://www.nytimes.com/2012/01/26/business/ieconomy-apples-ipad-and-the-human-costs-for-workers-in-china.html?pagewanted=all (accessed April 22, 2017).

Chris Morrison, "Insanely Great Marketing," *CBS MoneyWatch*, August 10, 2009, http://www.cbsnews.com/news/insanely-great-marketing/ (accessed April 22, 2017).

Claire Milne, Nominet UK Dispute Resolution Service Decision of Independent Expert, March 10, 2005, http://www.nominet.org.uk/digitalAssets/766_itunes.pdf (accessed June 8, 2011).

Daisuke Wakabayahsi and Robin Sidel, "Fraud Starts to Take a Bit out of Apple Pay," *The Wall Street Journal*, March 3, 2015, http://www.wsj.com/articles/fraud-starts-to-take-a-bite-out-of-apple-pay-1425430639 (accessed April 22, 2017).

Daisuke Wakabayashi, "Apple Seeks Japan iWatch Trademark," *The Wall Street Journal*, July 2, 2013, B5.

Dan Farber, "When iPhone Met World, 7 Years Ago Today," CNet, January 9, 2014, http://www.cnet.com/news/when-iphone-met-world-7-years-ago-today/ (accessed April 22, 2017).

David Meyer, "Apple Has Paid the $14.3 Billion It Owes the Irish Tax Authorities—But the Check Hasn't Cleared Yet," *Fortune*, September 19, 2018, https://fortune.com/2018/09/19/apple-ireland-tax-payments-escrow/ (accessed August 13, 2019).

Dawn Kawamoto, Ben Heskett, and Mike Ricciuti, "Microsoft to Invest $150 Million in Apple," *CNET*, August 6, 1997, http://news.cnet.com/MS-to-invest-i50-million-in-Apple/2ioo-iooi_3-202i43.html (accessed May 4, 2015).

Don Reisinger, "Apple Found Guilty of Illegal iPhone Price-Fixing in Russia," *Fortune*, March 15, 2017, http://fortune.com/2017/03/15/apple-iphone-price-fixing/ (accessed April 22, 2017).

Economist staff, "Bruised Apple," *The Economist*, September 3, 2016, p. 10.

Eva Dou, "Apple Shifts Supply Chain Away from Foxconn to Pegatron," *The Wall Street Journal*, May 29, 2013, http://www.wsj.com/articles/SB10001424127887323855804578511122734340726 (accessed April 22, 2017).

Gespard Sebag, Dara Doyle, and Alex Webb, "The Inside Story of Apple's $14 Billion Tax Bill," *Bloomberg*, December 15, 2016, https://www.bloomberg.com/news/articles/2016-12-16/the-inside-story-of-apple-s-14-billion-tax-bill (accessed April 22, 2017).

Greg Sandoval, "This Is Why DOJ Accused Apple of Fixing e-Book Prices," *CNET*, April 11, 2013, http://news.cnet.com/8301-13579_3-57412369-37/this-is-why-doj-accused-apple-of-fixing-e-book-prices/ (accessed April 22, 2017).

Henry Foy and Madhumita Murgia, "Apple Found Guilty of Price-Fixing in Russia over iPhone Prices," *Financial Times*, March 14, 2017, https://www.ft.com/content/e27e4f4a-08be-11e7-97d1-5e720a26771b (accessed April 22, 2017).

Issie Lapowsky, "Supreme Court Deals Blow to Apple in Antitrust Case," *Wired*, May 13, 2019, https://www.wired.com/story/supreme-court-apple-decision-antitrust/?verso=true (accessed August 3, 2019).

J. Taylor Kirklin, "Second Circuit Hears Oral Argument in Apple E-Book Appeal," *Antitrust Update*, December 19, 2014, http://www.antitrustupdateblog.com/blog/second-circuit-hears-oral-argument-apple-e-book-appeal (accessed April 22, 2017).

Jack Nicas, "Apple Cracks Down on Apps That Fight iPhone Addiction," *The New York Times*, April 27, 2019, https://www.nytimes.com/2019/04/27/technology/apple-screen-time-trackers.html?module=inline (accessed August 3, 2019).

Jack Purcher, "France is First to Introduce a New Digital 'GAFA Tax' (Google, Apple, Facebook and Amazon Tax) with the EU to Follow," *Patently Apple*, April 8, 2019, https://www.patentlyapple.com/patently-apple/2019/04/france-is-first-to-introduce-a-new-digital-gafa-tax-google-apple-facebook-and-amazon-tax-with-the-eu-to-follow.html (accessed August 13, 2019).

Jamie Fullerton, "Suicide at Chinese iPhone Factory Reignites Concern Over Working Conditions," *Telegraph*, January 7, 2018, https://www.telegraph.co.uk/news/2018/01/07/suicide-chinese-iphone-factory-reignites-concern-working-conditions/ (accessed August 13, 2019).

Jeffrey Ball and Lisa Jackson, "Lisa Jackson on Apple's Green Initiatives," *The Wall Street journal*, March 30, 2015, http://www.wsj.com/articles/lisa-jackson-on-apples-green-initiatives-1427770864 (accessed April 22, 2017).

Jim Aley, "The Beginning," *Bloomberg Businessweek, Special Issue on Steve Jobs*, October 2011, 20–26.

Joanna Stern, "Apple and Foxconn Make Progress on Working Conditions at Factories," *ABC News*, August 21, 2012, http://abcnews.go.com/blogs/technology/2012/08/apple-and-foxconn-make-progress-on-working-conditions-at-factories/ (accessed April 22, 2017).

Joe Palazzolo, "Apple E-book Ruling Heaps New Doubt on 'MFN' Clauses," *The Wall Street Journal*, July 15, 2013, B1.

Joel Rosenblatt, "Jobs Threatened Suit If Palm Didn't Agree to Hiring Terms," *Bloomberg*, January 22, 2013, http://www.bloomberg.com/news/2013-01-23/jobs-threatened-suit-if-palm-didn-t-agree-to-hiring-terms.html (accessed April 22, 2017).

John Brownlee, "What It's Like to Work at Apple," *Cult of Mac*, July 7, 2010, http://www.cultofmac.com/what-its-like-to-work-at-apple (accessed April 22, 2017).

John Ribeiro, "Apple, Samsung Agree to Settle Patent Disputes Outside US," *PC World*, August 5, 2014, http://www.pcworld.com/article/2461940/apple-samsung-agree-to-settle-patent-disputes-outside-us.html (accessed April 22, 2017).

Julia Angwin, "Apple, Google Take Heat," *The Wall Street Journal*, May 11, 2011, https://www.wsj.com/articles/SB10001424052748703730804576315121174761088 (accessed April 22, 2017).

Kalyeena Makortoff, "Apple to Pay 10 Years of Back Taxes to France," *The Guardian*, February 5, 2019, https://www.theguardian.com/technology/2019/feb/05/apple-to-pay-10-years-of-back-taxes-to-france (accessed August 12, 2019).

Kevin Johnson, Jon Swartz, and Marco della Cava, "FBI Hacks into Terrorist's iPhone without Apple," *USA Today*, March 28, 2016, https://www.usatoday.com/story/news/nation/2016/03/28/apple-justice-department-farook/82354040/ (accessed April 22, 2017).

Kieren McCarthy, "Apple Threatens iTunes.co.uk Owner," *The Register*, December 6, 2004, http://www.theregister.co.uk/2004/12/06/apple_itunescouk_domain_dispute/ (accessed April 22, 2017).

Kif Leswing, "Android and iOS Are Nearly Tied for U.S. Smartphone Market Share," *Gigaom*, February 4, 2015, https://gigaom.com/2015/02/04/android-and-ios-are-nearly-tied-for-u-s-smartphone-market-share/ (accessed April 22, 2017).

Kit Eaton, "Steve Jobs vs. Tim Cook: Words of Wisdom," *Fast Company*, August 26, 2011, http://www.fastcompany.com/1776013/steve-jobs-vs-tim-cook-words-wisdom (accessed April 22, 2017).

Louis Columbus, "The 50 Most Innovative Companies of 2014: Strong Innovators Are Three Times More Likely to Rely on Big Data Analytics," *Forbes*, November 3, 2014, https://www.forbes.com/sites/louiscolumbus/2014/11/03/the-50-most-innovative-companies -of-2014-strong-innovators-are-three-times-more-likely-to-rely-on-big-data-analytics/#1b143e0d52ac (accessed April 22, 2017).

Louise Matsakis, "The Pepper v. Apple Supreme Court Case Will Decide if Apple's App Store Is a Monopoly," *Wired*, June 18, 2018, https://www.wired.com/story/pepper-v-apple-supreme-court-app-store-antitrust/?verso=true (accessed August 3, 2019).

Marguerite Reardon and Tom Krazit, "Cisco Sues Apple over Use of iPhone Trademark," *CNET*, January 10, 2007, http://news.cnet.com/Cisco-sues-Apple-over-use-of-iPhone-trademark/2100-1047_3-6149285.html (accessed April 22, 2017).

Martyn Williams, "Timeline: iTunes Store at 10 Billion," *ComputerWorld*, February 24, 2010, http://www.computerworld.com/article/2520037/networking/timeline--itunes-store-at-10-billion.html (accessed April 22, 2017).

Matt Hamblen, "Tablet Sales Growth Slows Dramatically," *ComputerWorld*, October 15, 2014, http://www.computerworld.com/article/2834238/tablet-sales-growth-slows-dramatically.html (accessed April 22, 2017).

Michael Potuck, "Apple's 2019 Environmental Responsibility Report Touts 35% Lower Carbon Footprint than 2015, Progress Towards Mining-Free Future, More," *9to5Mac*, April 18, 2019, https://9to5mac.com/2019/04/18/2019-apple-environment-report/ (accessed August 13, 2019).

Miguel Helft, "Will Apple's Culture Hurt the iPhone?" *The New York Times*, October 17, 2010, http://www.nytimes.com/2010/10/18/technology/18apple.html (accessed October 17, 2019).

Nathan Reiff, "Top 7 Companies Owned by Apple," *Investopedia*, May 16, 2019, https://www.investopedia.com/investing/top-companies-owned-apple/ (accessed August 12, 2019).

Nick Statt, "Apple Wins $539 Million from Samsung in Latest Chapter of Ongoing Patent Trial," *The Verge*, May 24, 2018, https://www.theverge.com/2018/5/24/17392216/apple-vs-samsung-patent-trial-539-million-damages-jury-verdict (accessed August 13, 2019).

Nick Wingfield, "As Apple's Battle with HTC Ends, Smartphone Patent Fights Continue," *The New York Times*, November 11, 2012, http://www.nytimes.com/2012/11/12/technology/as-apple-and-htc-end-lawsuits-smartphone-patent-battles-continue.html?_r=o (accessed April 22, 2017).

Nilay Patel "Confirmed: Apple and AT&T Signed Five-Year iPhone Exclusivity Deal — But Is It Still Valid?" *Engadget*, May 10, 2010, https://www.engadget.com/2010/05/10/confirmed-apple-and-atandt-signed-five-year-iphone-exclusivity-de/?guccounter=1 (accessed August 4, 2019).

Nilofer Merchant, "Apple's Startup Culture," *Bloomberg Businessweek*, June 24, 2010, https://www.bloomberg.com/news/articles/2010-06-14/apples-startup-culture (accessed April 22, 2017).

Paul Andrews, "Apple-Microsoft Lawsuit Fizzles to a Close—'Nothing Left' to Fight About," *The Seattle Times*, June 2, 1993, http://community.seattletimes.nwsource.com/archive/?date=19930602&slug=1704430 (accessed April 22, 2017).

Paul Elias, "Samsung Ordered to Pay Apple $1,05B in Patent Case," *Yahoo! Finance*, August 25, 2012, http://finance.yahoo.com/news/samsung-ordered-pay-apple-1-004505800.html (accessed April 22, 2017).

Pete Williams, "Supreme Court May Let Consumers Sue Apple over App Store Monopoly Claims," *NBC News*, November 26, 2018, https://www.nbcnews.com/politics/supreme-court/supreme-court-may-let-consumers-sue-apple-over-app-store-n940141 (accessed August 4, 2019).

Peter Burrows, "The Wilderness," *Bloomberg Businessweek, Special Issue on Steve Jobs*, October 2011, 28–34.

Reuters, "Apple to Pay $450m Settlement over US eBook Pricing," *The Guardian*, March 7, 2016, https://www.theguardian.com/technology/2016/mar/07/apple-450-million-settlement-e-book-price-fixing-supreme-court (accessed April 22, 2017).

Reuters, "Apple, Cisco Agree Both Can Use iPhone Name," February 22, 2007, http://www.reuters.com/article/us-apple-cisco-idUSWEN460920070222 (accessed April 22, 2017).

Rob Hassett, Impact of Apple vs. Franklin Decision, 1983, http://www.internetlegal.com/impactof.htm (accessed April 22, 2017).

Robert Paul Leitao, "Apple's 25% Solution," *Seeking Alpha*, November 7, 2011, http://seekingalpha.com/article/305849-apple-s-25-solution (accessed April 22, 2017).

Rocco Pendola, "Amazon vs. Apple: Jeff Bezos Just Squashed Tim Cook," *CNBC*, September 7, 2012, http://www.cnbc.com/id/48945231 (accessed April 22, 2017).

Saheli Roy Choudhury, "Apple Denies Claims It Broke Chinese Labor Laws in iPhone Factory," *CNBC*, September 9, 2019, https://www.cnbc.com/2019/09/09/apple-appl-claims-it-broke-china-labor-laws-at-iphone-factory-mostly-false.html (accessed October 24, 2019).

Sam Schechner, "Apple Hits Back over EU Irish-Tax Decision," *The Wall Street Journal*, December 19, 2016, https://www.wsj.com/articles/eu-raises-pressure-on-apples-tax-deal-in-ireland-1482162608 (accessed April 22, 2017).

Sara Salinas, "Apple Stock is up 43,000% Since Its IPO 38 Years Ago," *CNBC*, December 12, 2018, https://www.cnbc.com/2018/12/12/apple-stock-is-up-43000percent-since-its-ipo-38-years-ago.html (accessed August 13, 2019).

Scott Martin, "Apple Invites Review of Labor Practices in Overseas Factories," *USA Today*, January 16, 2012, 3B.

Scott Martin, "Apple's Mac Sales Reported Down Again," *USA Today*, October 9, 2013, http://www.usatoday.com/story/tech/2013/10/09/apples-mac-sales-reported-down-again/2955735/ (accessed April 22, 2017).

Scott Martin, "How Apple Rewrote the Rules of Retailing," *USA Today*, May 19, 2011, lB.

Simon Sharwood, "Apple to EU: It's Our Job to Design Ireland's Tax System, Not Yours," *The Register*, February 21, 2017, https://www.theregister.co.uk/2017/02/21/apple_vs_ec_tax_case_defence_filed/ (accessed April 22, 2017).

Steven Musil, "Apple Reportedly Tinkering with Larger Screens for iPhone, iPad," *CNet*, http://www.cnet.com/news/apple-reportedly-tinkering-with-larger-screens-for-iphone-ipad/ (accessed April 22, 2017).

Tim Worstall, "Ireland to Close Apple's Tax Break, Not That It Will Make the Slightest Difference to Anything at All," *Forbes*, October 16, 2013, https://www.forbes.com/sites/timworstall/2013/10/16/ireland-to-close-apples-tax-break-not-that-it-will-make-the-slightest-difference-to-anything-at-all/#3be790a455d4 (accessed April 22, 2017).

Tracy Lien, Brian Bennett, Paresh Dave, and James Queally, "Apple CEO Says Helping FBI Hack into Terrorist's iPhone Would Be 'Too Dangerous,'" *Los Angeles Times*, February 29, 2016, http://www.latimes.com/local/lanow/la-me-apple-san-bernardino-terror-20160218-story.html (accessed April 22, 2017).

Vanessa Houlder, Vincent Boland, and James Politi, "Tax Avoidance: The Irish Inversion," *Financial Times*, April 29, 2014, https://www.ft.com/content/d9b4fd34-ca3f-11e3-8a31-00144feabdc0 (accessed April 22, 2017).

Yukari Iwatani Kane and Ethan Smith, "Apple Readies iCloud Service," *The Wall Street Journal*, June 1, 2011, B1.

Yukari Iwatani Kane and Ian Sherr, "Apple: Samsung Copied Design," The Wall Street Journal, April 19, 2011, https://www.wsj.com/articles/SB10001424052748703916004576271210109389154 (accessed April 22, 2017).

Zack Whittaker, "Apple Card Will Make Credit Card Fraud a Lot More Difficult," *TechCrunch*, March 25, 2019, https://techcrunch.com/2019/03/25/apple-credit-card-fraud/ (accessed August 12, 2019).

Zack Whittaker, "Apple Expands Its Bug Bounty, Increases Maximum Payout to $1M," *TechCrunch*, August 8, 2019, https://techcrunch.com/2019/08/08/apple-hackers-macos-security/ (accessed August 12, 2019).

CASE 12

The Hershey Company's Bittersweet Success

Introduction

Chocolate is enjoyed by millions, mainly in decadent desserts, candies, and drinks. Dark chocolate, chocolate with at least 70 percent cocoa, is known for its health benefits, such as reducing blood pressure, improving blood flow, and increasing good cholesterol. As society learns more about the health benefits of dark chocolate, demand for the product continues to grow. Developing countries are discovering that cocoa beans improve their sweet treats and candies, thus creating even greater worldwide demand. Cocoa beans grow mostly in tropical climates, mainly in West Africa, Asia, and Latin America, with the largest exporters being Ghana and the Ivory Coast.

With more than $7.7 billion in annual sales, the Hershey Company is one of the world's largest producers of chocolate and candy products. Hershey's products are sold in more than 70 countries and include Hershey's Kisses and Hershey's Milk Chocolate Bars, as well as brands such as Reese's, Whoppers, Almond Joy, and Twizzlers. Although Hershey strives to be a model company and has several philanthropic, social, and environmental programs, the company has struggled with ethical problems related to labor issues in West African cocoa communities. These issues have included child labor. Hershey has developed several initiatives to improve the lives of West African cocoa workers and is involved with a number of organizations that are involved in cocoa communities. However, critics argue that Hershey is not doing enough to stop labor exploitation on cocoa plantations. This case examines some of the issues related to the Hershey Chocolate Company and West African cocoa communities.

Hershey's History

The Hershey Chocolate Company was founded in 1894 by candy manufacturer Milton Hershey in Lancaster, Pennsylvania. As a candy entrepreneur, he had two bankruptcies before his eureka moment while making candy caramels with fresh milk. Hershey's chocolate business started off as a side project, a way to create sweet chocolate coatings for his caramels; however, the company soon began producing baking chocolate and cocoa and then selling the extra product to other confectioners. The successful sale of Hershey's excess products was enough to make the chocolate department its own separate entity.

Despite the company's immediate success, Milton Hershey still craved more chocolate, especially milk chocolate. At the time, milk chocolate was perceived as a treat only the wealthy could afford to enjoy. Hershey set out to find a less expensive way to produce milk chocolate while still maintaining its quality. In 1896, Hershey bought a milk processing plant in Derry Township, Pennsylvania, and began working day and night until 1899 when he created the perfect milk chocolate recipe—a recipe that could be manufactured cheaply and efficiently while maintaining a high level of quality. The company soon opened a factory and began introducing new chocolate treats. The most popular of these was the Hershey's Kiss, a small dollop-shaped chocolate candy wrapped in foil.

The Hershey's Kiss was only the beginning. Hershey soon came out with Mr. Goodbar and Krackel, both of which remain popular today. In 1923, Hershey began collaborating with another famous confectioner: H.B. Reese. H.B. Reese was a former employee at the Hershey Company who started his own candy company that focused on a single product, the peanut butter cup. Due to his ties with the Hershey Company, the chocolate coating for the Reese's peanut butter cups was supplied by Hershey.

Throughout the mid-twentieth century, the Hershey Chocolate Company continued to expand. The company's entrepreneurial spirit continued after Milton Hershey's death in 1945. The company acquired several other firms, including Reese's, and was renamed the Hershey Foods Corporation in 1968. From 1969 to 2004, the company grew from $334 million to $4.4 billion in net sales. The company changed its name to the Hershey Company in 2005.

Today, Hershey employs more than 14,930 people worldwide, with the company headquarters in Hershey, Pennsylvania. The company has a formal "Code of Conduct" and was ranked number 252 on *Forbes'* "Best Employer List." In March 2017, Michele Buck was named President & CEO, making her Hershey's first female chief executive. She was later named to *Fortune's* "50 Most Powerful Women" list. Hershey's stock price has increased 40 percent since Buck joined the company.

Hershey, which had $7.7 billion in sales in 2018, now includes the following brands: Hershey's, Kisses,

This material was developed by Dianne Kroncke, Harper Baird, and Sarah Sawayda under the direction of O.C. Ferrell and Linda Ferrell, © 2019. Shelby Wyatt provided updates. It is intended for classroom discussion rather than to illustrate effective or ineffective handling of administrative, ethical, or legal decisions by management. Users of this material are prohibited from claiming this material as their own, emailing it to others, or placing it on the Internet.

Reese's, Kit Kat, 5th Avenue, Almond Joy, Brookside, Cadbury, Heath, Mounds, Mr. Goodbar, Krackel, Whatchamacallit, Skor, Symphony, York, Whoppers, Allan, Good & Plenty, Jolly Rancher, Pelon Pelo Rico, Twizzlers, Breath Savers, Bubble Yum, ICE BREAKERS, Milk Duds, PAYDAY, Rolo, Zagnut and Zero. In September 2018, Hershey acquired Pirate Brands, which includes *Pirates Booty, Smart Puffs,* and the *Original Tings,* for $42 million and Amplify, the parent company of SkinnyPop, for nearly $1 billion.

After 125 years of business, Hershey is still innovating. The company plans to make a larger dent in the $88 billion snacking industry by introducing more snack products, evidenced by their acquisition of SkinnyPop's parent company, Amplify, Hershey's largest acquisition to date. Hershey is evolving to accommodate changing consumer preferences, including changes in the way people shop. In 2019 Hersey introduced stand-up packaging, which was designed to look good on the shelf in a store as well as appear appealing on mobile devices. By encouraging retailers to implement creative cross-selling solutions to their e-commerce platforms that encourage shoppers to add candy to their carts, Hershey hopes to appeal to online shoppers who purchase groceries online and order in bulk.

Thanks to Milton Hershey, the company has a long history of philanthropy and stewardship. He supported education, building the Milton Hershey School, a private school for lower income children. He also built parks and a hospital, as he put his employees' well-being over his personal profits. At the time of his death, he bequeathed most of his estate to the Hershey School.

Ethics, Values, and Social Responsibility

Hershey's commitments to their stakeholders through ethical behavior are outlined in the Code of Ethical Business Conduct. The code covers issues from conflicts of interest and antitrust to fair trade, sustainable supply chain management, and workplace diversity. The company encourages ethics reporting through a variety of channels, including management, human resources, executives, and third-party reporting. All employees go through ethics training and certify their adherence to the code every year. Hershey's Ethical Business Practices Committee provides oversight and guidance in all ethical issues at the company.

Values

Hershey's four core values are centered on the idea of "One Hershey":

1. **Open to Possibilities:** "We are open to possibilities by embracing diversity, seeking new approaches and striving for continuous improvement."

2. **Growing Together:** "We are growing together by sharing knowledge and unwrapping human potential in an environment of mutual respect."
3. **Making a Difference:** "We are making a difference by leading with integrity and determination to have a positive impact on everything we do."
4. **One Hershey:** "We are One Hershey, winning together while accepting individual responsibility for our results."

Corporate Social Responsibility Strategy

Hershey's corporate social responsibility (CSR) strategy, called Shared Goodness Promise, centers on engagement with their stakeholders and continually improving their CSR performance. The company also incorporates their values into their programs and initiatives. The company believes that "The Hershey Company's commitment to CSR is a direct reflection of our founder's life-affirming spirit." Hershey uses their value chain to categorize their social responsibility activities into four groups: Shared Futures, Shared Planet, Shared Business, and Shared Communities.

Shared Futures

Hershey's Shared Futures pillar focuses on helping children succeed through education and nutrition. Hershey introduced The Heartwarming Project in 2018 aimed at helping children build meaningful connections while promoting inclusivity and empathy. Hershey partnered with organizations such as The Boys & Girls Club of America and WE Charity to reach more than 6 million children in the program's first year.

Additionally, Hershey aims to bring nourishment to children around the world with a variety of nutrition programs. In 2015 Hershey introduced ViVi, a fortified nutritional supplement, to students in Ghana to improve nutrition as well as increase school attendance. In 2018, a study by the University of Ghana showed that anemia rates decreased by 11 to 81 percent and attendance rates improved by 84 to 95 percent in the 57,700 children that received ViVi daily. In 2018 Hershey partnered with Annamrita, a nonprofit in India, to provide school lunches to more than 6,400 children. Additionally, they conducted an assessment of the nutrition of children in underserved areas of Mumbai with the purpose of creating a snack to address any nutritional needs identified. These efforts, among others, demonstrate Hershey's commitment to improving access to food and nutrition in its communities worldwide.

Shared Planet

Maintaining the environment is important to Hershey, and they are taking many steps to reduce their impact on the environment, including sustainable product designs, sustainable sourcing, and efficient business operations. Some specific programs include the following:

- **Sustainable palm oil sourcing:** Palm oil comes from the African oil palm tree and is used in a wide variety of products, including Hershey's chocolate. However, the production of palm oil is highly controversial because of its impact on ecosystems. To combat concerns, Hershey became a member of the Roundtable of Sustainable Palm Oil (RSPO) and purchases their palm oil only from suppliers that are also RSPO members.
- **Sustainable paper:** In 2011, Hershey began to purchase paper for their office from suppliers that use sustainable forestry practices and are Forest Stewardship Council or Sustainable Forestry Initiative certified.
- **Recyclable packaging:** More than 80 percent of Hershey's packaging is recyclable, including syrup bottles, foil, paper wrappers, and boxes. Additionally, Hershey aims to reach a company-wide recycling rate of 95 percent by 2025.
- **Zero waste-to-landfill facility:** The Reese's manufacturing plant is a zero-waste-to-landfill facility, meaning that none of the plant's routine waste goes to a landfill. Today, 15 Hershey manufacturing plants and facilities have achieved zero waste-to-landfill. The waste that is not recycled goes to an energy incinerator and is used as a source of fuel.

Shared Business

Hershey strives to conduct business fairly and ethically by focusing on the integrity of their supply, consumer well-being, and alignment with customers. For Hershey, the integrity of supply includes not only the ingredients but also the people and processes used to grow, process, and acquire those ingredients (the entire supply chain). Cocoa is of particular concern to Hershey, and the company is involved in a number of cocoa-sector initiatives and partnerships to make progress in sustainable cocoa farming and fair labor. These issues are explored in greater detail later in this case.

The company sponsors several consumer health initiatives and programs, including Moderation Nation, a national consumer education initiative that promotes balanced lifestyles, which is sponsored by the Hershey Center for Health & Nutrition (HCHN) and the American Dietetic Association (ADA). The company also hosts Hershey's Track and Field Games across the U.S. to encourage children ages 9–14 to engage in sports and a healthy lifestyle.

Shared Communities

Hershey's idea of shared communities begins with employee engagement and volunteerism and extends to investing in the communities in which Hershey operates. Hershey wants to provide value to their employees and make the company a desirable place to work by focusing on safety, wellness, openness, and inclusion. The company has strong diversity policies and focuses on continuous safety improvements in their manufacturing

facilities. However, this does not mean that Hershey never faces workplace issues. In 2011, over 400 foreign students working for Hershey went on strike after Excel, one of the company's subcontractors, misled and underpaid them. OSHA later fined the subcontractor $283,000 for health and safety violations.

Hershey has continued to improve their workplace practices. In 2015, the company was listed in *Corporate Responsibility* magazine as one of America's "Best Corporate Citizens." The firm launched an initiative called the Manufacturing Apprenticeship Program to recruit, train, and retain employees with physical or intellectual disabilities for their manufacturing plants. In 2019, Hershey was named one of the "Best Places to Work for LGBTQ Equality" by the Human Rights Campaign.

Hershey's biggest philanthropic contribution is through their Milton Hershey School. Milton Hershey and his wife, Catherine, started the school in 1909 to help orphan boys receive an education while living in a nurturing environment that included meals and clothes. The school was a cause dear to the couple's heart because they were unable to have children of their own. After his wife's death, Milton Hershey created the Hershey Trust Fund, to which he donated most of his money to be used for the support of the school. To this day, the fund remains the company's biggest shareholder and largest beneficiary. It holds a 30 percent stake in Hershey.

Although the school is Hershey's biggest philanthropic contribution, the company also donates to and supports over 1,400 organizations, including the American Red Cross, Habitat for Humanity, Junior Achievement, Dress for Success, and the Children's Miracle Network. The company has also designed a way to get their employees involved in the community. Hershey designed a program called "Dollars for Doers" in which employees who participate in 50 hours of community service over one year are rewarded $250, by the company, to donate to an organization of their choice.

Board Changes

Despite their strong record of social responsibility, in 2016, Hershey experienced a board upheaval when the Hershey Trust Company settled with the Pennsylvania attorney general's office. The attorney general's office had begun investigating concerns that board members were overpaid, received reimbursements for excessive travel expenses, and exceeded 10-year term limits. There were also questions about whether board members of the trust were acting in the best interests of the Milton Hershey School. The board had rejected different offers by other firms to acquire Hershey. The local community of Hershey, Pennsylvania, encouraged Hershey to remain independent, but some believed that selling the company would have been the most beneficial option for the school. The Hershey Trust holds 81 percent of the voting power, which gives it the power to control votes on mergers or acquisitions.

The allegations were serious enough that Hershey agreed to make corporate governance changes. Some of the board members resigned. In addition, Hershey developed a legal document that caps board member terms as well as compensation. This lapse in corporate governance was a slight blow to Hershey's reputation, but it also offered the firm an opportunity to learn from their mistakes and develop more sound leadership for the future.

Labor Issues in the Cocoa Industry

Although The Hershey Company strives to engage in ethical and responsible behavior, the realities of the cocoa industry present several ethical challenges related to the fair and safe treatment of workers, especially children. Chocolate is one of the world's most popular confections, but few people consider the sources of the chocolate they consume.

The process of making chocolate spans several countries and companies even before the ingredients arrive at the manufacturing plant. It starts with the cocoa bean, which is found within the *Theobroma cacao*, also known as the cocoa pod (fruit). The harvest process is labor-intensive and starts when the seeds (cocoa beans) are extracted by splitting the pod with a machete. Each pod can contain anywhere from 20 to 50 beans, and around 400 beans are needed to produce one pound of chocolate. After the beans have been extracted, they are laid out to dry in the sun for several days in order to acquire the flavor needed for chocolate. The beans are then packed into bags and sent out for shipment.

The cocoa bean supply chain is extensive and elaborate; at times, the cocoa bean can go through up to 12 different stages before getting to the chocolate manufacturers, and the price per pound of cocoa beans changes significantly throughout the supply chain. By the time the beans reach the chocolate manufacturers, they are a mix of beans from hundreds of cocoa plantations.

Although the process of manufacturing chocolate requires many steps before it can begin, most of the major ethical and legal issues are related to the source of the cocoa bean. Cocoa plantations are found in areas with rainy, hot, tropical climates and high amounts of vegetation. The global cocoa market is currently supplied by mostly poor nations, with 70 percent supplied by Africa (Ivory Coast, Ghana, Nigeria, and Cameroon). The Ivory Coast supplies 40 percent of the entire global market, and Ghana supplies 20 percent. This is followed by 19 percent from Asia and Oceania (Indonesia, Papua New Guinea, Malaysia), and 11 percent from South America (Ecuador, Brazil, Colombia).

With the majority of the global cocoa supply coming from Africa, the need for workers on plantations never dwindles. This has brought about the booming business of child labor, slavery, and human trafficking across African borders. Many cocoa farms do not own the cocoa plantation and pay the landowner 50 to 66 percent of each year's crop. To keep costs low, farmers often use their own family members as a source of labor.

Children who work on cocoa plantations are usually somewhere between 12 and 15 years old but can be as young as five years old. Many of them work in hazardous conditions on the plantations, with workdays often lasting eight to twelve hours. Poverty in the Ivory Coast and Ghana causes parents to rely on their children to help provide for the family's basic survival. The average number of children in a household range from 5 to 17. Children work in all segments of cocoa production including land preparation, planting, farm maintenance, harvesting, and post-harvest. They clear land; fell and chop trees and brush; burn; spray insecticides; and apply fertilizers and fungicides.

It is not uncommon for traffickers to abduct small children from the neighboring African countries of Burkina Faso and Mali, some of the poorest countries in the world. Boys are sent to the fields, often in hot, humid conditions with little food and water. They are taught to use chainsaws to cut through the forest, while others climb and work on trees higher than 9 feet. They use machetes to cut the cocoa bean pods, and then put the pods in sacks that weigh up to 100 pounds. The children are then required to either drag or carry the sacks out of the forest. Other children receive the pods and use their machetes or cutlasses to open the pod's hard shell to harvest the cocoa beans.

Once the cocoa seeds have been removed, young girls assist women in processing or grinding the beans by hand. Some girls work on the farms for a few months, while others stay for the rest of their lives. This labor-intensive operation has been done by hand for centuries. Along with the physical demands, workers experience poor health services, little access to drinkable water, food insecurity, and lack of education.

Insect and pest control is a major problem for the growers. To mitigate this issue, children are sent to spray the pods with large amounts of industrial and toxic chemicals and pesticides, without the benefit of protective clothing. Exposure to these poisons creates damage to their neurological and physical development.

Although governments and corporations are aware of this problem, no accurate information, aside from estimates, exists regarding the true number of children working on cocoa plantations. The difficulty of obtaining accurate data can be attributed to the immense quantity of cocoa plantations across Africa, totaling well over 1,000,000 small plantations (average size 2 to 4 hectares), with between 600,000 and 800,000 plantations located throughout the Ivory Coast.

Nonetheless, it is estimated that two-thirds of African farms use child labor. Research conducted by the International Labor Organization (ILO) stated that in 2007 there were 284,000 children who worked in hazardous conditions related to cocoa in the Ivory Coast. Furthermore, according to surveys conducted by both Tulane University and the Government of the Ivory Coast, an estimated 819,921 children in the Ivory Coast alone are working in some area of the cocoa business. According to an ILO investigation in 2002, an estimated 12,000 child laborers in the Ivory Coast had no relatives anywhere near the plantations, which suggests that they may have been trafficked.

In addition to child labor, many cocoa plantations engage in the exploitation of other workers. While some non-family workers are paid, others may be enslaved or work in abusive conditions. They may have been trafficked from neighboring countries or tricked into owing large amounts of money to their employers. The workers are often threatened with physical punishment or death if they attempt to leave the plantation. Hershey introduced a human rights policy in 2019 as a sign of its commitment to human rights issues in the supply chain such as child labor, women's rights and empowerment, living wage and income, and forced labor. The goal of the policy is to create awareness around human rights issues across the company, identify training needs, and improve the company's supplier code conduct and social audit program.

Global Help and a Little Green Frog

The issues of child labor, human trafficking, and forced labor in West Africa have drawn the attention of many organizations, as well as the companies that procure products from that region. They have implemented many different initiatives, laws, and other precautionary measures in order to reduce the use of children for cocoa farming in terms of manual labor. In Africa, individuals under the age of 14 are not allowed by law to work within the business sector, which does not include family farms. This law seems to be effective, but in reality, it does almost nothing when considering the large number of family cocoa farms and the ease of hiding non-family laborers.

To help change labor practices without relying on governmental or legal support, several organizations are working to encourage the ethical sourcing of cocoa. Most of these organizations focus on the fair treatment and education of cocoa producers and raising voluntary support from companies. The following are some of the global organizations and programs that are working to combat the labor problem within the cocoa industry:

- **World Cocoa Foundation (WCF):** An organization devoted to improving cocoa farmers' lives through sustainable and responsible cocoa farming practices.
- **Sustainable Tree Crops Program (STCP):** Farmers learn to improve their cocoa crop yields and earn more money through nine-month field training courses.

- **Harkin-Engel Protocol:** An initiative enacted in 2001 to commit the chocolate industry to fighting the worst cases of child labor. The agreement was signed by eight chocolate manufacturers, including The Hershey Company.
- **International Cocoa Initiative (ICI):** An independent foundation established in 2002 under the Harkin-Engel Protocol to address the worst forms of child labor and adult forced labor on cocoa farms in West Africa. The organization works to inform and educate communities on child labor and how to create community-based solutions.
- **International Labor Organization (ILO):** An organization working to combat the various child labor-related problems within West Africa. The different programs initiated by the ILO have focused on creating sustainable ways of removing children from child labor in the cocoa business, improving community initiatives to fight child labor, and increasing overall income for the adult sector to prevent the need for child labor.

The International Cocoa Organization was established in 1973 by the United Nations. Membership is composed of cocoa producers and representatives from countries that import cocoa. It developed seven formal economic agreements that address funding of projects, sustainable development, disputes, consultations, and research and marketing. It also established a set of standards for a "Sustainable World Cocoa Economy."

Today, there are three main certifying organizations for cocoa: Fair Trade USA, UTZ, and Rainforest. Their mission is to provide assurance that the product is produced in a sustainable manner. They have a formal "Code of Conduct" and "Certifications" that address farming methods, working conditions, and care of the environment.

Fair Trade USA

Fair Trade Certified is a non-profit organization that was founded in 1981 by the Institute for Agricultural Trade Policy and involves a network of producers, companies, consumers, and organizations that are concerned about the environment and making people a priority. Fair Trade sets standards and criteria that protect ecosystems and stipulate farmers work in safe conditions and receive a harvest price while protecting the environment. Fair Trade guarantees a minimum price to farmers and a guaranteed premium payment per ton. While this is an improvement in financial remuneration to the farmers, it is still not enough to eliminate poverty for families. Their certification provides child labor monitoring, as well as remediation programs for those farmers who are caught abusing child labor laws. Fair Trade USA was a member of Fairtrade International until September 2011 when they resigned their membership because of disagreements as to the "best paths forward" in their certification and expansion missions.

Today, more than two billion people live on less than two dollars a day according to U.N. poverty statistics. Fair Trade created Co-Op Link to provide cooperatives with funding for capital access and increased quality standards. It also limits child labor, the use of pesticides, herbicides, and genetically modified products (GMOs), and establishes standards for contracts and importers that must be met before certification. It also allows a set of standards for democratic decision-making, so farmers will have an opportunity to have input into how the Fairtrade premiums are invested.

Universal Trade Zone and Rainforest Alliance

Universal Trade Zone (UTZ) was founded in 2002 as UTZ Kapeh, or "good coffee," by Nick Bocklandt, a Belgian-Guatemalan coffee grower, and Ward de Groote, a Dutch coffee roaster. Both men were committed to implementing sustainable farming practices. In October 2007, cocoa certifications were added. Today, more than 750,000 cocoa farmers from 21 countries producing 1.5 million tons of cocoa are now UTZ certified. UTZ has a "Certified Code of Conduct" and includes traceable growing practices that address farm management, farming practices, labor and living conditions, and the environment. UTZ is also a full member of the ISEAL Alliance, the global sustainability standards association.

Rainforest Alliance

Rainforest Alliance ensures that agriculture, rain forests, and farm workers and their families meet standards that protect against environmental and social hazards. Cocoa certified by the Sustainable Agriculture Network (SAN)/Rainforest Alliance makes up more than 13.4 percent of the world's cocoa supply. SAN is a non-profit conservation organization that has partnered with the Rainforest Alliance to help sustainable cocoa farming become mainstream. The SAN/Rainforest Alliance certification program was created to protect natural ecosystems and teach farmers about sustainable agricultural principles. This includes how to protect against insect infestations, prevent disease of cocoa trees, and safe farming techniques that protect workers as well as the environment.

Rainforest Alliance addresses the use of child labor by prohibiting minors under 15 years of age from working on the farms as part of its certification process. Young people between 15 and 18 are allowed to work but are restricted in the tasks they are allowed to perform. It also ensures that workers have access to education for their children along with access to medical services for farmers, workers, and their families.

On January 9, 2018, the Rainforest Alliance officially merged with UTZ. The certification merger includes coffee, cocoa, tea, and hazelnuts. With 182,000 farmers being certified in one or both of the organizations, the new merger is the largest certification organization in the world. This merger also reduced administrative costs and duplications in the first year as each organization continued with their separate and standard certifications and audits. In 2019, a new single program was instituted and marketed as a single certification brand. Currently, neither UTZ nor Rainforest have a system that protects farmers from market fluctuations or addresses fixed premiums for farmers.

Hershey's Efforts to Improve Labor Conditions

Hershey has made several commitments to help reduce labor issues in their own supply chain and in the chocolate industry. Hershey is involved in West Africa and the organizations that fight child labor in West African cocoa farming. The company is a member of the WCF, ICI, and is one of the eight corporations that signed the Harkin-Engel Protocol. Involvement in these programs and organizations requires Hershey to commit to certain standards and contribute to fighting child labor.

The Hershey Company is dedicated to sustainably and ethically supplying the cocoa needed for their products, as well as educating their suppliers. One program that integrates these two concepts is Hershey's CocoaLink program. CocoaLink uses mobile technology to share practical information with rural cocoa farmers. Farmers receive free text or voice messages that cover topics such as improving farming practices, farm safety, child labor, health, crop disease prevention, post-harvest production, and crop marketing. Farmers can also share information and receive answers to specific cocoa-farming questions.

In 2012, Hershey launched the Hershey Learn to Grow (LTG) farm program in Ghana, which provides local farmers with information on best practices in sustainable cocoa farming. Specifically, the program seeks to encourage ethical farming practices as well as leadership and empowerment. Both men and women are being trained on how to improve crop yields. Those who meet acceptable certification standards receive extra money. Hershey estimates that this program influenced over 31,000 farmers by 2015.

Hershey also produces some of their products using ethical and sustainable cocoa. Hershey Bliss, one of the company's specialty chocolates, is made with 100 percent Rainforest Alliance Certified cocoa. In 2006, Hershey acquired Dagoba from Knoppers, a German chocolate wafer snacks company. In 2012, Hershey purchased certified organic cocoa from the Rainforest Alliance for their Bliss and Dagoba premium brand chocolates.

Hershey launched their Learn to Grow Farmer and Family Development Center in Assin Fosu in Ghana's central cocoa region in 2012. Source Trust, a non-profit organization in Ghana, was created for the education of farmers to help improve their revenues by teaching better farming techniques. It also includes a supply system that allows for the tracing of a product back to the farm of origination. Source Trust has an alliance with the Cocoa Livelihoods Program and with the Bill and Melinda Gates Foundation to address food security for farming communities. Hershey partnered with Source Trust to expand the Learn to Grow program.

In March 2013, the Hershey Company instituted their Raise the Bar campaign that included a timeline to begin a transition to certified cocoa as part of their 21st Century Cocoa Plan. Hershey made a commitment to source their cocoa through UTZ, Fairtrade USA, and Rainforest Alliance. The goal is to source 100 percent sustainable cocoa in the near future.

In 2016, Hershey initiated the One for All Cocoa Project, with its Dagoba brand organic chocolate. The Project's mission is to advance women and to assist in the economic development of cocoa farming communities. Women are taught management skills and customized farming techniques that enable a sustainable environment.

Hershey also supports Women in Cocoa and Chocolate Network, a program that supports women farmers who now make up a quarter of the cocoa farm population in West Africa. This organization provides extension, business management, and certification services. They work to improve the economic lives in the cocoa communities as well as empower women throughout the cocoa supply chain.

One of Hershey's latest endeavor, The Cocoa for Good campaign, was introduced to West African farming communities in April 2018. Hershey pledged $500 million by 2030 to address the cocoa community's issues of poverty, lack of nutrition, child labor, at-risk youth, and sustainable ecosystems.

Criticism of Hershey's Efforts

Some critics argue that Hershey is not doing enough to combat labor exploitation and improve communities in West Africa. Over the past few years, Mars, Mondelez, Nestlé, Cargill, and other competitors have worked to adopt fair trade certification and/or release information regarding their suppliers. Despite many requests for public disclosure of its cocoa suppliers, Hershey still declines to name them. It is well known that Hershey acquires most of its cocoa from West Africa, but the specific sources are more difficult to identify.

According to a report titled "Time to Raise the Bar: The Real Corporate Social Responsibility for the Hershey Company":

> Hershey has no policies in place to purchase cocoa that has been produced without the use of labor exploitation, and the company has consistently refused to provide

public information about its cocoa sources... Hershey's efforts to further cut costs in its cocoa production has led to a reduction in good jobs in the United States.

The report, compiled by Global Exchange, Green America, the International Labor Rights Forum, and Oasis USA, accused Hershey of not embracing fair trade practices despite having a U.S. market share of over 40 percent. It also accused Hershey of greenwashing, or creating a false public impression regarding their eco-friendly behavior, by donating to various programs without actually changing their policies to ensure that their cocoa is ethically produced. Green America even created a coalition called Raise the Bar, Hershey! to urge the company to address child labor and trafficking in the supply chain.

Since then, relations between Hershey and Green America seem to have improved somewhat. The organization was pleased with Hershey's pledge to source 100 percent of its cocoa from sustainable sources (free from child labor) by 2020. However, the company has many obstacles to overcome, and Green America has ranked Hershey's competitors higher than Hershey in their approach to solving the child labor problem. Green America developed a Big Chocolate Scorecard to grade chocolate manufacturers on the sustainability of their supply chains. Hershey ranked behind their major competitors Nestlé, Mars, Mondelez, and Ghirardelli (owned by Lindt); Hershey received a C- according to the scorecard's ranking criteria. However, even Nestlé—the highest ranked among the top chocolate manufacturers—only scored a C+. A representative from Green America maintains that Hershey scored lower because they rely more on third-party certification rather than direct engagement. The organization believes that while third-party certification is a step in the right direction, it is only part of the solution to combatting child labor.

Through the years, Hershey has had to address numerous litigations regarding child labor, human rights, and abuse of civil liberties in their supply chains, particularly in developing countries. Two class action lawsuits were files against Hershey in 2018. They alleged The Hershey Company and Mars knowingly imported cocoa beans from the Ivory Coast, a country that uses child labor, slave labor, and child trafficking. The lawsuits also contended that Hershey has failed to address these issues with their suppliers. Though the lawsuits were dismissed in 2019, a similar lawsuit was filed by Perkins Coie, an international law firm, on behalf of three California residents who alleged the Hershey Company, along with the Mars and Nestle Company, committed false advertising by failing to disclose the use of child slavery on their packaging. They also contended that these companies deceived consumers into "unwittingly supporting child labor and violations of human rights." The suit sought monetary damages for California residents who purchased the chocolate. They also petitioned to revise the Hershey packaging to acknowledge that child slaves were used in the production of the product.

Conclusion

The labor issues in the chocolate industry are complex and are connected to the poverty within West Africa. The exploitation of cocoa communities is intertwined with the meager incomes for the majority of the population, a lack of education and opportunity, governmental corruption, and other conditions in the region. With more than 2.1 million children used in the cocoa production just in the Ivory Coast, the magnitude of this corruption is vast. Improving the overall well-being of West Africa is an important part of any attempt to effectively fight the problems associated with labor cocoa plantations.

The Hershey Company recognizes the need to improve labor conditions in the supply chain and has developed several initiatives to help create positive change in the cocoa industry. However, despite the company's large financial contributions, the company trails behind competitors Nestlé, Mars, Mondelez, and Ghirardelli on efforts to address sustainability, poverty, and child labor. On the other hand, the company appears to have improved significantly in combatting child labor after initiating the 21st Century Cocoa Plan.

In the end, labor exploitation in the chocolate industry cannot be solved by one company alone. There are many possible solutions, and it will take many years and a large amount of investment from the chocolate industry before conditions change. However, by making small changes to West African cocoa communities, the quality of life for thousands of cocoa workers will slowly improve.

Questions for Discussion

1. Should Hershey be held ethically responsible for child labor conditions in the West African cocoa communities?
2. If it is not possible for Hershey to gain control of their supply chain for a required raw material (cocoa beans) in the final product, what are its alternatives?
3. In your opinion, is Hershey doing enough in terms of corporate social responsibility, given that the company is lagging behind competitors? If not, what could they do to improve?

Sources

"Hershey Co.," MarketWatch, https://www.marketwatch.com/investing/stock/hsy/financials (accessed August 23, 2019).

"'Bitter' Chocolate Report: Hershey Dominates U.S. Market, But Lags Behind Competitors in Avoiding Forced Labor, Human Trafficking, and Abusive Child Labor," *PR Newswire*, September 13, 2010, http://www.prnewswire.com/news-releases/bitter-chocolate-report-hersheydominates-us-market-but-lags-behind-competitors-in-avoiding-forced-labor-human-trafficking-and-abusive-childlabor102803859.html (accessed July 21, 2016).

"2018 Cocoa Barometer Released, Thursday, April 19, 2018. *Coco Barometer Organization*, 19, April 2018, https://www.voicenetwork.eu/2018/04/2018-cocoa-barometer-released/ (accessed September 25, 2018).

"Chocolate Makers Hershey's and Mars Hit with Lawsuits Over Alleged Use of Child and Slave, Labor," *Hagens Berman*, February 26, 2018, https://www.hbsslaw.com/cases/hershey-chocolate-slave-labor/pressrelease/hershey-chocolate-slave-labor-chocolate-makers-hersheys-and-mars-hit-with-lawsuits-over-alleged-use-of-child-and-slave-labor (accessed October 11, 2018).

"Dagoba," *Merriam-Webster Dictionary*, https://www.merriam-webster.com/dictionary/dagoba, (accessed August 20, 2018).

"Hershey '21st Century Cocoa Plan' Outlines Commitments to Sustainable Cocoa and Improving Cocoa Communities," *Business Wire,* March 21, 2013, http://www.businesswire.com/news/home/20130321006184/en/Hershey%E2%80%9821 StCentury-Cocoa-Plan%E2%80%99-Outlines-Commitment (accessed July 21, 2016).

"Hershey Revenue 2006-2019 HSY," *Macrotrends*, https://www.macrotrends.net/stocks/charts/HSY/hershey/revenue (accessed August 5, 2019).

"Hershey to Acquire Pirate Brands from B&G Foods," *MarketWatch*, September 12, 2018, https://www.marketwatch.com/press-release/hershey-to-acquire-pirate-brands-from-bg-foods-2018-09-12 (accessed September 18, 2018).

"International Programme on the Elimination of Child Labour (IPEC)" International Labour Organization, http://www.ilo.org/public//english//standards/ipec/themes/cocoa/download/2005_02_cl_cocoa.pdf (accessed July 21, 2016).

"Name Change at Hershey," *Prepared Foods Network*, April 26, 2005, http://www.preparedfoods.com/articles/name-change-at-hershey (accessed July 21, 2016).

"Survey Research on Child Labor in West African Cocoa Growing Areas 2013/14," *Tulane University*, July 30, 2015, http://www.childlaborcocoa.org/images/Payson_Reports/Tulane%20University%20-%20Survey%20Research%20on%20Child%20Labor%20in%20the%20Cocoa%20Sector%20-%2030%20July%202015.pdf (accessed October 08, 2018), 8–13.

"Survey Research on Child Labor in West African Cocoa Growing Areas 2013/14," *Tulane University*, July 30, 2015, http://www.childlaborcocoa.org/images/Payson_Reports/Tulane%20University%20-%20Survey%20Research%20on%20Child%20Labor%20in%20the%20Cocoa%20Sector%20-%2030%20July%202015.pdf (accessed October 08, 2018), 54–73.

"Survey Research on Child Labor in West African Cocoa Growing Areas 2013/14," *Tulane University*, July 30, 2015, http://www.childlaborcocoa.org/images/Payson_Reports/Tulane%20University%20-%20Survey%20Research%20on%20Child%20Labor%20in%20the%20Cocoa%20Sector%20-%2030%20July%202015.pdf (accessed October 08, 2018), 84–87.

"The Hershey Company Recognized as One of America's '100 Best Corporate Citizens'," *Business Wire*, April 12, 2013, http://www.businesswire.com/news/home/20130412005450/en/Hershey-Company-Recognized-America%E2%80%99s%E2%80%98100-Corporate-Citizens%E2%80%99 (accessed July 27, 2016).

"Tulane Report Survey Research on Child Labor in West Africa in Cocoa Growing Areas." *Tulane University News*, July 30, 2018, http://www2.tulane.edu/news/releases/tulane-releases-report-on-child-labor-in-west-african-cocoa-production.cfm (accessed August 18, 2018).

Abby Haglage, "Lawsuit: Your Candy Bar Was Made By Child Slaves," *Daily Beast,* September 30, 2015, https://www.thedailybeast.com/lawsuit-your-candy-bar-was-made-by-child-slaves (accessed August 20, 2019).

Alan Panebaker, "Dagoba Sales to Hershey Draws Mixed Reaction from Locals," *Ashland Tidings*, October 21, 2006, https://ashlandtidings.com/news/business/dagoba-sale-to-hershey-draws-mixed-reaction-from-locals (accessed August 20, 2019).

Annie Gasparro, "Hershey Trust to Reach Settlement with Pennsylvania Attorney General's Office," *The Wall Street Journal*, July 22, 2016, http://www.wsj.com/articles/hershey-trust-to-reach-settlement-with-pennsylvania-attorney-generals-office-1469224460 (accessed July 27, 2016).

Anti-Slavery International, "The Cocoa Industry in West Africa: A History of Exploitation," 2004, http://www.antislavery.org/includes/documents/cm_docs/2008/c/cocoa_report_2004.pdf (accessed July 21, 2016).

Antonie Fountain and Friedel Huetz-Adams, *Cocoa Barometer* 2018, April 19, 2018, http://www.cocoabarometer.org/Cocoa_Barometer/Download_files/2018%20Cocoa%20Barometer%20Executive%20Summary.pdf (accessed September 25, 2018).

Brian O'Keefe, "Inside Big Chocolate's Child Labor Problem," *Fortune,* March 1, 2016, http://fortune.com/big-chocolate-child-labor/ (accessed July 21, 2016).

Brian O'Keefe, "Was Your Easter Chocolate Made with Child Labor?" *Fortune,* March 25, 2016, http://fortune.com/2016/03/25/easterchocolate-child-labor/ (accessed July 21, 2016).

Briana Elliott, "Cassava: Benefits and Dangers," *Healthline Website,* March 24, 2017, https://www.healthline.com/nutrition/cassava (accessed August 17, 2018).

Chocolate Manufacturers Association, "Protocol for the Growing and Processing of Cocoa Beans and Their Derivative Products in a Manner That Complies with ILO Convention 182 Concerning the Prohibition and Immediate Action for the Elimination of the Worst Forms of Child Labor," http://www.cocoainitiative.org/images/stories/pdf/harkin percent20engel percent20protocol.pdf (accessed May 25, 2012).

Christian Alexandersen, "Hershey Co. a Sweet Place to Work for LGBT Community, Report Finds," *Penn Live,* November 18, 2015, http://www.pennlive.com/news/2015/11/hershey_co_a_sweet_place_to_wo.html (accessed July 27, 2016).

Crystal Lindell, "How the 125-year-old Hershey Company Continues to Innovate," *Candy Industry,* May 14, 2019, https://www.candyindustry.com/articles/88674-how-the-125-year-old-hershey-company-continues-to-innovate (accessed October 28, 2019).

Danielle Dresden, "What to Know about Cassava: Nutrition and Toxicity," *Medical News Today*, November 20, 2018, https://www.medicalnewstoday.com/articles/323756.php (accessed August 20, 2019).

Douglas Yu, "Cocoa Farmers' Fear of Being Reported Drives Child Labor Issue Underground, says ICI," *Confectionery News,* June 14, 2018, https://www.confectionerynews.com/Article/2018/06/13/Cocoa-farmers-fear-of-being-reported-makes-child-labor-issue-worse (accessed August 10, 2018).

Food Manufacturing, "Hershey to Acquire Pirate Brands from B&G Foods, Food Manufacturing," *Food Manufacturing,* August 13, 2018, https://www.manufacturing.net/news/2018/09/hershey-acquire-pirate-brands-b-g-foods (accessed August 20, 2019).

Green America, "2016 Chocolate Scorecard," http://www.greenamerica.org/programs/fairtrade/whatyoucando/2010Scorecard.cfm (accessed July 21, 2016).

Green America, "Thank You, Hershey! Please Keep Your Promise to Address Child Labor in Your Supply Chain," http://www.greenamerica.org/takeaction/hershey/ (accessed July 21, 2016).

Human Rights Campaign, "Best Places to Work 2019," https://www.hrc.org/resources/best-places-to-work-2019 (accessed August 22, 2019).

International Cocoa Organization, "Articles," August 2, 2016, https://www.icco.org/component/content/category/7-about-icco.html (accessed August 20, 2019).

Jan Conway, "Number of Full-Time Employees (FTE) of the Hershey Company Worldwide from 2008 to 2018," *Statista*, https://www.statista.com/statistics/370346/number-of-employees-hershey-company/ (accessed August 5, 2019).

Jenara Nerenberg, "Hershey Gets a Not-So-Sweet Kiss for Fair Trade Month," *Fast Company*, October 5, 2010, http://www.fastcompany.com/1693089/hershey-gets-a-not-so-sweet-declaration-for-fair-trade-month (accessed July 21, 2016).

Joseph James Whitworth, "Hershey Reveals 500m Sustainable Cocoa Strategy," *Confectionery News*, April 5, 2018, https://www.confectionerynews.com/Article/2018/04/05/Hershey-to-invest-0.5bn-by-2030-for-sustainable-cocoa-supply (accessed August 18, 2018).

Julia Preston, "Hershey's Packer Is Fined Over Its Safety Violations," *The New York Times*, February 21, 2012, http://www.nytimes.com/2012/02/22/us/hersheys-packer-fined-by-labor-department-for-safety-violations.html (accessed July 21, 2016).

Kathryn Manza, "Making Chocolate Sweeter: How to Encourage Hershey Company to Clean up Its Supply Chain and Eliminate Child Labor," Boston College *International and Comparative Law Review,* May 20, 2014, https://lawdigitalcommons.bc.edu/iclr/vol37/iss2/6/ (accessed August 2, 2018).

Kris Gunnars, "7 Proven Health Benefits of Dark Chocolate," *Healthline*, June 25, 2018, https://www.healthline.com/nutrition/7-health-benefits-dark-chocolate (accessed September 26, 2018).

Lauren Hirsch, "After 124 Years, Hershey Tries to Be More Than Just a Chocolate Company (Again)," *CNBC*, April 24, 2018, https://www.cnbc.com/2018/04/24/not-just-a-chocolate-company-hershey-plots-its-future-in-snacking.html (accessed October 28, 2019).

Marc Gunther, "Hershey & Other Chocolate Companies Using More Certified Cocoa, but African Farmers Still Mired in Poverty," *The Guardian*, July 14, 2015, https://www.business-humanrights.org/es/node/125592 (accessed August 11, 2018).

Marc Gunther, "Hershey's Uses More Certified Sustainable Cocoa, but Farmers May Not Be Seeing the Benefits," *The Guardian*, July 6, 2015, https://www.theguardian.com/sustainable-business/2015/jul/06/hersheys-mars-ferrero-cocoa-farming-fair-trade-global-exchange (accessed August 18, 2018).

Marjie Sackett, "Forced Child Labor and Cocoa Production in West Africa," *Topical Research Digest: Human Rights and Contemporary Slavery,* November 30, 2009, https://www.du.edu/korbel/hrhw/researchdigest/slavery/africa.pdf 84–86.

Mark Funk, "Child Labor in Cocoa: What You Need to Know," *Green America*, August 18, 2018. https://www.greenamerica.org/end-child-labor-cocoa-choose-fair-labor/taking-bite-out-child-labor (accessed August 18, 2018).

Oliver Nieburg, "Cocoa Child Labor Lawsuits against Mars and Hershey filed," *Confectionary News*, February 5, 2018, https://www.confectionerynews.com/Article/2018/02/28/Cocoa-child-labor-lawsuits-against-Mars-and-Hershey-filed (accessed August 11, 2018).

Paul Robson, "Ending Child Trafficking in West Africa," *Anti-Slavery International*, December 2010, http://www.antislavery.org/includes/documents/cm_docs/2011/c/cocoa_report_for_website.pdf (accessed July 21, 2016).

Payson Center for International Development and Technology Transfer, "Oversight of Public and Private Initiatives to Eliminate the Worst Forms of Child Labor in the Cocoa Sector in Cote d'Ivoire and Ghana," *Tulane University*, March 31, 2011, http://www.childlabor-payson.org/Tulanepercent 20Finalpercent20Report.pdf (accessed May 25, 2012).

Rainforest Alliance , "Joining Forces: The Rainforest Alliance and UTZ," *Rainforest Alliance Organization*, January 9, 2018, https://www.rainforest-alliance.org/business/utz-merger (accessed August 18, 2018).

Rainforest Alliance, "Our Very Lives Depend on Them," August 15, 2018. https://www.rainforest-alliancne.org/issues/forests (accessed August 15, 2018).

Rainforest Alliance, "What Does Rainforest Alliance Certified™ Mean?" October 15, 2018. https://www.rainforest-alliance.org/faqs/what-does-rainforest-alliance-certified-mean (access August 15, 2018).

Robert H. Shmerling, "Your Brain on Chocolate," *Harvard Medical School,* August 16, 2017, https://www.health.harvard.edu/blog/your-brain-on-chocolate-2017081612179 (accessed August 8, 2018).

Sudarsan Raghavan and Sumana Chatterjee, "A Taste of Slavery," *Stop Chocolate Slavery*, http://vision.ucsd.edu/~kbranson/stopchocolateslavery/atasteofslavery.html (accessed July 21, 2016).

Susan Adams, "Hershey Fudges Labor Relations Image," *Forbes*, August 26, 2011, http://www.forbes.com/sites/susanadams/2011/08/26/hershey-fudges-labor-relations-image (accessed July 21, 2016).

The European Chocolate & Cocoa Industry, "Cocoa Farming: An Overview," http://www.cocoafarming.org.uk/cocoa_farming_bw_v8_uk.pdf (accessed July 21, 2016).

The Hershey Company, "Environmental Sustainability," https://www.thehersheycompany.com/en_ca/responsibility/good-business/environmental-sustainability.html (accessed August 23, 2019).

The Hershey Company, "Cocoa For Good," https://www.the-hersheycompany.com/en_us/shared-goodness/shared-business/cocoa-for-good.html (accessed August 18, 2018).

The Hershey Company, "Cocoa Sustainability Strategy," https://www.thehersheycompany.com/en_us/responsibility/good business/creatinggoodness/cocoa-sustainability.html (accessed July 21, 2016).

The Hershey Company, "Milton S. Hershey From Humble to Hero,' https://www.thehersheycompany.com/en_us/this-is-hershey/milton-hershey.html (accessed August 18, 2018).

The Hershey Company, "Share Goodness: 2018 Sustainability Report," 2018, https://www.thehersheycompany.com/content/dam/corporate-us/documents/pdf/Hershey-SR-2018.pdf (accessed October 28, 2019).

The Hershey Company, http://www.thehersheycompany.com (accessed July 21, 2016).

United States Department of Labor, Bureau of International Labor Affairs, "Child Labor, Forced Labor & Human Trafficking," https://www.dol.gov/agencies/ilab/our-work/child-forced-labor-trafficking (accessed August 11, 2018).

UTZ Organization, "Certification," https://utz.org/what-we-offer/certification/ (accessed August 8, 2018).

UTZ Organization, "Joining Forces: UTZ and the Rainforest Alliance," https://utz.org/merger/ (accessed August 8, 2018).

World Cocoa Foundation, "Cocoa Market Update," April 1, 2014, http://www.worldcocoafoundation.org/wpcontent/uploads/CocoaMarket-Update-as-of-4-1-2014.pdf (accessed July 21, 2016).

CASE 13

Corporate Social Responsibility from the Outside In at Patagonia

Introduction

How can businesses make a difference in a world of decreasing resources? Patagonia, a privately held outdoor clothing company based out of Ventura, California, is working toward finding an answer to that question. Patagonia's clothing has been developed and marketed toward a variety of outdoor sports, travel, and everyday wear. The company has integrated core beliefs and values into every product they produce and is known for their innovative designs, exceptional quality, and environmental ingenuity. Their high integrity and commitment to the environment has regularly placed Patagonia on the Ethisphere Institute's "World's Most Ethical Companies" list.

History of Patagonia

Like many successful companies, Patagonia stems from one entrepreneur's passion. In 1953, Yvon Chouinard, founder of Patagonia, developed a passion for rock climbing. His passion brought him West to the San Fernando Valley in California, where he became an expert at climbing and rappelling. Unfortunately, his passion was limited by a lack of appropriate climbing gear. The only available climbing gear were pitons, metal spikes that were driven into cracks or seams in rocks. These pitons were left in the rock, meaning that a long climb could require hundreds of these tools.

Recognizing a need for better, more environmentally friendly equipment, Chouinard began to make his own reusable pitons that were stronger than what was currently on the market. Word of Chouinard's invention spread and he began selling his pitons out of the back of his car for $1.50 each. By 1965, Chouinard decided to partner with Tom Frost to create Chouinard Equipment. For nearly a decade, Chouinard and Frost made improvements on nearly every climbing tool. Soon Chouinard and his wife Malinda were selling clothing as a way to support the hardware business. By 1972, the clothing line had expanded to become a business venture. The name of the line was Patagonia and was intended to reflect the mysticism of far-off lands and adventurous places located beyond the map.

The clothing line was successful for many years. Financial hardships, coupled with Chouinard's strong focus on the environment, resulted in a change in the product material. The company switched to more expensive and durable organic cotton in 1996, a risky business move considering it increased the firm's supply costs. The more durable the product, the fewer customers need to purchase from the company. However, the change had a net positive effect; consumers were more willing to do business with Patagonia due to their environmental consciousness and the fact that they could trust Patagonia's products to last a long time.

As the change to organic cotton shows, Patagonia puts the values of integrity, accountability, and trust into practice in their business by backing their mission with action. As of late 2019, recycled materials account for 69 percent of their clothing. The company plans to hit 100 percent by 2025. Patagonia's environmentally friendly fibers include hemp, organic cotton, recycled nylon, 100% recycled down, recycled polyester, recycled wool, Yulex, reclaimed cotton, denim made from organic cotton, sustainably source wool, and cellulose-based fibers REFIBRA lyocell and TENCEL lyocell. In addition to clothing, Patagonia has also spoken out about sustainability practices in other areas. For example, the company has produced films about the environmental impacts of common business practices. One of these films, *Artifishal*, discusses the need for more natural salmon fishing rather than reliance on the controversial practices of fish hatcheries.

Today Patagonia is debt-free and is still willing to bend the rules. For instance, the firm—which constantly remarks that they place the environment over profits—has embarked upon a "Buy Less" campaign, among other initiatives that seem like they might discourage revenue growth. On the contrary, annual revenue has hit $1 billion in recent years.

Patagonia's Purpose and Core Values

When Patagonia was first developed, Yvon and Malinda agreed that the company would produce only products of the highest quality and manufactured in the most responsible way. They selected the following mission statement for the company: "Build the best product, cause no unnecessary harm, use business to inspire

This case was prepared by Mark Zekoff and Sarah Sawayda for and under the direction of O.C. Ferrell and Linda Ferrell, © 2019. It was prepared for classroom discussion rather than to illustrate either effective or ineffective handling of an administrative, ethical, or legal decision by management. All sources used for this case were obtained through publicly available material.

and implement solutions to the environmental crisis." Patagonia strives to live out their mission statement every day. To make their mission into a reality, Patagonia has adopted four core guiding principles for their operations: quality, integrity, environmentalism, and not bound by convention.

For Patagonia, this means working with friends, hiring self-motivated, intelligent employees, and giving them flexible time to enjoy surfing, climbing, and spending time with their families. Another important value involves finding ways to be responsible by restoring or reusing, which has prompted the company to open retail locations in old buildings that have been restored. After the company nearly went out of business during the 1990s, Yvon Chouinard vowed to never again stray from the core values that he had adopted to develop Patagonia. These values are strongly embedded into all company operations and activities.

Patagonia's Leadership And Management Style

Yvon Chouinard set out to create a company that was proactive in their approach to how business is conducted by embracing a progressive corporate culture. As stated, Patagonia believes that employees should be out enjoying nature or tending their children when sick. Such a culture has made the company widely popular with employees and has steered the company toward innovation and success on a global platform.

Although Yvon Chouinard owns Patagonia, he surrounds himself with talented leaders to help advance the company's goals. Patagonia's leadership is well-known for ethical conduct and for guiding the company according to their corporate mission and values. Patagonia's CEO, Rose Marcario, is committed to Patagonia's vision of environmentalism and is one of Business Insider's 100 "People Transforming Business." Originally the company's CFO in 2008, she earned the CEO position in 2014. She has been influential in driving the company to continue pursuing their environmental and social responsibility goals.

Environmental Initiatives

Over the years, Patagonia has teamed up with other corporations to develop and create initiatives aimed at reducing the environmental footprint businesses leave behind. They have pioneered revolutions in clothing technology development and manufacturing. Patagonia has also been an innovative force in creating programs that deal with the environmental crisis head-on.

1% for the Planet

The organization 1% for the Planet is an alliance of businesses that donate part of their proceeds to environmental organizations to support sustainability and the preservation of the environment. Since 1985, Patagonia has committed to donate 1 percent of their sales to environmental organizations around the world that work to conserve and restore the natural environment. Since they started to support 1% for the Planet, Patagonia has contributed $74 million in donations. In addition to 1% for the Planet, Patagonia regularly contributes additional dollars to environmental groups. For example, in 2018, following corporate tax cuts, Patagonia took the money they saved and donated $10 million to non-profit environmental organizations.

Worn Wear Initiative

After years of hosting Worn Wear pop-up events where customers could bring used clothing for either repair or exchange, Patagonia launched a permanent Worn Wear store on their site in 2017. Now, customers can buy, sell, and trade Patagonia gear second-hand. Patagonia also educates their customers on how to repair their purchases. This initiative embraces the concept of extending the life of each product, allowing customers to reuse, recycle, repair, resell, or recycle to keep products out of the landfill.

Conservation Alliance

The Conservation Alliance was co-founded by Patagonia in 1989. The purpose of the Conservation Alliance is to encourage businesses in the outdoor industry to contribute to environmental organizations. Throughout the years, the Conservation Alliance has grown beyond their four founders to include 180 businesses. The Conservation Alliance has donated over $10 million and Patagonia remains actively involved with the alliance, maintaining a seat of the board.

The bluesign® System

Patagonia has worked with bluesign technologies in their quest to reduce resource consumption since 2000 and became the first official bluesign system partner in 2007. For those resources that cannot be reduced, bluesign helps Patagonia use more sustainable resources that will have less of a negative impact on the environment. Patagonia's goal is to have "bluesign approved fabrics" on 100 percent of their products in the future. There are now more than 400 partners of the bluesign System including brands, manufacturers, and suppliers.

Corporate Social Responsibility

In addition to their many environmental initiatives satisfying stakeholder groups throughout the community, Patagonia also focuses on satisfying their employees. As described earlier, Patagonia believes in a work/life balance philosophy. Because of this strong relationship with their workforce, the company has a 4 percent turnover rate compared to the industry average of 13 percent. Patagonia averages 900 applications per job opening, providing them with the opportunity to hire the best talent. Patagonia also works with factories to ensure that their products are being produced in alignment with Patagonia's corporate values and environmental integrity. In 1990, Patagonia developed the Contractor Relationship Assessment, a scorecard used to rate a factory's performance. In 1996, Patagonia became a founding member of the FLA (Fair Labor Association), which conducts audits and training on factory conditions. In 2007, the firm joined the Fair Factory Clearinghouse (FLC), which is a database that helps Patagonia collect and manage supplier data that deals with social and environmental issues. This information is shared with other firms in Patagonia's industry and can help establish benchmarks for best practices.

Patagonia keeps a close eye on their supply chain with regular factory audits. They also score factories based on how they measure up to social responsibility and environmental goals. For their materials suppliers such as mills, Patagonia has Environmental Health and Safety requirements as well as a Raw Materials Social Responsibility program. Under this program, Patagonia's materials suppliers must audit their factories to measure whether they are compliant with safety, social responsibility, and environmental criteria as well as areas of improvement. By raising the bar for social and environmental responsibility among their suppliers and factories, Patagonia is attempting to incorporate corporate social responsibility among all of their stakeholders.

In 2019, Patagonia made a controversial decision to limit the sales of their custom vests, only selling them to companies that "prioritize the planet," according to the company's announcement. The vests, which have become trendy among business people often feature company logos on the chest opposite the Patagonia logo. The move, which only impacts new partners, protects the Patagonia brand from being associated with environmentally-unfriendly companies and holds other companies to a higher standard.

What the Future Holds for Patagonia

Patagonia shows no signs of slowing down and neither does Yvon Chouinard. The company remains dedicated to advancing environmental awareness among businesses—even if it entails partnering with some unlikely companies. For instance, Patagonia partnered with Walmart and Adidas to form the Sustainable Apparel Coalition. Patagonia realizes that to create lasting change, they must not only improve their sustainability operations but also assist in helping other businesses learn how to reduce their impact on the environment. By 2025, Patagonia hopes to be carbon neutral and would like to be carbon positive in the future.

Chouinard continues to see himself as an innovator rather than just an inventor. Under his influence and the influence of company leaders such as CEO Rose Marcario, Patagonia seeks to make a difference and create a revolution in how businesses view sustainability. Rather than taking from the environment, the goal for Patagonia is to educate consumers and businesses about how they can help to preserve it. Patagonia demonstrates how strong corporate values and ethical leadership can create a company that is both successful and a role model for those who desire to make a positive difference.

Questions for Discussion

1. How has Patagonia been able to promote sustainability among other businesses?
2. Do you think it is beneficial for Patagonia to branch out into ventures other than apparel?
3. Does Patagonia—a privately held, debt-free company—have an advantage over public companies with shareholders by being socially responsible?

Sources

Ashley Lutz, "A Clothing Company Discourages Customers from Buying Its Stuff—and Business Is Booming," 14, *Business Insider,* September, 2016, 1–2 (accessed October 31, 2017).

Associated Press, "Patagonia Gives $10 Million GOP Tax Windfall to Environmental Groups," *CNBC,* November 29, 2018, https://www.nbcnews.com/business/business-news/update-patagonia-gives-gop-tax-windfall-environmental-groups-n941551 (accessed October 25, 2019).

Bradford Wieners, "Solving Climate Change with Beer from Patagonia's Food Startup," *Bloomberg Business Week,* October 3, 2016, https://www.bloomberg.com/news/features/2016-10-03/solving-climate-change-with-beer-from-patagonia-sfood-startup (accessed October 31, 2017).

Daniel Bentley, "Doing Good and Making a Profit: These Apparel Companies Are Proving They Aren't Mutually Exclusive," *Fortune,* January 23, 2019, http://fortune.com/2019/01/23/patagonia-art-eden-sustainability/ (accessed August 10, 2019).

Daniela Sirtori-Cortina, "From Climber to Billionaire: How Yvon Chouinard Built Patagonia into a Powerhouse in Own Way," *Forbes,* March 20, 2017, 1, https://www.forbes.com/sites/danielasirtori/2017/03/20/from-climber-to-billionaire-how-yvon-chouinard-builtpatagonia-into-a-powerhouse-his-own-way/#387feacf275c (accessed November 2, 2017).

Hailey Gunderson, "Patagonia's Strategic Management, "Patagonia's Code of Ethics," Blog, 25, April, 2012, 1, http://hrgunderson08.blogspot.com/ (accessed August 10, 2019).

Hailey Gunderson, Patagonia's Strategic Management, "How Patagonia Satisfies Customer Wants," Blog, 01, May, 2012, 1. http://hrgunderson08.blogspot.com/ (accessed August 10, 2019).

J. B. MacKinnon, "Patagonia's Anti-Growth Strategy," *The New Yorker,* 21, May, 2017, 1–2). https://www.newyorker.com/business/currency/patagonias-anti-growth-strategy (accessed August 10, 2019).

Jeff Beer, "How Patagonia Grows Every Time It Amplifies Its Social Mission," *Fast Company,* February 21, 2018, https://www.fastcompany.com/40525452/

how-patagonia-grows-every-time-it-amplifies-its-social-mission (accessed August 10, 2019).

Katherine Martinko, "Patagonia Launches Worn Wear, an Online Store for Used Gear," *TreeHugger*, September 21, 2017, https://www.treehugger.com/sustainable-fashion/patagonia-launches-worn-wear-online-store-used-gear.html (accessed October 25, 2019).

Lila MacLellan, "At Patagonia, Exit Interviews Are Rare—but They Go Deep," *Quartz*, https://qz.com/work/1574375/patagonias-hr-leader-has-been-moved-to-tears-in-exit-interviews/ (accessed August 10, 2019).

Nick Paumgarten, "Patagonia's Philosopher-King," *The New Yorker*, September 19, 2017, 1–22, https://www.newyorker.com/magazine/2016/09/19/patagonias-philosopher-king (accessed August 10, 2019).

Patagonia, "100% for the Planet," https://www.patagonia.com/100-percent-for-the-planet.html (accessed August 10, 2019).

Patagonia, "bluesign® System," https://www.patagonia.com/bluesign.html (accessed October 25, 2019).

Patagonia, "Materials & Technologies," https://www.patagonia.com/materials-tech.html (accessed October 25, 2019).

Patagonia, "Mission Statement – and about Us," http://www.patagonia.com/home/ (accessed August 10, 2019).

Patagonia, "The Conservation Alliance: One Hundred Eighty Companies in the Outdoor Industry Give Back to the Natural World," https://www.patagonia.com/conservation-alliance.html (accessed August 10, 2019).

Patagonia, "What We're Doing about Our Plastic Problem," June 13, 2019, https://www.patagonia.com/blog/2019/06/what-were-doing-about-our-plastic-problem/ (accessed October 17, 2019).

Richard Feloni, "Patagonia's CEO Says 'Capitalism Needs to Evolve' If We Want to Save the Planet," *Business Insider*, April 16, 2019, https://www.businessinsider.com/patagonia-ceo-rose-marcario-says-capitalism-must-evolve-to-save-earth-2019-4 (accessed August 10, 2019).

Scott Mautz, "Patagonia Has Only 4 Percent Employee Turnover Because They Value This 1 Thing So Much," *Inc.*, https://www.inc.com/scott-mautz/how-can-patagonia-have-only-4-percent-worker-turnover-hint-they-pay-activist-employees-bail.html (accessed August 10, 2019).

Stephanie Spear, "10 Most Profound Passages from 'Let My People Go Surfing," *EcoWatch*, September 19, 2016, 1. https://www.ecowatch.com/let-my-people-go-surfing-2008599492.html (accessed August 10, 2019).

Susan Reda, "Waste Not, Want Not," *Stores Magazine*, January 4, 2016, 1, https://nrf.com/blog/waste-not-want-not (accessed October 31, 2017).

Tessa Byars, "Patagonia Releases a Documentary about The High Cost of Fish Hatcheries, Fish Farms and Human Ignorance," *Patagonia Works*, April 12, 2019, http://www.patagoniaworks.com/press/2019/4/18/patagonia-releases-a-documentary-about-the-high-cost-of-fish-hatcheries-fish-farms-and-human-ignorance (accessed August 10, 2019).

CASE 14

Johnson & Johnson Experiences the Pain of Recalls

Introduction

When it comes to a corporate crisis, Johnson & Johnson (J&J) and their subsidiary Tylenol have historically demonstrated what a company should do in responding to stakeholder concerns. With their handling of the Tylenol tampering in the early 80s, J&J secured their status in the history books for effective crisis management. Since then, J&J has won numerous accolades for consumer safety and for their social responsibility initiatives. In 2019, *Fortune* named J&J one of the world's most admired companies, their seventeenth year on the list. Targeted at top investors, the survey ranked winners according to their strength of management, business strategy, ethical business practices, competitive edge, shareholder orientation, and consistent revenue/profit growth.

As with most major companies, however, J&J has received their share of criticism regarding Tylenol and other medicinal products. The 2012 waves of Tylenol recalls and other over-the-counter medications, resulting from bacterial contamination, nauseating smells, and metallic flakes, cost the company financially and reputationally. The Food & Drug Administration (FDA) criticized J&J's slow response time in addressing the issue. The problems escalated so much that the House Committee on Oversight, Government Reform, and the Justice Department began investigating the company.

Similarly, J&J experienced criticism over the allegations that ingredients in their products may cause ovarian cancer and mesothelioma. Although the company had developed a reputation for baby-safe and natural products, they are taking a hit from a string of lawsuits and litigation proceedings. This case will analyze some of these crucial issues as well as how J&J attempts to maintain their industry-leading reputation through their day-to-day operations and commitment to their Credo, a set of values and beliefs meant to inspire and guide the actions of all J&J employees.

Company Background

Robert Wood Johnson began his career as a pharmaceutical apprentice. During the Civil War, the world of healthcare and innovative medicine piqued his interest because he saw huge room for improvement. After witnessing countless infectious outbreaks and poor medicinal practices, he knew that he could make a difference.

In 1886, Robert and his two younger brothers, Edward Mead and James Wood, began this journey to improvement by beginning Johnson & Johnson. Opening their first manufacturing plant in New Brunswick, New Jersey, the company launched with 14 employees, eight women, and six men. After manufacturing the world's first mass-produced, sterile surgical supplies, J&J soon discovered that a large part of the issue stemmed from the lack of knowledge of various medical professionals. In 1888, J&J published *Modern Methods of Antiseptic Wound Treatment*, teaching medical professionals how to perform antiseptic surgery and best practices for medical safety. This publication became widely distributed across the U.S. throughout the remainder of the year, thus beginning J&J's commitment to the development and innovation of products to serve consumers.

Today, J&J is an international company, still headquartered in New Brunswick, with locations in more than 60 countries with more than 265 operating companies. The firm maintains 135,000 employees, $81.6 billion in sales, and is ranked number 37 in the Fortune 500. In addition to developing a company code of ethics, J&J has their Credo, penned by Robert Wood Johnson in 1943, etched in stone outside their headquarters building.

J&J has three main business segments:

1. **Consumer** – includes many everyday drugstore lines for skin and hair products, including Neutrogena and AVEENO, as well as wound care such as the Band-Aids brand and baby care.
2. **Pharmaceutical** – drugstore line of products such as Tylenol, Motrin, and Benadryl. It also includes controlled pharmaceutical drugs for hospitals and prescribed use medicines for vaccines, infectious diseases, and therapies for cardiovascular, arthritis, oncology, and hypertension.
3. **Medical Devices and Diagnostics** – specialized equipment and surgical instruments; technology; and surgical products used by hospitals, physicians, and healthcare professionals.

Johnson & Johnson Credo

While many organizations have developed ethics initiatives only recently, J&J was a pioneer in developing a sound code of ethics. Robert Wood Johnson, the son of co-founder Robert Johnson who acted as chairman of J&J from 1932 to 1963, developed the Credo of values

This case was prepared by Dianne Kroncke, Jennifer Sawayda, and Shelby Wyatt for and under the direction of O.C. Ferrell and Linda Ferrell, © 2019. It was prepared for classroom discussion rather than to illustrate either effective or ineffective handling of an administrative, ethical, or legal decision by management. All sources used for this case were obtained through publicly available material.

in 1943 before Johnson & Johnson became publicly traded company. J&J recognized that a set of company morals would not only maintain an ethical corporate culture but also help to ensure business success. The J&J Credo emphasizes putting the consumer first—a concept that would make all the difference during the mass Tylenol recalls in the early 80s. The Credo identifies four primary stakeholders and addresses the company's duty to each group. These groups include consumers, employees, communities, and stockholders.

Consumers

The J&J Credo begins by addressing the groups they see as their most important stakeholder: "We believe our first responsibility is to the doctors, nurses and patients, to mothers and fathers and all others who use our products and services. In meeting their needs everything we do must be of high quality…"

The Credo seeks to serve consumers by (1) keeping costs low so reasonable prices can be maintained and (2) promptly and accurately servicing customer orders. Access to medicines and medical care is also an issue that J&J is addressing. The company is conducting studies to research a universal prevention tool to prevent the spread of tuberculosis and HIV. They are also partnering with governments and organizations, including Rwanda, to increase access to mental healthcare in Sub-Saharan Africa where access to treatment is low. Because of these initiatives, Johnson & Johnson was ranked third among pharmaceutical companies on the "Access to Medicine" index from the Access to Medicine Foundation.

Employees

The second section of the Credo addresses J&J employees: "We are responsible to our employees, the men and women who work with us throughout the world. Everyone must be considered as an individual. We must respect their dignity and recognize their merit…"

To address the needs of their employees, the Credo maintains that J&J will provide (1) a sense of job security, (2) fair and adequate compensation, and (3) clean and safe working conditions.

Job security became more problematic during the recent global recession of 2008, but J&J believed their bonus overhaul in 2010 would make the pay system more equitable by tying in bonuses to performance. To create a more open workplace environment, employee suggestions and complaints are encouraged. Internally, J&J operates numerous programs that seek to help the physical and mental well-being of their employees. For example, J&J offers employee assistance programs that help employees in matters pertaining to mental health. Under this program, employees have access to resiliency training; employee assistance programs, which include counseling and intervention; and work-life programs including flexible schedules, compressed work weeks, telecommuting, and flextime.

Communities

After addressing consumers and employees, J&J's Credo goes on to address itself within the community: "We are responsible to the communities in which we live and work and to the world community as well. We must help people be healthier by supporting better access and care in more places around the world. We must be good citizens…"

J&J defines good citizens as those who "support good works/charities and who accept their fair share of taxes, with the belief that these will encourage civic improvement and lead to better health and education within each community." To improve communities, J&J places a special emphasis on environmental and disaster relief initiatives.

Reviewed and updated every five years since 1990, J&J's environmental goals seek to reduce the company's environmental footprint. J&J works with various stakeholders, including government officials, environmental groups, and academic leaders, to achieve their environmental goals, which are organized into categories such as energy use, product stewardship, and external manufacturing. Thus far, the program has seen positive results. For example, when the program first began in 1990, J&J set a goal of reducing their carbon dioxide emissions by 7 percent within the next 20 years. By 2007, the company had already surpassed their goal. In 2019, J&J earned the Energy Star Partner of the Year Award for demonstrating best practices in energy efficiency. Among their many goals, J&J has pledged to make 100 percent of their products reusable, recyclable, or compostable by 2025.

As part of their Credo, J&J also works to provide disaster relief, both domestically and internationally. Within one month of Hurricane Katrina, J&J had contributed $5 million in cash and $250,000 in disaster relief products. After the 2010 earthquakes in Haiti and Chile, J&J leveraged their international connections and partnered with several nonprofit companies to quickly transport resources to victims. The company has pledged to support long-term efforts to provide health care services for women and children within these countries. The company also donated money to Japan after the 2011 earthquake and tsunami. In addition, J&J maintains their U.S. Matching Gifts Program, in which employee's personal contributions are double matched by the company.

Stockholders

The last section of the J&J Credo addresses stockholders: "Our final responsibility is to our stockholders. Business must make a sound profit. We must experiment with new ideas…"

J&J emphasizes the importance of innovation in generating a fair return for stockholders. To develop new ideas, J&J is committed to (1) conducting research and developing new programs, (2) purchasing new equipment and facilities to aid in launching new products, and (3) creating reserves for protection in adverse times. A small, but significant, section of the Credo states that mistakes must be paid for. This was widely demonstrated during the 1982 Tylenol recalls that will be discussed later in the case.

Despite J&J's recent problems, the company's long-term and consistent returns have continued to maintain the positive relationship they have with stockholders. Combined with their Credo and their actions during the 1982 product recalls, J&J has earned a stellar reputation that is demonstrated through stockholder returns.

Tylenol Products and Recalls

Tylenol sells a variety of self-healthcare products to tackle some of the most common issues of a cold or flu, including relieving pain, reducing fevers, and relieving the symptoms of allergies and coughs. Tylenol's goal has been to become the leader in over-the-counter (OTC) products worldwide. The Tylenol product line consists of hundreds of products that fit into categories such as Head & Body (back pain, headaches, muscle aches, and cramps); Arthritis; Sinus and Allergy; Cold and Flu (coughs, sore throats, congestion, and multi-symptoms); Pain and Sleeplessness; and Children (fever, aches, cold, cough, flu, and non-medicated). In addition to tablets, J&J has come out with Tylenol chewables, drops, and meltaways.

While it isn't unusual for pharmaceutical companies to experience crisis situations, it is highly unusual and frightening for firms to experience the type of crisis that J&J faced during the 1980s. Despite the fear that gripped the nation, J&J tried to maintain a sense of calm and concern for consumer well-being that reassured their customers. While J&J certainly lost money in the short run, their quick actions served to create a favorable reputation as a firm that pursued the right course even when it cost them financially. Indeed, J&J's effective crisis management perhaps even increased their market share in the long term because customers could feel confident that the company had their best interests at heart.

Tylenol Poisonings

The crisis started on September 29, 1982, in the Chicago area when 12-year-old Mary Kellerman was pronounced dead at a hospital after her parents found her on the bathroom floor. Adam Janus was later found collapsed on his living room floor in another part of town and died in the hospital shortly thereafter. Adam's brother Stanley and sister-in-law Theresa gathered at his house. Suffering from a headache, they found a bottle of Extra-Strength Tylenol on the kitchen counter and took some capsules. They also collapsed soon afterward and died later at the hospital. Three more deaths were reported the next day. All these deaths occurred after the victims had consumed Tylenol. The news of the incident spread quickly, causing a nationwide panic.

Investigations revealed that the sudden deaths were a result of cyanide poison discovered in the Tylenol capsules. The capsules had been opened and filled with 65 mg of cyanide—up to 10,000 times that which was needed to kill a person. Since the tampered bottles came from different factories and the seven deaths had all occurred in the Chicago area, the possibility of sabotage during production was eliminated. Instead, the culprit was believed to have entered various supermarkets and drug stores over a period of weeks, pilfered packages of Tylenol from the shelves, poisoned their contents with cyanide at another location, and then replaced the bottles. In addition to the five bottles which led to the victims' deaths, three other tampered bottles were discovered. These poisoned bottles were discovered at different stores in the Chicago area.

Johnson & Johnson's Reaction

The crisis was every company's worst nightmare. Some predicted that Tylenol would never sell again. What followed, however, is one of the most often used examples of effective crisis management. J&J took the consumer responsibility outlined in their Credo seriously. They immediately recalled 31 million bottles of Extra-Strength Tylenol worth over $100 million from all retail stores across the United States. In addition, the company offered to exchange all Tylenol capsules already purchased by the public with solid tablets. J&J also distributed warnings to hospitals and distributors that Tylenol production and advertising would be halted until further notice. According to an analyst, J&J suffered a loss of $1.24 billion due to the depreciation of the company's brand value. Immediately after the crisis, Tylenol's share fell from 37% of the U.S. over-the-counter pain reliever market to just 7% by late 1982. Yet, rather than drop the brand as a lost cause, J&J President James Burke poured millions into reviving the struggling brand. Within six months, their share was back up to 30 percent.

Tylenol managed the crisis in two steps: public relations (reacting to the crisis) and their comeback stage. Even though the deaths were not a fault of the company, they took responsibility and, unlike many companies in similar predicaments, put consumer safety over profit. In addition to their countrywide recall, J&J partnered with the FBI, the Chicago Police, and the FDA to track down the culprit, even offering a $100,000 reward for anyone who could volunteer information about the killer. Perhaps most importantly, J&J did not deny the link between the deaths and their products, a mistake that many companies make immediately following a product crisis.

In Tylenol's comeback stage, J&J needed to find a way to restore consumers' trust in the brand. The company took several actions to demonstrate Tylenol's safety. Tylenol products were introduced with new triple-seal tamper resistant packaging. They also offered a $2.50 off coupon on the purchase of their Tylenol products, which could be found in newspapers or by calling a toll-free number. A new pricing program was introduced that provided discounts of up to 25 percent.

In addition, more than 2,250 salespeople made presentations to members of the medical community. J&J's actions effectively restored customer goodwill toward the company. In fact, in a survey taken shortly after the crisis, 90 percent of respondents stated that J&J was not to blame for the situation.

Unfortunately, product tampering did not stop with the 1982 Tylenol poisonings. In 1986, the company faced another crisis after a woman died after taking Extra-Strength Tylenol capsules. Once more, cyanide was to blame. This time Tylenol was not alone. The incidence of product tampering appeared to rise after the 1982 Tylenol murders, including incidents of poisoned chocolate milk, orange juice, Excedrin, and Sudafed. J&J responded with another recall and a promise to only release Tylenol in caplet or tablet form.

Additional Tylenol Recalls Cause More Pain

Although J&J has been praised countless times for their quick actions during the Tylenol poisoning crisis of 1982, the company encountered criticism for not reacting quickly enough to another crisis. In 2009, J&J recalled many of their children's Tylenol common cold and allergy medications. Nearly two dozen varieties of their children's Tylenol were voluntarily pulled off the shelves because of a bacterial contamination in their Fort Washington, Pennsylvania facility. J&J took precautionary steps to voluntarily recall some of the Tylenol product line after an internal lab test found bacteria in the raw material that went unused in the making of their product. Although the bacteria Burkholderia cepacia was found in a portion of the raw material that went unused, none of the bacteria was found in finished products. As a precaution, however, all products were recalled that had used any of the raw material manufactured at the same time as the raw material that tested positive for the bacteria. The effects of the bacteria can be dangerous for those with weakened immune systems or chronic lung diseases, with symptoms ranging from none to serious respiratory infections.

Unfortunately, the bacterial contamination didn't stop there. In addition to the previous recalls, J&J also recalled millions of bottles of Tylenol, Benadryl, Zyrtec, and Motrin in April 2010. The recall was issued because of possible safety violations in the medications, including too much of an active drug, metal specks, or ingredients that had failed testing requirements. Due to the massive amounts of recalls and seeming lack of oversight on the part of J&J's subsidiary McNeil Healthcare, the issue was investigated by a Congressional committee. Documents were recovered revealing that in 2009, McNeil Consumer Healthcare hired private companies to buy defective Motrin products from stores, without reporting it to the FDA. A McNeil spokeswoman said that since the products did not prove to be a safety risk (they were defective in other ways), it was not a recall and thus did not have to be reported to the FDA. With accusations of rampant misconduct by governmental agencies, McNeil Laboratories and their executives (VP of Quality and VP of Operations) were charged with failure to comply with federally mandated manufacturing practices. In March of 2011, the FDA gave McNeil two options: to agree to a "consent decree" or to succumb to a lawsuit. McNeill chose the consent decree, which requires adherence to a strict timetable for bringing their facilities into compliance.

Additionally, Tylenol Arthritis Pain was recalled due to complaints of moldy odors, nausea, vomiting, and diarrhea. The scent was found to be a result of 2,4,6-tribromoanisole, a component of pesticides and flame retardants that were used to treat wooden storage pallets at McNeil's plant in Las Piedras, Puerto Rico. These are only a few examples of 50 products that were recalled in a matter of 50 weeks. In addition, it was found that J&J had known of the odors for more than a year, but only recalled the product after an FDA investigation. The investigation also uncovered unsanitary conditions at the Fort Washington, Pennsylvania, facility. Thick dust and grime were found covering certain equipment. There was also a hole in the ceiling and duct tape-covered pipes.

J&J traced many of the problems to the Tylenol plant in Fort Washington, Pennsylvania. The company responded by shutting down the plant and submitting a plan to regulators addressing how they will fix the problems. Some of the proposed solutions included installing new equipment and revamping their operations to reduce the opportunity for product contamination. J&J stressed their commitment to upgrading the plant, which would remain closed until after these renovations. Such changes caused an elimination of 300 jobs at the plant. To prevent future recalls—and the resulting negative publicity—J&J also made changes in their management, hired an outside expert to help in redoing the plant, and improved their employee training and operational processes.

Organizational Issues

As the recalls demonstrate, despite J&J's reputation of effective crisis handling over the last few decades, the firm continues to be impacted by myriad costly issues. Some analysts say the causes of these issues lie in three possible areas: heavy profit focus, decentralization, and lapses in leadership oversight. Critics have suggested that each division of J&J has their own separate culture, indicating that there is no overall sense of coherence in leadership or operations. Analysts also proposed that J&J is cutting too many costs to increase profits, thus sacrificing customer safety and increasing risk in this area. Then CEO of J&J William Weldon disagreed. Weldon claimed that the company had not placed profits over the customer, and he also discounted the idea that decentralization was the problem. He said that if decentralization was the issue, all of the divisions would have experienced problems and not just McNeil.

Other accusations levied against J&J include paying kickbacks, using financial incentives to encourage unauthorized use of drugs and devices, and taking actions to avoid a recall by sending employees into stores to buy up tainted products. J&J also created a strain on their relationship with FDA regulators throughout their investigations by not being immediately compliant. J&J denied claims regarding a lack of oversight. However, their annual report for 2010 outlined government criminal and civil investigations as well as thousands of private lawsuits covering a wide range of drugs, devices, and business practices.

Talcum Powder Creates Painful Litigation

Since 1971 when scientists found talc particles in ovarian and cervical tumor tissue, talc has been a health concern and talc content in consumer products has been closely monitored. Talc makes up talcum powder, which is commonly used in cosmetic products such as baby powder and other products. Personal Care Products, Inc. (formerly known as Cosmetic, Toiletry and Fragrance Association) sets the purity standard for the amount of talc ore in cosmetic products. This is the accepted testing level for personal care products (commonly known as cosmetic grade), which is also the accepted standard by the U.S. Food and Drug Administration. Although J&J maintains that their products follow or even beat these standards, recent events have put the company's credibility on the line.

J&J has always touted that their products are safe enough, even for babies. Yet in 2015, Jacqueline Fox of Tarant, Alabama, a small town near Birmingham, filed the first lawsuit alleging that J&J's Baby Powder caused ovarian cancer. Beasley and Allen, a law firm in Montgomery, Alabama, represented Mrs. Fox and contended that J&J knew the hazards of their product for decades and sought to cover up the health risks by getting female oncologists to help defend against potential lawsuits. A St. Louis jury ultimately awarded Mrs. Fox

$72 million, ruling that J&J's Baby Powder and Shower to Shower, J&J products she used for feminine hygiene for more than 35 years, caused her ovarian cancer. The Fox family was awarded $10 million in actual damages and $62 million in punitive damages. J&J was found guilty of negligence, conspiracy, and fraud.

In July 2018, a jury in St. Louis awarded $4.69 billion to 22 women who sued J&J, alleging that their ovarian cancer was caused by the J&J Baby Powder after using the product as part of their daily health and hygiene care. Compensatory damages of $550 million and punitive damages of $4.14 billion were awarded, making it the largest verdict against the 130-year-old company. This award is currently under appeal. J&J continues to state that clinical research does not show increased cancer rates by users of talcum powder. They cite The Nurse's Health Study, funded by the U.S. government, that investigated the risk factors for 78,630 individuals who were studied for 24 years. About 40 percent (31,789) of nurses answered that they had used talc on their genital areas, and the results reported no overall rate of ovarian cancer, regardless of how the product was used.

Another study by the Women's Health Initiative was conducted in 1991 involving 61,576 women. Of these, 32,219 (53 percent) of the women admitted to using powder on their genitals. Once again, no evidence of an overall increase for ovarian cancer appeared. J&J contends that other products or risk factors contributed to the ovarian cancers and a product recall was not needed. The firm removed 50 percent of ingredients from their baby care product line in 2018 and now refers to these products as natural and safe. J&J stands by their products, continuing to deny that they cause ovarian cancer or mesothelioma.

The fight is not over for Johnson & Johnson. The company also faces lawsuits related to asbestos in the baby powder. The lawsuits allege that J&J knew that their baby powder could be contaminated by asbestos because it is found underground near talc, but did not warn consumers. A lawsuit was filed by Stephen Lanzo III and his wife. Mr. Lanzo claimed he had used J&J Talcum Baby powder since infancy, and it had caused him to develop mesothelioma, a rare and often fatal cancer connected with asbestos. He was awarded $37 million in compensatory damages by a jury in New Jersey in 2018. Additionally, a California jury awarded a woman $29 million in March 2019 for her asbestos lawsuit against J&J. J&J plans to appeal the verdict. To make matters worse, in October 2019 Tylenol recalled 33,000 bottles of baby powder due to concerns of asbestos contamination. The FDA purchased a 22-ounce bottle online, tested the powder, and found traces of chrysotile asbestos in the sample. Stores such as Target, CVS, and Walgreens removed products from the lot number in question from store shelves. The asbestos that was found was no more than 0.00002 percent, and it has not been confirmed that the test sample came from a sealed bottle. The FDA defended the quality of the test and claimed that they were not aware of any adverse events that would have exposed the bottle to cross-contamination. Whether the product contained asbestos or not, J&J faces an uphill battle to assure the public that their baby power products are safe.

There are 14,200 claims related to Johnson's Baby Powder, with approximately 12,000 pending in federal courts. J&J has made a motion to exclude expert witness opinions, saying the biologists, physicians, and epidemiologists used by the plaintiffs' attorneys have made "unsupported leaps of logic." If J&J succeeds with their motion, it could result in many of the lawsuits being dismissed.

Opioid Crisis

In addition to the baby powder lawsuits, J&J also faces 2,000 lawsuits from both state and local governments alleging that the company contributed to the opioid crisis with their marketing of pain medications such as Duragesic and Nucynta. Pharmaceutical companies began to promote prescription opioid pain relievers in the late 1990s, which many believe led to increased rates of opioid overdoses. This public health crisis has attracted widespread attention and has been called the worst drug crisis in U.S. history by The White House. In 2017, President Donald Trump declared the opioid crisis was a public health emergency. Major drug distributors such as McKesson Corp., AmerisourceBergen Corp., Cardinal Health, Teva, and J&J have attracted the attention of sweeping litigation. In October 2019, J&J offered $4 billion to settle all lawsuits in the United States, potentially resolving all outstanding lawsuits. J&J will need to continue to protect their reputation as the opioid lawsuits and baby powder lawsuits continue.

Conclusion

After their successful handling of the 1982 Chicago Tylenol murder crises, J&J was largely acknowledged as an industry leader in business and ethics. Until recently, J&J's management of their reputation has been effective. However, the company's recent product recalls of Tylenol and other medications, along with the thousands of allegations of harmful baby products, has brought into question the quality of their products.

It would appear that J&J has slipped some in their careful handling of product development and consumer safety. These developments demonstrate that ethics is an ongoing process necessary for all companies, and it is a process that begins upstream. Even companies like J&J who have gained a reputation for ethically-sound management must work hard to ensure the integrity of their products and operations. Like in the past, the company must now commit their resources to rebuilding

the trust of consumers, government regulatory agencies, and other stakeholders. As the litigation continues and the lawsuits are settled, the way in which J&J handles themselves and the situation will better show how committed the company is to their Credo and values.

Questions for Discussion

1. Johnson & Johnson was a leader in recognizing key stakeholders and in developing a credo for appropriate conduct. Why do you think that there have been a number of failures in product safety even though the company has tried to be responsible?
2. Why do you think Johnson & Johnson has continued to receive awards for ethically and socially responsible conduct despite product recalls?
3. Johnson & Johnson's over-the-counter drugs such as Tylenol products have many risks associated with them in product quality and safety. How would you suggest Johnson & Johnson gain more control and decrease the possibility of misuse, safety defects, and other harmful consequences?

Sources

"Does Talc Contain Asbestos?" *Bergman Draper Oslund*, August 7, 2018, https://www.bergmanlegal.com/talc-contain-asbestos/ (accessed July 28, 2019).

"J&J Covered Talc Cancer Risk Decades," *Beasley Allen Law Firm*, August 9, 2018, http://www.beasleyallen.com/news/jj-covered-talc-cancer-risks-for-decades/ (accessed July 28, 2019).

"Johnson & Johnson Update on Hurricane Katrina Relief Efforts," *Medical News Today*, September 5, 2006, http://www.medicalnewstoday.com/articles/30206.php (accessed July 28, 2019).

"Johnson and Johnson to Pay $57M in Compensatory Damages in Talc Mesothelioma Case," *Beasley Allen Law Firm*, April 6, 2018, https://www.beasleyallen.com/news/johnson-and-johnson-to-pay-37m-in-compensatory-damages-in-talc-mesothelioma-case/ (accessed July 28, 2019).

"Maximum Tylenol Dose Lowered to Prevent Overdoses," *The Huffington Post*, July 28, 2011, http://www.huffingtonpost.com/2011/07/28/tylenol-maximum-dose-lowered_n_912629.html (accessed November 19, 2012).

"The Johnson & Johnson Tylenol Controversies," *IBS Center for Management Research*, http://www.icmrindia.org/casestudies/catalogue/Business%20Ethics/BECG015.htm (accessed July 28, 2019).

"Tylenol Scandal and Crisis Management," University of Florida Interactive Media Lab, http://iml.jou.ufl.edu/projects/Fall02/Susi/tylenol.htm (accessed March 12, 2010).

Access to Medicine Foundation, "Johnson & Johnson," 2018, https://accesstomedicinefoundation.org/access-to-medicine-index/report-cards/johnson-johnson (accessed July 28, 2019).

Alex Nussbaum, David Voreacos, and Greg Farrell, "Johnson & Johnson's Quality Catastrophe," *Bloomberg Businessweek*, March 31, 2011, https://www.bloomberg.com/news/articles/2011-03-31/johnson-and-johnsons-quality-catastrophe (accessed July 28, 2019).

Alison Young, "Children's Tylenol Plant Cited for Tainted Ingredient in 2009," *USA Today*, June 1, 2010, http://www.

usatoday.com/news/health/2010-05-26-tylenol-plant_N.htm (accessed July 28, 2019).

Amanda Kelly, "The Green Graph: 8 Innovative Ways Johnson & Johnson Is Helping the Environment," Johnson & Johnson, April 21, 2019, https://www.jnj.com/caring-and-giving/8-innovative-ways-johnson-johnson-is-helping-the-environment (accessed July 28, 2019).

American Cancer Society, "Signs and Symptoms of Ovarian Cancer," August 09, 2018, https://www.cancer.org/cancer/ovarian-cancer/detection-diagnosis-staging/signs-and-symptoms.html (accessed July 28, 2019).

American College of Obstetricians and Gynecologists, "Salpingectomy for Ovarian Cancer Prevention," February 2016, https://www.acog.org/Clinical-Guidance-and-Publications/Committee-Opinions/Committee-on-GynecologicPractice/Salpingectomy-for-Ovarian-Cancer-Prevention (accessed July 23, 2015).

Associated Press, "J&J to Cut 7,000 to 8,000 jobs Globally," *MSNBC*, November 3, 2009, http://www.msnbc.msn.com/id/33600017 (accessed November 19, 2012).

Jane Akre, "J&J's McNeil Expands Tylenol Benadryl Recall," *The Injury Board National NewsDesk*, June 16, 2010, http://news.injuryboard.com/jjs-mcneil-expands-tylenol-benadryl-recall.aspx?googleid=282298 (accessed November 19, 2012).

Johnson & Johnson, "Johnson & Johnson Named a 2019 Fortune World's Most Admired Company," January 22, 2019, https://www.jnj.com/latest-news/johnson-johnson-on-2019-fortune-worlds-most-admired-companies-list (accessed August 22, 2019).

Johnson & Johnson, "A History of Johnson & Johnson," June 26, 2013, https://pharmaphroum.com/articles/a-history-of-johnson-johnson/ (accessed July 28, 2019).

Johnson & Johnson, "Help for Earthquake Victims," http://www.jnj.com/connect/caring/patient-stories/help-for-earthquake-victims-in-haiti/ (accessed November 19, 2012).

Johnson & Johnson, "Johnson & Johnson Earns a Top Spot on the 2018 Access to Medicine Index," November 20, 2018, https://www.jnj.com/latest-news/johnson-johnson-earns-a-top-spot-on-the-2018-access-to-medicine-index (accessed July 28, 2019).

Johnson & Johnson, "Johnson & Johnson's Official Statement in Response to Today's Verdict in St. Louis Trial," July 12, 2018, https://www.jnj.com/johnson-johnsons-official-statement-in-response-to-todays-verdict-in-st-louis-trial (accessed July 28, 2019).

Johnson & Johnson, "Our Credo Values," http://www.jnj.com/connect/about-jnj/jnj-credo/ (accessed July 28, 2019).

Johnson & Johnson, "What We Do," August 1, 2018, https://www.careers.jnj.com/business-structure-and-mission-page (accessed July 28, 2019).

Johnson & Johnson, "What You Need to Know about Johnson & Johnson's 2018 Full-Year Earnings Report," January 22, 2019, https://www.jnj.com/latest-news/what-you-need-to-know-about-johnson-johnsons-2018-full-year-earnings-report (accessed July 28, 2019).

Johnson & Johnson, *2011 Responsibility Report*, https://www.jnj.com/sites/default/files/pdf/2011-responsibilty-report.pdf (accessed July 28, 2019).

Johnson & Johnson, *2018 Health for Humanity Report: Progress in Citizenship & Sustainability,* http://healthforhumanityreport.jnj.com/_document/johnson-johnson-2018-health-for-humanity-report-summary?id=0000016a-c2ca-ddc4-affe-cefa24f70000 (accessed July 28, 2019).

Jonathon D. Rockoff, "WSJ: J&J Submits Plans to Fix Problems at Tylenol Plant," *Fox Business*, July 15, 2010, http://www.foxbusiness.com/markets/2010/07/15/wsj-jj-submits-plan-fix-problems-tylenol-plant/ (accessed August 10, 2010).

Kent Faulk, "Family of Alabama Woman Awarded $72 Million over Talc Powder Link to Ovarian Cancer," *Birmingham News*, February 24, 2018, https://www.al.com/news/birmingham/2016/02/family_of_alabama_woman_awarde.html (accessed July 28, 2019).

Kristen Rogers, "Retailers Are Pulling Johnson's Baby Powder from Store Shelves," *CNN*, October 15, 2019, https://www.cnn.com/2019/10/25/health/johnsons-baby-powder-retailers-recall/index.html?no-st=1572287803 (accessed October 28, 2019).

Linda A. Johnson, "J&J Changing Bonus Plan to Reward Performance More," *ABCNews/Money*, February 18, 2010, http://abcnews.go.com/Business/wireStory?id=9875436 (accessed March 16, 2010).

Mark L. Mitchell, "The Impact of External Parties on Brand-Name Capital: The 1982 Tylenol Poisonings and Subsequent Cases," *Economic Inquiry*, 2007, 601–618.

McNeil Consumer Healthcare Company, "History of Tylenol," 2009, http://www.nancywest.net/pdfs/McNeilConsumerHealthcareCompany.pdf (accessed July 28, 2019).

Natasha Singer, "F.D.A. Weighs Penalties in Drug Recall," *The New York Times*, May 27, 2010, http://www.nytimes.com/2010/05/28/business/28drug.html?ref=johnson_and_johnson (accessed July 28, 2019).

Natasha Singer, "More Disputes over Handling of Drug Recall," *The New York Times*, June 11, 2010, http://www.nytimes.com/2010/06/12/business/12drug.html?ref=johnson_and_johnson (accessed July 28, 2019).

Parija Kavilanz, "Bacteria Identified in Tylenol Recall," *CNNMoney*, May 5, 2010, http://money.cnn.com/2010/05/05/news/companies/childrens_tylenol_recall_bacteria/index.htm (accessed July 28, 2019).

Parija Kavilanz, "Johnson & Johnson CEO: 'We Made a Mistake,'" *CNNMoney*, September 30, 2010, http://money.cnn.com/2010/09/30/news/companies/hearing_johnson_fda_drug_recalls/index.htm (accessed July 28, 2019).

Parija Kavilanz, "Tylenol Recall: FDA Slams Company," *CNNMoney*, January 15, 2010, http://money.cnn.com/2010/01/15/news/companies/over_the_counter_medicine_recall/ (accessed July 28, 2019).

Parija Kavilanz, "U.S. Takes Over Three Tylenol Plants," *CNNMoney*, March 11, 2011, http://money.cnn.com/2011/03/10/news/companies/johnson_mcneil_fda_action/index.htm (accessed July 28, 2019).

Peter Loftus and Sara Randazzo, "Johnson & Johnson Faces Key Test in Defense Against Talc-Safety Lawsuits," *The Wall Street Journal*, July 21, 2019, https://www.wsj.com/articles/johnson-johnson-faces-key-test-in-defense-against-talc-safety-lawsuits-11563701400 (accessed August 22, 2019).

Peter Loftus and Sara Randazzo, "J&J Offers $4 Billion Opioid Litigation Settlement," *The Wall Street Journal*, October 16, 2019, https://www.wsj.com/articles/j-j-offers-4-billion-opioid-litigation-settlement-11571247596 (accessed October 17, 2019).

Rachael Bell, "The Tylenol Terrorist." *truTV*, http://www.trutv.com/library/crime/terrorists_spies/terrorists/tylenol_murders/index.html (accessed November 19, 2012).

Reuters, "Johnson & Johnson Loses Another Lawsuit Linking Its Talc-Based Products to Ovarian Cancer," *Fortune*, August 21, 2017, http://fortune.com/2017/08/21/johnson-and-johnson-baby-powder-cander-suit/ (accessed August 1, 2018).

Sandra Dalton, "Big Wins for Ovarian Cancer Victim after More Data on Tac Is Revealed," *US Recall News*, May 24, 2016, https://usrecallnews.com/category/drug-recalls/talcum-powder/ (accessed August 3, 2018).

Sandra Dalton, "St. Louis Court Rules in Favor of J&J in Talc Ovarian Cancer Lawsuits," *US Recall News*, March 08, 2017, https://www.usrecallnews.com/category/drug-recall/talcum-powder/ (accessed August 3, 2018).

Sara Randazzo, "Drug Distributors in Talks to Settle Opioid Litigation for $18 Billion," *The Wall Street Journal*, October 15, 2019, https://www.wsj.com/articles/drug-distributors-in-talks-to-settle-opioid-litigation-for-18-billion-11571170730?mod=article_inline (accessed October 17, 2019).

Steve Reinberg, "FDA Advisers Urge Smaller Doses of Acetaminophen," *U.S. News & World Report*, June 30, 2009, http://health.usnews.com/healthnews/family-health/pain/articles/2009/06/30/fda-advisers-urge-smaller-doses-of-acetaminophen.html (accessed July 28, 2019).

Susan Heavey, "FDA Finds Grime at J&J Plant, Urges Use of Generics," *Reuters*, May 4, 2010, http://www.reuters.com/article/2010/05/04/us-johnsonandjohnson-recall-idUSTRE64367Z20100504?feedType=RSS&feedName=topNews (accessed July 28, 2019).

Tamara Kaplan, "The Tylenol Crisis: How Effective Public Relations Saved Johnson & Johnson," Aero Biological Engineering, http://www.aerobiologicalengineering.com/wxk116/TylenolMurders/crisis.html (accessed June 21, 2010).

The American College of Obstetricians and Gynecologists, "Talc Use and Ovarian Cancer," September 11, 2017, https://www.acog.org/About-ACOG/News-Room/Statements/2017/Talc-Use-and-Ovarian-Cancer?IsMobileSet=false (accessed July 28, 2019).

The White House, "Ending America's Opioid Crisis," https://www.whitehouse.gov/opioids/ (accessed October 17, 2019).

Tiffany Hsu, "Johnson & Johnson Hit with $29 Million Verdict in Case over Talc and Asbestos," *The New York Times*, March 14, 2019, https://www.nytimes.com/2019/03/14/business/johnson-johnson-powder-cancer.html (accessed August 22, 2019).

Tiffany Hsu, "July Award $4.7 Billion in Baby Powder Lawsuit," *The New York Times*, July 13, 2018, https://www.nytimes.com/2018/07/12/business/johnson-johnson-talcum-powder.html (accessed July 28, 2019).

Tylenol, "Our Products," http://www.tylenol.com/page.jhtml?id=tylenol/products/main.inc (accessed February 28, 2010).

U.S. Food and Drug Administration, "Talc," U.S. Food and Drug Administration, July 20, 2018, https://www.fda.gov/cosmetics/productsingredients/ingredients/ucm293184.htm (accessed July 28, 2019).

Vanessa O'Connell and Shirley S. Wang, "J&J Acts Fast on Tylenol," *The Wall Street Journal*, July 9, 2009, http://online.wsj.com/article/SB124709897531615407.html (accessed July 28, 2019).

Vince Lattanzio, "McNeil Laying off 300 Employees from Montco Plant," *NBC 10 Philadelphia*, July 15, 2010, http://www.nbcphiladelphia.com/news/local/McNeilLaying-Off-300-Employees-From-Montco-Plant-98547729.html (accessed July 28, 2019).

CASE 15

Herbalife Nutrition: Managing Risks and Achieving Success

Introduction

Herbalife Nutrition is a leading nutritional health company that has had a successful and sustainable business model over the last 40 years. In 2018, Herbalife Ltd. changed their name to Herbalife Nutrition Ltd. ("Herbalife"). The name change was a strategic decision that represented Herbalife's commitment to making the world a healthier place and their strategic transformation into a leader in the nutrition industry. However, despite Herbalife's long-term success, there have been concerns over the company's direct selling business model. The objective of this case is to provide insight into the opportunities for success and to examine the need to manage risks associated with direct selling using a multilevel compensation system. The involvement of the regulatory and political system in addressing charges of misconduct and the efficacy of the direct selling business model is examined in the context of William Ackman and Pershing Square Capital Management's attack on Herbalife. How Herbalife managed this conflict, including the negative publicity by news media, demonstrates the importance of understanding, documenting, and successfully defending the operations of a business. The investigation into the operations of Herbalife opens the door to an improved understanding of how direct selling can be an effective business model that provides benefits to all stakeholders.

Before presenting the Herbalife story, we first explore the direct selling business model that the firm uses to distribute its products. This business model is often misunderstood and questioned as being unsustainable. While there is misconduct in all business models, direct selling misconduct is often associated with the entire industry rather than the firm that perpetrated the misconduct.

The Direct Selling Business Model

Before discussing the direct sales model, it is important to note that all products are "sold" to consumers. Beyond direct selling, many products are sold at retail stores or through online sources. Some are sold via salespeople, either at a retail location or directly to the consumer. Specific to this case, "direct selling" is defined as the marketing of products to end consumers through person-to-person sales presentations at non-retail locations such as consumer homes, the workplace, or online. The practice of direct selling should not be confused with more traditional on-site selling, such as at car dealerships, where customers come to the salesperson. In a direct selling model, salespeople seek out the consumer (at their home, work, socially, or online), to sell the product, rather than the consumer coming to them. Direct selling is not a new business model; in fact, it is one of the oldest ways to distribute products. In the nineteenth century it was a widespread method because many consumers did not have access to retail stores. In addition, direct sellers are generally not employees of the companies they represent but rather autonomous individuals who enter into independent contractor agreements with a company to sell their products. In return, companies do the research and development (also known as R&D), manufacturing, packaging, shipping, quality control, servicing of customers, website development, social media promotions, making for low-risk, low-cost of entry and exit for the direct sellers. Thus, for the remainder of this case, think of companies such as Avon, Juice Plus+, and Herbalife Nutrition as examples of direct sellers.

Single and Multilevel Direct Selling

Direct selling has two compensation methods. There are single- and multilevel compensation models of direct selling. Single-level compensation occurs when direct sellers only earn commissions for sales they make themselves. Multilevel compensation is when direct sellers earn income from their own sales of products as well as commissions from sales made by those they have recruited to sell the product. Forms of multilevel direct selling operate in nearly all countries, but the practice is often strictly regulated and/or closely scrutinized because pyramid schemes have given this form of selling a negative connotation. In most cases, multilevel marketing companies are legitimate because they sell products to consumers and do not require direct sellers to recruit others in order to earn a profit. Thus, properly monitored and managed multilevel direct selling models are not pyramid schemes, as they offer companies a sustainable way to directly sell their products through a hardworking salesforce of individuals who believe in the

This case was developed by O.C. Ferrell, Auburn University; Bryan Hochstein, University of Alabama; and Linda Ferrell, Auburn University, © 2019. It was prepared for classroom discussion rather than to illustrate either effective or ineffective handling of an administrative, ethical, or legal decision by management. All sources used for this case were obtained through publicly available material.

products they sell. In fact, most direct selling representatives are champions for the products and often become independent contractors to get discounts and provide the products to friends and neighbors. The vast majority of representatives are involved part time and are not trying to earn a living. Many well-established companies operate using a multilevel direct sales model (see Table 1 for the top ten global direct selling companies based on 2018 sales revenue).

Pyramid Schemes

Any business model can be used to conduct fraud. Some store retailers can engage in consumer fraud through pricing, promotion, or inferior products. A major concern that has plagued multilevel direct selling is that it can be used by unethical actors to develop fraudulent pyramid schemes. A pyramid scheme is a fraudulent business model that eventually collapses, with the vast majority of participants losing their investments. Pyramid schemes can develop from multilevel sales models as well as other schemes that take money with the promise of large gains. However, in reality, there is no legitimate product. The only way to keep the scheme going is to find new investors. The four defining characteristics of a pyramid scheme are laid out by the Koscot Test, which is used to determine whether a business is a pyramid scheme. These characteristics are: (1) people pay the company to participate; (2) in return, they gain the right to sell a product or service; (3) they are compensated for recruiting others; and (4) this compensation is unrelated to whether or not any of the product or service is actually sold. In other words, participants in pyramid schemes have little or no incentive to sell products, but rather have a much greater incentive to aggressively recruit others into the scheme. Each person recruited pays an up-front fee (usually expensive), and these fees trickle up the pyramid to be collected by leaders at the top. These schemes become problematic because newcomers are promised large profits for buying in and continuing to recruit others. As the network grows, the ability to deliver payment for recruitment becomes impossible and the scheme fails, leaving most in the network in a position where they lose their initial investment. The Federal Bureau of Investigation (FBI) warns of pyramid schemes that come in the form of marketing and investment opportunities where the individual is offered a contractorship or franchise to market a product. The key is where the real profit is earned; if it is not earned by the actual sale of a legitimate product but by the sales of new contractorships, it is likely a pyramid scheme. Therefore, a pyramid scheme is not sustainable in the long run. Multilevel direct selling companies that sell quality products to consumers and have existed for decades are not pyramid schemes.

Pyramid schemes can be hard to identify clearly, but the FTC has warned consumers about two red flags. The first is inventory loading, which is when a new participant purchases a large amount of nonrefundable inventory that they are unlikely to use or consume within a reasonable period of time; this is a requirement and not a choice like with internal consumption (sellers using the products). If the product is low quality, it is clear how this requirement invites fraud. As such, inventory loading is prohibited by the Direct Selling Association's (DSA) Code of Ethics (see Table 2). Legitimate firms follow the DSA's code by offering a refund policy and buyback process for a contractor who no longer wants to sell. The second warning sign of a pyramid scheme is a lack of sales external to the selling network. If the only people buying the product are the ones selling it, there is a clear problem with the business. Businesses that require inventory loading and don't rely on external sales are likely to be pyramid schemes.

Self-Regulation of Direct Selling

To overcome the concerns of multilevel marketing, some direct selling firms choose to self-regulate their multilevel direct sales practices through membership in self-regulatory organizations. For example, many firms follow the principles of the World Federation of Direct Selling Association (WFDSA) and national-level

Table 1 Top Ten Direct Selling Companies

	Company Name	Product Types	2018 Revenue (USD Billions)
1	Amway	Nutrition, Beauty, Bath and Body, Home, Jewelry, Food and Beverage, Fragrances	$8.80
2	Avon	Cosmetics, Skin Care, Fragrance, Personal Care, Hair Care, Jewelry, Gifts	$5.57
3	Herbalife	Nutrition, Weight Loss Management, Personal Care	$4.90
4	Infinitus	Health Products	$4.50
5	Vorwerk	Household Appliances and Cosmetics	$4.30
6	Natura	Cosmetics	$3.67
7	Nu Skin	Cosmetics	$2.68
8	Coway	Air Filtration Systems	$2.50
9	Tupperware	Food Storage and Preparation, Cookware, Serving Items, Cosmetics, Beauty Products	$2.00
10	Young Living	Cosmetics, Home Care, Personal Care, Wellness	$1.90

Source: "2019 DSN Global 100 List," *Direct Selling News*, 2019, https://www.directsellingnews.com/dsn-announces-the-2019-global-100/ (accessed August 5, 2019).

direct selling associations such as the United States Direct Selling Association (DSA) in the United States. The WFDSA promotes ethical practices in direct selling globally through advocacy and strong relationships with governments, consumers, and academia. The U.S. DSA also emphasizes ethical business practices and consumer protection measures and requires that members adhere to the DSA's Code of Ethics (See Table 2). This Code of Ethics recognizes the importance of a fair and responsible approach to direct selling since direct selling requires sensitive and personal one-on-one interaction that can lead to undue pressure placed upon consumers. The Code (1) prohibits deceptive or unlawful practices regarding recruits and customers; (2) requires that direct sellers provide accurate and truthful information about the price, quality, and promotion of the products;

(3) illuminates and enforces the need for a clear record of the sales made by contractors; (4) necessitates that warranties be fully explained; (5) requires direct sellers to clearly identify themselves to customers and maintain the confidential information of their customers; (6) prohibits pyramid scheme practices; and (7) provides guidelines on inventory purchases, earnings reporting, inventory loading, start-up fee payments, and training practices.

The DSA and the Council for Better Business Bureaus (CBBB), the network hub for BBBs in the United States, Canada, and Mexico, have created a third-party, self-regulatory program, the Direct Selling Self-Regulatory Council (DSSRC), for the direct selling industry, which was launched in January 2019. The DSSRC monitors the entire direct selling channel—including DSA member

Table 2 Direct Selling Association Code of Ethics

As a consumer you should expect salespeople to:
Tell you who they are, why they're approaching you, and what products they are selling.
Promptly end a demonstration or presentation at your request.
Provide a receipt with a clearly stated cooling off period permitting the consumer to withdraw from a purchase order within a minimum of three days from the date of the purchase transaction and receive a full refund of the purchase price.
Explain how to return a product or cancel an order.
Provide you with promotional materials that contain the address and telephone number of the direct selling company.
Provide a written receipt that identifies the company and salesperson, including contact information for either.
Respect your privacy by calling at a time that is convenient for you.
Safeguard your private information.
Provide accurate and truthful information regarding the price, quality, quantity, performance, and availability of their product or service.
Offer a written receipt in language you can understand.
Offer a complete description of any warranty or guarantee.

As a salesperson, you should expect a DSA member company to:
Provide you with accurate information about the company's compensation plan, products, and sales methods.
Describe the relationship between you and the company in writing.
Be accurate in any comparisons about products, services, or opportunities.
Refrain from any unlawful or unethical recruiting practice and exorbitant entrance or training fees.
Ensure that you are not just buying products solely to qualify for downline commissions.
Ensure that any materials marketed to you by others in the salesforce are consistent with the company's policies, are reasonably priced, and have the same return policy as the company's.
Require you to abide by the requirements of the Code of Ethics.
Safeguard your private information.
Provide adequate training to help you operate ethically.
Base all actual and potential sales and earning claims on documented facts.
Encourage you to purchase only the inventory you can sell in a reasonable amount of time.
Repurchase marketable inventory and sales aids you have purchased within the past 12 months at 90 percent or more of your original cost if you decide to leave the business.
Explain the repurchase option in writing.
Have reasonable startup fees and costs.

Source: Direct Selling Association, *Consumer Protection Toolkit,* http://www.dsef.org/wp-content/uploads/2015/03/DSEF-Consumer-Protection-Toolkit.pdf (accessed May 25, 2017).

and non-member companies. The new, third-party, self-regulatory organization monitors the entire U.S. direct selling industry and embodies the following principles:

- Clear industry standards on issues such as product and earning representations;
- Identification of relevant best practices from other self-regulatory models;
- Creation of a process that both monitors and enforces strict business principles;
- Enacts measures to raise the bar of excellence for DSA members and the entire direct selling channel

Herbalife is a leading supporter of the DSSRC. This demonstrates the company's commitment and leadership in supporting ethical conduct in the direct selling industry.

Herbalife Nutrition

Herbalife Nutrition, Ltd. is the third-largest multilevel marketing company in the world. The story of Herbalife includes direct selling, but the company's success has come through the acceptance of their products by consumers, much like any other company. One difference between Herbalife and most companies is that their products are not sold in retail stores; rather, consumers interact with independent sellers to order products. Herbalife is a publicly traded company headquartered in Los Angeles, California, that has loyal customers around the world.

Herbalife focuses on the sale of products related to nutrition, weight management, and personal care, with independent contractors selling in more than 90 countries. Mark Hughes founded the company in 1980 out of a desire to create a safe alternative to other weight loss products. Herbalife's first sales were conducted from the trunk of Hughes's car in Los Angeles. Two years later, the company reached $2 million in sales. Herbalife became a publicly traded company in 1986 when it joined the NASDAQ stock exchange. Since then, Herbalife has become a sustainable multibillion-dollar global company. Throughout their growth, Herbalife has experienced many changes to leadership and ownership structure.

Foundational Products

Herbalife sells products for weight management, nutrition, energy, fitness, and personal care that support a healthy lifestyle. The weight management line consists of Formula 1 protein shakes, supplements, weight loss enhancers, protein bars, and snacks, all serving the purpose of helping customers to attain their weight goals. For instance, the Personalized Protein Powder and the Protein Drink Mix offerings provide an alternative to traditional meals while supplying energy and curbing hunger cravings, whether consumers want to lose or maintain their weight or build muscle mass. Targeted

nutrition products include dietary and nutritional supplements that contain herbs, vitamins, minerals, and other natural ingredients to strengthen specific areas of the body that tend to be problematic for many people. For example, Tri-Shield helps the heart stay healthy by maintaining good cholesterol levels and providing antioxidants, and Ocular Defense Formula and Joint Support Advanced offer nutritional aid for the eyes and joints of aging adults. The energy and fitness product options are designed for those engaged in sports and fitness activities. Customers can choose from drink mix-ins such as the H^3O Fitness Drink, which enhances clarity and rehydrates the body, or utilize supplements such as N-R-G (Nature's Raw Guarana Tablets), which also promote mental clarity. Herbalife's personal care products include skin cleansers, moisturizers, lotions, shampoos, and conditioners. In this product line, Herbalife offers program sets called Herbalife SKIN, containing groups of cleansers, moisturizers, and creams customized for different types of skin, from dry to oily. Overall, Herbalife follows a strategy of producing high quality products that enhance customer health and well-being.

Herbalife's Implementation of the Direct Selling Model

People are attracted to becoming direct sellers for many reasons. Some are passionate about a product and want to promote the company. Others want to receive a discount on their personal orders, a common benefit of being a direct seller. Many find working as a direct seller to be a flexible, part-time opportunity for extra income. There are 2.3 million independent contractor direct sellers of Herbalife products. Most, if not all, of them personally use these products.

Direct sellers are attracted to the low startup cost of selling Herbalife. For about $94 a kit, new sellers receive a Herbalife Member Pack, which includes forms, applications, a tote bag, and samples of various Herbalife products. The pack includes informational and training materials that educate the new seller on using and retailing the products, business basics, and how to build a sales and marketing plan. The member kit is the only purchase required to become an Herbalife network member and seller. Herbalife does not require their distributors to pay a "fee" to join, and the only up-front money spent represents the true value of the kit.

As soon as a seller joins Herbalife, they receive benefits. Sellers enjoy discounts on products ranging from 25 to 50 percent depending on the level of contractorship (contractors move up levels by achieving certain sales goals). Contractors can sell products at any price they set and make decisions on how they want to position and sell the Herbalife products (within legal and company guidelines). The more successful an Herbalife seller, the greater the discounts and commissions on product sales.

In the event that a contractor no longer wants to sell Herbalife products, the company will buy back any remaining inventory of the seller. In fact, Herbalife goes beyond the Direct Selling Association's ethical guidelines for buying back products by reimbursing the distributor for everything he or she initially purchased (100 percent buyback policy). The company also limits the amount of inventory a seller can initially purchase. Herbalife's membership structure is designed to clearly differentiate their legitimate multilevel marketing model from fraudulent schemes.

The Herbalife business model has succeeded due to the company's products and support. Most Herbalife distributors do not have a physical store location, as they practice direct selling from home. However, there are strict company policies and legal requirements that regulate product information, sales techniques, advertising, lead generation, social media, and related issues. Herbalife also created a centralized e-commerce section for contractors on their GoHerbalife website that also controls branding and product claims. Distributors each have their own page on the platform, which they can use to attract customers. Customers are only randomly connected through the platform if they don't have a Distributor who can provide them service. Thus, direct sellers are independent, yet are required to represent Herbalife through ethical business practices.

Herbalife Customer Base

Herbalife serves a broad external customer base. To illustrate, an independent survey conducted by Nielsen, a global information and measurement company, sampled 10,525 consumers and indicated that 3.3 percent of the general U.S. population made an Herbalife purchase sometime within a three-month period (approximately 7.9 million customers). The external sales volume is a good indicator of the strength and legitimacy of the company's business. Additionally, the study showed that those who had made a purchase in the last three months were loyal and tended to make purchases approximately every two months. A strength of Herbalife over their long history as a company is a sustained customer base that uses and repurchases their products based on the quality, usefulness, and value they provide.

Challenges to Herbalife's Multilevel Model

Herbalife, like many multilevel marketing companies, has been accused of being a pyramid scheme. However, considering the firm's long and successful history, these claims were not taken seriously until 2012 when prominent hedge fund manager and billionaire investor William Ackman announced that he and his company, Pershing Square Capital Management, had spent a year studying Herbalife and concluded the firm was, in fact, an elaborate pyramid scheme. Ackman is known as an "activist investor" and claimed it was his civic duty to expose Herbalife as fraudulent. Of note, Ackman's company also stood to profit heavily, having invested $1 billion in a short sale of Herbalife's stock (a complex investment strategy that earns money if the stock price falls, rather than rises). Ackman's target stock price for Herbalife was $0. In other words, he believed the company should and would fail. Ackman continued to campaign and advocate against Herbalife, which plunged Herbalife into a controversy over the potential legitimacy of their business. The problem was, the investment community and mass media did not understand a sustainable direct selling business model. The investigation led by Ackman focused on the low earnings of independent contractors and was the result of months of research and analysis by his team. The accusations against Herbalife included the following: (1) the majority of contractors for Herbalife lose money, (2) Herbalife pays more to recruit new contractors than sell actual products, and (3) only the top one percent of contractors earn most of the money. Ackman argued that Herbalife recruits contractors under false pretenses by unrealistically suggesting they can earn a large income. Furthermore, he alleged that the real money in Herbalife comes not from selling products but from recruiting other contractors, as all the top earners make the vast majority of their income through downline commissions from the sales of those in their recruiting chain. Although Herbalife has published results showing that the majority of their profit is made through product sales, Ackman believed this information to be false and misleading, as he estimated sales to be only 3 percent of Herbalife's revenue, with the rest made via recruiting. In reality, Herbalife does not charge a fee for becoming an independent contractor and earns their profits from selling products.

Herbalife has also been accused of issuing false accounting statements, although there has never been any official legal claim brought about their accounting records. According to allegations, all products sold to contractors are shown as retail sales, without tracking whether the contractor consumes the products (internal consumption) or to whom the contractor sold the products. Critics believe the company should not record sales revenue for internal consumption but only from sales made to end users. This argument falls into the larger backdrop of the defense and legitimacy of internal consumption. Ackman and other critics have used these arguments to emphasize that the majority of Herbalife contractors are not successful in selling their products (other than to themselves). Herbalife's records show that only one percent of their registered contractors will make $100,000 or more from the business in their lifetime. This statistic shows that many who try direct selling are either not willing or lack the business knowledge to put in sufficient effort to make a living. In most cases, those who sell Herbalife do so as a side job and only work part time, depending on how much extra money they want to make.

Ackman's allegations launched an unprecedented storm of controversy for Herbalife. Four days after Ackman's initial presentation, the company's stock fell 43 percent. Ackman launched a well-financed mass media and publicity campaign and engaged in political lobbying to drive down the price of the stock. The debate over the company became polarized, with prominent investors, analysts, public interest groups, and loyalists presenting heated arguments both for and against Herbalife's legitimacy. Recognizing the seriousness of the situation, Herbalife responded in force, including hiring a lobbying team and launching one of the largest marketing campaigns in the company's history to bolster and strengthen the Herbalife brand. Over the length of the dispute, both Ackman and Herbalife spent multiple millions of dollars supporting their positions and attacking each other. The media showcased the Ackman and Herbalife conflict.

FTC Investigation and Settlement of Claims

In March of 2014, the Federal Trade Commission (FTC) opened a civil investigation of Herbalife. The investigation was prompted by Ackman's reports to the public and lobbying efforts that brought the "pyramid scheme" message to Congress. Ackman made political contributions to legislators who advocated for his position. Ackman believed the FTC would rule against the company and force the firm to cease operations. However, Herbalife welcomed the investigation and was very cooperative with the FTC. At the onset of the investigation, Herbalife stated they were confident in their compliance with laws, their financial stability, and their success as a company over the past 34 years. In 2016, the FTC settled its case with Herbalife, dismissing the accusation of Herbalife being a pyramid scheme.

Nevertheless, the settlement did result in major changes for Herbalife. The FTC mandated a restructure of Herbalife's business practices, affecting how the company reports sales of members (consumers) and independent contractors selling to retail consumers. Changes were made to the level of involvement participants were allowed to have in selling products. An aspect of the settlement is a mandate that Herbalife must derive 80 percent of sales from legitimate end-user purchases to maintain their distributor compensation program. In addition, Herbalife must now prohibit participants from leasing or purchasing physical business locations to sell Herbalife products until they have completed a year as a distributor and completed a business-training program.

The FTC also required Herbalife to pay $200 million to individuals who had lost money through involvement in selling Herbalife products. It was deemed that Herbalife's use of advertising through testimonials had misled potential participants about the realities of

financial success through involvement with Herbalife. The settlement requires Herbalife to make truthful claims about how much people are likely to make and ensure the claims are backed by facts.

The company was able to comply with the FTC order. In 2017, Herbalife exceeded the settlement guidelines, proving 90 percent of sales were documented sales by consumers outside the distribution network. Additionally, Herbalife proved 400,000 discount buyers or "preferred" members were not pursuing the business opportunity and thus were simply customers of Herbalife through retail sales. These successes counteract Ackman's claims of Herbalife having no "real" consumers. Investor Carl Icahn, a supporter of Herbalife throughout the controversy, stated, "I think it's ironic, but factual, that as a result of the propaganda against the company that it now has a much better idea of who their customers are and it opens the door for Herbalife to greatly benefit." By 2019, Herbalife fully emerged from the FTC investigation. The company achieved a stock price of $59 in January 2019, from a low of $15 in 2015. Overall, Herbalife learned several lessons throughout the investigation and has improved business practices as a result of the FTC settlement. The investigation confirmed that Herbalife has maintained a 40-year sustainable business model.

Impact of FTC Settlement on Pershing Capital

The end of Pershing Capital's crusade against Herbalife came to a "bruising defeat" as described by *The Wall Street Journal*. Ackman's hedge fund management company Pershing Square Capital lost hundreds of millions of dollars over his five-year bet against Herbalife. While disappointed that the pyramid scheme accusation was found to be false, Ackman contended that several of his claims were confirmed in the FTC case. Since the settlement, Pershing Capital reported losses for four years in a row. As such, a large number of Pershing Capital's largest investors have left the fund and Ackman has reduced staff to return the firm to their roots as a smaller organization. Ackman has publicly admitted to making mistakes in his bets with Herbalife but states confidence in his portfolio and the future of Pershing Capital.

New Opportunities: Consumer Megatrends

Herbalife has overcome many challenges throughout their history. In addition to the FTC settlement and general societal misconceptions about multilevel marketing, Herbalife has always had to adapt to changes in consumer preferences. It is no secret that today's consumers spend more time shopping for and researching products online and less time shopping in stores or interacting with salespeople than in the past. In addition, the digitization of society has led consumers to have greater demands that infringe upon their personal life. Fortunately, for Herbalife, solutions that address many societal changes termed megatrends are well aligned with the company's products. According to a recent investor's presentation, Herbalife leadership views the trends of (1) increasing obesity of the population, (2) aging of the population, (3) increasing healthcare costs, and (4) expanding interest in entrepreneurship as opportunities that position the company for long-term success. In addition, as consumers become more dependent on social recommendations, Herbalife expects their model of individual and social exchange (i.e., direct selling consultation) to help consumers looking for coaching and experience that helps them in making decisions related to personal well-being.

Specifically, societal megatrends largely relate to a need for better nutrition, well-being, and fulfillment across society. Concerns over obesity and healthcare costs affect both older consumers and younger ones. In both cases, recovery and prevention are an important ingredient to enjoying a fulfilling life. Older adults need options to help offset health problems, and younger adults are increasingly interested in preventing the problems that they see in older generations. Thus, Herbalife's strategy to rebrand themselves as a nutrition company that develops, manufactures, and delivers products of unquestioning quality fits closely to consumer segments responding to alarming societal trends. These consumers are also well informed and willing to invest time and energy to make sure they are purchasing products that will actually deliver on claims. Herbalife is embracing these trends by building upon their direct sales model through social media and new initiatives that position direct sellers as trusted consultants that connect people who learn from and support each other. In addition, Herbalife's well-established direct selling model fits well with consumer interest in entrepreneurship. Similar to Uber, Lyft, and other "gig" opportunities, direct selling allows an individual to work at their own schedule and with the intensity they desire. Pairing high quality products with flexible, self-driven earning opportunities positions Herbalife well to respond to changing consumer markets. The following sections outline selected specifics of Herbalife's (1) product quality strategy, (2) engagement strategy termed "nutrition clubs," which started in Mexico in 2004, and (3) commitment to social responsibility through their mission to encourage nutrition and well-being to external and internal communities.

Product Quality Strategy

To ensure quality, Herbalife invests in continuous research and development of their product lines. For example, recent use of genetic technology advances allows Herbalife to confirm quality raw materials for the manufacture of their products. Steven Newmaster, PhD and trained ethnobotanist, speaks on behalf of the DNA testing Herbalife uses to ensure the quality of plants they use. Newmaster states the natural supply chain they use has been tested from the producer to the manufacturer. Through DNA barcode technology, Herbalife can confirm the ingredients used in their products are authentic, healing, and nutritious. DNA testing is conducted by raw ingredients being matched to a comprehensive library of thousands of botanical species around the globe to determine high DNA-level quality. Herbalife is undertaking these changes in their product development because consumers desire transparency of product origins prior to purchase.

To support consistent product quality through technology, Herbalife has six research and development facilities and seven labs that test for quality. The company also has a global operations team of almost 2,000 people including more than 300 research scientists that support their products. This team sets the uniform global standard for quality and oversees all elements of product development and production. Herbalife's ISO 17025 accreditation indicates adherence to strict standards in technical competency of laboratory personnel, accuracy of testing methods, use of proper equipment, and it assures consumers that the tests are trustworthy.

To further ensure product quality, Herbalife closely controls their supply chain through their "Seed to Feed" strategy. Since 2009, Herbalife has invested $250 million in vertical manufacturing and infrastructure to increase the in-house production of key product units from less than 5 to 70 percent, in essence managing products from raw seed to feed the manufacturing process. COO, David Pezzullo, elaborates on the strategy: "We use a stage-gate product development process with hundreds of steps and more than 60 sign-offs along the way to ensure that every aspect of the product, from quality assurance, safety, science and regulatory to sensory and label design, conforms to our specifications." This process can take up to 18 months to complete and involves the work of more than 300 technical employees. All manufacturing facilities, whether in the United States or abroad, must comply with FDA regulations for manufacturing practices, which specify how production facilities in food, dietary supplements, and acidified foods must operate. Herbalife undertakes all of these steps as they strive for "best in class" regarding product excellence.

Engagement Strategy

Herbalife has achieved success through direct and personal attention to consumer needs; nutrition clubs build on this through support communities. The first Herbalife Nutrition Club opened in Mexico in 2004. The Nutrition Club was formed to bring together people interested in nutrition and the support of a like-minded community. Originally, the club served as a physical location where the community could meet and purchase the products they needed in cost-effective portions that were more convenient than bulk purchasing. In addition to convenience, the club also provides a connection to enjoy and learn about the products in the company of other people with similar goals in their weight loss journey. Over time, Nutrition Clubs have also incorporated fitness classes to address a healthy lifestyle. Herbalife has embraced the Nutrition Club concept as an answer to societal megatrends and to further differentiate the company from others in their industry. Nutrition Clubs allow independent distributors to provide personalized nutrition plans, motivation, and accountability to customers. Since 2004, the concept has thrived, with Herbalife supporting over 17,500 Nutrition Clubs in the United States and nearly 118,000 worldwide.

Research shows that healthy habits are best formed in a social setting that offers support, advice, and reinforcement of the habits. Members who attend the clubs can receive nutrition and fitness tips and encouragement from the independent distributors running the establishments. Herbalife Executive Vice President explains, "The Nutrition Club owners typically charge an attendance fee on a daily, weekly or monthly basis. Invited members can enjoy shakes, teas and aloe and participate in activities like group workouts, fitness walks and weight-loss challenges." Nutrition Clubs are the perfect solution to those seeking influence in their nutrition lifestyle while also giving them community support in a positive environment. To ensure quality and consistency, Nutrition Club operators (independent Herbalife distributors) must undergo extensive training before commencing operations. Herbalife's training for operators provides them with the resources and education to create a budget and business plan and learn the local laws. Additionally, Herbalife compliance staff monitors and performs site visits regularly to ensure regulations are upheld. Overall, the Nutrition Club strategy has enhanced Herbalife's direct selling model and has been instrumental in gaining consumer trust in the company's product line and its informed and helpful resellers.

Social Responsibility

Herbalife takes their responsibility as a corporation seriously. The company summarizes their values through a commitment to doing "the right, honest and ethical thing." More specifically, CEO Michael Johnson stated that the "company's reputation is its greatest asset," so much emphasis is placed on ethical business conduct. According to Herbalife's Corporate Code of Business Conduct and Ethics, employees must engage in fair interaction with everyone associated with the company, including external stakeholders. The code has guidelines in place as to how contractors and employees of Herbalife should interact with suppliers, competitors, business partners, and regulatory authorities. The company discourages conflicts of interest and offers three methods of reporting unethical behavior: through the company hotline, through the company website, or by contacting the general counsel. Those who violate these standards are disciplined, suspended, or terminated, which demonstrates Herbalife's commitment to their ethics code and ethical conduct.

Herbalife is committed to their external and internal community. To the external community, the Herbalife Family Foundation (HFF) and the Casa Herbalife program provide funds and volunteerism to charities committed to supporting at-risk children. Herbalife Nutrition Foundation also provides support to nutrition initiatives and disaster relief. For instance, Herbalife's partnership with the Global Alliance for Improved Nutrition (GAIN) focuses on providing essential nutrients to improve the health of women and children worldwide. To their internal community, Herbalife proactively embraces employee wellness and eco-friendly initiatives. The company incentivizes employees to be healthy and participate in fitness activities. Such incentives include providing complementary products and reduction of individual health insurance costs. As such, the company has been recognized by *Men's Fitness* magazine as "One of the 15 Fittest Companies in America." In terms of being environmentally conscious, Herbalife's headquarters have received accolades for their LEED certification and environmentally friendly design. The firm also encourages distributors to increase their own sustainability activities.

Conclusions

Herbalife Nutrition has navigated many challenges and capitalized on many opportunities since their formation in 1980. Important to this case is Herbalife's direct sales, multilevel compensation model. This model is responsible for Herbalife's exceptional growth and success, as committed and engaged sellers have delivered value through products and expertise to the company's large customer base. However, the same model has led to concerns over the stability and sustainability of the company, as some have assumed their operations to be a pyramid scheme destined to fail. Despite Herbalife's investigation and resulting restructuring, the company has emerged well positioned to continue their success by aligning the core competencies of their products and business model with changing consumer preferences and needs. This case illustrates that referring to direct selling firms as pyramid schemes is a misrepresentation of a highly effective sustainable business model that has existed for hundreds of years.

Herbalife will face the same challenges other members of the retail industry must address in the future. Internet sales are now 10 percent of retail sales and Amazon has more than 50 percent of the online retail market. Herbalife may be better positioned to face this competition because they do not have the overhead of expensive retail stores. The need for assistance and consultation in buying nutritional products provides the opportunity for person-to-person interaction. Maintaining a strong ethical culture and building trust with consumers is the glue that holds relationships together. The multilevel compensation method in the direct selling business model will continue to be debated and scrutinized, but Herbalife provides a strong example of how this system can benefit all stakeholders.

Questions for Discussion

1. Describe the differences between a legitimate direct selling business model and a pyramid scheme.
2. Evaluate how Herbalife managed their regulation and public relations risks.
3. Why has Herbalife continued to be successful after the attack by Ackman and an FTC investigation?

Sources

"Direct Selling Methods: Single Level and Multilevel Marketing," *More Business*, March 26, 2007, http://www.morebusiness. com/running_your_business/management/Direct-Sales.brc (accessed May 25, 2017).

"Frauds of the Century," in O.C. Ferrell, John Fraedrich, and Linda Ferrell, *Business Ethics: Ethical Decision Making and Cases*, 10th ed. (Mason, OH: South-Western Cengage Learning, 2015).

"Herbalife Announces Results of Study on Contractors and End Users in the U.S.," *Yahoo! Finance*, June 11, 2013, http:// finance.yahoo.com/news/herbalife-announces-results-study-contractors-214500826.html (accessed June 12, 2013).

"Herbalife Ltd.," Hoover's Company Records—In-depth Records, April 17, 2013.

"Herbalife Review," *Vital Health Partners RSS*, Web, April 23, 2013.

"Herbalife Says Survey Indicates 7.9M Customers in the U.S.," *Yahoo! Finance*, June 12, 2013, http://finance.yahoo.com/ news/herbalife-says-survey-indicates-7-103428808.html (accessed June 16, 2015).

"New Pyramid Scheme Allegations against Herbalife that Might Just Stick," Shortzilla LLC, April 11, 2013, http://www. shortzilla.com/new-pyramid-scheme-allegations-against-herbalife-that-might-just-stick/ (accessed July 25, 2013).

"Top Herbalife members contacted by law enforcement agencies: report," *The Globe and Mail*, April 6, 2015, http://www. theglobeandmail.com/report-on-business/top-herbalife-members-contacted-by-law-enforcement-agencies-report/ article23804675/ (accessed June 16, 2015).

Agustino Fontevecchia, "Investors Side with Carl Icahn: Herbalife Soars after Epic TV Battle with Ackman," *Forbes*, January 25, 2013, https://www.forbes.com/sites/afontevecchia/2013/01/ 25/investors-side-with-carl-icahn-herbalife-soars-after-epic-tv-battle-with-ackman/#a2f65903585a (accessed May 25, 2017).

Agustino Fontevecchia, "The Anti-Ackman Effect: Herbalife Surges Then Plunges as Hedge Fund Billie Omits It from Ira Sohn Speech," *Forbes*, May 8, 2013, http://www.forbes.

com/sites/afontevecchia/2013/05/08/the-anti-ackman-effect-herbalife-surges-then-punges-as-hedge-fund-billie-omits-it-from-ira-sohn-speech/ (accessed May 25, 2017).

Alexandra Stevenson and Ben Protess, "Bruised, Herbalife Swings Back at Accuser," *The New York Times*, June 2, 2015, https:// www.nytimes.com/2015/06/03/business/dealbook/herbalife-steps-up-lobbying-to-counter-ackmans-attacks.html (accessed May 25, 2017).

Anita Balakrishnan, "Herbalife, Ackman Cleared by Government Probes: Report," *CNBC*, February 1, 2016, http://www.cnbc. com/2016/02/01/herbalife-ackman-cleared-by-government-probes-report.html (accessed May 25, 2017).

Anne T. Coughlan, "Assessing an MLM Business," Herbalife, July 2012, http://ir.herbalife.com/assessing-MLM.cfm (accessed July 10, 2013).

Business Wire, "Pershing Square Responds to Recent Ruling in *FTC V. BurnLounge, Inc.*" June 3, 2014, http://www. businesswire.com/news/home/20140603006090/en/Pershing-Square-Responds-Ruling-FTC-V.-BurnLounge#.VX8X7kYj-A (accessed May 25, 2017).

Carlton English, "Herbalife CEO Calls Critics 'Fake News' After Strong Quarter," *New York Post*, May 4, 2017, http://nypost. com/2017/05/04/herbalife-ceo-calls-critics-fake-news-after-strong-quarter/ (accessed May 25, 2017).

Dan McCrum, "Herbalife Faces Challenge of Greater Transparency over Sales," *Financial Times*, June 17, 2013, https://www. ft.com/content/9289508c-d2e6-11e2-aac2-00144feab7de (accessed May 25, 2017).

Dan McCrum, "Keep an Eye on the FTC vs Burnlounge," *Financial Times*, March 21, 2014, https://ftalphaville.ft.com/ 2014/03/21/1806772/keep-an-eye-on-the-ftc-vs-burnlounge/ (accessed May 25, 2017).

Daniel Yi and Tom Petruno, "Herbalife Investor Bids for Rest of Firm," *Los Angeles Times*, February 3, 2007, http://articles. latimes.com/2007/feb/03/business/fi-herbalife3 (accessed May 25, 2017).

Devika Krishna Kumar, "This Is Not What Bill Ackman Needed for Herbalife," *Business Insider*, October 31, 2014, http:// www.businessinsider.com/r-herbalife-to-pay-15-million-to-settle-class-action-lawsuit-2014-10 (accessed May 25, 2017).

Duane D. Stanford and Kelly Bit, "Herbalife Drops after Ackman Says He's Shorting Shares," *Bloomberg*, December 20, 2012, http://www.bloomberg.com/news/2012-12-19/herbalife-drops-after-cnbc-says-ackman-is-short-company.html (accessed June 16, 2015).

Economist staff, "The House of Cards Put," *The Economist*, March 15, 2014, http://www.economist.com/news/ finance-and-economics/21599055-activist-investing-meets-activist-government-house-cards-put (accessed May 25, 2017).

Facts about Herbalife, http://www.factsaboutherbalife.com/ (accessed May 25, 2017).

Federal Trade Commission, "FTC Action Leads to Court Order Shutting Down Pyramid Scam Thousands of Consumers Burned by BurnLounge," March 14, 2012, http://www.ftc.gov/ news-events/press-releases/2012/03/ftc-action-leads-court-order-shutting-down-pyramid-scamthousands (accessed May 25, 2017).

Herbalife, "Herbalife Ltd. Announces Record Fourth Quarter 2013 and Record Full Year Results, and Raises 2014 Earnings Guidance," February 18, 2014, http://ir.herbalife.com/ releasedetail.cfm?ReleaseID=826429 (accessed May 25, 2017).

Herbalife, "Herbalife Partners with Global Health Strategies Institute to Improve Children's Nutrition in India," April 7, 2015, http://ir.herbalife.com/releasedetail.cfm?ReleaseID=905163 (accessed May 25, 2017).

Herbalife, "I Am Herbalife FAQs," http://iamherbalife.com/faq/ (accessed May 25, 2017).

Herbalife, "Product Catalogue," http://catalog.herbalife.com/Catalog/en-US (accessed June 16, 2015).

Herbalife, "Social Responsibility," http://company.herbalife.com/social-responsibilty (accessed May 25, 2017).

Herbalife, "Statement of Average Gross Compensation Paid by Herbalife to United States Contractors in 2013," http://opportunity.herbalife.com/Content/en-US/pdf/business-opportunity/statement_average_gross_usen.pdf (accessed May 25, 2017).

Herbalife, *Sales & Marketing Plan and Business Rules*, 2013, https://www.myherbalife.com/Content/en-US/pdf/distributorForms/Book4_SalesandMarketing.pdf (accessed May 25, 2017).

Herbalife, The Real Bill Ackman website, http://www.therealbillackman.com/ (accessed May 25, 2017).

Herbalife, United States—Official Site, http://www.herbalife.com/ (accessed May 25, 2017).

Investopedia, "Short Selling: What Is Short Selling?" *Investopedia*, http://www.investopedia.com/terms/s/shortselling.asp (accessed May 25, 2017).

Javier E. David, "Herbalife CEO Casts Doubt on Ackman's Motives in Shorting Stock," *CNBC*, January 10, 2013, http://www.cnbc.com/id/100369698 (accessed July 25, 2013).

Jen Wieczner, "Why Herbalife's CEO Says He's Done with Bill Ackman's 'Hogwash'," *Fortune*, February 24, 2017, http://fortune.com/2017/02/24/herbalife-stock-earnings-bill-ackman/ (accessed May 25, 2017).

Joe Nocera, "For Better or Worse, Ackman's Still Betting Against Herbalife," *Bloomberg*, March 1, 2017, https://www.bloomberg.com/view/articles/2017-03-01/for-better-and-worse-ackman-s-still-betting-against-herbalife (accessed May 25, 2017).

Julia La Roche, "California Congresswoman Asks the FTC to Investigate Herbalife," *Business Insider*, June 13, 2013, http://www.businessinsider.com/sanchez-asks-ftc-to-probe-herbalife-2013-6 (accessed May 25, 2017).

Juliet Chung, "In Herbalife Fight, Both Sides Prevail," *The Wall Street Journal*, March 31, 2013, https://www.wsj.com/articles/SB10001424127887323361804578388682197247250 (accessed May 25, 2017).

Kaja Whitehouse, "Bill Ackman's Herbalife Short is Backfiring—Again," *USA Today*, March 23, 2015, http://americasmarkets.usatoday.com/2015/03/23/bill-ackmans-herbalife-short-is-backfiring-again/ (accessed June 16, 2015).

Karen Gullo, "BurnLounge Ruling in FTC Case Seen as Good for Herbalife," *Bloomberg*, June 2, 2014, http://www.bloomberg.com/news/2014-06-02/burnlounge-shutdown-by-ftc-upheld-by-federal-appeals-court-1-.html (accessed June 3, 2014).

Kevin Thompson, "Inventory Loading: When Does a Company Cross the Line?" *Thompsonburton.com*, March 20, 2010, https://thompsonburton.com/mlmattorney/2010/03/20/inventory-loading-when-does-a-company-cross-the-line/ (accessed May 25, 2017).

Kevin Thompson, "The BurnLounge Court Decision Clears the Air on Many Issues," *Direct Selling News*, August 2014: 64–66.

Lehman, Lee, and Xu. "Direct Sale," Lehman Law, http://www.lehmanlaw.com/practices/direct-sale.html (accessed May 25, 2017).

Linette Lopez, "REPORT: The FBI Is Interviewing People and Asking for Documents about Bill Ackman and Herbalife," *Business Insider*, March 12, 2015, http://www.businessinsider.com/the-fbi-is-investigating-bill-ackman-over-herbalife-2015-3 (accessed May 25, 2017).

Martin Russell, "Herbalife Scam: Let's Review the Claims," Careful Cash RSS, March 4, 2011, http://www.carefulcash.com/herbalife-scam-lets-review-the-claims/ (accessed May 25, 2017).

Martinne Geller, "Group Says Herbalife Products Have Too Much Lead," *Reuters*, May 19, 2008, http://www.reuters.com/article/us-this-hold-toni-herbalife-idUSN1955645920080520 (accessed May 25, 2017).

Michael S. Schmidt, Eric Lipton, and Alexandra Stevenson, "After Big Bet, Hedge Fund Pulls the Levers of Power," *The New York Times*, March 9, 2014, http://www.nytimes.com/2014/03/10/business/staking-1-billion-that-herbalife-will-fail-then-ackman-lobbying-to-bring-it-down.html?_r=0 (accessed May 25, 2017).

Michelle Celarier, "BurnLounge Shutdown Has Implications for Herbalife," *New York Post*, June 2, 2014, http://nypost.com/2014/06/02/burnlounge-shutdown-has-implications-for-herbalife/ (accessed May 25, 2017).

Michelle Celarier, "Little-Known Deal Could Be the Downfall of Herbalife," *The New York Post*, February 6, 2015, http://nypost.com/2015/02/06/little-known-deal-could-be-the-downfall-of-herbalife/ (accessed May 25, 2017).

Michelle Celarier, "NYC Pol: It's Herb-sploitation," *New York Post*, June 14, 2013, http://www.nypost.com/p/news/business/nyc_pol_it_herb_sploitation_zr63x783q4YqvSA3hReQEM (accessed May 25, 2017).

Michelle Urban and Jennifer Sawayda, "The Network Marketing Controversy," Daniels Fund Ethics Initiative website, 2013, https://danielsethics.mgt.unm.edu/pdf/network-marketing-di.pdf (accessed May 25, 2017).

Miles Weiss, "Icahn Says No Respect for Bill Ackman after Herbalife Bet," *Bloomberg*, January 25, 2013, http://www.bloomberg.com/news/2013-01-24/icahn-says-no-respect-for-bill-ackman-after-herbalife-bet.html (accessed May 25, 2017).

Nathalie Tadena, "Ackman: Herbalife Should Come Clean on Surveys," *The Wall Street Journal*, June 18, 2013, http://blogs.wsj.com/moneybeat/2013/06/18/ackman-herbalife-should-come-clean-onsurveys/?mod=yahoo_hs (accessed May 25, 2017).

Nathan Bomey, "Herbalife Agrees to $200M Settlement," *USA Today*, July 15, 2016, https://www.usatoday.com/story/money/2016/07/15/federal-trade-commission-herbalife/87119208/ (accessed May 25, 2017).

Nathan Vardi, "Carl Icahn and Herbalife are Crushing Bill Ackman," *Forbes*, May 21, 2013, http://www.forbes.com/sites/nathanvardi/2013/05/21/carl-icahn-and-herbalife-are-crushing-bill-ackman/ (accessed May 25, 2017).

O. C. Ferrell and Linda Ferrell, "Defining a Pyramid Scheme," PowerPoint presentation, University of New Mexico, 2013.

Paul R. La Monica, "Herbalife Stock Is Having an INSANE Month," *CNN Money*, March 24, 2015, http://money.cnn.com/2015/03/24/investing/herbalife-stock-bill-ackman-carl-icahn/ (accessed May 25, 2017).

Pyramid Scheme Alert, "China Leads the World in Fighting the Global Scourge of Pyramid Schemes," September

2009, http://pyramidschemealert.org/PSAMain/news/ChinaLeadsPyramidFight.html (accessed May 25, 2017).

Pyramid Scheme, "Funk & Wagnalls New World Encyclopedia," *EBSCOhost* (accessed April 20, 2013).

Rebecca McClay, "Herbalife Strikes Back at Ackman amid Reports of Federal Investigation," TheStreet, April 6, 2015, http://www.thestreet.com/story/13102435/1/herbalife-strikes-back-at-ackman-amid-at-reports-of-federal-investigation.html (accessed May 25, 2017).

Reuters and Fortune Editors, "Ackman renews attacks on Herbalife, says it will be gone within a year," *Fortune*, January 13, 2015, http://fortune.com/2015/01/13/ackman-renews-attacks-on-herbalife-says-it-will-be-gone-within-a-year/ (accessed May 25, 2017).

Richard Lee and Jason D. Schloetzer, "The Activism of Carl Icahn and Bill Ackman," Director Notes: The Conference Board, May 2014, No. DN-V6N10.

Scott Warren, "MLM Laws in China," Wellman & Warren Attorneys at Law, February 3, 2014, http://w-wlaw.com/mlm-laws-in-china/ (accessed May 25, 2017).

Steve Schaefer, "Ackman Takes Ax to Herbalife, Company Says It Is 'Not an Illegal Pyramid Scheme'," *Forbes*, 2012, 4.

Steve Schaefer, "Herbalife Posts Record Results, Raises Guidance," *Forbes*, April 29, 2013, http://www.forbes.com/sites/steveschaefer/2013/04/29/herbalife-posts-record-results-raises-guidance/ (accessed May 25, 2017).

Steven Pfeifer, "Latinos Crucial to Herbalife's Financial Health," *Los Angeles Times*, February 15, 2013, http://articles.latimes.com/2013/feb/15/business/la-fi-herbalife-latino-20130216 (accessed May 25, 2017).

Stuart Pfeifer, "Herbalife Now Making Its Products Available through Company Website," *Los Angeles Times*, April 6, 2015, http://www.latimes.com/business/la-fi-herbalife-online-20150407-story.html (accessed May 25, 2017).

Stuart Pfeifer, "Herbalife Shares Surge Past Price When Ackman Made Allegations," *Los Angeles Times*, May 6, 2013, http://articles.latimes.com/2013/may/06/business/la-fi-mo-herbalife-stock-price-20130506 (accessed May 25, 2017).

Stuart Pfiefer, "Consumer Group Urges FTC to Investigate Herbalife," *Los Angeles Times*, March 12, 2013, http://articles.latimes.com/2013/mar/12/business/la-fi-mo-consumer-group-urges-ftc-to-investigate-herbalife-20130312 (accessed May 25, 2017).

Stuart Pfiefer, "Rep. Linda Sanchez Asks FTC to Investigate Herbalife," *Los Angeles Times*, June 14, 2013, http://articles.latimes.com/2013/jun/14/business/la-fi-herbalife-ftc-20130614 (accessed May 25, 2017).

Svea Herbst-Bayliss, "Ackman Outspent by Herbalife in Lobbying," *Reuters*, March 9, 2014, http://www.reuters.com/article/2014/03/09/us-herbalife-idUSBREA280OH20140309 (accessed May 25, 2017).

Svea Herbst-Bayliss, "Ackman Says Herbalife Execs Are Hiring Their Own Lawyers," *Reuters*, April 13, 2015, http://www.reuters.com/article/2015/04/13/us-herbalife-ackman-idUSKBN0N428420150413 (accessed May 25, 2017).

Tabinda Hussain, "Hispanic Federation Urges FTC to Investigate Herbalife," *Value Walk*, May 20, 2013, http://www.valuewalk.com/2013/05/hispanic-federation-urges-ftc-to-investigate-herbalife/ (accessed May 25, 2017).

theflyonthewall.com, "Congresswoman asks FTC to Investigate Herbalife, NY Post Reports," *Yahoo! Finance*, June 13, 2013, http://finance.yahoo.com/news/congresswoman-asks-ftc-investigate-herbalife-101651927.html (accessed May 25, 2017).

William Pride and O.C. Ferrell, *Foundations of Marketing*, 5th ed. (Mason, OH: South-Western Cengage, 2013), 444.

World Federation of Direct Selling Association, "Objectives," http://www.wfdsa.org/about_wfdsa/?fa=objectives (accessed June 16, 2015).

Zachary Scheidt, "Capture Major Upside as Nu Skin Launches New Product," *Beta Fool*, June 14, 2013, http://beta.fool.com/traderzach/2013/06/14/capture-50-profits-as-nu-skin-launches-new-product/37167/?source=eogyholnk0000001 (accessed June 17, 2013).

Glossary

acid rain a phenomenon when nitrous oxides and sulfur dioxides emitted from manufacturing facilities react with air and rain

Act on the Protection of Personal Information (APPI) Japanese data regulation stipulating that all businesses servicing individuals in Japan, whether based in Japan or not, are required to disclose how personal data is being used and correct, suspend, or delete data if requested by a user

Affordable Clean Energy (ACE) rule a rule (replacing the EPA's Clean Power Plan that set mandatory guidelines on power plant emissions) giving more power at the state level to reduce emissions

algorithm a set of rules providing a procedure or formula for problem solving

ambient advertising a form of advertising where unconventional or unexpected messages are placed in a target market's social environment

artificial intelligence machines learning and performing tasks that typically require human intelligence by using algorithms

Better Business Bureau (BBB) a self-regulatory association supported by businesses

big data large structured and unstructured sets of data that can be analyzed to reveal information and associations

biodiversity the variety of living organisms found in a given area on Earth or on Earth as a whole and the ecological systems in which they live

bioenergy renewable energy made from biological waste

bioethics the study of ethical issues in the fields of medical treatment and research, including medicine, nursing, law, philosophy, and theology

biometric data digital data used for personal verification or identification that includes fingerprints, facial scans, retina scans, voice, and DNA

blockchain decentralized record-keeping technology that stores an immutable record of data blocks over time

board of directors a group of members who represent shareholders and oversee the firm's operations and legal and ethical compliance

boycott a form of consumer action in which consumers abstain from using, purchasing, or dealing with a company or other organization

bribery the practice of offering something, such as money, entertainment, travel, or other gifts to gain an illicit advantage from someone in authority

Bureau of Consumer Protection a bureau within the Federal Trade Commission (FTC) charged with protecting consumers against unfair, deceptive, or fraudulent practices

business ethics the principles and standards that guide behavior in the world of business

business ethics the principles and standards that guide the behavior of individuals and groups when carrying out tasks to meet business objectives

cap and trade programs programs that set carbon emissions limits (caps) for businesses, countries, or individuals. To legally emit beyond that limit, carbon credits must be purchased from another entity that did not pollute to its own limit

cause-related marketing ties an organization's products directly to a social concern

Caux Round Table Principles for Business principles for moral capitalism created by business leaders from all regions of the world who have a strong desire and interest in promoting socially responsible capitalism

Center for Global Development a nonprofit think tank in Washington, D.C., and London that works to reduce global poverty and improve lives through innovative economic research that drives better policy and practice by the world's top decision-makers

Certified Information Privacy Professional (CIPP) an information privacy credential from the International Association of Privacy Professionals (IAPP)

chief diversity officer (CDO) the corporate executive responsible for diversity and inclusion initiatives and results

chief privacy officer (CPO) high-level executives who are given broad powers to establish policies to protect consumer privacy and, in so doing, protect their companies from negative publicity and legal scrutiny

Children's Online Privacy and Protection Act (COPPA) a U.S. law which prohibits websites and internet providers from seeking personal information from children under the age of 13 without parental consent

civil regulations pressures exerted in society to encourage and persuade organizations to address issues in the social and physical environment

Clayton Antitrust Act   created to clarify the Sherman Antitrust Act and limit mergers and acquisitions, prohibit price discrimination, tying agreements, exclusive agreements, and the acquisition of stock in another corporation where the effect may be to hinder competition or create a monopoly

climate change   the alteration of weather patterns and temperature in an area or across the entire Earth due to global warming

Coalition for Environmentally Responsible Economies (CERES)   a union of businesses, consumer groups, environmentalists, and other stakeholders, who have established a set of goals for environmental performance

code of conduct   a written collection of the rules, principles, values, and expectations of employee behavior

codes of conduct   formal statements that describe what an organization expects of its employees; also called codes of ethics

collective bargaining   a negotiating process where employees work through their unions to establish employment contracts and conditions with their employers

Commitment to Development Index (CDI)   a ranking, produced by the Center for Global Development, of 27 developed nations by their contributions to and support of development in poorer, developing countries

Common Cause   a nonprofit, nonpartisan organization that fights corrupt government and special interests

common good   the development of social conditions that allow for societal welfare and fulfillment to be achieved

Communication on Progress   a required annual report of how a company that has committed to the Global Compact implements the 10 principles and supports the UN's developmental goals

community relations   the organizational function dedicated to building and maintaining relationships and trust with the community

community   members of society who are aware of, concerned with, or in some way affected by the operations and output of an organization

compliance officer   one who develops and oversees corporate compliance programs to ensure compliance with state and federal regulations

conflict of interest   an issue that arises when an individual has competing interests and must choose whether to advance his or her own interests, those of his or her organization, or those of some other group

conflicts of interest   using one's position within an organization to obtain personal gain, at the expense of the organization

consequentialism   a class of moral philosophy that considers a decision right or acceptable if it accomplishes a desired result, such as career growth, the realization of self-interest, or utility in a decision

Consumer Bill of Rights   a group of four consumers rights (to choose, to safety, to be informed, and to be heard) first introduced by U.S. President John F. Kennedy in 1962

Consumer Financial Protection Bureau (CFPB)   an independent agency within the Federal Reserve System that was established by the Dodd-Frank Act to regulate banks and other financial institutions by monitoring consumer financial products and services

consumer fraud   intentional deception to derive an unfair economic advantage over an organization

Consumer Product Safety Commission   the U.S. government commission charged with protecting the public from unreasonable risks of injury or death associated with the use of thousands of types of consumer products under the agency's jurisdiction

consumer protection laws   regulations enacted to protect vulnerable members of society with formal safeguards for consumers

consumer protest   a form of consumer action that involves the organized and public display of consumers' disapproval of a firm's actions

consumer relations   a firm's process for creating and maintaining a positive relationship with consumers by meeting customer needs

consumerism   the movement to protect consumers from an imbalance of power on the side of business and to maximize consumer welfare in the marketplace

consumers   individuals who purchase, use, and dispose of products for themselves and their households

conventional business partnerships (CBPs)   partnerships that promote efficiency in markets where competition does not exist; assumes government is inefficient and that a business organization provides the best solution

copyright infringement   the unauthorized execution of the rights reserved by a copyright holder

core competencies   unique advantages that differentiate a firm from its competitors

core practices   recognized best practices that are often encouraged by regulatory forces and industry trade associations

corporate accountability partnerships (CAPs)   focus on accountability and the setting of requirements and standards based on what society expects

corporate culture   shared values, attitudes, and beliefs that characterize members of an organization

corporate governance   a company's formal system of accountability, oversight, and control

corporate governance   formal system of oversight of, accountability for, and control over organizational decisions and resources

corporate public affairs activities   actions that build a relationship between a corporation and a governmental body or politician to mold and influence the decisions that the government makes to be in the best interest of corporations

corporate social responsibility partnerships (CSRPs)   voluntary and business-centered partnership providing resources for social initiatives, such as job training and entrepreneurial development, that contribute to a citizen's livelihood and therefore a stronger workforce and economic contagion

crisis management   the process of handling a high-impact event characterized by ambiguity and the need for swift action

cross-training   the process of ensuring that employees have the knowledge and skills to perform more than a single set of job duties

crowdfunding   the practice of funding a project or by securing relatively small donations from a large number of people

cultural intelligence (CQ)   the ability to interpret and adapt successfully to different national, organizational, and professional cultures

cybersquatter   an individual who deliberately registers web addresses that match or relate to other firms' trademarks and then attempts to sell the registration to the trademark owners

Data and Marketing Association (DMA)   a self-regulatory resource that assists its business members in becoming more efficient and up to date in marketing by relying on accurate consumer data and adjusting to new technology

dead zone   an area in a large body of water that has a reduced level of oxygen and increased algae blooms due to excessive nutrient pollution from human activities, which negatively affects marine life and can be toxic to humans as well

deep learning   a subset of AI that simulates how humans learn from experience by using algorithms that relate to the structure and function of the brain

Department of Labor   the U.S. federal agency charged with fostering, promoting, and developing the welfare of wage earners, job seekers, and retirees in the United States; improving working conditions; advancing opportunities for profitable employment; and assuring work-related benefits and rights

deregulation   changing or deleting existing laws or regulations to provide less oversight of business activities, operation, and outcomes

development   improvement in the economic, environmental, educational, and health conditions of a country

disruptive technology   new technology that displaces an established technology and changes an industry or a unique new product that creates a completely new industry

Dodd–Frank Wall Street Reform and Consumer Protection Act   legislation created to prevent financial crisis by increased financial deregulation, additional oversight of the industry, and preventative measures against unhealthy risk-taking and deceptive practices

downsizing   the process of making permanent reductions in an organization's labor force

duty of care   (also known as duty of diligence) the obligation of directors and officers to avoid ethical misconduct and provide leadership to prevent ethical misconduct in the organization

duty of loyalty   the obligation of directors and officers to make decisions in the interests of the corporation and its stakeholders

economic regulation   protection of competition to provide opportunity for organizations and individuals to be financially successful in order to create a strong economy

egoism   a philosophy that defines right or acceptable conduct in terms of the consequences for the individual

emotional intelligence   an important characteristic possessed by ethical leaders, referring to the skills to manage themselves and their relationships with others effectively

employee assistance program (EAP)   workplace program that provides employees with services to improve mental health and well-being

employee engagement   the connection that employees have with their employers that influences behavior, effort, and commitment

employee engagement   the psychological state in which employees feel a vested interest in the company's success and are motivated to perform at levels that exceed job requirements

employee stock ownership plans (ESOPs)   employment benefits programs that confer stock ownership to employees providing the opportunity to contribute to and benefit from organizational success

employee well-being   the health and wellness of employees, including how workers feel about their work and their working environment

employer of choice   an organization of any size in any industry that is able to attract, optimize, and retain the best employee talent over the long term

employment at will   a common-law doctrine that allows either the employer or the employee to terminate the relationship at any time, so long as it does not violate an employment contract so long as it does not violate an employment contract or law

enlightened capitalism   a theory of capitalism originally proposed by Adam Smith as "promoting the happiness of mankind" that emphasizes stakeholder concerns and issues

Environmental Protection Agency (EPA)   the most influential regulatory agency that deals with environmental issues and enforces environmental legislation in the United States

ergonomics   the design, arrangement, and use of equipment to maximize productivity and minimize fatigue and physical discomfort

ethical climate   the part of a firm's culture that focuses specifically on issues of appropriate conduct and right and wrong

ethical conflict   a situation where individuals and groups within a company do not embrace the same set of values

ethical culture   refers to the character of the decision-making process that employees use to determine if their responses to ethical issues are right or wrong

ethical diversity   refers to the fact that employee values often differ from person to person

ethical formalism   also known as *deontology*, class of moral philosophy that focuses on the rights of individuals and on the intentions associated with a particular behavior rather than on its consequences

ethical issue   a problem, situation, or opportunity requiring an individual, group, or organization to choose among several actions that must be evaluated as right or wrong, ethical or unethical

ethical misconduct disaster (EMD) an unexpected organizational crisis that results from employee misconduct, illegal activities such as fraud, or unethical decisions and that significantly disrupts operations and threatens or is perceived to threaten the firm's continuity of operations

Ethics & Compliance Initiative (ECI) a community of organizations that educates about regulatory compliance and best ethical practices

ethics codes guidelines that businesses create to maintain their company's values and hold employees and employers accountable to ethical standards

ethics officer a high-ranking person known to respect and understand legal and ethical standards

extrinsic motivation wanting to take action based on external factors

Fair Labor Association (FLA) works to end sweatshop conditions for factory workers; organizes universities, social groups, and socially responsible organizations to protect workers' rights

fair trade a trading partnership based on dialogue, transparency, and respect that seeks greater equity in international trade and contributes to sustainable development

Federal Communications Commission (FCC) the U.S. government commission charged with regulating interstate and international communications by radio, television, wire, satellite, and cable in all 50 states, the District of Columbia and U.S. territories

Federal Sentencing Guidelines for Organizations (FSGO) a set of standards developed by the U.S. Sentencing Commission and approved by Congress in November 1991 to streamline sentencing and punishment for organizational crimes and holds companies and employees responsible for misconduct

Federal Trade Commission (FTC) the U.S. government agency charged with protecting consumers and competition by preventing anticompetitive, deceptive, and unfair business practices through law enforcement, advocacy, and education about unduly burdening legitimate business activities

Federal Trade Commission Act a law enacted to further strengthen the antitrust provisions of the Sherman Antitrust Act and broadly prohibit unfair methods of competition

fiduciaries persons placed in positions of trust who use due care and loyalty in acting on behalf of the best interests of the organization

Food and Drug Administration (FDA) the U.S. government agency charged with protecting the public health by ensuring the safety, efficacy, and security of foods, drugs, cosmetics, biological products, medical devices, tobacco, veterinary products, and electronic products that give off radiation

Foreign Corrupt Practices Act (FCPA) maintains that it is illegal for individuals, firms, or third parties doing business in U.S. markets to, in the words of the law, "make payments to foreign government officials to assist in obtaining or retaining business"

Foreign Corrupt Practices Act prohibits bribery of foreign officials and requires accounting transparency

fraud any false communication that deceives, manipulates, or conceals facts to create a false impression when others are damaged or denied a benefit

full employment occurs when the available labor force is fully utilized and employers have difficulty finding employees to fill available positions

General Data Protection Regulation (GDPR) a European Union (EU) law that requires businesses to protect the personal data of EU citizens by standardizing laws and increasing privacy; U.S. organizations processing the data of individuals in the EU must comply with the regulation

genetically modified (GM) organisms organisms created through manipulating plant and animal DNA so as to produce a desired effect like resistance to pests and viruses, drought resistance, or high crop yield

gerrymandering the practice of manipulating district boundaries for partisan political advantage which ultimately has the power to greatly influence legislation

gig economy a labor market in which independent contractors offer their services to large and small companies or individuals for an agreed level of compensation

Global Compact an agreement which encourages organizations to commit to 10 common principles regarding human rights, labor, environment, and anticorruption, whereby effective and responsible business can be conducted on a global scale

Global Reporting Initiative (GRI) an independent international organization that provides standards for businesses and other organizations to assess their performance across an array of social responsibility indicators and seeks to provide transparency and accountability in sustainability reporting akin to that found in financial reporting

green marketing a strategic process involving stakeholder assessment to create meaningful, long-term relationships with customers while maintaining, supporting, and enhancing the natural environment

greenhouse effect when Earth's atmosphere becomes thick with carbon dioxide, other gasses, and substances which trap the Sun's heat making Earth's surface warmer

greenwashing misleading a consumer into thinking that a product is more environmentally friendly than it is

group polarization the tendency for a team to decide on a more extreme solution than an individual might choose on their own

groupthink a phenomenon whereby individuals go along with group decisions even when those decisions run counter to one's own values

hostile work environment sexual harassment a type of sexual harassment that involves epithets, slurs, negative stereotyping, intimidating acts, graphic materials that show hostility toward an individual or group, and other types of conduct that affect the employment situation

hostile work environment a kind of workplace environment where the conduct is unwelcome; severe, pervasive, and hostile such as to affect conditions of employment; and offensive to a reasonable person

identity fraud the use of someone's personal information to access money online

identity theft the access and theft of personal information, leading to identity fraud

impact investing investments made with the intention of generating positive and measurable social and environmental impact, as well as financial returns

insider trading the act of purchasing or selling a public company's security with access to nonpublic information about the company

intellectual property the ideas and creative materials developed to solve problems, carry out applications, educate, and entertain others

International Association of Privacy Professionals (IAPP) U.S. group responsible for developing and launching the first broad-based credentialing program in information privacy

Internet Corporation for Assigned Names and Numbers (ICANN) a nonprofit organization overseen by the U.S. Department of Commerce and charged with overseeing basic technical matters related to addresses on the internet

Internet of Things (IoT) the connectivity of devices such as security systems and electric appliances to provide the ability to send and receive information over the internet

interorganizational networks a set of organizations that are associated through shared or mutual affiliations and interests

intersectionality theory a theory which focuses on the multidimensional nature of identity, including class, gender, and race, and its effects on social dimensions of differences

intrinsic motivation wanting to take action based on internal factors

ISO 14000 a comprehensive set of environmental standards that encourage a cleaner, safer, and healthier world developed by the International Organization for Standardization

justice theory a class of moral philosophy that relates to evaluations of fairness, or the disposition to deal with the perceived injustices of others

Kyoto Protocol a treaty among industrialized nations aimed at slowing global warming

leader–follower congruence when leaders and their followers (i.e., employees) share the same organizational vision, ethical expectations, and objectives

legal responsibility the most basic expectation that a company must comply with the law

legitimacy the perception or belief that a stakeholder's actions are proper, desirable, or appropriate in a given context

license to operate permission to conduct a business activity, subject to regulation by the licensing authority

living wage an hourly wage on which it is possible to live according to minimum standards

lobbying the process of working to persuade public and/or government officials to favor a particular position in decision-making

Machiavellianism the use of duplicity or cunning to achieve business goals

machine learning a subset of AI that explains the application of AI using algorithms and data in order to allow the computer to learn without being programmed for a specific task

mandated boundaries externally imposed boundaries of conduct, such as laws, rules, regulations, and other requirements

marketplace of ideas the assumption that ideas compete against one another for truth and acceptability

microlending small loans provided to individuals and businesses, typically in impoverished areas, that are unable to obtain loans from traditional lending institutions

minimum wage the lowest hourly wage that may be legally paid to employees

mission statement a summary of a company's aims and values

monopoly a market type in which just one business provides a good or service in a given market

moral philosophies principles, or rules, which individuals apply in deciding what is right or wrong; *morals* refers to individuals' philosophies about what is right or wrong

National Advertising Division (NAD) an investigatory branch of the National Advertising Review Council (NARC) that provides reviews of advertisements for accuracy and truthfulness and resolves disputes

neighbor of choice an organization that builds and sustains trust with the community through employment opportunities, economic development, and financial contribution to education, health, artistic, and recreational activities of the community

nongovernmental organizations (NGOs) nonprofit, citizen-based groups that function independent of government

normative approaches provide a vision and recommendations for improving ethical decision-making; are concerned with how organizational decision-makers *should* approach an ethical issue

Occupational Safety and Health Administration (OSHA) the U.S. government agency charged with ensuring safe and healthful working conditions for working men and women by setting and enforcing standards and by providing training, outreach, education, and assistance

opportunity a set of conditions that limits barriers or provides rewards

organizational ethics and compliance programs programs developed by an organization to establish, communicate, and monitor ethical values and legal requirements that characterize its history, culture, industry, and operating environment

organizational values   abstract ideals distinct from individual values

organizational, (corporate) culture   a set of values, beliefs, and artifacts shared by members or employees of an organization

outsourcing   the practice of hiring an outside individual or organization to perform tasks and functions traditionally performed by company employees

ozone   a highly reactive form of oxygen that is a critical component of the stratosphere where it encircles the Earth in a deep layer that protects the planet from the Sun's ultraviolet radiation

particulate matter (PM)   a mixture of solid particles and liquid droplets found in the air; also known as particle pollution

patent laws   laws that grant the developer a period of time (usually 20 years) during which no other firm can use the same technology without the patent holder's consent

philanthropic activities   efforts made by a company to improve human welfare

philanthropy   acts such as donations to charitable organizations to improve quality of life, reduce government involvement, develop employee leadership skills, and create an ethical culture to act as buffer to organizational misconduct

philanthropy   the desire to improve the welfare of others through donations of money, resources, or effort

political action committees (PACs)   organizations that solicit donations from individuals and then contribute these funds to candidates running for political office

power   the extent to which a stakeholder can gain access to coercive, utilitarian, or symbolic means to impose or communicate its views to an organization

primary stakeholders   people or groups who are fundamental to a company's operations and survival; these include shareholders and investors, employees, customers, suppliers, and public stakeholders, such as government and the community

Principle of Equal Freedom   asserts that all persons must have equality under the law

principles   specific and pervasive boundaries for behavior that are universal and absolute and often form the basis for rules

privacy issues   issues that businesses must address that include the monitoring of employees' use of available technology, consumer privacy, and online marketing

private interest groups   people with a shared interest who work to influence public policy in their favor

privatization   a process that occurs when public operations are sold to private entities. Public-private partnerships count as partial privatization

product liability   a business's legal responsibility for the performance of its products

product placement   a type of advertising in which a company pays for its product to be viewed in a movie, television show, or other form of media

proxy access   the ability of long-term shareholders to nominate alternative candidates for the board of directors on the company's annual shareholder meeting ballot

proxy   an agent legally authorized to act on behalf of another person/party. Used as a voting mechanism when a shareholder is not present at a shareholder's meeting

psychological contract   largely unwritten, it includes beliefs, perceptions, expectations, and obligations that make up the agreement between individuals and the organizations that employ them

Public Company Accounting Oversight Board (PCAOB)   required by the Sarbanes-Oxley Act, a private, nonprofit company that provides oversight of the accounting firms that audit public companies and sets standards for the auditors in these firms.

puffery   exaggerated statements that no reasonable person would believe to be fact

quality of life   a measure of social, physical, economic, and environmental health conditions affecting an individual or group

quid pro quo sexual harassment   a type of sexual extortion where there is a proposed or explicit exchange of job benefits for sexual favors

recycling   the reprocessing of materials, especially steel, aluminum, paper, glass, rubber, and some plastics, for reuse

regulation   the act of creating and enforcing rules for a specific purpose

reputation management   the process of building and sustaining a company's good name and generating positive feedback from stakeholders

resource advantage theory   a theory stating that the value of a resource is viewed relative to its potential to create competitive differentiation or customer value

reverse mentoring   organizational mentoring program where less experienced employees mentor more experienced employees

rightsizing   the process of reorganizing or restructuring an organization's labor force

risk management   hedging uncertainty while ensuring that leadership is taking the appropriate steps to move the organization and its strategy forward

Sarbanes-Oxley (SOX) Act   legislation created to protect investors by improving the accuracy and reliability of corporate disclosures

secondary stakeholders   people or groups who do not typically engage in direct transactions with a company and thus are not essential for its survival; these include the media, trade associations, and special-interest groups

self-regulation   when an industry-level organization, such as a trade association or professional society, creates a set of rules and enforces regulations within its industry

sexual harassment   any repeated, unwanted behavior of a sexual nature perpetrated upon one individual by another; it may be verbal, visual, written, or physical and can occur between people of different genders or those of the same gender

sexual harassment unwelcome sexual advances, requests for sexual favors, and other verbal or physical conduct of a sexual nature which, when submitted to or rejected, explicitly or implicitly affects an individual's employment, unreasonably interferes with an individual's work performance, or creates an intimidating, hostile, or offensive work environment

shareholder lawsuits lawsuits brought against a key member of a company by a shareholder or group of shareholders suing on behalf of the corporation

shareholder model of corporate governance founded in classic economic precepts, a model that focuses on making decisions toward what is in the best interest of investors

shareholder resolutions nonbinding, yet important, statements about shareholder concerns

shareholder any person or entity that owns at least one share of a company's stock

sharing economy a labor market in which independent contractors "rent out" underutilized resources such as their cars or lodging to earn extra income

Sherman Antitrust Act the principal tool used to prevent businesses from restraining trade and monopolizing markets

significant others superiors, peers, subordinates, and others in an organization who influence the ethical decision-making process

single-use plastics also known as *disposable plastics*, these materials are used only once before they are discarded or recycled

smart devices devices connected to other devices on networks that are capable of communication and computation for different wireless protocols, such as Wi-Fi and Bluetooth, operating interactively

social audit the process of assessing and reporting a firm's performance in adopting a strategic focus for fulfilling the economic, legal, ethical, and philanthropic social responsibilities expected of it by its stakeholders

social capital an asset that resides in relationships and is characterized by mutual goals and trust

social contract an implicit agreement between members of society that establishes the rights and duties of each party to the agreement

social economy partnerships (SEPs) partnerships that pursue alternatives to conventional corporations and profit maximization and have a distinctly social purpose, use democratic governance, and cooperate with other social economy partnerships

social entrepreneurship when an entrepreneur founds a business with the purpose of creating social value rather than making money

social exchange theory a theory stating that social behavior is determined by social exchanges between different parties

social regulation protection and support for consumers providing safe work conditions, equal opportunity, and healthcare

social responsibility a strategic focus for fulfilling economic, legal, ethical, and philanthropic responsibilities, can also be referred to as corporate social responsibility (CSR) when adopted by a business

stakeholder engagement the organizational process of involving stakeholders who may be affected by the decisions it makes or may influence the content and implementation of its decisions

stakeholder interaction model a model that conceptualizes the two-way relationships between a firm and a host of stakeholders

stakeholder map a company-specific map that names its primary and secondary stakeholders, identifies key issues, and examines relationships and networks between the organization and stakeholders

stakeholder model of corporate governance a model where the business is accountable to all its stakeholders, not just shareholders

stakeholder orientation the aim to benefit all parties affected by the success or failure of an organization

stakeholder orientation the degree to which a firm understands and addresses stakeholder demands

stakeholders constituents who have an interest or stake in a company's products, industry, markets, and outcomes

stock option a financial tool that gives a shareholder the right to buy or sell a stock at a set price for a certain amount of time

strategic philanthropy the synergistic use of an organization's core competencies and resources to address key stakeholders' interests and to achieve both organizational and social benefits

subcontracting the practice of hiring an outside individual or organization to perform specific tasks and functions in partial fulfillment of a larger company contract

supply chain management the coordination of all the activities involved with the flow of supplies and products from raw materials through to the end customer

sustainability a company's economic, environmental, and social performance

sustainability the potential for long-term well-being of the natural environment, including all biological entities, as well as the interaction among nature and individuals, organizations, and business strategies

sustainable business practices actions a company takes to reduce their environmental impact and that may lower costs and improve competitive advantage, stakeholder relationships, and the company's reputation and branding

technology assessment a procedure used by companies to calculate the effects of new technologies by foreseeing the effects new products and processes will have on their firm's operations, on other business organizations, and on society in general

technology the application of knowledge, including the processes and applications to solve problems, perform tasks, and create new methods to obtain desired outcomes

time theft a major form of observed misconduct including late arrivals, long lunch breaks, leaving early, day dreaming, excessive socializing, and use of social media that costs companies billions annually

Title VII of the Civil Rights Act of 1964   prohibits employment discrimination on the basis of race, national origin, color, religion, and gender, and applies to employers with 15 or more employees, including state and local governments

trade associations   groups formed by members of industries to promote the interests of their industry through means such as lobbying, publishing, and advertising

transactional leadership   a leadership style that attempts to create employee satisfaction through negotiating for levels of performance or "bartering" for desired behaviors

transformational leadership   a leadership style that tries to raise the level of commitment of employees and creates greater trust and motivation

Troubled Assets Recovery Program (TARP)   a law authorizing the U.S. Treasury to purchase up to $700 billion of troubled assets such as mortgage-based securities

trusts   organizations established to gain control of a product market or industry by eliminating competition

U.S. Global Climate Change Initiative   a voluntary protocol for reporting greenhouse gases

U.S. Securities and Exchange Commission (SEC)   the government agency that oversees the operations and protection of securities markets and investors

unconscious bias   a lack of awareness of one's own unconscious attitudes and associations

underemployment   occurs when employees engage in work that requires skills or education below their qualifications, or when employees want to work on a full-time basis but can find only part-time positions

unemployment rate   the percentage of the available labor force that is currently unemployed

urgency   the time sensitivity and the importance of the claim to the stakeholder

utilitarianism   a consequentialist philosophy that is concerned with seeking the greatest good for the greatest number of people

values   norms that are socially enforced, such as integrity, accountability, and trust

vesting   the legal right to pension plan benefits

virtue ethics   adhering to general ideas, social values, and good character for appropriate ethical behavior

vision statement   a description of a company's current and future objectives to help align decisions with their philosophy and goals

voluntary practices   the beliefs, values, and voluntary responsibilities of an organization

volunteerism   when employees spend company-supported time in support of social causes

warranty   a written guarantee issued at the time of purchase that promises to repair or replace the purchased product within a certain time frame

whistleblower   a person who exposes an employer's wrongdoing to outsiders, such as the media or government regulatory agencies

work/life programs   programs that assist employees in balancing work responsibilities with personal and family responsibilities

Worker Adjustment and Retraining Notification (WARN) Act   a federal law requiring that U.S. employers give at least 60 days' advance notice if a layoff will affect 500 or more employees or more than one-third of the workforce

workforce reduction   the process of eliminating employment positions

workplace diversity   recruiting and retaining individuals regardless of age, gender, ethnicity, physical or mental ability, or other characteristics

workplace inclusion   organizational (corporate) culture that ensures that policies, procedures, and practices are fair, transparent, supportive, and empowering for all employees

zero tolerance   the practice of applying penalties to even minor infractions of policy

Notes

Chapter 1

1. Adele Peters, "Ikea Is Quickly Shifting to a Zero-Emissions Delivery Fleet," *Fast Company*, September 13, 2018, https://www.fastcompany.com/90236539/ikea-is-quickly-shifting-to-a-zero-emissions-delivery-fleet (accessed September 24, 2018); "New WRI Project to Bring Clean Electricity to 1 Million People in India and East Africa," *IKEA Foundation*, May 23, 2018, https://www.ikeafoundation.org/pressrelease/new-wri-project-to-bring-clean-electricity-to-1-million-people-in-india-and-east-africa/ (accessed September 24, 2018); "Why CSR Is Becoming a Crucial Part of IKEA's Long-Term Recruitment Strategy," *Satell Institute*, January 31, 2018, https://www.satellinstitute.org/why-csr-is-becoming-a-crucial-part-of-ikeas-long-term-recruitment-strategy/ (accessed September 24, 2018); "IKEA Vision, Culture, and Values," *IKEA*, https://ikea.jobs.cz/en/vision-culture-and-values/ (accessed September 24, 2018); "IKEA Address Ethical and Social Responsibility Challenges," *Daniels Funds Ethics Initiative*, 2014, https://danielsethics.mgt.unm.edu/pdf/ikea.pdf (accessed September 24, 2018); "History," IKEA Foundation, https://www.ikeafoundation.org/about-us-ikea-foundation/history/ (accessed September 26, 2018).
2. O. C. Ferrell, Dana E. Harrison, Linda Ferrell, and Joe F. Hair, "Business Ethics, Corporate Social Responsibility, and Brand Attitudes: An Exploratory Study," *Journal of Business Research* 95 (February 2019): 491–501.
3. UNM Daniels Fund Ethics Initiative, "VW Cheats Environmental Expectations," 2015, https://danielsethics.mgt.unm.edu/pdf/vw-mini-case.pdf (accessed June 24, 2016); William Boston and William Wilkes, "Volkswagen's Ex-CEO Martin Winterkorn Faces Probe over Emissions Scandal," *The Wall Street Journal*, June 18, 2016, http://www.wsj.com/articles/former-volkswagen-ceo-martin-winterkorn-faces-market-manipulation-probe-in-germany-1466432926 (accessed June 24, 2016); "How VW Paid $25 Billion for 'Dieselgate'—and Got Off Easy," *Fortune*, February 6, 2018, http://fortune.com/2018/02/06/volkswagen-vw-emissions-scandal-penalties/ (accessed November 10, 2018).
4. "BDS Movement Targets Caterpillar, Volvo After Israeli Forces Attack Protesters in Khan Al-Ahmar," *TeleSUR*, October 20, 2018, https://www.telesurenglish.net/news/BDS-Movement-Targets-Caterpillar-Volvo-After-Israeli-Forces-Attack-Protesters-in-Khan-Al-Ahmar-20181020-0009.html (accessed August 10, 2019).
5. Allen St. John, "Equifax Settlement: What's in It for Consumers," *Consumer Reports*, July 22, 2019, https://www.consumerreports.org/credit-bureaus/equifax-settlement/ (accessed August 14, 2019).
6. "The FTC Is Investigating the Equifax Breach. Here's Why That's a Big Deal," *Washington Post*, September 14, 2017, https://www.washingtonpost.com/news/the-switch/wp/2017/09/14/the-ftc-confirms-its-investigating-the-equifax-breach-adding-to-a-chorus-of-official-criticism/?utm_term=.e512a5f9f9c4 (accessed August 10, 2019).
7. "Ethisphere Announces 2011 World's Most Ethical Companies," *BusinessWire,* March 15, 2011, http://www.businesswire.com/news/home/20110315006776/en/Ethisphere-Announces-2011-World%E2%80%99s-Ethical-Companies#.U5iTXKLb4R4 (accessed June 24, 2016).
8. Federal Trade Commission, "Bureau of Consumer Protection," https://www.ftc.gov/about-ftc/bureaus-offices/bureau-consumer-protection (accessed November 10, 2018).
9. "Deconstructing CSR: Corporate Philanthropy," http://www.ethicalcorp.com/deconstructing-csr-corporate-philanthropy (accessed November 10, 2018).
10. Dima Jamali and Ramez Mirshak, "Corporate Social Responsibility (CSR): Theory and Practice in a Developing Country Context," *Journal of Business Ethics*, 72(3), 243–262.
11. E. R. Pedersen, "Modelling CSR: How Managers Understand the Responsibilities of Business Towards Society," *Journal of Business Ethics*, 2010, 91(2), 155–166.
12. Milton Friedman, *Capitalism and Freedom* (Chicago: University of Chicago Press, 1962).
13. Clive Crook, "Why Good Corporate Citizens Are a Public Menace," *National Journal*, April 24, 1999, 1087; Charles Handy, "What's a Business For?" *Harvard Business Review* 80 (December 2002): 49–55.
14. BMW, "BMW Social Responsibility," https://www.bmwusfactory.com/sustainability/social-responsibility/ (accessed August 10, 2019).
15. Associated Press, "BBB Expels Largest Bureau over Pay-to-Play Charges," Fox News, March 12, 2013, http://www.foxnews.com/us/2013/03/12/bbb-expels-largest-bureau-over-pay-to-play-charges.html (accessed June 24, 2016).
16. Nancy J. Miller and Terry L. Besser, "The Importance of Community Values in Small Business Strategy Formation: Evidence from Rural Iowa," *Journal of Small Business Management* 38 (January 2000): 68–85; James Knight and Mary Kate O'Riley, "Local Heroes," *Director* 55 (February 2002): 28.
17. "2018 Small Business Profile," U.S. Small Business Administration, https://www.sba.gov/sites/default/files/advocacy/2018-Small-Business-Profiles-US.pdf (accessed September 17, 2019).
18. Hershey, "About Hershey: Corporate Social Responsibility," http://www.hersheypa.com/about_hershey/about_csr.php (accessed June 24, 2016).
19. Herman Miller, "Our Values," https://www.hermanmiller.com/our-values/ (accessed July 31, 2019).
20. "Press—Awards," Herman Miller Inc., http://www.hermanmiller.com/about-us/press.html (accessed June 3, 2014).
21. Jim Carlton, "New Leaf: Once Targeted by Protestors, Home Depot Plays Green Role," *The Wall Street Journal*, August 6, 2004, A1.
22. Starbucks, "Starbucks Ethical Sourcing of Sustainable Products," https://www.starbucks.com/responsibility (accessed July 31, 2019).
23. Archie Carroll, "The Four Faces of Corporate Citizenship," *Business and Society Review* (January 1, 1998): 1; Naomi Gardberg and Charles Fombrun, "Corporate Citizenship: Creating Intangible Assets Across Institutional Environments," *Academy of Management Review* 31 (April 2006): 329–336.
24. The Coca-Cola Company, "An Ambitious Goal: Reducing Carbon in Our Value Chain," https://www.coca-colacompany.com/stories/an-ambitious-goal-reducing-carbon-in-our-value-chain (accessed July 31, 2019).
25. Transparency International, "Corruption Perceptions Index 2013," http://cpi.transparency.org/cpi2013/results/ (accessed June 24, 2016).
26. Direct Selling Association, "Code of Ethics," https://www.dsa.org/consumerprotection/code-of-ethics (accessed July 30, 2019); World Federation of Direct Selling Associations, "Direct Selling Code of Ethics," https://wfdsa.org/download/resources/resources_for_dsas_and_member_companies/Code-of-Ethics-Booklet-2017.pdf (accessed July 31, 2019).
27. UPS Foundation, *2017 Social Impact Report*, https://sustainability.ups.com/media/2017-social-impact-report.pdf (accessed August 12, 2019).
28. Barbara W. Altman, "Transformed Corporate Community Relations: A Management Tool for Achieving Corporate Citizenship," *Business & Society Review* 102/103, no. 1 (March 1999): 43; Carroll, "Four Faces of Corporate Citizenship."

29. Christopher N. Osher and Jennifer Brown, "Drug Firms Have Used Dangerous Tactics to Drive Sales to Treat Kids," *Denver Post*, April 14, 2014, http://www.denverpost.com/investigations/ci_25561024/drug-firms-have-used-dangerous-tactics-drive-sales (accessed June 24, 2016).

30. Aaron Kessler, Elizabeth Cohen, and Katherine Grise, "The More Opioids Doctors Prescribe, the More Money They Make," *CNN*, https://www.cnn.com/2018/03/11/health/prescription-opioid-payments-eprise/index.html (accessed August 12, 2019).

31. S. D. Hunt, *A General Theory of Competition: Resources, Competences, Productivity, Economic Growth* (Thousand Oaks, CA: SAGE Publications, 2000).

32. "Method: Our Story," https://methodhome.com/about-us/ (accessed August 10, 2019).

33. R. Edward Freeman, *Strategic Management: A Stakeholder Approach* (Boston: Pitman, 1984).

34. C. J. Palus and V. Asif, *Exploring Shared Value: Use Inter-Organizational Networks as a Strategy for Business Success and Positive Societal Impact* (Greensboro, NC: Center for Creative Leadership, 2014).

35. Kingfisher, "Delivering Value," http://www.kingfisher.com/files/reports/annual_report_2012/business_review/delivering_value/ (accessed June 24, 2016); Kingfisher, "Net Positive," http://www.kingfisher.com/netpositive/index.asp?pageid=1 (accessed June 24, 2016).

36. Edward S. Mason, "Introduction," in *The Corporation in Modern Society*, ed. Edward S. Mason (Cambridge, MA: Harvard University Press, 1959), 1–24.

37. Isabelle Maignan and O. C. Ferrell, "Measuring Corporate Citizenship in Two Countries: The Case of the United States and France," *Journal of Business Ethics* 23 (February 2000): 283; Robert J. Samuelson, "R.I.P.: The Good Corporation," *Newsweek*, July 5, 1993, 41.

38. Charles W. Wooten and Christie L. Roszkowski, "Legal Aspects of Corporate Governance in Early American Railroads," *Business and Economic History* 28 (Winter 1999): 325–326.

39. Ralph Estes, *Tyranny of the Bottom Line* (San Francisco: Berrett-Koehler, 1996); David Finn, *The Corporate Oligarch* (New York: Simon & Schuster, 1969).

40. Marina v. N. Whitman, *New World, New Rules* (Boston: Harvard Business School Press, 1999).

41. Mason, "Introduction."

42. Carl Kaysen, "The Corporation: How Much Power? What Scope?" in *The Corporation in Modern Society*, ed. Edward S. Mason (Cambridge, MA: Harvard University Press, 1959), 85–105.

43. David M. Gordon, *Fat and Mean: The Corporate Squeeze of Working Americans and the Myth of Managerial "Downsizing"* (New York: Free Press, 1996).

44. Richard Leider, *The Power of Purpose: Creating Meaning in Your Life and Work* (San Francisco: Barrett-Koehler, 1997).

45. David J. Lynch, "Big Banks: Now Even Too Bigger to Fail," *Businessweek*, April 19, 2012, http://www.businessweek.com/articles/2012-04-19/big-banks-now-even-too-bigger-to-fail (accessed June 24, 2016).

46. Sara Castellanos, "By 2025, Machines Will Perform Half of Today's Workplace Tasks," *The Wall Street Journal*, September 18, 2018, https://blogs.wsj.com/cio/2018/09/18/by-2025-machines-will-perform-half-of-todays-workplace-tasks/ (accessed October 1, 2018).

47. "Here to Help," *The Economist*, March 31, 2018: 40–41.

48. Vipal Monga, "Need an Accountant? Try a Robot Instead," *The Wall Street Journal*, March 7, 2017, https://blogs.wsj.com/cfo/2017/03/07/need-an-accountant-try-a-robot-instead/ (accessed October 1, 2018).

49. Jimmy Song, "Why Blockchain is Hard," *Medium*, https://medium.com/@jimmysong/why-blockchain-is-hard-60416ea4c5c (accessed October 2, 2018).

50. Angus Loten, "Walmart Makes Blockchain a Requirement for Veggie Suppliers," *The Wall Street Journal*, September 25, 2018, https://blogs.wsj.com/cio/2018/09/25/the-morning-download-walmart-makes-blockchain-a-requirement-for-veggie-suppliers/ (accessed October 1, 2018).

51. Zach Church, "Blockchain, Explained," MIT Sloan School of Management, http://mitsloan.mit.edu/newsroom/articles/blockchain-explained/ (accessed August 28, 2018).

52. Martin Wolf, "Comment and Analysis: The Big Lie of Global Inequality," *Financial Times*, February 9, 2000, 25.

53. Edelman, *2016 Edelman Trust Barometer Global Report*, http://www.edelman.com/insights/intellectual-property/2016-edelman-trust-barometer/global-results/ (accessed June 24, 2016).

54. M. N. Graham Dukes, "Accountability of the Pharmaceutical Industry," *Lancet*, November 23, 2002, 1682–1684; Elizabeth Olson, "Global Trade Negotiations Are Making Little Progress," *The New York Times*, December 7, 2002, C3; Robert Pear, "Investigators Find Repeated Deception in Ads for Drugs," *The New York Times*, December 4, 2002, A22.

55. John Dalla Costa, *The Ethical Imperative: Why Moral Leadership Is Good Business* (Reading, MA: Addison-Wesley, 1998).

56. Nestlé, "Nestlé's Corporate Business Principles," http://www.nestle.com/investors/corporate-governance/businessprinciples (accessed August 12, 2019).

57. The Coca-Cola Company, "Regional Sustainability Reports," October 23, 2013, http://www.coca-colacompany.com/sustainability/regional-sustainability-reports (accessed June 3, 2014).

58. S. A. Anwar, "APEC: Evidence and Policy Scenarios," *Journal of International Marketing and Marketing Research* 27 (October 2002): 141–153; Richard Feinberg, "Two Leading Lights of Humane Globalisation," *Singapore Straits Times*, February 21, 2000, 50.

59. Nicole Fallon, "15 Great Examples of Socially Responsible Businesses," *Business News Daily*, November 21, 2013, http://www.businessnews-daily.com/5499-examples-socially-responsible-businesses.html (accessed June 24, 2016); SurveyMonkey, "SurveyMonkey Contribute," http://help.surveymonkey.com/articles/en_US/kb/SurveyMonkey-Contribute (accessed June 24, 2016).

60. Ibid.

61. Andreas Georg Scherer and Guido Palzaao, *Handbook of Research on Global Corporate Citizenship* (Cheltenham, UK: Edward Elgar, 2008).

62. Nielsen, "Nielsen Identifies Attributes of the Global, Socially-Conscious Consumer," March 27, 2012, http://www.nielsen.com/us/en/press-room/2012/nielsen-identifies-attributes-of-the-global--socially-conscious-.html (accessed June 24, 2016).

63. Frederick Reichheld, *The Loyalty Effect* (Cambridge, MA: Harvard Business School, 1996); Jeffrey S. Harrison and R. Edward Freeman, "Stakeholders, Social Responsibility, and Performance: Empirical Evidence and Theoretical Perspectives," *Academy of Management Journal* 42 (October 1999): 479.

64. Stephen R. Covey, "Is Your Company's Bottom Line Taking a Hit?" *PRNewswire*, June 4, 1998, http://www.prnewswire.com; Terry W. Loe, "The Role of Ethical Climate in Developing Trust, Market Orientation, and Commitment to Quality," unpublished Ph.D. dissertation, University of Memphis, 1996.

65. Ethics Resource Center, *National Business Ethics Survey of the U.S. Workforce* (Arlington, VA: Ethics Resource Center, 2014).

66. Cone Communications, *2013 Cone Communication Social Impact Study* (Boston: Cone Communications Public Relations and Marketing, 2013), 15.

67. Carmen I. Mal, Gary Davies, and Audra Diers-Lawson, "Through the Looking Glass: The Factors That Influence Consumer Trust and Distrust in Brands," *Psychology and Marketing* 35 (December 2018): 936–947.

68. Ibid.

69. Alsop, "Corporate Reputations Are Earned with Trust, Reliability, Study Shows," http://interactive.wsj.com.

70. "Richard Branson Reveals His Customer Service Secrets," *Forbes*, May 8, 2013, http://www.youtube.com/watch?v=Fy4lYDN1gz4 (accessed July 6, 2016).

71. Rachel W. Y. Yee, Andy C. L. Yeung, and T. C. Edwin Cheng, "An Empirical Study of Employee Loyalty, Service Quality and Firm Performance in the Service Industry," *International Journal of Performance Economics* 124, no. 1 (March 2010): 109–120.

72. C. B. Bhattacharya, Sankar Sen, and Daniel Korschun, "Using Corporate Social Responsibility to Win the War for Talent," *MIT Sloan Management Review*, Winter 2008, http://sloanreview.mit.edu/article/using-corporate-social-responsibility-to-win-the-war-for-talent/ (accessed July 6, 2016).

73. Tony Schwartz and Christine Porath, "Why You Hate Work," *The New York Times*, May 30, 2014, http://www.nytimes.com/2014/06/01/opinion/sunday/why-you-hate-work.html?_r=0 (accessed July 6, 2016).

74. Jane Collier and Rafael Esteban, "Corporate Social Responsibility and Employee Commitment," *Business Ethics: A European Review* 16 (January 2007):19–33.

75. John Galvin, "The New Business Ethics," *SmartBusinessMag. com*, June 2000, 97.

76. Paul Ziobro, "Target Earnings Slide 46% After Data Breach," *The Wall Street Journal*, February 26, 2014, http://online.wsj.com/news/articles/

SB100014240527023042556045794066 94 182132568 (accessed July 6, 2016).

77. Dan Burrows, "Warren Buffett Buys a Stake in Verizon, Sells a Chunk of GM," *Investor Place*, May 16, 2014, http://investorplace. com/2014/05/warren-buffett-verizon-vz-stock-gm/#.V32MCnkUVVI (accessed July 6, 2016).

78. David Rynecki, "Here Are 8 Easy Ways to Lose Your Shirt in Stocks," *USA Today*, June 26, 1998, 3B.

79. "Investment Club Numbers Decline; Crisis of Confidence Caused Many to Take Their Money and Run," *Investor Relations Business*, September 23, 2002, 1; Charles Jaffe, "Securities Industry Aims to Renew Trust; Leaders Face Challenge of Rebuilding Investor Confidence Amid Slump," *Boston Globe*, November 8, 2002, E1.

80. Isabelle Maignan, O. C. Ferrell, and G. Tomas Hult, "Corporate Citizenship: Antecedents and Business Benefits," *Journal of the Academy of Marketing Science* 24, no. 4 (1999): 455–469.

81. S. B. Graves and S. A. Waddock, "Institutional Owners and Corporate Social Performance: Maybe Not So Myopic After All," *Proceedings of the International Association for Business and Society*, San Diego, 1993; Ronald M. Roman, Sefa Hayibor, and Bradley R. Agle, "The Relationship Between Social and Financial Performance," *Business and Society* 38 (March 1999); W. Gary Simpson and Theodor Kohers, "The Link Between Corporate Social and Financial Performance: Evidence from the Banking Industry," *Journal of Business Ethics* 35 (January 2002): 97–109; Curtis Verschoor and Elizabeth A. Murphy, "The Financial Performance of U.S. Firms and Those with Global Prominence: How Do the Best Corporate Citizens Rate?" *Business and Society Review* 197 (Fall 2002): 371–380; S. Waddock and S. Graves, "The Corporate Social Performance-Financial Performance Link," *Strategic Management Journal* 18 (1997): 303–319.

82. Chris C. Verschoor, "A Study of the Link Between a Corporation's Financial Performance and Its Commitment to Ethics," *Journal of Business Ethics* 31 (October 1998): 1509.

83. Shawn L. Berman, Andrew C. Wicks, Suresh Kotha, and Thomas M. Jones, "Does Stakeholder Orientation Matter? The Relationship Between Stakeholder Management Models and Firm Financial Performance," *Academy of Management Journal* 42 (October 1999): 502–503.

84. Roman et al., "The Relationship Between Social and Financial Performance."

85. Melissa A. Baucus and David A. Baucus, "Paying the Payer: An Empirical Examination of Longer-Term Financial Consequences of Illegal Corporate Behavior," *Academy of Management Journal* 40 (1997): 129–151.

86. Marc Orlitzky and Diane L. Swanson, *Toward Integrative Corporate Citizenship: Research Advances in Corporate Social Performance* (New York: Palgrave Macmillan, 2008).

87. K. J. Arrow, *The Limits of Organization* (New York: W. W. Norton, 1974), 23, 26; D. C. North, *Institutions, Institutional Change, and Economic Performance* (Cambridge: Cambridge University Press, 1990).

88. Shelby D. Hunt, "Resource-Advantage Theory and the Wealth of Nations: Developing the Socio-Economic Research Tradition," *Journal of Socio-Economics* 26 (1997): 335–357.

89. North, *Institutions*, 9.

90. L. E. Harrison, *Who Prospers? How Cultural Values Shape Economic and Political Success* (New York: Basic Books, 1992), 16.

91. Edelman, "2019 Edelman Trust Barometer." https://www.edelman.com/ sites/g/files/aatuss191/files/2019-02/2019_Edelman_Trust_Barometer_ Global_Report.pdf (accessed August 12, 2019).

92. Hunt, "Resource-Advantage Theory and the Wealth of Nations," 351–352.

93. Cummins, "Sustainability at Cummins," http://www.cummins. com/ global-impact/sustainability (accessed July 6, 2016); Ethisphere Institute, "World's Most Ethical Companies® Honorees," 2016, http:// worldsmostethicalcompanies.ethisphere. com/honorees/ (accessed July 6, 2016); Cummins, Cummins Engines website, https:// cumminsengines.com/ (accessed July 6, 2016).

94. Cummins, "Cummins Named to Ethical Companies List for 12th Year in a Row," https://www.cummins.com/news/2019/03/05/cummins- named-ethical-companies-list-12th-year-row (accessed July 31, 2019); Cummins, "Ethics and Compliance," https://www.cummins.com/ company/ethics-and-compliance (accessed July 31, 2019).

95. Ibid.

96. Better Business Bureau, "BBB Expels 5 Firms for Accreditation Violations," April 2, 2015, http://www.bbb.org/stlouis/news-events/ news-releases/2015/04/bbb-revokes-accreditation-for-5-firms/ (accessed July 6, 2016).

97. "19th Annual Technical Excellence Awards," *PC Magazine*, November 19, 2002, http://www.pcmag.com (accessed December 20, 2002); Glenn R. Simpson, "Raytheon Offers Office Software for Snooping," *The Wall Street Journal*, June 14, 2000, B1.

98. Robin Sidel, "Cyberthieves' Latest Target: Your Tax Forms," The *Wall Street Journal*, April 3, 2016, http://www.wsj.com/articles/online- thieves-target-employee-tax-information-1459715329 (accessed July 6, 2016).

99. S&P Dow Jones Indices, "Dow Jones Sustainability World Index," 2014, http://eu.spindices.com/indices/equity/dow-jones-sustainability- world-index (accessed June 4, 2014); Dow Jones Sustainability Indices, "Overview," http://www.sustainability-indices.com/index-family- overview/djsi-diversified-family-overview/index.jsp (accessed June 4, 2014).

100. William B. Werther and David Chandler, "Strategic Corporate Social Responsibility as Global Brand Insurance," *Business Horizons* 48 (July–August 2005): 317–324.

Chapter 2

1. Whole Foods Market, "Life at Whole Foods Markets," http://www. wholefoodsmarket.com/careers/why-were-great-place-work (accessed December 26, 2018); Whole Foods Market, "Whole Foods Market's Core Values," www.wholefoodsmarket.com/values/corevalues. php#supporting (accessed December 26, 2018); Kerry A. Dolan, "America's Greenest Companies 2011," *Forbes*, April 18, 2011, www. forbes.com/2011/04/18/americas-greenest-companies.html (accessed December 26, 2018); Joseph Brownstein, "Is Whole Foods' Get Healthy Plan Fair?" *ABC News*, January 28, 2010, https://abcnews.go.com/ Health/w_DietAndFitnessNews/foods-incentives-make-employees- healthier/story?id=9680047 (accessed August 19, 2019); Whole Foods Market, "Whole Foods Market Unveils Top 10 Food Trends for 2019," November 15, 2018, https://media.wholefoodsmarket. com/news/whole-foods-market-unveils-top-10-food-trends-for-2019 (accessed August 19, 2019); Whole Foods Market, "Amazon Prime," https://media.wholefoodsmarket.com/video-library/videos/amazon (accessed August 19, 2019); Sarah Halzack, "Amazon Hasn't Exactly Blown up the Grocery Business Yet," *Bloomberg*, April 3, 2018, https://www.bloomberg.com/opinion/articles/2018-04-03/amazon-s- whole-foods-buy-no-grocery-game-changer-yet (accessed August 19, 2019); Dan Malovany, "Mackey: Whole Foods Set Free by Amazon Acquisition," *Food Business News*, September 26, 2017, https://www. foodbusinessnews.net/articles/10655-mackey-whole-foods-set-free- by-amazon-acquisition (accessed August 19, 2019); Whole Foods, "Whole Foods Market celebrates 20 years as one of FORTUNE's '100 Best Companies to Work For,'" March 9, 2017, https://media. wholefoodsmarket.com/news/whole-foods-market-celebrates-20-years- as-one-of-fortunes-100-best-companie (accessed September 25, 2019); "The 100 Best Companies to Work For," *Fortune*, 2018, https://fortune. com/best-companies/2018/ (accessed September 25, 2019).

2. Scott J. Reynolds, Frank C. Schultz, and David R. Hekman, "Stakeholder Theory and Managerial Decision-Making: Constraints and Implications of Balancing Stakeholder Interests," *Journal of Business Ethics* 64, no. 3 (March 2006): 285–301.

3. Vikas Anand, Blake E. Ashforth, and Mahendra Joshi, "Business as Usual: The Acceptance and Perpetuation of Corruption in Organizations," *Academy of Management Executive* 18, no. 2 (2004): 39–53.

4. Chris Marsden, "The New Corporate Citizenship of Big Business: Part of the Solution to Sustainability?" *Business and Society Review* 105 (Spring 2000): 9–25; James E. Post, Lee E. Preston, and Sybille Sachs, *Redefining the Corporation: Stakeholder Management and Organizational Wealth* (Stanford, CA: Stanford University Press, 2002).

5. D. L. Swanson and W. C. Frederick, "Denial and Leadership in Business Ethics Education," in *Business Ethics: New Challenges for Business Schools and Corporate Leaders*, ed. R. A. Peterson and O. C. Ferrell (New York: M. E. Sharpe, 2004), 222–240.

6. American Productivity & Quality Center, *Community Relations: Unleashing the Power of Corporate Citizenship* (Houston: American Productivity & Quality Center, 1998); Thomas

Donaldson and Lee E. Preston, "The Stakeholder Theory of the Corporation: Concepts, Evidence, and Implications," *Academy of Management Review* 29 (January 1995): 65–91; Jaan Elias and J. Gregory Dees, "The Normative Foundations of Business," Harvard Business School Background Note 897-012, June 1997.

7. G. A. Steiner and J. F. Steiner, *Business, Government, and Society* (New York: Random House, 1988).

8. Milton Friedman, "Social Responsibility of Business Is to Increase Its Profits," *The New York Times Magazine*, September 13, 1970, 122–126.

9. "Business Leaders, Politicians, and Academics Dub Corporate Irresponsibility 'An Attack on America from Within,'" Business Wire, November 7, 2002, via America Online.

10. Adam Smith, *The Theory of Moral Sentiments*, Vol. 2 (New York: Prometheus, 2000), 32–45.

11. Theodore Levitt, *The Marketing Imagination* (New York: Free Press, 1983).

12. Norman Bowie, "Empowering People as an End for Business," in *People in Corporations: Ethical Responsibilities and Corporate Effectiveness*, ed. Georges Enderle, Brenda Almond, and Antonio Argandona (Dordrecht, the Netherlands: Kluwer Academic Press, 1990), 105–112.

13. "Is Corporate Social Responsibility Profitable?" *Boss Magazine,* March 31, 2017, https://thebossmagazine.com/csr-profitability/ (accessed November 28, 2018).

14. Adapted from Isabelle Maignan, O. C. Ferrell, and Linda Ferrell, "A Stakeholder Model for Implementing Social Responsibility in Marketing," *European Journal of Marketing* 39 (September–October 2005), 956–977.

15. Ibid.

16. Thomas Barrabi, "Tax Reform Windfall: These Companies Are Hiking Pay, Delivering Bonuses," *Fox Business,* March 7, 2018, https://www.foxbusiness.com/markets/tax-reform-windfall-these-companies-are-hiking-pay-delivering-bonuses (accessed November 28, 2018).

17. BSR, "Twin Metals Minnesota: Using Early Stakeholder Engagement to Improve Strategy," https://www.bsr.org/en/our-insights/case-study-view/twin-metals-minnesota-using-early-stakeholder-engagement (accessed August 15, 2019); Dean DeBeltz, "Let's Have Honest Conversations About Copper-Nickel Mining," *Duluth News-Tribune*, August 16, 2019, https://www.duluthnewstribune.com/opinion/columns/4610947-Local-View-Column-Lets-have-honest-conversations-about-copper-nickel-mining (accessed August 17, 2019).

18. Isabelle Maignan and O. C. Ferrell, "Corporate Social Responsibility: Toward a Marketing Conceptualization," *Journal of the Academy of Marketing Science* 32 (2004): 3–19.

19. David L. Schwartzkopf, "Stakeholder Perspectives and Business Risk Perception," *Journal of Business Ethics* 64, no. 4 (April 2006): 327–342.

20. Maignan and Ferrell, "Corporate Social Responsibility."

21. Cloetta, "Corporate Responsibility," http://www.cloetta.com/en/corporate-responsibility/stakeholders-and-materiality-issues/ (accessed March 15, 2019).

22. Ibid.

23. This section is adapted from Isabelle Maignan, Bas Hillebrand, and Debbie Thorne McAlister, "Managing Socially Responsible Buying: How to Integrate Non-Economic Criteria into the Purchasing Process," *European Management Journal* 20 (December 2002): 641–648.

24. Johnson, Julie, "Animal Rights Protestors with Direct Action Everywhere Plead Not Guilty to Felony Charges Stemming from Demonstration at Petaluma Egg Farm," *The Press Democrat*, February 4, 2019, https://www.pressdemocrat.com/news/9246649-181/animal-rights-protesters-with-direct (accessed March 14, 2019).

25. Andrew L. Friedman and Samantha Miles, "Developing Stakeholder Theory," *Journal of Management Studies* 39 (January 2002): 1–21; Ronald K. Mitchell, Bradley R. Agle, and Donna J. Wood, "Toward a Theory of Stakeholder Identification and Salience: Defining the Principle of Who and What Really Counts," *Academy of Management Review* 22 (October 1997): 853–886.

26. Will Burns, "Walmart Brand Doubles Down on 'Live Better' with Commitment to American Manufacturing," *Forbes*, February 19, 2014, http://www.forbes.com/sites/will-burns/2014/02/19/walmart-brand-doubles-down-on-live-better-with-commitment-to-american-manufacturing/ (accessed July 7, 2016); Jason Furman, "The Fifth Anniversary of the American Recovery and Reinvestment

Act," *White House,* February 17, 2014, https://www.whitehouse.gov/blog/2014/02/17/fifth-anniversary-american-recovery-and-reinvestment-act (accessed July 7, 2016).

27. Amitai Etzioni, *Modern Organizations* (Upper Saddle River, NJ: Prentice Hall, 1964).

28. Treasury Advisory Committee on International Child Labor Enforcement, "Notices," *Federal Register*, March 6, 2000, 65 FR 11831.

29. Brian Scott, "3 Arrested in Denton Fracking Protest," NBC, June 1, 2015, https://www.nbcdfw.com/news/local/3-Arrested-in-Denton-Fracking-Protest-305759361.html (accessed March 14, 2019); Frances Perraudin, "Blackpool Activists Jailed for Anti-Fracking Protest," *The Guardian*, September 26, 2018, https://www.theguardian.com/environment/2018/sep/26/anti-fracking-activists-jailed-for-blackpool-cuadrilla-protest (accessed March 14, 2019).

30. Mark C. Suchman, "Managing Legitimacy: Strategic and Institutional Approaches," *Academy of Management Review* 20 (July 1995): 571–610.

31. Sharon Kelly, "Responding to Investor Pressure, ExxonMobil Agrees to Disclose Fracking Risks," *DeSmog Blog*, April 6, 2014, http://www.desmogblog.com/2014/04/06/exxonmobil-agrees-disclose-fracking-risks-investors (accessed July 7, 2016); Sharon Kelly, "Risks of Fracking Boom Draw Renewed Attention from Investors," *DeSomg Blog*, February 4, 2014, http://www.desmogblog.com/2014/02/04/risks-fracking-boom-draw-renewed-attention-investors (accessed March 14, 2019).

32. Ruma Paul, "Protests Rage over Bangladesh Factory Fire, Supervisors Arrested," *Reuters*, November 28, 2012, http://www.reuters.com/article/us-bangladesh-fire-idUS-BRE8AQ0WE20121128 (accessed July 7, 2016); Joanne Chiu and Tripti Lahiri, "Factory Fire Draws Protests in Bangladesh," *The Wall Street Journal*, November 26, 2012, http://online.wsj.com/news/articles/SB10001424127887324469304578142053199783698 (accessed July 7, 2016).

33. UNM Daniels Fund Ethics Initiative, "Should Pharmacies Sell Harmful Products?" https://danielsethics.mgt.unm.edu/pdf/cvs-debate-issue.pdf (accessed July 7, 2016); Truth Initiative, "Who Sells Cigarettes?" https://truthinitiative.org/research-resources/tobacco-industry-marketing/who-sells-cigarettes-tobacco-free-status-major (accessed August 15, 2019).

34. Ronald Alsop, "Corporate Reputations Are Earned with Trust, Reliability, Study Shows," *The Wall Street Journal*, September 23, 1999, http://interactive.wsj.com; John F. Mahon, "Corporate Reputation: A Research Agenda Using Strategy and Stakeholder Literature," *Business and Society* 41 (December 2002): 415–445.

35. Diana Marszalek, "New Research Claims That Purpose Drives Corporate Reputation," *The Holmes Report,* November 19, 2018, https://www.holmesreport.com/latest/article/new-research-claims-that-purpose-drives-corporate-reputation (accessed April 3, 2019).

36. Manto Gotsi and Alan Wilson, "Corporate Reputation Management: 'Living the Brand,'" *Management Decision* 39, no. 2 (2001): 99–105; Jim Kartalia, "Technology Safeguards for a Good Corporate Reputation," *Information Executive* 3 (September 1999): 4; Prema Nakra, "Corporate Reputation Management: 'CRM' with a Strategic Twist?" *Public Relations Quarterly* 45 (Summer 2000): 35–42.

37. Jeanne Logsdon and Donna J. Wood, "Reputation as an Emerging Construct in the Business and Society Field: An Introduction," *Business and Society* 41 (December 2002): 265–270; "Putting a Price Tag to Reputation," Council of Public Relations Firms, http://www.prfirms.org (accessed December 20, 2002); Allen M. Weiss, Erin Anderson, and Deborah J. MacInnis, "Reputation Management as a Motivation for Sales Structure Decisions," *Journal of Marketing* 63 (October 1999): 74–89.

38. Christy Eidson and Melissa Master, "Who Makes the Call?" *Across the Board* 37 (March 2000): 16; Logsdon and Wood, "Reputation as an Emerging Construct."

39. Alison Rankin Frost, "Brand vs. Reputation," *Communication World* 16 (February–March 1999): 22–25.

40. Glen Peters, *Waltzing with the Raptors: A Practical Roadmap to Protecting Your Company's Reputation* (New York: Wiley, 1999).

41. Margie Kuchinski, "Corporate Responsibility Magazine Announces 2018 100 Best Corporate Citizens," *3BL Association*, May 3, 2018, https://www.3blassociation.com/insights/corporate-responsibility-magazine-announces-2018-100-best-corporate-citizens (accessed March 25, 2019); Microsoft Corporation, "About," 2019, https://www.microsoft.com/en-us/about (accessed March 25, 2019); Vincent

Shih, "Contributing to Taiwan's Ambitious Renewable Energy Targets," *Microsoft*, February 12, 2018, https://blogs.microsoft.com/green/2018/02/12/contributing-taiwans-ambitious-renewable-energy-targets/ (accessed March 25, 2019); Microsoft Corporation, "Corporate Social Responsibility," 2019, https://www.microsoft.com/en-us/corporate-responsibility/ (accessed March 25, 2019); Microsoft Corporation, "Airband Initiative," 2019, https://www.microsoft.com/en-us/airband (accessed March 25, 2019); Microsoft Corporation, "An Update on Connecting Rural America: The 2018 Microsoft Airband Initiative," *Microsoft*, 2018, https://query.prod.cms.rt.microsoft.com/cms/api/am/binary/RWptEB (accessed March 25, 2019).

42. Daniel E. Ho and Frederick Schauer, "Testing the Marketplace of Ideas," *New York University Law Review* 90 (October 2015): 1160–1228; Ben Medeiros, "Evaluating the Reputation Management Industry through the Lens of Public Relations Ethics," *Journal of Media Ethics*, 34 (July–September 2019): 160–170.

43. Edelman, "2019 Edelman Trust Barometer: Global Report," https://www.edelman.com/sites/g/files/aatuss191/files/2019-03/2019_Edelman_Trust_Barometer_Global_Report.pdf?utm_source=website&utm_medium=global_report&utm_campaign=downloads (accessed March 25, 2019); Reputation Institute, "These Companies Have the Best Corporate Reputations in the World," March 7, 2019, https://www.reputationinstitute.com/blog/these-companies-have-best-corporate-reputations-world (accessed March 25, 2019); Epstein, Adam, "The Reign of the Middle-Aged White Man Is Over, At Least in 'House of Cards'," *Quartz*, September 27, 2018, https://qz.com/quartzy/1404649/house-of-cards-season-6-netflix-touts-kevin-spaceys-removal/ (accessed March 25, 2019).

44. Adapted from Lisa A. Mainiero, "Action or Reaction? Handling Businesses in Crisis After September 11," *Business Horizons* 45 (September–October 2002): 2–10; Robert R. Ulmer and Timothy L. Sellnow, "Consistent Questions of Ambiguity in Organizational Communication: Jack in the Box as a Case Study," *Journal of Business Ethics* 25 (May 2000): 143–155; Robert R. Ulmer and Timothy L. Sellnow, "Strategic Ambiguity and the Ethic of Significant Choices in the Tobacco Industry's Crisis Communication," *Communication Studies* 48, no. 3 (1997): 215–233; Timothy L. Sellnow and Robert R. Ulmer, "Ambiguous Argument as Advocacy in Organizational Crisis Communication," *Argumentation and Advocacy* 31, no. 3 (1995): 138–150; Peter V. Stanton, "Ten Communication Mistakes You Can Avoid When Managing a Crisis," *Public Relations Quarterly* 47 (Summer 2002): 19–22.

45. Seth Arenstein, "How Southwest Communicated News and Empathy in the Aftermath of Flight 1380," *PR News*, April 18, 2018, https://www.prnewsonline.com/prnewsblog/how-southwest-communicated-news-and-empathy-in-the-aftermath-of-flight-1380/ (accessed April 3, 2019).

46. Lynn Brewer, Robert Chandler, and O. C. Ferrell, *Managing Risks for Corporate Integrity: How to Survive an Ethical Misconduct Disaster* (Mason, OH: Texere/Thomson, 2006), 2–3.

47. Tara S. Bernard, Tiffany Hsu, Nicole Perlroth, and Ron Lieber, "Equifax Says Cyberattack May Have Affected 143 Million in the U.S.," *The New York Times*, September 7, 2017, https://www.nytimes.com/2017/09/07/business/equifax-cyberattack.html (accessed April 3, 2019).

48. Krystina Gustafson, "Lord & Taylor Settles Deceptive Advertising Charges," CNBC, March 15, 2016, http://www.cnbc.com/2016/03/15/ (accessed July 7, 2016).

49. Paul Argenti, "Crisis Communication: Lessons from 9/11," *Harvard Business Review* 80 (December 2002): 103–109; L. Paul Bremer, "Corporate Governance and Crisis Management," *Directors and Boards* 26 (Winter 2002): 16–20; Christine M. Pearson and Judith A. Clair, "Reframing Crisis Management," *Academy of Management Review* 23 (January 1998): 59–76.

50. Ben DiPietro, "Crisis of the Week: Disney Responds to Alligator Killing Boy," *The Wall Street Journal*, June 28, 2016, http://blogs.wsj.com/riskandcompliance/2016/06/28/crisis-of-the-week-disney-responds-to-alligator-killing-boy/ (accessed July 7, 2016).

51. Michael John Harker, "Relationship Marketing Defined?" *Marketing Intelligence and Planning* 17 (January 1999): 13–20; Robert M. Morgan and Shelby D. Hunt, "The Commitment-Trust Theory of Relationship Marketing," *Journal of Marketing* 58 (July 1994): 20–38.

52. Jordan Kahn, "Apple Kicks off Its Big In-Store iPhone Upgrade Event," 2014, *9to5Mac*, http://9to5mac.com/2014/05/09/apple-kicks-off-its-big-in-store-iphone-upgrade-event/ (accessed July 7, 2016).

53. Paula Andruss, "Secrets of the 10 Most-Trusted Brands," *Entrepreneur*, March 20, 2012, http://www.entrepreneur.com/article/223125 (accessed July 7, 2016).

54. Jörg Andriof and Sandra Waddock, "Unfolding Stakeholder Engagement," in *Unfolding Stakeholder Thinking: Theory, Responsibility and Engagement*, ed. Jörg Andriof, Sandra Waddock, Bryan Husted, and Sandra S. Rahman (Sheffield, UK: Greenleaf Publishing, 2002), 19–42; James Coleman, "Social Capital in the Creation of Human Capital," *American Journal of Sociology* 94 (1988): S95–S120; Carrie R. Leana and Harry J. Van Buren III, "Organizational Social Capital and Employment Practices," *Academy of Management Review* 24 (July 1999): 538–555.

55. Barbara Gray, "Social Capital: The Secret Behind Airbnb and Uber," *BrandyCap*, June 4, 2014, http://bradycap.com/social-capital-the-secret-behind-airbnb-and-uber/ (accessed July 7, 2016).

56. Adapted from Maignan et al., "A Stakeholder Model for Implementing Social Responsibility in Marketing," 956–977.

57. "REI Overview," REI, https://www.rei.com/about-rei/business (accessed April 3, 2019).

58. Corporate Social Responsibility at Starbucks, http://www.starbucks.com/aboutus/csr.asp (accessed July 7, 2016).

59. Robinson Meyer, "How the U.S. Protects the Environment, from Nixon to Trump," *The Atlantic*, March 29, 2017, https://www.theatlantic.com/science/archive/2017/03/how-the-epa-and-us-environmental-law-works-a-civics-guide-pruitt-trump/521001/ (accessed April 3, 2019).

60. Dave Lieber, "Texas Business Owners Say Negative Comments on Yelp Hurt Bottom Line," *Dallas News*, November 7, 2013, http://www.dallasnews.com/investigations/watchdog/20131107-watchdog-texas-business-owners-say-negative-comments-on-yelp-hurt-bottom-line.ece (accessed June 6, 2014).

61. Michael Pirson and Deepak Malhotra, "Unconventional Insights for Managing Stakeholder Trust," *Sloan Management Review* 49 (Summer 2008): 42–50.

62. Taylor Ray, "World Watches as Coca-Cola Launches Flagship EKOCENTER in Rwanda," *Coca-Cola Journey*, June 24, 2016, http://www.coca-colacompany.com/coca-cola-unbottled/world-watches-as-coca-cola-launches-flagship-ekocenterin-rwanda (accessed July 7, 2016); Adeline Chong, "Coke Combats Sustainability and Nutrition Critics with Rural Ekocenters," *BrandChannel*, October 8, 2013, http://brand-channel.com/2013/10/08/coke-combats-sustainability-and-nutrition-critics-with-rural-ekocenters/ (accessed July 7, 2016).

63. Max B. E. Clarkson, "A Stakeholder Framework for Analyzing and Evaluating Corporate Social Performance," *Academy of Management Review* 20 (January 1995): 92–117.

64. Ibid.

65. Ibid.

66. Jörg Andriof, "Managing Social Risk Through Stakeholder Partnership Building," unpublished Ph.D. dissertation, Warwick Busines School, 2000; Andriof, "Patterns of Stakeholder Partnership Building," 215–238.

67. Nick Chaloner and David Brontzen, "How SABMiller Protects Its Biggest Asset—Its Reputation," *Strategic Communication Management* 6 (October–November 2002): 12–15.

Chapter 3

1. 2020 Women on Boards, "About," https://www.2020wob.com/about (accessed April 19, 2019); Julie B. Davis, "Why Companies Are Adding More Women Board Members to Their Rosters," *American Express*, December 10, 2018, https://www.americanexpress.com/en-us/business/trends-and-insights/articles/why-companies-are-adding-more-women-board-members-to-their-rosters/ (accessed April 19, 2019); Erica Hersh, "Why Diversity Matters: Women on Boards of Directors," Harvard T. H. Chan School of Public Health, July 21, 2016, https://www.hsph.harvard.edu/ecpe/why-diversity-matters-women-on-boards-of-directors/ (accessed April 19, 2019); Terence Jeffrey, "Women Earn 57% of US Bachelor's Degrees—For 18th Straight Year," *CNS News*, June 8, 2019, https://www.cnsnews.com/news/article/terence-p-jeffrey/women-earn-57-us-bachelors-degrees-18th-straight-year (accessed April 19, 2019).

2. Rafael LaPorta and Florencio Lopez-de-Silanes, "Investor Protection and Corporate Governance," *Journal of Financial Economics* 58 (October–November 2000): 3–38.

3. Sean McLain, "Nissan's Corporate Governance Needs to Be Overhauled, Committee Says: Former Chairman Carlos Ghosn Wielded

Too Much Power, Special Committee Says," *The Wall Street Journal*, March 27, 2019, https://www.wsj.com/articles/nissans-corporate-governance-needs-to-be-overhauled-committee-says-11553691956 (accessed April 4, 2019); Michael Volkov, "Wells Fargo: Corporate Board Lessons Learned?" *Ethical Boardroom*, June 4, 2018, https://www.housingwire.com/articles/48617-wells-fargo-ceo-tim-sloan-abruptly-steps-down (accessed April 8, 2019); David Trainer, "Poor Governance Makes These Companies Acquisition Targets," *Forbes*, November 1, 2018, https://www.forbes.com/sites/greatspeculations/2018/11/01/poor-governance-makes-these-companies-acquisition-targets/#22ac52d63331 (accessed April 15, 2019).

4. *Dodge v. Ford Motor Co.*, 204 Mich. 459, 179 N.W. 668, 3 A.L.R. 413 (1919).

5. Susan Heavy, "Tyson Poultry Pleads Guilty over Missouri Spill, to Pay $2 Mln Fine," *Reuters*, September 27, 2017, https://www.reuters.com/article/legal-tyson-foods-missouri/tyson-poultry-pleads-guilty-over-missouri-spill-to-pay-2-mln-fine-idUSKCN1C22FN (accessed April 8, 2019).

6. Alfred Marcus and Sheryl Kaiser, *Managing Beyond Compliance: The Ethical and Legal Dimensions of Corporate Responsibility* (Garfield Heights, OH: North Coast Publishers, 2006), 79.

7. Jeffrey Dastin and Alwyn Scott, "Activist Investors Question United Airlines CEO's Board Role, Pay," *Reuters*, March 14, 2016, http://www.reuters.com/article/us-ual-board-idUSKC-N0WF0EA (accessed July 8, 2016); Sean McLain, "Nissan's Corporate Governance Needs to Be Overhauled, Committee Says: Former Chairman Carlos Ghosn Wielded Too Much Power, Special Committee Says," *The Wall Street Journal*, March 27, 2019, https://www.wsj.com/articles/nissans-corporate-governance-needs-to-be-overhauled-committee-says-11553691956 (accessed April 4, 2019); Mengqi Sun, "More U.S. Companies Separating Chief Executive and Chairman Roles," *Wall Street Journal*, January 23, 2019, https://www.wsj.com/articles/more-u-s-companies-separating-chief-executive-and-chairman-roles-11548288502 (accessed April 15, 2019).

8. Min-Jeong Lee, "Samsung Insider-Trading Probe Involves President-Level Executives," *The Wall Street Journal*, December 7, 2015, http://www.wsj.com/articles/samsung-insider-trading-probe-involves-president-level-executives-1449478252 (accessed July 8, 2016).

9. Ben W. Heineman Jr., "Are You a Good Corporate Citizen?" *The Wall Street Journal*, June 28, 2005, http://online.wsj.com/article/0,SB111991936947571125,00-search.html (accessed July 8, 2016).

10. Joann S. Lublin, "McKesson Makes Corporate-Governance Changes," *The Wall Street Journal*, January 21, 2014, http://online.wsj.com/news/articles/SB10001424052702304027204 579335081375388634 (accessed July 8, 2016).

11. Erik Berglöf and Stijn Claessens, "Enforcement and Good Corporate Governance in Developing Countries and Transition Economies," *The World Bank Research Observer*, February 21, 2006, http://wbro.oxfordjournals.org/cgi/content/full/21/1/123 (accessed July 8, 2016); Darryl Reed, "Corporate Governance Reforms in Developing Countries," *Journal of Business Ethics* 37 (May 2002): 223–247; McKesson Corporation, "Corporate Governance," 2019, https://www.mckesson.com/investors/corporate-governance/ (accessed April 19, 2019).

12. Bryan W. Husted and Carlos Serrano, "Corporate Governance in Mexico," *Journal of Business Ethics* 37 (May 2002): 337–348.

13. Robert A. G. Monks, *Corporate Governance in the Twenty-First Century: A Preliminary Outline* (Portland, ME: LENS, 1996), http://www.lens-library.com/info/cg21.html.

14. James McRitchie, "Ending the Wall Street Walk: Why Corporate Governance Now?" *Corporate Governance*, https://www.corpgov.net/1996/05/ending-the-wall-street-walk-why-corporate-governance-now-2/ (accessed September 18, 2019).

15. David A. Cifrino and Garrison R. Smith, "NYSE and NASDAQ Propose to Review Corporate Governance Listing Standards," *Corporate Governance Advisor* 10 (November–December 2002): 18–25.

16. Julia Carpenter and Jackie Wattles, "California Has a New Law: No More All-Male Boards," CNN, October 3, 2018, https://www.cnn.com/2018/09/30/business/california-requires-women-board-of-directors/index.html (accessed April 15, 2019); Alison Smale and Claire C. Miller, "Germany Sets Gender Quota in Boardrooms," *The New York Times*, March 6, 2015, https://www.nytimes.com/2015/03/07/world/europe/german-law-requires-more-women-on-corporate-boards.html (accessed April 15, 2019).

17. Timothy Devinney, "Is the Socially Responsible Corporation a Myth? The Good, the Bad, and the Ugly of Corporate Social Responsibility," *Academy of Management Perspectives* 23, no. 2 (May 2009): 44–56; Luke Mullins, "Obama's Financial Regulation Reform: 7 Things You Need to Know," *U.S. News & World Report*, June 17, 2009, http://money.usnews.com/money/blogs/the-home-front/2009/06/17/obamas-financial-regulation-reform-7-things-you-need-to-know (accessed July 8, 2016).

18. Ada Demb and Franz-Friedrich Neubauer, *The Corporate Board: Confronting the Paradoxes* (Oxford: Oxford University Press, 1992).

19. Jenny Strasburg, Giles Turner, and Eyk Henning, "Executive Who Committed Suicide Anxious Amid Deutsche Bank Probes," *The Wall Street Journal*, March 26, 2014, C1, C2; Chad Bray, "Deutsche Bank Warns Investors on Currency Investigation," *The New York Times*, June 5, 2014, http://dealbook.nytimes.com/2014/06/05/deutsche-bank-warns-investors-on-currency-investigation/ (accessed July 8, 2016). Kathrin Jones and Thomas Atkins, "No End in Sight for Deutsche Bank Libor Probe: Sources," *Reuters*, May 12, 2014, https://www.reuters.com/article/us-deutsche-bank-libor/no-end-in-sight-for-deutsche-bank-libor-probe-sources-idUSBREA4B09220140512 (accessed July 8, 2016).

20 Organisation for Economic Co-operation and Development, *The OECD Principles of Corporate Governance* (Paris: Organisation for Economic Co-operation and Development, 1999).

21. Jennifer McKevitt, "Modern Slavery Allegations Burn Clothing Supply Chains," *SupplyChainDive*, October 26, 2016, https://www.supplychaindive.com/news/modern-slavery-clothing-retail-supply-chain/429021/ (accessed April 19, 2019); Daniel Zager, Angeles Solis, and Sonia Adjroud, "These Georgetown Students Fought Nike—and Won," *The Nation*, September 15, 2017, https://www.thenation.com/article/these-georgetown-students-fought-nike-and-won/ (accessed April 12, 2019).

22. "Corporate Governance," International Finance Corporation: World Bank Group, http://www.ifc.org/corporategovernance (accessed July 8, 2016).

23. Clive Crook, "Why Good Corporate Citizens Are a Public Menace," *National Journal*, April 24, 1999, 1087.

24. Reuters, "Citigroup Board Names New Chairman, Keeps Post Separate from CEO," *The Economic Times*, November 6, 2018, https://economictimes.indiatimes.com/news/international/business/citigroup-board-names-new-chairman-keeps-post-separate-from-ceo/articleshow/66520405.cms?from=mdr (accessed April 22, 2019).

25. Melvin A. Eisenberg, "Corporate Governance: The Board of Directors and Internal Control," *Cordoza Law Review* 19 (September–November 1997): 237.

26. Halah Touryalai, "Jamie Dimon's Power Struggle: Loses Bank Chairman Role, a Bigger Blow May Come Next," *Forbes*, October 4, 2013, http://www.forbes.com/sites/halahtouryalai/2013/10/04/jamie-dimons-power-struggle-loses-bank-chairman-role-a-bigger-blow-may-come-next/#43b1afa84729 (accessed July 12, 2016).

27. New York Stock Exchange (NYSE), "303A.01 Independent Directors," *NYSE Manual*, http://nysemanual.nyse.com/lcm/Help/mapContent.asp?sec=lcm-sections&title=sx-ruling-nyse-policymanual_303 A.01&id=chp_1_4_3_2 (accessed July 12, 2016).

28. New York Stock Exchange (NYSE), "303A.00 Corporate Governance Standards," *NYSE Manual*, http://nysemanual.nyse.com/lcm/sections/lcm-sections/chp_1_4/default.asp (accessed July 12, 2016).

29. Louis Lavelle, "The Best and Worst Boards," *Business Week*, October 7, 2002, 104.

30. Harvey L. Pitt, "Retaining Ethical Cultures During a Weak Economy," *Compliance Week*, June 30, 2009, https://www.complianceweek.com/blogs/harvey-l-pitt/retaining-ethical-cultures-during-a-weak-economy#.V4V9_LgrLIU (accessed July 12, 2016).

31. "Biz Deans Talk-Business Management Education Blog," January 2, 2009, http://www.deanstalk.net/deanstalk/2009/01/warren-buffetts.html (accessed June 7, 2014); "Volcker Rule Resource Center," Securities Industry and Financial Markets Association, http://www.sifma.org/issues/regulatory-reform/volcker-rule/overview/ (accessed July 12, 2016).

32. Adrian Cadbury, "What Are the Trends in Corporate Governance? How Will They Impact Your Company?" *Long-Range Planning* 32 (January 1999): 12–19.

33. "How Shareholder Proposals Work," The Equality Project, http://www.equalityproject.org (accessed June 7, 2014); Barry Burr, "Shareholder Activism Hot in Poor Business Climate," *Pensions & Investments*,

July 8, 2002, 4, 32; Siddharth Cavale, "P&G Appoints Peltz to Board Despite Losing Proxy Battle," *Reuters,* December 15, 2017, https://www.reuters.com/article/us-procter-gamble-trian/pg-appoints-peltz-to-board-despite-losing-proxy-battle-idUSKBN1E92ZA (accessed April 12, 2019).

34. Lauren Tara LaCapra, "BofA's Board Shuffle an Ode to Stakeholders," *The Street,* June 22, 2009, http://www.thestreet.com/story/10523721/1/bofas-board-shuffle-an-ode-to-shareholders.html (accessed July 12. 2016).

35. "Internal Auditors: Integral to Good Corporate Governance," *Internal Auditor* 59 (August 2002): 44–49.

36. Donna Kardos, "KPMG Is Sued over New Century," *The Wall Street Journal*, April 2, 2009, http://online.wsj.com/news/articles/SB123860415462378767 (accessed July 12, 2016).

37. Eisenberg, "Corporate Governance."

38. Tom Hamburger and BenPershing, "Car Company with Ties to Terry McAuliffe Probed by SEC," *The Washington Post*, August 2, 2013, http://www.washingtonpost.com/politics/company-with-ties-to-terry-mcauliffe-is-under-sec-investigation/2013/08/02/da483b36-f956-11e2-b018-5b8251f0c56e_story.html (accessed July 12, 2016); Becky Yerak, "GreenTech Automotive Files for Bankruptcy," The *Wall Street Journal*, February 27, 2018, https://www.wsj.com/articles/greentech-automotive-files-for-bankruptcy-1519775795 (accessed April 22, 2019).

39. Lynn Brewer, Robert Chandler, and O. C. Ferrell, *Managing Risks for Corporate Integrity: How to Survive an Ethical Misconduct Disaster* (Mason, OH: Texere/Thomson, 2006), 72.

40. Ray A. Goldberg, *Kraft General Foods: Risk Management Philosophy* (Boston: Harvard Business School Press, 1994).

41. Heather Timmons, "Financial Scandal at Outsourcing Company Rattles a Developing Country," *The New York Times,* January 7, 2009, http://www.nytimes.com/2009/01/08/business/worldbusiness/08outsource.html (accessed July 12, 2016).

42. Brewer et al., *Managing Risks for Corporate Integrity,* 75; John Browne and Robin Nuttall, "Beyond Corporate Social Responsibility: Integrated External Engagement," McKinsey & Company, March 2013, http://www.mckinsey.com/insights/strategy/beyond_corporate_social_responsibility_integrated_external_engagement (accessed July 12, 2016).

43. Brewer et al., *Managing Risks for Corporate Integrity,* 75.

44. Jim Billington, "A Few Things Every Manager Ought to Know About Risk," *Harvard Management Update,* March 1997, 10–11; Lee Puschaver and Robert G. Eccles, "In Pursuit of the Upside: The New Opportunity in Risk Management," *PW Review,* December 1996.

45. Scott Alexander, "Achieving Enterprisewide Privacy Compliance," *Insurance & Technology* 25 (November 2000): 53; M. Joseph Sirgy and Chenting Su, "The Ethics of Consumer Sovereignty in an Age of High Tech," *Journal of Business Ethics* 28 (November 2000): 1–14.

46. Ed Silverstein, "CEO 'Pay' Definition Remains Unclear as SEC Struggles to Meet Dodd-Frank Deadlines," *Inside Counsel,* May 2, 2014, http://www.insidecounsel.com/2014/05/02/ceo-pay-definition-remains-unclear-as-sec-struggle (accessed July 12, 2016); Alyce Lomax, "Is Shareholder 'Say on Pay' Working?" *The Motley Fool*, April 3, 2014, http://www.fool.com/investing/general/2014/04/03/is-shareholder-say-on-pay-working.aspx (accessed July 12, 2016); U.S. Securities and Exchange Commission Press Release, "SEC Adopts Rule for Pay Ratio Disclosure: Rule Implements Dodd-Frank Mandate While Providing Companies with Flexibility to Calculate Pay Ratio," U.S. Securities and Exchange Commission, August 5, 2015, https://www.sec.gov/news/pressrelease/2015-160.html (accessed April 22, 2019).

47. Sarah Anderson, John Cavanaugh, Scott Kinger, and Liz Stanton, "Executive Excess 2008: How Average Taxpayers Subsidize Runaway Pay," Institute for Policy Studies, United for a Fair Economy, http://faireconomy.org/files/executive_excess_2008.pdf (accessed July 12, 2016).

48. "Executive Paywatch," AFL-CIO, https://aflcio.org/paywatch (accessed August 14, 2019).

49. Tony Wolverton, "Uber Gave CEO Dara Khosrowshahi $45 Million in Total Pay Last Year, But It Paid Its COO Even More," *Business Insider*, April 11, 2019, https://www.businessinsider.com/uber-ceo-dara-khosrowshahi-salary-total-compensation-45-million-in-2018-2019-4 (accessed April 15, 2019).

50. Kara Scanell, "SEC Ready to Require More Pay Disclosures," *The Wall Street Journal*, June 3, 2009, http://online.wsj.com/article/

SB124397831899078781.html (accessed July 12, 2016); "Food Security Catastrophe Bonds," *Sustainable Investing Challenge,* April 26, 2013, http://sustainableinvestingchallenge.org/wp-content/uploads/2013/03/FSC-Bonds.pdf (accessed July 12, 2016); "From SRI to ESG: The Changing World of Responsible Investing," Commonfund Institute, September 2013, https://www.commonfund.org/investor-resources/publications/white%20papers/white-paper_sri%20to%20esg%202013%200901.pdf (accessed June 7, 2014).

51. Gary Strauss, "America's Corporate Meltdown," *USA Today,* June 27, 2002, 1A, 2A.

52. Louis Lavelle, "CEO Pay, the More Things Change…," *BusinessWeek,* October 16, 2000, http://www.businessweek.com/2000/00_42/b3703102.htm (accessed June 7, 2014).

53. Ted Mann, "GE's Immelt Misses Part of Five-Year Performance Target," *The Wall Street Journal*, February 17, 2016, http://www.wsj.com/articles/ges-immelt-misses-part-of-five-year-performance-target-1455753884 (accessed July 12, 2016).

54. Stephen Gandel, "The Only Thing Up on Wall Street Is Pay," *Fortune,* March 22, 2016, http://fortune.com/2016/03/22/wall-street-ceo-pay/ (accessed July 12, 2016); Shana Lebowitz, "132 Top CEOs Now Have a Median Salary of $1 Million a Month—Here Are the CEOs Whose Pay Has Been Most Widely out of Sync with Company Performance," *SFGATE*, March 18, 2019, https://www.sfgate.com/technology/businessinsider/article/The-25-CEOs-whose-pay-is-most-wildly-out-of-sync-13638134.php (accessed April 22, 2019).

55. "Measuring Corporate Governance Standards," *Asiamoney,* December 2000–January 2001: 94–95.

56. Barbara Crutchfield George, Kathleen A. Lacey, and Jotta Birmele, "The 1998 OECD Convention," *American Business Law Journal* 37 (Spring 2000): 485–525; Ira Millstein, "Corporate Governance: The Role of Market Forces," *OECD Observer* (Summer 2000): 27–28; "About OECD," Organisation for Economic Co-operation and Development, http://www.oecd.org/pages/0,3417,en_36734052_36734103_1_1_1_1_1,00.html (accessed June 7, 2014).

57. Sean McLain, Shefali Anand, and Biman Mukherji, "Frustrated by Indian Policy, Foreign Investors Pull Back," *The Wall Street Journal,* July 19, 2013, https://www.wsj.com/articles/SB10001424127887323993804578613730684912770 (accessed September 18, 2019).

58. Sonu Bhasin, "View: A Generational Shift in Corporate Governance," *The Economic Times,* August 9, 2018, https://economictimes.indiatimes.com/news/company/corporate-trends/view-a-generational-shift-in-corporate-governance/articleshow/65331646.cms (accessed April 23, 2019).

59. Fareed Zakaria, "A Capitalist Manifesto: Greed Is Good (to a Point)," *Newsweek,* June 13, 2009, http://www.newsweek.com/id/201935 (accessed July 12, 2016).

60. Adam M. Brandenburger and Barry J. Nalebuff, *Co-opetition: 1. A Revolutionary Mindset That Redefines Competition and Cooperation; 2. The Game Theory Strategy That's Changing the Game of Business* (New York: Doubleday, 1997); Hamburger and Pershing, "Car Company with Ties to Terry McAuliffe Is Under SEC Investigation.

61. Maria Maher and Thomas Andersson, "Corporate Governance: Effects on Firm Performance and Economic Growth," Organisation for Economic Co-Operation and Development, 1999, https://www.oecd.org/sti/ind/2090569.pdf (accessed September 25, 2019).

62. Monks, *Corporate Governance in the Twenty-First Century.*

63. "Three Skills for Today's Leaders," *Harvard Management Update* 4 (November 1999): 11.

64. Catherine M. Daily, Dan R. Dalton, and Albert A. Cannella Jr., "Corporate Governance: A Decade of Dialogue and Data," *Academy of Management Review* 28 (July 2003): 371–382.

65. Carol Hymowitz, "How to Fix a Broken System," *Wall Street Journal*, February 24, 2003, R1–R3.

66. Monks, *Corporate Governance in the Twenty-First Century,* 82.

Chapter 4

1. Sam Schechner and Valentina Pop, "Google Fined $1.7 Billion in EU for Restricting Rivals' Ads," *The Wall Street Journal*, March 20, 2019, https://www.wsj.com/articles/google-fined-1-7-billion-in-eu-over-ad-restrictions-11553080506 (accessed May 13, 2019); Kelvin Chan and Raf Casert, "EU Fines Google $1.7 Billion for Abusing Online Advertising Market," *USA Today*, March 20, 2019, https://www.usatoday.com/story/money/business/2019/03/20/google-fine-eu-online-advertising/3224834002/ (accessed May 13, 2019); Bill Chappell,

"EU Fines Google $1.7 Billion over 'Abusive' Online Ad Strategies," *NPR*, March 20, 2019, https://www.npr.org/2019/03/20/705106450/eu-fines-google-1-7-billion-over-abusive-online-ad-strategies (accessed May 13, 2019); Dave Graham and David Ljunggren, "New NAFTA Deal 'In Trouble', Bruised by Elections, Tariff Rows," *Reuters*, April 7, 2019, https://www.reuters.com/article/us-trade-nafta-analysis/new-nafta-deal-in-trouble-bruised-by-elections-tariff-rows-idUSKCN1RJ0BS (accessed May 13, 2019); Inu Manak, "ITC Report on Economics of USMCA Out; Next Up, Politics," Cato Institute, April 19, 2019, https://www.cato.org/blog/itc-report-economics-usmca-out-next-politics (accessed May 13, 2019); Jen Kirby, "USMCA, Trump's New NAFTA Deal, Explained in 500 Words," *Vox Media*, February 5, 2019, https://www.vox.com/2018/10/3/17930092/usmca-nafta-trump-trade-deal-explained (accessed May 13, 2019); Phil Levy, "Is the New NAFTA Any Good?" *Forbes*, March 31, 2019, https://www.forbes.com/sites/phillevy/2019/03/31/is-the-new-nafta-any-good/#30fcf8525d0c (accessed May 13, 2019); Jessica Murphy and Natalie Sherman, "USMCA Trade Deal: Who Gets What from 'New NAFTA'?" BBC News, October 1, 2018, https://www.bbc.com/news/world-us-canada-45674261 (accessed May 13, 2019); Kimberly Amadeo, "Multilateral Trade Agreements with Their Pros, Cons, and Examples: 5 Pros and 4 Cons to the World's Largest Trade Agreements," *The Balance*, December 14, 2018, https://www.thebalance.com/multilateral-trade-agreements-pros-cons-and-examples-3305949 (accessed May 13, 2019).

2. Robert Litan, "Regulation," Library of Economics and Liberty, https://www.econlib.org/library/Enc/Regulation.html (accessed June 7, 2019).

3. David Goldman, "Obama Vows Antitrust Crackdown," CNN Money, May 11, 2009, http://money.cnn.com/2009/05/11/news/economy/antitrust/index.htm (accessed July 15, 2016).

4. Steve Lohr, "High-Tech Antitrust Cases: The Road Ahead," *The New York Times,* May 13, 2009, http://bits.blogs.nytimes.com/2009/05/13/high-tech-antitrust-the-road-ahead/ (accessed July 15, 2016); Jonathan Tepper, "The Conservative Case for Antitrust," *The American Conservative*, January 28, 2019, https://www.theamericanconservative.com/articles/the-conservative-case-for-antitrust-jonathan-tepper/ (accessed April 29, 2019); Nihal Krishan, "Justice Department Loses Antitrust Appeal to AT&T-Time Warner Deal," *Mother Jones*, February 26, 2019, https://www.motherjones.com/politics/2019/02/doj-loses-antitrust-appeal-att-time-warner-deal-trump/ (accessed April 29, 2019).

5. Natalia Drozdiak and Sam Schechner, "EU Files Additional Formal Charges Against Google," *The Wall Street Journal*, July 14, 2016, http://www.wsj.com/articles/google-set-to-face-more-eu-antitrust-charges-1468479516 (accessed July 15, 2016).

6. Danielle Douglas, "Second-Largest Swiss Bank Pleads Guilty to Tax Evasion," *Washington Post*, May 19, 2014, https://www.washingtonpost.com/business/economy/credit-suisse-charged-in-tax-evasion-case/2014/05/19/772afeb2-dfb0-11e3-9743-bb9b59cde7b9_story.html (accessed September 19, 2019).

7. Alan S. Blinder, "Keynesian Economics," Library of Economics and Liberty, http://www.econlib.org/library/Enc/Keynes-ianEconomics.html (accessed July 15, 2016).

8. Robert L. Formaini, "Milton Friedman—Economist as Public Intellectual," *Economic Insights* 7, no. 2 (2002).

9. Jeffry Bartash, "John Maynard…Trump? President's Tax Cuts, Spending Spree Evoke Liberals' Favorite Economist," *MarketWatch*, February 9, 2019, https://www.marketwatch.com/story/john-maynard-trump-presidents-tax-cuts-spending-spree-evoke-liberals-favorite-economist-2018-02-09 (accessed April 29, 2019); Chris Pandolfo, "Trump Infrastructure Plan Reeks of Keynes, Not Reagan," *Conservative Review*, March 29, 2018, https://www.conservativereview.com/news/trump-infrastructure-plan-reeks-keynes-not-reagan/ (accessed April 29, 2019).

10. Robert Litan, "Regulation," *Library of Economics and Liberty*, https://www.econlib.org/library/Enc/Regulation.html (accessed June 7, 2019).

11. Will Kenton, "Natural Monopoly," *Investopedia*, April 17, 2018, https://www.investopedia.com/terms/n/natural_monopoly.asp (accessed June 7, 2019); BusinessDictionary, "Natural Monopoly," http://www.businessdictionary.com/definition/natural-monopoly.html (accessed June 7, 2019); MyAccountingCourse.com, "What Is a Natural Monopoly?" https://www.myaccountingcourse.com/accounting-dictionary/natural-monopoly; https://www.economicshelp.org/blog/glossary/natural-monopoly/ (accessed June 7, 2019).

12. Lisa Rein, "Electric Rates No Bright Spot for O'Malley as Election Nears," *Washington Post*, July 6, 2009, http://www.washingtonpost.com/wp-dyn/content/article/2009/07/05/AR2009070502697.html (accessed July 15, 2016).

13. Joseph Walker, "Drugmakers' Pricing Power Remains Strong," *The Wall Street Journal*, July 14, 2016, https://www.wsj.com/articles/drugmakers-pricing-power-remains-strong-1468488601 (accessed September 19, 2019); Luke Timmerman, "A Timeline of the Turing Pharma Controversy," September 23, 2015, http://www.forbes.com/sites/luketimmerman/2015/09/23/a-timeline-of-the-turing-pharma-controversy/#30c633297b94 (accessed July 15, 2016).

14. Jorge L. Ortiz, "Fatal Flights: What We Know About Boeing MAX 8 Crashes in Ethiopia and Indonesia," *USA Today*, April 4, 2019, https://www.usatoday.com/story/news/nation/2019/04/04/boeing-max-8-plane-crashes-what-we-know-two-fatal-flights/3371347002/ (accessed June 5, 2019); David Gelles and Natalie Kitroeff, "Before Ethiopian Crash, Boeing Resisted Pilots' Calls for Aggressive Steps on 737 Max," *The New York Times*, May 14, 2019, https://www.nytimes.com/2019/05/14/business/boeing-737-max-ethiopian-plane-crash.html (accessed June 5, 2019); Leslie Josephs, "Boeing's Rocky Road to Win Back Trust After Deadly 737 Max Crashes: 'We Know We Have Work to Do'," *CNBC*, June 5, 2019, https://www.cnbc.com/2019/06/04/boeing-has-a-rocky-road-to-win-back-trust-after-deadly-737-max-crashes.html (accessed June 5, 2019).

15. Todd E. Napolitano, "Bioengineered and Genetically Modified Foods: 4 Key Questions Answered," *Merieux NutriSciences*, July 24, 2018, http://foodsafety.merieuxnutrisciences.com/2018/07/24/bioengineered-genetically-modified-foods-4-key-questions-answered/ (accessed June 5, 2019); "Center for Science in the Public Interest Greg Jaffe Cornell and GMOs," *Corporate Crime Reporter*, January 7, 2019, http://www.corporatecrimereporter.com/news/200/center-science-public-interest-greg-jaffe-cornell-gmos/ (accessed June 5, 2019); "About U.S. Right to Know," U.S. Right to Know, https://usrtk.org/about/ (accessed June 5, 2019); Greg Jaffe, "Biotech Blog: The Final National Bioengineered Food Disclosure Standard," Center for Science in the Public Interest, April 8, 2019, https://cspinet.org/news/biotech-blog-final-national-bioengineered-food-disclosure-standard (accessed June 5, 2019); "Long-Awaited Final Regulations for GMO Food Labeling Leave Millions of Americans in the Dark," Center for Food Safety, December 20, 2018, https://www.centerforfoodsafety.org/press-releases/5487/long-awaited-final-regulations-for-gmo-food-labeling-leave-millions-of-americans-in-the-dark (accessed June 6, 2019); U.S. Department of Agriculture, "Establishing the National Bioengineered Food Disclosure Standard," December 20, 2018, https://www.usda.gov/media/press-releases/2018/12/20/establishing-national-bioengineered-food-disclosure-standard (accessed June 6, 2019); "Consumer, Environmental, Farmer Groups Demand Strong GMO Food Labeling Standards," July 3, 2018, https://www.centerforfoodsafety.org/press-releases/5374/consumer-environmental-farmer-groups-demand-strong-gmo-food-labeling-standards (accessed June 6, 2019); "GMO Facts," Non-GMO Project, https://www.nongmoproject.org/gmo-facts/ (accessed June 6, 2019); NowFindOrganic.com, "Countries That Ban GMOs," https://www.nowfindorganic.com/countries-that-ban-gmos/ (accessed June 6, 2019).

16. Aaron Cadena, "Hemp vs. Marijuana: The Difference Explained (2019 Update)," *CBDOrigin*, September 10, 2018, https://medium.com/cbd-origin/hemp-vs-marijuana-the-difference-explained-a837c51aa8f7 (accessed June 6, 2019); John Hudak, "The Farm Bill, Hemp Legalization and the Status of CBD: An Explainer," Brookings Institution, December 14, 2018, https://www.brookings.edu/blog/fixgov/2018/12/14/the-farm-bill-hemp-and-cbd-explainer/ (accessed June 6, 2019); Michael Nepveux, "2018 Farm Bill Provides a Path Forward for Industrial Hemp," American Farm Bureau Federation, February 28, 2019, https://www.fb.org/market-intel/2018-farm-bill-provides-a-path-forward-for-industrial-hemp (accessed June 6, 2019); "33 Legal Medical Marijuana States and DC," ProCon.org, 2019, https://medicalmarijuana.procon.org/view.resource.php?-resourceID=000881 (accessed June 6, 2019).

17. "SOPA (Stop Online Piracy Act) Debate: Why Are Google and Facebook Against It?" *Washington Post*, November 17, 2011, http://www.washingtonpost.com/business/sopa-stop-online-piracy-act-debate-why-are-google-and-facebook-against-it/2011/11/17/gIQAvLubVN_story.html (accessed July 15, 2016).

18. S. Bono, A. Rubin, A. Stubblefield, and M. Green, "Security Through Legality," *Communications of the ACM* 49 (June 2006): 41–43.

19. Federal Trade Commission, "Mobile Advertising Network InMobi Settles FTC Charges It Tracked Hundreds of Millions of Consumers'

Locations Without Permission," June 22, 2016, https://www.ftc.gov/news-events/press-releases/2016/06/mobile-advertising-network-inmobi-settles-ftc-charges-it- tracked (accessed July 15, 2016); "What Are Some of the Laws Regarding Internet and Data Security?" Symantec Corporation, 2019, https://us.norton.com/internetsecurity-privacy-laws-regarding-internet-data-security.html (accessed April 29, 2019).

20. Leslie Meredith, "Internet Safety for Kids: Almost All Children Under 2 Have a Digital Footprint," *Huffington Post,* January 10, 2013, http://www.huffingtonpost.com/2013/01/10/children-internet-safety_n_2449721.html (accessed July 15, 2016); "Children's Access to and Use of the Internet," National Center for Education Statistics, May 2017, https://nces.ed.gov/programs/coe/indicator_cch.asp (accessed April 30, 2019).

21. Bob Zukis, "Regulators Want CEOs to Go to Jail For Cyber Failings, Should You?" *Forbes,* April 10, 2019, https://www.forbes.com/sites/bobzukis/2019/04/10/regulators-want-ceos-to-go-to-jail-for-cyber-failings-should-you/#4b6fa3ee19fa (accessed May 10, 2019); Brian Deagon, "More Than 10% of Facebook Users Have Quit the Platform," *Investor's Business Daily,* April 9, 2019, https://www.investors.com/news/technology/facebook-users-quit-ibd-poll-privacy/ (accessed May 10, 2019); Richard Nieva, "Google, Plagued by Data and Privacy Issues, Still Rakes It In," *CNET,* February 4, 2019, https://www.cnet.com/news/google-alphabet-earnings-fourth-quarter-2018/ (accessed May 10, 2019).

22. Jon Watson, "70+ Common Online Scams Used by Cyber Criminals and Fraudsters," *Comparitech,* July 8, 2018, https://www.comparitech.com/vpn/avoiding-common-scams-schemes/ (accessed April 29, 2019); Internet Crime Complaint Center (IC3), "2018 IC3 Annual Report: IC3 Complaint Statistics 2014-2018," 2018, https://www.ic3.gov/media/annualreport/2018_IC3Report.pdf (accessed April 29, 2019).

23. Susan Dudley and Melinda Warren, "Regulators' Budget: More for Homeland Security, Less for Environmental Regulation, An Analysis of the U.S. Budget for Fiscal Years 1960 Through 2019," Weidenbaum Center on the Economy, Government, and Public Policy, May 2018, https://wc.wustl.edu/files/wc/imce/2019_regulators_budget_40_final.pdf (accessed April 29, 2019).

24. Kymberly Escobar, "Government Regulation: Costs Lower, Benefits Greater than Industry Estimates," *Pew,* May 26, 2015, https://www.pewtrusts.org/en/research-and-analysis/fact-sheets/2015/05/government-regulation-costs-lower-benefits-greater-than-industry-estimates (accessed June 13, 2019); Diane Coyle, "3 Ways That Regulation Benefits Economies," World Economic Forum, July 18, 2018, https://www.weforum.org/agenda/2018/07/three-cheers-for-regulation/ (accessed June 13, 2019).

25. William M. Pride and O. C. Ferrell, *Marketing: Concepts and Strategies,* 12th ed. (Boston: Houghton Mifflin, 2003), pp. 54–55; Better Business Bureau, "About BBB," 2019, https://www.bbb.org/about-bbb (accessed April 29, 2019); Better Business Bureau, "What We Do," 2019, https://www.bbb.org/washington-dc-eastern-pa/get-to-know-us/about-us/what-we-do/ (accessed April 29, 2019).

26. Better Business Bureau, "Accreditation Revoked," April 22, 2016, http://www.bbb.org/southeast-texas/news-events/bbb-in-the-news/2016/04/revocation/ (accessed July 15, 2016).

27. ASRC, "About NAD," http://www.asrcreviews.org/ (accessed June 6, 2019). Better Business Bureau, "National Advertising Division (NAD)," https://bbbprograms.org/programs/nad/ (accessed June 6, 2019); Council of Better Business Bureaus, "Self-Regulation: Leadership and Support," ASRC, 2019, http://www.asrcreviews.org/supporting-advertising-industry-self-regulation/ (accessed June 6, 2019). D. McPherson, "NAD: Testimonials on Pinterest Need Disclaimers," Response, 2012, 10. C. Lee Peeler, "Four Decades Later, Ad Industry's Self-Regulation Remains the Gold Standard, Yet the Program Does Not Enjoy Broad-Based Financial Support," *Advertising Age,* March 13, 2013, http://adage.com/article/guestcolumnists/40-years-adland-s-regulation-remains-gold-standard/240245/ (accessed June 6, 2019). John E. VillaFranco and Katherine E. Riley, "So You Want to Self-Regulate? The National Advertising Division as Standard Bearer," *Antitrust* 27(2), 2013, 79–84.

28. "Our History: What Is DMA?" *Marketing Edge,* 2019, https://www.marketingedge.org/about-us/what-is-dma (accessed June 6, 2019); Allison Torres Burtka, "For Marketing Association, Name Change Highlights Data," *Associations Now,* October 24, 2016, https://associationsnow.com/2016/10/marketing-association-name-change-highlights-data/ (accessed June 6, 2019); BusinessDictionary, "Direct Marketing Association (DMA)," http://www.businessdictionary.com/definition/Direct-Marketing-Association-DMA.html (accessed June 6, 2019); "The Code," DMA: Data and Marketing Association, https://dma.org.uk/uploads/misc/dma-code-v3.pdf (accessed June 7, 2019).

29. European Union, "EU Member Countries," http://europa.eu/about-eu/countries/member-countries/index_en.htm (accessed July 15, 2016).

30. Europa, "Structural Reform of the EU Banking Sector," January 29, 2014, http://europa.eu/rapid/press-release_IP-14- 85_en.htm?locale=en (accessed July 15, 2016); Europa, "Commission Roadmap to Meet the Long-Term Financing Needs of the European Economy," March 27, 2014, http://europa.eu/rapid/press-release_IP-14-320_en.htm?locale=en (accessed July 15, 2016); Europa, "New Measures to Restore Confidence in Benchmarks Following LIBOR and EURIBOR Scandals," September 18, 2013, http://europa.eu/rapid/ press-release_IP-13-841_en.htm?locale=en (accessed July 15, 2016).

31. *Financial Times* Reporters, "Why Did We Leave the EU? and Other Brexit FAQs," *Financial Times,* June 28, 2016, http://www. ft.com/cms/s/0/f1300fb4-3c5a-11e6-8716-a4a71e8140b0.html#axzz4EUqkbcax (accessed July 15, 2016); Brian Wheeler and Paul Seddon, "Brexit: All You Need to Know About the UK Leaving the EU," *BBC News,* April 18, 2019, https://www.bbc.com/news/uk-politics-32810887 (accessed April 29, 2019).

32. James Kanter, "E.U. Objects to U.S. Regulations on Capital Requirements," *The New York Times,* April 22, 2013, http:// www.nytimes.com/2013/04/23/business/global/eu-objects-to-us-regulations-on-capital-requirements.html (accessed July 15, 2016).

33. Brandon Mitchener, "Global Antitrust Process May Get Simpler," *Wall Street Journal,* October 27, 2000, p. A17; Debbie Thorne LeClair, O. C. Ferrell, and Linda Ferrell, "Federal Sentencing Guidelines for Organizations: Legal, Ethical, and Public Policy Issues for International Marketing," *Journal of Public Policy and Marketing* 16 (Spring 1997): 30.

34. Matthew Kahn, "George H.W. Bush Understood That Markets and the Environment Weren't Enemies," *The Conversation,* December 3, 2018, https://theconversation.com/george-h-w-bush-understood-that-markets-and-the-environment-werent-enemies-108011 (accessed June 7, 2019); Peter Bondarenko, "North American Free Trade Agreement," *Encyclopedia Britannica,* https://www.britannica.com/event/North-American-Free-Trade-Agreement (accessed June 7, 2019); Miller Center, "George H.W. Bush–Key Events," University of Virginia, https://millercenter.org/president/george-h-w-bush/key-events (accessed June 14, 2019).

35. NAFTA Signed into Law," *History,* July 28, 2019, https://www.history.com/this-day-in-history/nafta-signed-into-law (accessed August 26, 2019).

36. Marilyn Geewax, "'Clintonomics' Ruled the 1990s; 'Hillarynomics' Would Be Different," *NPR,* April 14, 2015, https://www.npr.org/sections/itsallpolitics/2015/04/14/399353192/clintononics-ruled-the-1990s-hillarynomics-may-be-different (accessed August 26, 2019).

37. Kimberly Amadeo, "Glass-Steagall Act of 1933, Its Purpose and Repeal," *The Balance,* July 10, 2019, https://www.thebalance.com/glass-steagall-act-definition-purpose-and-repeal-3305850 (accessed August 26, 2019).

38. Troy Segal, "Troubled Asset Relief Program (TARP)," *Investopedia,* May 5, 2019, https://www.investopedia.com/terms/t/troubled-asset-relief-program-tarp.asp (accessed June 7, 2019); U.S. Department of the Treasury, "TARP Programs," https://www.treasury.gov/initiatives/financial-stability/TARP-Programs/Pages/default.aspx# (accessed June 7, 2019); Kimberly Amadeo, "TARP Bailout Program: Did TARP Help You or the Banks?" *The Balance,* November 15, 2018, https://www.thebalance.com/tarp-bailout-program-3305895 (accessed June 7, 2019); "Troubled Asset Relief Program (TARP)," History.com, August 21, 2018, https://www.history.com/topics/21st-century/troubled-asset-relief-program (June 7, 2019); Chris Isidore, "U.S. Ends TARP with $15.3 Billion Profit," *CNN Business,* December 19, 2014, https://money.cnn.com/2014/12/19/news/companies/government-bailouts-end/ (accessed June 7, 2019).

39. Robert Scheer, "Obama Pulls a Clinton on Deregulation," *The Nation,* January 19, 2011, https://www.thenation.com/article/obama-pulls-clinton-deregulation/ (accessed August 26, 2019).

40. Kimberly Amadeo, "Obama's Stimulus Package and How Well It Worked," *The Balance,* August 7, 2019, https://www.thebalance.com/what-was-obama-s-stimulus-package-3305625 (accessed August 26, 2019).

41. Barack Obama, "Toward a 21st-Century Regulatory System," *Wall Street Journal,* January 18, 2011, https://www.wsj.com/articles/SB100

01424052748703396604576088272112103698 (accessed August 26, 2019).

42. Sam Batkins, "Deregulation Under Obama and Trump," *American Action Forum*, June 28, 2017, https://www.americanactionforum.org/insight/deregulation-obama-trump/ (acccessed August 26, 2019).

43. The White House, "President Donald J. Trump Is Delivering on Deregulation," December 14, 2017, https://www.whitehouse.gov/briefings-statements/president-donald-j-trump-delivering-deregulation/ (accessed August 26, 2019).

44. Ana Swanson, "U.S. Delays Some China Tariffs Until Stores Stock up for Holidays," *The New York Times*, August 13, 2019, https://www.nytimes.com/2019/08/13/business/economy/china-tariffs.html (accessed August 26, 2019).

45. Thomas Mitchell, "Trump Signs Farm Bill, Officially Legalizing Industrial Hemp," *Westword*, December 20, 2018, https://www.westword.com/marijuana/trump-signs-bill-officially-legalizing-industrial-hemp-11069764 (accessed August 26, 2019).

46. Richard W. Rahn, "Why Do We Regulate?" *Washington Times*, August 10, 2005, https://www.washingtontimes.com/news/2005/aug/10/20050810-092828-2104r/ (accessed May 27, 2019); Will Kenton, "Dodd-Frank Wall Street Reform and Consumer Protection Act," *Investopedia*, May 10, 2019, https://www.investopedia.com/terms/d/dodd-frank-financial-regulatory-reform-bill.asp (accessed June 11, 2019).

47. William Dunkelberg, "Why Deregulation Is Important," *Forbes*, March 23, 2018, https://www.forbes.com/sites/williamdunkelberg/2018/03/23/why-deregulation-is-important/#f94adfc1c184 (accessed June 11, 2019).

48. "5 Benefits of Energy Deregulation," American Power and Gas, September 1, 2015, https://www.americanpowerandgas.com/5-benefits-of-energy-deregulation/ (accessed June 11, 2019).

49. Kimberly Amadeo, "Deregulation Pros, Cons, and Examples: Why Airline Travel Is So Miserable, and Other Effects of Deregulation," *The Balance*, January 28, 2019, https://www.thebalance.com/deregulation-definition-pros-cons-examples-3305921 (accessed June 12, 2019).

50. Alfred E. Kahn, "Airline Deregulation," Library of Economics and Liberty, http://econlib.org/library/Enc1/AirlineDeregulation.html (accessed June 11, 2019).

51. "The Growth Potential of Deregulation," Council of Economic Advisors, October 2, 2017, https://www.whitehouse.gov/sites/whitehouse.gov/files/documents/The%20Growth%20Potential%20of%20Deregulation.pdf (accessed June 12, 2019).

Chapter 5

1. Will Brinson, "Frontline PBS Doc 'League of Denial' Examines NFL Concussion Problem," *CBS Sports*, October 8, 2013, https://www.cbssports.com/nfl/news/frontline-pbs-doc-league-of-denial-examines-nfl-concussion-problem/ (accessed June 21, 2019); Travis Waldron, "What Does the NFL's Concussion Settlement Mean for the Future of Football?" *Think Progress*, August 29, 2013, https://thinkprogress.org/what-does-the-nfls-concussion-settlement-mean-for-the-future-of-football-d8650489ea7e/ (accessed June 21, 2019); Michael McCann, "Will New CTE Findings Doom the NFL Concussion Settlement?" *Sports Illustrated*, August 15, 2017, https://www.si.com/nfl/2017/08/15/new-cte-study-effect-nfl-concussion-settlement (accessed June 21, 2019); Tom Huddleston Jr., "The Football Industrial Complex Is in Big Trouble," *Fortune*, September 7, 2017 (accessed June 21, 2019); "NFL Concussions Fast Facts," *CNN*, August 26, 2018, https://www.cnn.com/2013/08/30/us/nfl-concussions-fast-facts/index.html (accessed June 21, 2019); Steve Almasy and Jill Martin, "Judge Approves NFL Concussion Lawsuit Settlement," *CNN*, April 22, 2015 (accessed June 21, 2019); Susan Scutti, "NFL Announces $100 Million Concussion Initiative," *CNN*, September 14, 2016, https://www.cnn.com/2016/09/14/health/nfl-concussion-safety-initiative/index.html (accessed June 21, 2019); Lorenzo Reyes, "NFL Says Player Concussions Dropped by 29 Percent in 2018 Regular Season," *USA Today*, January 24, 2019 (accessed June 21, 2019); Mark Wilson, "Why NFL Helmets Will Never Be Concussion-Proof," *Fast Company*, January 5, 2016, https://www.fastcompany.com/1671752/why-nfl-helmets-will-never-be-concussion-proof (accessed June 21, 2019); Melissa Locker, "NFL Concussions: On Super Bowl Weekend, Here's the Latest Head Injury Data," *Fast Company*, February 2, 2019, https://www.fastcompany.com/90300790/nfl-concussion-statistics-2018-2019-on-super-bowl-day-heres-the-latest-head-injury-data

(accessed June 21, 2019); Lauren Ezell, "Timeline: The NFL's Concussion Crisis," *PBS*, October 8, 2013, https://www.pbs.org/wgbh/pages/frontline/sports/league-of-denial/timeline-the-nfls-concussion-crisis/ (accessed October 1, 2019); Eric Branch, "Making Football Safer," *San Francisco Chronicle*, October 25, 2018, https://www.sfchronicle.com/sports/article/Football-wrestles-with-its-violent-nature-Can-it-13319237.php (accessed October 1, 2019).

2. Noam N. Levey, "Trump Officials Tell One Court Obamacare Is Failing and Another It's Thriving," *Los Angeles Times*, July 8, 2019, https://www.latimes.com/politics/la-na-pol-trump-obamacare-lawsuit-20190708-story.html (accessed July 10, 2019).

3. Rachel Augustine Potter, "Regulatory Lobbying Has Increased Under the Trump Administration, but the Groups Doing the Lobbying May Surprise You," Brookings Institution, July 11, 2018, https://www.brookings.edu/research/regulatory-lobbying-has-increased-under-the-trump-administration-but-the-groups-doing-the-lobbying-may-surprise-you/ (accessed August 26, 2019).

4. National Archives, "Chapter 23. Records of the Joint Committees of Congress 1789–1968 (Record Group 128)," 1989, http://www.archives.gov/legislative/guide/house/chapter-23-joint-organization-of-congress-1944-1946.html (accessed June 11, 2014); National Archives, "Congressional Records," http://www.archives.gov/legislative/research/ (accessed June 11, 2014); "Driving Mr. Gephardt," *Newsweek*, August 21, 2000, 48.

5. "About the FEC," Federal Election Commission, http://www.fec.gov/about.shtml (accessed July 15, 2016).

6. "A Brief History of Money and Politics," Campaign Legal Center, http://www.campaignlegalcenter.org/attachments/BCRA_MCCAIN_FEINGOLD/BCRA_REGULATIONS/1223.pdf (accessed June 11, 2014).

7. Gregory J. Krieg, "What Is a Super PAC? A Short History," ABC News, August 9, 2012, http://abcnews.go.com/Politics/OTUS/super-pac-short-history/story?id=16960267 (accessed July 15, 2016).

8. Michael Wines, "What Is Gerrymandering? And Why Did the Supreme Court Rule on It?" *The New York Times*, June 27, 2019, https://www.nytimes.com/2019/06/27/us/what-is-gerrymandering.html (accessed July 9, 2019).

9. "About Common Cause," Common Cause, https://www.commoncause.org/about-us (accessed April 29, 2019).

10. "Our Work," Common Cause, https://www.commoncause.org/our-work/ (accessed July 9, 2019).

11. Karl Evers-Hillstrom, "Trade Takes over K Street as Lobbyists Take Aim at Trump Tariffs," *Open Secrets*, April 26, 2019, https://www.opensecrets.org/news/2019/04/trade-takes-over-k-street-as-lobbyists-take-aim-at-trump-tariffs/ (accessed July 9, 2019).

12. Peter Eavis, "U.S. Reforms No Pushover for Banks," *The Wall Street Journal*, June 22, 2009, http://online.wsj.com/article/SB124563161642335927.html (accessed July 15, 2016); Deborah Solomon and Damian Paletta, "U.S. Eyes Bank Pay Overhaul," *The Wall Street Journal*, May 13, 2009, http://online.wsj.com/article/SB124215896684211987.html (accessed July 15, 2016); Silla Brush, "Top 10 Lobbying Fights over Financial Reform Overhaul Legislation," *The Hill*, March 16, 2010, http://thehill.com/business-a-lobbying/87225-top-10-lobbying-fights-over-financial-reform-overhaul (accessed July 15, 2016); Larry D. Wall, "Supervising Bank Compensation Policies," Federal Reserve Bank of Atlanta, November 2013, http://www.frbatlanta.org/cenfis/pubscf/nftv_1311.cfm (accessed July 15, 2016).

13. Timothy Smith, Walden Asset Management, and John Keenan, "2019 Lobbying Disclosure Resolutions," Harvard Law School Forum on Corporate Governance and Financial Regulation, March 14, 2019, https://corpgov.law.harvard.edu/2019/03/14/2019-lobbying-disclosure-resolutions/ (accessed July 25, 2019).

14. Jake Sherman, "Legislators Framing Climate Bills Hold Energy Stock," *The Wall Street Journal*, June 17, 2009, http://online.wsj.com/news/articles/SB124519704993421187 (accessed July 15, 2016).

15. Maggie Severns, "Reckless Stock Trading Leaves Congress Rife with Conflicts," *Politico*, May 14, 2017, https://www.politico.com/story/2017/05/14/congress-stock-trading-conflict-of-interest-rules-238033 (accessed June 10, 2019).

16. "Can Congress Members Sit on Corporate Boards? It's Allowed," CBS News, August 10, 2018, https://www.cbsnews.com/news/congress-member-sitting-on-corporate-board-its-allowed/ (accessed July 10, 2019).

17. Sandra Day O'Connor, "Judicial Independence and 21st-Century Challenges," *The Bencher: The Magazine for the American Inns of Court*, July/August 2012, 14; used information from the Annenberg Public

Policy Institute; Richard H. Levenstein, "Making a Difference: Educating the Public About the Importance of a Fair, Impartial, and Independent Judiciary One Judge and One Lawyer at a Time," *The Bencher: The Magazine for the American Inns of Court*, July/August 2012, 22; used information from a Harris Interactive Poll of Florida's adult population commissioned by the Florida Bar in December 2005; Doug Schuler, *Business and Government: Some Introductory Thoughts*, Rice University, Washington Campus Microsoft PowerPoint © 2013; Jeffrey Toobin, "Money Unlimited: How Chief Justice John Roberts Orchestrated the Citizens United decision," *The New Yorker*, May 21, 2012, http://www.newyorker.com/reporting/2012/05/21/120521fa_fact_toobin?currentPage=all (accessed July 15, 2016).

18. Léa Coulet, "The Value of Engagement with Trade Associations in Policymaking, Regulation, and Standardization," Regulatory Affairs Professionals Society, June 10, 2019, https://www.raps.org/news-and-articles/news-articles/2019/6/the-value-of-engagement-with-trade-associations-in (accessed July 8, 2019).

19. Daniel Castro, "Benefits and Limitations of Industry Self-Regulation for Online Behavioral Advertising," Information Technology & Innovation Foundation, December 2011, https://www.itif.org/files/2011-self-regulation-online-behavioral-advertising.pdf (accessed June 19, 2019); Jerrold G. Van Cise, "Regulation—By Business or Government? *Harvard Business Review*, March 1966, https://hbr.org/1966/03/regulation-by-business-or-government (accessed June 19, 2019); Anil K. Gupta and Lawrence J. Lad, "Industry Self-Regulation: An Economic, Organizational, and Political Analysis," *Academy of Management Review* 8, no. 3 (1983): 417.

20. Christopher Cheney, "5-Part Guideline Set to Address Impaired Physicians," *Health Leaders*, June 3, 2019, https://www.healthleadersmedia.com/clinical-care/5-part-guideline-set-address-impaired-physicians (accessed July 8, 2019).

21. "Public Affairs," PR Council, https://prcouncil.net/inside-pr/public-affairs/ (accessed June 19, 2019).

22. Anup Shah, "General Electric's Influence," *Global Issues*, December 26, 2004, www.globalissues.org/article/162/some-examples#General ElectricsInfluence (accessed July 8, 2019).

23. "5 Ways Social Media Has Changed Public Relations," 5W Public Relations, https://www.5wpr.com/new/social-media-public-relations/ (accessed July 8, 2019).

24. "The Sherman Antitrust Act," Antitrust Case Browser, http://www.stolaf.edu/people/becker/antitrust/statutes/sherman.html (accessed July 15, 2016); Federal Trade Commission, "The Antitrust Laws," https://www.ftc.gov/tips-advice/competition-guidance/guide-antitrust-laws/antitrust-laws (accessed July 10, 2019).

25. Jan Wolfe, "Here's Why the Justice Department Wants to Go After Google," CNBC, June 2, 2019, https://www.cnbc.com/2019/06/02/heres-why-the-justice-department-wants-to-go-after-google.html (accessed July 8, 2019).

26. Madeleine Joung, "Google, Amazon, Facebook, and Apple Could Face Antitrust Investigations. How Do Those Work?" *TIME*, June 5, 2019, https://time.com/5601245/google-amazon-facebook-apple-antitrust/ (accessed July 8, 2019).

27. U.S. Department of Justice, "Antitrust Enforcement and the Consumer," http://www.justice.gov/atr/public/div_stats/antitrust-enfor-consumer.pdf (accessed July 15, 2016).

28. Corporate Research Project of Good Jobs First, "Violation Tracker Individual Record: Tachht, Inc. and Teqqi, LLC," *Good Jobs First*, 2019, https://violationtracker.goodjobsfirst.org/violation-tracker/-tachht-inc-and-teqqi-llc (accessed April 29, 2019); Federal Trade Commission, "FTC Sending Refund Checks Totaling More Than $437,000 to Consumers Who Bought Bogus Weight-loss Products," Federal Trade Commission: Press Releases, March 15, 2018, https://www.ftc.gov/news-events/press-releases/2018/03/ftc-sending-refund-checks-totaling-more-437000-consumers-who (accessed April 29, 2019).

29. Manatt Phelps and Phillips LLP, "LASIK Providers Need Corrective Advertising, *Lexology*, January 28, 2013, http://www.lexology.com/library/detail.aspx?g=1cfa731f-3821-4e40-b270-bc5b9d8d813d (accessed July 15, 2016).

30. Federal Trade Commission, "FTC Approves Final Consent Order in Moonlight Slumber, LLC Advertising Case," *Federal Trade Commission: Press Releases*, December 12, 2017, https://www.ftc.gov/news-events/press-releases/2017/12/ftc-approves-final-consent-order-moonlight-slumber-llc (accessed April 29, 2019); "Illinois Firm Barred from Making Misleading Baby Mattress Claims," Federal Trade Commission, September 28, 2017, https://www.ftc.gov/news-events/press-releases/2017/09/illinois-firm-barred-making-misleading-baby-mattress-claims (accessed April 29, 2019).

31. Janna Herron, "Consumer Protection Wanes Under Trump, Report Finds," *USA Today*, March 13, 2019, https://www.usatoday.com/story/money/2019/03/13/consumer-protection-actions-cfpb-ftc-and-cpsc-decline-under-trump/3142905002/ (accessed April 29, 2019).

32. Richard Conaboy, "Corporate Crime in America: Strengthening the Good Citizen Corporation," in *Corporate Crime in America: Strengthening the "Good Citizenship" Corporation* (Washington, DC: U.S. Sentencing Commission, 1995), 1–2.

33. Win Swenson, "The Organizational Guidelines' 'Carrot and Stick' Philosophy, and Their Focus on 'Effective' Compliance," in *Corporate Crime in America: Strengthening the "Good Citizenship" Corporation* (Washington, DC: U.S. Sentencing Commission, 1995), 17–26.

34. U.S. Sentencing Commission, "Overview of Federal and Criminal Cases," 2018, https://www.ussc.gov/sites/default/files/pdf/research-and-publications/research-publications/2019/FY18_Overview_Federal_Criminal_Cases.pdf (accessed July 15, 2019).

35. Katherine Blunt, "A Judge Wants to Control PG&E's Dividends Until It Reduces Risk of Fires," *The Wall Street Journal*, March 31, 2019, https://www.wsj.com/articles/a-judge-wants-to-control-pg-es-dividends-until-it-reduces-risk-of-fires-11554049719 (accessed July 15, 2019).

36. O. C. Ferrell and Linda Ferrell, "Current Developments in Managing Organizational Ethics and Compliance Initiatives," white paper, University of Wyoming, 2006, Daniels Fund Ethics Initiative.

37. Open Compliance Ethics Group, "2005 Benchmarking Study Key Findings," http://www.oceg.org/view/Benchmarking2005 (accessed June 12, 2014).

38. "U.S. Sentencing Guidelines Changes Become Effective November 1," *FCPA Compliance and Ethics Blog*, November 2, 2010, http://tfoxlaw.wordpress.com/2010/11/02/us-sentencing-guidelines-changes-become-effective-november-1/ (accessed June 12, 2014).

39. Paula Desio, deputy general counsel, *An Overview of the Organizational Guidelines,* http://www.ussc.gov/sites/default/files/pdf/training/organizational-guidelines/ORGOVERVIEW.pdf (accessed February 25, 2015).

40. Ferrell and Ferrell, "Current Developments."

41. "Benchmarking SOX Costs, Hours, and Controls," Protiviti, 2018, https://www.protiviti.com/sites/default/files/united_states/insights/sarbanes-oxley_survey_2018_protiviti.pdf (accessed May 1, 2019); Protiviti, "SOX Compliance Trends," YouTube, August 9, 2018, https://www.youtube.com/watch?v=glP1f60Lw6Y (accessed May 1, 2019).

42. *Report to the Nations: 2018 Global Study on Occupational Fraud and Abuse*, Association of Certified Fraud Examiners, 2018, https://s3-us-west-2.amazonaws.com/acfepublic/2018-report-to-the-nations.pdf (accessed May 1, 2019).

43. Barack Obama, "Remarks by the President on 21st-Century Financial Regulatory Reform," White House, June 17, 2009, https://www.whitehouse.gov/the-press-office/remarks-president-regulatory-reform (accessed July 15, 2016).

44. Michelle Price, "U.S. Markets Regulators Reach Deal on Dodd-Frank Swaps Capital Rules," *Reuters*, June 21, 2019, https://www.reuters.com/article/usa-sec-swaps/us-markets-regulators-reach-deal-on-dodd-frank-swaps-capital-rules-idUSL4N23R3YN (accessed July 9, 2019).

45. Joshua Gallu, "Dodd-Frank May Cost $6.5 Billion and 5,000 Workers," *Bloomberg*, February 14, 2011, http://www.bloomberg.com/news/articles/2011-02-14/dodd-frank-s-implementation-calls-for-6-5-billion-5-000-staff-in-budget (accessed July 15, 2016); Binyamin Appelbaum and Brady Dennis, "Dodd's Overhaul Goes Well Beyond Other Plans," *Washington Post*, November 11, 2009, http://www.washingtonpost.com/wp-dyn/content/article/2009/11/09/AR2009110901935.html?hpid=topnews&sid=ST2009111003729 (accessed July 15, 2016).

46. Maria Bartiromo, "JPMorgan CEO Jamie Dimon Sees Good Times in 2011," *USA Today*, February 21, 2011, http://www.usatoday.com/money/companies/management/bartiromo/2011-02-21-bartiromo21_CV_N.htm (accessed July 15, 2016).

47. Alan Rappeport and Emily Flitter, "Congress Approves First Big Dodd-Frank Rollback," *The New York Times*, May 22, 2018, https://www.nytimes.com/2018/05/22/business/congress-passes-dodd-frank-rollback-for-smaller-banks.html (accessed July 25, 2019).

48. "Office of Financial Research," U.S. Department of the Treasury, http://www.treasury.gov/initiatives/ofr/Pages/default.aspx (accessed July 15, 2016).

49. "Initiatives: Financial Stability Oversight Council," U.S. Department of the Treasury, http://www.treasury.gov/initiatives/Pages/FSOC-index.aspx (accessed July 15, 2016).

50. "Financial Stability Oversight Council Created Under the Dodd-Frank Wall Street Reform and Consumer Protection Act: Frequently Asked Questions," October 2010, http://www.treasury.gov/initiatives/wsr/Documents/FAQs%20-%20Financial%20Stability%20Oversight%20Council%20-%20October%202010%20FINAL%20v2.pdf (accessed July 15, 2016).

51. "Subtitle A—Bureau of Consumer Financial Protection," One Hundred Eleventh Congress of the United States of America, 589.

52. "Wall Street Reform: Bureau of Consumer Financial Protection (CFPB)," U.S. Department of the Treasury, http://www.consumerfinance.gov/ (accessed July 15, 2016); Sudeep Reddy, "Elizabeth Warren's Early Words on a Consumer Financial Protection Bureau," *The Wall Street Journal*, September 17, 2010, http://blogs.wsj.com/economics/2010/09/17/elizabeth-warrens-early-words-on-a-consumer-financial-protection-bureau/ (accessed July 15, 2016); Jennifer Liberto and David Ellis, "Wall Street Reform: What's in the Bill," *CNN*, June 30, 2010, http://money.cnn.com/2010/06/25/news/economy/whats_in_the_reform_bill/index.htm (accessed July 15, 2016).

53. Jean Eaglesham, "Warning Shot on Financial Protection," *The Wall Street Journal*, February 9, 2011, http://online.wsj.com/article/SB10001424052748703507804576130370862263258.html?mod=googlenews_wsj (accessed July 15, 2016).

54. Liz Rappaport, Liz Moyer, and Anupreeta Das, "Goldman Sets Funds for 'Volcker'," *The Wall Street Journal,* February 8, 2013, C1–C2.

55. Eaglesham, "Warning Shot on Financial Protection."

56. Will Kenton, "Consumer Financial Protection Bureau (CFPB)," *Investopedia*, March 11, 2019, https://www.investopedia.com/terms/c/consumer-financial-protection-cfpb.asp (accessed June 19, 2019); Joe Valenti, "Why We Need a Strong CFPB, in 5 Numbers," Center for American Progress, January 18, 2017, https://www.americanprogress.org/issues/economy/news/2017/01/18/296539/why-we-need-a-strong-cfpb-in-5-numbers/ (accessed June 19, 2019); "Consumer Financial Protection Bureau Fines Wells Fargo $100 Million for Widespread Illegal Practice of Secretly Opening Unauthorized Accounts," Consumer Financial Protection Bureau, September 8, 2016, https://www.consumerfinance.gov/about-us/newsroom/consumer-financial-protection-bureau-fines-wells-fargo-100-million-widespread-illegal-practice-secretly-opening-unauthorized-accounts/ (accessed June 19, 2019).

57. Jean Eaglesham and Ashby Jones, "Whistleblower Bounties Pose Challenges," *The Wall Street Journal*, December 13, 2010, C1, C3.

58. "SEC Announces First Whistleblower Payout Under Dodd-Frank Bounty Program," *Compliance Corner,* August 2012, http://compliancecorner.wnj.com/?p=177 (accessed July 15, 2016).

59. Jamie Dimon, "A Unified Bank Regulator Is a Good Start," *The Wall Street Journal*, June 29, 2009, http://www.wsj.com/articles/SB124605726587563517 (accessed July 15, 2016).

60. Jane J. Kim and Aaron Lucchetti, "Big Change in Store for Brokers in Obama's Oversight Overhaul," *The Wall Street Journal*, June 19, 2009, http://online.wsj.com/article/SB124536973514629609.html?mod=googlenews_wsj (accessed July 15, 2016).

61. Joe Flint, "Justice Department Sides with Broadcasters in Fight Against Aereo," *Los Angeles Times,* March 3, 2013, http://articles.latimes.com/2014/mar/03/entertainment/la-et-ct-justice-department-aereo-supreme-court-brief-20140303 (accessed July 15, 2016) (accessed June 26, 2014); Keach Hagey, "Supreme Court Ruling a Likely Death Knell for Aereo," *The Wall Street Journal*, June 25, 2014, http://www.wsj.com/articles/supreme-court-ruling-a-likely-death-knell-for-aereo-1403707884 (accessed July 15, 2016).

62. Don Reisinger, "Here's How Much Cash You'll Collect from Apple's Price-Fixing Case," *Fortune,* June 21, 2016, http://fortune.com/2016/06/21/apple-lawsuit-price-fixing/ (accessed July 15, 2016).

Chapter 6

1. Stephanie Armour, "Drug Prices to Be Disclosed in TV Ads Soon," *The Wall Street Journal*, May 8, 2019, https://www.wsj.com/articles/drug-prices-to-be-disclosed-in-tv-ads-soon 11557335295 (accessed May 29, 2019); "Should Drug Prices Be Disclosed in Ads Targeted Directly to Consumers?" *The Wall Street Journal*, April 29, 2019, https://www.wsj.com/articles/should-drug-prices-be-disclosed-in-ads-targeted-directly-to-consumers-11556589840 (accessed May 29, 2019); "How Are Prescription Drugs Prices Determined?" *American Medical Association*, April 9, 2019, https://www.ama-assn.org/delivering-care/public health/how-are-prescription-drug-prices-determined (accessed May 29, 2019); Yoni Blumberg, "Here's Why Many Prescription Drugs in the US Cost So Much—and It's Not Innovation or Improvement," *CNBC*, January 14, 2019, https://www.cnbc.com/2019/01/10/why-prescription-drugs-in-the-us-cost-so-much.html (accessed May 29, 2019); Wayne Winegarden, "The Bizarre World of Drug Pricing," *Forbes*, November 19, 2018, https://www.forbes.com/sites/waynewinegarden/2018/11/19/the-bizarre-world-of-drug-pricing/#6abe5d9064c6 (accessed May 29, 2019); Scott W. Atlas, "How to Reduce Prescription-Drug Prices: First, Do No Harm," *The Wall Street Journal: Opinion*, February 13, 2019, https://www.wsj.com/articles/how-to-reduce-prescription-drug-prices-first-do-no-harm-11550100537 (accessed May 29, 2019); Denise Roland, "A $2 Million Drug Is About to Hit the Market," *The Wall Street Journal*, May 07, 2019, https://www.wsj.com/articles/a-2-million-drug-is-about-to-hit-the-market-11557221401?mod=hp_lead_pos6 (accessed May 28, 2019); Linda A. Johnson, "Here Are the 6 Reasons Why Prescription Drugs are So Expensive," *Business Insider,* September 25, 2015, http://www.businessinsider.com/ap-multiple-factors-cause-high-prescription-drug-prices-in-us-2015-9 (accessed July 3, 2019); Peter Loftus, "Gilead Knew Hepatitis Drug Price Was High, Senate Says," *The Wall Street Journal,* December 1, 2015, http://www.wsj.com/articles/gilead-knew-hepatitis-drug-price-was-high-senate-says-1449004771 (accessed July 3, 2019); Amy Nordrum, "Why Are Prescription Drugs So Expensive? Big Pharma Points to the Cost of Research and Development, Critics Says That's No Excuse," *International Business Times,* May 19, 2015, http://www.ibtimes.com/why-are-prescription-drugs-so-expensive-big-pharmapoints-cost-research-development-1928263 (accessed July 3, 2019); Andrew Pollack, "Drug Goes from $13.50 a Tablet to $750, Overnight," *The New York Times,* September 20, 2015, http://www.nytimes.com/2015/09/21/business/a-huge-overnight-increase-in-a-drugs-price-raises-protests.html?_r=0 (accessed July 3, 2019); Reuters, "Turing Names New CEO to Replace Shkreli," *CNBC*, December 18, 2015, http://www.cnbc.com/2015/12/17/turing-pharmaceuticalsceo-shkreli-arrested-by-fbi-reuters.html (accessed July 3, 2019); Jonathan D. Rockoff, "Express Scripts Turns to a Compounder to Avoid a Turing Drug," *The Wall Street Journal,* December 1, 2015, http://www.wsj.com/articles/express-scripts-seeks-lower-price-alternative-to-daraprim-1448946061 (accessed July 3, 2019); Jeanne Whalen, "Why the U.S. Pays More Than Other Countries for Drugs," *The Wall Street Journal,* December 1, 2015, http://www.wsj.com/articles/why-the-u-s-pays-more-than-other-countries-for-drugs-1448939481 (accessed July 3, 2019).

2. Deirdre Campbell, "2019 Trust in Financial Services," Edelman Holdings, April 24, 2019, https://www.edelman.com/research/trust-in-financial-services-2019 (accessed June 25, 2019).

3. Raytheon website, "Ethics," https://www.raytheon.com/ourcompany/ourculture/ethics (accessed June 25, 2019); CSRHUB, "Raytheon Company CSR/ESG Ranking," https://www.csrhub.com/CSR_and_sustainability_information/Raytheon-Company (accessed June 25, 2019); Raytheon, "The Lessons in the Stories: Communication is Critical to Identifying and Resolving Ethical Concerns," December 15, 2017, https://www.raytheon.com/news/feature/lessons-stories (accessed June 25, 2019).

4. Devin Thorpe, "Why CSR? The Benefits of Corporate Social Responsibility Will Move You to Act," *Forbes*, May 18, 2013, http://www.forbes.com/sites/devinthorpe/2013/05/18/why-csr-the-benefits-of-corporate-social-responsibility-will-move-you-to-act/#108178db5e1c (accessed August 3, 2016).

5. Investopedia, "5 Most Publicized Ethics Violations by CEOs," *Forbes*, February 5, 2013, https://www.forbes.com/sites/investopedia/2013/02/05/5-most-publicized-ethics-violations-by-ceos/#149669694bbc (accessed June 25, 2019); Peter Yang, "The Most Outrageous Resume Lies Employers Have Seen—and the 4 Secret Tactics They Use to Catch a Liar," *CNBC*, March 19, 2019, https://www.cnbc.com/2019/03/19/the-most-outrageous-resume-lies-and-4-secret-tactics-hiring-managers-use-to-catch-a-liar.html (accessed June 25, 2019).

6. 1% for the Planet, "About Us, " https://www.onepercentfortheplanet.org/about (accessed June 25, 2019); Patagonia, "Giving Back," https://www.patagoniaprovisions.com/pages/giving-back (accessed June 25, 2019); Patagonia, "1% for the Planet," https://www.patagonia.com/one-percent-for-the-planet.html (accessed June 25, 2019); Anthony

Shields, "Good Business: 10 Companies with Ethical Corporate Policies," *Minyanville*, February 16, 2013, http://www.minyanville.com/sectors/consumer/articles/Good-Business253A-Corporations-with-Great-Ethical/2/16/2013/id/48045?refresh=1 (accessed August 3, 2016).

7. Cassidy Morrison, "FDA Struggles with Limited Powers on E-Cigarettes," *Washington Examiner*, March 29, 2019, https://www.washingtonexaminer.com/news/fda-struggles-with-limited-powers-on-e-cigarettes (accessed June 25, 2019); Elizabeth Klinefelter, "FDA in Brief: As Part of Continuing Efforts to Advance Robust Framework for Oversight of E-Cigarettes, FDA Finalizes Compliance Policy for Certain Activities Conducted by Vape Shops That Modify E-Cigarettes," U.S. Food and Drug Administration, March 22, 2019, https://www.fda.gov/news-events/fda-brief/fda-brief-part-continuing-efforts-advance-robust-framework-oversight-e-cigarettes-fda-finalizes (accessed June 25, 2019); Gigen Mammoser, "How the New FDA E-Cig Rules Could Affect You," *Healthline*, March 14, 2019, https://www.healthline.com/health-news/how-the-new-fda-e-cig-rules-could-affect-you (accessed June 25, 2019).

8. Debbie Thorne McAlister and Robert Erffmeyer, "A Content Analysis of Outcomes and Responsibilities for Consumer Complaints to Third-Party Organizations," *Journal of Business Research* 56 (April 2003): 341–352.

9. "Drugmakers Allegedly Inflated Prices over 1,000% and 44 States Are Now Suing," *CNBC*, May 11, 2019, https://www.cnbc.com/2019/05/11/us-states-accuse-teva-and-other-drugmakers-of-colluding-to-inflate-prices-over-1000percent.html (accessed June 25, 2019).

10. "Biz Deans Talk—Business Management Education Blog," January 2, 2009, http://www.deanstalk.net/deanstalk/2009/01/warren-buffetts.html (accessed August 3, 2016).

11. Barry Newman, "An Ad Professor Huffs Against Puffs, but It's a Quixotic Enterprise," *Wall Street Journal*, January 24, 2003, A1.

12. Kathy Caprino, "If Your Values Clash with How You're Working, You'll Suffer—Here's How To Fix That," *Forbes*, August 4, 2016, https://www.forbes.com/sites/kathycaprino/2016/08/04/if-your-values-clash-with-how-youre-working-youll-suffer-heres-how-to-fix-that/#77028f796601 (accessed June 27, 2019); Leslie Peters, "Organizational Values Are Important. What About Personal Values?" *Forbes*, August 9, 2018, https://www.forbes.com/sites/lesliepeters/2018/08/09/organizational-values-are-important-what-about-personal-values/#773bd80d5df9 (accessed June 27, 2019).

13. Guendalina Donde, "Ethics at Work: 2018 Survey of Employees Europe," Institute of Business Ethics, 2018, https://www.ibe.org.uk/userassets/publicationdownloads/ibe_survey_report_ethics_at_work_2018_survey_of_employees_europe_int.pdf (accessed September 24, 2019).

14. Thomas Sullivan, "Medtronic Settles $2.8 Million Off-Label Suit over Neurostimulator Promotion," Rockpointe, Inc.: Policy & Medicine, May 5, 2018 (last updated), https://www.policymed.com/2015/02/medtronic-settles-with-doj-for-28-million-to-resolve-false-claims-act-allegations-related-to-spinal.html (accessed June 28, 2019); U.S. Department of Justice: Office of Public Affairs, "Medtronic Inc. to Pay $2.8 Million to Resolve False Claims Act Allegations Related to 'SubQ Stimulation' Procedures," February 6, 2015, https://www.justice.gov/opa/pr/medtronic-inc-pay-28-million-resolve-false-claims-act-allegations-related-subq-stimulation (accessed June 28, 2019).

15. Daniel Press, "Consumer Financial Protection Bureau Should Define 'Abusive'," Competitive Enterprise Institute, June 5, 2019, https://cei.org/blog/consumer-financial-protection-bureau-should-define-abusive (accessed June 28, 2019).

16. Chris Woolston, "Bad Bosses: Dealing with Abusive Supervisors," *Knowable Magazine*, July 17, 2018, https://www.knowablemagazine.org/article/society/2018/bad-bosses-dealing-abusive-supervisors (accessed June 28, 2019).

17. "These Stats on Stealing Might Surprise You," Mars Hill Church, November 8, 2013, http://marshill.se/marshill/2013/11/08/these-stats-on-stealing-might-surprise-you (accessed August 3, 2016).

18. Erin Osterhaus, "43% of Employees Commit Time Theft: How Software Can Reduce Payroll Losses," *Software Advice*, April 23, 2015, https://www.softwareadvice.com/hr/industryview/time-theft-report-2015/ (accessed June 28, 2019).

19. Steven Mintz, "Unethical Employee Behaviors in the Workplace," *Workplace Ethics Advice Blog*, November 2, 2016, https://www.workplaceethicsadvice.com/2016/11/unethical-employee-behaviors-in-the-workplace.html (accessed June 28, 2019).

20. Boeing, "Ethical Business Conduct Guidelines: Using Resources," http://www.boeing.com/resources/boeingdotcom/principles/ethics_and_compliance/pdf/ethical_business_conduct_guidelines.pdf (accessed June 28, 2019).

21. Liz Wagner, Jeremy Carroll, Michael Horn, and Kevin Nious, "Conflict of Interest? Agreement Allowed Google to Pay Wages for Sunnyvale City Employees," NBC, February 25, 2019, https://www.nbcbayarea.com/investigations/Agreement-Allows-Google-to-Pay-Wages-of-Sunnyvale-City-Employees-506249411.html (accessed June 28, 2019).

22. Kate Sheppard, "Keystone XL Contractor's Potential Conflicts of Interest Not Mentioned in State Department Documents," *Huffington Post*, October 25, 2013, http://www.huffingtonpost.com/2013/10/25/keystone-xl-contractor_n_4159685.html (accessed August 3, 2016).

23. Christine Ferretti, "IT Firm, Ex-CEO Banned from Doing Business with Detroit After Bribery Case," *Detroit News*, https://www.detroitnews.com/story/news/local/detroit-city/2019/06/11/firm-and-ex-ceo-banned-city-contracts/1422668001/ (accessed June 28, 2019).

24. Samuel Rubenfeld and Dave Michaels, "Two Former Cognizant Executives Charged in Bribery Probe," *The Wall Street Journal*, February 15, 2019, https://www.wsj.com/articles/cognizant-to-pay-25-million-to-settle-bribery-claims-11550252878 (accessed June 28, 2019).

25. Stephen Johnson, "Corruption Is Costing the Global Economy $3.6 Trillion Every Year," World Economic Forum, December 13, 2018, https://www.weforum.org/agenda/2018/12/the-global-economy-loses-3-6-trillion-to-corruption-each-year-says-u-n (accessed June 29, 2019); Stephen Johnson, "The Global Economy Loses $3.6 Trillion to Corruption Each Year, Says U.N.," *Big Think*, December 10, 2018, https://bigthink.com/politics-current-affairs/corruption-costs-world-3-6-trillion (accessed June 29, 2019).

26. Patrick Thomas, "Health-Care Executive Tied to Admissions Scandal Found Guilty in Separate Fraud Case," *The Wall Street Journal*, April 5, 2019, https://www.wsj.com/articles/health-care-executive-tied-to-admissions-scandal-found-guilty-in-separate-fraud-case-11554499141 (accessed June 28, 2019).

27. U.S. Department of Justice, "Foreign Corrupt Practices Act Antibribery Provisions," http://www.justice.gov/criminal/fraud/fcpa/ (accessed August 3, 2016).

28. William H. Frey, "The US Will Become 'Minority White' in 2045, Census Projects," Brookings Institution, March 14, 2018, https://www.brookings.edu/blog/the-avenue/2018/03/14/the-us-will-become-minority-white-in-2045-census-projects/ (accessed June 29, 2019).

29. Katie Clarey, "Back to Basics: Everything HR Needs to Know About the EEOC," *HR Dive*, July 30, 2019, https://www.hrdive.com/news/back-to-basics-everything-hr-needs-to-know-about-the-eeoc/559549/ (accessed August 26, 2019).

30. Mark H. Anderson, "Business Gets Stronger Hand in Age Cases," *The Wall Street Journal*, June 18, 2009, http://online.wsj.com/article/SB124535060326328507.html (accessed August 3, 2016).

31. Annie Nova, "Older Workers Could Soon Find It Easier to Prove Age Discrimination," *CNBC*, June 11, 2019, https://www.cnbc.com/2019/06/11/older-workers-could-soon-find-it-easier-to-prove-age-discrimination.html (accessed July 1, 2019); Alessandra Malito, "This Bipartisan Proposal Aims to End Age Discrimination for a Graying Workforce," *MarketWatch*, February 16, 2019, https://www.marketwatch.com/story/this-bipartisan-proposal-aims-to-end-age-discrimination-for-a-graying-workforce-2019-02-15 (accessed July 1, 2019).

32. Rachel Bachman, "U.S. Women's Team Sues Soccer Federation, Alleging Gender Discrimination," *The Wall Street Journal*, March 8, 2019, https://www.wsj.com/articles/u-s-womens-soccer-team-alleges-gender-discrimination-11552059299 (accessed June 28, 2019).

33. Paula N. Rubin, "Civil Rights and Criminal Justice: Primer on Sexual Harassment Series: NIJ Research in Action," National Criminal Justice Reference Service, October 1995, https://www.ncjrs.gov/txtfiles/harass.txt (accessed August 3, 2016).

34. U.S. Equal Employment Opportunity Commission, "Facts About Sexual Harassment," https://www.eeoc.gov/eeoc/publications/fs-sex.cfm (accessed July 1, 2019); Workplace Fairness, "Sexual Harassment—Legal Standards," https://www.workplacefairness.org/sexual-harassment-legal-rights#9 (accessed July 1, 2019); U.S. Equal Employment Opportunity Commission, "Facts About Retaliation," https://www.eeoc.gov/laws/types/facts-retal.cfm (accessed July 1, 2019).

35. "Charges Alleging Sexual Harassment FY 2010–FY 2018," U.S. Equal Employment Opportunity Commission, https://www.eeoc.gov/eeoc/statistics/enforcement/sexual_harassment_new.cfm (accessed July 1, 2019).

36. *Zabkowicz v. West Bend Co.,* 589 F. Supp. 780, 784, 35 EPD Par.34, 7 66 (E.D. Wis.1984).

37. Reed Abelson, "Theranos Founder Elizabeth Holmes Indicted on Fraud Charges," *The New York Times,* June 15, 2018, https://www.nytimes.com/2018/06/15/health/theranos-elizabeth-holmes-fraud.html (accessed June 28, 2019).

38. *Report to the Nations: 2018 Global Study on Occupational Fraud and Abuse,* Association of Certified Fraud Examiners, https://s3-us-west-2.amazonaws.com/acfepublic/2018-report-to-the-nations.pdf (accessed July 1, 2019); Beth Pinsker, "Expense Report of the Future Reduces Fraud and Headaches," *CNBC,* March 25, 2019, https://www.cnbc.com/2019/03/25/reuters-america-expense-report-of-the-future-reduces-fraud-and-headaches.html (accessed July 1, 2019).

39. *Report to the Nations.*

40. Nora J. Rifon, Robert LaRose, and Sejung Marina Choi, "Your Privacy Is Sealed: Effects of Web Privacy Seals on Trust and Personal Disclosures," *Journal of Consumer Affairs* 39, no. 2 (2002): 339–362.

41. Te-Ping Chen, "Workers Push Back as Companies Gather Fingerprints and Retina Scans," *Wall Street Journal,* March 27, 2019, https://www.wsj.com/articles/workers-push-back-as-companies-gather-fingerprints-and-retina-scans-11553698332?mod=hp_lead_pos11 (accessed June 28, 2019).

42. Mitch Wagner, "Google's Pixie Dust," *InformationWeek,* no. 1061 (2005): 98.

43. Internet Health Report 2018, *The Good, the Bad, and the Ugly Sides of Data Tracking,* April 2018, https://internethealthreport.org/2018/the-good-the-bad-and-the-ugly-sides-of-data-tracking/ (accessed July 1, 2019); "How Do Websites Track Users? Technologies and Methods, GDPR Compliance," *Cookiebot,* https://www.cookiebot.com/en/website-tracking/ (accessed July 1, 2019).

44. Kate Rogers, "One New Identity Theft Victim Every 3 Seconds in 2012," Fox Business, February 20, 2013, http://www.foxbusiness.com/features/2013/02/20/one-new-identity-theft-victim-every-3-seconds-in-2012.html (accessed August 4, 2016); *The Good, the Bad and the Ugly Sides of Data Tracking;* "How Do Websites Track Users?"

45. Seena Gressin, "The Marriott Data Breach," *Federal Trade Commission: Consumer Information,* December 4, 2018, https://www.consumer.ftc.gov/blog/2018/12/marriott-data-breach (accessed June 28, 2019).

46. Amitai Etzioni and Oren Etzioni, "AI Assisted Ethics," *Ethics and Information Technology,* 18, no. 2(2016), 149–156, doi:10.1007/s10676-016-9400-6.

47. Virginia Dignum, "Ethics in Artificial Intelligence: Introduction to the Special Issue," *Ethics and Information Technology,* 20, no. 1 (2018): 1–3, doi:10.1007/s10676-018-9450-z.

48. PJ Jakovljevic, "Demystifying Blockchain: The Technology and Its Providers," Technology Evaluation Centers, January 2, 2018, https://www3.technologyevaluation.com/research/tec-report/demystifying-blockchain-the-technology-and-its-providers.html (accessed January 17, 2019).

49. Luzi-Ann Javier, "Yes, These Chickens Are on the Blockchain," *Bloomberg,* April 9, 2018, https://www.bloomberg.com/news/features/2018-04-09/yes-these-chickens-are-on-the-blockchain (accessed August 26, 2019).

50. Matthew Howard, "The Future of AI Relies on a Code of Ethics," *TechCrunch,* June 21, 2018, https://techcrunch.com/2018/06/21/the-future-of-ai-relies-on-a-code-of-ethics/ (accessed June 26, 2019); Jared Council, "Investors Urge AI Startups to Inject Early Dose of Ethics," *The Wall Street Journal,* June 16, 2019, https://www.wsj.com/articles/investors-urge-ai-startups-to-inject-early-dose-of-ethics-11560682800?mod=searchresults&page=1&pos=7 (accessed June 25, 2019). James Tenser, "Are Ethics Compatible with AI?" *RetailWire,* January 29, 2018, www.retailwire.com/discussion/are-ethics-compatible-with-ai/ (accessed June 26, 2019); Dignum, "Ethics in Artificial Intelligence: Introduction to the Special Issue."

51. Tiffany Kary, "Corporate America Can't Afford to Ignore Gen Z," *Bloomberg,* March 29, 2019, https://www.bloomberg.com/news/articles/2019-03-29/how-gen-z-s-different-than-millennials-companies-try-asmr-memes (accessed July 1, 2019).

52. Immanuel Kant, "Fundamental Principles *of the Metaphysics of Morals,*" in *Problems of Moral Philosophy: An Introduction,* 2nd ed., ed. Paul W. Taylor (Encino, CA: Dickenson, 1972), 229.

53. Stefanie E. Naumann and Nathan Bennett, "A Case for Procedural Justice Climate: Development and Test of a Multilevel Model," *Academy of Management Journal* 43 (October 2000): 881–889.

54. Joel Brockner and P. A. Siegel, "Understanding the Interaction between Procedural and Distributive Justice: The Role of Trust," in *Trust in Organizations: Frontiers of Theory and Research,* ed. R. M. Kramer and T. R. Tyler (Thousand Oaks, CA: SAGE, 1995), 390–413.

55. Debbie Thorne LeClair, O. C. Ferrell, and John Fraedrich, *Integrity Management: A Guide to Managing Legal and Ethical Issues in the Workplace* (Tampa, FL: University of Tampa Press, 1998), 37.

56. John Fraedrich and O. C. Ferrell, "Cognitive Consistency of Marketing Managers in Ethical Situations," *Journal of the Academy of Marketing Science* 20 (1992): 242–252.

57. Shalom H. Schwartz, "Cultural Value Differences: Some Implications for Work," *Applied Psychology: An International Review* 48 (1999): 23–47.

58. Michel Callon, Pierrre Lascoumes, and Yannick Barthe, *Acting in an Uncertain World: An Essay on Technical Democracy* (Cambridge, MA: MIT Press, 2009).

59. Joel Gehman, Linda K. Treviño, and Raghu Garud, "Values Work: A Process Study of the Emergence and Performance of Organizational Values and Practices," *Academy of Management Journal* 56, no. 1 (2013): 84–112.

60. Joseph W. Weiss, *Business Ethics: A Managerial, Stakeholder Approach* (Belmont, CA: Wadsworth, 1994), 13.

61. Matt Levine, "Fake Accounts Still Haunt Wells Fargo," *Bloomberg: Opinion,* October 23, 2018, https://www.bloomberg.com/opinion/articles/2018-10-23/fake-accounts-still-haunt-wells-fargo (accessed June 28, 2019).

62. Carol Loomis, "Derivatives: The Risk That Still Won't Go Away," *Fortune,* June 6, 2009, 55–60.

63. Marc Gunther, "Brewing Success (The Fun Way)," *B the Change,* October 31, 2016, https://bthechange.com/brewing-success-the-fun-way-5bd9e5e187a1 (accessed August 26, 2019).

64. New Belgium Brewing, "Energy," https://www.newbelgium.com/sustainability/environmental-metrics/energy/ (accessed August 26, 2019).

65. New Belgium Brewing, "We Are 100% Employee Owned," December 29, 2012, https://www.newbelgium.com/blogs/new-belgium-brewing/2013/01/16/we-are-100-employee-owned/ (accessed August 26, 2019).

66. Ethics Resource Center, *2013 National Business Ethics Survey of the U.S. Workforce* (Arlington, VA: Ethics Resource Center, 2014).

67. George Diepenbrock, "Ethics and Compliance Officers Face Challenges to Their Legitimacy, Study Finds," University of Kansas, May 17, 2017, https://news.ku.edu/2017/05/12/ethics-and-compliance-officers-face-challenges-their-legitimacy-study-finds (accessed July 3, 2019); Adam Hayes, "Compliance Officer," *Investopedia,* June 12, 2019, https://www.investopedia.com/terms/c/compliance-officer.asp (accessed July 3, 2019).

68. O. C. Ferrell, Larry G. Gresham, and John Fraedrich, "A Synthesis of Ethical Decision Models for Marketing," *Journal of Macromarketing* 9 (Fall 1989):58–59.

69. Robert Gatewood, Robert Taylor, and O. C. Ferrell, *Management* (Homewood, IL: Richard D. Irwin, Inc., 1995).

70. Ethics and Compliance Initiative, *2016 Global Business Ethics Survey: Measuring Risk and Promoting Workplace Integrity* (Arlington, VA: Ethics and Compliance Initiative, 2016), 43; Ethics and Compliance Initiative, *2018 Global Business Survey: 2018 Global Benchmark on Workplace Ethics,* https://www.ethics.org/knowledge-center/interactive-maps/ (accessed June 28, 2019).

71. "Employee Theft No Longer an If—Now It Is How Much!" Kessler International, April 26, 2013, http://www.investigation.com/press/press118.htm (accessed August 4, 2016).

72. Yuval Feldman, "Companies Need to Pay More Attention to Everyday Unethical Behavior," *Harvard Business Review,* March 1, 2019, https://hbr.org/2019/03/companies-need-to-pay-more-attention-to-everyday-unethical-behavior (accessed June 28, 2019).

73. Jeffrey L. Seglin, "Forewarned Is Forearmed? Not Always," *The New York Times,* February 16, 2003, www.nytimes.com/2003/02/16/business/yourmoney/16ETHI.html (accessed August 4, 2016); Barbara Ley Toffler, *Final Accounting: Ambition, Greed, and the Fall of Arthur Andersen* (New York: Broadway Books, 2003).

74. General Electric, "Ecomagination," http://www.ge.com/about-us/ecomagination (accessed June 30, 2014); General

Electric, "Healthymagination," http://www.ge.com/about-us/ecomagination (accessed August 4, 2016); Business Wire, "GE Releases 2013 Progress Against Sustainability Commitments," June 30, 2014, http://www.businesswire.com/news/home/20140630006140/en/GE-Releases-2013-Progress-Sustainability-Commitments (accessed August 4, 2016).

75. Amanda Hess, "Dov Charney Was Fired for Losing, Not Sexual Harassment," *Slate,* June 27, 2014, http://www.slate.com/blogs/xx_factor/2014/06/27/dov_charney_firing_american_apparel_ceo_was_fired_for_financial_reasons.html (accessed August 4, 2016).

76. Ferrell et al., "A Synthesis of Ethical Decision Models."

77. Muel Kaptein, "From Inaction to External Whistleblowering: The Influence of the Ethical Culture of Organizations on Employee Responses to Observed Wrongdoing," *Journal of Business Ethics* 98 (2011): 513–530.

78. Gehman et al., "Values Work."

79. Bert Scholtens and Lammertjan Dam, "Cultural Values and International Differences in Business Ethics," *Journal of Business Ethics* 75 (2007): 273–284.

80. "2011 Annual Report," *Marriott,* 2011, http://investor.share-holder.com/mar/marriottAR11/pdf/marriott11ar.pdf (accessed August 4, 2016).

81. Gary R. Weaver and Linda K. Trevino, "Compliance and Values Oriented Ethics Programs: Influences on Employees' Attitudes and Behavior," *Business Ethics Quarterly* 9, no. 2 (1999): 315–335.

82. O. C. Ferrell, J. Fraedrich, and L. Ferrell, *Business Ethics: Ethical Decision-Making and Cases,* 12th ed. (Stamford, CT: Cengage, 2019).

83. Fraedrich and Ferrell, "Cognitive Consistency of Marketing Managers in Ethical Situations."

Chapter 7

1. Ryan Jenkins, "Rita Crundwell Recovery Funds to Fuel New Projects in Dixon," *WQAD 8,* March 14, 2019, https://wqad.com/2019/03/14/rita-crundwell-recovery-funds-to-fuel-new-projects-in-dixon/ (accessed June 1, 2019); Gravitas Ventures, "All the Queen's Horses," *Netflix,* http://www.allthequeenshorsesfilm.com/ (accessed June 1, 2019); Matt Pearce, "How One of the Biggest Swindlers in American History Built a Horse-Breeding Empire," *Los Angeles Times,* http://www.latimes.com/nation/la-na-horse-swindler-crundwell-20151030-story.html (accessed June 1, 2019); Rachel Rodgers, "Crundwell Recovery: 5 Years Later," *saukvalley.com,* April 14, 2017, http://www.saukvalley.com/2017/04/14/crundwell-recovery-5-years-later/a7nasm0/ (accessed June 1, 2019); The Fifth Estate, "Rita Crundwell—Fraud in Dixon, Illinois: Small Town Shakedown," *YouTube,* July 25, 2016, https://www.youtube.com/watch?v=WAYtaFxlw3M (accessed June 1, 2019); Melissa Jenco, "Dixon to Get $40 Million in Settlement of Embezzlement Case," *Chicago Tribune,* September 25, 2013, https://www.chicagotribune.com/news/ct-xpm-2013-09-25-chi-dixon-to-get-40-million-in-settlement-of-embezzlement-case-20130925-story.html (accessed June 1, 2019); Dick Carozza, "Dixon's Quiet Hero," *Fraud Magazine,* November/December 2018, https://www.fraud-magazine.com/article.aspx?id=4295003585 (accessed June 1, 2019).

2. Facebook Investor Relations, "Code of Conduct," *Facebook,* https://investor.fb.com/corporate-governance/code-of-conduct/default.aspx (accessed July 1, 2019); "Facebook," Better Business Bureau, https://www.bbb.org/us/ca/menlo-park/profile/social-media-marketing/facebook-1116-385674 (accessed July 1, 2019); Miles Howard, "Facebook, Yet Again, Violates Our Privacy. The Government Should End the Company's Monopoly," *WBUR,* December 20, 2018, https://www.wbur.org/cognoscenti/2018/12/20/facebook-privacy-violation-miles-howard (accessed July 1, 2019).

3. Umair Irfan and Julia Belluz, "Olympic Swimmer Ryan Lochte Broke Doping Rules. It Happens Far More Than You Think," *Vox,* July 27, 2018, https://www.vox.com/2018/7/24/17603358/ryan-lochte-doping-ban-olympics-instagram (accessed July 1, 2019).

4. "Third of Employees See Unethical Behaviour Being Rewarded by Managers," *Insurance Edge,* October 19, 2018, https://insurance-edge.net/2018/10/19/third-of-employees-see-unethical-behaviour-being-rewarded-by-managers/ (accessed July 1, 2019).

5. Starbucks, "Business Ethics and Compliance: Standards of Business Conduct," http://www.starbucks.ph/media/Business-Ethics-and-Compliance-eng_tcm70-11290.pdf (accessed July 1, 2019); Texas Instruments, "Our Values: Code of Conduct," http://www.ti.com/about-ti/company/our-values.html (accessed July 1, 2019); Martin

Jacobs, "How Ethical Is Levi's?" *Good on You,* September 4, 2017, https://goodonyou.eco/levis-ethical/ (accessed July 1, 2019).

6. David Grossman, "7 Critical Traits for Building Trust in Companies," Grossman Group, January 22, 2018, https://www.yourthoughtpartner.com/blog/7-critical-traits-for-building-trust-in-companies (July 3, 2019).

7. Adam Hayes, "Code of Ethics," *Investopedia,* May 31, 2019, https://www.investopedia.com/terms/c/code-of-ethics.asp (accessed July 13, 2019).

8. Lauren Hamer, "CEO Controversy: These Prominent CEOs Were Forced to Leave Their Own Companies," *Showbiz Cheat Sheet,* March 20, 2018, https://www.cheatsheet.com/money-career/ceo-controversy-prominent-ceos-forced-leave-companies.html/ (accessed July 1, 2019); Marisa Kendall, "Sexual Harassment Scandal: Silicon Valley VC Resigns over Claims of Inappropriate Conduct," *Mercury News,* June 26, 2017, https://www.mercurynews.com/2017/06/26/sexual-harassment-scandal-silicon-valley-vc-resigns-over-claims-inappropriate-conduct/ (accessed July 1, 2019).

9. Robert Reiss, "CEOs and Ethics," *Forbes,* March 19, 2019, https://www.forbes.com/sites/robertreiss/2019/03/19/ceos-and-ethics/#42c221682163 (accessed July 3, 2019); Ethisphere Institute, "2019 World's Most Ethical Companies," February 26, 2019, https://ethisphere.com/128-worlds-most-ethical-companies-for-2019/ (accessed July 3, 2019); Ethisphere Institute, "The 2019 World's Most Ethical Companies Honoree List," February 26, 2019, https://www.worldsmostethicalcompanies.com/honorees/ (accessed July 3, 2019); Ethisphere Institute, "The Methodology Behind the Selection Process," https://www.worldsmostethicalcompanies.com/ (accessed July 3, 2019).

10. "Integrity Survey 2013," KPMG, 2013, http://www.kpmg.com/CN/en/IssuesAndInsights/ArticlesPublications/Documents/Integrity-Survey-2013-O-201307.pdf (accessed July 3, 2019).

11. "How Am I Doing?" *Business Ethics,* Fall 2005, 11.

12. Texas Instruments, "Code of Conduct: Our Values and Ethics," 2019, http://www.ti.com/lit/ml/szza066c/szza066c.pdf (accessed July 3, 2019).

13. Texas Instruments, "Code of Conduct: Ethics Quick Test," 2019, http://www.ti.com/lit/ml/szza066c/szza066c.pdf (accessed July 3, 2019).

14. Adil Munim, "18 of the Best Code of Conduct Examples," *i-Sight,* https://i-sight.com/resources/18-of-the-best-code-of-conduct-examples/ (accessed July 3, 2019).

15. Mark S. Schwartz, "A Code of Ethics for Corporate Code of Ethics," *Journal of Business Ethics* 41 (2002): 37.

16. "National Business Ethics Survey of the U.S. Workforce," Ethics Resource Center, 2013, http://www.ethics.org/downloads/2013NBESFinalWeb.pdf (accessed June 23, 2014).

17. Lockheed Martin, "Code of Ethics and Business Conduct," October 2017, https://www.lockheedmartin.com/content/dam/lockheed-martin/eo/documents/ethics/code-of-conduct.pdf (accessed July 3, 2019).

18. Ethics & Compliance Initiative, "About ECI," https://www.ethics.org/about/ (accessed July 3, 2019).

19. Alynda Wheat, "Keeping an Eye on Corporate America," *Fortune,* November 25, 2002, 44–45.

20. "Rise of the Chief Ethics Officer," *Forbes,* March 27, 2019, https://www.forbes.com/sites/insights-intelai/2019/03/27/rise-of-the-chief-ethics-officer/#71c178dd5aba (accessed July 3, 2019).

21. Jeffrey Rhodes, "Transgender Ethics Training Prompts Religious-Discrimination Claim," SHRM, March 26, 2019, https://www.shrm.org/resourcesandtools/legal-and-compliance/employment-law/pages/court-report-transgender-ethics-training.aspx (accessed July 3, 2019).

22. Caroline Whitbeck, *Ethics in Engineering Practice and Research* (New York: Cambridge University Press, 1998), 176.

23. Debbie Thorne LeClair and Linda Ferrell, "Innovation in Experiential Business Ethics Training," *Journal of Business Ethics* 23 (2000): 313–322.

24. Jaclyn Jaeger, "Benchmark Report Provides Holistic Look at Compliance Best Practices," *Compliance Week,* June 18, 2019, https://www.complianceweek.com/surveys-and-benchmarking/benchmark-report-provides-holistic-look-at-compliance-best-practices/27265.article (accessed July 3, 2019); Navex Global, "The Standard in Ethics and Compliance Management," https://www.navexglobal.com/en-us/products (accessed July 4, 2019).

25. "Ethics," Boeing, http://www.boeing.com/boeing/companyof-fices/aboutus/ethics/index.page (accessed July 3, 2019).

26. NAVEX Global, "Hotline Reporting Is More Important than Ever: The Latest Findings from the 2018 Hotline Benchmark Report,"

https://assets.corporatecompliance.org/Portals/1/PDF/Resources/past_handouts/Regional/2018/atlanta/330-430_penman_2.pdf (accessed July 9, 2019).

27. *Ibid.*

28. Caroline Spiezio, "Airbnb's General Counsel Shows up and Gets Creative to Promote Employee Ethics," *CorporateCounsel*, June 13, 2019, https://www.law.com/corpcounsel/2019/06/13/airbnbs-general-counsel-shows-up-and-gets-creative-to-promote-employee-ethics/?slreturn=20190518145359 (accessed July 4, 2019).

29. Kristin Broughton, "SEC Grants $50 Million Award to Two JPMorgan Whistleblowers," *Wall Street Journal*, March 28, 2019, https://www.wsj.com/articles/sec-grants-50-million-award-to-two-whistleblowers-11553633544?mod=hp_minor_pos10 (accessed July 4, 2019).

30. Kevin McCarty, "Pierce County Whistleblower to Get Big Cash Settlement," *KIRO-TV*, October 1, 2019, https://www.kiro7.com/news/south-sound-news/pierce-county-whistleblower-to-get-big-cash-settlement/992423068 (accessed October 2, 2019).

31. Ethics Resource Center, *National Business Ethics Survey of the U.S. Workforce* (Arlington, VA: Ethics Resource Center, 2013), 34.

32. Government Accountability Project, "SEC Proposes Changes to Whistleblower Reward Program," August 1, 2018, https://www.whistleblower.org/uncategorized/sec-proposes-changes-to-whistleblower-reward-program/ (accessed July 9, 2019).

33. Darren Dahl, "Learning to Love Whistleblowers," *Inc.*, March 2006, 21–23.

34. Associated Press, "South Korea Seeks Arrest of Samsung Chief Suspected of Bribery," *NBC News*, January 15, 2017, https://www.nbcnews.com/news/world/prosecutors-seek-arrest-samsung-chief-suspected-bribery-n707246 (accessed July 4, 2019); Samsung, "Ethics: Fair and Transparent Corporate Culture," https://www.samsung.com/us/aboutsamsung/sustainability/ethics/ (accessed July 4, 2019).

35. O. C. Ferrell, John Fraedrich, and Linda Ferrell, *Business Ethics: Ethical Decision Making and Cases,* 10th ed. (Mason, OH: South-Western Cengage Learning, 2015), 94.

36. *Ibid.*, 94–97.

37. Paul K. Shum and Sharon L. Yam, "Ethics and Law: Guiding the Invisible Hand to Correct Corporate Social Responsibility Externalities," *Journal of Business Ethics* 98 (2011): 549–571.

38. Cornell University School of Hotel Administration, "Best Practices in US Lodging Industry Introduction," 2014, https:// www.hotelschool.cornell.edu/research/chr/pubs/best/project/intro.html (accessed July 2, 2014).

39. Kia Kokalitcheva, "These 8 Employers Will Pay You to Volunteer," *Fortune*, March 21, 2016, https://fortune.com/2016/03/21/companies-that-offer-paid-time-off-to-volunteer/ (accessed July 10, 2019).

40. "Employee Volunteering: 'Take Action'," Novo Nordisk, https://www.novonordisk.com/sustainable-business/performance-on-tbl/responsibility-in-the-workplace/employee-engagement/volunteering.html (accessed July 10, 2019).

41. R. Eric Reidenbach and Donald P. Robin, *Ethics and Profits* (Englewood Cliffs, NJ: Prentice-Hall, 1989), 92.

42. Chris Golis, "Emotional Intelligence: Did Myers-Brigg Destroy Arthur Andersen?" CBS, April 16, 2011, http://www.cbsnews.com/news/emotional-intelligence-did-myers-briggs-destroy-arthur-andersen/ (accessed July 13, 2019).

43. R. Edward Freeman and Lisa Stewart, "Developing Ethical Leadership," Business Roundtable Institute for Corporate Ethics, 2006, http://www.corporate-ethics.org.

44. James B. Avey, Michael E. Palanski, and Fred O. Walumbwa, "When Leadership Goes Unnoticed: The Moderating Role of Follower Self-Esteem on the Relationship Between Ethical Leadership and Follower Behavior," *Journal of Business Ethics* 98 (2011): 573–582.

45. John Rampton, "How Bill Gates Became a Leadership Legend," *Entrepreneur*, September 9, 2016, https://www.entrepreneur.com/article/250607 (accessed July 4, 2019); Bill and Melinda Gates Foundation, "All Lives Have Equal Value," https://www.gatesfoundation.org/ (accessed July 11, 2019).

46. Constance E. Bagley, "The Ethical Leader's Decision Tree," *Harvard Business Review*, January–February 2003, 18.

47. O. C. Ferrell and Larry G. Gresham, "A Contingency Framework for Understanding Ethical Decision Making in Marketing," *Journal of Marketing* 49 (1985): 90–91.

48. Andreas Cremer and Tom Bergin, "Fear and Respect: VW's Culture Under Winterkorn," *Reuters*, October 11, 2015, https://www.reuters.com/article/us-volkswagen-emissions-culture-idUSKCN0S40MT20151010 (accessed August 5, 2016).

49. "Integrity Survey 2013," *KPMG*, http://www.kpmg.com/CN/en/IssuesAndInsights/ArticlesPublications/Documents/Integrity-Survey-2013-O-201307.pdf (accessed August 4, 2016).

50. "Global Business Ethics Survey: The State of Ethics & Compliance in the Workplace," Ethics & Compliance Initiative, March 2018, http://www.boeingsuppliers.com/GBES2018-Final.pdf (accessed July 11, 2019).

51. John R. P. French and Bertram Ravin, "The Bases of Social Power," in Dorwin Cartwright, ed., *Group Dynamics: Research and Theory* (Evanston, IL: Row, Peterson, 1962), 607–623.

52. Virginia Tech, "Employee Incentives Can Lead to Unethical Behavior in the Workplace," *ScienceDaily*, December 11, 2018, https://www.sciencedaily.com/releases/2018/12/181211122456.htm (accessed July 4, 2019).

53. Lynn Brewer, Robert Chandler, and O. C. Ferrell, *Managing Risks for Corporate Integrity: How to Survive an Ethical Misconduct Disaster* (Mason, OH: Texere/Thomson, 2006), 35.

54. Susan Pulliam, "How Following Orders Can Harm Your Career," *CFO Magazine*, October 3, 2003, http://ww2.cfo. com/human-capital-careers/2003/10/how-following-orders-can-harm-your-career/ (accessed August 4, 2016).

55. Southwest Airlines, "Welcome to Adopt-a-Pilot," http://www.southwest.com/adoptapilot/ (accessed July 11, 2019); Carmine Gallo, "Southwest Airlines Founder Herb Kelleher Was the Brand's Storyteller-in-Chief," *Forbes*, January 4, 2019, https://www.forbes.com/sites/carminegallo/2019/01/04/southwest-airlines-founder-herb-kelleher-was-the-brands-storyteller-in-chief/#2ca9525e620b (accessed July 11, 2019).

56. Ferrell and Gresham, "A Contingency Framework."

57. Janet Wiscombe, "Don't Fear Whistle-Blowers," *Workforce*, July 2002, 26–32.

58. Ferrell et al., "Business Ethics," 313–315.

59. Freeman and Stewart, "Developing Ethical Leadership."

60. James M. Burns, *Leadership* (New York: Harper & Row, 1985).

61. John P. Kotter, "What Leaders Really Do," *Harvard Business Review*, December 2001, https://hbr.org/2001/12/what-leaders-really-do (accessed July 13, 2019).

62. Stephen R. Covey, *The 7 Habits of Highly Effective People* (New York: Simon & Schuster, 1989).

63. Archie B. Carroll, "Ethical Leadership: From Moral Managers to Moral Leaders," in O. C. Ferrell, Sheb True, and Lou Pelton, eds., *Rights, Relationships, and Responsibilities*, vol. 1 (Kennesaw, GA: Kennesaw State University, 2003), 7–17.

64. Jim Collins, "Leadership Lessons," *Leadership Excellence* 29, no. 2 (February 2012): 10.

65. Kotter, "What Leaders Really Do."

66. Newman's Own Foundation, "Newman's Own Foundation Provides over $1.7 Million to Support Nutrition Initiatives," *Cision PR Newswire*, October 2, 2018, https://www.prnewswire.com/news-releases/newmans-own-foundation-provides-over-1-7-million-to-support-nutrition-initiatives-300722394.html (accessed July 12, 2019); Li Yen, "Paul Newman's Incredible Philanthropic Legacy Is Larger than Life Itself," *The Epoch Times*, February 23, 2019, https://www.theepochtimes.com/paul-newmans-incredible-philanthropic-legacy-is-larger-than-life-itself_2807952.html (accessed July 12, 2019).

67. Carroll, "Ethical Leadership," 11.

68. "100 Best Companies to Work for: NetApp," *Fortune*, 2013, http://archive.fortune.com/magazines/fortune/best-companies/2013/snapshots/6.html (accessed July 13, 2019).

69. Michael W. Grojean, Christian J. Resick, Marcus W. Dickson, and Brent D. Smith, "Leaders, Values and Organizational Climate Regarding Ethics," *Journal of Business Ethics* 55, no. 3 (December 2004): 223–241.

70. Whole Foods, "Our Core Values," http://www.wholefoodsmarket.com/mission-values/core-values (accessed July 12, 2019); Ross Brooks, "10 Companies with Core Values That Actually Reflect Their Culture," *Peakon.com*, August 2, 2018, https://peakon.com/us/blog/workplace-culture/best-company-core-values/ (accessed July 12, 2019); Palbir Nijjar, "How Whole Foods Market Lives Its Values," *Motley Fool*, November 21, 2018 (updated), https://www.fool.com/investing/general/2016/01/24/how-whole-foods-market-lives-its-values.aspx (accessed July 12, 2019).

71. Ferrell et al., "Business Ethics," 315–316.

72. Daniel J. Brass, Kenneth D Butterfield, and Bruce C. Skaggs, "Relationship and Unethical Behavior: A Social Science Perspective," *Academy of Management Review* 23 (January 1998): 14–31.

73. Linda Klebe Trevino, Gary R. Weaver, David G. Gibson, and Barbara Lay Toffler, "Managing Ethics and Legal Compliance: What Works and What Hurts," *California Management Review* 41 (1999): 131–151; Michael E. Brown and Linda K. Trevino, "Ethical Leadership: A Review and Future Directions," *The Leadership Quarterly* 17, no. 6 (December 2006): 595–616.

74. Mitchell J. Neubert, Dawn S. Carlson, K. Michele Kacmar, James A. Roberts, and Lawrence B. Chonko, "The Virtuous Influence of Ethical Leadership Behavior: Evidence from the Field," *Journal of Business Ethics* 90 (2009): 157–170.

75. Sean Valentine, Lynn Godkin, Gary M. Fleischman, Roland E. Kidwell, and Karen Page, "Corporate Ethical Values, Group Creativity, Job Satisfaction and Turnover Intention: The Impact of Work Context on Work Response," *Journal of Business Ethics* 98 (2011): 353–372.

76. The Container Store, "What We Stand For: Our Employee First Culture," http://standfor.containerstore.com/putting-our-employees-first/ (accessed July 12, 2019); "The Container Store: An Employee-Centric Retailer," UNM Daniels Fund Business Ethics Initiative, http://danielsethics.mgt.unm.edu/pdf/Container%20Store%20Case.pdf (accessed July 12, 2019).

77. Remi Trudel and June Cotte, "Does It Pay to Be Good?" *MIT Sloan Management Review* 50, no. 2 (2009): 60–68.

78. Dan Shewan, "Ethical Marketing: 5 Examples of Companies with a Conscience," *WordStream*, November 28, 2018, https://www.wordstream.com/blog/ws/2017/09/20/ethical-marketing (accessed July 13, 2019).

79. Edelman, "2019 Edelman Trust Barometer Global Report," January 2019, https://www.edelman.com/sites/g/files/aatuss191/files/2019-03/2019_Edelman_Trust_Barometer_Global_Report.pdf?utm_source=website&utm_medium=global_report&utm_campaign=downloads (accessed July 12, 2019).

80. Tae Hee Choi and Jinchul Jung, "Ethical Commitment, Financial Performance, and Valuation: An Empirical Investigation of Korean Companies," *Journal of Business Ethics* 81, no. 2 (2008): 447–463.

81. Jin-Woo Kim, "Assessing the Long-Term Financial Performance of Ethical Companies," *Journal of Targeting, Measurement and Analysis for Marketing* 18, no. 3/4 (2010): 199–208.

82. Win Swenson, "The Organizational Guidelines' 'Carrot and Stick' Philosophy, and Their Focus on 'Effective' Compliance," in *Corporate Crime in America: Strengthening the "Good Citizenship" Corporation* (Washington, DC: U.S. Sentencing Commission, 1995), 17–26.

83. Coca-Cola Company, "2017 Sustainability Report: Stakeholder Engagement," *Coca-Cola Journey*, August 27, 2018, https://www.coca-colacompany.com/stories/stakeholder-engagement (accessed July 12, 2019); Maggie McGrath, "World's Largest Food And Beverage Companies 2018: Anheuser-Busch, Nestle and Pepsi Top the List," *Forbes*, June 6, 2018, https://www.forbes.com/sites/maggiemcgrath/2018/06/06/worlds-largest-food-and-beverage-companies-2018-anheuser-busch-nestle-and-pepsi-top-the-list/#1928e1e91b08 (accessed July 12, 2019).

84. Ferrell et al., "Business Ethics," 329–332.

85. Brass et al., "Relationship and Unethical Behavior."

86. Cam Caldwell, Linda A. Hayes, and Do Tien Long, "Leadership, Trustworthiness, and Ethical Stewardship," *Journal of Business Ethics* 96 (2010): 497–512.

87. Al Lewis, "Lewis: A Good Man Who Did a Bad Thing," *Denver Post*, October 25, 2012, http://www.denverpost.com/2012/10/25/lewis-a-good-man-who-did-a-bad-thing/ (accessed July 13, 2019).

88. Tara Duggan, "Transformation Leadership Examples in Business," *AZCentral*, April 23, 2018, https://yourbusiness.azcentral.com/transformational-leadership-examples-business-4571.html (accessed July 12, 2019); James Chen "Peter Lynch," *Investopedia*, June 21, 2018, https://www.investopedia.com/terms/p/peterlynch.asp (accessed July 12, 2019).

89. Jim Collins, "Be Great Now." *Inc.*, June 2012, 72–73.

90. Robert Kerr, John Garvin, Norma Heaton, and Emily Boyle, "Emotional Intelligence and Leadership Effectiveness," *Leadership & Organizational Development Journal* 27, no. 4 (2006): 265–279.

91. "Seventy-one Percent of Employers Say They Value Emotional Intelligence over IQ, According to CareerBuilder Survey," CareerBuilder, August 18, 2011, http://www.careerbuilder.com/share/aboutus/pressreleasesdetail.aspx?id=pr652&sd=8/18/2011&ed=8/18/2099 (accessed August 4, 2016).

92. Brewer et al., *Managing Risks for Corporate Integrity*.

93. Richard Boyatzis and Annie McKee, *Resonant Leadership: Renewing Yourself and Connecting with Others Through Mindfulness, Hope, and Compassion* (Boston: Harvard Business Review Press, 2005); Bruce Rosenstein, "Resonant Leader Is One in Tune with Himself, Others," *USA Today*, November 27, 2005, http://usatoday30.usatoday.com/money/books/reviews/2005-11-27-resonant-book-usat_x.htm (accessed July 13, 2019).

94. Peter Ubel, "Do Starbucks Employees Have More Emotional Intelligence than Your Physician?" *Forbes*, November 2, 2012, http://www.forbes.com/sites/peterubel/2012/11/02/do-starbucks-employees-have-more-emotional-intelligence-than-your-physician/#65a9b2a96beb (accessed July 12, 2019); Micah Solomon, "Thanks a Latte: How to Fix a Customer Service Failure, per Starbucks, Marriott and Me," *Forbes*, November 19, 2017, https://www.forbes.com/sites/micahsolomon/2017/11/19/thanks-a-latte-how-to-fix-a-customer-service-failure-per-starbucks-marriott-and-me/#16eae448462a (accessed July 12, 2019).

95. Burns, *Leadership*.

96. Royston Greenwood, Roy Suddaby, and C. R. Hinings, "Theorizing Change: The Role of Professional Associations in the Transformation of Institutionalized Fields," *Academy of Management Journal* 45 (January 2002): 58–80.

97. Shuili Du, Valérie Swaen, Adam Lindgreen, and Sankar Sen, "The Roles of Leadership Styles in Corporate Social Responsibility," *Journal of Business Ethics* 114 (2013): 155–169.

98. Eric Pillmore, "How Tyco International Remade Its Corporate Governance," speech at Wharton Business School, September 2006.

99. New Belgium Brewing, "Purpose and Core Values and Beliefs," https://www.newbelgium.com/Human-Powered-Business/core-values-and-beliefs/ (accessed July 13, 2019).

100. Bill George, Peter Sims, Andrew M. McLean, and Diana Mayer, "Discovering Your Authentic Leadership," *Harvard Business Review*, February 2007, https://hbr.org/2007/02/discovering-your-authentic-leadership (accessed July 13, 2019).

101. Stephen R. Covey, *Principle-Centered Leadership* (New York: Franklin Covey Co., 1991), 102–105.

102. Ferrell et al., "Business Ethics," 326–327.

103. S. K. Collins and K. S. Collins, "Micromanagement—A Costly Management Style," *Radiology Management* 24, no. 6 (2002): 32–35.

104. Gary Yukl, "Managerial Leadership: A Review of Theory and Research," *Journal of Management* 15 (June 1989): 251–289.

105. Ryan S. Bisel, Katherine M. Kelley, Nicole A. Ploeger, and Jake Messersmith, "Workers' Moral Mum Effect: On Facework and Unethical Behavior in the Workplace," *Communication Studies* 62, no. 2 (2011): 153–170.

106. Ferrell et al., "Business Ethics," 322–326.

107. Gary T. Hunt, *Communication Skills in the Organization* (Upper Saddle River, NJ: Prentice-Hall, February 1989).

108. *Ibid*.

109. Robert Gatewood, Robert Taylor, and O. C. Ferrell, *Management* (Homewood, IL: Richard D. Irwin, Inc., 1995).

110. Sally Planalp and Julie Fitness, "Interpersonal Communication Ethics," in George Cheney, Steve May, and Debashish Munshi, eds., *The Handbook of Communication Ethics* (New York: Taylor and Francis, 2011), 135–147.

111. Jack R. Gibb, "Defensive Communication," *Journal of Communication* 11, no. 3 (September 1961): 141–148.

112. Hunt, *Communication Skills in the Organization*.

113. Mary Ellen Guffey, Kathleen Rhodes, and Patricia Rogen, *Business Communication: Process and Product* (Toronto: Nelson Education Ltd., 2010).

114. Cass R. Sunstein, "The Law of Group Polarization," John M. Olin Law & Economics Working Paper No. 91(1999) (2D Series), https://chicagounbound.uchicago.edu/cgi/viewcontent.cgi?referer=https://www.google.com/&httpsredir=1&article=1541&context=law_and_economics;The (accessed July 13, 2019).

115. Gatewood et al., *Management*, 530.

116. Jan Gleisner, "Nonverbal Communication Percentage," *Silent Communication*, March 20, 2016, https://www.silentcommunication.org/single-post/2016/03/20/17-Non-verbal-communication-percentage (accessed July 13, 2019); Ashley Hamer, "Is Communication Really

80 Percent Nonverbal?" *Curiosity.com,* November 13, 2017, https://curiosity.com/topics/is-communication-really-80-percent-nonverbal-curiosity/ (accessed July 13, 2019).

117. Hunt, *Communication Skills in the Organization.*

118. Susan M. Heathfield, "Top Ten Employee Complaints," *About.com,* http://humanresources.about.com/od/retention/a/emplo_complaint.htm (accessed July 13, 2019).

119. *Ibid.*

Chapter 8

1. 100 Best Companies to Work For 2018," *Fortune,* http://money.cnn.com/magazines/fortune/bestcompanies/2010/snapshots/36.html, (accessed June 10, 2019); Susan Berfield, "The Clutter in Kip Tindell," *Bloomberg Businessweek,* February 23, 2015, 40–45; Anne Fisher, "Want to Build a Great Brand? Keep It Simple," *Fortune,* http://search.ebscohost.com/login.aspx?direct=true&db=bsu&AN=116667078&site=ehost-live&scope=site (accessed June 8, 2019); Great Place to Work, "The Container Store," https://www.greatplacetowork.com/certified-company/1000436 (accessed June 15, 2019); Heather Martin, "The Container Store Redefines Loyalty. *FierceRetail,* http://search.ebscohost.com/login.aspx?direct=true&db=bsu&AN=114636344&site=ehost-live&scope=site (accessed June 10, 2019); Vicki Powers, "Finding Workers Who Fit," Business 2.0, November 1, 2004, http://money.cnn.com/magazines/business2/business2_archive/2004/11/01/8189362/index.htm (accessed June 10, 2019); The Container Store, "Our Foundation Principles," https://standfor.containerstore.com/our-foundation-principles/ (accessed June 13, 2019); Kip Tindell and Garrett Boone, "Containing a Counter Culture," *Inc.,* March 1, 2002, http://www.inc.com/articles/2002/03/23988.html (accessed June 10, 2019).

2. Joanne B. Ciulla, *The Working Life: The Promise and Betrayal of Modern Work* (New York: Times Books, 2000).

3. *Ibid.*; Adriano Tilgher, *Work: What It Has Meant to Men Through the Ages,* trans. Dorothy Canfield Fisher (New York: Harcourt, Brace & World, 1958).

4. These facts are derived from Brenda Paik Sunoo, "Relying on Faith to Rebuild a Business," *Workforce* 78 (March 1999): 54–59.

5. Polartec LLC, "About Polartec/FAQ," http://polartec.com/about/faq.aspx (accessed July 15, 2016); "Polartec LLC," *Bloomberg Businessweek,* http://investing.businessweek.com/research/stocks/private/snapshot.asp?privcapId=728315 (accessed July 15, 2016); Sunoo, "Relying on Faith to Rebuild a Business"; Justin Pope, "Malden Mills Emerges from the Bankruptcy, Still Under Financial Cloud," *Houston Chronicle,* August 15, 2003, B1. Janet B. Rodie, "Textile World News," *Textile World* 152 (January 2002): 12.

6. "Worldatwork Finds One-Third of Companies Downsized After 9/11," *Report on Salary Surveys* 2 (December 2002): 12; Stephanie Armour, "Companies Chisel Away at Workers' Benefits," *USA Today,* November 18, 2002, 1B–3B; Lynn Gresham, "Winning the Talent War Requires a Fresh Benefits Approach," *Employee Benefit News,* April 15, 2006, 9.

7. Neil Conway and Rob B. Briner, *Understanding Psychological Contracts at Work* (London: Oxford University Press, 2006); Denise M. Rousseau, *Psychological Contracts in Organizations: Understanding Written and Unwritten Agreements* (Thousand Oaks, CA: SAGE, 1995).

8. Denise M. Rousseau, "The Individual–Organization Relationship: The Psychological Contract." In S. Zedeck, ed., *Handbook of Industrial and Organizational Psychology, Vol. 3* (Washington, DC: American Psychological Association, 2011), 191–220.

9. Jacqueline Coyle-Shapiro, "A Psychological Contract Perspective on Organizational Citizenship Behavior," *Journal of Organizational Behavior* 23 (December 2002): 927–946; William H. Turnley and Daniel C. Feldman, "The Impact of Psychological Contract Violations on Exit, Voice, Loyalty, and Neglect," *Human Relations* 52 (July 1999): 895–922.

10. Denise M. Rousseau, Samantha D. Hansen, and Maria Tomprou, "A Dynamic Phase Model of Psychological Contract Processes," *Journal of Organizational Behavior* 39 (November 2018): 1081–1098.

11. Ans De Vos and Annelies Meganck, "What HR Managers Do Versus What Employees Value," *Personnel Review* 38 (2009): 45–60.

12. Kimberly D. Elsbach and Greg Elafson, "How the Packaging of Decision Explanations Affects Perceptions of Trustworthiness," *Academy of Management Journal* 43 (February 2000): 80–89; David E.

Guest and Neil Conway, "Communicating the Psychological Contract: An Employer Perspective," *Human Resource Management Journal* 12, no. 2 (2002):22–38.

13. AON, "2018 Trends in Global Employee Engagement," https://www.aon.com/2018-global-employee-engagement-trends/index.html (accessed June 15, 2019).

14. Gillian Flynn, "Looking Back on 100 Years of Employment Law," *Workforce* 78 (November 1999): 74–77.

15. "A Guru Ahead of Her Time," *Nation's Business* 85 (May 1997): 24.

16. Steve Sayer, "Cleaning Up the Jungle," *Occupational Health and Safety* 66 (May 1997): 22.

17. Flynn, "Looking Back on 100 Years of Employment Law."

18. "Employee Relations in America," *IRS Employment Review* (March 1997): E7–E12; Roger LeRoy Miller and Gaylord A. Jentz, *Business Law Today* (Cincinnati: West Legal Studies in Business, 2000).

19. Clark Davis, *Company Men: White-Collar Life and Corporate Cultures in Los Angeles, 1892–1941* (Baltimore: Johns Hopkins University Press), 2000.

20. C. Wright Mills, *White Collar: The American Middle Classes* (New York: Oxford University Press, 1951).

21. Ciulla, *The Working Life;* William H. Whyte, *The Organization Man* (New York: Simon & Schuster, 1956).

22. U.S. Department of Health, Education, and Welfare, *Work in America: Report of a Special Task Force to the Secretary of Health, Education, and Welfare* (Cambridge, MA: MIT Press, 1973).

23. Ciulla, *The Working Life.*

24. Taina Savolainen, "Leadership Strategies for Gaining Business Excellence Through Total Quality Management: A Finnish Case Study," *Total Quality Management* 11 (March 2000): 211–226.

25. L. L. Bollinger, "Is Subcontracting the Answer?" *Harvard Business Review* 20 (Winter 1942): 171.

26. Anonymous, "Outsourcing: Make It Work for Your Company," *Journal of Accountancy* 190 (October 2000): 20; James Brian Quinn, Thomas L. Doorley, and Penny C. Paquette. "Beyond Products: Services-Based Strategy." *Harvard Business Review* 68 (March 1990): 58–67.

27. "Younger Employees Want Security," *USA Today,* October 3, 2001, 1B.

28. U.S. Department of Labor, "Labor Force Statistics from the Current Population Survey," July 15, 2016, http://data.bls.gov/timeseries/LNS14000000 (accessed July 15, 2016).

29. "The Great Jobs Boom; Work." (2019, May 25). *The Economist,* 431(9144), 13(US), http://link.galegroup.com/apps/doc/A586391431/GPS?u=txshracd2550&sid=GPS&xid=76d61ec1 (accessed June 12, 2019)

30. A. Schaefers, "Tourism Jobs Take a Hit as Hawaii Unemployment Rises," March 9, 2019, *Honolulu Star-Advertiser,* http://search.ebscohost.com/login.aspx?direct=true&db=n5h&AN=2W6478456949&site=eds-live&scope=site (accessed June 12, 2019).

31. U.S. Department of Labor, "Employment and Unemployment Among Youth Summary," Bureau of Labor Statistics, August 18, 2015, http://www.bls.gov/news.release/youth.nr0. htm (accessed July 15, 2016); Veronique De Rugy , "Youth Unemployment Is Down But Are Young People Actually Working?" *Reason* 51 (June 2019): 11.

32. Juri Zuzanek and Margo Hilbrecht, "Enforced Leisure: Time Use and Its Well-Being Implications," *Time & Society* 28 (2019): 657–679.

33. This section is adapted from Debbie Thorne LeClair, "The Ups and Downs of Rightsizing the Workplace," *ABACA Profile,* November–December 1999, 25.

34. Priti Pradhan Shah, "Network Destruction: The Structural Implications of Downsizing," *Academy of Management Journal* 43 (February 2000): 101–112; Steve Lohr, "Cutting Here, but Hiring Over There," *The New York Times,* June 24, 2005, C3.

35. Elizabeth Weise, "Intel to Lay Off 11% of Workforce in Big Shift from PCs," *USA Today,* April 20, 2016, http://www.usatoday.com/story/tech/2016/04/19/intel-lay-offs-12000-11/83242832/ (accessed July 18, 2016).

36. Colum Wood, "GM Says It Needs $16.6 Billion MORE: Will Cut 47,000 Jobs and Close 5 U.S. Plants to Get It," *Auto Guide,* February 17, 2009, http://www.autoguide. com/auto-news/2009/02/gm-says-it-needs-166-billion-more-will-cut-47000-jobs-and-close-5-us-plants-to-get-it.html (accessed June 28, 2014); *The New York Times Special Report: The Downsizing of America* (New York: Times Books, 1996); Victor B. Wayhan and Steve Werner, "The Impact of Workforce Reductions on Financial Performance: A Longitudinal Perspective," *Journal of Management* 26 (2000): 341–363.

37. Thomas G. Cummings and Christopher G. Worley, *Organization Development and Change* (Cincinnati: South-Western Cengage Learning, 2009).

38. Harry J. Van Buren III, "The Bindingness of Social and Psychological Contracts: Toward a Theory of Social Responsibility in Downsizing," *Journal of Business Ethics* 25 (January 2000): 205–219; Davis J. Flanagan and K. C. O'Shaughnessy, "The Effects of Layoffs on Firm Reputation," *Journal of Management* (June 2005): 445.

39. Geoff Colvin, "Layoffs Cost More Than You Think," *Fortune,* March 30, 2009, 24.

40. Steve Beigbeder, "Easing Workforce Reduction," *Risk Management* 47 (May 2000): 26–30; Matthew Camardella, "Legal Considerations of Workforce Reduction," *Employment Relations Today* 29 (Autumn 2002): 101–106.

41. U.S. Department of Labor, "The Worker Adjustment and Retraining Notification Act," http://www.doleta.gov/programs/factsht/warn.htm (accessed July 18, 2016).

42. "Community Ventures Receives National Economic Development Award," https://www.michigan.gov/som/0,4669,7-192-29701_74909_74922-479682--,00.html (accessed June 10, 2019).

43. Angelo J. Kinicki, Gregory E. Prussia, and Francis M. McKee-Ryan, "A Panel Study of Coping with Involuntary Job Loss," *Academy of Management Journal* 43 (February 2000): 90–100.

44. Wayhan and Werner, "The Impact of Workforce Reductions on Financial Performance."

45. Nicholas Stein, "Winning the War to Keep Top Talent," *Fortune,* May 29, 2000, pp. 132–138.

46. Carlyn Kolker, "Survivor Blues," *American Lawyer* 24 (October 2002): 116–118; Susan Reynolds Fisher and Margaret A. White, "Downsizing in a Learning Organization," *Academy of Management Review* 25 (January 2000): 244–251. Mattias Brauer and Martin Zimmermann, "Investor Response to Workforce Downsizing: The Influence of Industry Waves, Macroeconomic Outlook, and Firm Performance," *Journal of Management* 45 (May 2019): 1775–1801.

47. Susan Beck, "What to Do Before You Say 'You're Outta Here,'" *BusinessWeek,* December 8, 1997, 6.

48. U.S. Department of Labor, *Employment Law Guide,* http://www.dol.gov/compliance/guide/ (accessed July 18, 2016).

49. Robert Harding, "Minimum Wage Debate: What Supporters, Opponents Say About Effects of Raising the Minimum Wage," *Auburn Citizen,* May 14, 2014, http://auburnpub.com/news/local/minimum-wage-debate-what-supporters-opponents-say-about-effects-of/article_102e4516-f582-552d-a02e-3b71896c76aa.html (accessed July 18, 2016).

50. Jason Brennan, "Should Employers Pay a Living Wage?" *Journal of Business Ethics* 157 (June 2019): 15–26; Eric Ravenscraft, "What a Living Wage Actually Means," *The New York Times,* https://www.nytimes.com/2019/06/05/smarter-living/what-a-living-wage-actually-means.html (accessed June 8, 2019).

51. "Minimum Wage Laws in the States," U.S. Department of Labor, https://www.dol.gov/whd/minwage/america.htm (accessed June 25, 2019); U.S. Department of Labor, "History of Federal Minimum Wage Rates Under the Fair Labor Standards Act, 1938–2009," https://www.dol.gov/whd/minwage/chart.htm (accessed June 15, 2019).

52. Flynn, "Looking Back on 100 Years of Employment Law."

53. Robert J. Nobile, "HR's Top 10 Legal Issues," *HR Focus* 74 (April 1997): 19–20.

54. Miller and Jentz, *Business Law Today.*

55. Flynn, "Looking Back on 100 Years of Employment Law."

56. "Commonly Used Statistics," Occupational Safety and Health Administration, https://www.osha.gov/oshstats/commonstats.html (accessed June 15, 2019).

57. Judith N. Mottl, "Industry Fights OSHA's Proposed Ergonomic Rule," *Informationweek,* June 19, 2000, 122; Daniel R. Miller, "OSHA Goes Too Far with Ergonomics Rules," *National Underwriter,* May 8, 2000, 59; John D. Schulz, "Trucking Wants Out," *Traffic World,* May 29, 2000, 21–22; Robin Suttell, "Healthy Work," *Buildings* 96 (October 2002): 56–58; "Enforcement," U.S. Department of Labor, https://www.osha.gov/SLTC/ergonomics/faqs.html (accessed July 18, 2016).

58. Gildan Activewear Inc., "Safe and Healthy Workplace," https://www.genuineresponsibility.com/en/priorities/caring-for-people/safe-and-healthy-workplace/ (accessed June 25, 2019).

59. "Workplace Violence," Occupational Safety and Health Administration, https://www.osha.gov/SLTC/workplaceviolence/ (accessed June 18, 2019).

60. Rod Hart and Denise Heybrock. "Workplace Violence and Components of a Psychologically Healthy Workplace." *Benefits Quarterly* 33 (207): 8–12; "Top Security Threats and Management Issues Facing Corporate America, Securitas, 2019, https://www.securitasinc.com/stand-alone/top-security-threats/ (accessed June 18, 2019); "Workplace Violence," Occupational Safety and Health Administration.

61. "Workplace Violence," Society for Human Resource Management, https://www.shrm.org/resourcesandtools/pages/workplace-violence.aspx (accessed June 18, 2019).

62. Joshua Berlinger and Dana Ford, "Kansas Shooting: Gunman Kills 3, Wounds 14 at Lawn Care Company," *CNN,* February 26, 2016, http://www.cnn.com/2016/02/25/us/kansas-shooting/ (accessed July 18, 2016); Steve Almasy and Rebekah Riess, "At Least 12 Dead after Disgruntled Employee Opens Fire at Virginia Beach Municipal Center," *CNN,* June 1, 2019, https://www.cnn.com/2019/05/31/us/virginia-beach-shooting/index.html (accessed October 1, 2019).

63. Carrie Coolidge, "Risky Business," *Forbes,* January 6, 2003, 54; Todd Henneman, "Ignoring Signs of Violence Can Be Fatal, Costly Mistake," *Workforce Management,* February 27, 2006, 10; John Leming, "New Product Covers Losses Related to Workplace Violence," *Journal of Commerce,* April 6, 2000, 15.

64. U.S. Equal Employment Opportunity Commission, "Pregnancy Discrimination Charges," https://www.eeoc.gov/eeoc/statistics/enforcement/pregnancy_new.cfm (accessed June 19, 2019).

65. Judy Greenwald, "Employers Confront AIDS in Africa," *Business Insurance* 35 (July 23, 2001): 15; Michael T. Parker, "Fighting AIDS Stigma in the Workplace," *Business Mexico* 15 (August 2005): 43–44.

66. "Global Diversity Mission," Coca-Cola, http://www.coca-colacompany.com/our-company/diversity/global-diversity-mission (accessed July 18, 2016).

67. U.S. Equal Employment Opportunity Commission, "Facts About Sexual Harassment," http://www.eeoc.gov/eeoc/publications/fs-sex.cfm (accessed July 18, 2016).

68. Donald J. Petersen and Douglas P. Massengill, "Sexual Harassment Cases Five Years After *Meritor Savings Bank v. Vinson,*" *Employees Relations Law Journal* 18 (Winter 1992–1993): 489–516.

69. "Code of Practice to Clamp Down on Sexual Harassment at Work," European Commission, http://europa.eu/legislation_summaries/employment_and_social_policy/equality_between_men_and_women/c10917b_en.htm (accessed July 18, 2016).

70. Robert D. Lee and Paul S. Greenlaw, "The Legal Evolution of Sexual Harassment," *Public Administration Review* 55 (July 1995): 357–364.

71. Ibid.

72. George D. Mesritz, "Hostile Environment Sexual Harassment Claims: When Once Is Enough," *Employee Relations Law Journal* 22 (Spring 1997): 79–85; Laura Hoffman Roppe, "*Harris v. Forklift Systems, Inc.*: Victory or Defeat?" *San Diego Law Review* 32 (Winter 1996): 321–342.

73. Susan Antilla, "Women Charge Bias and Harassment in Suit Against Sterling Jewelers," *The New York Times,* March 28, 2014, http://www.nytimes.com/2014/03/29/business/women-charge-bias-and-harassment-in-suit-against-sterling-jewelers.html (accessed July 18, 2016); Brendan Pierson, "U.S. Judge Excludes 70,000 Women from Sterling Jewelers Sex Bias Lawsuit," *Reuters,* January 16, 2018, https://www.reuters.com/article/us-sterlingjewelers-lawsuit/u-s-judge-excludes-70000-women-from-sterling-jewelers-sex-bias-lawsuit-idUSKBN1F603J (accessed October 1, 2019).

74. "Ashley Alford's Verdict: $95M for Sex Harassment," *Reuters,* June 14, 2011, http://www.reuters.com/article/tagblogs-findlawcom2011-freeenterprise-idUS71042601620110614 (accessed July 18, 2016).

75. Jonathan W. Dion, "Putting Employers on the Defense: The Supreme Court Develops a Consistent Standard Regarding an Employer's Liability for a Supervisor's Hostile Work Environment Sexual Harassment," *Wake Forest Law Review* 34 (Spring 1999): 199–227; Darlene Orlov and Michael T. Roumell, *What Every Manager Needs to Know About Sexual Harassment* (New York: AMACOM, 1999).

76. Joann Lublin, "Retaliation over Harassment Claims Takes Focus," *Wall Street Journal,* April 17, 2006, p. B4.

77. Howard Koplowitz, "Texas Man Wins Sexual Harassment Case Against Female Boss: Jury Awards James Gist $567K in Pam Matranga Case," *International Business Times,* March 24, 2014, http://www.ibtimes.com/texas-man-wins-sexual-harassment-case-against-female-boss-jury-awards-james-gist-567k-pam-matranga (accessed July 18, 2016).

78. Janet P. Near and Marcia P. Miceli, "Organizational Dissidence: The Case of Whistleblowing," *Journal of Business Ethics* 4 (January 1985): 1–16.

79. This section is adapted from Randy Chiu, Richard Tansey, Debbie Thorne, and Michael White, "Is Procedural Justice the Dominant Whistleblowing Motive Among Employees?" unpublished manuscript.

80. Phaedra Haywood, "County Whistleblower Doesn't Regret Standing 'Up for What Is Right'," *Santa Fe New Mexican*, June 28, 2014, http://www.santafenewmexican.com/news/local_news/county-whistleblower-doesn-t-regret-standing-up-for-what-is/article_b5c02633-8e86-52d3-b5e5-2a2e09b11e1a.html (accessed July 18, 2016).

81. Lorri Freifeld, "Jiffy Lube Revs up to No. 1," *Training Magazine*, https://trainingmag.com/trgmag-article/jiffy-lube-revs-no-1 (accessed July 18, 2016).

82. "Helping Employees Develop Professionally," University of California, Berkeley, http://hrweb.berkeley.edu/toolkits/managers-supervisors/helping-employees-develop (accessed June 30, 2014).

83. Scott Westcott, "Good Bye and Good Luck," *Inc.* 28 (April 2006): 40–41.

84. Betsy Cummings, "Training's Top Five," *Successful Meetings* 49 (October 2000): 67–73; Adam J. Grossberg, "The Effect of Formal Training on Employment Duration," *Industrial Relations* 39 (October 2000): 578–599; Kathryn Tyler, "Extending the Olive Branch," *HR Magazine* 47 (November 2002): 85–89.

85. Association for Talent Development, "2018 State of the Industry," https://www.td.org/research-reports/2018-state-of-the-industry (accessed June 25, 2019).

86. Starbucks, "Starbucks College Achievement Plan," http://www.starbucks.com/careers/college-plan (accessed July 18, 2016).

87. Katherine Y. Williams and Charles A. O'Reilly III, "Demography and Diversity in Organizations: A Review of 40 Years of Research," *Research in Organizational Behavior* 20 (January 1998): 77–140.

88. David Pollitt, "Diversity Is About More Than Observing the Letter of the Law," *Human Resource Management International Digest* 13 (2005): 37–40.

89. Boris Groysberg and Katherine Connolly, "Great Leaders Who Make the Mix Work." *Harvard Business Review* 91 (September 2013): 68–76; Wei Shi, Seemantini Pathak, Lynda Jiwen Song, and Robert E. Hoskisson, "The Adoption of Chief Diversity Officers Among S&P 500 Firms: Institutional, Resource Dependence, and Upper Echelons Accounts." *Human Resource Management* 57, (January 2018): 83–96.

90. Alina Tugend, "Intersectionality in the Workplace," *The New York Times*, September 30, 2018, https://www.nytimes.com/2018/09/30/us/the-effect-of-intersectionality-in-the-workplace.html (accessed June 15, 2019).

91. Marilyn Loden and Judith B. Rosener, *Workforce America! Managing Employee Diversity as a Vital Resource* (Burr Ridge, IL: Irwin/McGraw-Hill, 1991).

92. DiversityInc, "Kaiser Permanente: No. 4 in the DiversityInc Top 50," http://www.diversityinc.com/kaiser-permanente/ (accessed July 8, 2014); Lincoln Cushing, "Alva Wheatley: Champion of Kaiser Permanente Diversity," Kaiser Permanente, February 18, 2014, http://kaiserpermanente.org/our-story/our-history/alva-wheatley-champion-of-kaiser-permanente-diversity/ (accessed September 28, 2019).

93. Ira Teinowitz, "Courting Change," *Advertising Age* 72 (May 14, 2001): 16–20; Michelle Saettler, "General Mills, Clorox Target Hispanic Mobile Shoppers Via Bilingual Promotions App," *Mobile Marketer*, April 14, 2014, http://www.mobilemarketer.com/cms/news/strategy/17575.html (accessed July 18, 2016).

94. New York Life Insurance Company, "New York Life Appoints Kathleen Navarro as Chief Diversity Officer," December 15, 2014, http://www.newyorklife.com/about/about/nyl-appoints-kathleen-navarro-chief-diversity-officer.

95. "Employers of the Year," *Equal Opportunity Publications,* 2014, http://www.eop.com/awards-CD-employers.php (accessed July 18, 2016).

96. Aneesya Panicker, Rakesh Agrawal, and Utkal Khandelwal, "Inclusive Workplace and Organizational Citizenship Behavior," *Equality, Diversity and Inclusion* 37 (2018): 530–550; Meghna Sabharwal, Helisse Levine, Maria D'Agostino, and Tiffany Nguyen, "Inclusive Work Practices: Turnover Intentions Among LGBT Employees of the U.S. Federal Government," *American Review of Public Administration* 49 (May 2019): 482–494.

97. Phil Gorman, Teresa Nelson, and Alan Glassman, "The Millennial Generation: A Strategic Opportunity," *Organizational Analysis* 12, no. 3 (2004): 255–270; Ron Zemke, Claire Raines, and Bob Filipczak, *Generations at Work: Managing the Clash of Veterans, Boomers, Xers, and Nexters in Your Workplace* (New York: AMACOM, 2000).

98. Baird, "Baird Recognized on the 2019 Fortune 100 Best Companies to Work For List," http://www.rwbaird.com/news/baird-recognized-on-fortune-2019-100-best-companies-to-work-for-list (accessed June 15, 2019); Cheryl Cran, "Reverse Mentoring By Millennials: Flipping the Mentoring Relationship to Collaborate and Leverage Each Other's Strengths," *Leadership Excellence* 36 (April 2019): 5–6; Josh Levs, "The Fortune at the Bottom of the Org Chart," *Strategy + Business* https://www.strategy-business.com/blog/The-fortune-at-the-bottom-of-the-org-chart (accessed June 18, 2019).

99. Arthur P. Brief, Elizabeth Umphress, Joerg Dietz, Rebecca Butz, John Burrows, and Lotte Scholten, "Community Matters: Realistic Group Conflict Theory and the Impact of Diversity," *Academy of Management Journal* 48 (October 2005): 830–844.

100. Eric Patton, "Autism, Attributions, and Accommodations: Overcoming Barriers and Integrating a Neurodiverse Workforce." *Personnel Review* 48 (2019): 915–934.

101. Cora Daniels, "To Hire a Lumber Expert, Click Here," *Fortune,* April 3, 2000, 267–270.

102. Georgia Wells, "Facebook Blames Lack of Available Talent for Diversity Problem," *Wall Street Journal*, July 14, 2016, http://www.wsj.com/articles/facebook-blames-lack-of-available-talent-for-diversity-problem-1468526303 (accessed July 15, 2016).

103. Tyrone A. Holmes, "How to Connect Diversity to Performance," *Performance Improvement* 44 (May–June 2005): 13–17.

104. Keon West and Asia Eaton, "Prejudiced and Unaware of It: Evidence for the Dunning-Kruger Model in the Domains of Racism and Sexism," *Personality and Individual Differences* 146 (August 2019): 111–119.

105. Jeffrey R. Edwards and Nancy P. Rothbard, "Mechanisms Linking Work and Family," *Academy of Management Review* 25 (January 2000): 178–199.

106. Dalton Conley, *Elsewhere, USA: How We Got from the Company Man, Family Dinners, and the Affluent Society to the Home Office, Blackberry Moms, and Economic Anxiety* (New York: Pantheon, 2009).

107. Douglas M. McCracken, "Winning the Talent War for Women: Sometimes It Takes a Revolution," *Harvard Business Review* 78 (November–December 2000): 159–167; Sally Roberts, "Work/Life Programs No Longer a 'Woman's Issue'," *Business Insurance*, August 8, 2005, 3–4; Stephanie Pappas, "Work-Life Balance Affects Men And Women Alike, Study Finds," *Huffington Post*, March 15, 2013, http://www.huffingtonpost.com/2013/03/15/work-life-balance-affects-men-women-alike-same_n_2884315.html (accessed July 18, 2016).

108. Mark C. Crowley, "How SAS Became the World's Best Place to Work," *Fast Company*, January 22, 2013, http://www.fastcompany.com/3004953/how-sas-became-worlds-best-place-work (accessed July 18, 2016).

109. "Work Stress on the Rise: 8 In 10 Americans Are Stressed About Their Jobs, Survey Finds," *Huffington Post*, April 10, 2013, http://www.huffingtonpost.com/2013/04/10/work-stress-jobs-americans_n_3053428.html (accessed July 18, 2016).

110. Bruce Horovitz, "All Stressed Out? Businesses Will Sell You Some Peace," *USA Today*, August 5, 2013, http://www.usatoday.com/story/money/business/2013/08/04/stress-deepak-chopra-dreamweaver-relaxation-drinks-american-psychological-association/2513655/ (accessed July 18, 2016).

111. Shai Oster, "They're Dying at Their Desks in China as Epidemic of Stress Proves Fatal," *Bloomberg*, http://www.bloomberg.com/news/articles/2014-06-29/is-work-killing-you-in-china-workers-die-at-their-desks (accessed July 18, 2016); Kumiko Nemoto, "Long Working Hours and the Corporate Gender Divide in Japan," *Gender, Work & Organization* 20 (September 2013): 512–527.

112. Charles R. Stoner, Jennifer Robin, and Lori Russell-Chapin, "On the Edge: Perceptions and Responses to Life Imbalance," *Business Horizons* (July–August 2005): 48–54.

113. Anne Roche, Victoria Kostadinov, Jacqui Cameron, Ken Pidd, Alice McEntee, and Vinita Duraisingam, "The Development and Characteristics of Employee Assistance Programs Around the Globe." *Journal of Workplace Behavioral Health* 33 (July 2018): 168–186.

114. Charles Benayon, "Providing Support: How EAPs Can Help in Times of Crisis," *HR Professional* 36 (February 2019): 17–18.

115. SAS, "2018-2019 Corporate Overview," https://www.sas.com/content/dam/SAS/documents/corporate-collateral/annual-report/company-overview-annual-report.pdf (accessed June 20. 2019); SAS, "Awards,"

https://www.sas.com/en_us/news/awards.html (accessed June 25, 2019).

116. E. Jeffrey Hill, Andrea Jackson, and Giuseppe Martinengo, "Twenty Years of Work and Family at International Business Machines Corporation," *American Behavioral Scientist* 49 (May 2006): 1165–1183.

117. Jessica Leong, "What Candidates Want: Improving the Applicant Screening Process," *Findly*, September 18, 2013, http://www.findly.com/blog/what-candidates-want-improving-the-applicant-screening-process/ (accessed July 18, 2016).

118. Selena Maranjian, "These Companies Do Work-Life Balance Right," *Daily Finance*, July 24, 2013, http://www.dailyfinance.com/2013/07/24/glassdoor-work-life-balance-report/ (accessed July 18, 2016).

119. Ibid.

120. Ryan Scott, "How Corporate Volunteer Programs Increase Employee Engagement," *Cause Cast*, February 16, 2012, http://www.causecast.com/blog/how-corporate-volunteer-programs-increase-employee-engagement (accessed July 18, 2016).

121. Blue Cross Blue Shield, "Blue Cross and Blue Shield Companies Host Seventh Annual National Walk@Lunch Day," April 24, 2013, http://www.bcbs.com/healthcare-news/bcbsa/bcbs-companies-host-seventh-annual-nwld.html (accessed July 8, 2014).

122. CA Technologies, "CA Technologies Springs into Twelfth Season of Giving Through Annual Volunteer Initiative," April 23, 2018, https://www.ca.com/us/company/newsroom/press-eleases/2018/ca-technologies-springs-into-twelfth-season-of-giving-through-annual-volunteer-initiative.html.

123. Sammi Caramela, "15 Cool Job Perks That Keep Employees Happy," *Business News Daily*, June 8, 2016, http://www.businessnewsdaily.com/5134-cool-job-benefits.html (accessed July 18, 2016).

124. AECOM, "About AECOM," https://www.aecom.com/about-aecom/corporate-responsibility/ (accessed June 18, 2019); Roger E. Herman and Joyce L. Gioia, *How to Become an Employer of Choice* (Winchester, VA: Oakhill Press, 2000).

125. Roger E. Herman and Joyce L. Gioia, *How to Become an Employer of Choice* (Winchester, VA: Oakhill Press, 2000); Da Joseph Kornik, "The Morale Majority," *Training* 43 (January 2006): 4.

126. "The Employee Ownership 100: America's Largest Majority Employee-Owned Companies," The National Center for Employee Ownership, June 2014, http://www.nceo.org/articles/employee-ownership-100 (accessed July 18, 2016).

127. "ESOP (Employee Stock Ownership Plan) Facts," National Center for Employee Ownership, 2014, http://www.esop.org (accessed July 18, 2016).

128. Kris Frieswick, "ESOPs: Split Personality," *CFO*, July 7, 2003, 1; Ronald Mano and E. Devon Deppe, "We Told You So: ESOPs Are Risky," *Ohio CPA Journal* 61 (July–September 2002): 67–68; Matthew Mouritsen, Ronald Mano, and E. Devon Deppe, "The ESOP Fable Revisited: Employees' Exposure to ESOPs and Enron's Exit," *Personal Financial Planning Monthly* 2 (May 2002): 27–31.

129. Lara Moroko and Mark D. Uncles, "Employer Branding and Market Segmentation," *Sloan Management Review*, March 23, 2009, http://www.researchgate.net/publication/247478730_Employer_branding_and_market_segmentation (accessed July 18, 2016).

130. "The Nike Case and Corporate Self-Censorship," *Business & the Environment with ISO 14000 Updates* 15 (March 2004): 6–7; Isabelle Maignan, Bas Hillebrand, and Debbie Thorne McAlister, "Managing Socially Responsible Buying: How to Integrate Non-economic Criteria into the Purchasing Process," *European Management Journal* 20 (December 2002): 641–648.

131. Nike, Inc., "Awards & Recognition," http://nikeinc.com/pages/awards-recognition (accessed July 22, 2014).

Chapter 9

1. Peter Frost, "Protein Bar Founder Goes All-In on 'Performance' Coffee," *Crain's*, April 19, 2016, http://www.chicagobusiness.com/article/20160419/NEWS07/160419844/protein-bar-founder-goes-all-in-on-performance-coffee (accessed July 18, 2016).

2. Mark Brandau, "Protein Bar," *Nation's Restaurant News*, June 27, 2011, http://nrn.com/nrn-50/breakout-brands-protein-bar (accessed July 18, 2016); Protein Bar, http://www.theproteinbar.com/ (accessed July 18, 2016).

3. Whole Foods, "Whole Foods Market Reports Second Quarter Results," May 4, 2016, http://investor.wholefoodsmarket.com/investors/

press-releases/press-release-details/2016/Whole-Foods-Market-Reports-Second-Quarter-Results-542016/default.aspx (accessed July 18, 2016); Sarah Halzack, "Why Supermarkets Are in Trouble," *Washington Post*, October 3, 2014, https://www.washingtonpost.com/news/business/wp/2014/10/03/why-supermarkets-are-in-trouble/ (accessed July 18, 2016).

4. "Buy Nothing Day: Participating by Not Participating," https://www.environment.co.za/environmental-issues-news/buy-nothing-day-participate-by-not-participating.html (accessed June 19, 2019); Buy Nothing Project, "About," https://buynothingproject.org/about/ (accessed June 20, 2019).

5. Jennie Bell, "The Long Game," *FN: Footwear News*, 75 (May 6, 2019): 35–39.

6. Kim Lane Scheppele, *Legal Secrets: Equality and Efficiency in the Common Law* (Chicago: University of Chicago Press, 1988).

7. "The Aggro of the Agora," *The Economist*, January 14, 2006, 76; F. Knox, "The Doctrine of Consumer Sovereignty," *Review of Social Economy* 63 (September 2005): 383–394.

8. Li Zeng, Lijie Zhou, Po-Lin Pan, and Gil Fowler, "Coping with the Milk Scandal," *Journal of Communication Management* 22 (2018): 432–450.

9. Duncan Graham and Andreas D. Arditya, "Heading to the Mall? Let the Buyer Beware," *Jakarta Post*, August 25, 2013, http://www.thejakartapost.com/news/2013/08/25/heading-mall-let-buyer-beware.html (accessed July 18, 2016).

10. Lee E. Norrgard and Julia M. Norrgard, *Consumer Fraud: A Reference Handbook* (New York: ABC-CLIO, 1998).

11. David M. Gardner, Jim Harris, and Junyong Kim, "The Fraudulent Consumer," in Gregory Gundlach, William Wilkie, and Patrick Murphy, eds., *Marketing and Public Policy Conference Proceedings*, 48–54 (Chicago: American Marketing Association, 1999).

12. Ana Serafin Smith, "Retail Inventory Shrinkage Increased to $45.2 Billion in 2015," National Retail Federation, June 13, 2016, https://nrf.com/media/press-releases/retail-inventory-shrinkage-increased-452-billion-2015 (accessed July 18, 2016). National Retail Federation, "National Retail Security Survey," https://nrf.com/research/national-retail-security-survey-2018 (accessed June 3, 2019).

13. "ASA Bans Boots Anti-Cellulite Ads," *Soap, Perfumery, & Cosmetics* 78 (October 2005): 5; Lisa McLaughlin, "Cloaking Cellulite," *Time*, May 24, 2004, 90; Christine Doyle, "How to Beat Cellulite—Part Two: Do Anti-Cellulite Creams, Lotions, and Massage Really Work, or Do Women Just Like to Think They Do?" *Ottawa Citizen*, May 23, 2000, D8.

14. Federal Trade Commission, "Imposter Scams Top Complaints Made to FTC in 2018," February 28, 2019, https://www.ftc.gov/news-events/press-releases/2019/02/imposter-scams-top-complaints-made-ftc-2018 (accessed October 2, 2019).

15. "Bureau of Consumer Protection," Federal Trade Commission, http://www.ftc.gov/bcp/index.shtml (accessed July 20, 2016).

16. Paula Span, "F.T.C.'s Lumosity Penalty Doesn't End Brain Training Debate," *The New York Times*, January 15, 2016, http://www.nytimes.com/2016/01/19/health/ftcs-lumosity-penalty-doesnt-end-brain-training-debate.html?_r=0 (accessed July 20, 2016).

17. "You Have Rights as a Consumer in Texas. Understanding Them Will Ensure That You Are Better Equipped to Avoid Scams and Get a Fair Shake," The Deceptive Trade Practices Act, https://www.texasattorneygeneral.gov/consumer-protection/file-consumer-complaint/consumer-rights (accessed August 9, 2019).

18. "Consumer Affairs and Outreach Division," Federal Communications Commission, http://transition.fcc.gov/cgb/cgb_offices.html (accessed July 20, 2016).

19. "Consumer Protection," Montana Department of Justice, https://doj.mt.gov/consumer/ (accessed October 7, 2019).

20. Robert B. Downs, "Afterword, in Upton Sinclair," *The Jungle* (New York: New American Library, 1960).

21. Abby W. Schachter, "Deconstructing the IKEA Dresser Recall," *Wall Street Journal*, July 13, 2016, http://www.wsj.com/articles/deconstructing-the-ikea-dresser-recall-1468449602 (accessed July 20, 2016). E. Price, "Ikea Issues Second Recall of Popular Dresser After 2-Year-Old's Death," *Fortune*, 2017, https://fortune.com/2017/11/21/ikea-issues-second-recall-of-popular-dresser-after-2-year-olds-death/ (June 2, 2019); U.S. Consumer Product Safety Commission, "IKEA Reannounces Recall of MALM and Other Models of Chests and Dressers Due to Serious Tip-over Hazard; 8th Child Fatality Reported; Consumers Urged to Choose Between Refund or Repair,"

https://cpsc.gov/Recalls/2018/IKEA-Reannounces-Recall-of-MALM-and-Other-Models-of-Chests-and-Dressers-Due-to-Serious-Tip-over-Hazard (accessed October 8, 2019).

22. James E. McNulty, Luis Garcia-Feijoo, and Ariel Viale, "The Regulation of Mortgage Servicing: Lessons from the Financial Crisis," *Contemporary Economic Policy* 37 (January 2019): 170–180.

23. Nadia Khomami, "Coronation Street signs product placement deals with Co-op and Costa," *The Guardian,* January 30, 2018, https://www.theguardian.com/media/2018/jan/30/coronation-street-product-placement-deal-co-op-costa-coffee (accessed June 19, 2019).

24. Brigitte Naderer, Jörg Matthes, and Ines Spielvogel, "How Brands Appear in Children's Movies. A Systematic Content Analysis of the Past 25 Years," *International Journal of Advertising* 38 (January 2019): 237–257.

25. Rene Lynch, "Sketchers Lawsuit: How to Get Your Piece of the $40-Million Payout," *Los Angeles Times,* May 17, 2012, http://articles.latimes.com/2012/may/17/nation/la-na-nn-skechers-20120517 (accessed July 20, 2016); Federal Trade Commission, "Reebok to Pay $25 Million in Customer Refunds to Settle FTC Charges of Deceptive Advertising of EasyTone and RunTone Shoes," September 28, 2011, http://www.ftc.gov/news-events/press-releases/2011/09/reebok-pay-25-million-customer-refunds-settle-ftc-charges (accessed July 20, 2016).

26. "Sensa and Three Other Marketers of Fad Weight-Loss Products Settle FTC Charges in Crackdown on Deceptive Advertising," Federal Trade Commission, January 7, 2014, http://www.ftc.gov/news-events/press-releases/2014/01/sensa-three-other-marketers-fad-weight-loss-products-settle-ftc (accessed July 2, 2014).

27. Wine Institute, "Direct Wine Shipments," http://www.wineinstitute.org/programs/shipwine/main.htm (accessed July 20, 2016). Emma Balter, "Supreme Court Debates Wine Laws," *Wine Spectator* 44 (April 30, 2019):13.

28. "Lemon Law Information and Sites," http://autopedia.com/html/HotLinks_LemonLaw.html (accessed July 20, 2016).

29. Xiaolin Wang, Min Xie, and Lishuai Li, "On Optimal Upgrade Strategy for Second-Hand Multi-Component Systems Sold with Warranty," *International Journal of Production Research* 57 (February 2019): 847–864.

30. Peter Neumann and Calvin Ding, "China's New Tort Law: Dawn of the Product Liability Era," *China Business Review,* March 1, 2010, http://www.chinabusinessreview.com/chinas-new-tort-law-dawn-of-the-product-liability-era/ (accessed July 20, 2016).

31. Jennifer Levitz, "J&J Settles Many Surgical-Tool Lawsuits," *The Wall Street Journal,* March 19–20, 2016, A3.

32. Ibid.

33. Viviane Adame, "Consumers' Obsession Becoming Retailers' Possession: The Way That Retailers Are Benefiting from Consumers' Presence on Social Media," *San Diego Law Review* 53 (Summer 2016): 653–700.

34. Renee Reints, "FCC Takes Major Step Toward Limiting Robocalls and Scammers," Fortune.com, June 7, 2019, http://fortune.com/2019/06/07/fcc-robocalls-fake-caller-id/ (accessed June 15, 2019).

35. Federal Trade Commission, "FTC Charges Operator of Crowdfunding Scheme," https://www.ftc.gov/news-events/press-releases/2019/05/ftc-charges-operator-crowdfunding-scheme (accessed June 3, 2019).

36. "Regulatory Watch," *Business China,* February 27, 2006, 11.

37. Sandra N. Hurd, Peter Shears, and Frances E. Zollers, "Consumer Law," *Journal of Business Law* (May 2000): 262–277.

38. Irene M. Kunii, "Stand Up and Fight," *Business Week,* September 11, 2000, 54–55.

39. Suk-ching Ho, "Executive Insights: Growing Consumer Power in China," *Journal of International Marketing* 9 (Spring 2001): 64–84.

40. Kenneth J. Meier, E. Thomas Garman, and Lael R. Keiser, *Regulation and Consumer Protection: Politics, Bureaucracy, and Economics* (Houston: Dame Publications, 1998).

41. Allan Asher, "Going Global: A New Paradigm for Consumer Protection," *Journal of Consumer Affairs* 32 (Winter 1998): 183–203; Benet Middleton, "Consumerism: A Pragmatic Ideology," *Consumer Policy Review* 8 (November–December 1998): 213–217; Audhesh Paswan and Jhinuk Chowdhury, "Consumer Protection Issues and Non-governmental Organizations in a Developing Market," in Harlan E. Spotts and H. Lee Meadow, eds., *Developments in Marketing Science,* 171–176 (Coral Gables, FL: Academy of Marketing Science, 2000).

42. Paul N. Bloom and Stephen A. Greyser, "The Maturing of Consumerism," *Harvard Business Review* 59 (November–December 1981): 130–139.

43. Consumer Reports, "Advocacy," https://advocacy.consumerreports.org/ (accessed June 19, 2019): Rhoda H. Karpatkin, "Toward a Fair and Just Marketplace for All Consumers: The Responsibilities of Marketing Professionals," *Journal of Public Policy and Marketing* 18 (Spring 1999): 118–123.

44. Gary Sankary, "Location Intelligence and Big Data: Managing the Retail Disruption," *Design: Retail,* 31 (April 2019): 45.

45. "Empowerment to the Consumer," *Marketing Week,* October 21, 1999, 3; Pierre M. Loewe and Mark S. Bonchek, "The Retail Revolution," *Management Review* 88 (April 1999): 38–44; Jim Guest, "Grassroots Advocacy Is Still in Style," *Consumer Reports* 70 (August 2005): 5; "About Us," Consumers Union, http://consumersunion.org/about/ (accessed July 20, 2016).

46. National Consumers League, "Coding Bootcamps: How to Spot a Fraud Before You Enroll," https://www.nclnet.org/coding_bootcamps (accessed June 10, 2019).

47. "Consumer Bill of Rights and Responsibilities: Report to the President of the United States," Advisory Commission on Consumer Protection and Quality in the Health Care Industry, November 1997, http://www.hcqualitycommission.gov/cborr/ (accessed July 2, 2014).

48. Mary Jane Fisher, "Pressure Mounts for Patient Rights Agreement," National Underwriter/Life & Health Financial Services, May 22, 2000, 3–4; Michael Pretzer, "New Mind 'Patient Relations': Get Ready for 'Consumer Rights'," *Medical Economics,* February 23, 1998, 47–55.

49. "Comprehensive Consumer Rights Bill Addresses Bank Fees, Identity Theft," *Consumer Financial Services Law Report,* May 15, 2000, 2.

50. Lori Sandoval, "Google Deletes Search Results in Europe, Abides by 'Right to Be Forgotten' Rule," *Tech Times,* June 30, 2014, http://www.techtimes.com/articles/9370/20140630/google-deletes-search-results-in-europe-abides-by-right-to-be-forgotten-rule.htm (accessed July 20, 2016).

51. Lin Zhu, Deepa Anagondahalli, and Ai Zhang, "Social Media and Culture in Crisis Communication: McDonald's and KFC Crises Management in China," *Public Relations Review* 43 (September 2017): 487–492.

52. Roger Yu, "FCC to Fine AT&T $100M for Slowing Speeds," *USA Today,* June 17, 2015, http://www.usatoday.com/story/money/2015/06/17/fcc-fines-att-100-million/28863455/ (accessed July 20, 2016).

53. WebMD LLC, "URAC Health Website Accreditation," *WebMD,* http://www.webmd.com/about-webmd-policies/urac-center (accessed July 20, 2016). URAC, "About URAC," https://www.urac.org/ (accessed June 10, 2019).

54. Better Business Bureau, "Dispute Resolution Processes and Guides," https://www.bbb.org/bbb-dispute-handling-and-resolution/dispute-resolution-rules-and-brochures/dispute-resolution-processes-and-guides/ (accessed June 20, 2019).

55. Federal Trade Commission, "Privacy and Data Security Update 2018," https://www.ftc.gov/reports/privacy-data-security-update-2018 (accessed June 20, 2019).

56. PR Newswire, "Service Line Warranties of America Named the 2013 Winner of the Western Pennsylvania Torch Award for Marketplace Ethics," *The Business Journals,* January 15, 2014, http://www.prnewswire.com/news-releases/service-line-warranties-of-america-named-the-2013-winner-of-the-western-pennsylvania-torch-award-for-marketplace-ethics-240310951.html (accessed July 20, 2016); "About Us," Service Line Warranties, http://www.slwofa.com/slw-about.html (accessed July 20, 2016).

57. Making Change at Walmart, "About Us," http://changewalmart.org/about-us/ (accessed June 7, 2019); Wendy Zellner, "Wal-Mart: Why an Apology Made Sense," *BusinessWeek,* July 3, 2000, 65–66; Wendy Zellner and Aaraon Bernstein, "Up Against the Wal-Mart," *BusinessWeek,* March 13, 2000, 76.

58. Michael Peel, "Wealthy Thais Vent Anger over Sanction with European Goods Boycott," *Financial Times,* June 27, 2014, http://www.ft.com/cms/s/0/0f6e80b8-fdde-11e3-bd0e-00144feab7de.html#axzz38Ea1c4Xc (accessed July 20, 2016).

59. Andrea Seikaly, "Kim Kardashian Weighs in on Beverly Hills Hotel Boycott," *Variety,* June 23, 2014, http://variety.com/2014/biz/news/kim-kardashian-weighs-in-on-beverly-hills-hotel-boycott-1201243471/ (accessed July 20, 2016).

60. E. E. L. Twarog (2017). *'What Do Housewives Do All Day? The Suburbanization of Meat Boycotts and Supermarket Protests* (New York: Oxford University Press).

61. Nick Snow, "Groups Express Concerns as Crude Oil Pipeline Protests Escalate," *Oil & Gas Journal,* October 12, 2106, https://www.ogj.com/pipelines-transportation/article/17250808/groups-express-concerns-as-crudeoil-pipeline-protests-escalate (accessed June 20, 2019).

62. "David Lansky to Join the Markle Foundation," Markle Foundation, September 28, 2004, http://www.markle.org/news-events/media-releases/david-lansky-join-markle-foundation (accessed July 20, 2016); Foundation for Accountability, "FACCT Legacy Documents," http://www.policyarchive.org/collections/markle/index?section=8 (accessed July 20, 2016).

63. Business in the Community, "Responsible Small Business of the Year 2018," https://www.bitc.org.uk/resources-training/resources/impact-stories/responsible-small-business-year-salary-finance-small (accessed June 10, 2019).

64. Adam Wooten, "Top 10 Intercultural Blunders of 2011," *Deseret News,* December 16, 2011, http://www.deseretnews.com/top/326/3/PUMA-shoe-design-disrespects-UAE-flag-Top-10-intercultural-blunders-of-2011.html (accessed July 20, 2016).

Chapter 10

1. Danielle Abril, "Google Is Paying Employees for Six Months of Charity Work," *Fortune.com,* January 16, 2019, https://fortune.com/2019/01/16/google-employees-charity-work/ (accessed June 30, 2019); "Introducing the Google.org Fellowship," Google.org, https://blog.google/outreach-initiatives/google-org/googleorg-fellowship/ (accessed June 20, 2019); Thorn, https://www.thorn.org/child-sexual-exploitation-and-technology/ (accessed July 1, 2019); Nicole Wallace, "Google to Donate 50,000 Hours of Pro Bono Tech Help to Charities This Year," *Chronicle of Philanthropy,* January 15, 2019 (accessed June 30, 2019).

2. J. P. Morgan Corporate Challenge, https://www.jpmorganchasecc.com/series/corporate-challenge (accessed June 25, 2019).

3. *U.S. News & World Report,* "Best Countries: Quality of Life," https://www.usnews.com/news/best-countries/quality-of-life-rankings (accessed June 27, 2019).

4. Yuka Fujimoto, Fara Azmat, and Nava Subramaniam, "Creating Community-Inclusive Organizations: Managerial Accountability Framework." *Business & Society* 58 (April 2019): 712–748; Jessica Shankleman, "Can Asia Pulp & Paper Really End Deforestation?" BusinessGreen.com, October 14, 2013, www.businessgreen.com/bg/feature/2299889/can-asia-pulp-paper-reallyend-deforestation (accessed June 29, 2019).

5. American Productivity and Quality Center, *Community Relations: Unleashing the Power of Corporate Citizenship* (Houston: American Productivity and Quality Center, 1998); Edmund M. Burke, *Corporate Community Relations: The Principle of the Neighbor of Choice* (Westport, CT: Praeger, 1999).

6. Bradley K. Googins, "Why Community Relations Is a Strategic Imperative," *Strategy & Business* (Third Quarter 1997): 14–16.

7. "Community," Merck, https://www.msdresponsibility.com/our-giving/community/ (accessed June 25, 2019).

8. "Academic Collaborations," Dow Chemical Company, https://corporate.dow.com/en-us/science-and-sustainability/collaboration/academic (accessed June 30, 2019).

9. Business for Social Responsibility, "Community Involvement," www.bsr.org/resourcecenter/ (accessed December 4, 2000); Sandra A. Waddock and Mary-Ellen Boyle, "The Dynamics of Change in Corporate Community Relations," *California Management Review* 37 (Summer 1995): 125–138; Barron Wells and Nelda Spinks, "Communicating with the Community," *Career Development International* 4, no. 2 (1999): 108–116.

10. "CECP Presents 2014 Excellence Award to Direct Relief for Exemplary Collaboration with FedEx," Committee Encouraging Corporate Philanthropy (CECP), May 20, 2014, http://cecp.co/pdfs/2014summit/EA_PR_May20_Final.pdf (accessed July 28, 2016); Direct Relief, "FedEx Direct Relief Deliver Essential Medicines to Flood Inundated Paraguay," June 11, 2019, https://www.directrelief.org/2019/06/fedex-direct-relief-deliver-essential-medicines-to-flood-inundated-paraguay/ (accessed June 30, 2019).

11. Giving USA, "Giving USA: 2015 Was America's Most-Generous Year Ever," June 13, 2016, http://givingusa.org/giving-usa-2016/ (accessed July 28, 2016); PepsiCo, "Strategic Grants," http://www.pepsico.com/Purpose/Global-Citizenship/Strategic-Grants (accessed July 28, 2016).

12. Alyson Warhurst, "The Future of Corporate Philanthropy," *BusinessWeek,* December 9, 2008, 16.

13. "Corporate Responsibility," Takeda, https://www.takeda.com/en-us/corporate-responsibility/ (accessed June 30, 2019); Top Employers Institute, "Takeda," https://www.top-employers.com/en/globalcompanyprofiles/takeda-global/ (accessed June 15, 2019).

14. "Community Needs Assessment Survey Guide," Utah State University Extension, http://extension.usu.edu/files/uploads/surveyguide.pdf (accessed July 28, 2016).

15. "Target Sucks," http://www.ihatetarget.net (accessed July 28, 2016); "I HATE Ryan Air...," http://ihateryanair.co.uk/ (accessed July 28, 2016).

16. Global Exchange, "Top Ten Corporate Criminals Alumni," http://www.globalexchange.org/corporateHRviolators/alums (accessed July 28, 2016); "Top Ten Corporate Criminals of 2018," Global Exchange, 2018, https://globalexchange.org/2018/11/23/ten-top-corporate-criminals-of-2018/ (accessed May 30, 2019).

17. Julie Jargon, "Starbucks Tries Franchising to Perk up Europe Business," *The Wall Street Journal,* November 29, 2013, http://online.wsj.com/news/articles/SB10001424052702304607104579209971318755960 (accessed July 28, 2016).

18. "AT&T Pebble Beach Pro-Am," AT&T, https://about.att.com/pages/pebble_beach (accessed June 30, 2019).

19. "Quad/Graphics Closing Plant in Woodstock, Cutting 540 Jobs," *Chicago Tribune,* July 8, 2014, https://www.chicagotribune.com/business/ct-xpm-2014-07-08-chi-illinois-layoffs-20140708-story.html (accessed October 1, 2019).

20. Lauren Sage Reinlie, "Construction Company Cited for Serious Safety Violations," *News and Information for the Emerald Coast,* June 20, 2014, http://www.nwfdailynews.com/business/local-business-news/construction-company-cited-for-serious- safety-violations-1.335694 (accessed July 5, 2014); "U.S. Department of Labor Cites Contractors for Safety Violations Following Two Fatalities at Florida Hotel Worksite," Occupational Safety and Health Administration, https://www.osha.gov/news/newsreleases/region4/03062019 (accessed May 30, 2019).

21. Wendy Zellner and Aaron Bernstein, "Up Against the Wal-Mart," *Bloomberg Businessweek,* March 13, 2000, 76–78.

22. Diane Hess, "An Upper West Side Retailer Survives by Being a Good Neighbor," *Crain's New York,* February 6, 2019, https://www.crainsnewyork.com/gotham-gigs/upper-west-side-retailer-survives-being-good-neighbor (accessed June 30, 2019).

23. Daniel B. Kline, "Amazon, Target and More: Here are the Companies Committed to $15 Hourly Minimum Wage," USAToday.com, October 2, 2018 https://www.usatoday.com/story/money/business/2018/10/02/minimum-wage-which-companies-15-hour/1498923002/ (accessed July 1, 2019).

24. Sarah Nassauer, "Wal-Mart Store Managers Make $175,00 a Year on Average," *Wall Street Journal* (Online), May 8, 2019, https://www.wsj.com/articles/walmart-store-managers-make-175-000-a-year-11557339360 (accessed July 1, 2019).

25. "Daniels Fund Grants Program," https://www.danielsfund.org/grants/overview (accessed May 30, 2019).

26. "Grants Program," New Belgium Brewing Company, https://www.newbelgium.com/sustainability/community/grants/ (accessed June 20, 2019).

27. "Research," Corporation for National and Community Service, https://www.nationalservice.gov/serve/via/research (accessed July 1, 2019).

28. Corporate for National and Community Service, "Benefits of Volunteering," http://www.nationalservice.gov/about/volunteering/benefits.asp (accessed July 5, 2014).

29. "About Employee Volunteering," National Center for Volunteering, http://www.ncvo.org.uk (accessed July 5, 2014).

30. "Volunteerism," Exelon, https://www.exeloncorp.com/community/volunteerism (accessed July 1, 2019).

31. "Corporate Partnerships," World Vision, https://www.worldvision.org/corporate/ (accessed June 25, 2019).

32. Ingrid Murro Botero, "Charitable Giving Has 4 Big Benefits," *Business Journal of Phoenix,* January 1, 1999, www.bizjournals.com/phoenix/stories/1999/04/smallb3.html (accessed July 28, 2016).

33. Steve McLaughlin, "Insights from Giving USA 2018," *npENGAGE,* https://npengage.com/nonprofit-fundraising/giving-usa-2018-insights/ (accessed July 1, 2019).

34. "Giving USA 2019," Giving USA, https://givingusa.org/giving-usa-2019-americans-gave-427-71-billion-to-charity-in-2018-amid-complex-year-for-charitable-giving/ (accessed June 27, 2019).

35. Shalene Gupta, "When Marriages Between Nonprofits and Corporations Sour," *Fortune,* June 26, 2014, http://fortune.com/2014/06/26/rocky-marriage-non-profits-corporations/ (accessed July 28, 2016).

36. Leon Kaye, "The Business Case for Strategic Philanthropy," *Triple Pundit,* August 8, 2013, http://www.triplepundit.com/2013/08/business-case-strategic-philanthropy/ (accessed July 28, 2016).

37. Michael E. Porter and Mark R. Kramer, "The Competitive Advantage of Corporate Philanthropy," *Harvard Business Review* 80 (December 2002): 56–68; Robbie Shell, "Breaking the Stereotypes of Corporate Philanthropy," *The Wall Street Journal,* November 26, 2002, B2.

38. Jennifer Keishin Armstrong, "Setting a High Bar," *Fast Company,* February 2014, 40–42; Nicole Goodkind, "KIND CEO: How We Became the Fastest-Growing Nutrition Bar in America," *Yahoo! Finance,* April 6, 2015, http://finance.yahoo.com/news/kind-bar-ceo-our-social-impact-doesn-t-persuade-customers-133322809.html (accessed July 28, 2016).

39. Noel M. Tichy, Andrew R. McGill, and Lynda St. Clair, eds., *Corporate Global Citizenship: Doing Business in the Public Eye* (San Francisco: New Lexington Press, 1997).

40. Jessica Stannard and Tamara Backer, "How Employee Volunteers Multiply Your Community Impact, PART 2," OnPhilanthropy.com, December 29, 2005, http://cwop.convio.net/site/News2?page=NewsArticle&id=5470 (accessed July 5, 2014).

41. J. P. Morgan Chase, "Generating Positive Impact Alongside Financial Return," https://www.jpmorganchase.com/corporate/Corporate-Responsibility/social-finance.htm (accessed July 28, 2016). Global Impact Investing Network, "Bridges Social Entrepreneurs Fund," https://thegiin.org/research/profile/bridges-social-entrepreneurs-fund (accessed June 20, 2019).

42. Paula Caligiuri, "When Unilever Bought Ben & Jerry's: A Story of CEO Adaptability," *Fast Company,* August 14, 2012, http://www.fastcompany.com/3000398/when-unilever-bought-ben-jerrys-story-ceo-adaptability (accessed July 28, 2016); David Gelles, "How the Social Mission of Ben & Jerry's Survived Being Gobbled Up," *The New York Times,* August 21, 2015, http://www.nytimes.com/2015/08/23/business/how-ben-jerrys-social-mission-survived-being-gobbled-up.html?_r=0 (accessed July 28, 2016).

43. Curt Weeden, *Corporate Social Investing* (San Francisco: Berrett-Koehler, 1998), 116–123.

44. Avon, "Avon Breast Cancer Crusade," Avon Foundation for Women, https://www.avonfoundation.org/programs/breast-cancer/ (accessed July 28, 2016).

45. Tichy et al., *Corporate Global Citizenship.*

46. Katharine M. Howie, Lifeng Yeng, Scott J. Vitell, Victoria Bush, and Doug Vorhies, "Consumer Participation in Cause-Related Marketing: An Examination of Effort Demands and Defensive Denial," *Journal of Business Ethics,* 2015, http://link.springer.com/article/10.1007%2Fs10551-015-2961-1 (accessed July 28, 2016).

47. Kevin T. Higgins, "Marketing with a Conscience," *Marketing Management* 11 (July–August 2002): 12–15; P. Rajan Varadarajan and Anil Menon, "Cause-Related Marketing: A Coalignment of Marketing Strategy and Corporate Philanthropy," *Journal of Marketing* 52 (July 1988): 58–74.

48. Population Services International, *2017 Annual Report,* https://www.psi.org/wp-content/uploads/2019/02/PSI_Annual-Report_Print_2017_v1_FINAL.pdf (accessed July 2, 20190; Population Services International, "What We Do," https://www.psi.org/work-impact/ (accessed July 2, 2019).

49. Steve Hoeffler and Kevin Lane Keller, "Building Brand Equity Through Corporate Societal Marketing," *Journal of Public Policy & Marketing* 21 (Spring 2002): 78–89; Sue Adkins and Nina Kowalska, "Consumers Put 'Causes' on the Shopping List," *M2 PressWire,* November 17, 1997; Matt Carmichael, "Stat of the Day: 83% Want Brands to Support Causes," *Ad Age,* January 18, 2012, http://adage.com/article/adagestat/stat-day-83-brands-support/232141/ (accessed July 28, 2016).

50. Jennifer Mullen, "Performance-Based Corporate Philanthropy: How 'Giving Smart' Can Further Corporate Goals," *Public Relations Quarterly* 42 (June 22, 1997): 42; Michal Strahilevitz, "The Effects of Prior Impressions of a Firm's Ethics on the Success of a Cause-Related Marketing Campaign," *Journal of Nonprofit & Public Sector Marketing* 11, no. 1 (2003): 77–92.

51. Stan Friedman and Charles Kouns, "Charitable Contribution: Reinventing Cause Marketing," *Brand Week,* October 27, 1997.

52. "Nonprofit Corporation," *Entrepreneur,* http://www.entrepreneur.com/encyclopedia/nonprofit-corporation (accessed July 28, 2016).

53. Samer Abu-Saifan, "Social Entrepreneurship: Definition and Boundaries," *Technology Innovation Management Review,* February 2012, 22–27.

54. H. Haugh, "Social Enterprise: Beyond Economic Outcomes and Individual Returns," in J. Mair, J. Robinson, and K. Hockerts, eds., *Social Entrepreneurship* (Basingstoke, UK: Palgrave Macmillan, 2006).

55. Raymond Dart, "The Legitimacy of Social Enterprise," *Non-profit Management & Leadership* 14, no. 4 (Summer 2004): 411–424.

56. Oregon Public Broadcasting, *The New Heroes,* PBS, 2005, http://www.pbs.org/opb/thenewheroes/whatis/ (accessed July 28, 2014); Pablo Muñoz and Jonathan Kimmitt, "Social Mission as Competitive Advantage: A Configurational Analysis of the Strategic Conditions of Social Entrepreneurship," *Journal of Business Research* 101 (August 2019): 854–861.

57. Institute for Social Entrepreneurs, *Evolution of the Social Enterprise Industry: A Chronology of Key Events,* August 1, 2008, http://socialent.org/documents/EVOLUTIONOFTHE-SOCIALENTERPRISEINDUSTRY--ACHRONOLOGY-OFKEYEVENTS.pdf (accessed July 28, 2016); Linda Perriton, "The Parochial Realm, Social Enterprise, and Gender: The Work of Catharine Cappe and Faith Gray and Others in York, 1780–1820." *Business History* 59 (January–March 2017): 202–230.

58. Oregon Public Broadcasting, *The New Heroes.*

59. Adam Ludwig, "Ashoka Chairman Bill Drayton on the Power of Social Entrepreneurship," *Forbes,* March 12, 2012, http://www.forbes.com/sites/techonomy/2012/03/12/ashoka-chairman-bill-drayton-on-the-power-of-social-entrepreneurship/#8add3bc3d34c (accessed July 28, 2016); Yonatan Gordis, "On the Value or Values of Jewish Social Entrepreneurship," *Journal of Jewish Communal Service* 84, no. 1/2 (Winter/Spring 2009): 37–44.

60. Anand Giridharadas and Keith Bradsher, "Microloan Pioneer and His Bank Win Nobel Peace Prize," *The New York Times,* October 13, 2006, http://www.nytimes.com/2006/10/13/business/14nobelcnd.html?_r=0&adxnnl=1&pagewanted=1&adxnnlx=1406646197-P8A97M3K4GY-HoZx4UHWYWA (accessed July 29, 2014); Grameen Bank website, http://www.grameen-info.org/ (accessed October 1, 2019).

61. Giridharadas and Bradsher, "Microloan Pioneer and His Bank Win Nobel Peace Prize."

62. *Ibid.;* Grameen Bank, "Credit Delivery System," http://www.grameen.com/index.php?option=com_content&task=view&i d=24&Itemid=169 (accessed July 28, 2016).

63. Muhammed Yunus, "Is Grameen Bank Different from Conventional Banks?" Yunus Centre, April 2009, http://www.muhammadyunus.org/index.php/design-lab/previous-design-labs/43-news-a-media/books-a-articles/232-is-grameen-bank-different-from-conventional-banks (accessed July 28, 2016); "Microcredit and Grameen Bank," *New Internationalist,* https://newint.org/books/reference/world-development/case-studies/poverty-microcredit-grameen-bank/ (accessed July 28, 2016).

64. "Grameen Bank at a Glance," Yunus Centre, http://www.muhammadyunus.org/index.php/design-lab/previous-design-labs/37-about/about/371-grameen-bank-at-a-glance (accessed July 28, 2016).

65. Giridharadas and Bradsher, "Microloan Pioneer and His Bank Win Nobel Peace Prize."

66. Grameen Bank, "General Questions on Grameen Bank FAQ," http://www.grameen.com/index.php?option=com_easyfaq&ta sk=cat&catid=80&Itemid=524 (accessed July 28, 2016); Mohammad I. Azim and Ron Kluvers, "Resisting Corruption in Grameen Bank." *Journal of Business Ethics* 156 (May 2019): 591–604.

67. "DEG Provides Loan for Egyptian Agri-Sector," *Trade Finance* 12 (8): 76; SEKEM, https://www.sekem.com/en/index/ (accessed July 1, 2019); Christian Seelos and Johanna Mair, "Social Entrepreneurship: Creating New Business Models to Serve the Poor," *Business Horizons* 48 (May/June 2005): 241–246.

68. Oregon Public Broadcasting, *Meet the New Heroes: Mimi Silbert,* PBS, 2005, http://www.pbs.org/opb/thenewheroes/meet/silbert.html (accessed July 29, 2014); Delancey Street Foundation, "Who Are the Constituents?" http://www.pbs.org/opb/thenewheroes/meet/silbert.html (accessed July 29, 2014).

69. TOMS, "What We Give," https://www.toms.com/what-we-give (accessed August 19, 2019).

70. Sseko Designs, "Our Impact," https://ssekodesigns.com/impact (accessed August 19, 2019).

71. Sean Stannard-Stockton, "The Effective Strategic Philanthropist," *Tactical Philanthropy,* March 16, 2011, http://www.tacticalphilanthropy.com/2011/03/the-effective-strategic-philanthropist/ (accessed October 2, 2019); Sean Stannard-Stockton, "The Social Entrepreneur," *Tactical*

Philanthropy, March 15, 2011, http://www.tacticalphilanthropy. com/2011/03/the-effective-social-entrepreneur/ (accessed July 29, 2014).

72. Ruth McCambridge, "WSJ Chart on 2014 Corporate Giving Explains Some Things," *Nonprofit Quarterly,* June 25, 2015, https:// nonprofitquarterly.org/2015/06/25/wall-street-journal-chart-on-2014-corporate-giving-explains-some-things/ (accessed July 28, 2016); Ruth McCambridge, "Giving USA 2019: Most Nonprofits Will Need to Work Harder for Their Money," *Nonprofit Quarterly,* June 18, 2019, https://nonprofitquarterly.org/giving-usa-2019-most-nonprofits-will-need-to-work-harder-for-their-money/ (accessed August 19, 2019).

73. Walker Information, *Corporate Philanthropy National Benchmark Study, Employee Report* (Chicago: Walker Information, 2002).

74. Caroline Stephens, "Do Good, Find Talent," *HR Professional* 36 (February 2019): 61–62.

75. Ryan Langan and Anand Kumar, "Time Versus Money: The Role of Perceived Effort in Consumers' Evaluation of Corporate Giving," *Journal of Business Research* 99 (June 2019): 295–305.

76. Robert J. Williams and J. Douglas Barrett, "Corporate Philanthropy, Criminal Activity, and Firm Reputation: Is There a Link?" *Journal of Business Ethics* 26 (2000): 341–350.

77. Roger Bennett, "Corporate Philanthropy in France, Germany, and the UK," *International Marketing Review* 15 (June 1998): 469; Rosa Chun, Antonio Argandoña, Christine Choirat, and Donald S. Siegel, "Corporate Reputation: Being Good and Looking Good," *Business & Society* 58 (July 2019): 1132–1142.

78. American Productivity and Quality Center, "Community Relations: Unleashing the Power of Corporate Citizenship," November 24, 1998, https://www.apqc.org/resource-library/resource-listing/community-relations-unleashing-power-corporate-citizenship-best (accessed October 2, 2019).

79. "BNP Paribas Foundation," BNP Paribas, http://www.bnppa-ribas.com/ en/bnp-paribas-foundation/objectives (accessed July 28, 2016); Forbes Corporate Communications Staff, "BNP Paribas Wealth Management Publishes BNP Paribas Individual Philanthropy Index by Forbes Insights," *Forbes,* February 11, 2014, http://www.forbes.com/sites/ forbespr/2014/02/11/bnp-paribas-wealth-management-publishes-bnp-paribas-individual-philanthropy-index-by-forbes-insights/#f24078c63c54 (accessed July 28, 2016).

80. Weeden, *Corporate Social Investing.*

81. Reprinted with permission of the publisher. From *Corporate Social Investing,* copyright ©1998 by Curt Weeden, Berrett-Koehler Publishers, Inc., San Francisco, CA. All rights reserved. www. bkconnection.com.

82. Walter W, Wymer Jr. and Sridhar Samu, "Dimensions of Business and Nonprofit Collaborative Relationships," *Journal of Nonprofit & Public Sector Marketing* 11, no. 1 (2003): 3–22.

83. Give.org, *Better Business Bureau Wise Giving Alliance,* http://www. give.org/ (accessed July 2, 2019); Joelle Harms, "Giving Back This Holiday Season," *LP/Gas* 78 (December 2018): 20.

84. John A. Byrne, "The New Face of Philanthropy," *Business Week,* December 2, 2002, 82–86; Stephanie Strom, "Ground Zero: Charity, a Flood of Money, Then a Deluge of Scrutiny for Those Handing It Out," *The New York Times,* September 11, 2002, B5; Panel on the Nonprofit Sector, "Principles for Good Governance and Ethical Practice: A Guide for Charities and Foundations," http://www.nonprofitpanel.org/Report/ principles/Principles_Executive_Summary.pdf (accessed July 12, 2009).

85. Marc Holley, "The Role of Evaluation in Strategic Philanthropy," *Nonprofit Quarterly,* March 7, 2013, http://nonprofitquarterly.org/ philanthropy/23808-the-role-of-evaluation-in-strategic-philanthropy. html (accessed April 28, 2016).

Chapter 11

1. "Drones, The Great Ally of Sustainability," *Active Sustainability,* https://www.activesustainability.com/sustainable-development/ drones-the-great-ally-of-sustainability/ (accessed July 20, 2019); C. Thompson, "Whole Earth, Cataloged," *Wired,* 27(07), 26–28; "The Role of Technology in Sustainability," First Carbon Solutions, 2019, https://www.firstcarbonsolutions.com/resources/newsletters/may-2015-the-role-of-technology-in-sustainability/the-role-of-technology-in-sustainability/ (accessed July 20, 2019); Nils Naujok, Henry Le Fleming, and Naveen Srivatsav, "Digital Technology and Sustainability: Positive Mutual Reinforcement," *strategy+business,* August 1, 2018, https://www.strategy-business.com/article/Digital-Technology-and-Sustainability-Positive-Mutual-Reinforcement?gko=7ce3e (accessed

July 20, 2019); Geotab, "About Us," 2019, https://www.geotab.com/ about/ (accessed July 20, 2019); Craig Michael, "What Is Telematics?" Geotab, January 8, 2018, https://www.geotab.com/blog/what-is-telematics/ (accessed July 20, 2019); Environmental Defense Fund, "Future Fleets: The Potential for Vehicle Based Pollution Mapping," Environmental Defense Fund, 2019, http://business.edf.org/projects/ featured/futurefleets (accessed July 20, 2019); CleanTechnica, "How Tech Is Turbocharging Corporate Sustainability," October 3, 2018, https://cleantechnica.com/2018/10/03/how-tech-is-turbocharging-corporate-sustainability/ (accessed July 20, 2019).

2. Yang Fan and Bi Zimo, "China Blocks Chat Apps, Deletes Social Media Accounts," translated into English by Luisetta Mudie, *Radio Free Asia,* July 2, 2014, http://www.rfa.org/english/news/china/ blocks-07022014152248.html (accessed August 4, 2016); Niall McCarthy, "China Now Boasts More Than 800 Million Internet Users and 98% of Them Are Mobile," *Forbes,* August 23, 2018, https:// www.forbes.com/sites/niallmccarthy/2018/08/23/china-now-boasts-more-than-800-million-internet-users-and-98-of-them-are-mobile-infographic/#722384ae7092 (accessed June 28, 2019).

3. Dieter Bohn, "Amazon Says 100 Million Alexa Devices Have Been Sold—What's Next?" *The Verge,* January 4, 2019, https://www. theverge.com/2019/1/4/18168565/amazon-alexa-devices-how-many-sold-number-100-million-dave-limp (accessed June 28, 2019).

4. Robert Valdes, "How Broadband over Powerlines Works," *How Stuff Works,* http://computer.howstuffworks.com/bpl.htm (accessed August 4, 2016); Stephen Shankland, "Fast Fiber-optic Broad-band Spreads Across Developed World," *CNET,* January 11, 2014, http://www. cnet.com/news/fast-fiber-optic-broadband-spreads-across-developed-world/#! (accessed August 4, 2016).

5. Ernest Tucker, "Researchers Developing Supercomputer to Tackle Grid Challenges," *Renewable Energy World,* July 7, 2014, http://www. renewableenergyworld.comarticles/2014/07/researchers-developing-supercomputer-to-tackle-grid-challenges.html (accessed August 4, 2016); Peerzada Abrar, "Russia Offers to Develop Supercomputer with India to Counter Chinese Supremacy," *Economic Times,* April 8, 2014, http://articles.economictimes.indiatimes. com/2014-04-08/ news/48971401_1_us-supercomputer-tianhe-2-indian-institute (accessed August 4, 2016); "Big Data," SAS, http://www.sas.com/en_us/ insights/big-data/what-is-big-data.html (accessed August 4, 2016).

6. Bernard Marr, "The Amazing Ways Instagram Uses Big Data and Artificial Intelligence," *Forbes,* March 16, 2018, https://www.forbes. com/sites/bernardmarr/2018/03/16/the-amazing-ways-instagram-uses-big-data-and-artificial-intelligence/#6cb271c5ca63 (accessed June 27, 2019); Mehboob Feelani, "Watson, Come Here. I Want You," *Fortune,* October 27, 2014, 36.

7. Gyln Taylor, "The Future Is Coming Much Faster Than We Think. Here's Why," *That's Really Possible,* July 4, 2014, http://www. thatsreallypossible.com/exponential-growth/ (accessed August 4, 2016).

8. GoToMeeting, "WebEx vs. GoToMeeting Comparison," https://www. gotomeeting.com/comparison/webex (accessed August 27, 2019).

9. Charles Graeber, "Ten Days in Kenya with No Cash, Only a Phone," *Bloomberg Businessweek,* June 5, 2014, http://www.businessweek. com/articles/2014-06-05/safaricoms-m-pesa-turns-kenya-into-a-mobile-payment-paradise (accessed July 11, 2014).

10. Josh Gottheimer and Jordan Usdan, "Low-Cost Broadband and Computers for Students and Families," Federal Communications Commission, November 10, 2011, https://www.fcc.gov/news-events/ blog/2011/12/14/low-cost-broadband-computers-millions-students-families (accessed August 4, 2016); "Cheap Internet Service Providers Offer High-Speed Broadband Internet to Americans at $9.95/month," *Cheap Internet,* http://www.cheapinternet.com (accessed August 4, 2016).

11. Dwight Silverman, "Comcast Offering $10 Internet for Low-Income Families Who Qualify," *The Chron,* August 8, 2011, http://blog.chron. com/techblog/2011/08/comcast-offering-10-internet-for-low-income-families-who-qualify/ (accessed August 4, 2016).

12. "Charting the Future of the Net," MSNBC, July 7, 2000, www.msnbc. com (accessed August 8, 2006).

13. The White House, "Technology and Economic Growth: Producing Real Results for the American People," http://clinton3.nara.gov/WH/ EOP/OSTP/html/techgrow.html (accessed August 4, 2016); Nicholas Bloom and Josh Lerner, "The NBER Productivity, Innovation, and Entrepreneurship Program," National Bureau of Economic Research, 2013, http://www.nber.org/programs/pr/pr.html (accessed August 4, 2016).

14. Alan Greenspan, "Remarks to the Economic Club of New York," Federal Reserve Board, January 13, 2000; Nicholas Bloom and Josh Lerner, "The NBER Productivity, Innovation, and Entrepreneurship Program."

15. Elana Varon, "B2B E-Commerce: What You Need to Know About Public and Private Exchanges," *CIO*, http://www.cio.com/article/30483/B_B_E_Commerce_What_You_Need_to_Know_about_Public_and_Private_Exchanges (accessed August 4, 2016); Elana Varon, "The ABCs of B2B," http://www.cchristopherlee.com/news/2001/010820b.htm (accessed August 4, 2016); Allison Enright, "B2b e-Commerce Is Poised for Growth," *Internet Retailer,* May 31, 2013, https://www. internetretailer.com/2013/05/31/b2b-e-commerce-poised-growth (accessed August 4, 2016).

16. Kelly Thomas, "Supply Chain Segmentation: Ten Steps to Greater Profits," *Supply Chain Quarterly*, Quarter 1, 2012, http://www.supplychainquarterly.com/topics/Strategy/201 201segmentation/#fnr1 (accessed August 4, 2016); University Alliance, "Walmart: Keys to Successful Supply Chain Management," University of San Francisco, http://www. usanfranonline.com/resources/supply-chain-management/walmart-keys-to-successful-supply-chain-management/#. U8HAtVaWsds (accessed August 4, 2016); Danielle Kucera, "Amazon Ramps up $13.9 Billion Warehouse Building Spree," *Bloomberg*, August 21, 2013, http://www.bloomberg. com/news/articles/2013-08-20/amazon-ramps-up-13-9-bil-lion-warehouse-building-spree (accessed August 4, 2016); "Amazon Global Fulfillment Center Network," *MWPVL*, 2014, http://www.mwpvl.com/html/amazon_com.html (accessed August 4, 2016).

17. David He and Venessa Guo, "4 Ways AI Will Impact the Financial Job Market," World Economic Forum, September 14, 2018, https://www.weforum.org/agenda/2018/09/4-ways-ai-artificial-intelligence-impact-financial-job-market/ (accessed June 26, 2019).

18. "IT Failing One in Four Small Businesses," http://smallbiztechnology.com/archive/2009/08/it-failing-one-in-four-small-b.html (accessed August 4, 2016).

19. Norris Dickard and Diana Schneider, "The Digital Divide: Where We Are," *Edutopia*, July 1, 2002, http://www.edutopia. org/digital-divide-where-we-are-today (accessed August 4, 2016).

20. Greenspan, "Remarks to the Economic Club of New York."

21. Center for Advanced Purchasing Studies, "The Future of Purchasing and Supply: A Five- and Ten-Year Forecast," http://http://onlinelibrary. wiley.com/doi/10.1111/j.1745-493X.2000.tb00066.x/abstract?userIsAuthenticated=false&deniedAccessCustomisedMessage= (accessed August 5, 2016).

22. David Field, "Some E-ticket Fliers Can Print Boarding Passes on PC," *USA Today*, December 5, 2000, 12B.

23. Glenda Chui, "Mapping Goes Deep: Technology Points the Way to a Revolution in Cartography," *San Jose Mercury News*, September 12, 2000, 1F.

24. "Internet Top 20 Countries," Internet World Stats, March 31, 2019, https://www.internetworldstats.com/top20.htm (accessed June 25, 2019).

25. Internet Assigned Numbers Authority, "TLDs Alpha by Domain," http://data.iana.org/TLD/tlds-alpha-by-domain.txt (accessed August 27, 2019).

26. William M. Pride and O. C. Ferrell, *Marketing: Concepts and Strategies*, 12th ed. (Boston: Houghton Mifflin, 2003), 493.

27. "E-Commerce Fraud Loss Reaches $57.8 Billion," *Security Magazine*, October 30, 2017, https://www.securitymagazine.com/articles/88451-e-commerce-fraud-loss-reaches-578-billion (accessed June 28, 2019).

28. Kimberly Palmer, "How Credit Card Companies Spot Fraud Before You Do," *USA News*, July 10, 2013, http://money. usnews.com/money/personal-finance/articles/2013/07/10how-credit-card-companies-spot-fraud-before-you-do (accessed August 5, 2016).

29. Steve Turner, "2019 Data Breaches—The Worst So Far," *IdentityForce*, January 3, 2019, https://www.identityforce.com/blog/2019-data-breaches (accessed June 28, 2019).

30. Federal Bureau of Investigation, "Online Auction Fraud," http://www.fbi.gov/page2/june09auctionfraud_063009.html (accessed July 14, 2014).

31. Cisco, "Internet of Things at a Glance," 2016, https:// www.cisco.com/c/dam/en/us/products/collateral/se/internet-of-things/at-a-glance-c45-731471.pdf (accessed August 27, 2019).

32. "A Non-Geek's A-to-Z Guide to the Internet of Things," SAS, https://www.sas.com/content/dam/SAS/en_us/doc/whitepaper1/non-geek-a-to-z-guide-to-the-internet-of-things-108846.pdf (accessed June 25, 2019).

33. "Home, Hacked Home," *The Economist: Special Report on Cyber-Security*, July 12, 2014, 14–15; "Prevention Is Better than Cure," *The Economist: Special Report on Cyber-Security*, July 12, 2014, 16.

34. Federal Trade Commission, "Protecting Consumer Privacy," https://www.ftc.gov/news-events/media-resources/protecting-consumer-privacy (accessed August 5, 2016).

35. Pride and Ferrell, *Marketing: Concepts and Strategies,* 600–601.

36. "Identity Theft Reports—Federal Trade Commission," *Tableau Public*, April 8, 2019, https://public.tableau.com/profile/federal.trade.commission#!/vizhome/IdentityTheftReports/StatebyState (accessed June 28, 2019).

37. Verizon, *2018 Data Breach Investigations Report,* April 2018, https://enterprise.verizon.com/resources/reports/DBIR_2018_Report.pdf, 5.

38. "How Common Is Identity Theft? (Updated 2018) The Latest Stats," Lifelock, April 13, 2018, https://www.lifelock.com/learn-identity-theft-resources-how-common-is-identity-theft.html (accessed June 28, 2019).

39. Dan Strumpf, "Trump Punches Huawei and Global Tech Firms Get a Bloody Nose," *The Wall Street Journal*, June 28, 2019, https://www.wsj.com/articles/trump-punches-huawei-and-american-tech-firms-get-a-bloody-nose-11561744203?mod=searchresults&page=1&pos=2 (accessed July 2, 2019); Kate O'Flaherty, "Huawei Security Scandal: Everything You Need to Know," *Forbes*, February 26, 2019, https://www.forbes.com/sites/kateoflahertyuk/2019/02/26/huawei-security-scandal-everything-you-need-to-know/#dfede7f73a55 (accessed July 2, 2019).

40. Rupert Jones, "Barclays to Sell Customer Data," *The Guardian*, June 24, 2013, http://www.theguardian.combusiness/2013/jun/24/barclays-bank-sell-customer-data (accessed August 5, 2016); Daniel Bates, "New Privacy Fears as Facebook Begins Selling Personal Access to Companies to Boost Ailing Profits," *Daily Mail Online*, October 3, 2012, http://www.dailymail.co.uk/news/article-2212178/New-privacy-row-Facebook-begins-selling-access-users-boost-ailing-profits.html (accessed August 5, 2016); Olga Kharif and Scott Moritz, "Carriers Sell Users' Tracking Data in $5.5 Billion Market," *Bloomberg*, June 6, 2013, http://www.bloomberg. com/news/2013-06-06/carriers-sell-users-tracking-data-in-5-5-billion-market.html (accessed August 5, 2016).

41. Federal Trade Commission, "Children's Online Privacy Protection Act of 1998," www.ftc. gov/ogc/coppa1.htm (accessed August 5, 2016).

42. Federal Trade Commission, "Snapchat Settles FTC Charges That Promises of Disappearing Messages Were False," May 8, 2014, https://www.ftc.gov/news-events/press-releases/2014/05/snapchat-settles-ftc-charges-promises-disappearing-messages-were (accessed August 5, 2016).

43. Josh Constine, "Facebook and Instagram Change to Crack Down on Underage Children," *TechCrunch*, July 19, 2018, https://techcrunch.com/2018/07/19/facebok-under-13/ (accessed June 28, 2019).

44. Cecilia Kang, "Preteens' Use of Instagram Creates Privacy Issue, Child Advocates Say," *Washington Post*, May 15, 2013, http://www.washingtonpost.com/businesstechnology/preteens-use-of-instagram-creates-privacy-issue-child-advocates-say/2013/05/15/9c09d68c-b1a2-11e2-baf7-5bc2a9dc6f44_story.html (accessed August 5, 2016).

45. Senator Al Franken, "The Location Privacy Protection Act of 2014—Summary," 2014, http://www.franken.senate.gov/files/documents/140327Locationprivacy.pdf (accessed August 5, 2016).

46. Federal Trade Commission, "Mobile Privacy Disclosures: Building Trust Through Transparency," February 2013, https://www.ftc.gov/reports/mobile-privacy-disclosures-building-trust-through-transparency-federal-trade-commission (accessed August 5, 2016).

47. Olivia B. Waxman, "The GDPR Is Just the Latest Example of Europe's Caution on Privacy Rights. That Outlook Has a Disturbing History," *Time*, May 24, 2018, https://time.com/5290043/nazi-history-eu-data-privacy-gdpr/ (accessed June 28, 2019); Rebecca Hill, "That's the Way the Cookies Crumble: Consent Banners up 16% Since GDPR," *The Register*, August 21, 2018, https://www.theregister.co.uk/2018/08/21/boffins_say_cookie_consent_banners_up_16_postgdpr/ (accessed July 2, 2019).

48. Jon Porter, "Google Fined €50 Million for GDPR Violations in France," *The Verge*, January 21, 2019, https://www.theverge.com/2019/1/21/18191591/google-gdpr-fine-50-million-euros-data-consent-cnil (accessed July 2, 2019).

49. Liam Tung, "GDPR, USA? Microsoft Says US Should Match the EU's Digital Privacy Law," *ZDNet*, May 21, 2019, https://www.zdnet.com/article/gdpr-usa-microsoft-says-us-should-match-the-eus-digital-privacy-law/ (accessed June 28, 2019).

50. Privacy Commissioner of Canada, "An Overview of Canada's New Private Sector Privacy Law: The Personal Information Protection and

Electronic Documents Act," http://www.priv.gc.ca/speech/2004/vs/vs_sp-d_040331_e.cfm (accessed July 8, 2014).

51. "Electronic Network Consortium," http://www.nmda.or.jp/enc/index-english.html (accessed August 5, 2016).

52. Andrada Coos, "Data Protection in Japan: All You Need to Know About APPI," *Endpoint Protector*, February 1, 2019, https://www.endpointprotector.com/blog/data-protection-in-japan-appi/ (accessed June 29, 2019).

53. Tom Davies, "European Commission Adopts Adequacy Decision on Japan, Creating the World's Largest Area of Safe Data Flows," *PrivSec Report*, January 24, 2019, https://gdpr.report/news/2019/01/24/european-commission-adopts-adequacy-decision-on-japan-creating-the-worlds-largest-area-of-safe-data-flows/ (accessed June 28, 2019).

54. Neil MacFarquhar, "Russia Quietly Tightens Reins on Web with 'Bloggers Law'," *The New York Times*, May 6, 2014, https://www.nytimes.com/2014/05/07/world/europe/russia-quietly-tightens-reins-on-web-with-bloggers-law.html (accessed August 1, 2019); Mike Butcher, "Russia Moves to Ban Online Services That Don't Store Personal Data in Russia," *Tech Crunch*, July 2, 2014, https://techcrunch.com/2014/07/02/russia-moves-to-ban-online-services-that-dont-store-personal-data-in-russia/ (accessed July 30, 2019).

55. David Meyer, "Russia's 'Big Brother' Data Law Now in Force: Kremlin Spies Are the Big Winners," *ZDNet*, July 2, 2018, https://www.zdnet.com/article/russias-big-brother-data-law-now-in-force-kremlin-spies-are-the-big-winners/ (accessed June 30, 2019).

56. TRUSTe.com, www.truste.com (accessed August 5, 2016); Chris Connelly, "Trustmark Schemes Struggle to Protect Privacy," *Galexia*, 2008, http://www.galexia.com/public/research/assets/trustmarks_struggle_20080926/trustmarks_struggle_public.pdf (accessed August 5, 2016).

57. Erik Larson, "American Airlines Drops Google Trademark Lawsuit (Update 1)," *Bloomberg*, July 18, 2008, http://www.bloomberg.com/apps/news?pid=newsarchive&sid=aNtnl9vC6QLc (accessed July 22, 2014); Terry Baynes, "Rosetta Stone and Google Settle Trademark Lawsuit," *Reuters*, October 31, 2012, http://www.reuters.com/article/2012/10/31/us-usa-court-rosettastone-google-idUSBRE89U1GE20121031 (accessed August 5, 2016).

58. "Trends in Proprietary Information Loss," *ASIS International*, June 2007, https://foundation.asisonline.org/FoundationResearch/Publications/Documents/trendsinproprietaryinformationloss.pdf (accessed August 5, 2016).

59. National Bureau of Asian Research. "The IP Commission Report: The Report of the Commission on the Theft of American Intellectual Property," May 2013, http://www.ipcommission.org/report/IP_Commission_Report_052213.pdf (accessed August 5, 2016).

60. Software Alliance, "Software Management: Security Imperative, Business Opportunity," June 2018, https://gss.bsa.org (accessed June 30, 2019).

61. "But Can the WTO Really Sock It to Software Pirates?" Business Software Alliance, June 2014, http://globalstudy.bsa.org/2013/downloads/studies/2013GlobalSurvey_Study_en.pdf (accessed August 5, 2016); Business Software Alliance, "Seizing Opportunity Through License Compliance," 2016, http://globalstudy.bsa. org/2013/downloads/studies/2013GlobalSurvey_Study_en.pdf (accessed August 5, 2016).

62. Microsoft, "Microsoft Settles 3,265 Software Piracy Cases in US and Abroad," Press Release, July 9, 2013, http://www.microsoft. com/en-us/news/press/2013/jul13/07-09casespr.aspx (accessed August 5, 2016); Chester Davis, "Microsoft Corporation Launches Cheaper Office Software," *Liberty Voice*, March 16, 2014, http:/guardianlv.com/2014/03/microsoft-corporation-launches-cheaper-office-software/ (accessed August 5, 2016).

63. U.S. Copyright Office, "The Digital Millennium Copyright Act of 1998," December 1998, http://www.copyright.gov/legislation/dmca.pdf (accessed August 5, 2016).

64. Ted Johnson, "Content Groups Fear Supreme Court Decision Will Make It More Difficult to Curb Piracy," *Variety*, March 4, 2019, https://variety.com/2019/politics/news/supreme-court-copyright-1203154603/ (accessed June 30, 2019).

65. William T. Neese and Charles R. McManis, "Summary Brief: Law, Ethics, and the Internet: How Recent Federal Trademark Law Prohibits a Remedy Against 'Cyber-Squatters'," *Proceedings from the Society of Marketing Advances*, November 4–7, 1998.

66. *Ibid.*

67. World Intellectual Property Organization, "WIPO Cybersquatting Cases Grow by 12% to Reach New Record in 2018," March 15, 2019, https://www.wipo.int/pressroom/en/articles/2019/article_0003.html (accessed June 30, 2019).

68. Martyn Williams, "Update: ICANN President Calls for Major Overhaul," *Computer World*, February 25, 2002, https://www.computerworld.com/article/2587971/update--icann-president-calls-for-major-overhaul.html (accessed October 7, 2019).

69. Thomas A. Guida and Gerald J. Ferguson, "Strategy ICANN Arbitration vs. Federal Court: Choosing the Right Forum for Trademark Disputes," *Internet Newsletter*, November 7, 2002.

70. ".XXX—What's It All About?" *XDnet*, July 27, 2011, http://xdnet.co.uk/blog/2011/07/27/xxx-whats-it-all-about/ (accessed July 23, 2014).

71. "ICANN Hears Concerns About Accountability, Control," http://www.pcworld.com/businesscenter/article/151736icann_hears_concerns_about_accountability_control.html (accessed August 5, 2016); Rana Foorohar, "The Internet Splits Up. The Web Changed the World. Politics Is Now Changing It Back," *Newsweek*, May 15, 2006, 1.

72. John McCormick, "Opposition to Police Use of Facial Recognition Grows," *The Wall Street Journal*, July 1, 2019, https://www.wsj.com/articles/opposition-to-police-use-of-facial-recognition-grows-11561973401 (accessed July 2, 2019).

73. Virginia Dignum, "Ethics in Artificial Intelligence: Introduction to the Special Issue," *Ethics and Information Technology*, 20-1, 2018, 1–3, doi:10.1007/s10676-018-9450-z.

74. "A Simple Way to Understand Machine Learning vs. Deep Learning," *Zendesk*, July 18, 2017, https://www.zendesk.com/blog/machine-learning-and-deep-learning/ (accessed July 2, 2019).

75. Irfan Ahmad, "How Much Data Is Generated Every Minute? (Infographic)," *Social Media Today*, June 15, 2018, https://www.socialmediatoday.com/news/how-much-data-is-generated-every-minute-infographic-1/525692/ (accessed August 2, 2019).

76. Bernard Marr, "The Amazing Ways Instagram Uses Big Data and Artificial Intelligence," *Forbes*, March 16, 2018, https://www.forbes.com/sites/bernardmarr/2018/03/16/the-amazing-ways-instagram-uses-big-data-and-artificial-intelligence/#5ef05b225ca6 (accessed August 2, 2019).

77. Ron Miller, "Walmart Is Betting on the Blockchain to Improve Food Safety," *TechCrunch*, September 24, 2018, https://techcrunch.com/2018/09/24/walmart-is-betting-on-the-blockchain-to-improve-food-safety/ (accessed August 27, 2019).

78. P. J. Jakovljevic, "Demystifying Blockchain: The Technology and Its Providers," Technology Evaluation Centers, January 2, 2018, https://www3.technologyevaluation.com/research/tec-report/demystifying-blockchain-the-technology-and-its-providers.html (accessed January 17, 2019).

79. S. Salzman. "Electronic Medical Records: Holy Grail for Blockchain," *Media Page Today,* August 22, 2018, https://www.medpagetoday.com/practicemanagement/informationtechnology/74695.

80. Tyler Wetzel, "A Concensus-Based Definition of 'Blockchain' to Be Used by the U.S. Congress," *Medium*, October 10, 2018, https://medium.com/@twwetzel76/a-blockchain-is-a-digital-mechanism-capable-of-not-only-storing-data-and-information-but-also-2458403252a5 (accessed July 2, 2019).

81. "Drone Technology Used to Better Prepare for 2019 Hurricane Season," CBS Miami, June 3, 2019, https://miami.cbslocal.com/2019/06/03/miami-dade-fire-rescue-drone-prepare-hurricane/ (accessed July 2, 2019).

82. "How Drone Technology Boosts P&C Customer Satisfaction," *Kespry*, August 27, 2017, https://www.kespry.com/how-drone-technology-boosts-pc-customer-satisfaction/ (accessed January 24, 2019).

83. Jeremiah Karpowicz, "4 Ways Drones Are Being Used in Maritime and Offshore Services," *Commercial UAV News*, August 9, 2018, https://www.expouav.com/news/latest/4-ways-drones-maritime-offshore-services/ (accessed June 26, 2019).

84. Tanya M. Anandan, "Robotics Industry Insights," Robotics Industry Association, March 21, 2019, https://www.robotics.org/content-detail.cfm/Industrial-Robotics-Industry-Insights/Automate-2019-Preview/content_id/7788 (accessed June 26, 2019).

85. Ivar Mendez, "How Robots Are Helping Doctors Save Lives in the Canadian North," *Robohub*, January 7, 2019, https://robohub.org/how-robots-are-helping-doctors-save-lives-in-the-canadian-north/ (accessed July 2, 2019).

86. Sven-Olof Husmark, "4 Ways Social Robots Improve Customer Experience in Retail Stores," *Customer Think*, October 20, 2016, http://www.customerthink.

com/4-ways-social-robots-improve-customer-experience-in-retail-stores/ (accessed June 26, 2019).

87. Tom Huddleston, Jr. "Walmart Will Soon Use Hundreds of A.I. Robot Janitors to Scrub the Floors on US Stores," CNBC, December 5, 2018, https://www.cnbc.com/2018/12/05/walmart-will-use-hundreds-of-ai-robot-janitors-to-scrub-store-floors.html (accessed July 3, 2019).

88. Amitai Etzioni and Oren Etzioni, "AI Assisted Ethics," *Ethics and Information Technology*, 18-2, 2016, 149–156, doi:10.1007/s10676-016-9400-6.

89. James Tenser, "Are Ethics Compatible with AI?" *RetailWire*, www.retailwire.com/discussion/are-ethics-compatible-with-ai/.

90. Matthew Howard, "The Future of AI Relies on a Code of Ethics," *TechCrunch*, June 21, 2018, https://techcrunch.com/2018/06/21/the-future-of-ai-relies-on-a-code-of-ethics/ (accessed January 24, 2019).

91. Arthur L. Caplan and Glenn McGee, "An Introduction to Bioethics," *Bioethics*, http://www.bioethics.net/bioethics-resources/bioethics-glossary/introduction/ (accessed August 5, 2016).

92. Lucette Lagundo, "Drug Companies Face Assault on Prices," *The Wall Street Journal*, May 11, 2000, B1.

93. Shamard Charles, "No End in Sight to Rising Drug Prices, Study Finds," NBC, May 31, 2019, https://www.nbcnews.com/health/health-care/no-end-sight-rising-drug-prices-study-finds-n1012181 (accessed June 30, 2019).

94. "Persuading the Prescribers: Pharmaceutical Industry Marketing and Its Influence on Physicians and Patients," Pew Charitable Trusts, November 11, 2013, http://www.pewtrusts.org/en/research-and-analysis/fact-sheets/2013/11/11/persuading-the-prescribers-pharmaceutical-industry-marketing-and-its-influence-on-physicians-and-patients (accessed August 5, 2016); Beth Mole, "Big Pharma Shells Out $20B Each Year to Schmooze Docs, $6B on Drug Ads," *Ars Technica*, January 11, 2019, https://arstechnica.com/science/2019/01/healthcare-industry-spends-30b-on-marketing-most-of-it-goes-to-doctors/ (accessed June 30, 2019).

95. Biotechnology Industry Association, "Biotechnology Industry Facts," http://www.bio.org/articles/what-biotechnology (accessed August 5, 2016); Heidi Chial, PhD, "DNA Sequencing Technologies Key to the Human Genome Project," *Scitable by Nature Education*, http://www.nature.com/scitable/topicpage/dna-sequencing-technologies-key-to-the-human-828 (accessed August 5, 2016).

96. "The Biotechnology Industry in the United States," *Select USA*, http://selectusa.commerce.gov/industry-snapshots/biotechnology-industry-united-states (accessed July 16, 2014); Mark Terry, "PhRMA Releases Annual Survey, Shows Highest R&D Spending Ever," *BioSpace*, August 15, 2018, https://www.biospace.com/article/phrma-releases-annual-survey-shows-highest-r-and-d-spending-ever/ (accessed June 30, 2019).

97. Andrew Dunn, "Drugmakers Say R&D Spending Hit Record in 2017," *BioPharma Dive*, August 13, 2018, https://www.biopharmadive.com/news/phrma-research-development-spending-industry-report/529943/ (accessed July 31, 2019).

98. Veronica Acosta, "Oro Valley, Pima County Partner for Biotech Incubator Facility," KGUN 9, June 26, 2019, https://www.kgun9.com/news/local-news/oro-valley-pima-county-partner-for-biotech-incubator-facility (accessed June 30, 2019).

99. Barbra Streisand, "Barbra Streisand Explains: Why I Cloned My Dog," *The New York Times*, March 2, 2018, https://www.nytimes.com/2018/03/02/style/barbra-streisand-cloned-her-dog.html (accessed June 30, 2019).

100. John Leavitt, "What Will Human Clones Be Like?" *Connecticut Law Tribune*, January 24, 2003, 5.

101. Sarah Knapton, "Breakthrough in Human Cloning Offers New Transplant Hope," *The Telegraph*, April 17, 2014, http:/www.telegraph.co.uk/science/science-news/10774097/Break-through-in-human-cloning-offers-new-transplant-hope.html (accessed July 16, 2014); Laura Ungar, "Stem-Cell Advances May Quell Ethics Debate," *USA Today*, June 22, 2014, http://www.usatoday.com/story/news/nation/2014/06/22/stem-cell-advances-may-quell-ethics-debate/11222721/ (accessed August 5, 2016).

102. Andy Coghlan, "Cloning Special Report: Cloning Without Embryos," *New Scientist*, January 29, 2000, 4.

103. Natasha McDowell, "Mini-pig Clone Raises Transplant Hope," *New Scientist*, http://www.newscientist.com/article/dn3257 (accessed August 5, 2016).

104. Rachel Nowak, "Australia OKs Human Embryo Research," *New Scientist*, http://www.newscientist.com/article/dn3149 (accessed July 16, 2014); "Stem Cell Research FAQs," *Research America*, http://www.researchamerica.org/stemcell_faqs (accessed August 5, 2016).

105. Ricki Lewis, PhD, "A Brief History of DNA Patents," *PLOS Blogs*, June 20, 2013, http://blogs.plos.org/dnascience/2013/06/20/a-brief-history-of-dna-patents/ (accessed August 5, 2016); Maggie Koerth-Baker, "Making Sense of the Confusing Supreme Court DNA Patent Ruling," *BoingBoing*, June 17, 2013, http://boingboing.net/2013/06/17/making-sense-of-the-confusing.html (accessed August 5, 2016).

106. Garry Peterson et al., "The Risks and Benefits of Genetically Modified Crops: A Multidisciplinary Perspective," *Conservation Ecology*, 4(1), 2000, 13.

107. Bill Gates, "Will Frankenfood Feed the World?" Microsoft, June 11, 2000, http://www.microsoft.com/presspass/ofnote/06-11time.mspx (accessed August 5, 2016); Natasha Gilbert and Nature Magazine, "A Hard Look at 3 Myths About Genetically Modified Crops," *Scientific American*, May 1, 2013, http://www.scientificamerican.com/article/a-hard-look-at-3-myths-about-genetically-modified-crops/ (accessed August 5, 2016).

108. John Robbins, "Can GMOs Help End World Hunger?" Food Revolution Network, December 10, 2012, http://foodrevolution.org/blog/gmos-world-hunger/ (accessed August 5, 2016); Joel Dunn, "Genetically Modified Crops and Hunger—Another Look at the Evidence," Permaculture Research Institute, May 31, 2013, http://permaculturenews.org/2013/05/31/genetically-modified-crops-and-hunger-another-look-at-the-evidence/ (accessed August 5, 2016).

109. David Baulcombe, "It's Time to Rethink Europe's Outdated GM Crop Regulations," *The Guardian*, March 14, 2014, http://www.theguardian.com/environment/2014/mar/14/europe-gm-crop-regulations (accessed August 5, 2016); "GM Crops and Foods in Britain and Europe," Gene Watch, http://www.genewatch.org/sub-568547 (accessed August 5, 2016).

110. Peterson et al., "The Risks and Benefits of Genetically Modified Crops."

111. Paul Magnusson, Ann Therese, and Kerry Capell, "Furor over Frankenfood," *BusinessWeek*, October 18, 1999, 50, 51; "Japan Asks That Imports of Corn Be StarLink-Free," *The Wall Street Journal*, October 30, 2000, A26; Naveen Thukral and Risa Maeda, "Japan Cancels GMO Wheat Order After Concerns over U.S. Grain Developed by Monsanto," *Huffington Post*, May 30, 2013, http://www.huffingtonpost.com/2013/05/30/japan-gmo-wheat-food-concerns_n_3357240.html (accessed August 5, 2016).

112. Heather Haddon, "Congress Passes GMO Labeling That Supersede Tough State Measures," *The Wall Street Journal*, July 14, 2016, http://www.wsj.com/articles/congress-passes-gmo-labeling-rules-that-supercede-tough-state-measures-1468516761 (accessed July 15, 2016).

113. Carey Polis, "Whole Foods GMO Labeling to Be Mandatory by 2018," *Huffington Post*, March 8, 2013, http://www.huffingtonpost.com/2013/03/08/whole-foods-gmo-labeling-2018_n_2837754.html (accessed August 5, 2016); "All Products for Allegro Coffee Company," Non-GMO Project, http://www.nongmoproject.org/find-non-gmo/search-participating-products/search/?brandId=1202 (accessed August 5, 2016); "On GMOs," General Mills, https://www.generalmills.com/en/ChannelG/Issues/on_biotechnology.aspx (accessed August 5, 2016); "Genetically Modified Crops," Unilever, http://www.unilever.com/sustainable-living-2014/our-approach-to-sustainability/responding-to-stakeholder-concerns/genetically-modified-crops/ (accessed July 16, 2014).

114. "'Terminator' Victory a Small Step in Long War," CNN, October 7, 1999, www.cnn.com/NATURE/9910/07/terminator.victory.enn/index.html (accessed August 5, 2016).

115. Adam Liptak, "Supreme Court Supports Monsanto in Seed-Replication Case," *The New York Times*, May 13, 2013, http://www.nytimes.com/2013/05/14/business/monsanto-victorious-in-genetic-seed-case.html (accessed August 5, 2016).

116. "Viewpoints: Is Genetically Modified Food Safe to Eat?" PBS, http://www.pbs.org/wgbh/harvest/viewpoints/issafe.html (accessed August 5, 2016).

117. Katy Canada, "GMOs Now 90 Percent of Corn, Beets, and Soy in US," *The Pendulum*, February 2014, http://www.elon-pendulum.com/2014/02/gmos-now-90-percent-corn-beets-soy-us/ (accessed July 16, 2014).

118. "Monsanto Attempts to Balance Stakeholder Interests," in O. C. Ferrell, John Fraedrich, and Linda Ferrell, eds., *Business Ethics: Ethical Decision-Making and Cases*, 9th ed., 308–318 (Mason, OH: South-Western Cengage Learning, 2013); Ian Berry, "Pesticides Make a Comeback," *The Wall Street Journal*, May 21, 2013, http://online.wsj.com/article/SB10001424127887323463704578496923254944066.html (accessed August 5, 2016); "The Perils of Always Ignoring the

Bright Side," *The Wall Street Journal*, http://online.wsj.com/article/SB1 0000872396390444004704578030340322279 54.html (accessed August 5, 2016).

119. Greg Farrell, "Police Have Few Weapons Against Cyber-Criminals," *USA Today*, December 6, 2000, 5B; Edward Iwata and Kevin Johnson, "Computer Crime Outpacing Cybercops," *USA Today*, June 7, 2000, 1A.

120. Siobhan Gorman and Julian E. Barnes, "Cyber Combat: Act of War," *The Wall Street Journal*, May 31, 2011, http://online.wsj.com/news/articles/SB10001424052702304563104576355623135782718 (accessed August 5, 2016); David E. Sanger and Elisabeth Bumiller, "Pentagon to Consider Cyberattacks Acts of War," *The New York Times*, http://www.nytimes.com/2011/06/01/us/politics/01cyber.html (accessed August 5, 2016).

121. Eric Tucker and Colleen Long, "US Officials Say Foreign Election Hacking Is Inevitable," AP, May 22, 2019, https://www.apnews.com/5 39a88d8a53c499181a9970d6f753a99 (accessed August 27, 2019).

122. Sheila M. J. Bonini, Lenny T. Mendonca, and Jeremy M. Oppenheim, "When Social Issues Become Strategic," *The McKinsey Quarterly*, 2 (2006): 20.

Chapter 12

1. "Cascade Engineering—Corporate Social Responsibility Example," 602 Communications, n.d., http://602communications.com/cascade-engineering-corporate-social-responsibility-example/ (accessed July 27, 2019); Adam Bluestein, "Regulate Me. Please." *Inc.*, May 2011, 72–80; Cascade Engineering, www.cascadeng.com (accessed July 27, 2019); B Corporation, "B Impact Report: Cascade Engineering," https://bcorporation.net/directory/cascade-engineering (accessed July 27, 2019); B Corporation, "About B Corps," https://bcorporation.net/about-b-corps (accessed July 27, 2019); "Cradle-to-Cradle," *Sustainability Dictionary*, https://sustainabilitydictionary.com/2005/12/03/cradle-to-cradle/ (accessed July 27, 2019); Lynn Golodner, "Welfare to Career: Plastics Company Helps People Break Barriers to Success," *Corp Magazine*, December 23, 2015, https://www.corpmagazine.com/industry/human-resources/welfare-career-plastics-company-helps-people-break-barriers-success/ (accessed July 27, 2019); Tim Fernholz, "Best Practices: Cascade Engineering Makes Welfare-to-Career a Reality," *Good*, September 28, 2011, https://www.good.is/articles/best-practices-cascade-engineering-makes-welfare-to-career-a-reality (accessed July 27, 2019); Cascade Engineering, "Welfare to Career," http://www.cascadeng.com/welfare-career (accessed July 27, 2019).

2. CGS, "CGS Survey Reveals 'Sustainability' Is Driving Demand and Customer Loyalty," 2019, https://www.cgsinc.com/en/infographics/CGS-Survey-Reveals-Sustainability-Is-Driving-Demand-and-Customer-Loyalty (accessed July 17, 2019).

3. Environmental Protection Agency, "Green Power Partnership Fortune 500 Partners List," April 22, 2019, https://www.epa.gov/greenpower/green-power-partnership-fortune-500r-partners-list (accessed July 17, 2019).

4. O. C. Ferrell, John Fraedrich, and Linda Ferrell, *Business Ethics: Ethical Decision-Making and Cases*, 10th ed. (Mason, OH: South-Western Cengage Learning, 2015), 347.

5. Kevin Gibson, "Stakeholders and Sustainability: An Evolving Theory," *Journal of Business Ethics* 109, no. 1 (2012): 15–25.

6. Ferrell et al., *Business Ethics*.

7. *Ibid.*

8. Ford, "Our Future Is in Motion: Ford Motor Company Reflects on 20 Years in Sustainability with New Goals Ahead," June 6, 2019, https://media.ford.com/content/fordmedia/fna/us/en/news/2019/06/06/ford-motor-company-20-years-sustainability.html (accessed July 17, 2019).

9. Patrick E. Murphy, Magdalena Öberseder, and Gene R. Laczniak, "Corporate Societal Responsibility in Marketing: Normatively Broadening the Concept," *AMS Review* 3, no. 2 (2013).

10. Jennifer Maloney, "Coke and Pepsi Want to Sell You Bottled Water Without the Bottle," *Wall Street Journal*, June 21, 2019, https://www.wsj.com/articles/coke-and-pepsi-want-to-sell-you-bottled-water-without-the-bottle-11561114805 (accessed July 17, 2019).

11. Cathy Siegner, "AB InBev's New Accelerator Zeroes in on Sustainability-Focused Startups," *Food Dive*, August 6, 2018, https://www.fooddive.com/news/ab-inbevs-new-accelerator-zeroes-in-on-sustainability-focused-startups/529376/ (accessed July 17, 2019).

12. Office of Air Quality Planning and Standards, Environmental Protection Agency, "Air Quality," https://www3.epa.gov/airquality/cleanair.html (accessed August 5, 2016).

13. World Health Organization, "Air Pollution," https://www.who.int/airpollution/en/ (accessed July 17, 2019).

14. Olivia Goldhill, "Air Pollution in India Caused 1.2 Million Deaths Last Year," *Quartz*, December 8, 2018, https://qz.com/1489086/air-pollution-in-india-caused-1-2-million-deaths-last-year/ (accessed July 17, 2019).

15. "Asthma Disease Market Expected to Reach USD 29.6 Billion by 2026—Analysis by Asthma Type, Trigger, Drug Class, and Therapy," *Rise Media*, July 16, 2019, https://risemedia.net/2019/07/16/asthma-disease-market-expected-to-reach-usd-29-6-billion-by-2026-analysis-by-asthma-type-trigger-drug-class-and-therapy/ (accessed July 17, 2019).

16. Environmental Protection Agency, "Overview of the Clean Air Act and Air Pollution," https://www.epa.gov/clean-air-actoverview (accessed August 5, 2016).

17. Sophia Yan, "China Declares 'War' on Pollution," CNN Money, March 6, 2014, http://money.cnn.com/2014/03/06/news/economy/china-pollution/ (accessed August 5, 2016). Katrina Yu, "The Good News (and Not So Good News) About China's Smoggy Air," NPR, December 18, 2018, https://www.npr.org/sections/goatsandsoda/2018/12/18/669757478/the-good-news-and-not-so-good-news-about-chinas-smoggy-air (accessed July 17, 2019).

18. Environmental Protection Agency, "Effects of Acid Rain," https://www.epa.gov/acidrain/effects-acid-rain (accessed August 5, 2016).

19. Dan Bobkoff, "Acid Rain Aftermath: Damaged Ecology, Damaged Politics," *Marketplace*, July 16, 2014, http://www.marketplace.org/2014/07/16/sustainability/we-used-be-china/acid-rain-aftermath-damaged-ecology-damaged-politics (accessed August 5, 2016).

20. U.S. Environmental Protection Agency, "Air Quality—National Summary," https://www.epa.gov/air-trends/air-quality-national-summary (accessed July 17, 2019).

21. Adam Mann, "Hole Found in Natural Protective Layer of Earth's Atmosphere," *Wired*, April 7, 2014, http://www.wired.com/2014/04/oh-hole-washing-machine/ (accessed August 5, 2016); Union of Concerned Scientists, "Is There a Connection Between the Ozone Hole and Global Warming?" http://www.ucsusa.org/global_warming/science_and_impacts/science/ozone-hole-and-gw-faq.html (accessed August 5, 2016).

22. U.S. Energy Information Administration, *International Energy Outlook 2016*, May 11, 2016, http://www.eia.gov/forecasts/ieo/exec_summ.cfm (accessed August 5, 2016).

23. "The Largest Producers of CO2 Emissions Worldwide in 2015, Based on Their Share of Global CO2 Emissions," *Statista*, 2015, http://www.statista.com/statistics/271748/the-largestemitters-of-co2-in-the-world/ (accessed August 5, 2016).

24. Johnny Wood, "The Countries Are Driving Global Demand for Coal," World Economic Forum, February 6, 2019, https://www.weforum.org/agenda/2019/02/these-countries-are-driving-global-demand-for-coal/ (accessed July 17, 2019).

25. Peter Baker and Coral Davenport, "Obama Orders New Efficiency for Big Trucks," *The New York Times*, February 18, 2014, http://www.nytimes.com/2014/02/19/us/politics/obama-to-request-new-rules-for-cutting-truck-pollution.html (accessed August 5, 2016); Coral Davenport, "Obama to Take Action to Slash Coal Pollution," *The New York Times*, June 1, 2014, http://www.nytimes.com/2014/06/02/us/politics/epato-seek-30-percent-cut-in-carbon-emissions.html (accessed August 5, 2016).

26. Sean O'Kane, "Automakers Still Want to Lower Emissions Standards in the U.S.," *The Verge*, June 7, 2019, https://www.theverge.com/2019/6/7/18656986/automakers-lower-emissions-standards-us-environment-pollution-trump (accessed July 17, 2019).

27. Alejandra Borunda, "The Last Five Years Were the Hottest Ever Recorded," *National Geographic*, February 6, 2019, https://www.nationalgeographic.com/environment/2019/02/2018-fourth-warmest-year-ever-noaa-nasa-reports/ (accessed July 17, 2019).

28. Doyle Rice, "'Breaking' the Heat Index: U.S. Heat Waves to Skyrocket as Globe Warms, Study Suggests," *USA Today*, July 16, 2019, https://www.usatoday.com/story/news/nation/2019/07/16/heat-waves-worsen-because-global-warming-study-says/1734127001/ (accessed July 18, 2019).

29. Environmental Protection Agency, "Climate Change Indicators in the United States," 2015, https://www.epa.gov/climate-indicators/us-and-global-temperature (accessed August 5, 2016).

30. "Climate Change Moves Border," *Planet Ski*, June 28, 2009, http://www.planetski.eu/news/535 (accessed August 5, 2016).

31. Doyle Rice, "Ancient Antarctic Ice Sheet Collapse Could Happen Again, Triggering a New Global Flood," *USA Today*, December 20, 2018, https://www.usatoday.com/story/news/2018/12/20/antarctic-ice-sheet-collapse-could-lead-global-flood/2375523002/ (accessed July 17, 2019).

32. Bradley Hope and Nicole Friedman, "Climate Change Is Forcing the Insurance Industry to Recalculate," *Wall Street Journal*, October 2, 2018, https://www.wsj.com/graphics/climate-change-forcing-insurance-industry-recalculate/ (accessed July 18, 2019).

33. Andrew Freedman, "How Global Warming Made Hurricane Sandy Worse," *Climate Central*, November 1, 2012, http://www.climatecentral.org/news/how-global-warming-madehurricane-sandy-worse-15190 (accessed August 5, 2016); "Extreme Weather: Impacts of Climate Change," *Natural Resources Defense Council*, January 15, 2014, http://www.nrdc.org/globalwarming/climate-change-impacts/ (accessed August 5, 2016).

34. Andrew Childers, "EPA Underestimates Fracking's Impact on Climate Change," *Bloomberg*, May 9, 2014, http://www.bloomberg.com/news/2014-05-09/epa-underestimatesfracking-s-impact-on-climate-change.html (accessed July 18, 2014); Emily Gosden, "Fracking Can Be Part of the Solution to Global Warming, Say UN Climate Change Experts," *The Telegraph*, April 13, 2014, http://www.telegraph.co.uk/news/earth/environment/climatechange/10763844/Fracking-canbe-part-of-the-solution-to-global-warming-say-UN-climatechange-experts.html (accessed August 5, 2016); Bobby Magill, "Fracking Hurts US Climate Change Credibility, Say Scientists," *The Guardian*, October 11, 2013, http://www.theguardian.com/environment/2013/oct/11/fracking-usclimate-credibility-shale-gas (accessed July 18, 2014); Fred Pierce, "Fracking Could Accelerate Global Warming," *New Scientist*, August 12, 2013, http://www.newscientist.com/article/dn24029-fracking-could-accelerate-global-warming.html#.U80ba5RdVc (accessed August 5, 2016).

35. Tracy Loew, "Oregon Senate Passes 5-Year Fracking Moratorium for Oil, Natural Gas," *Statesman Journal*, May 29, 2019, https://www.statesmanjournal.com/story/news/2019/05/29/oregon-senate-passes-5-year-fracking-moratorium/1271400001/ (accessed July 17, 2019).

36. Mark Alpert, "Protections for the Earth's Climate," *Scientific American* 293 (December 2005): 55.

37. "Status of Ratification of the Kyoto Protocol," United Nations Framework Convention on Climate Change, http://unfccc.int/kyoto_protocol/status_of_ratification/items/2613.php (accessed August 5, 2016); "Kyoto Protocol," United Nations Framework Convention on Climate Change, http://unfccc.int/kyoto_protocol/items/2830.php (accessed August 5, 2016).

38. United Nations Treaty Collection, "Doha Amendment to the Kyoto Protocol," https://treaties.un.org/Pages/ViewDetails.aspx?src=TREATY&mtdsg_no=XXVII-7-c&chapter=27&clang=_en (accessed July 17, 2019).

39. "California, Canada Sidestep Trump, Ink Deal on Emissions," KTLA, June 26, 2019, https://ktla.com/2019/06/26/california-canada-sidestep-trump-ink-deal-on-emissions/ (accessed July 17, 2019).

40. Jim Tankersley, "EPA Gives California Emissions Waiver," *Los Angeles Times*, June 30, 2009, http://articles.latimes.com/2009/jun/30/nation/na-california-waiver30 (accessed August 5, 2016).

41. Energy Star, "Energy Star by the Numbers," https://www.energystar.gov/about/origins_mission/energy_star_numbers (accessed July 17, 2019).

42. Ferrell et al., *Business Ethics*, 352.

43. Richard Harris, "Climate Change Bill Heads for House Vote," NPR, May 22, 2009, http://www.npr.org/templates/story/story.php?storyId=104436991 (accessed August 5, 2016).

44. World Resources Institute, "Regional Cap and Trade Programs," https://www.wri.org/resources/maps/regional-cap-and-trade-programs (accessed July 18, 2019).

45. U.S. Environmental Protection Agency, "Acid Rain Program," http://www.epa.gov/airmarkets/progsregs/arp/basic.html (accessed August 11, 2014).

46. Gloria Gonzalez and Ben McCarthy, "US EPA Gives Major Boost to Cap-and-Trade, But Not Offsets," *Ecosystem Marketplace*, June 2, 2014, http://www.ecosystemmarketplace.com/pages/dynamic/article.page.php?page_id=10379&section=news_articles&eod=1 (accessed August 5, 2016).

47. U.S. Environmental Protection Agency, "EPA Finalizes Affordable Clean Energy Rule, Ensuring Reliable, Diversified Energy Resources While Protecting Our Environment," June 19, 2019, https://www.epa.gov/newsreleases/epa-finalizes-affordable-clean-energy-rule-ensuring-reliable-diversified-energy (accessed July 18, 2019); Umair Irfan, "Trump's EPA Just Replaced Obama's Signature Climate Policy with a Much Weaker Rule," *Vox*, June 19, 2019, https://www.vox.com/2019/6/19/18684054/climate-change-clean-power-plan-repeal-affordable-emissions (accessed July 18, 2019).

48. Cathy Siegner, "Impossible Burger Boasts Much Smaller Carbon Footprint Than Beef," *Food Dive*, March 22, 2019, https://www.fooddive.com/news/impossible-burger-boasts-much-smaller-carbon-footprint-than-beef/551073/ (accessed July 18, 2019).

49. Adele Peters, "These Startups Are Trying to Reduce the Massive Carbon Footprint of Concrete," *Fast Company*, January 14, 2019, https://www.fastcompany.com/90290780/these-startups-are-trying-to-reduce-the-massive-carbon-footprint-of-concrete (accessed July 18, 2019).

50. "Buildings and Emissions: Making the Connection," Center for Climate and Energy Solutions, http://www.c2es.org/technology/overview/buildings (accessed August 5, 2016).

51. "GHGRP 2012: Reported Data," Environmental Protection Agency, 2012, https://www.epa.gov/ghgreporting/ghgrp2012-reported-data (accessed August 5, 2016).

52. "UN-Water Thematic Factsheets," UN Water, 2013, http://www.unwater.org/statistics/thematic-factsheets/en/ (accessed June 5, 2016); UN Water, "Water Scarcity," https://www.unwater.org/water-facts/scarcity/ (accessed July 18, 2019).

53. Kevin Begos, "4 States Confirm Water Pollution from Drilling," *USA Today*, January 5, 2014, http://www.usatoday.com/story/money/business/2014/01/05/some-states-confirm-waterpollution-from-drilling/4328859/ (accessed August 5, 2016).

54. "The Water Crisis," Water.org, https://water.org/our-impact/water-crisis/ (accessed July 18, 2019).

55. Annmargaret Warner, "The 11 Most Polluted Beaches in the US," *Business Insider*, June 28, 2013, http://www.businessinsider.com/most-polluted-beaches-in-us-2013-6?op=1 (accessed August 8, 2016); Natasha Geiling, "America's Cleanest and Most-Polluted Beaches," *Smithsonian*, June 27, 2014, http://www.smithsonianmag.com/travel/cleanest-and-dirtiest-beachesAmerica-180951869/?no-ist (accessed August 8, 2016).

56. "Water Quality Facts," Environmental Protection Agency, http://water.epa.gov/aboutow/owow/waterqualityfacts.cfm (accessed July 22, 2014); National Ocean Service, "What Is a Dead Zone?" https://oceanservice.noaa.gov/facts/deadzone.html (accessed July 18, 2019).

57. Michelle Chen, "Trump Moves to Gut the Clean Water Act," *The Nation*, December 13, 2018, https://www.thenation.com/article/trump-clean-water-act/ (accessed July 18, 2019).

58. Maggie Fox, "Lead in Water: Study Shows Many Schools Have Far Too Much," *NBC News*, January 9, 2019, https://www.nbcnews.com/health/health-news/lead-water-study-shows-many-schools-have-far-too-much-n956851 (accessed July 18, 2019); Amanda Sawit, "New Report Shows Only 15 States and D.C. Have Laws for Testing Lead in School Water," U.S. Green Building Council, November 12, 2018, https://www.usgbc.org/articles/new-report-shows-only-15-states-and-dc-have-laws-testing-lead-school-water (accessed July 18, 2019).

59. Dawn Fallik, "This New Study Found More Drugs in Our Drinking Water Than Anybody Knew," *New Republic*, December 11, 2013, http://www.newrepublic.com/article/115883/drugs-drinking-water-new-epa-study-finds-more-we-knew (accessed August 8, 2016); U.S. Environmental Protection Agency, "Concentrations of Prioritized Pharmaceuticals in Effluents from 50 Large Wastewater Treatment Plants in the US and Implications for Risk Estimation," https://www.epa.gov/water-research/concentrations-prioritized-pharmaceuticals-effluents-50-large-wastewater-treatment (accessed July 18, 2019).

60. Thomas Hartwell, "Plant Manager Sentenced for Violating Clean Water Act," *Plant Services*, July 17, 2019, https://www.plantservices.com/industrynews/2019/plant-manager-sentenced-for-violating-clean-water-act/ (accessed July 18, 2019).

61. Levi Strauss & Co., "How Levi's Is Saving Water," March 25, 2019, https://www.levistrauss.com/2019/03/25/world-water-day-2019-saving-h2o/ (accessed July 18, 2019); Levi Strauss & Co., "Use and Reuse,"

https://www.levistrauss.com/how-we-do-business/use-and-reuse/ (accessed July 18, 2019).

62. Caroline Tell, "AYR Launches Sustainable Aloe Jean," *Forbes*, November 2, 2017, https://www.forbes.com/sites/caroline-tell/2017/11/02/ayr-launches-sustainable-aloe-jean/#1d4bafb11c82 (accessed July 19, 2019).

63. Jan Wesner Childs, "Climate Change Will Make Droughts Hotter and Longer, NOAA Study Says," Weather Channel, July 18, 2019, https://weather.com/science/environment/news/2019-07-18-climate-change-making-droughts-longer-hotter (accessed July 18, 2019).

64. Susan Berfield, "There Will Be Water," *BusinessWeek*, June 23, 2008, 40; "U.S. Drought Monitor Update for July 15, 2014," National Climatic Data Center, July 15, 2014, http://www.ncdc.noaa.gov/news/us-drought-monitor-update-july-15-2014 (accessed July 22, 2014); U.S. Environmental Protection Agency, "Residential Toilets," https://www.epa.gov/watersense/residential-toilets (accessed July 18, 2019); NOAA National Centers for Environmental Information, *State of the Climate: Drought for June 2016, July 2016*, http://www.ncdc.noaa.gov/sotc/drought/201606 (accessed August 8, 2016).

65. Robert Lee Hotz, "U.S. Government Report Warns of Economic Losses From Climate Change," *Wall Street Journal*, November 23, 2018, https://www.wsj.com/articles/u-s-government-report-warns-of-economic-losses-from-climate-change-1543009853 (accessed July 18, 2019).

66. Ferrell et al., *Business Ethics*, 354.

67. Josh Chin and Brian Spegele, "China Details Vast Extent of Soil Pollution," *Wall Street Journal*, April 17, 2014, http://online.wsj.com/news/articles/SB10001424052702304626304579507040557046288 (accessed July 22, 2014); Danson Cheong, "Study: 20% of China's Polluted Land Cleaned Up," *The Straits Times*, April 19, 2019, https://www.straitstimes.com/asia/east-asia/study-20-of-chinas-polluted-land-cleaned-up (accessed July 19, 2019).

68. Lauren Eiko Fujino, "China's Soil Pollution Law Triggers New Compliances for Businesses," *China Briefing*, November 19, 2018, https://www.china-briefing.com/news/china-soil-pollution-law-environmental-compliance-businesses/ (accessed July 19, 2019).

69. "US Court Rules for Chevron in Ecuador Rainforest Damage Case," *Los Angeles Times*, August 8, 2016, https://www.latimes.com/business/la-fi-chevron-ecuador-20160808-snap-story.html (accessed July 19, 2019).

70. "The Costs of Fracking," Environment America Research and Policy Center, September 20, 2012, http://www.environmentamerica.org/reports/ame/costs-fracking (accessed August 8, 2016); Hans Asfeldt, "'This Land Is Everything to Us': A Story of Fracking in Alberta," *Resilience*, September 26, 2013, http://www.resilience.org/stories/2013-09-26/this-land-is-everything-to-us-a-story-of-fracking-in-alberta (accessed August 8, 2016); Academy of Medicine, Engineering, and Science of Texas, "Land Impacts," https://tamest.org/shale-task-force/land/ (accessed July 19, 2019).

71. U.S. Environmental Protection Agency, "Facts and Figures About Materials, Waste, and Recycling," https://www.epa.gov/facts-and-figures-about-materials-waste-and-recycling/national-overview-facts-and-figures-materials (accessed July 19, 2019); "Landfills: Hazardous to the Environment," http://www.zerowasteamerica.org/landfills.htm (accessed August 8, 2016).

72. Confederation of European Waste-to-Energy Plants, "Waste-to-Energy: Energizing Your Waste," 2018, www.cewep.eu/wp-content/uploads/2018/07/Interactive-presentation-2018-New-slides.pdf (accessed July 19, 2019).

73. "In the Bin," *The Economist*, April 22, 2015, http://www.economist.com/blogs/democracyinamerica/2015/04/recyclingamerica (accessed August 8, 2016); Center for Biological Diversity, "10 Facts About Single-Use Plastic Bags," https://www.biologicaldiversity.org/programs/population_and_sustainability/sustainability/plastic_bag_facts.html (July 19, 2019).

74. Whole Foods, "Whole Foods Market to Further Reduce Plastics Across all Stores," May 20, 2019, https://media.wholefoodsmarket.com/news/whole-foods-market-to-further-reduce-plastics-across-all-stores (accessed June 19, 2019); U.S. Environmental Protection Agency, "Facts and Figures About Materials, Waste and Recycling."

75. Rick Leblanc, "E-Waste Recycling Facts and Figures," *The Balance*, December 31, 2018, https://www.thebalancesmb.com/e-waste-recycling-facts-and-figures-2878189 (accessed July 19, 2019).

76. Nithin Coca, "Dell Continues to Close the Loop on E-Waste," *The Bridge to Better Brands*, January 21, 2019, https://sustainablebrands.com/read/waste-not/dell-continues-to-close-the-loop-on-e-waste (accessed July 19, 2019).

77. Wendy Koch, "More States Ban Disposal of Electronics in Landfills," *USA Today*, December 18, 2011, http://usatoday30.usatoday.com/tech/news/story/2011-12-18/electronicsrecycling/52055158/1 (accessed August 8, 2016).

78. Saabira Chaudhuri, "P&G Faces Backlash over Diaper, Sanitary Waste," *Wall Street Journal*, April 3, 2019, https://www.wsj.com/articles/p-g-faces-backlash-over-diaper-sanitary-waste-11554283800 (accessed July 19, 2019).

79. "Rainforests," The Nature Conservancy, http://www.nature.org/ourinitiatives/urgentissues/rainforests/rainforests-facts.xml (accessed August 8, 2016); Justin Worland, "Here's How Many Trees Humans Cut Down Each Year," September 2, 2015, http://time.com/4019277/trees-humans-deforestation/ (accessed August 8, 2016).

80. Colin Drury, "Global Tree Cover Has Increased 7% Since 1982, Finds Biggest Ever Study," *Independent*, August 10, 2018, https://www.independent.co.uk/environment/tree-cover-increase-world-deforestation-farming-rainforests-forests-a8486096.html (accessed July 19, 2019).

81. "Amazon Rainforest Deforestation 'Worst in 10 Years', Says Brazil," BBC News, November 24, 2018, https://www.bbc.com/news/world-latin-america-46327634 (accessed July 19, 2019).

82. Bryan Walsh, "Study: Economic Boost of Deforestation Is Short-Lived," *TIME*, June 12, 2009, http://www.time.com/time/health/article/0,8599,1904174,00.html?iid=tsmodule (accessed August 8, 2016).

83. Martha Cuba, "Deforestation Now Driven by Profit, Not Poverty," *Forest News*, August 2, 2012, http://blog.cifor.org/10382/deforestation-now-driven-by-profit-not-poverty#.U8-x6laWsds (accessed August 8, 2016).

84. World Wildlife Federation, "How Many Species Are We Losing?" wwf.panda.org/our_work/biodiversity/biodiversity/ (accessed July 19, 2019).

85. Samantha Jakuboski, "Global Crisis: Honeybee Population on the Decline," *Green Science*, June 24, 2013, http://www.nature.com/scitable/blog/green-science/global_crisis_honeybee_population_on (accessed August 8, 2016).

86. Center for Biological Diversity, "White-Nose Syndrome: Questions and Answers," https://www.biologicaldiversity.org/campaigns/bat_crisis_white-nose_syndrome/Q_and_A.html (accessed July 19, 2019).

87. Matthew Fisher, "Ground Zero of Amphibian 'Apocalypse' Finally Found," *National Geographic,* May 10, 2018, https://news.nationalgeographic.com/2018/05/amphibians-decline-frogs-chytrid-fungi-bd-animals-science/ (accessed July 19, 2019).

88. Ian Berry, "Pesticides Make a Comeback," *Wall Street Journal*, May 21, 2013, http://online.wsj.com/article/SB10001424127887323463704578496923254944066.html (accessed August 8 2016).

89. "Genuity Drought Gard Hybrids," Monsanto, http://www.monsanto.com/products/pages/droughtgard-hybrids.aspx (accessed August 8 2016).

90. U.S. Food and Drug Administration, "FDA Approves Orphan Drug ATryn to Treat Rare Clotting Disorder," February 6, 2009, http://www.fda.gov/NewsEvents/Newsroom/PressAnnouncements/2009/ucm109074.htm (accessed August 8, 2016).

91. "About Genetically Engineered Foods," Center for Food Safety, http://www.centerforfoodsafety.org/issues/311/gefoods/about-ge-foods (accessed August 8, 2016).

92. "Wal-Mart Says No to Milk from 'Juiced' Cows," *Triple Pundit*, March 28, 2008, http://www.triplepundit.com/2008/03/walmart-says-no-to-milk-from-juiced-cows/ (accessed August 8, 2016).

93. Maggie Caldwell, "5 Surprising Genetically Modified Foods," *Mother Jones*, August 5, 2013, http://www.motherjones.com/environment/2013/08/what-are-gmos-and-why-should-i-care (accessed August 8, 2016).

94. The NonGMO Project, "GMO Facts," https://www.nongmoproject.org/gmo-facts/ (accessed July 19, 2019).

95. Sybille de La Hamaide, "French, German Farmers Destroy Crops After GMOs Found in Bayer Seeds," *Reuters*, February 6, 2019, https://www.reuters.com/article/us-france-gmo-bayer/french-german-farmers-destroy-crops-after-gmos-found-in-bayer-seeds-idUSKCN1PV1RG (accessed July 19, 2019).

96. Charlie Dunmore and Olivia Kumwenda, "As Health Fears Ebb, Africa Looks at Easing GM Crop Bans," Reuters, June 6, 2013, http://www.reuters.com/article/2013/06/06/

eu-africagmo-idUSL5N0EG3K520130606 (accessed August 8, 2016); Reuters, "South Africa to Ease Some GM Crop Rules to Avert Food Crisis," *The Guardian*, February 23, 2016, https://www.theguardian.com/environment/2016/feb/23/south-africa-to-ease-some-gm-crop-rules-to-avert-food-crisis (accessed August 8, 2016); Nkechi Isaac and Joan Conrow, "Nigeria Approves Its First GMO Food Crop," *Alliance for Science*, January 28, 2019, https://allianceforscience.cornell.edu/blog/2019/01/nigeria-approves-first-gmo-food-crop/ (accessed July 19, 2019).

97. James Owen, "Bulging Mutant Trout Created: More Muscle, More Meat," *National Geographic*, March 29, 2010, http://news.nationalgeographic.com/news/2010/03/100329-sixpack-mutant-trout-genetically-engineered-modified-gm/ (accessed August 8, 2016).

98. U.S. Food and Drug Administration, "AquAdvantage Salmon Fact Sheet," https://www.fda.gov/animal-veterinary/animals-intentional-genomic-alterations/aquadvantage-salmon-fact-sheet (accessed July 19, 2019); AquaBounty, "Ask Your Supermarket to Stock GMO Salmon," March 20, 2019, https://aquabounty.com/ask-your-supermarket-to-stock-gmo-salmon/ (accessed July 19, 2019).

99. "Supreme Court Hands Monsanto Victory over Farmers on GMO Seed Patents, Ability to Sue," *RT Question More*, http://rt.com/usa/monsanto-patents-sue-farmers-547/ (accessed August 8, 2016); John Entine, "'No Such Thing as GMO Contamination' Rules Australian Court in Landmark Decision, Rebuffing Organic Activists," *Forbes*, May 28, 2014, http://www.forbes.com/sites/jonentine/2014/05/28/nosuch-thing-as-gmo-contamination-rules-australian-court-inlandmark-decision-rebuffing-organic-activists/#5de7d56522cb (accessed August 8, 2016); Wood Prairie Farm, "Organic Farmers vs. Monsanto: Final Appeal to U.S. Supreme Court to Protect Crops from GMO Contamination," *Eco Watch*, December 24, 2013, http://ecowatch.com/2013/12/24/farmers-monsanto-gmo-contamination/ (accessed August 8, 2016); "Oregon May Allow Lawsuits over Genetically Engineered Crops," AP, May 8, 2019, https://www.apnews.com/c55395def8524f918f9ccf71fe0a9545 (accessed July 19, 2019).

100. U.S. Environmental Protection Agency, "Our Mission and What We Do," https://www.epa.gov/aboutepa/our-mission-andwhat-we-do (accessed August 8, 2016).

101. U.S. Environmental Protection Agency, "Strategic Plan 2019–2023," https://www.epa.gov/sites/production/files/2019-03/documents/_epaoig_epaoig_strategicplan2019-2023_3-12-2019.pdf (accessed July 19, 2019).

102. U.S. Environmental Protection Agency, "EPA Publishes Notice Identifying Hardrock Mining Industry for Financial Responsibility Requirements," July 13, 2008, http://yosemite.epa.gov/opa/admpress.nsf/d0cf6618525a9efb85257359003fb69d/90a65f473216e941852575f2004807eb!OpenDocument (accessed August 8, 2016).

103. James R. Healey, "The Big Squeeze Has Begun," *USA Today*, August 29, 2012, 1B–2B.

104. Chris Woodyard and James Healey, "Ford Looking to Aluminum for Pickups?" *USA Today*, July 26, 2012, http://www.usatoday.com/money/autos/story/2012-07-26/aluminum-fordf-150/56515524/1 (accessed August 8, 2016).

105. U.S. Environmental Protection Agency, "The Plain English Guide to the Clean Air Act," https://www.epa.gov/clean-air-act-overview/plain-english-guide-clean-airact (accessed August 8, 2016).

106. *The Economist* Staff, "Breathing Room," *The Economist*, September 8, 2012, http://www.economist.com/node/21562248 (accessed August 8, 2016).

107. Ferrell et al., *Business Ethics*, 361.

108. Congressional Research Service, "Clean Air Act Issues in the 116th Congress," April 18, 2019, https://fas.org/sgp/crs/misc/R45451.pdf (accessed July 19, 2019).

109. U.S. Environmental Protection Agency, "Summary of the Endangered Species Act," http://www2.epa.gov/laws-regulations/summary-endangered-species-act (accessed August 8, 2016).

110. U.S. Fish and Wildlife Service, "Environmental Conservation Online System: Listed Species Summary (Boxscore)," http://ecos.fws.gov/ecp0/reports/box-score-report (accessed July 22, 2019).

111. Jeremy Roebuck, "Feds Charge N.J. Man with Illegal Purchase of $6,800 Tiger-Skin Rug," *Philadelphia Inquirer*, June 28, 2019, https://www.inquirer.com/news/tiger-skin-rug-endangered-species-loren-varga-20190628.html (accessed July 22, 2019).

112. Dustin Stephens, "On the Brink: The Endangered Species Act," CBS News, July 21, 2019, https://www.cbsnews.com/news/on-the-brink-the-endangered-species-act/ (accessed July 22, 2019).

113. Tiffany Gabbay, "Man Faces Two Years in Prison for Shooting Grizzly While Defending Family," *The Blaze*, August 26, 2011, http://www.theblaze.com/stories/2011/08/25/man-faces-2-years-in-prison-for-shootinggrizzly-while-defending-family/ (accessed August 8, 2016).

114. U.S. Environmental Protection Agency, "Summary of the Toxic Substances Control Act," http://www2.epa.gov/lawsregulations/summary-toxic-substances-control-act (accessed August 8, 2016).

115. Jonathan Stempel, "U.S. States Sue EPA for Stricter Asbestos Rules," Reuters, July 1, 2019, https://www.reuters.com/article/us-usa-asbestos-lawsuit/us-states-sue-epa-for-stricter-asbestos-rules-idUSKCN1TW3N6 (accessed July 22, 2019).

116. U.S. Environmental Protection Agency, "Summary of the Clean Water Act," http://www2.epa.gov/laws-regulations/summary-clean-water-act (accessed August 8, 2016).

117. Kiah Collier, "Federal Judge Rules Against Formos Plastics in Pollution Case, Calling Company a 'Serial Offender'," *Texas Tribune*, June 28, 2019, https://www.texastribune.org/2019/06/28/federal-judge-rules-lawsuit-formosa-plastics-texas-pollution-case/ (accessed July 22, 2019).

118. U.S. Environmental Protection Agency, "Summary of the Food Quality Protection Act (FQPA)," https://www.epa.gov/lawsregulations/summary-food-quality-protection-act (accessed August 8, 2016).

119. Nicolas Loris and David W. Kreutzer, "Economic Realities of the Electric Car," Heritage Foundation, January 24, 2011, http://www.heritage.org/research/reports/2011/01/economic-realities-of-the-electric-car (accessed August 8, 2016).

120. Associated Press, "Bush Signs $12.3 Billion Energy Bill into Law," *NBC*, August 8, 2005, http://www.nbcnews.com/id/8870039/ns/politics/t/bush-signs-billion-energy-bill-law/ (accessed October 7, 2019).

121. U.S. Energy Information Administration, "Frequently Asked Questions," http://www.eia.gov/tools/faqs/faq.cfm?id=32&t=6 (accessed July 22, 2019).

122. U.S. Energy Information Administration, "EIA Forecasts Renewables Will Be Fastest Growing Source of Electricity Generation," January 18, 2019, https://www.eia.gov/todayinenergy/detail.php?id=38053 (accessed July 22, 2019).

123. Alyssa Danigelis, "Top 10 Countries on Wind Power," *Discovery*, January 25, 2013, http://news.discovery.com/tech/alternative-power-sources/top-10-countries-windpower-130130.htm (accessed July 28, 2014); "World's Top 10 Countries in Wind Energy Capacity," https://energy.economictimes.indiatimes.com/news/renewable/worlds-top-10-countries-in-wind-energy-capacity/68465090 (accessed August 28, 2019).

124. U.S. Department of Energy, *2017 Wind Technologies Market Report*, https://www.energy.gov/sites/prod/files/2018/08/f54/2017_wind_technologies_market_report_8.15.18.v2.pdf (accessed August 28, 2019), viii.

125. Seth Borenstein, "No Free Lunch for Renewables: More Wind Power Would Warm U.S.," *AP*, October 4, 2018, https://www.apnews.com/82f436aa913a4ddf87e3cee8d3915924 (accessed July 22, 2019).

126. Sarah Golden, "Cargill, GM, P&G Among Group Calling for Market-Ready Renewable Thermal Energy," *GreenBiz*, March 21, 2019, https://www.greenbiz.com/article/cargill-gm-pg-among-group-calling-market-ready-renewable-thermal-energy (accessed July 22, 2019).

127. Alexander Richter, "The Top 10 Geothermal Countries 2018," *Think Geoenergy*, January 3, 2019, www.thinkgeoenergy.com/the-top-10-geothermal-countries-2018-based-on-installed-generation-capacity-mwe/ (accessed July 22, 2019).

128. Justin Walton, "The 5 Countries That Produce the Most Solar Energy," *Investopedia*, June 25, 2019, https://www.investopedia.com/articles/investing/092815/5-countries-produce-most-solar-energy.asp/ (accessed August 28, 2019).

129. Jeff Watterson, "California Is Producing Too Much Solar Energy—That's Not a Good Thing," *USA Herald*, July 15, 2019, https://usaherald.com/california-producing-much-solar-energy-thats-not-good-thing/ (accessed July 22, 2019).

130. Office of Energy Efficiency and Renewable Energy, "SunShot 2030," https://www.energy.gov/eere/solar/sunshot-2030 (accessed July 22, 2019); U.S. Energy Information Administration, https://www.eia.gov/tools/faqs/faq.php?id=427&t=3/ (accessed August 28, 2019).

131. Walmart, "Walmart, US Solar Announce Agreement for 36 Community Solar Gardens," June 11, 2019, https://corporate.walmart.com/newsroom/2019/06/11/walmart-us-solar-announce-agreement-for-36-community-solar-gardens (accessed July 22, 2019).

132. World Nuclear Association, "Nuclear Power in the USA," June 2019, https://www.world-nuclear.org/information-library/country-profiles/countries-t-z/usa-nuclear-power.aspx (accessed July 22, 2019).

133. "Noted: The Supply Chain in Brief," *Inbound Logistics*, June 2019, 22.

134. Dan Reed, "A Wild Hare of an Idea: Japanese Airline ANA Will Test Biofuel Derived from Rabbit Poop," *Forbes*, June 28, 2019, https://www.forbes.com/sites/danielreed/2019/06/28/a-wild-hare-of-an-idea-japanese-airline-will-test-biofuel-derived-from-rabbit-pellets/#1d6105405152 (accessed July 22, 2019).

135. U.S. Geological Survey, "Hydroelectric Power Water Use," May 13, 2009, http://ga.water.usgs.gov/edu/wuhy.html (accessed August 8, 2016); Institute for Energy Research, "Hydroelectric," https://www.usgs.gov/special-topic/water-science-school/science/hydroelectric-power-water-use?qt-science_center_objects=0#qt-science_center_objects (accessed July 22, 2019).

136. Tatyana Shumsky, "More Companies Link Executive Pay to Sustainability Targets," *Wall Street Journal*, June 24, 2019, https://www.wsj.com/articles/more-companies-link-executive-pay-to-sustainability-targets-11561379745 (accessed July 22, 2019).

137. Saabira Chaudhuri, "LEGO Struggles to Find a Plant-Based Plastic That Clicks," *Wall Street Journal*, June 12, 2019, https://www.wsj.com/articles/lego-struggles-to-find-a-plant-based-plastic-that-clicks-11560331800 (accessed July 22, 2019).

138. Walmart, "Walmart's Sustainability Index Program," https://www.walmartsustainabilityhub.com/sustainability-index (accessed July 22, 2019).

139. Miguel Bustillo, "Wal-Mart Plans Environmental Labels for Products," *Wall Street Journal*, July 16, 2009, http://online.wsj.com/article/SB124766892562645475.html#mod=testMod (accessed August 8, 2016).

140. "Values and Stories," New Belgium Brewing, http://www.newbelgium.com/sustainability (accessed August 8, 2016).

141. "The EU Eco-label," http://ec.europa.eu/environment/ecolabel/ (accessed August 8, 2016).

142. Ferrell et al., *Business Ethics*, 369.

143. "The Seven Sins of Greenwashing," *Terra Choice*, http://sinsofgreenwashing.org/ (accessed August 8, 2016).

144. Paul Hawken and William McDonough, "Seven Steps to Doing Good Business," *Inc.*, November 1993, 79–90.

145. Timothy N. Carson and Lata Gangadharan, "Environmental Labeling and Incomplete Consumer Information in Laboratory Markets," *Journal of Environmental Economics and Management* 43, no. 1 (January 2002): 113–134.

146. Kent Walker and Fang Wan, "The Harm of Symbolic Actions and Green-Washing: Corporate Actions and Communications on Environmental Performance and Their Financial Implications," *Journal of Business Ethics* 109 (2012): 227–242.

147. Steven Li, "Zara Makes a Bold Commitment to Sustainability. Is It Greenwashing?" *The Rising*, July 18, 2019, https://therising.co/2019/07/18/zara-makes-a-bold-commitment-to-sustainability-is-it-greenwashing/ (accessed July 22, 2019).

148. "FTC Issues Revised 'Green Guides'," Federal Trade Commission, October 1, 2012, http://www.ftc.gov/news-events/press-releases/2012/10/ftc-issues-revised-green-guides (accessed August 8, 2016).

149. Paper Recycles, "U.S. Paper Recovery for Recycling Rate Reaches Record 68.1 Percent in 2018," May 8, 2019, https://www.paperrecycles.org/media/news/2019/05/08/u.s.-paper-recovery-for-recycling-rate-reaches-record-68.1-percent-in-2018 (accessed July 22, 2019).

150. MillerCoors, "Waste Reduction," https://www.millercoors.com/sustainability/sustainably-brewing/waste-reduction (accessed July 22, 2019).

151. WasteWise, "About WasteWise," https://www.epa.gov/smm/wastewise (accessed August 8, 2016).

152. Ana Campoy, "'Water Hog' Label Haunts Dallas," *Wall Street Journal*, July 15, 2009, http://online.wsj.com/article/SB124762034777142623.html (accessed August 8, 2016).

153. Green Globes, http://greenglobe.com/ (accessed August 8, 2016).

154. Ibid.

Chapter 13

1. Amrita Khalid, "Alibaba Opens E-commerce Platform to Sellers Outside of China," *Engadget*, May 9, 2019, https://www.engadget.com/2019/05/09/alibaba-opens-ali-express-to-retailers-outside-china/ (accessed July 29, 2019); CB Insights Research Briefs, "Alibaba vs. Amazon: How the E-Commerce Giants Stack up in the Fight to Go Global," *CB Insights*, March 2, 2018, https://www.cbinsights.com/research/amazon-alibaba-international-expansion/ (accessed July 29, 2019); Rebecca McClay, "10 Companies Owned by Alibaba," *Investopedia*, May 17, 2019, https://www.investopedia.com/insights/10-companies-owned-alibaba/ (accessed July 29, 2019); Sharon Kwok, "Alibaba Tops E-commerce Market Share While Facing Fresh Competition in China," *Marketing-Interactive.com*, November 7, 2018, https://www.marketing-interactive.com/alibaba-tops-e-commerce-market-share-while-facing-fresh-competition-in-china/ (accessed July 29, 2019); Xinhua, "Number of Online Shoppers in China Hits 610 million," *China Daily*, March 2, 2019, https://www.chinadailyhk.com/articles/62/250/44/1551506282401.html (accessed July 29, 2019); Dan Western, "Jack Ma Net Worth," *Wealthy Gorilla*, 2019, https://wealthygorilla.com/jack-ma-net-worth/ (accessed July 29, 2019); Bill George, "Jack Ma on Alibaba, Entrepreneurs, and the Role of Handstands," *The New York Times*, September 22, 2014, http://dealbook.nytimes.com/2014/09/22/jack-ma-on-alibaba-entrepreneurs-and-the-role-of-handstands/?_r=0 (accessed July 29, 2019); Frank Langfitt, "From a Chinese Apartment to Wall Street Darling: The Rise of Alibaba," NPR, September 8, 2014, http://www.npr.org/blogs/parallels/2014/09/08/326930271/from-a-chinese-apartment-to-wall-street-darling-the-rise-of-alibaba (accessed July 29, 2019); Daniel Keyes, "Amazon Is Struggling to Find Its Place [in] China," *Business Insider*, August 30, 2017, http://www.businessinsider.com/amazon-is-struggling-to-find-its-place-china-2017-8 (accessed July 29, 2019); Kathy Chu, "Alibaba to Act Faster Against Counterfeits," *The Wall Street Journal*, May 15, 2014, B1; *Economist* staff, "E-commerce with Chinese Characteristics," *The Economist*, November 15, 2007, http://www.economist.com/node/10125658 (accessed July 29, 2019); Eric Markowitz, "From Start-up to Billion-Dollar Company," *Inc.*, April 6, 2012, https://www.inc.com/eric-markowitz/alibaba-film-dawn-of-the-chinese-internet-revolution.html (accessed July 29, 2019); Shannon Liao, "Amazon Admits Defeat Against Chinese E-commerce Rivals Like Alibaba and JD.com," *The Verge*, April 18, 2019, https://www.theverge.com/2019/4/18/18485578/amazon-china-marketplace-alibaba-jd-e-commerce-compete (accessed August 2, 2019); Paul R. La Monica, "Alibaba Will Let American Companies Sell on Its Site," CNN, July 23, 2019, https://www.cnn.com/2019/07/23/investing/alibaba-b2b-us-retailers/index.html (accessed August 2, 2019).

2. Center for Cultural Intelligence, "What Is Cultural Intelligence (CQ)?" http://www.cci.ntu.edu.sg/ (accessed August 9, 2016).

3. Mary Lou Egan and Marc Bendick, "Combining Multi-Cultural Management and Diversity into One Course on Cultural Competence," *Academy of Management Learning and Education* 7, no. 3 (2008): 387–393.

4. Moses Opobo, "Cultural Awareness Training Comes to Rwanda," *The New Times*, August 5, 2019, https://www.newtimes.co.rw/news/cultural-awareness-training-comes-rwanda (accessed August 5, 2019).

5. P. Christopher Early and Elaine Mosakowski, "Cultural Intelligence," *Harvard Business Review* 82 (October 2004): 1–9.

6. Mary Johnson, "Executive MBA Program Emphasizes International Business," *Tampa Bay Business Journal*, July 12, 2019, https://www.bizjournals.com/tampabay/news/2019/07/12/executive-mba-program-emphasizes-international.html (accessed August 5, 2019).

7. Early and Mosakowski, "Cultural Intelligence."

8. Marieke K. de Mooj, *Consumer Behavior and Culture* (Thousand Oaks, CA: SAGE, 2003).

9. Business Knowledge Source, "Overseas Manufacturing Pros and Cons," www.businessknowledgesource.com (accessed July 28, 2014).

10. Brandi Buchman, "Walmart Settles Brazil Corruption Case for $138M," Courthouse News Service, June 20, 2019, https://www.courthousenews.com/walmart-settles-brazil-corruption-case-for-138m/ (accessed August 5, 2019).

11. Andrew Singer, "United Parcel Service Translates and Transports an Ethics Code Overseas," *Ethikos and Corporate Conduct Quarterly*,

May/June 2001, http://www.singerpubs.com/ethikos/html/ups.html (accessed August 5, 2019).

12. Susan Raymond, "Global Philanthropy Part 2: Philanthropy in Latin America," *On Philanthropy*, March 6, 2008, www.onphilanthropy.com (accessed July 29, 2014).

13. "Global Sullivan Principles of Social Responsibility," www. thesullivanfoundation.org/gsp/default.asp (accessed August 9, 2016).

14. Caux Round Table, "Staff & Board," https://www.cauxroundtable.org/staff-board/ (accessed October 7, 2019).

15. Mercer, "Global Talent Trends 2019," https://www.mercer.com/content/dam/mercer/attachments/private/gl-2019-global-talent-trends-study.pdf (accessed August 5, 2019).

16. Kelsey Gee, "The New Labor Movement: Pushing Employers to Be Socially Active," *Wall Street Journal*, June 25, 2019, https://www.wsj.com/articles/the-new-labor-movement-pushing-employers-to-be-socially-active-11561476199 (accessed August 5, 2019).

17. "Global Code of Ethics for Tourism," World Tourism Organization, http://ethics.unwto.org/en/content/global-code-ethics-tourism (accessed August 9, 2016).

18. "Fairtrade Tops $9 Billion in Global Sales for First Time on 8% Growth," *Globe Newswire*, October 29, 2018, https://www.globenewswire.com/news-release/2018/10/29/1638502/0/en/Fairtrade-Tops-9-Billion-in-Global-Sales-for-First-Time-on-8-Growth.html (accessed August 5, 2019).

19. Jean E. Palmieri, "J. Crew to Introduce Fair Trade Certified Denim Collection," *WWD*, January 29, 2019, https://wwd.com/business-news/retail/j-crew-fair-trade-certified-denim-collection-1202990699/ (accessed August 5, 2019).

20. "Fair Trade," GreenAmerica, http://www.greenamerica.org/programs/fairtrade/ (accessed August 9, 2016).

21. "New Standard Development Project Plan: Agricultural Production Standard," Fair Trade USA, May 2014, http://fairtradeusa.org/sites/all/files/wysiwyg/filemanager/standards/Public_Summary_APS_Project_Plan_May2014.pdf (accessed August 9, 2016); Fair Trade Certified, "The Impact of Fair Trade Certification," https://www.fairtradecertified.org/why-fair-trade/our-impact (accessed August 5, 2019).

22. Amartya Sen, *Development as Freedom* (Random House: New York, 1999).

23. Austen Hufford and Bob Tita, "Manufacturers Move Supply Chains out of China," *The Wall Street Journal*, July 14, 2019, www.wsj.com/articles/manufacturers-move-supply-chains-out-of-china-11563096601 (accessed July 30, 2019); David J. Lynch, Heather Long, and Damian Paletta, "Trump Says He Will Impose New Tariffs on $300 Billion of Imports from China Starting Next Month, Ending Brief Cease-Fire in Trade War," *Washington Post*, August 1, 2019, https://www.washingtonpost.com/business/economy/trump-says-he-will-impose-new-tariffs-on-300-billion-in-chinese-imports-starting-next-month-ending-brief-cease-fire-in-trade-war/2019/08/01/d8d42c86-b482-11e9-8949-5f36ff92706e_story.html?utm_term=.8269e3b256cc (accessed August 2, 2019).

24. United Nations, "News on Millennium Development Goals," https://www.un.org/millenniumgoals/ (accessed August 9, 2016).

25. United Nations Global Compact, https://www.unglobalcompact.org/ (accessed August 5, 2019).

26. Ananya Mukherjee Reed and Darryl Reed, "Partnerships for Development: Four Models of Business Involvement," *Journal of Business Ethics* 90, supplement 1 (May 2009): 3–37.

27. Uwafiokun Idemudia, "Oil Extraction and Poverty Reduction in the Niger Delta: A Critical Examination of Partnership Initiatives," *Journal of Business Ethics* 90, supplement 1 (May 2009): 91–116.

28. "Socialism in Reverse," *The Wall Street Journal*, July 29, 2006, http://online.wsj.com/news/articles/SB115412585898220871 (accessed August 9, 2016); Arijit Mukherjee and Kullapat Seutrong, "Privatization, Strategic Foreign Direct Investment and Host-Country Welfare," *European Economic Review* 53(7), 2009, 775–785.

29. Anna-Catherine Brigida, "Campaigners Fear Creeping Privatisation of El Salvador's Water," *The Guardian,* September 25, 2018, https://www.theguardian.com/global-development/2018/sep/25/campaigners-fear-creeping-privatisation-el-salvador-water (accessed August 2, 2019).

30. "About the Microcredit Summit Campaign," Microcredit Summit, http://www.microcreditsummit.org/about-the-campaign2.html (accessed August 9, 2016).

31. Freedom from Hunger, "Microcredit Summit Campaign and Freedom from Hunger Form Alliance to Benefit 3.7 Million of the World's Poor Through Combining Microfinance and Health," January 23, 2019, https://www.freedomfromhunger.org/sites/default/files/mcs-ffh_alliance_news_release_english.pdf (accessed August 5, 2019).

32. Grameen Bank, "The Nobel Peace Prize 2006," http://www.grameen-info.org/index.php?option=com_content&task=view&id=197&Itemid=197 (accessed July 30, 2014); World Bank, "10 Years of World Bank Support for Microcredit in Bangladesh," http://web.worldbank.org/WBSITE/EXTERNAL/NEWS/0,,contentMDK:21153910~pagePK:34370~piPK:34424~theSitePK:4607,00.html (accessed July 30, 2014).

33. Fair Labor Association, "Participating Companies," https://www.fairlabor.org/affiliates/participating-companies (accessed August 6, 2019).

34. Michael Posner, "The Fair Labor Association: A Useful Tool for Investors," *Forbes*, June 28, 2019, https://www.forbes.com/sites/michaelposner/2019/06/28/the-fair-labor-association-a-useful-tool-for-investors/#1b6a00ca2799 (accessed August 5, 2019).

35. Fair Labor Association, "FLA Highlights Underlying Challenges of Child Labor After Extensive Investigation of Nestlé Cocoa Supply Chain," June 29, 2012, http://www.fairlabor.org/blog/entry/fla-highlights-underlying-challenges-child-labor-after-extensive-investigation-nestl%C3%A9 (accessed August 9, 2016); Peter Whoriskey and Rachel Siegel, "Cocoa's Child Laborers," *Washington Post*, June 5, 2019, https://www.washingtonpost.com/graphics/2019/business/hershey-nestle-mars-chocolate-child-labor-west-africa/ (accessed August 6, 2019).

36. Self-Employed Women's Association, Home Page, http://www.sewa.org (accessed August 9, 2016).

37. Center for Global Development, "The Commitment to Development Index," 2018, https://www.cgdev.org/commitment-development-index-2018 (accessed August 6, 2019).

38. Global Reporting Initiative, "GRI and Sustainability Reporting," https://www.globalreporting.org/information/sustainability-reporting/Pages/gri-standards.aspx (accessed August 6, 2019).

39. Patrick Temple-West, "US Congress Rejects European-Style ESG Reporting Standards," *Financial Times*, July 12, 2019, https://www.ft.com/content/0dd92570-a47b-11e9-974c-ad1c6ab5efd1 (accessed August 6, 2019).

40. Global Reporting Initiative, https://www.globalreporting.org/standards/ (accessed August 6, 2019).

Index

Page numbers followed by f and t indicate figures and tables, respectively.